HANDBOOK OF
SOFTWARE
ENGINEERING

HANDBOOK OF SOFTWARE ENGINEERING

Edited by

C. R. Vick, Ph.D.
Department of Electrical Engineering
Auburn University

C. V. Ramamoorthy, Ph.D.
Department of Electrical Engineering
and Computer Science
University of California at Berkeley

Van Nostrand Reinhold Electrical/Computer Science and Engineering Series

VNR VAN NOSTRAND REINHOLD COMPANY
New York

Copyright © 1984 by Van Nostrand Reinhold Company Inc.

Library of Congress Catalog Card Number: 82-24784
ISBN: 0-442-26251-5

Manufactured in the United States of America

Published by Van Nostrand Reinhold Company Inc.
135 West 50th Street,
New York, N.Y. 10020

Van Nostrand Reinhold Company Limited
Molly Millars Lane
Wokingham, Berkshire RG11 2PY, England

Van Nostrand Reinhold
480 Latrobe Street
Melbourne, Victoria 3000, Australia

Macmillan of Canada
Division of Gage Publishing Limited
164 Commander Boulevard
Agincourt, Ontario MIS 3C7, Canada

15   14   13   12   11   10   9   8   7   6   5   4   3   2

Library of Congress Cataloging in Publication Data

Main entry under title:
Handbook of software engineering.

   (Van Nostrand Reinhold electrical/computer
science and engineering series)
   Includes index.
   1. Electronic digital computers—Programming—Hand-
books, manuals, etc.   I. Vick, Charles R. (Charles
Ralph)   II. Ramamoorthy, C. V. (Chittoor V.), 1926–
III. Series.
QA76.6.H3335 1983   001.64′25   82-24784
ISBN 0-442-26251-5

Van Nostrand Reinhold
Electrical/Computer Science and Engineering Series
Sanjit Mitra, Series Editor

HANDBOOK OF ELECTRONIC DESIGN AND ANALYSIS PROCEDURES USING PROGRAMMABLE CALCULATORS, by Bruce K. Murdock

COMPILER DESIGN AND CONSTRUCTION, by Arthur B. Pyster

SINUSOIDAL ANALYSIS AND MODELING OF WEAKLY NONLINEAR CIRCUITS, by Donald D. Weiner and John F. Spina

APPLIED MULTIDIMENSIONAL SYSTEMS THEORY, by N. K. Bose

MICROWAVE SEMICONDUCTOR ENGINEERING, by Joseph F. White

INTRODUCTION TO QUARTZ CRYSTAL UNIT DESIGN, by Virgil E. Bottom

DIGITAL IMAGE PROCESSING, by William B. Green

SOFTWARE TESTING TECHNIQUES, by Boris Beizer

LIGHT TRANSMISSION OPTICS, Second editon, by Dietrich Marcuse

REAL TIME COMPUTING, edited by Duncan Mellichamp

HARDWARE AND SOFTWARE CONCEPTS IN VLSI, edited by Guy Rabbat

MODELING AND IDENTIFICATION OF DYNAMIC SYSTEMS, by N. K. Sinha and B. Kuszta

COMPUTER METHODS FOR CIRCUIT ANALYSIS AND DESIGN, by Jiri Vlach and Kishore Singhal

HANDBOOK OF SOFTWARE ENGINEERING, edited by C. R. Vick and C. V. Ramamoorthy

SWITCHED CAPACITOR CIRCUITS, by Phillip E. Allen and Edgar Sanchez-Sinencio

SOFTWARE SYSTEM TESTING AND QUALITY ASSURANCE, by Boris Beizer

Contributors

Boris Beizer, Data Systems Analysis, Inc.

Bharat Bhargava, University of Pittsburgh

B. W. Boehm, TRW Systems, Inc.

S. C. Chang, Northwestern University

Wesley W. Chu, University of California, Los Angeles

George E. Cole, Jr., John Hopkins Hospital

Alex Paul Conn, Digital Equipment Corp.

Merril Cornish, Texas Instruments, Inc.

Michael J. Flynn, Stanford University

Sakti P. Ghosh, IBM Research Laboratory

Robert Glaser, Telesaver

Jerome C. Huck, Stanford University

Steven M. Jacobs, TRW Defense Systems Group

K. H. Kim, University of South Florida

Robert E. Larson, Optimization Technology Inc.

R. C. T. Lee, National Tsing Hua University, Taiwan

Vincent Y. Lum, IBM Research Laboratory

Paul L. McEntire, Optimization Technology, Inc.

M. P. Mariani, TRW Systems

Edward F. Miller, Jr., Software Research Associates

Tadao Murata, University of Illinois

John D. Musa, Bell Laboratories

Jack G. O'Reilly, Systems Control Technology, Inc.

Don Oxley, Texas Instruments, Inc.

D. F. Palmer, General Research Corporation

C. V. Ramamoorthy, University of California, Berkeley

S. H. Saib, General Research Corporation

Bill Sauber, Texas Instruments, Inc.

K. S. Shankar, IBM Federal Systems Division

C. W. Shen, First International Computer Corporation, Taiwan

S. W. Smoliar, Schlumberger-Doll Research

Hon H. So, Bell Laboratories

W. N. Toy, Bell Laboratories

Joseph E. Urban, University of Southwestern Louisiana

C. R. Vick, Auburn University

N. A. Vosbury, System Development Corporation

Benjamin W. Wah, Purdue University

Howard O. Welch, System Development Corporation

R. D. Williams, TRW/DSSG

R. W. Wolverton, TRW Systems, Inc.

A. W. Wymore, University of Arizona

Raymond T. Yeh, University of Maryland

Pamela Zave, Bell Laboratories

Bernard P. Zeigler, Wayne State University

Preface

As "Software Engineering" enters a second decade as an acknowledged engineering discipline it is appropriate to consider the current state of the art and reflect on the contributing technology that has brought us this far. The fundamental premise of the term *software engineering* is the widely recognized need to interpret and apply sound engineering discipline and practice to the design, development, testing, and maintenance of software systems. Bauer gave us an early indication of the software engineering objective: "the establishment and use of sound engineering principles (methods) in order to obtain, economically, software that is reliable and works on real machines." In their recent book, Jeffery and Linden have asserted that "software engineering is not just a collection of tools and techniques, it is engineering. . . . software engineering has more in common with other kinds of engineering than is usually appreciated. Software engineering can learn from other engineering disciplines. . . ."

It is in the spirit of such definitions that we have undertaken the development of this documentary. The book begins with chapters of a more theoretical nature including topics covering modeling and simulation, graph theory and Petri net applications, theory of algorithms and complexity, and real-time control and system theory. A transition to hardware/software tradeoffs is made via a chapter on the topic of emulation. A sequence of chapters follows on various system software topics, ranging from computer languages and translation to operating systems and data base design and management. The related topics of software testing, formal verification, software reliability, and software fault tolerance are then covered, followed by a treatment of software management, costing and life cycle factors. The subjects of requirements engineering and process design are then addressed, and the book concludes with unique software development issues for a range of computer architecture.

C. R. VICK and C. V. RAMAMOORTHY

Introduction:
A Software Engineering Environment

C. R. Vick
Auburn University

1. THE NEED FOR A SOFTWARE ENGINEERING ENVIRONMENT

In spite of the concerted effort in software engineering research during the 1970s, critical issues and problems are yet to be found in virtually every aspect of the software life cycle. Cost remains excessive, schedules are unpredictable, and quality has improved very little. This is not to say that progress has not been made in software engineering, quite the contrary. There is widespread awareness of the contribution that a concerted effort in the requirements phase can make [24]. There is no disagreement regarding the benefits of structured design, verification, and validation across the total development cycle [16] and numerous other fundamental principles that have become commonplace. However the cost of software continues to escalate and major improvements in quality have not been realized. Productivity is not meeting demands, and operation and maintenance costs amount to substantially more than half of the life cycle investment. The 1970s will be remembered as the decade of awareness of software engineering. Industry, government, and academia carried out numerous R&D projects designed to deal with the "software crises." We must ask ourselves why more progress has not been realized. The problem lies not in the quantity and quality of research and development but in fragmentation. It is simply not sufficient to support the development, operation, and maintenance of a software system across the life cycle with an incomplete heterogeneous collection of tools and practices applied more randomly than not. The *software engineering system* is as complex as the *software system* that it supports, and the quality of the end product will largely depend on the quality and completeness of the supporting system. If quality assurance and operation/maintenance issues continue to be ignored during the development phase, an inproportionate amount of the life cycle cost will continue to be assessed for operation and maintenance. If the software engineer is not provided with comprehensive and integrated tools, techniques and disciplines that support *all* activities of the development life cycle, productivity and quality cannot be expected to make substantial gains. If the software manager is not provided with comprehensive and high-visibility management tools and practices, cost overruns and schedule infractions will continue to be imposed [21]. Much of the technology needed for such a comprehensive approach is currently available. For the remaining technological requirements, a large body of knowledge exists. What has not been accomplished is a comprehensive and systematic treatment of the life cycle issues in their entirety, their interrelations and potential solutions. Once this has been completed an orderly development of an environment with well-defined objectives can proceed.

2. SCOPE OF A SOFTWARE ENGINEERING ENVIRONMENT

Much has been said about programming environments, but significantly less attention has been devoted to the comprehensive *software engineering environment.* Programming represents but one facet of the discipline required of software engineers, and is one of the most studied and better understood activities. We must reach far beyond the programming environment to solve the problems associated with a total software engineering environment [6, 23, 24]. The starting point is the *user* or *customer environment.* A systematic and effective means must be developed to establish a user/developer dialogue, supporting analysis of the requirements and qualification of parameters. Well-founded disciplines must be applied to the subsequent development of system and subsystem requirements providing the assurance of accuracy, consistency, and traceability as they take on more detail. The issue of testing and quality assurance during the requirements phase must receive as much attention as the programming environment now receives. Standards for documentation, configuration control, and product assurance must be developed and applied. Predictive models for estimation of cost [22], schedule [23], productivity, and reliability [18] must be an integral part of the software engineering environment, providing the manager as well as the software engineer with vital decision-making information. Metrics must be established for application across the various stages of development as the software evolves from user requirements to operational code. Automated instrumentation, data collection and analysis must support each phase as well as computer aided in test case design, generation, and application. Standards and tools must be developed for the verification and validation activity.

As previously pointed out, many of the tools, techniques and disciplines exist to accomplish the foregoing objectives. Of these, however, many are inadequate and/or outdated. In no case have they been integrated into a consistent system for supporting the total life cycle of software.

3. THE SOFTWARE LIFE CYCLE

The software life cycle may be fundamentally partitioned into the *development phase* and the *operations and maintenance (O&M) phase.*

The development phase includes those activities from the recognition of a *required operational capability* by the user through acceptance testing of the final product. The O&M phase includes operational testing and activities such as error correction, modification, and product improvement. The majority of research and development in software engineering during the 1970s concentrated on the development phase. We have noted earlier the staggering percentage of life cycle cost allocated to the O&M phase. This can be blamed on the fact that it has largely ignored software engineering tools, techniques, and disciplines. If software doesn't meet the expected quality standards as it leaves the development phase, chances are it never will. The O&M phase was never meant to include "testing" quality into software. A significant and in most cases a majority of O&M costs are due to product improvement as opposed to error correction. This may imply a modification of the original structure. Such an undertaking should take place from the top-down as opposed to the bottom-up (or just the bottom, as is true in most cases). If the software system is not traceable with well-designed structure, top-down modification is impossible. It stands to reason that the O & M activity has as many requirements for software engineering support as the development phase. In fact, the tools, techniques, and disciplines should simply be an extension of the development support. The conclusion must be that if substandard software is transferred to the O&M phase with little or no software engineering support for error correction, modification, product improvement, or configuration control, one should expect software deficiencies as are now experienced to continue.

The Development Life Cycle of Software

There are numerous interpretations of the various development phases of software. The shortcoming of most is that software is viewed as an isolated discipline. A more realistic life cycle chart shown in Figure 1 views the *software life cycle* embedded within a *system life cycle.* Many of the software systems that a software engineering environment will be ex-

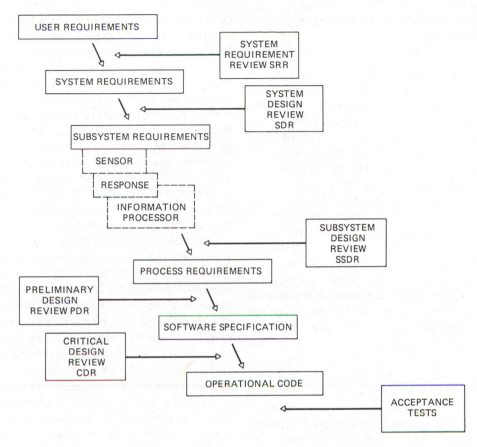

Figure 1. States of the development phase.

pected to support are what have come to be called *embedded systems.* This simply means that the software (and hardware) of the computing system must interface with and support other subsystems such as sensors and/or responsive devices. This viewpoint is far from restrictive, for it is proper to view many computing systems as embedded, for instance, process control, air traffic control, defense applications, etc., all can be classified as embedded systems. A large majority of the requirements that will be placed on an embedded computing system will be derived from an external source (e.g., through tradeoff studies with other subsystem elements).

User Requirements to System Requirements

User requirements constitute a top-level model of the entire system [1], required whether the system is embedded or not. The model of the system at the user requirements level must support analysis and validation of the required operational capability as well as dialogue and understanding between the user (or customer) and developer. The evolving *system requirements* model must be quantitative but must also recognize the limitation of "system understanding" at this juncture. Subsequent phases will further enlarge upon and produce more quantitative requirements values. The semantical issue of "requirements versus specifications" will be dealt with in more detail later, but it should be pointed out from the outset that requirements define *what* should be accomplished as opposed to specifications which detail *how* to accomplish it. System requirements must consistently, comprehensively, and accurately represent and be traceable to the user requirements.

System Requirements to Subsystem Requirements

This phase supports analysis of all subsystems from a system viewpoint (e.g., sensors, communications, responsive devices, as well as the computing subsystem). The point of departure for this phase is the system requirements, and the objective is to provide requirements for each of the subsystems. This involves conducting tradeoff studies on the overall system model to arrive at a complementary set of requirements for each subsystem that will in an integrated state collectively provide the behavior identified in the system requirements. The system model must of course contain more detail, and there is a great danger at this point that (at least some) specifications rather than requirements will be the outcome. There are cases where this cannot be avoided to some degree, but care must be taken not to make this a "specification" phase. If, for example, the system involves interfacing a computing subsystem with an *existing sensor,* one may be in a position to provide some or all of the specifications for the interfaces to the computing subsystem. The "operational" tradeoffs that dictate eventual system behavior may be much more restrictive in these cases, but in no sense should software specifications be produced at this point. Often specific computing machinery and operational algorithms are prematurely identified during this phase when the state of computer subsystem analysis and understanding is far from sufficient to support the required decisions.

Computer Subsystem Requirements to Process Requirements

Given the *computing subsystem requirements* the software development life cycle becomes more focused. We should not refer to simply the software life cycle, however, for it is during the *subsystem requirements phase* that the requirements for both hardware and software are determined. If the hardware has been specified as part of the project, this issue is academic. However, if the project calls for the acquisition or development of computing hardware, one has the opportunity to optimize the computing subsystem. It is important at this point to emphasize the meaning of the term *process* as opposed to the more general term *software*. By process we mean that profile in memory, both instructions and data, that is defined during *execution of the program* and explicitly describes the requirements that should be placed on a software design to derive a given system behavior. On the other hand, software is taken to mean the static collection of programs, both instructions and data. With these definitions in mind it is obvious that *requirements* must describe the process, whereas *specifications* derived from the process requirements will provide the *how* with regard to implementing the programs. A detailed analysis of computing subsystem requirements with the objective of determining process requirements and software specifications is *necessary* to explicitly determine hardware requirements. The process represents the eventual operational behavior of the system as prescribed in the system requirements. If the hardware is not sufficient to support the process, one cannot expect the system performance or behavior to meet requirements. The notion of "software first" or better yet "process requirements first" is feasible in today's hardware environment. It should be emphasized that the concept of software or process first goes far beyond the throughput estimating exercises that have repeatedly recommended undersized systems. The process and software requirements and specifications should be carried to a depth that support definition of the *architecture* of the supporting hardware system. Considering the hardware resources available today this is a completely feasible option. The analysis required to produce the process requirements includes decomposition of the subsystem requirements and partitioning of the decomposed system into a logical computation space. Finally the partitioned system must be allocated to a physical computation space. The allocation process may be constrained by a specified hardware subsystem or exercise the latitude of defining a hardware structure.

Process Requirements to (Software, Hardware) Specification

The next phase of the development life cycle will produce the software and hardware specification and will focus on *how* the requirements will be implemented. At this point the architecture and characteristics of the computing hardware will be clarified. The software specifications must take these attributes into account, (e.g., timing, accuracies, memory space, etc.). The software specifications define a physical computing space while the process requirements define a logical computing space. Also the operating system and other system software (if it exists) must be taken into account when deriving the software specifications. If the system software must also be developed, it will be specified in the software specification.

Software Specifications to Operational Code

At this point a *software development computer* may be utilized to provide the environment and attributes of the *eventual computer* such that software developed and tested on it will be transportable to the target machine.

4. OVERVIEW OF SOFTWARE ENGINEERING AND VERIFICATION/ VALIDATION

A graphical overview of typical software development activities is given in Figure 2 structured about the life cycle phases identified in the preceding paragraphs. The identified *intermediate* and *end item deliverables* are shown to interface with the activities of software engineering and verification and validation. The deliverables are actually a product of software engineering and serve as the principle input to verification and validation. The software engineering and verification and validation activities are discussed further in the following paragraphs.

Software Engineering

Much has been written concerning the formal definition of software engineering and many opinions offered. All agree however that the fundamental objective is that of providing sound engineering principles, practice, and tools in support of all phases of the software life cycle. As each phase of the software engineering cycle is considered a basic theme common to all can be summarized as follows: (1) ensure that the performance or behavior required by the preceding stage is met, and (2) minimize the errors passed on to the successor stage. As with the differentiation between requirements and specifications, we draw a distinction between performance and quality. Software of the highest quality (with regard to indigenous errors, efficiency, reliability, etc.) can and often does deliver unacceptable performance or operational behavior. Likewise, software can meet performance requirements precisely until a single error surfaces because of poor quality that causes the system to fail. A software engineering environment must emphasize both in the development of software engineering and quality assurance support. A further instance of the common theme is the supporting tools and their application. At each stage, a model of the system should be constructed to examine its dynamic behavior at that point. This model will implement the requirements or specifications from the preceding stage and support appropriate extension to the successor stage. This hierarchical collection of models will characterize the evolution of the system from the initial statement of user need to operational code. It will be the vehicle upon which principles such as demonstration of consistency, comprehensiveness, and traceability depend. In order to construct a model that can be examined with respect to dynamic behavior, it must ultimately be translated to a form that will execute on a computer. Rather than transforming a design description of the model (generally in English) through a procedural or simulation language to a state that can then be translated to an executable form, the model should be initially described in an unambiguous language appropriate to the par-

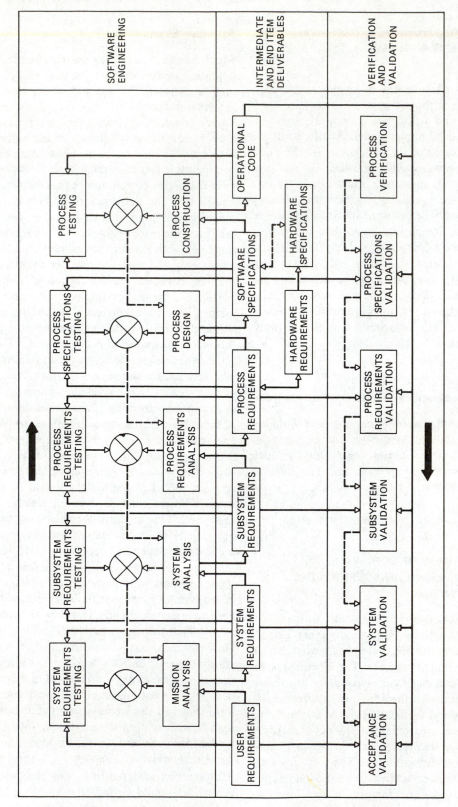

Figure 2.

ticular stage of development. In other words, a user-oriented computer language should be used to describe the model such that when it is appropriately translated, it exists in executable form.

In summary, given the user requirements as an input, a model of the system will be constructed. At this point very little is known concerning the *details* of system implementation. The model will be utilized for mission analysis and dialogue between the user and the system developer. It will be utilized for system feasibility and tradeoff studies and should be supported by resources that provide rapid turnaround. It will be the first and possibly most important bridge between the user and developer, for it is upon this model that a basis of fundamental understanding will be reached. The primitives of the language in which the model is described and the system that supports its implementation should be "user friendly"; that is, they should focus on and support the language and abilities of the user and the system designer. The objective of the *mission analysis phase* is to develop system requirements. Rather than simply using the user requirements as a guideline for producing the system requirements, the system requirements should be a *direct derivative* of and *explicitly traceable* to the user requirements. As implied in Figure 2, it is imperative that system requirements testing demonstrate a consistent and comprehensive implementation of the user requirements. Similar arguments can be made for each subsequent stage of the software life cycle.

Verification and Validation

The mistake is often made of implementing a *verification and validation (V&V) activity* that simply duplicates the testing program implemented for software development, the only difference being that it may be done by an independent source. This serves little purpose. When we refer to V&V we are in general addressing the ultimate goal of testing the deliverable end item software. As may be seen in Figure 2, the end item software should be tested from a V&V viewpoint with respect to the "intermediate" requirements and specifications, working backward toward user requirements. However, it should not be assumed that software V&V is a process that of necessity works from the bottom-up or proceeds to acceptance testing sequentially, for a well-planned V&V program can proceed through the phases concurrently with development. The V&V program should be planned and initiated at the outset of the development program. Even though the actual software testing activity cannot be initiated until end item products become available, the testing of requirements and specifications and the design of software test cases and test tools should proceed concurrently with the phases of the development program. Each V&V phase should be identified and the objectives of each clarified. Responsibilities for test case design and execution as well as error correction should be established for each phase and the responsibilities and procedures for regression testing established. Test tools should be identified for each phase, and a plan for their development or acquisition and implementation developed. Finally, a completion criteria for each phase of V&V should be developed.

5. ASSORTED USER REQUIREMENTS

It is reasonable to assume that there will be a need to apply elements of a software engineering environment to programs that may be in different stages of the software life cycle. Of course the most appealing time is to start at the outset of a development program, which permits the application of all software engineering elements across the entire life cycle. There are many programs however that are either in or entering the O&M phase for which sound arguments can be presented for introducing software engineering support. This is especially true for programs with a long life expectancy or projected product improvement programs. Programs in which no formal system was utilized to develop the requirements and specifications will more than likely be deficient in traceability. The most significant issues that surface in such cases are: (1) When an error is corrected at the operational code level, the reflection of that correction on other elements of the system may not be apparent and as a consequence introduce errors, and (2) when major modifications or product improvements are implemented it may be necessary to operate at the lowest levels of the development phases rather than implement an orderly redesign from the top down. The preceding are convincing arguments for introducing tools from a software engineering environment no matter what stage the development is in. As the elements of a software engineering environment are identified in the following sections, it will become obvious that many can be lifted and possibly modified for application to unique and individual problems. The significant factor that must be kept in mind, however, is that elements of a software engineering environment must be developed with a comprehensive objective in mind.

The question has often been raised concerning the use of software engineering disciplines for small development programs. There is indeed a lower bound at which a software engineering environment in its entirety might not be useful. However, the techniques for testing and standards for documentation, configuration control, etc. would be of benefit. Where does this boundary lie? The answer lies in the size and complexity of the problem. The need to apply a software engineering environment to a project increases dramatically as the ability to comprehend the total system exceeds the capacity of a few individuals. This may be dealt with to some extent through management techniques, but when the development team exceeds 10 individuals, a software engineering environment should be considered.

A software engineering environment must also be able to be applied in all hardware environments. As indicated in previous paragraphs, it should support an environment in which a target computer has been identified and exists, one in which the target computer is being concurrently developed, and finally an architectural integration approach where the hardware system is constructed from off-the-shelf components.

6. DETAILS OF REQUIREMENTS ENGINEERING

The following section will treat the various elements and activities of a proposed software engineering environment in some detail. It will first address the issue of requirements and specifications with respect to the development phase. The discussion will not be limited to the modeling activity introduced in the previous paragraphs, but will address the intellectual aspects of requirements and specification design as well as testing. The same approach will be taken for addressing the process and software design phases of the development cycle. The relationship of different test activities will be defined and supporting predictive models indentified.

Requirements Engineering

Requirements have been identified as the means for conveying *what* must be done toward the solution to a problem, whereas specifications relate *how* one would implement the solution [24]. A further definition of these two entities is as follows: Requirements are defined to be quantitative models of requisite conditions that bound but do not specify a solution space. Specifications are defined to be quantitative models enumerating specific solutions in response to a requirements space. Requirements may be further defined as functional or nonfunctional. Functional requirements for computing subsystems are requirements that when met specify system behavior with respect to the sequence of events, accuracy, and timeliness of the implemented solution. Nonfunctional requirements for computing subsystems are requirements that when met specify the attributes (reliability, cost, growth, size, etc.) expected of the media (hardware, software) that will implement the functional requirements. There are three categories of activity in the top-down design of a system that are closely associated with the previously defined notions of requirements and specifications. The first is *decomposition,* which is defined to be analysis leading to increasingly definitive elaboration or expression of a system at successively lower (more detailed) levels of abstraction. The second is *partitioning,* which is defined to be the synthesis or grouping of *elements of decomposition* according to some well-defined criteria or relation into sets that collectively form a logical computation space. The third is *allocation,* which is defined as the mapping of partitioned logical sets onto physical computing media.

Functional Requirements and Decomposition

When we refer to decomposition we are alluding to a heirarchy of increasingly definitive elaborations in which each level defines a complete and consistent *behavioral model* of the system. Figure 3 displays a simplified abstract notion of requirements decomposition in terms of *solution sets.* The predecessor requirement is shown at the upper level as a two dimensional function that is capable of being decomposed into three successor functions. The three successor functions are associated by relations R_i, the composite of which defines the predecessor function. The dotted vertical lines are bounds of feasibility or tradeoff regions. The bounds are established such that any solution falling within the range constitute an acceptable and implementable response. As indicated in Figure 3, there may indeed exist more than one collection of points which when mapped onto the solution set will constitute a correct response. For that matter there may be a *fam-*

ily of solution sets that constitute a correct decomposition. It may be said that when a set of tradeoff decisions is made such that the composite relation of the solution set yields an operating point within the bounds of feasibility in the predecessor level, that set of decisions becomes a *specification set* for the predecessor level and a *requirements set* for the successor level. Decomposition is strongly related to functional requirements and more weakly related to nonfunctional requirements. An example of the consequences of faulty decomposition is that a complete level of elaboration or abstraction may be ignored or levels may be mixed. These errors destroy the problem space structure, introduce discontinuities in traceability, and render determination of consistency and comprehensiveness impossible.

A Decomposition Model

Figure 4 proposes a decomposition model, identifying tools and techniques that support the activity. The input is assumed to be a set of *quantitative requirements* (user, system, subsystem, etc.). For example, at the beginning of the *development life cycle* this need would be filled by the user requirements. The objective is decomposition to the next level of abstraction, and it should be noted that there is a *statement language* to support description of the derived model. The insight into decomposition is largely based on human intuition

▲ SOLUTION 1
● SOLUTION 2

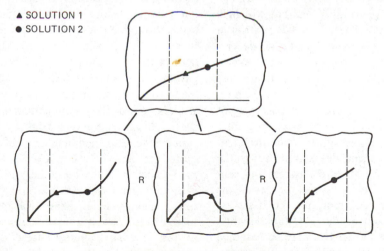

Figure 3. Solution sets.

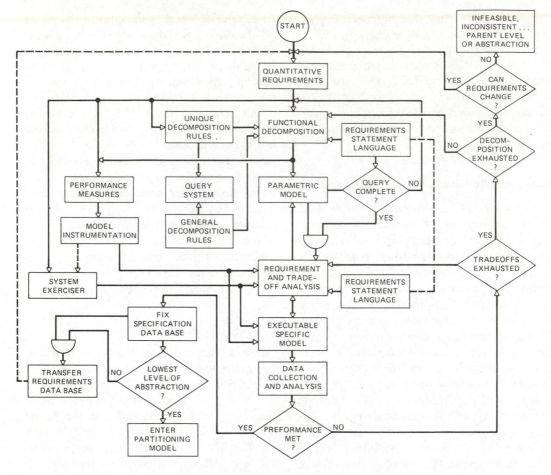

Figure 4. A generalized decomposition model.

and intellect, which among other things depends on analytical ability and past experience. However, there are rules that will help produce guidelines. These have been shown in Figure 4 as "unique" and "universal" decomposition rules (e.g. a knowledge based expert system). Unique rules are those that are specific to the system being decomposed. This includes establishing the bounds of feasibility of functions under consideration as well as other constraints due to predefined structures and subsystems. Universal rules deal more with the abstract decomposition of the system and consist of rules that are applicable in general. The criteria for decomposistion may be based on elaboration of control, data, or functionality. In realistic cases the criteria may be based on a composistion of these approaches. Rules may

be derived that will provide guidance to the designer. Such rules are introduced into the system not only as an aid to the designer but as a check through a query system on the parametric model that is being produced to assure that none of the rules have been violated. Once the parametric model has been developed, one is ready to establish operating points within the bounds of feasibility. The statement language that was used for model construction should support the refinement and tradeoff activity required to arrive at an *executable specific model*. Performance measures will have been identified at the outset from the input quantitative requirements. These will provide the measures for establishing the degree of success as well as a basis for test case design, instrumentation, and coverage analysis. The requirements themselves will provide the basis for the design of the *system exercisor* identified in Figure 4. If the executable specific model meets the required performance, the decomposition by definition becomes a specification data base for the input requirements and a requirements data base for the next lower level. It should be obvious how traceability can be maintained through levels of decomposition, but the issues of consistency and comprehensiveness can only be demonstrated with the assistance of testing. Two levels of testing are required at each level of decomposition. The first is the set of tests from the predecessor level. Even though the executable model is in more detail and is capable of and will provide more analytic results, it must be capable of reproducing the results from the predecessor level tests to demonstrate consistency. The second-level tests are keyed to the current level of requirements but must be a derivative of and consistent with the first-level tests. As is evident the activity of test case design must take as a principle objective the demonstration of consistency and comprehensiveness of requirements. (Test case design will be treated later.)

Requirements Partitioning

Partitioning has been defined as the synthesis or grouping of *elements of decomposition* according to a well-defined criteria into a logical computation space. It is more strongly related to nonfunctional than to functional requirements. Recall that functional requirements deal with system behavior or performance Performance should not be confused with throughput! One may minimize the complexity of the control/data interface to maximize throughput, but if adequate resources are available, logical behavior of the system is only indirectly related to partitioning. If by the time one begins the partitioning activity the behavior of the system isn't established, no amount of partitioning will accomplish it. One may also wish to maximize reliability. This may be accomplished through the partitioned structure of the logical system or optimization for fault-tolerance. Another tradeoff may be the

maximization of maintainability through optimization of testability, modifiability, or portability. Others include maximization of growth potential or the ability to dynamically reconfigure the system. One must also decompose the partitioning tradeoffs until measurable entities exist. It is not sufficient to have maximization of throughput as an objective. One might identify as an objective for throughput maximization the minimization of control and data interfaces. This might further be decomposed to more measurable attributes such as minimization of data relations and precedence or successor relations as well as isolation of recursive structures, inherently different types of computation, disjoint control segments, etc.

Allocation of Specifications

Allocation is the activity of mapping the logical computation space onto physical computing resources. Physical resources may be interpreted as an *extended machine* [11] where the sum of operating-system privileged instructions and basic hardware instructions collectively form the instruction set of the extended machine. Key functions needed by system modules are separated into an inner extended machine while certain modules can be separated out and executed on the extended machine much the same as application processes. The logical computation space is interpreted as a "logical control structure" and "specifications for application algorithms." The logical computation space must be transformed to computer programs that will produce a correct process when executed on the extended machine. The computer programs will consist of application algorithms, operating-system processes that execute on the outer machine, and kernel functions that operate on the inner machine. The application algorithms should exhibit a one-to-one correspondence with the specifications for a partitioned entity of the logical computation space. The logical control structure is subject to a transformation depending on the architecture of the eventual hardware. The design of the control structure and associated application algorithms is called *process design.* Process design has a fundamental responsibility to preserve the integrity of the process on the extended machine (i.e., predecessor/successor relations, space, timing, and accuracy). The interpretation of the logical control structure relies on the design of the operating system kernel, and this is the element that must bridge the gap between the logical computation space and the physical resources. An extreme example would be the implementation of the same process on a fully distributed versus a centralized architecture.

7. THE REQUIREMENTS ENGINEERING SYSTEM

Figure 4 indicated a decomposition model supporting the design of requirements and specifications. This model is valid, with slight modification, for all requirements phases of the development cycle from user requirements through process requirements (see Figure 1).

There are two significantly different types of technology that must support requirements and specification engineering. These might be classified as (1) tools and (2) techniques. The first (tools) is an easier notion to grasp, yet the requirements for them must be fully analyzed. The second (techniques) is not so straightforward as we are dealing with methodology and abstractions, standards and proof techniques. The benefits of one are extremely limited without the other. SREM is an example of a tool with limited techniques; SADT is an example of techniques but few tools [24, 25].

Requirements Expression Language

A common contributor to the deficiencies of requirements is that they are generally expressed in highly ambiguous English text. A corollary is that any formal analysis involving further interpretation may lead to furthur ambiguity. Even though one might resort to simulation as an analysis aid, a human is required to interpret the English text. Furthermore it implies that at some point the human mind(s) must embrace the total complexity of design if comprehensive analysis of the system is to be accomplished. These are fundamental reasons for a supporting unambiguous design language capable of automated translation to machine executable form which is suitable for analysis. Given such a language, the executable model previously referred to would be a *direct* product of the translated expression of design. Several endeavors in this direction have been made, but none have been fully successful. The language may have to become richer as one proceeds from user requirements to process requirements, but modern concepts of language and language processor design make this a realizable task [9, 10]. Likewise the syntax or grammar of the language must support meaningful English-like phrases or strings of text. A set of graphic symbols is a useful adjunct for envisioning the logical control structure. These should be one to one translatable to text and should include analytic aids such as Petri nets, graph theoretical analysis, etc. [2]. The language should include primitives for expressing parallelism, concurrency [3], intercommunication, logical data set access, interrupt schemes, and instrumentation for data collection, analysis, and proofs.

Foremost in this issue is the analysis that leads to identification of the primitives or the statements of the language. One must remember the different levels of requirements definition that this language will be serving. Current languages should be surveyed for their positive attributes (e.g., RSL, PSL, SADT) [9, 24, 25] and expression capability. As pointed out earlier, the user must feel comfortable with the language. The foregoing task is critical to the success of the entire requirements engineering task.

The language should support structured expression (e.g., PASCAL) [9]. One must remember that an eventual objective is to produce a simulation. Consideration must also be given to the primitive attributes of good simulation languages (e.g., timing, events, etc.). It must be kept in mind that vital to the effort is a wideranging instrumentation capability for data collection and analysis. The requirement to support textual documentation must also be considered.

Requirements Expression Data Base and Language Translator

The design as expressed in the *requirements expression language* is a static model of requirements, and the text serves as requirements documentation (which may be enriched with comments). The requirements expression source statements along with comments should be recorded in an interactive relational data base system that supports addition, deletion, modification, reading, and writing as well as other analysis aids (e.g., set operations, algebraic operations, etc.) The data base should be supported by a DBMS System [13] with interactive graphic access. Analysis of the static data base is possible with tools similar to static code analyzers (i.e., inspection of Program A with Program B without executing Program A, where the input to Program B is the text of Program A). Program B will search for syntactical and semantical errors, execute consistency checks, and perform a thorough graphical analysis of the implied logical control structure. This static data base is the vehicle for traceability with regard to further decomposition (i.e., an elaborated version of the subject data base). The consistency checks referred to above should not be confused with consistency checks between levels of requirements abstraction previously identified. Here we are speaking of horizontal consistency as opposed to vertical consistency. The static data base must eventually be placed under strict configuration control at each level of abstraction. The requirements expression source statements in the data base serve as the input to the *requirements expression language translator,* which will produce an executable model for dynamic analysis. As one evolves more detail from user requirements, several issues must be understood. In the beginning there was little more than a fundamental logical control structure with gross quantitative estimations of system behavior. Further elaboration will not only refine and expand the logical control structure but produce quantitative models of application algorithms [4, 5]. The application models will of course have an imbedded control structure that is an expansion of the system control structure. The object simulation provides the means for analysis of the dynamics of the expressed requirements. The analytical possibilities critically depend on four interrelated factors: (1) test case design, (2) model instrumentation, (3) coverage analysis, and (4) system exercisors. The language translator must be capable of inserting software test probes into the executable object code of the model. These probes may be data collection routines or calls to in-line analytical programs. There must also be a feature for the analyst to add instrumentation during analysis. Coverage analysis is a means by which one minimizes the set of test cases during design and through a report generator analyzes the extent of analytical coverage due to test case execution. There is a growing formalism in the area of test case design and coverage analysis that can be applied to requirements and specifications, but it should be recognized that it is not nearly as advanced as similar supporting tools for application code. The system exercisor must provide the stimuli (control signals and input data) that will cause the simulation model to execute. Its design is based on the requirements document and the design test cases. The system exercisor will in general be composed of software modules, although hardware-in-the-loop should not be excluded, especially at lower levels of system realization [7]. At each level of system elaboration one can associate a given level of system exercisor fidelity. Since the system exercisors must rely on software for implementation, it too is subject to be designed and implemented within the software engineering environment's domain.

Summarizing, the *requirements data base* is the repository for requirements design. The requirements written in the requirements expression language will be maintained there, and analysis on the data base itself will be of a static nature. As previously mentioned the data base will be supported by an interactive *data base management system.* It is the media that contains the evolutionary design and must be the instrument for configuration control. A static analyzer for syntactic and semantic (and other structural) analysis should support the data base. The data base will contain the requirements expressions (including comments) and will be the input source to the language translator. Since there may be multiple access users, the data base must have a security and privacy protection [14, 15]. The language translator will accept as input source statements *requirements expressions* from the requirements statement data base and should employ all of the capabilities of modern compilers [10]. Various requirements routines (as well as analysis routines) will have to be linked together and loaded into the system. The product of the language translator will be an executable simulation of the requirements and the object code will be instrumented with data collection probes or calls to in-line analysis routines.

Decomposition and Partitioning

The development of rules to be implemented by the designer in decomposition is one of the more difficult intellectual tasks. It will require heuristics derived from experience as well as elements of formal decomposition theory. Issues that must be addressed are (1) the establishment of guidelines that insure that all elements in a given level of abstraction or system elaboration belong there, (2) the types of relations required for creating composite expressions, (3) the requirements placed on the language for decomposition, since the decomposed state is to be expressed in the requirements expression language, (4) identification of fundamental axioms or rules for hierarchical structures that should be identified as a decomposition standard (universal rules), (5) identification of classes of systems for which decomposition standards can be identified (unique rules), (6) proof of consistency of decomposition from level to level (multilevel repeatable testing as addressed earlier), (7) proof of comprehensiveness: once a level is proven comprehensive, consistency proofs will support proof of successive levels. Comprehensiveness proofs must rely on test case design and semantic analysis, requiring an interactive process among levels, (8) traceability proofs that rely on the formal expression language and consistency proofs, (9) a stopping rule, that is, a rule stating when decomposition has

progressed to the point that partitioning should be initiated.

Partitioning is a great deal more straightforward. It is an optimization exercise and will require multicriterion optimization techniques. The principle partitioning issue is identification of partitioning objectives (the performance objectives will be derived from nonfunctional requirements, e.g., reliability, growth, cost, size, transportability, etc.). It must be recognized that the performance objectives must also be decomposed. For example, reliability must rely on inherent failure rate, fault tolerance, and so forth. The problem is a mathematical programming problem of optimization. The partitioning activity will produce restructuring of the requirements data base and will place requirements on the requirements expression language. This activity will result in what has been referred to as the logical computation space.

Test Case Design and Coverage Analysis

Test case design for requirements and specifications falls in the black box category, since one is interested in the performance or behavior of the model as opposed to its structure. The techniques of equivalence partitioning and cause-effect graphing are possible candidates to impose a degree of formalism on test case design. However, without automation these techniques are likely to get out of hand for large systems at lower levels of elaboration or abstraction. Cause-effect graphing could not only provide an aid to selecting an optimized set of test cases but might also provide the basis for coverage analysis. These two techniques as well as others should be analyzed for automation possibilities and expanded or modified to support requirements and specifications. The test cases will identify the data collection requirements and instrumentation points of the model.

System Exercisor

The system exercisor for requirements and specifications analysis must support the test cases selected for a given coverage. Since the test cases are performance-oriented, the test stimuli must be designed to produce output that will exhibit the behavior of the model as characterized by the instrumentation coverage. Care must be taken not to overdesign the system exercisor in terms of analytic stimuli for a given level of elaboration. A principal difference between system exercisors for requirements and specifications and those for process design is that there is no requirement to derive a real-time response. Also, there is no reason to require a fully interactive test driver as in process design. One may modularize the test cases by equivalence partitioning, which would identify the modularization of the system exercisor. There must be an overall superstructure of test cases that assures the integrity of the interfaces among modules both in the requirements model and the system exercisor. The family of system exercisors must be hierarchically consistent and eventually form the basis for a fully interactive integrated system exercisor for process design.

Predictive Models

During the early requirements and specifications phases there are certain predictive models of interest. One is interested in cost [22], schedule [23], and performance models throughout the entire development life cycle. Predictive models pertaining to reliability [18] and growth that are principally dependent on partitioning must wait until derivations of the logical computation space are available. There are numerous cost and schedule models available; however, none are based on a total systems approach. One will have to be well into the development cycle and have the support of some empirical data before the cost and schedule models will begin to take shape. Performance models have been addressed in previous sections and are a critical element in every phase. There are numerous software reliability models—each based on different principles. All credible models should be in a system library. Each will place requirements on data collection, both in the dynamic execution of the requirements models and empirical data (e.g., frequency of error detection, mean time

to failure, duration of correction time, inserted errors during correction, etc.). Growth models may be one of the most straightforward to implement. Its use during the requirements phase is not so much to predict growth as to serve as a design aid during partitioning. Performance models are much broader than system behavior prediction at the partitioning level. At this point one wants to take into account reconfigurability, both static and dynamic, a first estimate of resource requirements, and so on. In fact, the mathematical programming models of partitioning serve themselves as predictive models [5].

8. SOFTWARE PROCESS ENGINEERING

Software process engineering is the set of activities associated with developing the operational software from the *software specification* [25]. One is concerned with mapping the process specifications onto physical computing resources (i.e., the extended machine). The logical control structure of the process must remain invariant in the mapping but the physical control structure of the operational process may vary from architecture to architecture [27, 28, 29, 30]. We must insist that the physical control structure implies the logical control structure. This permits design freedom on the part of the processor designer. The principles of creating a process model prior to implementation is as valid for process design as it is for requirements and specification analysis. One is interested in insuring that operational events will occur in order and within time constraints that support the comprehensive requirements of the system as realized on a given hardware architecture (i.e., time and space tradeoffs are possible, and different, for different types of architecture). One is also interested in the accuracy with which the application algorithms produce results and the efficiency (of both time and space) of their design. All of these issues are interrelated. The fundamental purposes of the process model is to optimize process performance prior to analytic implementation.

Systematic Process Design

Modern programming language environments
offer numerous practices and tools to support
process design, and these should be specified as
a development standard. Some of the older
languages, however, especially assembly languages, do not have an adequate environment.
One should enforce standards that will promote readability, productivity, transportability, and maintainability. A good example of a
modern programming environment is that of
Ada* [9]. Given process design aids and standards, one should turn attention to procedure.
Given the logical control structure, operational
algorithm specifications, and hardware specifications, the process designer has sufficient
data to construct an operational model of the
process. The process model should *not* be considered a simulation model but a functional
model of the actual process. The physical control structure should be designed in analytic
detail at the outset with application algorithms
called or embedded as functional models. This
will provide several benefits: (1) One can make
time and space tradeoffs on the operational
control structure while the process remains at
a functional level, (2) the entire process can be
analyzed at a comprehensible level, and (3) as
algorithms are designed in detail they can replace their functional counterpart in the process model and can immediately be analyzed
in a full system context. This approach causes
several attendant issues to surface. One must
have a system exercisor at a level of detail sufficient to execute the operational code for behavioral analysis. This system exercisor must
be an analytic version of the family of system
exercisors identified earlier for requirements.
Since at some point the application algorithm
will be represented in the process model as a
mixture of functional and analytic implementations, an executive overlay must in some
cases provide analytic data transfers to application algorithms from functional algorithms
that are insufficient to produce the detail required. The functional and analytic versions of
application algorithms should reside in a data

*Ada is a trademark of Dod

base under configuration control and a *process
construction language* utilized to generate the
system.

The phases from user requirements to process requirements advanced the development
state to a logical computation space. The logical computation space exists as a partitioned
structure optimized around criteria provided
by nonfunctional requirements. Allocation of
the logical computation space to physical elements (i.e., the extended machine) will result
in both hardware and software specification.

Hardware Allocation

If the hardware architecture and physical
components have been prespecified, that specification will serve as a constraint on the partitioning process and allocation will be restricted to that of software development for
specified hardware. The structure of the logical computation space will provide the hardware architectural requirements, and further
analysis of the process requirements (leading
to software specifications) will provide the resource requirements of individual physical
components. In the case where the hardware is
prespecified, a situation may surface where the
functional or nonfunctional requirements (or
both) cannot be met. At this point one must
either decide to modify the prespecified hardware constraint or relax the functional/non-
functional requirements. The formal process of
design will allow the necessary tradeoffs to be
made while maintaining overall system integrity [8]. The optimum situation is one in which
the latitude exists to specify the hardware architecture and physical components. The physical components may be designed and developed, selected at large or from a family of
common building blocks. In any case one
should proceed with process development on a
software development machine. Allocation is
the transformation from a logical to a physical
computation space. While the mapping of elements in the logical computation space may
not be one to one, the logical integrity of the
logical computation space must be maintained
in the *physical computation space*.

Process Engineering

Process design may be defined as the activity of deriving software specifications from process requirements. The tools and techniques required for process design are similar to those needed for *requirements design*. One should have the capability to construct an operational model of the process before proceeding to detailed implementation. To assist in constructing, analyzing, and optimizing the model one must have a *process design and construction language*. To maintain the design in its most current state in an accessible form and to provide traceability to requirements and specifications requires a *process data base*. The *process model* differs from the *requirements model* in that certain structures of the most elementary form (first level) of the process model will be present in the final software. The design of a process is treated as an evolutionary activity where functional features are replaced and analytic counterparts are integrated into the model as they become understood and are available. In its final form the process model will indeed be the operational process encoded in the specified procedural language. The first realization of the process model will focus on the control structure. It will take into account the architectural specifications of the hardware as derived from the logical computation space. The application algorithms as well as the physical data base will be treated initially as functional models. The parameters for the functional models will be taken from the process requirements. As the analytic applications algorithms and data structures are developed, they will replace their functional counterparts in the process model. Issues that will be analyzed with the process model (all with respect to the eventual hardware architecture) are time and space attributes, including (1) the ordering and timing of events (e.g., handling of process race conditions, synchronization, concurrency control, predecessor/successor conditions, interrupt handling) with as much flexibility as possible within the limits of the hardware architecture and the objective of the optimized physical resource requirements, yet capable of producing the behavior required by the process requirements, (2) optimized use of physical resources (sharing of files, interprocess communication, optimized data structures, commonality in algorithms, etc.), (3) fault detection, isolation and resolution [20], (4) process reconfiguration, (5) growth (new requirements placed on the control structure, algorithms, or data), and (6) modification (e.g., changes and additions to or deletions from the resident control structure, algorithms, or data).

Process Design/Construction Language

Since the process model will evolve into the *operational process,* the control structure and analytic application algorithms should be written in the specified procedural programming language. The functional models of the application algorithms may be written in a simulation language for efficiency and effectiveness of modeling required behavior [1], but care must be taken in such an intermediate step to assure that the model correctly implements the process requirements in specification derivation and that the analytic algorithm provides the behavior specified by the model. The process design/construction language is a tool with which the designer manipulates the design. The primitives are pseudo-operations (instructions to the language processors, editors, loaders, preprocessors, etc.) and macroinstructions. They must support the implementation of a simulation executive and the provision of truth data (quantitative data that an analytic algorithm needs to execute which a functional model cannot provide). The requirements for a process design/construction language must take into account the following factors: (1) the kernel of process design as the control structure into which functional models and analytic counterparts will be integrated, (2) individuals who will likely have no knowledge of the overall process (e.g., a large team of programmers), (3) a process which is *completely* executable at all times (first functional with an intermediate functional/analytic-life, and finally fully analytic), requiring a simulation executive and truth data, (4) tradeoffs and optimization which may require a great deal of modification, in turn implying a need for strict configuration control, and rapid turnaround and assistance in constructing, modifying and deleting control, communication and data dependencies during analysis and modification, (5) the need to produce functional models, (6) the need to rapidly and correctly replace functional models with analytic counterparts, (7) the need to instrument the process model for analysis [19], and (8) the need to rapidly and correctly construct an operational process from a process data base [12].

Process Design / Construction Data Base

The process design and construction data base differs from the requirements and specification data base in several respects. The *process design and construction data base* is a repository in which models of processes and real processes will be created and will also provide the means for configuration control. The functional models and their analytic counterparts, as they become available, will reside there. The physical control structure will also reside there. Finally the process under configuration control (fully functional, functional/analytic, fully analytic) will reside there. The data base system for requirements and specifications will serve the requirements of process design and construction and the process design/construction psuedo-operations should provide access to the data base to generate the specified process.

Test Case Design and Coverage Analysis

Test case design for the process design phase involves both black box and white box testing [16]. Black box tests must be designed using much the same techniques as those used for requirements and specifications testing to assure that the process model and eventually the operational code provides the required behavior. The test cases identified for process requirements testing should serve this purpose with possible elaboration on the detail of the stimuli. White box static tests will be required to examine the internal structure of the process

both for correctness and efficiency, while dynamic tests will observe behavior of the final product.

System Exercisors

There are several requirements for system exercisors to be considered for the process design phase [30]. One will be concerned with classical phases of unit, integration and system testing. One principle must be maintained at each level, that is, that the system exercisor is a derivative of and correctly implements its predecessors in requirements and specifications. This again points to the fact that the system exercisor should be subject to the same software engineering procedures as the application software. Unit tests and test drivers must not be left to the whims of application algorithm designers but must be constructed from the process requirements. Integration tests require a system exercisor that can correctly execute a functional/analytic process; it must be capable of providing the system with "truth data."

9. DEVELOPMENT TESTING

Referring to Figure 2, a testing activity is indicated with respect to each phase of the software engineering development life cycle. This subsection will address each phase, following a few introductory remarks.

Test Case Design

Black box testing refers to an examination of behavior or performance derived from and with regard to requirements and specifications. Black box testing does not take into account nor does it care *how* the performance is derived but merely addresses the end result. On the other hand *white box testing* relates to tests from which the test data are derived from examination of the internal structure (for example, the logic of programs). It does not dwell on behavior or performance (i.e., *what* the system is doing), but rather on the validity of the implementation. It should be acknowledged at the outset that exhaustive or complete testing is impossible. One simply cannot within realistic terms of time, cost, and intellectual capacity generate a complete coverage of test cases. The objective then has to be that of selecting and implementing a subset of test cases that has the highest probability of detecting the most errors.

Test Completion or Stopping Rules

The issue of when one should discontinue testing in a development test program is not only the most difficult but the most critical. One simply cannot guarantee the absence of residual errors in a program; in fact it is safe to assume that residual errors exist. This imposes the necessity for a well-established test completion criteria for each phase of the development test program. One might establish the exhaustion of defined test cases as a criterion. Further commitment might be made to find x errors. This of course implies that one assumes x errors exist and that x errors represent an acceptable percentage of the total. While one cannot be certain in establishing such a value, techniques exist for arriving at such a value. A technique known as error seeding is one such method. It draws on the notion of the equal likelihood of finding a residual error as a known or seeded error. Given such an assumption and a detection history of residual and seeded errors, the model predicts the number of residual errors. Numerous other statistical methods exist that rely on the error detection rate and so forth. Error detection rates should be plotted and trends observed. The best possible completion criterion is a combination of techniques, like that just mentioned.

Test Tools and Practices

Numerous test tools exist, but most of them focus on white box testing. *Static flow analysis* tools exist as a program that examines a program in its static state [16]. Such tools may identify unreachable code, endless loops, undefined variables, etc. Test coverage monitors examine programs during execution, indicat-

ing numbers of branches, statement execution numbers, and so on. Symbolic execution is a technique where algebraic symbols are inserted in a program rather than letting variables take on numeric values [17]. Other techniques include program inspections and walkthroughs that involve the manual inspection or reading of code in a highly structured and organized team effort. Black box testing relies heavily on system exercisors or simulation drivers that impose tests that derive the behavior of the program in its intended environment. As one progresses from system requirements testing to process testing, the system exercisors become more analytic in nature. This reinforces the necessity of initiating the testing effort at the outset of a development program. System exercisors at each level of complexity should be consistent with their predecessor.

10. DEVELOPMENT TEST PHASES

The development tests shown in Figure 2 are in five phases. Each will be addressed in the following paragraphs.

System Requirements Testing

This phase is associated with assuring that the derived system requirements meet the criteria established by the user requirements and that the user requirements are feasible in a system context. At this juncture the system will not be well defined as subsystems, and concern is principally aimed at overall system response. The tests will be black box tests directed at examining, optimizing, and predicting system behavior. Known parameters will principally be those related to sensors and responsive devices (stimuli and responses), while the information processing will for the most part be inferred.

Subsystem Requirements Testing

The translation from system requirements to *subsystem requirements* implies that logical and physical interfaces are established between partitioned elements of the system (i.e., sensor, information processor, reactionary device). The subsystem of interest here is the information processor, which includes the hardware and software elements of the computing subsystem. The inferred requirements of the previous phase will be reduced to computing subsystem requirements. Testing at this juncture will again be at a black box level concerned with the integrated behavior of the subsystems and their collective ability to satisfy system requirements. At this point a fairly detailed structure of system events and timing will begin to take shape. The information processor has the principal responsibility for implementing that structure. It is necessary that the "system" model of the subsystems treat each subsystem as a distinct model to insure integrity of the interfaces.

Process Requirements Testing

The transition from computing subsystem requirements to *process requirements* will advance the level of requirements from a comprehensive information processing model to a logical computation space. A logical control structure for the process will be developed that will implement the event and timing requirements of the system. Requirements for application algorithms which will provide the accuracy required to provide the required system performance will also be developed. Testing is still at a black box level aimed at ensuring that the timing and event sequences of the logical control structure coupled with the accuracy required of the application algorithms produce acceptable computing system performance.

Software Specification Testing

The transition from process requirements to *software specifications* must take into account the definition of the extended machine. As indicated earlier, if the machine has been specified, this consideration is trivial. However, if one must identify or develop the hardware, this involves a significant tradeoff. It should be recognized that until one reaches the process design stage, data sufficient to make a low-risk

selection or define an optimized system simply is not available. In either case one can proceed with software development on a "development machine." It is during the transition from process requirements to software specifications that the nonfunctional attributes of the logical computation space surface. As a consequence testing must now extend beyond behavioral interests to include tests for requirements such as fault tolerance, growth, size, testability, and the like. Testing must also take into account the structure of the specified computing hardware and the ability of the specified software to collectively meet the process requirements.

Process Testing

The transition from software specifications to *operational code* involves the activity identified as process design. Here both black box and white box testing must be applied. One is concerned not only with performance but with quality and effectiveness as well as efficiency. The code must be exercised for behavioral analysis not only in producing expected performance but in areas of nonfunctional requirements such as fault tolerance. It must be structurely examined for indigeneous errors, efficiency of solutions, and use of resources.

11. QUALITY ASSURANCE AND INDEPENDENT VERIFICATION AND VALIDATION

The tools and techniques identified in the previous section for *development testing* are identical to those needed for a *quality assurance (QA)* or *independent verification and validation* (IV&V) program. The difference lies in objectives, psychological attitude, and test case design sources. The attitude taken by the development test team must be one that supports design. It is an integral part of the development process and must be positively utilized to support tradeoff analysis and expected performance. It is used to convey design consistency and comprehensiveness among the various levels of system realization. On the other hand QA and IV&V are concerned with independently establishing the integrity of delivered products. Quality assurance is more attentive to the quality of delivered products than their operational behavior. It has classically been concerned with the assurance that standards have been met, that documentation is appropriate, and that configuration control is exercised. Quality assurance however should extend beyond these issues. It should be concerned with the adequacy of the means by which the development team assured consistency and comprehensiveness among the design phases, and it certainly should be concerned with the proof of quality of the end product, namely, the operational code (e.g., efficiency, freedom from implementation errors, etc.). Quality assurance should be concerned with the development test plans and resulting quality of development tests, if they were adequate, comprehensive, and consistent, as well as the adequacy of the system exercisors. It should be concerned with the nonfunctional attributes of the system (e.g., can growth requirements be met, has the maintainability issue been adequately addressed, etc.). While QA extends its authority into the development process, the IV&V interface begins and ends with the requirements, specifications, and operational code produced from the development phases. The psychological attitude of IV&V may be classified as destructive from the viewpoint that the principle objective is to find performance deficiencies and implementation errors. IV&V should not be priviledged to test cases executed during development testing; it should establish its own test coverage criteria and should not be responsible for error correction or regression testing. Both QA and IV&V should be implemented at the outset of the development program, QA extending its analysis into the development process and IV&V designing and implementing independent test cases as each deliverable is made available.

12. SUPPORTING ELEMENTS

The previous paragraphs of this section have identified the superstructure of a software engineering environment for the development life cycle. But there are a number of supporting elements that must be imposed on the super-structure. These will be addressed in the following paragraphs.

Predictive Models

The problems of predicting and controlling the cost and schedule of software projects possibly remain as two of the most difficult issues to grasp. However, if one takes into account the lack of structure and discipline that has characterized software development projects, little more should be expected. The disciplines and structure outlined in the preceding paragraphs compare to past practices somewhat as the development of an automobile in a modern automated plant does to one produced in a hobby shop. Without discipline and tools upon which productivity can be based, predictions of cost and schedule become rule-of-thumb estimates. Once the superstructure of a software engineering environment is understood, productivity models of each phase can be developed. This will of course require that parameters and measures be identified as inputs to a model of each stage [19]. This can only be realistically known as the system evolves. The issue of performance models has been covered in detail in the preceding paragraphs. It is important to reemphasize, however, that a running account of performance must be maintained (test cases and results saved) as one proceeds from stage to stage. Once the stage of process design has been reached and actual coding commenced, it is important to initiate models of software reliability. A number of such models exist [18] based on different attributes, and an automated data collection facility can provide predictions under automated control.

Management Overlay

The predictive models addressed in the previous paragraph provide the basis for a management overlay [21] which must also include access to the test cases and data of each development phase. The discipline and structure of a software engineering environment must provide the means by which a highly automated management system can be developed.

Standard and Metrics

As the various elements and phases of a software engineering environment are developed, standards for design, development, and testing must also be developed. This will be critical to enforcing the disciplines of the system. Automated checking of adherence to standards must be embedded in the superstructures. Metrics that are meaningful, and (in fact) measurable, must also be identified in support of each phase. Metrics are not only necessary for application to functional and nonfunctional requirements but to the predictive models identified earlier.

13. SUMMARY

The preceding discussion has outlined a software engineering environment that supports the total life cycle of software. Many of the required tools, techniques, and disciplines required for implementation of such an environment, the majority of which are addressed in this handbook, exist today.

REFERENCES

1. B. P. Zeigler, "Theory and Application of Modeling and Simulation: A Software Engineering Perspective," C. R. Vick and C. V. Ramamoorthy (eds.), *Handbook of Software Engineering,* Van Nostrand Reinhold, New York, 1983.
2. H. H. So, "Graph Theoretic Modeling and Analysis in Software Engineering," ibid.
3. T. Murata, "Modeling and Analysis of Concurrent Systems," ibid.
4. B. W. Wah and C. V. Ramamoorthy, "Theory of Algorithms and Computational Complexity with Applications to Software Design," ibid.
5. R. E. Larson, P. L. McEntire, and J. G. O'Reilly, "Application of Real Time Control Theory to Software Engineering," ibid.
6. A. W. Wymore, "Application of System Theory to Software Engineering," ibid.
7. M. J. Flynn and J. C. Huck, "Emulation," ibid.
8. W. N. Toy, "Hardware/Software Tradeoffs," ibid.
9. J. E. Urban, "Computer Languages," ibid.
10. R. C. T. Lee, C. W. Shen, and S. C. Chang, "Compilers," ibid.
11. S. M. Jacobs, "Operating Systems," ibid.
12. K. S. Shankar, "Data Design: Types, Structures, and Abstractions," ibid.
13. S. P. Ghosh and V. Y. Lum, "Data Base Management," ibid.
14. W. W. Chu, "Distributed Data Base Systems," ibid.
15. B. Bhargava, "Concurrency Control and Reliability in Distributed Data Base Management Systems," ibid.
16. E. F. Miller, "Software Testing Technology—An Overview," ibid.
17. S. H. Saib, "Formal Verification," ibid.
18. J. D. Musa, "Software Reliability," ibid.
19. B. Beizer, "Software Performance," ibid.
20. K. H. Kim, "Software Fault Tolerance," ibid.
21. R. D. Williams, "Management of Software Development," ibid.
22. R. W. Wolverton, "Software Costing," ibid.
23. B. W. Boehm, "Software Lifecycle Factors," ibid.
24. R. T. Yeh, P. Zave, A. P. Conn, and G. E. Cole, "Software Requirements: A Report of the State of the Art," ibid.
25. N. A. Vosbury, "Process Design," ibid.
26. S. W. Smoliar, "Application and Functional Programming," ibid.
27. R. Glaser, "Software Development for Micro/Mini Machines," ibid.
28. H. O. Welch, "Software Development for Array Machines," ibid.
29. D. Oxley, B. Sauber, and M. Cornish, "Software Development for Data Flow Machines," ibid.
30. M. D. Mariani and D. F. Palmer, "Software Development for Distributed Computing Systems," ibid.

Contents

HANDBOOK OF SOFTWARE ENGINEERING

1

Theory and Application of Modeling and Simulation: A Software Engineering Perspective

Bernard P. Zeigler
Department of Computer Science
Wayne State University
Detroit, Michigan

1.1. INTRODUCTION

A Short History of Development

Modeling and simulation (M&S) is an emerging field whose boundaries are not well defined. Model building can be traced back at least as far as the Newtonian era, but the tremendous enhancement it received with the advent of the electronic computer is, of course, a relatively recent phenomenom. Moreover, there are at least two main sources of approaches and techniques—from physical science and from operations research—that are yet in the process of confluence and unification.

Physical scientists—especially in the applied and engineering branches—were faced with increasingly complex equations, combinations of general laws, and empirical relationships for which analytic solutions are of limited usefulness. In response, mechanical solvers of differential equations were developed whose operation was based on the integration capabilities of some particular natural medium. Currently, the predominant form of such analog devices is the electronic analog computer whose capacitors integrate by storing inflowing charge. Analog computers saw

heavy and significant use in the chemical and aerospace industries, among others, but limitations of problem size, stability of equipment, and accuracy of computation led to harnessing of the emerging digital computer to achieve equivalent capabilities. The latter performs integration numerically, using principles that originated with long-known manual approximation methods. However, what gave the digital computer eventual primacy was its information processing abilities, which meant that languages could be designed that would provide for convenient specification and processing of differential equation models.

The second source of approaches and techniques lay in operations research with its desire to ameliorate industrial processing networks plagued by congestion, unproductive waiting, and underutilization of resources. New concepts such as *event* and *activity* were developed which (in the beginning) had little to do with the classical modeling concepts. An associated development was the incorporation of direct experimentation subject to chance outcomes within the computation, originally known as the Monte Carlo methods. Lacking the four-hundred year experience of its older brother, the discrete modeling approach saw its tools being developed before there was adequate practical experience or theory to support them. (Shannon [1] gives an excellent classification of computer simulation languages and reviews their development.)

---
[1]Work was supported in part by Grant No. DAERO-78-G-088 of the European Research Office of the U.S. Army.

A Software Engineering Perspective

As the field matures the emphasis is shifting from that of "simulation," as a set of computational techniques, to that of "modeling," whether it be in continuous or discrete form, or indeed, in forms that combine the two. Limitations and pitfalls are being better appreciated but so are the enormous potentials. This chapter attempts to provide a basic appreciation of the M&S area for the software engineer. From this perspective the field is rather unique: it is both a source of tools open for use in software engineering as well as a source of large-scale software systems that require software engineering principles for their design.

The chapter will proceed with a general characterization of M&S and will discuss a case study of simulation modeling for computer system performance evaluation. With this as background, general concepts and tools of M&S will then be introduced. To bring out the software engineering perspective, an extensive treatment is given of simulation modeling in relation to the design process. Finally, proposals for next-generation M&S support systems are reviewed that will tax state-of-the-art software engineering concepts and methodology.

1.2. CHARACTERIZATION OF MODELING AND SIMULATION

The Definitions Approach

Definitions of modeling and simulation abound [2], which partly reflect the many origins of the area. Perhaps the most representative of them is that of Shannon [1]:

Simulation is the process of designing a model of a real system and conducting experiments with this model with the purpose of either understanding the behavior of the system or of evaluating various strategies (within the limits imposed by a criterion or set of criteria) for the operation of the system.

Shannon emphasizes the experimental orientation of simulation techniques but widens the term *simulation* to include modeling activities not necessarily related to simulation. Other definitions try to characterize simulation more narrowly so as to distinguish it from other computational techniques as in Reference 2:

Simulation modeling assumes that we can describe a system in terms acceptable to a computing system. In this regard, a key concept is that of system state description. If a system can be characterized by a set of variables, with each combination of variable values representing a unique state or condition of the system, then manipulation of the variable values simulates the dynamic behavior of the system by moving it from state to state in accordance with well-defined operating rules.

Indeed, it is characteristic of simulation tools that they facilitate a (hypothetical) description of the internal structure of a real system to a richness in detail as arbitrarily close to that which the modeler perceives to pertain to reality. It is this power of representation that distinguishes simulation from analytical techniques but that also places a new burden of choices on the modeler: what level of detail to choose that is compatible with the objectives of the modeling effort, the data available on the real system, and the computational and manpower resources at one's disposal. To write a detailed description of a system (i.e., a model) acceptable to a computer is one thing. To verify that it reflects one's intentions and then to validate it as a true description of a real system is another.

The Framework for Activities Approach

It should be recognized that such informal definitions can go only so far in conveying concepts and methods. A formal framework that founds a structure of definitions and theorems upon a set-theoretic basis was provided by Zeigler [3]. A subsequent series of papers [4, 5, 6] developed a top-down structuring of M&S that emphasizes the many activities entailed by good practice. The hierarchy states that the modeling and simulation process may be decomposed into the following activities:

- Model generation/referencing
- Model processing
- Behavior processing
- Real system experimentation
- Model acceptability assessment

Each of these activities is further decomposable, but we shall only briefly discuss the broad categories at this point. As we proceed, the reader should gain a perspective of the full range of activities encompassed by the term *modeling and simulation* (a range which defies attempts at a one-paragraph definition).

1. Model generation/referencing refers to the generation of models (i.e., system descriptions) either by construction from scratch or by employing models retrieved from model data base components to be coupled together.
2. Model processing refers to the manipulation of model texts (e.g., to produce documentation, to check consistency, etc.) and to the generation of model behavior, of which simulation, restricted hereafter to mean computerized experimentation with models, is a predominant form.
3. Behavior processing refers to the analysis and display of behavior in a static setting (e.g., in equilibrium) or in a dynamic mode (i.e., concerning state trajectories) or in a structural mode (i.e., tracking of changes in model structure).
4. Real-system experimentation refers to the gathering of behavioral data from the real system or any of its component systems of interest.
5. Model acceptability assessment refers to the verification and validation of models but also to a host of other tests of the relationships in which models participate.

1.3. CASE STUDY: MODELING AND SIMULATION OF AN EXISTING OPERATING SYSTEM

In order to provide a background for later discussion of concepts and tools we shall briefly review a concrete M&S application. A simulation study of the MVT operating system of the IBM 370/165 under HASP serving a major university computing center was carried out [7]. In addition to its potential to add to the understanding of the operating system (OS) in its workload environment, there was a desire by the computing center management for the model to support the prediction of the amount of new core memory which would be needed to relieve memory congestion. We shall describe the study under several headings as follows:

Objectives

The objectives of the study were:

1. To construct, verify and calibrate a model capable of reproducing OS performance under typical daily load conditions, and
2. To employ this model to predict the effect of increasing core memory in the existing installation.

Available Data

The main source of data was the IBM System Management Facility, which monitored the OS operation over a working period of 8.42 hours. A total of 1,505 jobs were identified comprising 12,431 steps. The latter were taken as the indivisible program units of the study. The facility produced tables of the following quantities for each HASP class:

1. Average CPU (central processing unit) time per step
2. Histogram giving for each core memory class, the frequency of steps using the given core memory
3. Histogram giving for each priority level, the frequency of steps having the given priority
4. Average number of tape/disk channel programs

Preparation of the Data for Input to the Model

Tables were constructed from this data for each HASP class giving:

1. Its relative frequency (total number of steps in a given class/total number of steps over all classes)
2. The distribution of memory size requests by steps within the class
3. The distribution of priority levels assigned to steps within a given class
4. Average CPU time per step of a given class
5. Average number of I/O requests per step of a given class

Modeling the Input Stream Process

The aforementioned tables were used to specify a generator for the input stream of steps. The arrival process was assumed to be Poisson (see Reference 8 or 9 among many others for stochastic process background) with an arrival rate parameter equal to the total number of steps per observation period. Each step was given the following attributes:

- An identification number
- A class
- A priority
- A memory requirement
- A number of I/O operations
- An assigned initiator

The class assignment was sampled from a probability distribution identical to the observed class frequency distribution. Similarly, the priority, memory requirement, and I/O number were sampled from corresponding class-dependent distributions. Initiators (to be described later) were selected with equal probability from subsets known to be associated with classes from the operations manual.

Modeling the OS Proper

Figure 1.1 displays the decomposition adopted to represent the internal operation of the operating system. In outline, upon arrival, a step appears at the queue of its assigned initiator, which in the real OS is responsible for conducting it through its entire processing in the system. After waiting its turn for the initiator, the step queues up for memory. Having satisfied its memory requirements it shuttles back and forth between the CPU stage and the I/O stage, the number of such cycles being given by its number of I/O operations attribute. However, in the former (CPU), the step may preempt the currently processed step if it has higher priority. When a step leaves the system it frees its assigned initiator and the memory space it had acquired.

Calibratable Parameters

The foregoing description fixes all aspects of the model dynamics except the service times assigned to steps in the CPU and I/O stages. In both cases, and for somewhat different reasons, data were not available to estimate their distributions a priori (in contrast to the memory distribution, for example). Thus, parameters were constructed whose values would have to be estimated in the context of the overall model behavior, i.e., in a process of model calibration (see below).

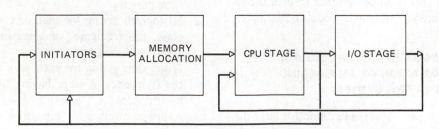

Figure 1.1. An operating system model.

In the case of the CPU stage, the class-dependent average CPU time was available (see above), and this value divided by the number of CPU operations (equal to one more than the number of I/O operations) was assigned as the step processing time. However, while processing a step, the CPU is actually intermittently engaged in many other activities (including the OS housekeeping operations such as memory assignment which the model assumes are somehow carried out!). Thus an overhead parameter (CPOVH) was defined such that the processing time is dilated by a factor $(1 + CPOVH/100)$ to become the CPU service time. Since this factor was not known a priori, it was left for calibration.

In the case of the I/O stage, no reliable data were available on the tape and disk program execution times. It was decided to assign a class-independent constant (EXCPL), as the I/O service time, giving a second parameter for model calibration.

Simulation Language Employed

The model was expressed in the discrete-event simulation language GPSS (General Purpose System Simulator), one of the more widely employed languages of this type. Excellent expositions of the language are available (e.g., Ref. 10; see also the discussion of languages, Section 1.5). To give the flavor of the GPSS implementation, refer to Figure 1.2 which displays an extract of the program, somewhat modified for readability.

In the GPSS implementation, a step is represented by a "transaction" that can be visualized as a control pointer moving sequentially through the statements and causing the indicated executions. Each transaction also has its own memory space, segmented into "parameters" that hold the values of the attributes of the step. As can be seen, GPSS statements are actually high-level macroinstructions for carrying out typical queuing operations among

	GENERATE STEP	generate a new transaction called STEP
	.	
	.	(assignment of parameter values to STEP)
	.	
	SEIZE *INITIATOR	seize the facility referenced by the INITIATOR parameter
CPU	QUEUE CPUQ	register in the queue called CPUQ
	PREEMPT CPU	preempt the facility called CPU according to priority
	DEPART CPUQ	deregister from CPUQ
	ADVANCE CPSERVTIME	wait here for a duration CPSERVTIME to mimic the time spent in CPU service
	RETURN CPU	return the CPU facility to preempted step
	TEST FINISHED, OUT	if finished (no more CPU operations left) go to label OUT
	QUEUE IOQ	register in IOQ
	.	
	.	(implementation of I/O stage)
	.	
	TRANSFER CPU	go to label CPU for next CPU operation
	RELEASE *INITIATOR	free the facility referenced by the
OUT		INITIATOR parameter
	.	
	.	(exit of step from system)
	.	

Figure 1.2. Extract of GPSS program describing OS model.

others. The most distinctive operation, as far as discrete-event simulation is concerned, is the ADVANCE statement. This causes the transaction to be linked into the FUTURE EVENTS CHAIN (FEC). Transactions in the FEC are ordered by increasing "departure times" (the clock time when the transaction was placed in the FEC + a specified advance time). In the appropriate FEC processing phase, the imminent transactions are removed and reactivated. The simulation clock is accordingly advanced to this earliest departure time. Such a scheduling mechanism is typical of so-called next-event languages and is especially efficient when events are sparsely distributed in time (note how gaps of inactivity are skipped; see Section 1.4).

Simulation Experiments

A number of runs of the model were made under different initialization and parametric value assignments. Each run simulated a real duration of 2,000 seconds during which between 250 and 450 steps flowed through the system. The following aspects were considered:

1. *Test for Equilibrium.* Every simulated 100 seconds the accumulated averages of all queue lengths were tested for convergence. When sufficient constancy was attained (this always occurred within the initial 1,000-second interval) the system was considered to be in stochastic equilibrium. After clearing out their accumulated values, statistics gathered during the remainder of the run were taken to represent the true equilibrium values. (For a discussion of the problem of stochastic equilibrium determination, see Refs. 8 and 9.)
2. *Replication of Runs.* Runs were replicated four times under exactly the same conditions except for the initial setting of the seeds of the pseudo random-number generators. Each seeded run under the same conditions represents a realization of the same stochastic process governed by these conditions. (For a discussion of pseudo random-number generators, see Refs. 9 and 1.)
3. *Model Calibration.* The available data from the real OS allowed a computation of CPU utilization over the observation period (fraction of the period in which the CPU was engaged in step processing). In the simulation, a set of experiments was performed in which most of the combinations of a set of levels for EXCPL (ranging from 3 to 400 milliseconds) and for CPOVH (ranging from 0 to 100%) were sampled. (For a discussion of experimental design, see Refs. 8, 11, and 1.) The CPU utilizations of the four runs for each pair of (EXCPL, CPOVH) settings were averaged to provide an estimate of the CPU utilization corresponding to this pair. It was found that only values in a small region of the parameter plane around the point (EXCPL = 400 milliseconds, CPOVH = 50%) could reproduce the observed utilization of .505. Confirmation of the calibration was obtained from the fact that at this setting, the mean number of engaged initiators (5 out of 15) agrees with system operators' experience. (For a discussion of the problem of estimating the statistical confidence in estimates of the mean, see Refs. 9 and 8.)
4. *Use of the Model.* After calibration of the model, a series of runs was made to study the effect of augmenting core memory beyond its then current capacity. A least value of additional memory which relieves memory congestion in the model was found and conveyed to the computing center management as a suggested basis for memory acquisition.
5. *Model Validation.* The project did not allow for further data acquisition or follow-up on the fate of the memory augmentation prediction. Unfortunately, the prematurity of termination is characteristic of many projects. The problems of model validation in the context of limited project planning will be considered further in the sequel.

This concludes our discussion of a case study in computer system modeling and simulation. A basis is now available for a wider exposition of M&S from a software engineering perspective.

1.4. SYSTEMS THEORETIC MODEL REPRESENTATION

A great deal of clarity can be achieved in appreciating the place of M&S and its basic concepts and tools by adopting a systems viewpoint. A fundamental hierarchy of systems descriptions has been identified [12, 13, 3] that organizes such descriptions according to their position along a behavior-to-structure axis. We shall limit this discussion to three main levels: behavioral, state-structured, and composite-structured. Regarding a model as a means of specifying a system at any one of the above levels enables us to understand and organize the diverse formalisms available for system specification.

Levels of System Description

1. *Behavior Level*. At this level one describes a system as if one were viewing it as a black box and recording measurements done on it in their chronological order. For this one needs a "time-base," which is usually a subinterval of the real-number axis (continuous time) or the integers (discrete time). An elementary descriptive unit is a "trajectory," which is a mapping from a subinterval of the time base to some set of values representing possible observation results. Typical trajectories are illustrated in Figure 1.3. A "behavioral" description consists of a set of such trajectories. Such a description may also be called the "behavior" of the system.

2. *State-structure Level*. At this level one describes a system as if one were providing a mechanism for its internal workings. Such a description is sufficient to generate, by iteration over time, a set of trajectories (i.e., a behavior). The basic device that enables such iteration is the "state set," which represents the possible configurations at any time, and the "state transition function," which provides the rule for computing the next state given the current state. The state set is "structured" when it is given as a subset of the cross product of more elementary sets.

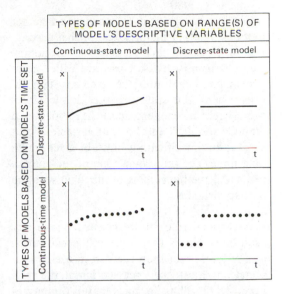

Figure 1.3. Types of models and their trajectories.

Such a state structuring may arise in the following manner: suppose that we wish to provide an iterative procedure (transition function) for generating a set of trajectories. Consider a subset of trajectories over the same time interval, i.e., that represent simultaneous observations. Let us assign to each such concurrent trajectory a variable whose "range set" (set of possible values) is the observation set of the trajectory. One possibility for a state set is the cross product of these range sets. However, such a set of variables may not contain the information required to sufficiently summarize "past behavior" (restriction of the trajectories to the subinterval bounded by the initial time and the current time) for the purpose of uniquely computing the future behavior (remaining portions of the trajectories). A set of variables capable of representing this information is called a set of "state variables" and the cross product of their range sets constitutes a "state space."

Note that a summary of the past sufficient for uniquely computing the future is at the very essence of the state concept. Unfortunately, although most authors recognize the centrality of the state concept in simulation, the foregoing system theoretic basis is usually missed. (For a full exposition of the state concept, see Ref. 3.)

3. *Composite-Structure Level*. At this level one describes a system as if one were specify-

ing how to construct it by connecting together more elementary black boxes. Such a description may also be called a network description. The elementary black boxes are called components, and each must be given a system description at the state-structure level. Moreover, each component must have identified "input variables" and "output variables," and a "coupling specification" must be given which determines the interconnection of the components and the interfacing of the input with the output variables.

A cardinal rule for the construction of any such hierarchy is that given any specification at any level other than the lowest, one can associate at most one specification at the next lower level. Thus, a meaningful composite-structure description will have a unique state-structure description (reflecting the result of the coupling) and a unique behavioral description. In this case, one can speak of one and the same system having a network structure, a state structure, and a behavior.

Indeed, M&S is characterized by the approach in which one postulates a structure (composite or state) and allows the simulation to carry out the generation of its behavior. An alternative approach, called "inductive modeling," starts with observed behavior and tries to induce higher-level structures that will reproduce this behavior. Since the reverse associations of state structure with behavior and composite structure with state structure is not one to one, such level-climbing runs into combinatorial complexity limitations (see Refs. 12 and 14 for inductive modeling and Ref. 13 for a comparison of the two approaches).

Modeling Formalisms

A *modeling formalism* is a set of conventions for specifying a subset of system descriptions. A formalism is more abstract and general than a simulation language, which can be said to provide convenient means for expressing models of a given formalism. Oren [15] has provided a classification of modeling formalisms based upon the type of trajectories produced by models in the formalism class. This

Trajectory of model's descriptive variables			Time set of model	Modelling formalism	Range of variables	
					Cont.	Discr.
COMBINED [CHANGE] MODEL	CONTINUOUS [CHANGE] MODEL		CONTINUOUS-TIME MODEL	Partial Differential Equation		
				Ordinary Differential Equation		
	DISCRETE [CHANGE] MODEL	DISCONTINUOUS [CHANGE] MODEL	DISCRETE-TIME MODEL	Activity Scanning		
				Difference Equation		
				Finite-State Machine		
				Markov Chain		
			CONTINUOUS-TIME MODEL	Discrete Event		
				Process Interaction		

(Attributes within [ ] may be omitted)

Figure 1.4. Classification of model formalisms.

classification is reproduced in Figure 1.4, and its trajectory basis may be understood from Figure 1.3.

It can be seen that the differential equation formalisms underlying classical simulation are distinguished as generating (piecewise) continuous trajectories. Discrete-change models, on the other hand, generate piecewise constant trajectories, the jumps in which are called "events."

Discrete-Change Formalisms. In a discrete-change model described either at the state- or composite-structure level, the information needed to activate events is contained (by definition) within the model state. Indeed, at these levels, an event can be viewed as a state transition. Such a formalism facilitates the specification of the state transition function via the following information:

1. *The Set of External (Exogenous) Event Types.* These are types of events which

are caused externally to the model and to which the model reacts. In the OS model of Section 1.3, this set is the set of steps where each step is a list of values for attributes.

2. *The State Set.* In the OS model, this set is given as a cross product of the ranges of the following variables (partial list):

a. For each INITIATOR

   i. INITIATOR.QUEUE: a list variable holding the set of steps awaiting service

   ii. STATUS: indicating whether the INITIATOR is free or engaged

b. For the MEMORY_HANDLER

   i. FREE.MEMORY: the memory not yet allocated to any steps

   ii. MEMORY.QUEUE: list of steps ordered by priority awaiting memory allocation

   iii. ALLOCATION_TIME_LEFT: time left until next allocation of memory (set to infinity to represent handler not active)

c. For the CPU_STAGE

   i. CPU.QUEUE: list of triples (step, cpu_time_left, i/o_ops_left) with the triple at the head of the list representing the step in process

d. For the I/O_STAGE

   i. IO.QUEUE: list of pairs (step, i/o_ops_left) with the pair at the head of the list representing the step in process

   ii. IO_TIME_LEFT: time left before the step in process will be finished

3. *Time Advance Function.* This gives for each state the time that the model will stay in this state if not interrupted by an external event. In the OS model this is the minimum of the time_left type variable values.

4. *Autonomous Transition Function.* This gives for each state the next state the model should enter if not interrupted by an external event. For example, when the IO_TIME_LEFT is the unique minimum of the time_left values, the next state will be one in which the (step, io_ops_left) pair at the head of the IO.QUEUE is removed and sent to the CPU.QUEUE. When such an event occurs it is called an internal event and is said to have been caused autonomously.

5. *External Transition Function.* This gives for each external event type, and value of elapsed time in this state, the state that the model will be in immediately after the occurrence of an event of that type. For example, when a step arrives at the OS, its main effect is to add itself to the INITIATOR.QUEUE of its assigned INITIATOR.

Note that while the formal description of a model and its program representation are necessarily related, they are distinct objects. This is evident by comparing the above formalization of the OS model (see also Ref. 7) and its GPSS implementation in Figure 1.2. Indeed, this distinction is the starting point for logical methods of simulation program verification [16, 3].

Discrete-Change World Views

Three major approaches to discrete modeling underlie the development of simulation languages for operations research (Section 1.1) [17, 9, 18, 19]. While it was recognized that these approaches represented distinct decomposition methodologies (so-called world views), it was only recently that any attempt was made to set down clearly the underlying formalisms [3]. In Figure 1.4 these formalisms appear under the names "discrete event," "activity scanning," and "process interaction," although other terminology is often used. In particular, discrete event may often refer to the whole class of discrete-change models, in which case next event replaces discrete event as the subclass designation.

While the more general discrete-change formalism is given at the state-structure level, each of the specialized formalisms are meaningful only at the composite-structure level. That is, they specify a system in terms of an interaction of "atoms" such as events, activities, or processes. The following is a brief description (for further discussion see [3]).

Discrete-Event (Next Event) Formalism.   In this formalism, events are explicitly and unconditionally "scheduled." This amounts to a restriction on the general formalism whereby the autonomous transition function is decomposable into "event functions" which must be applied to produce a state transition when the corresponding time_left variable has reached zero. The OS model above is an example of such a formulation. In a simulation language implementation (see below) the event functions are realized by "event routines" and the role of the time_left variable is played by the placement of a corresponding "event notice" on the future events list, of which the FEC of GPSS (Section 1.3) is an example. SIMSCRIPT [20] and GASP [21] are well known languages of this type.

Activity Scanning Formalism.   In contrast to the above, the activity scanning formalism requires that events be implicitly scheduled. Here, the autonomous transition is expressed as a set of functions called "activities", each having an "activation condition" and an "action". Also, the time advance function is restricted to take on either a fixed value (discrete time model), a zero value (time is not advanced), or an infinite value (no further events possible). At every time step, the "condition" segments are scanned (in some fixed order) and the first condition found to be true causes the immediate execution of its associated "action" segment. This scanning, testing, and execution continues until there are no conditions which are true of the resulting state. Then (and only then) is the model advanced to the next time step.

In a more general formulation, the time advance function is unrestricted as in the event formalism. In this case, one can think of activities persisting in time. Thus, an activity is "activated" when its activation condition becomes true, and the duration of this "activation" is schedulable as part of the action performed by

the activity. ECSL [17] is an activity-based language widely employed in the U.K.

Process Interaction Formalism.   This formalism can be looked upon as a combination and refinement of the above formalisms. A "process" is a set of activities which are mutually exclusive (at most one may be activated at any time) and connected in the sense that the termination of one activity enables the initiation of another in the set. Common forms of processes are linear sequences (single initial, single successor, and single terminal activity) and simple cycles (single successor activity). Processes "interact" both explicitly, as in the event formalism and implicitly, as in the activity formalism. SIMULA [22, 23] and GPSS (regarding each transaction as executing a process as it traverses the program) are widely employed process interaction languages.

Controversies Over World Views

Formalisms express a certain "world view," that is, a way of decomposing real systems. Historically, the isolated development of discrete simulation languages in England and the United States led to the local predominance of a particular approach, the activity view in the former and the event view in the latter. There also arose strong controversies about the merits of each view in terms of user psychology and machine efficiency. While recent integrative developments have somewhat outdated the either/or positions of the older proponents (see below), the issues of suitable model formalism still remain (for a statement of the issues and a spirited defense of the activities view see Ref. 24; also see Refs. 25, 26, 27 for balance).

1.5. SIMULATION SOFTWARE TOOLS

Having the basics of modeling theory and formalisms, we are in a position to survey the software tools currently available to facilitate the construction and analysis of simulation models. Our survey will first sweep across the horizon at large. After this we shall return to emphasize certain tools of immediate interest within a software engineering perspective.

Languages, Packages, Systems—A Taxonomy

It will help to attempt a preliminary classification of the support facilities currently provided by simulation software. We can distinguish facilities for:

1. Linguistic operations: provision of (a) syntax and semantics for model description/program specification, (b) error detection, and (c) translation (compilation) of programs in executable form
2. Simulation execution and its control: initialization of execution, termination, and rerunning of simulation experiments under user-specified control with user-specified data
3. Analysis and display of data: provision of functions for statistical analysis, optimization, graphical curve plotting, and so forth
4. Storage and retrieval of models, programs, data: provision of files, data bases, libraries, and the like accessible from within the simulation software rather than at the host operating-systems level.

On the basis of this classification, we can begin to delineate the facilities encompassed by the following software terms:

Simulation Languages. By definition, provide type 1 facilities (linguistic operations), usually provide a modicum of type 2 (execution control) and type 3 (analysis/display) facilities as well.

Simulation Packages. Provide routines for subsets of types 2, 3, and more recently 4, usually providing extensive support in some restricted domain.

Simulation Systems. Provide for integrated access to, and use of, facilities of types 1, 2, 3, and 4.

This taxonomy helps to set into focus the evolution of state-of-the-art simulation software toward comprehensive and integrated support of the full range of M&S activities outlined in Section 1.2. We shall now enumerate some trends that give evidence of this evolution and shall return to discuss the implied next-generation software systems in a later section. The trends are to be categorized roughly as being most associated with languages, packages or systems.

Simulation Languages.

Trend toward Independence of Model Specification from Procedural and Machine-Required Specifications. In the discrete-change domain, the evolution from machine language to FORTRAN to GASP to GPSS, SIMPS-CRIPT, and SIMULA (via ALGOL) manifests successive degrees of removal from machine-level considerations to higher-level model-oriented constructs. A parallel evolution occurred in the family of continuous system simulation languages standardized by the CSSL definition [28, 29]. CSMP, CSSL3, ASCL, and so on, contain functional constructs attempting to shield the user from many of the computational decisions involved in numerical integration. The principle that model description should be invariant with respect to hosting hardware underlies hybrid compiler design, as in HL1 [30] where ideally a model specification should be translatable into equivalent analog, digital, or hybrid programs. Much remains in the way of separating model description from program writing. The most explicit moves in this direction are probably represented by such languages as CAPS and DRAFT, which generate simulation programs from user input that is structured by questionnaires (see Ref. 17 for a review).

Trend toward Inclusion and Separation of Functional Elements in Simulation Programming. As hinted above, contemporary simulation languages are actually simulation packages in disguise. That is, they provide features going beyond the linguistic prescription of model structure. Programs tend to be jumbled mixtures of model description statements and commands for carrying out operations of types 2 (execution control) and 3 (analysis/display) [5]. The CSSL definition provides at least some segmentation (into INITIAL, DYNAMIC, and TERMINAL) but much more is possible [31, 5].

Trend toward Flexibility in Modeling Formalism. What were once thought to be noncommunicating formalisms expressing incompatible "world views"—"continuous" versus "discrete event," and within the latter, "event" versus "activity" versus "network"—are being brought together even in standard languages such as SIMSCRIPT, GASP, and SIMULA. Oren [32] surveys combined simulation software, and Nance [27] has critiqued the blurring of conceptual boundaries.

Simulation Packages.

Trend toward Extensive Support of Simulation-Related Activities. We mention the following examples:

Model Manipulation. DYMOLA [33] is a preprocessor that operates on model equations to impose an input/output orientation specified by the user or the environment. FORSIM [34] enables the user to conveniently convert a model specified as a set of partial differential equations into a system of ordinary differential equations and then to simulate this system. Formula manipulation tools such as FORMAC can be used, for example, to operate symbolically on a system of differential equations to produce the associated sensitivity derivative system. Via graphical means one can define and manipulate signal flow graphs (a restricted but important class of [linear] model descriptions) [35]. As yet these are the first instances of support in this potentially extensive model manipulation category.

Execution Control. Packages like WISSIM [36] enable the user to conveniently specify the initialization, execution, and termination

of FORTRAN programs employing commands similar to those contained in CSMP. APT [37] provides more extensive control for policy testing.

Statistical Processing. Packages like SAS, SPCS [38], and AUTOGRP [39] enable the user to invoke statistical operations on data, to compute statistics, correlations, confidence levels, and so forth.

Graphical Display. Packages such as SIMPAK [40] provide convenient display of simulated (real variable) trajectories, while "moving pictures" of model states can be produced by a SIMULA external class [41] (see also Section 1.6).

Optimization. Linear programming packages [42] provide tools for convenient description and solution of LP problems. Libraries such as ISML and NAG contain various direct-search routines. A more integrated package of such routines is available for CSSL-based languages [43].

Storage and Retrieval. Apparently the first general data base specifically designed for simulation output is SDL/1 [44]. Libraries of models in particular domains such as agricultural [45] and transportation models [46] are developing.

Trend toward Interfacing of Activities. Packages such as DYNASTAT [47] interface linguistic operations of simulation languages with capabilities for statistical processing and optimization. SDL/1 was designed from the start to be callable within SLAM, thus linking simulation directly to data storage and retrieval. Cellular space simulation packages [5] provide model specification, execution control, and graphical display capabilities.

Trend toward Increased Interactivity. Support of interaction between man and machine becomes crucial for packages providing a range of tools for selection. Most of the packages and languages mentioned above are interactive or possess recently completed interactive versions.

Simulation Systems.

Trend toward Integration and Comprehensiveness. As indicated previously, we distinguish systems from packages by the degree to which they provide a comprehensive and integrated set of facilities. Such systems are still comparatively rare but there have already been some significant developments. SCENARIO [48] provides an interactive setting in which models of airplanes, control systems, sensors, and so forth, resident in the Avionic Simulation Laboratory of USAF can be interfaced and simulated, then displayed and analyzed. An engineer may employ models at various levels of refinement of components, depending on his questions or interest.

Econometric modeling is an area where software systems have developed [49, 50], providing tools for data management, model construction, filing of models, simulation and parameter estimation. MBS [51] (model bank system) is a more ambitious enterprise noteworthy for its facilities for linking socio-economic models developed under various methodologies, such as systems dynamics (DYNAMO) and econometric approaches.

Trend toward Incorporation into Larger Contexts. Modeling and simulation activities are being incorporated into larger computer-based systems such as management information systems, corporate planning systems, and financial planning systems [52, 53].

1.6. THE SIMULATION MODELING/ SOFTWARE ENGINEERING INTERFACE

Progress in M&S methodology has much in common with developments in the areas of software engineering and in data base/information systems design.

On the one hand simulation programs and tools constitute a class of software (with some quite distinctive characteristics) and should therefore benefit from the concepts and tools being developed in structured programming (e.g., top-down design [54]), data structuring (e.g., abstract data types [55]), and data base management system design (e.g., data model concepts [56]).

On the other hand, modeling and simulation methodology is playing an increasingly important role in software and data base design methodologies. Indeed there is an intimate interreliance of design and modeling methodologies on each other, and their activities are also partially analogous (with some essential differences; see editor's introduction to Ref. 67). It is not surprising then that computer-based software design systems [57, 58, 59] resemble the simulation support systems that have been proposed in architectural philosophy, if not in facilities provided. Likewise data models developed in the data base field resemble the schemes for data representation provided by simulation languages (indeed, a data base management system built upon SIMSCRIPT principles is nearing completion [Markowitz, personal communication 1981].

As developments proceed in these areas, points of commonality can be shared to mutual advantage [60, 16, 61, 62].

M&S Issues and Tools in Software Engineering

We shall now consider some of the general issues and tools reviewed above within the specific context of software engineering applications.

Modeling of computer systems (as indeed, of any man-made system) can take place throughout the design process. For simplicity, let us just consider the categories "modeling during design" and "modeling after construction." The objectives in modeling may be quite varied, but again let us use the simple categorization "logical" and "performance." In the former we refer to modeling done primarily to test the correctness of a system relative to its required behavior (does it work as it should?). In the latter we refer to modeling done primarily to assess extra-logical aspects of a system, for instance, efficiency, cost, reliability, and so forth. This taxonomy generates the following matrix:

	DURING DESIGN	AFTER CONSTRUCTION
Logical	1	2
Performance	3	4

Most effort in the literature has been concentrated in areas 1 and 4. Recently it has been suggested that improved and more economical designs might be obtained if performance as well as logical correctness could be predicted well before actual construction. Thus there is increasing interest in area 3. The use of simulation models in testing the behavior of a functioning system (area 2) is an intriguing possibility that does not seem to have been taken up yet in the literature (although there is a resemblance to fault-detection approaches). Let us then consider the modeling of computer systems within the foregoing framework.

System Boundaries. A computer system is naturally decomposable into subsystems involving hardware, software, and an external data environment. Each of these is further decomposable as illustrated in Figure 1.5. System boundaries refer to the subsystem toward which the modeling effort is oriented. All influence of the computer system outside the boundaries must be represented by suitable input to the model. For example, the operating system model previously addressed excludes all processing of batch jobs before being placed in the job queue. Thus the arrival process used as input to the model represents the characteristics of the data environment as seen by the OS (and not as seen by the overall computer system). In general, the volume and frequency of arrival of the incoming data, i.e., the workload, constitutes the key source of input variables for performance models [63].

In the literature, system boundaries have

```
1 : ENTITY COMPUTER SYSTEM
  2 : ASPECT STRUCTURAL.DECOMPOSITION
   3 : ENTITY HARDWARE
    4 : ASPECT HARDWARE _ DECOMPOSITION
     5 : ENTITY CENTRAL _PROCESSORS
     5 : ENTITY CENTRAL MEMORY
     5 : ENTITY MASS _ STORAGE
      6 : ASPECT STORAGE _ DECOMPOSITION
       7 : ENTITY DISCS
       7 : ENTITY TAPES
       7 : ENTITY DRUMS
     5 : ENTITY I/O _ PROCESSORS
     5 : ENTITY I/O CHANNELS
     5 : ENTITY UNIT _ RECORD _ DEVICES
      6 : ASPECT U _ R _ D _ TYPES
       7 : ENTITY LINE _ PRINTERS
       7 : ENTITY CARD _ READERS/PUNCHERS
     5 : ENTITY COMMUNICATIONS _ DEVICES
   3 : ENTITY SOFTWARE
    4 : ASPECT SOFTWARE _ DECOMPOSITION
     5 : ENTITY SYSTEMS _ SOFTWARE
      6 : ASPECT S _ S _ DECOMPOSITION
       7 : ENTITY OPERATING _ SYSTEM
       7 : ENTITY DATA _ BASE SYSTEM
     5 : ENTITY APPLICATIONS _ SOFTWARE
 * 3 : ENTITY EXTERNAL _ DATA _ ENVIRONMENT
    4 : ASPECT ENVIRONMENTAL _ DECOMPOSITION
     5 : ENTITY TERMINAL _ ORIGINATING _ COMMANDS/DATA
     5 : ENTITY BATCH _ JOB _ STREAM
     5 : ENTITY PROCESS _ CONTROL _ MEASUREMENTS
```

Figure 1.5. Standard decomposition of a computer system.

been set all the way from that of the distributed computer network to the single-device level. (For a recent sampling of modeled subsystems, primarily for performance evaluation, see Ref. 64).

Level of Detail/Decomposition/Aggregation. Having chosen a system boundary, there yet remains a panorama of choices as to the detail that should be included in the model. The level of detail is manifested in the depth to which a subsystem is decomposed and the variables used to describe its state. The deeper the decomposition, the more variables are available for description; that is, the more detailed is this description. Thus when a decomposition process is halted, one can think of the variables available as representing "aggregations," that is, summaries, of the variables which would have been available had the decomposition been continued to a greater depth.

Choice of level of detail is an issue no matter which subsystem is involved. In hardware for example, a disk subsystem may be represented as an undifferentiated unit with a certain data-rate bandwidth, or it may be decomposed into a sequence of three components: an I/O channel with a certain data-rate bandwidth, a disk moving arm with a certain access time, and a disk platter with a certain rotational latency. In software, the strategy for virtual memory management may be accounted for only in the CPU overhead (as in the OS model), or it may be represented by a conditional sequence of operations for page faulting, task switching, and memory management. Finally, the environmental workload may be characterized by a set of numbers indicating average arrival rates of transactions and their work demands, or by a stochastic process (as in the OS model), or by an actual trace history of incoming transactions measured during some previous period [65].

Level of Abstraction. The issue of level of aggregation should be carefully distinguished from the notion of level of abstraction as commonly employed in the design context. Both notions are tied to the more fundamental notion of system decomposition mentioned above.

However in the case of abstraction the author is usually referring to the fact that the component in question is being described at the behavioral level (or perhaps state-structure level) rather than at the level of composite structure, which would be possible if it were decomposed. Such a distinction will become increasingly important as efforts are made to link both performance and logical modeling to the design process (see below).

Computer System Modeling Methodology. The choice of system boundaries, decomposition, and aggregation level is a universal problem of modeling and indeed has been recognized as a prime problem in computer system modeling [66]. An approach to modeling for performance evaluation has been suggested [65] that employs three kinds of component descriptions: workload characteristics, process descriptions, and system resource descriptions. From this point of view, a computer system is a set of processes that cooperate with each other to process data and compete with each other for resources.

The kinds of considerations that arise in choosing descriptions for workload, processes, and resources are outlined in Figure 1.6. In each case, the level of aggregation, as discussed above is a crucial choice. A heuristic guideline, which has its justification in modeling theory [67], is that the level of aggregation should be governed by the questions being addressed by the model. Thus one component should not be more detailed than another merely because the details of its operation are available in greater extent to the modeler. Indeed, it is the natural tendency to provide greater disaggregation to the description of a well-understood component, even if this component turns out to play a minor role in those aspects of the system operation related to one's questions of interest.

The "bottleneck technique" is an antidote to this tendency. In this approach one first formulates all process descriptions at the "load" level rather than the "instruction" level. Simulation of the model then is done to reveal the location of the "bottlenecks;" that is, parts of the system where contention for resources is so

Workload Descriptions
—Describes external data environment
—Can be trace-driven or modeled by stochastic arrival pattern
—Normal and stress conditions are important

Process Descriptions
—Pattern of resource utilization and interprocess interactions
—Instruction versus load level of modeling
—Bottleneck technique

Resource Descriptions
—Physical versus logical level of resource model
—Accuracy of representation or resource allocation policy
—Treatment of overhead due to allocation policy execution

Figure 1.6. Aggregation-level choices in computer system modeling.

intense that throughput of processing is greatly impaired. This begins an iterative procedure in which the bottleneck components are represented in greater detail until no changes in throughput at these locations are observed. The same approach can be applied in principle to any performance measure whose values have an associated importance. For instance, it is more important to faithfully model points of high contention than those of low contention because of their strong effect on overall throughput.

Measurement Tools. Key factors in the progress of modeling effort are the availability and quality of real system data. Thus modeling is a prime motivator for the design of measuring instruments (one rarely knows what to measure before a model cries out in need for specific data). The software literature is still sparse on this subject but the following summary can be given [68]:

Hardware monitors, electronic probes attached to the computer, can measure any variable reducible to its electromagnetic state. For example, CPU or I/O channel status (busy/free) or number of operations performed can be detected. However, such probes are necessarily blind to software-level attributes.

Software monitors are data collection programs, the most prevalent of which are for accounting purposes. Such accounting monitors, however, do not necessarily provide the kind and detail of data required for modeling. As a result, system-oriented monitors have been designed that record the usage of various hardware and software resources, often giving operating-system-related data such as paging rates or multiprogramming levels as well. Such data may be sampled periodically, or may be recorded only in certain conditions of the system under the control of the operating system.

As in all measurement, there is an overhead cost in monitoring and a possibility of significant interference (the measured system may not represent what the free system was like).

Queuing-Based Performance Models

Queuing network models have become a major source of computer system models largely for studies of performance after construction. With rare exceptions, the literature tends to diverge into two forms of such models: analytical and simulation. Perhaps the only real distinction between the two is in the intent of the modeler—in the first case to solve the model analytically (i.e., with paper and pencil) or in the second, to analyze it via simulation experimentation. The OS model is an example of a relatively simple simulation model. Actually, even this distinction is becoming more subtle since with attempts to extend the range of application of analytic models, these models have required computerized numerical solution. Kleinrock [69, 70] has given an extensive treatment to queuing systems in general, and an excellent survey of applications to computer systems is available [68]. A slightly modified classification scheme based on the latter work will now be given in order to convey an idea of the models that have come under the analytical domain (Table 1.1).

Analytic models are usually analyzed for their equilibrium behavior. Such performance measures as server utilizations, customer throughput, mean queue lengths, and mean waiting times are of interest. A basic solution technique is to seek product form solutions, that is, to express the probability of a network state as a product of the probabilities of the states of each of the queues. However, since the class of models amenable to such a solution

Table 1.1. Analytical Queueing Model Classification Scheme.

Arrival Process:
  Open (external arrivals and departures)
    Exponential interarrival time distribution (Poisson process)
    General interarrival time distribution
  Closed (initial customers recycled, no new arrivals)
  Mixed

Network Structure:

  Single server
    Without feedback
    With feedback
  Central server (customers always return to designated server)
  General network (customers arbitrarily routed among servers)
  Hierarchical (single center is represented by a network at a deeper level of decomposition)

Workload Class:
  Single class of customers
  Multiple classes of customers (no class changes)
  Multiple classes with possibility for customer to change class

Service Demand:
  Workload vector (giving mean total service required by customer of each class at each service center)
  Routing matrix ($p(c, i, j)$) = the probability that customer of class c when finished at service center i will next
            visit service center j.
  Service distribution
        exponential
        hypoexponential
        general

Queuing Discipline:
  Class-independent work-conserving first-in-first-out (FIFO)
  Station balance
        preemptive last-in-first-out (LIFO)
        processor sharing
        no-queuing
        strict priority (based on customer class)

Server Characteristic:
  Load-independent server
  Load-dependent server

is quite restrictive, much effort has been expended in obtaining good approximate solutions to more general networks. Despite this mathematical effort, Kienzle and Sevcik [68] report that each of the more than 20 case studies that they surveyed were based primarily on models with product form solutions.

Now let us consider some of the relative merits of analytical and simulation models:

1. *Expressive power.* As indicated in Section 1.1, the capacity of simulation models to capture the workings of real systems is virtually unlimited. On the other hand, tractable analytic models are subject to severe constraints including:

a. Inability to handle simultaneous contention for more than one resource; that is, a job can not engage two or more servers at the same time (e.g., an initiator, a memory handler, and a CPU as in the OS model)

b. Inability to treat correlated sets of jobs, which occurs for example when a job is split into several concurrent steps that converge upon completion

c. Inability to model blocking of jobs because of finite resource capacities and finite queue sizes

d. All of the above are manifestations of the more general inability to handle global-state conditioned waiting as in the activities formalism

2. *Computational complexity.* Even if not hand solvable, some of the analytic solution methods are computationally very efficient. This is especially true of yet more simplified models satisfying the conditions of local balance [71] and operational analysis [72]. Simulation is by its nature a more brute-force operation although much can be done to achieve acceptable time and cost within the constraints of the basic paradigm.

3. *Quantity and quality of output.* As indicated, analytical models are solvable for the most part for equilibrium properties and even in this case may yield only a restricted set of indicators. To the extent that free parameters are retained in the solution, however, an understanding may be gained of the effect of a parameter across its full range.

On the other hand, a simulation experiment provides but a single realization of a process, and so samples only a point in some parameter space. However, each such experiment may produce readings for an unlimited set of indicators both for transient as well as equilibrium behavior. Indeed, it is commonly assumed that equilibrium behavior is most representative of real system operation (see, e.g., Ref 1). This assumption has been strongly questioned by Kleijnen [11], who argues that many questions of interest concern specific time intervals (e.g., rush hour or peak load periods) or intervals that terminate upon occurrence of a specific event (e.g., the failure of a piece of equipment). In such cases, the problems of eliminating start-up and end-effect biasing in simulation runs is obviated since these are part of the behavior of interest.

4. *Ease of construction, verification, and calibration.* Due to their relative simplicity, analytic models are readily designed and implemented (this is more true of models taking on standard forms than of innovative ones). Moreover, because of their relatively small number of parameters, their calibration data requirements are relatively easy to meet. Simulation models, on the other hand, are usually tuned closely to specific system details and therefore require significant effort to construct and implement. Moreover, as for all software, simulation programs have to be verified with respect to the abstract model being implemented. Finally, since they may have many free parameters, the so-called parameter identification problem may be nontrivial. This problem may involve a nonlinear optimization search over a large space and may result in a multiplicity of optimal points (in contrast to the case for the OS model). While the literature in computer system modeling is sparse on this subject, it has been of intense interest in natural systems modeling (see Part IV of [3]).

5. *Model credibility.* While simplicity affords to analytic models advantages in computation and in calibration, it also brings with it potential hazards as well. Credibility, an all important but subjective factor, may be difficult to achieve for what may appear to be an oversimplified representation of real complexity. And indeed while easily tunable to sparse data, a model may fail to capture the underlying structure of the real system so that it is worthless for prediction of the effects of fundamental design modification. (For an experimental investigation of the success of analytical models in predicting performance of modified computer systems, see Ref. 73). Of course, the same problems apply to simulation models. In the case of an existing system whose operation is well understood, however, one may be quite confident in the credibility of a detailed model. This leads us to a brief general discussion of model validation.

Simulation Model Validation

The general subject of model validity is a difficult one. There exists a hierarchy of levels of validity that corresponds to that of the level of system descriptions. In increasing order of strength and difficulty of achievement, a model may be valid at the behavioral level (i.e., is able to reproduce the observed behavior of the real system), at the state-structure level (i.e., is able to be synchronized with the real system into a state from which unique prediction of future behavior is possible), or at the composite-structure level (i.e., can be shown to uniquely represent the internal workings of the real system). Moreover, validity should always be considered relative to an "experimental frame" formalizing one's objectives.

Sargent [74] has reviewed the various approaches that have been taken to model "validation," the ascertaining of the degree to which a model is accepted as valid. Basically, all such validation must be reducible to a comparison of model and real system behavior. For such a comparison a metric (distance measure) must be chosen that (inevitably) reflects a certain weighting of features of the behavior. A second choice must be made if the real system data is believed to be stochastically generated (for example, noisy) and/or if the model is taken to represent a stochastic process (i.e., has random number generators). In this case, statistical tests must be chosen in order to assess the probability that the degree of agreement (or disagreement) found between the model and the real system with the finite data available is truly representative of the stochastic processes from which the data was sampled. Such tests are described in References 9, 8, and 1 and applications to computer system simulation are discussed in References 75 and 76.

It may happen that the use of statistical tests in certain situations is questionable, for example where variability in the data is extreme [77]. Greig [78] demonstrates that the choice of significance level in standard statistical tests is itself problematic and should be linked to the relative cost of accepting an invalid model versus the cost of rejecting a valid one—the greater this ratio, the stricter the test should be. It would seem that on this decision theoretic basis, the standard significance levels (.05) are not strict enough (should be 0.5 for example). In any event, confidence in model validity should not be based on positive test results alone.

A variety of more "subjective" tests of validity apply judgment, intuition, and experience in one form or another. In order to bypass the ego investment of the modeler, a panel of outside "experts" may be called in [79]. A particularly intriguing form of such evaluation is the Turing test (originally suggested by Turing for testing machine intelligence). Here, "experts" are randomly presented with samples of real and simulated data to see if they can distinguish the two sources. In this case, the experts should, and need only, be persons directly familiar with the operation of a system (e.g., users of a computer system) but not its mechanics. Of course, the data must be presented in a form which is familiar and is within the persons' scope of experience.

While intrinsically unsolvable when restricted to a single model in a limited time frame, the validation problem may be more tractable when viewed within the context of a family of models being developed over an extended time. In this case, validity becomes the internal consistency of the models with each other as well as the external consistency of each with its real subsystem counterpart. A more stable basis for model construction and validation results [80, 81].

Simulation Modeling During Design

As suggested above increasing interest is being shown in supporting simulation modeling during design both in performance as well as logic evaluation. We shall now briefly review some of the software being developed along these lines.

Queuing Network Software. Software packages for queuing network analysis are reviewed in Reference 82 and were found to be of limited capability in facilitating rapid setup and flexible scanning of a wide range of design alternatives. The goals the authors stress for such software are:

1. To provide a selection of solution methods, both analytical and simulation
2. In the case of simulation, to provide facilities for confidence interval estimation and equilibrium detection
3. In the case of analytic methods, to provide only those producing exact results

when applicable, and to enable the user to introduce approximation methods at his own risk (thereby safeguarding the credibility of the package)

4. To provide a comfortable user interface for model definition
5. To provide a general (relative to queuing networks) and powerful set of primitives, compatible with the given solution methods
6. To support hierarchal modeling [83] and model reuse

RESQ (Research Queuing Package) is being developed to meet these goals [82], which indeed are compatible with those of the proposals for comprehensive and integrated simulation systems.

Computer System Modeling Languages. Special purpose simulation systems are being developed for hardware modeling and system software development. As in all such special purpose designs, there are basically two approaches: (a) start from scratch or (b) specialize a general purpose simulation system. The queuing network software reviewed above provides examples of the start-from-scratch approach. On the other hand, development of a special purpose system may be greatly accelerated if one can exploit existing facilities of a general purpose system. The general purpose simulation language SIMULA has proven to be very attractive from this point of view. As indicated previously, SIMULA supports the process interaction world view of discrete-change simulation. However, its most important, and highly influential, contribution to programming languages in general is its "class concept." A SIMULA class is a specification of static and dynamic attributes (i.e., local variables, procedures, and functions) that can generate any number of independent instances, called objects of the class, upon demand. Moreover, one can specialize a class by declaring that a package of static and dynamic attributes is to be added to it. The result is a new class, called a subclass of the first. Such specialization can be repeated indefinitely. Thus the core of SIMULA, together with a hi-

erarchy of specifically designed classes, constitutes a special purpose language.

One example of such an approach is the OASIS (Operating System Implementation and Simulation) language [84]. It provides a set of SIMULA classes for writing and simulating the operation of small operating systems at the device management and higher levels. For example, MODULE and PROCESSOR are classes that represent programs and processors, respectively. MODULE is a specialization of the SIMULA core class LINK, so that its objects may be linked into various chains. PROCESSOR is a specialization of core class PROCESS so that its objects are processes. In addition to having the dynamic attributes of PROCESS objects (e.g., procedures for activation and deactivation), PROCESSOR objects have specialized attributes for association with MODULE objects (to represent execution of particular programs on particular processors). A user may further specialize these classes to construct his own model. In this way, alternative architectures of both hardware and system software can be modeled and evaluated for both logical and performance properties.

Design Oriented Modeling Systems. A computer system modeling language, while convenient for design evaluation, still leaves the burden of the design itself entirely to the user. Support systems are under development with the object of assisting in the iterative design process, and in which modeling plays an integral role. The modeling languages of such systems attempt to provide constructs that are abstract in nature but that may be successively elaborated until the code level is reached. Such high-level model constructs contrast with those embodied in Petri net and like formalisms [85], which provide for detailed, single- (low) level description. The SIMULA class concept (sans SIMULA) has been adopted in the form of structural template definitional facilities in such design languages as TOPD (Tools for Program Development) [86] and DDN (DREAM Design Notation) [87].

Sanguinetti [88] discusses the considerations involved in providing simulation analysis of model descriptions at the high levels of abstraction characteristic of early design phases. At the lower levels characteristic of the end phase, one may wish to integrate existing hardware or software into the model, for example, replacing stochastically predicted scheduling of a computation completion by its actual completion time. AIMER (Automatic Integration of Multiple Element Radars) [89] has apparently achieved such an integration of conventional simulation with microprocessor emulation by employing a future events executive based on that of GPSS.

1.7. M&S METHODOLOGY-BASED SUPPORT SYSTEMS

Our review of state-of-the-art simulation software has suggested that there is an evolution toward systems that attempt to provide sets of tools for comprehensive and integrated assistance in carrying out the activities involved in M&S. Such support systems are especially desirable in ongoing, large-scale, multifaceted system studies, of which computer systems are examples. Concurrent with this natural evolution has been an increasing impact of research into the methodology of M&S on the design of such support systems. After briefly discussing this research we shall outline current proposals for advanced M&S support systems.

Research into M&S Methodology

Methodological research is a critical, theoretical, or conceptual examination of the modeling and simulation process viewed as an ongoing, purposeful, cumulative, and integrated set of activities.

The methodologist seeks to structure the modeling process—to decompose it into component activities, their interrelations, and the objects manipulated by these activities. His goal is to improve the manner in which the modeling process is carried out and hence indirectly, to improve its products—the models. To do this he seeks to bring about a more optimal division of labor between man and machine and enhance the performance of both. Wherever the modeling process is ill-struc-

tured and error prone, he seeks to develop new concepts, theories and paradigms. These new approaches, even if more effective in the long run, may be unfamiliar and difficult to execute without aid. Thus new computer-based tools must be developed to support the advocated methodologies.

Thus, in the end, methodological research should propose new architectures—software and hardware—for improved man-machine symbiosis. The human must be the ultimate decision maker in this interaction. But the machine must stand ready to suggest possible courses of action and to carry out those component activities of the process that it can best perform.

We have discussed many of the issues confronting the M&S methodologist. A collection of central works in the area is available in Reference 67. We shall now outline the kinds of architectures being developed for M&S support systems, which are inspired by methodologically based concepts and theory.

Architectures for M&S Support Systems

An architectural framework [6] has users interacting with the computer system through interfaces that enable them to initiate or engage in activities. The sequencing of activities may be partly fixed and partly open to users' control. An activity is executed by one or more processors (in conjunction with the user) and acts upon one or more data bases (where the "data" may be of various kinds to be described). In executing an activity, information is stored in the bases. The information so generated is accessible to the user through the interfaces.

Model and Experimental Frame Bases. As illustrated in Figure 1.7, one may view the modeling process as being initiated by the incidence of "objectives" and terminating in the construction of models to meet these objectives. If we think of the modelling process as part of the overall process of decision making, then the objectives derive from requests by decision makers for models with which to assess the efficacy of proposed policies. ("Decision

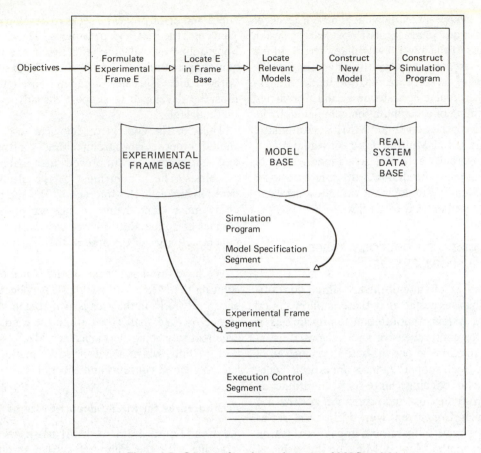

Figure 1.7. Concepts for advanced support of M&S activities.

maker" and "policy" are intended here in a broad sense to include engineer, designer, manager, etc., and implementation, design, tactic, strategy, etc., respectively.) Such objectives are supposed to be formulated as a series of questions regarding a real system or its components and ultimately to be formulated as "experimental frames." An experimental frame is a specification of the kind of data a model should produce in order to answer the questions of interest. The concept, however, must be meaningful both for the real system as well as for model experimentation since, in principle, the same data could be obtained from the real system (although there are many reasons why models are preferred in practice).

It should be noted that the experimental frame is a key concept in model assessment since model validity is properly formulated as a relation involving a model, a real system, and a frame in which the behavioral data of the

two are compared. For definitions and applications of the experimental frame concept see References 3, 80, 81, 90.

In the scheme of Oren and Zeigler [5], the M&S support system should maintain a base of previously defined experimental frames and help to locate a new frame among them. A model base of previously developed models should also be maintained that should be referenceable from the frames base. That is, knowing which resident frames are similar to the new frame should provide an entree to the existing models which are relevant to it. Such models, after adaptation and simplification, should serve as components to be interfaced to form a model to which the new frame is applicable.

Hierarchical System Structure Organizer. At the center of the organization of models and frames should be a hierarchical structure of system decompositions. A node in this structure represents a component of one or more decompositions and points to the models and frames that concern the real subsystem associated with this component. An interactive tool for defining and manipulating such structures has been developed [91]. Figure 1.5 presents an example of such a structure.

Model-Oriented Language Interface. In such a modeling support system, a simulation language may be regarded as interface through which the user directs the writing of simulation programs. The suggested structure of a simulation program, as illustrated in Figure 1.7, comprises model specification experimental frame and execution control segments. The GEST78 simulation language [31, 32] is being designed to reflect these fundamental distinctions in a simulation program's tasks. Ultimately, the model specification and experimental frame segments should originate from their respective bases.

Other languages that should be compatible with the interface role are PROSIM78 [92] and COSY [93]. It is characteristic of all three that they are model oriented (i.e., support the model specification/execution control distinction) and truly general purpose in the sense of providing constructs for combining discrete event and continuous formalisms.

Integration of Data Management and Simulation. The design of SDL/1 [44] is aimed at integrating a conventional data base management system with a state-of-the-art simulation software system. The relational data base can be defined to hold both simulation-generated data as well as real-system data. Simulation programs can store and retrieve data on line by invoking FORTRAN subprograms; statistics and plots can be produced and operations invoked for statistical analyses and validation purposes. The integrated data base/simulation/statistical software system is thus open to a variety of users including decision makers, statisticians, and simulation modelers whose activities may be mutually synergistic.

Space precludes all but the mention of the systems-theory-based proposals of Dekker [94] and Klir [34, 12].

1.8. PROSPECTS FOR THE FUTURE

It should be clear that there is, indeed, a significant interface between the simulation modeling and software engineering fields of activity. The software engineer would expect to see increasing use of M&S tools and concepts throughout all phases of the design process both for logical and performance evaluation objectives. Conversely, the development of systems for supporting the on-going modeling and simulation of large-scale, multifacetted systems will tax state-of-the-art software engineering methodology.

REFERENCES

1. R. E. Shannon, *System Simulation: The Art and Science,* Prentice Hall, New Jersey, 1975.
2. A. A. Pritsker, "Compilation of Definitions of Simulation," *Simulation 33* (August 2, 1979).
3. B. P. Zeigler, *Theory of Modelling and Simulation,* Wiley, New York, 1976.
4. T. I. Oren, "Computer-Aided Modelling Systems," in *Proceedings of Simulation,* Interlaken, Switzerland, 1980.
5. T. I. Oren and B. P. Zeigler, "Concepts for Advanced Simulation Methodologies," *Simulation 32*(3) (1979).
6. B. P. Zeigler, "Concepts and Software for Advanced Simulation Methodologies," *Proceedings/Winter Simulation Conference,* Orlando, Fla., 1980.
7. D. Evenczyk and B. P. Zeigler, "Formalization and Confirmation of the Boyd-Epley Operating System Model," *Comp. & Maths. with Appl. 3* (1977).
8. J. P. C. Kleijnen, *Statistical Techniques in Simulation,* Marcel Dekker, New York, 1974–75.
9. G. S. Fishman, *Concepts and Methods in Discrete Event Simulation,* Wiley, New York, 1973.
10. T. J. Schriber, *Simulation Using GPSS,* Wiley, New York, 1974.
11. J. P. C. Kleijnen, "The Role of Statistical Methodology in Simulation," in Zeigler et al., *Methodology in Systems Modelling and Simulation,* North Holland Publishing Company, Amsterdam, 1979.
12. G. J. Klir, "General Systems Problem Solving Methodology," in ibid.
13. B. P. Zeigler, "A Conceptual Basis for Modelling and Simulation," *International Journal General Systems 1* (1974).
14. H. J. J. Uyttenhove, *Computer-Aided Systems Modelling: An Assemblage of Methodological Tools for Systems Problem Solving,* Ph.D. Dissertation, State University of New York, Binghamton, New York, 1978.
15. T. I. Oren, "Concepts for Advanced Computer Assisted Modelling," in Zeigler et al., *Methodology in Systems Modelling and Simulation,* North Holland Publishing Company, Amsterdam, 1979.

16. M. M. Cutler, *A Formal Program Model for Discrete Event Simulation and Its Use in the Verification and Validation of System Models and Implementations,* Ph.D. Dissertation, UCLA, Los Angeles, 1980.
17. N. R. Davies, "Interactive Simulation Program Generation," in Zeigler et al., *Methodology in Systems Modelling and Simulation,* North Holland Publishing Company, Amsterdam, 1979.
18. H. S. Krasnow, "Simulation Languages," *The Design of Computer Simulation Experiments,* Duke University Press, North Carolina, 1969.
19. W. Kreutzer, "Comparison and Evaluation of Discrete Event Simulation Programming Languages for Management Decision Making," *Simulation,* Acta Press, Zurich, 1975.
20. H. M. Markowitz, *The SIMSCRIPT II.5 Programming Language,* ed. E. C. Russell, CACI, Los Angeles, 1973.
21. A. A. B. Pritsker and R. E. Young, *Simulation with GASP PL/1,* Wiley, New York, 1975.
22. O. J. Dahl and K. Nygaard, "SIMULA—An ALGOL-Based Simulation Language," *CACM 9*(1) (1966).
23. W. R. Franta, *The Process View of Simulation,* Elsevier-North Holland, New York, 1977.
24. K. D. Tocher, Keynote Address, *Proceedings/Winter Simulation Conference,* San Diego, 1979.
25. S. Atkins, "A Comparison of SIMULA and GPSS for Simulation of Sparse Traffic," *Simulation 38*(3) (1980).
26. P. Hogeweg, "Simulating the Growth of Cellular Forms," *Simulation 32*(3) (1978).
27. R. E. Nance, "The Time and State Relationships in Simulation Modelling," Technical Report, Combat Systems Department, Dahlgren, Va., 1980.
28. Y. Chu, *Digital Simulation of Continuous Systems,* McGraw-Hill, New York, 1969.
29. "The SCi Continuous System Simulation Language (CSSL)," *Simulation 9*(6) (1967).
30. M. S. Elzas, "HL1 or Towards a Unique Language for All Continuous System Simulation," *Proceedings/7th AICA Conference,* Prague, 1973.
31. M. S. Elzas, "What is Needed for Robust Simulation?" in Zeigler et al., *Methodology in Systems Modelling and Simulation,* North Holland Publishing Company, Amsterdam, 1979.
32. T. I. Oren, "Software for Simulation of Combined Continuous and Discrete Systems: A State of the Art Review," *Simulation 28*(2) (1977).
33. H. Elmqvist, "DYMOLA—A Structured Model Language for Large Continuous Systems," *Proceedings/Summer Computer Simulation Conference,* Toronto, July 1978, pp. 8–14.
34. R. Cavallo and G. J. Klir, "A Conceptual Foundation for Systems Problem Solving," *International Journal Systems Science 9*(2) (1978).
35. D. Tavangarian and K. Waldschmidt, "Interactive Graphical Network Simulation," Technical Report, U. Dortmund, W. Germany, 1978.
36. *WISSIM Guide,* IIASA Report, RM-76-24, 1976.
37. M. Mesarovic, "World Modelling: An Assessment of Policies Tool," *Proceedings/Winter Simulation Conference,* U.S.A., 1976, pp. 563–576.
38. C. H. Hull and N. H. Nie, *SPSS Update,* McGraw-Hill, New York, 1979.
39. R. Mills, "AUTOGRP: An Interactive Computer System for the Analysis of Health Care Data," *Medical Care 14*(7) (1976).
40. L. G. Birta, "A Parameter Optimization Module for CSSL-Based Simulation Software," *Simulation 28*(4) (1977).
41. J. Palme, "Moving Pictures in SIMULA," Technical Report, Swedish National Defense Institute, Stocholm, 1976.
42. W. Orchard-Hays, Several chapters on mathematical programming systems in *Design and Implementation of Optimization Software,* H. J. Greenberg (ed.), Sijthoff and Noorddhoff, Holland, 1978.
43. L. G. Birta, A. M. Haggani, and J. Raymord, "SIMPAK: An Interactive/Graphics Program for Continuous System Simulation," *Simulation 27*(4) (1976).
44. A. A. B. Pritsker and C. R. Standridge, "Using Data Base Capabilities in Simulation," *Proceedings/Simulation '80,* Interlaken, Switzerland, 1980.
45. M. H. Abkin and T. W. Caroll, "Library for Agricultural Systems Simulation," Technical Report, Department of Agricultural Economics, Michigan State University, Michigan, 1976.
46. B. Conrad and D. A. D'Esopo, "Simulation of a Rail Rapid Transit System at Several Levels of Detail," *Proceedings/Winter Simulation Conference,* U.S.A., 1978, pp. 585–594.
47. *DYNASTAT,* Pugh Associates, Boston, 1978.
48. J. K. Clema and F. Scarpino, "A General Purpose Tool for Interactive Simulations," *Proceedings/Winter Simulation Conference,* U.S.A., 1976, pp. 475–486.
49. M. Norman, "Software Package for Economic Modelling," Technical Report, RR-76-21, IIASA, Austria, 1976.
50. K. Plasser, "IAS-System Reference Guide," Technical Report, Institute of Advanced Studies, Vienna, 1978.
51. "MBS: Version 0.2," Technical Report IPES-GMD, St. Augustin, W. Germany, 1978.
52. R. H. Bonczek, C. W. Holsapple, and A. B. Whinston, "The Evolving Roles of Models within Decision Support Systems," *Decision Sciences 11* (1980).
53. E. A. Stohr and M. Tannira, "The Design of a Corporate Planning System Simulator," *Proceedings/Winter Simulation Conference,* U.S.A., 1978, pp. 919–930.
54. E. W. Dykstra, *A Discipline of Programming,* Prentice Hall, New Jersey, 1976.
55. B. Liskov and S. Zilles, "Programming with Abstract Data Types," *ACM Sigplan Notices 9* (1974).
56. G. M. Nijssen (ed.), *Architecture and Models in Data Base Management Systems,* North Holland Publishing Company, Amsterdam, 1977.

57. G. Estrin, "A Method for Design of Digital Systems Supported by SARA at the Age of One," *Proceedings/AFIPS Conference,* NCC, 1978.

58. E. Hershey and D. Teichrow, "PSL/PSA: A Computer-Aided Technique for Structure Documentation and Analysis of Information Processing Systems," *IEEE Trans. Soft. Eng.,* 3/1, 1978.

59. R. Yeh (ed.), *Current Trends in Programming, Volume 1: Software Specification and Design,* Prentice Hall, New Jersey, 1977.

60. J. N. Beauchamp and R. C. Field, "Simulation Modelling by Stepwise Refinement," *Proceedings/Winter Simulation Conference,* San Diego, 1979.

61. K. T. Ryan, "Software Engineering and Simulation," *Proceedings/Winter Simulation Conference,* San Diego, 1979.

62. G. Rzevski, "Systematic Design of Simulation Software," *Proceedings/Simulation '80,* Interlaken, Switzerland, 1980.

63. M. N. MacDougall, "Computer System Simulation: An Introduction," *Computer Surveys 2*(3) (1970).

64. G. J. Nutt and P. F. Roth (eds.), "Conference on Simulation, Measurement and Modeling of Computer Systems," *Simuletter 11*(1) (1979).

65. G. Wong, "Modelling Methodology for Computer System Performance-Oriented Design," in Zeigler et al., *Methodology in Systems Modelling and Simulation,* North Holland Publishing Company, Amsterdam, 1979.

66. H. D. Schwetman, "Hybrid Simulation Models of Computer Systems," *CACM 21*(9) (1978).

67. B. P. Zeigler, M. S. Elzas, G. J. Klir, and T. I. Oren, *Methodology in Systems Modelling and Simulation,* North Holland Publishing Company, Amsterdam, 1979.

68. M. G. Kienzle and K. C. Sevick, "Survey of Analytic Queueing Network Models of Computer Systems," in Nuttt and Roth, 1979.

69. L. Kleinrock, *Queueing Systems, Vol. 1: Theory,* Wiley, New York, 1975.

70. L. Kleinrock, *Queueing Systems, Vol. 2: Applications,* Wiley, New York, 1976.

71. K. M. Chandy, J. H. Howard, and D. F. Towsley, "Product Form and Local Balance in Queueing Networks," *JACM,* Apr. 1977.

72. R. Blake, "TAILOR: A Simple Model that Works," Nutt and Roth, 1979.

73. L. Dekker, "Parallel Simulation Systems," *Proceedings/IMACS Simulation of Systems Conference,* Sorrento, Italy, 1979.

74. R. G. Sargent, "Validation of Simulation Models," *Proceedings/Winter Simulation Conference,* IEEE, 1979.

75. R. G. Sargent, "Statistical Analysis of Simulation Output Data," *ACM Proceedings/Symposium on the Simulation of Computer Systems IV,* 1976.

76. T. Teorey, "Validation Criteria for Computer Systems Simulation," *Proceedings/Symposium on the Simulation of Computer Systems III,* 1975.

77. H. A. Anderson and R. G. Sargent, "Investigation in Scheduling for an Interactive Computer System," *IBM Journal of Research and Development 18*(2) 1974.

78. I. D. Greig, "Validation, Statistical Testing, and Decision to Model," *Simulation 33*(2) (1979).

79. S. I. Gass, "Evaluation of Complex Models," *Comp. & O.R. 4:*1977.

80. B. P. Zeigler, "Structuring the Organization of Partial Models," *Int. Journal of General Systems 4*(1) (1978).

81. B. P. Zeigler, "Structuring Principles for Multifaceted System Modelling," in Zeigler et al., *Methodology in Systems Modelling and Simulation,* North Holland Publishing Company, Amsterdam, 1979.

82. E. A. Macnair and C. H. Sauer, "Queuing Network Software for Systems Modelling," *Software Practice and Experience 9* (1979).

83. M. B. Carver, "The FORSIM VI Distributed System Simulation Package," in Zeigler et al., *Methodology in Systems Modelling and Simulation,* North Holland Publishing Company, Amsterdam, 1979.

84. J. R. Parker and B. W. Unger, "An Operating System Implementation and Simulation Language (OASIS)" in Nutt and Roth, 1979.

85. J. L. Peterson, "Petri Nets," *Computer Surveys 9*(3) 1977.

86. P. Henderson, "The TOPD System," Technical Report 77, Computing Lab., University of Newcastle upon Tyne, U.K., 1975.

87. W. E. Riddle and J. H. Sayler, "Modelling and Simulation in the Design of Complex Software Systems," in Zeigler et al., *Methodology in Systems Modelling and Simulation,* North Holland Publishing Company, Amsterdam, 1979.

88. J. Sanguinetti, "A Technique for Integrating Simulation and Systems Design," Conference on Simulation, Measurement and Modeling of Computer Systems, *Sigmetrics/Simuletter,* Fall 1979.

89. D. A. Bennett and C. A. Landauer, "Simulation of a Distributed System for Performance Modelling," in Nutt and Roth, 1979.

90. B. P. Zeigler, "Multi-Level, Multi-Formalism Modelling: An Ecosystem Example," in E. Halfon (ed.), *Theoretical Systems Ecology* Academic Press, New York, 1979.

91. A. Bolshoi, D. Belogus, and B. P. Zeigler, "ESP: An Interactive Tool for System Structuring," *Proceedings/European Meeting on Cyb. & Sys. Res.,* Vienna, 1980.

92. O. deGans and R. Sierenberg, *PROSIM78 Textbook.* Delft Institute of Technology, (in preparation).

93. F. E. Cellier, *Combined Continuous/Discrete System Simulation by Use of Digital Computers: Techniques and Tools,* Ph.D. Dissertation, ETH, Zurich, Switzerland, 1979.

94. L. Dekker, "Parallel Simulation Systems," *Proceedings/IMACS Simulation of Systems Conference,* Sorrento, Italy, 1979.

2

Graph Theoretic Modeling and Analysis in Software Engineering

Hon H. So
Bell Laboratories

2.1. INTRODUCTION

The concept of a graph is simple, yet extremely general. Moreover, it is the fundamental notion in the study of all forms of "structures" in almost any branch of science and engineering [1]. A graph is, mathematically, a collection of nodes and pairs of nodes called arcs. The nodes are often used to represent the elements of a structure and the arcs their interrelations. The reader is assumed to have some knowledge of elementary graph theory. However, some basic notions will be defined in order to introduce a uniform set. This chapter discusses the major graph models and applications of graph theoretic techniques in the design and analysis of computers and software. This moderate scope of applied graph theory is already too large to be covered extensively here. A wide range of models will be treated, however, and we will illustrate the most significant analysis techniques. The following classes of models and techniques are discussed: directed graph models of sequential programs, analysis of program structure, and computing network models of reliability.

2.2. PROGRAM GRAPHS

Analysis of Basic Program Structure

The conventional sequential computer program is most naturally modeled by a graph, with its branch (or decision points) represented by nodes, and the program codes between branch points represented by arcs. Figure 2.1 gives a flow chart of a program and its directed graph representation.

Connectivity, Reachability, and Well-Formed Program Graphs. By reducing the program to a directed graph, several important structural properties of the program (e.g., flow of control) can be studied via the connectivity analysis of the graph. We illustrate one of the most basic, yet important, graph theoretic techniques via the notion of *well-formation* of a program structure. The more elementary ideas of *connectivity* and *reachability* need to be introduced first.

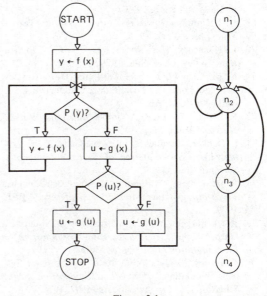

Figure 2.1.

Definition 1. The *connectivity matrix* $\mathbf{C}[i,j]$ of a directed graph $\mathbf{G}(\mathbf{A},\mathbf{N})$, where $\mathbf{A}$ is the set of arcs and $\mathbf{N}$ is the set of nodes $\{x_1, \ldots, x_n\}$, is defined as follows:

$$\mathbf{c}_{ij} = \begin{cases} 1 & \text{if there is an arc from } x_i \text{ to } x_j \\ 0 & \text{otherwise} \end{cases}$$

Node x_j is said to be reachable from node x_i if a path exists from x_i to x_j. The *reachability matrix* $\mathbf{R}[i,j]$ is defined as:

$$\mathbf{r}_{ij} = \begin{cases} 1 & \text{if there exists a path from } x_i \text{ to } x_j \\ 0 & \text{otherwise} \end{cases}$$

$\mathbf{R}$ is the *reflexive transitive closure* of $\mathbf{C}$ and is related to $\mathbf{C}$ as follow: $\mathbf{R} = \mathbf{I} \cup \mathbf{A}$, where $\mathbf{I}$ is the identity matrix and $\mathbf{A} = \bigcup\limits_{k=1}^{n} \mathbf{C}^k$.* The matrix $\mathbf{A}$ is the *transitive closure* of matrix $\mathbf{C}$. The computation of the transitive closure of a matrix is involved in many graph-theoretic algorithms, and its computational efficiency is oftentimes crucial. One of the earliest algorithms was authored by Warshall and is based on Boolean matrix representation of a graph [2].

For a given graph, with respect to two nodes *s* and *t* (the start and terminal nodes, respectively), we say that a node *x* is essential if (1) it is reachable from node *s* and (2) it can reach the terminal node *t* [3]. With this interpretation applied to actual software, it is desirable to verify that every node in the program is essential, that is every statement may be executed starting from the entry statement, and that it will lead to normal termination by exiting via the terminal statement. Even more el-

---

*Given two $n \times n$ matrices $\mathbf{A}$ and $\mathbf{B}$, their union $\mathbf{S} = \mathbf{A} \cup \mathbf{B}$ is defined as:

$$\mathbf{s}_{ij} = \begin{cases} 1 & \text{if } a_{ij} = 1 \text{ or } b_{ij} = 1, \\ 0 & \text{otherwise} \end{cases}$$

and their product $\mathbf{P}_n = \mathbf{AB}$ is defined as

$$\mathbf{p}_{ij} = 1 \quad \text{if } \sum_{k=1}^{n} a_{ik} b_{ij} > 0$$
$$0 \quad \text{otherwise}$$

and $\mathbf{C}^k = \mathbf{C}(\mathbf{C}^{k-1})$.

ementary, it may be desirable to check that the terminal node is reachable by the entry node. These two properties: (1) existence of a path from *s* to *t* and (2) no inessential node, together define the *well-formation property* of a program graph, and can be verified easily by inspecting the reachability matrix $\mathbf{R}$.

Algorithm 1. Verification of graph well-formation

Input: Reachability matrix $\mathbf{R}$, start node = x_1, terminal node = x_n.

Output: A Boolean variable *w* will be TRUE if the graph is well formed, and FALSE otherwise.

Algorithm.

1. If $\mathbf{R}_{in}$ is 0 then $w \leftarrow$ FALSE, stop.
2. If Row 1 and Column *n* do not contain all 1's, then $w \leftarrow$ FALSE, else $w \leftarrow$ TRUE.

Partitioning of a Program Graph into Maximal Strongly Connected Components. Another important structural property of a graph based on its connectivity can be studied by its reachability matrix. A subset $\mathbf{S}$ of the nodes together with the arcs involving the nodes of $\mathbf{S}$ only is said to be strongly connected if every node in $\mathbf{S}$ can reach every other node in $\mathbf{S}$. $\mathbf{S}$ is a *maximal strongly connected component* (MSCC) of the graph $\mathbf{G}$ if $\mathbf{S}$ is *strongly connected* and $\mathbf{S}$ is not a proper subset of another strongly connected subgraph, $\mathbf{S}'$ (i.e., there is no $\mathbf{S}'$ such that $\mathbf{S} \subsetneq \mathbf{S}'$ and $\mathbf{S}'$ is strongly connected). It is sometimes useful to identify the maximal strongly connected components. It is rather easy to see that the MSCCs of a graph partition it, that is, they are pairwise disjoint, and every node of the graph belongs to precisely one of the components. Otherwise, suppose x_i belongs to two distinct components; then by the transitivity property of the "reachable" relation, every element of one component can reach any one in the other. It means the union of the two components is itself a strongly connected subset, violating the assumption of their maximality; thus the MSCCs partition a graph. The following algorithm identifies the MSCCs of a graph.

Algorithm 2.   Partitioning of a graph into its MSCCs

Input: Reachability matrix **R**.
Output: A partition of the graph **C** into its MSCCs.
Algorithm:

1. $\mathbf{M} \leftarrow \mathbf{R} \cup \mathbf{R}^T.$* The number of MSCCs is given by the number of distinct non-zero rows of **M**. If $\mathbf{M}_i \neq 0$ (a vector of all zeros), then the nodes of the MSCC correspond to the nonzero columns of $\mathbf{M}_i$. If all nonzero row vectors are treated in a similar way, the membership of every MSCC can be determined.

Example 1.   Given the reachability matrix **R** of the graph in Figure 2.2, and performing the computation specified in the algorithm, we obtain:

$$\mathbf{R} = \begin{bmatrix} 1 & 1 & 1 & 1 & 1 & 1 & 1 & 1 & 1 & 1 & 1 \\ 0 & 1 & 1 & 1 & 0 & 1 & 0 & 0 & 1 & 0 & 1 \\ 0 & 1 & 1 & 1 & 0 & 1 & 0 & 0 & 1 & 0 & 1 \\ 0 & 0 & 0 & 1 & 0 & 0 & 0 & 0 & 0 & 0 & 1 \\ 0 & 1 & 1 & 1 & 1 & 1 & 1 & 1 & 1 & 1 & 1 \\ 0 & 1 & 1 & 1 & 0 & 1 & 0 & 0 & 1 & 0 & 1 \\ 0 & 1 & 1 & 1 & 1 & 1 & 1 & 1 & 1 & 1 & 1 \\ 0 & 1 & 1 & 1 & 1 & 1 & 1 & 1 & 1 & 1 & 1 \\ 0 & 1 & 1 & 1 & 0 & 1 & 0 & 0 & 1 & 0 & 1 \\ 0 & 1 & 1 & 1 & 1 & 1 & 1 & 1 & 1 & 1 & 1 \\ 0 & 0 & 0 & 1 & 0 & 0 & 0 & 0 & 0 & 0 & 1 \end{bmatrix}$$

$$\mathbf{R} \cap \mathbf{R}^T = \begin{bmatrix} 1 & 0 & 0 & 0 & 0 & 0 & 0 & 0 & 0 & 0 & 0 \\ 0 & 1 & 1 & 0 & 0 & 1 & 0 & 0 & 1 & 0 & 0 \\ 0 & 1 & 1 & 0 & 0 & 1 & 0 & 0 & 1 & 0 & 0 \\ 0 & 0 & 0 & 1 & 0 & 0 & 0 & 0 & 0 & 0 & 1 \\ 0 & 0 & 0 & 0 & 1 & 0 & 1 & 1 & 0 & 1 & 0 \\ 0 & 1 & 1 & 0 & 0 & 1 & 0 & 0 & 1 & 0 & 0 \\ 0 & 0 & 0 & 0 & 1 & 0 & 1 & 1 & 0 & 1 & 0 \\ 0 & 0 & 0 & 0 & 1 & 0 & 1 & 1 & 0 & 1 & 0 \\ 0 & 1 & 1 & 0 & 0 & 1 & 0 & 0 & 1 & 0 & 0 \\ 0 & 0 & 0 & 0 & 1 & 0 & 1 & 1 & 0 & 1 & 0 \\ 0 & 0 & 0 & 1 & 0 & 0 & 0 & 0 & 0 & 0 & 1 \end{bmatrix}$$

---

*The transpose of a matrix **R**, denoted by $\mathbf{R}^T$, is defined by $\mathbf{r}_{ij}^T = \mathbf{r}_{ji}$.

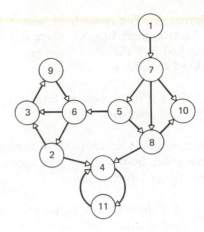

Figure 2.2.

The number of distinct nonzero rows, hence the number of MSCCs, is equal to 4. The nodes of these MSCCs are $\{x_1\}$, $\{x_2,x_3,x_6,x_9\}$, $\{x_5,x_7,x_8,x_{10}\}$, and $\{x_4,x_{11}\}$.

The study of the connectivity and strongly connected subgraphs forms the basis of many properties of a structure and relations among its components. The reader is referred to Reference 3 for a more thorough treatment of this subject.

Set Covering of Program Graph and Application to Program Testing.   Consider now the problem of test data generation. It may be extremely difficult to thoroughly test sizable programs. Several (sometimes arbitrary) criteria have been proposed on the selection of test cases based on the program graph structure. For example, one requires that each statement in the program must be executed at least once. Let us for the moment not worry about the adequacy of this criterion. Instead, we concentrate on satisfying the criterion with the minimal number of test cases. For a given test case, it will lead to the execution of the program along a particular sequence of statements, referred to as a program path. The problem then is to identify the minimal set of program paths so that collectively they cover every statement, and then to find the test cases that exercise those paths. The first path can be reduced to a graph-theoretic problem called the *set covering problem* (SCP).

Given a set $\mathbf{R} = \{x_1, \ldots, x_m\}$, and a family $\mathbf{S} = \{S_1, \ldots, S_n\}$ of subsets of **R**, (i.e.,

$S_j \subset R$,) any subfamily $S' = \{S_{j1}, S_{j2}, \ldots, S_{jk}\}$ of S such that

$$\bigcup_{i=1}^{k} S_{ji} = R$$

is called a set covering of R, and the S_{ji} are called the covering sets. If with each $S_j \in S$, there is associated a positive cost c_j, the SCP is to find a set-covering of R that has minimum cost, the cost of $S' = \{S_{j1}, \ldots, S_{jk}\}$ being $\sum_{i=1}^{k} c_{ji}$.

The problem can be formulated as a (0–1) linear programming problem:

$$\text{Minimize } Z = \sum_{j=1}^{N} C_j \xi_j$$

$$\text{subject to } \sum_{j=1}^{N} t_{ij} \xi_j \geq 1 \; i = 1, 2, \ldots, M$$

where $c_j \geq 0$, ξ_j is 1, (0) depending on $S_j \in S'$, ($S_j \notin S'$) and $t_{ij} = 1$, (0) depending on $x_i \in S_j$, ($x_i \notin S_j$).

Next we see how the test case generation problem can be reduced to the SCP. The elements of R, $\{x_1, \ldots, x_m\}$, can be identified as the arcs of the program path. Each subset S_j identifies a feasible program path whose elements are the arcs on the particular path. Each path S_j is associated with a cost of 1. Even though the problem is transformed to an SCP, its solution is not easy. Generation of all feasible paths is difficult, if not unsolvable. Furthermore, the solution of an integer (0–1) program can be extremely time-consuming. In realistic test case generation, other techniques, usually faster heuristics, are actually used, (see Refs 4 and 5).

We further illustrate the use of graph analysis to program testing with the problem of generating a *program execution profile*. In the simple case, the execution profile can be thought of as the frequency of execution of each statement of a program after a selected set of test runs.

To count the number of times a particular statement is executed, the most straightforward approach is to insert the following to every program statement:

count(statement__number) ← count(statement__number) + 1.

It is obvious that this approach is excessively expensive. For within a block of "straight-line code" (i.e., with no branch statements of any kind in between), the number of times each statement is executed will be the same for the whole block. Thus, using the program graph model, only the arc frequencies need be counted. In this straightforward approach, a counter is associated with each arc (block of straight-line code). It is, however, possible to reduce the number of counters by noting that on each node there is a conservation relation between the counts on the incoming and outgoing arcs. The total counts on the incoming arcs should be equal to the total counts on the outgoing arcs. With this dependency among the arc frequencies, it is possible to eliminate redundancy in the counting. In the graph shown in Figure 2.3.a with the known arc frequencies $a_4 = 1$, $a_5 = 2$, $a_6 = 1$, and $a_{10} = 8$, the unknown arc frequencies a_1, a_2, a_3, a_7, a_8, and a_9 can be deduced from the conservation equations below:

$$
\begin{aligned}
\text{node 1: } & a_1 + a_2 + a_3 & = 8 \\
\text{node 2: } & a_1 & = 1 \\
\text{node 3: } & a_2 - a_5 & = 2 \\
\text{node 4: } & a_3 - a_7 & = 0 \\
\text{node 5: } & a_8 & = 3 \\
\text{node 6: } & a_7 - a_9 & = 1 \\
\text{node 7: } & a_8 + a_9 & = 8
\end{aligned}
$$

Note that there are seven equations and six unknowns. The equations are not linearly independent, but they yield a unique solution, which is $a_1 = 1$, $a_2 = 3$, $a_3 = 4$, $a_7 = 4$, $a_8 = 3$, and $a_9 = 5$ (see Figure 2.3.b).

The previous example prompts the questions: What is the minimal number of counters needed to obtain the arc frequencies of any given graph and where should the counters be located? The answer to these questions, as well as the process to find the minimal counter set, is summarized in the following theorem [6].

Theorem 1. The knowledge of the frequencies of execution of all of the directed arcs not in an undirected spanning tree of the program

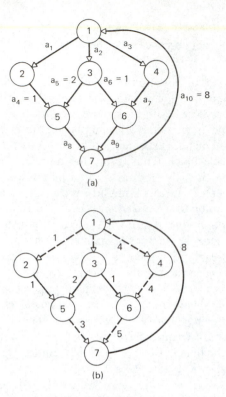

(a)

(b)

Figure 2.3.

graph is both necessary and sufficient to determine the frequencies of execution of all the directed arcs in the program graph.

We will not prove the theorem. Since, however, the spanning tree plays a central role, we will discuss this concept and describe an algorithm to construct the spanning tree of a graph.

Definition 2. An *undirected tree* is a connected graph $T = (A, N)$ with no cycle. A *cycle* is a sequence of nodes $n_1, \ldots, n\gamma$ such that $(n\gamma, n_1) \in A$ and $(n_i, n_{i+1}) \in A$, for all $i = 1, \ldots, \gamma - 1$. A graph is connected if, for any pair of nodes $n_i, n_j \in N$, there exists nodes $n_1, \ldots, n_\gamma$, in N such that $(n_i, n_1), (n_1, n_2), \ldots, (n_{\gamma-1}, n), (n_\gamma, n_j) \in A.$

Definition 3. Let $G = (A, N)$ be an undirected graph. A *spanning tree* of G is an undirected tree $T = (A', N)$.

Intuitively, a spanning tree of a graph is a connected subgraph with no cycles and covers all nodes of the original graph. Figure 2.3.b

shows the spanning tree (dotted arcs) of a graph (ignoring the direction of the arcs).

Theorem 1 implies that the locations of arc frequency counters are at the complement of an undirected spanning tree. It is readily observed that a graph can have a number of different spanning trees. Each spanning tree will have exactly n nodes and $n - 1$ arcs, where n is the number of nodes of the program path. The number of counters needed will be $a - n + 1$, where a is the number of arcs. If the cost associated with inserting a counter is the same for all arcs, then finding any spanning tree will directly determine the optimal locations of counters. We consider a more general case in which a cost c_i is associated with each arc. The cost will be characterized by the following factors: storage and execution time, interference by monitoring the arc, measurement overhead for every activation of the monitor, and frequency of activation of the monitor on the arc, and so forth.

If an estimate of the costs for each arc can be made, then the optimal counter locations can be found by finding a maximal (cost) spanning tree (and locating counters on the complement of the tree).

The algorithm starts by selecting all nodes of the graph, then progressively joining them to form a tree. To obtain the maximal cost spanning tree, the arcs are examined in the order of their cost to determine whether they should be included in the tree. This is also an illustration of a "greedy" algorithm that yields the optimal solution.

Algorithm 3. Maximal cost spanning tree

Input: Graph $G = (A, N)$ and c_i associated with each arc.
Output: Spanning tree $T = (A', N)$.

Algorithm:

begin
   $A' \leftarrow \emptyset$;
   $V \leftarrow \emptyset$(V is a set of sets);
   for each node $v \in N$ **do** add the singleton set {v} to V;
   while $|V| > 1$ **do**

```
begin
    choose (v,w) ∈ A of the greatest cost;
    delete (v,w) from A;
    if v and w are in different sets W₁ and
then   W₂ in V
    then begin
        replace W₁ and W₂ in V by W₁ ∪ W₂;
        add (v,w) to A';
        end
    end
end
```

Program Flow Analysis.   Program flow analysis is an example of a graph theory application of great practical importance in computer science. Flow analysis usually incorporates both control-flow and data-flow analyses and deals with the "flow" and "propagation" of various information about the program, namely, the flow of control (sequence of execution) and the flow of data (the availability of information and communication of information). The primary motivations for performing flow analysis on a program (usually in a step before compilation of the program) are to (1) derive some characteristics of the program that can be very illuminating, for instance, unreachable code, unused parameters, variables that are used before being defined, and (2) increase program execution efficiency, such as eliminating useless code and redundant computation, and even providing register allocation information to achieve a most efficient use of faster memory. As such, flow analyses contribute to quality enhancement in both aiding to uncover problem areas and indicating possibilities for efficiency improvement.

Control-Flow Analysis.   Control-flow analysis is usually prerequisite to data-flow analysis because the latter requires information about the sequence of statement execution.

An extremely important analysis on the control-flow graph is the interval analysis. It is also fundamental to an efficient data-flow analysis algorithm, which is discussed later.

To understand both the data flow and control flow of a program, especially a large one, it is necessary to establish some form of hierarchy. The most natural hierarchy in this context is the propagation of local information to progressively larger and larger radii of influence. Information originates from the local area and radiates to its immediate surroundings, and so on. Central to this is the notion of a *loop*. There can be alternative notions of a loop in terms of a (control) flow graph, such as a cycle or a strongly connected region. These do not, however, give rise to a natural hierarchy. A construct known as an *interval* [7] will be shown to be more appropriate.

Definition 4.   Given a node h, an *interval* $I(h)$ is the maximal, single-entry subgraph in which h is the only entry node and in which all closed paths contain h. The unique interval node h is called the *interval head*. An interval can be expressed in terms of the nodes within it $I(h) = (n_1, n_2, \ldots, n_m)$.

Alternatively, an interval can be defined algorithmically, which may be more illuminating. Let the flow graph be $G = (A, N, s)$, where $s \in N$ is the start node of the graph.

Algorithm 4.   Construction of an interval

```
I(h)    ← h (Initially)
while   there is m ∈ N such that
        m ∉ I(h) ∧ m ≠ s ∧ (for all (k,m)
        ∈ A, k ∈ I(h))
do I(h) ← I(h) ∪ {m}
```

The body of the *do-while* loop selects those nodes that are not the start node, not already in the interval, and whose immediate predecessors are already in the interval.

An important property of the interval is that we can partition the control-flow graph into a set of intervals. A new graph is constructed by replacing each of the intervals with a node and retaining those arcs that go from a node in one interval to one in another interval. The interval partition process continues until a terminal graph is obtained that contains the same number of intervals as the number of nodes. To understand this process, we first introduce an algorithm that partitions a given control-flow graph into a set of intervals.

Algorithm 5. Partition a control-flow graph
G = (**A, N,** *s*)

```
var H: set (set of potential header nodes)
    L: set (set of intervals)
begin
   H ← {s}
   L ← ∅
   while H ≠ ∅ do
     begin
     Select and delete h from H;
     Compute I(h) from Algorithm 4
     Add I(h) to L;
     Add to H any node that has a
predecessor
         in I(h), but that is not already in H
         or in one of the intervals of L;
     end
     Output L;
end
```

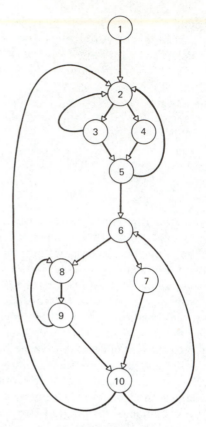

Figure 2.4.

Example 2. If Algorithm 5 is applied to the graph **G** in Figure 2.4, the interval partition (in broken boxes) will be found.

The intervals obtained in this way are known as the *first-order intervals,* and the graph from which these intervals are derived is accordingly called the *first-order graph* **G**^{1}. The *second-order graph* is derived from the first-order graph and its intervals by making each first-order interval into a node and each interval edge into an edge in the second-order graph. *Second-order intervals* are the intervals in the second-order graph. Successive higher-order graphs are obtained by the same process. Figure 2.5 shows the process carried out on the graph in Figure 2.4.

In this example, the limiting or terminal graph **G**^{5} is a single node. A flow graph satisfying this property is called *reducible;* otherwise, it is *irreducible.*

In practice (realistic program graphs), irreducibility is rarely encountered. In particular, programs produced from structured programs constructs are reducible.

Data-Flow Analysis. Program data-flow analysis attempts to answer the following types of questions: (1) When a program variable is set to a new value in a certain part of the pro-

gram (definition of a data item), what later uses of this data item might be affected by this particular definition? (2) What are the data definitions that are no longer needed from a certain point onward (life-death analysis)?

In program data-flow analysis, the program is modeled by a directed graph, but is slightly different from what is done in connectivity analysis (in Figure 2.1). The nodes in this graph model represent blocks of program code, normally a piece of straight-line code (but a single-entry, single-exit block of code can be represented by a single node). The arcs represent the possible flow of control between blocks of code (nodes).

A data item *x* is said to be *defined* in a node if it is assigned a new value, represented by *x* = in the graph. A data item is said to be *used* if its value is referenced in a certain computation, represented by = *x* in the graph. Figure 2.6 shows an example with this notation.

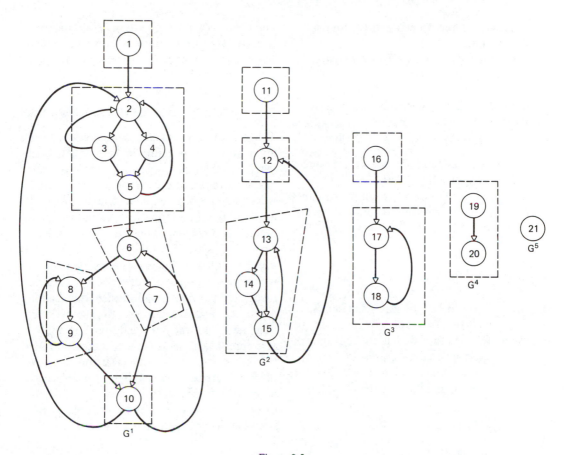

Figure 2.5.

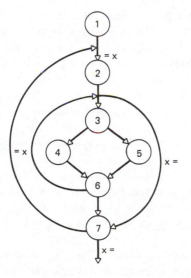

Figure 2.6.

The following definitions are necessary for proceeding further:

R_i = The set of definitions that may *reach* node *i*. This is the set we want to determine for each node in the graph to ascertain the effect of other parts of the program on a specific block of code.

A_i = The set of *available definitions* at node *i*. Contrasted to R_i, A_i includes the effect of the data definitions and uses that may destroy some definitions reaching node *i*.

DB_i = The set of *locally available definitions* through node *i*. This is the set of definitions created in the block of code represented by node *i* and is preserved (i.e., not redefined again) through the node.

PB$_i$ = The set of *definitions preserved* through node i.

With these definitions, it is fairly easy to verify that the reach set that we are seeking is defined recursively as $\mathbf{R}_i = \bigcup_{p \in P} \mathbf{A}_p$, where **P** is the set of all immediate predecessors of node i, and $\mathbf{A}_p = (\mathbf{R}_p \cap \mathbf{PB}_p) \cup \mathbf{DB}_p$.

The following algorithm is a simple straightforward iterative algorithm to obtain the set of available definitions $\mathbf{R}_i$ for each node of a graph.

Algorithm 6.   Basic reach algorithm

Input: **PB**$_i$ and **DB**$_i$ for each node in the control-flow graph
Outputs: **R**$_i$, the set of definitions that reach each node in the graph. The set **A**$_i$ of definitions available from each node is generated in the algorithm.

Algorithm:

1. A$_i \leftarrow \emptyset$ and R$_i \leftarrow \emptyset$ for all i;
2. Perform Step 3 until there is no change in any R$_i$ or A$_i$;
3. Apply R$_i \leftarrow \bigcup_{p \in P} A_p$, where P is the set of all immediate predecessors of node i, and A$_i \leftarrow (R_i \cap PB_i) \cup DB_i$ to all nodes of the graph.

It can be shown that the algorithm stabilizes. How fast it settles, however, depends very much on the order in which the nodes of the graph are examined.

A number of iterations are needed before the information stabilizes because cycles exist whereby it is not possible to process a node after all its predecessors have been processed. In the search for the "best" order of processing the nodes, the notion of an interval introduced in the previous section seems to offer the solution. The data-flow analysis algorithm developed by Allen and Cocke [7] is based on interval analysis. The technique used in the algorithm is typical of a large class of graph-analytic algorithms used in computer science; however, a detailed treatment of this topic would be very lengthy.

2.3. NETWORK MODELING AND ANALYSIS

The role of networks and computers in future applications, especially in large-scale problems, is becoming increasingly important. One of the more important considerations in a network is reliability, expressed in terms of the availability of communication paths among the computers composing the nodes of the network. This type of consideration readily lends itself to the application of graph-theoretic techniques. Computer networks are naturally modeled by graphs with nodes representing computers and arcs representing communication links. The study of the design and analysis of computer networks is then centered around (1) formulating reliability measures in graph-theoretic terms, (2) analyzing the graph model in terms of these measures, and (3) attempting to synthesize networks optimal to such measures, subject to certain constraints.

Network Reliability Measures

Reliability measures constitute the richest class of all measures developed. Reliability questions are asked in terms of the impact on computation if communications between one or more of the nodes or arcs are eliminated (destroyed). In particular, the most often used criterion is when and how a portion of the network is disconnected from the rest.

In the following discussion, relevant graph-theoretic concepts are formulated followed by a discussion of associated reliability measures.

Attention is restricted to undirected graphs corresponding to the situation where communication between nodes is either half or full duplex communication links. A computer network is modeled by a graph $\mathbf{G} = (\mathbf{A}, \mathbf{N})$, where $\mathbf{N}$ = set of nodes and $\mathbf{A}$ = set of arcs. For any node x_i, the degree d_i of the node is equal to the number of arcs incident on it. A path is a sequence of distinct nodes ($x_i, \ldots, x_l$) such that any two consecutive nodes x_i and

x_j, $(x_i, x_j) \in \mathbf{A}$. Any two paths between two nodes x_i, x_j are said to be *node disjoint (edge distinct)* if they have no common nodes (arcs, respectively).

The number of node-disjoint paths gives an indication of the multiplicity of ways communication can exist between any two given nodes. It also indicates the vulnerability of their ability to communicate following destruction of links on their communication paths. A similar observation can be made regarding the effect caused by the destruction of the nodes. Consider the network in Figure 2.7. With respect to nodes 2 and 5, paths (2, 9, 5) and (2, 3, 4, 5) are both node disjoint and edge disjoint, whereas paths (2, 3, 9, 4, 5) are edge disjoint from (2, 9, 5) but not node disjoint (node 9 being the common node).

It is often more convenient to work with the following concept of a *cut-set,* although it is not as intuitively straightforward. A graph $\mathbf{G}$ = $(\mathbf{A}, \mathbf{N})$ is said to be connected if there is at least one path between every pair of nodes, x_i and $x_j \in \mathbf{N}$. A (minimal) set of arcs such that their removal will render the graph disconnected is called a *(prime) node cut-set* of the graph. With respect to a pair of nodes x_i and x_j, a set of arcs whose removal will break all paths between them is called an *i-j edge cut.* The minimal number of elements in any *i-j edge cut,* denoted by C_{ij}^e, is known as the *edge connectivity* between nodes x_i and x_j. The edge connectivity of a graph $\mathbf{G}$ is defined as $C^n(\mathbf{G})$ = $\min_{ij} C_{ij}^n(\mathbf{G})$, and if $C^n(\mathbf{G}) \geq m$, $\mathbf{G}$ is said to be *m-connected.*

The simplest reliability measures of a network are the edge connectivity and the node connectivity of the graph, corresponding to its ability to maintain communication despite the destruction of some of its communication links or computers.

The basic results for this class of analysis are as follows: C_{ij}^n is equal to the maximum number of node-disjoint paths between nodes x_i and x_j, and C_{ij}^e is equal to the maximum number of edge-disjoint paths between x_i and x_j. This establishes the relation between the connectivity of the graphs and the existence of communication paths. Furthermore, the following relation holds between the various quantities.

$$C^n(\mathbf{G}) \leq C^e(\mathbf{G}) \leq \min_i d_i \leq \left| \frac{2|\mathbf{A}|}{|\mathbf{N}|} \right|$$

where $|\mathbf{A}|$ and $|\mathbf{N}|$ equal the number of arcs and nodes, respectively. For any given graph, it is possible to obtain the edge and node connectivity by the algorithm to find the maximum flow between pair of nodes [8], and hence a network can be evaluated in terms of these criteria. These results can also be applied in the design of a network. If successful communication between all node pairs is equally important, a maximally reliable network of $|\mathbf{A}|$ = a arcs and $|\mathbf{N}|$ = n nodes is one in which

$$C^m = C^e = \min_i d_i = \left| \frac{2a}{n} \right|$$

This leads to the design of a homogeneous network. In the case that communication between pairs of nodes is not equally important, specific connectivities between all pairs of nodes have to be specified, and the general problem becomes a more difficult one.

Another reliability criterion has been defined [9] based on the minimum number of arcs, $\delta(m)$, that must be removed from a graph in order to isolate any subgraph of m nodes from the rest of the graph.

A variant of the above criterion is based on the concern that even though a network may not be completely disconnected because of destruction of some of its nodes or arcs, it may

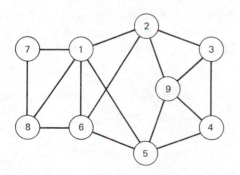

Figure 2.7.

increase the length of the communication paths between a critical pair of nodes that may have an adverse impact on the performance of the overall network. This criterion can be formulated in terms of the *diameter* of the graph, which is defined as the maximum length of the shortest path between any two nodes x_i and x_j. The measures $D^e(k, \lambda)$ and $D^n(k,\lambda)$, being the minimum number of arcs or nodes that must be removed from a graph of diameter k in order that the diameter of the resulting graph exceeds λ, may become the design objective and evaluation criterion of a network.

The reliability measures discussed so far are based on static and deterministic properties of the graph model. In certain design situations, we may be interested in how communication may be maintained subject to the possibility that individual links and computers may fail independently, or in a situation where the network is subject to random attack so that the removal of elements is probabilistic. As an example of this measure, network survivability is defined as the largest fraction of surviving nodes that can communicate with each other after a random attack. Techniques for handling this class of problem rely heavily on Monte Carlo simulation, which lies outside graph theoretic analysis.

Set Partitioning

To illustrate another class of problems in the application of graph modeling in computer networks, let us consider the following general problem of graph partitioning. Given a graph $G = (A, N)$ with costs c_{ij} for arc (x_i, x_j), associated with its arcs, partition A into subsets $A_1, \ldots, A_k$, each of them no larger than a given maximum size, i.e., $|A_j| \leq p \ \forall j = 1, \ldots, k$, so as to minimize the total cost of the arcs cut, that is,

$$\min \Sigma c_{ij}$$
$$(x_i, x_j) \in A, x_i \in A_p, x_j \in A_q, \text{ and } A_p \neq A_q$$

Numerous examples of practical design situations can be formulated in the form of the above problem. Since G is a finite graph, there is only a finite number of partitions of A, and

we can evaluate each possible partition for the cost of the arcs cut. However, the number of partitions with $N = n$, given below, is prohibitively large for moderate values of n and p.

$$\frac{1}{k!} \binom{n}{p} \binom{n-p}{p} \cdots \binom{2p}{p} \binom{p}{p}$$

The practical solution cannot be based on this exhaustive search. In most cases, we can rely only on heuristic methods that produce a "good" solution fast. Kernighan and Lin proposed such a heuristic algorithm [10], briefly described below.

The algorithm is based on an extension of the idea of heuristically solving the simpler problem of *two-way uniform partitioning*. This simpler problem requires one to partition a given set into two equal subsets, in each of which the sum of the cost associated with the cut is minimal. The algorithm begins with an arbitrary partition of A and B, and then in each iteration, subsets X and Y, of equal size, are chosen from A and B, respectively, and interchanged. Figure 2.8 graphically illustrates this step. X, Y are found by sequentially identifying their elements. Define, for each $a \in A$, $E_d = \Sigma_{y \in B} c_{ay}$ the external cost and $I_a = \Sigma_{x \in A} c_{ax}$, the internal cost of $D_a = E_a - I_a$. Similarly, E_b, I_b, and D_b can be defined with respect to subset B. Consider interchanging $a \in A$ and $b \in B$. The initial cost $T = z + E_a + E_b - c_{ab}$ (where z is the cost due to all connections between A and B that do not involve a or b), and the cost after interchange, $T' = z + I_a + I_b + c_{ab}$. Therefore, the reduction in cost due to the interchange of a and b is $D_a + D_b - 2c_{ab}$.

The algorithm begins with a selection of a_i and b_i initially to maximize $g_1 = D_{a,i} + D_{b,i} - 2C_{a,i,b,i}$. The a_i and b_i are set aside, and the

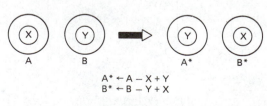

$$A^* \leftarrow A - X + Y$$
$$B^* \leftarrow B - Y + X$$

Figure 2.8.

D values of the rest of the elements are updated by

$$D_x \leftarrow D_x + 2c_{xa,i} - 2c_{xb,i} \qquad x \in \mathbf{A} - \{a_i\}$$
$$D_y \leftarrow D_y + 2c_{yb,i} - 2c_{ya,i} \qquad y \in \mathbf{B} - \{b_i\}$$

and the next maximum gain g_2 is obtained by the same procedures, and so on, until g_n is calculated (n = number of elements in $\mathbf{A}$ or $\mathbf{B}$). Some g_i's will be negative and the first g_k is chosen so that $\sum_{i=1}^{k} g_i$ is maximum over all $i = 1, \ldots, n$. If $g_k = 0$ in an iteration, a local optimal has been obtained. Figure 2.9 shows this algorithm.

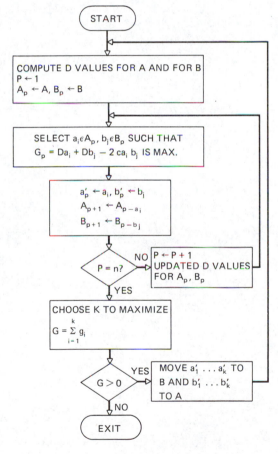

Figure 2.9.

2.4. CONCLUSION

This short survey of graph theoretic models and analysis techniques for software and computer systems engineering is hardly complete. A large area of omission, for example, is in the scheduling of tasks with precedence constraints on multiprocessor systems. Many other applications of the most basic graph algorithms have also been attempted in addressing questions of code optimization, routing in computer network, deadlock situation in resources allocation, and so on. In fact, almost all areas of graph theory may find some applications in software engineering. The reader should consult the fundamental texts [11, 12, 13]. For a good survey in graph models in programming systems, see Reference 14, and for a comprehensive coverage of the applications in computer networks, consult the collection of papers edited by Boesch [15].

REFERENCES

1. D. Cartwright, F. Harary, and R. Z. Norman, *Structural Models: An Introduction to the Theory of Directed Graphs*, Wiley, New York, 1965.
2. S. Warshall, "A Theorem on Boolean Matrices," *Journal ACM*, vol 9, no. 1, Jan. 1962.
3. C. V. Ramamoorthy, "Analysis of Graphs by Connectivity Considerations," *Journal ACM*, Apr. 1966.
4. W. T. Chen, S. F. Ho, and C. V. Ramamoorthy, "On the Automated Generation of Program Test Data," *IEEE Transactions on Software Engineering*, vol. SE-2, no. 4, Dec. 1976.
5. R. K. Deb, "On Generation of Test Data and Minimal Cover of Directed Graphs," *IFIP'77*, 1977.
6. R. C. Cheung, *A Structural Theory for Improving Software Reliability*, Ph.D. Dissertation, Department of Electrical Engineering and Computer Sciences, University of California, Berkeley, 1974.
7. F. E. Allen and J. Cocke, "A Program Data Flow Analysis Procedure," *Comm. ACM*, vol. 16, no. 3, Mar. 1973.
8. T. C. Au and R. E. Gomory, "Multiterminal Network Flows," *SIAM Journal of Applied Mathematics*, vol. 9, Dec. 1961.
9. F. T. Boesch and R. E. Thomas, "On Graphs of Invulnerable Communication Nets," *IEEE Transactions on Circuit Theory*, vol. CT-17, May 1970.
10. B. W. Kernighan and S. Lin, "An Efficient Heuristic Procedure for Partitioning Graphs," *Bell System Technical Journal*, vol. 49, Feb. 1970.
11. F. Harary, *Graph Theory*, Addison-Wesley, 1969.
12. N. Christofides, *Graph Theory: An Algorithmic Approach*, Academic Press, Inc., New York, 1975.
13. L. R. Ford and D. R. Fulkerson, *Flows in Networks*, Princeton University Press, Princeton, 1962.
14. J. L. Baer, "Graph Models in Programming Sys-

tems," *Current Trends in Programming Methodology, Volume III: Software Modeling,* Prentice-Hall, Inc., 1978.

15. F. T. Boesch, ed., "Large-Scale Networks: Theory and Design," *IEEE,* 1976.

3

Modeling and Analysis of Concurrent Systems

Tadao Murata
University of Illinois at Chicago

3.1. INTRODUCTION

Informally speaking, a concurrent system is one in which several activities progress in parallel. Examples of concurrent systems include distributed computing systems, operating systems of large computers, industrial process control systems, and social or organizational systems in which individuals or subgroups engage in many different activities while exchanging information among themselves. In programming, concurrency problems can arise when a task involves several users, processes or processors proceeding in parallel. Concurrency has been a fundamental issue in operating systems for many years. Only recently, however, has the concept of concurrent programming been introduced into the user's program by such languages as Concurrent Pascal, Modula, and others. The field is still so young that few practical modeling techniques have emerged.

This chapter is concerned with modeling and analysis of concurrent systems using Petri nets. In modeling and simulation for computer systems, existing techniques of queuing theory and graph theory are thus far inadequate, both in terms of their representational ability and their computational tractability. However, it is a general consensus [1] that Petri nets and similar formalisms offer some promise in the modeling of *asynchronous, concurrent* execution of cooperating processes. Petri nets and similar graph models can be used by both practitioners and theoreticians. Thus, these nets provide an ideal means of learning from each other; that is, practitioners can learn from theoreticians ways to make their models more methodical, and theoreticians can learn from practitioners ways to make their models more realistic.

3.2. WHAT IS A PETRI NET?

A graph model now known as a Petri net originated in C. A. Petri's dissertation in 1962 [2] and was developed by Holt et al. [3] into a model applicable to many areas in the information processing field. Petri observed that the basic properties of asynchronously communicating processes (or automata) are representable by purely combinational-topological means. He states in Reference 4 that some present and intended applications of the nets go back to the year 1959 when WAIT and SPLIT (which correspond to the input and output of what he calls a transition) were introduced as programming language primitives. He intended to show that these were the only language constructs that are theoretically needed.

The behavior of many systems can be described in terms of system states and their changes. A state may be regarded as holding a certain set of conditions. A state change means the termination of some of the conditions and the beginning of others. An elementary (atomic) state change is called an *event*. Petri nets are graph models for describing system behavior using the notions of conditions and events.

A *Petri net* (or place/transition net) is formally defined as a 6-tuple $N = (P, T, E, M_0, K, W)$. The first three sets $\{P, T, E\}$ are used to describe the static graph structure of a Petri net, where P and T are two disjoint sets of vertices called *places* (or P elements) and *transitions* (or T elements), respectively, and **E** is the edge or arc set consisting of directed edges from a place to a transition or from a transition to a place. In modeling, using the concept of conditions and events, places represent the former and transitions the latter. A transition (an event) has *input and output places* representing the preconditions and postconditions of the event, respectively. For example, in the simple Petri net shown in Figure 3.1a, places $\{p_1, p_2, p_3\}$ represent input places (preconditions) and places $\{p_4, p_5\}$ represent output places (postconditions) of the transition (the event of a marriage ceremony). As illustrated in Figure 3.1, places are usually depicted as circles, and transitions as boxes (or bars when transitions are to represent indivisible "atomic" events). In order to simulate the dynamic behavior of a system or the flow of control and/or data, tokens are used in a Petri net. The presence of a certain number of tokens in a place may be interpreted as holding that number of data items or conditions associated with the place. A token distribution over places may be considered as a system state. $\mathbf{M}_0$ in the tuple N denotes the initial token distribution called the *initial marking,* and it is a function, $\mathbf{M}_0\colon \mathbf{P} \to N$, from **P** (the set of places) to N (the set of non-negative integers). $\mathbf{M}_0(p)$ denotes the number of tokens in a place p. **K** is a function from **P** to $N \cup \{\infty\}$ and $\mathbf{K}(p)$ denotes the capacity of place p, the maximum number of tokens that a place p may hold. Unless otherwise stated, we assume here that $\mathbf{K}(p)$ is infinite for all places, since a net with a finite capacity

constraint can be transformed into its equivalent net without the constraint, as will be shown later in this section. **W** is a function from **E** to N and $\mathbf{W}(e)$ denotes the weight or multiplicity assigned to arc e. An arc with weight $\mathbf{W}(e)$ represents a set of $\mathbf{W}(e)$ parallel unit-weight arcs as illustrated in Figure 3.2, where $\mathbf{W}(a) = \mathbf{W}(c)$ and $\mathbf{W}(b) = 1$. The weight of a unit-weight arc is usually omitted when a net is drawn.

So far, we have described the static structure of a Petri net. In order to simulate the dynamic behavior of a system, a token distribution or *marking* is changed as an event takes place according to the following rules of operation, called the *transition rules:*

1. A transition is said to be *enabled* or *firable* if each of its input places has at least as many tokens as the weight of the respective incoming arc to the transition. (A transition without any input places is always enabled by definition.)
2. An enabled transition may or may not *fire* (depending on whether the event corresponding to the transition may or may not take place).
3. When an enabled transition fires, the number of tokens in each of its input places decreases by the weight of the respective incoming arc to the transition, and the number of tokens in each of its output places increases by the weight of the outgoing arcs from the transition.

Example 1. The transitions shown in Figure 3.1a and Figure 3.2b are enabled, and when

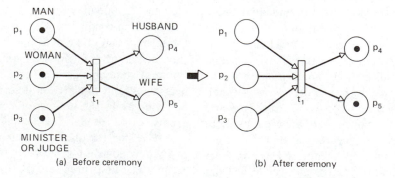

(a) Before ceremony

(b) After ceremony

Figure 3.1. A Petri net representation of the event of a marriage ceremony and illustration of the transition rule.

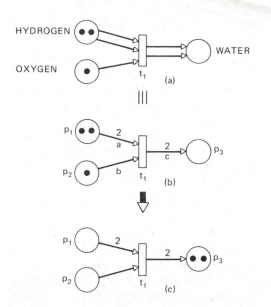

Figure 3.2. A Petri net representation of the chemical reaction $2H_2 + O_2 \rightarrow 2H_2O$, and illustration of the transition rule.

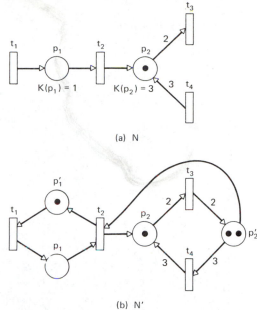

Figure 3.3. Transformation of a net N with the strict transition rule to its equivalent net N′ with the weak transition rule.

they fire, the markings will be changed to those shown in Figure 3.1b and Figure 3.2c, respectively.

The above rule is referred to as the *weak transition rule* and applies to Petri nets with infinite capacity ($K(p) = \infty$ for all p). For Petri nets with finite capacity ($K(p) < \infty$), there is an additional condition for a transition to be enabled so that the number of tokens in each of the output places will not exceed its capacity after firing. The latter rule is referred to as the *strict transition rule* [5]. However, a Petri net N with the strict transition rule can be transformed to its equivalent Petri net N′ with the weak transition rule as follows.

For each place p with finite capacity $K(p)$ and initial marking $M_0(p)$ in N:

1. Add a complementary place p' having initial marking $M_0(p') = K(p) - M_0(p)$.
2. Draw an arc $a' = (p',t)$ from p' to each of the input transitions t of p, where $W(a') = W(a)$ and $a = (t,p)$ is the arc from t to p.
3. Draw an arc $b' = (t,p')$ to p' from each of the output transitions t of p, where $W(b') = W(b)$ and $b = (p,t)$ is the arc from p to t.

Example 2. The above transformation is illustrated in Figure 3.3. The strict transition rule applies to the net N shown in Figure 3.3a, where $K(p_1) = 1$ and $K(p_2) = 3$, and the weak transition rule applies to the net N′ shown in Figure 3.3b. It can be verified that N and N′ are equivalent with respect to the behavior of all possible firing sequences (for example, $(t_1t_2t_3t_4 \ldots)$ is a possible firing sequence in both N and N′, and so on).

3.3. MODELING OF CONCURRENT SYSTEMS

A wide variety of systems have been modeled by Petri nets. In this section, we present several examples of Petri net models that are germane to computer software. From this representation of simple models, the reader will gain an understanding of the representational ability of Petri nets for the large class of concurrent systems.

Figure 3.4 is a Petri net representation of a sequential program. It is easy to see from this figure how the structured programming constructs such as IF-THEN-ELSE and DO-

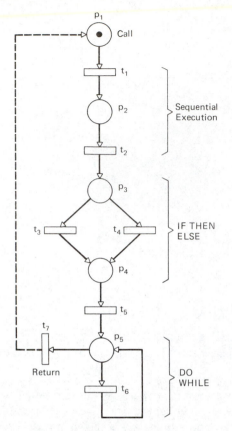

Figure 3.4. A structured sequential program and illustration of a state machine and conflict (decision).

WHILE can be modeled by the Petri net. Note that each transition in this net has exactly one incoming arc and one outgoing arc. The subclass of Petri nets with this property is known as *state machines*. All sequential programs or their flow of control can be modeled by state machines. The transitions t_3 and t_4 in Figure 3.4 are said to be *in conflict,* since when place p_3 has a token, either t_3 or t_4 can fire but not both. A conflict is a fundamental concept of Petri nets and represents a decision from the viewpoint of modeling. State machines can represent decisions but not concurrency.

The concurrent execution constructs such as PARBEGIN/PAREND, FORK/JOIN, and SPLIT/WAIT can be modeled by the Petri net shown in Figure 3.5. The two transitions t_1 and t_2 (or t_1 and t_3 or t_2 and t_3) are said to be *concurrent* since they are causally independent, that is, one transition may fire before or

after or in parallel with the other. Note that each place in the net shown in Figure 3.5 has exactly one incoming arc and one outgoing arc. The subclass of Petri nets with this property is known as *marked graphs*. Marked graphs can model concurrency but not decisions (conflicts).

Petri nets can represent not only the flow of control as shown in the above two examples, but also the flow of data. The net shown in Figure 3.6 illustrates the principle of a data-flow computation. A data-flow computer is one in which instructions are enabled for execution by the arrival of their operands, and may be executed concurrently. In the Petri net representation of a data-flow computation or program, tokens denote the values of current data as well as the availability of data. In the net and marking shown in Figure 3.6, the instructions represented by transitions t_1 and t_2 may be executed concurrently and the resulting data $(a + b)$ and $(a - b)$ will appear in the respective output places. A program for a data-flow computer is normally expressed as a data-flow graph—a directed graph with tokens whose nodes represent instructions and whose arcs represent data paths or data dependencies among instructions [6, 7, 8].

Communication protocols are another area where Petri nets and similar graph models can

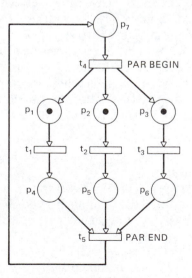

Figure 3.5. Concurrent execution constructs and illustration of a marked graph and concurrency.

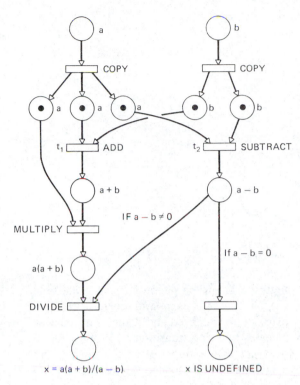

Figure 3.6. A data-flow computation for $x = a(a + b)/(a - b)$.

and makes use of the data flow and interpretation domains to reduce the state space.

In distributed computing systems, resources and information are shared among several processes. This sharing must be controlled or synchronized to insure correct operations of the overall system. Petri nets have been used by many authors to model and solve a variety of *synchronization problems* such as the mutual exclusion problem, the readers/writers problem, the producer/consumer problem, and the dining philosophers' problem [12–14]. For example, the Petri net in Figure 3.8 shows a method of mutual exclusion, where the two processes cannot enter concurrently their critical sections. Figure 3.9 is a representation of the producer-consumer bounded-buffer interprocess communication mechanism operating in a one-producer two-consumer system. A readers/writers system is shown in Figure 3.10, where n tokens in the place p_1 represent n processes that may read and write in a shared memory. Several processes may be reading concurrently, but when a process is writing, no other process can be reading or writing. In the net of Figure 3.10, it is easily verified that as many as n tokens (processes) may be in place p_3 (reading) if no token is in place p_5 (no process is writing), and that only one token (process) can be in place p_5 (writing) since all the n tokens in place p_6 will be removed when t_5 fires (see Example 6).

Dijkstra's dining philosophers' problem is stated as follows. Five philosophers are sitting around a round table where there are only five

be used to represent and specify essential features of a system. The liveness and safeness (see Section 3.4) properties of a Petri net are often used as correctness criteria in communication protocols. Figure 3.7 shows a simple communication protocol between two processes [9, 10]. The SARA graph model of communication protocols [11] is based on UCLA graph models equivalent to Petri nets

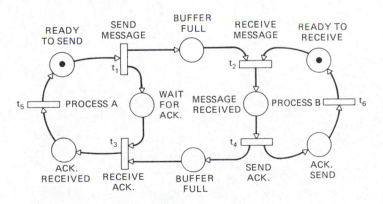

Figure 3.7. A communication protocol between two processes.

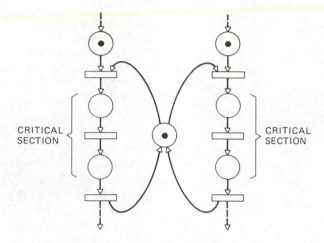

Figure 3.8. Mutual exclusion.

forks as shown in Figure 3.11a. The philosophers may think or eat. To eat, a philosopher needs the two forks nearest him. Thus two neighbors cannot eat at the same time. (This problem corresponds to the synchronization problem involving five processes and five resources.) A modified Petri net representation of this system is shown in Figure 3.11b. To reduce the size of the net model, we have made the following two modifications: (1) Each token has a color, and (2) each arc has a label to specify which token(s) are removed or added when a transition fires. For example, in

Figure 3.11b when philosopher no. 2 starts to eat, token c_2 in place p_1 and tokens f_2 and f_3 in place p_3 are removed and token c_2 is added to place p_2 by firing transition t_1. While philosopher no. 2 is eating (token c_2 is in p_2), his neighbors (tokens c_1 and c_3) cannot eat because tokens f_2 and f_3 are not in p_3, although pilosopher no. 4 or no. 0 may eat. This modified Petri net is a special case of a predicate/transition net [15]. The standard Petri net representation of the net in Figure 3.11b can be obtained by duplicating the net for each of five colors, where place p_3 is shared by two dupli-

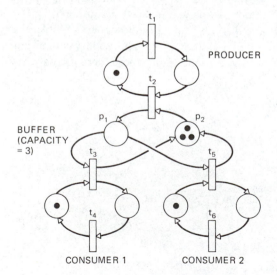

Figure 3.9. A bounded buffer producer-consumer system.

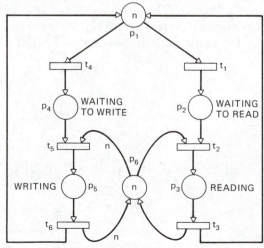

Figure 3.10. A reader-writer system and the Petri net used for Examples 6 and 11.

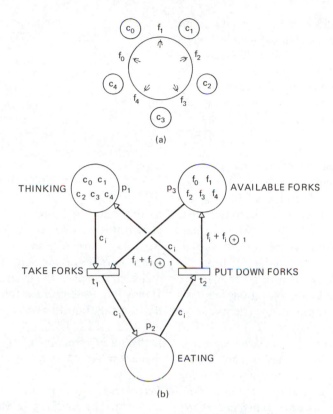

Figure 3.11. A modified Petri net representation of the dining philosophers' system, where $\oplus$ denotes modulo 5 addition.

cated nets since a fork is shared by two neighboring philosophers.

3.4. ANALYSIS PROBLEMS FOR PETRI NETS

The previous section provided a glimpse of the representational ability of Petri nets. A major strength of Petri nets is not just their ability to represent concurrent systems graphically, but their ability to support analysis of many properties and problems associated with concurrent systems. The following properties and questions are most commonly discussed in the literature on Petri nets.

Reachability. The firing of an enabled transition will change the token distribution (marking) in a net according to the transition rule described in Section 3.2. A sequence of firings results in one marking after another. We say that a marking M_1 is *reachable* from a marking M_0 if there exists a sequence of firings that transforms M_0 to M_1. Henceforth $R(M_0)$ denotes the set of all possible markings reachable from a marking M_0. Reachability is a fundamental property used for studying the dynamic behavior of any system. Although the reachability problem for Petri nets has been shown exponential-space hard [16], it appears decidable according to a recent report by Mayr [17].

Boundedness. A Petri net is said to be *k-bounded* for the initial marking M_0 if each place of the net gets, at most, a finite number k of tokens for every marking reachable from M_0. For example, the net shown in Figure 3.9 is 3-bounded, and the net in Figure 3.10 is *n*-bounded.

Safeness. A Petri net is said to be *safe* if it is 1-bounded, that is, $M(p) \leq 1$ for each place p and every marking M in $R(M_0)$. The Petri nets in Figures 3.4, 3.5, and 3.7 are all safe for the respective marking shown. Places in a Petri net are often used to represent buffers and registers for storing intermediate data. By verifying that the net is bounded or safe, it is guaranteed that there will be no overflows in the buffers or registers, regardless of firing sequences chosen.

Liveness. The concept of liveness is closely related to the complete absence of deadlocks in operating systems. A Petri net is said to be *live* for the initial marking M_0 if, no matter what marking has been reached from M_0, it is possible ultimately to fire any transition of the net by progressing through some further firing sequence. Thus, a Petri net with a live marking guarantees deadlock-free operations, regardless of firing sequences chosen. The markings of the nets shown in Figures 3.7, 3.9, and 3.10 are all live. However, the marking shown in Figure 3.12 is not live, although each transition can be fired once in the order of firing transitions t_2, t_4, t_5, t_1, and t_3. These transitions in Figure 3.12 are sometimes called *potentially firable* [18] or live at level 1 (L1) according to the following classification of levels of liveness [19]. A transition is *dead* (L0) if it can never be fired. A transition t is *live at level 1* (L1) if t appears in some firing sequence starting at M_0. A transition t is *live at level 2* (L2) if, for every positive integer n there is a firing sequence in which t appears at least n times. A transition t is *live at level 3* (L3) if there is an infinite firing sequence in which t appears in-

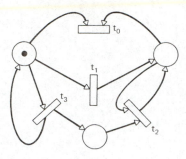

Figure 3.13. Different levels of liveness: Transition t_i is live at level i for $i = 0, 1, 2,$ and 3.

finitely often. A transition t is *live at level 4* (L4) if it is L1 for every marking in $R(M_0)$. A Petri net is live at level i if every transition is live at level i. Liveness at level 4 is strongest and corresponds to the liveness defined earlier. It may be a good exercise for the reader to verify that the transitions t_0, t_1, t_2, and t_3 in Figure 3.13 are L0, L1, L2, L3, respectively. Lautenbach [20] proposes another classification of liveness different from the above.

Persistence. A Petri net is said to be *persistent* if at any marking in $R(M_0)$ an enabled transition can be disabled only from its own firing. A safe persistent Petri net can be transformed into a marked graph by duplicating some transitions and places [21].

Coverability. A marking M is said to be *coverable* if there exists a marking M_1 reachable from initial marking M_0 such that $M_1(p) \geq M(p)$ for each place p. Coverability is closely related to potential firability. Let M be the marking that enables a transition t with the minimum number of tokens. Then, t is potentially firable if and only if M is coverable, or t is dead if and only if M is not coverable.

Reversibility. A Petri net is said to be *reversible* if for each marking M in $R(M_0)$, M_0 is in $R(M)$. The reversibility problem of Petri nets has been shown decidable in Reference 22.

Synchronic Distance. Roughly speaking, the synchronic distance $d(t_1, t_2)$ between two transitions t_1 and t_2 is a measure of mutual dependencies between two events t_1 and t_2. It is formally defined by

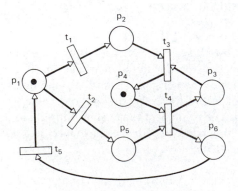

Figure 3.12. A Petri net that is safe, but not live (since no transitions are enabled after firing t_1).

$$d(t_1,t_2) = \text{Max}\{|\#(\sigma,t_1) - \#(\sigma,t_2)|\} \quad (1)$$

where the maximum is taken over all possible firing sequences and subsequences, and $\#(\sigma,t_i)$ denotes the number of appearances of t_i, $i = 1, 2, \ldots$, in a firing sequence σ. For example, in the Petri net shown in Figure 3.4 $d(t_1,t_2) = d(t_1,t_5) = 1$ and $d(t_1,t_6) = d(t_3,t_4) = \infty$. In the net shown in Figure 3.5, $d(t_1,t_2) = 2$ because after firing t_2 and t_3 there is the firing subsequence $(t_1t_5t_4t_1)$ in which t_1 appears twice without t_2. The synchronic distance is an important metric that can be used to implement "fairness" in resource-sharing concurrent systems. The weighted synchronic distance and other details are discussed in Reference 15.

The Petri net properties discussed so far depend not only on the graph structure of a given net but also on the initial marking M_0. There are Petri net properties that depend only on their structure and are independent of initial markings. These properties are referred to as structural properties. Some of these structural properties are consistency, conservativeness, controllability, and repetitiveness, which will be discussed in Section 3.7.

3.5. ANALYSIS METHODS

As pointed out earlier, a major strength of Petri nets is its ability to support analysis. This section presents two approaches to Petri net analysis.

The Coverability Tree

For the initial marking M_0 in a Petri net, some transitions may be enabled. Firing each transition enabled in M_0, we may obtain as many different markings as the number of the enabled transitions. For each new marking resulting from M_0, there may be more enabled transitions. If the above firings of enabled transitions are repeated at each new marking, one can construct a tree representation of markings. Here, nodes represent markings generated from M_0 [the root] and its successors, and each arc represents a transition firing showing

which marking will result from which as the result of the firing.

The above tree representation, however, will grow too large to handle or become infinite if the net is unbounded. To reduce the size of the tree or to keep it finite, we use a special symbol ω, which can be thought of as "infinity." For each integer n, ω has the properties that $\omega > n$, $\omega \pm n = \omega$ and $\omega \geq \omega$. The coverability tree for a Petri net is constructed as follows:

1. Label the initial marking M_0 the root and tag it "new."
2. While new markings exist do the following:
   2.1. Select a new marking M.
   2.2. If M is identical to another marking in the tree, then tag M "old" and go to another new marking.
   2.3. If no transitions are enabled in M, tag M "terminal."
   2.4. While there exist enabled transitions in M, do the following for each transition t enabled in M:
   2.4.1. Obtain the marking M' that results from firing t in M.
   2.4.2. If there exists a marking M'' in the path from the root to M such that $M' \geq M''$ and $M' \neq M''$, then replace $M'(p)$ by ω whenever $M'(p) > M''(p)$.
   2.4.3. Introduce M' as a node, draw an arc from M to M' labeled t, and tag M' "new."

Example 3. Consider the Petri net shown in Figure 3.14. For the initial marking $M_0 = (1, 0, 0)$, t_1 is the only enabled transition and can be fired an arbitrary number of times, resulting in a new marking $M_1 = (1, 0, \omega)$. In M_1, t_1 and t_2 are enabled. Firing t_1 results in the old marking M_1, and firing t_2 results in a new marking $M_2 = (0, 1, \omega)$. In M_2, t_3 and t_4 are enabled, and their firings result in the old markings M_2 and M_1, respectively. Thus, we have the coverability tree shown in Figure 3.15.

It is easy to see that a Petri net is bounded iff (if and only if) the symbol ω never appears in its coverability tree, and that it is safe iff

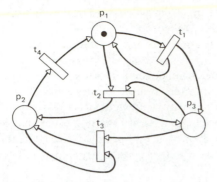

Figure 3.14. A live Petri net for Example 3.

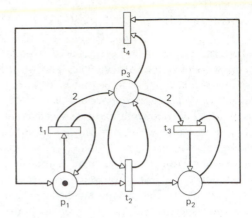

Figure 3.16. A nonlive Petri net that has the coverability tree shown in Figure 3.15.

there are only 0 and 1 in the markings represented by the nodes of its coverability tree. If a Petri net is bounded, it is a finite state system, and all the analysis problems mentioned in Section 3.4 can be solved by the coverability tree or state diagram, although it is an exhaustive method. However, because of the information lost by the use of the symbol ω (which may represent only even or odd numbers, etc.), the reachability and liveness problems of unbounded Petri nets cannot be solved by the coverability tree method. For example, the two different Petri nets shown in Figures 3.14 and 3.16 [23] have the same coverability tree shown in Figure 3.15, but the one in Figure 3.14 is a live Petri net, whereas the one in Figure 3.16 is not (because no transitions are enabled after firing t_1, t_2, and t_3).

Although it is an exhaustive method, the coverability tree can also be used for the coverability problem [24] and to test if the weighted sum of tokens are the same for all markings in $\mathbf{R(M_0)}$.

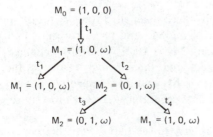

Figure 3.15. The coverability tree of the Petri nets shown in Figures 3.14 and 3.16.

Matrix State Equations [37]

The dynamic behaviors of many electrical and mechanical systems can be described by differential equations, or linear equations if the system is linear. It would be ideal to have an analogue for Petri nets. In this spirit, this section will discuss some matrix equations that govern the dynamic behavior of concurrent systems modeled by Petri nets. However, solvability of these equations is somewhat limited partly because of the nondeterministic nature inherent in Petri net models and because of the constraint that solutions must be found in nonnegative integers.

Incidence Matrix. For a Petri net with n transitions and m places, the incidence matrix $\mathbf{A} = [a_{ij}]$ is an $n \times m$ matrix of integers, and its typical entry a_{ij} is given by:

$$a_{ij} = a_{ij}^+ - a_{ij}^-$$

where a_{ij}^- = the weight of arc to transition i from its input place j, and a_{ij}^+ = the weight of arc from transition i to its output place j. (For a marked graph, the above matrix $\mathbf{A}$ reduces to the well-known incidence matrix of a directed graph. For this reason, we use $\mathbf{A}$ as the incidence matrix of a Petri net instead of its transpose used by many authors.)

It is easy to see from the transition rule described in Section 3.2 that a_{ij}^-, a_{ij}^+ and a_{ij} represent the numbers of tokens removed, added, and changed in place j, respectively, when transition i fires; and that transition i is enabled in marking $\mathbf{M}$ iff $a_{ij}^- \leq \mathbf{M}(j)$ for $j = 1,2, \ldots, m$. A pair consisting of transition i and place j such that $a_{ij}^+ = a_{ij}^- \neq 0$ is called a *self-loop*. It is assumed that Petri nets considered henceforth have no self-loops (or have been made self-loop-free by adding another pair of a transition and a place on a self-loop).

State Equation. We denote marking $\mathbf{M}_k$ as the $m \times 1$ column vector whose jth entry is $\mathbf{M}_k(j)$ (= the number of tokens in place j). Let $\mathbf{M}_k$ be the marking resulting from another marking $\mathbf{M}_{k-1}$ by firing one transition i at the kth firing. To denote the transition i fired at the kth firing, we define the elementary firing vector $\mathbf{U}_k$ as the $n \times 1$ column vector all of whose entries are zero except for the ith entry being equal to 1. Since the ith row of the incidence matrix $\mathbf{A}$ denotes the change of the marking as the result of firing transition i, we have the following matrix state equation:

$$\mathbf{M}_k = \mathbf{M}_{k-1} + \mathbf{A}^T\mathbf{U}_k \quad k = 1,2,3,\ldots \quad (2)$$

where superscript T denotes the matrix transpose. As long as a firing is *legal*, that is, only an enabled transition is fired, it is guaranteed that

$$\mathbf{M}_{k-1} + \mathbf{A}^T\mathbf{U}_k \geq 0 \quad \text{for each } k \quad (3)$$

that is, $\mathbf{M}_k$ remains a vector of non-negative integers.

Example 4a. The incidence matrix and the state equation (2) are illustrated below, where the marking $\mathbf{M}_1$ results from the initial marking $\mathbf{M}_0$ by firing transition t_2 in the Petri net shown in Figure 3.17:

$$
\begin{array}{c}
p_1 \\ p_2 \\ p_3 \\ p_4
\end{array}
\underbrace{\begin{bmatrix} 2 \\ 0 \\ 0 \\ 1 \end{bmatrix}}_{\mathbf{M}_1}
= \underbrace{\begin{bmatrix} 1 \\ 1 \\ 0 \\ 0 \end{bmatrix}}_{\mathbf{M}_0}
+ \underbrace{\begin{bmatrix} -1 & 1 & 1 \\ 0 & -1 & 0 \\ 1 & 0 & -1 \\ -1 & 1 & 1 \end{bmatrix}}_{\mathbf{A}^T}
\underbrace{\begin{bmatrix} 0 \\ 1 \\ 0 \end{bmatrix}}_{\mathbf{U}_1}
$$

Necessary Condition for Reachability: Suppose a marking $\mathbf{M}_d$ is reachable from $\mathbf{M}_0$ by the firing sequence $\mathbf{U}_1, \mathbf{U}_2, \ldots, \mathbf{U}_d$. Then, we have the following d equations from (2):

$$\mathbf{M}_1 = \mathbf{M}_0 + \mathbf{A}^T\mathbf{U}_1$$
$$\mathbf{M}_2 = \mathbf{M}_1 + \mathbf{A}^T\mathbf{U}_2$$
$$\mathbf{M}_d = \mathbf{M}_{d-1} + \mathbf{A}^T\mathbf{U}_d$$

Combining the above d equations, we get

$$\mathbf{M}_d = \mathbf{M}_0 + \mathbf{A}^T\Sigma_{k=1}^d\mathbf{U}_k$$

or simply

$$\mathbf{A}^T\Sigma = \Delta\mathbf{M} \quad (4)$$

where $\Delta\mathbf{M} = \mathbf{M}_d - \mathbf{M}_0$ and $\Sigma \triangleq \Sigma_{k=1}^d\mathbf{U}_k$ is an $n \times 1$ column vector of nonnegative integers called the *firing count vector*. The ith entry of Σ denotes the number of times that transition i must fire to transform marking $\mathbf{M}_0$ to $\mathbf{M}_d$.

Let r be the rank of the incidence matrix $\mathbf{A}$ and partition A in the following form:

$$
\mathbf{A} = \begin{bmatrix} \mathbf{A}_{11} & \mathbf{A}_{12} \\ \mathbf{A}_{21} & \mathbf{A}_{22} \end{bmatrix} \begin{matrix} \updownarrow r \\ \updownarrow n - r \end{matrix} \quad (5)
$$

where $\mathbf{A}_{12}$ is a nonsingular square matrix of order r. Now consider the following system of

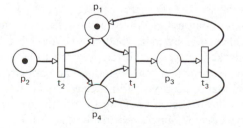

Figure 3.17. A Petri net used for Examples 4 and 12.

equations, which is the transposed homogeneous system corresponding to Eq. (4)

$$\mathbf{A}\mathbf{y} = 0 \tag{6}$$

where an integer solution $\mathbf{y}$ of Eq. (6) is called *S-invariant* of the Petri net (see Section 3.7). A set of $(m - r)$ linearly independent solutions $\mathbf{y}$ of Eq. (6) can be given as the rows of the following $(m - r) \times m$ matrix $\mathbf{B}_f$:

$$\mathbf{B}_f = [\mathbf{I}_\mu : - \mathbf{A}_{11}^T (\mathbf{A}_{12}^T)^{-1}] \tag{7}$$

where $\mathbf{I}_\mu$ is the identity matrix of order $\mu = m - r$. Note that $\mathbf{A}$ and $\mathbf{B}_f$ are orthogonal to each other, that is,

$$\mathbf{A}\mathbf{B}_f^T = 0 \tag{8}$$

and that $\mathbf{B}_f$ corresponds to the fundamental circuit matrix in the case of a marked graph.

It is well known in matrix algebra [25] that the system Eq. (4) is consistent (i.e., has a solution Σ over the rational field) iff $\Delta\mathbf{M}$ is orthogonal to every solution of its transposed homogenous system (6), that is,

$$\mathbf{B}_f\Delta\mathbf{M} = 0 \tag{9}$$

Thus, if $\mathbf{M}_d$ is reachable from $\mathbf{M}_0$, then the corresponding firing count vector Σ must exist and Eq. (4) must be consistent. Therefore, we have the following necessary condition for reachability [37]:

Theorem 1. If $\mathbf{M}_d$ is reachable from $\mathbf{M}_0$ in a Petri net, then $\mathbf{B}_f\Delta\mathbf{M} = 0$, where $\Delta\mathbf{M} = \mathbf{M}_d - \mathbf{M}_0$ and $\mathbf{B}_f$ is given by Eq. (7).

The converse of Theorem 1 provides the following sufficient condition for nonreachability [37].

Theorem 2. In a Petri net, a marking $\mathbf{M}_d$ is not reachable from $\mathbf{M}_0$ ($\neq \mathbf{M}_d$) if their difference is a linear combination of the rows of $\mathbf{B}_f$, that is,

$$\Delta\mathbf{M} = \mathbf{B}_f^T \mathbf{V} \tag{10}$$

where $\mathbf{V}$ is a nonzero $\mu \times 1$ column vector.

Proof. If Eq. (10) holds, then $\mathbf{B}_f\Delta\mathbf{M} = \mathbf{B}_f\mathbf{B}_f^T\mathbf{V} \not\equiv 0$ since $\mathbf{V} \not\equiv 0$ and $\mathbf{B}_f\mathbf{B}_f^T$ is a $\mu \times \mu$ nonsingular matrix (because the rank of $\mathbf{B}_f = \mu = m - r$). Therefore by Theorem 1 $\mathbf{M}_d$ is not reachable from $\mathbf{M}_0$.

Example 4b. For the Petri net shown in Figure 3.17, $r = \text{rank } \mathbf{A} = 2$, and $\mathbf{A}$ can be partitioned in the form of Eq. (5):

$$
\mathbf{A} = \begin{array}{c} \\ t_1 \\ t_2 \\ \\ t_3 \end{array}
\begin{array}{cc} \begin{array}{cccc} p_1 & p_2 & p_3 & p_4 \end{array} \\
\left[\begin{array}{cc|cc} -1 & 0 & 1 & -1 \\ 1 & -1 & 0 & 1 \\ \hline 1 & 0 & -1 & 1 \end{array} \right] \end{array}
$$

Thus, $\mathbf{B}_f$ for this Petri net can be obtained by Eq. (7):

$$
\mathbf{B}_f = \left[\begin{array}{cc} 1 & 0 \\ 0 & 1 \end{array} - \begin{pmatrix} -1 & 1 \\ 0 & -1 \end{pmatrix} \begin{pmatrix} 1 & 0 \\ -1 & 1 \end{pmatrix}^{-1} \right]
$$

$$
= \left[\begin{array}{cc|cc} 1 & 0 & 0 & -1 \\ 0 & 1 & 1 & 1 \end{array} \right]
$$

It is easy to verify that $\mathbf{B}_f\Delta\mathbf{M} = 0$ holds for $\mathbf{M}_0 = (1\ 1\ 0\ 0)^T$ and $\mathbf{M}_1 = (2\ 0\ 0\ 1)^T$ where $\Delta\mathbf{M} = \mathbf{M}_1 - \mathbf{M}_0 = (1\ -1\ 0\ 1)^T$, since $\mathbf{M}_1$ is reachable from $\mathbf{M}_0$ (Theorem 1).

The matrices and equations presented in this section can be used for analysis of many more properties and problems of Petri nets, as will be discussed later. For the time being, we will restrict ourselves to a subclass of Petri nets called marked graphs.

3.6. DECISION-FREE CONCURRENT SYSTEMS

As stated in Section 3.3, marked graphs are a subclass of Petri nets that can model *concurrency* but not decisions (or conflicts). Thus, concurrent systems that can be modeled by marked graphs are often referred to as decision-free concurrent systems. The comparison of marked graphs with general Petri nets is similar to that of linear systems with nonlinear systems, or finite state machines with Turing machines. There is a trade-off between them; that is, the former is more amenable to analysis and the latter has more modeling power. Because analytic techniques for the latter model are intractable or unavailable, we often find that the former model is useful for quick analysis and can be the basis for analyzing more general models.

Analysis of Marked Graphs

Since each place in a marked graph has exactly one incoming and one outgoing arc of unit weight, a marked graph can be drawn as a marked directed graph, where nodes correspond to transitions, arcs to places, and tokens are placed on arcs. For example, the Petri net of a communication protocol shown in Figure 3.7 can be redrawn as the marked directed graph shown in Figure 3.18. The firing of a node (transition) in a marked graph consists of removing one token from each of its incoming arcs (input places) and adding one token to each of its outgoing arcs (output places). If a node is on a directed circuit (or loop), then exactly one of its incoming arcs and one of its outgoing arcs belong to the directed circuit. If a node does not lie on the directed circuit in question, none of the arcs incident to that node will belong to the directed circuit. Thus, we have the following token invariance property [26]:

Property 1.   The token count in a directed circuit is invariant under any node firing.

By Property 1, if there are no tokens on a directed circuit at an initial marking, then this directed circuit remains token-free and the nodes on this directed circuit must forever be nonfirable. It can also be shown by back-tracing unmarked arcs that if a node cannot be made firable by any firing sequence, then this node must belong to a token-free directed circuit. Therefore, we have:

Property 2 (liveness).   A marked graph $\mathbf{G}$ is live for a marking $\mathbf{M}_0$ iff $\mathbf{G}$ has no token-free directed circuit in $\mathbf{M}_0$.

Using the min-max theorem in References 27 and 28 or Eq. (19) in the next section we can show that:

Property 3.   Max $\{\mathbf{M}(e) \mid \mathbf{M} \in \mathbf{R}(\mathbf{M}_0)\}$ = Min $\{\mathbf{M}_0(\mathbf{C}) \mid e \in \mathbf{C}\}$, where $\mathbf{M}_0(\mathbf{C})$ denotes the token count of a directed circuit $\mathbf{C}$.

From Property 3, we can say that an arc e will have, at most, one token iff this arc e belongs to a directed circuit having a token count of one, and does not belong to any token-free directed circuit for initial marking $\mathbf{M}_0$. Thus, we have:

Property 4 (safeness).   A live marking is safe in a marked graph $\mathbf{G}$ iff every arc in $\mathbf{G}$ belongs to a directed circuit with token count one.

It is interesting to know that live-and-safe markings are related to minimal (but not minimum) feedback arc sets [29], and that the maximum live and safe marking is akin to a maximum-cost minimum-flow problem [26].

Let $\mathbf{A}$ and $\mathbf{B}_f$ be the node-to-arc incidence matrix and the fundamental circuit matrix of the directed graph underlying a marked graph $\mathbf{G}$. It is well known in graph theory [30] that

$$\mathbf{B}_f \mathbf{A}^T = 0 \qquad (11)$$

Thus, if $\mathbf{M}_d$ is reachable from $\mathbf{M}_0$, we have from Eqs. (11) and (4) that

$$\mathbf{B}_f \Delta \mathbf{M} = 0 \text{ or } \mathbf{B}_f \mathbf{M}_d = \mathbf{B}_f \mathbf{M}_0 \qquad (12)$$

Conversely, if Eq. (12) holds, then it can be shown [31] that two live markings $\mathbf{M}_d$ and $\mathbf{M}_0$ are mutually reachable from one to the other. When $\mathbf{M}_0$ is not live, $\mathbf{G}$ has some token-free directed circuits. If the nodes on these token-free directed circuits need not be fired, that is, if the zero entries of the minimum firing count vector Σ satisfying Eq. (4) correspond to the nodes of the token-free directed circuits, then

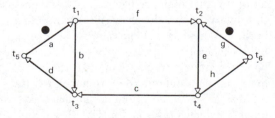

Figure 3.18. The marked graph representation of a communication protocol shown in Figure 3.7 and used for Example 10.

it has been shown in Reference 31 that M_d is reachable from M_0 iff Eq. (12) holds. Stated above is a *necessary and sufficient condition for reachability* of marked graphs in the most general case. If G is strongly connected, then condition in Eq. (12) is equivalent to saying that M_d and M_0 have identical token counts on every directed circuit in G. If G is a tree, Eq. (12) holds for any two markings since there are no circuits in a tree and $B_f = 0$.

Example 5. Consider the marked graph G shown in Figure 3.19, where G is not strongly connected and the two markings M_0 and M_d are not live. Condition (12) holds since $\Delta M = M_d - M_0 = (0\ 0\ 1\ -2\ -1\ -1)^T$ and

$$\underbrace{\begin{bmatrix} a & b & c & d & e & f \\ 1 & 0 & 0 & -1 & 1 & 1 \\ 0 & 1 & 0 & 1 & -1 & -1 \\ 0 & 0 & 1 & 0 & 1 & 0 \end{bmatrix}}_{B_f} \begin{bmatrix} 0 \\ 0 \\ 1 \\ -2 \\ -1 \\ -1 \end{bmatrix} = \begin{bmatrix} 0 \\ 0 \\ 0 \end{bmatrix}$$

where $\{d,e,f\}$ are chosen as the reference spanning tree for the above B_f. Equation (4) for this marked graph is given by

$$\underbrace{\begin{matrix} & 1 & 2 & 3 & 4 \\ a & \begin{bmatrix} 1 & 0 & 0 & -1 \\ b & -1 & 0 & 0 & 1 \\ c & 0 & 1 & -1 & 0 \\ d & 1 & -1 & 0 & 0 \\ e & 0 & -1 & 1 & 0 \\ f & 0 & 0 & -1 & 1 \end{bmatrix} \end{matrix}}_{A^T} \begin{bmatrix} \sigma_1 \\ \sigma_2 \\ \sigma_3 \\ \sigma_4 \\ \Sigma \end{bmatrix} = \underbrace{\begin{bmatrix} 0 \\ 0 \\ 1 \\ -2 \\ -1 \\ -1 \end{bmatrix}}_{\Delta M}$$

Setting $\sigma_4 = 0$ and solving the following equation corresponding to the spanning tree $\{d,e,f\}$:

$$\begin{matrix} d \\ e \\ f \end{matrix} \begin{bmatrix} 1 & -1 & 0 \\ 0 & -1 & 1 \\ 0 & 0 & -1 \end{bmatrix} \begin{bmatrix} \sigma_1 \\ \sigma_2 \\ \sigma_3 \end{bmatrix} = \begin{bmatrix} -2 \\ -1 \\ -1 \end{bmatrix}$$

we have $\sigma_1 = 0$, $\sigma_2 = 2$, and $\sigma_3 = 1$ or $\Sigma = (0\ 2\ 1\ 0)^T$. Since all the zero entries in Σ correspond to the nodes 1 and 4 of the token-free

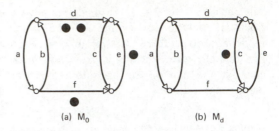

(a) M_0 (b) M_d

Figure 3.19. The marked graph used for Example 5.

directed circuit $\{a,b\}$, M_d is reachable from M_0 (by firing nodes 2, 3, and 2).

Synthesis of Marked Graphs

From the well-known relationship $B_f C_f^T = 0$ [30], it can be seen that Eq. (12) holds if ΔM is a row of the fundamental cutset matrix C_f. In fact, it can be shown [31] that:

Property 5. In a marked graph G, two live markings M_0 and M_d are mutually reachable iff $\Delta M = M_d - M_0$ is a linear combination of a set of fundamental cutsets of G.

In system design, we are often given a set of states that are mutually reachable. If a state is coded with a p-tuple of 0s and 1s, then the given set of states can be regarded as a set of (possibly safe) markings in a marked graph with p edges. Can we find a marked graph, with the given set of binary p-tuples as mutually reachable markings? Using Property 5 this synthesis problem can be converted to that of realizing cutset matrices of directed graphs [31].

The above synthesis method yields live (but not necessarily safe) marked graphs. A modular synthesis approach described in Reference 27 makes use of Petri net transformations [32–35] that preserve liveness and safeness. In addition to guaranteeing liveness and safeness, this approach can also prescribe several other properties such as: (1) the number of reachability classes, (2) the maximum resource (temporary storage) requirement, (3) the maximum computation rate (performance), (4) the number of states, and (5) the number of system components (arcs and nodes). The details can be found in Reference 27.

3.7. STRUCTURAL PROPERTIES

Structural properties are those that depend only on the topological structures of Petri nets and are independent of initial marking $\mathbf{M}_0$. Thus these properties can often be characterized in terms of the incidence matrix $\mathbf{A}$ and its associated algebraic linear equations. In this section, we discuss the following structural properties of Petri nets: controllability, structural boundedness, conservativeness, repetitiveness, consistency, and S- and T-invariants. As before, let m and n be the numbers of places and transitions of a Petri net, respectively.

Controllability. A Petri net is said to be *completely controllable* if any marking is reachable from any initial marking. Applying the well-known controllability condition of dynamic systems [36] to the state equation of Petri nets, Eq. (2), it is easy to show [37] that if a Petri net with m places is completely controllable, then we have

$$\text{Rank } A = m \qquad (13)$$

Because of the requirement that the firing vectors $\mathbf{U}_k$ be vectors of nonnegative integers, Eq. (13) is only a necessary condition for controllability of Petri nets. However, it is necessary and sufficient for marked graphs since for a connected marked graph $\mathbf{G}$ having n nodes, it is known that

$$\text{Rank } A = n - 1 \qquad (14)$$

From Eqs. (13) and (14), we have $m = n - 1$, that is, there are only $(n - 1)$ arcs to connect the n nodes, and no circuits in $\mathbf{G}$. So, $\mathbf{G}$ is a tree. Therefore, from Eq. (12), it is easy to see that a marked graph is completely controllable iff it is a tree or a forest (a collection of trees). This shows that trees are a structure amenable to analysis, and it may explain why tree structures are employed in representing and analyzing many computer algorithms.

Structural Boundedness. A Petri net is said to be *structurally bounded* if it is bounded for any initial marking $\mathbf{M}_0$ ($<\infty$).

Theorem 3. A Petri net is structurally bounded iff there exists an m-vector $\mathbf{y}$ of positive integers such that $\mathbf{Ay} \leq 0$.

Proof: ($\leftarrow$) Suppose the stated condition is true. Let $\mathbf{M} \in \mathbf{R}(\mathbf{M}_0)$. Then from Eq. (4) we have

$$\mathbf{M} = \mathbf{M}_0 + \mathbf{A}^T \mathbf{\Sigma} \quad \mathbf{\Sigma} \geq 0 \qquad (15)$$

Consider the inner product of vectors $\mathbf{M}$ and $\mathbf{y}$:

$$\mathbf{M}^T \mathbf{y} = \mathbf{M}_0^T \mathbf{y} + \mathbf{\Sigma}^T \mathbf{Ay} \qquad (16)$$

Since $\mathbf{Ay} \leq 0$ and $\mathbf{\Sigma} \geq 0$, we have

$$\mathbf{M}^T \mathbf{y} \leq \mathbf{M}_0^T \mathbf{y} \qquad (17)$$

Thus, $\mathbf{M}(p)$, the number of tokens in any place p is bounded by

$$\mathbf{M}(p) \leq (\mathbf{M}_0^T \mathbf{y})/\mathbf{y}(p) \qquad (18)$$

where $\mathbf{y}(p)$ is the pth component of $\mathbf{y}$.

($\rightarrow$): Suppose the stated condition is not true. Then from Farkas's lemma [38], there exists an n-vector $\mathbf{x} \geq 0$ such that $\mathbf{A}^T \mathbf{x} \gneqq 0$. (For two vectors $\mathbf{x}_1$ and $\mathbf{x}_2$, $\mathbf{x}_1 \gneqq \mathbf{x}_2$ means $\mathbf{x}_1 \geq \mathbf{x}_2$ and $\mathbf{x}_1 \neq \mathbf{x}_2$). Then there exist two markings $\mathbf{M}$ and $\mathbf{M}_0$, and a firing count vector $\mathbf{x}$ such that $\mathbf{M} - \mathbf{M}_0 = \mathbf{A}^T \mathbf{x} \gneqq 0$ or $\mathbf{M} \gneqq \mathbf{M}_0$. Choose $\mathbf{M}_0$ large enough and repeat the firing sequence $\mathbf{x}$ indefinitely. The net will be unbounded.

Conservativeness. A Petri net is said to be *conservative* or an *S-invariant net* if there exists a *positive* integer $\mathbf{y}(p)$ associated with each place p such that the weighted sum of tokens, $\Sigma_{p=1}^{m} \mathbf{M}(p)\mathbf{y}(p) = \mathbf{M}^T \mathbf{y} = \mathbf{M}_0^T \mathbf{y}$ is a constant for any fixed initial marking $\mathbf{M}_0$ and any marking $\mathbf{M} \in \mathbf{R}(\mathbf{M}_0)$. Note that if $\mathbf{y}(p) = 1$ for all places p, then the weighted sum is the total number of tokens in the net. It is clear from Eq. (16) that:

Theorem 4. A Petri net is conservative iff there exists an m-vector of positive integers $\mathbf{y}$ such that $\mathbf{A}\mathbf{y} = 0$.

Repetitiveness. A Petri net is said to be *repetitive* if there exists a marking $\mathbf{M}_0$ and a firing sequence σ from $\mathbf{M}_0$ such that every transition occurs infinitely often in σ.

Theorem 5. A Petri net is repetitive iff there exists an n-vector $\mathbf{x}$ of positive integers such that $\mathbf{A}^T\mathbf{x} \geq 0$.

Proof. If there exists an $\mathbf{x} > 0$ such that $\mathbf{A}^T\mathbf{x} \geq 0$, then there exist two markings $\mathbf{M}$ and $\mathbf{M}_0$, and a firing count vector $\mathbf{x}$ (choose $\mathbf{M}_0$ large enough) such that

$$\mathbf{M} - \mathbf{M}_0 = \mathbf{A}^T\mathbf{x} \geq 0$$

Since $\mathbf{M} \geq \mathbf{M}_0$, the firing sequence of the firing count vector $\mathbf{x}$ can be repeated indefinitely to obtain a firing sequence σ in which every transition occurs infinitely often. The converse is also true.

Consistency. A Petri net is said to be *consistent* or a *T-invariant net* if there exist a marking $\mathbf{M}_0$ and a firing sequence σ from $\mathbf{M}_0$ back to $\mathbf{M}_0$ such that every transition occurs at least once in σ.

Theorem 6. A Petri net is consistent iff there exists an n-vector $\mathbf{x}$ of positive integers such that $\mathbf{A}^T\mathbf{x} = 0$.

Proof. If a Petri net is consistent, then there exists $\Sigma = \mathbf{x} > 0$ and $\mathbf{M} = \mathbf{M}_0$ in Eq. (15), such that $\mathbf{M}_0 = \mathbf{M}_0 + \mathbf{A}^T\mathbf{x}$ or $\mathbf{A}^T\mathbf{x} = 0$. The converse is also true.

It is obvious that conservativeness is a special case of structural boundedness, and that consistency is a special case of repetitiveness.

S- and T-invariants. An m-vector $\mathbf{y}$ (n-vector $\mathbf{x}$) of integers is called an *S-invariant (T-invariant)* if $\mathbf{A}\mathbf{y} = 0$ ($\mathbf{A}^T\mathbf{x} = 0$). The following two properties are obvious from the preceding discussion.

Property 6. An m-vector $\mathbf{y}$ is an S-invariant iff $\mathbf{M}^T\mathbf{y} = \mathbf{M}_0^T\mathbf{y}$ for any fixed initial marking $\mathbf{M}_0$ and any $\mathbf{M} \in \mathbf{R}(\mathbf{M}_0)$.

Property 7. An n-vector $\mathbf{x} \geq 0$ is a T-invariant iff there exist a marking $\mathbf{M}_0$ and a firing sequence from $\mathbf{M}_0$ back to $\mathbf{M}_0$ whose firing count vector is $\mathbf{x}$.

The subset of places (transitions) corresponding to nonzero entries of an m-vector $\mathbf{y}$ (an n-vector $\mathbf{x}$) is called the *support* and is denoted by $\|\mathbf{y}\|$ ($\|\mathbf{x}\|$). A support is said to be *minimal* if no proper subset of the support is another support. An improved upper bound for $\mathbf{M}(p)$ can be obtained if we replace $\mathbf{y}$ in Eq. (18) by the minimal S-invariants $\{\mathbf{y}_i \geq 0, i = 1, 2, \ldots\}$ associated with the minimal supports containing place p [39]:

$$\mathbf{M}(p) \leq \underset{i=1,2,\ldots}{\text{Min}} \ [(\mathbf{M}_0^T\mathbf{y}_i)/\mathbf{y}_i(p)] \quad (19)$$

For a marked graph, a directed circuit is a minimal support and its associated minimal S-invariant $\mathbf{y}_i$ has nonzero entries $\mathbf{y}_i(p) = 1$ iff arc p belongs to the directed circuit. Thus, Eq. (19) reduces to Property 3 in Section 3.6.

Example 6. Consider the Petri net of a reader/writer system shown in Figure 3.10. Its incidence matrix $\mathbf{A}$ is given by

	p_1	p_2	p_3	p_4	p_5	p_6
t_1	-1	1	0	0	0	0
t_2	0	-1	1	0	0	-1
t_3	1	0	-1	0	0	1
t_4	-1	0	0	1	0	0
t_5	0	0	0	-1	1	$-n$
t_6	1	0	0	0	-1	n

$\mathbf{A} = $ (matrix above)

It is easy to verify the following:

1. $\mathbf{A}\mathbf{y}_1 = 0$ and $\mathbf{A}\mathbf{y}_2 = 0$ for $\mathbf{y}_1 = (1\ 1\ 1\ 1\ 0)^T$ and $\mathbf{y}_2 = (0\ 0\ 1\ 0\ n\ 1)^T$. Thus $\mathbf{y}_1$ and $\mathbf{y}_2$ are minimal S-invariants, and their minimal supports are $\|\mathbf{y}_1\| = \{p_1, p_2, p_3, p_4, p_5\}$ and $\|\mathbf{y}_2\| = \{p_3, p_5, p_6\}$.
2. Consider Eq. (19) for place p_5 and $\mathbf{M}_0 = (n\ 0\ 0\ 0\ 0\ n)^T$. $\mathbf{M}(p_5) \leq \text{Min}\ [\mathbf{M}_0^T\mathbf{y}_1/$

$y_1(p_5)$, $M_0^T y_2/y_2(p_5)]$ = Min $[n/1, n/n]$ = 1. Thus, at most one user is writing.

3. $A^T x_1 = 0$ and $A^T x_2 = 0$ for $x_1 = (1\ 1\ 1\ 0\ 0\ 0)^T$ and $x_2 = (0\ 0\ 0\ 1\ 1\ 1)^T$. Thus x_1 and x_2 are minimal T-invariants and their minimal supports are $\|x_1\| = \{t_1, t_2, t_3\}$ and $\|x_2\| = \{t_4, t_5, t_6\}$.

4. This Petri net is not completely controllable since Rank $A = 4 (\neq 6 = m)$.

5. The net is structurally bounded and conservative since there exists $y = y_1 + y_2 = (1\ 1\ 2\ 1\ n+1)^T > 0$ such that $Ay = 0$. For $M_0 = (n\ 0\ 0\ 0\ 0\ n)^T$ and any $M \in R(M_0)$ we have the constant weighted sum of tokens, $M^T y = M_0^T y = 2n$.

6 The net is repetitive and consistent since there exists $x = x_1 + x_2 = (1\ 1\ 1\ 1\ 1\ 1)^T > 0$ such that $A^T x = 0$.

There are many more rich mathematical results on the structural properties of Petri nets reported in References 39, 37, and 40–44. Table 3.1 is a summary of the results related to the structural properties discussed in this section. In the table, **N** and (**N**, M_0) denote Petri nets with unspecified and specified initial marking M_0, respectively, and $\exists$ means "there exists".

Example 7. For the Petri net shown in Figure 3.12, there exists $y = (1\ 1\ 0\ 0\ 1\ 1)^T \geq 0$ such that $Ay = (0\ 0\ -1\ 0\ 0)^T \nleq 0$. Therefore, by Case 2 in Table 3.1, this Petri net is not live for any initial marking.

Siphon and Trap. Let **N** be a Petri net where each arc has unit weight. A subset of places P_s is called a *siphon* (or *deadlock*) of **N** if every transition having an output place in P_s has an input place in P_s. A subset of places P_t is called a *trap* of **N** if every transition having an input place in P_t has an output place in P_t. A siphon having lost all of its tokens can never obtain a token again, and a trap containing at least one token can never lose all of its tokens by firing any transitions. If a vector **y** of 0s and 1s is an S-invariant, then its support $\|y\|$ is both a siphon and a trap (and the total number of tokens in $\|y\|$ is the same for all reachable markings).

Example 8. The subsets of places $\{p_1, p_2\}$ in Figure 3.20a and b are a siphon and a trap, respectively. The subset $\{P_1, P_3, P_4\}$ is both a siphon and a trap in both Figure 3.20a and b.

The concepts of a siphon and a trap have been used to derive the following necessary and sufficient condition for liveness of free-choice nets [19]. *Free-choice nets* are a subclass of Petri nets in which every arc from a place is either a unique outgoing arc of a place or a unique incoming arc to a transition.

Table 3.1. Additional Structural Properties.

CASE	IF	THEN
1	**N** is structurally bounded and $\exists$ a live M_0 for **N**	**N** is both conservative and consistent.
2	$\exists\ y \geq 0\ Ay \leqq 0$	$\exists$ no live M_0 for **N**. **N** is not consistent.
3	$\exists\ y \geq 0\ Ay \gneqq 0$	(**N**, M_0) is not bounded for a live M_0. **N** is not consistent.
4	$\exists\ x \geq 0\ A^T x \leqq 0$	$\exists$ no live M_0 for structurally bounded **N**. **N** is not conservative.
5	$\exists\ x \geq 0\ A^T x \gneqq 0$	**N** is not structurally bounded. **N** is not conservative.

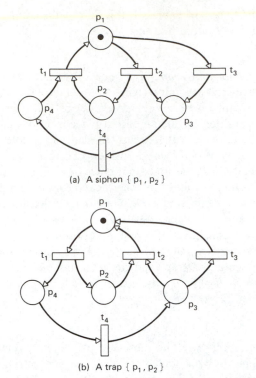

(a)   A siphon { p_1 , p_2 }

(b)   A trap { p_1 , p_2 }

Figure 3.20.   Illustration of (a) a siphon and (b) a trap.

Theorem 7.   A free-choice net is live iff every siphon contains a marked trap.

Property 2 is a special case of Theorem 7 since a directed circuit in a marked graph is both a siphon and a trap.

Example 9.   The Petri net in Figure 3.12 is a nonlive free-choice net, since a siphon $\{P_1, P_5, P_6\}$ contains no trap (although a siphon $\{P_3, P_4\}$ contains a marked trap $\{P_3, P_4\}$).

3.8.   APPLICATIONS

In this section, we present some applications of Petri nets and related graph models.

Distributed Database Systems

Consider a duplicate distributed database system in which a set of n database managers, $\{d_1, d_2, \ldots, d_n\}$ communicate to each other through a set of message buffers. Figure 3.21 shows a simplified model of this system using a special case of the predicate/transition nets

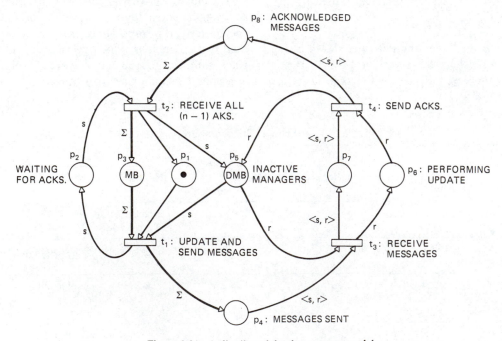

Figure 3.21.   A distributed database system model.

(adapted from Refs. 14, 15 and 66). The interpretation of this model is as follows. Just like the net in Figure 3.11b, each token has a distinct name or color, and arc labels indicate which token(s) are removed or added when a transition fires. The arc labels shown in Figure 3.21 denote the following: s = a sender; r = a receiver; $\langle s,r \rangle$ = a message from s to r; Σ = $\Sigma_{r \neq s} \langle s,r \rangle$ = the sum of the $(n - 1)$ messages; and s,r $\in \{d_1, d_2, \ldots, d_n\}$. Let $M(p)$ denote the set of tokens expressed as a formal sum in place p under marking M. Let the initial marking (state) M_0 be as follows:

$M_0(p_1) = 1$ (i.e., no manager is updating)

$M_0(p_3)$ = the sum of all possible $n(n - 1)$ ordered pairs taken from $\{d_1, d_2, \ldots, d_n\}$

$\quad \overset{\Delta}{=} MB$ (i.e., no one is using the database)

$M_0(p_5) = d_1 + d_2 + \ldots + d_n$

$\quad \overset{\Delta}{=} DMB$ (i.e., all managers are inactive)

$M_0(p) = 0$ for all other places p

The states of the message buffers are represented by the following four places: p_3 (unused), p_4 (message sent), p_7 (message received), and p_8 (acknowledged). The states of database managers are represented by the following three places: p_2 (waiting for acknowledgment), p_5 (inactive), and p_6 (performing update).

Since at this initial state, no one is using the database and all managers are inactive, a manager s can start updating his own data segment. This is done by firing transition t_1, resulting in $M_1(p_4) = \Sigma_{r \neq s} \langle s,r \rangle$ (i.e., s sends the messages to all other managers), $M_1(p_2) = s$ (i.e., s waits for acknowledgments), and $M_1(p_1) = 0$ (i.e., an update is in progress). When a manager r receives the message $\langle s,r \rangle$ (t_3 fires), he performs the update. After each of the $(n - 1)$ managers has performed the update (t_4 has fired $n - 1$ times), all the acknowledgments, $\Sigma_{r \neq s} \langle s,r \rangle$ are present in the

message buffer of place p_8. Then, the sending manager s can return to place P_5 (the system goes back to the initial marking M_0 by firing t_2). After that (but not before), another manager may start an update. Note that, at each firing, $n - 1$ tokens move through a heavy line arc, whereas one token moves through a light line arc in the model of Figure 3.21.

Let us analyze this model by applying some of the analysis techniques discussed in Section 3.7. First, the transition-to-place incidence matrix A of the net shown in Figure 3.21 is given by:

$$A = \begin{array}{c} \\ t_1 \\ t_2 \\ t_3 \\ t_4 \end{array} \begin{array}{c} \begin{matrix} p_1 & p_2 & p_3 & p_4 & p_5 & p_6 & p_7 & p_8 \end{matrix} \\ \left[\begin{matrix} -1 & s & -\Sigma & \Sigma & -s & 0 & 0 & 0 \\ 1 & -s & \Sigma & 0 & s & 0 & 0 & -\Sigma \\ 0 & 0 & 0 & -sr & -r & r & sr & 0 \\ 0 & 0 & 0 & 0 & r & -r & -sr & sr \end{matrix} \right] \end{array}$$

where $sr = \langle s,r \rangle$ and $\Sigma = \Sigma_{r \neq s} \langle s,r \rangle$. For the above incidence matrix A, there are the following independent S-invariants:

$$\begin{aligned} y_1 &= (0 \quad 1 \quad 0 \quad 0 \quad 1 \quad 1 \quad 0 \quad 0)^t \\ y_2 &= (0 \quad 0 \quad 1 \quad 1 \quad 0 \quad 0 \quad 1 \quad 1)^T \\ y_3 &= (s \quad 1 \quad 0 \quad 0 \quad 0 \quad 0 \quad 0 \quad 0)^T \\ y_4 &= (0 \quad 0 \quad 0 \quad 0 \quad 0 \quad sr \quad -r \quad 0)^T \\ y_5 &= (0 \quad \Sigma \quad s \quad 0 \quad 0 \quad 0 \quad 0 \quad 0)^T \end{aligned}$$

There is one independent T-invariant: $x_1 = (1 \ 1 \ n-1 \ n-1)^T$.

Using the analysis techniques and terminology described in Section 3.7, we can make the following observations:

1. The net is structurally bounded and conservative since there exists

$$y = y_1 + y_2 + y_3 = (s \ 2 \ 1 \ 1 \ 1 \ 1 \ 1 \ 1)^T$$
$$> 0 \text{ such that } Ay = 0.$$

2. The net is repetitive (thus deadlock-free) and consistent since there exists $x_1 > 0$ such that $A^T x_1 = 0$.

3. Since $y_1^T M = y_1^T M_0$ for every $M \in R(M_0)$, we get

$$M(p_2) + M(p_5) + M(p_6) = DMB$$

that is, each database manager d_i is in exactly one of its three states: "inactive", "waiting", and "performing."

4. From $y_2^T M = y_2^T M_0$, we get

$$M(p_3) + M(p_4) + M(p_7) + M(p_8) = MB$$

that is, each message buffer is in exactly one of its four states: "unused," "sent," "received," and "acknowledged."

5. From $y_3^T M = y_3^T M_0$, we get

$$sM(p_1) + M(p_2) = s$$

that is, while the update of one manager s is in progress, no manager can initiate another update.

6. The S-invariants y_4 and y_5 can be combined with other S-invariants to derive additional observations [14, 15].

In the above, we have used a simpler model of a database system for the purpose of illustrating the use of our modified Petri nets and the application of the analysis techniques discussed in earlier sections. The reader who is interested in more detailed models of distributed database systems is referred to the predicate/transition net models discussed in References 15 and 45 and the colored Petri nets models in Reference 46.

Performance Evaluation by Timed Nets

How to introduce or not to introduce the concept of time in Petri nets has been a controversial issue. This is because it may not be practical to assume the availability of a universal time scale in distributed concurrent systems. Nevertheless, the introduction of delay times associated with transitions and/or places yields some results useful for performance evaluation and scheduling problems. Such a Petri net is called a timed Petri net. In this section, we look into some of the results of timed marked graphs and the more general timed Petri nets.

Timed Marked Graphs. Let $\tau(C_i)$ be the delay associated with each directed circuit C_i in a marked graph model of a decision-free concurrent system, where $\tau(C_i)$ is the total sum of the delays of all nodes and/or arcs belonging to C_i, depending on the interpretation of the model. From the fact that $x = (1\ 1\ \ldots\ 1)^T$ is the only independent solution of $A^T x = 0$ for marked graphs, it can be shown that a live initial marking in a marked graph is reproduced iff each node fires an equal number of times. Thus, in a timed marked graph all the nodes can fire periodically with the same period T, and it is easily shown [21, 47–49] that the minimum value of period T is given by

$$T_{\min} = \text{Max } \{\tau(C_i)/M_0(C_i)\}, \quad (20)$$

where the maximum is taken over all directed circuits and $M_0(C_i)$ is the number of tokens on directed circuit C_i. $T_{\min}$ may be interpreted as the maximum computation rate or a measure of performance in the sense that one cycle of a process or job can be executed at best in every $T_{\min}$ unit of time.

Example 10. In the marked graph shown in Figure 3.18, there are three directed circuits: $C_1 = \{a,b,d\}$, $C_2 = \{g,e,h\}$, and $C_3 = \{a,f,e,c,d\}$. Since there is only one token in each circuit, $T_{\min}$ is equal to the delay of the slowest among the three directed circuits.

Timed marked graphs with finite capacity ($K < \infty$) are used in Reference 48 to study scheduling problems such as the existence of admissible firing schedules, algorithms for the earliest and latest schedules, and the maximum computation rate. The results are applicable to scheduling decision-free parallel computations, as well as generalized PERT charts (activity networks) with feedback loops.

Timed Petri Nets. Due to the nondeterminism inherent in Petri nets, it is very difficult to evaluate the performance of systems modeled by timed Petri nets. It has been shown that the performance prediction for conservative timed Petri nets is an *NP*-complete problem [21]. As in timed marked graphs, we are interested in finding how fast one cycle of a computation can be performed in a given timed Petri net, where the one cycle is defined as a firing sequence leading back to the initial marking after firing each transition at least once. Thus, it is assumed that the net under consideration is consistent, that is,

$$A^T x = 0 \quad x > 0 \qquad (21)$$

where the ith entry of x denotes the frequency of firing transition i in the one cycle. Suppose that we are given the minimum delay d_j associated with each place j; that is, a token spends at least d_j time in place j, and that the delay associated with each transition is zero (if not, split this transition into two, add a place between them, and assign the delay to this place). Comparing the mean number of tokens in each place with that of tokens arriving at that place, Sifakis [49] has shown that the following relation must hold for each S-invariant $y_k \geq 0$:

$$y_k^T M_0 \geq y_k^T D(A^+)^T x \quad k = 1,2 \ldots ,\mu \quad (22)$$

where D is the diagonal matrix of delays d_j, A^+ = A with all negative entries replaced by zeros, and μ is the number of independent S-invariants. Therefore, the maximum vector x satisfying Eqs. (21) and (22) yields the maximum rate of computation. In particular, the vector x satisfying Eqs. (21) and (22) with equality is the maximum possible rate of computation, if it exists.

For a timed marked graph, $x = (x_0 \; x_0 \ldots x_0)^T > 0$ satisfies Eq. (21) and each directed circuit C_k corresponds to an S-invariant y_k. Thus, Eq. (22) reduces to

$$M_0(C_k) \geq \tau(C_k) x_0 \quad k = 1,2, \ldots ,\mu \quad (23)$$

or the period T is given by

$$T = 1/x_0 \geq \tau(C_k)/M_0(C_k) \qquad (24)$$
$$k = 1,2, \ldots ,\mu$$

Therefore, we have Eq. (20) as a special case of Eq. (22).

Example 11. Consider the Petri net of a reader/writer system shown in Figure 3.10, where it is assumed that delays $d_1, d_2, \ldots$, d_6 are associated with the six places. We have found in Example 6 that $y_1 = (1\;1\;1\;1\;1\;0)^T$ and $y_2 = (0\;0\;1\;0\;n\;1)^T$ are the two independent S-invariants, and $x = [x_0]_{6\times 1}$, $x_0 > 0$ satisfies Eq. (21). Thus, applying Eq. (22) to y_1 and y_2 yields

$$n \geq (2d_1 + d_2 + d_3 + d_4 + d_5)x_0$$
$$n \geq [d_3 + nd_5 + (n + 1)d_6]x_0$$

Therefore, we have

$$T = 1/x_0 \geq \{(2d_1 + d_2 + d_3 + d_4 + d_5)/n, \quad [d_3 + nd_5 + (n + 1)d_6]/n\}$$

and the maximum possible computation rate is given by

$$T_{min} = \max \{(2d_1 + d_2 + d_3 + d_4 + d_5/n, \quad [d_3 + nd_5 + (n + 1)d_6]/n\}.$$

Fault Detection and Isolation

In Section 3.5, it has been shown that if a marking M_k is reachable from M_0, then Eqs. (4) and (9) must hold, that is,

$$\Delta M = M_k - M_0 = A^T \Sigma \qquad (25)$$

and

$$B_f \Delta M = 0 \qquad (26)$$

Thus, by checking if Eqs. (25) and/or (26) hold at some place(s) after executing some operations (firings), it may be possible to detect and/or isolate fault(s) in the system modeled by a Petri net. There are two methods: one is based on Eq. (25) and the other on Eq. (26). Both methods have advantages and disadvantages.

Method a. This method is based on Eq. (25).

1a. Store the initial marking $\mathbf{M}_0$ and the incidence matrix $\mathbf{A}$ of a given Petri net model of a system.

2a. At each or some stage k, record the kth firing count vector $\mathbf{\Sigma}_k = [\sigma_i]$, where σ_i is the number of times that transition i has fired up to stage k, and compute $\mathbf{V}_k = \mathbf{A}^T \mathbf{\Sigma}_k$.

3a. At each or some stage k, record the marking vector $\mathbf{M}_k = [m_j]$, where m_j is the number of tokens in place j at stage k.

4a. Compute $\mathbf{\Delta T}_k = \mathbf{M}_k - \mathbf{M}_0 - \mathbf{V}_k$.

5a. If the jth entry of the m-vector $\mathbf{\Delta T}_k$ is different from zero, then a fault is suspected in the subsystem involving place j.

Method b.   This method is based on Eq. (26).

1b. In addition to step 1a, compute $\mathbf{B}_f$ with Eq. (7).

2b. Do step 3a.

3b. Compute $\mathbf{\Delta S}_k = \mathbf{B}_f(\mathbf{M}_k - \mathbf{M}_0)$.

4b. If the ith entry of the μ-vector $\mathbf{\Delta S}_k$ is different from zero, then a fault is suspected in the subsystem involving the support of the ith S-invariant $\mathbf{y}_i$.

It is required to record the firing count vector in method a but not in method b. However, the former has a better resolution of isolating faults than the latter. Not all faults can be detected by these methods (nor many other methods), since Eqs. (25) and (26) are only necessary conditions for reachability, and certain combinations of multiple faults would yield $\mathbf{\Delta T}_k = 0$ and $\mathbf{\Delta S}_k = 0$. In a geographically distributed system, it may be difficult to find a global system state such as $\mathbf{M}_k$. Nevertheless, we can apply the above methods to a local subsystem by computing $\mathbf{V}_k$ in step 2a, $\mathbf{M}_k$ in step 3a, and $\mathbf{\Delta T}_k$ in step 4a *only for a locally affected subset of places,* and by computing $\mathbf{\Delta S}_k$ in step 3b *only from the subset of places* corresponding to the support of an S-invariant (assuming that the local initial marking is updated whenever there is a flow of tokens in and out of the local places). The above methods are simple and suitable for real-time

fault analysis since they require a very small amount of computation (essentially a few vector subtractions and multiplications at each test).

Example 12.   Consider the Petri net shown in Figure 3.17, for which the matrix $\mathbf{B}_f$ has been computed in Example 4. Suppose a marking $\mathbf{M}_2 = (2\ 0\ 1\ 1)^T$ is detected at a certain stage when the initial marking was $\mathbf{M}_0 = (1\ 1\ 0\ 0)^T$. By Method b, we compute

$$\mathbf{\Delta S}_k = \mathbf{B}_f(\mathbf{M}_2 - \mathbf{M}_0)$$

$$= \begin{bmatrix} 1 & 0 & 0 & -1 \\ 0 & 1 & 1 & 1 \end{bmatrix} \begin{bmatrix} 1 \\ -1 \\ 1 \\ 1 \end{bmatrix} = \begin{bmatrix} 0 \\ 1 \end{bmatrix}.$$

It shows that there is a fault in $\{p_2, p_3, p_4\}$, the support of the second S-invariant, while there is no fault in $\{p_1, p_4\}$, the support of the first S-invariant. Thus, it is likely that there is a fault in the subsystem involving $\{p_2, p_3\}$.

As for other methods of fault diagnosis using Petri nets, Sifakis [50] has presented an elegant method of applying error-correcting code techniques to the design of fault-tolerant systems based on Petri nets. Also, Merlin and Farber [51] have shown the use of "time Petri nets" (where each transition is allowed to fire only in a certain time interval) for the design of a message protocol that will automatically recover from an error caused by a loss of a token in a place. For details of these methods, refer to the original papers.

Other Applications

In addition to those mentioned earlier, Petri nets and related graph models have been applied to a wide variety of areas such as code optimizations in compilers [52, 53], legal systems [54], operating systems [55], asynchronous control structures [56–58], automation of office procedure [59], software requirements and specifications [60], formal language theory [61, 62] and representation of mathematical knowledge [63]. Groups in France have been doing a great deal of research on applications of Petri-net-based models and a survey of their work up to 1979 can be found in Reference 64. Due to space limitation, it is not possible to cite all the work done in the field. Interested readers are referred to *A Bibliography of Net Theory* [65] which lists over 500 papers and research reports on Petri nets and related topics.

ACKNOWLEDGMENT

This work was supported in part by the National Science Foundation under grants ENG 78-05933 and ECS 81-05649.

REFERENCES

1. R. H. Eckhouse, Jr., J. A. Stankovic, and A. van Dam, "Issues in distributed processing—An overview of two workshops," *Computer,* vol. 11, no. 1, Jan. 1978, pp. 22–26.

2. C. A. Petri, "Kommunikation mit Automaten," Dissertation, Univ. of Bonn, 1962; translation by C. E. Greene, Jr., "Communication with automata," *Supplement to Tech. Doc. Rep. #1,* Rome Air Dev. Center, Contract #AF30 (602)-3324, 1965.

3. A. W. Holt, et al., "Information system theory project: Final report," *Tech. Rep. RADC-TR-68-305,* Rome Air Dev. Center, Sept. 1968.

4. C. A. Petri, "Communication disciplines," *Computing System Design: Procs. of the Joint IBM and U. of Newcastle upon Tyne Seminar,* B. Shaw (ed.), 1977, pp. 171–183.

5. H. J. Genrich, and E. Stankiewicz-Weichno "A dictionary of some notations of net theory," in W. Brauer (ed.), *Net Theory and Applications, Lecture Notes in Computer Science,* vol. 84, Springer-Verlag, New York, 1980, pp. 519–531.

6. J. B. Dennis "Data Flow Supercomputers," *Computer,* vol. 13, Nov. 1980, pp. 48–56.

7. S. H. Yu and T. Murata, "Modeling and simulating data flow computations at machine language level," *Procs. of Conf. on Simulation, Measurement and Modeling of Computer Systems,* ACM, New York, Aug. 1979, pp. 207–213.

8. M. Sowa and T. Murata, "A data flow computer architecture with program and token memories," *Procs. of the 14th Asilomar Conf. on Circuits, Systems, and Computer,* IEEE Comp. Society, Long Beach, Cal., Nov. 1980. Also IEEE Trans. on Computers, Sept. 1982, pp 820–824.

9. P. M. Merlin, "A methodology for the design and implementation of communication protocols," *IEEE Trans. on Comm.,* vol. COM-24, no. 6, June 1976, pp. 614–621.

10. P. Azema, J. M. Ayache, and B. Berthomieu, "Design and verification of communication procedures: A bottom-up approach," *Proc. 3rd IEEE Conf. on Software Eng.,* Atlanta, May 1978, pp. 168–174.

11. R. Razouk and G. Estrin, "Modeling and verification of communication protocols in SARA: The X.21 Interface," *IEEE Trans. on Computers,* vol. C-29, no. 12, Dec., 1980, pp. 1038–1052.

12. K. Lautenbach and H. A. Schmid, "Use of Petri nets for proving correctness of concurrent systems," *Proceedings of IFIP Congress 74,* North Holland Pub. Co., 1974, pp. 187–191.

13. R. E. Miller, "Some relationships between various models of paralellism and synchronization," *Report RC-5074,* IBM T. J. Watson Res. Center, Yorktown Heights, N.Y., Oct. 1974.

14. K. Jensen, "Coloured Petri Nets and the Invariant Method," *Report DAIMI PB-104,* Computer Science Department, Aarhus University, Denmark, Oct. 1979. *Theoretical Comp. Sci., 14,* 1981, pp. 317–336.

15. H. J. Genrich, K. Lautenbach, and P. S. Thiagarajan, "Elements of General Net Theory," *Net Theory and Applications, Lecture Notes in Computer Science,* vol. 84, Springer-Verlag, New York, 1980, pp. 21–164.

16. R. Lipton, "The Reachability Problem Requires Exponential Space," *Report 62,* Department of Computer Science, Yale University, New Haven, Jan. 1976.

17. E. W. Mayr, "An Algorithm for the General Petri Net Reachability Problem, Procs, of the 13th Annual ACM Symposium on Theory of Computing, May 1981, pp.238–246.

18. M. Hack, "Decidability Questions for Petri Nets," *Report TR-161,* MIT Laboratory for Computer Science, Cambridge, Mass., June 1976.

19. F. Commoner, "Deadlocks in Petri Nets," *Report CA-7206-2311,* Massachusetts Computer Association, Inc., Wakefield, Mass., June 1972.

20. K. Lautenbach, "Liveness in Petri Nets," *Report 02.1/75-7-29,* GMD, Bonn, 1975.

21. G. S. Ho and C. V. Ramamoorthy, "Performance Evaluation of Asynchronous Concurrent Systems Using Petri Nets," *IEEE Transactions on Software Engineering,* vol. SE-6, no. 5, Sept. 1980, pp. 440–449.

22. T. Araki and T. Kasami, "Decidable Problems on the Strong Connectivity of Petri Net Reachability Set," *Theoretical Comp. Sci.,* vol. 4, no. 1, February 1977, pp. 99–119.

23. J. L. Peterson, *Petri Net Theory and the Modeling of Systems,* Prentice-Hall, Englewood Cliffs, N.J., 1981.

24. R. M. Karp and R. E. Miller, "Parallel Program Schemata," *Journal of Comp. and Syst. Sci.,* vol. 3, no. 2, May 1969, pp. 147–195.

25. F. E. Hohn, *Elementary Matrix Algebra,* Macmillan, New York, 1958.

26. F. Commoner, S. Even, A. W. Holt, and A. Pnueli,

"Marked Directed Graphs," *Journal of Comp. and Syst. Sci.,* vol. 5, Oct. 1971, pp. 511–532.

27. T. Murata, "Synthesis of Decision-Free Concurrent Systems for Prescribed Resources and Performance," *IEEE Transactions on Software Engineering,* vol. SE-6, no. 6, Nov. 1980, pp. 525–530.

28. T. Murata, "Relevance of Network Theory to Models of Distributed/Parallel Processing," *Journal of the Franklin Institute,* vol. 310, no. 1, 1980, pp. 41–50.

29. A. T. Amin and T. Murata, "A Characterization of Live and Safe Markings of Directed Graphs," *Proceedings of the 1976 Conference on Info. Sci. and Syst.,* Johns Hopkins University, Baltimore, March 1976.

30. N. Deo, *Graph Theory with Applications to Engineering and Computer Science,* Prentice-Hall, Englewood Cliffs, N.J., 1974.

31. T. Murata, "Circuit Theoretic Analysis and Synthesis of Marked Graphs," *IEEE Transactions on Circuits and Systems,* vol. CAS-24, no. 7, July 1977, pp. 400–405.

32. T. Murata and J. Y. Koh, "Reduction and Expansion of Live and Safe Marked Graphs," *IEEE Transactions on Circuits and Systems,* vol. CAS-27, no. 1, Jan. 1980, pp. 68–70.

33. R. Johnsonbaugh and T. Murata, "Additional Methods for Reduction and Expansion of Marked Graphs," *IEEE Transactions on Circuits and Systems;* idem, "Analysis of Resource Requirements in Marked Graph Computation Models," *Proceedings of the 1980 International Symposium on Circuits and Systems,* Apr. 1980, pp. 342–345.

34. R. Valette, "Analysis of Petri Nets by Stepwise Refinements," *Journal of Comp. Syst. Sci.,* vol. 18, no. 1, Feb. 1979, pp. 35–46.

35. T. Murata and I. Suzuki, "A Method for Hierarchically Representing Large Scale Petri Nets," *Proceedings of the IEEE International Conference on Circuits and Computers,* Oct. 1980, pp. 620–623.

36. C. T. Chen, *Introduction to Linear System Theory,* Holt, Rinehart and Winston, Inc., New York, 1970.

37. T. Murata, "State Equation, Controllability, and Maximal Matchings of Petri Nets," *IEEE Transactions on Automatic Control,* vol. AC-22, no. 3, June 1977, pp. 412–416.

38. T. C. Hu, *Integer Programming and Network Flows,* Addison-Wesley, Reading, Mass., 1970.

39. G. Memmi and G. Roucairol, "Linear Algebra in Net Theory," *Net Theory and Applications, Lecture Notes in Comp. Sci.,* vol. 84, Springer-Verlag, New York, 1980, pp. 213–224.

40. J. Sifakis, "Structural Properties of Petri Nets," *Math. Fund. of Comp. Sci., Lecture Notes in Comp. Sci.,* vol. 64, Springer-Verlag, New York, 1978, pp. 474–483.

41. Y. E. Lien, "Termination Properties of Generalized Petri Nets," *SIAM Journal of Comp.,* vol. 5, no. 2, June 1976, pp. 251–265.

42. E. Best and H. A. Schmid, "Systems of Open Paths in Petri Nets," *Math. Fund. of Comp. Sci., Lecture Notes in Comp. Sci.,* vol. 32, Springer-Verlag, New York, 1975, pp. 186–193.

43. F. Commoner, and A. W. Holt, "Final Report for the Project-Development of Theoretical Foundations for Description and Analysis of Discrete Information Systems," vol. II, *Mathematics, CADD-7405-2011,* Massachusetts Computer Association, Inc., Wakefield, Mass., May 1974.

44. M. Jantzen and R. Valk, "Formal Properties of Place/Transition Nets," *Net Theory and Applications, Lecture Notes in Comp. Sci.,* Springer-Verlag, vol. 84, New York, 1980, pp. 165–212.

45. K. Voss, "Using Predicate/Transition Nets to Model and Analyze Distributed Database Systems," *IEEE Transactions on Software Engineering,* vol. SE-6, no. 6, Nov. 1980, pp. 539–544.

46. K. Jensen, "How to Find Invariants for Coloured Petri Nets," *Report DAIMI PB-120,* Computer Science Department, Aarhus University, Denmark, May 1980.

47. C. Ramchandani, "Analysis of Asynchronous Concurrent Systems by Timed Petri Nets," *Report TR-120,* Project MAC, MIT, Cambridge, Mass., Feb. 1974.

48. T. Murata and K. Tani, "Scheduling Parallel Computations with Storage Constraints," *Proceedings of the 12th Asilomar Conference on Circuits, Systems, and Computers,* IEEE Computer Society, Long Beach, Cal., Nov. 1978.

49. J. Sifakis, "Use of Petri Nets for Performance Evaluation," *Measuring, Modelling and Evaluation Computer Systems,* H. Beilner and E. Gelenbe (eds.), North Holland, Amsterdam, 1977, pp. 75–93.

50. J. Sifakis, "Realization of Fault-Tolerant Systems by Coding Petri Nets," *Journal of Design Automation and Fault-Tolerant Computing,* vol. IV, no. 1, 1979, pp. 93–107.

51. D. J. Farber and P. M. Merlin, "Recoverability of Communication Protocols: Implications of a Theoretical Study," *IEEE Trans. Comm.,* vol. COM-24, no. 9, Sept. 1976, pp. 1036–1043.

52. R. M. Shapiro and H. Saint, "A New Approach to Optimization of Sequencing Decisions," *Annual Review of Automatic Programming,* vol. 6, no. 5, 1970, pp. 257–288.

53. J. L. Baer and C. S. Ellis, "Model, Design, and Evaluation of a Compiler for a Parallel Processing Environment," *IEEE Transactions on Software Engineering,* vol. SE-3, no. 6, Nov. 1977, pp. 394–405.

54. A. W. Holt and J. A. Meldman, "Petri Nets and Legal Systems," *Jurimetrics Journal,* vol. 12, no. 2, Dec. 1971, pp. 66–75.

55. J. D. Noe and G. J. Nutt, "Macro E-Nets for Representation of Parallel Systems," *IEEE Trans. on Comp.,* vol. C-22, no. 8, Aug. 1973, pp. 718–727.

56. J. R. Jump, "Asynchronous Control Arrays," *IEEE Trans. on Comp.,* vol. C-23, no. 10, Oct. 1974, pp. 1020–1029.

57. S. S. Patil, "Micro-Control for Parallel Asynchro-

nous Computers," Euromicro Workshop, Nice, June 1975. idem, *Comp. Struct. Group Memo #120,* Project MAC, MIT, Cambridge, Mass., March 1975.

58. S. S. Reddi, "A Parallel Computer with Centralized Control," *IEEE Comp. So. Repository, R76-22,* Feb. 1976.

59. C. A. Ellis and G. J. Nutt, "Office Information Systems and Computer Science," *ACM Computing Surveys,* vol. 12, no. 1, Mar. 1980, pp. 27–60.

60. C. V. Ramamoorthy and H. H. So, "Software Requirements and Specifications, Status and Perspectives," *Tutorial: Software Methodology,* IEEE Catalog no. EHO 142-0, 1978, pp. 43–164.

61. M. Hack, "Petri Net Languages," *Report TR-159,* MIT Laboratory for Computer Science, Cambridge, Mass., March 1976.

62. J. L. Peterson, "Computation Sequence Sets," *Jour-nal of Comp. and Syst. Sci.,* vol. 13, no. 1, August 1976, pp. 1–24.

63. H. J. Genrich, "The Petri Net Representation of Mathematical Knowledge," *Report ISF-76-05, GMD, Bonn, 1976.*

64. A. M. Diaz, C. Girault, and J. Sitakis, "Survey of French Research and Applications Based on Petri Nets," *Net Theory and Applications, Lecture Notes in Comp. Sci.,* vol. 84, Springer-Verlag, New York, 1980, pp. 321–346.

65. E. Pless and H. Plünnecke, "A Bibliography of Net Theory," *Report ISF,* ISF-79-04, GMD, Bonn, August 1979.

66. W. Reisig, "A Note on the Drawing of Nets," Special Interest Group on Petri Nets and Related System Models, Gesellshaft für Informatik, *Newsletter No. 10, Feb. 1982, pp. 6–9.*

4

Theory of Algorithms and Computation Complexity with Applications to Software Design

Benjamin W. Wah

Purdue University

C. V. Ramamoorthy

University of California, Berkeley

4.1. INTRODUCTION

What Is an Algorithm?

The word *"algorithm"* is explained in the latest Webster's dictionary as "any special method of solving a certain kind of problem." However, this word has special significance in computer science. It means a finite sequence of definite steps, each of which may consist of one or more operations, that can be carried out systematically to solve a problem. In this context, a *problem* is a general question to be answered, usually possessing several *parameters* or free variables, whose values are left unspecified. An *instance* of a problem is obtained by specifying particular values for the problem parameters.

The method of implementation of an algorithm is not very important. It can be hardware, software, firmware, or a combination of these. However, implementation using software is usually implied and to say that *a problem is solvable algorithmically* means, informally, that there is a computer program, which when given enough space and time, will produce the correct answer.

There are three notable characterisitics in the definition of an algorithm. First, the steps must be definite, that is, they precisely indicate what must be done. For example, adding 5 to 7 is very definite whereas incrementing a var-

iable a number of times is not. Second, the method of carrying out the algorithm is systematic, that is, the steps of the algorithm are always carried out in a defined order. The implication of the first and second characteristics is that the results of the execution of the algorithm are identical no matter how many times the algorithm is executed if the inputs are identical. Lastly, the algorithm should terminate in a finite number of steps. This last characteristic is not required in some algorithms. For example, the scheduling algorithm in the operating system of a computer never terminates. We assume that the algorithms to be discussed will terminate eventually.

To say that an algorithm terminates is not to say that the algorithm is good, because it may take hundreds or thousands of years for the fastest computer to complete the algorithm. For example, in deciding the order in which a travelling salesman should visit a set of n cities, an explicit enumeration would examine $n!$ possible combinations in order to determine the combination with the minimum cost. If each combination can be evaluated in one microsecond and n = 20, it would take 771 centuries to solve the problem. On the other hand, there are algorithms that can solve the same problem efficiently in seconds. It is, therefore, important to study the properties of algorithms and to design good algorithms that

64

run efficiently. The following questions are generally asked when an algorithm is designed.

1. How to design algorithms?
2. How to express algorithms?
3. How can algorithms be improved?
4. What is the "best" algorithm to solve the problem?
5. How to validate algorithms?
6. What criteria may be used to select between different algorithms for the same application?
7. How to analyze algorithms?

We plan to answer some of the above questions in this chapter by classifying algorithms according to their complexity. Questions 2, 6, and 7 are answered in this section. The remainder of this chapter classifies problems according to the complexity of the algorithms needed to solve them. The topics discussed include problems solvable in polynominal time (Section 4.2), *NP*-complete problems (Section 4.3), strongly *NP*-complete problems (Section 4.4), *NP*-hard problems (Section 4.5), enumeration techniques (Section 4.6), and approximation algorithms (Section 4.7). These discussions provide answers to Questions 1, 3, and 4. Question 5 depends mainly on the proof techniques developed to verify that an algorithm meets the requirements, and is beyond the scope of this chapter. More complete treatment of the topic can be found in References 1–5 and other references cited in the ensuing discussions.

It is the goal of this chapter to introduce the theory of algorithms and some of the existing algorithms that can be used for a wide variety of applications. It is hoped that this will provide an introduction and pointers to other references that can be used to guide the design of new algorithms.

Methods to Express Algorithms

Algorithms are generally expressed by some algorithmic language such as a high-level language. The overall structure of the algorithm can be classified as iterative or recursive. This section gives an overview of the methods used to express algorithms.

High-Level Language. Although algorithms can be designed for a wide variety of applications, they can universally be represented in the form of a program. Various programming languages have been used. Knuth used an assembly-language-like programming language (MIX) to represent algorithms [6–8]. Other authors tend to use a high-level language such as pidgin Algol, which is a Pascal-like language [9], to represent algorithms [1–5]. Using a high-level language to represent algorithms makes it easier to achieve the goals of simplicity, readability, and correctness. However, the measure of complexity may not be as accurate as that of a low-level language and some constants may be combined in the process of abstraction. The high-level language is useful when the order of magnitude of complexity is desired. In this chapter, our main objective is to discuss algorithms and present their complexity. Exact algorithms will not be discussed. Some algorithms will be presented in pidgin Algol with some part of the algorithm replaced by nonalgorithmic descriptions in order to simplify the structure.

In summary, a piece of software represents an algorithm and an algorithm is represented in the form of a program. The words *software* and *algorithm* are, therefore, sometimes taken to be synonymous in computer science. In the remainder of this chapter, an execution of an algorithm is taken to mean the execution of the corresponding program representing the algorithm.

There are two standard ways in which an algorithm can be represented—iteration and recursion.

Iteration. Very few algorithms are executed from the beginning to the end in a single pass without reusing some of the statements in the original program. A part of the program is frequently represented in the form of an iteration or loop so that statements in the loop can be repeated. An example of this is shown in the computation of $n!$.

```
FUNCTION FACT (N: INTEGER) :
INTEGER;
    VAR I: INTEGER;
    BEGIN
        FACT : = 1;
        IF N > 1 THEN
        FOR I : = 1 TO N DO
            FACT : = FACT * I
END
```

It is very easy to see that the number of multiplications equals *n*. Besides using iteration, a program can be formulated as one which calls itself directly or indirectly. This is called recursion.

Recursion.   Procedures and functions may include a call to themselves, referred to as *recursion*. When procedures and functions call other procedures or functions which then cause the original procedures or functions to be reinvoked, this is referred to as *indirect recursion*. It can be shown very easily that for any algorithm written in an iterative form, there is a corresponding algorithm with identical behavior and written in a recursive form, and vice versa [4]. For example, the computation of *n!* can be redone in a recursive form.

```
FUNCTION FACT (N: INTEGER) :
INTEGER;
    BEGIN
        IF N < = 1
        THEN
            FACT : = 1
        ELSE
            FACT : = N * FACT (N-1)
    END ;
```

Some computers such as stack computers [10] are capable of executing recursive programs directly. Other computers transform recursive programs into iterative algorithms before execution. Readers interested in the transformation process can refer to examples in Reference 11.

Besides differing in implementation, recursive and iterative programs also differ in the analysis of the number of operations. In the case of an iterative program, the number of operations can be calculated by direct counting of the number of times that a particular loop is executed. For example, the number of times the FOR loop is executed in calculating *n!* iteratively is *n* and the operation performed in each iteration is a multiplication. In the case of a recursive program, the number of operations required is written in a recurrence relation. A *recurrence relation* for a function is an equation relating the value of the function on the argument *n* to values of the function on small arguments. For example, for the computation of *n!* in the recursive form, let $f(n)$ be the number of multiplications required to compute *n!*. The recurrence relation for $f(n)$ is

$$f(n) = 1 + f(n - 1)$$

with the boundary condition $f(0) = 0$. This recurrence relation can be solved very easily to show that $f(n) = n$. Programs using recursion are usually easier to write and simpler to understand. However, the corresponding recurrence relation may be difficult to solve. Knuth has shown numerous examples of solving recurrence relations on sorting and searching [8].

The Analysis of Algorithms

Question 7, raised earlier, was, How can algorithms be analyzed? Before we answer this, the following question may be raised: Why do we have to analyze algorithms? The major reasons for doing so are to allow different algorithms of the same problem to be compared and to characterize problems so that their inherent difficulty can be identified. If a problem has been characterized as difficult and requires a large amount of execution time before a solution is found, then continual search for faster algorithms will be fruitless. The analysis of algorithms is, therefore, aimed at determining the complexity of the algorithm and classifying problems of similar complexity together.

Measuring Problem Size.   In order to analyze algorithms and determine the time needed to execute them, the features or parameters characterizing an algorithm must be found. The time requirements of an algorithm are normally expressed in terms of the *size* of a problem instance, which is the amount of input data needed to describe the instance. Generally, this size is expressed in an informal way. For example, if a graph, which is a set of n nodes linked together by a maximum of $\frac{n(n-1)}{2}$ edges, is used as input to an algorithm, the size of the input includes the one number to represent the number of nodes and a maximum of $n(n-1)$ ordered pairs to represent the edges.

In order to characterize the time requirements more precisely, we have to know the size of each number and this depends on the *encoding scheme*. For example, if a number m is encoded in binary form, then the size of the number is $\lceil \log_2 m \rceil$ bits where $\lceil x \rceil$ is the smallest integer larger than x. In general, the input length will be different for different encoding schemes. However, if the encoding scheme is "reasonable," then the input lengths will be "polynomially related." Informally, an encoding scheme is reasonable if it describes the problem instance with natural brevity and without any unnatural padding. Further, the decoding scheme for obtaining the original problem instance is very fast. (We have not characterized algorithms that are very fast; these algorithms are polynomial algorithms and will be described later.) *Polynomially related* means that the size of the encoded input is a polynomial function of the original input. Given a reasonable encoding scheme, the encoded input will be used as a parameter to measure how complex the algorithm is. There can, of course, be other characterizing parameters, for instance, number of nodes, number of edges, and so forth. But they usually do not reflect the size of all the inputs operated upon by the algorithm.

The Notion of Complexity. There are many ways to characterize the behavior of an algorithm, the most important of which are the time needed to execute an algorithm as a function of the input length, and the amount of

memory space needed for the execution of the algorithm. The *complexity* of an algorithm measures the time or space or a combination of both needed to execute the algorithm. We can identify two phases for this analysis: a priori analysis and a posteriori analysis. In *a priori analysis,* the complexity of the algorithm is expressed as a function of the input length that bounds the algorithm's computing time and memory space. In *a posteriori analysis,* actual statistics are collected during the execution of the algorithm when given some initial input data, on the frequency of execution of the different operations, and on the time to execute each operation. Since these measures would be dependent on the configuration and the architecture of the computer executing the algorithm, it would be difficult to generalize for different computer systems. A general computer system with a simple language must be designed in order for this analysis not to be restrictive. A typical example is illustrated in the book by Knuth [6] where a language called MIX was designed to represent algorithms. In general, the algorithm analyst uses a priori analysis but resorts to a posteriori analysis for actual testing of the algorithm. Since a prior analysis is more powerful and less restrictive, it is taken to be the measure for algorithm complexity in this chapter.

A priori analysis usually calculates the order of magnitude of the complexity, which measures up to a constant multiplier of the actual complexity. Let f and g be two functions with domain N, the natural numbers. We say that $f(n) = 0(g(n))$ (f is less than or equal to the order of g) iff there are positive constants C and n_o such that $f(n) \leq C g(n)$ for all $n > n_o$. Thus, $0.5n = 0(5n) = 0(5n^2)$, but $5n^2 \neq 0(n)$. The set of functions of the same order as g, $\theta(g(n))$, includes all functions $g(n)$ such that $g(n) = 0(f(n))$ and $f(n) = 0(g(n))$. This means that the functions $g(n)$ in $\theta(g(n))$ differ from $f(n)$ by a constant factor. In general, $f(n) = 0(g(n))$ is taken to mean that $f(n) \in \theta(g(n))$. A sorting algorithm can, therefore, be said to have time complexity $0(n*\log_2 n)$ with n inputs. Likewise, a scheduling algorithm can be said to have time complexity $0(2^n)$ and space complexity $0(n^2)$. This means that there are constants C_1, C_2 and C_3 such that the sorting algorithm can be executed in time $C_1 n * \log_2 n$ and the scheduling algorithm can be executed in time $C_2 2^n$ using a memory space of $C_3 n^2$. The sorting algorithm is said to be executable in *polynomial time* and the scheduling algorithm is said to executable in *exponential time* and *polynomial space*.

Some of the common orders of magnitude and their relative sizes are: $0(1) < 0(\log n) < 0(n) < 0(n \log n) < 0(n^m) < 0(2^n)$ where m is a constant.

The obvious disadvantage of using the order of magnitude complexity measure or the a priori analysis is that it is difficult to compare two algorithms with the same orders of magnitude. For example, two sorting algorithms may be analyzed to have time complexity $0(n \log_2 n)$; this implies that the execution times differ in a constant factor that is not reflected in the complexity measures. In order to compare two algorithms with the same order of magnitude, a posteriori analysis has to be used.

Worst-Case and Average-Case Analysis. The measure of complexity indicates the amount of time or space needed to execute an algorithm. Since there may be infinitely many possible input combinations that can be used for an algorithm, it would be impossible to have a complexity measure for each possible input. The complexity measures for all the possible input combinations must be combined together into a single complexity measure. There are two popular ways of achieving this: the worst-case and average-case complexity measures.

Let I be a member of the input set D_n, where n is the size of the input, and $p(I)$ is the probability that I occurs. Let $t(I)$ be the complexity measure of the algorithm under input I, ($t(I)$ can be the number of basic operations performed under I for the time complexity, or it can be the memory space required under I for the space complexity). The *worst-case behavior* $W(n)$ is defined as the maximum time or space required for any possible input.

$$W(n) = \max_{I \in D_n} t(I)$$

The worst-case complexity, therefore, puts a lower bound on the performance of the algorithm.

Similarly, the *average-case behavior* $A(n)$ is defined as the expected time or space required by all inputs.

$$A(n) = \sum_{I \in D_n} p(I) \cdot t(I)$$

There are merits and demerits in using either method. The worst-case is usually easier to compute, but can underestimate the behavior of the algorithm. For example, an algorithm can behave very poorly for a small set of inputs, but perform very well in general. In this case, the average behavior is a more accurate measure. In contrast, the average-case complexity measures the weighted average of the performance of the algorithm and thus reflects the performance more realistically. However, the probability that an input I occurs is usually not easy to measure accurately. The function p must be determined from experience and/or special information about the application. In addition, the analysis of the average behavior can become complex and more simplifying assumptions have to be made in order for the analysis to be mathematically tractable.

The following example illustrates the average- and worst-case analyses.

Example. *Problem:* Given a set A of n numbers, search the set to determine if the number X is in the set. It is assumed that the set is not ordered in any fashion.

Algorithm: A linear search is performed which compares elements in the set with X successively. The search stops when X is found or when the set is exhausted.

Input length: K$*n$ where K is a constant representing the size of each number.

Worst-time analysis: The number of operations performed or the time required to perform the algorithm is directly proportional to the number of comparisons. The number of comparisons made depends on the position of X in the set. Before complexity analysis can be done, D_n must be defined. Since each number in the set can be of any value, the total number of possible input configurations is infinite. However, this can be reduced because it is only important to know the position of X in the set and the values of the other numbers that do not equal X and do not affect the outcome. There are n possible positions for X to occur. A special case happens when X is not in the set. Therefore, $D_n = \{X$ in 1st postition, $\ldots$, X in nth position, X is not in the set$\}$ and $|D_n| = n + 1$. The maximum number of comparisons is needed when X is the last element examined or when X is not in the set. Therefore, $W(n) = 0(n)$.

Worst-space analysis: Memory space is needed to store X and the set. The worst-space required is therefore $0(n + 1) = 0(n)$.

Average-time analysis: In order to find the average time for the algorithm, the probabilities, $p(I)$, for all $I \in D_n$ must be known. As an illustration, assume that there is a probability $(1 - p_X)$ that X does not occur in the set. If X occurs in the set (with probability p_X), then X is equally likely to be at any position in the set. The execution time $t(I)$ of the algorithm on input I, depends on the position of X in I.

Suppose X is at position i, $1 \le i \le n$. Then $t(I)\alpha i$. The average time required is

$$A(n) = \alpha \sum_{i=1}^{n} i\,\frac{p_x}{n} + n(1 - p_x)$$

$$= n\left(1 - \frac{p_x}{2}\right) + \frac{p_x}{2}$$

$$= 0(n)$$

Average space analysis: The average memory space needed is the same as the worst-case space needed, $0(n + 1) = 0(n)$.

Optimality of Algorithms.   After analyzing an algorithm to get the complexity measure, it would also be useful to know whether this is the best or optimal algorithm among all algorithms that can be designed to solve the same problem, using the same complexity measure. Once an algorithm has been proven to be optimal, further improvement of the algorithm cannot be done.

The general method of proving an algorithm to be optimal is to prove for some function F a theorem stating that for any algorithm in the class under consideration there is some input of size n for which the algorithm would result in a complexity measure of $F(n)$. $F(n)$ is, therefore, the lower bound of the complexity measure for any algorithm in this class. If the complexity measure for the algorithm analyzed equals $F(h)$, then the algorithm is optimal. Sometimes, the equality may be shown with respect to the orders of magnitude, and this implies that the algorithm can only be improved with a constant factor.

Using the example we have in the last section, the lower bound in the number of comparisons is $0(n)$ because every number has to be compared once in order to determine whether X is in the set. Therefore, the algorithm shown is optimal.

Models of Computation.   Algorithms can always be represented in a high-level language like PASCAL, and the order of magnitude of the complexities can be analyzed. However, in order to analyze algorithms more accurately, a theoretical model of computation or the structure of the computer must be specified. Only a brief introduction to these models will be given here. Interested readers can refer to the corresponding references.

The *Deterministic Turing Machine (DTM)* [12, 13, 14], is a basic model of computation. It is useful in proving the minimum time required by an algorithm. The general DTM has k tapes, which are infinite to the right. A tape is divided into cells, each of which holds a finite number of tape symbols. Each tape has a read/write head that can read the current symbol from the tape and feed it to a finite state control. After interpreting the symbols read from each tape, the finite state control commands the write heads to write a new symbol in the current position of each tape and moves the read/write heads to the left or right by one position. The finite state control is always in one of the finite number of states, which can be regarded as positions in a program. The finite state control, therefore, implements an algorithm, called a *deterministic algorithm*.

A second and equally powerful computational model is the *Random Access Machine (RAM)* [15, 16]. A RAM models a one-accumulator computer in which instructions are not allowed to modify themselves. It consists of a read-only tape, a write-only tape, a program memory, a location counter pointing to the currently executed instruction in the program memory, and a set of registers $r_0, r_1, \ldots, r_k, \ldots$ where all the basic computations are done in the accumulator r_0. The input and the output tapes are accessed unidirectionally, that is, once a symbol has been read from the input tape, or written to the output tape, it cannot be reread or rewritten. Simple, assembly-language-type instructions, such as ADD, MULT, JUMP, and so forth, are defined to control the operations of the RAM.

A generalization of the RAM is the *Random Access Stored Program Machine (RASP)* in which programs are allowed to modify themselves. RASP does not assume a separate program memory and register file. The program of RASP resides in the register file and, therefore, can be self-modified.

It can be shown that the RAM and RASP, under a reasonable scheme, compute an algorithm in times of the same order of magnitude, that is, the times differ by a constant factor. Similarly, the time required on a multitape DTM is polynomially related to the time required on a RAM or RASP. Two functions $f_1(n)$ and $f_2(n)$ are polynomially related if there are polynomials $p_1(x)$ and $p_2(x)$ such that for all values of n, $f_1(n) \leq P_2(f_2(n))$ and $f_2(n) \leq P_1(f_1(n))$. Note that n^4 and 2^n are not polynomially related. It is shown that the maximum time needed on a DTM is $(f(n))^4$ where $f(n)$ is the time needed to execute the same algorithm on a RAM or RASP [17]. In summary, if an algorithm can be computed in polynomial (or exponential) time or space, the RAM, RASP, or DTM computational model will be able to indicate this. Thus, all these models can be used interchangeably to analyze an algorithm. We will use the Turing machine in our discussion in this chapter.

Designing Algorithms

There is basically no algorithm to design an algorithm for an application—the process is never fully automated. However, there are guidelines and design strategies that have been devised for many application areas, and it is the responsibility of the designer to either search for an existing algorithm to fit his application or design a new algorithm based on experience accumulated in other applications. We plan to answer the following question in this section: What are the criteria that may be used to select algorithms for the same application? The answer involves tradeoffs between space and time and decisions about optimality and suboptimality.

Time and Space Tradeoff. In many problems, there exist different algorithms that can solve the same problem using different time and space complexity. A famous example is the matrix multiplication problem described in Section 4.2. In multiplying together two $n \times n$ matrices **A** and **B**, a conventional method takes $0(n^3)$ multiplications and constant space in addition to that needed by matrices **A** and **B** and the result matrix. On the other hand, Strassen's matrix multiplication method [18] takes approximately $0(n^{2.81})$ time complexity and $0(n^2)$ space complexity in addition to that needed by matrices **A** and **B** and the result matrix. There is, therefore, a tradeoff between time and space in designing algorithms. Another example is illustrated in the branch and bound algorithm to be described in Section 4.6 [19]. Different search criteria uses different time and space complexity. The breadth-first search and depth-first search criteria use constant space and exponential time. The best-first search uses exponential space and the minimum time, but is, nonetheless, exponential. The heuristic search [20] uses space and time between the extremes of best-first search and depth-first or breadth-first searches.

In general, an algorithm that requires a large amount of memory space usually solves the same problem faster than an algorithm that uses a small amount of memory space. The algorithm designer must always realize that space and time can be traded in designing algorithms of various complexities for the same problem.

Exact and Approximate Algorithms. Besides trading between space and time, the algorithm designer also has at his disposal, the tradeoff between optimality and nonoptimality of the algorithm. Some problems have very large time complexity (e.g., exponential); therefore, when the problem size is large, it cannot be computed in real time. In order to solve the problem, a fast algorithm or *heuristic* may be designed to solve it in a reasonable amount of time.

Heuristics that do not guarantee performance are usually easy to design. The results gained through these algorithms do not have a bound on the deviation from the optimal solution. Depending on the starting condition of the algorithm, different local optima can be obtained, and the final result is taken to be the best local optimum.

On the other hand, fast polynomial-time heuristics with guaranteed performance are difficult to design and are problem-dependent. Very few problems have been studied with respect to fast approximation schemes. The experience obtained through these problems has very little impact on generalizing the design of fast approximation algorithms for any type of problem. More of these will be discussed in Section 4.7 when we cover approximation algorithms for *NP-complete problems*.

In the following sections, we discuss problems solvable in increasing complexities. We start with problems solvable in polynomial time, followed by *NP*-complete problems that are solvable in exponential time. Problems that are strongly *NP*-complete and *NP*-hard will also be discussed.

4.2. SOME PROBLEMS SOLVABLE WITH POLYNOMIAL-TIME ALGORITHMS

Polynomial-time algorithms are algorithms that are executable in time bounded by a polynomial of the input size. All of these algorithms are considered good because the time complexities do not increase very rapidly with the input size (the orders of the polynomials must be low enough for this to be true). Because of this, we do not attempt to classify algorithms according to the orders of the polynomials.

In this section, a few of the problems that can be solved by polynomial-time algorithms

are described. These problems illustrate the general approach to the design of polynomial-time algorithms. The problems described include substring searching, fast Fourier transform, and matrix multiplication.

Substring Searching

Substring searching is an essential problem in many text-editing, data-retrieval, and symbol-manipulation problems. A simple version of the problem is to determine all the occurrences of the pattern string x in a text string y. The pattern string can be any concatenation or alternation of other pattern strings. However, we are going to present the substring search algorithm where the pattern string is a simple string of characters. A more rigid theoretical treatment of the problem can be found in Reference 2.

A simple algorithm to perform substring searching, with a pattern string of m characters and a text string of n characters, has a time complexity of $0(m*n)$. The algorithm starts by anchoring the leftmost character of the pattern string under the leftmost character of the text string and performing a comparison of m characters to determine if the pattern is matched in this position. If there is a mismatch, the pattern string is moved one character to the right and the matching is done again. This process is repeated a maximum of $n - m + 1$ times. Therefore, for $n \gg m$, the algorithm has a worst-time complexity of $0(n*m)$.

A much faster algorithm is presented by Knuth et al. [21]. The pattern string is preprocessed into a data structure that represents "program." This takes $0(m)$ time to perform. The "program" then searches the text string in time linear in $i + m$ where i is the position of the leftmost character in the first occurrence of the pattern in the text string. In particular, the algorithm inspects each of the first $i + m - 1$ characters of text string precisely once. The wst-case complexity is $0(n + m)$.

Boyer and Moore [22] devised an even faster algorithm with the same worst-case complexity but a faster average-case behavior. By utilizing some simple observations, they made it unnecessary to examine every element of the text string. This algorithm is an order of magnitude faster than the naive algorithm.

Fast Fourier Transform (FFT)

The continuous FFT algorithm can be viewed as a transformation of a function in the time domain into the frequency domain, or the decomposition of a function into its sinusoidal components. The discrete FFT algorithm is a transformation of a set of n reals into another set of n reals. This problem has applications in signal processing, interpolation methods, multiplication of integers, and so on. We will examine the discrete FFT algorithm.

The naive version of the Fourier transform algorithm corresponds to the evaluation of a polynomial at n points and each evaluation required $0(n)$ multiplications and additions. The algorithm has a complexity of $0(n^2)$.

The FFT algorithm, first proposed by Cooney and Tukey [23] computes these n values using $0(n \log n)$ operations. It was observed that the points at which the polynomial have to be evaluated are the primitive n'th root of unity. The FFT algorithm partitions the polynomial into two sets, each of which represents the evaluation of the polynomial at a previously evaluated point. The method belongs to the general divide and conquer method and has a complexity of $0(n \log n)$.

Matrix Multiplication

To multiply two $n \times n$ matrices $\mathbf{A}$ and $\mathbf{B}$ normally takes $0(n^3)$ multiplications and additions. Each matrix can be partitioned into four $n/2$ by $n/2$ submatrices. The original matrix multiplication is, therefore, reduced to the multiplication of two 2×2 matrices where each element of the 2×2 matrices is an $n/2 \times n/2$ submatrix. The multiplication of two $n/2 \times n/2$ submatrices can be partitioned further, recursively. A naive method of multiplying two 2×2 matrices needs 8 multiplications and 4 additions. An addition of two $n/2$ by $n/2$ matrices takes $0(n^2)$ time. The time complexity $T_1(n)$ of the matrix multiplication problem can be formulated as a recurrence equation

$$T_1(n) = \begin{cases} b & n \le 2 \\ 8T_1\left(\dfrac{n}{2}\right) + cn^2 & n > 2 \end{cases}$$

where b and c are constants. A solution for this is $T_1(n) = 0(n^3)$.

A faster method of multiplying two 2×2 matrices together is presented by Strassen [18]. Only 7 multiplications, but 18 additions are needed. The multiplication is done by computing seven temporary values.

$$\begin{bmatrix} a & b \\ c & d \end{bmatrix} \times \begin{bmatrix} e & f \\ g & h \end{bmatrix} = \begin{bmatrix} w & x \\ y & z \end{bmatrix}$$

$$t_1 = (b - d) * (g + h)$$
$$t_2 = (a + d) * (e + h)$$
$$t_3 = (a - c) * (e + f)$$
$$t_4 = (a + c) * h$$
$$t_5 = a * (e - f)$$
$$t_6 = d * (g - e)$$
$$t_7 = (c + d) * e$$

By combining these seven values, we obtain

$$w = t_1 + t_2 - t_4 + t_6$$
$$x = t_4 + t_5$$
$$y = t_6 + t_7$$
$$z = t_2 - t_3 + t_5 - t_7$$

The recurrence equation for the time complexity, $T_2(n)$, using Strassen's method is

$$T_2(n) = \begin{cases} b & n \le 2 \\ 7T_2\left(\dfrac{n}{2}\right) + dn^2 & n > 2 \end{cases}$$

where b and d are constants. A solution to this recurrence is

$$T_2(n) = 0(n^{\log_2 7}) \simeq 0(n^{2.81})$$

Due to the additional amount of matrix additions, Strassen's method is not always more efficient than the conventional method. Experimental results have shown that Strassen's method is slightly faster when n is greater than about 40.

Strassen's method also requires a larger intermediate storage, namely, t_1 through t_7. The space complexity is $7n^2(1/4 + 1/16 + 1/64 + \ldots) \leq 0(7n^2/3)$. By carefully reusing the space, some of this additional space may be saved.

Other Examples

There are numerous other problems that can be solved by polynomial-time algorithms, including sorting of n numbers [8], searching of a number in a list [8], finding the shortest path between two points in a graph [24], the transitive closure of a matrix [25], LU-decomposition of a matrix [26], and maximum-flow-minimum-cut network flows [27]. There is very little similarity among these algorithms except that they all compute the solutions in a time bounded by some polynomial of the input lengths. From these, very little can be said about the design of polynomial-time algorithms. The algorithm designer has to search intelligently the design of such algorithms, or to transform his problem into another problem with polynomial algorithms.

The existence of a polynomial algorithm is proven by the design of such an algorithm. The nonexistence of a polynomial algorithm is proven by showing its *NP*-completeness, which will be the topic of discussion in the next section. There also exists open problems in which the existence or nonexistence of polynomial algorithms cannot be established. In this case, a polynomial algorithm to solve the problem has not been found and the *NP*-completeness of the problem has not been proven. As a consequence, the algorithm designer has to work in both directions, namely, to find the polynomial algorithm, and to prove the *NP*-completeness, in order to determine the complexity of the problem.

4.3. *NP*-COMPLETE PROBLEMS

Basic Concepts

The theory of NP-completeness was first established by Karp [28]. Informally, a problem is said to be *NP-complete* if there is no known optimal algorithm to solve the problem with a computation time that increases polynomially with the size of the problem. The computation time for all known optimal algorithms for this class of problems increases exponentially with the problem size, that is, if n represents the size of the problem, then the computation time goes up as k^n where $k > 1$. We have seen previously that, for problems with exponential-time complexity, the computation time goes up tremendously as the problem size is increased.

A more formal definition of *NP*-completeness requires the use of an abstract model of computation similar to those discussed in Section 4.1. This theory is discussed with respect to the recognition of languages by one-tape Turing machines. Let Σ^* be the set of all finite strings of 0s and 1s. A subset of Σ^* is called a *language*. A language is said to be *recognized* by a one-tape deterministic Turing machine if the deterministic algorithm implemented on the machine is terminating and the result produced is ACCEPT whenever the string $\in \Sigma^*$. P is the class of languages recognizable in polynomial time by a one-tape deterministic Turing machine. The class P models problems that are computable in polynomial time.

On the other hand, a language is said to be recognized by a one-tape *Nondeterministic Turing Machine (NDTM)* if the nondeterministic recognition algorithm implemented on the machine is terminating and the result produced is ACCEPT whenever the string $\in \Sigma^*$. *NP* is the class of languages recognizable in polynomial time by one-tape nondeterministic Turing machines. The class *NP* models problems that are computable in exponential or hyperexponential time.

A *nondeterministic algorithm* can be regarded as a process that when encountered with the decision of two or more alternatives, creates two or more copies of itself and pursues the alternatives concurrently. Repeated splitting of the algorithm can lead to an exponential growth in the number of copies. The input string is accepted whenever any one of the copies leads to acceptance. Another way to view a nondeterministic Turing machine is to assume that there is a guessing stage in the nondeterministic algorithm, which always makes the correct choice when encountered with two or more alternatives. In this case, one tape is sufficient for the execution of the algorithm. The nondeterministic Turing machine, like the deterministic Turing machine, is a hypothetical model of computation that cannot be implemented in practice. They are defined so that the properties of algorithms can be studied.

The recognition of a language by a Turing Machine is an example of a decision problem. Formally, a *decision problem* Π consists of a set D_Π of instances and a subset $Y_\Pi \subseteq D_\Pi$ of *yes* instances. Given any $I \in D_\Pi$, an algorithm to solve a decision problem returns *no* if Y_Π is empty and otherwise returns *yes*.

In general, problems encountered in practice are optimization problems. A *combinatorial optimization problem* Π is a minimization (or maximization) problem and contains a set D_Π of instances; a finite set $S_\Pi(I)$ of candidate solutions for each $I \in D_\Pi$; and a function m_Π that maps each $I \in D_\Pi$ and each $\sigma \in S_\Pi(I)$ into a positive rational number $m_\Pi(I,\sigma)$ called the solution value σ [1]. If π is a minimization (or maximization) problem, then the *optimal solution* for each $I \in D_\Pi$ is a candidate solution $\sigma^* \in S_\Pi(I)$ such that, for all $\sigma \in S_\Pi$, $m_\Pi(I,\sigma^*) \leq m_\Pi(I,\sigma)$ (or $m_\Pi(I,\sigma^*) \geq m_\Pi(I,\sigma)$). The search of a tour with the minimum cost in the TRAVELING SALESMAN problem is an example of an optimization problem. Basically, an optimization problem can be transformed into a decision problem. If an optimization problem asks for a solution with the minimum (or maximum) cost, we can associate a value B with the corresponding decision problem that asks whether there is a solution with value no more than (or at least as large as) B. Therefore, we can treat optimization problems as special cases of decision problems. The theory of NP-completeness is developed with respect to decision problems, and can be applied to optimization problems as well.

To determine whether a language is recognizable by a Turing machine, one can write the algorithm that performs the recognition process on the Turing machine. This is very time-consuming and difficult if it has to be done for every language. A better way is to define a standard problem that can be reduced to the problem at hand. The problem studied, therefore, assumes the same properties as the standard problem. Let L and M be languages. L is said to be *reducible* to M (i.e., $L \propto M$) if there is a function f that is computable in polynomial time by a one-tape deterministic Turing machine, such that $f(x) \in M \leftrightarrow x \in L$. The reduction process is, therefore, a polynomial time transformation process that maps L into M. L and M are equivalent iff $L \propto M$ and $M \propto L$. The property of transitivity also holds for the reduction process, that is, if $L_1 \propto L_2$ and $L_2 \propto L_3$, then $L_1 \propto L_3$.

The importance of reducibility is that if $M \in P$ and $L \propto M$, then $L \in P$. That is, if M is a polynomial-time algorithm and $L \propto M$, then L is also a polynomial-time algorithm. In contrast, proving that a problem is not solvable in polynomial time cannot be done in a similar fashion, because the nonexistence of a polynomial algorithm cannot be proven by showing that the language is reducible from a language in NP. It must be shown that every language in NP is reducible to the language on hand. An additional requirement to show the nonexistence of a polynomial-time algorithm is the property that P does not equal NP, otherwise all problems in NP could be solved in polynomial time and there are no problems in NP that require exponential-time algorithms. In other words, if we can establish that P does not equal NP and we can find a language $M \in NP - P$ and $L \propto M$, then $L \in NP$. However, the question of $P = NP$ is still open [1] and, therefore, we have to focus on proving results of the weaker form, "if $P \neq NP$, then $L \in NP - P$."

We define a class of languages L to be *NP-complete* if $L \in NP$ and every language in NP is reducible to L. This means that if any single NP-complete problem can be solved in polynomial time, then all problems in NP can be solved in polynomial time. Similarly, if any problem in NP is solvable in exponential time, then all NP-complete problems are solvable in exponential time. The class of NP-complete problems forms an equivalence class that is distinguished by the property that it contains the most difficult languages to recognize in

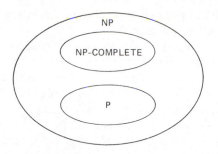

Figure 4.1. The relationship between problems in NP, P, and NP-complete.

NP. The relationship among the problems in *NP*, *P* and *NP*-complete is shown in Figure 4.1.

Cook's Theorem

The requirement that reduction has to be performed on every problem in *NP* is very stringent because there are many possible languages contained in *NP*. However, if one of the problems *M* in *NP* can be proved to be *NP*-complete, then a set of problems in *NP* can be proved to be *NP*-complete by direct reduction to the standard *NP*-complete problem. Similarly, any problem in *NP* can be proved to be *NP*-complete by direct reduction to any problem that has been proved to be *NP*-complete, because this implies that there exists a sequence of reductions from the problem in question to the standard *NP*-complete problem. The identification and proof of a standard *NP*-complete problem is shown by Cook [29], and the standard problem is the *SATISFIABILITY* problem.

Satisfiability. *Input:* A set $X = \{X_1, X_2, \ldots, X_m\}$ of Boolean variables of values {TRUE, FALSE} and a collection $C = \{C_1, C_2, \ldots, C_p\}$ of clauses where each C_j is a subset of the complemented or uncomplemented variables in X and represents the disjunction of the variables. If $X_i \in C_j$ and X_i is TRUE, then C_j is TRUE; if $\overline{X_i} \in C_j$ and X_i is FALSE, then C_j is TRUE. C_j is *satisfied* by a truth assignment iff one of the variables is TRUE under the assignment.

Question: Is the conjunction of the given clauses C satisfiable? That is, is there a truth assignment for C such that all the C_js are satisfied?

Cook's Theorem. SATISFIABILITY is *NP*-complete. The proof of this follows the standard way of proving *NP*-completeness, that is, by showing that it can be evaluated in polynomial time by a *NDTM* and by showing that for all languages L in *NP*, $L \propto$ SATISFIABILITY. As mentioned before, the number of possible languages is infinite and the proof is impossible if a transformation has to be carried out for each one of them. The proof is done by classifying the languages in *NP* into classes and giving a polynomial time *NDTM* program that recognizes each class of languages. Readers interested in the proof should refer to the paper by Cook [29].

Using Cook's theorem, a new definition can be made for *NP*-completeness. The language L is *NP complete* if (1) $L \in NP$ and (2) SATISFIABILITY $\propto L$. The second condition can be satisfied if there is an *NP*-complete problem M such that $M \propto L$. If M has been shown to be *NP*-complete, it must be true that SATISFIABILITY $\propto M$ and this implies SATISFIABILITY $\propto L$.

In the next section, examples of *NP*-complete problems and their corresponding reductions are shown.

Examples of *NP*-Complete Problems

In this section, we present three examples and illustrate the proofs of *NP*-completeness. The three examples of *NP*-complete problems are 0–1 INTEGER PROGRAMMING, CLIQUE, and VERTEX COVERING. All of these problems are in *NP* because an *NDTM* can guess the solution in polynomial time. In the following examples, we will only show that the problem is reducible to the SATISFIABILITY problem or other problems proven to be *NP*-complete. Karp [28] and Garey and Johnson [1] give an extensive list of *NP*-complete problems and their corresponding proofs.

(A) 0–1 INTEGER PROGRAMMING is NP-Complete. The 0–1 INTEGER PRO-

GRAMMING problem is the selection of the elements of a 0–1 vector $\mathbf{X}$ such that for a given integer matrix $\mathbf{C}$ and integer vector $\mathbf{d}$, $\mathbf{CX} = \mathbf{d}$.

To prove that SATISFIABILITY $\propto$ 0–1 INTEGER PROGRAMMING, we have to choose the matrix $\mathbf{C}$ and the vector $\mathbf{d}$ such that the solution vector $\mathbf{X}$ represents a solution to the SATISFIABILITY problem. $\mathbf{C}$ and $\mathbf{d}$ can be set as:

$$
\mathbf{C}_{i,j} = \begin{cases} 1 \text{ if } \mathbf{X}_j \in \mathbf{C}_i & i = 1,2,\ldots,p \\ -1 \text{ if } \overline{\mathbf{X}}_j \in \mathbf{C}_i & j = 1,2,\ldots,n \\ 0 \text{ otherwise} \end{cases}
$$

$\mathbf{d}_i$ = number of uncomplemented variables in $\mathbf{C}_i, i = 1,2,\ldots,p$

If $\mathbf{X}_j$ is set to be TRUE (or FALSE) in SATISFIABILITY, then $\mathbf{X}_j$ has to be chosen to be 1 (or 0) in the 0–1 INTEGER PROGRAMMING problem. The SATISFIABILITY problem is, therefore, a special instance of the 0–1 INTEGER PROGRAMMING problem. If the SATISFIABILITY problem is *NP*-complete, then so is that of the 0–1 INTEGER PROGRAMMING.

(B) CLIQUE is NP-Complete. The CLIQUE problem searches in an undirected graph $\mathbf{G} = \{\mathbf{V},\mathbf{E}\}$ whether there is a fully connected subgraph of k vertices. $\mathbf{V}$ is the set of vertices and $\mathbf{E}$ is a set of unordered pairs of vertices that represent the edges joining two vertices together.

We can construct a special instance of the CLIQUE problem from the general SATISFIABILITY problem by specifying the sets $\mathbf{V}$ and $\mathbf{E}$.

$\mathbf{V} = \{\sigma_{i,j} \mid \mathbf{X}_i \text{ is a variable that occurs in } \mathbf{C}_j\}$
$\mathbf{E} = \{(\sigma_{i,k}, \sigma_{j,l}) \mid \mathbf{X}_i \neq \overline{\mathbf{X}}_j \text{ and } \mathbf{C}_k \neq \mathbf{C}_l\}$
$k = p$, the number of clauses

If there is a satisfying assignment of variables in the SATISFIABILITY problem, then there exist k vertices in the graph such that this subgraph is fully connected. If the SATISFI-

ABILITY problem is *NP*-complete, then so is the CLIQUE problem.

A problem that is very similar to the CLIQUE problem is the INDEPENDENT SET problem, which can also be shown to be *NP*-complete. The *INDEPENDENT SET* problem searches in an undirected graph $\mathbf{G} = (\mathbf{V}, \mathbf{E})$ whether there is a subset $\mathbf{V}' \subseteq \mathbf{V}$ such that for all $u, v \in \mathbf{V}'$, the edge $\{u, v\}$ is not in $\mathbf{E}$. Therefore, if $\mathbf{V}$ is a vertex cover for $\mathbf{G}$, then $\mathbf{V} - \mathbf{V}'$ is an independent set of $\mathbf{G}$.

(C) VERTEX COVERING is NP-Complete

The VERTEX COVERING problem decides in an undirected graph $\mathbf{G}' = \{\mathbf{V}', \mathbf{E}'\}$ whether there is a set of ℓ or less vertices such that all the edges in the graph are covered. (By *cover* is meant that all the edges in the graph emanate from at least one of the included vertices. That is, there is a subset $\mathbf{R} \subseteq \mathbf{V}'$ such that $|\mathbf{R}| \leq \ell$ and every arc in $\mathbf{E}'$ is incident with some node in $\mathbf{R}$.)

To prove that the VERTEX COVERING problem is *NP*-complete, we can show that CLIQUE $\propto$ VERTEX COVERING. By transitivity, SATISFIABILITY $\propto$ VERTEX COVERING. The CLIQUE and VERTEX COVERING problems are equivalent because we can choose for the VERTEX COVERING problem,

$\mathbf{V}' = \mathbf{V}$
$\mathbf{E}' = \{(i, j) \mid i, j \in \mathbf{V} \text{ and } (i, j) \notin \mathbf{E}\}$
$\ell = |\mathbf{N}| - k$

The existence of a clique in graph $\mathbf{G}$ implies the existence of a vertex cover in graph $\mathbf{G}'$. If CLIQUE is *NP*-complete, then so is VERTEX COVERING.

We have seen three examples of proving *NP*-completeness. These examples are meant to be illustrative and do not intend to present the different techniques of proving *NP*-completeness. Reference 1 shows three general methods of proving *NP*-completeness: (1) restriction, (2) local replacement, and (3) complement design. Interested readers can refer to it for details.

There are many practical problems that are *NP*-complete. To name a few, problems like the TRAVELING SALESMAN, WAREHOUSE LOCATION, JOB-SHOP SCHEDULING, GRAPH PARTITIONING for VLSI design, dynamic storage allocation, consistency of data base frequency tables, and feasible register assignment for program optimization are *NP*-complete. In fact, a lot of the nontrivial practical problems are *NP*-complete. The search for good, efficient algorithms to solve these problems is, therefore, very important.

4.4. STRONG *NP*-COMPLETE PROBLEMS

Basic Concepts

To illustrate the concept of strong *NP*-completeness, we will discuss the solution of applying a dynamic programming algorithm to solve the 2-PARTITION problem.

The inputs to the 2-PARTITION problem consist of a set of positive integers, $\{c_1, c_2, \ldots, c_n\}$ and $\sum_{i=1}^{n} c_i = B$. The problem is to discover whether there is a subset $I \subseteq \{1, 2, \ldots, n\}$ such that $\sum_{i \in I} c_i = \sum_{i \notin I} c_i$. This problem can be shown to be *NP*-complete by a sequence of reductions from the SATISFIABILITY problem.

The dynamic programming approach to solve the 2-PARTITION problem can be written in the iterative form. (The dynamic programming method will be discussed further in Section 4.6.) Let $t(i,j)$, $1 \leq i \leq n$, $0 \leq j \leq B/2$, be a binary variable such that $t(i,j) = 1$ if there is a subset of $\{a_1, a_2, \ldots, a_i\}$ for which the sum of the item sizes is exactly j and 0 otherwise.

$$t(i,j) = \max \{t(i-1,j), t(i-1, j-a_j)\}$$

with the boundary conditions of

$$t(1,j) = \begin{cases} 1 & j = 0 \text{ or } j = a_i \\ 0 & \text{Otherwise} \end{cases}$$

and

$$t(i,j) = 0 \text{ for } j < 0$$

The answer to the 2-PARTITION problem is *yes* if $t(n, B/2) = 1$ and *no* otherwise. A computational method to compute $t(n, B/2)$ is to construct a two dimensional table of size $n \times B/2$ and compute each entry of the table accordingly. The complexity of this computation is $0(n*B)$ and this looks like a polynomial algorithm in n. However, the input length required to represent the 2-PARTITION problem has a value of $0(n*\log_2 B)$ since each c_i has a maximum value of B. As $0(n*B)$ is not bounded by any polynomial function of $0(n*\log_2 B)$, this means that the dynamic programming algorithm applied is not truly a polynomial-time algorithm.

Nonetheless, if an upper bound is imposed on the maximum value of the input set such that each value is polynomial in the total input length, then the dynamic programming algorithm is a polynomial-time algorithm. The 2-PARTITION problem is an example that is solvable when an upper bound is put on inputs and is *NP*-complete otherwise. Such an algorithm is called a pseudo-polynomial-time algorithm.

Formally, an algorithm is a *pseudo-polynomial-time algorithm* if the time complexity function is bounded above by a polynomial function of two variables, length of input, length[I], and maximum value of each individual input item, Max[I] [30]. For many of the problems considered, Max[I] is bounded above by a polynomial function of Length[I] and there is no distinction between polynomial- and pseudo-polynomial-time algorithms. For example, the maximum clique size is the number of vertices in the graph. For the 2-PARTITION problem, the use of a pseudo-polynomial-time algorithm is important because the problem is solvable in either polynomial time or is *NP*-complete.

A problem that cannot be solved by a pseudo-polynomial-time algorithm unless $P = NP$ is said to be *strongly NP-complete*. Problems that are strongly *NP*-complete are, therefore, even harder to solve than problems that are *NP*-complete because no restrictions can be put on these problems in order for them to be polynomially solvable. Problems that are strongly *NP*-complete have also been termed as *unary NP-complete* [31] and problems that are *NP*-complete in the normal sense are termed as *binary NP-complete*. This means that if a problem is strongly *NP*-complete, then the corresponding language is *NP*-complete even when the inputs are represented in the unary notation (that is, a number n is represented as a string of n 1s).

Proving Strong *NP*-Completeness

The purpose of this section is to introduce some aspects of proving strong *NP*-completeness. Readers interested in the details of this topic should refer to References 1 and 31.

A *number problem* Π is defined as a decision problem such that there is no polynomial p and $\text{Max}[I] \leq p(\text{Length}[I])$ for all possible inputs. The 2-PARTITION problem is an example of a number problem. A new decision problem Π_p is obtained by restricting the inputs to those with $\text{Max}[I] \leq p(\text{Length}[I])$. Therefore, Π_p is not a number problem. If Π is solvable by a pseudo-polynomial-time algorithm, it is easy to see that Π_p is solvable by a polynomial-time algorithm.

To prove that a problem is strongly *NP*-complete, it is necessary to prove that for some polynomial p, Π_p is *NP*-complete. This method of proof involves two aspects. First, a restricted problem Π_p must be found such that $\text{Max}[I] \leq p(\text{Length}[I])$. Second, this problem has to be proved to be *NP*-complete. This rather inconvenient method requires the identification of the polynomial p. An easier way is to use a similar method in proving *NP*-completeness and to transform the problem in question to a problem that is known to be strongly *NP*-complete. Suppose there are two decision problems Π and Π' with domains D_Π and $D_{\Pi'}$, yes sets of Y_Π and $Y_{\Pi'}$ and specified functions Max, Length, Max' and Length', respectively. Define a *pseudo-polynomial transformation* from Π to Π' as a function $f: D_\Pi \rightarrow D_{\Pi'}$ such that

1. For all $I \in D_\Pi$, $I \in Y_\Pi$ iff $f(I) \in Y_{\Pi'}$
2. f can be computed in time polynomial in $\text{Max}[I]$ and $\text{Length}[I]$

3. There exist two polynomials q_1 and q_2 such that for all $I \in D_\Pi$,

$$q_1(\text{Length}'[f(I)]) \geq \text{Length}[I]$$
$$\text{Max}'[f(I)] \leq q_2(\text{Max}[I], \text{Length}[I])$$

It can be shown that if Π is strongly *NP*-complete, $\Pi' \in NP$, and there is a pseudopolynomial transformation from Π to Π', then Π' is strongly *NP*-complete.

We will only mention without proof a few of the strongly *NP*-complete problems. These problems are the TRAVELING SALESMAN problem, the 3-PARTITION problem, the 4-PARTITION problem, and SEQUENCING WITH INTERVALS. Readers interested in the proofs can refer to Reference 30.

4.5. *NP*-HARD PROBLEMS

The problems we have encountered so far belong to *NP*, that is, they can be evaluated in polynomial time by a *NDTM*. There also exist problems that do not belong to *NP*. An example of this is the K'th LARGEST SUBSET problem.

The *K'th LARGEST SUBSET* problem assumes inputs of a finite set A, a size $s(a) \in Z^+$ for each $a \in A$, and two non-negative integers $B \leq \sum_{a \in A} s(a)$ and $K \leq 2^{|A|}$. It asks the question whether there are K distinct subsets $A' \subseteq A$ that satisfy $S(A') = \sum_{a \in A'} s(a) \leq B$.

It has been shown in Reference 32 that this problem can be solved in time bounded by a polynomial function of $|A| * K \lceil \log S(A) \rceil$ and is a pseudo-polynomial-time algorithm. Thus for any fixed value of K, this problem can be solved in polynomial time. However, if the question is formulated asking for the maximum number of distinct subsets, a *NDTM* will guess the K distinct subsets. In order the the *NDTM* to execute in polynomial time, the number of output symbols must be a polynomial in the input length, and it seems to be impossible for the *NDTM* to guess K distinct subsets in time polynomial in $|A| \lceil \text{Log } K \rceil$ $\lceil \text{Log } s(a) \rceil$. Therefore, this problem does not belong to *NP*.

For any decision problem that is not a member of *NP*, but is reducible from an *NP*-complete problem, this problem cannot be solved in polynomial time unless $P = NP$. The problem is termed *NP-hard*, that is, it is as hard as any other *NP*-complete problems [33].

The definition of *NP*-hardness can be extended to search problems. The K'th LARGEST SUBSET problem discussed above is such an example. A *search problem* Π consists of a finite set of input objects, D_{Π}, and for each $d \in D_{\Pi}$, of a set $S_{\Pi}[d]$ of objects called solutions for d. Given any $d \in D_{\Pi}$, an algorithm to solve a search problem returns *no* if $S_{\Pi}[d]$ is empty and otherwise returns any solution belonging to $S_{\Pi}[d]$. To define the *NP*-hardness of search problems, the concept of polynomial transformation must be generalized. A *polynomial-time Turing reduction* for a search problem Π to a search problem Π' is an algorithm A that solves Π by using the algorithm S to solve Π' as a subroutine such that if S is a polynomial-time algorithm for Π', then A is a polynomial-time algorithm to solve Π. This definition is more general than the definition of reducibility defined in Section 4.3 and can be applied to both search problems and decision problems.

A search problem is defined to be *NP-hard* if SATISFIABILITY (or any other *NP*-complete problems) is Turing reducible in polynomial time to the problem in question [34]. This definition is as popular as the definition given earlier. That is, a decision problem Π is termed *NP*-hard if SATISFIABILITY $\propto \Pi$ [33]. The implications of these two different definitions are equivalent. That is, no problem in this class can be solved in polynomial time unless $P = NP$, and hence can be no easier than any other *NP*-complete problems; and if $P = NP$, all problems in this class can be solved in polynomial time.

The K*th* LARGEST SUBSET problem defined earlier is *NP*-hard. The problem does not belong to *NP*, and there is no known transformation from an *NP*-complete problem to this problem. However, it can be shown that the *NP*-complete PARTITION problem can be Turing-reduced to the K*th* LARGEST SUBSET problem [36].

4.6. SOME ENUMERATIVE ALGORITHMS FOR SOLVING *NP*-COMPLETE PROBLEMS

So far, we have studied algorithms that are *NP*-complete or are as hard as any *NP*-complete problems. In this section, we discuss two of the most general methods to obtain a solution of a decision, search, or optimization problem, namely, the branch and bound algorithm and dynamic programming method. These methods are general enough to be applied to any type of *NP*-complete or polynomial-time problems. In the case of an *NP*-complete problem, an optimal solution is usually desired.

The algorithms are discussed with respect to the constrained optimization problem,* which can be put into the following form:

Minimize	$C_0(\mathbf{x})$
subject to	$g_1(\mathbf{x}) \geq 0$
	$g_2(\mathbf{x}) \geq 0$
	.
	.
	.
	$g_m(\mathbf{x}) \geq 0$
and	$\mathbf{x} \in \mathbf{X}$

where $\mathbf{X}$ represents the domain of optimization defined by the m constraints, normally an Euclidean n-space and $\mathbf{x}$ denotes a vector $(x_1, x_2, \ldots, x_n)$. A solution vector that lies in $\mathbf{X}$ is said to be a *feasible solution* and a feasible solution for which $C_0(\mathbf{x})$ is minimal is said to be an *optimal solution*.

Branch and Bound Algorithm

The branch and bound algorithm is an organized and intelligently structured search of the space of all feasible solutions and is a general form of the backtracking method. It has been extensively studied in areas such as artificial intelligence and operations research [5, 19, 36, 37]. It has been applied extensively to solve such problems as scheduling [40, 41], knapsack [40, 41], traveling salesman [42, 43, 44], facility allocation [45, 46], integer program-

---

*These problems may or may not be *NP*-complete.

ming [47, 48], and many others. Dominance relations similar to those used in dynamic programming have been used to prune search tree nodes [49, 50, 51].

Theoretical properties of the branch and bound algorithm have been developed in References 20, 37, and 52–56. It is shown in Reference 53 that depth-first search, breadth-first search, and best-first search are special cases of heuristic search. In heuristic search, an evaluation function $f(n)$ for a subproblem n is computed as the sum of the cost of an optimal path from a given start node to n and the cost of an optimal path from n to a goal. An ordered search algorithm picks up a subproblem with the minimum value of f for expansion each time. Any general heuristic functions can be included in the computation, and the choice of a heuristic function depends on the application.

In the branch and bound algorithm, the space of all feasible solutions is repeatedly partitioned into smaller and smaller subsets, and both the lower and upper bounds are calculated for the cost of solutions within each subset. After each partitioning, subsets with a lower bound (in the case of minimization) that exceeds either the cost of a known feasible solution or the least upper bound of all the subsets are excluded from all further partitioning. The partitioning process continues until a feasible solution is found such that the cost is no greater than the lower bound for any subset.

The state of the partitioning process at any time can be represented as a partial tree (Figure 4.2). Each node in the tree represents a partition and is termed a *subproblem*. The partitioning process selects a partition and breaks it up into smaller partitions, which in essence extend the node in the partial tree representing this partition by one level, and uses the sons to denote the smaller partitions. In Figure 4.2, node j is expanded in the partitioning process into k other partitions that are represented as sons of node j in the partial tree.

There are two essential features of a branch and bound algorithm, namely, the branching rule and the bounding rule. Let us discuss these with respect to the tree in Figure 4.2. Each node in the partial tree has two numbers

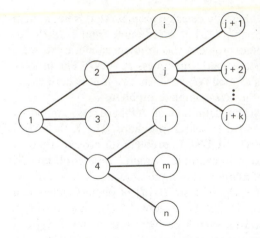

Figure 4.2. A branch and bound tree.

associated with it—the upper bound and the lower bound of the subproblem. The leaf nodes in the partial tree are candidates for partitioning. We say that a leaf node of the partial tree whose lower bound is less than both the value of a known feasible solution and the greatest upper bound of all leaf nodes is *active;* otherwise it is designated as *terminated* and need not be considered in any further computation.

The branching algorithm examines the set of active leaf nodes and selects one for expansion based on some predefined criterion. If the set of active nodes is maintained in a first-in-first-out (FIFO) list, the algorithm is called a *breadth-first search.* If the set is maintained in a last-in-first-out list, then the algorithm is termed *depth-first-search.* Lastly, if the node selected for expansion is one with the minimum lower bound, then the search algorithm is called a *best-first search.* In a breadth-first search, the nodes of the tree will always be examined in levels; that is, a node at a lower level will always be examined before a node at a higher level. This search will always find a goal node nearest to the root. However, the sequence of nodes examined is always predetermined and therefore the search is "blind." The depth-first search has a similar behavior except that a subtree is generated completely before the other subtrees are examined. In both of these algorithms, since the next node to be examined is known, the state of the parent node leading to the next node does not have to be kept because the path leading to the next node from the root node is easily found and unique. These two algorithms are, therefore, space-economical. On the other hand, best-first search is space-consuming because all the active subproblems must be stored as intermediate data in the computer. However, the total number of nodes expanded is minimized as any branching operation performed under this policy must also be performed under other policies, provided that all the bounds are unique [19].

Once the subproblem has been selected for partitioning, the next task is to select some undetermined parameters in the subprogram in order to define alternatives for these parameters and create multiple sub-problems. For example, in the traveling salesman problem, the undetermined alternatives are the set of untraversed edges. In expanding a subproblem, an untraversed edge (i,j) is selected and two alternatives can be created, namely, the edge is traversed and that the salesman goes directly from city i to city j and vice versa. The parameter chosen is usually done in a rather ad hoc fashion.

After new subproblems are created, the bounding algorithm is applied to evaluate the upper and lower bounds of a subproblem. In general, only the lower bound is evaluated because the merits of using the upper bound are very small. The bounding algorithm design is highly dependent on the problem. For example, in an integer programming problem, a linear program with the integer constraints relaxed can be used as a lower bound [57]; in a traveling salesman problem, an assignment algorithm [58] or a spanning-tree algorithm [43, 44] can be used as the bounding algorithm. We apply the branch and bound algorithm on an *NP*-complete problem, the VERTEX COVERING problem discussed in Section 4.3.

In the VERTEX COVERING problem, the problem is to find, in an undirected graph, the minimum number of vertices that are needed to "cover" all the edges in the graph. (By "cover," it means that all the edges in the graph emanate from at least one of the included vertices). The branching rule uses the best-first search and branches on an unselected vertex with the largest out-degree. Two subproblems can be created, one including this vertex in the set and one excluding it. The lower bound in the bounding rule is chosen to be the minimum number of unselected vertices such that the total out-degree is greater than or equal to the number of uncovered edges. Notice that edges emanating from different vertices in the lower bound calculation may overlap and, therefore, this vertex does not necessarily cover all the uncovered edges. Further, if a vertex has been excluded in a previous stage and there are uncovered edges emanating from this excluded vertex in the current subproblem, the unselected vertex covering these edges must be included in the minimal set first. As an example, the branch and bound tree for the graph in Figure 4.3a is shown in Figure 4.3b.

Many results have been proved for the branch and bound algorithm [20, 52, 53, 54, 55]. It has been shown that the best-first search is the best branching rule and minimizes the number of subproblems expanded [19]. Furthermore, the branch and bound al-

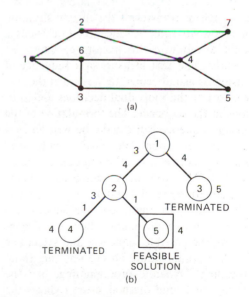

Figure 4.3a. An example graph.
Figure 4.3b. The branch and bound tree for Figure 4.3a. (The number in the node indicates the order of evaluation; the number outside the node indicates the lower bound; the number on the edge indicates the included or excluded node).

gorithm can be used as a general purpose heuristic to compute solutions that differ from the optimum by no more than a prescribed amount [19]. Suppose it were decided at the outset that a deviation of 10% from the optimum is tolerable. If a feasible solution of 150 is obtained, then all subproblems with lower bounds of 136.4 or more (= 150/1.1) will be terminated. This technique significantly reduces the amount of intermediate storage and the time to arrive at a suboptimal solution. A technique is also available to find the best solution in a given length of time [19]. It consists basically of searching for an optimal solution for a length of time equal to $T/2$. If one is not found, then the search is continued for a suboptimal solution that differs from the optimal by no more than 5% in time of length $T/4$. The time for searching is halved each time while the precision of the solution is reduced until a solution is found.

Dynamic Programming

Dynamic programming is an optimization procedure that can be used to solve problems requiring a sequence of interrelated decisions. Each decision transforms the current situation into a new situation. A sequence of decisions is sought to minimize (or maximize) some cost measures. The cost measure of a sequence of decisions is usually equal to the sum of the cost measures of the individual decisions and situations in the sequence. The formulation of the decision sequence can usually be written as a recurrence equation. We have already seen such an example when the solution of the 2-PARTITION problem is written as a recurrence equation (Section 4.4).

Since there are many possible decision sequences, an explicit enumeration would generate all the possible sequences and select one with the optimal value. This can be very time-consuming. Dynamic programming, like the branch and bound method, often reduces the total number of decision sequences by avoiding the enumeration of some decision sequences that cannot possibly lead to the optimal solution. The criterion used—the *principle of optimality*—is different from the criterion used in the branch and bound method. The princi-

ple states that an optimal sequence of decisions has the property that whatever the initial situations and decisions are, the remaining decisions must consititute an optimal decision sequence with regard to the situation resulting from the first set of decisions [59, 60, 61]. Decision sequences that violate the principle of optimality cannot be optimal and, therefore, will not be generated.

Let us illustrate the application of dynamic programming with two problems. The first problem, the SHORTEST PATH problem, has an execution time that is a polynomial of the input size [24]. The *SHORTEST PATH* problem searches in a directed (or undirected) graph $G = (V,E)$, for the shortest path from a source vertex $s \in V$ to a sink vertex $t \in V$. V is the set of vertices of G, and E is the set of edges connecting the vertices. The cost of a path is defined as the sum of weights on the edges forming the path.

The second problem, the KNAPSACK problem, is *NP*-complete and has an execution time that is exponential of the input size [63]. The *KNAPSACK* problem has as inputs a knapsack of size M, and n objects where object i has a weight $w_i > 0$ and a profit $p_i > 0$ if it is put in the knapsack. The problem seeks a subset of the objects that has the maximum profit and the sum of weights is less than M; that is, they fit in the knapsack.

Application of Dynamic Programming to Solve the SHORTEST PATH Problem The SHORTEST PATH problem involves a sequence of decisions. The ith decision chooses the ith vertex to be included in the shortest path. To see how the principle of optimality can be applied, consider the shortest path from s to t along the path $s,i_1,i_2, \ldots ,i_n j_i,j_2, \ldots ,j_m,t$. The decisions made in choosing the path $s \rightarrow j_i$ have no effect on the remaining path to be chosen. The path $j_1 \rightarrow t$ must be the shortest path; otherwise a new path $j_1,j_2', \ldots ,j_q',t$ can be chosen such that $s,i_1,i_2, \ldots ,i_n j_1 j_2', \ldots ,j_q',t$ is the shortest path. By extending this reasoning, if vertex j_1 is included in the shortest path, then the shortest path must consist of the shortest path from s to j_1 and the shortest path from j_1 to t.

To obtain a recursive formulation of the

problem, let A_s be the set of adjacent vertices to the source vertex. The value of the shortest path from s to t, $SP(s,t)$, is

$$SP(s,t) = \min_{j \in A_s} \{w_{s,j} + SP(j,t)\} \quad (1)$$

where $w_{s,j}$ is the weight on the edge (s,j).

The evaluation of the above recurrence equation starts with the boundary condition $SP(t,t) = 0$ and evaluates backwards by first examining the vertices adjacent to t. Let this set be A_t and the shortest path for each element of A_t is computed using Eq. (1). This is then repeated for the adjacent vertices of each element of A_t until all the vertices are included in the expanded tree. For n vertices of G, the time complexity can become 2^n.

A faster method is to use the principle of optimality and to eliminate unnecessary repeated nodes in the expanded tree. This is done by computing the shortest path for each vertex of G. Since the shortest path for a vertex j in G equals

$$\min_{r \in A_j} \{w_{j,r} + SP(r,t)\}$$

and the minimization has to be carried out over all adjacent vertices of j. Since this is repeated for n vertices of G and each edge of G is examined twice, the time complexity of the modified algorithm is $0(n + e)$ where n is the total number of vertices and e is the total number of edges. This is, therefore, a polynomial-time algorithm.

Application of Dynamic Programming to Solve the KNAPSACK Problem. The KNAPSACK problem also involves a sequence of n decisions, where n is the number of objects in the problem. At the ith decision, the algorithm has to decide whether the ith object is to be included in the knapsack. If the ith object is included, it will incur a weight $w_i > 0$ in the knapsack and return a profit of $p_i > 0$. Let x_i be a binary variable such that

$$x = \begin{cases} 0 & \text{object } i \text{ is not included in knapsack} \\ 1 & \text{object } i \text{ is included in knapsack} \end{cases}$$

The objective is to maximize

$$\sum_{i=1}^{n} = p_i x_i$$

subject to $\Sigma_{i=1}^{h} w_i x_i \leq M$. That is, we want to choose a subset of the objects such that the total weight is less than or equal to M, while the returned profit is maximum.

Consider a particular sequence of decisions $y_1, y_2, \ldots, y_n$. If $y_1 = 0$ (or $y_1 = 1$), then the choice for $y_2, \ldots, y_n$ must be the optimal decision for filling in the knapsack of size M (or $M - w_1$ for $y_1 = 1$) using only objects 2 to n. Otherwise, another sequence $z_2, \ldots, z_n$ can be found such that

$$\sum_{i=2}^{n} P_i y_i < \sum_{i=2}^{n} p_i z_i,$$
$$\sum_{i=2}^{n} w_i z_i \leq M \text{ (or } M - w_1 \text{ for } y_1 = 1)$$

and the sequence $y_1, z_2, \ldots, z_n$ has a larger profit. The principle of optimality therefore applies.

To obtain the recursive formulation of the problem, let $K_i(X)$ be the total profit values obtained on objects i to n for a knapsack of capacity X. In the first decision, object 1 is decided upon. Hence,

$$K_0(M) = \min \{K_1(M), p_1 + K_1(M - w_1)\} \quad (2)$$

The evaluation of Eq. (2) starts with the boundary condition $K_{n+1}(X) = 0$ for all values of X. It evaluates backwards to obtain K_n, $K_{n-1}, \ldots$, until $K_0(M)$ is obtained. To obtain the optimal decision sequence, the decision from K_1 leading to $K_0(M)$ in the optimal decision sequence is found. It traces in a forward fashion until K_{n+1} is reached. The time complexity of this algorithm is 2^n.

The time complexity can be reduced by a constant factor by applying dominance rules. Dominance rules are rules for discarding unnecessary expansions. Suppose that in a partial decision sequence, objects j to n have been decided upon in a decision sequence $y_j, \ldots, y_n$ and $\Sigma_{k=j}^{n} y_k w_k > M$. This means that there is no way to decide upon the remaining objects such that $\sum_{k=1}^{n} y_k w_k < M$. This decision sequence should be eliminated from further considerations. Another dominance rule can also be applied in a partial decision sequence d when i decisions have been made. There is a maximum of 2^i possible decision sequences when i decisions have been made. Suppose there are two decision sequences $d_j = y_{n-i+1}$, $y_{n-i+2}, \ldots, y_n$ and $d_k = y'_{n-i+1}, y'_{n-i+2}, \ldots, y'_n$ on the last i objects and

$$P_j = \sum_{l=n-i+1}^{n} p_l y_l, \ W_j = \sum_{l=n-i+1}^{n} w_l y_l,$$

$$P_k = \sum_{l=n-i+1}^{n} p_l y'_l, \ W_k = \sum_{l=n-i+1}^{n} w_l y'_l$$

with the property that $P_j \leq P_k$ and $W_j \geq W_k$. Decision sequence j can be discarded because for any decision sequence $y_1, \ldots, y_{n-i}$ such that

$$W_j + \sum_{l=1}^{n-i} y_l w_l \leq M,$$

it is true that

$$W_k + \sum_{l=1}^{n-i} y_l w_l \leq M \text{ and}$$

$$P_j + \sum_{l=1}^{n-i} p_l y_l \leq P_k + \sum_{l=1}^{n-i} p_l y_l$$

Decision sequence d_j can never lead to a better solution than decision sequence d_k and, therefore, should be discarded. The dominance rules described here are very effective in discarding a large number of the decision sequences.

The time and space complexities of the algorithm when dominance rules are applied can be shown to be $O(\min\{2^n, n\sum_{i=1}^{n} P_i, nW\})$ [63].

Although it is true that in some cases like the KNAPSACK problem, dynamic programming algorithms still lead to an exponential number of decision sequences. The application of dominance rules and the principle of optimality eliminates a large number of suboptimal sequences. Because of these, dynamic programming algorithms often have a polynomial-time complexity.

Other Algorithms

A number of other algorithms are available to solve both the polynomial time and NP-complete problems; among them are linear and nonlinear programming algorithms [64], integer programming algorithms [48], geometric programming algorithms [65], algebraic simplification and transformation [5], divide and conquer methods, maximum-flow-minimum-cut network-flow algorithms [27], and so on. For algorithms that run in time exponential with the input size, they have limited application when the problem size is large.

One way to speed up the processing of NP-complete problems but to sacrifice optimality is to use heuristics to solve these problems. *Heuristics* are fast (usually polynomial-time) algorithms that solve the problem, and may or may not have a performance guarantee on the solution. Algorithms with guaranteed performance are called approximation algorithms and are discussed in the next section. They are usually problem-dependent and are difficult to design. On the other hand, algorithms without a performance guarantee have to be verified by simulations. An example of heuristics without performance guarantee is the *greedy method*. This is similar to the branch and bound and dynamic programming algorithms except that in this case, only one decision sequence that will most likely lead to the optimal solution is expanded in each stage. The choice of the "best" decision sequence without global information constitutes a local decision and, therefore, generally does not lead to the optimal solution.

4.7. APPROXIMATION ALGORITHMS FOR *NP*-COMPLETE PROBLEMS

This section introduces the use of approximation algorithms for combinatorial optimization (usually NP-complete). Recall the definition of combinatorial optimization in Section 4.3. These approximation algorithms execute in polynomial time while guaranteeing some performance measures, usually the deviation from the optimal solution. An algorithm A is an *approximation algorithm* for Π if it finds a solution $A(I) = \sigma \in S_{\Pi}(I)$ for a given $I \in D_{\Pi}$. This solution does not have to be the optimum. An algorithm OPT is an *optimization algorithm* for Π if for every $I \in D_\Pi$, it finds the optimal solution $\text{OPT}(I) = \sigma^* \in S_\Pi(I)$. A *performance measure of approximation algorithm* is the fractional deviation from the optimal solution,

$$
\begin{array}{c}
\text{Performance} \\
\text{measure of} \\
\text{approximation} \\
\text{algorithms}
\end{array} = \frac{|A(I) - \text{OPT}(I)|}{\text{OPT}(I)} \quad (3)
$$

Although some general properties can be cited about these algorithms, a large part of the design relies on the ingenuity of the algorithm designers. There are five types of approximation algorithms [66, 67], and they are discussed in the remainder of this section.

Absolute Approximations

An algorithm A is an *absolution approximation algorithm* for Π iff for each $I \in D_\Pi$, $|A(I) - \text{OPT}(I)| \leq k$ for some constant k. That is, the deviation from the optimal value is independent of the optimal value. There are very few problems that are known to have absolute approximation algorithms and the problem of determining whether an absolute approximation algorithm exists for many *NP*-complete problems is *NP*-hard itself.

An absolute approximation algorithm can be used to find the minimum number of colors to color a planar graph $G = (V, E)$ so that no two vertices joined by the same edge has the same color. The graph is 0-colorable if $|V| = 0$. The graph is 1-colorable if $|E| = 0$. The graph is 2-colorable if it is bipartite, which can be determined in time $0(|V| + |E|)$ [2]. Every planar graph is 4-colorable [2]. To determine whether a graph is 3-colorable is *NP*-complete. Therefore, an approximation algorithm can return the minimum number of colors in polynomial time when the graph is 0-, 1- or 2-colorable. Otherwise, the algorithm returns 4 if the graph is 3- or 4-colorable. The maximum error made is $|A(I) - \text{OPT}(I)| = 1$ for all $I \in D_\Pi$ independent of the optimum value. The algorithm discussed is, therefore, an absolute approximation algorithm.

For many *NP*-complete problems, the problem of determining whether an absolute approximation algorithm exists is *NP*-hard itself. Examples of these *NP*-complete problems are the KNAPSACK problem [68], maximum CLIQUE problem, and maximum INDEPENDENT SET problem [1]. The only property used in proving *NP*-hardness is that the solution values can be multiplied by an arbitrarily large constant without changing the candidate solutions. By choosing the constant of the absolute approximation to be K and setting the constant to be multiplied to the solution values to be K + 1, it is easily seen that any suboptimal solutions differ from the optimal solution by at least K + 1. (They differ by at least 1 in the original problem assuming all solution values are integers.) An absolute approximate algorithm would always obtain the optimal solution in the modified problem because it always obtains a solution with a maximum deviation of K from the optimal solution. This contradicts the assumption that $P \neq NP$.

ϵ-Approximations

An algorithm A is an *ϵ-approximation algorithm* for Π iff for each $I \in D_\Pi$, $|A(I) - \text{OPT}(I)|/\text{OPT}(I) \leq \epsilon$ for some constant $\epsilon \leq 1$ and assuming that $\text{OPT}(I) > 0$. As before, some *NP*-complete problems can be shown to have ϵ-approximation algorithms, whereas for some others, the problem of determining whether an ϵ-approximation algorithm exists is *NP*-hard. We will state without proof some examples of these problems.

The problem of *scheduling N independent tasks on m, m $\leq$ 2, processors with the minimum finish time* is *NP*-complete. An algorithm developed by Graham [69] called the *Longest Processing-Time (LPT)* algorithm is a $\frac{1}{3}(1 - \frac{1}{m})$ − approximation algorithm. Whenever a processor becomes free, the LPT algorithm assigns to this processor the job with the longest processing time from the remaining set of jobs.

The *BIN PACKING* problem of determining the minimum number of bins, each of capacity L, to accommodate n objects where object i requires L_i of the bin capacity, is strongly *NP*-complete (it contains 3-partition as a special case). There are four possible ϵ-approximation algorithms for the BIN PACKING problem [70].

1. *First-fit:* The objects are considered in the order $1, 2, \ldots, n$. and the bins are indexed as $B_1, B_2, \ldots$. The algorithm places the next item into the lowest indexed bin in which it will fit (without exceeding the bin capacity). It uses no more than $\frac{17}{10} \text{OPT}(I) + 2$ bins.
2. *Best-fit:* The algorithm places the next items into the lowest indexed bin that has current contents closest to, but not exceeding the maximum capacity. The capacity of the bin chosen must not be exceeded when the item is placed into the bin. As before, it uses a maximum of $\frac{17}{10} \text{OPT}(I) + 2$ bins.
3. *First-fit-decreasing:* The objects are reindexed so that $l_i \geq l_{i+1}$ before the First-fit algorithm is applied. It uses a maximum of $\frac{11}{9}\text{OPT}(I) + 4$ bins.
4. *Best-fit-decreasing:* The objects are reindexed so that $l_i \geq l_{i+1}$ before the Best-fit algorithm is applied. It uses no more than $\frac{11}{9}\text{OPT}(I) + 4$ bins.

Another example that can be solved by an ϵ-approximation algorithm is a special case of the TRAVELING SALESMAN problem satisfying triangular inequality [71, 72].

For some *NP*-complete problems, the problem of determining whether an ϵ-approximate algorithm exists is *NP*-hard. Examples of these *NP*-complete problems include the ϵ-approximate TRAVELING SALESMAN problem [72], ϵ-approximate INTEGER PROGRAMMING, and ϵ-approximate QUADRATIC ASSIGNMENT problem [5]. The proof technique is similar to the technique discussed for proving the *NP*-hardness of absolute approximations.

Polynomial-Time Approximation Schemes

An algorithm A is an *approximation scheme* for Π iff for each $I \in D_\Pi$ and an accuracy requirement $\epsilon > 0$, A outputs a candidate solution $A(I, \sigma) \in S_\Pi(I)$ such that $|A(I, \sigma) - \text{OPT}(I)|/\text{OPT}(I) \leq \epsilon$. It is assumed that $\text{OPT}(I) > 0$. The term *scheme* is used because A actually provides a range of approximation algorithms for Π, one for each fixed value of $\epsilon > 0$. An algorithm A is a *polynomial-time approximation scheme* iff for each fixed $\epsilon > 0$, A has an execution time that is polynomial in the problem size. To illustrate the use of polynomial-time approximation schemes, let us study two examples.

The first example is the m processor, N independent tasks scheduling problem discussed at the beginning of this section. Suppose k is a specific and fixed integer ($k < N$). An optimal algorithm is applied to solve the problem of scheduling k longest tasks (such as branch and bound with complexity $0(m^k)$). The remaining $N - k$ tasks are scheduled using the LPT rule discussed earlier. This takes time with complexity $0(N \log N)$. For a given input instance, it is shown in Reference 69 that

$$\frac{|A(I) - \text{OPT}(I)|}{\text{OPT}(I)} \leq \frac{1 - 1/m}{1 + \lfloor k/m \rfloor}$$

For any given input ϵ, a value of k can be computed so that

$$\epsilon \leq \left(1 - \frac{1}{m}\right) \Big/ \left(1 + \frac{k}{\lfloor m \rfloor}\right)$$

Solving for k, we obtain

$$k = \frac{\lceil m - 1 \rceil}{\epsilon} - m$$

The total complexity of the algorithm is

$$0(N \log N + m^{\lceil m-1/\epsilon - m \rceil}).$$

This algorithm is, therefore, a polynomial-time approximation scheme (for any given m) since the time complexity is polynomial in N.

The second example is the heuristic for the KNAPSACK problem studied by Sahni [68]. The algorithm fills the knapsack for a fixed integer k, with combinations of at most k of the

N objects with total weights less than or equal to M. This requires a total time complexity of $\Sigma_{j=0}^{k} \binom{N}{j} = 0(N^k)$. The remaining capacity of the knapsack is filled with the remaining $N - k$ objects using the following rule. The remaining objects are ordered in nonincreasing order of p_i/w_i. If object i fits in the remaining capacity of the knapsack, then object i is included in the knapsack, otherwise it is discarded. This has a time complexity of $0(N)$. The total time complexity is $0(N^{k+1})$. It is shown by Sahni that

$$\frac{|A(I) - \mathrm{OPT}(I)|}{\mathrm{OPT}(I)} < \frac{1}{1 + k}$$

and this bound is tight [68]. For a given ϵ, k can be chosen to be $\lceil 1/\epsilon - 1 \rceil$ in order to satisfy the inequality $\epsilon \leq 1/(1 + k)$. The time complexity is, therefore, $0(N^{1/\epsilon})$ which is linear in N. This algorithm is a polynomial-time approximation scheme.

There are open problems on determining whether a polynomial-time approximation scheme exists for some NP-complete problems. An example is to find the minimum number of colors to color a (planar or nonplanar) graph. We know that an absolute approximation algorithm exists for planar graphs. For nonplanar graphs, the best polynomial time coloring algorithm A currently known has a performance of

$$\frac{|A(I) - \mathrm{OPT}(I)|}{\mathrm{OPT}(I)} \leq \frac{C|V| - \log|V|}{\log|V|}$$

where C is a positive constant and $|V|$ is the number of vertices of the graph [73]. For other NP-complete problems such as finding a maximum set of independent vertices in a graph and finding a minimum traveling salesman tour when the triangle inequality is not satisfied, it is still open whether a polynomial-time approximation algorithms exist.

In order to prove the nonexistence of a polynomial-time approximation schemes, one can prove that there is some $\epsilon > 0$ such that there is no polynomial-time approximation algorithm A for Π that has

$$\frac{|A(I) - \mathrm{OPT}(I)|}{\mathrm{OPT}(I)} < \epsilon, \text{ unless } P = NP$$

A theorem stated in Reference 1 shows that if Π is a minimization problem having solution values in Z^+ and suppose that for some fixed $K \in Z^+$, the decision problem "Given $I \in D_\Pi$, is $\mathrm{OPT}(I) \leq K$?" is NP-hard. Then if $P \neq NP$, no polynomial-time approximation algorithm A for Π can satisfy $[A(I) - \mathrm{OPT}(I)]/\mathrm{OPT}(x) < 1/K$, and Π cannot be solved by a polynomial-time approximation scheme.

Fully Polynomial Time Approximation Schemes

A *fully polynomial time approximation scheme* is an approximation scheme whose computing time is polynomial both in the problem size and in $1/\epsilon$. Two previously studied examples, namely, the polynomial-time approximation schemes for the m PROCESSOR SCHEDULING problem and the KNAPSACK problem are not fully polynomial approximation schemes because the time complexities are polynomial in N, but not polynomial in $1/\epsilon$.

A useful property in proving the nonexistence of fully polynomial approximation schemes is shown by Garey and Johnson [30]. It is shown that if there exists a two-variable polynomial q such that for all instances of $I \in D_\Pi$, $\mathrm{OPT}(I) < q(\mathrm{Length}(I), \mathrm{Max}(I))$, then the existence of a fully polynomial-time approximation scheme for Π implies the existence of a pseudo-polynomial optimization algorithm for Π. The inverse of the above premise, which follows as a corollary, states that if Π is NP-hard in the strong sense, which means that Π does not have a pseudo-polynomial-time optimization algorithm, then Π cannot be solved by a fully polynomial-time approximation scheme unless $P = NP$. In summary, proving strong NP-completeness implies the nonexistence of fully polynomial-time approximation schemes.

In order to prove the existence of a fully polynomial-time approximation schemes for a problem, such an algorithm must be designed.

Sahni has shown three general techniques for designing fully polynomial-time approximation schemes, namely, rounding, interval partitioning, and separation [50]. These techniques are discussed in the remainder of this section.

Rounding is a technique that starts with a given problem instance I and transforms it into another problem instance I' that is easier to solve. This transformation preserves the accuracy of the solution so that

$$\frac{|A(I) - A(I')|}{A(I)} \leq \epsilon \text{ for a fixed } \epsilon > 0$$

where A is a pseudo-polynomial-time algorithm. Ibarra and Kim have shown a method of converting the pseudo-polynomial-time algorithm for solving the KNAPSACK problem into a polynomial-time approximation algorithm by rounding and scaling with only a limited loss of accuracy [74]. This method is illustrated with the following example.

Suppose $N = 4$, $M = 512$, $(p_1,p_2,p_3,p_4) = (w_1,w_2,w_3,w_4) = (1,3,10,500)$ for the KNAPSACK problem. A straightforward enumeration would need to examine $2^4 = 16$ combinations of the objects. The optimal solution is $(x_1,x_2,x_3,x_4) = (1,0,1,1)$ with a value of 511. If the weights of objects are scaled and rounded by a factor of $K = 5$, we obtain $(p_1,p_2,p_3,p_4) = (1,2,10,500)$ and $(w_1,w_2,w_3,w_4) = (0,0,2,100)$. Only 4 combinations of weights have to be examined, and we include every object in the knapsack with a total profit of 514. The solution is $(x_1,x_2,x_3,x_4) = (1,1,1,1)$ with an error of $(514 - 511)/511 < 0.01$. We are therefore able to solve the problem in a much shorter time while achieving a prescribed degree of accuracy. Readers interested in the details of this algorithm should refer to the paper by Ibarra and Kim [74].

Interval partitioning solves the problem instance I by generating a restricted class of feasible assignments for $S^{(0)},S^{(1)}, \ldots ,S^{(n)}$. Let P_i be the maximum $\Sigma_{j=1}^{i} p_j x_j$ among all feasible assignments generated for $S^{(i)}$. The profit interval $[0,P_i]$ is divided into subintervals each of size $P_i\epsilon/(n - 1)$. All feasible assignments in the same subinterval are regarded as having

the same $\Sigma_{j=1}^{i} p_j x_j$, and the dominance rules are used to discard all but one of them. This algorithm runs in $0(n^2/\epsilon)$ time with a maximum fractional error of $[A(I) - \text{OPT}(I)]/\text{OPT}(I) < \epsilon$.

Separation is similar to interval partitioning except that further elimination of unnecessary expansion is done. For example, if an $S^{(i)}$ with feasible solutions of $\Sigma_{j=1}^{i} p_j x_j$: 0, 2.7, 4.1, 6.0 and the interval size is $P_i\epsilon/(n - 1) = 2$, the subintervals are (0,2), (2,4), (4,6), (6,8). Since each value falls in a different subinterval, no feasible solutions can be eliminated. By the use of separation, the solution with value 4.1 can be eliminated because its separation with the previous solution having a value of 2.7 is less than the interval size, 2. Simulation results demonstrate that separation performs better than interval partitioning.

Probabilistically Good Algorithms

An algorithm A is a *probabilistically good algorithm* if the algorithm "almost always" generates either an exact solution or a solution with a value that is "exceedingly close" to the value of the optimal solution. An algorithm A solves a problem Π *almost everywhere* (abbreviated a.e.) if when $X = x_1,x_2, \ldots ,x_n, \ldots$ is drawn from the sample space $S_1 \times S_2 \times \ldots \times S_n \times \ldots$, the number of x_i on which the algorithm fails to solve Π is finite with probability 1 [75, 76].

This definition provides a means for evaluating the average performance of algorithms. Some algorithms have very good average-case behavior, but have very bad worst-case behavior. For example, Johnson [77] has performed Monte Carlo simulations on evaluating first-fit and first-fit-decreasing algorithms for the bin-packing problem under a number of assumptions about the distribution of item sizes. First-fit has an average deviation from the optimal solution of 7%, whereas the worst-case behavior has a deviation of 70%. First-fit-decreasing has an average deviation from the optimal solution of 2%, whereas the worst-case behavior is 22%. Analytical average behavior of algorithms has been studied in a limited set of problems, including the problems of finding a

Hamiltonian cycle [78], INDEPENDENT SET [79], GRAPH COLORING [80], BIN-PACKING [81], and deciding the path for the TRAVELING SALESMAN problem [79]. In these analytical studies, theorems are proved about the expected behavior of approximation algorithms under some predefined probability distributions. Unfortunately, some simple distribution functions must be used in order for the analysis to be mathematically tractable. Furthermore, distribution functions used in real applications may be highly unstructured and are difficult to capture mathematically. The techniques developed so far are very problem-dependent, and very few generalizations can be made at this time. This is a growing field of research, and we expect to see some additional results in the future.

4.8. CONCLUDING REMARKS

Besides the theory of algorithms we have presented in this chapter, there is also the theory developed on algorithms outside of the domain of *NP*. This deals with the space requirement on the computer. The problem of linear space, logarithmic space, and *NP*-space are studied with respect to a model of computation such as the Turing machine. These problems are very rare in practice, and at this time, they are mainly studied for theoretical interest. The discussion of this matter is beyond the scope of this chapter. Interested readers can refer to the book by Garey and Johnson for a useful introduction to the topic [1].

We have covered a wide spectrum of the methods for algorithm design. Problems can be classified according to their computing time required to solve them optimally. They can also be classified as polynomial or *NP*-complete. Deciding that a problem can be solved in polynomial time then requires the design of a polynomial-time algorithm. These algorithms are usually problem-dependent and must be investigated individually. Sometimes, the problem studied can be transformed into another problem that has a polynomial-time algorithm. On the other hand, to decide that a problem is *NP*-complete, it must be proved to be a member of the class *NP* and is reducible to a problem known to be *NP*-complete. By making an assumption that $P \neq NP$, we know that these problems cannot be solved optimally in polynomial time. In this case, the only hope to solve the problem is by designing either pseudo-polynomial-time algorithms, polynomial-time approximation algorithms, probabilistically optimal algorithms, or heuristics. Heuristics are fast algorithms with no performance guarantee and are often used.

Although a lot of theory has been developed for designing good algorithms, simulations are still widely used in practice because of the difficulty in verifying the performance of algorithms analytically. In this case, random instances of the problem are generated, and statistics about the performance of the solutions are collected. No mathematical proof is necessary and the algorithm may perform badly when an unanticipated problem instance comes up. Nonetheless, this is widely used because of its simplicity and fast design time. However, we expect that in the future, better proof methods can be developed to aid the design of algorithms.

In retrospect, it is hoped that we have succeeded in this chapter in providing an introduction to a very difficult topic. We have provided answers to the questions that we raised in Section 4.1. The theory of algorithms is still somewhat abstract, but it is becoming increasingly important to software designers.

REFERENCES

1. M. R. Garey and D. S. Johnson, *Computers and Intractability: A Guide to the Theory of NP-Completeness*, W. H. Freeman and Company, San Francisco, 1979.
2. A. V. Aho, J. E. Hopcroft, and J. D. Ullman, *The Design and Analysis of Computer Algorithms*, Addison-Wesley, 1974.
3. E. M. Reingold, J. Nierergelt, and N. Deo, *Combinatorial Algorithms: Theory and Practice*, Prentice Hall, Englewood Cliffs, N.J., 1977.
4. S. Baase, *Computer Algorithms: Introduction to Design and Analysis*, Addison-Wesley, 1978.
5. E. Horowitz and S. Sahni, *Fundamentals of Computer Algorithms*, Computer Science Press, 1978.
6. D. E. Knuth, *The Art of Computer Programming*, Vol. 1, *Fundamental Algorithms*, Addison-Wesley, 1969.
7. D. E. Knuth, *The Art of Computer Programming*,

Vol. 2, *Semi-numerical Algorithms*, Addison-Wesley, 1973.

8. D. E. Knuth, *The Art of Computer Programming*, Vol. 3, *Sorting and Searching*, Addison-Wesley, 1973.

9. K. Jensen and N. Wirth, *PASCAL User Manual and Report*, 2d ed., Springer-Verlag, 1974.

10. D. M. Bullman, "Stack Computers: An Introduction," *IEEE Computer*, vol. 10, no. 5, pp. 18–28, May 1977.

11. E. Horowitz and S. Sahni, *Fundamentals of Data Structures*, Computer Science Press, Inc., 1976.

12. A. M. Turing, "On Computable Numbers with an Application to the Entscheidungsproblem," *Proceedings London Mathematical Society Series 2*(42) pp. 230–265, 1935. Corrections, ibid. (43) pp. 544–546, 1937.

13. M. Minsky, *Computation: Finite and Infinite Machines*, Prentice-Hall, Englewood Cliffs, N.J., 1967.

14. J. E. Hopcroft and J. D. Ullman, *Formal Languages and Their Relation to Automata*, Addison-Wesley, 1969.

15. J. C. Shepherdson and H. E. Sturgis, "Computability of Recursive Functions," *JACM 10*(2):217–255(1963).

16. S. A. Cook and R. A. Reckhow, "Time-bounded Random Access Machines," *Journal of Computer and System Sciences 7*(4):354–375(1973).

17. M. Blum, "A Machine Independent Theory of the Complexity of Recursive Functions," *JACM 14*(2):322–336(1967).

18. V. Strassen, "Gaussian Elimination is Not Optimal," *Numerische Mathematik*, vol. 13, pp. 354–356, 1969.

19. E. L. Lawler and D. W. Wood, "Branch and Bound Methods: A Survey," *Operations Research*, vol. 14, pp. 699–719, 1966.

20. T. Ibaraki, "Computational Efficiency of Approximate Branch and Bound Algorithms," *Math. of Oper. Res.*, vol. 1, no. 3, pp. 287–298, 1976.

21. D. E. Knuth, J. H. Harris and V. R. Pratt, "Fast Pattern Matching in Strings," *SIAM Journal of Computing*, vol. 6, no. 2, pp. 323–350, 1977.

22. R. S. Boyer and J. S. Moore, "A Fast String Searching Algorithm," *CACM*, vol. 20, no. 10, pp. 762–772, Oct. 1977.

23. J. M. Cooley and J. W. Tukey, "An Algorithm for the Machine Calculations of Complex Fourier Series," *Math. Comp.*, vol. 19, pp. 297–301, 1965.

24. R. Floyd, "Algorithm 97: Shortest Path," *CACM*, vol. 5, no. 6, p. 345, 1962.

25. S. Warshall, "A Theorem on Boolean Matrices," *JACM*, vol. 9, no. 1, pp. 11–12, 1962.

26. R. Moenck and A. B. Borodin, "Fast Modular Transforms via Division," *Conference Record, IEEE 13th Annual Symposium on Switching and Automata Theory*, pp. 90–96, 1972.

27. L. R. Ford and D. R. Fulkerson, *Flows in Networks*, Princeton University Press, Princeton, 1974.

28. R. M. Karp, "Reducibility Among Combinatorial Problems," *Complexity of Computer Computations*, R. E. Miller and J. W. Thatcher (eds.), Plenum Press, New York, pp. 85–104, 1972.

29. S. A. Cook, "The Complexity of Theorem-Proving Procedures," *Proceedings Third Annual ACM Symposium on Theory of Computing*, pp. 151–158, 1971.

30. M. R. Garey and D. S. Johnson, "Strong NP-Completeness Results: Motivations, Examples and Implications," *JACM*, vol. 25, pp. 499–508, 1978.

31. B. J. Lageweg, J. K. Lenstra and A. H. G. Rinnooy Kan, "Minimizing Maximum Lateness on One Machine: Computational Experience and Some Applications," *Statistica Neerlandica*, vol. 30, pp. 25–41, 1978.

32. E. L. Lawler, "A Procedure for Computing the K Best Solutions to Discrete Optimization Problems and its Application to the Shortest Path Problem," *Management Science*, vol. 18, pp. 401–405, 1972.

33. D. E. Knuth, "A Terminological Proposal," *ACM SIGACT News*, vol. 6, no. 1, pp. 12–18, 1974.

34. D. E. Knuth, "Postscript about NP-hard Problems," *ACM SIGACT News*, vol. 6, no. 2, pp. 15–16, 1974.

35. D. B. Johnson and S. D. Kashdan, "Lower Bounds for Selection in X + Y and Other Multisets," Report no. 183, Computer Science Department, Pennsylvania State University, Pa., 1976.

36. L. Mitten, "Branch and Bound Methods: General Formulation and Properties," *Operations Research*, vol. 18, pp. 24–34, 1970.

37. N. J. Nilsson, *Problem Solving Methods in Artificial Intelligence*, McGraw Hill, New York, 1971.

38. J. Lenstra, "Sequencing by Enumerative Methods," *Math. Centre. Tract 69*, Mathematisch Centrum, Amsterdam, 1976.

39. B. Lageweg, J. Lenstra and A. Rinnooy Kan, "Job-shop Scheduling by Implicit Enumeration," *Management Science*, vol. 24, no. 4, pp. 441–500, 1977.

40. G. Ingargiola and J. Korsh, "A Reduction Algorithm for Zero-one Single Knapsack Problems," *Management Science*, vol. 20, no. 4, pp. 460–663, 1973.

41. G. Ingargiola and J. Korsh, "A General Algorithm for One Dimensional Knapsack Problems," *Operations Research*, vol. 25, no. 5, pp. 752–759, 1977.

42. R. Garfinkel, "On Partitioning the Feasible Set in a Branch and Bound Algorithm for the Asymmetric Travelling Salesman Problem," *Operations Research*, vol. 21, no. 1, pp. 340–342, 1973.

43. M. Held and R. Karp, "The Travelling Salesman Problem and Minimum Spanning Trees," *Operations Research*, vol. 18, pp. 1,138–1,162, 1970.

44. M. Held and R. Karp, "The Travelling Salesman Problem and Minimum Spanning Trees, Part II," *Math. Prog.*, vol. 1, pp. 6–25, 1971.

45. G. Sa, "Branch and Bound and Approximate Solutions to the Capacitated Plant Location Problem," *Operations Research*, vol. 17, no. 6, pp. 1,005–1,016, 1969.

46. M. A. Efroymson and T. C. Ray, "A Brand and Bound Algorithm for Plant Location," *Operations Research,* vol. 14, pp. 361–368, 1966.

47. A. M. Geoffrion and R. E. Marsten, "Integer Programming Algorithms: A Framework and State-of-the-Art Survey," *Management Science,* vol. 18, no. 9, pp. 465–491, May 1972.

48. R. S. Garfinkel and G. L. Nemhauser, *Integer Programming,* Wiley, New York, 1972.

49. M. Held and R. Karp, "A Dynamic Programming Approach to Sequencing Problems," *Journal of SIAM,* vol. 10, pp. 196–210, 1962.

50. S. Sahni, "General Techniques for Combinatorial Approximations," *Operations Research,* vol. 25, no. 6, pp. 920–936, 1977.

51. T. Morin and R. Marsten, "Branch and Bound Strategies for Dynamic Programming," *Operations Research,* vol. 24, pp. 611–627, 1976.

52. W. Kohler and K. Steiglitz, "Characterization and Theoretical Comparison of Branch and Bound Algorithms for Permutation Problems," *JACM,* vol. 21, no. 1, pp. 140–156, 1974.

53. T. Ibaraki, "Theoretical Comparisons of Search Strategies in Branch and Bound Algorithms," *Int. Jr. of Comp. and Info. Sci.,* vol. 5, no. 4, pp. 315–344, 1976.

54. T. Ibaraki, "On the Computational Efficiency of Branch and Bound Algorithns," *J. of Oper. Res. Soc. of Japan,* vol. 20, no. 1, pp. 16–35, 1977.

55. T. Ibaraki, "The Power of Dominance Relations in Branch and Bound Algorithms," *JACM,* vol. 24, no. 2, pp. 264–279, 1977.

56. T. Ibaraki, "Depth-m Search in Branch-and-Bound Algorithms," *Int. Jr. of Comp. and Inf. Sci.,* vol. 7, no. 4, pp. 315–343, 1978.

57. A. H. Land and A. Doig, "An Automatic Method for Solving Discrete Programming Problems," *Econometrica,* vol. 28, pp. 497–520, 1960.

58. W. L. Eastman, "A Solution to the Traveling Salesman Problem," presented at the American Summer Meeting of the Econometric Society, Cambridge, Mass., Aug. 1958.

59. R. E. Bellman and S. E. Dreyfus, *Applied Dynamic Programming,* Princeton University Press, Princeton, 1962.

60. G. Nemhauser, *Introduction to Dynamic Programming,* Wiley, New York, 1966.

61. S. E. Dreyfus, *The Art and Theory of Dynamic Programming,* Wiley, New York, 1978.

62. G. Nemhauser and Z. Ullman, "Discrete Dynamic Programming and Capital Allocation," *Management Science,* vol. 15, no. 9, pp. 494–505, 1969.

63. E. Horowitz and S. Sahni, "Computing Partitions with Applications to the Knapsack Problem," *JACM,* vol. 21, pp. 277–292, 1974.

64. M. S. Bazaraa and J. J. Jarvis, *Linear Programming and Network Flows,* Wiley, New York, 1977.

65. C. S. Beightler and D. T. Philips, *Applied Geometric Programming,* Wiley, New York, 1976.

66. M. Garey and D. Johnson, "Approximate Algorithms for Combinatorial Problems: An Annotated Bibliography," *Algorithms and Complexity: Recent Results and New Directions,* J. Traub (ed.), Academic Press, New York, 1976.

67. S. Sahni and E. Horowitz, "Combinatorial Problems: Reducibility and Approximation," *Operations Research,* vol. 26, no. 4, 1978.

68. S. Sahni, "Approximate Algorithms for the 0/1 Knapsack Problem," *JACM,* vol. 22, pp. 115–124, 1975.

69. R. L. Graham, "Bounds for Certain Multiprocessing Anomalies," *Bell System Tech. Journal,* vol. 45, pp. 1,563–1,581, 1966.

70. D. S. Johnson, A. Denvers, J. D. Ullman, M. R. Garey, and R. L. Graham, "Worst-Case Performance Bounds for Simple One-Dimensional Packing Algorithms," *SIAM Journal on Computing,* vol. 3, pp. 299–325, 1974.

71. D. J. Rosenkrantz, R. E. Stearns, and P. M. Lewis, "An Analysis of Several Heuristics for the Travelling Salesman Problem," *SIAM Journal of Computing,* vol. 6, pp. 563–581, 1977.

72. N. Christofedes, "Worst-Case Analysis of a New Heuristic for the Travelling Salesman Problem," Management Science Research Report #388, Carnegie Mellon University, 1976.

73. D. S. Johnson, "Worst-Case Behavior of Coloring Algorithms," *Proceedings Southwestern Conference on Combinatorics, Graph Theory and Computing,* Utilitas Mathematica Publishing, Winnipeg, pp. 513–527, 1974.

74. O. Ibarra and C. Kim, "Fast Approximation Algorithms for the Knapsack and Sum of Subsets Problems," *JACM,* vol. 22, pp. 463–468, 1975.

75. R. M. Karp, "The Fast Approximate Solution of Hard Combinatorial Problems," *Proceedings Sixth Southeastern Conference on Combinatorics, Graph Theory and Computing,* Winnipeg, 1975.

76. R. M. Karp, "The Probabilistic Analysis of Some Combinatorial Search Algorithms," University of California, Berkeley, Memo No. ERL-M581, 1976.

77. D. S. Johnson, *Near-Optimal Bin Packing Algorithms,* Doctoral Thesis, Department of Mathematics, Massachusetts Institute of Technology, Cambridge, Mass., 1973.

78. L. Posa, "Hamiltonian Circuits in Random Graphs," *Discrete Mathematics,* vol. 14, pp. 359–364, 1976.

79. R. M. Karp, "Probabilistic Analysis of Partitioning Algorithms for the Travelling Salesman Problem in the Plane," *Math. of Oper. Res.,* vol. 2, no. 3, pp. 209–224, 1977.

80. G. R. Grimmet and C. J. H. McDiarmid, "On Coloring Random Graphs," *Math. Proc. Cambridge Philos. Soc.,* vol. 77, pp. 313–324, 1975.

81. S. D. Shapiro, "Performance of Heuristic Bin Packing Algorithm with Segments of Random Length," *Information and Control,* vol. 35, pp. 146–158, 1977.

5

The Theory of Real-Time Control

R. E. Larson

P. L. McEntire

J. G. O'Reilly

Optimization Technology, Inc.

5.1. INTRODUCTION

The theory of real-time control (RTC) provides a framework for the design and operation of time-critical data processing systems. The RTC methodology maximizes the utilization of limited system resources on the basis of real-time information about system loading and hardware availability. This chapter will summarize the state of the art in RTC for both centralized and distributed systems.

The basic concept of RTC arises because of the time-varying nature of most computational processes. A process here denotes a set of software functions that is to be executed on a particular set of hardware (processors, memories, etc.). In the design of a system, an allocation is made as to which functions are to be performed on which hardware. If the system is static, it is not necessary to change this allocation during execution, and there is no need for RTC. But in many systems there are significant variations in the computational resources required for performing individual functions, for instance, because of the dependence of the functions on external data. Furthermore, there may also be changes in the availability of the hardware components, perhaps because of a component failure. In these two cases, as well as in other situations of dynamic behavior, RTC can be used to reallocate the functions to the hardware in real-time so as to achieve the most effective utilization of the available resources.

A critical question that arises in RTC is what level of detail to use in performing this reallocation—in other words, what granularity of functions should be reallocated to what granularity of hardware and how often should the reallocation be performed? Clearly, the answer is problem dependent; the examples discussed later in the chapter provide some guidance in this area. There are also some general principles that can be applied to this decision, some of which will now be considered.

One important principle is related to the amount of hardware resources required to implement the RTC calculations themselves: Once the amount of resources for RTC becomes comparable with the total resources in the system, the overhead has reached a point where the value of the RTC is questionable.

Another set of principles can be deduced by examining the relationship of RTC to two other important concepts in computer systems, namely, the system design and the real-time operating system. Both of these concepts are discussed extensively in other chapters of this handbook. Conceptually, the relationships are as shown in Figure 5.1.

The system design provides a framework for RTC by specifying both the functions that the system is to perform and the hardware available to perform them. Generally, the system design also imposes restrictions on the method of RTC, for instance, a particular function may have to be performed on a subset of the hardware. Such constraints are helpful in re-

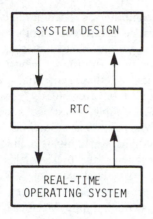

Figure 5.1. Relationship of RTC to system design and real-time operating system.

ducing the alternatives that the RTC method must consider, but if they do not take into account the actual dynamics of the system, they may degrade system performance unnecessarily. Of course, as already noted, in the extreme case of a static system where there are no variations at all, the design allocation is never varied and RTC is not applied.

The application of RTC theory influences the system design by providing improved performance in the face of variations in function loading and hardware availability. This improved performance then enters the trade-offs in the total design process. For example, a better RTC method can maintain system performance at a fixed level while using less hardware. Hence, RTC can provide improved performance with the same level of hardware, or it can maintain system availability using

less reliable hardware. Axiomatic requirements engineering (ARE), a quantitative approach for performing these trade-offs, including the trade-offs with RTC, is described elsewhere [1]. This approach uses multiattribute utility theory [2] and "indifference curves," which show how one system attribute changes with respect to another, with all other attributes held constant. An indifference curve for RTC complexity versus hardware cost, with system performance held constant, is shown in Figure 5.2.

Methods of RTC relate to the real-time operating system by providing direction on the basis of observed system loads, observed hardware failures, and other dynamic events. The methods, then, are closely related to the executive of the real-time operating system. In fact, the RTC method may actually serve this purpose in a specific implementation. In that case, the structure of the controlling method within the real-time operating system is as shown in Figure 5.3.

Basically, a specific RTC methodology is augmented by real-time data-gathering functions that interact directly with the detailed real-time operating system functions to obtain information about function loading, hardware status, and other dynamic factors. The methodology provides for the utilization of this information to reallocate the software functions to the hardware. These reallocations are then translated into inputs to the detailed real-time operating system functions by another group of functions specifically designed for this pur-

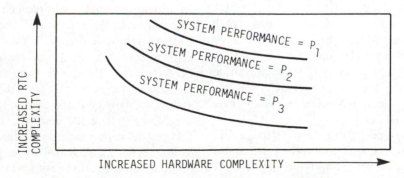

Figure 5.2. Indifference curves showing lines of constant system performance plotted against hardware cost and RTC complexity.

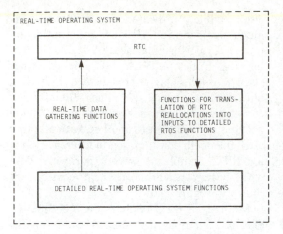

Figure 5.3. Role of RTC within a real-time operating system.

pose. Thus, RTC deals with the highest levels of functions within the real-time operating system, and it specifically responds to major dynamic events caused by external events, such as a function overload or a hardware failure. This viewpoint is often helpful in delineating the levels of detail of decisions in the RTC method.

Another critical aspect of RTC is the extent to which the real-location decisions anticipate the future. A truly optimal RTC approach would make projections of future loads and other dynamic effects, and attempt to compensate for them. However, this is rarely done in practice for two reasons. First, the computational requirements for this type of dynamic control are very high; and second, it is often very difficult to obtain data that supports an accurate projection of the future. What is usually done instead is to use a quasistatic or open-loop feedback control (OLFC) approach; the idea is to solve a sequence of static problems, but to update the parameters of the static problems based on real-time information. By far, the majority of past applications have used the quasistatic approach; one truly dynamic application is presented as an example later in this chapter.

A development that makes work in the RTC area particularly important is the trend toward distributed data processing (DDP) systems. As discussed elsewhere in this book, this trend is motivated by new technologies in microproces-

sors, minicomputers, data communication, and other areas. As is also noted in these chapters, distributed systems have numerous potential advantages over traditional centralized systems. Many of these potential advantages either require or are greatly enhanced by RTC. For example, increased system availability is widely cited as a potential advantage of DDP systems. Certainly, if redundant hardware components are present, this potential advantage exists. However, unless some mechanism is provided for recognizing hardware faults and switching in replacement hardware, this potential advantage will not be realized. In fact, the probability that a hardware failure occurs somewhere in the system increases with the number of components. Thus, the presence of an RTC system to perform these fault-recognition and hardware-replacement functions is critical to the effective implementation of increased availability in DDP systems.

The RTC approach can also enhance DDP in the general area of system performance. For example, RTC can improve response time by detecting queue buildups in the system and reallocating the hardware resources to those functions where the queues are arising. Also, RTC methods can enhance the effective system throughput by constantly anticipating increased loading, and reallocating hardware to handle these loads.

Both availability and system performance in distributed systems can also be achieved in a brute-force fashion by simply adding more and more hardware. Because of the low cost of microprocessors and other hardware, it is tempting to take this approach and to ignore RTC. In a truly dynamic environment, however, there are real advantages to applying RTC. Certainly, the cost of providing sufficient hardware to meet the worst-case requirements at every function, along with enough redundant components for each function to maintain total system availability at the desired level, will be much higher than the cost of a system with RTC, at least in a case with dynamic system loading. This much hardware may well turn out to be excessive, even with a low cost of individual components. More important, the complexity of the communication network to connect all this hardware may induce considerable added costs and a major penalty in availability. Thus, from an overall systems viewpoint, RTC may be very important in achieving the proper balance between system performance, availability, and cost; the ARE methodology identified above provides a powerful quantitative approach to achieving this balance.

The remainder of this chapter is organized as follows. The next major section discusses the basic theory and presents several possible formulations of the RTC problem. The section after that describes several techniques for solving this problem, including enumeration of decision alternatives, integer programming, methods based on graph theory, heuristic approaches, and spatial dynamic programming. These examples illustrate some of the areas where RTC has been applied successfully. Although most of the examples are based on a quasistatic approach, one truly dynamic RTC scheme is discussed. Many of the examples concern distributed systems. The final section presents conclusions and projects future trends in this area.

5.2. PROBLEM FORMULATION

The RTC problem for a computer system is basically one of resource scheduling. Given a set of processes that must be executed in a certain order under time and hardware constraints, an RTC method should be capable of scheduling these processes in an acceptable, if not optimal, way. As stated, this problem has a large number of variables and a correspondingly high degree of difficulty. Hence, the methods to solve it must be selected with great care.

Essentially, the strategy for handling an RTC problem can be decomposed into a series of steps:

Problem Formulation

- The goals and limits of the problem must be defined in light of the eventual applications of the system.

- The functional interdependence of system parameters must be determined and resources should be evaluated as to their finite or infinite availability.
- A system performance index must be defined so that the relative values of different problem solutions can be calculated.

Technique Selection

- A method must be selected that can yield the desired solution (optimal or just "good") based on the performance index chosen and all associated constraints.

Solution

- The technique selected must be applied to the problem in the presence of resource or other constraints.
- The solution must be evaluated as to its practicality. That is, does the solution make sense and can it actually be implemented? If not, a return to the problem formulation stage is warranted.

The above steps summarize the general path leading from the introduction of an RTC problem to its successful solution. Although the steps have a surface simplicity, there are many subtleties that can and usually do arise. The remainder of this chapter will examine several of these problems and present the reader with viable options. Specifically, this section will emphasize the first step, *problem formulation*.

Absolutely crucial to solving any RTC problem is the "correct" definition of an index to measure the value of the system solution, that is, a system performance index. It is this parameter that one hopes to optimize over all possible states of the system. Although there is a large amount of freedom in the selection of this factor, the "correct" one is the one that embodies the elements most important to the system. Since the systems being controlled are often time-critical, a possible performance index is one that is time dependent. Two commonly applied indices are:

1. Time of completion of a particular process
2. Time of completion of the final process in the series

Denoting the chosen (time-dependent) performance index by J, the RTC problem can then be stated as:

$$\text{Min } \{J(T)\}. \tag{1}$$

Since process execution is generally stochastic, it is not possible to compute an exact value of such performance indices. Hence, either mean or maximum ("worst case") times of completion can be used in Formula (1).

Another viewpoint in the formulation of system performance measures involves modeling subsystem interactions. In the case of scheduling modules to run on processors, either individual processors or groups of connected processors can be regarded as subsystems of the overall system. Here, an assignment of modules to processors involves intermodule communication which, if the communicating modules are in different processors, requires data transfer across a link. This data flow can be viewed as a subsystem interaction that

- Requires time to complete
- Induces system overhead required for message handling
- Makes the system vulnerable to link failure or interruption
- May induce errors in the transmitted data*

A common objective in highly interconnected systems is to minimize the total interprocessor communication. This can be represented as

$$\text{Min } \{J(C_t)\}$$

where C_t represents the time required for data transfer, or by

$$\text{Min } \{J(C_v)\}$$

Where C_v represents the "volume" of data that is to be transferred.

In addition to the *time of completion* and *interprocessor communication* formulations, other performance indices are feasible. Since a chosen performance index will be either maximized or minimized with respect to the system limitations, an extension of the index to encompass such constrained parameters is possible. For example, an index could be constructed that gives a high value to a solution utilitizing a minimum fraction of the available resources. Or, if the tasks to be allocated are time dependent, then the index could reward completion prior to a preset deadline. In any case, the selected performance index is not constrained to fit a predetermined format. Rather, the index is free to be problem oriented and, in this respect, can be quite heuristic. In fact, the measure may even take unique details of a particular problem into account by intermixing parameters such as time and component cost. In the end, the only requirement is that the system performance measure allow different problem solutions to be evaluated on equal (and correct) grounds.

There exists no standard RTC problem upon which all other RTC problems can be modeled. Rather, differences between these problems are as widely varying as are the physical systems they represent. Such differences can arise from both the inherent characteristics of the modeled subsystems and from the desired method(s) of measuring system performance.

Because of system differences, there is no single method of solving RTC problems. Rather, many different solution techniques are available. These methods often take advantage of certain system characteristics, such as sparsity, to provide acceptable or optimal solutions to certain classes of RTC problems. The person intending to solve an RTC problem should have all possible techniques at his disposal so that the one best suited to the problem can be selected. With this end in mind, several methods of solution are examined in the following section.

---

*Additionally, data transfer over a link raises data security questions. Hence, overhead may be incurred for data encryption.

5.3. THEORY AND METHODS OF SOLUTION

Enumeration

The least sophisticated mathematical technique for scheduling problems is enumeration. Here, all the possible assignment combinations are tried, and a performance measure for each is calculated. Although the method has the distinct advantage of guaranteeing a globally optimum solution, the time required for it to do so is prohibitively large. As an example, consider the assignment of n modules with deterministic execution times to be executed on a system of m processors. If the modules are not constrained by precedence relationships, then there are

$$\frac{(n + m - 1)!}{(m - 1)!}$$

possible module arrangements that must be considered. For a relatively small system consisting of 25 modules and 5 processors, then there are 3.7×10^{29} possibilities.

Estimating that each assignment requires 10^3 machine instructions to be evaluated (a low estimate) then a post-1990 Josephson junction computer capable of 2.5×10^8 instructions per second would require 4.7×10^{16} years to examine all combinations. For comparison, the age of the earth is approximately 5.0×10^9 years.

Restricting the possible module assignment order by imposing precedence relationships on the modules reduces the number of combinations to a minimum of m^n. Of course, the actual number of combinations depends on the severity of the precedence constraints. Again, for $n = 25$ and $m = 5$ there are at least 3.0×10^{17} possibilities to be tested. Although this number is smaller than that of the unconstrained case, it is still not a workable situation. Clearly, enumeration is not a feasible method of solution for scheduling problems consisting of more than a few modules and processors.

Integer Programming

Various mathematical programming methods are typically used to solve large, constrained optimization problems. Integer programming is particularly appropriate for such problems since the assignment of a software module to a hardware unit can be represented by a binary decision variable. The objective function (or performance index) chosen for allocation evaluation may be either linear or nonlinear. In either case, the performance index is a function of a set of binary decision variables representing the state of the system. Solution of the equations is generally done in the presence of linear and/or nonlinear constraints and results in a determination of the values of the decision variables. Hence, the optimal state of the system is determined.

As an example, we will consider a set of software modules (without precedence relationships) that is to be mapped onto a set of connected memories and processors. The modules, however, are allowed to communicate with each other. For simplicity, we assume that associated with each processor is one and only one memory; that is, the memories are dedicated. Furthermore, we constrain the memories to have finite storage capacities. A possible architecture for this system is shown in Figure 5.4. We define the decision variable x_{ik}:

$$x_{ik} = \begin{cases} 1 \text{ if module } i \text{ is assigned to} \\ \quad \text{processor } k \\ 0 \text{ otherwise} \end{cases}$$

Also, we define:

t_{ik} = execution time of module i on processor k

$C_{ijk\ell}$ = communication time for modules i and j when i is assigned to processor k, and j is assigned to processor ℓ

m_i = memory requirement of module i

M_k = capacity of the memory associated with processor k

We have several choices for an objective function but, recalling Formula (1), we choose to

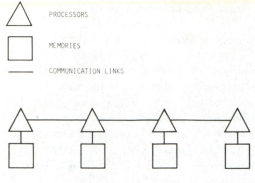

PROCESSORS

MEMORIES

COMMUNICATION LINKS

Figure 5.4. A system of processors and dedicated memories.

define T as the time required for all modules to complete. Thus, it is desired to

$$\text{Min } \{T\} \tag{2}$$

subject to:

$$\sum_i \left[x_{ik}t_{ik} + \sum_{j \neq i} \sum_{\ell \neq k} C_{ijk\ell}x_{ik}x_{j\ell} \right] \leq T \quad \text{for all } k \text{ (time constraint)} \tag{a}$$

$$\sum_i m_i x_{ik} \leq M_k \quad \text{for all } k \text{ (memory constraint)} \tag{b}$$

$$\sum_k x_{ik} = 1 \quad \text{for all } i \text{ (all modules be assigned once)} \tag{c}$$

$$x_{ik} = 0,1 \quad \text{(binary assignment variable)} \tag{d}$$

This is an integer programming problem (T will assume integer values if all the parameters are integers), with quadratic constraints and a linear objective function. The intermodule communication transforms what would have otherwise been a linear objective function into a quadratic one containing the term $x_{ik}x_{j\ell}$. Such objective functions are representative of the so-called quadratic assignment problem first discussed by Koopmans and Beckman in 1957 [3]. Since then the problem has been treated by many authors [4,5,6,7,8].*

Quadratic assignment problems can be linearized by the inclusion of additional constraints. Once this has been done, standard in-

teger programming methods such as "branch-and-bound" can be applied. E. L. Lawler [9] provides a review of the linearization and solution procedure.

The main disadvantage in applying the integer programming methodology to RTC problems is that module precedence relationships cannot be efficiently modeled. Indeed, if there are such constraints, then other scheduling algorithms must be used. Such methods also rely on integer programming methods by redefining the decision variable x:

$$x_{ik} \rightarrow x_{ikt}$$

where

$$x_{ikt} = \begin{cases} 1 \text{ if module } i \text{ runs on processor } k \\ \quad \text{at time } t \\ 0 \text{ otherwise} \end{cases}$$

Here, the object is to minimize a function similar or identical to (2), subject to linear and/or nonlinear constraints.

Graph Theory

An interesting graph theoretic approach to the module allocation problem has been taken by H. S. Stone and S. H. Bokhari [10,11,12]. The components of their system consist of several connected processors ($N \leq 3$) and a set of software modules with deterministic execution times. The modules communicate with each other but are not subject to precedence relationships. System performance is defined to be the total time taken for all of the modules to complete. The time taken for a single module i to complete consists of two components: the time for the actual execution of the module code t_i and the time required for the module to

---

*Quadratic objective functions often arise in multicommodity problem formulations. Also, the famous "traveling salesman problem" is a special case of a quadratic assignment problem.

communicate c_{ij} with all other modules j. The objective is to find the module to processor mapping that minimizes:

$$\sum_i t_i + \sum_i \sum_{\substack{j \\ j \neq i}} C_{ij}$$

Although Stone and Bokhari's model is quite simplified, their solution technique guarantees a global optimal solution for the two processor case and allows bounds to be set on the optimality of the three processor system solution.

Stone and Bokhari have extended their model to include "quasidynamic" module execution. Here, modules have their execution ordered but are constrained so that only one module in the system can execute at any instant in time. Although they are able to arrive at methods of solving the resulting equations, they do not provide for an extension of the model to more realistic situations. In fact, it is not apparent that their model can be extended to include either model precedence relationships or true dynamic operation. Hence, the graph theory approach seems to provide little in the way of solving RTC problems.

Heuristic Methods

The methods of solution thus far presented have well-based mathematical foundations. They are all limited, however, in the scope of problems that they can solve. At this point in time the development of solid mathematical techniques to solve RTC problems appears lagging behind the growing complexity of the application requirements. Hence, many researchers have developed heuristic methods for finding solutions to allocation and scheduling problems.

For the most part, heuristic algorithms follow no specific development pattern, are usually ad hoc, and can't guarantee optimal solutions. However, in general, they are computationally very efficient and often yield excellent solutions to very complex problems.

Heuristic methods often take the form of "greedy" algorithms in which at every step the objective function is improved as much as possible.

For example, consider a module-to-processor allocation with intermodule communication but without precedence relationships. A simple greedy algorithm might take the following form:

1. Order the modules in decreasing numbers of instructions.
2. Assign each module in turn to the processor which will minimize the maximum execution time so far in the assignment process. Ties are broken arbitrarily.

This algorithm encourages pairs of modules with high communication costs to share the same processor. It also encourages load balancing among processors.

Unlike the integer programming and graph theory approaches, heuristic methods do allow both memory constraints and precedence relationships to be included in the model. Hence, they have a major advantage over the other two methods in regard to RTC.

Maximum Marginal Return

In general, heuristic methods do not guarantee optimal solutions for arbitrary problems. However, there are a few methods that provide such solutions for surprisingly wide classes of problems. One of these methods, *maximum marginal return* (MMR), is based on a greedy algorithm. The method is particularly useful for resource allocation problems and has been shown to yield optimal allocations for concave benefit functions.

Consider the case of a resource allocation problem where it is desired to maximize the function $F(x)$ where

$$F(x) = \sum_{i=1}^{n} F_i(x_i)$$

Here, the x_i denote n discrete state variables of the system each with δ as the unit of discretization. $F_i(x_i)$ represents the benefit functions for the x_i and $F(x)$ is the benefit function of the entire system. Furthermore, due to limited resources, the x_i are constrained:

$$C(x) = \sum_{i=1}^{n} x_i \le R$$

$$x_i \ge 0$$

where R is a scalar.

Given the discrete nature of the state variables, one can determine an n dimensional state space that is populated by points representing allowed value combinations of x_i. In Figure 5.5 is shown such a space where there are just two integer state variables (i.e., $\delta = 1$) constrained by the equation

$$C(x) = x_1 + x_2 \le 5.$$

Associated with every allowed point in the state space is the benefit function $F(x)$. These values can be included as another dimension in Figure 5.5. Thus, the $F(x)$ would constitute a "discrete surface." The problem, of course, is to find the maximum point on the surface. The MMR heuristic methodology is intended to do just that.

There are 3 steps in the MMR procedure, as follows:

1. Set $x_i^0 = 0$ for all i and find $F(x_i = 0)$.*
2. Let $x_I^{k+1} \to x_I^k + \delta$ where I is the index where the marginal return

$$\Delta F_i = \frac{1}{\delta}(F_i(x_i^k + \delta) - F_i(x_i^k))$$

   is greatest. (Here, k is the kth stage in the computation.) Let $x_i^{k+1} = x_i^k$ for the remaining indices.
3. If $C(x^{k+1}) > R$ then x^k is the resultant. Otherwise return to step 2. Ties are broken arbitrarily.

In this way discrete steps are made in the direction that yields the maximum marginal return.

---
*The superscripts on x_i represent x_i at the different stages in the computation. For example, x_1^0 is the initial value of x_1.

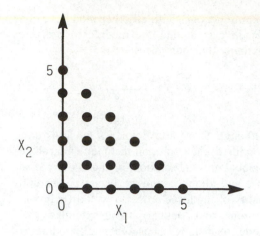

Figure 5.5. Possible state space values.

We can illustrate the MMR methodology by considering the example represented in Figure 5.5. Define the functions

$$F_1(x_1) = x_1$$

and

$$F_2(x_2) = 5(1 - e_2^{-x^2})$$

which are plotted in Figure 5.6. Again, we have the constraint

$$C(x) = x_1 + x_2 \le 5$$

Using the MMR method we first set $x_1 = x_2 = 0$ and calculate $F(x_1,x_2) = 0$. We then separately increase x_1, and x_2 by their increments and compare the resulting benefit function values. For convenience, Table 5.1 contains the function values for $F_1(x_1)$ and $F_2(x_2)$. Thus,

$$F_1(x_1 = 1) = 1.00 \Rightarrow \Delta F_1 = 1.00$$

and

$$F_2(x_2 = 1) = 3.16 \Rightarrow \Delta F_2 = 3.16$$

Hence, the new values of the state variables are taken to be $x_1 = 0$ and $x_2 = 1$. Repeating the procedure we find that the next step is to $x_1 = 0$, $x_2 = 2$ since

$$F_1(x_1 = 1) = 1.00 \Rightarrow \Delta F_1 = 1.00$$
$$F_2(x_2 = 2) = 4.32 \Rightarrow \Delta F_2 = 1.16$$

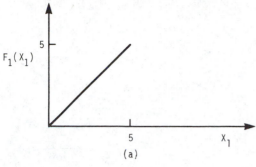

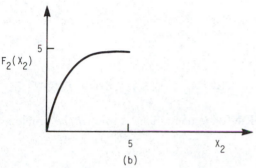

Figure 5.6. Plots of (a) $F_1(x_1)$ and (b) $F_2(x_2)$.

Here, the marginal return still favors x_2 over x_1, and the new state variables are $x_1 = 0$ and $x_2 = 2$.

Repeating the procedure we find

$$F_1(x_1 = 1) = 1.00 \Rightarrow \Delta F_1 = 1.00$$
$$F_2(x_2 = 3) = 4.75 \Rightarrow \Delta F_2 = 0.43$$

That is, the increment to x_1 resulted in a larger marginal return than did the increment to x_2. Hence, the current state variables are $x_1 = 1$ and $x_2 = 2$.

Repeated application of the methodology results in finding the optimal variable values $x_1 = 3$, $x_2 = 2$. Although larger values of the benefit function are possible, the procedure was terminated because of the constraint:

Table 5.1. Function Values for x_1 and x_2.

X_1	$F(X_1)$	X_2	$F(X_2)$
0	0	0	0
1	1	1	3.16
2	2	2	4.32
3	3	3	4.75
4	4	4	4.91
5	5	5	4.97

Table 5.2. Step-by-Step Solution to the MMR Problem.

STEP #	X_1	ΔF_1	X_2	ΔF_2	$F(X_1,X_2)$
1	0	1.00	1	3.16	3.16
2	0	1.00	2	1.16	4.32
3	1	1.00	2	0.43	5.32
4	2	1.00	2	0.43	6.32
5	3	1.00	2	0.43	7.32

$$C(x) = x_1 + x_2 \leq 5.$$

In Table 5.2 are the marginal return values for all the steps in the example. In Figure 5.7 the step-by-step progression to the result is shown.

In the above problem the increment δ was set equal to one for both x_1 and x_2. However, the MMR methodology allows different values of δ to be used for each state variable. Differing increments might be desired in the case where, for example, a particular benefit function has a range that differs widely from those of the other functions. Freedom in the selection of a δ can also be exploited by setting δ to an arbitrarily small value so that any degree of precision may be obtained.

The MMR methodology can be shown to yield optimum solutions for problems in which the benefit functions are concave [13,14]. Moreover, the method provides optimal solutions for certain classes of nonconcave functions [15]. In a later section MMR is applied to a resource grouping problem.

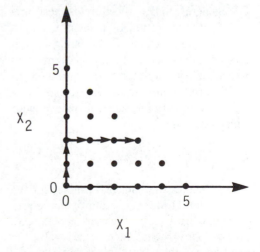

Figure 5.7. Steps leading to the solution of the MMR problem.

Spatial Dynamic Programming

The network structure inherent in software engineering problems is particularly well suited for solution by dynamic programming techniques. In the 1950s Bellman's work with constrained linear systems provided the first results in this area [16]. These results were later extended by Nemhauser [17] and by Bertelé and Brioschi [18] to include more generally structured networks. More recently, the relationships between dynamic programming and mathematical programming have been presented by Mine and Ohno [19, 20], Bonzon [21], and Chong, McEntire, and Larson [22].

Of particular importance to a wide variety of network problems is spatial dynamic programming (SDP). Developed by McEntire and Larson [23], SDP is a technique for solving large-scale control problems for a system or interconnected subsystems. Although traditional dynamic programming and SDP are analogous, they differ in regard to their decompositional methods. Whereas standard dynamic methods involve temporal system decomposition, SDP is unique in that it is based upon the spatial decomposition of a system. Application of SDP does not require that the system be composed of weakly interacting subsystems. However, full exploitation of the methodology is most easily achieved if the subsystem interaction matrix is sparse. Many distributed data processing systems exhibit such sparsity.

The general SDP procedure is best presented by consideration of a short example. Figure 5.8 shows a system consisting of four connected subsystems. Intersubsystem links denote all subsystem interactions and the variables $\{Z_i\}$ are the interaction variables.

One natural form for the performance index for this system is

$$J = f_1(S_1) + f_2(S_2) + f_3(S_3) + f_4(S_4)$$

where S_i denotes the control variables for the ith subsystem. However, spatial dynamic programming can also solve the more general case where the performance index can involve the interaction variables for a subsystem, that is,

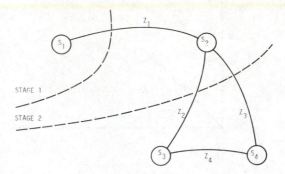

Figure 5.8. Decomposition of a system consisting of four connected subsystems.

$$J = f_1(S_1,Z_1) + f_2(S_2,Z_1,Z_2,Z_3)$$
$$+ f_3(S_3,Z_2,Z_4) + f_4(S_4,Z_3,Z_4).$$

The fundamental idea is to solve the problem

$$\begin{array}{c} \text{Max } \{J\} \\ \{S_i\} \\ \{Z_i\} \end{array}$$

by decomposing the problem into a sequence of smaller problems. At each stage of the process another subsystem is introduced, and only a cumulative performance index is needed to summarize the results of the computations for the previous stages. Hence, the system is decomposed spatially.

If we choose to use J as our performance index, then the initial step is to compute J_1:

$$J_1(Z_1) = \max_{S_1} f_1(S_1,Z_1).$$

The function $J_1(Z_1)$ is stored and is then available as input to the second stage of the process. Supposing that subsystem 2 is to be added at the second stage, the computations for stage 2 would be

$$(J_2Z_2,Z_3) = \max_{\substack{S_2 \\ Z_1}} \{J_1(Z_1) + f_2(S_2,Z_1,Z_2,Z_3)\}.$$

This process is continued until the final subsystem is added, yielding the optimal value for the global performance index. Finally, a rapid trace back is performed to determine the optimal subsystem controls.

Experience has shown that SDP is straightforward to program. Because of the requirements for "parameterizing" over the interaction variables, the efficiency of this solution technique is particularly impressive for systems with sparse interactions. The execution time tends to grow linearly with the size of the network. However, for problems possessing such sparsity, the method offers an approach that (1) finds a global optimum, (2) allows nonlinear objectives and constraints, and (3) can be implemented on a distributed computer network to exploit the ability to do concurrent computations. A realistic application of SDP to a network problem is contained in Section 5.3 of this chapter. Although both that problem and the one just considered are static, a version of the SDP methodology has been developed that treats dynamic problems. Other practical applications of SDP are contained in the literature [27].

5.4. CURRENT APPLICATIONS TO DISTRIBUTED SYSTEMS

The development of distributed systems methodologies in the context of military systems has provided a large arena for testing of the algorithms in realistic situations. Hence, many of the applications that have been most thoroughly examined and are most often used as examples involve military systems. The intent of the remainder of this section is to use these and other available examples to demonstrate the RTC methodologies presented in the previous section.

Ballistic Missile Defense Systems

One of the major problems facing system engineers for and next decade will be the design of computing systems capable of handling the processing demands of the magnitude of those required for ballistic missile defense (BMD) systems. In addition to requiring system throughput of several hundred MIPS, BMD systems also require an extremely high reliability and a very fast response time. These latter two factors can be appreciated when the overall operation of the system is considered.

The basic goal of a BMD site is to utilize sensor data to detect and track an incoming warhead so that a kill mechanism (e.g., missile) may be used against it. Once such a site is operational, its controlling computer system will proceed with standard "search/verify" methods on objects contained in its allocated airspace. In the "dormant" situation prevailing most of the time, the system will remain comparatively unused. However, in the event of an enemy attack the demands on the system will increase dramatically. Although an incoming missile might contain only a few warheads, it might also have several dozen decoys. Additionally, in the case of a low-altitude BMD site, missiles directed to nearby regions might be passing through this site's airspace, and hence constitute "cross-traffic."

This sudden increase in the number of objects places a tremendous load upon the site's computing system. The system must respond immediately to this increased throughput requirement and must do so with an extremely high degree of reliability. The length of queues must be kept at a minimum and "hang-ups" in system performance prevented. The duration of the threat may be only a few seconds, but if a system problem occurs that is not immediately solvable, then there may be no second chance. Indeed, the BMD computing requirements constitute an example of the need for a well-designed, distributed processing system.

The problem of a simplified BMD system can be formulated using the techniques discussed in Section 5.2. We assume that there are three types of objects that must be processed: warheads, decoys, and cross-traffic. Each object is processed sequentially by four functions until it is deemed either to be a warhead or not to be a warhead. The four functions are:

1. Search/verify
2. Track initiation
3. Track
4. Classify

Objects that pass through all four functions without being "dropped" are said to be "engaged."

An attack in which all the objects are bunched together in time is assumed. In Figure 5.9 are shown typical processing requirements for the attack. The requirements for each of the four functions are shown individually. The double pulse in Figure 5.9a is due to the fact that both a *search* and *verify* have to be performed on each object.

The problem to be considered is simply: What is the "best" way to assign the functions to be executed on processors? Two methods of solving the problem will be examined:

1. Static allocation
2. Spares on demand

Static Allocation. The static-allocation solution to the BMD problem is that of assigning sufficient dedicated processors to each function so that peak loads can be handled. The processor assignment based on the throughput requirements of Figure 5.9 is shown in Figure 5.10. (For convenience, all the processors will be considered to be identical and capable of operation at 0.5 MIPS.) In all, 11 processors are required. During off-peakload periods, however, the processors remain partially available. This situation is clearly not optimum and can be improved using an RTC method.

Spares on Demand. The spares-on-demand method is a real-time approach to the control of BMD computing resources. It is a simple but effective procedure in which processors are taken from and returned to a spare pool as needed. C. Vick has studied this method in detail [25].

In Figure 5.11 is shown the time variation of the total system throughput requirements. From the figure it is clear that in the spares on demand approach, only 10 processors are required for the given attack. (The peak computational demand is 5.0 MIPS. Hence, one needs, at most, (5.0 MIPS)/(0.5 MIPS/processor) = 10 processors.) In fact, by some sharing of processors possibly 9 or even 8 processors would suffice. Although the sharing

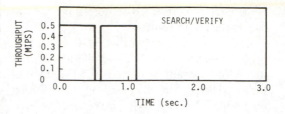

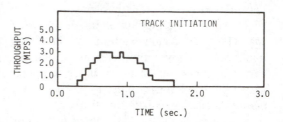

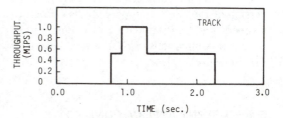

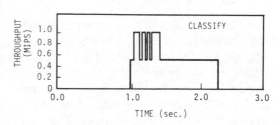

Figure 5.9. Throughput requirements for the four BMD system functions.

might cause a processing delay due to the extra computation, the situation could still be superior to the last problem.

In the current-assignment procedure, it was assumed that any processor could be assigned to any function. In actual practice such generality would require considerable overhead in terms of communication and switching equipment. However, a close examination of Figure 5.11 will show that together *track initiation* and *classify* never require more than 7 processors and track initiation alone never requires

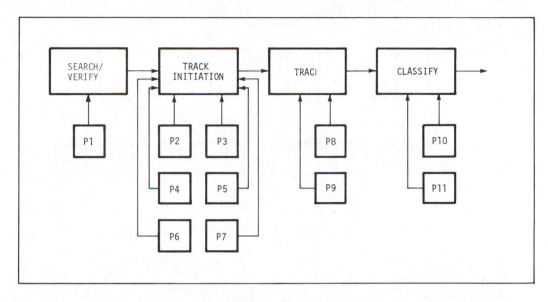

Figure 5.10. Processor assignment found by the static allocation method.

more than 6. This result suggests the following: Assign permanently five processors to track initiation, two processors to track, one processor to search/verify, and one processor to classify. Finally, a tenth processor is assigned to process either track initiation or classify with its actual assignment determined in real time. This assignment is illustrated in Figure 5.12.

In an actual BMD problem a number of typical attack patterns would be analyzed. One could then decide on a permanent assignment of processors to one or more functions in such a manner so as to minimize communication and switching requirements. Those processors without a unique a priori assignment would then be assigned in real time to appropriate functions. While in the present example the

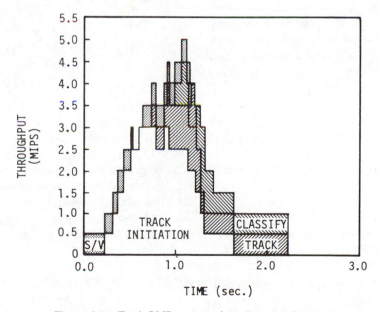

Figure 5.11. Total BMD system throughput require-ments.

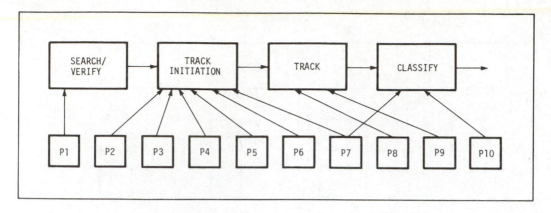

Figure 5.12. Processor assignment found by the spares on demand approach.

real time assignment is trivial, more realistic situations would require use of an optimization procedure such as SDP.

Software to Processor Assignment

A generic extension of the BMD problem provides an excellent opportunity for application of the SDP methodology. Consider the assignment of a set of software tasks to a system of distinct processors. Although we seek a solution for the static case, the method can be applied to dynamic versions of the same problem. Each processor divides its time among the tasks it is allowed to work on. The tasks each processor is allowed to work on are indicated by a network, with nodes for tasks and processors, and arcs for each allowable pair. A task that is not connected by an arc to a processor cannot run on that processor.

The total amount of processing resources allocated to a task determines a benefit. The goal is to find an efficient allocation that maximizes the overall benefits. Formally, we define, with a notation modified slightly from that used previously,

$$f_{ij} = \text{the fraction of processor } i$$
$$\text{allocated to task } j, \text{ and}$$
$$B_j(x) = \text{the benefit function for task } j$$

The goal is to maximize the total system benefits, as expressed by

$$\text{MAX}_{f_{ij}} \sum_j \left(\sum_i f_{ij} \right)$$

Subject to:

$$0 \le f_{ij} \le \bar{f}_{ij} \qquad \text{for all } i \text{ and } j$$
$$\sum_j f_{ij} = 1 \qquad \text{for all } i$$

and subject to the restrictions imposed by the network topology.

As an example, consider the network of eight processors and five tasks shown in Figure 5.13. The task benefits are

$$B_A(x) = -5x^2 + 49x$$
$$B_B(x) = -5x^2 + 53x$$
$$B_C(x) = -5x^2 + 40.6x$$
$$B_D(x) = -5x^2 + 51.4x$$
$$B_E(x) = -5x^2 + 43x$$

The allocation upper bounds $\bar{f}_{ij}$ were all assumed to be 1, except $\bar{f}_{5E} = \bar{f}_{4B} = .5$.

By inspection $f_{1A} = f_{3B} = f_{8E} = 1$. The dotted lines indicate the stages—one stage for each task node. To illustrate the method, consider the first two stages. At stage 1, the resource amount allocated to task A is $1 + f_{2A} + f_{6A}$, for a benefit of

$$J(f_{2A}, f_{6A}) = -5(1 + f_{2A} + f_{6A})^2$$
$$+ 49(1 + f_{2A} + f_{6A}).$$

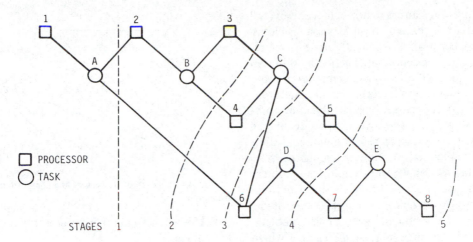

Figure 5.13. Network for the processor assignment problem.

At stage 2, the resource amount allocated to B is:

$$1 + (1 - f_{2A}) + f_{4B} = 2 - f_{2A} + f_{4B}$$

The total benefit is

$$J(f_{6A}, f_{4B}) = \max_{f_{2A}} J(f_{2A}, f_{6A})$$
$$- 5(2 - f_{2A} + f_{4B})^2 + 53(2 - f_{2A} + f_{4B})$$

The optimal f_{2A} is found to be $(\frac{1}{10})(3 - 5f_{6A} + 5f_{4B})$, and so:

$$J(f_{6A}, f_{4B}) = -5(\tfrac{13}{10} + \tfrac{1}{2}f_{6A} + \tfrac{1}{2}f_{4B})^2$$
$$+ 49(\tfrac{13}{10} + \tfrac{1}{2}f_{6A} + \tfrac{1}{2}f_{4B})$$

$$- 5(\tfrac{17}{10} + \tfrac{1}{2}f_{6A} + \tfrac{1}{2}f_{4B})^2$$
$$+ 53(\tfrac{17}{10} + \tfrac{1}{2}f_{6A} + \tfrac{1}{2}f_{4B}).$$

This problem was solved on a computer by discretizing the variables. Repeated applications of SDP with decreasing grid sizes allowed an eventual discretization in units of 0.01. The solution is shown in Figure 5.14. Notice that f_{4B} is at its upper bound and as a result, not all the tasks have the same marginal benefit (benefit from an additional unit of resource).

Resource-Grouping Problem

Distributed scheduling problems are of common occurrence in many applications; the

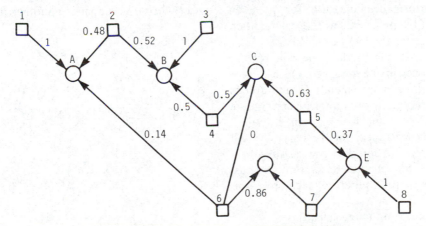

Figure 5.14. Solution to the processor assignment problem.

grouping of resources to best achieve an overall objective is a common form for such problems. System constraints frequently arise from requirements for coordinated action by different entities, or by the sharing of computer or other spatial resources. When the spatial structure is appropriately sparse, spatial dynamic programming is an effective solution technique and frequently avoids the formulational difficulties associated with alternative methods.

In this section we will examine the problem of grouping a set of resources in an optimal fashion. This problem is a special case of the canonical distributed scheduling problem, which consists of N subsystems, each of which has a list of possible tasks to perform. A typical global performance index is written as a sum of indices for each subsystem; the performance index at the ith subsystem, however, does not depend only upon the tasks performed by that subsystem. There are constraints between certain subsystems that affect their mutual freedom of choice of tasks.

Consider the problem of N processors A_1, $A_2, \ldots, A_N$, each of which has a set of tasks to perform. Assume that the processors may aid neighboring processors, but may not time-share. The allowable groupings must conform to a specified network structure; two processors can cooperate only if they are connected to each other via a communication link. For example, in the 7 processor system shown in Figure 5.15, processor 1 can cooperate only with processors 2, 3, or 4.

The performance measure for a given grouping of the processors will be a summation of the scores for the tasks completed.

To illustrate the method, we will require that the processors be grouped into single processors working independently or into groups of three processors working together. In the latter case the group will be termed a *triad*, and the processor receiving the assistance will be termed the *master*. The two assisting processors will be referred to as *slaves*. Thus, there are three possibilities for each processor:

1. It is operating independently
2. It is a master with assistance from two neighboring processors

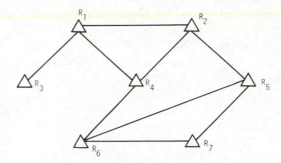

Figure 5.15. A group of processors and their communication links.

3. It is assisting another processor in a slave mode

The component of the score function for a given processor will assign nonzero scores in cases 1 and 2 but a score of 0 in case 3. Although the requirement to group processors in this particular manner is artificial, it is typical of the types of combinatorial problems that occur in actual systems because of design "externalities."

The SDP methodology will be applied to a simplified scheduling problem involving 9 processors with 14 possible links. This problem is diagrammed in Figure 5.16. Associated with each node (processor) is an ordered pair of values (scores), where the first value is the score assigned when the processor is acting independently and the second value is the score assigned when the processor is acting as a master in a triad. A score of zero is assigned to a processor when it is supporting another processor

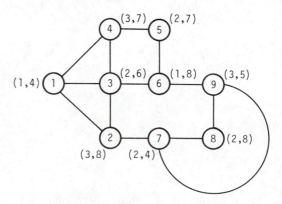

Figure 5.16. Processor scheduling problem.

in a triad. The objective is to group the processors so that the sum of the scores is maximized. For this problem the scores are given above the nodes.

Associated with each pair of processors that may cooperate is a variable x_{ij}, where i and j are the numbers of the processors and $i < j$. These variables may take one of three values, which will be denoted 1, 2, and 3.

$$x_{ij} = \begin{cases} 1 \text{ if } i \text{ and } j \text{ do not cooperate} \\ 2 \text{ if } j \text{ assists } i \\ 3 \text{ if } i \text{ assists } j \end{cases}$$

At the stage in the SDP procedure associated with processor k, the parameterization is over all possible values of x_{kj}, where $j > k$, as well as over all x_{ij} where $i < k < j$. For each of the possible values, the optimal values of all of the x_{ik}, where $i < k$, are found.

In the example, the first stage is shown in Figure 5.17. The variables associated with this stage are x_{12}, x_{13}, and x_{14}. Since each variable may take three values, there are $3^3 = 27$ values for the set. However, the constraints on the problem eliminate 20 of these possibilities, so that only 7 remain. In general, if there are n processors that can cooperate with processor i, there are $(n^2 + n + 2)/2$ possible values of the associated x_{ji} and x_{ij}. This can be derived from the following three cases:

1. i operates independently; all x_{ij} and x_{ji} equal 1: 1 possibility
2. i is a master; two of the x_{ij} or x_{ji} equal 2, the rest equal 1: $\binom{n}{2} = n(n-1)/2$ possibilities
3. i is a slave; one of the x_{ij} or x_{ji} equals 3, the rest equal 1: n possibilities

For the current example, the seven possibilities and their scores for processor 1 are given in Table 5.3.

The remaining stages are shown in Figure 5.18. At stage 2, for example, the parameterization is over x_{23}, x_{27}, x_{13}, and x_{14}. The objective is now

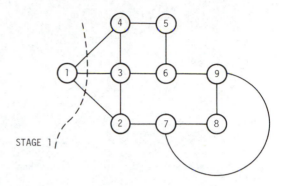

Figure 5.17. Illustration of first SDP stage.

Table 5.3. Values of $J_1(x_{12}, x_{13}, x_{14})$.

x_{12}	x_{13}	x_{14}	J_1
0	0	0	1
0	1	1	4
1	0	1	4
1	1	0	4
0	0	2	0
0	2	0	0
2	0	0	0

$$J_2(x_{23}, x_{27}, x_{13}, x_{14}) = \max_{x_{12}} (J_1(x_{12}, x_{13}, x_{14}) + f_2(x_{12}, x_{23}, x_{27}))$$

where f_2 is the score function at node 2. There are 20 different feasible values of x_{23}, x_{27}, x_{13}, and x_{14}. In this case the values of these variables uniquely determine an x_{12}, but in general

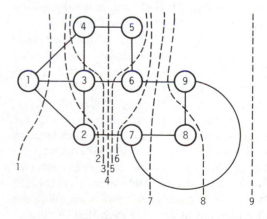

Figure 5.18. Illustration of all the SDP stages.

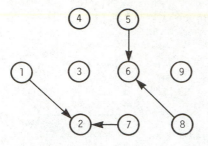

Figure 5.19. Solution to the processor scheduling problem.

Table 5.4. Radar and Computer Resources.

PAIR TYPE	RADAR RESOURCES	COMPUTER RESOURCES	SURVIVAL PROBABILITY
1	8	5	0.90
2	9	4	0.75
3	6	9	0.65
4	7	7	0.80
5	8	7	0.85

some optimization will have to be done. The remaining stages are done in the same manner.

The final solution to the problem is illustrated in Figure 5.19. The scores for the two indicated triads are 8 and 8, while processors 3, 4, and 9 yield a total of $2 + 3 + 3$ to give an overall score of 24. In the figure, directed arrows indicate the direction of cooperation from a slave processor to a master processor, while a processor by itself indicates that it is operating independently. A computer program on a PDP-11 using enumeration took 3.5 hours to get this solution, whereas a program using SDP took about 12 seconds.

Resource Allocation via Maximum Marginal Return

The method of maximum marginal return can be used to solve another version of an allocation problem. The problem considered has been solved by Bellman and Dreyfus [26] using dynamic programming (see also Casti and Carson [27]). Both their method and ours lead to identical (optimal) solutions.

Consider the situation in which both radar and computer resources have to be allocated for use in a hostile environment. We assume that there are five types of radar units that act together in a specific mode of operation. To insure proper system operation, at least one radar of each type is required. Associated with each radar is a fixed amount of computer resource. Moreover, each radar-computer pair has a specified probability of survival (benefit function). The problem is to find an allocation of additional radar units such that the probability of survival is maximized. The allocation

to be made is constrained by upper limits on the computer and radar resources.

Given in Table 5.4 are the radar and computer resources and the radar-computer pair survival probabilities p_i. We choose to set upper limits on the additional radar and computer resources as 104 and 100, respectively. (Care must be taken in the application of the MMR methodology to problems with activities which have differing resource requirements. In general, optimality is not guaranteed unless each activity requires identical resources).

We define x_i to be the number of additional radar-computer pairs of type i in the allocation. Thus, the constraint on radar and computer resources can be written:

$$C_1 = 8x_1 + 9x_2 + 6x_3 + 7x_4 + 8x_5$$
$$\leq 104 \text{ (radar)}$$
$$C_2 = 5x_1 + 4x_2 + 9x_3 + 7x_4 + 7x_5$$
$$\leq 100 \text{ (computer)}$$

In the allocation the survival probability of x_i (additional) radar-computer pairs of type i is:

$$F_i(x_i) = 1 - (1 - p_i)^{x_i + 1}$$

Thus, the probability of at least one of each of the 5 types of radar-computer pairs surviving an attack is:

$$F(x) = \prod_{i=1}^{5} F_i(x_i)$$

We wish to find the values of the x_i that result in a maximum survival probability while satisfying the radar and computer resource constraints. The MMR solution to the problem requires 15 steps; the first three of which are presented below:

Step 1: From Table 5.4 we find:

$$F_1(x_1 = 0) = 0.90$$
$$F_2(x_2 = 0) = 0.75$$
$$F_3(x_3 = 0) = 0.65$$
$$F_4(x_4 = 0) = 0.80$$
$$F_5(x_5 = 0) = 0.85$$

and $F(x) = .30$.

Step 2: We calculate:

$$F_1(x_1 = 1) = 0.99 \Rightarrow F = 0.33; \Delta F = 0.03$$
$$F_2(x_2 = 1) = 0.94 \Rightarrow F = 0.38; \Delta F = 0.08$$
$$F_3(x_3 = 1) = 0.88 \Rightarrow F = 0.40; \Delta F = 0.10$$
$$F_4(x_4 = 1) = 0.96 \Rightarrow F = 0.36; \Delta F = 0.06$$
$$F_5(x_5 = 1) = 0.98 \Rightarrow F = 0.34; \Delta F = 0.04$$

Thus, x_3 is selected as the variable to be incremented:

$$x = (x_1, x_2, x_3, x_4, x_5) = (0,0,1,0,0)$$

Currently, $F(x) = 0.40$.

Step 3: We calculate:

$$F_1(x_1 = 1) = 0.99 \Rightarrow F = 0.44; \Delta F = 0.04$$
$$F_2(x_2 = 1) = 0.94 \Rightarrow F = 0.51; \Delta F = 0.11$$
$$F_3(x_3 = 2) = 0.96 \Rightarrow F = 0.44; \Delta F = 0.04$$
$$F_4(x_4 = 1) = 0.96 \Rightarrow F = 0.48; \Delta F = 0.08$$
$$F_5(x_5 = 1) = 0.98 \Rightarrow F = 0.47; \Delta F = 0.07$$

Thus, since the maximum ΔF is associated with an increment in x_2 the new set of x is: $x = (0,1,1,0,0)$. Also, $F(x) = 0.51$.

A similar procedure, when applied in subsequent steps, leads to the step-by-step result shown in Table 5.5. The final allocation is found to be:

$$x_1 = 2$$
$$x_2 = 3$$
$$x_3 = 4$$
$$x_4 = 3$$
$$x_5 = 2$$

This allocation uses the maximum number of radar resources (104) while using 93 of the possible 100 computer resources. The resulting (maximized) system survival probability is 0.98.

Dynamic Resource Allocation

Many situations to which distributed computers are applied have the characteristic of continually processing streams of input data. In the BMD case, for example, we saw that the different objects constituted a data stream and that each object had to be processed by four software functions. The "static" assignment of processors to each function led to acceptable performance at the expense of processing "overkill." In the present example we will examine the dynamic reassignment of processors to the functions that require them.

The function i, shown in Figure 5.20, has a single input and a single output. The input is such that the function takes equal amounts of time (E_i time units) to complete calculations on the input data (Figure 5.21).

If the time required for i to complete pro-

Table 5.5.

STEP	$i = 1$	$i = 2$	$i = 3$	$i = 4$	$i = 5$	$F(X)$
1	0	0	0	0	0	—
2	0	0	1	0	0	0.40
3	0	1	1	0	0	0.50
4	0	1	1	1	0	0.60
5	0	1	1	1	1	0.69
6	1	1	1	1	1	0.76
7	1	1	2	1	1	0.83
8	1	2	2	1	1	0.88
9	1	2	2	2	1	0.90
10	1	2	3	2	1	0.93
11	1	2	3	2	2	0.95
12	1	3	3	2	2	0.96
13	1	3	4	2	2	0.97
14	2	3	4	3	2	0.98
15	2	3	4	3	2	0.98

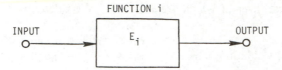

E_i = number of time periods required by function i
to process one object.

Figure 5.20. Typical software function.

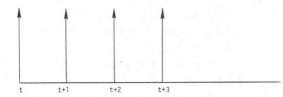

Figure 5.21. Input data sequence to function i.

Figure 5.22. Output data sequence from function i.

cessing a single input is less than the input data rate then the function can keep up with the data. That is, no queue results if $E_i \leq 1$. The output data sequence in such an instance is shown in Figure 5.22. However, if $E_i > 1$ then the function cannot keep up with the processing requests and an infinite queue will build up.

We can now extend our model to C_i identical processors performing function i. We assume that no sharing of computers is allowed, that is, one computer must completely process one input. In this situation an input sequence at rate R can be handled by C_i computers with no queue buildup if $RE_i \leq C_i$. For example, at unit input rate ($R = 1$) a function that requires 2 time units to complete must be assigned at least $RE_i = (1)(2) = 2$ computers to prevent a queue from building up.

A further extension of the model to a series of functions is also possible. In Figure 5.23 is shown a serial arrangement of n functions. For example, the output for function i constitutes the input to function $i + 1$. Here, any function that does not satisfy $RE_i < C_i$ will cause a queue to accumulate and hence will prevent the system from operating at the desired capacity. This is an example of the "bottleneck" principle. In a form similar to this, the processing requirement to prevent a queue from building up is:

$$\text{Min} \left\{ \frac{C_i}{E_i} \right\} \geq R \text{ for all } i \qquad (3)$$

The delay from input to output is:

$$\sum_{i=1}^{n} E_i \qquad (4)$$

An alternative to the case of serial function processing is parallel processing. Shown in Figure 5.24 are n functions arranged in a par-

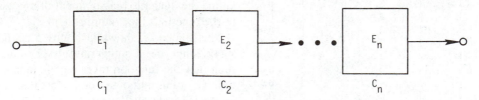

Figure 5.23. Serial functions.

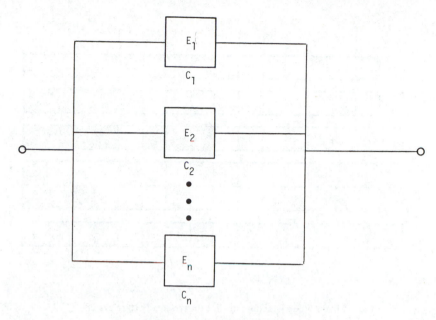

Figure 5.24. Parallel functions.

allel system. Here, the processing requirement to prevent queue buildup is identical to the case for serial functions:

$$\text{Min } \frac{C_i}{E_i} \geq R \text{ for all } i$$

However, the delay to perform all functions is:

$$\text{Max } \{E_i\}. \tag{5}$$

We can now examine a more meaningful example of a set of serial functions of varying requirements. We define a set of five functions such that the times required for execution are:

$$E_i = \tfrac{1}{2} \text{ (time units)}$$
$$E_2 = 1$$
$$E_3 = \tfrac{1}{2}$$
$$E_4 = \tfrac{3}{2}$$
$$E_5 = \tfrac{1}{2}$$

For an input object frequency $R = 1$ we can use (4) to determine the number of processors required to prevent a bottleneck situation. Hence we find:

$$C_1 = 1$$
$$C_2 = 1$$
$$C_3 = 1$$
$$C_4 = 2$$
$$C_5 = 1$$

Thus, a total of 6 processors is needed to satisfy the demands of this steady-state system. This arrangement is shown in Figure 5.25. In Figure 5.26 is shown the timeline for all of the functions. There are five input objects A, B, C, D, and E.

In practical systems the input is not constant. Thus, we can add a degree of realism to our example by perturbing the input. This will be done by increasing the input object rate to

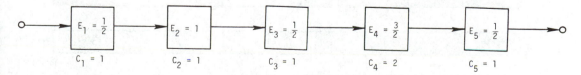

Figure 5.25. Steady-state function assignment.

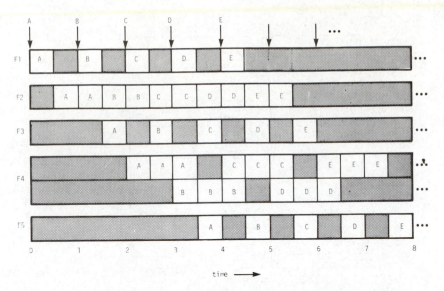

Figure 5.26. Function timeline for the steady-state system.

2 for 2 time units. After this period the rate will return to its original value of 1. The function timelines for the new case are shown in Figure 5.27.

Function timeline for the increased input frequency system.

From the figure it is clear that there is a backlog of objects building up at the second function. In the previous example this function was barely capable of keeping up with the input rate. However, when this rate was increased, a queue built up. From the figure it can be seen that the queue causes a maximum delay of 2 time units. This is due to the fact that the input object rate eventually returns to its lower value of 1 from its temporary value

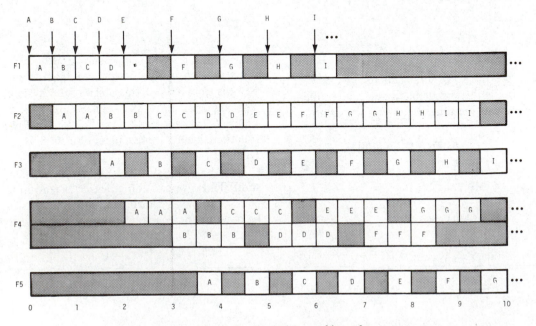

Figure 5.27. Function timeline for the increased input frequency system.

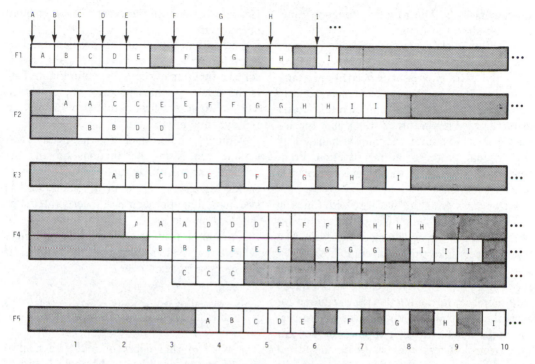

Figure 5.28. Function timeline for the system with two processors at function two.

of 2. If it had not done so, the length of the queue would have continued to grow. Still, the second function is fully taxed and is not capable of reducing the queue, and hence the queue remains for the duration of the system operation. An ad hoc solution to this problem is to make an additional processor available for function 2. This increases the total number of

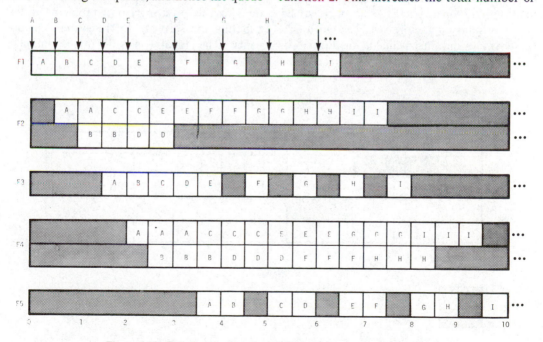

Figure 5.29. Function timeline for the dynamically reconfigured system.

processors to 7. The resulting function timelines are shown in Figure 5.28.

With the extra processor available for function 2 there is no queue build up there. Moreover, the extra processor is needed only temporarily. That is, it is needed only to help
recover from the increased input rate. Shortly
after the rate has returned to normal, the situation is steady state and can be handled by
the original processor at the function. From
this point on ($t > 3$) the second processor is
idle.

However, a problem does arise with function
4. Here, a queue accumulates due to the increased rate at the beginning of the cycle. The
input objects take time to accumulate but, by
$t = 3$ there is a queue. Although the system
recovers by $t = 7$ the net effect of the queue
is to increase the completion time required for
several of the first objects. Hence, system performance is not optimal. The power of the real-
time control of resources can be demonstrated
by realizing the fact that for $t > 3$, the idle
processor associated with function 2 can be dynamically reassigned to function 4. The result
of this is shown in Figure 5.29. The reassignment succeeds in preventing a queue buildup
at function 4 by exactly meeting the excess object computation demands. After the peak load
period has passed, the previously assigned processor is idle and thus available for further ob-

ject reassignment in the event of another input
object spurt.

The critical aspect of this problem (and its
solution) is the allocation of the spare processor as a function of time. Shown in Figure 5.30
is the resulting state space for the processor.
This solution was first obtained by using spatial dynamic programming.

Although the method of dynamically reas-
signing processors to functions on an "as-
needed" basis is conceptually easy, it is, nonetheless, an extremely powerful technique. The
system design approach that incorporates such
methods should result in computing systems
that are more responsive, less costly, and more
reliable than systems based on static or similar
design approaches.

5.5. CONCLUSIONS AND FUTURE OUTLOOK

The birth of the theory of real-time control
was dictated by the technological breakthroughs that permitted computers to evolve
from large single-processor, single-memory
units to systems of many smaller, more flexible
processors and memories. The capability of
constructing such distributed hardware systems resulted in a myriad of problems in distributing the software to the system components. The theory is still in its infancy,

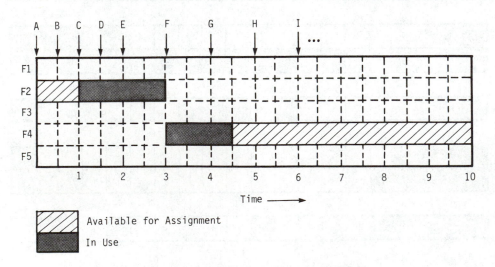

Figure 5.30. State space of the spare processor.

however, and as yet does not provide a standard methodology for either formulating or solving real-time control problems. Rather, problems that arise in the design and development of distributed systems must be handled on an individual basis with the utilization of proper problem-solving techniques. To aid the systems analyst or designer in achieving this goal the preceding sections have presented several of these problems, mathematical tools for attacking them, and examples illustrating their solutions.

Although most of the examples considered in this chapter have been static problems involving distributed systems, the RTC methodologies apply to a far wider range of problems. For example RTC can be applied in centralized systems to optimize scheduling of finite resources. Also, dynamic problems can be decomposed to a series of static problems which can then be solved separately with respect to temporal boundary conditions. Indeed, this particular strategy holds outstanding potential for use in real-time systems where stringent time constraints exist. In these situations, the desire for a rapid resolution of the system assignment may be greater than the need for a total dynamic restructuring of the system assignments. It is precisely for reasons such as these that the need is ever increasing for fast, efficient RTC methodologies.

REFERENCES

1. S. J. Javid, R. E. Larson, and T. L. Steding, "A Systems Theory Approach to Axiomatic Requirements Engineering," *IEEE Computer Society Conference (COMPCON)*, Feb. 1978.
2. R. L. Keeney and H. Raiffa, *Decisions with Multiple Objectives: Preferences and Value Tradeoffs*, Wiley, New York, 1976.
3. M. J. Beckmann and T. C. Koopmans, "Assignment Problems and the Location of Economic Activities," *Econometrica*, vol. 25, pp. 52–76, 1957.
4. P. C. Gilmore, "Optimal and Suboptimal Algorithms for the Quadratic Assignment Problem," *J. Soc. Indus. Appl. Math.*, vol. 10, pp. 305–313, 1962.
5. G. W. Graves and A. B. Whinston, "A New Approach to Discrete Mathematical Programming," *Mgmt. Sci.*, vol. 15, pp. 177–190, 1968.
6. A. G. Doig and A. H. Land, "A Problem of Assignment with Interrelated Costs," *Opnal. Res. Quart.*, vol. 14, pp. 185–199, 1965.
7. S. C. Jaisingh and R. S. Lashkari, "A Heuristic Approach to the Quadratic Assignment Problem," *J. Opl. Res. Soc.*, vol. 31, pp. 845–850, 1980.
8. R. F. Love and J. Y. Wong, "Solving Quadratic Assignment Problems with Rectangular Distances and Integer Programming," *Mgmt. Sci.*, vol. 13, pp. 42–57, 1976.
9. E. L. Lawler, "The Quadratic Assignment Problem," *Mgmt. Sci.*, vol. 9, pp. 586–599, 1963.
10. S. H. Bokhari and H. S. Stone, "Control of Distributed Processes," *Computer*, vol. 11, pp. 97–106, July 1978.
11. H. S. Stone, "Multiprocessor Scheduling with the Aid of Network Flow Algorithms," *IEEE Trans. Software Eng.*, SE-3, pp. 85–94, 1977.
12. T. C. Hu, G. S. Rao and H. S. Stone, "Assignment of Tasks in a Distributed Processor System with Limited Memory," *IEEE Trans. Computers*, vol. C-28, pp. 291–299, 1979.
13. B. Fox, "Discrete Optimization via Marginal Analysis," *Mgmt. Sci.*, vol. 13, pp. 210–216, 1966.
14. M. J. Magazine, G. L. Nemhauser and L. E. Trotter, "When the Greedy Solution Solves a Class of Knapsack Problems," *Opns. Res.*, vol. 23, pp. 207–217, 1975.
15. A. Cohen, "Resource Allocation by Maximum Marginal Return," Systems Control, Inc., Technical Memorandum TM 5164–12, 1977.
16. R. E. Bellman, "On the Computational Solution of Linear Programming Problems Involving Almost-Block-Diagonal Matrices," *Management Science*, vol. 3, no. 4, pp. 403–406, July 1957.
17. G. L. Nemhauser, *Introduction to Dynamic Programming*, Wiley, New York, 1966.
18. U. Bertelé and F. Brioschi, *Nonserial Dynamic Programming*, Academic Press, New York, 1972.
19. H. Mine and K. Ohno, "Decomposition of Mathematical Programming Problems by Dynamic Programming and Its Application to Block-Diagonal Geometric Programs," *J. Math. Anal. Appl.*, vol. 32, pp. 370–385, 1970.
20. M. Fukushima, H. Mine, and K. Ohno, "Multilevel Decomposition of Nonlinear Programming Problems by Dynamic Programming," *J. Math. Anal. Appl.*, vol. 53, pp. 7–27, 1970.
21. Bonzon, "Necessary and Sufficient Conditions for Dynamic Programming of Combinatorial Type," *J. Assoc. Comp. Mach.*, vol. 17, pp. 675–682, 1970.
22. C. Y. Chong, R. E. Larson, and P. L. McEntire, "Decomposition of Mathematical Programming by Dynamic Programming," *Proceedings/Second Lawrence Symposium on Systems and Decision Sciences*, Berkeley, Calif., Oct. 1978.
23. R. E. Larson and P. L. McEntire, "Optimal Resource Allocation in Sparse Networks," Proceedings of IFAC/81, Kyoto, Japan.
24. B. Friedlander, "A Decentralized Strategy for Resource Allocation," *Proceedings/19th IEEE Conference on Decision and Control*, Albuquerque, N.M., Dec. 1980.

25. C. R. Vick, *A Dynamically Reconfigurable Distributed Computing System,* Ph.D. thesis, Auburn University, Dec. 1979.

26. R. Bellman and S. Dreyfus, *Applied Dynamic Programming,* Princeton University Press, Princeton, N.J., 1962.

27. J. L. Casti and R. E. Larson, *Principles of Dynamic Programming,* Marcel Dekker, New York, 1978.

6

Theory of Systems

A. W. Wymore
University of Arizona

6.1. INTRODUCTION

Mathematical system theory is the appropriate basis for software engineering, just as physics is the appropriate basis for classical engineering. Every aspect of software engineering is expressible in system theoretic terms. That many aspects of software engineering have not by now been expressed in system theoretic terms is a comment on the current state of the art of software engineering and of its theoretical basis, not evidence of the impossibility or disutility of applying mathematical system theory to software engineering. It is the objective of this chapter to indicate how the problems of software engineering might be expressible in system theoretic terms and to demonstrate the relevance of mathematical system theory to the problems of software engineering.

For the purpose of the discussions in this chapter, mathematical system theory will mean any rigorous mathematical construct that purports to describe dynamic phenomena in terms of inputs, states, and outputs. The emphasis is on the word *mathematical*. It is the purpose here to limit the discussion only to rigorous mathematical constructs and to exclude any other forms of system theory or levels of detail of system theory. From this point of view, mathematical system theory subsumes the theories and applications of finite-state machines, discrete automata, push down machines, Turing machines, and almost all the classical models of physics and engineering based on differential equations. Included also would be, for examples, statistical mechanics and topological dynamics.

This chapter on the theory of systems will be devoted to two brief sketches, one of an appropriately general mathematical theory of systems and another of a theory of the design of systems based on mathematical system theory. It is in these theoretical contexts that the above assertions concerning the relevance and utility of mathematical system theory to the foundations of software engineering will be found to be valid.

6.2. SYSTEM THEORY

From the wide scope of potential applications for mathematical system theory within software engineering, it is fairly clear that if a common definition of the word *system* in mathematical terms is to be adopted, it cannot be specialized to discrete systems, for the word would not then apply to the systems traditionally studied by means of the theory of differential equations or, generally, to the models of engineering phenomena with which software engineers frequently must deal. Thus, the first issue in defining a system must be to specify the time scale T of the system, whether the time scale is to be represented by the integers, by the set of all real numbers, or by some other set used to model time. Any abstract definition of the word *system* must allow such variability in system definitions. There seems to be little justification, however, to allow as the time scale any but a subset of the set of nonnegative real numbers.

Once the time scale T has been chosen, it is then necessary to consider possibilities for the set P of inputs. Since eligible time scales include discrete time scales represented by subsets of integers, and continuous ones represented by subsets of the set of all real numbers that are topological continua, the idea of an input *trajectory* is also important: a function defined over the time scale T with values in the input set P. When speaking strictly of discrete time automata, many authors do not worry about input trajectories; they talk about input strings without reference to a time scale. But if one is to try to incorporate the idea of input strings into a class of models where input trajectories can be continuous, then it is necessary to attach some sort of a time marking to input strings even in discrete cases. Hence, the idea of an input trajectory is important in every case. Thus far then, in order to define a system, one must choose a time scale T, one must identify the set P of all inputs, and then one must identify the set F of appropriate input trajectories that will be considered.

The next step in defining a system is to identify the set S of states that describe the internal workings of the system. Choice of the set of states must satisfy two criteria, roughly stated as follows:

1. Knowing the state of the system at any time s, say, and the input trajectory between time s and some future time t, then the state of the system at time t must be completely determined by these two factors: the state of the system at time s and the input trajectory between s and t. These two pieces of knowledge must completely and uniquely define the state of the system at time t.
2. Each state of the system must carry the information that is needed or desirable as an output of the system.

Once the set S of states, the set T of time values, the set P of inputs, and the set F of input trajectories have been defined, then it is necessary to define the state transition function z, a function defined over the Cartesian product F $\times$ S $\times$ T with values in S. The interpretation of the value of z at a point (f,x,t) ϵ F $\times$ S $\times$ T is that z(f,x,t) is the state of the system Z at time t given the input trajectory f and the initial state x.

With the definition of z, the fundamental behavior of the system Z has been postulated. Now the set Q of outputs and the readout function ζ that will link the behavior of the system to its output can be defined. In the literature, three principal types of readout functions ζ are postulated. These will be called Mealy [1], Moore [2], and Desoer [3]: A Mealy readout function is defined over the Cartesian product of the set S of states and the set P of inputs; a Moore readout function is defined over the set S of states; a Desoer readout function is defined over the Cartesian product of the set S of states, the set P of inputs, and the set T of time values. Since all three readout functions lead to equivalent theories, it is best to adopt the simplest: the Moore readout function. Furthermore, the Moore readout function is closer to reality in the sense that the only information available about a given real system is some information about its state. Finally, and most persuasively, the Mealy and Desoer readouts inject spurious ambiguity into the study of systems resultant from the coupling of system components through input/output relationships. Such a study must be the principal tool in the development of system design methodologies based on mathematical system theory.

Thus a system can be defined as a 7-tuple, Z = (S,T,P,F,z,Q,ζ), where S is the set of states; T is the time scale; P is the set of inputs; F is the set of input trajectories; z is the state transition function that gives the state of the system at every time value t given the state of the system at time 0, and the input trajectory between 0 and t; Q is the set of outputs; and ζ is the (Moore) readout function.

All the sets involved in the definition just given are arbitrary, except the time scale T and the set F of input trajectories. The time scale T must be some subset of the set R[0, ∞) of nonnegative real numbers. The set F of input trajectories must be a subset of the set F(T,P) of all functions defined over T with values in P.

Usually some consistency conditions and additional structure are required on the various sets and functions involved. For example, the set of input trajectories is usually assumed to be closed under concatenation. That is, if one takes an input trajectory f, follows it by another g at some time value s, then one assumes that the new input trajectory thus obtained is also legitimate for the system. The concatenation of the input trajectories f and g at the point s is denoted *cat*(f,s,g) and defined as follows:

$$(cat(f,s,g))(t) \quad \begin{aligned} &= f(t) \text{ if } t < s \\ &= g(t - s) \text{ if } t \geq s \end{aligned}$$

Furthermore, if independence of the origin of the time scale is to be sought, then it must be assumed that the set of input trajectories is closed under translation of the origin of the time scale. If f is an input trajectory and s is a time value, then the translation of f to the point s is denoted $f \rightarrow s$ and is defined as follows: $(f \rightarrow s)(t) = f(s + t)$. These conditions imply, one way or another, some other aspects of the structure of the time scale, again, some closure properties: if s and t are time scale members, then s + t is a member of the time scale T; if both s and t are positive and s is less than t, then t − s is also an element of the time scale.

Consistency requirements on the class of system models usually devolve around the state transition function z. One requires that the state of the system at time 0 be the initial state of the system. This has to be postulated; that is, if f is any input trajectory and x is any state, then z(f,x,0) is equal to x. Another consistency requirement usually demanded is called the semigroup property; it simply says that if s and t are time values, and if the state of the system at time s, z(f,x,s), is determined by an input trajectory f and an initial state x, and one performs a new experiment on the system starting at time 0 with the system in the state z(f,x,s) and continues the input f where the first experiment left off at time s, now denoted $f \rightarrow s$ on the time scale of the new experiment, then at time t one would arrive at the state z(f → s,z(f,x,s),t) of the system, and one insists that this state be the same as the state z(f,x,s + t) that the system would have arrived at had one allowed the first experiment to continue to time s + t. The final consistency condition that

is usually demanded is the nonanticipatory requirement: the state of the system at time t cannot depend upon inputs at or after time t nor inputs before time 0. This requirement is usually expressed as follows: if f and g are two input trajectories that agree between 0 and t, then they determine the same state at time t given the same state at time 0, that is, if *res*(f,T[0,t)) = *res*(g,T[0,t)), then z(f,x,t) = z(g,x,t) for every x ϵ S.

In the literature of computer science (see for examples, Refs. 4 and 5), the systems involved are characterized as finite-state machine, discrete automata, Turing machines, and push down machines. All of these can be fitted into the definition of system given above. In almost all of these constructs, it is assumed that the set F of input trajectories is the set *F*(T,P) of all functions defined over the time scale T with values in the set P and that the state transition function is characterized by a next-state function ν such that for any input trajectory f, initial state x, and time t, the state transition function z is defined as follows:

$$z(f,x,t)$$
$$= x \text{ if } t = 0;$$
$$= \nu(z(f,x,t - 1),f(t - 1)) \text{ if } t \neq 0.$$

The next-state function ν within the system definition given above, can be characterized as follows: if x ϵ S, and p ϵ P, then $\nu(x,p) = z(con(p),x,1)$ where *con*(p) is the constant input trajectory equal everywhere to p. This ν is a function defined over S X P with values in S, which is the basic idea of the next state function.

It is shown in Reference 6 that any discrete automaton can be represented as a system in the definition given above, that any sequential machine can be represented as a system, that Turing machines can also be so represented, and that phenomena definable by systems of differential equations can be included in the system theoretic definition given above with a continuous scale. When subsequent use is made here of the word *system*, a system theoretic model or a mathematical construct, as defined above, is meant. The discussion here is concerned almost exclusively with the manipulation of mathematical models of systems for design purposes. The reader who prefers to think more concretely may visualize a computer simulation of a real system and computer runs of the simulation when the text here speaks of system and manipulations of a system, or experiments on a system. Even more concretely, but perhaps somewhat more dangerously, the reader may visualize a real system with which he is familiar when the text speaks of a system. The source of the danger is that there are real differences between a system theoretic model and a real system. Operationally, within the discussion, the most important difference is that with respect to system theoretic models, it can be assumed that the discussants are omniscient and, at least intellectually, omnipotent: It is possible to see and to know everything there is to see and know about system theoretic models throughout their lifetime, and manipulate them arbitrarily. This assumption is unacceptable and invalid for real systems.

Further basic concepts that will be discussed hereafter are those associated with the names of input port, output port, coupling recipe, resultant of a coupling recipe, subsystem, homomorphism, isomorphism, and simulation.

In the complex system theoretic models that one encounters in software engineering, the inputs to a given system may not be of a single kind; there may be system models that accept inputs of several different kinds, and the inputs may arrive simultaneously and independently from different sources in the overall system of which the given system is a component. Such a situation gives rise to the concept of an input port. The set P of inputs of a system then might be a Cartesian product of several input ports, indicating that there are different kinds of inputs to the system that make up the total set of inputs to the system.

For example, a system Z may have three input ports each denoted with an unique symbol, say, A^1, A^2, and A^3, all of which might accept the same set of inputs or each of which might accept a different set: Say, at A^1 only elements of the set $\{0,1\}$ are acceptable, at A^2 any integer is acceptable, and at A^3 any real number is acceptable. Then the input port

structure of Z might be defined as follows: $P = A^1 \times A^2 \times A^3$ where $A^1 = \{0,1\}$, $A^2 = I$, and $A^3 = R$. If $p = (0, -4, \sqrt{2})$, then $p \in P$.

Projection funtions over Cartesian products are denoted consistently by the symbol π with the appropriate subscripts or by the symbol π followed by appropriate specifications in parenthesis as the following examples adequately exhibit: if $p \in P = A^1 \times A^2 \times A^3$ and $p = (0, -4, \sqrt{2})$, then

$$\pi_2(p) = (\pi(A^2))(p) = -4$$
$$\pi_{2,3}(p) = (\pi(\{A^2, A^3\}))(p) = (-4, \sqrt{2})$$

Similar conventions are established to define output ports and the output port structure of the system Z. For example, the output port structure of the system Z might be defined as follows: $Q = B^1 \times B^2$ where $B^1 = B^2 = R$. The set of input ports of Z is denoted $IP(Z)$ and is defined as the set of sets of which P is the Cartesian product. The set of output ports of Z is denoted $OP(Z)$ and is defined as the set of sets of which Q is the Cartesian product. One of the reasons that this kind of description is important is to allow the detailed and precise description of input/output relationships among system components of an overall resultant system.

The mathematical construct that corresponds to the familiar block diagram cartoon of interconnected systems is the coupling recipe. A coupling recipe is a pair $K = (Z, k)$, where Z is a connectable set of systems and k is a connectivity function for Z. The set Z is a connectable set of systems: Z is not empty, and every element is a system; all the systems in Z have the same time scale; no two systems in Z have a common input port symbol or a common output port symbol. The connectivity function k has the following properties: it is a 1-to-1 function; its domain is a subset of the set of all input ports of the component systems in Z; its range is a subset of the set of all output ports of the system components in Z; if (A,B) is an element of k where A is an input port of a system Z' in Z and B is an output port of a system Z'' in Z, then A and B have to be symbols for the same set; that is, the set of elements acceptable to the system Z' at the input port A must be the same as the set of outputs eligible to be produced by the system Z'' at its output port B. The set of input ports that are in the domain of the connectivity function k are called the occupied input ports; similarly, the output ports that are in the range of the connectivity function k are the occupied output ports. Those input ports that are not in the domain of the connectivity function k are said to be unoccupied and denoted $UI(K)$. Unoccupied output ports are similarly defined and similarly denoted: $UO(K)$.

The coupling recipe K is conjunctive provided the connectivity function is empty—there are no interconnections between the components. If K is a conjunctive coupling recipe then the system resultant Z^Z determined by K is particularly easy to define: If $Z = \{Z^1, \ldots, Z^n\}$, then S^Z is the Cartesian product of the sets of states of the components, $S^Z = S^1 \times \ldots \times S^n$; the time scale T^Z of Z^Z is the same as for any component system in Z; the set of input ports of Z^Z is simply the union of the sets of input ports of the system components: $IP(Z^Z) = U \{IP(Z'): Z' \in Z\}$; the set F^Z of input trajectories of Z^Z is determined by the Cartesian product of the sets of input trajectories of the system components, $F^Z = \{f: f \in F(T^Z, P^Z);$ there exists $g \in F^1 \times \ldots \times F^n$ such that if $Z^i \in Z$ and $A \in IP(Z^i)$, then $\pi(A) \circ f = \pi(A) \circ \pi_i (g)\}$; the state transition function z^Z of Z^Z is defined as if each component transforms independently: $\pi_i(z^Z(f,x,t)) = z^i(\pi(IP(Z^i)) \circ f, \pi_i(x), t)$; the set of output ports of Z^Z is the union of the sets as output ports of the system components, $OP(Z^Z) = U \{OP(Z^1): Z' \in Z\}$; the readout function of ζ^Z of Z^Z is simply the readout function that is obtained by reading out each individual component, independently: $\zeta^Z = \{(x,q): z \in S^Z; q \in Q^Z;$ if $Z' \in Z$ and $B \in OP(Z')$, then $\pi(B)(q) = \pi(B) (\zeta'(\pi(Z')(x)))\}$. Note that any coupling recipe can determine a conjunctive coupling recipe by simply using the same set of components with an empty connectivity function. Thus, associated with each coupling recipe is the conjunction of the components as if they were not connected.

When the systems are interconnected it be-comes difficult to deduce directly what the inputs to occupied input ports actually must be under operating conditions. This difficulty leads to the postulation of a coupling function κ associated with a coupling recipe K. The coupling function κ determines, as a function of the input trajectory supplying unoccupied input ports and the initial state of the resultant, what is going into each input port of any system component in the coupling recipe *under the connectivity conditions*. Ordinarily, for a given input trajectory f supplying unoccupied input ports and an initial state x of the resultant, the input trajectory $\kappa(f,x)$ supplying all the input ports is determined by solving a set of equations.

Coupling recipes can be defined for which the coupling function does not exist and for which the coupling function is not unique. All such pathological cases have continuous time scales. If all the systems in Z are discrete, then the coupling function exists and can be defined uniquely, recursively.

In terms of a coupling function κ, a system Z^* can be defined that is the resultant of the coupling recipe K under nontrivial coupling conditions. The set S^* of states Z^* is the same as the set of states of the conjunction of the systems in Z, $S^* = S^Z$; the time scale T^* is the same as the time scale of the conjunction, $T^* = T^Z$; the set of input ports of Z^* is the set of unoccupied input ports $IP(Z^*) = UI(K)$; the set F^* of input trajectories is the projection of the set of input trajectories of Z^Z on the unoccupied input ports, $F^* = \pi(UI(K)) \circ F^Z$; the state transition $z^*(f,x,t)$ of the resultant, with input f into the unoccupied input ports, initial state x, at time t, is the same as the state transition $z^Z(\kappa(f,x),x,t)$ of the conjunction with input trajectory $\kappa(f,x)$, initial state x, at time t; the set of output ports of the resultant is simply the set of unoccupied output ports $OP(Z^*) = UO(K)$; and the readout function ζ^* for the resultant is the projection on the unoccupied output ports following the readout function of the conjunction, $\zeta^* = \pi(UO(J)) \circ \zeta^Z$. The fact that Z^* is the resultant of K will be denoted $Z^* = RES(K)$.

The coupling recipe K is said to be regular if there exists a coupling function κ for Z that is unique. It can be proved that the system resultant always exists and is unique for regular coupling recipes. Coupling recipes with discrete components are regular.

Consider the cartoon of a coupling recipe given in Figure 6.1. Here, three system components Z^1, Z^2, and Z^3 are to be interconnected by I/O relationships. The sets of input ports of the three system components are: $IP(Z^1) = \{A^{11}, A^{12}\}$, $IP(Z^2) = \{A^{21}, A^{22}, A^{23}\}$, $IP(Z^3) = \{A^{31}, A^{32}, A^{33}, A^{34}\}$, and the sets of output ports are: $OP(Z^1) = \{B^{11}, B^{12}, B^{13}\}$, $OP(Z^2) = \{B^{21}, B^{22}\}$, $OP(Z^3) = \{B^{31}, B^{32}, B^{33}\}$. To complete the definitions of the input port structures and the output port structures, specific set assignments would have to be defined for A^{11}, Z^{12}, A^{21}, . . . , A^{34} and B^{11}, B^{12}, B^{13}, B^{21}, . . . , B^{33}.

A formal coupling recipe K corresponding to the cartoon of Figure 6.1 is defined as follows: $K = (Z,k)$ where $Z = \{Z^1, Z^2, Z^3\}$, $k = \{(A^{11}, B^{32}), (A^{21}, B^{31}), (A^{22}, B^{11}), (A^{23}, B^{12}), (A^{31}, B^{22}), A^{32}, B^{13})\}$. Completion of K would require that for each $i \in I[1,3]$, Z^i be defined in the form $Z^i = (S^i, T^i, P^i, F^i, z^i, Q^i, \zeta^i)$ where each artifact is defined explicitly.

If the component systems in Z are all discrete, then the resultant system Z^* is discrete and defined as follows: $Z^* = RES(K)$, $S^* = S^1 \times S^2 \times S^3$, $T^* = I[0,\infty)$, $IP(Z^*) = \{A^{11}, A^{33}, A^{34}\}$, $F^* = F(T^*, P^*)$, $OP(Z^*) = \{B^{21}, B^{33}\}$, the readout function ζ^* is defined by projections on output ports as follows: $\pi(B^{21}) \circ \zeta^* = \pi(B^{21}) \circ \zeta^2 \circ \pi_2$, and $\pi(B^{33}) \circ \zeta^* = \pi(B^{33}) \circ \zeta^3 \circ \pi_3$; the next state function ν^* is also defined by projections on state components as follows: if $x = (x_1, x_2, x_3) \in P^*$ and $p = (p_{12}, p_{33}, p_{34}) \in P^*$, then

$$\pi_1(\nu^*(x,p)) = \nu^1(x_1, ((\pi(B^{32}))(\zeta^3(x_3)), p_{12}))$$
$$\pi_2(\nu^*(x,p)) = \nu^2(x_2, ((\pi(B^{31}))(\zeta^3(x_3)),$$
$$(\pi(B^{11}))(\zeta^1(x_1)), (\pi(B^{12}))(\zeta^1(x_1))))$$
$$\pi_3(\nu^*(x,p)) = \nu^3(x_3, ((\pi(B^{22}))(\zeta^2(x_2)),$$
$$(\pi(B^{13}))(\zeta^1(x_1)), p_{33}, p_{34}))$$

Although these expressions are complicated in appearance, all they really say (very precisely, to be sure) is that each coordinate of the next state of the resultant is determined by the next-state function of the corresponding com-

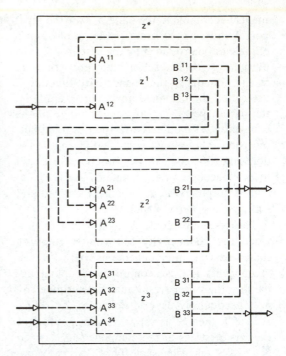

Figure 6.1. Caricature of a computer recipe.

ponent evaluated at the present state of the component and the present input to the component under the coupling conditions. Thus, for example, the present input to the Z^3 component under the coupling conditions is expressed as follows: at the input port A^{31} is the output of Z^2 from its output port B^{22}, namely, $(\pi(B^{22}))(\zeta^2(x_2))$; at the input port A^{32} is the output of Z^1 from its output port B^{13}, namely, $(\pi(B^{13}))(\zeta^1(x_1))$; at the input port A^{33} and A^{34} are the inputs from outside Z^*, namely, p_{32} and p_{34}, respectively.

The concepts of coupling recipes and their resultants are of utmost importance for the applications of mathematical system theory to the problems of software engineering, for these concepts are central (implicitly in the present state of the art) to the processes of modeling, simulation, design, and development of software and the design and management of organizations to produce software.

If Z^* is the resultant of a coupling recipe ($K = (Z,k)$, then each system in Z is said to be both a component of K and a component of Z^*. The components of a computer system interconnected by I/O relationships might be considered to be the hardware boxes: mainframe, operator's console, tape drives, discs, and so forth, or, the operating system, compilers, subroutines and so forth, in a software system.

The idea of subsystem of a system is distinct from the idea of component. A subsystem of a real system is usually generated by restricting the input in some way, and such a subsystem is called a mode of operation. For example, a software package can be designed to operate in a routine mode for most inputs and then to exit into an exceptional mode for exceptional inputs. From the system theoretic point of view these modes might be characterized as the routine subsystem and the exceptional subsystem.

Formally, a system Z^1 is a subsystem of a system Z^2 if S^1 is a subset of S^2, T^1 is a subset of T^2, P^1 is a subset of P^2, F^1 is a subset of the set of restrictions of input trajectories of Z^2 to T^1, if (f^1,x,t) is an element of $F^1 \times S^1 \times T^1$, then there exists f^2 in F^2, such that the restriction of f^2 to T^1 is f^1, and $z^1(f^1,x,t)$ is $z^2(f^2,x,t)$, Q^1 must be a subset of Q^2 and ζ^1 must be the restriction of ζ^2 to S^1.

Note that the component concept is an entirely different relationship than the subsystem relationship given in the above definition. The system components of Z^* are not subsystems of Z^* except in trivial cases, nor are subsystems of Z^* components of Z^*. The common parlance of software engineering tends to obscure this difference between components and subsystems.

Two systems Z^1 and Z^2 are essentially the same system if the time scales, T^1 and T^2, the sets F^1 and F^2 of input trajectories, the sets S^1 and S^2 of states, and the sets Q^1 and Q^2 of outputs are (pairwise) equivalent as sets, and the state and output behaviors of the systems Z^1 and Z^2 are the same given the equivalence of the set artifacts. These heuristics are transformed into a formal definition as follows: The system Z^1 is isomorphic to the system Z^2 if and only if there exist mappings ρ, μ, θ, and λ such that each is 1-to-1, ρ maps T^1 *onto* T^2; μ maps F^1 *onto* F^2 such that $\mu(f \rightarrow s) = \mu(f) \rightarrow \rho(s)$ and $\mu(cat(f,s,g)) = cat(\mu(f),\rho(s),\mu(g))$ for every $f\epsilon F^1$, $g\epsilon F^1$, and $s\epsilon T^1$; θ maps S^1 *onto* S^2 such that $\theta(z^1(f,s,t)) = z^2(\mu(f),\theta(x),\rho(t))$ for every $(f,x,t)\epsilon F^1 \times S^1 \times T^1$; and λ maps Q^1 *onto* Q^2 such that $\lambda \circ \zeta^1 = \zeta^2 \circ \theta$.

If the mappings ρ, μ, θ, and λ are not 1-to-1 then Z^2 is said to be a homomorphic image of Z^1. In this case, Z^2 is thought of as a simplification of Z^1. If a flow diagram, a corresponding FORTRAN program, and the compiled machine-language program are modeled respectively as systems Z^1, Z^2, and Z^3, then Z^1 must be a homomorphic image of Z^2, and Z^2 must be a homomorphic image of Z^3, if the FORTRAN programming and compiling have been done correctly.

The concept of simulation will be defined here as a relationship between system models as opposed to common parlance that refers to simulation as a relationship between a computer program and a real system. Suppose Z^{real} represents the real system, and Z^r is a system theoretic model of Z^{real}, Z^c is a system theoretic model of the computer, and Z^s is Z^c operating under control of a program written to simulate Z^{real}. Then Z^s must be a subsystem of Z^c, and Z^c can be said to simulate Z^{real} only if Z^r is a homomorphic image of Z^s. The real system cannot be part of this definition because it is outside the theory but is represented inside the theory by Z^r.

Generally, then, a system Z^1 simulates a system Z^2 if there is a subsystem Z^{1s} of Z^1 of which Z^2 is a homomorphic image.

6.3. SYSTEM DESIGN THEORY

On the basis of the mathematical theory of systems sketched above, a mathematical theory of system design is propounded. The theory that will be sketched is called in Reference 7 the tricotyledon theory of system design (T3SD). The central notion of T3SD is that of a system design problem. A system design problem is a 6-tuple, $P = (X,T,\alpha,\beta,\gamma,D)$, where X is an I/O specification, T is a technology, α is a merit ordering over the I/O cotyledon, β is a merit ordering over the technology cotyledon, γ is a merit ordering over the feasibility cotyledon that is a tradeoff (T/O) between the feasibility extensions of α and β, and D is a system test plan. Each of these terms will be defined and discussed briefly.

An I/O specification is itself a 6-tuple $X = (V,X,G,Y,H,\eta)$ where V is the time scale of the I/O specification X; X is called the set of inputs; G is a set of input trajectories defined over V with values in X; Y is the set of outputs; H is a set of output trajectories defined over V with values in Y; and η is a function defined over G whose values are subsets of H; that is, η matches with each given input trajectory g the set of all output trajectories that might, or could be, or are eligible to be, produced by *some* systems experiencing the given input trajectory g as input.

As with systems, the set X of inputs of the I/O specification X and the set Y of outputs of the I/O specification X can have an input port structure and an output port structure, respectively. Thus, the I/O specification X has the set $IP(X)$ of input ports and the set $OP(X)$ of output ports.

The I/O specification is intended to be a technology-free statement of the basic reason for existence of the system, establishing the input/output boundaries of the system, describing the inputs that the system is designed to handle and the outputs that the system is designed to produce. For example, an I/O specification for a transportation system might include as inputs the desires of people to travel from one point to another but would not include the inputs of fuel and spare parts. Fuel and spare parts are necessary inputs for certain types of implementations but are not the inputs that the system is designed to manage.

An I/O specification is not a system, but it determines the set of all systems that satisfy the I/O specification. A system satisfies an I/O specification X if the system accepts as input any input trajectory of X and produces an output trajectory consistent with X. Formally, a system Z satisfies the I/O specification X if there is a state y of Z and some subset U not empty of the time scale T of Z, such that for every input trajectory g in G, one of those that is defined as part of the I/O specification X, there is an output trajectory h in H, one of those output trajectories matched with g by η such that the output trajectory generated by Z, started in the state y, experiencing the input trajectory g, will agree with the values of the output trajectory h over the time set U. That is, $\zeta(z(g,y,t)) = h(t)$ for every $t \in U$.

The I/O cotyledon generated by the I/O

specification X is denoted $C(X)$ and is the set of all triples of the form (Z,y,U) where Z is a system that satisfies X with respect to the initial state y over the time subscale U. The I/O cotyledon consists of all systems that are essentially functional solutions of the problem. These systems accept the proper kind of inputs and produce the proper kind of outputs but may not be implementable in any technology. The concept of a technology is needed, therefore, to represent what is available to build solutions to the problem.

A technology is any set not empty of systems. The role played by the technology T in a system design problem is to represent the set of models of components that are available on the shelf to build the system which will be a solution to the problem. A system Z is buildable in a technology T if Z is a resultant of a coupling recipe K with respect to a coupling function κ of K, where all the components of K are in the technology T. The technology cotyledon is denoted $C(T)$ and is the set of all triples, (Z,K,κ) where Z is a system buildable in T with respect to K and κ.

Thus, the dichotomy between ends and means is clearly established and corresponding issues distinguished in T3SD. The I/O specification X and the I/O cotyledon $C(X)$ represent the ends that the system is to serve. The technology T and the associated technology cotyledon $C(T)$ represent the means that are available to solve the problem.

Now it is necessary to postulate some relationship between the systems that satisfy the I/O specification X, that is, systems that are functional solutions of the problem, and systems that are builable in the technology, that is, systems that are acceptable solutions to the problem in the sense of existing technology. The appropriate relationship is called implementability. A system Z is *implementable* in a technology T if there is some system Z^r that is buildable in the technology T that simulates Z. If Z is a system in the I/O cotyledon and Z^r is a system in the technology cotyledon, then Z^r is an implementation of Z provided that Z^r simulates Z.

On the basis of this notion of implementability, the feasibility cotyledon is defined. The assertion of an implementation relationship between a system Z in the I/O cotyledon and a system Z^r in the technology cotyledon requires eleven parameters: the system Z, an initial state y, and a time subscale U, the system Z^r, that is the resultant of a coupling recipe K with respect to the coupling function κ, and five additional parameters for the simulation assertion, namely, a subsystem Z^s of Z^r of which Z is a homomorphic image with respect to mappings ρ, μ, θ, and λ. Thus, the feasibility cotyledon generated by the I/O specification X and the technology T is denoted $C(X, T)$ and is defined as the set of all 11-tuples, $(Z, y, U, Z^r, K, \kappa, \rho, \mu, \theta, \lambda)$ where $(Z, y, U) \epsilon C(X)$, $(Z^r, K, \kappa) \epsilon C(T)$ and Z^r simulates Z with respect to the subsystem Z^s of Z^r, the time scale mapping ρ, the input trajectory mapping μ, the state mapping θ, and the output mapping λ.

Thus, three cotyledons are determined: (1) the I/O cotyledon, (2) the technology cotyledon, and (3) the feasibility cotyledon. These are essentially structural relationships among classes of systems. Within this context, to design a system means to choose a point in the feasibility cotyledon. If this point has the form $(Z, y, U, Z^r, K, \kappa, Z^s, \rho, \mu, \theta, \lambda)$, then Z represents the chosen functional solution to the problem in the sense of I/O performance, Z^r represents the system that implements Z in the technology T, and K can be regarded as a set of blueprints that shows how to build Z^r in the real world; K shows which components (Z) to procure and how to connect them together (k). The parameters Z^s, ρ, μ, θ, and λ specify the relation between Z and Z^r. The system Z^r also represents utilization of real-world resources.

The selection of a point in the feasibility cotyledon might be accomplished by choosing a point (Z, y, U) in the I/O cotyledon on the basis of preferred I/O performance and an implementation Z^r of Z in the technology cotyledon on the basis of preferred utilization of resources. All these choices should be made optimally, if possible. The notions of preferability and optimality imply the possibility of comparison: comparison of elements, pairwise, in the I/O, technology and feasibility cotyledons. Such comparisons are usually made on the basis of figures of merit. In the I/O coty-

ledon, typical figures of merit are: expected speed of service, expected quality of service, expected amount of service, probability of providing service, efficiency of service, and so forth, whatever the service might be that the system is to perform. Any figure of merit definable in terms of the inputs and outputs specified by the I/O specification can be utilized. In the technology cotyledon, typical figures of merit are: capital investment requirements, operating and maintenance costs, life cycle costs, expected energy consumption, expected air, water, noise and esthetic pollution, expected time of development, reliability, and so forth, any figure of merit that represents utilization of resources (U/R) in designing, developing and running the system. Typical figures of merit in the feasibility cotyledon are: expected profit, expected benefit/cost, and any of a large class of possible relationships between the I/O and U/R figures of merit.

Given two systems Z^1 and Z^2 in the I/O, technology, or feasibility cotyledons, one computes or estimates the values of the appropriate figures of merit for each system and decides, somehow, which system is preferred or that the systems are equivalent, or that the systems are not comparable. Ideally, the decision maker follows a prescribed algorithm in making the comparison. In T3SD, in a complete statement of the problem of the design of a system, such algorithms are required to be stated explicitly. Mathematically, the algorithms are represented by (partial) orderings over the three cotyledons.

An ordering over an arbitrary set E is a function υ defined over E^2, the set of pairs of elements of E, with values in the set $\{0,1\}$ of only two elements. It is required that υ be reflexive, $\upsilon(a,a) = 1$, and transitive, $\upsilon(a,b) = \upsilon(b,c) = 1$ implies $\upsilon(a,c) = 1$. Then the following conventions are established: $a \underset{\upsilon}{\leq} b$ if $\upsilon(a,b) = 1$; $a \underset{\upsilon}{<} b$ if $\upsilon(a,b) = 1$ and $\upsilon(b,a) = 0$; $a \underset{\upsilon}{\cong} b$ if $\upsilon(a,b) = \upsilon(b,a) = 1$; a *not* $\underset{\upsilon}{} b$ if $\upsilon(a,b) = \upsilon(b,a) = 0$.

T3SD requires an ordering α to be defined over the I/O cotyledon, an ordering β to be defined over the technology cotyledon, and an ordering γ to be defined over the feasibility cotyledon. The orderings α and β can be defined arbitrarily in terms of figures of merit as indicated above. Both α and β have extensions to the feasibility cotyledon because every element v in the feasibility cotyledon has projections on both the I/O and technology cotyledons: if $v = (Z,y,U,Z^r,K,\kappa,Z^s,\rho,\mu,\theta,\lambda)$ then π $(C(X))(v) = (Z,y,U) \epsilon C(X)$ and $\pi(C(T))(v)$ $= (Z^r,K,\kappa) \epsilon C(T)$, and the feasibility extensions $\overline{\alpha}$ and $\overline{\beta}$, of α and β, respectively, are defined as follows for $(v^1,v^2)\epsilon(C(X,T)^2)$: $\overline{\alpha}(v^1,v^2) = \alpha(\pi(C(X)) (v^1), \pi(C(X))(v^2))$; $\overline{\beta}(v^1,v^2) = \beta(\pi(C(T))(v^1), \pi(C(T))(v^2))$.

The ordering γ over the feasibility cotyledon $C(X,T)$, determined by an I/O specification X and a technology T, must be defined in such a way to represent the comparison of elements in the feasibility cotyledon based on a tradeoff (T/O) between I/O performance, represented by α, and the utilization of resources (U/R), as represented by β. The ordering γ is a tradeoff between orderings $\overline{\alpha}$ and $\overline{\beta}$, if and only if: if $\overline{\alpha}(a,b) \times \overline{\beta}(a,b) = 1$ and $\overline{\alpha}(b,a) \times \overline{\beta}(b,a) = 0$, then $\gamma(a,b) = 1$ and $\gamma(b,a) = 0$; or, to put it another way, if $a < b$, then $a < b$. Check

$$\overline{\alpha}\times\overline{\beta} \qquad \gamma$$

that the classical tradeoffs, profit and benefit/ cost, satisfy this condition.

In general, and intuitively, to design a system means to develop a model from which a real system can be built. Traditionally, the models involved have been oral descriptions or sketches or blueprints or some other kind of model that is acceptable to people who construct or develop physical objects. In the case of the design of large-scale, complex, man/ machine systems including software systems, the models must be at the same time more powerful and more precise; T3SD requires system theoretic models.

After a system is designed in the T3SD context, that is, a point v* has been selected in the feasibility cotyledon, then, if the models in T (or more specifically, in Z^*) have been developed appropriately to represent current (or foreseeable) technology, a real system, denoted Z^{real}, can be built. Thus, the end item of the system design process is a real system Z^{real} that is actually constructed, developed, deployed, or otherwise brought into existence, in operational form, on the basis of the element v* = $(Z^*,y^*,U^*,Z^{r*},K^*,\kappa^*, Z^{s*}, \rho^*,\mu^*,\theta^*,\lambda^*)$, in the feasibility cotyledon $C(X,T)$, where the coupling recipe K^* plays the role of production blueprints specifying how the real system is to be constructed from the set Z^* of system components in the technology T. It is a plan for testing this system Z^{real} that must be included in the statement of the problem of the design of Z^{real}.

Recall that a system design problem is a 6-tuple, $P = (X,T,\alpha,\beta,\gamma,D)$, where D is the system test plan. That D should be a part of the statement of the problem of the design of a system is a crucial point, especially when the merit orderings α, β, and γ may be defined in terms of figures of merit having precise mathematical definitions, but somewhat imprecise operational definitions. For example, one might define a figure of merit for systems in the technology cotyledon as the portability of software packages from one computer to another. Now, mathematically, the figure of merit representing portability can be defined as a number between 0 and 1; such a definition is valid and easy to manipulate in abstract fashion. But given a real software package, how does one actually determine what the value of the portability figure of merit is for that software package? This question might be answered operationally in several ways: One might convene a panel of experts to study the software package and ask each expert to assign a number between 0 and 1 to the package representing the degree of portability of the package; one could then use the average of the estimates as the value of the figure of merit (or one could use some more sophisticated methodology to extract a group estimate). At the other extreme, one could define a series of controlled experiments involving teams of programmers chosen at random installing the package on different computers chosen at random. Thus, if portability is an important figure of merit for a system design problem involving software packages, then the way in which portability of the packages is actually to be tested might make a difference to the way the system would be designed.

The structure of the system test plan is developed in the following context: The point v* in the feasibility cotyledon has been chosen as the desirable design of the system, a development team has taken the coupling recipe $K^* = (Z^*,k^*)$ and selected from the shelf or developed various hardware and software packages specified by Z^* and put them together according to k^* to arrive at the real system Z^{real}. There is no way that the theory being developed here can incorporate formally, mathematically, in the same discussion, system theoretic models and real systems composed of human beings, software and hardware in the real world. Therefore, the real system Z^{real} that has been built on the basis of a chosen design v* will also be represented in the theory being developed here by a system theoretic model denoted typically Z^{real}.

The components that have been used to build Z^{real} are in one-to-one correspondence with the components used to define Z^{r*}, the implementation of Z^* in the technology T. It can be assumed that the only difference between the components (as system theoretic models) that are used to build Z^{real} and the components (in Z^*) used to define Z^{r*} is that the state transitions of the components of Z^{real} might be different from the state transitions of the components of Z^{r*}. Otherwise, it can be assumed that states, input ports, output ports, and all other artifacts of the components of Z^{real} and the components of Z^{r*} can be precisely identified by means of some sort of an engineering manual which points out, for example, places in hardware corresponding to input ports and different aggregations of measurements, observations, and readings that constitute an observation of the state in the real system.

Thus, the concept of testable system representation is propounded. A system Z^1 is a testable system representation of a system Z^2 if everything about Z^1 and Z^2 is exactly the same, with the possible exception of the state transition function. A system Z^1 is a testable *component* representation of a system Z^2 if both Z^1 and Z^2 are resultants of coupling recipes K^1 and K^2, in which Z^1 and Z^2 are equivalent sets, such that corresponding pairs consisting of one system component from Z^1 and a system component Z^2 are testable system representations. It will be assumed that Z^{real} is a testable component representation of Z^{r*}.

When testing actually begins further downstream in the system design and development cycle, the situation at that time will be that a point v* in the feasibility cotyledon will have been chosen. If a system Z^{real} will have been built on the basis of a coupling recipe K^{real} whose set Z^{real} of components is equivalent with respect to a mapping e to the set Z^* of components of the coupling recipe K^*, such that if $Z^2 \epsilon Z^{real}$ and $Z^2 = e(Z^1) \epsilon Z^*$, then Z^1 is a testable system representation of Z^2. Testing can take place for each collection of such artifacts, namely, a point v* in the feasibility cotyledon, a system Z^{real} that is a testable component representation of the buildable system artifact Z^{r*} of v*. Testing can consist of any combination of manipulation of Z^{real} or, through simulation studies, of the model Z^{r*} or of Z^*, itself. A feasible test item is a quadruple $(v^*,Z^{real},K^{real},e)$.

Traditionally, there are three testing functions: performance testing, conformance testing, and acceptance testing. These are all terminal types of tests to be performed on the system that is built at the end of the system design and development cycle. There is no attempt here to formalize interim testing which may be essential to the development of technological components or thought to be desirable during the design or development cycle itself. What is being formalized here is the client's idea of what the system is to do and how it is to be tested, in order, in some measure, to help clarify operationally more abstract concepts that went into the definition of the I/O specification X, the technology T, and the merit orderings, α, β, and γ.

In the area of performance testing it is possible to decide that the performance of Z^{real} is or is not acceptable: that is, the outcome could be simply *go* or *nogo*. That is a traditional testing outcome. Think of an inspector testing widgets as they pass his station on a conveyor belt. The inspector may simply pick up a widget, apply to it a *go* or *nogo* kind of device, and either allow the widget to continue to its next station or discard it at that point. Frequently, however, it is desirable to have more detailed information about the performance of the system as the outcome of performance testing. The performance of the model Z^{r*}, on the basis of which the system Z^{real} is built, during the course of the system design process, will have been considered an element in the feasibility cotyledon and judged by various figures of merit that comprise the definition of the feasibility merit ordering γ. So there would be for Z^{r*}, for example, various estimates of quality of service, quantity of service, speed of service—those kinds of figures of merit associated with a system model Z^r on the basis of which Z^{r*} was chosen as the preferred system design.

Now, Z^{real} is given as a real-world implementation of Z^{r*}, and it is reasonable to ask what is the performance of Z^{real}? Has the performance of Z^{real} been adequately predicted by the theoretical performance of Z^{r*}? One way to summarize the performance of Z^{real} is to try to locate Z^{real} in the feasibility cotyledon in the following sense. There is a class of systems or elements, actually, in the feasibility cotyledon that are all equivalent with respect to γ to the system Z^{r*}. It might be possible, through testing, to determine to which equivalence class the system Z^{real} belongs, in some operational sense.

As a rule the equivalence classes of the feasibility cotyledon as determined by γ are much too fine. Through statistical tests with small sample sizes, through statistical estimations, and other manipulations of the system Z^{real}, it might be impossible to obtain the kind of exact, detailed information necessary to decide to which element in the feasibility cotyledon the system Z^{real} is equivalent. Therefore, the system test plan itself will postulate a much coarser equivalence relationship over the feasibility cotyledon, one, however, that is consistent with γ. The equivalence relationship over the feasibility cotyledon is typically denoted δ and called the test tolerance ordering. Being consistent with γ means that any equivalence class of γ is contained in an equivalence class of δ. Usually, the equivalence classes of δ are assumed to be finite in number, as pointed out above. One of the simplest test tolerance orderings is determined by dividing the feasibility cotyledon into *go* or *nogo* classes.

A system test plan is denoted $D = (\delta, d)$, where δ is a test tolerance ordering and d is a function defined over the set of all feasible test items whose value for any feasible test item is a triple. The triple consists first of all of an equivalence class with respect to δ, which represents an assertion about the performance of Z^{real}; secondly, there is a number 0 or 1 reflecting whether or not Z^{r*} is an adequate model of Z^{real}; and, thirdly, there is a number 0 or 1 reflecting whether or not the system Z^{real} is acceptable. That is all that is required mathematically of a testing function. In the real world, of course, the testing function might be extremely complicated. The testing function may specify that some tests are performed by simulation on Z^{r*} and some are performed in the real world on Z^{real}. That is the reason for the second 0 or 1 element in the range of d. It is important to report whether or not Z^{r*} is an adequate model of Z^{real}. This might be called the blueprint checking or conformance testing function; that is, one checks over the blueprints and the real system to make sure that the real system has been built according to the blueprints. Because Z^{real} is usually much more complicated than the blue prints, the question is asked backwards from the usual way: Is Z^{r*} an adequate model of Z^{real}? What is meant by adequate and which are the criteria for an adequate model are points to be discussed and negotiated with the client. Conformance testing certainly will involve estimating values of I/O figures of merit, U/R figures of merit, and T/O figures of merit.

Thus, a system design problem can be defined rigorously as a 6-tuple, $P = (X, T, \alpha, \beta, \gamma, D)$ where X is an I/O specification, T is a technology, α is a merit ordering over the I/O cotyledon, β is a merit ordering over the technology cotyledon, γ is a merit ordering over the feasibility cotyledon that is a tradeoff between the feasibility extensions $\bar{\alpha}$ and $\bar{\beta}$ of the orderings α over the I/O cotyledon and β over the technology cotyledon, respectively, and a system test plan D for the I/O specification X, the technology T, and the tradeoff merit ordering γ.

The orderings α and β are included primarily for methodological reasons; secondarily for design considerations. During the design process it is the merit ordering γ that will be used ultimately and perhaps almost exclusively in order to choose a system design represented by a point in the feasibility cotyledon. The merit orderings α and β, however, need to have been developed by the engineering team in conjunction with the client. They are developed separately and independently simply because it is methodologically desirable to keep the issues involved with the I/O cotyledon distinct from the issues involved with the technology cotyledon. All 6 of the artifacts defining a system design problem P should be developed in negotiation with the client in order to incorporate his or her value judgments in the definitions.

6.4. CONCLUSION

The theories developed in the last two sections, *system theory* and *system design theory*, can be used to develop tools and techniques for software engineering.

The creation of a model of a given phenomenon and a simulation package corresponding to that model should not be regarded as simply an exercise in modeling and programming. Such a problem must be regarded as the problem of the design of an information system. The inputs to that information system are queries about the phenomenon in question, and the output must be responses to such queries. The design of that system may involve a model or several models of the phenomenon in question. It is clear that given any sort of a complex phenomenon, there are a great many models that could be used to represent it, from very simple to very complex. Thus, one can easily see that it is a design decision to select a model that is no more complicated and expensive than is absolutely necessary to provide the desired information with appropriate accuracy. Thus, one can already begin to see emerging from this discussion, the basic elements, X, T, α, β, γ, D, of a T3SD problem statement for the development of a software package for the modeling and simulation of a given phenomenon.

A system theoretic approach can be helpful in the modeling process itself. It turns out usually to be effective to identify component systems of a given complex phenomenon being modeled, to develop system theoretic models of these simpler components, and then to define a system coupling recipe whose resultant is the desired model of the original phenomenon. A compiler, DIGEST, has been developed at the University of Arizona based on this concept. The use of such a compiler effectively combines modeling and programming activities rather than confusing and confounding them.

One of the principal benefits of the application of T3SD in software engineering would be much better communication between clients and software engineers. Communication has been a terrible stumbling block to the successful development of software because the client and the software engineers do not have a clear common understanding of what is to be developed. The use of a formal system design problem statement such as T3SD would help to specify what is to be done in terms understandable to both the clients and the software engineers. Furthermore, the development of each artifact in the T3SD problem statement would allow the client to interject his value judgments in the form of weights, utility functions, and other value-dependent parameters into the statement of the problem.

Once the problem is stated in the T3SD format, it is quite clear what is to be done and how the final design is to be chosen, and contracts between clients and software engineering can be developed with precision and clear understanding. These benefits are not achieved without cost, of course. The use of T3SD requires that a great deal more software development time be spent on the statement of the problem and less time be spent on the development of a particular solution to the problem. That this investment of time results in a better end product, more economically achieved, is taken on faith, but it is clear that most people feel a great deal better about the design process if they are operating under a T3SD problem statement.

Another advantage to the application of T3SD to problems in software engineering, is that T3SD provides a rigorous and uniform context and set of notation for the documentation of the design and development process. All of the decisions that are made in the course of the development of a software package can be precisely documented within the T3SD problem statement structure. Future generations of software engineers who must modify or develop the next generation of the system can see clearly why the present software package was designed the way it was and can see how that design can be improved through modification of the T3SD problem statement. For example, it is possible that improvement can be achieved by incorporating more figures of merit in the definitions of α, β, and γ than were included previously or by changing the weights or utility functions that go into the standard roll-ups of such figures of merit.

Many of the benefits so far of the application of system theory to the problems of software engineering have been somewhat negative. Thus, it has been proved, through the use of finite state machines, automata, and Turing machines, that certain kinds of functions are not computable and that certain kinds of decisions are undecidable. Actually, these results have little application to software engineering because they deal with problems within logic rather than reality. For example, the halting problem should be restated, not as an abstract mathematical problem, but as an engineering design problem. As an engineering problem, the halting problem has a solution. Experienced machine operators and even operating systems make the undecidable decisions every day. All such computability and unsolvability problems should be recast as engineering design problems and realistic system designs created for their implementation.

Another area for the application of T3SD is to the design of the engineering decision/information system that will be used in any given system design project. For example, suppose that a T3SD problem statement has been negotiated between the engineering team and the client. The next question that arises is, how is the engineering team to make the decision as to what the best point is in the feasibility cotyledon? There is a spectrum of answers to this question: One could ask his boss; one could convene a panel of experts to estimate figures of merit and choose between system designs, one could design elaborate models and simulations and sophisticated experiments to compute figures of merit rather precisely on the basis of very large samples. This shows that there is a wide range of possibilities for the design of the engineering decision/information system, and T3SD can be used to design that system.

Mathematical system theory is the only hope for a universal theoretical context for computer science and software engineering. The importance of system theory has already been indicated through the application of finite-state machines, discrete automata, push down machines, Turing machines, and so on, on the one hand, and the stability, controllability, observability, kinds of applications of system theory in the engineering sense [8] on the other hand. It would seem that an effort to describe uniformly the problems of computer science in a system theoretic language employing a universally acceptable set of notation would have a great deal of benefit for the field.

In terms of these ideas the future already begins to look fairly bright. Within the T3SD structure a theory has been developed of the resolution of a given system design problem into an interrelated set of system component design problems [9]. This involves defining the concept of a coupling recipe among I/O specifications and then trying to deduce component design problems $P^i = (X^i, T^i, \alpha^i, \beta^i, \gamma^i, D^i)$ from the top level design problem $P^o = (X^o, T^o, \alpha^o, \beta^o, \gamma^o, D^o)$. Resolutions must be accomplished with several objectives in mind. One of the objectives is that a suitable set of solutions to the component design problems must determine a solution to the next higher level problem. The second objective is to ensure that the merit orderings of the component design problems have relationships to the merit orderings of the top level problem. It turns out there are several such relationships that might be appropriate. The third objective is to ensure specific functional relationships of system test plans of the component design problems to the system test plan of the top level problem. Such resolutions might provide a theoretical basis for the organization of a software development group into teams, each team working on a different component of the problem, hoping that when they are finished the different solutions can be put together in some sense to form a solution to the overall problem and that comparisons of solutions of component design problems will be consistent with comparisons of correspondingly determined solutions of the top level problem and that testing of solutions of component design problems will provide testing information for and confidence in the corresponding top level solution.

It is certain that, in due course, there will be many other important contributions to the theory and practice of software engineering forthcoming from mathematical system theory.

REFERENCES

1. G. H. Mealy, "A Method for Synthesizing Sequential Circuits," *Bell System Technical Journal*, vol 34, pp. 1045–1079, 1955.

2. E. F. Moore, "Gedanken Experiments on Sequential Machines," pp. 129–153 of *Sequential Machines, Selected Papers,* Addison Wesley, Reading, Mass., 1964.

3. C. A. Desoer, *Notes for a Second Course on Linear Systems,* Van Nostrand Reinhold Company, New York, 1970.

4. P. J. Denning, J. B. Dennis, and J. E. Qualitz, *Machines, Languages and Computation,* Prentice-Hall, Englewood Cliffs, 1978.

5. J. E. Hopcroft and J. D. Ullman, *Introduction to Automata Theory, Languages and Computation,* Addison Wesley, Reading, Mass., 1979.

6. A. W. Wymore, *A Mathematical Theory of Systems Engineering—The Elements,* Robert E. Krieger Publishing Co., Huntington, N.Y., 1977.

7. A. W. Wymore, *Systems Engineering Methodology for Interdisciplinary Teams,* Wiley, New York, 1976.

8. M. A. Arbib, P. L. Falb, and R. E. Kalman, *Topics in Mathematical System Theory,* McGraw Hill, New York, 1969.

9. A. W. Wymore, "Resolution of System Design Problems," *Proceedings of COMPSAC 79,* The IEEE Computer Society, Long Beach, Cal., 1979.

7

Emulation

Michael J. Flynn and Jerome C. Huck

Stanford University
Computer Systems Laboratory

7.1. INTRODUCTION

The instruction set of a computer is frequently called its architecture and as such defines the boundary between many software and hardware issues. Recently, and with increasing frequency, the interpretation of the architecture (instruction set) itself is programmed, thus making the understanding of both architectural (instruction set) and interpretative (interpretation of the instruction set) issues all the more important for the software engineer.

To define a few terms: a *machine* is an instruction set (architecture), a storage (a space of named objects over which the instruction set exercises control), and a mechanism for interpretation of the instruction set (i.e., one that causes the correct state transition in the storage as specified by the instruction set). This mechanism is frequently a machine itself; that is, it has its own instruction set, its own storage (outside of the original storage), and its own interpretive mechanism. The important aspect of this is that the emulator is the program associated with the mechanism that causes the interpretation of the instruction set.

7.2. FURTHER DEFINITIONS AND TERMS

For our purposes, interpretation and emulation are synonyms for a process that executes commands (a vector of bits representing identifiers) according to a set of semantic rules. The execution process usually involves a number of intermediate state transitions, that is, transformations and storage before the execution of the command is complete.

The machine whose storage is reconfigured,

that is, undergoes the designated state transitions to cause the execution, is called the *host machine*. The program that causes these state transitions to correctly interpret a particular command is called the *emulator*. The set of commands that are interpreted define the *architecture* or for our purposes the *image machine* (Figure 7.1). The image machine is more frequently referred to as the target machine or occasionally as the virtual machine. We prefer the use of image here because the terms *target and virtual machines* are used extensively in other contexts.

The number of possible state transitions is a measure of the complexity of the host machine, and indirectly of its cost. For a given image machine, increasing the complexity of the host machine decreases the number of state transitions necessary to interpret commands. In some very high-performance machines, the host machine becomes indistinguishable from the image machine. By mapping the host machine's state transitions into the image machine's commands, the emulator is eliminated.

Significant savings both in machine cost and development time is realized by correctly trading off a very complex host machine and a little or nonexistent emulator with a simple host machine and a potentially large and sophisticated emulator. This trade-off is similar to a programmer's decision to encapsulate high-level statements into subroutines. Floating-point capability is often implemented as a relatively simple emulator routine, but optionally is replaced with a much faster and more expensive hardware module. Emulation also allows image machine development and en-

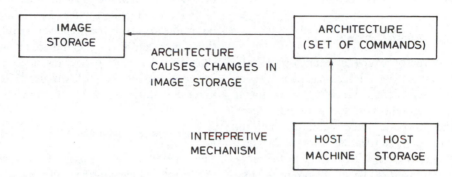

Figure 7.1. The image machine.

hancement by simple program changes, thus precluding the need for hardware redesign.

The host machine is an interesting object in itself. It contains the registers, storage elements, and data transformational devices that actually transform data and execute state transitions. The control of these state transitions is accomplished by the emulator program, which consists of a sequence of commands, each one of which reconfigures the internal storage of the host. Since the state transition in the host (generally the internal cycle time of a physical machine) is made as fast as possible by the designer, it is naturally important to have equally fast access to the storage for commands that determine which state transition is to occur. The programmable means to control these state transitions is frequently called the *microinstruction,* and sequences of these microinstructions or host-machine instructions are what actually accomplish the emulation of the image machine command or *image instruction.* The emulator storage is termed *control* or *microstore.* This requirement for fast access has over the years led designers to use a variety of special storage devices. Sometimes read-only memory was used. With the advance of bipolar technology, however, small bipolar read/write memories have largely replaced nonsilicon-based read-only technology as emulator storage.

Frequently emulator storage is arranged so that objects (either variables or constants) sig-nificant to the emulator or interpreter can also lie in the storage as well as the emulator program itself. The fast-access requirement, of course, implies a limited capacity for the interpretive storage since invariably very large storages will not be very fast. The host has other physical constraints, but certainly several very important characteristics are its general correspondence to a particular image machine; whether the designer has an *a priori* understanding of the particular image machine that is to be interpreted, and whether or not there is a requirement for interpretation of image machines that are not known at the time of the design of the host machine.

The analysis of the performance of image machines is greatly enhanced by emulation. Traditionally monitoring facilities are located in either the hardware or the software. Hardware monitoring, although extremely accurate, requires custom built components with their associated costs. Software monitors that are reasonably simple to program either greatly degrade the performance of the system or rely on statistical sampling techniques that have questionable validity. By embedding the monitor into the emulator, an accurate and inexpensive data collection facility is realized.

7.3. KINDS OF IMAGE MACHINES

The image machine architecture may be designed about two kinds of image objects: those found in the high-level language (HLL) or those found in the host. The first image type is a language-oriented image architecture, whereas the second is the traditional ALU-memory-oriented architecture.

Language-Oriented Image

In the directly executed language (DEL) [1,2], a simple one- or two-pass compilation process is envisioned, resulting in an image machine representation that is in close correspondence to the source program in which the values are bound to the identifiers and in which all encoding is done with respect to the scope of definition used in the source program (Figure 7.2). Thus, whatever the action used in the high-level language, *add, multiply, SIN,* and so forth, a correspondence is made to instructions of the image machine. This one-to-one correspondence between high-level language objects and image objects is a necessary characteristic of a well-designed, directly executed language. In general, the goals of the DEL strategy are to provide a concise program representation within the limitation of transparency of representation. *Transparency* is a property of an image machine representation whereby the source program is readily reconstructible from the image representation. It is somewhat of an intuitive notion since—presuming the existence of an elaborate decompilation process—even a low-level representation can be reconstructed into a probable source form. However, the spirit of the DEL is to retain a one-to-one correspondence between actions, object identifiers (variables), and labels so that the reconstruction process is facilitated. Within the transparency limitation, coding of the image program representation is as concise as possible, generally $\log_2$ of the number of objects in a particular environment or scope of definition. The number of objects to be interpreted is also kept at a minimum to be in line with the transparency requirement; thus, each action in the high-level language should evoke exactly one instruction in the image processor. We will discuss DEL forms in more detail later in this chapter.

Host-Oriented Image Machines

The instructions in the DEL form correspond to semantic objects in the source program; the traditional image machine creates instructions about transformations presumed to be present in the host, and the floating-point operations as well as traditional arithmetic transformations are defined in terms of the presumed host hardware (Figure 7.3). Similarly, coding of objects (addresses) is also formed about host-oriented notions—physical word size and maximum number of objects that can be stored determining the resolution and range of the image identifier. In the host-oriented image, if the host has registers, then the image will have commands to load and store these registers. If condition codes are present, then the image will have instructions to test and set these codes. The host-oriented image naturally requires a traditional compilation process that can be somewhat complex. It also requires a nontrivial interpretation. A process may be regarded as trivial if the instruction can be fetched in one state transition and executed in the next. This is generally not true in a host-oriented image command since a series of state transitions is required to perform the execution of an instruction. The following shows a typical sequence of state transitions for a host-oriented image.

- The operation must be decoded.
- A one- or two-state transition may be required to form the effective address of the object to be operated on.
- That object must be fetched.
- Finally, the operation may be executed.

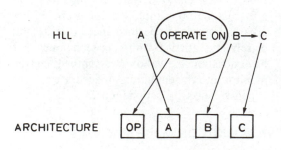

Figure 7.2. Language-oriented image.

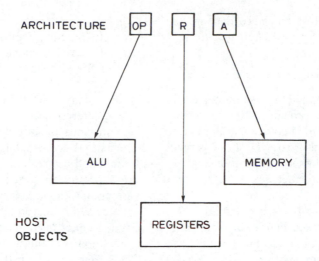

Figure 7.3. Host-oriented image.

Typically in traditional host-oriented image machines, between 5- and 10-state transitions are required for interpretation.

7.4. KINDS OF HOST-IMAGE MAPPING [3]

The number of cycles actually required to perform the interpretation of an image instruction is an important measure of the correspondence between the host and the image machine. In inspecting a host or, for example, a host-oriented image instruction, one expects a certain number of state transitions or cycles to be required by a host for the interpretation of this instruction. The expected number of state transitions is largely determined by the logical structure of the instruction. Thus, in the case of a System 360 instruction, the following sequential state transitions are expected to occur logically:

- Fetch instruction.
- Decode instruction.
- Generate effective address of the operand.
- Fetch operand.
- Execute operation.

Thus, if the instruction and data could each be fetched in one state transition, the total interpretation of a 360 instruction would average about five cycles (excluding multiplication, division, etc.). We would not be surprised if the 5 cycles were actually more like 8 or 10, since a word boundary alignment problem might require additional access cycles. Many of the operations will be multicycle; setting up the condition code and inspection of machine status for pending interrupts might take an additional cycle, and so on. If the host machine actually executes the System 360 instruction in accordance with our expectation, we call such a mapping a *well-mapped machine* or a well-mapped correspondence between image and host.

If the designer simply does not know what the image would look like when he is designing his host machine, the interpretation process will by necessity be significantly more complex. Each field in the instruction is now separately decoded to determine the proper interpretation. Thus, we expect the total number of cycles for the interpretation for such a correspondence to at least double the expected well-mapped total. Since the designer cannot anticipate all the required attributes needed by the host's data paths, the doubled number of state transitions usually is somewhat of a lower bound, and more commonly about four times the expected number of state transitions will be required for even the best host to interpret a typical traditional image. *Best* in this sense means that the host is designed for interpretation; it can rapidly access arbitrary bit fields and manipulate them as required during the decoding process. Host machines that are so equipped are called *universal host machines*.

7.5. HOST MACHINE CHARACTERISTICS

In looking at well-mapped hosts and universal host machines, it is probably most useful to start with the very broad common ground that both implementations share. Hosts of recent vintage, at least, will generally contain (Figure 7.4) the elements described below.

1. A large read-write microprogram storage. As mentioned before, bipolar technology has found an ideal niche in use as a microprogram control storage. Since the technology supports write applications, it is becoming increasingly popular to include at least a portion of writable control store as part of the microstorage. The remainder, of course, may be read-only memory (ROM) to support fixed and a priori well-defined image machines. The microstorage may be a pure storage or be used in conjunction with *programmable logic arrays* (PLAs). Since PLAs in general cannot be reconfigured, the PLA is limited to a replacement of the read-only memory part of the microprogram function. The use of PLA/microprogram storage in place of "hard wire" control implementation is a simple, practical fact of technology. Realization and implementation of control functions with standard traditional components (AND, OR, XOR Gates) require many components and a complex set of interconnections. PLAs and bipolar components provide customized components that dramatically reduce the parts count and use regular interconnections.

2. A single access to the bipolar or microprogram storage corresponds to a complete ALU interpretation; that is, the time it takes to complete a register ALU operation is of the same order as the access time for the next microinstruction. This allows a fetching of a control action (microinstruction) in one cycle, with its interpretation and the prefetching of the next microinstruction in the following cycle.

3. Rather than having a complex multistate transition as the basis for effective address generation, the architecture of the host supports simple, direct addressing and use of immediate operands in the microinstruction. While this limits somewhat the placement of objects in microprogram storage, since the ability to dynamically relocate is limited, the simplicity of the addressing structure is a

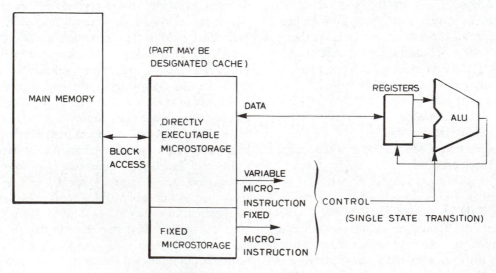

Figure 7.4. Host processor.

natural consequence of the single microprogram access for ALU interpretation
requirement mentioned in the previous
item.

4. Main memory is increasingly becoming a
block-oriented access device for bulk
storage in a multilevel hierarchical storage system. The multiple levels may require support varying from simple to very
elaborate interpretations in the movement of environments from remote levels
to executable levels of storage.

Note that these characteristics are common to
recent vintage host machines; they are largely
derived from technology and the economics of
technology.

There are, of course, significant differences
between host machines in spite of the above
commonality. Well-mapped machines are
biased to a particular image machine and the
interpretation of its instruction set. This biasing may be toward a host-oriented image, that
is, a traditional machine, or conceivably it
could be toward a directly executed language
of DEL-based system. The former, of course,
is the ubiquitous traditional implementation of
host image architectures. The latter is largely
experimental but holds promise for the future,
at least where economics indicate that a large
linguistic environment can be identified.

For universal host systems, the structure is
unbiased. This is the universal host machine,
in the sense that it has no particular support
for any designated image but rather is designed either as a special-purpose interpretive
or execution engine. Special hardware is provided to support interpretation when it is designated as the purpose of the host. The unbiased host's structure may be designed to
support a strictly interpretive environment as
in the case of supporting either HLL-image or
DEL-image machines, or as an executor of
precompiled encoded microinstructions as in
the case of image basis. While the unbiased
hosts of either type have further commonality
when compared to the image-biased host, the
latter will differ largely in its treatment of
storage.

7.6. CLASSIFICATION OF EMULATIONS [4]

Comparison among various host machines,
when one is emulating a specific image machine or various image machines, forms an important basis for host machine performance
evaluation. With the increasing availability of
universal host machines and the use of these
machines in the emulation of a variety of images, subtle differences in the interpretation of
a specific image may give rise to significant differences in performance of emulation.

Even with a single manufacturer, different
models designed to interpret the same image
may have subtle inconsistencies in the image
machine emulation. Consider, for example,
System 360 and such models as the Model 20,
Model 44, Model 67, and Model 91, each of
which differs from the stated definition of the
System 360 image.

Performance comparisons are made even
more difficult in nonproduction, nonopera-
tional image environments when the hosts are
used basically for architectural experimental
purposes. Since the amount of image source
material run through such systems is limited,
performance claims resulting from significantly different underlying image assumptions
give rise to inconsistent performance data.

Classification

A classification scheme for comparisons of emulations has been proposed:

Class A. Transforms all image programs
precisely as a true image machine
(e.g., duplicates failure modes). A
class *A* emulation, therefore,
would pass Turing's test in that a
user would be unable to distinguish between a class *A* emulation
of the image and "the true machine" except perhaps for the
physical time for interpretation.

Class B. Transforms all image programs
corresponding to "correct programs" as would a true image machine (i.e., the emulation may fail
differently from the true image

machine). Class *B* emulations are useful for interpreting archival code that is known to be correct. Of course, this leaves substantially open the issue of what is a "correct program." However, programs that violate memory protection, arithmetic overflow, address range, and so forth, can be assumed to be incorrect.

Class C. Transforms a selected subset of image programs as would the true image machine. The class *C* emulator perhaps excludes certain difficult features or instructions unique to a particular environment. It is assumed here that the "subset of image programs" is in fact statistically significant over the broad user set of image programs.

Class D. Transforms a selected subset of image programs in a manner such that the behavior of the true image machine could be predicted for this subset. For example, a class *D* emulation may make certain subtle differences in the implementation of arithmetic functions and also make certain changes in the definition of a particular data type. The importance of the class *D* emulation lies in its value as a research tool. An image floating point add, for example, will still correspond to a class *D* emulation of that add despite the slight modification of the floating point format. The class *D* emulation requires that the statistical significance be preserved in important machine architectural parameters such as the number of instructions interpreted, the number of memory references required, the address patterns remain the same, and so on.

Class E. For some functions or subroutines in an image machine, transformation is performed on a different basis in the emulation. These subroutines are effectively reinterpreted so that integrity is preserved only with respect to entry and exit of the routine. It is a lower class emulation than class *D* since one can no longer predict machine behavior parameters by observing the performance of the emulation.

Class F. Class *F* emulations include anything other than the above classes.

Environment

The classification is further distinguished by two separate environments—the problem environment and the supervisory environment. Thus, problem state code may be interpreted with a class *A* emulation, whereas the supervisory state, or operating systems code, may be interpreted at some lower level, perhaps even a class *E* emulation: A new operating system is written to support a particular image machine but the operating system routine calls (e.g., in 360 SVCs) have their own interpretation in this new operating system. Another example might be a class *A* emulation in the problem state and a class *C* emulation in the supervisory state, where certain operating system functions or features are not supported in the emulator but others are available.

7.7. EMULATION OF TRADITIONAL ARCHITECTURES

Two sample emulations are described: an image-biased host (i.e., a 360/65 emulating another image machine or image architecture) (IBM 7090) and a universal host machine emulation.

Emulation of Conventional Machine Languages

In the past, emulation has mainly involved the interpretation of lower-level machine language DELs, using microprogramming techniques for instruction interpretation. It is relatively easy for a single physical system to interpret more than one machine language. It is possible to write an emulator for one image machine in terms of another image machine language; thus, one can conceive of layers of emulators. The more common usage of the term *emulator,* however, implies that the interpretive set of programs is written in the microlanguage of the host processor.

Probably the most widely known use of emulation is the IBM System 360. Most of the models of System 360 and System 370 are microprogrammed [5], with the notable exception of Models 91 and 195. Each model of the System 360 and System 370 series is a distinct machine with widely differing performance characteristics, data paths, size, and price. However, each shares a common DEL, the machine language of System 360. In all the microprogrammed models of the System 360, the interpretation of this machine language is done by an emulator that resides in microstorage. This emulator consists of a series of routines, and each routine represents a particular System 360 instruction.

The emulation of a machine other than a 360 is not so straightforward. Consider a Model 65 that emulates a 7090. The emulation of a 7090 on a Model 65 is more accurately described as a simulation of the 7090 using a combination of techniques including 360 instructions, special instructions, and 7090-type instructions. The hybrid approach to emulation reduces the amount of microstorage needed to provide emulation of the 360 and the 7090. In the Model 65, each 7090 instruction is interpreted by an emulation subroutine contained in a main memory (Figure 7.5a). This subroutine uses special instructions as well as conventional System 360 instructions. One of the special instructions is the *do interpretive loop* (DIL), which is a microprogrammed routine that does a fetch and interpretation of the next 7090 instruction. In addition to the DIL instruction, a number of other subroutines are added to the microstorage to assist in emulating specific 7090 instruction. The emulation of three 7090 instructions is shown in Figure 7.5b.

Emulation with a Universal Host

The less that is known of the image machine, the more difficult the emulation could potentially become when done on an unbiased or universal host. Because no natural correspondence exists between the image and the host, the programmer, in writing the emulation, must make all the required accommodations without any hardware assistance. Consider an example of System 360 emulation on the Stanford Emmy [6,7].

The Stanford Emmy

Designed for interpretation, the Emmy is classified as a universal host. Organized as three

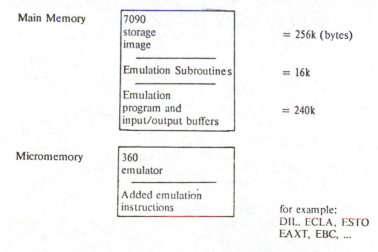

Figure 7.5a. Memory layout for IBM 7090 emulation on a System 360/65.

7090 Instruction	360 Emulation Routine	
AXT Address to index true	EAXT	Microroutine that does AXT
	DIL	Microroutine that does fetch and interpretation of next instruction
AXC Address to index complemented	LCR	360 instruction that complements the address
	EAXT	Microroutine
	DIL	Microroutine
TIM Transfer if minus	ESTO	Microroutine that puts the value into a work area of the 360 (the simulated accumulator)
	TM	360 instruction, test under mask (to obtain the sign bit)
	EBC	Microroutine that does a 7090 branch if the test is satisfied

Figure 7.5b. Example 7090 emulation.

independent machines, it achieves parallelism by separating the functions of data transformation, instruction fetch, and storage access. These components are termed the T-machine, I-machine, and A-machine, respectively. The microinstruction controls the operation of each machine (Figure 7.6). Much in the same way as traditional machine instructions have formats and fields, the Emmy microinstruction is divided into two halves. The "left side" operation (T-op) normally controls the transformation of data located in the register file. The "right side" operation (A-op) deals primarily with the transfer of data between the various

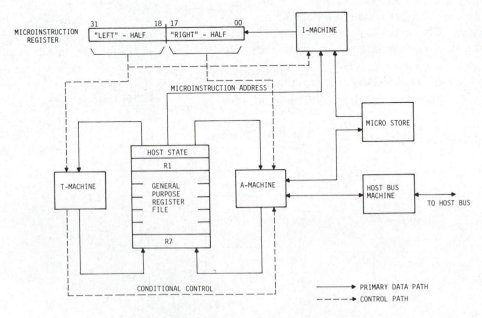

Figure 7.6. Structure of the Emmy processor.

storage resources. There is a special format, both for the T-op and the A-op, that can conditionally (or unconditionally) change the normal I-machine sequencing. The T-machine has additional control for canceling A-machine execution to allow an immediate data path for the T-side operation.

The storage mechanisms are organized around a large writable control (or micro) storage. All the microinstructions and various portions of the image machine state are contained therein. The register file contains seven general purpose registers and one special purpose state register. The state register contains the microprogram counter and two sets of condition indicators. One set, termed the C-codes, is a complete set of condition codes. The other set termed the I-codes, are easily tested indicators for arbitrary use. Often image state information, regularly used, is stored there (e.g., interrupt pending).

The *host bus machine* depicted in Figure 7.6 can be conceived of as a synchronized distributed slave processor for the A-machine. For example, the main memory system is programmed with a command byte appended to the address field to control the interpretation of the address and the format of the data [8]. The address can be either of one, two, or four byte objects; data can be justified. Sign can be extended and can vary in length from one to four bytes.

T-machine operations use the register file exclusively. The syntax of the T-machine microinstructions is shown in Figure 7.7. Logical, arithmetic, and shift/rotate instructions func-

tion similar to conventional machines. The traditional multiply, divide, and decimal instructions are too closely tied to specific data formats and word widths. So the "extended" class of T-op's provides primitives with which the more complex operations may be done. For example, the multiply step instruction conditionally adds a multiplier to a multiplicand. By appropriate repetitions signed or unsigned multiplication of various word widths can be performed.

Interpretation often requires isolating or packing fields of bits. With the last T-op format, the extract/insert instruction, groups of bits can either be extracted and stored into a cleared register or isolated and inserted into various fields of another register. While most useful in instruction decode, extract/insert instructions are often used in floating point, decimal arithmetic, and image state emulation (e.g. PSW formation).

Instructions that control A-machine operation (Figure 7.8) fall into the following classes:

- Load address
- Direct register/microstore transmission
- Internal Access (indirect)
- External Access (indirect).

Since the microprogram counter is the low part of general register 0, the load address instruction (from an immediate field in the microinstruction) is most frequently used for program jumps. Although only affecting the low part of the register, load address instructions can place short constants and pointers into reg-

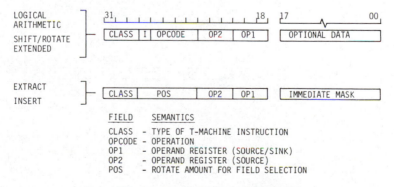

Figure 7.7. Syntax of T-machine microinstructions.

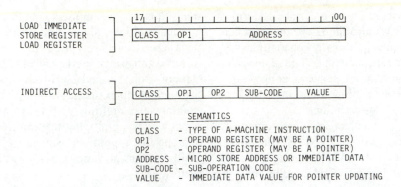

Figure 7.8. Syntax of A-machine microinstructions.

isters. Direct class microinstructions transfer data between control store and registers with the address directly specified in an immediate field. Internal and external access instructions reference control store and main memory (and memory mapped I/O), respectively. Registers are used as pointers for the internal and external access formats. For these later operations the pointer may be updated by a small value (-8 to $+7$) to facilitate block-style transfers.

Normal I-machine sequencing is suspended either by directly modifying the state register, RO, or by execution of an I-machine instruction (Figure 7.9). Conditional instructions (T-side replacement) when "true," signal the A-machine to abort the current instruction. This is similar to the traditional "skip or condition" instruction. Short-distance conditional jumps are performed by branch or loop control instructions (A-side replacements). Branch instructions have the same wide range of testing

capability as the conditional instruction. Loop control instructions on the other hand can only test the sign or zero sense of a register, but simple arithmetic can be done allowing programmed looping. Emmy interrupts are handled by the I-machine and force a state register swap with a source-dependent, control-store word pair.

A 360 Emulation

In the case of a biased host, the System 360 host or model 65 host, while primarily biased toward System 360, required some significant hardware concessions for supporting a 7090 image. Thus, the emulator had significant hardware support although not as much as the 360 image. The task of emulation with an unbiased host is even more difficult [9].

Consider the diagram of emulation in Figure 7.10. The mapping of the image state

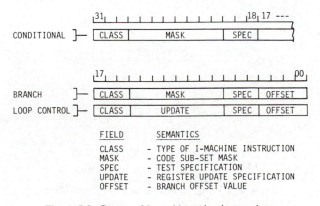

Figure 7.9. Syntax of I-machine microinstructions.

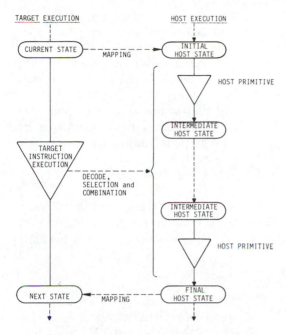

Figure 7.10. The general interpretive process.

Using the Emmy as the unbiased host, main memory maps directly into the Emmy's main memory system. Image registers are mapped into the low 16 words of control store. Using that portion of control store allows direct addressing of the image registers with the register specification found in the image instruction. Notice that addressing a 360 floating point register will require an additional offset by its base address in control store.

The 360 PSW is a 64 bit quantity indicating the current mode, condition codes, program counter, and so forth. Because the PSW is only accessible to the program through special instructions, it can be mapped into arbitrary places in the Emmy. When necessary the various components are packed together to form the true PSW. The program counter is stored in one of the Emmy general purpose registers, while the condition codes are stored in a control store location. Since condition codes are formed more often than tested, they are stored in Emmy format and translated into 360 format only if needed. Components such as the ILC are formed by the appropriate PSW swap routine.

(termed target in the figure) into the host state is often straightforward. The 360 state consists of main memory, registers, and a PSW (optional control registers, memory protection, virtual memory, etc., will not be considered).

The instruction decode of the 360 parses

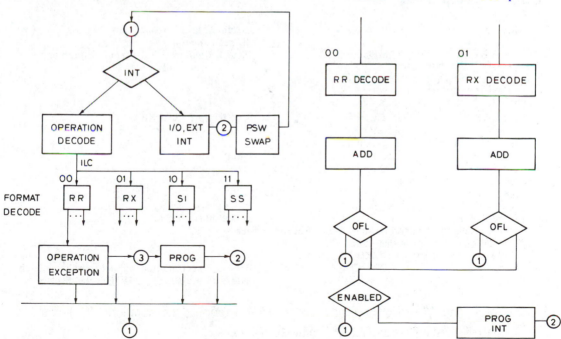

Figure 7.11. System 360 instruction decode.

from left to right as shown by the RR and RX add example in Figure 7.11. The high-order byte determines the operation, and the 256 way branch transfers control to the routine (termed the semantic routine) that executes the instruction. To avoid repeated code for address generation, register specification, isolation, and so on, the format class (high 2 bits of instruction) selects alternate code paths for execution before the semantic routine is called.

Figure 7.12 shows the Emmy microcode implementing initial decode and the format decode for RR- and RX-type instructions. The following table shows the registers when ready to execute at DECODELOOP.

MPC   Emmy microprogram counter
PC360   360 program counter
XR   Instruction register extension: preloaded with all ones by the previous instruction's semantic routine
IR   Instruction register: preloaded with the current instruction by previous instruction's semantic routine
P,Q,R,S   Uninitialized registers

The first statement isolates the format index (extended with ones) into XR and saves it in R. By placing the addresses of the semantic

```
.*****************
.* Main decode *
.*****************
DECODELOOP:
1    XR,IR << 2        ;R := XR                .Isolate format index into XR, and R
2    XR,IR << 6        ;S := M(XR)             .Isolate op-code in XR, and use it to
                                               . pick up semantic pointer
3    XR := 0           ;MPC := MPC - R         .Branch either 2, 3, 4, or 5 instructions forward
4    DC 0                                      .Not used
5    XR,IR << 4        ;MPC := SSEA            .Transfer to SS format decode; isolate R1 spec
6    XR,IR << 4        ;MPC := SIEA            .Transfer to SI format decode; isolate R1 spec
7    XR,IR << 4        ;MPC := RXEA            .Transfer to RX format decode; isolate R1 spec
.*************************
.* RR Format Decode *
.*************************
RREA:
8    XR,IR << 4        ;R := XR                .Isolate R1 spec and save, in R, for use
                                               . by semantic routine
9    XR := 0           ;MPC := S               .Clear XR and transfer to semantic routine
.*************************
.* RX Format Decode *
.*************************
RXEA:
10   R := XR           ;XR := 0                .Save R1 spec, clear XR
11   P := 0            ;Q := XR                .Clear P,Q
.Isolate index register spec, if zero skip next instruction
12   XR,IR << 4        ;Q := Q + XR (ZERO => *+2)
13   XR := 0           ;Q := M(Q)              .Pickup index register
.Isolate base register spec, if zero skip next 2 instructions
14   XR,IR << 4        ;P := P + XR (ZERO => *+3)
15   XR := 0           ;P := M(P)              .Pick up base register
16   Q := Q + P                                .Add to index register
.Extract the displacement field from bits 31:20, clear the register
. and load into the low part of that same register
17   IR(11:0) = IR(31:20) EXTRACT
18   MPC := S          ;Q := Q + IR            .Branch to semantic routine and complete effective
                                               . address calculation by adding in the displacement
```

Note: The ";" separates T-side and A-side operations; the notation M(...) is a control store access and X(...) is an external access.

Figure 7.12. Operation and format decode.

```
*************
.* Add (RR) *
*************
OP1A:
1      XR,IR << 4              ;P := M(XR)                   .Isolate R2 spec. and load its contents.
2      XR := -1                ;Q := M(R)                   .Load contents of R1 spec.
3      PC360 := PC360+2        ;IR := X(PC360)              .Update 360's PC and prefetch next instruction.
4      Q := Q + ᴾ              :M(CC) := MPC                .Perform operation and save condition codes.
5                              ;M(R) := Q                   .Store result using R1 spec.
6      ( NOT OVERFLOW =>       ;MPC := DECODELOOP)          .Return when no error.
************************
.* Arithmetic overflow *
************************
ARITHOFL:
7                              ;P := M(PSW+1)               .Load low 32 bits of PSW
8      P := P AND X'08000000'                               .Check for enabled exception.
9      ( ZERO =>               ;MPC := DECODELOOP)
10     XR := 8                                              .Indicate exception source.
11                             ;Q := M(PROGLOC)             .Indicate exception type.
12                             ;MPC := INTUR                .Go swap PSW's.
*************
.* Add (RX) *
*************
OP5A:
13     Q(31:24) = S(31:24) INSERT                           .Load memory control byte.
14                             :P := X(Q)                   .Fetch memory operand.
15     XR := -1                ;Q := M(R)                   .Load R1 spec. contents.
16     PC360 := PC360+4        ;IR := X(PC)                 .Update 360's PC and prefetch next instruction.
17     Q := Q + P              ;M(CC) := MPC                .Perform operation and save condition codes.
18                             :M(R) := Q                   .Save result in R1 spec.
19     (NOT OVERFLOW =>        ;MPC := DECODELOOP)          .Return when no error.
20                             ;MPC := ARITHOFL             .Process exception.
```

Figure 7.13. Add operation semantic routines.

routines in a table at the top of control store (termed the semantic pointer table), statements 2 and 3 will load the semantic pointer into S and branch to the appropriate format decode routine. Each format decode routine generates effective addresses if necessary and branches to the semantic routine.

Semantic routines must prefetch the next 360 instruction before returning to the initial decode loop. Figure 7.13 shows the Emmy microinstructions for the RR and RX "add" semantic routines. Consider now the RX add semantic routine starting at statement 13. First the high byte of the register, which was loaded by the format decode routine with the address of the operand (Q), is loaded with a memory control byte from the semantic pointer. For the opcode X'5A' (hex notation), add full-word, a 4 byte transfer is specified. For the opcode X'4A'—add half-word—the same routine is ex-

ecuted but with a 2 byte length specification in the semantic pointer. After the source operand is fetched (statement 14), then the destination register is loaded (15), the operation performed (17) and the result stored (18). The next instruction is prefetched (16) and the condition codes saved (17). Execution conditions are tested (19) and if not indicated, then control returns to the decode loop (19). Had an overflow occurred, the PSW would be interrogated and appropriate action taken (7–12).

Considering all the effort involved note that universal host machines can be respectable in their performance levels in image interpretation. Performances between 5 and 10 microseconds for image instruction on System 360 or PDP-11-type image machines have been reported by several independent experimenters of class *A* emulations of a least problem state code.

7.8. ARCHITECTURAL TRENDS AND LANGUAGE-ORIENTED ARCHITECTURES

If we exclude from further discussion the first strategy for high-level execution of direct interpretation of source program representation—because of its limited suitability to many of the traditional languages—we are left with three alternate strategies: the traditional host-oriented image machine, the language-oriented image, and the trivial strategy (somewhat modified) of direct compilation to microinstructions. A point that has become clear to many designers, the traditional host-oriented image is simply not a good program representation. Too many instructions are required to be interpreted, too many state transitions are required for program execution, and program size is excessive. Its great redeeming value is compatibility, which can economically outweigh all other considerations. Still modern machines as they are enhanced, modified, improved, and so on, are moving away from host-oriented image program representations. The change is subtle to be sure but present nonetheless. The earliest moves toward language-oriented image machines were largely directed at the COBOL source language environment. Companies such as Honeywell introduced an extended instruction set (EIS). NCR introduced a support language for COBOL, and Burroughs, through its B1700 S languages, introduced the most elaborate (for the early 1970s) language support system for COBOL, RPG, and for FORTRAN. More recently, DEC has upgraded its PDP-11 by introducing a 32 bit version called VAX, which also incorporates significant support for the FORTRAN language. Finally, IBM as well as many other companies, by microcoding elements of the operating system, effectively provides image machines for parts of the operating system.

REFERENCES

1. M. J. Flynn and L. W. Hoevel, "A Theory of Interpretive Architectures: Ideal Language Machines," Technical Report TR-170, Computer Systems Laboratory, Stanford University, Stanford, Calif., Feb. 1979.
2. M. J. Flynn and L. W. Hoevel, "A Theory of Interpretive Architectures: Some Notes on DEL Design and a Fortran Case Study," Technical Report TR-171, Computer Systems Laboratory, Stanford University, Stanford, Calif., Feb. 1979.
3. M. J. Flynn, "Computer Organization and Architecture," Lecture notes on advanced course on operating systems, Munich, Germany, July 28 to Aug. 5, 1977.
4. L. W. Hoevel and W. A. Wallach, "A Tale of Three Emulators," Computer Systems Laboratory, Technical Report TR-98, Stanford University, Stanford, Calif., Nov. 1975.
5. S. G. Tucker, "Emulation of Large Systems," *Communications of the ACM,* vol. 8, pp. 753–761, Dec. 1965.
6. W. A. Wallach, "EMMY/360 Functional Characteristics," Computer Systems Laboratory, Technical Report TR-114, Stanford University, Stanford, Calif., June 1976.
7. C. J. Neuhauser, "Emmy System Processor—Principles of Operation," Computer Systems Laboratory, Technical Note TN-114, Stanford University, Stanford, Calif., May 1977.
8. C. J. Neuhauser, "Emmy System Peripherals—Principles of Operation," Computer Systems Laboratory, Technical Note TN-77, Stanford University, Stanford, Calif., Dec. 1975.
9. C. J. Neuhauser, *An Emulation Based Analysis of Computer Architecture,* Ph.D. dissertation, Johns Hopkins University, Baltimore, Jan. 1980.

8
Hardware/Software Tradeoffs

W. N. Toy
Bell Telephone Laboratories

8.1. INTRODUCTION

In the fifties and early sixties, computer architecture was dictated to a large extent by the high cost of hardware. The heavy emphasis on minimizing hardware placed a heavy burden on software. Under the "hardware first" philosophy, the system was completely designed without fully appreciating the complexity of the software. Any inadequacies were assumed to be easily rectified by simple software changes. As a result, programmers, left to fend for themselves, occasionally worked with machines that led to insoluble conflicts or "spaghetti" programs [1]. The excessive cost of designing, updating, and maintaining software is very much evident by the lack of hardware support in simplifying software effort. Another major cause of software problems is the complexity of programming languages and the enormous size of system and application programs. These factors contribute to the creation of programs that are difficult to understand and highly susceptible to human error.

Hardware/Software Cost

Advances in computer technology offer opportunities for innovative hardware-software tradeoffs that reduce system development cost, improve performance, and enhance software reliability. Studies indicate that (1) software development costs about $10 per written line, or several times the cost of an IC (integrated circuit) chip, (2) approximately 70% of the total cost of a software product occurs after the product is delivered, and goes into debugging and maintenance, and (3) software mainte-

nance alone takes 50 to 80% of the data-processing budget at a typical installation [1]. The increasing importance of software is readily apparent from Figure 8.1 [2]. About 80% of costs was attributed to hardware and 20% to software in the mid 1950s. This ratio is expected to be reversed by 1985 by rapidly decreasing hardware costs and by the increasing rate of labor-intensive software costs.

Maintenance plays an important role in an computer installation. Its cost is continually rising and reflects the high labor-intensive effort. Figure 8.2 shows the maintenance price per $100K of purchase price for IBM processors and storage [3]. The monthly rate has increased by a factor of three from 1960 to 1975.

Advances in software engineering have not been as great as those in hardware. The price and performance of hardware have improved by leaps and bounds, put improvement in programmer productivity has been slow, as indicated in Table 8.1 [4]. This is reflected in the high cost of software development. In order to achieve the most cost effective arrangement, efforts are now being made to assure adequate

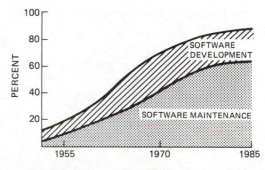

Figure 8.1. Hardware-software cost trends.

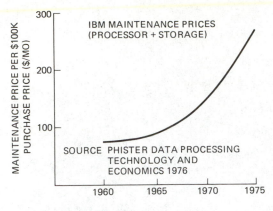

Figure 8.2. Maintenance cost.

performance via hardware-software tradeoffs in the design of both of these components of computer systems.

Hardware/Software Tradeoff Goals

A strong interest in hardware-software tradeoffs is directed toward new hardware architectures to aid the programming problem. A considerable amount of work has been focused on direct execution of higher-level languages, replacement of data base management software with data base machines [5], communications processors for distributed data processing systems, and implementation of parts of the operating system and procedural calls in microprogram memory. The flexibility of microprogram implementation offers other possible tradeoffs. It is now both economically and technologically attractive to implement many of the software functions in microcode.

Because of advances in hardware technology, it is not surprising that most of the tradeoff choices are from software to firmware or to hardware. Some of the tradeoff goals pointed out [6] are to:

1. Achieve higher performance (e.g., use hardware or microprograms for critical functions that require too much time in software, such as floating point arithmetic functions)
2. Reduce software complexity (e.g., provide special instructions needed for data base management)
3. Reduce programming effort (e.g., provide a large instruction repertoire and variety of methods of data representation and assume that their execution is sufficiently fast: avoid special needs to scale variables or to overlay memory space)
4. Improve reliability and fault-tolerance (e.g., provide built-in error diagnostics, recovery features, or error detection/correction codes)
5. Improve integrity and security (e.g., implement hardware features such as processor mode indicators, security tags, or memory protection bounds registers)
6. Reduce overall system life cycle cost (e.g., provide growth capability, improved performance measurement, and diagnostic aids).

8.2. TECHNOLOGY

Technological advances over the past decade have been phenomenal in cost-performance improvement, in reliability, and in alternative technologies open to the designer. Integrated circuit technology has doubled the number of components per chip about once every two years during the first 15 years or so, as shown in Figure 8.3 [7]. This trend is expected to continue well into the 1980s and will have a direct impact on processors, mass storage, terminals and peripherals, and system architectures. The 1980s will also see the next phase of

Table 8.1. Data Processing Industry Growth Trends.

	1955	1965	1975	1985
Industry	1	20	80	320
Machine performance	1	10^2	10^4	10^6
Programmer productivity	1	2.4	5.6	13.3
System reliability	1	5	24	120

SOURCE: Art Benjamin Associates

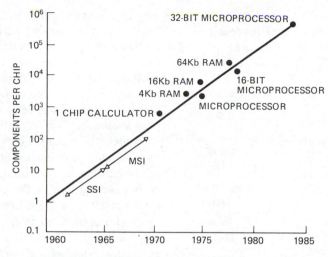

Figure 8.3. Advances in integrated circuit technology.

integration in semiconductors—that of very large-scale integration (VLSI). It will be possible to put 100,000 gates on a single chip [8].In 1981 Hewlett Packard announced their 32-bit microprocessor chip, containing 450,000 transistors and incorporated the chip as integral part of their commercial product, HP9000 computer systems in late 1982.

Device-level Impact

Progress in devices has played a significant role in identifying the computer generation. During the first generation, vacuum tubes were employed as logic elements; transistors were used during the second generation. The advent of integrated circuits (IC) ushered in the third generation, and at present, we are in the large-scale integration (LSI) stage. In the past 30 years, we have seen the average switching speed of a logic circuit increase about 10^7 times, from 10 ms for a relay to 1 ns for a logic gate in an LSI chip. No such rapid progress has been made in any other field, and these rapid developments have been a basic factor in the evolution of computers.

The complexity of an IC can be expressed in terms of active elements, a measure equivalent to logic gates and memory cells. The 64k bit dynamic random access memory (RAM) and 16 bit microprocessor are state-of-the-art devices today. The next generation devices will be 32 bit microprocessors and 256K bit dynamic RAMs [9]. It is projected that with new advances in electron beam lithography a 32 bit microcomputer chip with 1 megabit of read only memory (ROM) should be possible in the late 1980s. The impact is perhaps better understood by observing that such a chip would be equivalent to the CPU of an IBM 370/148 [3].

Lower cost is another important factor introduced with LSI technology. For example, the storage capacity per chip has increased as much as four times every two years: the 1k bit chip in 1972, 4k in 1974, 16k in 1976, 64k in 1980 and 256k in 1982, but the price per chip has increased only 20 to 30% during the same period [10]. Therefore, the price per bit has decreased remarkably. Improvement in microprocessor functions, cost, and speed has continued at a similar pace. The 64k devices, however, have not progressed as rapidly as earlier memory parts.

Improving computer reliability and miniaturization are additional benefits of using LSI circuits. The mean time between failures (MTBF) of a commercially available Motorola MC6800 CPU, a device with 3,000 gate complexity and packaged in ceramic, was 877 years in 1978 and reached 1,900 years in 1979, as indicated in Table 8.2 [9]. This clearly shows the reliability advantage of LSI as compared with computers designed with SSIs and

Table 8.2. Failure Rates and Mean Time Between Failure (MTBF) for the Motorola MC6800 Microprocessor.
(Ceramic Package 70° C Ambient Temperature)

YEAR	FAILURE RATE PERCENT 1000 HOURS	MTBF HOURS (YEARS)
1974	1.27	78,000 (9)
1975	0.5	200,000 (23)
1976	0.12	833,000 (95)
1977	0.08	1,700,000 (194)
1978	0.013	7,700,000 (877)
1979	0.006	16,666,666 (1900)

MSIs. The reliability of a given size IC chip does not vary appreciably with increases in the number of components on the chip. Consequently, the reliability per gate or per function is expected to increase tremendously with VLSI. As shown in Table 8.2, the reliability is increasing with a failure rate of 6×10^{-8} (failures/hour). With a million devices per chip (300,000 equivalent gates) and a failure rate of 6×10^{-8}, the corresponding failure rate is 2×10^{-13} per gate.

Function-level Impact

The capability of the semiconductor industry to make reliable VLSI is no longer seriously doubted. As a result, a difficult problem that will arise is what to do with all those transistors and gates on VLSI chips. The most obvious product area is in larger memory parts which are of lower cost, as well as better and faster processors. The recent trend has been increasing processor complexity, from 4 bits in 1972, to 8 bits in 1974, to 16 bits in 1978, to 32 bits by 1981 and 64 bits by 1985 [11].

A microprocessor chip by itself does not constitute all the parts required to implement a computer system. Performance is improved by increasing the bit width of the processor. In addition, functions will eventually be pulled into the microprocessor chip in order to reduce the number of parts required to implement a computer. There are two directions in which additional features are being incorporated into the microprocessor chip, as indicated in Figure 8.4. For many of the dedicated control functions such as a TTY controller or floppy disk controller, the program control sequences are relatively short, hence the memory needs are not large. It is logical to incorporate memory as an essential part of the chip. For example, the Intel 8051, 8 bit microcomputer, has 4k bytes of program memory and 128 bytes of data memory [12]. Such a device would increase the range of applications as more and more memories are included as a part of the chip. The inclusion of program and data memory within the microprocessor chip is referred to most appropriately as a microcomputer. The second direction, as indicated in Figure 8.4, is the inclusion of functions or features. This would enhance the performance capability of the microprocessor, not only in reducing the number of parts, but also in increasing its capability to compete with the minicomputer's spectrum of applications. For example, Intel is planning to incorporate in its next generation of microprocessors, iAPX 286 and iAPX 432, on-chip memory management and protection, multi-level software protection, an integral operating system kernel and other features that are currently available only in midi- and maxi-minicomputers [12]. The migration of software functions into hardware will extend the microprocessor capability into the high end of the minicomputer spectrum range.

At the mainframe high-performance level,

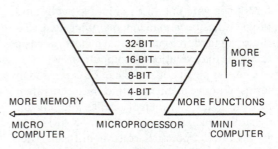

Figure 8.4. Microprocessor feature extensions.

the application of VLSI is more difficult. Among the chip techniques currently used are processor bit-slice, programmable logic arrays, gate arrays, and custom circuitry. Bit-slice processors contain only the arithmetic and logic functions of the central processor unit. They operate on a slice of data, typically 4 bits at a time. By cascading these chips we can design computers of various widths in multiples of 4 bits, for instance, eight 4 bit slices would give a 32 bit structure. Available since approximately 1975, the bit slices are just starting to show up in large numbers of computers. DEC, for example, uses the AMD 2901 (4 bit slice) in its DEC system-2020, and UNIVAC's 1100/60 model uses the Motorola 10800, also a 4 bit slice. Fairchild Camera and Instrument Corp. has recently come out with a family of LSI ECL 8 bit slices (F100220) designed for use in mainframe computers [13]. For VLSI there are two basic challenges: interconnections and product uniqueness. Because of the fact that the number of leads for a circuit has increased rapidly with the increase in circuit components, it is necessary to develope the interconnection capability beyond the current technology. The standard 14- or 40-pin dual-in-line packages are no longer adequate. The Intel iAPX 432 CPU will be packaged in 64-pin quad-in-line packages (QUIPs). It is expected that hundreds of pins are needed for custom logic VLSI chips. In addition, the product uniqueness problem results because the blocks tend to become unique; with a resulting explosion of different part types, each unit is needed only in small quantities. This is a challenge in developing cost-effective VLSI products.

System-level Impact

When improved basic technology becomes available, computers tend to evolve along two directions. Each model has two successors. In the first one, the performance is held constant, and the improved technology is used to build lower-priced machines that attract new applications, thus increasing the volume. This concept of a *minimal computer* expands the market, continually attracting new applications.

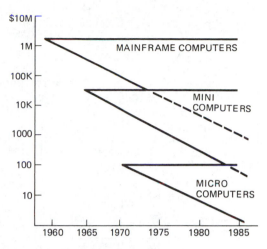

Figure 8.5. Computer evolution.

Each year, as the prices of the machines decline, new applications become economically feasible. The other model represents a constant cost with an increasing functionality or performance path. The improved technology is used to achieve better performance. The result of this evolutionary path is shown in Figure 8.5 [3]. As indicated in the figure, mainframe computers began their evolution around 1960; minicomputers, in the mid 1960s. The increase in performance capability of minicomputers began to intersect the low end of the mainframe computers in the mid 1970s. A tremendous growth of the superminis was evident during this period. The emergence of the microcomputers in the early 1970s promises to dominate the low end of the minicomputer market by 1985. The figure shows the performance level of the small mainframes in 1970 was provided by the superminis in 1975 and will probably be achieved by microcomputers in 1985.

8.3. LEVELS OF COMPUTER ARCHITECTURE

The word *architecture* is defined in Webster as "the art or science of building." We normally associate the term implicitly with designing and building inhabitable structures. Computer architecture explicitly means the art or science of designing and building computers. Both fields serve the needs of users in special ways.

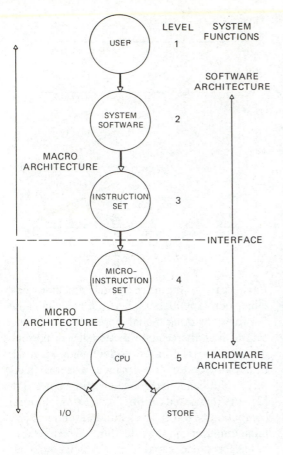

Figure 8.6. Levels of computer architecture.

The overall design of a computing system can be viewed functionally as a set of levels of interpreters [14] or abstractions [2]. This implies that there are distinct types of architecture within a computing system. The computer system is partitioned into various functional levels of components, which are illustrated in Figure 8.6. At the highest level or level 1, the system architecture determines which data processing functions are provided by the system and which ones belong to the external world, the end users. The communication between the system and the outside world is through two sets of interfaces: languages and system application programs (i.e., as utilities, sorts, and information retrieval programs). The system architecture includes the definition of both sets of interfaces.

Level 2 represents various functions within the system's software architecture. High-level languages and operating systems have necessarily played an important role in reducing software complexity and development effort and in increasing the programmer's productivity and software reliability. This is obtained at the expense of increasing memory space and program execution time. Most general operating system software provides a set of procedures that enables users to share computer hardware facilities efficiently. Automatic control over the resources is also provided. This helps free programmers from machine details such as the specific physical characteristics and protocol of peripheral devices used for input/output operations. The operating system does this by providing services such as memory management, process management, interrupt handling, file system management, system maintenance, and so forth. The next level, the instruction set, is the lowest level available to programmers. It is a collection of hardware features or characteristics such as the set of data operators, addressing modes, trap and interrupt sequences, register organization, and other features visible to software designers of the bare machine. The architecture of the instruction set and higher levels, as indicated in Figure 8.6, is the dividing line between the hardware and software architecture of a computer system. If the machine is microprogram-controlled, the microprogram that interprets the instruction set is termed *firmware,* and is considered part of the hardware architecture. The basic machine structure consists of the central processing unit (CPU), the storage unit, and the input/output unit. The interconnection of these three major units forms a digital computer, representing the hardware architecture.

Macro/Micro Architecture [15]

VLSI is drastically changing how computers are designed. The new integrated circuits are having the most impact on the hardware structure, that is, the configuration of registers, control circuitry, arithmetic and logic units, memories, and their interconnecting buses. This hardware structure is referred to as the microarchitecture of a computer. Considerable freedom is made possible in the invention of new microarchitectures. By building much more sophisticated microprocessor or ALU slices, this technique is extended into the VLSI realm. In the microarchitecture of very large mainframe systems, high-speed gate arrays continue to be the most appropriate technique of implementation.

Through all the changes in the hardware microarchitecture, there has been a concerted effort to maintain a constant macroarchitecture. By macroarchitecture, we mean the program-visible structure of the computer. Programmers or users are generally not aware of the buffers, ALUs, and buses, but see instead the instruction set, the types of data that can be manipulated (byte, half-word, full word, fixed or floating point, etc.) and the principles of operation at the user level. Any changes at the macroarchitecture level force a user to program or at least to convert the job the computer is to perform. If all programs were written in higher-level languages, the amount of recoding would be relatively small. Unfortunately, this is not the case with the code in the world today. Although a few people see the need for entirely new macroarchitectures, many wish to keep those that already exist. In fact, some advocate an industrywide standard macroarchitecture. The U.S. Army recognizes this proliferation of computer types. It causes unnecessary expense and makes development and support activities more complicated that they should be. A survey of 128 army systems indicated the use of 57 different computer types from 29 manufacturers for 92 of these systems [16]. Consequently, this led to the proposed standardization of the macroarchitecture for a family of military computers [16].

Because of the difficulty in introducing new macroarchitectures, alternative techniques are currently employed in order to achieve higher performance without requiring users to rewrite existing code. One successful technique is to build special purpose architectures and use them as attached processors to existing macroarchitectures. The same user interface is preserved while certain functions or applications are off-loaded for more efficient execu-

tion. This off-loading can be hidden from the user by the operating system. Potential tasks for this type of off-loading are data base management systems, scientific processing, front-end communications, input/output channel control, and systems control and maintenance. Such special processors are seen as predecessors of larger multiple-processor systems that could include units dedicated to particular programming languages, data base management, and so on. [17].

Greater freedom is possible in the invention of new microarchitectures for existing macroarchitectures. One significant challenge is to create a microarchitecture structure that can significantly aid the partitioning problem for the utilization of VLSI. To support the widely used System/370 macroarchitecture of the mainframes in its line, IBM designed two 4300 processors. Gate arrays are now being used for the first time in implementing a new microarchitecture. The variety of hardware microarchitectures that support the IBM System/370 macroarchitecture is increased as the number of the so-called IBM-plug compatible machine (PCM) vendors follow.

Architecture Trends

Computer architecture trends have passed through several distinct stages, as shown in Figure 8.7 [3]. During the early periods it is understandable that macroarchitecture played an important role in computer architecture. Since software investment had not been extensive, it was not excessively painful to change the software base. Consequently, there was considerable freedom in the macroarchitecture of computer systems. In the 1950s and early 1960s, the main emphasis was on the macroarchitecture design of the CPU with strong emphasis in minimizing hardware cost. By the mid 1960s the price prominence of the CPU had decreased substantially and the importance of software was recognized. IBM introduced its System/360 line of processors with constant macroarchitecture but each processor model was designed with a different microarchitecture in order to achieve the proper balance in cost/performance ratio. As more and

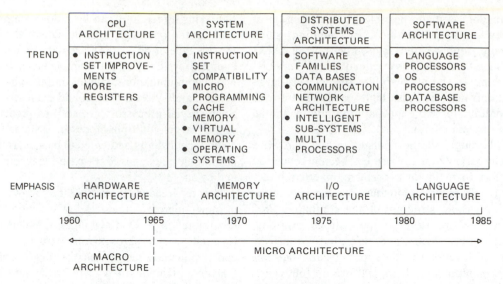

Figure 8.7. Architecture trends.

more application software was developed and accumulated, it became increasingly difficult to change the macroarchitecture. During the late 1960s, strong emphasis was placed on memory architecture as characteristized by microprogramming, cache memory, and virtual memory. These features took advantage of the rapid growth of semiconductor technology and integrated circuit technology in influencing the design of the microarchitecture. The advantages of instruction set compatibility was identified with resulting mainframe and minicomputer families. However, it was later recognized that instruction set compatibility was not completely sufficient for compatible software. Deliberately planned software is required for software compatibility [3].

Advances in microprocessors during the past years have shifted the emphasis toward distributed systems architectures. It is the main trend both in a network sense and in the organization of a computer system. Specific functions are off-loaded from the main processor to improve program execution. Progress is now beginning to be made in creating efficient architectures for manipulating data bases. Relational views of data are difficult to support within existing architectures. However, the data bases exhibit a high degree of regularity and inherent parallelism that can be exploited by specialized architectures supporting the main processor.

Similarly, intelligent peripherals and subsystems are economically attractive in expanding the capability of a computer system since the unbalanced speed and price of the CPU and peripherals is placing greater emphasis on I/O architecture.

The future trend is directed toward software architecture. It is already underway as indicated by increased sophistication of the microcoding functions for many of the system primitives for the operating system, interrupt handling, and language translation. Some of these functions will then migrate into hardware. By the early 1980s, processors tailored for languages, operating systems, and data bases will probably become a reality. Language architecture concepts for microprocessors are currently being explored by semiconductor manufacturers.

8.4. LANGUAGE SUPPORT

Importance of High-level Language

It is very clear that software dominates the cost of producing computer systems. As the range of computer applications increases and the application software grows larger and more complicated, a reduction in software development cost or an increase in software productivity is considered to be one of the more crucial problems in software development. Another factor that contributed to the high cost of software is its maintenance. Of the total cost of software, 70% occurs after the initial release [18] in debugging and maintaining a program through the life cycle. By implementing a straightforward, well-structured, and well-documented design, the total maintenance effort would be reduced.

The common approach to increasing software productivity and reducing maintenance cost is the extensive use of a high-level language suitable for each application. High-level languages offer the possibility that machine-independent code can be written so that software investment is less at the mercy of any one hardware vendor.

Rapid advances in integrated circuit technology have vastly expanded microprocessor capabilities. It is now far more convenient to implement system designs using software rather than hardwired logic. Minicomputer and microcomputer programmers often start out short on memory space and machine speed. This makes it imperative that assembly language be used to program their small machines. The same software problems of the earlier large machines are now appearing at the microcomputer level. The use of high-level language is gaining momentum in view of the cost benefits achievable by its adoption. Even more significantly, the software portability benefit of high-level language becomes more important as newer, more efficient microprocessors appear on the market. With the accelerated growth of integrated circuit technology, algorithms will have a far greater life expectancy than the hardware on which they are executed. The primary disadvantage of using a high-level language is that the assembled machine program that interprets the algorithm is generally less efficient in both speed and space than its functional equivalent, which is coded in assembler language. For this reason, most microprocessor programs have traditionally been written in native machine-level assembler language. Because of rapidly decreasing memory costs and continually increasing microprocessor power, this factor is becoming less important. The tradeoff is toward simplifying and reducing the software cost.

Semantic Gap of High-level and Machine Language [19]

Although current systems differ significantly from their predecessors in terms of cost, speed, reliability, internal organization, and circuit technology, the computer architecture of most current systems has not advanced beyond the basic von Neuman-type of structure. Some of the shortcomings of today's computer systems are attributable to a phenomenon known as the *semantic gap* [20]. The semantic gap is a measure of the difference between the concepts in high-level languages and the computer architecture supporting the machine-level assembler languages. The objects and operations provided in programming languages are not reflected in the framework of the hardware architecture. This undesirable large semantic gap contributes to software unreliability, performance problems, excessive program size, compiler complexity, and distortions of the programming languages, all of which contribute to the cost of data processing.

The large semantic gap introduces complexity into the design of a compiler. The code-generation portion must be extremely complex to generate code that bridges the semantic gap as efficiently as possible. As a result, a large number of instructions must be generated by the compiler from the rather primitive machine-instruction repertoire to implement the high-level language concepts. The larger size program correspondingly requires more storage. This has a negative effect on performance because it increases the number of instructions that must be executed. The information flow between the memory and the CPU is likewise increased. A good first-order measure in comparing the performance of different machines is the size of the compiled program. If the semantic gap is so large that it cannot be efficiently bridged by the compiler, then undesired restrictions must be placed on the definition of the language, the underlying machine shows through the language, and the language is misused.

The semantic gap contributes to software unreliability because sets of programming errors that could be prevented or detected by the computing system, are not detected in the cur-

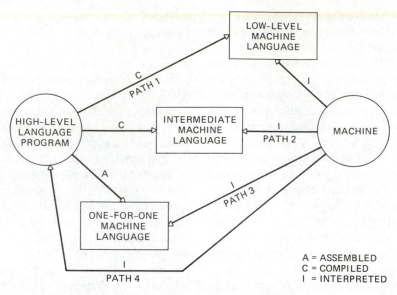

Figure 8.8. General language/machine relationships.

rent systems. As pointed out [19], one common programming error that arises in a large variety of circumstances is a reference to a variable that has an undefined value. The error is difficult to debug when program execution proceeds using some unpredictable value. This creates an error condition that usually is not repeatable.

Language-based Architecture

Many architectural features were designed to facilitate the construction of large programs in a multi-user operating environment. Innovation in addressing, memory management, and protection are key features in systems using capability- or object-based addressing/protection schemes. These mechanisms may be viewed as architectural concepts designed to narrow the gap between hardware structure and the requirements of modern programming methodology.

Figure 8.8 from Reference 19 illustrates some of the basic approaches to computer architecture in terms of a relationship between the high-level language program and the machine. The top path represents the conventional or traditional approach of an extensive compilation process of translating a high-level language program to a machine-level instruc-

tion program, which is then executed by the machine. An alternative is to develop a computer system architecture with a precise and complete intermediate or base language that the system will support at the machine level. Such a machine can support many user high-level languages, implemented by compilation of the source program into the base language, which is in turn interpreted by the machine. This approach is called *language direction architecture,* an alternative that aims at closing the semantic gap.

The first two paths in Figure 8.8 represent the category commonly referred to as *high-level language machines.* In path 3, the high-level language can be thought of as the assembly language of the system. There is a one-to-one correspondence between the statement types and operators in the high-level language and machine instructions. The source program is assembled rather than compiled. The bottom path in Figure 8.8 is the extreme approach in which the machine directly interprets high-level language programs, reducing the semantic gap to zero. However, such architecture is not practical from the viewpoint of cost, performance, and flexibility. It is also much less efficient than the previous approaches. Every time the machine executes a statement, it must perform a lexical analysis of the statement, parse the statement, convert symbols to addresses, and so on. All of these steps must be performed each time a statement is executed in comparison to once per statement by the compiler or assembler.

Properties of languages are directly represented in hardware by some machines that have been specially designed. Examples are the FORTRAN machine [21], the ALGOL machine [22], and the SYMBOL system [23]. They represent path 3 in Figure 8.8 high-level language machines. The latter machine implements the SYMBOL programming language (SPL) compiler directly in hardware. This restricts the system's flexibility and dedicates a large part of the hardware to performance of a function that is used only occasionally.

In the path 2 category, language-directed architecture includes the Burroughs B5500/6500/5700/7600 [24] and the KDF9 [25]. These machines introduced the "stack" mechanism to expressly support language features such as procedure activation and termination, including the allocation and deallocation of storage locations for local variables. This was motivated by the ALGOL 60 block structured-type of language, which provides for local variable declaration and permits recursive invocation of procedures.

Direct execution of high-level code ranks among the most significant developments in microcomputers. Pascal, a relative newcomer to the high-level language scene was proposed by Niklaus Wirth in 1968. Since then, it has been implemented as a compiler in a wide range of computers from large mainframes to microcomputers. The common implementation technique for Pascal follows path 2 of Figure 8.8. The source program in Pascal is compiled into an intermediate language called Pascal P-code. It is then interpreted into machine instruction. There is already the Western Digital Pascal MICROENGINE, a microprogrammed processor whose machine language is Pascal P-code. The same chip set as the PDP LSI-11 is used in the implementation but with a different microprogram. Sorrento Valley Associated claims that the MICROENGINE executes Pascal programs faster than an LSI-11 executes hand-turned machine code for the same operations [26].

Implementation Method or High-level Lanugage Machine

The compilation or interpretation time of a source program into machine-executable code is in general not an important factor, especially in the real-time environment. There the compiled object program continues to run for a long period without further recompilation. In some applications, however, such as a computation center, programs are constantly being compiled and run. In this situation, the compilation time will account for a large share of the computation time and has a direct impact on system performance. Various high-level language machines have been implemented. These can be classified into three categories, in terms of the implementation method, as follows:

1. Software: conventional compilers and interpreters
2. Firmware-implemented: firmware that processes high-level languages on the microinstruction level
3. Hardware-implemented: special hardware that directly executes high-level language programs

The most recently developed high-level language machines belong in the second category. They are mainly superior to a software high-level language processor in terms of performance and to a hardware-implemented high-level language machine in terms of flexibility. In addition, firmware-implemented high-level language machine performance can be improved by introducing appropriate hardware modules specialized for high-level language features. The cost/performance of three experimental high-level language machines (HLLMs): S-BASIC (software-implemented BASIC), F-BASIC (firmware-implemented), and H-BASIC (firmware-implemented with additional hardware) were compared on a common evaluation basis to analyze tradeoffs among software, firmware, and hardware [27]. Each BASIC machine translates a BASIC program into an intermediate language program, which is in turn interpreted into an object machine-language program. Experimental results show that performance is improved 17 times or more with the F-BASIC (firmware-implemented) and 3.6 times more with appropriate hardware functions in the H-BASIC. This is in comparison with the S-BASIC (software-implemented) in terms of translation and interpretation time required with each machine. The necessary memory capacity for a language processor is also reduced by adopting firmware and is reduced still more by introducing additional hardware. The addition of firmware and hardware, however, increases system cost by an estimated 4% [27]. Firmware implementation support of a high-level language machine appears to be more practical.

Instruction Enhancements for High-level Languages

Compiler and language designs have made dramatic advances in recent years. Processors like DEC's VAX 11/780 [28] and MCF (Military Computer Family) show a definite trend toward incorporating features in the instruction set that are designed specifically for supporting high-level languages. Similarly, new microprocessors like National's NS16000 group [29] and Motorola's 68000 [30] are following a similar trend. Some of these features are concerned with the following:

- Symmetrical resources
- Addressing modes
- Address manipulation
- Flexible data structure
- Stack instructions
- Procedural instructions

The assembly language instruction set is the basic machine for which code must be compiled. Enhancements in this area reduce the amount of memory required and correspondingly improve both compilation time and program execution time.

From the compiler's viewpoint, the most important attribute of a processor instruction set is regularity [31]. It is the key feature needed to abstract the various processor resources for uniform treatment by the compiler. Otherwise the compiler will be hampered by special case treatment of the nonregular instruction set. For example, some processors do not allow the general purpose register 0 to be used as an index register. In effect, the register field of the instruction whose value of nonzero or zero is used to indicate the decision of indexing or not avoids the need of one additional bit in the instruction to indicate whether or not there is an index. This means that the register 0 must be treated as a special case by the compiler. Another one of the more common restrictions involves multiplication and division where an even-odd register pair is required to hold the double word product or dividend. This allows a single register field n in the assembled instruction to specify two registers, n and $n + 1$ (where $n = $ even). The need for a second register field in the instruction encoding is eliminated, thereby simplifying the hardware logic and reducing the bit size of the instruction. From the compiler's viewpoint, however, allocation of temporary registers for intermediate values of expression computation is made more complicated. When temporary registers are allocated for a multiplication or division, the compiler cannot take any two free registers. It must find a contiguous even-odd register pair [32].

A wide range of address modes, that is, indexing, direct, indirect, covering various data structures is required to provide flexibility in address calculations, a very important function in high-level language programming. Variations in addressing memory take the form of operations performed on the address field before the operand is referenced in main storage. The capability of the architecture for applying a large range of addressing modes in identically accessing all data types, bytes, half words or full words, and instructions, without any exceptions, makes it possible to compile compact and efficient code. The Motorola 68000 and the National NS16000 microprocessors have incorporated features in their architecture that enable the general-purpose registers, address modes, data types. and instructions to be used symmetrically with respect to each other.

Several modern languages incorporate pointers as a basic data type. For example, the C programming language allows pointer arithmetic [33]. This provides a fast way of iterating through an array of objects without the implied multiplication of array indexing [31]. The processor instruction set must support arithmetic operations on addresses to take advantage of this feature, which is provided in the language. Such a facility would not present any problems if the address data is of the same size as the data word; then the arithmetic operation within the processor's ALU is the same. However, if processors have addresses wider than the ALU, that is, 16 bit arithmetic and 24 bit pointers, pointer operations would be rather awkward. The Motorola 68000 microprocessor (16 bit data, 24 bit addresses) provides a separate 24 bit ALU to handle address calculations. This increase in hardware is offset by improvement in execution time.

Another important attribute of the processor is the data structure. The Burroughs B1700 gives 100% variability in that operands may be any shape or size, without loss of efficiency. There are no word sizes or data formats. All information in a B1700 system is represented by fields, which are recursively defined to be either bit strings or strings of fields [34]. All memory is addressable to the bit, and all field lengths are expressible to the bit. Bytes and words are special cases of fields. The more current machines such as the VAX 11/780 provide a flexible data structure in terms of byte, word, and double-word and also supports arrays of bit fields. This facility allows elements or fields of variable lengths that are not limited to a word boundary.

One of the frustrating problems in designing languages and compilers to be used on different machines is that of byte order representation [31]. In transmitting data between machines, character string data is usually treated as a series of bytes; numerical data, or as a series of words. The current computers are not all consistent in byte count within a word. One group that consists of IBM machines, Interdata machines, and others, counts bytes within a word from the left. Another group consisting of the PDP 11 series, the INTEL 8086, and others, counts bytes from the right. The compiler lays out a structure in the natural byte and word order of each particular machine. For example, the word *WING* is represented as *GNIW* in a 32 bit word on right to left ma-

chines, and as *WING* on left to right machines. Thus, whenever communication is required between the PDP 11 and the IBM 370, additional data-dependent processing is required in order to send character strings as bytes and numerical values as words. The PDP 11 provides a special instruction to swap bytes in a word to handle this incompatibility. The best solution from the compiler's viewpoint is for all manufacturers to adopt a common standard, thereby simplifying the communication problem between machines.

The subroutine is one of the most important concepts in software. The principal idea in modular, structured programming is the partitioning of large programs into many small, understandable modules, which are known as procedures or subroutines. The best mechanism for the subroutine's call and return involves the stack. In a well-structured program, subroutine calls will be perfectly nested in a last-in first-out manner. Essentially all modern computers provide some sort of stacking facility to assist in the implementation of subroutine functions. Efficient instructions have been provided in many of the current mini- and microcomputers to handle subroutine entry and exit and stack manipulation. These instructions and the associated stack hardware are clear indications of software requirements affecting computer architecture all the way down to the microprocessor level.

Future Trends

In the years ahead, software productivity enhancements will be a major concern. It is expected that high-level languages will reduce initial program development and long-term maintenance costs and provide for greater software transportability from machine to machine. Progress in hardware and firmware technologies pushes toward a consistent computer system, where system implementation, debugging, execution, and maintenance are uniformly supported on the high-level language level. The movement of adopting a standard language has been strong at the microcomputer level. Many of the problems we have concerning mainframes we are now facing with microprocessors, except at an accelerated rate. The resulting software obsolescence can be minimized by use of a machine-independent transportable language—that is, a language and associated run-time support that may be maintained and transported to various architectures, even those that are yet to be developed.

Pascal is widely available and is undoubtedly the most popular new language. The rapid growth of Pascal has become a de facto standard in the microprocessor arena. Today, Pascal exists for all hardware, from micros to super computers, and its range of uses has been broadened considerably from its original role as a teaching tool. Current uses of Pascal range from real-time processing for NASA's Deep Space Network to general ledger systems on a minicomputer [35]. Machines like the Motorola 68000 and the National NS16000 were designed with Pascal in mind [30]. More specifically, the Pascal MICROENGINE from Western Digital Corp and the MK-16 from Mikros Systems Corp. were made to execute P-code, the immediate interpretive language generated by some Pascal compilers. Therefore, it is expected that Pascal will continue to be popular for some time to come.

Pascal was the basis of the Department of Defense (DOD) high-level language *Ada*. While it departs significantly from Pascal, most of the good features of Pascal have been retained [16]. The adoption of Ada as the standard language addresses the issue of software obsolescence with changes in hardware technology.

As evidenced by the strong interest in high-level languages, hardware support is beginning to play an increasingly important role in reducing the software development cost. Moreover, the problem of software transportability from machine to machine is a strong economic reason for upgrading technology and completely redoing software.

8.5. OPERATING SYSTEM SUPPORT

Needs of Operating Systems

The term *operating system* is defined by Madnick and Donovan [36] as "those program modules within a computer system that govern the control of equipment resources such as processor(s), main storage, secondary storage, I/O devices and files. These modules resolve conflicts, attempt to optimize performance and simplify the effective use of the system. They act as an interface between the user's programs and the physical computer hardware." In the earlier computer systems, each programmer personally operated the machine by loading decks, pushing buttons, running and debugging the program. The execution process involved the entire computer, and run times were quite long. As time passed, the demands upon the computer system far exceeded the amount of equipment available in a traditional computing center. Moreover, the equipment itself was expensive; no user could afford to pay for the entire machine during the period required to process his complete job. The primary objective of early operating systems was to utilize the physical equipment as efficiently as possible. This disparity in the processing speed of the central processing unit (CPU) and its I/O devices suggested the sharing of resources as a means of using them more efficiently. By maintaining a series of queues for various types of resources, the operating system could then coordinate and schedule all pending tasks so that all the devices were simultaneously busy most of the time. This tended to maximize the number of tasks per unit time that was completed and thereby distributed the cost of running the equipment among as many different jobs as possible.

In addition to managing the hardware resources, the operating system implements *software resources,* for example, files, processes, and message channels [37]. These resources are needed to provide a more useful and more reliable programming environment for the user. The term *virtual objects* is often used in referring to software resources. Though they appear to be simple objects to the user, they may in fact be created by the operating system by a complicated, underlying mechanism. Higher productivity in application programming is made possible by these high-level, simplified facilities. A file is an example of a virtual object. It appears to the programmer simply as a set of records that the user may update or read on command from his program. However, the operating system must format the records and store them in various storage media. In addition, the operating system must set up buffers and provide procedures to control the transfer of records between the main storage and secondary storage. It must also protect files from unauthorized access or accidental damage. Virtual objects can save the application programmer from a considerable amount of work that he/she would otherwise have to do. All the internal details of the objects and of the task of controlling the devices used to implement them are masked by the operating system. This results in greater protection on its part from misuse and in more reliable operation for all users. The development of operating systems plays an increasingly important role in modern computer systems.

Types of Operating Systems [38]

Operating systems can be classified into four categories: (1) the serial batch system, (2) the multiprogramming system, (3) the time sharing system, and (4) the real-time system. The key operating system functions are the scheduling of resources and dispatching of programs. The emphasis placed on the characteristics of these functions and policies of implementation are determined by the type of operating system. The handling of I/O facilities is also common to most operating systems, but the extent of the functions and their capabilities varies from category to category.

The serial batch system was the first type to be developed. It utilizes what is called sequential job scheduling. Jobs may come in from a card reader or may be stored on a fast intermediate device, usually direct access, and are collected into groups called batches. The operating system would process the jobs singly until all were done. There is no multiprogramming and the operating system is primarily used for scheduling input/output.

Multiprogrammed operating systems implement multiple, concurrently operating virtual machines. This enables the concurrent running of two or more batch jobs. Multiple jobs would be in the CPU at the same time contending for the resources of the system. While one job waits for an I/O event, another job has control of the CPU and is executing. This maximizes the usage of system resources. It is not at all unusual to see a system with 15 or more jobs running concurrently with most of them waiting for I/O events. Multiprogramming obviously offers a tremendous improvement over simple serial batch systems. The problem of wasting valuable CPU time while waiting for I/O operations was one of the reasons for its development. The key characteristic of a multiprogramming system is the importance that is placed on hardware utilization rather than user utilization.

A time-sharing operating system on the other hand places emphasis on user utilization. It is a type of system where there are many users, each treating the computer as though he/she had exclusive use of it. A time-sharing operating system is typically characterized by multiple terminal connections in the computer system. The terminal may be a teletypewriter or perhaps a video display unit with a keyboard. Often these users are located across large geographical distances and are connected through dial-up telephone lines to the central processing unit. Time-sharing has the effect of giving the user a complete computing system at his disposal at all times, but he pays only for the time he actually uses.

Another type of operating system is the real-time system. In many ways, real time seems much like time sharing. We may have multiple remote terminals initiating inputs; appropriate outputs are generated in response. The difference between the two is that in a time-sharing system, the users generally run different jobs. Each feeds his own requests into the computer, gets his program executed and backs out. In a real-time system, there is a common program running in the CPU that handles the remote terminals. The remote terminals feed data into this one program. It processes the data and sends the output back to the remote terminals. An electronic telephone switching system is a good example of a real-time system. The remote terminals are the telephone sets. Their inputs are "on-hook," "off-hook," and dialing information. A common call-processing program processes the inputs, provides the appropriate signaling, and sets up the connection paths. One of the major requirements imposed on the operating system is that input requests from remote terminals must respond within a certain prescribed time, namely, milliseconds—so-called real-time—otherwise the input data may be lost.

Operating-system Functions

There are several ways of examining the operating system structure. One of them is based on the view that the operating system is a manager of resources: namely, memory, processor(s), devices, and information (programs and data). It is the function of the operating system to allocate these valuable resources efficiently and to resolve conflicts among the users in using them. The programs that manage these resources are grouped into four resource categories: memory management, processor management, device management, and information management. Each manager must (1) keep track of the resources, (2) enforce the policy of distribution and scheduling of resources, (3) allocate the resource, and (4) reclaim the resource.

The main storage is an important resource handled by the memory manager. The complexity of this function depends very much upon the sophistication of the memory hierachical structure. Advanced operating systems operate on the concept of virtual memory. Such a scheme permits the user to treat the main memory and auxiliary storage, such as disk drives, as a homogeneous unit. It is the memory manager that moves information from the disk drives to the main memory and back, as needed for the processing program. These transfers are transparent to the user. Although the user's virtual addresses do not change, the physical location of information within the computer does. The memory manager must keep track of the ever changing internal addresses, which parts are in use and by whom, and which parts are not in use. In a multiprogramming environment, the manager decides which process (job) gets memory, when it gets it, and the amount. After the process no longer needs the memory or has been terminated, the manager must then reclaim the resource and make it available for allocation to other processes.

Another important system resource is the processor itself, the time allotted to a job or program by the CPU. The job scheduler selects from all the jobs submitted to the system and decides which one will be allowed into the system. The CPU time allocated to a job is the time when that task has control of the system resources and executes it program. Figure 8.9 shows a state model which a job may go through from submission to completion. In a multiprogramming system, the scheduling is divided into two parts: job scheduler and processor scheduler. The job scheduler chooses which jobs will run and creates processes for each job. The processor scheduler decides which of the ready processes receives a processor at what time and for how long. The life cycle of a process is represented by the transitions between the states shown on the right in Figure 8.9:

- Run: The process is running and its programs are executing in the processor.
- Wait: The process is blocked or put to sleep. It is waiting for some event, for instance, an I/O operation to be completed.
- Ready: The process is ready to run. It is waiting for a processor to be assigned.

Another program module within the processor manager, the traffic controller, keeps track of the status of the process. There is a similar state diagram for every process in a system.

In most computer installations, I/O devices account for over half of the system cost. They include disks, tapes, printers, card readers, and support devices such as control channels. It is desirable to employ them as efficiently as possible. The primary techniques of managing and allocating devices can be categorized into three major types: dedicated, shared, and virtual. A dedicated device is assigned to a job for its entire duration. This type of allocation is inefficient if the job does not fully and continually utilize the device. Most direct-access

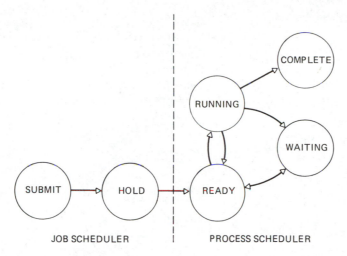

Figure 8.9. State model.

storage devices such as disks or drums may be shared concurrently by several processes. The interleaving capability of sharing a single device with different jobs in a multiprogramming environment permits the full utilization of the more expensive devices. However, the management of a shared device in terms of keeping track of its status, scheduling policy, and allocation can become rather complicated, particularly if a robust and efficient operation is desired. Some slow, sequential devices such as printers or card punches, lend themselves more readily to the dedicated mode of operation. They may be converted into shared devices through so-called SPOOLing techniques. The SPOOLing routine, for example, simply records the printer data onto a disk, and at some later time a routine would copy the information onto a printer at maximum speed. Since the disk may be shared by several users, a dedicated device is therefore converted to or gives the illusion of a shared device, changing one printer into many "virtual" printers. This approach of creating virtual devices provides a more flexible technique for managing and scheduling jobs and devices.

The information manager is concerned with generation, storage, and retrieval of data in a file system. The basic functions are (1) to keep track of the resource (information), that is, its location, status, size, use, access rights, and so forth, (2) to decide who has access to the re-

sources, enforce protection requirements, and provide accessing routines, (3) to allocate the resource, that is, open a file and (4) to deallocate the resource, that is, close a file. The management of a file system by the information manager frees the user from many of the problems associated with allocating space for the user's data, physical storage formats, and I/O accessing. In addition, sharing information among users and protection of information from unauthorized access are administrated by the information manager.

Figure 8.10 from Reference 36 shows the hierarchical structure of a kernel of the operating system. The modules of information management are placed in the outer ring. As pointed out in the reference, full implementation of this manager can be quite complicated. The file system is divided into layers and each follows structured programming techniques in that each level depends only on the level below it and only calls downward.

Hardware Enhancements

The primary function of an operating system as indicated in the previous section, is to manage hardware resources in such a way as to achieve their best possible utilization. Since physical equipment is limited, the operating system conceptually sets up virtual resources and competes for use of the physical resources.

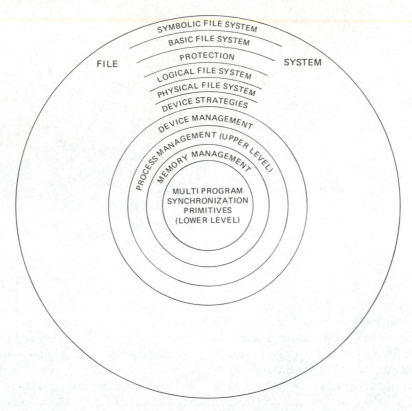

Figure 8.10. Resource management relationship.

However, only one assumes full control of the real resource. In order to enhance the operating systems ability to carry out its functions, studies have shown that certain hardware [39] and firmware [40, 41, 42] facilitate the administration and control of jobs through the system. These possible enhancements are discussed in the following sections.

Queue Administration.   If the number of resources is insufficient to satisfy all users, some queueing mechanism is needed to temporarily store the requests. As soon as a resource is free, the top one of the waiting list would be dispatched to assume control of the newly available resource. There are various queues throughout the system mainly for the purpose of time sharing the more expensive resources. For example, Figure 8.11a shows the general arrangement of processor management involving the hold, ready, and wait queues. The user submitted jobs arrive in the system and are temporarily stored on disk. The job manager places the selected job in the hold queue ac-

cording to some preestablished policy. As soon as resources and space are available in the ready queue, the top of the hold queue moves onto the ready queue. This in effect creates the process and assigns a virtual processor to the job (Figure 8.11b). The virtual processor is dedicated until the job is completed. After the process moves into the ready queue, the process manager administers and schedules the actual time sharing of the real processor. The process may be in one of three possible states.

A running process which has possession of the real processor will run until either the assigned time slice is used up or it cannot proceed any further. In the former case, the process will be reinserted into the ready queue and then will wait for its next time slice. In the latter case, the process will be put into the wait queue since it is blocked and must wait until the device becomes idle. As indicated in Figure 8.11a, the unblocked process is returned to the ready queue to wait its turn for the use of the processor.

In examining various ways of improving the

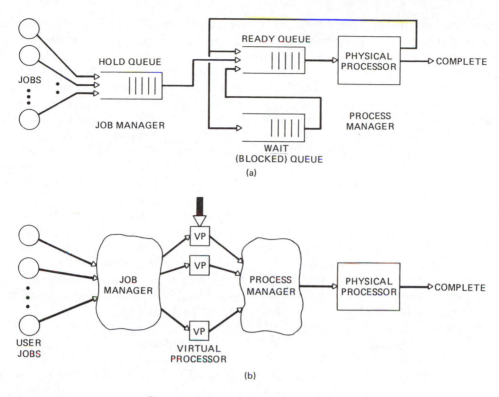

Figure 8.11. Process management structure.

performance of an operating system and after two years of study, the conclusions stated in Ref. [39] are (1) to support a good mechanism for holding the queues of processors waiting for resources and (2) to provide enough resources so that very few processes are waiting on queues. The hardware proposal for queue implementation is content addressable memories (CAMs) [43]. This will allow the operating system to post a request for service in one machine cycle and to return the highest priority request for servicing another cycle.

In a conventional software maintained queue, the queue manipulation functions are rather tedious and time consuming. For example, it would be necessary to keep the ready queue sorted by priority, search the queue for the highest priority process each time the operating system wishes to dispatch a process to run, or have a separate queue for each priority. When an I/O devices becomes idle, the operating system must search the wait (blocked) queue for the highest priority request waiting for this device and transfer the request to the ready queue where it competes with all other

requests for the CPU. The use of CAMs for queue implementation simplifies the situation. Both the ready and the wait queue can be combined and reside on the same CAM. This eliminates the need to move entries between them. When a process is ready for execution, a request is inserted into the CAM with the job number, process number, and priority as determined by the system and the status bit set to 0 or 1 depending on whether the process is known to be idle (ready to run) or busy (blocked). When the operating system is ready to dispatch a new process to be run, the entire CAM is examined simultaneously (one machine cycle) for the request for an idle process having the highest priority level. The selected one is dispatched and is removed from the CAM. If this process involves using an I/O device, for instance, a line printer, the updating of the device status to the busy state includes accessing the CAM and setting all processes requesting the use of the busy device to the busy state. As long as the device is in the busy state, none of the made-busy processes will be dispatched. When the device is released and becomes idle, the inverse operation changes the blocked processes to the ready state and again they are qualified as candidates for dispatching.

The software overhead can be reduced substantially using a CAM to implement system queues. The queue manipulation is especially time critical and one of the more frequently performed operations in the operating system.

Context Switching. The sharing of the processor is achieved by placing several processes together in main storage and providing a mechanism for switching the control of the processor from one process to another. The state of the active process is defined by a set of processor registers. *Context switching* is the swapping of the contents of these registers for another register image. Typically, it is invoked when an active process calls operating system functions or is unable to proceed further without requesting a service provided by the control program, such as I/O. It is also invoked when a process requires cooperation from another process.

Context switching is done frequently in a multiprogramming environment; hence, it is important that this operation of saving one process context and loading another be done rapidly. In modern computers such as the VAX 11/780, the instruction set includes *save hardware* context and *load hardware* context instructions [44]. This reduces operating system overhead in both system calls and in the dispatching of another process. In addition to providing specialized instructions to enhance context switching, dedicated hardware for the operating functions is provided to maintain the context of the operating system hardware. Two specific areas in which additional hardware is provided are (1) in the memory management unit and (2) in the hardware register set. A later section will discuss the hardware support for memory management units. In the area of hardware register sets, multiple copies have been provided to facilitate context switching. For example, in the UNIVAC 1100 series computer systems, there are three sets of 16 registers: *A, X,* and *R. A* registers are used for arithmetic, *X* registers for indexing, and *R*

registers for special functions. To reduce the register's *saves* and *restores,* another three sets of *A, X,* and *R* registers are provided for the operating system [45,46]. An interesting variation of multiple copies of register sets is the technique employed by Texas Instruments in the implementation of the 990 computer family [47]. Its general register set is placed in main memory and is realized as a 16 word area of memory that is considered as workspace. This area is defined by a workspace pointer that is not fixed, but may be changed dynamically under program control. The context saving and restoring the general register set deal with only the workspace pointer rather than with the registers themselves, which constitutes a substantial savings in terms of the number of words transferred in and out of main memory [47].

Interrupt Facilities. Context switching is also necessary upon interrupts. The time interval between the interrupt being requested and the interrupt software routines starting work on the problem is called the *latency time.* This latency time is basically the time required to change the context of the processor and to determine the interrupting source and branch into the selected interrupt handling routine. A stack facility is usually provided to facilitate saving and restoring the hardware context. The operating characteristic of a last-in-first-out stack mechanism provides a direct and straightforward manner for handling priority interrupts, that is, permitting higher-priority interrupts to interrupt or preempt lower ones. This nesting of interrupts is automatically serviced in the proper order as the interrupts unwind from higher to lower priority. The physical implementation of a stack may take one of three forms [48]:

- The stack may be located entirely in main memory.
- The stack may be configured entirely from a set of dedicated hardware registers.
- The stack may be implemented with hardware registers and extended into

main memory when the hardware stack is exceeded.

By providing a hardware stack facility, the saving and restoring of the processor context can be done quickly. The problem of exceeding the number of hardware registers allocated to form the stack may be removed if the hardware stack is allowed to expand into the main memory.

It is possible to achieve a very fast response time for individual priority interrupt requests by associating a separate hardware register set with each interrupt level. Using this technique, there is no need to save the registers on the stack each time a program is interrupted by a higher-priority request. The interrupt hardware simply switches from the register set associated with the interrupted program to the register set associated with the new priority level. The IBM System/7 uses this technique with four priority levels [49]. Each level has a complete set of internal registers. There may be as many as 16 sublevels of priority assigned to each priority level. Current processing is interrupted only by requests on a higher-priority level.

The procedure of identifying the interrupting device can be done either by software or hardware polling techniques. Software polling, of course, is a very time-consuming method in which a software routine interrogates each device sequentially from the top of the sequence and works down to the interrupting device. In hardware polling, the processor and its external set of devices are physically interconnected in such a manner that the CPU may interrogate all devices simultaneously to obtain the address of the interrupting unit. The address returned by this hardware handshaking procedure could be used as an index or vector that is added to the contents of a preassigned processor hardware register. The processor register acts as a base address, and the index points to a full memory word that is treated as an indirect address by the interrupt hardware. Each interrupting device has a unique index into the table. The address found at the table location pointed to by the index vectors is the location of the appropriate device service routine. The

use of hardware polling is very effective in determining the highest-priority interrupt that is pending and generates the program address that handles the selected interrupt.

Memory Management Hardware.   In virtual memory systems, the complete virtual-to-physical address translation tables are typically stored in main memory. A significant amount of time is required by the CPU in the repetitive task of dynamic address translation, using the main store tables. This translation time can be reduced substantially by storing the likely-to-be-used physical address translations in a high-speed cache-like address translation buffer (ATB). This is also commonly referred to as a translation lookaside buffer. Only one job is running at a time. If the ATB contains one set of translation entries just for that job, the ATB must be reset or "flushed" so as to take on new translation data when the processor switches to a new job. A separate set of ATBs dedicated to the operating system would reduce the amount of "flushing" and reloading of the ATB when the system is switching between a user's process and a system call. In the VAX 11/780, the cache containing 128 virtual-to-physical page address translations are divided into two equal sections: a 64 system space page translation and a 64 user process space page translation [44].

In the microcomputer area, memory management chips are currently available to extend the capability and improve the performance of the microprocessor spectrum of machines. The Motorola memory management chip, MC6829, contains 4 sets of preloaded mapping entries with 32 registers per set [50]. For many applications, 1 set can be dedicated to the operating system and the other 3 to separate processes. This allows for fast context switching between processes. Up to 8 of the MC6829s can be connected together, providing the capability of having 32 unique processes existing simultaneously in the system. Each process can accommodate up to 64k bytes of memory or 32 pages with each page containing 2k bytes. Another sophisticated memory management chip is National's NS16082 [51]. It is paired with the 16032

CPU to make this 16 bit microprocessor a virtual memory machine. The memory management unit (MMU) has an on-chip translation buffer that holds the 32 most recently referenced virtual pages with their translations. The most significant feature of this chip and the CPU chip is the aborting facility, which would support demand paging in the memory management scheme. In normal operation, the MMU examines each memory access and determines whether or not the word resides in main memory. If it does, the MMU translates the virtual address to a physical address and sends it to the main memory. However, if the desired word is not in memory, the MMU responds with an abort signal to the CPU. At this point the CPU will stop executing the instruction and restores any register that was altered by the instruction to its original state prior to the instruction execution. The operating system will then locate the needed page from the secondary storage and load it into the main memory. All of this transaction is transparent to the user. The combination of the CPU and MMU ensures that the aborted instruction can be reexecuted and proceed properly after the missing page has been transferred into the main memory.

Real-time Clock. Hardware support to maintain and update a timing list is another operating system function that can be quite time consuming when it is done entirely by software. Reference 39 indicates that the use of content-addressable memories (CAMs) in storing the clock wake up list is very desirable. Many processes need to be activated periodically or after a certain amount of time has elapsed. In the meantime, they must sleep quietly in the background using as few resources as possible. On each tick of a real-time clock, an interrupt is generated. The timers are updated to reflect the passing of another unit of time; the entire timer list is then examined to see if any job needs to be awakened at this time. The administration of the list must constantly be kept in the proper order or it must be searched. The use of a CAM simplifies this ordering or searching problem. A typical timing function available in a system is in the

form "wake me up after N time units have elapsed for m number of times." The m events could be once, a predetermined number, or every time. Since the clock interrupt will occur with high frequency, hardware support in this area will have relatively large payoffs in system efficiency.

An alternative to CAMs in implementing the timing list would be the use of a microcomputer, for instance, the Intel 8051. The on-chip program and data memory can be fully utilized to implement a set of timers and associated control sequence to administer the timing functions. They include the operations of inserting a new timer into the list, sorting the list into an ordered set, updating the timing count, signaling to the processor when a timeout occurs, and deleting the timer from the list when it is no longer needed. By allocating special hardware to perform the repetitive and time-consuming task, the main processor is deloaded. The system overhead of process activation and deactivation is reduced.

In the microprocessor area, timing functions are also needed in many applications. In order to relieve the CPU of the function of timing internal or external events, special programmable interval timer chips, such as the Intel 8253 are currently available, and are capable of direct interfacing with almost any microprocessor, including the 8080, 6800, Z80, PACE, SC/MP, 6502, and 8085 [52].

Microprogram Enhancements. Microprogramming is another technique to enhance operating system functions [53]. The benefits derived from casting some of the primitives in firmware are (1) improved performance, (2) decreased program development cost, and (3) security and program correctness. The primitives that are candidates for microprogram implementation are those that are used frequently throughout the operating system, that are unlikely to change with time, and that would suffer from the slower execution rate of software. A recent study by Brown et. al. [40] lists 14 functions that could be implemented as primitives through microprogramming. Some of these are: queue manipulation, context switching, program synchronizing, memory management control, process communication, reconfiguration, protection and checking, scheduling, and so on. As mentioned in earlier sections, some of these functions are also candidates for hardware implementation. In some cases, a combination of hardware and firmware is appropriate.

A subsequent paper by Brown et. al. [41] shows several things: (1) how to take advantage of the efficiency that may be gained from microprogramming operating system primitives, (2) how to select those primitives most appropriate for implementation, and (3) how to perform an analysis of the trade-offs between software, firmware, and hardware. Microprogramming provides another dimension in which operating system primitives can be implemented.

Future Direction

A wide range of operating systems exists today, ranging from the very simple to the very sophisticated. They are available even on the microprocessor level. The UNIX* time-sharing operating system [54] developed for minicomputers is currently running on various microprocessors, that is, the 8086, 68000, and Z8000. Because UNIX itself is written in the high-level C language [33], it is portable and can be made to work on a number of machines easily and quickly. All other software packages are directly usable with it, a tremendous asset in software capability without much development effort.

As pointed out by Madnick and Donovan [36], the functions and operations between the file system and the memory segmentation and paging mechanisms are similar. It appears that the future direction would be to unify and integrate both memory management and information management. Hardware can be designed to help merge these two important modules of the operating system. The evidence for this direction is shown in the recent IBM System/38. This system employs an address structure with 48 bits, which is sufficient to reference all main and secondary memory

*UNIX is a trademark of Bell Laboratories.

without reusing an address. All program codes and data to be manipulated are stored as an object. The user is not aware of the internal storage format once he defines the object's characteristics and initial values. This object-oriented high-level architecture is beginning to appear in new systems. Such a structure provides improved data integrity, protection, and security. Intel's iAPX 432 has an object-oriented architecture [12].

The major emphasis in the future will be on distributed functions and processing to take advantage of the new cost-effective microprocessors. From the operating system viewpoint, we are beginning to see the following [55]:

- Migration of frequently used system primitives into hardware or firmware
- Movement of I/O drivers into intelligent controllers
- Resource allocation distributed to attached dedicated function microprocessors or associated controllers
- Major file system functions done by a back-end processor

The overall objective of the distribution of functions is to allow more parallelism, thereby increasing the effective throughput of the system. Computer systems will be composed of general purpose processors as well as highly specialized processors. The architecture is evolving into a computer complex that may have hundreds of processors interconnected by means of a high-speed access interconnection switching mechanism. This means that a community of cooperating operating systems or a distributed operating system will be necessary. The challenge will be in designing an operating system that will manage the resources efficiently and provide a robust, high-level easy-to-interface environment for the application programs.

8.6. RELIABILITY AND MAINTENANCE SUPPORT

The Importance of Reliability

Reliability requirements can vary considerably from application to application. In the case of computers aboard missiles or unmanned space-craft where defective units cannot be repaired, continuous operation is essential for a successful mission. Nearly all commercial computers are accessible to maintenance personnel. When a fault occurs, the system must detect the trouble quickly, then shut down to await repair. For most scientific or accounting problems, the interruption of operation is annoying but not catastrophic. Inconveniences result from having a system out of commission for hours at a time, in which case the entire operating procedures of the installation could be disrupted. One maintenance objective of both scientific and business machines is to reduce drastically the maximum length of repair time. This objective requires fault diagnosis techniques that can isolate the trouble to within a few replaceable units or circuit packs.

For real-time applications, such as telephone switching or process control, uninterrupted operation is essential, requiring the system to function correctly even when a fault is present and maintenance is being performed. One approach to providing continuous operation is the use of redundant machines. In electronic switching systems (ESS), the central processor is duplicated and both units process the same input data [56, 57]. The outputs are taken from the active (on-line) machine. If the on-line machine fails, the outputs are promptly switched to the standby machine. The defective unit is then repaired and put back into operation. The system is completely shut down *only* if both machines are faulty.

The development of low-cost, small computer systems has expanded at a phenomenal rate. The hardware cost of a CPU was reduced through remarkable developments in integrated circuit technology. As a result, the use of minicomputers and microcomputers has spread to many areas of process control, data processing, telecommunication, automated testing, device control, and so on. The reliability needs are different for each of these various applications. For real-time systems such as a computer-controlled chemical process or some complex industrial process, there must be a reasonably high probability that no faults will occur, since such failures may result in defec-

tive products and a reduction in output at considerable cost to the company. In this type of application, it is also desirable to have continuous performance with minimal interruption. Consequently, fault detection and recovery techniques developed for telephone systems are also applicable to many real-time industrial control systems [58, 59].

Cost of Reliability

The most important consideration in the design of any equipment or system is usually cost, specifically the initial cost of the equipment. The heavy emphasis on initial cost, nevertheless, is very often a mistake. Maintenance cost should also be considered before the equipment has been designed or purchased. The maintenance and repair costs depend on the reliability of the equipment. As the reliability increases, maintenance costs decrease. However, the initial cost of the equipment will be higher since some form of hardware redundancy and/or more reliable devices must be used to obtain the higher reliability. A trade-off exists between the on-going maintenance costs of a system (i.e., how often must it be serviced and by what caliber of service personnel) and the initial cost of the computer system. Maintenance is a labor- and logistic-intensive expense that is most vulnerable to inflation. Labor rates for repair service doubled in the five year period 1975–1980 from about 30 to $60 an hour [60]. Because of its upward trend, maintenance cost has become more visible than ever before to users.

The most significant factor in selecting a given system with a high reliability requirement should not be limited to the initial cost of the system but should include the overall expense of operating and maintaining the system after its initial purchase. If the proper maintenance features have been added to the system, the actual total expense (initial cost plus on-going maintenance charges) can be held down significantly. By paying more initially to obtain more reliable equipment, maintenance costs can be made lower, and the total cost of purchasing and operating the system is reduced. The effect is shown in Figure 8.12 [61],

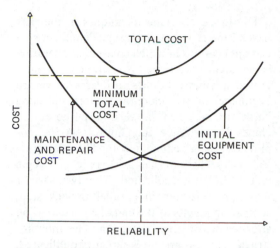

Figure 8.12. System equipment and maintenance cost.

where initial cost rises as reliability increases, and at the same time, maintenance and repair costs decrease. The total cost of purchasing and maintaining a system first falls with increasing reliability, and then rises again, showing that the most cost-effective system is at the minimum point represented by the dotted lines in the figure. In practice, the optimum economic reliability is difficult to realize because it involves many elusive variables in estimating production and maintenance costs.

Optimum economic reliability can be achieved with any reasonable accuracy only if there is a considerable amount of previous experience by the designers from which they can draw. In some cases, the minimum total cost is not always the determining factor in deciding the degree of a system's reliability. If the results of a failure are likely to be serious, it may be necessary to provide more redundancy to ensure continuous and reliable operation. In the other extreme, it may be necessary to reduce reliability to a minimum acceptable level for the buyer whose main consideration is initial cost. This, then, is the challenge: to design computer systems, particularly small computer configurations, that satisfy a wide range of applications with different reliability requirements.

Maintenance Components

Repair Time. In order to design and manufacture a system with a specified value of reliability for a given period of operation, it is essential not only to estimate the failure rate of individual components but also to predict the mean-time-to-repair (MTTR) for various fault conditions that could occur in the system. Such a prediction is usually based on past experiences of the designer and the resources (such as personnel and equipment) that will be available for repair work. The system repair time may be divided into two separate intervals called the *passive repair time* and the *active repair time*. The passive repair time is the time interval measured from the time a fault is first recognized in the system until the time that maintenance personnel arrive to initiate repair work. This interval is determined entirely by the administrative and logistic support provided by the user of the system.

The active part of the repair time is the actual time required by the maintenance personnel to recognize, isolate, and correct the trouble condition in the faulty system. This time is directly affected by the equipment design and may be further subdivided into the following intervals:

1. *Fault detection interval:* The period of time between the occurrence of a failure and the recognition by the system that a failure has occurred.
2. *Fault diagnosis interval:* The period of time required by the maintenance personnel to isolate the trouble to a few replaceable circuit boards. This interval is a function of both the sophistication of the equipment design and the technical skill of the maintenance personnel.
3. *Repair interval:* The time period required by the maintenance personnel to carry out the replacement of any suspected faulty circuit boards. This interval is also intimately related to the equipment design and the technical skill of the repair personnel.
4. *Verification interval:* The amount of time required by the maintenance personnel to verify that the repair of the fault has been effective in correcting the trouble condition and that the system is fully operational.

Again, the active repair time can be reduced by improvement of both hardware and software designs, with an eye toward minimizing the maintenance skills required to support the system. In view of the continued increase in labor costs, this is a particularly worthwhile philosophy to observe.

Fault Detection. In general, error detection can be accomplished through the use of hardware, firmware, and software, or a combination of all of these methods. The type of checking circuitry used depends on the logical structure of the machine, as well as the operational and functional use of the data and control signals. The built-in detection hardware is an integral part of a particular computer design. Coding techniques such as parity, Hamming correction code, cyclic redundancy check, and so forth are commonly used approaches for checking data storage and data transfer paths [62, 63]. Hardware techniques range from self-checking circuits at the gate level, through duplication at the module level, to replicated computers at the system level [58, 64]. Coding and hardware checking are concurrent techniques of error detection while the system is executing and performing its normal operations. In most instances the errors will not proliferate and contaminate the system before they are detected by the hardware checking logic.

On the other hand, resident software or firmware test techniques are nonconcurrent. The test sequences are scheduled to run periodically. During their execution, normal functional processing is not being done. This approach is low-cost since no additional special purpose hardware is required. The exact amount of time that may elapse between the occurrence of a fault and its detection depends on the frequency with which the tests are run. Because of the prolonged duration of an error state, the integrity of the system at the time of detection can no longer be trusted, which will adversely affect the system reliability. The motivation of periodic software or firmware tests is to achieve increased confidence that a computer is working correctly while executing its normal processing operations and to halt its execution as soon as a fault is detected.

Hardware checking techniques in the past have been predominately in the domain of special applications in which continuous operation is a system requirement. As the cost of integrated circuits continues to decrease, we are beginning to see more and more checking hardware designed in general purpose machines. For example, the Univac 1100/60 employs extensive redundancy for fault detection [65, 66]. The internal arithmetic and logic unit (ALU) is duplicated. The two sets of ALU are operated in parallel in lock step, comparing results at the end of each operation as a means of error detection. The microinstruction execution unit is similarly duplicated. Because of the redundancy built into the machine, failing portions can be disconnected, allowing the rest of the machine to operate while the repair is being made.

Fault Diagnosis. *Fault detection* determines whether or not a circuit is behaving correctly; *fault diagnosis* localizes or pinpoints the failure to a replaceable unit. The *replaceable unit* may be a component, a circuit, or a subsystem. The fault diagnosis routine utilizes fault detection hardware and test sequences to facilitate the task of locating the defective unit. When the replaceable unit is the logical entity indicating the detected fault, no other diagnostic action may be required since the fault may be corrected by simple replacement of the bad unit. However, if the detection circuit or diagnostic routine must examine a number of replaceable units, the fault diagnosis routine may be called in to further isolate the offending unit.

In a microprogrammed machine, microinstructions provide access to the individual micro-operations or control primitives of the processor. These control primitives represent the elementary control signals of the machine. Consequently, if a sequence of microinstructions is used to selectively activate the control primitives, a more detailed evaluation of the hardware may be performed rather than an evaluation generated by executing a sequence of macroinstructions. In a machine with built-in detection hardware, microdiagnostics are, in general, much more efficient than normal diagnostic programs without the hardware support. The error indication signals from the detection hardware may be controlled by a microinstruction that provides direct diagnostic information. A microdiagnostic sequence does not need to compare the results of each control operation and analyze internal test points for the occurrence of proper outputs. The microdiagnostic program needs only to interpret the error signal(s) from the detection circuits.

The cost of repair is directly related to the adequacy of diagnostics to pinpoint the faulty unit. Special attention has been focused in this area to simplify the repair procedure with additional maintenace hardware support. Computer Automation, Inc., implemented the so-called Isolite concept on the Naked Mini computers in late 1979 [60]. Isolite is an integrated hardware/software/firmware diagnostic technique for the purpose of curtailment and, in some cases, elimination of field service calls for routine circuit board failures. Isolite puts self-test logic in a read-only memory chip on each circuit board, along with an LED indicator that displays a go/no-go test result. The CPU board contains power-up option switches, and firmware that enables the self-test sequence to begin upon power-up. Each circuit board has a select switch for identification. The LED indicators at the edge of each card are lit when power is applied to indicate that the self-test sequence is working. If the board is good, the light goes out after completion of the test sequence. If the board is defective, the light remains on. The hardware support is for the sole purpose of making the system easy to maintain by unskilled individuals who repair the machine by replacing boards.

A commonly used procedure in performing fault diagnosis is based upon the bootstrap approach. The diagnosis starts from the point where the integrity of the hardcore has been ensured. The *hardcore* can be loosely defined as that part of the hardware that must be functioning correctly in order to initiate any diagnostic functions. The bootstrap approach involves using the hardcore portion of the processor to start diagnostic evaluation of another portion of the machine and to expand this validation process to the subsystem level as each successively larger level is found to be fault free. The basic idea is to start evaluating a small section of the processor and to expand the diagnostic process to include more and more hardware with each succeeding step until the entire machine has been completely tested. An effective method of validating the processor hardcore is to have the necessary diagnostic test sequences automatically run on the hardcore under the control of another intelligent controller, a so-called maintenance processor. In many current computer systems, a dedicated intelligent maintenance processor has been incorporated as an integral part of the system, mainly for diagnostic purposes [44, 66, 67, 68].

With the high cost of labor, the concept of remote and centralized maintenance appears to be an attractive solution. Using this approach, the expertise necessary to perform maintenance of a computer system is concentrated at a central location. Instead of dispatching technicians to the site of a faulty machine, fault diagnosis is done remotely by using standard telephone lines as data links to the centralized maintenance facility. Computer systems such as the VAX 11/780, IBM 4300, System/38, HP 3000 Series 33, all provide remote diagnostic capability [28, 66, 69].

Maintenance Function in High-reliability Real-time Systems*

Software and hardware maintenance features must effectively function together to insure reliability in a real-time system. Software features include such components as fault recovery programs, audits, and diagnostics, hardware features, redundant processors, self-checking circuits, maintenance access and controls, and diagnostic microcode. These components contribute to effective maintenance design. The relationship between hardware and software is continually changing in that some maintenance software will be implemented by hardware, appropriately assisted by firmware.

---

*This section is extracted from Reference 70.

Maintenance Hierarchical Structure.
Maintenance architecture is typically organized in a hierarchical structure. Figure 8.13 shows the hardware and software maintenance features that form the hierarchical system. It is partitioned into the following levels:

1. Hardware level: This is the lowest level, consisting of functions that are implemented directly in hardware. Examples are parity check circuits, maintenance access circuits for diagnostics, and redundant self-checking hardware.
2. Firmware level: This level consists of maintenance functions that are implemented in firmware, assuming that the system is a microprogrammed machine. An example of a microcoded function might be an initialization sequence for a disk controller.
3. Software nondeferrable level: The next level up in the hierarchical structure consists of software functions that must be handled immediately when a signal is received from the hardware. A common example would be an error interrupt handler. Another example would be a system reconfiguration program that switches redundant units into service when a fault is detected in an active unit.
4. Software deferrable level: The highest level consists of maintenance activities that are considered to be deferrable, noncritical in real time. Examples are diagnostics, audits, unit restoral, and human interface programs.

The upward flow of signals and status information from the hardware maintenance circuits is shown in Figure 8.13. A large part of this flow at the lowest level consists of error interrupts that are generated by hardware check circuits. These interrupts are initially processed by microcoded interrupt handlers. They in turn pass control to nondeferrable software handlers, and a software message is sent to the deferrable maintenance structure.

On the other hand, the control information flows down from the higher levels to the lower levels. Deferrable maintenance sends software control messages to nondeferrable maintenance. Nondeferrable maintenance issues commands that initiate microprogram sequences, and at the lowest level, microcode manipulates the hardware directly.

The flow of information up and down the maintenance hierarchical structure can be best illustrated with a specific example. In the Bell System No. 3ACC ESS processor [71, 72], a technique for correcting memory faults known as *double store read* is used. In this implementation, when bad parity is detected on a memory read, the processor automatically redirects the read operation to the off-line memory. The No. 3ACC processor is operated as a duplex pair in which the write operations are directed to both memories. Therefore, the off-line memory normally contains the same data as the on-line memory. The handling of the double store read operation that relates to Figure 8.13 is as follows:

1. A single bit error is detected by the parity detect circuit on a memory read. The error-indicating signal causes a microinterrupt. A signal is sent from the hardware to the firmware level to start the process.
2. The microcoded interrupt handler records the location of the error in a scratch register and then reinitiates the memory read operation to the off-line memory. This microinterrupt can occur between microinstructions within a complex in-

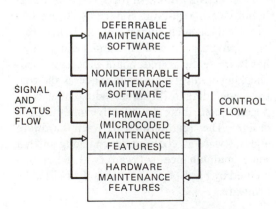

Figure 8.13. Functional hierarhical structure.

struction containing many store references. The microinterrupt handler causes a software interrupt that is handled within the nondeferrable maintenance structure. Note that at this point the bad word is still in memory even through the correct data was read from the off-line memory.

3. The nondeferrable error interrupt handler reads the scratch register to determine the location of the error. The memory module that contains the faulty word may be removed from service and be replaced with a backup module. This function takes longer than the memory reread described in step 2 (milliseconds versus microseconds). Nondeferrable maintenance notifies the deferrable maintenance of the error's presence via a software message.

4. Based on the message sent by nondeferrable maintenance, a memory diagnostic of the faulty module is initiated. This diagnostic requires many seconds to execute. Appropriate reconfiguration actions are then taken, and the results are reported to the craftperson via a teletypewriter message.

The above illustration shows a natural signal flow from the lowest to the highest level to accomplish all related maintenance functions.

There has been a greater use of structured design principles in defining the total maintenance subsystem from the highest levels to the lowest levels of hardware. This results in an overall structure that is not only inherently better partitioned at the hardware-software boundary, but also globally within the entire maintenance system. Although structured design was not entirely neglected in the past, it is the current emphasis on this approach that will lead to future systems that are both easier to maintain and more reliable.

Basic Maintenance System Structure. There are two basic system architectures that appear in various forms in many deployed systems. Figure 8.14 shows a hierarchical system. The highest level of this system would normally be a processor. The next level down might be a channel such as a DMA unit. Further down in the hierarchy are peripheral controllers, disk units, and so on. The lowest level in the structure might be a data terminal. This hierarchical arrangement is typically under control of a centralized CPU. The advent of

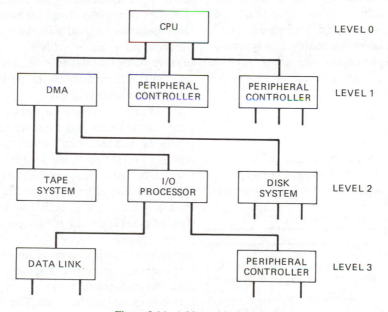

Figure 8.14. A hierarchical system.

inexpensive microprocessors, however, has led to a hierarchical system with more levels and considerably more intelligence at each node. This presents interesting maintenance control problems that are quite different from earlier problems. For example, it is no longer practical for the CPU at the top node to directly diagnose a bottom node. Instead, some sort of message must flow down the hierarchy with a diagnostic request, and then a response flows up with the result of the diagnostic.

Parallel or multiprocessing systems are at the opposite end of a spectrum from the hierarchical systems. Figure 8.15 shows a simple view of such a system arrangement. Proponents of parallel processing system architecture say that it is the way of the future. They base their belief on the premise that by simply paralleling n small processors that share a common (redundant) communication bus, a more effective large processor can be obtained that is both powerful and reliable. This is particularly true if there is no a priori assignment of tasks to the n processors.

Both hierarchical and parallel processing systems require the joint efforts of hardware and software designers in order to achieve an effective maintenance system design. The movement of software functions into hardware or firmware will continue. Microdiagnostics, self-checking circuits, error correction hardware, and well-structured hardware-software interfaces will allow maintenance programs to be greatly simplified and will allow software designers to take a more functional view of the hardware system.

Future Trends

A great deal of work in the area of fault-tolerant computing has been done in recent years, much of it in support of the U.S. space pro-

gram [73] and special applications such as electronic telephone switching systems [74]. Reliability is obviously of primary importance in the designs for these applications. A large collection of design techniques has been developed for their implementation. Some of them are [75]:

- Duplex self-checking configurations [58]
- Triple modular redundancy (TMR) with voting [76]
- Coding techniques for concurrent fault detection [62, 77]
- Self-checking circuits [64]
- Software-implemented fault tolerance [78]
- Memory systems tolerating multiple faults [79]

These and other techniques are components available to designers of fault-tolerant systems. The way they are used depends on the reliability requirements, technology level, and economics of a system.

On the other extreme, general purpose commercial computers have very few built-in maintenance features other than memory parity. Fault detection in such machines was often done by the user, having noted that the output had stopped altogether or was obviously incorrect. The prime objective of manufacturers of these machines was to minimize the machine purchase price. Since hardware was expensive in early years, maintenance features which did not contribute directly to the performance of the system were excluded.

As improved integrated circuit technology becomes available and users demand greater reliability, maintenance features are being integrated into the machine designs. Most fault-tolerant design techniques developed for space application and other real-time high-availability applications are directly applicable to designs of reliable and highly maintainable computer systems. Figure 8.16 shows the maintenance design trend of special and general purpose computers. The top curve represents the fault-tolerant computer systems dedicated to special applications. The cost of these systems will continually decrease with im-

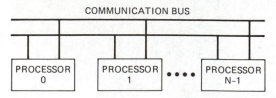

Figure 8.15. A parallel processing system.

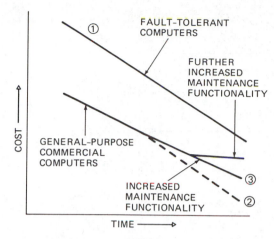

Figure 8.16. Maintenance functionality trend.

proved technology. The second curve represents general purpose commercial computers. It starts out with the same slope as the top curve assuming constant functionality. With greater demands from users, more maintenance features are incorporated into the system, increasing the functionality (more hardware), and the slope changes. With continued cost reduction of integrated circuits, new applications in the area of high reliability become economically feasible. The third curve is generated representing further increases in functionality (more hardware). For example, the NonStop Tandem computer is the first commercial fault-tolerant computer system [80]. It fills the need of those applications requiring nonstop computing operation. The market is ready for more computer companies to enter into this area, representing the third curve. The trend of the future will be more of the NonStop-type of computer systems.

8.7. PERSPECTIVE FOR THE FUTURE

The excessive cost of designing, updating, and maintaining software is responsible for the so-called software crisis [1]. Software issues are important for both computer systems and microsystems. Consequently, the fast-moving integrated technology is directed in solving these difficult problems in the 1980s by placing more software functions into hardware. Future processors tailored for languages, operating systems, and data bases will eventuality be a reality.

Intel Corporation has mapped out an elaborate and ambitious plan to solve many of these software problems over a wide range of applications ranging from microcontrollers to main frames. Figure 8.17 from Reference 24 shows Intel's planned iAPX product line to expand their market segment and to help to solve software problems. It is expected that the iAPX product line will use increasing levels of integration to significantly reduce software, hardware, and development costs. As indicated in Figure 8.17, the micromainframe iAPX 432 combines VLSI technology with integration of high-level language and operating system functionality into silicon.

Some key features of iAPX 432 are [12]:

- High-level, language-directed instruction set
- Operating system assisted instruction repertoire
- Hardware-supported multiprogramming and multiprocessing (synchronization and concurrency supports)
- Virtual memory
- Object-oriented architecture
- Self-dispatching processors with hardware-implemented process scheduling

The iAPX 432 is an object-oriented architecture that ensures protection, reliability, and integrity of system data in a multiprogramming environment. The system structure also provides efficient support of highly modular program and data structures in both systems and application software.

Distributed processing has become increasingly active throughout the universities and industry. The technology is "ripe" for using processors and microprocessors interconnected in a variety of schemes to configure a distributed system. The term *distributed processing* has two meanings: distribution of functions and distribution of load. Distribution of functions is accomplished by assigning different jobs, such as input/output processing, file processing, maintenance processing, and central processing to different processors. Although there

	CENTRAL PROCESSOR INTEGRATION	EXTERNAL MODULE INTEGRATION	O.S. NUCLEUS INTEGRATION	HLL & O.S. INTEGRATION
MICROMAINFRAME (32 BIT)	/////	/////	/////	iAPX 432
MICROMAXI (16/32 BIT)	/////	/////	iAPX 286	
MICROMIDI (16 BIT)	/////	iAPX 86	iAPX 186	
MICRO-COMPUTER (8/16 BIT)	8080	iAPX 88 8085	iAPX 188	
MICRO-CONTROLLER (8 BIT)		8051 8048 8022		

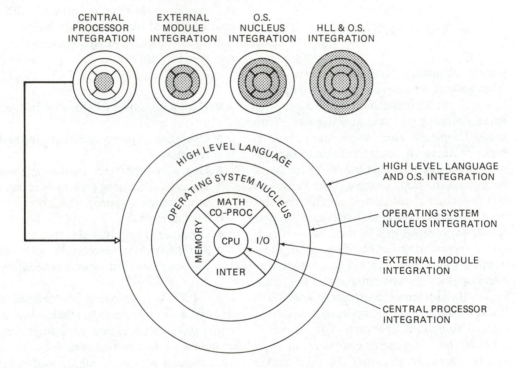

Figure 8.17. Intel iAPX system functionality and levels of integration.

is a multiplicity of processors physically and logically interconnected, only one of the processors will serve as the central processing unit in controlling the entire environment. Distribution of the load or load sharing, on the other hand, refers to assignment of a job to any of the processors in the system. Systemwide control and resources are completely decentralized. There is no single, central processing element in charge, nor is there a central state table. Systemwide cooperation among independent processing elements results in a single unified system. The challenge of a load-sharing type of distributed processing is extremely high. A great deal of technology, largely software, needs to be developed before load-sharing distributed processing becomes a realistic alternative. However, such an architecture potentially has a large payoff in reliability and extensibility. The decentralized control of a multiplicity of processing elements provides the potential for higher reliability than is now possible in systems that have more vulnerable centralized control. Whether such potential can be realized depends on a great number of factors such as error detection, error confinement, and system reconfiguration and recovery after an error. Because of the decentralization of control algorithms and state information, distributed processing systems have the potential for simpler and more economical growth in computing elements without changing any of the algorithms. By such ease of extensibility, a complete range of computing power can be realized in a single system simply by adding processing elements. These attributes are also applicable to functional distributed processing, but are somewhat more restrictive and less general than the load-sharing type of structure. The architecture design will be considerably less complex than in the general case of distributed processing. It is expected that many of the difficult problems associated with distributed processing of both types will be solved. Some forms of distributed processing will be successfully realized to enhance performance and reliability in the 1980s. The architecture of Intel iAPX 432 is pointed in that direction.

New I/O hardware support will be one of the more cost-effective areas for improvement. The user will probably see a lot of intelligence placed in I/O channels, or in intelligent front-ends on storage devices to perform functions such as sorting, retrieval, and so forth. In addition, the user should expect to see the I/O oriented toward new bus structures with intelligent peripherals available in wide functional and performance ranges [81].

Data base management software has grown both in complexity and size. This growth is caused by the increase in user requirements and by the recent change of a data processing mode from an off-line, batch, single-user environment to an on-line, concurrent, multi-user environment [82]. Large and complex software systems tend to be unreliable. The operation of data base management is concerned with the storage, retrieval, and management of large data bases. It requires a quick search and, sometimes, good update operation for concurrent access. The conventional von Neumann-type computers are awkward at handling data base management functions. Again, hardware support for data base management functions appears to be a certainty. The prospect of commercial data base machines utilizing specialized hardware to provide the performance and reliability required in handling large data bases is a strong possibility in the 1980s. The future trend will be directed to increase software productivity and reduce overall development and maintenance costs of software engineering.

REFERENCES

1. Robert Bernhard. Computers: Emphasis on software. *IEEE Spectrum* 17 (Jan. 1980): 32–37.
2. Peter Wegner, ed. *Research directions in software technology*. Cambridge, Mass.: MIT Press, 1979.
3. J. E. Juliussen and W. J. Watson. Problems of the '80's: Computer system organization. *Proceedings of the Conferences on Computing in the 1980's*. Portland, Oreg. pp. 14–23, 1978.
4. Electronics Staff, Computer technology shifts emphasis to software: A special report. *Electronics*, pp. 142–150, May 8, 1980.
5. R. I. Baum, D. K. Hsiao, and K. Kannan. The architecture of a database computer, part 1: Concepts and capabilities. *OSU-CISRC-TR-76-1*. Columbus, Ohio: Ohio State University, Sept. 1976.
6. R. Turn. Hardware-Software tradeoffs in reliable software development. *11th Annual Asilomar Conference on Circuits, Systems and Computers*, pp. 282–288, 1978.
7. Gordon Moore. VLSI: Some fundamental challenges: *IEEE Spectrum*, pp. 30–35.
8. R. N. Gossen, Jr. and G. H. Heilmeier. 100,000+ gates on a chip: Mastering the minute. *IEEE Spectrum*, pp. 42–47, March 1979.
9. Daniel Queyssac. Projecting VLSI's impact on microprocessors. *IEEE Spectrum*, pp. 38–41, May 1979.
10. Taiyu Kobayashi. Very large-scale integrated circuits (VLSI) and the future of the computer. *Fujitsu Scientific and Technical Journal*, pp. 1–19, Dec. 1977.
11. Roger Allan. VLSI: Scoping its future. *IEEE Spectrum*, pp. 30–37, April 1979.
12. *Microsystem 80 Advance Information*. INTEL, Corp., 1980.
13. C. F. Wolfe. Bit-slice processor come to main frame design. *Electronics*, pp. 118–123, Feb. 28, 1980.
14. C. G. Bell, J. C. Mudge and J. E. McNamara. *Computer Engineering*. Digital, 1978.
15. B. R. Borgerson. Computer systems in the '80's. *Proceedings of the Conference on Computing in the 1980's*. Portland, Oreg., pp. 3–8, 1978.
16. Instruction set architecture for the military computer family. *MIL-STD-1862*, May 28, 1980.

17. Anthony Durniak. VLSI shakes the foundations of computer architecture. *Electronics*, pp. 111–133, May 24, 1979.

18. Marvin Conrad. A High-level language for micros and minis. *Datamation*, pp. 153–56, July 1979.

19. G. J. Myers. *Advances in computer architecture*. New York: Wiley, 1978.

20. U. O. Gagliardi. Report of workshop 4-software-related advances in computer hardware. *Proceedings of a Symposium on the High Cost of Software*. Menlo Park, Calif.: Stanford Research Institute, pp. 99–120, 1973.

21. T. R. Bashkow, A. Sasson, and A. Kronfield. System design of a FORTRAN machine. *IEEE Transon Electronic Computers* EC-16, pp. 485–99, 1967.

22. L. S. Haynes. The architecture of an ALGOL 60 computer implemented with distributed processing. *Proceedings of the Fourth Annual Symposium on Computer Architecture*. New York: IEEE, pp. 95–104, 1977.

23. G. D. Cheslev and W. R. Smith. The hardware-implemented high-level machine language for SYMBOL. *Proceedings of the 1971 SJCC*. Montvale, N.J.: AFIFS, pp. 563–573, 1971.

24. E. A. Hauck and B. A. Dent. Burroughs B6500/7500 stack mechanism. *Proceedings of the 1968 SJCC*. Montvale, N.J., AFIPS, pp. 245–251, 1968.

25. G. M. Davis. The English electric KDF9 computer system. *Comp. Bull*, pp. 119–120, Dec. 1960.

26. M. Charlin. High-level languages for microcomputers. *Mini/Micro Systems*, pp. 89–110, Apr. 1980.

27. K. Kumano, Y. Nagai, M. Yamamoto, M. Umemura, M. Hattori, and K. Hakozaki. A quantitative evaluation of a high-level language machine. *NEC Research & Development* 50 (July 1978): 30–41.

28. Digital Equipment Corp. *VAX 11/780 Architecture Handbook*, 1977.

29. Subhash Bal, Yoav Lavi, Asher Kaminker, and Avram Menachem. Optimizing microprocessor performance. *Mini-Micro Systems*, pp. 103–108, June 1980.

30. J. G. Poso. Microprocessor and microcomputers. *Electronics*, pp. 144–157, Oct. 25, 1979.

31. R. W. Mitze. Hardware/software tradeoffs from the compiler design viewpoint. *COMPSAC 1978*. Chicago, Ill.

32. A. V. Aho, S. C. Johnson, J. D. Ullman. Code generation for expressions with common subexpressions. *JACM* 24(1): (Jan. 1977) 146–160.

33. B. W. Kernighan and D. M. Ritchie. *The C programming language*. Englewood Cliffs, N.J.: Prentice-Hall, 1978.

34. W. T. Wilner. Design of the Burroughs B1700. *1972 Proc. Fall Joint Comp. Conf. AFIPS* 41 (1972) 489–497.

35. Marvin Conrad. Pascal power. *Datamation*, pp. 142ff., July 1979.

36. S. E. Madnick and J. J. Donovan. *Operating systems*. N.Y.: McGraw Hill, 1974.

37. P. J. Denning. Operating systems principles for data flow networks. *Computer*, pp. 86–96, July 1978.

38. A. P. Savers, ed. *Operating systems survey*. N.Y.: Anerback, 1971.

39. C. C. Foster. Hardware enhancement of operating systems. *AD-A062462*, University of Massachusetts, Nov. 23, 1978.

40. G. E. Brown, R. Eckhouse, and R. P. Goldberg. Operating system enhancement through microprogramming. *SIGMICRO Newslett* 7 (March 1976) 28–33.

41. G. E. Brown, R. Eckhouse, and J. Estabrook. Operating system enhancement through firmware. *SIGMICRO Newslett* 8 (Sept. 1977) 119–133.

42. R. Chattergy. Microprogrammed implementation of a scheduler. *SIGMICRO Newslett* 7 (Sept. 1976) 15–19.

43. C. Y. Lee and M. C. Paull. A content addressable distributed logic memory with applications to information retrieval. *Proc. IEEE* 51 (June 1963) 924–932.

44. VAX 11/780. *Technical Summary*. Digital Corp., 1977.

45. B. R. Borgerson, M. D. Godfrey, P. E. Hagery, and T. R. Rykken. The architecture of the Sperry Univac 1100 series systems. *Proceedings of the Sixth International Symposium on Computer Architecture*, pp. 137–145.

46. D. R. Appelt. Making it compatible and better: Designing a new high-end computer. *Electronics*, pp. 131–136, Oct. 11, 1979.

47. *990 Computer Family Systems Handbook*, Manual No. 945250-9701. Houston: Texas Instrument, Inc., 1975.

48. G. D. Kraft and W. N. Toy. *Mini/microcomputer hardware design*. Englewood Cliffs, N.J.: Prentice-Hall, 1979.

49. *IBM System/7 System Summary*. Boca Raton, Fla.: IBM Corp., 1972.

50. Ian LeMair. Indexed mapping extends microprocessor addressing range. *Computer Design*, pp. 111–118, Aug. 1980.

51. Y. Lavi, A. Kaminker, A. Menachem, and S. Bal. 16-bit microprocessor enters virtual memory domain. *Electronics*, pp. 123–129, April 24, 1980.

52. D. Wicker. Programmable interval timer. *Digital Design*, pp. 32–36, May 1980.

53. T. G. Rauscher and P. M. Adams. Microprogramming: A tutorial and survey of recent developments. *IEEE Transactions on Computers* C-29 (Jan. 1980): 2–19.

54. D. M. Ritchie and K. Thompson. The UNIX time-sharing system. *CACM* 17(7) (July 1974) 365–375.

55. M. R. Georgen and K. W. Switzer. Hardware/software tradeoffs from an operating system design viewpoint. *COMPSAC*. Chicago: 1978.

56. H. J. Beuscher, G. E. Fessler, D. W. Huffman, P. J. Kennedy, and E. Nussbaum. Administration and maintence plan of the no. 2 ESS. *Bell System Technical Journal*, Oct. 1969.

57. R. W. Downing, J. S. Nowak, and L. S. Tuome-noksa. No. 1 ESS maintenance plan. *Bell System Technical Journal*, Sept. 1964.

58. W. N. Toy. Fault-tolerant design of local ESS processors. *Proc. IEEE* 66 (10) (Oct. 1978) 1126–1145.

59. P. J. Kennedy and T. M. Quinn. Recovery strategies in the no. 2 ESS. *Digest of 1972 Fault-Tolerant Computing*, June 1972.

60. Gene Danler and Richard McGowan. The case for self-testing computers. *Mini-Micro Systems*, pp. 97–101, July 1980.

61. G. D. Kraft and W. N. Toy. *Microprogrammed control and reliable design of small computers*. Englewood Cliffs, N.J.: Prentice-Hall Inc., 1981.

62. W. W. Peterson, Jr. *Error correcting codes*. Cambridge, Mass.: MIT Press, 1961

63. R. W. Hamming. Error detecting and error correcting codes. *Bell System Tech. J.*, pp. 47–160, 1950.

64. D. A. Anderson. Design of self-checking digital networks using code techniques. *CSL Report R527*, University of Illinois, PhD Thesis, Oct. 1971.

65. L. A. Boone, G. A. Champin, and B. A. Borgerson. The microarchitecture of UNIVAC's 1100/60. *Datamation*, pp. 173–178, July 1979.

66. A. Durniak. Computers. *Electronics*, pp. 164–177, Oct. 25, 1979.

67. Richard Coyle and John Doyle. A self-diagnosing minicomputer. *Mini-Mico Systems*, pp. 90–94, July 1980.

68. H. Cordero, Jr. 4341's intrastructure is new from the substrate up. *Electronics*, pp. 110–115, Nov. 8, 1979.

69. D. L. Nelson. A remote computer troubleshooting facility. *Hewlett-Packard Journal*, pp. 13–15, Sept. 1979.

70. D. C. Plisch and F. M. Goetz. Hardware vs software design tradeoffs for maintenance functions in high-/

reliability real time system. *COMPSAC 1978*. Chicago, pp. 607–613.

71. T. F. Storey. Design of a microprogram control for a processor in an electronic switching system. *Bell System Technical Journal*, Feb. 1976.

72. R. W. Cook, W. H. Sisson, T. F. Storey, and W. N. Toy. Design of a self-checking microprogram control. *IEEE Transactions on Computers*, March 1973.

73. A. Avizienis. Fault tolerance: The survival attribute of digital systems. *Proc. IEEE* 66 (10) (Oct. 1978): 1109–1125.

74. B. E. Briley, and W. N. Toy. Telecommunication processors. *Proc. of IEEE* 65 (9) (Sept. 1977).

75. D. A. Rennels. Distributed fault-tolerant computer systems. *Computer*, pp. 55–65, March 1980.

76. R. E. Lyons and W. Vanderkulk. The use of triple-modular redundancy to improve computer reliability. *IBM Journal Res. Dev.* 6 (2) (Apr. 1962): 200–209.

77. A. Avizienis. Arithmetic error codes: Cost and effectiveness studies for application in digital system design. *IEEE Trans Computers* c-20 (11) (Nov. 1971): 1322–1331.

78. J. H. Wensley. SIFT-Software Implemented Fault Tolerance. *Fall, Joint Comput. Conf.*, pp. 243–253, 1972.

79. W. C. Carter and C. E. McCarthy. Implementation of an experimental fault-tolerant memory systems. *IEEE Trans. Computers* C-25 (6) (June 1976): 557–568.

80. J. A. Katzman. System architecture for nonStop computing. *Compcon*, pp. 77–80, Feb. 1977.

81. K. J. Thurber and D. R. Anderson. Hardware/software trade-offs: Hardware design viewpoint. *Proceedings of COMPSAC 1978*, Chicago, pp. 601–606.

82. D. K. Hsiao. Data base machines are coming. *Computer*, pp. 7–9, March 1979.

9
Computer Languages

Joseph E. Urban
University of Southwestern Louisiana

9.1. INTRODUCTION

Perspectives on the State of Languages

The field of software engineering has witnessed a proliferation of computer languages over the past decade. As program development moved away from assembly/machine language use toward the preferred high-level language approach, programmers and managers witnessed the introduction of new languages, as well as the subsetting and supersetting of existing languages. Regardless of the language proliferation problem, the Cobol and Fortran programming languages have dominated language use in the areas of business applications and scientific programming, respectively. The proliferation was large enouph, however, that in 1975 the U.S. Department of Defense began to grapple with the language problem by initiating the Common High-Order Lanugage Effort.

The intent of this chapter is not to survey the set of existing languages. A survey of this nature is certainly beyond the scope of this chapter and this handbook. There are several excellent references [1, 2, 3, 4] that address, in a survey-like manner, the field of language design, implementation, and use. In addition, it is not the intent of this chapter to teach an individual to program in one or more languages. Instead, this chapter is primarily concerned with computer language issues in relation to the software life cycle, thereby establishing a framework from which to discuss current features in computer languages. Case studies are provided for two major computer lanaguages. The first language, Pascal, was selected for the

reason that it has had an important influence on language use and language design in the 1970s. The second language, Ada (Ada is a trademark of the U.S. Department of Defense), was selected for the reason that its recent introduction is expected to serve as an important influence on language design and use in the near future. In other words, Pascal and Ada can be viewed as delimiters that surround the decade of the 1970s.

The discussions on Pascal and Ada are not intended to serve as a comparison between the two languages. Each language has a separate and distinct set of goals and features that are of importance to this chapter. References to other languages are provided within the text of the discussion on both languages. The language descriptions focus on the histories, concepts, and implementations of each language. An assessment of each language is also included.

Languages and their Effects

Computer languages have had major effects in many related areas in software engineering. Six areas are identified below with cross-references to chapters in this handbook that provide further information. The related areas of consideration are language translation, abstraction and structuring, data base management systems, operating systems, verification and testing, and software metrics.

Relationship to Language Translation. Interpretation or compilation involves the processing of a language in order to achieve execution. Language translation is affected by the complexity of the language and the degree of optimization to be achieved. An intermediate language serves as a buffer or interface between the high-level language and the host machine. A high-level language can be translated into an intermediate language that has been designed to support a number of machine architectures. Optimization of a program can be accomplished on the intermediate representation.

Relationship to Abstraction and Structuring.

Software engineers require tools and techniques for dealing with the complexity of large software systems. One means of handling the complexity is through abstraction. Control structures, modularity, and data representations provide three degrees of orthogonality in computer languages and a means for dealing with large software systems. Control structures provide a means for representing the logical flow of execution through a program. Modularity in a computer language is a tool for managing the complexity of large programs. Data representations provide the ability to group data elements according to such characteristics as types of values, structures, and operations. This chapter discusses these three degrees of orthogonality in more detail.

Relationship to Data Base Management Systems.

There exists a dual relationship between data base management systems and computer languages. A computer language serves as a tool for implementing the data base management system. Additionally, language features incorporated in a data base management system serve as a means of communication between system and user. Recent research indicates that software support environments will be evolving in the future with data base support. These data bases are expected to serve as the crucial element for retaining information about a software system over the entire life cycle. Chapter 13 provides a foundation for data base management systems.

Relationship to Operating Systems.

As with data base management systems, a similar relationship exists between operating systems and computer languages. This point will be emphasized later in this chapter in the discussion on concurrency. Two examples of the system-language link can be found in the Pilot operating system/Mesa language [5, 6, 7, 8] and the UNIX operating system/C language [9, 10, 11, 12] (UNIX is a trademark of Bell Laboratories).

Relationship to Formal Verification and Testing.

The development of reliable software is of particular concern to software engineers. Formal verification and testing are two techniques that are available for increasing one's confidence that the software is performing as expected. In general, the problem is complex in nature and can be further compounded by features provided in a computer language. Euclid [13], Gypsy [14], and Aphard [15] are examples of languages that had verification as a language design goal.

Relationship to Software Metrics.

Finally, program behavior has been of interest since the inception of coding, but within the last decade, programmer behavior has surfaced as a means of understanding the programming process [16]. For example, for many years we have known that a rigidly enforced indentation policy enhances the readability of programs in group software engineering efforts. The discipline of structured programming has improved software development and maintenance. For many years, the previous statement was based on a qualitative assessment. We are now approaching the point where quantitative assessment can be drawn from controlled experiments on the programming process. A recent issue of *Computer* had human factors in software engineering as the featured theme, with several articles [17, 18, 19, 20, 21] devoted to the quantitative aspects of programming.

9.2. IMPACTS ON CURRENT LANGUAGE DESIGNS

The purpose of this section is to develop a foundation from which we can discuss the impact of computer languages on software engineering. This section includes several basic concepts that have influenced the introduction of language features in current computer languages. In addition, among the plethora of languages (including machine, assembly and high-order languages) that have been developed over the past three decades, we want to discuss several high-order languages that were significant enough to have influenced the current state of languages. A discussion is included that relates computer languages to several desired goals in software engineering. Finally, discussions of Pascal and Ada are provided as examples of two contemporary languages.

Computer Language Concepts

In this section, we discuss several basic concepts related to computer languages. These concepts include structured programming, data types, parameter passage and side effects, program verification, and parallel processing.

Structured Programming. The structured programming revolution had a significant impact on computer languages that emerged in the past decade. Structured programming is defined as a disciplined approach to computer program development. Structured programming couples the use of a limited number of control structures with a modular approach to program development. Bohm and Jacopini [22] developed some early work in proving a structure theorem that limits the number of control structures required in programming. Dijkstra [23] was one of the early proponents of limiting the use of the goto statement. A large number of publications have been devoted to the subject of structured programming. An early definitive work on structured programming can be found in Reference 24. Two examples of articles that appeared in the mid-1970s [25, 26] provide an indication of the controversy that arose over structured programming. An excellent recent tutorial article [27] also covers the subject of structured programming.

An important issue with respect to structured programming is the concept of a proper program. A proper program is one which (1)

can be flowcharted, (2) has one entry point and one exit point, and (3) is constructed so that each point in the program can be reached from the entry point. Proper programs can be constructed with the three control structures of sequence (compound statement), selection (conditional control), and interation (looping). Several additional control structures have been proposed that also satisfy the definition of a proper program.

The three control structures mentioned above are illustrated in Figure 9.1. Note that any process box (rectangle) in the control structures shown in Figure 9.1 can be substituted for by one of the other control structures. A proper program can therefore be decomposed by step-wise refinement, as described by Wirth [28]. The definition of a proper program is maintained by this approach.

Two example control structures, the repeat-until and case statement, are illustrated in Figure 9.2. The repeat-until and case statement have only one entry point/one exit point, and each point is reachable from the entry point.

Another concept associated with structured programming is modularity. The complexity of a large system can be controlled if the system is decomposed into small, understandable, and manageable parts. It has been recommended

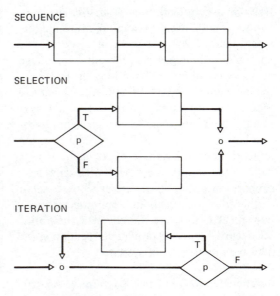

Figure 9.1. Three control structures for proper programs.

REPEAT-UNTIL

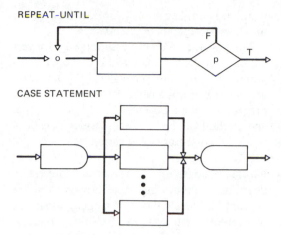

CASE STATEMENT

Figure 9.2. Additional control structures.

that module length be limited to one to two pages of high-level language code. Also important is the manner in which modules are structured in the hierarchical development of a software system. Interfacing modules, or module communication in terms of control and data, is a major concern in a modularized system. The interfacing problem is addressed later in this section.

Finally, group organization of personnel developing a software system is a concern in structured programming. The chief programmer team concept developed by Mills [29, 30, 31] is one approach to organizing and managing personnel on a software project. Credibility for the chief programmer team approach was provided by Baker [32, 33, 34].

Data Types. The declaration of the range of values that an object can acquire occurs in many computer languages. In some languages, such as Fortran and PL/I, it is possible to write programs in which the type of an object can be declared implicitly through the use of the object or explicitly through a specific declaration of the object. The concept of requiring an explicit declaration of the data type of an object was first introduced in ALGOL 60. A data type consists of a set of values and operations applicable to the values. More important, language processors can enforce adherence with objects having distinct properties. A recent tutorial [35] addresses the concept of data.

The idea of encapsulating data and operations as an abstraction was introduced as a classs in the Simula 67 language. An abstract data type provides a form for describing data abstractions such that the details of their representations are hidden. Recent work in data abstractions [36, 37] has focused on the formal specification of abstract data types. One technique for representing abstract data types that has received considerable attention is algebraic definitions. This technique involves the explicit statement of the functions that can be applied to a data structure and the axioms that hold for the functions.

Hoare [38] argues that the pointer type of data structures is closely analogous to the goto statement for control structures. He suggests that pointer variables can be misused in much the same manner that the goto can obscure the readability of program control. Furthermore, he proposes a set of data structuring methods that are sufficient for describing data without the use of the pointer. Jackson [39] has proposed a design methodology that uses the same data structuring methods as proposed by Hoare.

Parameter Passage and Side Effects. In providing a computer language with modularity, the interface that exists between program units becomes important. Three commonly used techniques for parameter passage are *call by value, call by reference,* and *call by name.* The crucial issue in parameter passing is the binding time of the actual and formal parameters.

In call by value, a copy of the contents of the location for the actual parameter is passed to the called subprogram. In call by reference, the location or address of the actual parameter is passed to the called subprogram. With the address of the actual parameters being passed in call by reference, there is the possibility that the parameter can be changed in the called subprogram. Call by value can potentially change the copy of the actual parameter and not the contents of the actual parameter. In call by name, the actual parameter is evaluated when it is needed during subprogram execution, allowing one to defer the binding of the actual parameter to the formal parameter for a long as possible.

Snobol 4 is an example of a language that performs call by value parameter passage. Fortran is an example of a language that uses call by reference. Pascal and PL/I support both value and reference parameter passage. Algol is an example of a language that allows for value and name parameters. Additional information related to parameter passage can be found in Reference 2.

The concept of block structure in a computer language is useful for limiting the scope in which an identifier is known within a program. An identifier is known throughout the block in which it is declared and is known in all sub-blocks, unless it is redeclared. In Algol, the scheme allows for efficient storage usage in that storage is allocated for variables declared on entry into the block and freed on exit from the block. An identifier in Algol that is declared to be *own* will maintain its storage location on exit from the block.

Program Verification. Program verification involves the mathematical demonstration that a program satisfies its assertions or specifications. A verification is developed through an input assertion which states the conditions that must be true on program entry and an output assertion which states the conditions that must be true on program exit. Intermediate assertions are included at the cut points of the program, which are conditions indicating the state of execution. A theorem is then constructed and proved which shows that the program satisfies the assertions. In terms of computer languages, various control and data structures place limitations on the applicability of program verification.

London [40] provides a tutorial article on program verification that covers the various methods employed, results that have been achieved, and future directions and limitations of the technology. One problem with verification is related to the difficulty and length of the proofs. When used as an a posteriori technique, a negative result can not salvage time and effort wasted on a software project. A positive benefit can be derived when program ver-

ification is applied to critical code during the top-down development of software.

The positive utility of pursuing program verification has been questioned in the open literature. Gerhart and Yelowitz [41] have revealed errors in published verifications of some programs. More recently, DeMillo, Lipton, and Perlis [42] have raised serious questions concerning program verification.

Parallel Processing. The current interest in distributed processing applications has increased the development of language features to support these systems. Exploiting concurrency in operations is important from the standpoint of increasing execution time efficiency. Several techniques and tools that allow for the handling of concurrency include semaphores [43], monitors [44], communicating sequential processes [45], and distributed processes [46].

The critical issues here involve protecting shared resources and ensuring that the deadlocking of processes or tasks does not occur in a software system. Deadlock can occur when two processes are unknowingly holding resources that the other requires and will not release the resources they are currently holding. The tools and techniques have been developed to ensure that both of the critical issues can be handled through computer language constructs.

As in the control structures mentioned earlier, the arguments have tended to subside concerning the set that are required in the development of software. This is not the case in terms of those tools and techniques needed to handle concurrency. For example, the Ada programming language, to be described later, uses features for describing parallel processing that are between semaphores and monitors in terms of expressive power. This area will continue to be of major concern as more software applications employ parallel processing.

Language Background and Influence

Wegner has produced two significant works in terms of providing taxonomies for language efforts. The taxonomies place the area of computer languages in historical perspective. An advantage of understanding the taxonomies is that they can provide an appreciation of the past and present, as well as, insight into the future.

Wegner [47] notes three distinctive phases in computer language design and development. These three phases cover the period from 1950 to the date of publication (1976). The phases, according to Wegner, were 1950 to 1960 for discovery and description, 1961 to 1969 for elaboration and analysis, and 1970 onward for technology. In the same reference, 30 milestones related to language development and programming concepts were established for a 25 year period. Wegner considered the 4 most important milestones in language development to be Fortran, Algol 60, Cobol, and Lisp.

In addition, Wegner [48] has provided a set of three generations of languages. The first-generation programming languages cover the period of 1950 to 1958 and include the language Fortran I, Algol 58, Flowmatic, and IPL 5. The second-generation languages cover the period of 1959 to 1961 and include the languages Fortran II, Algo 60, Cobol, and Lisp. The third-generation languages cover the period of 1962 to 1969 and include the languages PL/I, Algol 68, Snobol 4, Simula 67, Pascal, APL, and Basic.

In 1978, the ACM SIGPLAN History of Programming Languages Conference [49] served as a means for capturing in one reference the historical aspects of several major programming languages. The conference focused on the following languages: Algol 60, APL, APT, Basic, Cobol, Fortran, GPSS, JOSS, Jovial, Lisp, PL/I, Simula, and Snobol. Each language was presented in light of two aspects: (1) a summary of the language, and (2) a history of the language.

Software Design Goals. Several factors have influenced the way in which software systems are produced. These factors include goals in software development, reliability, maintainability, and efficiency. The remainder of the section discusses these goals in relation to computer languages.

Computer languages are important aspects in the development of software systems. Implementation of the program in a computer language is the step immediately following design in the software life cycle. The choice of language and corresponding language features has a strong bearing on the design and implementation of the system. The language features influence design decisions with respect to data structures available, use of control structures, and modular decomposition. Language designers, users, evaluators, and critics would benefit from Hoare's last hint in Reference 50: "A final hint: listen carefully to what language users *say* they want, until you have an understanding of what they *really* want. Then find some way of achieving the latter at a small fraction of the cost of the former."

We can define reliable software as software that performs according to its specifications. It is important to obtain a level of confidence that developed software satisfies the specifications. The complexity of the reliability problem makes it impossible to exhaustively test a software system for all possible inputs. Software testing and formal verification provide a means for increasing the confidence level of a software system.

The development of large software systems and the problem of software reliability result in software maintenance consuming a large percentage of the total system cost. The goal of maintainability is concerned with developing a system that will ease the burden of maintenance after it becomes operational. Swanson [51] provides a taxonomy of software maintenance activities, a description of a maintenance data base, and measures for evaluating maintenance performance.

The design goal of efficiency is multifaceted with respect to language design and use, as well as time and space constraints. Therefore, the term efficiency includes aspects related to compilers and programmers. Compiler developers need to be concerned with producing products that are efficient in the use of computer system resources from the standpoint of the actual compiler and the object code generated. Programmers need to be concerned with those language features that enhance productivity in individual and group efforts.

Sheppard, Curtis, Milliman, and Love [20] describe several experiments that were conducted on professional programmers in order to measure human factors aspects of programming activities.

Pascal

History. Pascal was reported by Wirth in the open literature in Reference 52. In his design of Pascal, Writh was heavily influenced by Algol 60 from a language standpoint. He was also interested in developing a language that could be used to teach programming concepts. Jensen and Wirth [53] note that an initial version of Pascal was developed in 1968. Two years later, the first Pascal compiler was available.

A key concept related to Pascal is language simplicity. The definition of the language is succinctly provided in one document [53] that contains the user manual (129 pages) and report (35 pages). Included in an appendix of the user manual is a small list of error messages. The use of syntax diagrams, as well as BNF notation, to describe the syntax of the language provide a means for desk-checking the syntactic correctness of Pascal programs. The semantics of Pascal have been formally defined in Reference 54. This formal definition, using the axiomatic approach, has been beneficial in further resolving questions related to the language. The formal definition parallels the user manual and report in terms of readability, clarity, and succinctness.

The language has been critiqued extensively in the open literature and is briefly discussed here. Habermann [55] commented on what he considered to be ill-defined constructs in the language. Lecarme and Desjardins [56] provided a response to the Habermann comments that clarified several points and raised further language-related questions. Wirth [57] assessed the language he designed from the standpoint of reliable programming. Finally, Welsh, Sneeringer, and Hoare [58] addressed ambiguity and insecurity questions about Pascal relevant to the work of compiler implementors.

During the 1970s Pascal surged as a language for teaching the concepts of structured programming. As mentioned earlier, one of Wirth's motivations for designing the language was for teaching programming. Pascal has been characterized as a self-documenting language. This point can be exploited in the classroom environment through numerous program examples and code-reading exercises.

Pascal has been plagued, however, with problems in attempting to standardize the language. It would appear that the description of the language provided in the Pascal User Manual and Report [53] has become the de-facto standard in lieu of any organized effort. Many dialects of Pascal have been introduced in the programming community. One prominent dialect of Pascal is Brinch Hansen's, Concurrent Pascal [59]. Recent languages, such as Modula [60], Euclid [13], and Ada [61] have been heavily influenced in their designs by Pascal.

Language Concepts. The Pascal language description that follows is based on the version that is defined in Jensen and Wirth [53]. A Pascal program consists of a heading and block. The heading serves as a means of stating the program identification and formal parameters. The block contains the following: label declaration part, constant definition part, type definition part, variable declaration part, procedure and function part, and statement part.

Identifiers are formed by an initial letter and an optional sequence of letters and/or digits. There are 35 identifiers that are reserved words in the language. We follow the convention of underlining reserved words, whenever used, throughout this section. The language requires that a variable declaration must occur before variable use in an executable statement. Comments are formed in the language by enclosing a sequence of characters within left and right braces, { and }. The semicolon ; is used to separate statements rather than terminate them as in PL/I.

Pascal provides for the following scalar types: boolean, integer, real, character, and enumeration. The four scalar types, boolean, integer, real, and character, are referred to as standard basic types provided in the language. The scalar type, enumeration, is user-defined as a grouping of enumerated literals. Subranges on scalar types are allowed in the language. Standard functions are defined for returning information related to scalar types, for instance, the function *ord* returns the ordinal number of an argument in the range of values.

The array and record types are structured types provided in the language. An array type consists of elements that are each of the same type. An array can be type defined as packed for the purpose of informing the compiler to conserve storage space. Obviously, the packing of an array is accomplished at an increased cost to execution time. A record type can be composed of heterogeneous components. The record type allows for a variant part, allowing a record structure to be formed (shaped) based on the value of the variant part.

The set type is provided in Pascal, along with the set operators of union, intersection, and difference. The relational operators defined on the set type are equality, inequality, inclusion, and membership. A file type is defined as a sequence of elements that are all of the same type. Dynamic variables are provided through the pointer type. Standard procedures, new and dispose, are used for the dynamic allocation and deallocation of variables.

As mentioned earlier, two areas of concern in computer languages are data abstraction and concurrency. Concurrent Pascal [59] includes three additional types of interest, which are *class, process,* and *monitor.* They allow for the encapsulation of data types and parallel processing.

Pascal includes unary and binary operators for constructing logical, relational, and arithmetic expressions. There is a language-defined precedence of operators. Parentheses can be used in expressions to override the precedence rules.

The assignment statement in Pascal allows for sequential control in programs. The goto statement is provided as a means for explicit transfer of control in programs. Conditional control is provided in Pascal through the if and case statements. The if statement has two forms, which are if-then and if-then-else.

Nested if statements are supported in the language. The case statement provides selective branching to case labels based on the evaluation of an expression. The result of the evaluation indicates which branch is selected for execution. An expression that follows the reserve word case is referred to as the selector and must be of the scalar type, with the exception of type real. Note that a case label must be an element of the selector, or the construct is in error.

Four forms of iteration are provided in Pascal. These include the while-do statement, repeat-until statement, and two forms of the for statement. The while-do statement has an expression test before the loop body that must evaluate to true for the loop body to be executed. The repeat-until has an expression test after the loop body that must evaluate to false for the loop body to be repeated. Note that the repeat-until statement guarantees at least one execution of the loop body. The two forms of the for statement include a loop control variable that can assume values in a range of explicitly stated initial and final values that are all of the same scalar type, with the exception of type real. The distinction between the two forms of the for statement specify whether the loop control variable acquires values from the initial value to the final value or downto the final value.

Two forms of program units are provided in the language, procedures and functions. Procedures and functions must be defined before being invoked within a program. It is possible to defer procedure and function definition with the identifier, forward, following a declaration of the program unit and corresponding formal parameter list. Recursive procedures and functions are supported in the language. Parameter passage requires a one-to-one correspondence between the actual parameters in the invocation and those formal parameters that are listed in program unit declaration. Value and result parameter passage mechanisms are provided in the language. Procedures and functions may be passed as parameters.

Three types of input/output operations are provided as procedures in the Pascal standard library. The get and put procedures are defined for input and output on user-defined sequential files. The read and write procedures are defined primarily for input and output on humanly readable textfiles, although it is possible for read and write to operate on files other than textfiles. Finally, readln and writeln procedures are similar to read and write, with the exception that an end-of-line character is utilized by the former input/output operations.

Implementation Issues. A Pascal compiler, written in Pascal, represents approximately 6,000 lines of code. The intermediate language, P-code, serves as a form for representing Pascal programs during the language translation process. Portability of the language has been widespread, in that system programmers rehosting a Pascal compiler are primarily involved in the translator or interpreter for P-code, as well as architecture-specific issues related to the standard program units and types.

The relatively small size of the language has benefited the development of a large number of Pascal compilers/interpreters on microprocessor-based computer systems. Pascal use in commercial applications has been hampered by the unavailability of compilers for production programming environments.

Language Assessment. Pascal has had a significant impact on computing in the 1970s. This impact can be viewed in a threefold manner: design, use, and education. This language has influenced new language designs from the standpoint of language features, description, and implementation. Secondly, Pascal has served as a vehicle for exercising the structured programming discipline.

Finally, the Pascal language has received considerable use in the teaching of programming. It is interesting to note that within some segments of industry, individuals who have been weaned on Pascal and structured programming concepts, can argue a strong case for improved software methodologies. These individuals can create an almost unsettling situation for senior staff members who have not kept up with the advances in the programming process.

Ada

History. The Ada programming language effort represents a five year period of language requirements formulation, design competition, testing, and refinement.* In 1975 a DOD High Order Language Working Group (HOLWG) was formed for the purpose of selecting a programming language suitable for DOD embedded computer systems [63, 64]. An *embedded* computer system is defined as a computer system within a larger system whose primary function is not data processing [65, 66]. The HOLWG was composed of representatives from the Army, the Navy, The Air Force, and other governmental organizations. The increasing cost for software development and maintenance was one of the motivating factors for undertaking the effort. The result of the effort was the development of the Ada programming language.

Two DOD management initiatives related to the acquisition of software systems were released in 1976. The first initiative, DOD Directive 5000.29, was aimed at establishing control in the life cycle management of major defense systems. The directive outlined milestones for software development and maintenance, as well as requiring that criteria be established to insure milestone completion. The second initiative, DOD Instruction 5000.31, provided a list of approved high-order languages for use in the development of new DOD software systems.

The requirements for a single programming language were developed over a period from 1975 to 1978. The language requirements were denoted STRAWMAN, WOODENMAN, TINMAN, IRONMAN, Revised IRONMAN, and STEELMAN [67]. These requirements documents received considerable review and comment by industry, academia, and the government. The STEELMAN document represented the final product of the HOLWG efforts in collecting, formulating, and reviewing the language requirements. Ad-

---

*The remainder of this section was developed from material in Reference 62.

ditionally, the STEELMAN document provided the requirements for the design of the DOD high-order language. It is an interesting and beneficial exercise to compare the language requirements in the STEELMAN document with the Ada programming language.

A language evaluation was conducted in 1976 to determine whether an existing high-order language could satisfy the DOD requirements. Since none of the languages evaluated satisfied the requirements, it was decided that a language would be designed with either Pascal, PL/I, or Algol 68 as a base language. A request for proposals was released in April 1977, seeking organizations to design the language. In July 1977, four organizations were awarded contracts to develop the language: CII-Honeywell Bull, Intermetrics, SofTech, and SRI International. The four design teams each selected Pascal as the base language from which to begin the language design. In April 1978, the language design competition was narrowed to two teams: CII-Honeywell Bull and Intermetrics. The preliminary language designs submitted by the contractors were extensively reviewed by industry, academia, and the government. In May 1979, the language design produced by CII-Honeywell Bull was selected by the HOLWG. The selected language was named Ada in honor of Ada Augusta.

A test and evaluation phase was conducted during the period from May 1979 to October 1979. Ada programs for a variety of applications were developed during the test and evaluation period. Language changes were recommended to the CII-Honeywell Bull design team based on the results generated from the experience gained in using Ada. A proposed standard for the Ada language [61] was produced in July 1980. This proposed standard had a debut in September 1980.

Concurrent with the language design effort, the HOLWG initiated the process of formulating requirements for the environments to support the Ada language. The requirements documents for the environments were denoted PEBBLEMAN, PEBBLEMAN Revised, Preliminary STONEMAN, and STONEMAN [68, 69]. The Army and Air Force have begun separate procurements for compilers and environments for the Ada language. A summary of the significant events that led to the development of Ada is provided in Table 9.1.

Language Concepts. The Ada language described in the remainder of this chapter is based on Reference 61. In general, a program unit in Ada consist of a declarative part and a sequence of statements. The delcarative part serves to identify the characteristics of objects to be used in the program unit. The sequence of statements serves to represent the execution of the program unit.

Identifiers are formed by an initial letter followed by an optional sequence of letters and/or digits. A single underscore character can be used as a separator between letters or digits in an identifier. The Ada language includes 62 identifiers that are designated as reserved words. Reserved words have specific uses in the language and as such must not be used as identifiers for other objects in the language.

Comments begin with 2 hyphens and are terminated by line boundaries. The semicolon is used to terminate language constructs rather than as a separator. Pragmas are used

Table 9.1. Ada—Significant Events in the Past.

STRAWMAN	Apr 75
WOODENMAN	Aug 75
DOD DIRECTIVE 5000.29	Apr 76
TINMAN	Jun 76
DOD INSTRUCTION 5000.31	Nov 76
IRONMAN	Jan 77
RFP	Apr 77
IRONMAN REVISED	Jul 77
CONTRACTS AWARDED	Jul 77
COMPETITION NARROWED	Apr 78
STEELMAN	Jun 78
PEBBLEMAN	Jun 78
PEBBLEMAN REVISED	Jan 79
LANGUAGE SELECTION	Apr 79
PRELIMINARY STONEMAN	Nov 79
STONEMAN	Feb 80
ADA	Jul 80
ADA DEBUT	Sep 80

in the language to convey information to the compiler. This information can be ignored by the compiler. There are 12 predefined language pragmas, and the capability exists for providing implementation defined pragmas.

Each identifier that occurs in an Ada program must be explicitly declared. A declaration achieves its effect by the process of elaboration. There are only three exceptions to the explicit declaration rule. Labels, block identifiers, and loop identifiers are declared implicitly upon elaboration of these objects.

The scalar types provided in the language are enumeration, character, boolean, integer, and reals (both fixed point and floating point). The fixed point type allows for specifying absolute bounds on errors, and the floating point type allows for specifying relative bounds on errors.

A homogeneous structure of components is provided in the array type. The record type may be used to create a hetergeneous structure of components. A variant part in a record type is similar to the Pascal variant part for shaping structures. Dynamic storage allocation is provided through the access type. Subtype declarations can be used to constrain the set of values of a declared type. There are 46 predefined attributes that return information related to an object, for instance, typing information on an object of scalar type.

The set type and corresponding set operations are not defined in Ada, although it would be possible to handle sets through the package and library features.

The language provides logical, relational, and arithmetic operators for constructing expressions. A language-defined operator precedence determines the order of expression evaluation. The precedence rules can be overridden by the use of parentheses.

Ada includes the classical set of three control structures that allow for sequential execution through sequence, selection, and iteration. The assignment statement implements the control structure for sequence. Also included is the goto statement for providing an explicit transfer of control mechanism.

Conditional control statements for the selection control structure include the if and case statements. Two common forms of the if statement provided are the if-then-end if and the if-then-else-end if. In addition, a multiple-branch if statement is provided in the if-then-elsif-end if construct. Note that there can be zero or more occurrences of the elsif clause, as well as an optional else clause.

Ada provides the ability to control the expression evaluation of an if statement through short-circuit evaluation. The short-circuit evaluation feature allows a programmer to take advantage of the evaluation of Boolean connectives and potentially minimizes the complete evaluation of a conditional expression.

The case statement provides a means for selective branching to one of the conditions explicitly specified in the execution of the statement. The reserved word others can be used as the last alternative condition on a case statement. The reserved word can then serve as a funnel for all alternatives that are not explicitly specified and require the same action to be performed.

Three iteration control structures are provided in Ada. These control structures are the loop, while, and for statements. The basic loop structure is a sequence of statements that are bracketed by the reserved words loop and end loop. This loop structure can be terminated with an exit statement or the statement exit when followed by a condition. The basic loop structure can be prefixed by an iteration clause. These iteration clauses include for loop parameter in discrete range, for loop parameter in reverse discrete range, and while condition.

Three types of program units are provided in Ada for achieving modularity. The program units available are subprograms, packages, and tasks. Subprograms include the procedure, which is analogous to a sequence of actions, and the function, which is analogous to the mathematical concept of a function. Procedure and function declarations must appear in a program unit before being called. Procedure calls appear as statements, and function calls appear as operators in an expression. Recursion is supported in Ada for procedures and functions.

Parameters are passed as either input, output, or input-output with the modes being consistent between the formal declarations and actual use. Positional and/or named notation may be used in the parameter list of a subprogram invocation. Positional parameter passage imposes a mapping of the actual parameters in the invocation to the formal parameters in the subprogram declaration. Named parameters allow the programmer to state explicitly in the invoking parameter list, both the formal and actual parameters. Positional and named parameter passage may be stated in the invoking parameter list. However, once one switches from positional to named parameter passage, the remainder of the parameter list must be provided in the named notation. A formal parameter may have a default value associated with it, such that, if the actual parameter is not provided then the default value is used.

This concludes the discussion of the basic language features of Ada. It is at this point in the language description that we begin to depart from those basic language features that are provided in both Pascal and Ada.

A package is a program unit that provides a mechanism for grouping a collection of logically related entities. In general, the package consists of a package specification, referred to as the visible part, and a package body, which serves as the implementation of the package. A package composed of a package specification and no body is useful for creating a group of common variables/constants or a common pool of data and types. The private type can appear in the package specification and is useful in implementing abstract data types. Several recent languages that have also embodied the concept of abstract data types are Mesa [5], Euclid [13], Alphard [15], Modula [60], and CLU [70].

A task is a program unit that can be executed in parallel with other tasks. Tasks are similar to packages in that they include a task specification, referred to as the visible part, and a task body, which serves as the implementation of the task. In addition, a task can be defined as a type. Communication between tasks is achieved by means of an entry declaration (similar to a subprogram declaration), an entry call (similar to a procedure call), and an accept statement (similar to a block of statements). The task specification contains entry declarations for all points of communication with other tasks. For each entry declaration in a task specification, there must be a corresponding accept statement within the task body. A calling task issues an entry call to communicate with another task. The link between the calling task and the called task is referred to as a *rendezvous*. The effects of a rendezvous include synchronization, parameter passage, and mutual exclusion. Associated with each entry is a queue where calling tasks can wait until the rendezous is completed with the called task. A select statement is available in the tasking features for handling multiple accept statements within a task.

The generic facility in Ada provides for possibly parameterized subprograms (procedures and functions) and packages. There is a two-step process to using a generic program unit. First, the generic program unit is instantiated (copied) and then invoked as a program unit. This facility is similar to generic subprograms in PL/I, with the exception that PL/I requires all possible parameter types to be explicitly described in a subprogram declaration.

Separate complication of program units is provided in Ada as a feature for controlling program development. The feature allows for top-down or bottom-up program development. It is through this feature that programmers can create program libraries and develop a software system in an orderly manner. Separate compilation of program units is a feature provided in a language such as Fortran.

The exception-handling facility in Ada provides for an action to occur should an unexpected error be encountered during program execution. There are five predefined language exceptions that cover a broad range of runtime errors. User defined exceptions can be declared, raised, and handled. In comparison, a facility for exception handling is provided in the language CLU [71, 72].

Representation specifications in Ada allow the programmer to control the mapping of types onto the host machine. There are specification features for length and address, as well as representation features for the enumeration and record types. The predefined pragma PACK is useful when the programmer wants the compiler to handle minimizing of storage for array and record types.

The input-output operations in Ada are provided through two packages, INPUT_OUTPUT and TEXT_IO. The package INPUT_OUTPUT is defined for providing file-processing operations. The package TEXT_IO is defined for providing operations on human-readable input and output. In addition, Ada includes low-level input-output operations for interfacing with non-standard devices.

Implementation Issues. There are currently several language processor efforts that are under development in industry and academia. The U.S. Army funded development of one of the earliest language processors, developed at New York University [73]. The interpreter developed at NYU was written in the very high-level language, SETL and executed on a DEC VAX 11/780.

An intermediate language for Ada compiler efforts has not been standardized. There have been compiler efforts within industry and academia, some of which are government funded and others are self-generated.

Language Assessment. The language requirements formulation and competitive design efforts for Ada were unique in the approach to developing a computer language. The short amount of time in which the language was designed and tested, however, is one significant drawback that can be attributed to the language. Ada is a large language, and this fact will affect the learnability of the language. Another area of concern is in relation to the development of packages to support the large domain of application areas. The Ada language was initially developed for a broad application domain, that is, embedded computer system applications. The applicability of the language to this domain and other areas is expected to be of major concern in the 1980s. In December 1980, an ACM-SIGPLAN Symposium on Ada [74] demonstrated the rapid and diverse interest that has surrounded the language.

A proposed Ada standard [61] has been sumitted to the American National Standards Institute (ANSI) for approval. The military services have begun the process of introducing regulations and directives that outline the use of Ada in embedded computer system applications. The DOD has maintained a strong position against subsetting and supersetting of the language. This position can, of course, be controlled within an organization, but not necessarily outside the scope of the organization. Obviously, because of the size of the language, one would expect that Ada programmers would work in mental subsets of the language.

As with Pascal and other languages, many critiques of Ada are now beginning to surface in the open literature. The ACM *SIGPLAN Notices* has served as a forum for critiques of Ada. The reader must be cautioned, however, that many of these comments are based on the preliminary Ada language design [75, 76] and not on the proposed standard.

9.3. FUTURE DIRECTIONS

This section covers six major areas in which computer languages are expected to influence future research in software engineering. These areas include requirements analysis/specifications, formal semantic models, design languages, language usage, software reliability, and software maintainability.

The interface between requirements analysis/specification techniques and computer languages is crucial to software engineering. Pioneering efforts in requirements analysis were performed in business applications with ISDOS [77] and in real-time applications with SREM [78, 79, 80]. There still remains, however, a large gap between the front-end requirements analysis/sepcification phases and the coding phase of the software life cycle.

A greater effort is needed in the development of formal semantic models for computer languages that can be used by the developers of language translators and language users. Language designers need formalisms in the area of semantics that will have the same impact that Backus-Naur Form notation has had for the representation of syntax. Marcotty, Ledgard, and Bochmann [81] provided an in-depth survey of four formal definition techniques: W-grammars, production systems coupled with the axiomatic approach, Vienna definition language, and attribute grammars. Milne and Strachey [82] have also elaborated a technique for the formal definition of computer languages.

A more extensive use of computer languages in the design phase of software systems is needed. Program design languages that are pidgin higher-order languages or stylized English forms of computer languages are receiving increased interest as an approach to representing the design of a system. Van Leer [83] has described the applicability of this approach to structured program development. Machine processing of a program design language would benefit programmer productivity.

Research into the human factors aspects related to language usage has been on the increase over the past decade. Weinberg spurred an interest in the human aspects of program development in an early work [84]. The introduction of a recent text by Shneiderman [85] also addresses the human aspects of language usage. In addition, the foundations in software science provided by Halstead [86] will give this area quantitative metrics with which to measure software.

Development of better techniques and tools to increase the level of confidence in software systems is a current area of research. Software testing [87], test data generation [88, 89, 90], symbolic execution [91, 92, 93], and formal verification [94] are dependent upon the constraints that are in computer languages.

Software maintenance cost is a major percentage of the total software life cycle cost, and this percentage is expected to increase through the near future. A significant advance in software engineering would be in decreasing the cost percentage for performing software manitenance. Lientz, Swanson, and Tompkins [95] have provided some insight into the tasks that are involved in software maintenance. Belady [96] has proposed software development based on generalized software components that could be coupled together to form a system. The software could then evolve in an orderly fashion based on user experience with a system. A major problem remaining with generalized software components is in identifying those functions to be generalized and then completely defining the component interface.

A significant amount of resreach has been accomplished in the approximately 30 years of computer language design, development, and use. The main benefit of this research is that software engineers can develop systems in confidence that the coding phase is the most understood of all life cycle phases, although there remain many topics of research in computer languages requiring further pursuit.

REFERENCES

1. M. Elson, *Concepts of Programming Languages,* Science Research Associates, Inc., Chicago, 1973.
2. T. W. Pratt, *Programming Languages: Design and Implementation,* Prentice-Hall, Inc., Englewood Cliffs, N.J., 1975.
3. E. I. Organick, A. I. Forsythe, and R. P. Plummer, *Programming Language Structures,* Academic Press, New York, 1978.
4. A. I. Wasserman, *Tutorial: Programming Language Design,* EHO 164-4, IEEE Computer Society, 1980.
5. C. M. Geschke, J. H. Morris, Jr., and E. H. Satterthwaite, "Early Experience with Mesa," *Communications of the ACM,* vol. 20, no. 8, Aug. 1977, pp. 540–553.
6. T. R. Horsley and W. C. Lynch, "Pilot: A Software Engineering Case Study," *Proceedings of the Fourth International Conference on Software Engineering,* Munich, Sept. 1979, pp. 94–99.
7. D. D. Redell, Y. K. Dalal, T. R. Horsley, H. C. Lauer, W. C. Lynch, P. R. McJones, H. C. Murray, and S. C. Purcell, "Pilot: An Operating System for a Personal Computer," *Communications of the ACM,* vol. 23, no. 2, Feb. 1980, pp. 81–92.
8. B. W. Lampson and D. D. Redell, "Experience with Processes and Monitors in Mesa," *Communications of the ACM,* vol. 23, no. 2, Feb. 1980, pp. 105–117.
9. D. M. Ritchie and K. Thompson, "The UNIX Time-Sharing System," *Communications of the ACM,* vol. 17, no. 7, July 1974, pp. 365–375.
10. D. M. Ritchie, S. C. Johnson, M. E. Lesk, and B. W. Kernighan, "The C Programming Language," *The Bell System Technical Journal,* vol. 57, no. 6, July–Aug. 1978, pp. 1991–2019.
11. B. W. Kernighan and D. M. Ritchie, *The C Programming Language,* Prentice-Hall, Inc., Englewood Cliffs, N.J., 1978.
12. B. W. Kernighan and J. R. Mashey, "The UNIX Programming Environment," *Computer,* vol. 14, no. 4, Apr. 1981, pp. 12–22, 24.
13. B. W. Lampson, J. J. Horning, R. L. London, J. G. Mitchell, and G. J. Popek, "Report on the Programming Language Euclid," *SIGPLAN Notices,* vol. 12, no. 2, Feb. 1977, p. 79.

14. A. L. Ambler, D. I. Good, J. C. Browne, W. F. Burger, R. M. Cohen, C. G. Hoch, and R. E. Wells, "GYPSY: A Language for Specification and Implementation of Verifiable Programs," *Proceedings of an ACM Conference on Language Design for Reliable Software,* available as *SIGPLAN Notices,* vol. 12, no. 3, March 1977, pp. 1–10.

15. M. Shaw, W. A. Wulf, and R. L. London, "Abstraction and Verification in Alphard: Defining and Specifying Iteration and Generators," *Communications of the ACM,* vol. 20, no. 8, Aug. 1977, pp. 553–563.

16. B. Shneiderman, "Exploratory Experiments in Programmer Behavior," *International Journal of Computer and Information Sciences,* vol. 5, no. 2, 1976, pp. 123–143.

17. J. D. Gannon, "Guest Editor's Introduction: Human Factors in Software Engineering," *Computer,* vol. 12, no. 12, Dec. 1979, pp. 6–7.

18. B. Shneiderman, "Human Factors Experiments in Designing Interactive Systems," *Computer,* vol. 12, no. 12, Dec. 1979, pp. 9–19.

19. V. R. Basili and R. W. Reiter, Jr., "An Investigation of Human Factors in Software Development," *Computer,* vol. 12, no. 12, Dec. 1979, pp. 21–38.

20. S. B. Sheppard, B. Curtis, P. Milliman, and T. Love, "Modern Coding Practices and Programmer Performance," *Computer,* vol. 12, no. 12, Dec. 1979. pp. 41–49.

21. H. E. Dunsmore and J. D. Gannon, "Data Referencing: An Empirical Investigation," *Computer,* vol. 12, no. 12, Dec. 1979, pp. 50–59.

22. C. Bohm and G. Jacopini, "Flow Diagrams, Turing Machines and Languages with only Two Formation Rules," *Communications of the ACM,* vol. 9, no. 3, May 1966, pp. 366–371.

23. E. W. Dijkstra, "Go To Statement Considered Harmful," *Communications of the ACM,* vol. 11, no. 3, March 1968, pp. 147–148.

24. O.-J. Dahl, E. W. Dijkstra, and C. A. R. Hoare, *Structured Programming,* Academic Press, New York, 1972.

25. H. Ledgard, "The Case for Structured Programming," *BIT,* vol. 14, 1974, pp. 45–57.

26. D. E. Knuth, "Structured Programming with go to Statements," *ACM Computing Surveys,* vol. 6, no. 4, December 1974, pp. 261–302.

27. R. W. Jensen, "Tutorial Series-6: Structured Programming," *Computer,* vol. 14, no. 3, March 1981, pp. 31–48.

28. N. Wirth, "Program Development by Stepwise Refinement," *Communications of the ACM,* vol. 14, no. 4, April 1971, pp. 221–227.

29. H. D. Mills, "Top-Down Programming in Large Systems," in R. Rustin (ed.), *Debugging Techniques in Large Systems,* Prentice-Hall, Inc., Englewood Cliffs, N.J., 1971, pp. 41–55,

30. H. D. Mills, *Mathematical Foundations for Structured Programming,* IBM Corporation, Gaithersburg, Md., Report No. FSC 72-6012, Feb. 1972.

31. H. D. Mills, "How to Write Correct Programs and Know It," *SIGPLAN Notices,* vol. 10, no. 6, June 1975, pp. 363–370.

32. F. T. Baker, "Chief Programmer Team Management of Production Programming," *IBM Systems Journal,* vol. 11, no. 1, 1972, pp. 56–73.

33. F. T. Baker, "System Quality Through Structured Programming," *AFIPS Conference Proceedings,* vol. 41, pt, I, 1972, pp. 339–343.

34. F. T. Baker, "Structured Programming in a Production Programming Environment," *SIGPLAN Notices,* vol. 10, no. 6, June 1975, pp. 172–185.

35. K. S. Shankar, "Tutorial: Data Structures, Types, and Abstractions," *Computer,* vol. 13, no. 4, Apr. 1980, pp. 67–77.

36. B. Liskov and S. Zilles, "An Introduction to Formal Specifications of Data Abstractions,". in *Current Trends in Programming Methodology,* vol. 1, *Software Specification and Design,* R. T. Yeh (ed.), Prentice-Hall, Inc., Englewood Cliffs, N.J., 1977, pp. 1–32.

37. J. Guttag, "Abstract Data Types and the Development of Data Structures," *Communications of the ACM,* vol. 20, no. 6, June 1977, pp. 396–404.

38. C. A. R. Hoare, "Data Reliability," *SIGPLAN Notices,* vol. 10, no. 6, June 1975, pp. 528–533.

39. M. A. Jackson, *Principles of Program Design,* Academic Press, New York, 1976.

40. R. L. London, "A View of Program Verification,". *SIGPLAN Notices,* vol. 10, no. 6, June 1975, pp. 534–545.

41. S. L. Gerhart and L. Yelowitz, "Observations of Fallibility in Applications of Modern Programming Methodologies," *IEEE Transactions on Software Engineering,* vol. SE-2, no. 3, Sept. 1976, pp. 195–207.

42. R. A. DeMillo, R. J. Lipton, and A. J. Perlis, "Social Processes and Proofs of Theorems and Programs," *Communications of the ACM,* vol. 22, no. 5, May 1979, pp. 271–280.

43. E. W. Dijkstra, "The Structure of the T.H.E. Multiprogramming System," *Communications of the ACM,* vol. 11, no. 5, May 1968, pp. 341–346.

44. C. A. R. Hoare, "Monitors: An Operating System Structuring Concept," *Communications of the ACM,* vol. 17, no. 10, Oct. 1974, pp. 549–557.

45. C. A. R. Hoare, "Communicating Sequential Processes," *Communications of the ACM,* vol. 21, no. 8. Aug. 1978, pp. 666–677.

46. P. Brinch Hansen, "Distributed Processes," *Communications of the ACM,* vol. 21, no. 11, Nov. 1978, pp. 934–941.

47. P. Wegner, "Programming Languages—The First 25 Years," *IEEE Transactions on Computer,* vol. C-25, no. 12, Dec. 1976, pp. 1207–1225.

48. P. Wegner, "10. Programming Languages—Concepts and Research Directions," in P. Wegner (ed.), *Research Directions in Software Technology,* The MIT Press, Cambridge, Mass. 1979

49. *Preprints: ACM SIGPLAN History of Programming Languages Conference,* Los Angeles, California, June 1978, available as *SIGPLAN Notices,* vol. 13, no. 8, Aug. 1978, p. 310.

50. C. A. R. Hoare, *Hints for Programming Language Design,* Stanford University, Computer Science Report STAN-CS-74-403, Stanford, Calif., Jan. 1974.

51. E. B. Swanson, "The Dimensions of Maintenance," *Proceedings of the Second International Conference on Software Engineering,* Oct. 1976, pp. 492–497.

52. N. Wirth, "The Programming Language Pascal," *Acta Informatica,* vol. 1, no. 1, 1971, pp. 35–63.

53. K. Jensen and N. Wirth, *PASCAL—User Manual and Report,* 2d ed., Springer-Verlag, New York, 1974.

54. C. A. R. Hoare and N. Wirth, "An Axiomatic Definition of the Programming Language Pascal," *Acta Informatica,* vol. 2, no. 4, 1973, pp. 335–355.

55. A. N. Habermann, "Critical Comments on the Programming Language Pascal," *Acta Informatica,* vol. 3, no. 1, 1973, pp. 47–57.

56. O. Lecarme and P. Desjardins, "More Comments on the Programming Language Pascal," *Acta Informatica,* vol. 4, no. 3, 1975, pp. 231–243.

57. N. Wirth, "An Assessment of the Programming Language Pascal," *IEEE Transactions on Software Engineering,* vol. 1, June 1975, pp. 192–198.

58. J. Welsh, W. J. Sneeringer, and C. A. R. Hoare, "Ambiguities and Insecurities in Pascal," *Software—Practice and Experience,* vol. 7, no. 6, Nov. 1977, pp. 685–696.

59. P. Brinch Hansen, "The Programming Language Concurrent Pascal," *IEEE Transactions on Software Engineering,* vol 1, June 1975, pp. 199–207.

60. N. Wirth, "Modula: A Language for Modular Multiprogramming," *Software—Practice and Experience,* vol. 7, no. 1, Jan. 1977, pp. 3–35.

61. U.S. Department of Defense, *Reference Manual for the Ada Programming Language, Proposed Standared Document,* July 1980.

62. J. E. Urban, *Introduction to Ada,* (2d ed.), Chapter Tutorial, IEEE Computer Society, 1981.

63. D. A. Fisher, "DoD's Common Programming Language Effort," *Computer,* vol. 11, no. 3, March 1978, pp. 24–33.

64. W. A. Whitaker, "The U. S. Department of Defense Common High Order Language Effort," *SIGPLAN Notices,* vol, 13, no. 2, Feb. 1978, pp. 19–29.

65. B. C. De Roze, "An Introspective Analysis of DOD Wespon System Software Management," *Defense Management Journal,* Oct. 1975, pp. 2–7.

66. J. H. Manley, "Embedded Computer System Software Reliability," *Defense Management Journal,* Oct. 1975, pp. 13–18.

67. U.S. Department of Defense, *Requirements for High Order Computer Programming Languages "STEELMAN,"* Jan. 1978.

68. U.S. Department of Defense, *Requirements for Ada Programming Support Environments "STONEMAN,"* Feb. 1980.

69. J. N. Buxton and L. E. Druffel, "Requirements for an Ada Programming Support Environment: Rationale for STONEMAN," *Proceedings of the IEEE Computer Society's Fourth International Computer Software & Applications Conference (COMPSAC80),* Chicago, Oct. 1980, pp. 66–72.

70. B. Liskov, A. Snyder, R. Atkinson, and C. Schaffert, "Abstraction Mechanisms in CLU," *Communications of the ACM,* vol. 20, no. 8, Aug. 1977, pp. 564–576.

71. B. Liskov and A. Snyder, "Exception Handling in CLU," *IEEE Transactions on Software Engineering,* vol. SE-5, no. 6, Nov. 1979, pp. 546–558.

72. B. Liskov, R. Atkinson, T. Bloom, E. Moss, C. Schaffert, B. Scheifler, and A. Snyder, *CLU Reference Manual,* MIT/LCS/TR-225, Cambridge, Mass., Oct. 1979. p. 166.

73. R. B. K. Dewar, G. A. Fisher, Jr., E. Schonberg, R. Froehlich, S. Bryant, C. F. Gross, and M. Burke, "The NYU Ada Translator and Interpreter," *Proceedings of the IEEE Computer Society's Fourth International Computer Software & Applications Conference (COMPSAC80),* Chicago, Oct. 1980, pp. 59–65.

74. *Proceedings of the ACM SIGPLAN Symposium on the Ada Programming Language,* Boston, Dec. 9–11, 1980, available as *SIGPLAN Notices,* vol. 15, no. 11, Nov. 1980, p. 242.

75. "Preliminary Ada Reference Manual," *SIGPLAN Notices,* vol. 14, no. 6, June 1979, pt. A.

76. J. D. Ichbiah, J. G. P. Barnes, J. C. Heliard, B. Krieg-Brueckner, O. Roubine, and B. A. Wichmann, "Rationale for the Design of the Ada Programming Language," *SIGPLAN Notices,* vol. 14, no. 6, June 1979, pt. B.

77. D. Teichroew and E. A. Hershey, III, "PSL/PSA: A Computer-Aided Technique for Structured Documentation and Analysis of Information Processing Systems," *IEEE Transactions on Software Engineering,* vol. SE-3, no. 1, Jan. 1977, pp. 41–48.

78. M. W. Alford, "A Requirements Engineering Methodology for Real-Time Processing Requirements," *IEEE Transactions on Software Engineering,* vol. SE-3, no. 1, Jan. 1977, pp. 60–69.

79. M. W. Alford, "Software Requirements Engineering Methodology (SREM) at the Age of Two," *Proceedings of the Second International Computer Software and Applications Conference 1978 (COMPSAC78),* Chicago, pp. 332–339.

80. M. W. Alford, "Software Requirements Engineering Methodology (SREM) at the Age of Four," *Proceedings of the Fourth International Computer Software and Applications Conference 1980 (COMPSAC80),* Chicago, pp. 866–874.

81. M. Marcotty, H. F. Ledgard, and G. V. Bochmann, "A Sampler of Formal Definitions," *ACM Computing Surveys,* vol. 8, no. 2, June 1976, pp. 191–276.

82. R. Milne and C. Strachey, *A Theory of Programming Language Semantics (Part A and B),* John Wiley, New York, 1976.

83. P. Van Leer, "Top-Down Development Using a Program Design Language," *IBM Systems Journal,* vol. 15, no. 2, 1976, pp. 155–170.

84. G. M. Weinberg, *The Psychology of Computer Programming,* Van Nostrand Reinhold, New York, 1971.

85. B. Shneiderman, *Software Psychology: Human Factors in Computer and Information Systems,* Winthrop Publishers, Inc., Cambridge, Mass. 1980.

86. M. H. Halstead, *Elements of Software Science,* Elsevier-North Holland Publishing Company, New York, 1977.

87. E. Miller, *Tutorial: Program Testing Techniques,* EHO 130-5, IEEE Computer Society, 1977.

88. C. V. Ramamoorthy and S. F. Ho, "Testing Large Software with Automated Software Evaluation Systems," *IEEE Transactions on Software Engineering,* vol. SE-1, no. 1, March 1975, pp. 46–58.

89. C. V. Ramamoorthy, K. H. Kim, and W. T. Chen, "Optimal Placement of Software Monitors Aiding Systematic Testing," *IEEE Transactions on Software Engineering,* vol. SE-1, no. 4, Dec. 1975, pp. 403–411.

90. C. V. Ramamoorthy, S. F. Ho, and W. T. Chen, "On the Automated Generation of Test Data," *IEEE Transactions on Software Engineering,* vol. SE-2, no. 4, Dec. 1976, pp. 293–300.

91. J. C. King, "A New Approach to Program Testing," *SIGPLAN Notices,* vol. 10, no. 6, June 1975, pp. 228–233.

92. J. C. King, "Symbolic Execution and Program Testing," *Communications of the ACM,* vol. 19, no. 7, July 1976, pp. 385–394.

93. J. A. Darringer and J. C. King, "Applications of Symbolic Execution to Program Testing," *Computer,* vol. 11, no. 4, Apr. 1978, pp. 51–60.

94. R. L. London, "8. Program Verification," in P. Wegner (ed.), *Research Directions in Software Technology,* The MIT Press, Cambridge, Mass. 1979.

95. B. P. Lientz, E. B. Swanson, and G. E. Tompkins, "Characteristics of Application Software Maintenance," *Communications of the ACM,* vol. 21, no. 6, June 1978, pp. 466–471.

96. L. A. Belady, "Evolved Software for the 80's," *Computer,* vol. 12, no. 2, Feb. 1979, pp. 79–82.

10

Compilers

R. C. T. Lee

National Tsing Hua University
Hsinchu, Taiwan

C. W. Shen

First International Computer Corporation
Taipei, Taiwan

S. C. Chang

Northwestern University
Evanston, Illinois

10.1. INTRODUCTION

A compiler is software that translates a high-level language program into a low-level language program which can be executed by a computer. In many compilers, the low-level language is the machine language. For our purpose, we assume that the compiler translates a high-level language into an assembly language simply because it is easier to comprehend assembly languages.

It is our experience that an individual, while learning a compiler writing technique, has to spend a major part of his time studying assembly language. This is rather unfortunate because the code generation part of a compiler is quite straightforward. One just has to remember many details. By spending too much time in learning assembly languages, one loses precious time for studying the other important techniques of compiler writing.

To ensure that one would not have to spend too much time studying languages, we decided to use a very simple assembly language, described in Section 10.5. As the reader will see, though it is very easy to learn, it contains enough instructions so that it will not be difficult to translate a high-level language into this assembly language.

If asked to write a compiler with this assembly language as its target language, one will not become bogged down by the details of the assembly language. Instead, one can concentrate on other important compiler writing skills.

As far as the high-level language is concerned, the same approach is used; we did not want to use a very complicated language, such as FORTRAN or PASCAL. Nor did we want to use a subset of FORTRAN for various reasons that will later become clear. We therefore designed a high-level language, called FRANCIS. FRANCIS is sufficiently complicated that writing a compiler for it is nontrivial, yet it is ideal for compiler writing. It was designed for this purpose, and the reader will gradually appreciate this point.

FRANCIS is very similar to FORTRAN, except that it contains some special features taken from PASCAL. It contains most of the well-known FORTRAN instructions, such as DIMENSION, SUBROUTINE, GO TO, and so on. As far as the IF statement is concerned, we have borrowed the IF ... THEN ... ELSE type of statement from PASCAL. However, to simplify the syntax analysis discussion, we do not initially allow an IF within an IF. Also all of the variables have to be declared—a feature again borrowed from PASCAL. We shall first assume that FRANCIS is not a recursive language in the sense that subroutines in FRANCIS cannot call themselves. After making sure that the basic concept of compiler writing is understood, we then add the recursive feature and also allow the IF statement to contain IF statements. By such time it will not be difficult to understand how this can be done.

The appendix contains all of the syntactical rules of FRANCIS. We have used the Backus Normal Form (BNF) to describe the syntax rules of our language. The following meta-symbols belong to BNF formalism and so do not appear in the FRANCIS language:

$$ ::= \ | \ \{ \} \ \langle \ \rangle $$

English words enclosed by ⟨ and ⟩ are elementary constructs in FRANCIS. The symbol ::= means "is equivalent to." The symbol | means "or" and the braces { and } denote possible repetition of the symbols zero or more times.

Let us consider an example. In FRANCIS, an identifier always starts with a letter and this letter is followed by letters, numbers, or nothing. This definition can be expressed as follows:

⟨identifier⟩ ::= ⟨letter⟩{⟨letter⟩|⟨digit⟩}.

In FRANCIS reserved words are used that cannot be used as ordinary identifiers. They are all underlined in the definition. For instance, the following expression describes the syntax rules of array declaration instruction:

⟨array declaration part⟩
   ::= DIMENSION⟨array declaration⟩ ;

For the definition of array declaration, consult the appendix.

10.2. A GLIMPSE AT COMPILERS

Before getting into the details of a compiler, let us consider a very simple program and investigate what the compiler should do.

```
VARIABLE INTEGER: X, Y, Z;
X = 7;
Y = 9;
Z = X − Y;
END;
```

For the first instruction declaring X, Y, and Z to be integers, the compiler will generate the following assembly language instructions:

```
X   DS   1
Y   DS   1
Z   DS   1
```

For the instruction

$$X = 7;$$

the compiler will create a constant (say, called I1,) and an assembly language code as follows:

```
I1  DC   7
    LD   I1
    ST   X
```

Similarly, for the instruction

$$Y = 9;$$

the compiler will generate the following code:

```
I2  DC   9
    LD   I2
    ST   Y
```

Finally, for the instruction

$$Z = X + Y;$$

the compiler will generate:

```
LD   X
AD   Y
```

```
ST   T1
LD   T1
ST   Z
```

The reader may wonder why the above sequence is so inefficient. It should simply be

```
LD   X
AD   Y
ST   Z
```

In fact, we deliberately showed a code that is not efficient for reasons that will become clear later.

Ultimately, the high-level language program will be translated into the following assembly language code:

```
X   DS   1
Y   DS   1
Z   DS   1
I1  DC   7
I2  DC   9
    LD   I1
    ST   X
    LD   I2
    ST   Y
    LD   X
    AD   Y
    ST   T1
    LD   T1
    ST   Z
```

This is what a compiler should do, but how does it do it?

Basically, a compiler is divided into three parts: the lexical analyzer, the syntax analyzer, and the code generator, as described in Figure 10.1.

1. The input of the lexical analyzer is a sequence of characters representing a high-level language program. The major function of the lexical analyzer is to divide this sequence of characters into a sequence of tokens. For instance, consider the statement

VARIABLE INTEGER: X, Y, Z;

The output of the lexical analyzer is

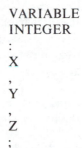

```
VARIABLE
INTEGER
:
X
,
Y
,
Z
;
```

2. The input of the syntax analyzer is a sequence of tokens that is the output of the lexical analyzer. The syntax analyzer divides the tokens into instructions. For each instruction, using the grammatical rules already stored, the syntax analyzer determines whether or not it is grammatically correct. If not, error messages will be produced. If correct, the instruction is decomposed into a sequence of basic instructions that are transferred to the code generator to produce an assembly language code.

For instance, consider the statement

$$X = Y + U * V;$$

The syntax analyzer would determine that this instruction is indeed correct and later produce three basic instructions as follows:

$$T1 = U * V$$
$$T2 = Y + T1$$
$$X = T2$$

3. The code generator accepts the output from the syntax analyzer. Every basic instruc-

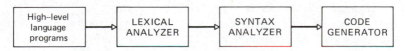

Figure 10.1.

tion is now translated into a sequence of assembly language instructions. This can be done easily because the code generator can examine the pattern of the basic instruction and determine which sequence of code it must generate.

To make sure that the code generator can recognize the pattern easily, we may assume that each basic instruction produced by the syntax analyzer is in a standard form. In our case, we assume that the standard form is a quadruple as follows:

$$(\text{Operator}, \text{Operand}_1, \text{Operand}_2, \text{Result}).$$

For instance, for the basic instruction

$$X = Y + Z,$$

the standard form will be

$$(+, Y, Z, X)$$

For the instruction

$$X = Y - Z,$$

the standard form will be

$$(-, Y, Z, X)$$

The code generator generates an assembly language code by examining the operator, the operands, and the result.

10.3. THE LEXICAL ANALYZER

As indicated above, the function of the lexical analyzer is to group the input sequence of characters into tokens. This is the major function. Actually, as the reader will see, the lexical analyzer does more than identify tokens.

The Identification of Tokens

As far as the language FRANCIS is concerned, the identification of tokens is trivial. Note that tokens are separated by delimiters, such as "+", "−", "=", and so forth, or blanks. Moreover, each delimiter itself is a token, and no token consists of more than one

delimiter. We therefore scan the input sequence sequentially and examine each character to see whether it is a delimiter or a blank. If it is a blank we identify the previous string formed, if it exists, as a token. If it is a delimiter, we have identified two tokens, the previous string formed is a token (assuming that it is not empty), and the current delimiter is also a token.

An algorithm to identify tokens for the language FRANCIS is shown in Figure 10.2.

Note that for some high-level languages, it is not as easy to identify tokens. For example, in FORTRAN, "." is sometimes a delimiter and sometimes it is not. In logical expressions, one may write

$$X.EQ.Y.$$

Here, "." is a delimiter. However, for a real number

$$35.76,$$

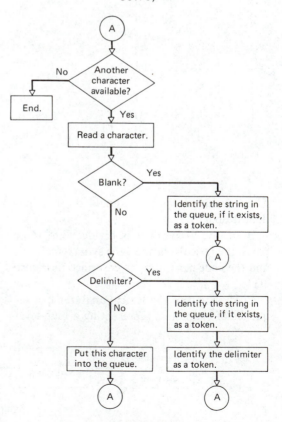

Figure 10.2.

the "." inside is not a delimiter. Thus, in FORTRAN, the detection of "." does not automatically mean that a token has been found.

Also, in FORTRAN, when we encounter the sign "*", we cannot say that this is a token because it may be a part of "**". In this case, we have to conduct some kind of look-ahead.

The high-level language has been deliberately defined to make sure that the identification of tokens is an easy job. In order to determine whether a character is a delimiter or not, a table called the *delimiter table* is set up. Since every input symbol will be checked against it, the delimiter table will be searched frequently; therefore we use hashing to store the data.

Table 10.1 shows all of the delimiters used in FRANCIS. Note that "." is not contained in Table 10.1.

The Types of Tokens Recognized by the Lexical Analyzer

In the previous section we showed how the lexical analyzer identifies tokens. In this section, we shall illustrate some other functions of the lexical analyzer.

Note that the major job of the lexical analyzer is to prepare everything for the syntax analyzer. Assume that the syntax analyzer encounters the following instruction:

VARIABLE INTEGER: X, Y, Z;

In this case, the syntax analyzer recognizes that this instruction is a declaration instruction

because it detects the token "VARIABLE". In FRANCIS, the word "VARIABLE" has a particular meaning and cannot be used in any other way. For instance, one cannot write the following instruction:

VARIABLE = VARIABLE + 1;

The word "VARIABLE" is a *reserved* word for FRANCIS. Similarly, the words IF, ELSE, and so on, are all reserved words in FRANCIS that cannot be used as ordinary variables.

It is appropriate to point out that in FORTRAN, there is not a reserved-word concept. Indeed, one may have

IF = IF + 1

in FORTRAN, whereas it is absolutely not allowed in FRANCIS.

Since the recognition of reserved words is so important for the syntax analyzer, it is appropriate for the lexical analyzer to do that job for it. Table 10.2 contains all of the reserved

Table 10.1. Delimiters.

1	;
2	(
3	)
4	=
5	+
6	−
7	*
8	/
9	↑
10	'
11	,
12	:

Table 10.2. Reserved Word Table.

1	AND
2	BOOLEAN
3	CALL
4	DIMENSION
5	ELSE
6	ENP
7	ENS
8	EQ
9	GE
10	GT
11	GTO
12	IF
13	INPUT
14	INTEGER
15	LABEL
16	LE
17	LT
18	NE
19	OR
20	OUTPUT
21	PROGRAM
22	REAL
23	SUBROUTINE
24	THEN
25	VARIABLE

words in FRANCIS. Since this table is also searched frequently, we may use hashing to store and retrieve the data.

In addition to recognizing reserved words, we may also easily recognize numerical constants in the lexical analyzer. If a token starts with a number, it must either be a real number or an integer. If it contains the ".", it must be a real number.

In summary, for any token, the lexical analyzer determines whether it is a delimiter, a real number, an integer, a reserved word, or an identifier. An identifier is a token that is not a delimiter, a real number, an integer, or a reserved word. In general, an identifier usually denotes a variable, an array, a label, the title of a program, or the title of a subroutine.

The Representation of Tokens

We now ask the question: How does the lexical analyzer let the syntax analyzer know the type of a token.

Before answering this question, let us note another problem. Our tokens are of different lengths, not an ideal situation for internal representation.

Note that a token, after the lexical analysis, is designated as belonging to one of the following types:

1. Delimiters
2. Reserved words
3. Integers
4. Real numbers
5. Identifiers

Each class of tokens has a table associated with it. We have already shown that delimiters are contained in Table 10.1 and reserved words in Table 10.2. Whenever a token is identified as an integer, we put this integer into Table 10.3. This is necessary because in the final analysis, the code generator is going to be used with this table to generate constants. For instance, consider the following instructions:

$$X = 5;$$
$$Y = 7;$$

After the execution of lexical analysis, Table 10.3 will contain two integers as shown below:

Table 10.3. Integer Table.

| 5 |
| 7 |
| • |
| • |
| • |

Similarly, later on, we shall designate a table containing real numbers (Table 10.6).

For each identifier, we shall put it into some location in the *identifier table* (Table 10.4). The identifier table is designated to contain three entries: the subroutine to which the identifier belongs, the type of the identifier, and a pointer pointing to some other tables. These will be explained in detail later. Meanwhile, we merely note the following:

1. Every identifier is hashed into Table 10.4
2. If an identifier appears more than once in the same subroutine, this identifier is put into Table 10.4 only once.
3. If the same identifier appears in different subroutines, it will occupy different locations in Table 10.4. We shall use the Table's second column to point to the subroutine in which the identifier appears.

Let us consider the following example:

PROGRAM MAIN;
VARIABLE INTEGER: U, V, W, Z;
U = 56;
V = 79;
W = U + V;
CALL A1 (W, 136, Z);
ENP;
SUBROUTINE A1 (INTEGER: X, Y, Z);
Z = X + 2.7 * Y;
ENS

In the above example, there are two subroutines: MAIN and A1 (The main program is also considered to be a subroutine). The identifiers that occur in the main program are

MAIN
U
V
W
Z

and the identifiers occurring in the subroutine A1 are

A1
X
Y
Z.

Table 10.4. Identifier Table.

	IDENTIFIER	SUBROUTINE	TYPE	POINTER
1				
2	W	3		
3	MAIN			
4	Z	3		
5	V	3		
6	X	8		
7				
8	A1			
9	U	3		
10	Y	8		
11	Z	8		

Note that the identifier Z occurs in both MAIN and A1 and will appear twice in Table 10.4. After the execution of the lexical analyzer, the contents of Table 10.4 are as shown. Consider the second entry of Table 10.4 which contains identifier W which in turn points to the third location of Table 10.4. Since the third location contains MAIN, the identifier W appears in subroutine MAIN. Similarly, in the tenth location, we have identifier Y pointing to the eighth location. Since the eighth location corresponds to subroutine A1, Y appears in subroutine A1.

We have shown that each token, after the lexical analysis phase, is found to be associated with a unique location in one of the tables from Table 10.1 to Table 10.4. The meaning of each table is summarized as follows:

1. Delimiter table
2. Reserved word table
3. Integer table
4. Real-number table
5. Identifier table

We may say that each token is characterized by two numbers i and j if it occupies the jth location of the ith table. Indeed, to solve the problem of different token lengths, we may simply use this 2-tuple (i, j) to represent the token. Note that this representation is one-to-one in the sense that given (i, j), we can uniquely identify the token. For instance, in Table 10.4, the 2-tuple (5, 2) denotes identifier W, and (5, 10) denotes Y.

Let us now give a complete example to illustrate the concept by considering the following programs:

PROGRAM MAIN;
VARIABLE INTEGER: U, V, M;
U = 5;
V = 7;
CALL S1(U, V, M);
ENP;
SUBROUTINE S1(INTEGER: X, Y, M);
M = X + Y + 2.7;
ENS;

After the execution of the lexical analyzer, the integer table will be as follows:

Table 10.5. Integer Table.

The real-number table will contain only one element (see Table 10.6).

Table 10.6. Real-Number Table.

Let us assume that after identifiers are put in Table 10.4, it looks like Table 10.7.

Assuming that Table 10.1 and 10.2 are as shown, the entire program will now be represented as shown below:

Table 10.7. Identifier Table.

	IDENTIFIER	SUBROUTINE	TYPE	POINTER
1	U		3	
2				
3	MAIN			
4	Y		10	
5	V		3	
6	M		3	
7				
8	X		10	
9	M		10	
10	S1			

case, we shall use quadruples to represent basic instructions.

4. Some other information obtained by the syntax analyzer will be put into the various tables of the compiler.

The first job of the syntax analyzer is to divide the input token stream into instructions. This is easy for FRANCIS because every instruction is terminated by the delimiter ";". We would like to point out that this is not the

```
PROGRAM MAIN;
(2,21)        (5,3)  (1,1)
VARIABLE INTEGER:      U  ,    V  ,    M  ;
(2,25)        (2,14)       (1,12) (5,1) (1,11) (5,5) (1,11) (5,6) (1,1)
U  =   5   ;
(5,1) (1,4) (3,1) (1,1)
V  =   7   ;
(5,5) (1,4) (3,2) (1,1)
CALL S1   (   U  ,    V  ,    M  )  ;
(2,3)   (5,10) (1,2) (5,1) (1,11) (5,5) (1,11) (5,6) (1,3)(1,1)
ENP ;
(2,6) (1,1)
SUBROUTINE S1   (    INTEGER :   X  ,   Y  ,   M  )  ;
(2,23)        (5,10) (1,2) (2,14)    (1,12)(5,8)(1,11)(5,4)(1,11)(5,9)(1,3)(1,1)
M  =  X  +  Y  +  2.7 ;
(5,9)(1,4)(5,8)(1,5)(5,4)(1,5)(4,1)(1,1)
ENS ;
(2,7) (1,1)
```

10.4. THE SYNTAX ANALYZER

The functions of the syntax analyzer are as follows:

1. The syntax analyzer divides the input tokens into instructions.
2. For each instruction, the syntax analyzer determines whether or not it is grammatically correct.
3. If the instruction is not grammatically correct, it is rejected and an error message is produced. Otherwise, it is decomposed into a sequence of basic instructions, each in a standard form. In our

case in FORTRAN. FORTRAN assumes that an instruction is contained in one card unless a symbol appears in the 6th column of the next card. This makes the job of determining the termination of an instruction much harder.

Note that even in PASCAL, the separation of tokens into instructions is more complicated. For instance, FRANCIS does not allow the instruction:

VARIABLE INTEGER :
X, Y, Z; REAL : U, V;

which is perfectly legal in PASCAL. In FRANCIS, we have the two instructions:

VARIABLE INTEGER : X, Y, Z;
VARIABLE REAL : U, V;

In PASCAL, compound statements are allowed. They start with BEG and end with END. Within BEG and END, there can be a sequence of instructions, each of which is terminated with ";". We deliberately designed FRANCIS to have such a syntax so that a compiler can be easily written. In FRANCIS, we allow an IF . . . THEN . . . ELSE instruction as follows:

IF P AND Q THEN X = X + 1
ELSE X = X − 1;

Note that the entire statement is only one instruction. It would not be difficult to modify the FRANCIS compiler to handle an instruction as follows:

IF P AND Q THEN BEG X = X + 1; Y = X + 2; END;
ELSE BEG X = X + 2; Y = X + L; END;

The Recognition of Different Types of Instructions

In FRANCIS, instructions may be classified in the following categories:

1. Program heading instructions
2. Subroutine heading instructions
3. Variable type declaration instructions
4. Label declaration instructions
5. Dimension declaration instructions
6. IF THEN ELSE instructions
7. GO TO instructions
8. Assignment instructions
9. CALL instructions
10. I/O instructions

Each type of instruction has its own syntax rules. The syntax analyzer has to recognize each instruction and branch to a subroutine to handle it. For instance, consider a GO TO instruction. This instruction must start with a reserved word GTO followed by a label. This label must be a type of identifier. That is, it must start with a letter followed by integers, letters, or nothing. Then, finally, we expect a

";" following this label. Since we have stipulated that every label must have been declared before it is used, we have to check whether the identifier following GTO is indeed a declared label. If the token following GTO is not an identifier or it was not declared as a label, an error message will be printed.

Let us consider another case. Imagine that we have already recognized the first token to be the reserved word VARIABLE. We then check whether the next token is INTEGER, REAL, OR BOOLEAN. If so, we proceed to check whether ":" follows. If not, an error message is printed. Upon finding ";", we expect a sequence of distinct identifiers, none of which appeared before and each of which is followed by ",". Finally, we expect a ";" to terminate this instruction. For each identifier appearing in this instruction, we have to take some semantic action that will be explained in detail later. If the variables are not distinct, or some variable is not followed by "," or some variable appeared before, error messages will be printed. The entire process of analyzing a variable-type declaration instruction can be illustrated, as shown in Figure 10.3.

The reader can see that it is absolutely necessary to recognize the type of instruction being analyzed. Let us temporarily assume that none of our instructions starts with a label (we shall discuss the handling of labeled instructions later). If this is the case, every instruction in FRANCIS, except the assignment instructions, starts with a reserved word. For instance, the program-heading instruction starts with the reserved word PROGRAM, and the IF THEN ELSE instructions start with the reserved word IF. In Table 10.8 we show how every instruction, except assignment instructions, starts with a particular reserved word. If an instruction does not start with a reserved word, then it must be an assignment instruction.

Again, we point out that in FORTRAN, we can not identify the type of instruction by checking the first token, because FORTRAN

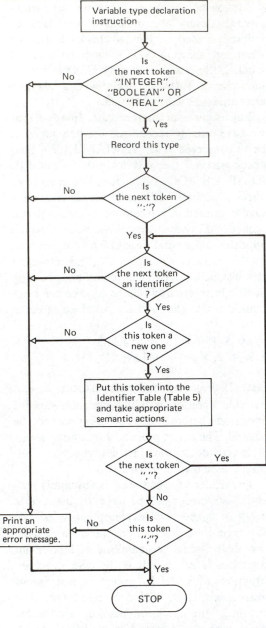

Figure 10.3.

Table 10.8. Correlation of Instructions and Reserved Words.

INSTRUCTIONS	RESERVED WORD
Program heading instructions	PROGRAM
Subroutine heading instructions	SUBROUTINE
Variable-type declaration instructions	VARIABLE
Label declaration instructions	LABEL
Dimension declaration instructions	DIMENSION
IF THEN ELSE instructions	IF
GO TO instructions	GTO
Assignment instructions	xxx
Call instructions	CALL
I/O instructions (read)	INPUT
I/O instructions (write)	OUTPUT

has no reserved words. However, those who are familiar with COBOL or BASIC will be able to note that every COBOL or BASIC instruction begins with a reserved word and this reserved word uniquely determines the type of the instruction.

Remember that in our compiler, every token is characterized by two integers. To check whether a token is a reserved word or not, we merely have to check whether the first integer is 2—recall that Table 10.2 contains all of the reserved words.

In our previous discussions we assumed that labels did not exist. This is, of course, not a valid assumption because we do allow labels. Actually, given an instruction, our first job is to check whether the beginning token is a label or not.

Note that labels were not detected in the lexical analysis phase; it was merely noted whether or not they were identifiers. Nevertheless, in FRANCIS, it is agreed that a label must have been declared before it is used. In other words, there must be an instruction I declaring label L before it is used. After instruction I is processed by the syntax analyzer, as will be seen later, the syntax analyzer will put a note in the identifier table to declare that identifier L is a label. This is done by putting an appropriate entry in the type entry of the identifier table, Later, whenever we want to know whether a token is a label or not, we merely have to check this token in the identifier table. If it is indeed a label, the type entry of this token in the identifier table will declare this fact.

At the top of the syntax analyzer, the type of each instruction is determined as follows:

1. Check the first token of an instruction. If it is a reserved word, the type is determined by this reserved word.

2. If the first token is not a reserved word, check whether the token is a label. If it is not a label, this instruction must be an assignment instruction.

3. If the first token is a label, the type of the instruction is determined by the second token. If the second token is a reserved word, then the type is determined by this token. Otherwise, it must be an assignment instruction.

The Processing of the Program Heading Instruction

There can be only one program heading instruction in the entire program, and this instruction must appear as the first instruction. The reserved word corresponding to this instruction is PROGRAM. After this instruction is processed, the heading of this program will now be classified as an identifier and put into the identifier table. In the identifier table, we do the following:

1. In the subroutine entry of the program heading in the identifier table, we have nothing. Having nothing appear in the subroutine entry of an identifier table indicates that this identifier is the name of a subroutine. Note that the main program can also be considered as a subroutine.

2. In the pointer entry, we put a 1 to indicate

that the quadruples corresponding to this program start from the first location of the quadruple table. The quadruple table is now illustrated in Fig. 10-4 b. For every subroutine, a sequence of quadruples are generated and stored consecutively in the quadruple table. In the identifier table, for every subroutine, there is a pointer aimed at the starting point of the corresponding sequence of quadruples.

The Processing of Variable-Type Declaration Instructions

The reserved word to identify a variable-type declaration instruction is VARIABLE. After processing such an instruction, the following actions are taken.

1. Let $X_1, X_2, \ldots, X_N$ be variables declared in this instruction. In the subroutine entry of X_i of the identifier table, direct a pointer to the subroutine X_i appears in. That is, suppose X_i belongs to subroutine S, which appears in location L_s in the identifier table; then put L_s in the subroutine entry corresponding to X_i in the identifier table.

2. Put a code indicating the type of X_i in the identifier table. We may arbitrarily set the codes as follows:

Array 1
Boolean 2

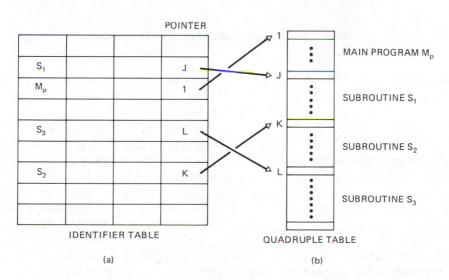

Figure 10.4.

Character	3
Integer	4
Label	5
Real	6

If the syntax analyzer finds out that the type of X_i is Boolean, 2 will be put into the type entry of X_i in the identifier table.

3. For each variable X_i, a quadruple is generated in the quadruple table. This quadruple will be used by the code generator later to assign the necessary space. Let the location in the identifier table occupied by X_i be L_i. Then the quadruple corresponding to X_i is $((5,L_i), , ,)$.

Let us assume that a certain variable X is declared as a real variable and the location occupied by this variable is 15 in the identifier table. Then the quadruple is $((5,15), , ,)$. In the type entry we have a 6, indicating that it is a real variable. The code generator, after noting the 2-tuple (5,15), will examine the 15*th* location of the identifier table. It will notice the existence of 6 in the type entry and thus will

record the type and dimensionality of the array and the size in each dimension. For instance, suppose the size of a real array is declared as (16,5). We now have to record the fact that the array is real, the dimensionality of this array is 2, the size of the first dimension is 16, and the size of the second dimension is 5. To store this information, we need a new one dimensional table called the *information table* (Table 10.9). In the above case, the information will be stored as follows:

Table 10.9. Information Table.

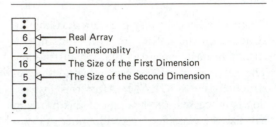

In the identifier table, a pointer will point to the information table as follows:

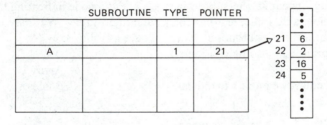

Figure 10.5. *a*, Identifier table and *b*, Information table.

generate the following assembly language code:

$$\text{X} \quad \text{DS} \quad 2$$

because a real-number variable will occupy two memory locations.

The Processing of Dimension Instructions

A dimension declaration instruction declares arrays. For every array declared, we have to

Let us summarize the actions taken by the syntax analyzer to handle a dimension declaration as follows:

1. Suppose A is declared an array. In the subroutine entry of A in the identifier table, place an appropriate pointer to indicate the subroutine to which it belongs.

2. In the type entry of A in the identifier table, place a 1, indicating that A is an array.

3. Assume that the type code of the array is j, the dimensionality of A is i, and the sizes of A corresponding to different dimensions of A are $s_1, s_2, \ldots, s_i$ respectively. Place j, i, s_1, s_2,

..., s_i into the information table. Assume that the next available location is N; then the information j, i, s_1, s_2, ..., s_i will be placed into locations N, N + 1, ..., N + i + 1 respectively; place N in the pointer entry of A.

4. In the quadruple table, generate a quadruple in which the first element identifies the location occupied by array A in the identifier table. That is, if the array occupies the 35th location of the identifier table, then the quadruple generated will be

$$((5,35), , ,).$$

The information table will not only contain information concerning arrays. For example, when we want to store other types of information, such as that concerning parameters of a subroutine, we can also use this table. We may view the information table as a warehouse where many people can store things. The only thing that we must do is keep pointers pointing to the location where the information is stored.

The reader may wonder why we don't keep separate tables for different types of information. For instance, why not keep one table to store information concerning arrays and another for information concerning subroutines? Note that if we keep several tables, we have to reserve quite a lot of memory locations, that is, we have to keep one array for each table. Since we do not know how large the size of each table should be, we would be forced to keep many rather large arrays only later to possibly find that many were largely empty, wasting a lot of memory space.

There is another important point to be made here. Suppose the compiler is written in FORTRAN; we can not have an array that will store integers as well as characters. The information table contains only integers. This is because the design, which dictates that every piece of information be represented by integers.

The Processing of Label Instructions

Label instructions are easily identified since they all start with a reserved word LABEL.

After recognition of a label, the following actions are taken.

1. Arrange a pointer to be placed into the subroutine entry of this label in the identifier table.
2. In the type entry, place 5 to indicate that it is a label.

The Processing of Labeled Instructions

In FRANCIS, labels must be declared before they are used, and also they must not be numbers. These instructions make it easier to process labeled instructions.

Let us assume that we have instructions as follows:

.
.
.

LABEL L100;

.
.
.

L100   X = Y + Z;

In this case, the following events must take place:

1. The lexical analyzer recognizes L100 as an identifier and hashes it into the identifier table.
2. The syntax analyzer recognizes the reserved word LABEL and consequently decides that identifier L100 must be a label. It then so indicates by putting 5 in the type entry of L100 in the identifier table, declaring that L100 is a label.
3. When the syntax analyzer encounters L100 again, it first checks through the identifier table and notices that it is a label. Suppose that in the quadruple table, the quadruple corresponding to

L100   X = Y + Z;

starts from location N; then put N into the pointer entry of L100 in the identifier table.

4. Suppose L100 is hashed into some location M in the identifier table, the first quadruple corresponding to this label instruction is

$$((5,M), \, , \,).$$

Later, when the code generator encounters this quadruple, it will realize that the next assembly language code generated should be labeled.

For

$$X = Y + Z$$

the assembly language code is

```
LD   Y
AD   Z
ST   X
```

Because this instruction is labeled, the code generator will generate a special label, say L3, in this case. Thus we may have

```
L3  LD   Y
    AD   Z
    ST   X
```

Assume that we later encounter an instruction as

```
GTO   L100;
```

In this case, the syntax analyzer checks the pointer entry of L100 in the identifier table and notices that the starting quadruple corresponding to the instruction labeled L100 starts from location N in the quadruple table. It will then generate a quadruple expressing GTO N when the code generator generates the following assembly language code:

```
JMP   L3.
```

The positive attributes of the fact that we do not use integers to represent labels, as is done in many languages, should be apparent. In FRANCIS, every integer recognized in the lexical analysis phase is indeed a number, and it is therefore appropriate to put it into the integer table. If we also used numbers to represent labels, we have to do some syntax analysis in the lexical analyzer, which means that the lexical analyzer and the syntax analyzer could not be clearly separated.

The Processing of Assignment Instructions

We will now discuss the most interesting and important part of the syntax analyzer: the processing of assignment instructions. As we noted before, assignment instructions are the only instructions that do not start with a reserved word and must contain an " = ".

In the following discussion, we shall first assume that the assignment instructions contain arithmetic expressions only. The method that will be presented can easily be extended to handle assignment instructions with logical expressions. Let us also temporarily assume that arrays do not appear in the assignment instructions.

Consider the instruction

$$X = Y + Z;$$

It is very easy for the syntax analyzer to recognize the operator " = " and generate the following quadruple:

$$(+,Y,Z,X).$$

It is appropriate to point out here that every entry is a token represented by a pair of integers. The plus sign " + " is represented by $(1,5)$ because it occupies the $5th$ location of Table 10.1, the delimiter table. Variables X, Y, and Z will all be represented by pairs of integers and the first integer of each pair is 5 because they are all identifiers (see Tables 10.4 and 10.7). Thus the quadruple will be:

$$((1,5), \, (5,3), \, (5,10), \, (5,13)),$$

If X, Y, and Z are stored in locations 13, 3, and 10 respectively in the identifier table.

To simplify the discussion, we shall use (+,Y,Z,X) instead of the above representation.

Unfortunately, a general assignment instruction is rather complicated since it may involve several operations and possibly parentheses. A typical assignment instruction may be

$$X = Y + U*V;$$

In this case, we must remember that we should perform the multiplication first and the addition next. That is, we should generate the following quadruples:

$$(*,U,V,T1)$$
$$(+,Y,T1,X)$$

where T1 is a temporary variable.

The question is: How does the computer know that we should first execute multiplication and then addition?

This problem can be solved by converting an assignment instruction into its Reverse Polish Notation. To obtain the Reverse Polish Notation of an assignment instruction involving arithmetic operations only, we shall first assume that there is an ordering of operations as follows:

$$\uparrow$$
$$*,/$$
$$+,-$$
$$(,)$$
$$=$$

The procedure to generate the Reverse Polish Notation for an assignment is as follows:

1. The symbols of the source string move left toward the junction.

2. When an operand (where the operand is a variable) arrives, it passes straight through the junction.

3. When an operator (where the operator is a delimiter) arrives, it pauses at the junction. If the stack is empty, this incoming operator slides down into the stack. Otherwise, it looks at the top of the stack. When the priority of

the incoming operator is not greater than that of the operator at the top of the stack, the operators in the stack will pop out and move to the left of the junction one by one. After the above process is finished, the incoming operator is pushed into the stack.

4. "(" always goes down to the stack.

5. When ")" reaches the junction, it causes all of the operators in the stack back as far as "(" to be shunted out, and then both parentheses disappear.

6. When all symbols have been moved to the left, all of the operators in the stack are popped out to the left junction.

Let us consider the case of

$$X = Y + U*V;$$

The steps of obtaining the Reverse Polish Notation of the above instruction are illustrated in Figure 10.6. The transformed Reverse Polish Notation is thus

$$X,Y,U,V,*,+,=.$$

After transforming an assignment instruction into its Reverse Polish Notation, one can decompose it into a sequence of basic instructions very easily. The procedure is as follows (although we assume that every operator is a binary operator here, it is easy to extend this method to handle unary operators):

1. Let $i = 1$
2. Pick the first operator from left to right. Let this operator be O_i.
3. Scan back and pick up two operands immediately preceeding O_i. Let these two operands be V_1 and V_2. Generate a basic instruction $O_i(V_1,V_2) = T_i$.
4. If the last symbol has already been scanned, stop. Otherwise, let $i = i + 1$ and go to step 2.

Let us again consider the assignment instruction

$$X = Y + U*V;$$

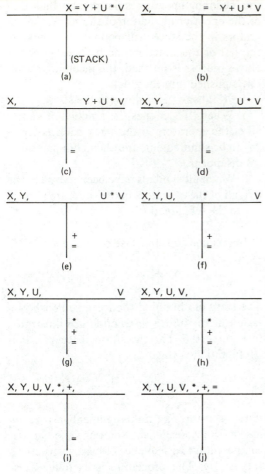

Figure 10.6.

The Reverse Polish Notation of the above instruction is

$$X,Y,U,V,*,+,=.$$

A sequence of basic instructions is now generated:

	BASIC INSTRUCTION	QUADRUPLE
X,Y,U,V,*,+,=	T1 = U*V	(*,U,V,T1)
X,Y,T1,+,=	T2 = Y+T1	(+,Y,T1,T2)
X,T2,=	X = T2	(=,T2, ,X)

Let us consider another example:

$$X = (Y+U)*V;$$

The Reverse Polish Notation of the above instruction is obtained as shown in Figure 10.7. The Reverse Notation for

$$X = (Y+U)*V$$

is thus

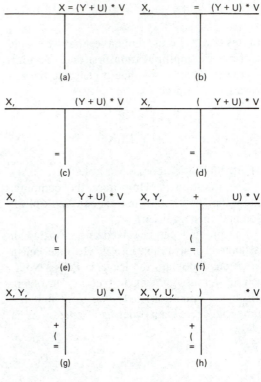

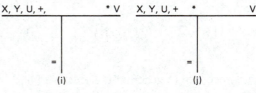

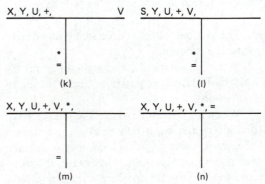

Figure 10.7.

$$X,Y,U,+,V,*,=.$$

A sequence of basic operations is generated as follows:

	BASIC INSTRUCTIONS	QUADRUPLES
X,Y,U,+,V,*,=	T1=Y+U	(+,Y,U,T1)
X,T1,V,*,=	T2=T1*V	(*,T1,V,T2)
X,T2,=	X=T2	(=,T2, ,X)

In the previous discussion, we dealt with assignment instructions with arithmetic operations only. In FRANCIS, we allow logical assignments as well. That is, we may have as an instruction

$$X=P \text{ AND } Q \text{ OR } R;$$

where P, Q, and R are Boolean variables. The reader can see that the above instruction can be transformed into its Reverse Polish Notation as follows:

$$X,P,Q,AND,R,OR,=$$

If we agree that AND should be performed before OR. The basic instructions are generated as shown below:

	BASIC INSTRUCTIONS	QUADRUPLES
X,P,Q,AND,R,OR,=	T1=P AND Q	(AND,P,Q,T1)
X,T1,R,OR,=	T2=T1 OR R	(OR,T1,R,T2)
X,T2,=	X=T2	(=,T2, ,X)

The Processing of Instructions Containing Arrays

In previous discussions, we assumed that arrays did not exist. If we allow for their existence, we have to take special actions. Consider the following instruction:

$$A(I) = B(2,3) + 4;$$

In this case, the parameters appear because of the arrays A and B, and they must be eliminated first.

Note that arrays must have been declared before they are used. Let us assume that A and B appear in the 7*th* and 16*th* locations in the identifier table respectively. Then A is represented by (5,7) and B is represented by (5,16). In the identifier table, both of these identifiers will be indicated as arrays. When the syntax analyzer encounters the symbol (5,7), it will examine the 7*th* location of the identifier table to find that this identifier represents an array. Immediately, it will branch to a subroutine to handle this array.

Let us consider a simple example first:

$$X = B(I,J) + 4;$$

In this case, we want to replace B(I,J) by a temporary variable. Let us assume that array B was defined as follows:

$$\text{DIMENSION INTEGER} : B(3,3);$$

The traditional method of memory management will arrange the array as follows:

B(1,1)
B(2,1)
B(3,1)
B(1,2)
B(2,2)
B(3,2)
B(1,3)
B(2,3)
B(3,3)

That is, B(I,J) will be the $((J-1)M+I)$ *th* Location of the B array if the dimensionalities of B are M and N respectively. Thus, to replace B(I,J), we have to generate the following quadruples:

(−,J,1,T1)	T1=J−1
(*,T1,M,T2)	T2=T1*M
(+,T2,I,T3)	T3=T2+I

Finally, we need the following quadruple:

$$(=,B,T3,T4),$$

which is interpreted as

$$T4 = B(T3).$$

The assembly language code corresponding to $(=,B,T3,T4)$ is

```
LD    B+T3-1
ST    T4
```

The entire sequence of quadruples for

$$X = B(I,J) + 4;$$

is

$(-,J,1,T1)$	$T1 = J-1$
$(*,T1,M,T2)$	$T2 = T1*M$
$(+,T2,I,T3)$	$T3 = T2+I$
$(=,B,T3,T4)$	$T4 = B(T3)$
$(+,T4,4,T5)$	$T5 = T4+4$
$(=,T5, ,X)$	$X = T5$

Let us consider an example in which an array appears at the left side of the equal sign:

$$A(I) = B(I,J);$$

In this case, B(I,J) is replaced by a temporary variable the same way as previously discussed. Suppose the temporary variable is T4, then:

$$A(I) = T4;$$

There are three types of quadruples for which the operators are all "=":

$(=,Y, ,X)$	$X = Y$
$(=,A,I,X)$	$X = A(I)$
$(=,X,A,I)$	$A(I) = X$.

The code generator will not be confused because A is a declared array whereas X and Y are not.

From the discussion of two dimensional integer arrays, the reader should be able to ex-

tend the concept to three, or four dimensional arrays and in fact to real arrays.

The Processing of IF THEN ELSE Instructions

IF THEN ELSE instructions can be easily recognized because they all start with the reserved word IF. A general format of this kind of instruction is

$$IF \ E \ THEN \ IN_1 \ ELSE \ IN_2;$$

where E is a logical expression and IN_1 and IN_2 are two simple instructions.

After analyzing the above instruction the syntax analyzer would generate the following quadruple:

$$(IF,P,QP_1,QP_2)$$

where P is a logical variable, evaluated to 1 or 0, depending on the expression E and the values of its variable during run time, and QP_i is the starting quadruple corresponding to IN_i. This quadruple will be interrupted as "If P is true, execute the code corresponding to QP_1; otherwise, execute the code corresponding to QP_2." Assume the quadruple corresponding to IN_1 starts from the 16th location of the quadruple table (Figure 10.4b): then QP_1 will be represented by (6,16).

Let us illustrate these ideas with an example. Consider

$$IF \ P \ THEN \ X = X + 1 \ ELSE \ X = X + 2;$$

The syntax analyzer will generate the following quadruples, assuming that the quadruples start from the 15th location of the quadruple table.

15	$(IF,P,(6,16),(6,19))$	
16	$(+,X,1,T1)$	
17	$(=,T1, ,X)$	
18	$(GTO, , ,(6,21))$	} $X = X + 1$
19	$(+,X,2,T2)$	
20	$(=,T2, ,X)$	
		} $X = X + 2$

When the first quadruple of the above sequence is generated, the syntax analyzer knows that QP_1 will start from the 16*th* location, but it does not know where QP_2 will start. Therefore, the syntax analyzer will have to wait for the generation of the 19*th* quadruple. When this quadruple is generated, the syntax analyzer comes back to quadruple 15 and fills in (6,19). The situation is the same for quadruple 18. When this quadruple is generated, the syntax analyzer does not know how long the sequence of quadruples corresponding to X = X + 2 will be. It therefore waits until all of the quadruples corresponding to X = X + 2 are generated.

Let us consider a more complicated case:

IF P AND Q THEN X = X + 1
ELSE X = X + 2;

In this case, we first have to evaluate P and Q, assuming that P and Q are Boolean variables. The quadruples for this instruction will be as follows:

15	(AND,P,Q,T1)
16	(IF,T1,(6,17),(6,20))
17	(+,X,1,T2)
18	(=,T2, ,X)
19	(GTO, , ,(6,22))
20	(+,X,2,T3)
21	(=,T3, ,X)

Quadruple 15 means that the value of T1 is the AND of P and Q. The assembly language codes for this quadruple are:

LD   P
AND Q
ST   T1

In general, a logical expression can be as complicated as follows:

X GT Y OR Y LT Z AND U EQ V.

To evaluate the above expression, we may use the Reverse Polish Notation to transform it into the following form (we have assumed that AND operations are to be evaluated before OR operations):

X, Y, GT, Y, Z, LT, U, V, EQ, AND, OR,

The sequence of quadruples generated are:

(GT,X,Y,T1)
(LT,Y,Z,T2)
(EQ,U,V,T3)
(AND,T2,T3,T4)
(OR,T1,T4,T5).

The Processing of GO TO Instructions

It is very simple to process GO TO instructions. For

GTO LX;

the syntax analyzer first has to find out whether LX is a label or not. This can be done by checking through the identifier table. If it has not been declared as a label or if it was declared to be something else, an error message is produced. If the LX is indeed a label, a check is made whether or not an instruction with this label has previously appeared. If so we may generate the following quadruple:

(GTO, , ,QP_X)

where QP_X is the starting quadruple corresponding to the instruction labeled with LX. Otherwise, we must wait until the syntax analyzer encounters the instruction with the label. If such an instruction never appears or appears more than once, an error message would be produced.

The Processing of CALL Instructions

When a CALL instruction is encountered, the syntax analyzer will record the name of the subroutine being called and the arguments appearing in the instruction. To do this, the information table is used.

A CALL instruction is of the following form:

CALL S1(P$_1$,P$_2$, . . . , P$_N$);

The quadruple corresponding to the above instruction will be of the following form:

Table 10.10. Information Table.

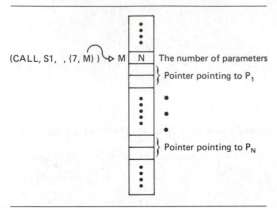

Since we store identifiers and numbers in tables, we have to use two numbers to represent each P$_i$. Let us assume that our CALL instruction is

CALL S1(W,136,A,57.9);

Assume that S1, W, and A occupy the 36*th*, 15*th*, and 27*th* locations of the identifier table (Table 10.7), respectively. Suppose 136 occupies the 3d location of the integer table (Table

10.5), and 57.9 occupies the 2d location of the real-number table (Table 10.6). Note that the reserved word CALL occupies the 3d location of the reserve word table (Table 10.2). Let us assume that the next available location in the information table is 59. The quadruple corresponding to the above instruction will be as shown in Table 10.11.

Examples

In this section two examples are presented to show how quadruples are generated and how the various tables (Tables 10.12–10.20) look after executing the syntax analyzer.

Example 1.

```
        PROGRAM A1;
        VARIABLE INTEGER: X,Y,I;
        DIMENSION INTEGER: A(12);
        LABEL L91, L92;
        I = 1;
        X = 5;
        Y = 11;
L91    IF X GT Y THEN GTO L92 ELSE
        X = X + 2;
        A(I) = X;
        I = I + 1;
        GTO L91;
L92    ENP;
```

Table 10.11. Information Table.

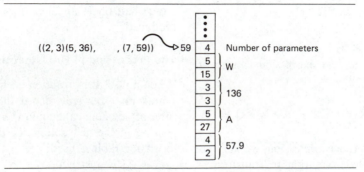

Table 10.12. Identifier Table.

	SUBROUTINE	TYPE	POINTER	
1				
2	I	5	4	
3				
4				
5	A1			1 → ▷ (Quadruple table)
6				
7	A	5	1	1 → ▷ (Information Table)
8	X	5	4	
9				
10				
11	Y	5	4	
12				
13				
14	L91	5	5	10 → ▷ (Quadruple Table)
15	L92	5	5	18 → ▷ (Quadruple Table)

Table 10.13. Integer Table.

1	12
2	1
3	5
4	11
5	2

Table 10.14. Information Table.

1	4	
2	1	} Array A
3	12	

Table 10.15. Quadruple Table.

1	((5, 8),	,	,	)	X
2	((5,11),	,	,	)	Y
3	((5, 2),	,	,	)	I
4	((5, 7),	,	,	)	A
5	((5,14),	,	,	)	L91
6	((5,15),	,	,	)	L92
7	((1, 4),	(3,2),	,	(5, 2))	I = 1
8	((1, 4),	(3,3),	,	(5, 8))	X = 5
9	((1, 4),	(3,4),	,	(5,11))	Y = 11
10	((2,10),	(5,8),	(5,11),	(0, 1))	T1 = X GT Y
11	((2,12),	(0,1),	(6,12),	(6,13))	IF T1 GO TO 12, ELSE GO TO 13
12	((2,11),	,	,	(6,19))	GTO L92
13	((1, 5),	(5,8),	(3, 5),	(0, 2))	T2 = X + 2
14	((1, 4),	(0,2),	,	(5, 8))	X = T2
15	((1, 4),	(5,8),	(5, 7),	(5, 2))	A(I) = X
16	((1, 5),	(5,2),	(3, 2),	(0, 3))	T3 = I + 1
17	((1, 4),	(0,3)	,	(5, 2))	I = T3
18	((2,11),	,	,	(6,10))	GTO L91
19	((2, 6),	,	,	)	L92 ENP

Example 2.

PROGRAM A2;
VARIABLE INTEGER: I,J,K:
DIMENSION INTEGER: A(20),B(4,5);
I = 2;
J = 3;
CALL A3(I,J,K);

A(K) = B(I,J) + 2.7;
ENP;
SUBROUTINE A3 (INTEGER: X,Y,K);
VARIABLE INTEGER: Z;
Z = 6;
K = (X − Z)↑2 + Y;
ENS;

Table 10.16. Identifier Table.

		SUBROUTINE	TYPE	POINTER	
1					
2	X	11	4		
3	I	6	4		
4					
5	A	6	1	1	▷ (Information Table)
6	A2			1	▷ (Quadruple Table)
7	K	6	4		
8	K	11	4		
9	B	6	1	4	▷ (Information Table)
10	J	6	4		
11	A3			16	▷ (Quadruple Table)
12					
13	Y	11	4		
14					
15	Z	11	4		
16					

Table 10.18. Integer Table.

1	20
2	4
3	5
4	2
5	3
6	6
7	1

Table 10.17. Information Table.

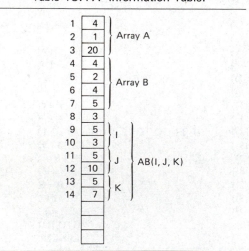

Table 10.19. Real-Number Table

1	2.7

Table 10.20. Quadruple Table.

Quadruples:

#						
1	((5, 3),	,	,	)	I	
2	((5,10),	,	,	)	J	
3	((5, 7),	,	,	)	K	
4	((5, 5),	,	,	)	A	
5	((5, 9),	,	,	)	B	
6	((1, 4),	(3, 4),	,	(5, 3))	I = 2	
7	((1, 4),	(3, 5),	,	(5,10))	J = 3	
8	((2, 3),	(5,11),	,	(7, 8))	CALL A3(I,J,K)	Program A2
9	((1, 6),	(5,10),	(3, 7),	(0, 1))	T1 = J − 1	
10	((1, 7),	(0, 1),	(3, 2),	(0, 2))	T2 = T1*4	
11	((1, 5),	(5, 3),	(0, 2),	(0, 3))	T3 = I + T2	
12	((1, 4),	(5, 9),	(0, 3),	(0, 4))	T4 = B(T3)	
13	((1, 5),	(0, 4),	(4, 1),	(0, 5))	T5 = T4 + 2.7	
14	((1, 4),	(0, 5),	(5, 5),	(5, 7))	A(K) = T5	
15	((2, 6),	,	,	)	ENP	
16	((5, 2),	,	,	)	X	
17	((5,13),	,	,	)	Y	
18	((5, 8),	,	,	)	K	
19	((5,15),	,	,	)	Z	
20	((1, 4),	(3, 6),	,	(5,15))	Z = 6	Subroutine A3
21	((1, 6),	(5, 2),	(5,15),	(0, 6))	T6 = X − Z	
22	((1, 9),	(0, 6),	(3, 4),	(0, 7))	T7 = T6↑2	
23	((1, 5),	(0, 7),	(5,13),	(0, 8))	T8 = T7 + Y	
24	((1, 4),	(0, 8),	,	(5, 8))	K = T8	
25	((2, 7),	,	,	)	ENS	

10.5. CODE GENERATION

The function of a code generator of a compiler is to generate assembly- or machine-language code. Conceptually, this is the easiest phase of compiler writing. In practice, however, it is always quite difficult because it is very machine dependent. One must be able to master the target assembly language, the operating system, the linkage editor, the file system, and many other features of the target machine. In order to simplify our discussion, we assume that we are implementing the compiler on a very simple machine whose assembly language instructions are shown below:

ADD	add
AND	and operation
ARG	argument
BN	branch if negative
BP	branch if positive
BZ	branch if zero
DC	define constant
DIV	divide
DS	define storage
EXP	exponential
END	end
INC	increase by one
JMP	unconditional jump
JSB	jump to subroutine
LD	load
LDI	load-indirect
MPY	multiply
NOP	no operation
OR	or operation
RTN	return
ST	store
STI	store-indirect
SUB	subtract
XI	input
XOR	exclusive or operation
XP	output

We shall first assume that our language is nonrecursive. The code generation of recursive languages will be discussed later. Let us consider Example 2 of the previous section. The code generator will first examine Tables 10.18

and 10.19 and generate the following instructions:

```
I1   DC   20
I2   DC   4
I3   DC   5
I4   DC   2
I5   DC   3
I6   DC   6
I7   DC   1
R1   DC   2.7
```

Then the code generator will examine the quadruples in Table 10-20 in one by one and erate a sequence of instructions for each quadruple. For instance, consider the first quadruple:

$$((5,3), , ,)$$

After examining this quadruple, the code generator will find out that this quadruple calls for the following instruction:

```
I   DS   1
```

because the third element in Table 10.16 corresponds to an identifier I which is an integer occupying one word of memory space.

Consider quadruple 4:

$$((5,5), , ,)$$

We first find that (5,5) corresponds to an array, as indicated by its type in Table 10.16. The other characteristics of this array can be found by its pointer pointing to Table 10.17. In Table 10.17, it is noted that array A is a one dimensional array and occupies 20 memory locations. Thus, the code generator will generate the following assembly instruction:

```
A   DS   20
```

Similarly, the assembly language instruction for quadruple ((5,9), , ,) will be

```
B   DS   20
```

Consider quadruple 6, which is:

$$((1,4),(3,4), ,(5,3)).$$

(1,4) will be found to correspond to "=", (3,4) will be found to correspond to 2, and (5,3) will be found to correspond to I. Thus this quadruple will be translated into the following assembly language instructions:

```
LD   I4
ST   I
```

Similarly, quadruple 11 will be translated into

```
LD   I
ADD  T2
ST   T3
```

The Code Generation for Subroutine Calls

Let us consider quadruple 8 of Example 2:

$$((2,3),(5,11), ,(7,8)).$$

The first 2-tuple corresponds to CALL, and (5,11) corresponds to A3. Thus the first assembly language instruction corresponding to the above quadruple will be:

```
JSB   A3.
```

A subroutine call will usually invoke the passing of arguments. The arguments of this jump-to-subroutine instruction can be found by examining the last element of the quadruple. Since the last element is (7,8), we examine the $8th$ element of Table 10.17. This will inform us that this calling instruction involves three parameters, namely, I, J, and K.

There are many methods of passing the arguments. Let us first introduce the simplest.

Method 1.—Call by Address. In this method, after the instruction

```
JSB   A3
```

we shall have a sequence of instructions to store the addresses of arguments that are to be passed.

```
        JSB   A3
        ARG   I
        ARG   J
        ARG   K
```

After these instructions, an instruction will follow corresponding to

$$T1 = J - 1$$

We have a sequence of assembly language instructions as follows:

```
        JSB    A3
L1      ARG    I
L2      ARG    J
L3      ARG    K
L4      LD     J
        SUB    ONE
        ST     T1
```

When the program is finally executed, the addresses of I, J, and K will be stored in L1, L2, and L3 respectively.

Let us now examine how the arguments are passed to the called subroutine A3 in this case. At the very beginning of the instructions corresponding to A3, we have a define-storage instruction

```
    A3   DS   1
```

When the calling instruction

```
    JSB   A3
```

is executed, the machine will store the address immediately after the JSB instruction, namely L1, into location A3. This action serves to create a link between a calling instruction and the called subroutine. As will later become clear, the arguments as well as the return addresses are all passed through this mechanism.

Note that in Example 2, we have to pass parameters I, J, and K to X, Y, and K (these

three variables are local ones), respectively. To pass I to X, we may use the following instructions:

```
        LDI   A3
        ST    X
```

The load-indirect instruction stores L1 into the register. Since the address of I is stored in L1, the store instruction puts the address of I into location X.

The other parameters can be transferred in a similar way. For instance, the transferring of J to Y will be as follows:

```
        INC   A3
        LDI   A3
        ST    Y
```

To transfer the last argument, we do the following:

```
        INC   A3
        LDI   A3
        ST    K
```

At the end of the code corresponding to the subroutine A3, there should be a return instruction:

```
        INC   A3
        RTN   A3
```

Note that A3 points to L4, eventually returning control to L4, as expected.

It is important to note that for every parameter inside a subroutine, which is not an ordinary variable, its address, not its value, is stored. Thus every time the subroutine refers to a parameter, it should use an indirect command so that the command will actually be referring to the variable in the calling procedure. For example, if Y is a parameter, then the statement

$$Y = Y + 1;$$

is translated into

```
LDI    Y
ADD    ONE
STI    Y
```

In this way, the argument Y is changed in the calling program, which is desired.

Method 2.—Call by Value. The above method of passing parameters during subroutine calls is called *call by address* because the address of a variable is used. Since the address is passed, it may sometimes cause trouble. For instance, consider the calling of ADD1(X) again.

```
SUBROUTINE ADD1(I: Integer);
I = I + 1;
RETURN;
END;
```

There is no problem if we have the following instructions:

```
X = 2;
CALL ADD1(X);
OUTPUT X;
```

In this case, 3 will be printed out.

Suppose we have the following program:

```
CALL ADD1(2);
J = 2;
OUTPUT J;
```

In this case, after

```
CALL ADD1(2)
```

is executed, the constant 2 will become 3. Therefore J will not be set to 2. Instead, it will become 3, which may be baffling to users.

In contrast to call by address, *call by value* avoids the above problem because only the temporary values of the parameters are passed. Thus the changes to the parameters will be local within the subroutine. They will not have any lasting effect.

To implement the call-by-value method, we shall store the values, instead of the addresses, of the parameters, immediately after the jump-to-subroutine instruction. For instance, in the above situation, we have:

```
     JSB    A3
L1   DC     I
L2   DC     J
L3   DC     K
```

Within the subroutine, we may use the load-indirect instruction to transfer the parameters to local variables. All instructions in the subroutine would then refer to these local variables.

Actually, if the language uses call by address, it is easy to simulate call by value by explicitly having the subroutine copy the arguments into local variables. The subroutine would then only refer to these copies, and never to the original variables.

One simple way to protect the variables from the undesirable effect of call-by-address is to simply rename the variables. For example, we may do the following:

```
Y = X;
CALL ADD1(Y);
```

or the subroutine may use a local variable Y with the statement

$$Y = X;$$

as the first statement and all Xs replaced by Ys in the program body. Then the calling programs would not need Y = X, and X is not changed by the subroutine call.

In what follows, we shall assume that call by address is used unless stated otherwise.

Code Generation for Recursive Languages

So far we have assumed that within a subroutine S, S is not called. If a subroutine calls itself, what will happen? To make sure that this question is understood, let us first consider the following problem.

Suppose that we want to compute the factorial function as defined below:

FACTORIAL (1) = 1
FACTORIAL (N) = N *
                        FACTORIAL (N−1)

where N is a positive integer.

The following FRANCIS program correctly computes the above function:

```
    PROGRAM FACTORIAL;
      VARIABLE INTEGER : N;
      VARIABLE REAL : FAC;
        INPUT N;
        CALL FSB(N,FAC);
AD₁ OUTPUT FAC;
    ENP;
    SUBROUTINE FSB(INTEGER: I,
    REAL: R);
      VARIABLE INTEGER: M;
      LABEL L1;
        IF I LE 1 THEN GTO L1;
        M = I − 1;
        CALL FSB(M,R);
AD₂  L₁  IF I LE 1 THEN R = 1.0
        ELSE R = R*I;
    ENS;
```

We have now denoted two addresses: AD_1 and AD_2. AD_1 is the return address for CALL FSB in the main program, and AD_2 is the return address for CALL FSB within itself. Imagine that the first CALL FSB is executed. In this case, AD_1 is stored indirectly as the return address. Then, within this subroutine, we have a CALL FSB instruction. This time, AD_2 is the return address. Since there is only one memory location prepared for the return address of subroutine FSB, AD_2 will necessarily override AD_1, in some sense. This is quite undesirable because we know that control has to eventually go back to AD_1.

Many programming languages, such as FORTRAN, solve this problem by simply prohibiting a subroutine from calling itself. A programming language that allows a subroutine to call itself is called a recursive programming language. ALGOL, LISP, and PASCAL are all famous recursive programming languages. We would like to emphasize here that a programming language can easily be made recursive. In fact, the authors have used many FORTRAN compilers that can handle recursive calls.

Let us now see why our program computes the factorial if the compiler is appropriately implemented. Imagine that N is equal to 3. The following actions take place:

1. FSB is first called, with N being equal to 3 and FAC unknown. The return address is AD_1.
2. Inside FSB, I is now set to 3. Since it is not less than or equal to 1, M is set to 2. FSB is called again and the return address is set to AD_2. It is important to note that I will be equal to 3. To simplify the discussion, let us denote this return address as AD_{21}.
3. Again, inside FSB, I is now equal to 2, M is set to 1, and FSB is called. The return address is set to AD_2 with I equal to 2. To simplify this discussion, let us now call this return address AD_{22}.
4. Finally, inside FSB, I is equal to 1. Control goes to AD_2 and R is computed to be equal to 1.0.
5. Control goes to AD_{22}. Since I is equal to 2, R is computed to be equal to 2.
6. Control then goes to AD_{21}. Since I is equal to 3 and R is equal to 2, R is computed to be equal to 3.
7. The value of FAC now becomes 6 and control goes to AD_1.

There is another problem in recursive program language compiler design. In a nonrecursive language compiler, a variable is assigned a fixed memory location. For a recursive language compiler, this obviously cannot be done. Consider the variable I within FSB. The first time the subroutine is called, I is equal to 3. This value has to be saved in some way because we are going to use it later when control comes back up to AD_2. If I is assigned to a fixed location, we shall have serious problems.

To facilitate these recursive language properties, we may use a stack. During run time, each time a subroutine is called, an activation record containing arguments and the appropriate return address is pushed into a stack. To build a link between the calling instruction and the called subroutine, a global variable pointing to the current activation record may be used. That is, this global variable changes each time a subroutine is called. All of the return addresses and parameters can be found by using this global variable. Let us now denote this global variable CURACT (current activation record). We shall also use another global variable, TOPSTACK, to denote the top of the stack.

Consider the above factorial program with the input N equal to 3. When the first

CALL FSB

is executed, an activation record will be pushed into the stack as shown below:

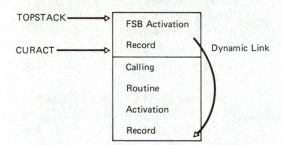

We shall note that the activation record may easily be of different lengths. Therefore, we shall store the stack as a linked list, so that we can pop it out later. The link for pointing to the calling procedure's activation record is called the dynamic link.

What should be stored in the activation record? Evidently, the following must be included:

1. The return address
2. The parameters that should be passed
3. The local variables
4. The dynamic link

We may arrange an activation record as follows:

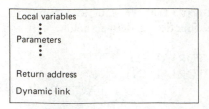

For instance, when the program is executed, the activation record will appear as below:

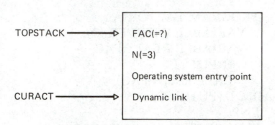

Note the difference between a nonrecursive language compiler and a recursive language compiler. In a recursive language compiler, the variables are assigned to locations in an activation record that is pushed into a stack. As will be explained later, every time a subroutine call is made, it is necessary to put all of its variables into an activation record pushed into a stack.

Suppose we have an activation record as follows:

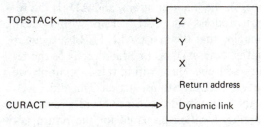

Let us consider the statement:

$$Z = X + Y;$$

We shall not use the following kind of instructions any more:

```
LD    X
ADD   Y
ST    Z
```

Instead, we shall do the following:

```
LD    CURACT(2)
ADD   CURACT(3)
ST    CURACT(4)
```

In other words, there is a table relating X, Y, and Z to the offsets from the address CURACT. This information may be easily stored in the identifier table.

When the first FSB is called, a new activation record is pushed into the stack as shown below:

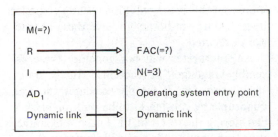

For this new activation record:

1. Dynamic link, AD_1, I, and R are put into the activation record before the

$$JSB \quad FSB$$

instruction.

2. M is put into the activation record by the code inside the subroutine.

3. Since we assume that call by address is used, I and R are pointers pointing to N and FAC, respectively.

The following instructions can be used to construct the new activation record and jump to the subroutine FSB. (The reader has to remember that before the new activation record is constructed, CURACT and TOPSTACK all refer to the old activation record.)

```
INC   TOPSTACK  ┌(The present TOP
LD    TOPSTACK  │ STACK is temporar-
ST    TEMP      ← ily stored.)
LD    CURACT
STI   TOPSTACK ←(The dynamic link is
INC   TOPSTACK   now put into the
```

```
LD    AD₁          new activation
                   record.)
STI   TOPSTACK←  (AD₁ is put into the
INC   TOPSTACK    new activation
                   record.)

LD    CURACT
ADD   TWO
STI   TOPSTACK←  (I is put into the
INC   TOPSTACK    new activation record
                   and it points to N.)

LD    CURACT
ADD   THREE
STI   TOPSTACK←  (R is put into the
LD    TEMP        new activation record
                   and it points to FAC.)

ST    CURACT   ←(The new CURACT
                   is now established.)

JSB   FSB      ←(Jump to FSB.)
```

Note that this new activation record is only partially constructed before the

$$JSB \quad FSB$$

instruction because there is no way for the code generator to know the exact size of the new activation record. The job of constructing this new activation record will be completed within subroutine FSB. In other words, within FSB, there will be instructions that put variable M into the new activation record.

After the new activation record is constructed, whenever a variable is mentioned, the code generator uses its offset with respect to CURACT. For instance, within FSB, the instruction

$$M = I - 1;$$

will be translated into the following code:

```
LD    CURACT(2)
SUB   ONE
ST    CURACT(4)
```

Finally, the stack will appear as follows:

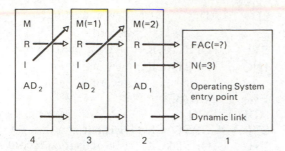

At this point, no further subroutine calls are necessary, and control goes to AD_2. R is computed to be equal to 1, and activation record 4 is popped out. I is pointing to 2 as registered in activation record 3. Activation record 3 is popped out with R computed to be equal to 2. Control goes to AD_2 with R computed to be equal to 6, and FAC is set to be equal to 6 because of an indirect store for R. Activation record 2 is now popped out. Control goes to AD_1, and FAC is printed out as equal to 6.

We would like to emphasize that FAC has to be permanently changed after the subroutine calls. Therefore call by address must be used here.

Interpreter

A compiler translates a high-level language into a low-level language to be executed later by the target machine. There are many cases where we do not want such a thorough translation because we can translate the source program into some intermediate code and directly execute this intermediate code. In such cases, we are not compiling; we are merely interpreting. After compiling, we have a machine-language object program, which we do not have after interpreting. Everytime we want to run a program, we have to interpret it again.

Interpreting can be explained by considering as an example the following high-level instruction:

$$X = Y + U*V$$

The intermediate code for the above instruction may consist of the following two quadruples:

$$(*, U, V, T1)$$
$$(+, Y, T1, X)$$

A compiler will examine the above quadruples and then generate assembly language instructions as follows:

```
LD     U
MPY    V
ST     T1
.
.
.
```

Note that this is the only thing that a compiler does. It does not bother to have these instructions executed.

An interpreter will not generate these assembly-language instructions. It is more straightforward; it simply executes the first quadruple by causing U to be multiplied by V and storing the result in T1. Later, it examines the second quadruple and will immediately execute it by adding Y to T1 and storing the result into X.

Since there is no object program generated, an interpreter requires much less space. This is why in many computers where memory space is limited, interpreters, instead of compilers, are used. The most famous language that uses the interpreter concept is BASIC.

When one is debugging a program, it is very useful to have an interpretive mode incorporated into the compiler. That is, we may give the user a choice between generating an object code program and interpreting it. This provides a quick way to find out whether a program executes or not. After the user is satisfied with his program, a request can then be made that the program be compiled.

The Relationship between a Compiler and the Operating System

Up to now, we have carefully avoided the issue of compiling input/output instructions. When we translate an input/output instruction into machine-dependent assembly-language code, use of the software facilities provided by the operating system is unavoidable. For instance, we never write our own input/output drivers unless it is absolutely necessary to do so, because we can and should use the drivers provided by the operating system. Besides, we probably could not ignore the input/output system provided by the operating system even if we wanted to. For example, nobody can arbitrarily write onto disks, since there are system programs as well as other users' data on the disk, and your access might destroy them totally and crash the system.

A compiler may also allow a user to use subroutines already defined and stored in the system or allow the use of overlay facilities. In either case a compiler writer has to know quite a lot about the operating system under which the compiler is going to work.

In conclusion, there is no way, in practice, to totally separate a compiler from the operating system. In this chapter, we have not touched on the problems because such issues cannot be easily discussed and the techniques used are usually considered as outside the category of compiler writing.

10.6. IMPLEMENTATION TECHNIQUES

In the previous sections compiler writing techniques were defined. We now ask a crucial question: What language should be used to write compilers? Should we use machine languages or some high-level language?

Of course, it is much easier to use a high-level language. The only reason for using some low-level language is that it produces a more efficient compiler. But the problem of maintaining such a compiler can be quite serious.

There are several problems arising from using high-level languages to write compilers. Let us assume that we want to write a PASCAL compiler and we have concluded that PASCAL is the ideal language to be used to write this compiler. We face the following dilemma: We do not have a PASCAL compiler yet. How can we use PASCAL to write any program?

To solve this problem, we may use some other language available to us to write a very small compiler that will work for a small subset of PASCAL instructions. We shall call the language comprising this PASCAL subset $PASCAL_1$. Using $PASCAL_1$, we can write a compiler for a larger subset of instructions in PASCAL. Thus a $PASCAL_2$ compiler is now produced. We may repeat this process until the entire set of PASCAL instructions is included in some compiler, and this compiler is a PASCAL compiler.

Let us consider another problem. Suppose we want to write a PASCAL compiler for PRIME 250. Yet, for some reason, we would like to use a VAX machine. One reason may be that there is a very good PASCAL compiler on the VAX machine, which means that we can use the PASCAL language to write our compiler.

If the PRIME 250 is available to us, we can use it to test the correctness of our compiler. That is, we can always execute the object code program on the PRIME 250. If the PRIME 250 is not available, we must have an emulator of the PRIME 250 on the VAX machine. We can use this emulator to test our compiled object program.

After the correctness of our compiler is established, we still have to transport it to the PRIME 250. How is this done? Remember that this compiler is written in PASCAL, which does not exist in the PRIME 250 machine. The solution is to compile our own compiler. The result is a PRIME 250 assembly-language program that is a PRIME 250 PASCAL compiler.

Can we build a compiler that works for several different machines? This appears to be a stupid question because the code generation part of a compiler is heavily machine dependent. Yet, this still can be done, and there is a trend toward building this kind of compiler. We may use some high-level language, say FORTRAN, to emulate a pseudomachine. Our compiler will generate the assembly language instructions of this pseudomachine. Since this pseudomachine is emulated by using a high-level language that works on many computers, our compiler is portable.

We may also use a high-level language to

build an interpreter that executes intermediate code. In this case, the compiler is almost like an interpreter except that we can save the intermediate code as our object code output. These kind of compilers are again portable because the interpreting part may be written by a portable high-level language.

There are clear advantages to developing machine-independent compilers. In a software house where many different compilers are produced, it is a standard practice to have a set of intermediate code that is for use with different compilers. That is, compilers for different languages will use the same set of intermediate code. Yet a price is paid in producing machine-independent compilers for they are usually quite inefficient.

Finally, let us ask a most important question. Can we automate the compiler writing process? Our answer is "no." Compiler writing can be automated only partially, not totally. We have succeeded in automating the parsing process of a compiler. That is, after the syntax rules of a language are specified, we can build an automatic parser that accepts a program and checks whether this program contains any syntactical error or not. However, we must note that syntax checking is not the only function of a parser; it must take semantic actions. The reader may now know that inside a compiler the data structure is quite crucial, and a compiler designer spends a large part of his or her time designing it. Such design work can never be automated.

APPENDIX: THE SYNTACTICAL RULES OF FRANCIS

⟨program⟩ := ⟨main program⟩⟨subroutine deck⟩
⟨main program⟩ := ⟨program heading⟩⟨block⟩ ENP;
⟨program heading⟩ := PROGRAM ⟨identifier⟩;
⟨identifier⟩ := ⟨letter⟩{⟨letter⟩|⟨digit⟩}
⟨block⟩ := ⟨array declaration part⟩
            ⟨variable declaration part⟩
            ⟨label declaration part⟩
            ⟨statement part⟩
⟨array declaration part⟩ := {DIMENSION ⟨array declaration⟩;}

⟨array declaration⟩ := ⟨type⟩:⟨subscripted variable⟩
            {,⟨subscripted variable⟩}
⟨subscripted variable⟩ := ⟨identifier⟩(⟨unsigned integer⟩)
            {;⟨unsigned integer⟩}
⟨unsigned integer⟩ := ⟨digit⟩{⟨digit⟩}
⟨type⟩ := INTEGER|REAL|BOOLEAN
⟨variable declaration part⟩ := {VARIABLE⟨variable declaration⟩;}
⟨variable declaration⟩ := ⟨type⟩:⟨identifier⟩ {,⟨identifier⟩}
⟨label declaration part⟩ := {LABEL⟨label⟩ {,⟨label⟩};}
⟨label⟩ := ⟨identifier⟩
⟨statement part⟩ := ⟨statement⟩{⟨statement⟩}
⟨statement⟩ := ⟨unlabelled statement⟩;|
            ⟨label⟩⟨unlabelled statement⟩;
⟨unlabelled statement⟩ := ⟨statement I⟩|⟨if statement⟩
⟨statement I⟩ := ⟨empty statement⟩|⟨assign statement⟩
            ⟨call statement⟩|⟨IO statement⟩|
            ⟨go to statement⟩
⟨empty statement⟩ :=
⟨assign statement⟩ := ⟨variable⟩ = ⟨expression⟩
⟨variable⟩ := ⟨identifier⟩|⟨identifier⟩(⟨unsigned integer⟩|
            ⟨identifier⟩))
⟨expression⟩ := ⟨simple expression⟩|⟨simple expression⟩
            ⟨relational operator⟩⟨simple expression⟩
⟨relational operator⟩ := EQ|NE|GT|GE |LT|LE
⟨simple expression⟩ := ⟨term⟩|⟨sign⟩⟨term⟩|
            ⟨simple expression⟩⟨adding operator⟩⟨term⟩
⟨adding operator⟩ := +|−|OR
⟨term⟩ := ⟨factor⟩|⟨term⟩⟨multiplying operator⟩⟨factor⟩
⟨multiplying operator⟩ := *|/|AND|↑
⟨factor⟩ := ⟨variable⟩|⟨unsigned constant⟩| (⟨expression⟩)
⟨unsigned constant⟩ := ⟨unsigned number⟩|⟨constant identifier⟩
⟨unsigned number⟩ := ⟨unsigned integer⟩|⟨unsigned real⟩
⟨unsigned real⟩ := ⟨unsigned integer⟩.{⟨digit⟩}
⟨sign⟩ := +|−
⟨constant identifier⟩ := ⟨identifier⟩

⟨call statement⟩ := <u>CALL</u>⟨subroutine identifier⟩
　　　　　　　　(⟨argument⟩ {,⟨argument⟩})
⟨subroutine identifier⟩ := ⟨identifier⟩
⟨argument⟩ := ⟨identifier⟩|⟨constant⟩
⟨constant⟩ := ⟨unsigned constant⟩|⟨sign⟩⟨unsigned constant⟩
⟨IO statement⟩ := <u>INPUT</u>⟨variable⟩
<u>OUTPUT</u>⟨variable⟩
⟨number size⟩ := ⟨unsigned integer⟩
⟨go to statement⟩ := <u>GTO</u>⟨label⟩
⟨if statement⟩ := <u>IF</u>⟨condition⟩<u>THEN</u>⟨statement
　　　　　　　　I⟩|
　　　　　　　　<u>IF</u>⟨condition⟩<u>THEN</u>⟨statement
　　　　　　　　I⟩
　　　　　　　　　　　<u>ELSE</u>⟨statement I⟩
⟨condition⟩ := ⟨condition variable⟩⟨relations⟩
⟨condition variable⟩
⟨condition variable⟩ := ⟨variable⟩|⟨constant⟩
⟨relations⟩ := ⟨relational operator⟩|<u>OR</u>|<u>AND</u>
⟨subroutine deck⟩ := {⟨subroutine declaration⟩}
⟨subroutine declaration⟩ := ⟨subroutine heading⟩
⟨block⟩<u>ENS</u>;
⟨subroutine heading⟩ := <u>SUBROUTINE</u>⟨identifier⟩(⟨parameter
　　　　　　　　group⟩
　　　　　　　　{⟨parameter group⟩});
⟨parameter group⟩ := ⟨type⟩:⟨parameter⟩{,⟨parameter⟩}
⟨parameter⟩ := ⟨identifier⟩|⟨array⟩
⟨array⟩ := ⟨array identifier⟩( )
⟨array identifier⟩ :=⟨identifier⟩

BIBLIOGRAPHY

Abramson, H., *Theory and Application of a Bottom-up Syntax Directed Translator,* ACM Monograph Series, Academic Press, New York, 1973.

Aho, A. V. and Ullman, J. D., *The Theory or Parsing, Translation and Compiling,* vol. I: *Parsing,* Prentice-Hall, Englewood Cliffs, N.J., 1972.

Aho, A. V. and Ullman, J. D., *The Theory of Parsing, Translation and Compiling,* vol. II: *Compiling,* Prentice-Hall, Englewood Cliffs, N.J., 1973.

Aho, A. V. and Ullman, J. D., *Principles of Compiler Design,* Addison-Wesley, Reading, Mass., 1977.

Backhouse, R. C., *Syntax of Programming Languages, Theory and Practice,* Prentice-Hall, Englewood Cliffs, N.J., 1979.

Barret, W. A. and Couch, J. D., *Compiler Construction, Theory and Practice,* Science Research Associates, Chicago, 1979.

Bauer, F. L. and Eickel, J., *Compiler Construction—an Advanced Course,* Springer-Verlag, New York, 1977.

Bornat, R., *Understanding and Writing Compilers,* The MacMillan Press, New York, 1980.

Callingart, P., *Assemblers, Compilers and Program Translation,* Computer Science Press, Rockville, Md.

Cleaveland, C. and Uzgalis, R. C., *Grammars for Programming Languages,* Elsevier, New York, 1977.

Elson, M., *Concepts of Programming Languages,* Science Research Associates, Chicago, 1973.

Ershov, A. and Koster, C. H. A., *Methods of Algorithmic Language Implementation,* Springer-Verlag, New York, 1977.

Foster, J. M., *Automatic Syntax Analysis,* Elsevier, New York, 1970.

Friedman, J., *Computer Model of Transformation Grammar,* Elsevier, New York, 1971.

Grau, A. A., Hill, U., and Langmaack, H., *Translation of ALGOL 60,* Springer-Verlag, New York, 1971.

Gries, D., *Compiler Construction for Digital Computers,* Wiley, New York, 1975.

Hecht, M. S., *Flow Analysis of Computer Programs,* Elsevier, New York, 1977.

Heindel, L. E. and Roberto, J. T., *Lang-Pak, an Interactive Language Design System,* Elsevier, New York, 1975.

Lee, J. A. N., *Anatomy of a Compiler,* Van Nostrand Reinhold, New York, 1974.

Lewi, P. M., Rosenkrantz, D. J., and Stearns, R. E., *Compiler Design Theory,* Addison-Wesley, Reading, Mass., 1976.

Magninis, J. R., *Elements of Compiler Construction,* Prentice-Hall, Englewood Cliffs, N.J., 1972.

Ollongren, A., *Definition of Programming Languages by Interpreting Automata,* Academic Press, New York, 1975.

Pollack, B. W., *Compiler Techniques,* Van Nostrand Reinhold, New York, 1972.

Rohl, J. S., *An Introduction to Compiler Writing,* Elsevier, New York, 1975.

Rustin, R., *Design and Optimization of Compilers,* Prentice-Hall, Englewood Cliffs, N.J., 1972.

Steele, D. R., *An Introduction to Elementary Computer and Compiler Design,* Elsevier, New York, 1978.

Weingarten, F. W., *Translation of Computer Languages,* Holden-Day, San Francisco, 1973.

Williams, J. H. and Fisher, D. A., "Design and Optimization of Programming Languages," *Proceedings of a DoD Sponsored Workshop,* Ithaca, N.Y. 1976; Springer-Verlag, New York, 1976.

Wulf, W., Johnson, R. K., Weinstock, C. B., Hobbs, S. O., and Geschke, C. M., *The Design of an Optimizing Compiler,* Elsevier, New York, 1975.

11

Operating Systems

Steven M. Jacobs

TRW Defense Systems Group

11.1. INTRODUCTION

Motivation

This chapter pertains to the portion of a computer system that controls the computer and acts as an intermediary between user and computer. Since the operating system controls the operation of a computer, it is as essential tool for the software engineer. This chapter combines a treatise on the basic concepts of operating system (OS) functions with a survey of many of the latest books and publications in the field.

The software engineer has many tools at his or her disposal in order to develop computer software, but most are not as machine dependent as the operating system. An operating system according to Madnick and Donovan [1] manages the resources of a computer system: its memory, processors, devices, and information. Computer programs that manage these resources include controllers, schedulers, memory management modules, I/O programs, and file systems—hence, the ironic fact that operating systems are indeed computer programs themselves. They are necessary for the smooth and efficient use of computer systems. The software engineer has tools available to develop application computer programs. Some of these software engineering tools are also useful in developing operating systems themselves.

Before continuing, there should be one note on terminology. What Madnick and Donovan refer to as an operating system, others may refer to as a monitor [2] a supervisor [3] or an executive [4]. These terms are all synonymous. Most often the difference in terminology reflects an author's or computer manufacturer's preference.

Background

Before operating systems were developed, the operator and programmer of the computer (usually the same person) prepared the I/O units to load in the computer program to be executed. The computer then executed the program and stopped. During this time, the computer was idle. A computer would sit idle much of the time during the day, in between each time it was used. Persons scheduled individual computer time, one person on the computer at a time. An operating system according to Murach [5] is designed to reduce the amount of time that a computer sits idle, therefore increasing the productivity of a computer system.

The fundamental operating system concept of *multiprogramming,* the simultaneous processing of more than one program at a time, was a new idea as recently as the mid-1960s, the years when the "third generation" of computers appeared, as described in Feingold [6]. *Virtual storage* was an innovation as recently as the 1970s and marked the "fourth generation" of computers. It is defined as a "means of expanding a computer's main storage by allowing a computer to directly access outside storage devices as though they were main storage itself" [6].

Scope

This chapter highlights operating system concepts. The reader will gain a working familiar-

234

ity with operating systems terminology and principles. An essential tool of the software engineer, the computer operating system is an interface between man and machine, allowing even the unsophisticated computer user easy use of a computer's capabilities. In addition recent developments in the software engineering literature illustrate new fundamentals for developing more sophisticated computer systems and operating systems.

Computer design decisions are discussed in terms of operating systems utilization and development. Computer architecture and hardware have changed because of operating systems. For example, privacy and security are now housed within operating system safeguards.

Numerous texts and publications cover the topic of operating systems. This chapter is an introduction to operating systems for software engineers and is necessary because operating systems are themselves computer software, requiring engineering practices in their design. Current work in operating system design is surveyed, with specific operating systems reviewed as examples. Future trends in this area are covered, in particular, distributed operating systems.

11.2. OPERATING SYSTEM CONCEPTS

Definitions

In the previous section, the terms *operating systems, multiprogramming,* and *virtual storage* were introduced. More terminology is necessary to comprehend basic operating system concepts. System parameters are specified to the computer using a *job control language* (JCL). *Instructions* and data are stored in a computer's *main storage* (or main memory). It is the fastest general purpose storage of a computer. *Central processing units* (CPUs) do arithmetic and manipulate data as well as execute instructions to control other processors. To enhance computing power, throughput, and so on, additional processors can be added to some computer systems forming *multiprocessor systems*. These additional processors can be used for specialized functions such as *input/output processors*. Multiprocessor systems can also include a large computer with several

smaller computers or a group of processors each of equal power. Often a sophisticated scheduling scheme is necessary to control such systems.

Computers often operate in a *privileged/nonprivileged* (master/slave) state where certain privileged instructions are not available to the ordinary user. *Interrupts* are hardware devices that are forced to take note of certain events that occur within a computer system.

Madnick and Donovan [1] conceptually subdivide the operating system functions into management of memory, processors, devices, and information—the resources of a computer installation. This is a useful format for discussion and is utilized in the section on detailed principles that follows.

A hierarchical view of an operating system appears below as Figure 11.1.

A process is a computation: data and a program that executes on the data. A *processor* is a physical component that can carry out a process. Sequential processes contain *sequential programs*. Sequential program statements are executed one at a time. Processes can execute with other processes concurrently, that is, their executions overlap in time. Methods for synchronizing *concurrent processes* are described in the next section. These methods include critical regions, semaphores, message buffers, and event queues. Figure 11.1 illustrates how all processes (in boxes) use the kernel and share all resources in the system. The relationship of some processes being "parents" of others is illustrated by the process layers.

A *kernel* is the basic subset of the operating system. In a leveled diagram such as in Figure 11.1, it is not definite which functions should be assigned to which levels, nor is it firm what is contained in the kernel. In hierarchical operating system implementation, a given level is allowed to call upon the services of lower levels, but not those of higher levels. These are decisions and trade-offs that must be made by the software engineer who designs operating systems.

Principles

This section will introduce detailed operating systems principles with the approach men-

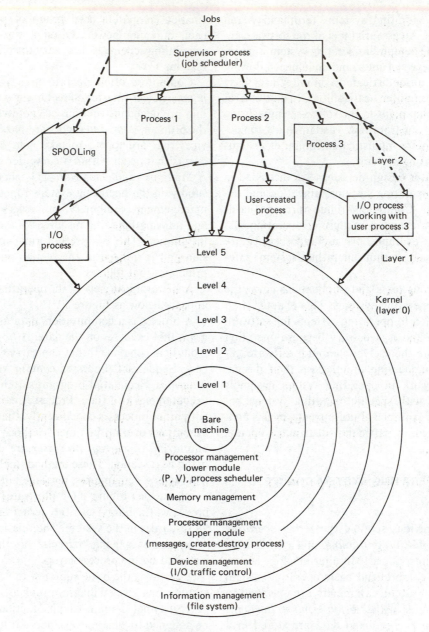

Figure 11.1. Hierarchical operating system structure [1].

tioned earlier, in terms of managing resources. The specific resource management areas include (1) memory management, especially in a multiprogramming environment, (2) processor management, with a *dispatching* function to allocate processor usage and a scheduling function to choose processor usage, (3) device management for I/O traffic control and scheduling, including *spooling* (simultaneous peripheral operations on-line), and (4) information management, usually in the form of a file system.

Memory can be managed by a number of methods. The simplest, most basic memory management is with a single, contiguous main memory. No multiprogramming can occur, and the operating system can only allocate memory for the single user job, leaving the remaining memory unused. A *job* is the activities needed by a user to do the work required. *Partitioned memory* is a memory management technique that supports multiprogramming. Main memory is divided into memory partitions. Four functions of this memory management technique are required: (1) keeping track of partition status (in-use, not in-use, size), (2) job scheduling (who gets memory), (3) allocating functions, and (4) deallocating functions. It can increase memory utilization efficiency, but requires a table of status of partitions, with a scheduler that performs allocation/deallocation functions. *Relocatable partitioned memory* prevents *fragmentation,* the development of a large number of separate free areas. Relocatable partitioned memory allows for *compaction* of memory whereby allocated memory is periodically moved so that it is contiguous, leaving the free areas as one large free area.

Paging memory can avoid the problem of keeping memory for user jobs contiguous. Paging involves breaking up jobs in main memory into smaller units called *pages*. This requires page map tables and memory block tables to monitor usage of pages of memory. *Demand paging* increases efficiency further by allowing a job, when scheduled, to receive the first page it needs only and receive the rest on demand. Algorithms such as first-in, first-out (FIFO) or least recently used (LRU) are necessary. FIFO removes a page in memory that has been there for the longest time, regardless of how often and when it was referenced. LRU removes the page that has been in memory for the longest time. Consideration may be needed for *swapping* time. Swapping is the exchange of jobs betweeen two levels of *storage.* Storage is a physical component where data and programs are stored for future use. *Main memory* (main storage) is sometimes called internal storage. *Secondary memory* is sometimes called backing storage and can be contained on (slower than main memory) drums or discs. The assignment of storage locations to programs and data *(storage allocation)* can be done at compile time *(fixed allocation),* prior to execution *(dynamic allocation),* or during execution *(dynamic relocation).* Buffers are used for transfers between main memory and secondary memory or I/O devices. *Buffer storage techniques* are utilized for storing information prior to output and following input from secondary memory or I/O devices, for storing messages and data communicated among active tasks, and for storing messages to and from remote terminals in a time-sharing environment. Demand paging and *segmented memory* management techniques are used in virtual memory systems.

Segmented memory techniques allow flexibility in the size of memory a user may require, in contrast to a fixed page size. Segments can be logical groups of information such as a subroutine or an array. *Segmentation* is the technique for managing segments. A segment is a logical unit of information often visible to a user program and varying in size. A page is a physical unit of information transparent to a user program and of fixed size. Segmentation has several advantages including the elimination of fragmentation and its capability for dynamically growing segments. Tables are necessary for segmentation implementation, including a segment map table. Segment "demand" interrupts handle the dynamic memory requirements in a segmented virtual system. A combination of segmented and demand paged memory management is often the most efficient combination of the above memory management techniques.

Processors need to be assigned to processes in an operating system. *Job scheduling* is required in processor management. The job scheduler assigns system resources to certain jobs. Scheduling policies such as FIFO or shortest job first (SJF) must be established by the operating system designer. Scheduling is often a policy issue. Someone in authority may decide which jobs are most "important" while being "fair" to other jobs. FIFO allows for jobs to be executed "first come, first served." SJF allows for the job with the smallest amount of processor requirements to execute ahead of the current jobs in the system. System resources are assigned to certain jobs using these policies. Processor scheduling takes place with the aid of a dispatcher or low-level scheduler. This includes the assignment of processes (within jobs) to processors. Priorities of jobs or a round-robin approach are part of what must be established by the operating system designer. Processor synchronization and coordination of shared resources is necessary to prevent *deadlock* (or "deadly embrace") where two or more processes are both waiting for resources held by each other. A "traffic control" function must be performed by processor management software.

Devices must be managed by the operating system. Portions of devices called *blocks* are referenced. Therefore, the status of blocks in I/O devices, for example, must be tracked. Policies for device use must be specified: dedicated, shared, or virtual allocation and deallocation of devices. I/O scheduling policies can be controlled by an I/O traffic controller that keeps track of the status of all the devices, control units, and channels. I/O device handlers are often used for control of each type of I/O device.

Information management in an operating system usually refers to the file system: the directory, tables, database software, and so forth, available to the system or the user for managing information.

Concurrent Programming

Two textbooks in the field of operating systems by Per Brinch-Hansen [7, 8] have had a significant impact on the theory and practice of operating system development. In Reference 8, Brinch-Hansen states that he would like to see operating systems writing become as disciplined and common as compiler writing. It is pointed out that there are often unpredictable demands on operating systems, and operating systems writers are often in a situation where they are forced to yield to the technical limitations of devices.

A key goal in operating is to write a system appropriate for the types of users. A *general purpose operating system* will perform an enormous number of functions for a large group of users. For example, a large university with a single computer installation may have the university professors and students utilize the system by day and the accounting depart-

ment at night. A single operating system must handle multiple types of users. There is also the *special purpose operating system,* such as the one in the computers on-board the Space Shuttle, which have separate, distinct, real-time functions for making the Space Shuttle operate properly and safely. In this case, the operating system must handle only one well-defined user.

Brinch-Hansen and others feel that there should be well-structured programming tools for the software engineers who design and develop operating systems. Operating systems in terms of sequential and concurrent processes, processor and store management, scheduling and resource protection are covered in Reference 5. I/O, data files, and programs left out of the first book are discussed in Reference 4.

An operating system is defined in Reference 8 as a set of "manual and automatic procedures that enable a group of people to share a computer installation efficiently." The key word "share" is emphasized in terms of competing for resources, cooperating by exchanging programs and data, making *policies* for order, enforcement and protection, developing accounting and measurement procedures, and using JCL.

Sequential processes and sequential programming are introduced. A modified version of Pascal [9] is proposed as an operating systems writing language so that time-dependent errors can be caught at compile time. The Pascal report subset is presented as a computer programming language used to represent operating systems functions, both sequential and concurrent, in a clear and structured manner. For example, an operating systems function representable in Pascal is the use of *critical regions,* a type of data structure concept used to denote a shared area within a computer system.

An example of a data structure used in concurrent processing is the *semaphore,* as described by Dijkstra [10], a signal that an event has occurred communicated by a certain process. *Process synchronization* occurs by the use of critical regions and semaphores. In addition, the concepts of message buffers, critical regions, and event queues are introduced. *Mes-*

sage buffers are "common" data structures used to exchange data between concurrent processes. "Common" refers to the data in common concept like that used in a FORTRAN programming language COMMON statement. Critical regions are a set of operations on a common data structure that exclude one another in time. Event queues are shared waiting areas for explicit process scheduling.

Per Brinch-Hansen introduces processor management in terms of process descriptions and scheduling queues maintained by a basic monitor. The problems of scheduling are next addressed. This is when concurrent processes occur on a limited number of processors. Levels of scheduling are proposed so that a scheduler program can assign priorities and collect measurements.

Thrashing can be avoided with preemption. Thrashing is the performance collapse that happens when there has been an attempt to over-commit main memory, according to Coffman and Denning [11]. There are two scheduling algorithms called *nonpreemptive* and *preemptive*. Preemptive scheduling forces processes to release resources temporarily in favor of other processes. Nonpreemptive scheduling allows processes to be the only entity that can release resources it acquired. *Resource* is a general term for processors, storage devices, data, and so forth in a shared environment. Various policies affect average response times for user requests. Resource protection is defined as the use of automatic methods to ensure that data and procedures are accessed properly.

The *class* concept is defined as an entity that checks resource access at compile time. *Capabilities,* an array of accessible resources and permissible operations, are used to check resource access at run time.

The theme of Reference 7 centers around writing high-quality concurrent computer programs. The goal is to:

write all concurrent programs in a language so structured that you can specify exactly what processes can do to shared variables and depend on a compiler to check that the program satisfy these assumptions. Concurrent Pascal is the first language to make this possible.

Concurrent Pascal extends sequential Pascal with concurrent processes and monitors. Language constructs and sequential and concurrent Pascal are introduced. The Solo OS serves as an example.

Model operating systems are presented with the illustration of a job stream system and a real-time scheduler. The concurrent Pascal report is included in the text.

11.3. COMPUTER SYSTEMS DESIGN

The act of designing computer systems will always include consideration of the type, versatility, and reliability of computer operating systems. This section digresses to describe some of the events that a computer system designer, installer, or manager may face with regard to the operating system. An efficient, easy-to-use system programming capability is, of course, imperative. Whether it is an on-line or real-time computer system has a strong influence. Computer architecture is affected by the operating system. The hardware required for an operating system to function has to be considered. Security and privacy capabilities are most often housed in the operating system.

This section will introduce concepts, clarify issues, and act as an over-all aid to the operating systems designer within the subject area of overall computer system design.

Designing Operating Systems

A large part of what is termed *systems programming* is the effective design, implementation, and use of operating systems. An excellent reference in the area of systems of programming is Donovan [12]. There are numerous user viewpoints of an operating system. To some, an operating system performs utility functions. To others, an operating system is represented by the control language. The systems programming viewpoint places importance on the structure and effectiveness of the operating system.

Recall that operating systems can be thought of as resource managers, the managers of memory, processors, devices, and information. Donovan describes in great detail the systems programming of operating systems in terms of (1) *I/O programming* and (2) systems programming to manage the four previously stated resources.

I/O programming consists in large part of interrupt processors and mechanisms. Donovan describes a 360/370 type I/O processor (IOP or, sometimes, I/O channel) as having memory and fetching instructions from a *channel command word*. In terms of the CPU/channel interface, I/O instructions are initiated by the CPU while the CPU can be interrupted by the channel. The state of the CPU is stored in a Program Status Word (PSW) or equivalent. An *interrupt* is a transfer of control in response to signals asynchronous with the instruction execution. There are different types of interrupts for such uses as I/O, machine check, or programmer error. Multiple processors, as the reader can easily imagine, make I/O programming more complex. The four areas of resource management are covered in Donovan from a systems programming perspective in great detail.

For the reader who does not have the time to investigate the details of operating systems development from the works previously described and referenced, it is somewhat difficult to grasp the full impact of the operating system on any given computer system.

For those who have the desire to learn more operating systems concepts by following a basic description and design of a simple, special purpose operating system, see Zelkowitz et al. [13]. This reference contains the design of a single-language, multiprogramming operating system. It is designed to run user programs written in a single, high-level language and execute a batch-mode operating system called SLOS. SLOS is multiprogrammed, and jobs are spooled for I/O.

Zelkowitz et al. describes the OS in terms of a process structure where there is a tree containing a job supervisor controlling a *loader* of jobs, the user jobs. There is a spool-in/spool-out function on a simple card reader/line printer, respectively. There is also a disk driver and an operator communication system. The base of the structure is a root that is an idle base process through which much of the system communication exists. He presents the SLOS design in a software design language. The design is clearly explained in a top-down manner and is an excellent example for the beginning operating system person to implement.

For the reader who requires more detail concerning the wide range of algorithms useful in the design of operating systems, see Coffman and Denning [11]. The algorithmic and analytical approach to operating system design in this text formally covers sequencing and control algorithms to avoid certain failures in concurrent processing systems and algorithms for scheduling, I/O devices, buffer storage, and storage management.

On-line and Real-time Systems

Yourdon states in Reference 14 the following paradox in the chapter entitled "The Functions and Structure of On-Line Operating Systems":

The more one tries to reduce overhead by minimizing the interference between the application programs and the operating system, the more one runs the risk of being outwitted by the operating system.

He continues:

One can be outwitted by an operating system if one does not understand it; conversely, one can do any effective job of writing application programs or designing data bases only if one does understand what an operating system is and how it works.

In an opinion similar to Donovan's, Yourdon feels that I/O handling is probably the most important function of an operating system. In addition to the I/O handling and resource management functions, Yourdon emphasizes communications and error recovery as functions of an operating system. He presents a leveled view of operating systems similar to that in Figure 11.1.

Error recovery and system failures involve reliability issues that every operating systems designer must face. Yourdon emphasizes that Murphy's Law can indeed occur in such computer system failure areas as:

Processor errors
Memory parity errors
Communication network problems
Peripherals
Programmer bugs
Operators
Power failures, etc.

Error recovery involves the graceful (one hopes) manner in which a computer system can recover from some failure. Such methods include bringing the system to a halt, stopping the task that caused the error, going to a less efficient mode, or passing control to a standby system that can resume operations in the face of disaster.

James Martin refers to operating systems as supervisory programs in *Design of Real-time Computer Systems* [15]. The supervisory programs are there to simplify the work of the applications programmers. Martin [16] suggests complex, multiprogrammed, real-time systems may require many of these functions:

I/O control
Communication line control
Message setup services
Handling displays
Communicating with the operator
Scheduling the message processing
Scheduling the machine processing
Queue control
Main storage allocation
Allocation of other equipment
Communication among computers
Control of off-line computers
Linkage between programs and subroutines
Handling interrupts
Selecting and calling in the required programs
Retaining working data, registers, etc. when control switches between programs
Controlling time-initiated actions
File security
Fault indication and reliability checks
Diagnostics
Switchover to back-up computers
Fallback for graceful system failure
Handling overloads
System testing aids and performance monitoring

Sometimes, in highly time-critical, real-time systems, manufacturer-supplied operating systems may need to be modified or, in special cases, replaced so that functions can execute within time-specific guidelines.

Architecture

An operating systems designer must be familiar with the particular computer's architecture. For example, base registers for addressing schemes are often hardware devices, but could be specified locations in computer memory. The operating system may occupy the low-numbered addresses in storage. A "relocating loader" as described in Foster [2] may exist so that each computer program has a *logical address* of "zero" when, physically, the program may reside anywhere in main storage.

Dynamic relocation can be performed in an execution-time table called a *program reference table*. It is updated by the operating system and is described in regard to stack computers in Stone [17]. Addressing mechanisms, types of available memory, and memory management schemes can be highly machine dependent. Thus, the OS designer must have a working familiarity with the capabilities and limitations of the computer hardware available.

Hardware Considerations

One of the few instances hardware is mentioned in this handbook is in the section on operating systems. When discussing computer systems, Hellerman [9] divides up hardware and software as in Table 11.1.

Storages are for both programs and data. Processing and control are for the functions normally CPU-resident and involve arithmetic, logic and control, and sequencing functions. Transducers are devices that translate information from one physical form to another such as a printer converting electric signals to printed characters on paper. Application programs have already been defined above, and system programs are compilers, operating systems, and so forth.

Certain operating system functions require

Table 11.1. Computer Systems.

HARDWARE (EQUIPMENT)	SOFTWARE (PROGRAMS)
Storages	Application programs
Processing and control logic	System programs
Transducers	

high speeds and are often implemented with hardware, according to Hellerman. They are listed in Table 11.2.

Clocks can be for time-of-day as well as for timing intervals, for example, for counting in order to allow computer programs n seconds of processing time. Interrupts, storage protection, and privileged mode may utilize hardware features. Physical features or markings and registers aid in storage protection. Privileged mode access may use interrupts.

Security

In dealing with matters pertaining to security in computer systems, Jensen and Tonies [18] say that "any program generated on a particular operating system can only be as secure as the operating system." Computer security is another area of software engineering about which numerous books and publications have been written, but this area creates special interest in light of security and privacy issues that touch all our lives such as tax records, credit, banking, law enforcement, and so forth. This section will cover some basic operating systems security methods in terms of protection methods and access specifications.

Protection mechanisms can be broken down into protection schemes of isolation, unrestricted sharing, and controlled sharing. Relocation registers are used for these schemes. This concept can be expanded to descriptor tables (or registers) for more users. A descriptor table entry is made up of read, write, and executive access flags, plus a base location and length.

Access specifications deal with user specification of access controls. *Descriptors* contain information so that the operating system can determine if information can be accessed. An *access matrix* contains access specifications that state whether certain files are allowed in a particular user or procedure domain. A *domain* can contain processes, files, or queues.

A *capability* (first introduced in Section 11.2) accesses an object by name whereas a descriptor accesses by location. Capabilities are protected in two ways. One is with a *tagged architecture,* an extra flag bit for every word in memory where 1 = capability and 0 = instruction or data. The other is to break each segment into (1) instructions and data or (2) capabilities.

Access control lists, familiar to many, assign users a name for an area of storage, and their user identification allows entry. In a dynamic authorization specification environment, access control lists must be weighed against capabilities for system efficiency as to which is better.

Examples and references appear in Jensen and Tonies with regard to general security features in three systems: IBM's OS/360, MIT's MULTICS, and Carnegie-Mellon's HYDRA.

11.4. SPECIFIC OPERATING SYSTEMS

Three specific operating systems are introduced in this section for clarity in understanding actual implemented operating systems. References to others are included.

T.H.E.

The puprose of the T.H.E. Multiprogramming System of E. W. Dijkstra described in Mc-Keag and Wilson [19] is "the smooth processing of a continuous flow of user programs as a service to the [Dijkstra's] University." The objectives are to reduce turn-around time, economically use peripherals, automatically utilize the backing store and economically use the CPU, assess the economic feasibility of using the machines for those applications that require a general purpose computer, and make

Table 11.2. Essential Operating System Hardware.

Clocks
Interrupts
Storage protection
Privileged mode

the system easy to use by operator and programmer alike. T.H.E. is known for its structuring and synchronization techniques.

The user sees a batch system with no file structures. Algol 60 is the only programming language input by paper-tape. A job can have two reader streams, two punch streams, one plot, and one print-out. There are no restrictions on run-time or store usage. The operator himself schedules the job on the Electrologica X8 machine. A virtual store is implemented by software paging.

Control of resources is done hierarchically. T.H.E. is designed as a "society of sequential processes" that progress in parallel. No reliance is placed on the fact that a particular event will occur at a particular time.

The mutual exclusion problem is addressed by the following methodology. When accessing shared data, other processes are excluded. Common data is stored in a critical section. Semaphores control critical sections. The semaphores can be private or general for single or multiple processes. A CPU dispatcher services system processes with a queue of drum, console, peripheral, and user processes.

Store management occurs with main and drum frame tables. The virtual store is a three dimensional representation (state space) of the range of:

i, number of pages for input files
o, number of pages for output files
p, number of pages for user programs

ensuring the bounds are not exceeded. This setup is called the "sugar lump."

The console control is performed by a console state function. A console process accepts an operator announcement, reads it when the console is free, checks if the message is applicable, and reroutes it. I/O occurs via the banker's algorithm (illustrated in McKeag and Wilson) to avoid deadlock.

UNIX

UNIX* is an interactive, general purpose operating system initially developed for certain

---

*UNIX is a trademark of Bell Laboratories.

Digital Equipment Corporation computer systems. It has an industry-wide reputation because of its hierarchical file system, simple tools and command language, and relative lack of complexity in comparison to features found in larger operating systems.

UNIX has compatible file, device, and interprocess I/O, the ability to initiate asynchronous processes, a system command language tailored for each user, over 100 subsystems including a dozen languages, and a high degree of portability, according to Ritchie and Thompson [20]. UNIX is mostly written in the programming language C.

Its file system is comprised of ordinary disk files of whatever a user wishes. Directories map between names of files and files themselves. Special files exist for each I/O device. Protection is by user ID.

For I/O, there is little designation of devices and the like. A directory entry contains only a name for the associated file and a pointer to the file itself. This pointer is the i-number (index) of the file. The i-number is used to index into a system table (i-list) stored in a known part of the device on which the directory resides. The entry found (i-node) contains the description of the file, including such things as user ID, protection bits, size, time of creation, and so forth.

An image is a computer execution environment containing the state of a "pseudo-computer," the open files, a memory image, directory, and so on. A process is an execution of an image. Processes can communicate with related processes using an interprocess channel called a *pipe*.

The *shell* is a command line interpreter. It is easy to use and is adequate for most users. The shell includes features such as control-flow primitives, parameter passing, variables, and string substitution. WHILE, IF-THEN-ELSE, CASE, and FOR constructs are available. The environment can be modified by the shell in which commands run. I/O can be redirected to files, and processes that communicate through pipes can be invoked. Bourne [21] describes more features in an introductory article on the UNIX shell. Thus, the shell is both a command language and a programming language that provides man-machine interface with the UNIX operating system. UNIX is influenced by MULTICS, and in particular, the I/O system calls. More on MULTICS can be found in Organick [22].

VAX/VMS

The Digital Equipment Corporation (DEC) VAX/VMS virtual memory operating system runs on VAX processors. It has a hardware-maintained context for each user program, 32 bit addresses, 4 processor access modes, a stack for each processor access mode, an interrupt stack, and native (normal) and compatibility (to act like certain other DEC machines) mode instruction sets. Details of the full range of VAX features can be found in the *VAX Architecture Handbook* [23].

VMS provides a virtual address space of 2^{32} bytes of memory. Memory management handles requests for physical memory within a process and among all processes in the system. A balance set consists of the set of processes resident in physical memory.

Process control occurs from within a process and among cooperating processes in the system. The I/O system consists of system services where an image can call to request I/O, ancillary control processes (ACPs) for file, directory, magnetic tape and network-related functions, and I/O drivers for devices.

VMS supports spooling, batch processing, and other system management and operation functions. VAX/VMS software and VAX hardware are developed to support real-time, multitasking systems. Multiple VAXs can be interconnected via a common shared memory (MA78D).

Figure 11.2 illustrates VAX/VMS in layered form. The figure also illustrates VAX/VMS support of time-critical applications. Since real-time applications are performance sensitive, VAX/VMS provides the application with a direct interface to the innermost core of the operating system.

VMS has event drive priority scheduling. It allows real-time applications to control their virtual memory paging and execution priority.

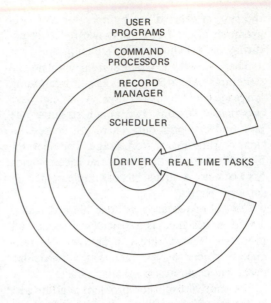

Figure 11.2. VAX/VMS layered OS [24].

Others

A special issue of the *Communications of the Association for Computing Machinery* [25] is dedicated to computer architecture. It contains articles detailing the evolution and architecture of the following computer systems:

1. Manchester Mark I and Atlas
2. MU5
3. Sperry Univac 1100
4. DECsystem 10
5. CRAY-1
6. IBM System/370

McKeag and Wilson contain, in addition to the T.H.E. system described earlier, a thorough description of the following operating systems:

1. Burroughs B5500 Master Control Program
2. CDC SCOPE 3.2
3. TITAN Supervisor

11.5. TRENDS IN OPERATING SYSTEMS

Operating system technological improvements are happening. Operating systems presented in this chapter indicate a trend toward more specialization for time-critical and other operating system applications. In addition, universities, manufacturers, and users are all striving for faster, more efficient operating systems for more taxing applications.

As the technology in hardware devices improves, so operating systems will be modified. One upcoming technology is in the area of distributed systems. Therefore, distributed operating systems are required. One of the key research issues for the 1980s according to Tanenbaum and Mullender [26] is the design of general purpose distributed operating systems. They have developed the Amoeba distributed OS with inspiration from UNIX. vanTilborg and Wittie have developed a Concurrent Pascal operating system for a network computer [27].

A networked computer system requires a cohesive control structure to bind its components and a local operating system for each of its node computers to execute. vanTilborg and Wittie have developed a control schema to describe a nodal operating system using Concurrent Pascal. The operating system consists of a packet switched subsystem that executes in the communications front-end processor of each node and a host processor operating system that manages local resources, interfaces with terminals, and executes tasks. A hierarchical control structure working with the nodal operating system comprises the system. Each node operating system is made up of a microprocessor front-end communication kernel, and the host processors control software. Details are contained in the reference article and a related article [28].

11.6. SUMMARY

Operating systems, a tool for the software engineer, are basically the managers of computer system resources: the memory, processors, I/O, and information. Pascal and Concurrent Pascal implementation of monitors, critical regions, semaphores, and other concepts make operating systems writing a practice that can be checked at compile time.

Operating systems must be considered by the computer system designer, manager, and installer. On-line and real-time requirements make operating systems choices difficult, sometimes requiring operating systems optimization, customization, or enhancement for special applications. Operating system designers need to acknowledge the hardware supporting the operating system. Microcomputer operating systems require special handling because of memory constraints. Security is often embodied in operating systems. There are many operating systems that have been developed and that are undergoing development. T.H.E., UNIX, and DEC's VAX/VMS were discussed in this chapter.

Operating systems research continues and is progressing along with the changing technologies of computer system devices, architectures, and distribution. Distributed operating systems will soon be common.

REFERENCES

1. S. E. Madnick and J. J. Dovan, *Operating Systems,* McGraw-Hill Book Co., New York, 1974.
2. C. C. Foster, *Computer Architecture,* Van Nostrand Reinhold Company, New York, 1970.
3. M. D. Abrams and P. G. Stein, *Computer Hardware and Software,* Addison-Wesley Publishing Co., Reading, Mass., 1973.
4. B. R. Borgerson, M. L. Hanson, and P. A. Hartley, "The Evolution of the Sperry Univac 1100 Series: A History, Analysis, and Projection," *Communications of the ACM,* volume 21, number 1, Jan. 1978.
5. M. Murach, *Principles of Business Data Processing,* Science Research Associates, Inc., Chicago, 1970.
6. C. Feingold, *Introduction to Data Processing,* Wm. C. Brown Company, Dubuque, Iowa, 1975.
7. P. Brinch-Hansen, *The Architecture of Concurrent Programs,* Prentice-Hall, Inc., Englewood Cliffs, N.J., 1977.
8. P. Brinch-Hansen, *Operating System Principles,* Prentice-Hall, Inc., Englewood Cliffs, N.J., 1973.
9. H. Hellerman, *Digital Computer System Principles,* McGraw-Hill Book Co., New York, 1973.
10. E. W. Dijkstra, "Cooperating Sequential Processes," F. Genuys (ed.), *Programming Languages,* Academic Press, New York, 1968.
11. E. G. Coffman and P. J. Denning, *Operating Systems Theory,* Prentice-Hall, Inc., Englewood Cliffs, N.J., 1973.
12. J. J. Donovan, *Systems Programming,* McGraw-Hill Book Co., New York, 1972.

13. M. V. Zelkowitz, A. C. Shaw, and J. D. Gannon, *Principles of Software Engineering and Design,* Prentice-Hall, Inc., Englewood Cliffs, N.J., 1979.

14. E. Yourdon, *Design of On-Line Computer Systems,* Prentice-Hall, Inc., Englewood Cliffs, N.J., 1972.

15. J. Martin, *Design of Real-Time Computer Systems,* Prentice-Hall, Inc., Englewood Cliffs, N.J., 1967.

16. J. Martin, *Programming Real-Time Computer Systems,* Prentice-Hall, Inc., Englewood Cliffs, N.J., 1965.

17. H. S. Stone (ed.), *Introduction to Computer Architecture,* Science Research Associates, Inc., Chicago, 1975.

18. R. W. Jensen and C. C. Tonies, *Software Engineering,* Prentice-Hall, Inc., Englewood Cliffs, N.J., 1979.

19. R. M. McKeag and R. Wilson, *Studies in Operating Systems,* D. H. R. Huxtable (ed.), Academic Press, New York, 1976.

20. D. M. Ritchie and K. Thompson, "The UNIX* Time Sharing System," *Communications of the ACM,* vol. 17, no. 7, July 1974.

21. S. R. Bourne, "An Introduction to the Unix Shell," in *UNIX Programmer's Manual,* 7th ed., volume 2A, Bell Telephone Laboratories Publication, Jan. 1979.

22. E. I. Organick, *The Multics System: An Examination of Its Structure,* The MIT Press, Cambridge, Mass., 1972.

23. *VAX Architecture Handbook,* Digital Equipment Corporation Publication, 1981.

24. *VAX11 Software Handbook,* Digital Equipment Corporation Publication, 1981.

25. *Communications of the ACM,* vol. 21, no. 1, Jan. 1978.

26. A. S. Tanenbaum and S. J. Mullender, "An Overview of the Amoeba Distributed Operating System," *ACM Operating Systems Review,* vol. 15, no. 3, July 1981.

27. A. M. vanTilborg and L. D. Wittie, "A Concurrent Pascal Operating System for a Computer Network," *Proceedings of COMPSAC 1980,* IEEE, Oct. 1980.

28. A. M. vanTilborg and L. D. Wittie, "Packet Switching Using Concurrent Pascal in a Network Computer," *Proceedings of Fall COMPCON 1980,* IEEE, Sept. 1980.

12

Data Design: Types, Structures, and Abstractions

K. S. Shankar

IBM Federal Systems Division

12.1. INTRODUCTION

The purpose of this discussion is to introduce the concepts of data structures, data types, and data abstractions, and to suggest how these ideas are related to each other. These three concepts are familiar to programmers, although their interrelationships as well as a unified way of looking at them might not be immediately recognizable. The objective of this chapter is to make explicit the connection among these three concepts and their interrelationships. We examine the concept of a data type in detail—in particular its specification, representation, and verification.

Of the three terms—data structures, data types, and data abstractions—probably the first two are most often used by programmers. This actually depends on the type of programming one does. Assembly language programmers use data structures very heavily, since that is how they can express the data content of their programs. Programmers coding in high-level languages like FORTRAN, ALGOL, PL/1, and Pascal are used to the concept of type (as defined by the language they are using) in addition to data structures. They normally use these two concepts in conjunction to organize the data in their programs. Few languages provide facilities to support data abstractions. Experience with such languages is limited as these are still experimental. Data structures, data types, and data abstractions are studied and analyzed in this chapter irrespective of the details of any particular language.

The term *data structures* [1] has been used since the earliest days of stored program computers; the earliest treatise on programming gave the basic algorithms for traversing these structures. The first structures to be used were arrays of information kept in consecutive memory locations. Then the idea of linked memory allocation of sequential lists appeared within computer programs along with dynamic insertion and deletion operations supported by dynamic storage management. The introduction of links to other elements of data is an extremely important concept in programming and is the key to the representation of data structures. In fact, this is one of the most important ways of building complex data structures.

Until the late 1950s, programming consisted of the detailed encoding of long sequences of instructions in binary, octal, or hexadecimal form. This is referred to as machine language programming. We all know how tedious and cumbersome it is to write programs in the machine language of a computer. The frustrations and agony of writing machine language programs led to the invention of the so-called high-level programming languages. A key idea in the development of these higher-level programming languages was the explicit specification and declaration of all variables used by the program by declaration statements. The use of this concept allowed compilation of function statements operating upon the declared variables and, as a side benefit, enhanced program readability. Such specification of variables is referred to as types. For example, in LISP the data types are ATOMS and LISTS, and in SNOBOL the basic data type is a character string, as SNOBOL is basically a string processing language. In most

247

languages, the association of a type with a variable is made by its declaration. In some instances, type information is implicit in the language (such as the initial letter of the variable in FORTRAN, which provides real versus integer type information).

The fundamental activity that must take place in programming is the recognition of abstractions. Programs must be developed by repeated analysis of a problem into subproblems to be solved by using various abstractions. Two kinds of abstractions are useful during the construction of programs, namely, procedural and data abstractions.

The *procedural abstraction* is a new name for a subroutine or function, used in programming for a long time. When a subroutine is invoked, it can be treated as a "black box." It performs a specified abstract function by an unprescribed algorithm. Thus, at the level where it is invoked, it can separate the relevant detail of *what* from the irrelevant detail of *how*. Similarly, at the level where it is implemented, it is usually unnecessary to complicate the *how* by considering the *why;* that is, the exact reasons for invoking a subroutine often need not be of concern to its implementor. By nesting subroutines, one may develop a hierarchy of abstractions. Subroutines, procedures, and functions that are well suited for describing abstract operations are not at all suitable for describing abstract objects. This is a serious problem as many applications (and hence their programs) are made complicated by the complexity of their data objects. For any complex data structure, the job of maintaining that structure and guaranteeing the consistency of the data stored there should not be distributed among all the programs that may need access to it. Instead, one abstraction should be responsible for maintaining it and guaranteeing its consistency, and other modules should be forced to access the data through this abstraction. Hence, a data abstraction can be defined as a set of operations (procedures) that are grouped around common data structures. This data structure must be hidden [2, 3] from operations that are not defined as part of the abstraction.

Like procedures, data should be designed in two stages. At the first stage, a data structure should be specified so that it is clear *what* it means, but not necessarily *how* it is implemented. This division of concerns, which clearly separates the specification and implementation, is useful because it enhances the use of abstractions and helps to control the complexity of the programming process.

In Sections 12.2, 12.3, and 12.4 we present the concepts of types, structures, and abstractions, respectively. After examining them, we present a unified way of looking at the three concepts in Section 12.5. After examining the concept of a data type, we present the concepts of type specifications (Section 12.6), type representation (Section 12.7), and type verification (Section 12.8). Section 12.9 is a short summary, followed, finally, by a selected reference list.

12.2. TYPES

It is customary in mathematics to classify variables according to certain important characteristics. For instance, a sharp distinction is made between real, complex, and logical variables or between an element, a set of elements, a set of sets, and so on. Whenever a mathematician introduces a new variable, the type of object it can stand for is immediately stated, for instance:

Let x and y be *real* variables.
Let c be a *complex* function of five *complex* variables.
Let S be a *set* of *integers*.

In programming (especially in high-level programming languages), the concept of type is of central importance. In this context, a type refers to the kinds of values a variable may assume in a programming language. For example, in FORTRAN some of the data types are REAL, INTEGER, LOGICAL, COMPLEX, and DOUBLE PRECISION. In SNOBOL and PL/1 there is also the data type CHARACTER. In most programming languages, before using a variable or function, an explicit declaration stating its type is required. In the implementation of the language, the type information determines the following:

1. Representation of the values of the variable
2. Amount of storage that must be allocated to it
3. Manner in which the operations are to be interpreted
4. Detection of errors by type checking

Hence, from the above we see that the set of values a variable may assume plays a very important role in the characterization of the variable that is called its type.

Experience in the design and use of high-level languages [4] has shown that the concept of types and especially the distinction between types and variables (which are typed) contribute significantly to the reliability and efficiency of software. More reliability is achieved because the type declaration provides a compiler with redundant information that is used in checking for the consistency of a program. The type declaration also aids the compiler in making a reasonable choice of representation of the object within the store of the computer. The capacity of storage allocated to a variable is chosen according to the size of the range of values that the variable may assume. If this information is known to a compiler, time-consuming dynamic storage allocation can be avoided. This is very often the key to an efficient realization of an algorithm.

12.3. STRUCTURES

A computer program consists of operations on some body of data. These operations transform the data in some way. If the body of data is a collection of predefined types (in assembly or a high-level language), then the operations in the computer program would consist of those defined for the types. For example, computing the average of a series of reals would involve reading the real numbers, summing them, and finally dividing the sum by the number of real numbers added.

In the above example, the program was operating on the values of the various data items only, but that is certainly not the only kind of transformation that can be performed. An example of a program that operates on the structure of the data is one for obtaining the derivative of an algebraic expression in symbolic form. The expression would be read in as a sequence of symbols and then be transformed according to the rules of differentiation.

Normally programs operate on aggregates of information. These aggregates consist of data elements with important structural relationships. Such entities are generally referred to as data structures. An example of a data structure is an ordered collection of data elements. If the element happens to be a bit we refer to it as a byte, word, and so on. If the element happens to have a structure of its own, then the data structure might be a vector, a matrix, an n dimensional array, a list, a tree, or a graph. Thus, a hierarchy of elements forms the data structure where the lowest-level element is a bit and each higher-level element (or data structure) is built from lower-level elements.

The study of data structures [1] involves the following:

- Properties of data structures
  —static
  —dynamic
  —representation
  —storage allocation and deallocation
  —density
- Operations on data structures
  —creation
  —access
  —alteration
  —duplication
  —change of structure.

It should be clear that the ultimate components in the construction of data structures are bits (Figure 12.1). Ultimate simply means that for the purposes of this discussion, we are not concerned about the structure of a bit. We really treat it as a black box, and all we need to know is that it can be in one of two states.

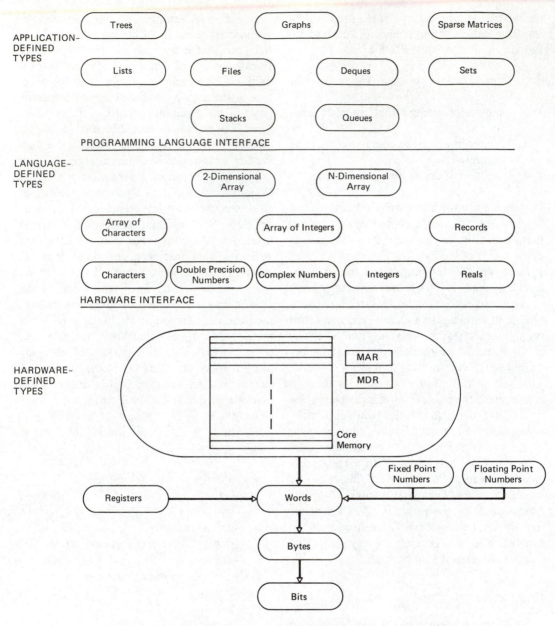

Figure 12.1. Types and structures.

We really do not care how the bit is implemented; we are interested only in the external characteristics or the visible behavior of a bit.

We show three levels and their interfaces in Figure 12.1: the hardware level, the programming language level, and the applications level, along with some sample data types.

Higher-level data objects are constructed using the bit as a basic building block. The next-level object we can build is by collecting some bits and treating them as a single unit. In many computers a collection of 8 bits is referred to as a byte. Using bytes, we can build words. Depending on the hardware characteristics (mainly access and speed) of these words, we can distinguish between two types of words. One we refer to as a register and the other as a memory word. What is really of interest is a collection of memory words, which we refer to as memory (core memory in Figure 12.1). We can construct other types of memory (for clarity, these are not shown in Figure 12.1). Hence up until now by using the bit as a basic building block, we have built the memory of a computer and by adding two registers—MAR (Memory Address Register) and MDR (Memory Data Register)—we can define the storing and retrieving operations for the data structure (memory).

We can also take words or collections of bits and give them more meaning by distinguishing fixed point and floating point objects. It is clear to everyone what fixed point and floating point numbers are. They can be looked upon as data structures (as we have been viewing them) as shown in Figures 12.2 and 12.3. In Figure 12.1, the floating point numbers are shown at the hardware level, although this may not be the case for all hardware, especially older models.

All the data structures we have designed so far have full hardware support in most computers and can be called *hardware data structures*. By this we mean that the representation and manipulation of these structures are solely done in hardware and that the manipulation is done by "hardware algorithms." Above the hardware interface level (Figure 12.1), we can make use of them to build more complicated data objects. When we use them to build higher-level objects, we are interested only in the external characteristics of these objects. Again, we treat them as black boxes (as we did before to build them from bits). The visible behavior of these black boxes is really given by the type of the objects.

Hence, we see that all types have structures. The only exception is the bit, where it would be more correct to say that the structure of a bit is of no interest to us as opposed to saying it has no structure. The bit is made of resistors,

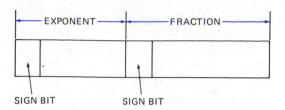

Figure 12.3. Floating-point numbers as a data structure.

transistors, wires, magnetic cores, and so forth, which in turn are made of atoms and molecules.

Using the hardware data objects, we can build more objects at the software level. The software level is divided into two parts: programming language and applications. The programming language level supports some data types, as shown in Figure 12.1. Their representation (structure) is part of language implementation and hence of no interest to the language user. For instance, the user does not care whether an array is stored by rows or columns as long as each element can be accessed.

11.4. ABSTRACTIONS

This section explores another concept pertaining to data, that is, data abstractions. First, however, the general concept of abstractions for programming should be examined.

Within the past few years, there has been a significant growth of concern about the quality of software, and a corresponding growth of interest in programming methodologies that can contribute to enhanced software quality. Two such methodologies have been described in the literature: *structured programming* [5, 6] and *modular design* [2, 7]. Both of these methodologies are concerned with those aspects of the software problem that result from human limitations in dealing with complexity.

Most programmers realize that the amount of complexity that the human mind can cope with, at any instant, is considerably less than that embodied in much of the software that one might wish to build. Thus, the key problem in the design and implementation of large software systems is reducing the amount of complexity or detail that must be considered at any one time. One way to do this is by the process

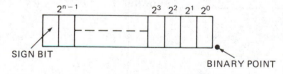

Figure 12.2. Fixed point numbers as a data structure.

of abstraction. What this means is to distinguish between the implementation and use of objects (data and procedure) in programming. These activities are usually referred to as the specification and the implementation phases.

A good example of the use of abstractions occurs in the specification of the hardware-software interface. Normally, the programmers (at the assembly/machine-language level) use only the instruction set of the machine to write programs. They are not concerned about how the instructions are implemented. They could be implemented using microprograms or in hardware or a combination of both, as shown in Figure 12.4. In this approach, we see a separation of the what and the how. The word *normally* is used above because sometimes this separation is not very clean. In other words, sometimes for certain instructions one may have to understand their implementation to use them effectively and correctly. The above example can be expanded to the operating system level. The users of operating system services do not care (and hence should not be told) how services are implemented. For instance, some of the functions may be implemented in microcode for efficiency reasons. The same example can further be extended to application programs. Details pertaining to the implementation of abstractions (parts of a program that embody a concept) should be hidden from their users. This

idea of abstractions is extremely powerful and useful, especially for large programs.

For the purpose of this discussion, two kinds* of abstraction have been found useful in programming. By looking at a program and its components, let us arrive at each kind and illustrate their usefulness. A program consists of two parts: its algorithm and data.

If the size of the program is small (less than 100 lines of a high-order language), then its algorithm and data parts can be understood as a whole (maybe by one person who is developing it). But as the size of the program increases, ways of breaking it into parts are needed for understanding, work assignments, and so forth. Three partitionings are obvious. Either the algorithm part, the data part, or both can be broken into pieces.

In the algorithm decomposition, only the algorithm is broken into pieces, which is the traditional way of handling complexity. When there is more emphasis on modularizing the algorithm, the data part is split into pieces and the algorithm is treated as a whole. This is particularly useful when the algorithm is simple and the data base is complex (size, diversity, etc.). A good example of this is a Query or Transaction System. The third decomposition

---

*A third kind of abstraction, namely, the control abstraction [8], has been found useful in programming but is not germane to the discussion here.

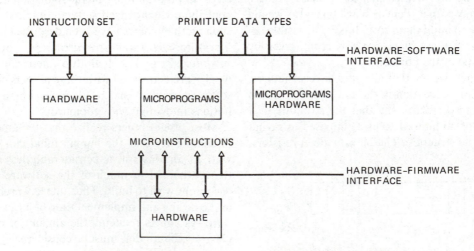

Figure 12.4. Use of abstractions at the hardware-software interface.

method is a combination of the first two. This is more realistic and in practice is how one normally handles complexity.

Before we investigate the organization of a program system by decomposing algorithms and data, let us examine procedure and data abstractions.

Procedure Abstraction

The purpose of a procedure abstraction is to permit the use of operations (algorithm parts) by just naming them without any knowledge of details of implementation. This kind of abstraction is naturally represented by subroutine or procedure. Other examples are listed below:

1. Machine instruction-hardware
2. Microinstruction-firmware
3. Subroutine-FORTRAN
4. Procedure-ALGOL, Pascal, PL/1
5. Function-FORTRAN, ALGOL
6. Macroassembly language

Data Abstraction

The nature of abstractions that may be achieved through the use of procedures is well suited to the description of abstract operations, but is not particularly well suited to the description of abstract objects. This is a serious drawback, for in many applications the complexity of the data objects to be manipulated contributes substantially to the overall complexity of the problem. Hence, an abstraction to model the data analog of a procedure would be useful and is what is provided by data abstraction.

The purpose of a data abstraction is to permit the use of data objects by naming them without any knowledge of details of implementation. The representation of data abstractions is not as obvious as the procedure abstractions. The ordinary representation, a description of the way the data objects will occupy storage, forces the user of the abstraction to be aware of its implementation. This defeats the purpose of abstraction.

In data structures there is no concept of two

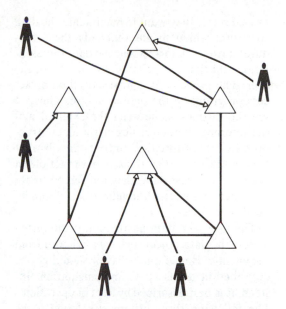

Figure 12.5. Data structure usage.

behaviors (internal and external). Everything is visible to all the users (Figure 12.5). They know all facts about its implementation and can write their own programs to manipulate any part of the data structure. In data abstraction, however, users never write their own programs to manipulate the data structure (Figure 12.6). Instead, they use a predefined set of

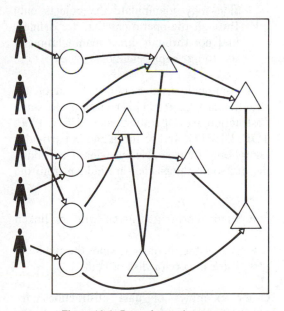

Figure 12.6. Data abstraction usage.

procedures if they want to manipulate the data structure, which means that only the procedures have to "know" about the data representation and the storage structures used, not the user. The procedures can be looked on as access programs to the data structure. Thus we see the distinction between the external and the internal characteristics of the data structure. In data abstraction, the data are abstract only in the sense that all users never get direct access to the raw data; they are forced to access them indirectly through a set of predefined procedures.

The user of a data abstraction is interested in how the data objects behave as viewed from the outside. Hence, the behavior should not be described in terms of its implementation. Instead, it is best described by a set of operations. The following three criteria are found to be useful to support data abstractions:

1. *Definition.* This must include the definitions of all operations applicable to objects in the data abstraction. These operations could be looked on as procedure abstractions.
2. *Information Hiding.* The user of a data abstraction need not know how the data objects are represented in storage [9, 10].
3. *Enforcement.* The user of a data abstraction may manipulate the objects only through the operations that are defined, and not through direct manipulation of its storage representation.

A commonly used example of a data abstraction is a *stack* [11]. The user of the stack abstraction sees operations like PUSH, POP, TOP, DEPTH, and so forth, and in particular knows only their visible behavior. The following are some things that are hidden from the user:

- Stack represented as an array or linked list
- Size of the memory to store the stack
- Stack in core or disk or both

Other examples of data abstractions are *queues, symbol tables,* and *file systems.* As the

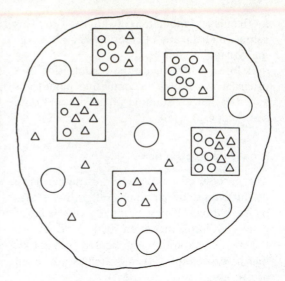

Figure 12.7. Program organization.

size and complexity of the data abstraction grow, it gets harder to specify it in a representation-independent fashion.

A program can then be organized using procedure and data abstractions as shown in Figure 12.7. Circles represent procedure abstractions, triangles represent the local or global data for the procedures, and squares represent data abstractions. The squares signify that the data enclosed in them can be accessed only by the procedures inside them.

Earlier we saw that all types are implemented as data structures. The data structure for an integer was shown in Figure 12.2. The implementations of the operations have to be "aware" of the data structure (of the type) since they manipulate them. The question now is, How does data abstraction fit in here? We saw before that three criteria were useful to support data abstractions, namely, the definition of operations, information hiding, and enforcement. The definition of operations for the various types causes no problems since the types are really quite primitive (basically, numbers, characters, and Boolean types). Information hiding is fairly easily achieved through the assembler or compiler since users never really care about the actual data representation of these primitive types. The third criterion of enforcement is not achieved in most of the older languages. For example, in

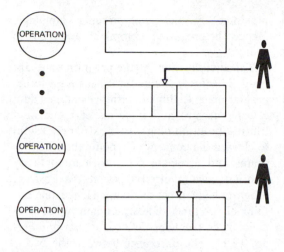

Figure 12.8. User manipulating the representation of an integer.

some higher-level languages (Figure 12.8), one can declare a variable as an integer and then start manipulating bits in the data representation (structure) of an integer. This cannot be done in typed languages like Pascal [12], AL-PHARD [13, 14], and CLU [8, 15].

Hence, we see that data abstraction fits in very nicely here, if all three criteria of data abstraction are met by a data type. Figure 12.9 shows an integer data type. The key point here is that in a data type there are many instances of the same type (e.g., integer), whereas in a data abstraction there is only one.

12.5. ABSTRACT DATA TYPE

We have seen the concepts of data type, data structure, and data abstraction and how they interrelate with each other. Our interest now is to unify the above concepts.

The unification is really straightforward because we can take a data type and its operations and implement it as a data abstraction supporting multiple instances and get an abstract data type. The only way to manipulate the objects of such a type is through its operations because the user of the abstract data type is unaware of its implementation. A data structure along with its operations can be implemented as a data abstraction and visualized as providing a data type with only one instance, but in practice, this is not often done. The three key concepts are data type, structure, and abstraction. That is, data are typed, have structure, and are abstract (by separating the use and implementation of data).

Data Type

The concept of type is of central importance in the design, implementation, and use of high-level programming languages. Hence, a programmer has to wait until reaching the last stages of refinement before he or she thinks of data in terms of its type (Figure 12.10). The stages of the stepwise refinement process can be partitioned into two levels: abstract and real programs. By abstract programs, we mean that the intermediate stages of the stepwise refinement process are represented as programs

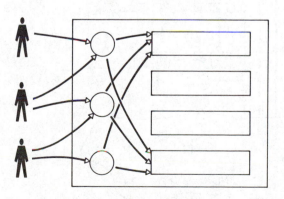

Figure 12.9. Integer data type.

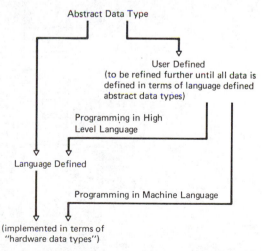

Figure 12.10. Kinds of abstract data types.

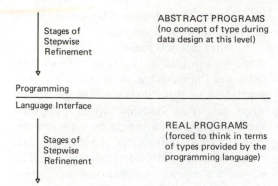

Figure 12.11. Data types and stepwise refinement.

that are complete except for the implementation of operators and operands. By real programs, we mean that all the operands and operators in the program are implemented in terms of the control structures and data types provided by the programming language. Hence, the program is compilable and ready to run.

This dividing line (at the programming language interface) is unnatural because it forces programmers to think in terms of untyped data (during design) and in terms of typed data (during programming). It is extremely useful to elevate the concept of type to abstract programs and associate types with all data by treating new required types at the abstract program level, if not available. Hence, one can think of two kinds of abstract data types: user-defined and language-defined, as shown in Figure 12.11. The difference between the two is that the user-defined abstract data type is still unrefined. At some level of stepwise refinement, it makes sense to talk in terms of that abstract data type. Eventually, all user-defined

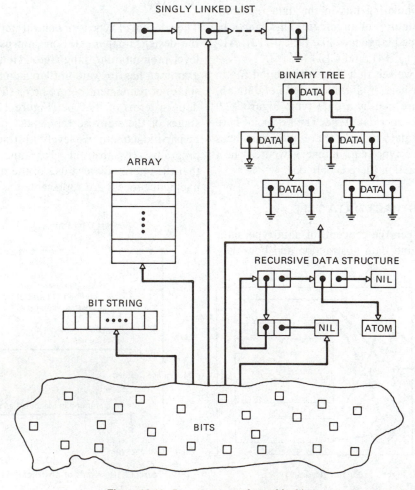

Figure 12.12. Data structures formed by bits.

abstract data types have to be refined and implemented in terms of the language-defined abstract data types, if programming is done using a high-level programming language. If not, all user-defined abstract data types are to be implemented in terms of the data types provided by hardware.

Data Structure

All data structures are really made out of bits; examples of this are shown in Figure 12.12. The first one is the ordered collection of bits from an array. A singly linked list can be formed out of bits such that they form a binary tree where each node has three fields: a left link (LLINK), a right link (RLINK), and a data field (DATA). The fifth example is that of a recursive data structure used in list processing by LISP. Data structures are not formed from bits in just one step. Instead, we have a hierarchy of data elements that form

the structure where the lowest-level element is a bit and each higher-level element (or data structure) is built from lower-level elements

We saw in the previous section that it is valuable to assign a type to each and every piece of data we are working with. In the section of types and structures, we observed that all types have structure. We can conclude from this that all typed data have structure (the same as that associated with the type).

Data Abstraction

It is desirable to separate the type and structure associated with a piece of data. Briefly, every type has structure (after refinement), and all variables (typed) have a structure corresponding to that type. Integrity of a data structure can be better maintained and guaranteed if it is always manipulated by a predefined set of procedures. All accesses and manipulations to these data structures must be

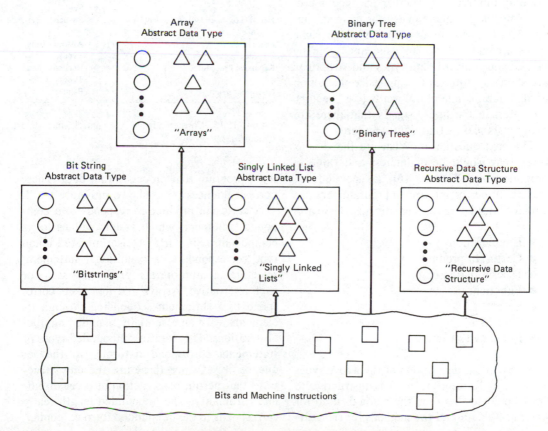

Figure 12.13. Data abstractions formed by bits and ma-chine instructions.

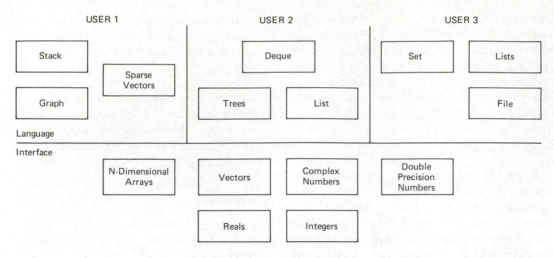

Figure 12.14. Use of abstract data types.

made through these access procedures. We can redraw Figure 12.12 to illustrate the concept of data abstraction as shown in Figure 12.13.

After seeing the concept of an abstract data type, one can envision all data as being typed; the only difference is whether the type is provided by the language or is user defined. Figure 12.14 shows an example in which some types are defined by language and some by users. Note that all data types and structures are shown in squares to emphasize the notion of abstraction. The plural words (e.g., vectors, sets, etc.) in the figure signify that there are many instances of that data structure.

The next question is, What are the various types that would be of interest and value in programming? Hoare [16] has pointed out that the types of interest to programmers are already familiar to mathematicians. They are:

- Enumeration
- Cartesian product
- Discriminated union
- Functions
- Sets
- Sequence
- Recursive structure

An excellent description of the above types is given in Reference 16. It is instructive to draw analogies between the methods used for structuring data and the methods for structur-

CONTROL STRUCTURE	DATA STRUCTURE
Compound Statement (do ... od)	Cartesian Product
Conditional Statement (if ... then ... else ... , case ...)	Type Union
Iterative (bounded) Statement (for ... do ...)	Array, Finite Set
Iterative (unbounded) Statement (while ... do ... , do ... until ...)	Sequence, Set
Procedure (proc ... corp)	Abstract Data Type
Recursive Procedures	Recursive Data Types
GoTo Statement	Pointer

Figure 12.15. Correspondence of control and data structures.

ing a program that processes that data. These correspondences are as shown in Figure 12.15.

A cartesian product corresponds to a compound statement, which assigns values to its components. Similarly, a discriminated union type corresponds to a conditional statement, selecting an appropriate processing step for each alternative. Arrays and finite sets correspond to a statement sequencing through its elements, with an essentially bounded number of iterations. The iterative unbounded types of statements correspond naturally to the sequence or set since these are the only structures that permit construction of types of infinite cardinality. The unbounded length really corresponds to the unbounded form of looping, with a condition to control termination. Procedure abstraction is analogous to data abstraction in the sense that the former hides algorithms and the latter hides data. Recursive procedures and recursive data types correspond since a recursive procedure is defined in terms of itself the same way a recursive data type is defined in terms of itself. The GoTo statement in the area of control structures and the pointer in the area of data structures are probably the most unstructured constructs in their two respective areas. With the former, one can jump anywhere in the program, whereas with the latter, one can reach any part of a data structure. The chances of misusing any of these constructs are very great, and the price paid in terms of software reliability is very high. That is why good programming practices dictate avoiding these constructs when possible. When they must be used, they must be used in a very restricted fashion.

12.6. SPECIFYING TYPES

The purpose of specifying new types is to enrich our programming environment by defining a new set of values and the mechanisms for operating on them. The type specification serves to document the intended type behavior and to communicate this behavior to the following:

1. Designer(s) of that type
2. User(s) of that type
3. Designer(s) of other types that use this type

The distinction between 2 and 3 is made on purpose since this usually seems to be a source of confusion. The user could be "human" or "other type." For example, an array type can be used by a human user directly or by a set type designer who is using the array type in its implementation. Hence, type specification constitutes the user's and designer's sole source of information about the type.

Two methods [17] of specifying the behavior of an abstract data type are abstract model specifications and axiomatic specifications. In the abstract model approach, the objects of a

type are represented in terms of other well-defined data objects with known properties. The operations of the type being defined can be specified in terms of operations of the known data objects. The operations are specified using the methods for specifying procedures. An alternative to using the abstract model is to implicitly define a module by giving a list of properties possessed by the objects and the operations on them. This approach can be formalized by expressing the properties as axioms for the type. Hence, in the axiomatic approach, the behavior of the type is described by giving axioms relating the operations.

It is not clear whether the abstract model or the axiomatic approach is better [18]. One major difference between the two techniques is the extent to which they exhibit a representation bias, that is, the extent to which the specification suggests a representation or implementation for the type abstraction being defined. The abstract model technique, which makes use of an existing mathematical discipline to specify an abstract model, has a representational bias depending on the abstract model chosen, whereas the axiomatic approach presents no representational bias at all. The axiomatic approach is seriously deficient with respect to comprehensibility however. It is difficult to see that all the axioms as a whole define a type abstraction. The abstract model specifications are easier for programmers to construct and understand since they are more like program specifications.

Given that criterion, we choose the abstract model approach to write type specifications. A type specification then consists of the following two parts:

1. Abstract model
2. Operations

Let us look briefly at each one of these and give a complete example of a type sepecification.

1. *Abstract model.* This part describes the model for data used to define the type, and the operations for the type are specified using the operations of the abstract model. It must be

emphasized that clarity and simplicity of description are important in choosing the abstract model, whereas implementation and efficiency are not. The latter are, however, highly important in the corresponding design and representation of the type. The standard mathematical concepts for sets, sequences, mappings, cartesian products, and so on, which are not supported by most programming languages, have been found convenient to use as abstract models for data. Careful choice of the abstract model can greatly simplify the specification for a type.

2. *Operations.* This section consists of all the procedures associated with that type. Each procedure has two parts: interface and behavior. In the interface we have a procedure name and all its parameters with their associated types specified, whereas in the behavior an abstract description of the function performed by the procedure is specified. Two ways to specify this behavior are: using pre- and postconditions [13] and using functions [6]. For illustration, we will be using the mathematical functions to specify behavior.

Let us now introduce an example we will carry through the remainder of the chapter in detail. Imagine while designing some program we found it desirable to use the notion of a set, in particular, a set whose elements are integers. We presume that the language being used does not contain sets (the way we want to

define it) as a primitive concept. So we want to introduce it as a new type abstraction. Suppose further that an a priori size limit is known or desired, so we need not define a general set type mechanism, only one in which the cardinality of all sets generated by the type do not exceed some predetermined maximum.

It is hard to write behavior without using any notations. We will only be using multiple and conditional assignment statements [6] to specify functions. The type specifications for the special set of integers (sint) are as shown in Figure 12.16.

Let us now read the intended function for add. Its overall structure is of the form

$$[p_1 \rightarrow f_1 | true \rightarrow f_2]$$

where

$$p_1 = i \notin s \wedge |s| < max$$
$$f_1 = s, c: = s \cup \{i\}, true$$
$$f_2 = c: = false$$

The function for add is expressed as a conditional rule. It says, if p_1 is true, the function of add is f_1; if p_1 if false, the function of add is f_2. The form of f_1 is a multiple assignment statement that says s becomes $sv \{i\}$ and c is assigned true. There is no sequence implied here. One can think all variables on the lefthand side are assigned the corresponding values on the righthand side concurrently.

Abstract model: We will use the concept of a mathematical set to model variables of type sint (finite set of integers limited to a constant maximum size of max); especially the operation ∪ (union), ∈ (membership test), − (subtraction) and || (cardinality) will be used. The operations also use variables of type integer and logical (can take on two values *true* or *false*).

Operations:
    proc add (*i*: integer, *s*: sint, *c*: logical)
        $[i \notin s \wedge |s| < max \rightarrow s, c: = s \cup \{i\}, true | true \rightarrow c: = false]$
    proc delete (*i*: integer, *s*: sint, *c*: logical)
        $[i \in s \rightarrow s, c: = s - \{i\}, true | true \rightarrow c: = false]$
    proc empty (*s*: sint, *c*: logical)
        $[c: = (s = \{ \})]$
    proc clear (*s*: sint)
        $[s: = \{ \}]$
    proc maxint (*s*: sint, *i*: integer, *c*: logical)
        $[\exists j \in s(\forall k \in s, k \leq j) \rightarrow i, c: = j, true | true \rightarrow c: = false]$

Figure 12.16. Type sint specification.

12.7. REPRESENTING TYPES

Once we have the specification for a type, the next step is to arrive at a more concrete data representation and restate the abstract functions by the more concrete representation. This is done as shown in Figure 12.17. The word *concrete* is used in a relative sense, since if it needs still further refinement it becomes abstract for the next lower level.

Hence, the representation of a type consists of the following two steps:

1. *Data refinement*. In general, the transformation from the abstract model to its concrete representation will be a relation [19]. Intuitively, this means that a data value of the abstract model can be represented by many possible values in its concrete representation or the inverse transformation from the concrete to the abstract referred to as data mapping will be a many-one function. In practice, we loosely justify this by noting that a specification has many possible implementations.
2. *Function restatement*. Once the data mapping has been formulated, the next step is to rewrite the operations for the type in terms of the more concrete representation.

The representation of a type then consists of the following three parts:

1. Concrete model
2. Map
3. Operations

These are identical to the contents of the type specification except for the map. Even though the map establishes a relationship between the two, it is considered part of the type representation because it arises during the refinement process.

1. *Concrete model*. This part describes the concrete representation of the data to be used for storing the objects of a type. In general, this is a collection or record of concrete variables. The concrete representation usually consists of several variables whose types are directly (or more directly) represented in computer store.
2. *Map*. The fundamental requirement for proving a type representation is to define the relationship between the objects of the concrete representation and the abstract model. Suppose that x is the concrete representation of an object of type T. The relation between x and the abstract object y that x represents may be expressed by a function; map $(x) = y$. Note the map may be many-one. The set of concrete objects in general will be defined by a predicate. Then the map could be expressed as a conditional rule and defined only when the predicate is true. Note that this predicate must be preserved by all procedures so that the concrete objects are always mappable to the abstract objects. Such a predicate is referred to as a concrete invariant [13, 19].
3. *Operations*. This section consists of all the procedures, one for each concrete operation. Each procedure has three parts: interface, behavior, and design. The interface and the behavior portions are the same as before, except that the behavior is written as functions operating on concrete variables. The design consists of the procedure body. We have not shown this in our examples for because of a lack of space. Interested readers are referred to Shankar [20].

We now design the type specification of sint given in Figure 12.16. For illustration purposes, we give two different representations. In fact, there are many others possible. For a few more, refer to Shankar [20].

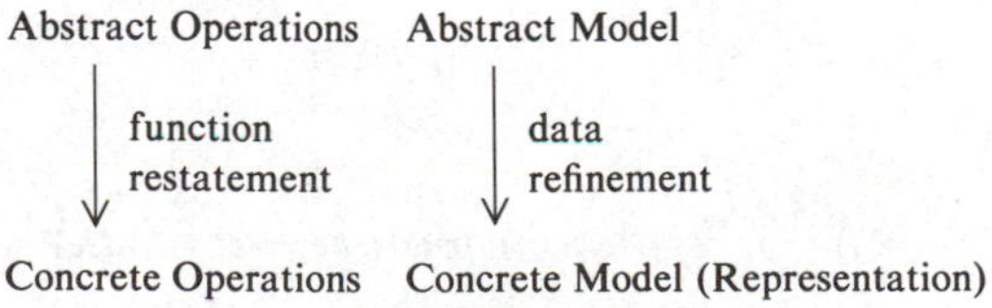

Abstract Operations   Abstract Model

   function   data
   restatement   refinement

Concrete Operations   Concrete Model (Representation)

Figure 12.17. Type representation.

a. *Array-pointer representation of sets.* This representation is useful when the possible number of set values is very large even though the actual set sizes are reasonably small. Under these circumstances, it is useful to use a one dimensional array (vector) to store the set. We use an additional integer, size, to keep track of how many elements are actually in use, and we'll require that these be stored, *without duplicates,* in the leftmost size positions in the vector. Since, we will never look at any elements whose indicies are greater than size, duplicates at the other end don't matter. Consider the set {−2, 0, 53, 76} and a max set size of 8. This will be represented as any of the following (and many others, how many?)

Vector = <−2, 0, 53, 76, 10, 6, 6, 6>, Size = 4

Vector = <0, −2, 76, 53, 77, 256, 0, 0>, Size = 4

Vector = <−2, 0, 53, 76, 0, −2, 0, −2>, Size = 4

Vector = <76, 53, 0, −2, −2, −2, 0, 53>, Size = 4

The type representation for sint is as shown in Figure 12.18.

b. *Bit vector representation of sets.* This representation is useful when we want to define sets whose members are drawn from a relatively small group of values, all of which are known in advance. The set is represented as a Boolean array *a* in which $a(i)$ indicates whether i is an element of the set or not. Consider the set {1, 2, 6} and a max set size of 8. The bit array representation of the set will be 00100011. Note in this case there is only one representation and hence the map is one-one.

The type representation for the special set of integers (sint) is as shown in Figure 12.19. In the representation shown, the integers in the set are in

---

Concrete Model
   type sint = *rec*
        size: 0.. max
        vec: *array* (1..max) *of* integer
        cer
map: let *r* be an instance of the concrete model and *s* be the object that *r* represents; then we have

$$(\forall((j, k), (1 \le j, k \le r.\text{size})), (j = k \lor r.\text{vec}(j) \ne r.\text{vec}(k)) \to s := \{r.\text{vec}(\ell)|1 \le \ell \le r.\text{size}\}$$

Operations
   proc add (*i*: integer, *s*: sint, *c*: logical)

    [/*j*, $1 \le j \le s$. size $\epsilon s.\text{vec}(j) = i \land s.\text{size} < \text{max} \to s.\text{size}, s.\text{vec}(s.\text{size} + 1), c := s.\text{size} + 1, i, true,$
    | *true* → *c* := *false*]

   proc delete (*i*: integer, *s*: sint, *c*: logical)

    [∃*j*, $1 \le j \le s.\text{size} \, \epsilon s.\text{vec}(j) = i \to s.\text{vec}(j), s.\text{size}, c := s.\text{vec}(s.\text{size}), s.\text{size} - 1, true, | true \to c := false]$

   proc empty (*s*: sint, *c*: logical)
    [*c* := (*s*.size = 0)]
   proc clear (*s*: sint)
    [*s*.size = 0]
   proc maxint (*s*: sint, *i*: integer, *c*: logical)
    [∃*j*, $1 \le j \le s.\text{size} \, \epsilon(\cdot k, (1 \le k \le s.\text{size}), s.\text{vec}(k) \le s.\text{vec}(j) \to i, c := s.\text{vec}(j), true | true \to c := false]$

Figure 12.18. Array-pointer representation of type sint.

Concrete Model:
  type sint = *array (mi . . . ma) of* logical

map: Let *a* be an instance of the concrete model and *s* be the object that *a* represents; then we have

$$s: = \{\ell \,|\, mi \leq \ell \leq ma \,\wedge\, a(\ell)\}$$

Operations
  proc add (*i*: integer, *s*: sint, *c*: logical)

$$[mi \leq i \leq ma \,\wedge\, \sim s(i), \; c: = true, \; true \,|\, true \to c: = false]$$

  proc delete (*i*: integer, *s*: sint, *c*: logical)

$$[s(i) \to s(i), \; c: = false, \; true \,|\, true \to c: = false]$$

  proc empty (*s*: sint, *c*: logical)

$$[c: = (\forall i, \, mi \leq i \leq ma, \, \sim s(i))]$$

  proc clear (*s*: sint)

$$[s: = false]$$

  proc maxint (*s*: sint, *i*: integer. *c*: logical)

$$[\exists j, \, mi \leq j \leq ma \, \epsilon s(j) \,\wedge\, (\forall k, \, (j + 1 \leq k \leq ma), \, \sim s(k) \to i, \; c: = j, \; true \,|\, true \to c: = false]$$

Figure 12.19. Bit vector representation of type sint.

the range $mi \leq i \leq ma$. Therefore, we have $ma - mi + 1 = \max$.

12.8. VERIFYING TYPES

Now that we have an understanding of type specification and type representation, the process of type verification consists of showing that the representation is correct with respect to its specifications. Intuitively, we wish to show that the behavior exhibited by the abstract model data and its operations and the concrete model data and its operations correspond. More specifically, we wish to show that it is safe for a designer using this type to prove the correctness of his design using only the type specification.

We saw earlier that a type specification consists of an abstract domain and a set of abstract operations, which we may label as T and $f_1, f_2, \ldots, f_n$. A type representation consists of a concrete domain, a set of concrete operations, and a map. Let us label them as T', f'_1, $f'_2, \ldots, f'_n$, and m. In the sequel, we often dis-

cuss an arbitrary function whose corresponding abstract and concrete operations are denoted by the symbols f and f', respectively; our remarks are, therefore, implicitly quantified over the set of such operations. Let us label the other inputs and outputs for the operations by domains I and O, respectively. We can represent all this pictorially as in Figure 12.20. We have also shown m^{-1}, which in general will be a relation.

We can further simplify the interconnections in Figure 12.20 by including input and output as part of the mapping on the two sides of the diagram.

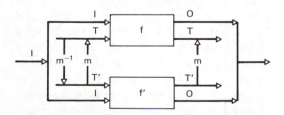

Figure 12.20. Type specification and representation relationship.

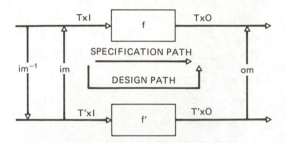

Figure 12.21. Simplified type specification and representation relationship.

We define another mapping function im as the outer product of m and the identity function on the input set. Let its transpose be denoted by im^{-1}. On the output side, likewise, we form the function om. These are as shown in Figure 12.21.

The user of a type is aware of T, I, O, and f. The specification of a type really says that given a value of $T \times I$, by application of f, a new value in $T \times O$ is produced. This is shown marked as a specification path in the figure. But that is not the path taken in reality because of data refinement. The design path, as shown in the figure, is roundabout. First $T \times I$ is refined to a corresponding value in $T' \times I$; then f' is applied to it, which yields a value in $T' \times O$; finally, this value is mapped back into a value in $T \times O$. Intuitively, then a type representation is correct, if the two paths lead to the same value in $T \times O$ given a value in $T \times I$. Assuming (c, i) is a starting value in $T \times I$, the value produced in $S \times O$ by the two paths can be formalized as follows:

Specification path : $f(c, i)$
Design path   : $om(f'\, (im^{-1}(c, i)))$

Since im^{-1} can be a relation, note there could be a multiplicity of design paths. For example, in the array-pointer representation of a set, note there will be 100! design paths for a 100 element set. In general, there will be $n!$ paths, where n is the cardinality of the set. There is nothing conceptually hard about showing this equality; it is just too laborious. However, one uncomfortable thing about it is that the proof depends on the sizes of the data structures. The type correctness question now

involves showing that each design path leads to the same value in $T \times O$, which the specification path produces. In practice, showing whether the module correctness proposition is true or false would be very difficult because im^{-1} could be a relation. Fortunately, we can use the following theorem to ease the problem.

Theorem: $f \circ im = om \circ f' \to f$
$\qquad\qquad\qquad = om \circ f' \circ im^{-1}$
Proof: $\qquad f = f \circ I$
$\qquad\qquad\quad = f \circ im \circ im^{-1}$
$\qquad\qquad\qquad (\because im \circ im^{-1} = I)$
$\qquad\qquad\quad = om \circ f' \circ im^{-1}$
$\qquad\qquad\qquad$ (by hypothesis $f \circ im$
$\qquad\qquad\quad = om \circ f')$
$\qquad\qquad\qquad$ Q.E.D.

Hence the proof of correctness of a type consists of showing the propositions $f \circ im = om \circ f'$.

In addition to showing the above propositions, one has to prove the implementation of each procedure with respect to its specification, that is, f'.

Initial Values. We have not yet mentioned one technical point of considerable importance—initial values when an an instance of the type is created. If the above propositions for type correctness have to be proven, it is very important that om be defined. More specifically, the predicate in the map (if any) must be true after applying the function f'; otherwise, we would be unable to map the final concrete values into the abstract. For example in the array-pointer representation of sets, the property no duplicates (between 1 and size) must be preserved by each procedure. The question then is, when a set is created (really an array and a pointer) the no duplicate may not be true. We must prove that once the predicate is established, no operation of the set invalidates it. This does not prove that the truth of the predicate was ever established; we have not, in effect, established a basis for our induction [21]. In order for our sets to work, they must first be initialized using the procedure clear.

One way out is to make sure that some standard initialization procedure is always invoked whenever we create a new variable of whatever type we are defining. Some languages will enforce this. Then, we need only establish that after this operation finishes, the map is defined. In the case of set, for example, "clear" could be designated as the initialization procedure. Such a procedure cannot, of course, assume that no duplicate predicate holds to start with.

For purposes of illustration, we will carry out two proofs. Both will prove the delete function from the two representations of sint (Figures 12.18 and 12.19).

Array-Pointer Representation "delete" Proof.

$$f = [i \in s \to s, c: = s - \{i\}, true \,|\, true \to c: = false]$$
$$f' = [\exists j, 1 \le j \le s.size \,\epsilon s.vec(j) = i$$
$$\to s.vec(j), s.size, c: = s.vec(s.size),$$
$$s.size - 1, true \,|\, true \to c: = false]$$
$$m = ((\forall(j, k), (1 \le j, k \le s.size)),$$
$$(j = k \lor s.vec(j) \ne s.vec(k))$$
$$\to s: = \{s.vec(\ell) \,|\, 1 \le \ell \le s.size\}$$

Let us rewrite m as follows

$$m = (nodup(s) \to s: = \{s.vec(\ell) \,|\, 1 \le \ell \le s.size\})$$

where $nodup(s)$ is the predicate

$$im = (nodup(s) \to s, i: = \{s.vec(\ell) \,|\, 1 \le \ell \le s.size\}, i)$$
$$om = (nodup(s) \to s, c: = \{s.vec(\ell) \,|\, 1 \le \ell \le s.size\}, c)$$

Let us rewrite f and f' as follows

$$f = (p_1 \to f_1 \,|\, p_2 \to f_2)$$
$$f' = (p_1' \to f_1' \,|\, p_2' \to f_2')$$

where
$$p_1 = i \in s$$
$$p_2 = i \notin s$$
$$f_1 = s, c: = s - \{i\}, true$$
$$f_2 = c: = false$$
$$p_1' = \exists j, 1 \le j \le s.size \,\epsilon s.vec(j) = i$$

$$p_2' = \exists j, 1 \le j \le s.size \,\epsilon s.vec(j) = 1$$
$$f_1' = s.vec(j), s.size, c: = s.vec(s.size),$$
$$s.size - 1, true$$
$$f_2' = c: = false$$

To show

$$(p_1 \to f_1 \,|\, p_2 \to f_2) \circ im$$
$$= om \circ (p_1' \to f_1' \,|\, p_2' \to f_2')$$

we must prove

$$p_i \land p_j \to f_i \circ im = om \circ f_j', 1 \le i, j \le 2$$

that is, we have to prove four equalities in all. This is as shown in the following matrix.

In this case, using the predicates and im, the crossed squares will always be false, that is, 2 out of 4 cases do not exist. Therefore, we have to show the other two, that is,

$$p_i \land p_i' \to f_i \circ im = om \circ f_i', 1 \le i \le 2$$
a. $p_1 \land p_1' \to f_1 \circ im = om \circ f_1'$

Let us start out in some concrete state S

$$f_1 \circ im = f_1(im((s.vec(1), s.vec(2), \ldots,$$
$$s.vec(s.size)), s.size), i)$$
$$= f_1(s), \text{ where } s \text{ is the set in the}$$
$$\text{abstract}$$
$$= (s - \{i\}, true)$$
$$om \circ f_1' = om(((s.vec(1). \ldots.$$
$$s.vec(size - 1),$$
$$s.size - 1,) true)$$
$$= (s - \{i\}, true)$$
b. $p_2 \land p_2' \to f_2 \circ im = om \circ f_2'$
(This is a trivial proof.)
Q.E.D.

Bit Vector Representation "delete" Proof.

$$f = [i \in s \to s, c: = s - \{i\}, true \,|\, true \to c: false]$$

$$f' = [s(i) \rightarrow s(i), c: = false, true | true$$
$$\rightarrow c: = false]$$
$$im = (nodup(s) \rightarrow s,i: = \{\ell \,|\, mi \leq \ell$$
$$\leq ma \wedge s(\ell)\}, i)$$
$$om = (nodup(s) \rightarrow s,c: = \{\ell \,|\, mi \leq \ell$$
$$\leq ma \wedge s(\ell)\}, i)$$

where $nodup(s) = (\forall(j, k), 1 \leq j, k \leq s.$
size$)$, $(j = k \vee s.vec(j) \neq s.vec(k))$
Let us rewrite $f = (p_1 \rightarrow f_1 | p_2 \rightarrow f_2)$ and f'
$= (p'_1 \rightarrow f'_1 | p'_2 \rightarrow f'_2)$
where

$$p_1 = i \in s$$
$$p_2 = i \notin s$$
$$f_1 = s,c: = s - \{i\}, true$$
$$f_2 = c: = false$$
$$p'_1 = s(i)$$
$$p'_2 = {\sim}s(i)$$
$$f_1 = s(i), c: = false, true$$
$$f'_2 = c: = false$$

To show

$$(p_1 \rightarrow f_1 | p_2 \rightarrow f_2) \circ im$$
$$= om \circ (p'_1 \rightarrow f'_1 | p'_2 \rightarrow f'_2)$$

We must prove

$$p_i \wedge p_j \rightarrow f_i \circ im = om \circ f_j, \quad 1 \leq i, j \leq 2$$

But examining im, p_1, p_2, p'_1, and p'_2, we find
that we have to only show

$$p_i \wedge p'_i \rightarrow f_i \circ im = om \circ f_i,$$
$$1 \leq i \leq 2$$
a. $p_1 \wedge p_i \rightarrow f_1 \circ im = om \circ f'_1$

Let us start out in some concrete state S

$$f_1 \circ im = f_1(im(s(mi), \ldots, s(ma)))$$
$$= f_1(s), \text{ where } s \text{ is the set in the}$$
$$\text{abstract}$$
$$= (s - \{i\}, true)$$
$$om \circ f: = om(f'_1(s(mi), \ldots, s(ma)), true)$$
$$= om(s(mi), \ldots, s(i) = false,$$
$$\ldots, s(ma)), true)$$
$$= (s - \{i\}, true)$$
b. $p_2 \wedge p'_2 \rightarrow f_2 \circ im = om \circ f'_2$
(trivial proof)
Q.E.D.

12.9. SUMMARY

We have considered the concepts of data types, data structures, and data abstractions separately. After this, we examined the relationships between data types and data structures, data structures and data abstractions, and data types and data abstractions. We then developed a unified way of looking at these concepts by creating the notion of an abstract data type. We then looked at methods for specifying, representing, and verifying data types.

Given a type specification, we showed how to carry out its design by refining data and reexpressing the functions of the type specification as functions operating on the more concrete data. The word *more* signifies that such refinements are carried out until one reaches a stage where all the data can be represented directly in terms of the data types of the implementation language being used. For example, if FORTRAN is used, one would stop when the lowest-level data are of types ARRAY, INTEGER, REAL, COMPLEX, and LOGICAL.

Once we have the representation for a type, we saw how its correctness can be checked with respect to its specifications. The concept of mapping function is crucial for type verification. Since formal verification of types gets very long and cumbersome, informal methods to verify types can be used [20]. These have the same basis as formal verification, but cut down on writing and a lot of algebraic manipulation.

REFERENCES

1. D. Knuth, *The Art of Computer Programming*, vol. 1, chap. 2, Addison-Wesley, Reading, Mass., 1972.
2. D. Parnas, "On the Criteria to be Used in Decomposing Systems into Modules," *CACM*, vol. 15, no. 2, Dec. 1972.
3. "Data: Abstraction, Definition, and Structure," *Proc. SIGPLAN/SIGMOD Conference* and *Supplement to the Proc.*, March 1976.
4. N. Wirth, "An Assessment of the Programming Language PASCAL," *Proc. of the International Conf. on Reliable Software*, Los Angeles, Apr. 1975.
5. E. W. Dijkstra, "Notes on Structured Programming," in *Structured Programming*, Academic Press, London, pp. 1–82.
6. R. C. Linger, H. Mills, and B. Witt, *Structured Pro-*

gramming: Theory and Practice, Addison-Wesley, Reading, Mass., 1979.

7. D. Parnas, "On the Design and Development of Program Families," *IEEE Transactions on Software Engineering,* SE-2, no. 1, March 1976.

8. B. Liskov et al., "Abstraction Mechanisms in CLU," *CACM,* vol. 20, no. 8, Aug. 1977.

9. B. Liskov and S. Zilles, "Specification Techniques for Data Abstractions," *IEEE Transactions on Software Engineering,* vol. SE-1, no. 1, March 1975.

10. J. Guttag, "Abstract Data Types and the Development of Data Structures," *CACM,* vol. 20, no. 6, June 1977.

11. D. Parnas, "Using Traces to Write Abstract Specifications for Software Modules," University of North Carolina, UNC Report No. TR77-012, Dec. 1977.

12. K. Jensen and N. Wirth, *PASCAL, User Manual and Report,* Springer-Verlag, 1976.

13. W. Wulf et al., "An Introduction to the Construction and Verification of Alphard Programs," *IEEE Transactions on Software Engineering,* vol. SE-2, no. 4, Dec. 1976.

14. W. Wulf et al., "An Information Definition of AL-PHARD," Carnegie Mellon University, Report CMU-CS-78-105, March 1978.

15. A. Snyder et al., "CLU Information Package," Computation Structures Group Memo 154, MIT, Nov. 1977.

16. C. A. R. Hoare, "Notes on Data Structuring," in *Structured Programming,* Academic Press, London, pp. 83–174.

17. B. H. Liskov and V. Berzins, "An Appraisal of Program Specifications," Computation Structures Group Memo 141-1, MJI, Apr. 1977.

18. J. Guttag, "Notes on Type Abstraction," *IEEE Software Engineering Transactions,* vol. SE-6, no. 1, Jan. 1980.

19. C. A. Hoare, "Proof of Correctness of Data Representations," *Acta Informatica,* vol. 1, 1972, pp. 271–281.

20. K. S. Shankar, "A Functional Approach to Module Verification," IBM FSD TR 79-0051, Gaithersburg, Md.

21. J. Spitzen and B. Wegbreit, "The Verification and Synthesis of Data Structures," *Acta Informatica,* vol. 4, 1975, pp. 127–144.

13

Data Base Management

Sakti P. Ghosh and Vincent Y. Lum
IBM Research Laboratory

13.1. INTRODUCTION

This chapter focuses on some major developments in the area of data base management systems (DBMS) for the past five years. Some of these concepts were already around in the early seventies but have established themselves firmly in DBMS in the past five years. Many concepts are in research-and-development stages and very likely will play a major role in DBMS in the future (e.g., security, locking, second generation of semantic models, distributed DBMS) but are not universally practiced at present, and so are not included. In this chapter we discuss the following topics: data base models, data base languages, access methods, data base design, and future trends. Each of these subjects contains a sufficient amount of results to cover a complete book; we shall discuss only some of the basic concepts in each area and hope this will create sufficient understanding and interest to stimulate the reader to go into the subjects in depth with the help of the cited materials.

13.2. DATA BASE MODELS

Data bases from the real world are frequently described within the framework of data models. Usually there are two classes of data models associated with data base management system software: one is referred to as the conceptual or semantic data model and the other is called the physical data model.

The conceptual model provides an environment to the user for interacting with the data base. The user can formulate his queries pertinent to the data base within the frame of the conceptual data model. Thus conceptual models are the basis for development of high-level query languages. The CODASYL [1] supporters usually refer to the conceptual model associated with the data base as the conceptual subschemas (usually an application program processes only a subset or a substructure of the data base).

The physical data model helps the data base administrator (i.e., users authorized to change the physical data) to organize the data and store them in the computer so that subsets of the data relevant to the user's request can be processed efficiently.

In the last five years the major thrust of research in the area of new concepts and software development for data base models has been focused on conceptual models rather than physical models. One of the major reasons for this is to accommodate the ever growing number of application programs directed at the data bases supported by data base management systems.

Three major types of conceptual models are widely used in data base management systems. These are the relational model, hierarchical model, and network model. The relational model is based on the concepts of relational theory and the hierarchical and network models are based on the concepts of graph theory. Each of these types of models has some advantages over the others.

There is another type of conceptual model called the entity set model, which is based on concepts of set theory. The entity set model does not have wide acceptance in the world of data base management systems, though many of its concepts are included in the query languages based on the relational, the hierarchical, and the network models. The SYSTEM 2000 (marketed by MRI Corporation [2]) and MODEL 204 (marketed by Computer Corporation of America [3]) have query languages that are based on concepts of the entity set model. In this section we discuss the basic concepts of the three major models with some citations of commercial data base management systems that make use of them. In the next section, where languages are discussed, we go into some details of DBMS.

Relational Model

The basic concepts of relational models were introduced by Codd in the early seventies. Since then, these concepts have been extended and augmented by many researchers and developers of data base management systems; today both experimental and commercial systems have been developed. In the relational model, the data are viewed as a collection of nonhierarchical time-varying relations. These are special constructs of mathematical relations and are different from the traditional data processing files and tables. This view of the data enables the user to apply the powerful operations and expressions of relational algebra to data manipulations. This model provides a means of describing data with its natural structure only, that is, without superimposing any additional structure for machine representation purposes. It provides a basis for a higher-level data language that yields maximal independence between the machine representation and organization of data. It also provides a sound basis for treating derivability, redundancy, and consistency of relations. In this model, relational algebra has been used to decompose a complex logical structure into a collection of simple relations so that complex relations of the real world can be expressed; also accessing and updating of data can be made simple and efficient.

Every relation has a unique name. In the relational model, data are viewed as an extension or intension of a table. The columns of the table contain the values of the attributes and the rows are referred to as elements of the relation and correspond to values associated with individuals in the real world; that is, a row corresponds to a record.

The columns are assigned distinct names. Each column takes values from a collection of values referred to as domain. A domain may contain more values than present in the corresponding column of the relation. The same value may appear multiple times in a column of a relation but appear only once in a domain. The degree of a relation is the number of attributes it contains.

The rows of a relation are referred to as tuples and all rows of a relation are distinct. In a relation there exists one or a collection of attributes that uniquely identify every tuple, and no subset can do the same. These attributes are called identifiers or keys. When every tuple of a relation is composed of single values from domains, then the relation is called a simple relation.

Example 1. Consider the simple relation STUDENT(SN, SA, BK#) where

$$STUDENT = \text{Name of relation}$$
$$SN = \text{Student name}$$
$$SA = \text{Student age}$$
$$BK\# = \text{Number of books belonging to a student}$$

The degree of this relation is 3. The data for this relation are given in the table shown in Figure 13.1. In this relation SN is an identifier.

If a value of a domain contains multiple types of values of a collection of domains, then the collection of domains is called a repeating group. Thus, if the STUDENT relation in Example 1 also has the domains CO = Course, and GR = Grade, then the tuple <CO,GR> forms a repeating group. Repeating groups make tabular representation difficult and are a

STUDENT(SN, SA, BK#)
Jim	16	3
Dick	17	13
Joan	16	10
Jean	18	8
Lance	16	17
Mary	17	15

Figure 13.1 A relation of degree 3.

major source of access delays for instances within repeating groups. In the relational model, this problem is eliminated by using operations of the relational calculus to create simple relational structures. These relational structures with simple domains are called first normal forms. The data represented in Example 1 are in first normal form. We shall provide here only a few examples of such relation manipulations. For further details, the reader should refer to papers written by Codd [4, 5, 6], Fagin [7, 8], Armstrong [9], and Bernstein [10]. We shall illustrate some of the relational operations using examples.

Example 2. Consider the following student-course (SC) data with a repeating group containing the domains (CO,GR,INS).

```
SC(SN,  SA, BK#, CO,  GR, INS),
    Jim  16   3    EE1  A   AJG
                   CS1  B   MJM
                   EE2  A   JBB
    Jean 18   8    EE1  B   AJG
                   EE4  A   DEK
                   CS2  A   JHD
```

where INS = Instructor.

The relation SC can be decomposed into two relations in first normal forms using projection operations on domains (SN,SA,BK#) and (SN,CO,GR,INS), respectively. The data in the two normal forms are:

```
STU(SN,  SA, BK#),
    Jim  16   3
    Jean 18   8
```

```
          COU(SN,  CO,  GR, INS),
               Jim  EE1  A   AJG
               Jim  CS1  B   MJM
               Jim  EE2  A   JBB
               Jean EE1  B   AJG
               Jean EE4  A   DEK
               Jean CS2  A   JHD
```

The identifier for the relation COU is (SN,CO).

First normal forms play a very important role in relational data bases and query languages based on them. There are three more types of normal forms, and to understand them we shall introduce the concept of functional dependency. Given a relation, if each value of an attribute, say, X, is associated precisely with one value of another attribute, say, Y, then we say that Y is functionally dependent on X. Functional dependence plays an important role in understanding the semantics of the data. The users of relational data bases usually decompose and recompose relations to express their requests (which includes insertion, deletion, and updating of tuples and domains) and achieve fast response. Thus, functional dependencies, as characterized through the different normal forms, dictate to the user what type of operations can be performed without destroying the semantics of the data. Functional dependence between attributes are also referred to as dependence. If the functional dependency between a set of attributes is transitive, then it is referred to as transative dependency. Because of a lack of space, only definitions of the normal forms will be stated here; for further details, the reader should refer to Ghosh [11] and Date [12].

A relation is in the second normal form if it is in the first normal form and has no dependency among the nonkey attributes.

A relation is in the third normal form if it is in the second normal form and there is no transitive dependency of any nonkey domain on a key domain.

A relation is in the fourth normal form if it is in the third normal form and, assuming there exists any multivalue dependency of an attribute, say, X, on attribute Y, if all attributes of the relation are functionally dependent on Y.

Few data base management systems based on relational models are currently available to the data base research community. The better known of these are: SYSTEM R [13] developed by IBM Research Lab at San Jose, the INGRES [14] system developed by University of California at Berkeley, the ADABAS [15] developed by Software AG, MAGNUM [16] by Tymshare, and ADL [17] by IBM.

Hierarchical Model

In the hierarchical model, data are viewed as a collection of relations (also called segments) that form a hierarchical relation.

A hierarchical relation is defined as a collection of relations that are connected together as a hierarchical tree (see Knuth [18]) by logical associations (i.e., a fan structure)—the hierarchical relation in a family tree. Each segment contains multiple instances; hence, even if the segments are connected as a chain by logical associations, the instance structure can be a fan structure with multiple branches. These logical associations are directional associations, the segment pointed to by the logical association is referred to as the child segment (referred to as member record type by CODASYL DBTG) [1] and the other segment is called the parent segment (owner record type according to DBTG).

Example 3. Consider the two segments with student enrollment as the logical association. The faculty segment is the parent segment and the student segment is the child segment. Suppose two students, John and Mary, are enrolled in courses taught by faculty Joan. Then the logical association between these instances will be represented as shown in Figure 13.2.

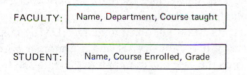

Though we have not shown it in this example, in general, the segments themselves could form a tree with multiple levels and multiple branches at each level.

The segment without a parent is called the root and the segments that have no children are called the leaves of the hierarchical model.

The hierarchical models are widely used as semantic models in practice because many real-world phenomenon are hierarchical in nature, for instance, administrative structures, biological structures, political and social struc-

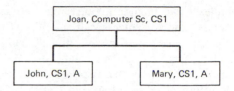

Figure 13.2. An instance of hierarchical relation.

tures. The hierarchical model is also widely used as a physical model because of the inherent hierarchical structure of the disk storage system, e.g. tracks, cylinders, disk packs, and so on.

Some commercial DBMSs, like IMB [19] and SYSTEM 2000 [2], are based on hierarchical models and have contributed to the wide popularity of this model. NOMAD [20] by NCSS is a recent system.

Network Model

A network model is the generalization of the hierarchical model. In the network model, a segment can have multiple parent segments. In general, the segments are grouped as levels but logical associations can exist between segments belonging to any level. Although the logical associations are directional in nature, any two levels can have both types of directional associations. In general, many-to-many logical associations can exist between any two segments and also their instances. The diagramatic representation of the different logical associations between the segments resembles a graph. In general, these logical associations between instances are implemented by pointers in the data set or by creating connecting relations that reflect the many-to-many associations between the instances.

Example 4. Consider the two segments of Example 3 and suppose that student John takes courses both in the computer science and electric engineering departments. That student instance will have at least two parent instances. Thus, the relation between the instances of the student and faculty segments is no longer hierarchical but a network.

This network model becomes even more

complex if we include another segment, say, 'Courses' and logical associations, like, 'Students Enrolled in Courses' and 'Faculties Teaching Courses'. In this extended model, a Student can be logically associated with multiple instances of Faculties and Courses. The same type of association can exist between the instances of the other segments.

The network models are used as semantic models rather than physical models because of their complexity. The network model was developed by the CODASYL's data base taskforce group (DBTG) [1], which has contributed to its wide familiarity. DBTG has developed in detail most of the concepts and techniques needed to build a DBMS based on a network model. The reader should refer to the DBTG report for details of one approach to implementation of the network model. The main contribution of the DBTG is the development of a systematic approach to describing, manipulating, and navigating through data with a network structure. Prior to their contribution it was extremely difficult to build a DBMS based on a network model. They introduced concepts like data definition language (DDL), data manipulation language (DML), and data navigational operators. Users of databases can define very complex real-world data structures using DDL. DML can be used to manipulate data to create complex structures suitable for a class of application programs. The navigational operators can be used in the application programs for navigating the search for data required by the programs. Because of space constraints, details of these concepts are omitted.

One main advantage of the network model is that it can capture complex views of the real world. This vastly increases, over the relational and hierarchical model, the class of applications programs that can be supported by DBMS. If properly used, this model is capable of supporting multiple views (subschemas) with very little increase in storage space. The model is complex and still very few users are good at using a substantial number of its features.

Some of the commercially available DBMSs based on the DBTG report are TOTAL (prod-

uct of Cincom Systems Inc.), IDMS (marketed by Cullinane Corp.), and EDMS (developed by Xerox Corp).

Second Generation of Models

In the past five years, researchers have been developing extensions of the existing models to accommodate new demands like consistency, integrity, security, authorization, and decentralization from DBMS. These models are in the early stages of development and because of lack of space, they will not be discussed here. The interested reader should find most of the materials in the New Orleans Data Base Design Workshop Report [21].

13.3. DATA BASE LANGUAGE

Development of data base models and high-level data base languages has been proceeding in parallel. The CODYSAL DBTG's recommendations started the trend to categorize data base languages into four subclasses, namely, DDL, DML, Query Language, and Data Access Control Language. Some DBMSs have the support of all four types of data base sublanguages; others a smaller subset. System R supports all four types.

Data Definition Language (DDL) consists of a vocabulary set and a grammar with which the user can define the data structure of the schema or subschema.

Data Manipulation Language (DML) consists of a vocabulary set and a grammar with which the user can manipulate the data set, for instance, insertion or deletion of instances in the data set.

Query Language (QL) is that subset of the data language with which the user can communicate to the DBMS the request to retrieve subsets of a data set.

Data Access Control Language (DACL) is the set of commands and sentences of the data languages with which the user can control access to the data sets.

SQL [22] is the data language associated with System R [13] and has all four sublanguages. SQL will be discussed in some detail here. QUEL is the data language for INGRES

[14] and is largely similar to SQL. QBE [22] is also a language based on a relational model but the interface with the user is a pictorial language. We shall discuss this language also. DL1 is a command type of sublanguage for communicating with IMS [19], which is imbedded in a host language. DEFINE is a DDL, and CONVERT is a DML of XPRS [26] which is based on a hierarchical model. We shall discuss only some features of these languages.

Structured English Query Language

Structured English Query Language (SQL) [23] was developed at IBM's Research Laboratory in San Jose. It is an external interface to SYSTEM R. It is based on relations in first normal form. It can be used for query, data manipulation, data definition, and data control. Statements written in SQL can be compiled into the host language by System R. We shall use a classical example to illustrate the different concepts of SQL.

Query Language Facilities.

Example 5. Consider the four relations shown in Figure 13.3.

The most important basic operation of SQL is mapping. It uses a known quantity (e.g., JOB = CLERK) to translate into a desired quantity (e.g., EMPNAME).

Q1. Find the names of the employees who are clerks.

        SELECT EMPNAME
        FROM   EMP
        WHERE JOB = 'CLERK'

In SQL it is possible to construct nested mapping, which is illustrated in the next query.

Q2. Find the names of all employees in the computer science department.

    SELECT EMPNAME
    FROM   EMP
    WHERE   DNO IN
            SELECT DNO
            FROM DEPT
            WHERE DEPTNAME =
            'COMPUTER SCIENCE'

One important feature of SQL is the capability to join two relations on the basis of values of two attributes from the two relations. This feature is reflected in Q2, where instances of relations EMP and DEPT are joined together if they have the same value of the attribute DNO.

The user can request the output to be ordered as in the following query.

Q3. List all the employee names, their jobs, and salaries from the computer science department in order of their salaries.

    SELECT   EMPNAME,JOB,SAL
    FROM   EMP
    WHERE   DEPTNAME = 'COMPUTER
                              SCIENCE'
    ORDER   BY SAL

The instances of a relation can be partitioned into groups according to the values of an attribute using GROUPD BY as shown in the next example.

Q4. List all departments and their managers.

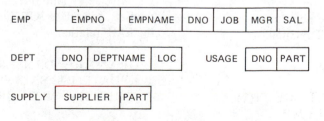

Figure 13.3. Four relations.

```
SELECT DNO,MGR
FROM EMP
GROUPD BY DNO
```

SQL has many built-in set functions, for instance, AVG,SUM,COUNT,MAX, and MIN. The next example illustrates the use of one of them.

Q5. Find the number of departments in San Jose.

```
SELECT COUNT(DNO)
FROM   DEPT
WHERE LOC = 'SAN JOSE'
```

SQL has many other query features, and the reader should refer to the cited materials.

Data Manipulation Facilities. Data manipulation includes insertion, deletion, update, and assignment. Insertion capability enables the user to insert new tuples into a relation, as shown in the next example.

M1. Insert the record of a new employee with employee number '246', name 'Mary' and department 'K53' in the relation EMP.

```
INSERT INTO
        EMP(ENO,EMPNAME,DNO);
        ⟨246,'MARY',K53⟩
```

Deletion, update, and assertion are shown next.

M2. Delete the employee records of 'JIM' from relation EMP

```
DELETE EMP
WHERE EMPNAME = 'JIM'
```

M3. Delete all the departments with no employees from DEPT relation.

```
DELETE DEPT X
WHERE
        (SELECT COUNT(*)
        FROM EMP
        WHERE DNO = X.DNO) = 0
```

M4. Update the EMP relation by giving all research employees a 10 salary raise.

```
UPDATE EMP
SET   SAL = SAL*1.1
WHERE JOB = RESEARCH
```

M5. Create a new relation named MANAGER with employee number, employee name, department, and salary.

```
ASSIGN TO MANAGER
  (EMPNO,EMPNAME,DEPT,SALARY):
SELECT EMPNO,EMPNAME,DNO,SAL
FROM EMP
WHERE EMPNO IN
      SELECT MGR
      FROM EMP
```

Data Definition Facilities. This facility is used to create and drop relations, define alternate subschemas of relations and specify the access aids, for instance, indices, as shown next.

D1. Create the supply relation.

```
CREATE TABLE SUPPLY
    (SUPPLIER(CHAR(20),NONULL),
      PART(CHAR(7))
```

Data Control Facilities. Data control facilities enable the user to exercise control over the integrity of data values and usage of the data by other users. In SQL a user may authorize access control to his data or view (subschema) using the GRANT command. The privileges include: READ, INSERT, DELETE, UPDATE (by column), EXPAND, IMAGE (to define subschemas on relation), LINK (to create links on relation), CONTROL, and so forth. The following is an example.

C1. Give Jerry and Jim the privilege to read, to insert, to update JOB and SAL columns on the EMP relation.

```
GRANT READ,INSERT,
UPDATE(JOB,SAL) ON EMP TO
JERRY,JIM WITH GRANT OPTION
```

REVOKE and ASSERT are similar.

TYPE	ITEM	COLOR	SIZE
	P.	P.	P.

Figure 13.5. Simple retrieval with multiple prints.

Query by Example

QBE [22] is a graphic language in which the programmer communicates with the system using two dimensional skeleton tables. This is accomplished by filling in the appropriate table space with examples of solutions and commands. The syntax of the system can distinguish between a constant element and an example element. As before, we shall introduce the concepts of the language using two classic examples of tables.

SALES (DEPT,ITEM)
TYPE (ITEM,COLOR,SIZE)

Initially the system displays a table skeleton to the user and the user has to fill in the name of a table present in the system. Then the system displays the table with all its columns. Suppose we are using the table TYPE. Then the user expresses the query making entries as shown in Figure 13.4.

The P. in a column indicates that the values of that column are output and are to be printed. BOOK is an example element and is underlined. It could be a possible answer. RED is a constant element that represents the required condition in the query and is not underlined. This diagram in QBE represents a query to find and print all red items such as BOOK. BOOK may not exist in the data base. The example element is to help the user to formulate his request; it may or may not be present in a diagram. The diagram represented in Figure 13.4 is referred to as simple retrieval. QBE also has the capability of specifying ordering of the output; this is achieved by typing AO (for ascending ordering) and DO (for descending ordering) after "P.". Multiple columns can be printed by inserting "P." in each column, as in Figure 13.5. This type of retrieval is also referred to as simple retrieval with multiple prints.

Figure 13.5 is also equivalent to printing the whole table, which could have been achieved by typing "P." only in the column for TYPE.

The qualification for retrieval can be prefixed with comparison operators, for example, $>$, $>=$, $<$, $<=$, and so on. These types of queries are referred to as qualified retrieval. Figure 13.6 illustrates the request for printing the items whose size is greater than 10 and that have the color RED.

An example element can be partially underlined to achieve the effect of a constant element for a string of characters. In Figure 13.7 all items whose color starts with D will be printed.

Similarly, QBE has many other capabilities including qualified retrieval using links, insertion, deletion, updates, and so forth. For details please refer to the cited publications [22].

Define

DEFINE is the DDL associated with Data Base Restructuring System [24] developed at IBM Research Laboratory in San Jose. It is designed to describe hierarchical data sets but relational data sets can also be defined. We shall give an example to illustrate how a hierarchical structure is defined in this language. Consider the hierarchical structure of Figure 13.8.

DEFINE has the capability to describe both a source file and a target file. Figure 13.9

TYPE	ITEM	COLOR	SIZE
	P.BOOK	RED	

Figure 13.4. Column headings and entries for display of red items.

TYPE	ITEM	COLOR	SIZE
	P.	RED	> 10

Figure 13.6. Qualified retrieval.

TYPE	ITEM	COLOR	SIZE
	P.	DRED	

Figure 13.7. Partially underlined qualified retrieval.

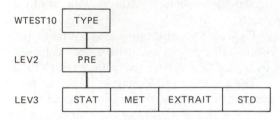

Figure 13.8. A hierarchical schema.

shows a DEFINE description for a target file. Each group is equivalent to a segment. It shows DEFINE's capability of creating new items (e.g., SEGCOD) and assigning values to them. The WRITE statement indicates when an instance of a segment is to be written out as a physical record. Thus, in this description every segment instance is written out as a separate record. DEFINE has many other capabilities, given in Reference 24.

Convert

CONVERT [25] is the DML associated with XPRS [26] and is used to manipulate data structures. It has the following commands:

SELECT - for selecting any qualified instances.
SLICE - for converting a hierarchical structure into a relation.
GRAFT - for grafting two structures.
MERGE - for merging two files.
SORT - for sorting a file.
ELIM-DUP - for eliminating duplicate records from a file.

```
DATA DESCRIPTION:
   TARGET FILE DESCRIPTION(WTEST10):
   GROUP WTEST10 :
        SEGCOD:            CHAR(2); ASSIGN '01';;
        TYPE:              CHAR(5);;
        WRITE;
        GROUP LEV2 :
          SEGCOD:          CHAR(2); ASSIGN '02';;
          PRE:             DEC(8,3);;
          WRITE;
          GROUP LEV3:
            SEGCOD:        CHAR(2); ASSIGN '03';;
            STAT:          CHAR(1);;
            MET:           BIT(4);
                           TRANSLATE (BIT'1010' TO BIT'1111'),
                             (BIT'1011' TO BIT'1111') ;;
            EXTRAIT:       BIT(4); ASSIGN BIT'1011';;
            STD:           CHAR(6);;
            WRITE;
          END LEV3;
        END LEV2;
      END WTEST10;
      END FILE WTEST10;
    END DATA DESCRIPTION;
```

Figure 13.9. Definition of a hierarchical data set in DEFINE.

CONSOLIDATE - for converting a relational data set into a hierarchical structure.

It also has built-in set functions such as SUM, MAX, MIN, AVG, COUNT. These commands can be used to manipulate data sets to create many different structures. We encourage interested readers to refer to the cited materials [24, 25, 26].

Data Base Task Group Data Language

The DBTG specifications describe an extensive data sublanguage for manipulating and retrieving data from a network structure. Their sublanguage is capable of accommodating a dynamic environment where data are being continually modified. It keeps track of the most recently accessed record occurrence, no matter what its type is, and is referred to as the *current of run-unit*. Some of the major DML statements used are given here.

FIND - locates an existing record occurrence and establishes it as the current of run-unit.

GET - retrieves the current of run-unit.

MODIFY—updates the current of run-unit.

CONNECT - inserts the current of run-unit into one or more set occurrences.

DISCONNECT - removes the current of run-unit from one or more set occurrences.

ERASE - deletes the current of run-unit.

STORE - Creates a new record occurrence and establishes it as the current of run-unit.

DL/1

The data base navigational language associated with IBM's IMS system [19] is called DL/1. The commands of this language are aimed at navigating through a hierarchical structured data base. This language is widely used by IMS users but is not popular with other users. Some of the major DML commands of this language are given here. Each of these commands can contain qualifiers based on segment names and values of attributes.

GU (Get Unique) - retrieves a unique instance that satisfies the qualifications.

GN (Get Next) - retrieves the next instance (in the hierarchical linear order) that satisfies the qualifications.

GNP (Get Next within Parent) - similar to GN but confines the search within an established parent instance.

INSERT - for insertion of instances.

DELETE - for deletion of instances.

REPLACE - for modification of instances.

DL/1 has many other facilities, and the interested reader is advised to read the IMS reference manuals.

13.4. DATA BASE ACCESS TECHNIQUES

A key component in any data base management system lies in its accessing the module (i.e., a collection of bytes that are accessed as an unit), because a system's performance depends on the implementation of the appropriate techniques to handle the accesses to its data.

Basic Access Techniques

Basically, there are four methods of accessing stored data: (1) serial or sequential accessing, (2) binary search, (3) indexed accessing, and (4) random accessing. We discuss each of these in turn.

Serial or Sequential Search. Sequential search is the oldest of all the access techniques in searching data in storage. When computers became broadly available for applications, the main mass storage device was tapes. The nature of this physical storage device necessitated the data to be stored and searched sequentially. As technology progressed, the principal mass storage device shifted to disk. Nevertheless, tapes remain a popular storage device today. Sequential search, however, can be applied to both tapes and disks and frequently is still the best technique to use in spite of its inflexible characteristics.

As shown in Figure 13.10a, the data, represented as records R1, R2, R3 . . . are stored in a device. To access any data record, say R5, one must first access R1, R2, R3, R4, and then R5, in that order. No record before R5 can be skipped. It is obvious that if the desired record is stored at the end of the file, one must read the whole file to get the record.

Due to the conceptual simplicity of this method one can easily see that the time to get to a particular record is equal to the time to read all the records stored before it. Physical storage devices are such that it takes a great deal more time to position the read head than to transmit the data; hence, the data records are usually blocked together to form a bigger physical record so that each time a read head is positioned, several records will be transmitted into a buffer where each record will then be searched sequentially. Apparently there is a trade off between the size of the block and the speed of accessing the data. Much earlier work in computer research was devoted to understanding these trade-offs among devices.

What about writing a record into a sequential file? The structure does not allow writing a record into the middle of the file, so in order to insert a record, one can either write the record at the end of the file, or one can copy all the records before the new record, then write the new record and copy over the rest of the file. For example, suppose that one wishes to write record RI between records R5 and R6. It becomes necessary to copy record R1, . . . , R5 onto a new file. Write record RI, and copy the rest of the records, namely R6, . . . from the original file. One can see that this access method is indeed totally inflexible in handling insertion of records.

A sequential file may be sorted with respect to a particular field. The advantage of having a sorted file is that in searching for a record with a given value in the sorted field, one does not have to search the whole file to determine whether that record is present. Assuming the file is sorted in ascending order, one needs only to search till the contained field value is larger than the given one, to be assured that no further search will be useful, as shown in Figure 13.10b.

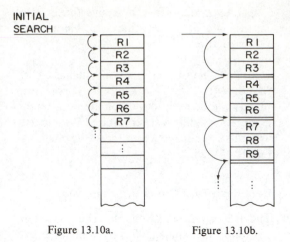

Figure 13.10a.   Figure 13.10b.

Refinement of this search technique to reduce average search time is possible. For example, having records most frequently searched at the beginning of the file will improve performance. Reference 19 goes into some detailed analysis of these aspects.

Binary Search. When a set of records are sorted in order with respect to a particular key field f and if the characteristics of the storage device permit random accessing of the stored data, one can use binary search to reduce the search time required to get the desired record. Basically, this method works as follows: As shown in Figure 13.11, suppose that record R with key ki is to be fetched. One goes first to the middle of the file to get the key of that record to compare it with ki. Assuming that the file is ordered in ascending order, the first step of finding k < ki leads us to the second step which is mid-way between the first step and the rest of the file. Again k < ki leads us to step 3. Having k > ki in step 3, it now becomes necessary to search backward at the midpoint between step 2 and 3, and one finally finds a match at step 5.

Binary search in itself is very inefficient with today's mass storage devices. However, the idea of dividing data into two halves at any time has useful applications, namely, in organizing binary search trees. A binary search tree, in the context of 'key search', is the graphic representation of a binary search. It is easy to see that the outcome of a comparison

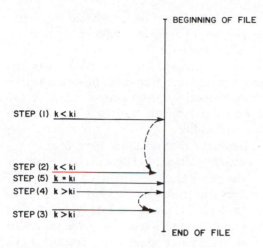

Figure 13.11.

between the sought key and the key in the accessed position is binary. Thus, binary search is analogous to tracing a path in a binary tree (for details see Ghosh's book [11]). The search algorithm for a binary tree is referred to as a binary search algorithm. A complete binary search tree has $2**M - 1$ nodes, where M is an integer. The number of comparisons needed to locate a key or decide that the sought key is not present in the list can vary between 1 and M. The number of comparisons in a binary search is also referred to as the path length of the search because it is similar to the path of a binary tree. The path length (or average path length) is often used as a measure to determine the goodness of a binary search algorithm. Ghosh's book [11] has an extensive discussion on the subject, and interested readers are invited to refer to it.

Indexed Search. Indexed search, which is frequently referred to as indexed sequential search, is the most versatile method in data search. It attempts to overcome the inflexibility of the sequential method and takes advantage of the directional capability in the binary search. Further, it has an inherent characteristic that allows an implementation to capitalize on the characteristics of today's principal storage devices, namely disks or devices with similar characteristics. The method works similar to the way we find information from a department store catalog, that is, one first finds

the subject index to determine the page to look for the desired item.

Let us suppose that a field f is the identifier of a record; that is, given a value of this field, there is a unique record in the file associated with this value. This field shall be referred to as the key field or the primary index field. To be more specific, let us suppose that this key field is the customer number assigned to a customer in a department store. To see how this search method works, we shall first construct an indexed sequential file via the department customer example (Figure 13.12).

First the customer file is sorted according to the key field, namely customer number, and is stored as a sequential file. Further, suppose that this file is blocked so that three customer records can be stored in each block. Let us extract the highest key value in each block, called the index value, namely 15, 24, 35, . . . , 76. For each of these numbers, we add a pointer to it so that the pointer points to the block containing this index value. Let us now store this index file as a sequential file. Further, suppose that this index file is blocked so that two index value-pointer pairs can be stored in a block. We repeat the process by extracting the highest value from each index block, that is, 24, 45, and 76 and associate with each a pointer that points to the appropriate index block. We again store the newly created

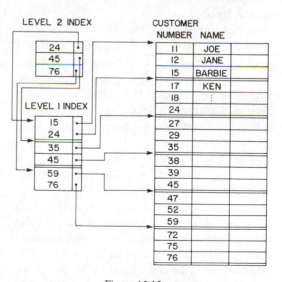

Figure 13.12.

index file as another sequential file. The end result of this process is that we have created three sequential files such that each one is smaller than the previous one, and they are connected in one direction by pointers. We have, in effect, created an indexed search structure for the customer file. We shall refer to the index file to customer file as the *level 1 index file,* and the index file to the level 1 index file, the *level 2 index file* (Figure 13.12).

We shall now examine how this search method works. Suppose that one wishes to find customer number 29. From the level 2 index file, a sequential search indicates that 29 is larger than 24 but smaller than 45. Hence, we follow the pointer associated with 45 to get us to the second block of the level 1 index file. From this block it is seen that 29 is less than 35. Hence, by following the pointer associated with 35, we get to the third block in the customer file. A sequential search of that block will locate the appropriate record.

Examining the steps that led us into creating the indexed search structure, it is apparent that a great number of variations can be applied. For example, one may have the customer file unblocked so that the level 1 index file will point to the exact location of the desired record. One may block the level 1 index in any size. One may create a large number of index files or very few index files. The following analysis helps to gain insight in the selection of levels.

Let us consider that these files are stored on disks. Disk search generally requires a position seek time to move the arm, latency time to position the head at the right spot on a track, and the time to transfer the data. Thus, even though a pointer indicates the exact location where the desired data are stored, the time to get to that data can be substantial. Further it is generally true that data transfer time is much less than seek time. Thus, if one builds an extra level of index, one must be sure that the gain outweighs the cost. A rule of thumb is to check if the time required to transfer the data in the nth level index file is much less than the seek and latency time of the device. Another factor to be considered is the size of an index file. If at any time an entire index file

can be read into a buffer without significant impact on the available buffer space, then one should not consider having another level of an index. In general, there should be very few index levels since each index block can store a large number of index-pointer pairs. A two level index structure can handle millions of records readily.

Indexed search methods have been implemented by software builders to take advantage of the physical characteristics of the storage devices. For example, the IBM ISAM access method (see Ghosh's book [11] for details) was implemented in such a way that the lowest level of the index points to the track in a cylinder where the desired data reside. The second level index file points to the cylinder where the data reside. Moreover, the track index file or the level 1 index file resides at the first track of the cylinder where the desired data are located. In this manner, when the device has accessed the track index, no further seek or arm movement is needed to get the data.

Suppose that one wishes to insert a customer record whose customer number is 31. It has been said that in a sequential file, if the sequence is to be kept, then the rest of the file containing items larger than the key to be inserted must be written over. This is an expensive operation. To avoid this, one can write the record in an overflow area and write a pointer in the record that is its predecessor—for example, the record whose customer number is 29 in this case (Figure 13.13). Subsequently records with keys equal to 73 and 33 are inserted. A pointer structure as shown in the diagram illustrates one possible way of accommodating the newcomers.

A question arises at this time, as to what to do if key 26 is to be inserted. One has at least two options: (1) Write a record whose key is 27 into an overflow area and write 26 in its place, or (2) write the new record in an overflow area with a pointer constructed in the record with key value 24 and pointing to the newcomer's record. At the same time change all the index files as needed to reflect the current status. The first option is more favorable as it requires less disturbance because two writes will always achieve the end result.

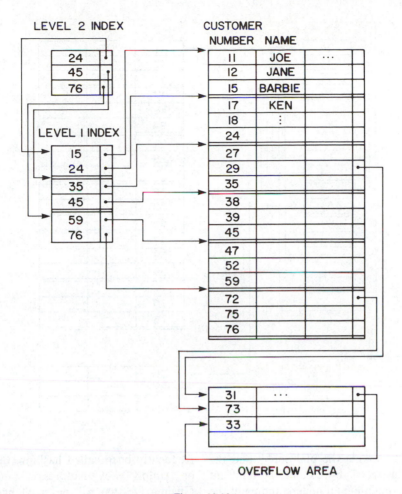

Figure 13.13.

One can see that such an insertion scheme can and will cause degradation in performance if a large number of records have been inserted. The reason is that under such circumstances, long chains necessitating long searches will be required. One strategy to avoid this is to create new blocks and new index entries to preserve the capability of an immediate access to data without going through a long chain. For example, suppose that a record with a key 31 is to be inserted. One can split the records to be stored into two blocks and split also the level 1 index file blocks as needed and update higher-level index files (Figure 13.14). By successively splitting the blocks as data records are inserted, one maintains the advantage of being able to immediately access the data records from the

index search. This strategy and philosophy is adopted in the IBM-VSAM and other vendors' access methods.

By now readers can see that there should be a variety of options and strategies that can be tailored to many devices to maximize the gains. For example, though storage may be relatively inexpensive, yet by customizing a device, substantial storage space saving is possible. On the opposite side of the coin, one may also use storage space to compensate for performance. For example, by repeating the same data on a track, one can reduce latency time, which is always substantial, in a random search of a record. Thus, some access methods have been implemented to replicate index file data within a track to strategically reduce access time. While the variations of indexed

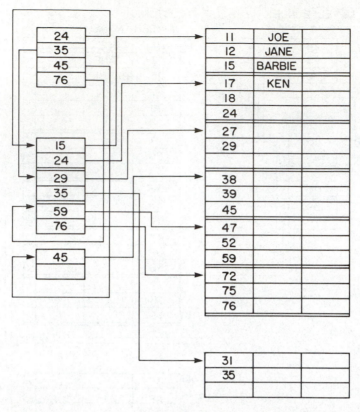

Figure 13.14.

search can be many, the philosophy and the strategies illustrated above should be sufficient to provide a fundamental understanding of the indexed search operations.

Direct Access.   Given an address on a device, one can directly access the data stored on that address. However, in normal data processing, one rarely starts with an address to retrieve the data. One frequently is given the key of a record and is required to find the data associated with that key. For example, a customer may wish to inquire about his bill which contains his customer number. The computer must then search for his record via this number. In this case, while an indexed search structure may be sufficient to do the job, it does require multiple searches to get to the data. An alternative method may reduce the number of searches in this situation.

Simply stated, the problem is to find a way of converting a key value into an address so that the data are found in that address. The process of converting this key to an address has

frequently been called hashing, randomizing, or simply key-to-address transformation. Given a file that will never change, a unique set of key values can be converted mathematically to a unique set of addresses so that each record can be retrieved in one access. For a dynamic file that will have insertion and deletion activities, there does not exist any solution that will preserve this property. This means, then, that given two distinct key values, a method may map these two keys to the same address. Thus we now have two problems: (1) to find a method that will give us the least likelihood of mapping two distinct key values to the same address, and (2) when two key values are mapped to the same address, a storage strategy is to be developed to preserve the overall good performance. We shall first discuss a few common hashing techniques and then the storage strategy (all of these methods are given in details in Ghosh's book [11]).

Division Hashing.   In this method, the given value of the key, whether numeric or alphanumeric, is treated as a number and is divided by another number approximately equal to the number of addresses used to hold the file. The remainder from the division is taken to be the address for this particular record key.

Thus if a file has 80 records and a key value is 507, one may choose a divisor equal to 83. In this case the address obtained is equal to 9.

Mid-Square Method.   The key value is multiplied by itself and the middle portion of the digits are kept as the address for that key. For example, with key value of 507, we have 507 times 507 equals 257049. Again suppose we have 80 records in this file. We shall keep the 3d and 4th digits from the right as an address and obtain a value of 70. Note that because two digits can give us more than 80 addresses, we may need to do another simple division to get to an acceptable address.

Shifting Method.   The length of a key is partitioned into sections, each of which is equal to the address length or less. Shift the sections to slide on top of each other and the results are added with or without carry. For example, with the number of addresses equal to 80, a key 71256 can be partitioned into 7 | 12 | 56 and shifting and adding we have

$$
\begin{array}{r}
56 \\
12 \\
\underline{07} \\
75
\end{array}
$$

The address will now become 75.

By now it should become obvious that one can almost arbitrarily invent any number of hashing methods. Indeed, there has been proposed a large number of such methods, including some where very sophisticated mathematics have been employed. Experimental and analytical results seem to indicate that the division method seems to provide very good performance in general. However, when using the division method, one must be careful to avoid using division that contains small prime numbers. Of course, the best way to choose a transformation is to actually take the key set, apply the hashing techniques and observe the result, as each method may provide a better perfor-

mance for a particular key distribution. Unfortunately, in practice, this is frequently not possible as the key sets may not be available.

As stated earlier, distinct keys may not produce distinct addresses. When the keys are hashed to the same address, it is called a collision and will produce overflow, as in the indexed search method. The number of methods proposed to handle overflows is almost as varied as the number of hashing techniques. Basically they fall into two categories: (1) store the overflow in the same storage area with all the rest of the records, or (2) set aside a separate area and put the overflow records in that area.

Within each category there are a large number of variations. The simplest of the first is open addressing where the overflow record is stored in the next address location if it is empty. If occupied, proceed to search for the next address and so on until the nearest empty address is found; the record will be stored there. If a group of records are mapped to a few consecutive locations, it becomes obvious that significant degradation in performance will occur because we have now a compounding effect. Thus methods have been proposed to store in addresses other than the adjacent spaces. Essentially these techniques propose to skip a number of addresses each time an empty address is being searched. The number of skips can be a function of the key or its hashed address or both. This alternative will alleviate the overflow problem.

If an overflow record is to be stored in a separate overflow area, chaining is usually used in that a pointer is stored in the home address to indicate where the overflow record is stored. If a second overflow record comes to the same address, it will be stored in the overflow area and a pointer is stored in the first overflow record to indicate the location of the second overflow record. Again, many variations of this scheme have been proposed to shorten the possibility of long chains.

A question may be raised concerning the performance of the hashing schemes in accessing records. Generally speaking, their performance can be considered good but not usually in one access. However, there are techniques that will help to produce results close to a single access per record. The two main factors that help in this respect are the loading factor and the bucket size. *Loading factor* is the ratio of records in the file to the records that can be stored in the address or storage space. A small loading factor, therefore, means more free space for future addition of records and decreases the chance of collisions and overflow conflicts. That is, because we have more space than needed, chances are that we do not find as many records all hashed to the same address. A rule of thumb in the selection of loading factor is to set it around 0.7 to 0.8. If performance is crucial, a smaller loading factor may have to be selected.

Bucket size is the number of records that can be stored in an address. If more than one record can be stored in the same address, then records with different keys hashed to the same address will not have to be moved to an overflow area. This obviously reduces the average number of accesses per record and thus improves performance. However, if bucket size is too large, then data transfer time will become a problem. It will contribute to the degradation of performance because each access now will have an additional overhead of transfering additional data that are not needed. This is particularly crucial if the record size is large. In general, an address should at least hold several records, and more if record size is small.

By adjusting the loading factor and bucket size, and by selecting appropriate hashing and overflow handling methods, one can get close to one access per record using hashing techniques.

In recent years, researchers have invented some new KAT techniques, referred to as extendible hashing (Fagin & Nievergelt [8]), virtual hashing (Litwin [27]), universal hashing (Carter & Wegman [28]), and so on.

Selection of Access Methods

Of the four basic access schemes discussed, binary search is the least useful for secondary storage, but is useful for in-core search. Binary tree organization, however, has found applications in storage devices, particularly for index file organization. Sequential search, though inflexible, is still used very frequently.

Three major reasons account for this phenomenon. First, in spite of the advances in storage devices, tape is still used widely. Second, many applications are naturally oriented to sequential processing. For example, customer billing processing in a utility company falls into this category. Third, if one is required to process more than 10 of the records in a file, sequential accessing may actually require less time than random or indexed accessing.

At the opposite end of the spectrum from sequential search is direct search. This method in reality is also inflexible because it is very inefficient to do sequential processing when an application demands it. Does this mean that one should always use the indexed search method? The answer is definitely *no*. Most DBMSs including major systems like IMS [19], System 2000 [2], and so forth, tend to use a combination of different access methods to their advantage. They frequently combine the different basic access schemes to form new access methods for storing users' data. For example, in IMS, a combination of indexed and sequential search techniques is used to create HISAM. At the same time, the system supports a modified random access method known as HDAM.

Not only do data base management systems permit different methods of accessing user data, they also use the same basic access techniques to manage their own data. For example, a data base system must store information to indicate where a user file is stored. To do this, an index file, known frequently as the directory, is created. If the directory is small, a sequential organization may be best. If the directory is large, then an indexed structure on a binary tree can be used to advantage. This data access structure is widely referred to as the B-tree [18]. The main advantage of B-trees is that insertion of data instances can be achieved with minimum difficulty. This latter technique is the way System R [13] has managed its directories and indexes.

Chaining

In the discussion of access methods, chaining was incidentally mentioned. Chaining is accomplished by including pointers with the data to indicate where to go next. In practice, chaining is used broadly. Nearly all data base management systems employ chains in one way or another. For example, IMS (21), System R [13], and System 2000 [2], ADABAS [15], and so on, all use pointers to create chains.

Why are chains so popular? The basic reason is that records can only be stored physically in a sequential manner with respect to only one field. Chaining is a mechanism that makes possible another sequence of search with respect to another field. A specific application of chains, for example, occurs in DBTG systems where rings or networks are created.

Secondary Index Structure

Secondary index files, also sometimes referred to as inverted index files, are broadly used in many DBMS systems. Some applications of secondary index files are discussed first.

In the discussion of indexed search, we showed how index files on a key field can be created to facilitate data search when a key value is given. However, suppose that in the organization of Figure 13.12 we wish to look for customer records that contain the name Jane. How are we to find such records? With nothing more than what has been shown in Figure 13.12, one will have to search the whole data file to find those records. Obviously this is a time consuming and expensive practice. To facilitate searches of this kind, secondary files are created.

In Figure 13.15, an index file on customer name is constructed. This file is very much like the index file on customer number and can have many levels. However, since the field may contain the value Jane in many records, the physical structure of this index file may be slightly different. For each value entry in the index file many pointers may have to be created, one for each record or block where the customer name is Jane. In this manner, the search when value "Jane" is given requires only the need to access the relevant data by first going to the index file and then following the pointers to the records where the data Jane will be found.

Secondary index file organization is a very powerful method for data search. Nearly all modern DBMS employ such a method. For example, System 2000 [2], IMS [19], ADABAS [15], System R [13], and so forth, all support secondary index search. Since basically the structure of secondary index files need not be different from the key or primary index file, some systems like System R do not make a distinction between primary and secondary index files.

Although the concept of secondary index file is simple, the method of selecting the field to be indexed is not. An index file occupies only a fraction of the space needed to store the data file, but a complete inversion (i.e., an index on every field) will generally require many times the space needed for the data file. This generally causes degradation in performance and is not tolerable. The subject has been the target of many research papers in recent years.

13.5. DATA BASE DESIGN

Although data base applications have been in existence for more than a decade, advances in techniques for data base design have not kept pace with the advances in DBMS development and their applications. As data base applications become more prevalent and more complex, problems in designing a data base to support the applications become more difficult. Furthermore, as end users of the data bases become more sophisticated, they place additional demands on design issues like integrity and consistency, which in earlier days were ignored, but now are an integral part of the design requirements.

Traditionally data base design has been separated into logical and physical design. Logical design covers that part of the design process wherein one designs a data base without the constraint of a DBMS and its storage and access techniques. Physical design is that part of the process that deals with the dependency of a DBMS. Unfortunately, although such a separation is desirable, in reality it is not quite achievable. One can easily see that it becomes difficult to evaluate the design without reference to any DBMS. Logical design will therefore be reduced to merely the specification of applications and the checking of the specifica-

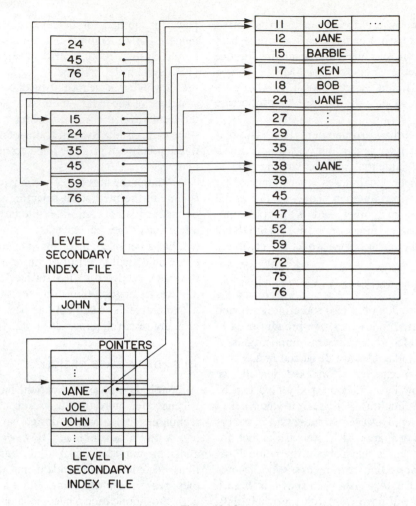

Figure 13.15.

tions for completeness and inconsistency. Nevertheless, the separation of the process into logical and physical design is useful in that the levels of the design will correspond to the levels of the DBMS.

Generally speaking, the steps in a data design process involve: (1) collecting information, which includes defining fields, assigning and resolving fields, defining usage, and so forth, (2) formulating the requirements, including performance, (3) forming records and files, (4) analyzing structure with respect to the needs in (2) and repetition of (3) if necessary, and (5) forming an overall structure for the data base that includes the specification of access paths and the placement of files in storage if needed. Of course, some steps can be combined and others augmented. For example,

steps 3 and 5 can be combined and another step 4 can be added after step 5.

A better and more organized separation as given in a 1978 New Orleans Data Base Design Workshop Report [32] is as follows: (1) corporate requirement analysis, (2) information analysis and definition, (3) implementation design, and (4) physical data base design.

Corporate Requirement Analysis

Corporate requirement analysis is the part of the process that concerns the gathering and specifying of information required for the design process. This part is intrinsically labor intensive and imprecise. It generally involves informal or formal interviews with people who may be managers, professionals, corporate officers, or clerks, and reading whatever documents that are available. Sometimes, a designer may even have to read code from old application programs to derive useful information not available elsewhere.

Currently, few tools or techniques are available to help designers to gather or specify information, although this may be changing. In recent years, some advances have been made to provide a more formal methodology and tools for specifying the required information. The best known and earliest work addressing this problem is PSL/PSA [29]. This system provides a language and a methodology with which designers and analysts can specify their applications in a more precise manner. More recent work to provide relief in this problem area includes the TELL [30] system. Neither of these two systems have been developed specifically for defining information for data base design. As a result, information given in these specifications will not be sufficient for the design process. Other work (Sheppard [31], etc.) that has been developed specifically for data base design tends to narrowly address one particularly proposed design method and is not generally applicable otherwise.

The most recent work designed specifically to solve this problem is the forms approach to specification by Shu et al. [32]. Here a specification is broken into two parts: information on data and constraints and information on processes. It has been recognized that factors to be considered in a data base design include not only performance but also integrity constraint enforcement, recovery, security, consistency, authorization, stability, growth capability, and so on. To be able to design a data base with these factors in mind, both the information on data and integrity constraints and the information on processes will be needed. This latest work is an attempt to provide a specification tool that captures enough information to permit designers to analyze some of these issues.

Information Analysis and Definition

Information captured in the requirement analysis may be transformed into a conceptual schema that defines the corporation's view of the data base needed to support the applications. In the previous step, specifications were defined for individual applications views of the data. These views must now be integrated to form a global view. Criteria must be defined during the integration process. Some of the criteria proposed include analyses of completeness, minimality in storage, correctness, independence, stability, and extendability. Completeness refers to the completeness of the data that is needed to support all applications. Minimality of storage refers to the amount of redundancy of the stored data. Correctness includes constraint enforcement both in data content and corporation rules. Independence here is taken to mean independence from a particular data base management system, and stability and extendability refer to the change in the design if requirements are modified or new applications are added. Though many of these aspects definitely are attributes to be considered in a design, unfortunately we understand very little about their application in the design process.

Basically, methods proposed for "view integration" have been done in three ways: Views are derived by (1) grouping items that are frequently referenced and accessed together, (2) applying functional dependencies among items to form groups of items so that items in a group are functionally dependent on an assigned key, and (3) finding matching objects or partially matched objects from the different views to determine the superimposed view.

Any approach to view integration must detect and find solutions to resolve conflicts among views. As a result of the lack of knowledge to specify a general approach toward a solution, one may propose some discrete cases that can be solved if the conditions are met. One recent proposal for a solution to this problem is given in El-Masri & Wiederhold [16]. This proposal may be indicative of the trend in searching for a solution.

Let us get a flavor of the approach with an example given by the authors. Suppose that two applications have two views as shown in Figure 13.16. The semantics in this diagram is as follows: In view 1, for each DEP# there may be none or many EMP# and vice versa. In view 2, each EMP# must have one DEP#

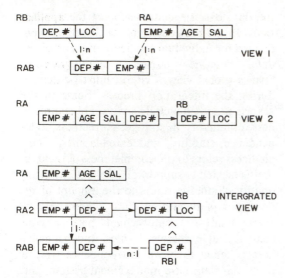

Figure 13.16.

as represented by the solid arrow. Further, in view 2, a deletion of a DEP# is permissible if and only if no EMP# refers to it. On the other hand, there is no restriction in view 1. Under such circumstances, we propose to have an integrated view as shown, where two subrelations, RA1 and RB1, have been created to support the two views. (RA1 subrelation means that the tuples in RA1 are all combined in RA). As a result, if view 1 or view 2 inserts a RB tuple, one RB and one RB1 tuple must be created in the integrated view. If view 2 inserts an RA tuple, then one RA and one RA2 tuple plus possibly RAB tuples will be created in the integrated view. Similar rules will hold for deletion.

As seen in the example, this technique uses subrelations to resolve conflicts. This paper analyzes a number of specific conflicts as given in the example above and proposes solutions in the same manner as Figure 13.16. Their approach is a concrete step toward a solution in view integration. However, it is not clear that such an approach will not lead to difficulties in the later steps of the design process because the introduction of more relations and rules makes the design more complex.

One aspect in the above example stands out, namely, that there is a need of having a rich model that can represent not only structure but constraints and semantics. This problem has been recognized by many researchers and many models have been proposed so that more meaning can be captured. However, as Codd [6] said, "the task of capturing meaning of data is a never-ending one.... The goal is nevertheless an extremely important one, because even small success can bring understanding and order into the field of data base design." A major problem related to the advances in this matter is the fact that there is not enough understanding in designing data bases. While there are concrete proposals of steps that lead to a good data base design, there is a lack of concrete general and broadly applicable algorithms that would methodically lead us to a good design. The lack of such algorithms makes it unclear to what extent specific information and meaning must be included in a model. For those interested in data models, the New Orleans Report [21] contains a large number of references.

Implementation Design

To design a schema (i.e., view) of a data base that is totally DBMS independent is not only difficult but may not be reasonable. In practice, every designer knows not only the applications but also the DBMS before he starts to design a data base. Perhaps the lack of progress in logical data base design was the result of early researchers' having placed too much emphasis on attempting to find a design that is system independent.

As stated in the New Orleans Report [21], it seems difficult to separate information analysis and definition from implementation design. The former should include completeness and consistency checking. The rest of the issues can probably be dealt with best in implementation design.

Data base design techniques that have been proposed for a relational environment generally deal with the design of data bases in normal forms, three of which have been given in Section 13.2. Relational enthusiasts have proposed several others. While the knowledge of the other normal forms are useful, it may be difficult in practice to go beyond the third normal form, as the splitting of relations will cause performance problems.

To do implementation design, one should

not only take advantage of the model but also more specific characteristics of a system. This approach has been done by Shu and Wong [33] who proposed a general design methodology suited for System R. When this approach is used, it resembles the process of physical design but with evaluations of a particular design at a grosser level.

Data base design in a hierarchically structured DBMS is not so well defined as in the relational environment. However, one well-known technique is to make use of the one-to-one or one-to-many relationships among fields. Fields with a one-to-one relationship can be grouped together to form segments. If segment A has a one-to-many relationship to segment B, then segment B will be in a higher level of the tree. For example, an instance of the department segment has many instances of the employee segment and each employee instance has many job history instances. Thus a tree can be constructed as shown in Figure 13.17. This principle and some specific rules were used to form the Data Base Design Aid by IBM for IMS data base design.

As in the hierarchical structure, data base design in the network environment uses the same one-to-one and one-to-many principle to arrive at a schema. The most notable work in this area has been that of Gerritsen [34]. He used the one-to-one, one-to-many, and many-to-many relationships to represent one, two, or three DBTG records, respectively, with the first two analyzed as in the above example and the third kind forming a structure as shown in Figure 13.18. In this figure, it was assumed that a department may have many projects and that a project may be in more than one department.

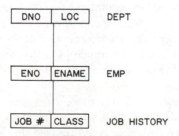

Figure 13.17.

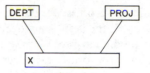

Figure 13.18.

Physical Data Base Design

Physical data base design is the last step in a design process and is the best understood area in the design process. This is the result of two major factors: (1) One must understand the physical design process before one can have insight into the other design steps. Consequently, nearly all earlier design studies have been concentrated in this area. (2) This aspect of the design lends itself to analysis. That is, results from a physical design can be analyzed in terms of tangible physical parameters like access time and storage space to get an evaluation of performance. As design objectives become clear, the problems become more definitive and soluble.

Physical data base design generally requires: (1) data characteristics such as volume, field size, data distribution, and so on, (2) information about the processes that will use the date including frequencies of application, the dominant processes, and the like, (3) the constraints on the processes and data, including application constraints, (4) the DBMS characteristics (for example, if a DBMS does not support direct accessing of data, it becomes meaningless to design a data base that requires direct access to achieve the required performance), and (5) hardware characteristics that are obviously needed to predict performance.

Although there are other problems to be addressed in physical design, the following are the three major ones: (1) record and file formulation, (2) file structure, and (3) secondary index selection.

Record and file formulation refer to the process of grouping fields together to form records and grouping records to form files. In an integrated data base, processes will use data in various ways. Generally one set of processes requires information that is not relevant to another set of processes. For example, a payroll process may require more fields than a retirement prediction process. Further the payroll process needs all the active employees, but the retirement prediction process may need only those employees who are, say, over 50 years old. Thus even with only these two processes, one may want to create more than one record type and more than one file, although one can use the same file to support both processes. The selection decision depends on the required performance.

As a data base generally supports a large number of applications and the decision of a design usually involves tradeoffs, the procedure leading to a decision is generally fairly complex. To be meaningful in the prediction of performance, one should build a model. Models can be divided into three categories: simulation, analytical, and heuristic.

Simulation models are built to reflect closely the actual behavior of a system. Heuristic models are built to reduce the large number of parameters and variations to a small subset that are believed to be crucial in that environment. Consequently, heuristic models are generally simpler. Analytical models cover both ends of the spectrum and therefore can be very simple or very complex. Generally, one would want to use a simple model to obtain "ball park" results quickly and would employ a more complex model only if accurate results are needed.

To understand further the trade-off between simple models and accuracy, let us examine for a moment the possible variations of an organization. With only the two applications above (payroll and retirement prediction), there are numerous possibilities. For example, one can have (1) one file for both applications, (2) two files in several ways (e.g. one file for each application or one file for, say, the retirement prediction and the other noncommon fields in the payroll application), and (3) three files in different ways (e.g. one file with common fields, another with noncommon fields in the retirement prediction application, and the third with noncommon fields in the payroll application. One can also have the two files in (2) but separate employees into two groups, below and above 55 years old, to form two files), and so on. To complicate the analysis further, one

has the options of placing files in storage in many ways and in many device types. One can also arrange a set of records to be near or far away from certain other records.

As a result of the many possibilities, designers tend to deal with only crucial issues and be satisfied with reasonable ball park figures in others. This approach to finding a solution is not limited to record or file formulation. Rather, it is a typical approach throughout the data base design process because there are too many variations.

File structure selection generally involves the selection of access methods and access paths supported by a particular DBMS. Not all of the access methods given in section 13.4 are supported by a selected DBMS, and most DBMSs create methods of their own by varying and combining the basic techniques given in Section 13.4. Typically for a given file, there exists a preferred access path along which data can be accessed more efficiently. For example, suppose that we have a sequential file, sorted in order of employee name. If we were to access records in the order of employee names, these records can be retrieved efficiently. However, if we were to address these same records in order ot employee number, we would encounter difficulty for we have no information on the ordering of employee number.

Even for a DBMS that supports a more versatile access method like the indexed access method, there still remains a preferred path. For example, if indexing is created to order records by employee number in the above file, it is still more expensive to access records in order of employee number than if the file had been stored in the sequence of employee name.

Obviously, record and file creation and access path and access method selection are highly system dependent. There has been a great number of techniques reported, both for a particular system environment as well as for a more general environment. The work of Senko [35, 36], Severance [37, 38], and Yao [39, 40, 41] are representative of some of these techniques.

The need to define more than one access path leads the design into the need to define secondary indexes. As discussed in section

13.4, secondary index files provide alternative access paths to the data base records and allow the records to be accessed in random or sequential manner. Techniques for this design process are typified by the works of Lum and Ling [42] and Schkolnick [43]. Basically, the creation of a secondary index file requires additional processing and maintenance. One would only create a secondary index if that sequence path is searched frequently and if the secondary index provides high resolution. For example, a secondary index file on the field 'sex' with possible values of male and female, will not likely improve performance. On the other hand, a secondary index file on employee number will. However, if the applications on the data base are such that a search by employee number occurs once a year, the provision of such an index will not produce the desired result. It is probably less expensive to search the file sequentially for that one time than to maintain the index file current because each insertion, deletion, or update may cause work on the index file.

Presently although physical data base design is fairly well understood, no comprehensive methods exist to integrate the various techniques. Neither do we have a technique that is directly applicable to a large number of systems that produces equally accurate results. Further, most of the techniques apply to a single file environment. Files in a data base are generally interrelated and not isolatable. Consequently, there does not exist any comprehensive design tool even for this aspect of the design process that we understand the most.

ACRONYMS

In this section we define some acronyms which some readers may not be familiar with.

CODASYL - Committee on Data Access, System, and Languages
DACL - Data Access and Control Language
DBMS - Data Base Management System
DBTG - Data Base Task Group
DDL - Data Definition Language
DML - Data Manipulation Language

HISAM - Hierarchical Index Sequential Access Method
HDAM - Hierarchical Direct Access Method
ISAM - Index Sequential Access Method
QBE - Query by Example
QL - Query Language
QUEL - Query like English Language
SQL - Simple Query Language
VSAM - Virtual Sequential Access Method
XPRS - Extraction, Processing, and Restructuring System.

REFERENCES

1. CODASYL Data Description Language Committee, NBS Handbook 113, 1974.
2. "SYSTEM 2000: MRI System Corp." in *System 2000 Publications,* MRI System Corp, Austin, Tex., 1972.
3. MODEL 204 Computer Corporation of America manuals.
4. E. F. Codd, "Normalized Data Base Structure: A Brief Tutorial," *Proc. 1971 ACM SIGFIDET Workshop on Data Description, Access and Control,* available from the Association for Computing Machinery (ACM), 1971.
5. E. F. Codd, "Recent Investigations into Relational Data Base Systems," *Proc. ACM Pacific Conference,* 1975.
6. E. F. Codd, "Extracting the Data Base Relational Model to Capture More Meaning," *ACM Trans. of Data Base Systems,* 1979.
7. R. Fagin, "Multivalued Dependencies and a New Formal Form For Relational Databases," IBM Research Report RJ 1812, 1976.
8. R. Fagin, J. Nievergelt, N. Pippenger, and H. R. Strong, "Extendible Hashing—A Fast Access Method for Dynamic Files," *ACM Trans. Data Base Syst.,* vol. 4, no. 3, 1979, pp. 315–344.
9. W. W. Armstrong, "Dependency Structure of Data Base Relationships," *Proc. IFIP Congress,* 1974.
10. P. A. Bernstein, J. R. Swenson, and D. C. Tsichtzis, "A Unified Approach to Functional Dependencies and Relations," *Proc. 1975 ACM SIGMOD International Conference on the Management of Data,* available from ACM, 1975.
11. S. P. Ghosh, *Data Base Organization for Data Management,* Academic Press, New York, 1977.
12. C. J. Date, An Introduction to Database System, 2d ed., Addison-Wesley, Reading, Mass., 1977.
13. M. M. Astrahan, et al., "System R: Relational Approach to Data Base Management," *ACM Trans. Data Base Sys.,* vol. 1, 1976, pp. 97–137.
14. M. R. Stonebraker, E. Wong, and P. Kreps, "The Design and Implementation of INGRES," *ACM Trans Data Base Sys.,* vol. 1, 1976, pp. 189–222.

15. Datapro Research Corp., "ADABAS—Software AG," *Datapro 70*, March, 1973.
16. Tymshare Inc., *MAGNUM Reference Manual*, 1975.
17. IBM Corp., *APL Data Language Programming Description/Operations Manual*, Form SB21-1805.
18. D. E. Knuth, *Sorting and Searching—The Art of Computer Programming*, vol. 3, Addison-Wesley, Reading, Mass., 1975.
19. IMS: *IBM Information Management System/360, Version 2 System/Application Design Guide*, Form SHO-0919.
20. National CSS Inc., *NOMAD Reference Manual*, Form No. 1004.
21. V. Y. Lum and S. P. Ghosh (eds.), *New Orleans Data Base Design Workshop Report*, IBM Research Report No. RJ 2554, 1978.
22. M. M. Zloff, "Query by Example: A Data Base Language," *IBM System Journal*, vol. 16, no. 4, 1977, pp. 324–343.
23. D. D. Chamberlin, "SQL 2: A Unified Approach to Data Definition, Manipulation, and Control," *IBM Journal of Research and Development*, vol. 20, 1976, pp. 560–575.
24. B. C. Housel, D. P. Smith, N. C. Shu, and V. Y. Lum, "DEFINE: A Nonprocedural Data Description Language for Defining Information Easily," IBM Research Report No. RJ 1526, 1975.
25. N. C. Shu, B. C. Housel, and V. Y. Lum, "CONVERT: A High Level Translation Definition Language For Data Conversion," *Comm. of ACM*, vol. 18, no. 10, 1975, pp. 557–567.
26. "Data Extraction Processing and Restructuring System: DEFINE and CONVERT Reference Manual," IBM Manual GC26-3838.
27. W. Litwin, "Virtual Hashing: A Dynamically Changing Hashing," *Proc. 4th Conf. on Very Large Databases*, Berlin, 1978, pp. 517–523.
28. J. L. Carter and M. Wegman, "Universal Classes of Hash Functions," IBM Research Report RC 6687, 1977.
29. D. Teichroew and E. A. Hershey III, "PSL/PSA: A Computer Aided Technique for Structured Documentation and Analysis of Information Processing Systems," *IEEE Trans. on Software Engineering*, vol. SE-3, no. 1, 1977.
30. P. G. Hebalkar and S. M. Silles, "Graphical Representation and Analysis of Information Systems Design," IBM Research Report RJ 2465, 1979.
31. D. L. Sheppard, "Data Base Design Methodology—Parts I & II," Auerbach Data Base Management Series, Portfolios #23-01-01 and 02, 1977.
32. N. C. Shu and H. K. T. Wong, "Relational Data Base Schema Design," IBM Research Report RJ 2688, 1979.
33. N. C. Shu, H. K. T. Wong, and V. Y. Lum, "Forms Approach to Application Specification for Data Base Design," IBM Research Report RJ 2687, 1979.
34. R. Gerritsen, "A Preliminary System for the Design of DBTG Data Structures, *Comm. of ACM*, vol. 18, no. 10, 1975, pp. 557–567.
35. M. E. Senko, V. Y. Lum, and P. J. Owen, "A File Organization Evaluation Model (FOREM)," *Proc. IFIP Congress, 1968*, pp. 514–519.
36. M. E. Senko, H. Ling, and V. Y. Lum, "Analysis of a Complex Data Base Management Access Method by Simulation," IBM Research Report RJ 647, 1969.
37. D. G. Severance, "A Parametric Model of Alternative File Structure," *Information Systems*, vol. 1, no. 2, 1975, pp. 51–55.
38. D. G. Severance and J. V. Carlis, "A Practical Approach to Selecting Record Access Paths," *Computing Surveys*, vol. 9, no. 4, 1977, pp. 259–272.
39. S. B. Yao and A. G. Merten, "Selection of File Organizations Using an Analytic Model," *Proc. of VLDB-1*, 1975, pp. 255–267.
40. S. B. Yao, "Optimization of Query Evaluation Algorithms," *ACM Trans. on Database Syst.*, vol. 4, no. 2.
41. S. B. Yao, S. B. Navathe, and J. L. Weldon, "An Integrated Approach to Logical Data Base Design," *Proc. of NYU Symposium on Database Design*, 1978.
42. V. Y. Lum and H. Ling, "An Optimization Problem on the Selection of Secondary Keys," *Proc. NCC*, 1971, pp. 349–356.
43. M. Schkolnick, "The Optimum Selection of Secondary Indices for Files," *Information Systems*, vol. 1, pp. 141–146, 1975.

14

Distributed Data Base Systems

Wesley W. Chu

University of California, Los Angeles

14.1. INTRODUCTION

With the advent of computer network technology, reliable, efficient and economical transfer of data among computers and terminals becomes feasible. The advances in this field provide us with a technological foundation for implementing distributed computing and distributed data base on a computer network. The motivation for connecting a group of geographically separate data bases into a network of data bases or a distributed data base is that these separate data bases need to process common information files. Examples of such systems are in transaction-oriented systems (such as credit checking, electronic funds transfer) and medical, business, and library management information systems. The advantages of linking all the remote data bases together include not only sharing of data bases, but also real-time retrieval, update, and distribution of large quantities of information. Such information handling capability over a geographically separated data base system not only provides more economical service, but also provides real-time information handling that was previously unachievable. For example, a user can instantaneously find out the current inventory level of a part from several geographically separate warehouses. Such a system also allows simultaneous file transactions against a common data base by users remotely located from each other. Because multiple copies of data bases may be contained in a distributed data base system, the system may still be operational even when a certain site is down, which provides fault tolerance capability.

In organizing a distributed data base, we first must allocate the individual data files to the computer (sites) in the network. This allocation is based on file usage rates, response time requirements of different files at different sites, communication and storage costs, and reliability requirements. The data base at each site forms a local data base and is maintained by itself. It also consists of a local directory that lists all the files in that computer. To list all sharable files in the distributed data base system for all the sites, a directory system is needed. When a user presents a transaction or a query to the system that involves files not stored at his local site, the system first examines the directory to obtain information on the physical, logical, security, as well as operational characteristics of the set of files relevant to the query. Based on information such as resource availability, access capabilities, and work load profile of the system, the system assigns resources and performs data translation if necessary to process the transaction. When a transaction or query involves several sites, the system, based on the directory information, also needs to determine the optimal sequence of operations and sites for processing the transaction or query.

In organizing and planning a distributed data base system, there arise many problems in need of solution, such as file allocation policy, directory design and distribution, avoidance of deadlock, integrity and consistency in updating multiple copies of data bases, optimal query processing policy, reliability and recovery as well as privacy and security issues. In this chapter, we shall present results for the above-mentioned areas and two prototype distributed database systems, with the exception of security and privacy.

14.2. FILE ALLOCATION

It is apparent that when a given information file is required in common by several computers, it may be stored in at least one of them and accessed by the others when needed. The overall operating cost related to the files is considered to consist of transmission and storage costs. The problem is the following. Given a number of computers that process common information files, how can one allocate the files so that the allocation yields minimum overall operating costs subject to the following constraints: (1) The expected time to access each file is less than a given bound, (2) the amount of storage needed at each computer does not exceed the available storage capacity, and (3) the availability of each file is above a certain level.

File Allocation Model

The file allocation problem can be formulated as an integer (0 or 1) programming model.

Let X_{ij} indicate that the jth file is stored in the ith computer:

$$X_{ij} = \begin{cases} 1 & j\text{th file stored in the }i\text{th} \\ & \text{computer} \\ 0 & \text{otherwise} \end{cases}$$

where

$i = 1, 2, \ldots, n$
$j = 1, 2, \ldots, m$
n = total number of computers in the distributed system
m = total number of distinct files in the distributed system

The availability of the jth file A_j is that portion of time when the system is in operation so that the jth file is available to users. It should be noted that the availability is independent of any queuing delay that may be experienced by the file. For example, $A_j = 0.9985$ means that within a 10,000-hour(h) period, the jth file is

available (operating) for 9,985 h and unavailable (system down) for 15 h. Clearly, the availability of the file is dependent upon the reliability of the computers, the reliability of the communication channels, their average repair times, the network-routing algorithm, and the number of redundant copies of the file stored in the interconnected computer network. Thus, given the required availability of a file and the reliability of the system (computer and communication channels), a given availability constraint can be satisfied by selecting the required number of redundant copies of the file.* For example, if the computers within the network are allowed to communicate only with their immediate neighboring computers, and all equipment in the system is assumed to have exponential failure distributions, and if all computers within the system have identical availability† a_p, and all channels have identical availability a_c, then the availability of the jth file given that r_j redundant copies are stored in the system is

$$A_j = a_p[1 - (1 - a_c a_p)^{r_j}] \qquad (1)$$

For example, if $a_p = 0.98$ and $a_c = 0.99$, then $A_j = 0.951$ for $r_j = 1$ and $A_j = 0.979$ for $r_j = 2$. Equation (1) states that the availability of the jth file is equal to the product of the availability of the requesting computer a_p and the availability of the r_j copies of the jth file, $1 - (1 - a_c a_p)^{r_j}$.

For storing r_j redundant copies of the jth file in the information system, we have

$$\sum_i X_{ij} = r_j \text{ for } 1 \leq j \leq m \qquad (2)$$

To assure that the storage capacity of each computer is not exceeded, we have

---

*The number of redundant copies of a file needed to be stored within a distributed data base system should also be based on other constraints such as response time requirements, cost, etc.

†The availability of a_p or a_c is equal to the ratio of mean time between failures to mean repair time plus mean time between failures of the equipment in question [1]. The availability function for other types of network-routing algorithms and/or other types of equipment-failure distributions will be more complex than Eq. (1).

$$\sum_j X_{ij} L_j \le b_i \text{ for } 1 \le i \le n \qquad (3)$$

where

L_j = length of the jth file,
b_i = available memory size of the ith computer

The expected time for the ith computer to retrieve and perform a transaction on the jth file from the kth computer (from initiation of request until start of reception) is denoted as a_{ijk}. The maximum allowable retrieval time of the jth file to the ith computer is T_{ij}. We require that a_{ijk} be no more than T_{ij}, that is,

$$(1 - X_{ij})X_{kj}a_{ijk}$$
$$\le T_{ij} \text{ for } i \ne k, 1 \le j \le m \qquad (4)$$

When $r_j = 1$ for all j, then from Eq. (2) we know that $X_{ij}X_{kj} = 0$ for $i \ne k$. Thus Eq. (4) reduces to

$$X_{kj}a_{ijk} \le T_{ij} \text{ for } i \ne k, 1 \le j \le m \qquad (5)$$

For a fully connected network, a_{ijk} is equal to the sum of the expected queuing delay at the ith computer for the channel to the kth computer W_{ik},* the expected queuing delay at the kth computer for the channel to the ith computer W_{ki}, and the expected computer processing time to the jth file t_{kj}. Hence,

$$a_{ijk} \doteq W_{ik} + W_{ki} + t_{kj} \qquad (6)$$

For a non fully connected network, the expected query response time a_{ijk} depends on network topology, routing, and flow control policy, which is difficult to estimate. However, under simplified assumptions such as Poisson message arrivals, nodes statistically independent from each other, and a known fixed routing policy (that is, a unique allowable path exists from origin to destination for each origin-destination pair), we are able to determine the message delay averaged over all messages flowing through the network [2].

*For an appropriate expression of W_{ik}, the interested reader should refer to Reference 3.

For a network with M communication links with equal transmission rate R, let the total offered traffic to the network be γ, and let the total traffic within the network be $\lambda = \sum_{s=1}^{M} \lambda_s$ where λ_s is the total traffic on the sth channel, which includes data traffic (with average message length ℓ) and control traffic (e.g., acknowledgment). Further, let the average time to transmit a message (control or data message) be $1/\mu'$, and the average time to transmit a data message (segment of a file required by a transaction) be $\dfrac{1}{\mu} = \dfrac{\ell}{R}$, nodal processing time t_n and query processing time t_q be the same for all computers, and propagation delay be t_p. Then the expected response time for a computer to perform a transaction on a file at a remote computer is

$$a_{ijk} \doteq A \doteq 2 \sum_{s=1}^{M} \frac{\lambda_s}{\gamma} \left[\frac{\lambda_s/\mu'}{\mu' - \lambda_s} + \frac{1}{\mu} + t_p + t_n \right] + t_q \qquad (7)$$

The factor of 2 in Eq. (7) is required to include the expected delay from the query originator to the destination and back to the originator.

Finally, we express the operating cost (objective function) in terms of the allocation (X_{ij}'s). Suppose we know the storage cost of the jth file per unit length and unit time at the ith computer C_{ij}, the communication cost* from the kth computer to the ith computer per unit length C'_{ik}, the request rate for the entire or part of the jth file at the ith computer per unit time u_{ij}, the frequency of modification of the jth file after a transaction at the ith computer P_{ij}, the average length of the segment of the jth file requested by a transaction ℓ_j, and the number of redundant copies of the jth file stored in the system r_j. Then the overall operating cost per unit time C for processing m distinct files required in common by n computers is

*In a non-fully-connected network, because of alternate routing, C'_{ik} should be viewed as the average communication cost from the kth computer to the ith computer per unit length C'_{ik}. In some packet switching systems, C'_{ik} are distance independent and can be simplified to a constant C'.

$$C = \sum_{i,j} C_{ij} L_j X_{ij}$$

(storage cost)

$$+ \sum_{i,j,k} \frac{1}{r_j} C'_{ik} \ell_j u_{ij} X_{kj} (1 - X_{ij})$$
$$+ \sum_{i,j,k} C'_{ik} \ell_j u_{ij} X_{kj} P_{ij} \qquad (8)$$

(communication cost)

which can be rearranged into the form

$$= \sum_{i,j} D_{ij} X_{ij} - \sum_{i,j,k} E_{ijk} X_{kj} X_{ij}$$
$$\text{where } D_{ij} > 0, \ E_{ijk} > 0. \qquad (9)$$

When $r_j = 1$, $1 \le j \le m$, then $X_{kj} X_{ij} = 0$ for $k \ne i$. Further, since $C'_{ii} = 0$, Eq. (9) reduces to

$$C = \sum_{i,j} D_{ij} X_{ij}$$

We want to minimize Eq. (9) subject to availability, storage, and access time requirement constraints given in Eqs. (1), (2), (3), and (4). As X_{ij} takes on values zero or one, the allocation problem becomes one of solving a nonlinear zero-one programming problem. The nonlinear zero-one equations can be reduced to a linear zero-one equation [3]. With this technique, the file allocation problem can be then solved by standard linear zero-one programming techniques [4].

A recent study [5] reported on solving the file allocation problem by the use of the APEX III system, an integer programming software package supported by CDC 6000 series computers. The system is capable of solving a problem consisting of 8,000 constraint equations and 2,500 unknowns. A file allocation problem with 15 computers and 15 files, consisting of 6,330 constraint equations and 1,801 unknowns, requires only a few minutes of computation time on that system.

Other file allocation studies performed in past years include channel switching [6] and assignment of channel capacity to achieve minimum operating cost [7]. Under the assumption that query response time is always satisfactory, Casey [8] studied the optimal number of copies of a file contained in the system such that it minimizes the cost of storing the copies of the file and of transmitting the file queries and updates. Let ρ be the minimum of the update to query traffic ratio for all sites in the network. An upper bound on the optimal number of copies is given by the minimum value of r that satisfies the expression $\rho \ge 1/(r - 1)$, where r is an integer. There are other factors such as file availability [9] and file response time [3, 7] that determine the optimal number of copies of a file. The higher the number of duplicate copies of a file in the system, the greater the availability of a file, and the lower the response time. However, duplicate copies also create problems of synchronization and consistency for concurrent updates, which will be discussed in Section 5 of this chapter.

Morgan and Levin [10] formulated a model for file allocation that considers interaction between programs and data files. Data files are accessed by programs that may not be located at the same site. The user-generated requests for access to a file utilize various programs with different probabilities. A mathematical model is developed that is based on parameters such as unit query communication cost, unit update communication cost, and file storage cost. The model distinguishes the lengths of messages traveling between users from programs and the lengths of messages traveling between programs and files.

After the files have been created and allocated in a network, a directory is needed to specify the physical, logical, operational, and security characteristics of the files so that the user or system can locate and access a shared file in the distributed data base. Directory organization and its distribution influence query and updating traffic patterns in the network. They not only affect the operating cost of the data base, but also the performance of the system in terms of security, reliability, and query response time.

14.3. FILE DIRECTORY SYSTEM DESIGN

A file directory is a listing of information about files available to users of the distributed data base in a computer network. Such a directory enables a user at any node to determine where in a network a specific sharable file is located. Such a directory can be considered to be similar to a card catalogue in a public library. Users at each node may offer to list their files in this directory of public files for sharing purposes. A user may consult this list to determine its contents or obtain information on the location and characteristics of specific sharable files. The nonshared files are assumed to be stored at the computer known to the user and are therefore not considered here. We assume each computer has its own directory which consists of information on all sharable files stored in that computer. To search for a file that is not listed in the directory at his or her computer, the user must consult the file directory system.

There are several ways to design the file directory system: centralized file directory system, multiple master directory systems, local file directory system, and distributed file directory system. Based on the computer network topology, operating cost (communication cost, storage cost, and code translation cost), directory query rate and directory update rate, mathematical models may be used to study the operating cost and response time of these directory systems as a function of directory query rate, directory update rate, and the ratio of storage cost to communication cost [11].

Information Contents of the Directory System

The directory system should consist of physical, logical, security, and operational information about a file, as shown in Table 14.1. Some directory examples are shown in [12].

The contents of the directory system may be logically partitioned and organized into several levels. Each level contains a certain amount of information and description about a file. The user terminates his query at the directory level when he acquires information sufficient to process his file. Since using the directory at different levels may require different access rights, this file directory system provides different degrees of security protection at different levels.

The directory may include a query-processing optimizer. When a user presents a query to the system, the directory first locates the files referenced by the query. Then based on the directory information, the current operating state of the data base, and resource requirements, the query-processing optimizer generates a procedure for retrieval and a choice of locations for processing the query that yields

Table 14.1. Content of a Directory System.

PHYSICAL (STATIC)	LOGICAL (DYNAMIC)	SECURITY	OPERATIONAL
Name of file	File status (R,W)	(File user, C)	Data reduction function (type of operation, query parameters)
Location (site)	Number of backlog jobs	C = read/write	Query processing optimizer
Creator	Computer site availability	Read only	Statistical data gathering algorithms
Version number of the file	Resource requirements	Write only	Deadlock avoidance algorithm
Processing cost	Consistency constraints		
Communication cost	Parsing information		
Translation cost			
File size			
Code format			
Number of duplicate copies of a file and their locations			
Date of last update			

minimum operating cost. An optimal query-processing model is presented in Section 14.7. Further, the information in the directory system is updated after each operation. The directory system thus presents the up-to-date status of the system and plays an important role in processing queries in a distributed data base.

Centralized Directory Systems. In the centralized file directory system, a master directory is located at one of the computers. Should a user require a file that is not listed by his local directory, he consults the master directory to find out the location and contents of the requested file. Further, the centralized directory must be updated when a new version of a file or a change in storage location is required. The advantage of such a system is its ease in updating. The disadvantage is the high communication cost of each transaction.

The extended centralized file directory is a variation of the centralized file directory. In this case whenever a user uses the centralized file directory, and once the user finds the location and description of a file, he can append this information to his local directory. Should the user use this file again, the directory information for this file can be obtained from his local directory, thereby reducing the communication cost as well as time for querying the master directory. However, when the information on that file at the master directory is updated, we also require updating the information on that file in the local directories. Therefore, for notification of future updates in the master directory, the list of local directories that have appended file information is recorded in the master directory. This directory system provides an adaptive feature. After a certain time period, each extended directory consists of directory information about frequently referenced files.

Multiple Master Directory System. When computers in a network are clustered in groups, it is often cost effective to provide a master directory for the entire network at each cluster. The savings in communication cost for queries in multiple master directory system could far outweigh the cost of storing and updating the file directories.

To organize the multiple directory system, we partition the n computers in the system into r clusters ($r \leq n$). During normal operation, computers in a given cluster will query the directory, which is located at a member of that cluster. One way to partition n computers into r clusters is to base the partitioning on the network topology so that the partitioned clusters yield minimum communication costs. Another way is to base the partitioning on directory query rates and directory update rates for achieving minimum directory query response time.

Local File Directory System. In the local file directory system, there is no master directory in the system. When a requested file is not stored in the user's local directory, the user queries all the other local directories in the system until the requested file has been located. Assuming the directory can be updated only by its owner, updating is done at its local directory, which does not entail communication costs. On the other hand, such a directory system involves high communication and translation costs, as well as search time for locating the file. For a system of n computers, it requires an average of $(n - 1)/2$ directory queries to locate a nonlocal file. However, if each of the computers contains a routing table that routes the directory query directly to the other computers rather than returning the negative query reply to the sender, the expected total communication cost can be greatly reduced, particularly if the routing sequence takes into consideration the probability of finding the file in the directory. The total operating cost can be reduced by a factor of ξ ($0 < \xi \leq 1$), which depends on the network topology and the policy used in the routing table. A simple implementation of the routing table is to let each computer contain a directory locator which specifies the directory locations of all the shared files in the system. Whenever a file is created, deleted, or changes its directory location, all the directory locators in the system will be updated to reflect this change. Since such changes are infrequent, the contents of the directory locator should be fairly static. With the aid of such a directory locator, the time required to search for a non local file is independent of the number of computers in the system. This greatly reduces the communication cost for searching the directory locations of the non-local files.

The advantage of such a directory is the ease of directory update as well as being particularly suitable for distributed database systems operating in a local network environment. The disadvantages are high communication cost and high directory query response time for locating and obtaining the file directory information if a directory locator is not used.

Distributed File Directory System. In the distributed directory case, each computer in the system has a master directory. The advantage of this system is its fast response time. The disadvantage of this system is the cost of storing master file directories at each computer in addition to the communication cost for updating all these directories.

Operating Cost Trade-off Among Directory Systems. Let P be the normalized directory update rate, which is defined as the ratio of the directory update rate to the directory query rate and which is assumed to be the same for all sites. Let $C_x(P)$ and $C_y(P)$ be the operating cost for directory systems x and y, respectively. The intersection of $C_x(P)$ and $C_y(P)$ represents the cost tradeoff point (in terms of normalized update rate) for directory systems x and y. If we assume that all computers in the system have identical directory update rates, then the operating cost is a linear function of P [11]. Thus $C_x(P)$ and $C_y(P)$ can be expressed as:

$$C_x(P) = a_x P + b_x$$

and

$$C_y(P) = a_y P + b_y \qquad (10)$$

where a_x and a_y are incremental costs (e.g., communication cost and translation cost), which increase with directory update rates,

and where b_x and b_y are fixed directory operating costs (e.g., storage cost), which are independent of directory update rates. The intersection of $C_x(P)$ and $C_y(P)$, $P(x,y)$, satisfies

$$P(x,y) = \frac{b_y - b_x}{a_x - a_y} \qquad (11)$$

Let us now consider the intersection of the cost curves for the centralized (C) and extended centralized (CE) directory systems. We assume that (1) communication cost is much higher than storage cost so that storage cost becomes negligible, (2) all computers in the system have the same directory query rate, and also use the same software code; thus translation cost is not required, and (3) the probability of updating each extended directory μ, given that the master directory has been updated, is the same for all computers. Then it can be shown that [11]

$$P(C,CE) \doteq \frac{2}{(n-1) \cdot \mu} \qquad (12)$$

For example, if $n = 10$ and $\mu = \frac{1}{3}$, then $P(C,CE) = \frac{2}{3} = 0.667$. Thus for a network with 10 computers operating in the above environment, when the directory update rate of each computer is less than 67% of its query rate, the extended centralized directory system yields a lower operating cost than that of the centralized directory system.

We will now consider the directory operating cost tradeoffs between the centralized directory system C and the distributed directory system D. If we assume that the directory query rate generated at each computer is the same and no translation cost is incurred, and that the communication cost between nodes i and k, C_{ik}^t, the communication cost between node i and the directory node C_{id}^t, the distance between nodes i and k, S_{ik}, and the distance between node i and the directory node, S_{id}, satisfy the condition $C_{ik}^t S_{ik} = C_{id}^t S_{id}$, then it can be shown that [11]

$$P(C,D) \doteq \frac{2}{(n-1)} \qquad (13)$$

For a network with 10 computers operating in the above environment, $P(C,D) \doteq 0.22$. This implies that when the directory update rate is less than 22% of its query rate, the distributed file directory yields a lower operating cost than the centralized file directory.

We will now consider the cost tradeoffs of the local file directory (L) cost curve with the distributed file directory cost curve. When the communication cost is high as compared to the storage cost, and when the directory update rate is less than the directory query rate, then the distributed file directory system yields a lower operating cost than that of the local file directory system; that is, when $C_{ik}^t \gg C_i^s$, then $P(L,D) \rightarrow 1$.

From performance studies based on the 10 node distributed network shown in Figure 14.1, we notice that the operating cost of the file directory depends greatly on the directory query rate and the directory update rate (Fig. 14.2). Because of the large amount of data communication and translation associated with the directory updates in the distributed directory system, the rate of increase in operating cost with respect to directory update rate for the distributed directory system is higher than that of the centralized directory system. In the local directory system, we need only update the local directory of the computer that generates the update, and no transmission is required. The operating cost is therefore independent of the directory update rate.

Assuming that the communication cost is higher than the storage cost, our study reveals

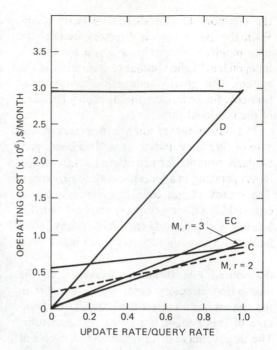

Figure 14.2. Performance of multiple directory systems for the distributed network $C^t/C^s = 10$ months/mile, and query rate = 1000 queries/month. For r = 2, master directories at computers 1 and 2; for r = 3, master directories at computers 1, 2, and 3.

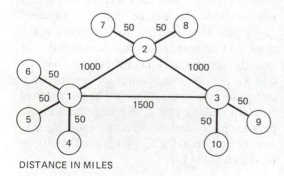

DISTANCE IN MILES

Figure 14.1. A distributed network for performance studies. Unit communication cost/unit storage cost = $C^t/C^s = 10$ months/mile.

that when the directory update rate is low (e.g., less than 10% of the query rate), the distributed directory system yields lower operating cost than the centralized directory system. As directory update rate increases, the centralized directory system yields lower operating cost than the distributed directory system.

Comparing the two types of centralized directory systems, the extended centralized directory yields a lower operating cost than the centralized directory at lower directory update rates (less than 50% of the query rate), and the performance reverses at high directory update rates. This is because of the excessive amount of data transmission required to update all the extended local directories. The cross-over point of the operating cost curves for these two types of directory systems depends on network topology and such parameters as storage cost, transmission costs, translation costs, and so forth. As the directory update rate increases, the performance characteristics of the extended centralized directory system become similar to those of the distributed directory system.

The influence of the distribution of the directory query traffic on the operating cost has also been studied [11]. In order to provide a common base for comparison, the total number of queries generated by the computers was kept constant, and the query traffic among the computers was varied. It was found that traffic distribution does not affect directory operating cost when all the computers are equal distances from each other, and does affect operating cost when distances among the computers are different.

Directory Query Response Time

Let us now consider the query response time for various directory systems. The expected response time for the ith computer to query its directory is defined as the time from initiation of a query at the ith computer until the start of the reception of the results of the query. The expected response time consists of the waiting time at the input queue of the directory for processing the query $t_1(i)$, the waiting time at the output queue of the directory for transmission $t_2(i)$, the time to transmit the query to and its reply from the directory $t_3(i)$, and the directory processing time $t_4(i)$. The processing time consists of code translation, searching, and accessing. It depends on the file structure of the directory as well as the access time of the storage device, which could be different from one system to another and which should be known to the users. Therefore, we consider only the delay incurred at the input queue and output queue(s) of the directory, and the time to transmit the query on the communication channel. Let us denote the sum of these components as $t_{i,d}$, known as the directory query response time from the ith computer to the directory. Thus

$$t_{i,d} = t_1(i) + t_2(i) + t_3(i) \qquad (14)$$

Clearly, the real query response time incurred by the users is equal to the sum of $t_{i,d}$ and $t_4(i)$.

The arrivals at the input queue of the directory are the queries and updates generated by all the computers. The arrivals at the output queue(s) of the directory are the query replies generated at the directory. Let us first consider the centralized directory system. The set of requests arriving at the directory consists of directory queries and updates from all computers in the system. Since the directory does not have to reply to update traffic and since each destination has its own output queue, the arrival rate at the output queue for the ith computer is equal to its directory query rate. For the computer that stores the master directory, $t_2(d) = t_3(d) = 0$. The expected query response time reduces to $t_1(d)$.

For multiple master directory systems, since the directory queries are shared by the multiple master directories, the waiting time for processing the directory queries at each master directory is much lower than the waiting time of the single master directory system. Therefore, the response time for the multiple master directory is lower than that of the single master directory system. The query reply rate at the output queue for the ith computer is equal to the directory query rate from the ith computer. When the directory queries are generated by those computers that store the master directories, these query replies do not require transmission. Thus the response time equals $t_1(d)$.

For the local directory system whose replies are returned directly to the sender (i.e., without routing), the ith computer may locate the information on the file before the request reaches the kth local directory. Therefore, on the average only half of the queries generated at the ith computer will reach the kth computer.

When a carefully designed routing strategy is used in a local directory system, the input traffic rate to each directory can be greatly reduced. As a result, the query response time for the system with routing or directory locator could be much smaller than that without routing.

For the distributed directory system, each computer has a master directory. File directory information can be obtained at each computer. Thus, $t_2(i) = t_3(i) = 0$. The input traffic to the directory consists only of queries generated from its own computer and the directory updates generated from the rest of the computers in the system.

An expression for $t_{i,d}$ for different types of directory systems can be generated from well-known queuing theory results, assuming that arrival rates at the directory input and output queues can be approximated as Poisson arrivals and that the communication lines have a fixed transmission rate. Then the query response times are shown in Figure 14.3. The queuing delay increases as the query rate increases. Except in the local directory case, the queuing delay increases as the directory update rate increases. This is because only the nonlocal update messages are considered as input traffic to the directory. Since the input traffic to the multiple master directory system is shared among the master directories, it yields lower queuing delay than the centralized directory system. For the range of query rates we have studied, the time spent in transmission to and from the directories constitutes a large portion of the delay. Since the distributed directory system does not require such transmission, it yields the lowest query response time.

Let us now consider the extended central-

ized directory system. For those files that have not yet been queried at the directory by the ith computer, the response time is similar to the centralized directory system except that the directory query rate is much smaller. The output queue at the centralized directory for a given computer should include the update traffic (generated by all the computers) for the extended directory of that computer. For those files whose directory information has already been appended to the local directory at that computer, there is no need for that computer to consult the master directory about these files. Therefore, the query response time has similar characteristics to that of the distributed directory system.

14.4. DEADLOCK IN DISTRIBUTED DATA BASES

A deadlock exists whenever two or more processes vying for the same resource reach an impasse. For example, suppose both processes 1 and 2 require resources A and B to complete their tasks. At a certain point in time, process 1 has locked resource A and requested resource B; likewise process 2 has locked re-

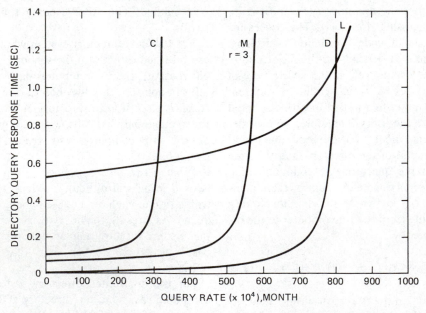

Figure 14.3. Expected directory query response time vs. directory query rate for various directory systems. Normalized directory update rate = 0.5. C = centralized directory, L = local directory, D = distributed directory, M = multiple master directories.

source B and requested A. Therefore, neither process 1 nor process 2 can obtain the necessary resources to complete its task. Thus a deadlock has occurred. When a deadlock occurs, if a job is aborted, the resulting partially completed process often represents a serious inconvenience to the user. He or she must, in many cases, reconstruct partially altered files. For this reason, deadlock is an important consideration in the design of operating systems, even though in practice it seldom occurs.

When the resources required by any process can be obtained prior to starting it, a deadlock prevention mechanism examines the resource requirements of all processes and allows a process to proceed only when a deadlock cannot occur. Therefore deadlock can be prevented. On the other hand, when the resources required by any process cannot be obtained a priori (or it is too costly to do so), or when the system uses dynamic resource allocation (e.g., virtual memory systems), resource requirements may change dynamically. In these cases, deadlock detection must be used. The system detects and resolves the deadlock by eliminating an offending process from contention. It is possible to combine these mechanisms so that certain resources are serviced by a detection mechanism while other resources are serviced by a prevention mechanism.

Many studies of deadlock protection schemes have been reported [13, 14, 15], but the emphasis in these studies has been on centralized data base systems. Here we will emphasize distributed data base systems, which are complicated by the necessity for coordinating several computers without impeding their progress.

Access Control.   In many cases, such as program libraries, it is necessary for two or more processes to have simultaneous access to the same file. However, a process that modifies a file cannot share with any other process access to that file at the same time. In order to provide users with this flexibility, a system must provide two methods of access to every file, either *shared* or *exclusive*. The user specifies which method of access is desired when the file is requested. If no process has been granted ex-

clusive access to a file, then a request for shared access to that file by any process can be granted. In the same manner, if no process has been granted either shared or exclusive access to a file, then a request for exclusive access to that file by any process can be granted. This protocol provides multiple readers *or* one writer with access to a specific file.

Deadlock Prevention Mechanisms

One way to implement deadlock prevention in a computer network is to assign a node (computer) as a monitor to examine the file requirements of all processes and allow a process to proceed when a deadlock cannot occur. This is rather inefficient since the monitoring node has to examine the file requirements before the process can be allowed to start, and a process will not be allowed to start if a future deadlock is possible. A more efficient way to implement deadlock prevention is to assign a fixed examining path in the network by assigning every node in the network a number [16]. Then the *examining path* is determined uniquely by the node number, as shown in Figure 14.4. When requests for files are passed around the network according to this path, intersite communication is greatly reduced. Further, node n_k (with node number k) has knowledge of the resource requests of the nodes that have node numbers lower than k, therefore node n_k is able to determine if the requeted resources will cause deadlock. Such distributed control scheme improves the efficiency of the deadlock prevention mechanisms.

Since the lower-numbered nodes have better

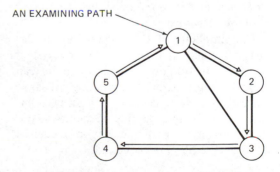

AN EXAMINING PATH

Figure 14.4. An examining path of a network.

access to the deadlock prevention mechanism than higher-numbered nodes, one way to assign the node numbers is to assign lower numbers to the nodes that contain files that have a high usage frequency and a high volume of data required per transmission.

A Simple Deadlock Prevention Mechanism
Deadlock prevention mechanisms require the user to specify the files that a process requires prior to initiation of that process. These requests are usually made through the job control language of the system. The information is used by the system to prevent a deadlock from occurring.

One means of preventing deadlock is for the system to obtain control of all the files requested by a process before initiating the process. For one process at a time, the system collects the requests for files and examines each one to determine if access to the file can be granted as outlined in the previous section. If all requests can be granted, the process is given access to the files and is initiated. Otherwise, the process is delayed until all processes that have access to requested files terminate. While the process is delayed, the requested files are available to other processes.

In a distributed data base, the system examines the requests for files to determine if all the requests are for local files. If they are, the requests are processed as outlined above. Otherwise, the requests for files are passed from node to node via the examining path, starting with the first node. Each node examines the requests for files located at that node as outlined above. As soon as all the requests for files have been granted, the node at which the requesting process resides is so informed and the process is allowed to proceed.

The simplicity of this mechanism enables easy implementation and requires low system overhead. In addition, interactive users can avoid waiting by simply terminating a delayed process, since such a process has not been initiated. Clearly, in a distributed data base system, intercomputer communication is required when remote files are requested.

Deadlock Prevention with Process Set [16]
In order to more effectively determine if access

to a file can be granted, processes having requests for the same file(s) can be grouped into process sets. A system may have any number of process sets. The membership criterion is, if a process requests exclusive access to a file, then that process and all other processes that have requested access (exclusive or shared) to that file are members of the same process set. Further, each process belongs to one process set.

Such a group of process sets is formed as follows: Whenever a new process arrives, certain process sets that have possession of file(s) that are requested by the new process are combined and the new process is added to the resulting process set. (Of course, if no process sets possess a file or a set of files requested by a new process, then the new process forms a process set by itself.) The rules for combining process sets are as follows. If shared access to a file is requested by the new process, the process set containing one or more processes that have requested exclusive access to that file is combined with the new process. If exclusive access to a file is requested by the new process, all the process sets containing one or more processes that have requested access (exclusive or shared) to that file are combined, and the new process is added to the resulting process set. When a process terminates, the remaining members of the process set may be reexamined with respect to each other by the same mechanism to reform their process set or sets.

The advantage of establishing process sets is that once a process has been allocated to a set, the progress of that process is independent of all processes in other process sets. Furthermore, in contrast with the simple deadlock prevention mechanism, a process in a process set does not require complete control of all its files. The use of process sets for deadlock prevention considerably reduces the amount of computation required to determine whether or not all the processes can be completed. However, there is a certain amount of overhead in forming the process sets.

Deadlock Detection

Deadlock detection allows the user to request access to files at any time. The system moni-

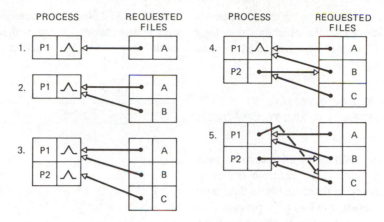

Figure 14.5. Deadlock detection in a distributed data base.

tors these requests by maintaining two lists, a list of processes P_1, P_2 ... , and a list of requested files A, B ... , as in Figure 14.5. The symbol $\wedge$ indicates the process is not waiting for a file. Lack of the symbol indicates the process is waiting for a file. Each element of the lists has a pointer that is used by the system to determine if a deadlock has occurred. When the system receives a request for access to a file from a process, if the request can be granted, the pointer of the corresponding file is set to point to that process and the process is allowed to proceed. Otherwise, the pointer of the process is set to point to the requested file. The file list and process lists starting from the requested file are traversed along the path formed by the pointers until either an open process pointer $\wedge$ is found, in which case the requesting process is delayed, or the pointers return to the requesting process, in which case a deadlock exists [14].

As an example, consider two processes that make the following series of requests for files:

Request 1   Process 1: requests for file A
Request 2   Process 1: requests for file B
Request 3   Process 2: requests for file C
Request 4   Process 2: requests for file B
Request 5   Process 1: requests for file C

The process and file lists are formed as shown in Figure 14.5. The open process pointer in request 4 is found when the path P2-B-P1 is detected. In this case P2 is delayed until P1 releases file B. If process P2 is not delayed, then the deadlock in request 5 is found when the loop P1-C-P2-B-P1 is detected by the detection algorithm. When a deadlock is detected, the system returns one of the processes involved to its initial state, releasing and restoring the files it controls. Since the files must be restored, a backup copy of each file must be available. The removed process is restarted at a later time.

The implementation of the deadlock detection mechanism in a distributed data base is accomplished by appointing one node of the network to monitor requests for files and detect deadlocks. The appointed node maintains the process and file lists, and every node is required to transmit to the appointed node information concerning the initiation and termination of each process and all requests for and releases of files. A process is allowed to proceed without waiting, even if a future deadlock is possible. For the purpose of improving reliability, a second node may be appointed as a back up to monitor requests for files.

Deadlock detection can be easily implemented and has an advantage in that the user is not required to know in advance which files a process requires. On the other hand, even though actual deadlocks are infrequent, when they do occur, considerable system overhead must be accounted for. For example, an interactive user who is restarted must resupply all the information he had given the process, since the original information has lost its integrity. Finally, although this mechanism requires considerable intercomputer communication even when local files are being used, processes will not be delayed by the mechanism as long as all its requests for files (made at various times) can be granted.

14.5. MUTUAL AND INTERNAL CONSISTENCY IN MULTICOPY DATA BASES

To improve the availability and response time of distributed data bases, multiple copies of files may be stored in the distributed data base system. As a result, the loss of a processor or channel link will not result in the loss of the entire data base, and storing data at those sites that use it frequently provides faster access. However, storing multiple copies of files in the system creates the problem of synchronization of concurrent updates. Many studies [17–35] have been done. We shall discuss a few of the methods.

The Problem. Every transaction that causes a change in any data item stored in the data base must be followed by update messages to all nodes (sites) that have a copy of the data. Each site has a data base management system (DBMS) that applies those updates to the data it maintains. As an extreme case we may have one complete copy of the data base in each node.

Considering a file that is stored in both sites A and B, an update may cause the loss of mutual consistency as shown in the following.

SITE A		SITE B	
PART #	PRICE	PART #	PRICE
.	.	.	.
.	.	.	.
.	.	.	.
1021	$10.00	1021	$10.00
.	.	.	.
.	.	.	.
.	.	.	.

At site A, a transaction may change the price of part #1021 from $10.00 to $13.00 and at site B an almost simultaneous transaction changes the price of the same item from $10.00 to $12.00. After these local executions and transmissions of the update messages to each other, a possible result is:

SITE A		SITE B	
PART #	PRICE	PART #	PRICE
.	.	.	.
.	.	.	.
.	.	.	.
1021	$12.00	1021	$13.00
.	.	.	.
.	.	.	.
.	.	.	.

The mutual consistency is not preserved because each site performs the local transaction before receiving the update message from the other site. Mutual consistency means that all copies of the same data must be identical to each other. It is not possible to have instantaneously identical copies at all times because of the communication delays. However they must converge to an identical final state when transaction activity is terminated.

Besides the problem of mutual consistency of the redundant copies of the data base, we also must consider the preservation of invariant relations among items within the data base, also known as integrity constraints. This is called internal consistency, or data integrity. The following example shows how internal consistency of each data base may be lost because of updates.

Suppose that we have a file consisting of three data fields (x, y and z) that must satisfy the condition $x + y + z = 3$. This file is stored at sites A and B, and initially these three variables have value 1. Now, if a user at site A executes $x = -1$, $y = 3$, and almost immediately another user at site B executes $y = 3$, $z = -1$, we have the following possible result:

SITE A		
	BEFORE UPDATE	AFTER UPDATE
x	1	−1
y	1	3
z	1	−1
x + y + z	3	1

SITE B		
	BEFORE UPDATE	AFTER UPDATE
x	1	−1
y	1	3
z	1	−1
x + y + z	3	1

Mutual consistency among the multiple copies is preserved here, but internal consistency of each data base is not. However, each transaction does preserve data integrity if it is executed alone.

In conclusion, we must then observe two criteria to preserve data consistency: mutual consistency between redundant copies of data bases and internal consistency of each copy.

Solutions to the Consistency Problem

To provide mutual consistency, any alteration of a data item must be performed in all the copies of the data base, and alterations to the same data item must be performed in the same order in all copies of the data base. To provide internal consistency on a distributed data base, a lock mechanism should be used to synchronize transactions, provided that each transaction when executed alone does not compromise data integrity.

Despite the delays in the communication lines, it is possible to force updates to take place in all the copies in the same order if we assign timestamps (TS) to them [21]. These timestamps are generated by a local clock at each site. Synchronization of these clocks is discussed in Reference 29. These timestamps represent the time that the local transactions, which generated the updates, happened and are propagated along with the update messages. Each data item in each copy of the distributed data base has also its own timestamp. (Using timestamps in this way clearly increases the storage requirements for the data base.) This timestamp represents the time that the data item was last updated. Upon arrival of an update message to a node, the local data management process compares the timestamp of the update message to the one assigned to the local data item. The update is performed only if the timestamp of the received update

message is more recent than that of the data item in the local copy.

Consider the following message for updating values of two data items in all redundant files in the distributed data base where the timestamp format is (year, month, day, hour, minute): $TS = (79, 3, 15, 21, 01)$

ID	VALUE
1021	$4.00
1035	$7.50

Consider one of the copies of the data base that has the following value:

ID	VALUE	TS
1021	$2.50	(77, 5, 15, 9, 12)
1035	$7.90	(79, 3, 15, 12, 14)

The second data item shown above will not have its value changed because its timestamp is more recent than that of the update message. It can be shown that by using timestamps, all copies of the data base converge to a final value as required by mutual consistency. However, the timestamp method is not sufficient to preserve internal consistency.

To provide internal consistency, the update transactions must be done with mutually exclusive access to every copy of the data items to be modified; that is, the transactions must be serialized. This is a direct extension of the problem in a centralized data base. The portions of the data base being read or written must be locked by the process executing the transaction. Further, there is a necessary restriction on the order of "lock" and "unlock" operations by a transaction. Suppose transaction A locks, reads, and unlocks a data item, then locks and reads a second data item. If another transaction, transaction B, updates both data items during the interval between the first unlock and the second lock of transition A, the set of data read by transaction A may be inconsistent. It can be shown that transactions must use "two-phase" locking to prevent such inconsistency [24]; that is, a transaction must consist of a "growing phase" where it sets all its locks and does not release any locks, followed immediately by a "shrinking phase" in which the locks are released and no locks can be set. Therefore, in two-phase locking, no lock may be set by a transaction after it has released a lock.

A straightforward algorithm implements the synchronization. For a network with n nodes, however, it requires $5n$ intercomputer messages which consist of n lock requests, n lock grants, n update messages, n update acknowledgments, and n lock releases. Because of the amount of communications involved, the method is time consuming and expensive.

A good synchronization algorithm must be deadlock free and speed independent, and allow partial operability. It must be speed independent because one cannot guarantee the order in which messages sent by two nodes will arrive at a third. The time required to transmit messages between any two nodes is not fixed. Partial operability implies the ability to operate even in case of failure of part of the network. In what follows, we will describe different approaches that reduce the amount of intercomputer communications.

Primary Site Locking [27]   PSL is a cost effective locking protocol for concurrency conntrol. In PSL, each file has a designated primary site (PS) that controls access to the file. For a task at a non PS to obtain read access, a lock request message for read only access is sent to the PS. The reading task then waits until the PS replies with a lock-grant message which indicates that all updates to the requested file are completed. Contained in the lock grant message is the sequence number of the last update made to the file. If the requesting site has not posted this update, then it waits until all outstanding updates have been posted before the reader is permitted to commence processing. Once the reader completes its processing, a lock release message is sent to the PS. If there is no other task using the file for read only access, then update access could be permitted at this time

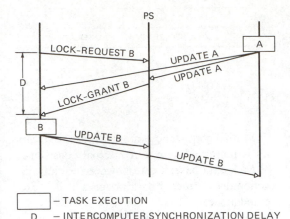

□ – TASK EXECUTION
D – INTERCOMPUTER SYNCHRONIZATION DELAY

Figure 14.6. Protocol diagram for primary site locking (PSL)

Figure 14.6 shows the file update protocol for PSL. If the requesting task does not reside at the PS of the file, a lock request message (for update access) is sent, and the PS must reply with a lock grant message before the requesting task can proceed. The requesting task may incur additional waiting if the sequence nunmber in the lock grant message indicates that there is an outstanding update message. Once the task completes its processing, its updates are distributed. The sequence number of the update is equal to the sequence number in the lock grant message plus one. A site receiving the update will post it if the update is in sequence. Otherwise, the new update is queued until outstanding updates arrive. At the PS, an update message has the additional interpretation of an implicit lock release.

In PSL, the number of messages required for file access varies with task assignment. In particular, if F_i is updated by a task assigned to F_i's primary site, then no lock request, lock grant, or lock release message is required.

The Majority Consensus Algorithm [21]. The majority consensus algorithm is based on the principle that an update can be performed only if the majority of the data base management systems in the network agree with a request for that update. The reason for this condition is because if two update requests have been accepted by a majority of the nodes, then at least one voted OK for both, and consequently they do not conflict. Each request contains the list of the variables that participate in the update computation with their respective timestamps and the values for the updated variables. Each DBMS upon receipt of a request must either vote OK, REJECT, PASS, or defer voting. A vote of REJECT is issued by a node if any of the variables in the request is already obsolete, that is, has a timestamp older than the one in that node's copy. A vote of OK is given if all variables are up-to-date and there is no conflict with any pending request. PASS is voted if the variables are up-to-date but there is a conflict with a higher-priority request. Voting is deferred if the variables are up-to-date but there is a conflict with a lower-priority request.

If the majority vote OK, the transaction is executed. In case of receiving a REJECT, the originating station must try again at a later time. If no REJECT is given but, because of PASS votes, the number of OK votes do not make the majority, the originating station must try again later.

For a network with n nodes, the number of transmissions to perform an update for a broadcast network is *2.5n*.

Speed independence is achieved by the use of timestamps, and the use of priorities along with timestamps makes the algorithm deadlock free. Partial operability is also guaranteed. However, if more than half the network is not accessible, no updates can be performed.

Variable Level of Synchronization Control [30]. Most synchronization techniques are ultimately equivalent to global locking by each transaction of the items in the data base that it reads or writes. However, a careful analysis of the conflicts between transactions shows that other synchronization mechanisms, weaker than global locking, can often be used instead. Such weaker synchronization mechanisms are faster and allow a greater degree of concurrency in transaction execution; thus, they bring about more efficient operation of the distributed database system. This work describes the design and implementation of a concurrency control that uses four different synchronization mechanisms. Conflicting transactions are run using the mechanism that

is most efficient and still generates consistent results.

The data base environment consists of transaction modules, which supervise execution of transactions, and data modules, each of which manages storage of a portion of the data base. Parts of the data base are duplicated in multiple data modules. A transaction in execution performs read operations on a set of items in the data base and write operations on another set of items. These sets are called the *read set* and the *write set* of the transaction. A conflict between two transactions occurs when the write set of one transaction intersects either the read set or the write set of another transaction.

The proposed synchronization mechanisms are called *protocols* and are expressed as rules for the relative sequencing of read and write operations in individual data modules. These read and write operations are generated by transactions that are being run concurrently. The relative sequence of read and write operations depends on the nature of the conflict between the transactions and on the transaction timestamp. Each transaction is assigned a globally unique timestamp by its transaction module.

The protocols define the relationship between transactions in execution; that is, one transaction runs under a particular protocol with respect to one or more conflicting transitions. Thus, transaction A may run under protocol 1 with respect to transaction B but (simultaneously) under protocol 3 with respect to transaction C. Four protocols are proposed and are numbered in order of the strictness of their synchronization requirements. Protocol 1 is for conflicts that occur only between the read set of one transaction and the write set of another. Protocol 2 is for read-only transactions that conflict with several other transactions. Protocol 3 is as strong as global locking, and synchronizes a pair of transactions where both the read set and write set of one transaction interfere with the other transaction. Protocol 4, for individual transactions that have a large number of conflicts with others, specifies that the transaction is to be run serially; that is, no conflicting transactions can be run concurrently with it.

In order to decide which of the protocols to use for synchronization at run-time, the transactions are first classified off-line according to their read sets and write sets. Each class has a read set and a write set. A transaction is a member of a particular class if its read set is contained in the class's read set and its write set is contained in the class's write set. The conflicts between classes are analyzed using a graphical technique called a conflict graph. The result of this analysis is a concurrency table that specifies which protocol to use when synchronizing transactions from conflicting classes. The table is referenced by transaction modules at run-time.

This concurrency control is implemented by the use of *read conditions*. A transaction module begins execution of a transaction by sending out read messages containing read conditions that specify that: (1) Read operations for the current transaction cannot be executed until the write operations generated by specified transaction classes have been completed, and (2) the read operations (except for protocol 1) must be executed before write operations for other transactions that might interfere with the executing transaction. Therefore Protocol 3 may often be more expensive than global locking. Protocol 4 requires an additional exchange of messages between transaction modules that takes place before the read messages are sent. A "concurrency monitor" at each data module schedules the read and write operations.

Atomic Transactions and Two-Phase Commit

Regardless of the mechanisms used to synchronize transactions, we must ensure that each transaction's execution is *atomic;* that is, the transaction either completes at all nodes of the network or does not happen at all. If the resulting database state at any node reflects a partial effect of the transaction, or if the transaction aborts at some nodes and completes at others, then consistency has not been preserved. Furthermore, it is undesirable to require any node to "back-out" or "undo" a transaction whose updates have already been written into that node's database.

Two-phase commit is a useful mechanism that provides transaction atomicity, and can be used effectively with many synchronization algorithms. We say that a node *commits* a transaction to its database when it writes the modifications and updates required by the transaction onto its permanent database storage, thus changing the database state. Two-phase commit provides a way to co-ordinate the decision of all nodes as to whether to commit or abort the transaction.

In two-phase commit, one node, acting as the *co-ordinator,* makes the final decision of whether to commit or abort the transaction. In the first phase, the co-ordinator sends a PREPARE message to all nodes. When receiving a PREPARE message, a node enters a state where it can recoverably either commit or abort the transaction. This is called the READY state, and normally requires that some local log entries be made at the node to facilitae recovery or a retry of the transaction, should it become necessary at a later time. It may also require that some local locks be set on the resources required to commit the transaction. The node then informs the co-ordinator that it is READY. Once a node enters the READY state, it cannot unilaterally decide whether to commit or abort; only the co-ordinator can make that decision. When the co-ordinator receives replies from all nodes, it then decides whether to commit or abort. The second phase then begins with a commit or abort message from the co-ordinator to all nodes. When receiving this second message, each node performs the appropriate action (commit or abort), releases resources required by the transaction and replies to the co-ordinator. This step either completes execution or aborts the transaction.

By leaving the final decision of whether to commit or abort in the hands of a single node, the two-phase commit procedure helps ensure consistency. Further, forcing all nodes to come to the READY state before commitment, where they are prepared to either commit or abort and to recover from either action, the procedure minimizes the possibility of expensive back-out or recovery operations which might be required otherwise, such as in the case where a node crashes while updating. For more extensive and detailed treatments of two-phase commit, the reader is referred to [32, 25].

The Exclusive Writer Protocol (EWP)

In the previous sections, we have discussed techniques for updating replicated files including locking and timestamps. While the processing costs and message volume of locking and timestamps can be substantial, this overhead may not be significant for database managment systems in which shared files reside on secondary storage. However, for real time systems in which files consist of data in RAM and which use no high level data model, the overhead of locking or timestamps may be prohibitive. Therefore, a new approach to data consistency has been introduced. In it, accesses to shared data are structured so that there is only one predetermined task which is allowed to write a shared data item. Referred to as the *exclusive-writer protocol* (EWP), this approach can provide a low cost technique for ensuring mutual consistency that is suitable for distributed real time systems.

In the EWP, a task can read a local copy of a data item at any time. However, *each shared data item is written by only one predetermined task which does not change during system operation.* To handle situations in which multiple tasks must write the same data (referred to as multiwriter situations), the following approach can be used (1) an exclusive-writer (EW) is designated for each shared data item, and (2) to update a shared data item, a task sends an update-request message to the data item's EW. Such an approach has been used by the Distributed Processing Architecture Design (DPAD) [34]. Here, we assume that exclusive-writers are dedicated to receiving update-request messages, distributing updates, and performing operations to ensure data consistency.

Using the EWP to ensure mutual consistency results in two advantages over employing non-exclusive writer techniques such as timestamps and locking. First, the EWP avoids delays due to locking protocol overhead and waits for locking synchronization. A second advantage relates to deadlocks. Since the

EWP does not use locking, the *EWP can eliminate deadlocks due to shared data access.*

Internal Consistency Considerations. Although the EWP can ensure mutual consistency, it does not necessarily ensure internal consistency as illustrated in the example (Section 14.5).

To ensure internal consistency in multiwriter situations without the use of locking or timestamps, the *interdependent data set (IDS) update rule* is proposed as follows:

1. When a data item is modified, the resulting update must include the values of all data for which the modified data item has an interdependency. (Applying the IDS update rule to the example in Section 14.5 assuming that site A is the exclusive writer, the user at site A must include z in its update, and the user at site B must include x, as shown in Figure 14.7). This implies that EWP updates may be larger than those for locking and timestamps.
2. When a site posts an update, it must guarantee that the entire update is processed atomically (i.e., without interruption). Under these conditions internal consistency (but not serializability) will be preserved.

Using the IDS update rule may increase the size of the update message. This motivates us to introduce the following variation of the EWP which does not use the IDS update rule. Each copy of a file has an update sequence number, SN. The update-request messages (rather than the entire IDS), contains the modified data and the SN. To determine if there was a conflict due to concurrent update-requests, the EW compares the SN in the update-request message with that of the corresponding file at its site. If they are not equal, then data conflict occurred. To avoid violating internal consistency, conflicting update-requests are discarded.* If no conflict occurred,

---

*For some applications (e.g. object discrimination in signal processing applications), occasional discard of updates may not be a problem.

EXCLUSIVE-WRITER'S SITE

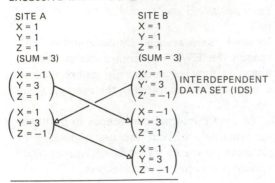

THE CONVERGED VALUES

X = 1	X = 1	MUTUAL AND
Y = 3	Y = 3	INTERNAL
Z = −1	Z = −1	CONSISTENCY
(SUM = 3)	(SUM = 3)	

Figure 14.7. Preserving internal consistency in the EWP with interdependent data set update rule.

the EW increases the SN by one and distributes the updates (which include the SN) as shown in Figure 14.8.

Discarding update requests may not be acceptable for some applications, so we extend the EWP to include a locking option (EWL). When an update conflict occurs, the EWP then switches to Primary Site Locking (PSL): the EW site is the primary site for all the files in the conflicting update-request, and the conflicting update-request is treated as a PSL lock request. Once all of the files required by the update request have been locked, the primary site issues a lock-grant message to the site that

originated the update-request message. The originating site then re-executes the transactions and increases the SN of the files it updates by one, and then distributes the updates. When the EW receives an update message, it is treated as a lock-release. The detailed protocol is shown in Figure 14.9.

To conclude, the EWP eliminates intercomputer synchronization delays but does not provide serializability (only internal and mutual consistency). The EWL does provide serializability (as well as internal and mutual consistency) and has the advantage of eliminating the intercomputer synchronization delay when there is no data conflict. Thus, the EWP and EWL have great appeal for updating replicated files in distributed real time systems. For more discussions on EWP, the interested reader should refer to [33].

14.6. FAULT TOLERANCE AND RECOVERY IN DISTRIBUTED DATA BASE SYSTEMS

Various techniques have been proposed to maintain the consistency of a multiple copy data base (that is, a distributed data base in which redundant copies of data are maintained at more than one site) in the event of site failures, and to facilitate proper recovery of a failed site. We shall first discuss techniques used to maintain consistency of the surviving copies of the data base if a crash occurs.

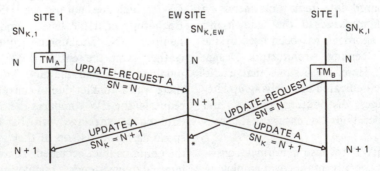

*UPDATE-REQUEST DISCARDED DUE TO DATA CONFLICT

$SN_{K,I}$ = UPDATE SEQUENCE NUMBER FOR THE COPY OF FILE F_K AT SITE I

(TM$_A$ AND TM$_B$ ONLY ACCESS FILE F_K)

Figure 14.8. Protocol diagram for the EWP with sequence numbers.

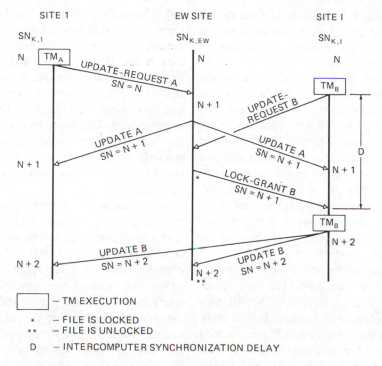

Figure 14.9. Protocol diagram for the EWL.

Maintaining Consistency of the Data Base if a Site Crashes. A number of approaches to this problem have been proposed. One of them is based on a scheme for organizing the computer network such that our host site is designated as a primary site and several others are designated as back-up sites. Protocols are used that guarantee that a resource-sharing service (such as multiple-copy update synchronization) will be disrupted only if n hosts fail simultaneously during a critical phase of the service, where n is determined by the design of the protocols. Such a scheme is said to satisfy the n-host resiliency criterion [17].

A number of simpler techniques can be used to maintain consistency. A two phase message-sending procedure for update messages was proposed in Reference 19. In this technique, the first phase of the procedure is the sending of a message to all sites informing them that an update message is to be forthcoming, including the names of the sites that should receive the message. The second phase is the update message itself sent to all sites. Any sites that received the first-phase message but do not receive the expected update message (pos-

sibly because of a failure of the originating site) will consult the other sites named in the first-phase message to ascertain whether any of them received the update. As a result of such consultation, the update will be applied either to all of the intended sites or to none of them, thus preserving mutual consistency.

An alternative technique [20] is to have each site keep a list of the last n updates generated by each site (where the choice of n depends on the characteristics of the system). Each site agrees not to initiate an update until its nth previous update has been acknowledged by all sites. When a site crashes, all the sites compare the lists of updates that were originated by the crashed site. This comparison indicates the possible inconsistencies resulting from the crash. The surviving sites can then be made mutually consistent.

Recovery of a Crashed Site [20]. When a crashed site recovers, it must be brought up to a state consistent with the other copies of the data base. There are two major problems here: The first is to make sure that the crashed site performs all the updates that originated at other sites while it was down, and the second is to complete any update transactions that were initiated by the crashed site and were interrupted by the crash.

Provided that the local data base copy was not destroyed by the crash, the first problem is solved by properly storing all the updates that occur while the site is down. This can be accomplished by using a history file at each site which records all updates to the data base and is marked to indicate the times when reconfigurations (crashes or recoveries) occurred. When a crashed site comes back up, one of the surviving sites sends a copy of the portion of the history file made between the time of the crash and the time of recovery.

If a site crashes before completing an update transaction, we have two consistency problems to contend with: (1) The site may have broadcast update messages before modifying its own data base, and (2) the site may have completed the updating of its local data base, but had not yet begun to send update messages. Problem 1 can be dealt with using the history file technique described above. For problem 2 we can require each site to record the updates to be made for a transaction before beginning to modify its own data base. This list of recent updates must survive any crash. When the site recovers, this list will be checked for outstanding updates so that the surviving sites can be made consistent with the crashed site.

In case the data base copy at a site is completely destroyed by a crash (e.g., disk head crash), another site must be selected to make a copy of its data base after the crashed site becomes operational. During the time-consuming process of generating the copy, the previously crashed site is still treated as inoperative. Once the copy is installed, the recovery procedure described above is followed, using history file segments to ensure that recent updates are entered.

14.7. OPTIMAL QUERY PROCESSING POLICY

In this section we discuss policy for query processing in a distributed data base [36, 37, 38, 39]. The main problem is the following: If a query can be decomposed into subqueries that require operations at geographically separated data bases, determine the sequence and the sites for performing this set of operations such that the operating cost (communication cost and processing cost) for processing this query is minimized. The problem is complicated by the fact that query processing policy depends not only on the query operations, but also on the parameter values associated with these operations.

In this section we present a method for generating the optimal query processing policy that jointly optimizes the processing cost and communication cost. Further, the method includes a variety of query operations.

We first discuss the representation of a query by a set of query trees and describe the procedure for generating the set of query processing graphs from the query trees. Next, theorems are given for optimal site selection for performing the operations and for determining local optimal query processing policies among the set of query processing graphs. Then a mathematical model is developed to compute the operating cost for a given query processing policy. Finally, an example is included to illustrate the procedure for finding the optimal query processing policy for processing a given query.

Query Trees

We assume that a given query can be decomposed into a sequence of operations with serial and parallel relationships, which will yield the correct result. We shall use a query tree as shown in Figure 14.10a to express these relationships. For example, in Figure 14.10a, the PROJECTION operation on F_2, and the PROJECTION and SELECTION operations on F_3 are performed in parallel and then input to the JOIN and PROJECTION operations, which are performed serially. The output from these operations together with F_1 are processed by UNION and SELECTION serially, and so on. In general, for a given query, there are many query trees that will produce the correct

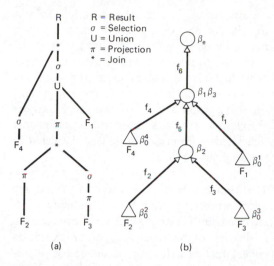

R = Result
σ = Selection
U = Union
π = Projection
* = Join

(a)   (b)

Figure 14.10. A query tree and a resulting query processing graph.

Query Processing Graphs

To reduce communication cost in distributed data-base systems, it is often desirable to perform a group of operations at a single site and then transmit the results to other site(s) for further processing. Therefore, we collect sets of connected operations in the query tree into groups (local operation groups). These groups have the property that any pair of operations in a group can be linked by a path in the query tree such that all the operations on the path are in the group. These groups may be selected as candidates to be performed at a single site. Further, under such arrangements the communication cost for processing this query becomes the algebraic sum of the commmunication cost among the selected groups. Therefore, this motivates us to transform the query tree into a graph representation. We shall call this new representation the *query processing graph*.

There are three types of operations in a query processing graph: initial operations, intermediate operations, and final operations.

Initial operations are designated by β_0^i, $i = 1, \ldots, s$, which mainly involve SELECTIONS and PROJECTIONS performed at the site that stores the file. Therefore, the initial operation selects the desired subset of the file for query processing. Intermediate operations are designated by β_i, which is either a single binary operation or a binary operation combined with one or more adjacent unary operations from a query tree to be executed at a single site. The final operation, β_e, presents the query result to the query initiator.

The query processing graph consists of execution nodes, storage nodes, and arcs, as shown in Figure 14.10b. The *execution node* (denoted by circles) represents execution of a local operation group (either a single operation β_j or multiple operations, $\beta_i \cdots \beta_j$) which are performed at a single site. The sites for execution by two neighboring execution nodes are distinct. Therefore, the *arcs* connecting the execution nodes represent data communication between sites. The *storage node* (denoted by triangles) represents a file permanently stored at a specific site. The arcs connecting storage nodes to execution nodes represent input data to the execution nodes. Therefore, a query processing graph not only represents a sequence of operations for processing the query, but also provides the information about a single operation or groups of operations to be performed at the same site or at different sites.

For example, β_2, an intermediate operation, in the query processing graph (Figure 14.10b) represents the join and projection operations of the query tree (Figure 14.10a) which is to be performed at a single site. β_0^3 in the query processing graph represents the initial operations of PROJECTION and SELECTION on file F_3 of the query tree. Files $f_1, \ldots, f_6$ are intermediate files that are transferred from one execution site to another. The transfer of intermediate file f_5 is represented by an arc between the site that performs β_2 and the site that performs β_1 and β_3. This graph represents the operation sequence $\beta_2\beta_1\beta_3\beta_e$ such that β_2 is executed at one site, followed by β_1 and β_3 at a second site, followed by β_e at the query originating site, which presents the final result file f_6 to the query initiator.

result of the query. We shall call these the set of feasible query trees for this query. Algorithms based on commutativity, associativity, and distributivity of operations are available to generate the set of feasible query trees.

In some cases the contents of a file are required to be sent to several sites for performing query operations; for example, in the SEMI-JOIN operation, part of the file stored at site Z may be sent to site X and the other part of the file may be sent to site Y for processing. Therefore, two arcs connecting different execution nodes (Z to X, and Z to Y) are needed to represent the communications for these query operations. Since sites X, Y, and Z represent different sites, adding an additional arc still satisfies the properties of the query processing graphs. In some cases, after performing the operation, site X may need to return some data to site Z (file storage location) for further processing. We need an additional execution node to represent the processing at site Z. Since the site for the processing of this additional execution node is different from the sites for the processing of its adjacent execution nodes, the additional graph still satisfies the properties of the proposed query processing graphs.

Since there are many possible ways for selecting local operation groups and for assigning sites for processing the operations, there are many possible query processing graphs for a given query tree.

Properties of Query Processing Graphs.
The operating cost for processing a query with a given policy consists of communication cost and processing cost. To apply a query processing graph to a given distributed data base, we assume that the communication cost between each pair of computers is proportional to the volume of data, that the unit communication costs among different pairs of computers are the same, and that the processing cost for all computers depends on the operation performed and on the volume of data. For a given operation the unit processing cost is the same for all the computers. Under these circumstances, we obtained the following theorems for site selection and computation reduction for the query processing graph [39].

Theorem 1. For each execution node of the query processing graph, selecting the site of the storage node execution that sends the largest amount of data to that operation node as the site for performing its operations yields a minimum operating cost for that graph.

If this site selection method generates an inconsistent site selection (selects the same site for two adjacent execution nodes of a graph), then the graph can be reduced to a simpler graph (one that has fewer execution nodes) that yields a lower operating cost than that of the original graph. ▲

Theorem 2. If the site selection for a given query processing graph based on Theorem 1 is inconsistent, then that graph can be reduced to a simpler graph (one with fewer execution nodes) that has the same sequence of operations. Furthermore, the reduced graph yields a lower operating cost than that of the original graph. ▲

If the set of operations at an execution node consists of more than one operation, we call it a multioperation execution node. Theorem 3 deals with graphs containing such execution nodes.

Theorem 3. For a given query processing graph that contains a multiple operation execution node that executes a set of operations $\{\beta_i \ldots \beta_j\}$, the sequence of operations from this set which has least processing cost is used by the policy that has least operating cost for this graph. ▲

Corollary. Theorem 3 is true for a query operation graph with more than one multiple operation execution node. ▲

Theorem 4. If the sequence of operations for processing a given query is fixed, then the query-processing policy that minimizes the communication cost (total volume of traffic) yields the lowest operating cost among the set of policies that uses this fixed sequence of operations. ▲

Theorems 1 and 2 together with the known file allocation information provide guidelines in site selection for performing operations. Theorem 3 can be used to select local optimal quering processing policies from certain query processing graphs that have multi-operation nodes, and Theorem 4 provides a way of locating local optimal query processing policies from the set of policies that perform the given fixed sequence of operations (that is, the set of query processing graphs generated from the same query tree). Using these theorems greatly reduces the computation requirements for determining the optimal query-processing policy.

Query Operating Cost Model

The operating cost for processing a query consists of the communication cost and the processing cost. The communication cost depends partially on the sites selected for the operations. Both the communication and processing costs depend on the data reduction functions, on the sequence of operations, and on the data volumes of the files involved. The data reduction function, $\alpha(\beta_j, \overline{F}, \overline{\gamma})$, is the ratio of the output data volume to the input data volume for the operation β_j, input files $\overline{F}$, and the query operation parameter $\overline{\gamma}$. The data reduction function further depends on the previous operations. The data reduction function of operation β_i preceded by operations $\overline{\beta}$ with input files $\overline{F}$ and query operation parameter $\overline{\gamma}$ is denoted as $\alpha(\beta_i \mid \overline{\beta}, \overline{F}, \overline{\gamma})$. $\alpha(\overline{\beta}_j, \overline{F}, \overline{\gamma})$ permits us to estimate the output temporary file length $\ell(f_i)$ for operation β_j from its input file size. Such data reduction functions may be estimated by simulation or measurement on a distributed data base [39] and their values are stored in the directory system [40,41].

Let C_0^i be the processing cost for operation β_0^i, and C_j be the processing cost for operation β_j per unit input file data (byte). Further, let C'_{ij} be the communication cost for transmitting a unit of data (byte) from the site that generates file f_i to the site of operation β_j. We will further define two indicating functions, Y_{ij} and Z_{ij}. We use Y_{ij} for indicating whether temporary file f_i is an input to operation β_j; that is,

$$Y_{ij} = \begin{cases} 1 \text{ if } f_i \text{ is an input to operation } \beta_j \\ 0 \text{ otherwise} \end{cases}$$

We use Z_{ij} for indicating whether f_i is available for processing at the site for performing β_j; that is,

$$Z_{ij} = \begin{cases} 1 \text{ if file } f_i \text{ is needed but is not} \\ \quad \text{available for processing at} \\ \quad \text{the site for performing } \beta_j \\ 0 \text{ otherwise} \end{cases}$$

Thus if $Z_{ij} = 1$, it is required to transmit file f_i to the site for performing β_j, $s(\beta_j)$. Z_{ij} is determined from the file allocation and the query-processing policy. The operating cost for processing a query with policy ψ equals

$$C(\psi) = \sum_{i=1}^{s} C_0^i \, \ell(F_i) + \sum_{j=1}^{k} C_j \sum_{i=1}^{q} \ell(f_i) Y_{ij}$$
$$+ \sum_{j=1}^{k} C'_{ij} \sum_{i=1}^{q} \ell(f_i) \, Z_{ij} \quad (15)$$
$$+ \delta_{ez} \cdot C'_{qe} \cdot \ell(f_q)$$

where

$\ell(F_i)$ = file length of F_i
$\ell(f_i)$ = file length of temporary file f_i
q = total number of temporary files required for processing of a given query
k = total number of operations β_j, $j > 0$, required for completing processing of a given query

$$\delta_{ez} = \begin{cases} 1 \text{ if } \beta_e \text{ is not at the same site of} \\ \quad \text{the last operation of } \psi, \beta_z \\ 0 \text{ otherwise} \end{cases}$$

C'_{qe} = unit communication cost for transmitting the query result to the originating site
f_q = result of the query

The first term of Eq. (15) is for the cost of the set of initial operations $\{\beta_0^i, i = 1, \ldots, s\}$ on the set of files $\{F_i, i = 1, \ldots, s\}$. The second term represents the total processing cost for performing operations β_j, $j = 1, \ldots, k$; the third term represents the total communication cost for transmitting temporary files, f_i, $i = 1, \ldots, q$, to the sites of operations β_j, $j = 1, \ldots, k$; and the last term represents the cost of transferring the final query result file to the result destination site. The δ_{ez} function indicates whether this transfer is necessary.

Different query-processing policies yield different sequences of query operations, as well as different locations for processing these operations. As a result, different policies yield different operating costs for processing a given query on a distributed data base. Eq (15) computes the operating cost for a given query-processing policy. With the aid of the theorems described in the last section and the use of Eq (15), we can determine the optimal policy that yields minimum operating cost for processing a given query.

Example

Consider a 4 node computer network (Figure 14.11) that contains an inventory relational data model and a data base consisting of 3 relations stored as files. The allocation and the descriptions of the files are given in Table 14.2.

The following query is initiated at node 4: "Generate a listing of ⟨part number, supplier name, quantity⟩ for all 'calculators' produced in Los Angeles in a quantity greater than 1,000 by any one supplier."

From this query an algorithm may be used to derive the required operations to construct the query tree, we have the tree as shown in Figure 14.12a. Based on the permutability of operations in the query tree, (i.e., adjacent JOIN operations are permutable), we can construct an additional tree for this query as shown in Figure 14.12a. Let us now generate the query graphs from each of the query trees.

In generating the processing query graphs from a query tree, we first generate the set of local operation groups from the operations in the query tree. Each of the local operation groups may be performed at an execution node in a query processing graph. Then we select the elements of the set of local operating groups and cascade them according to the sequence of operations in the query tree. The operations from the query trees are:

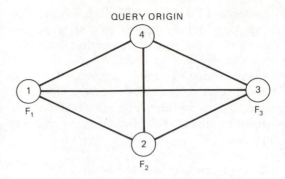

Figure 14.11. Computer network for the example.

- $\beta_0^1 = \sigma_1\pi_1$ are the initial SELECTION and PROJECTION operations on F_1.
- $\beta_0^2 = \sigma_2$ is the initial SELECTION operation on F_2.
- $\beta_0^3 = \sigma_3\pi_3$ are the initial SELECTION and PROJECTION operations on F_3.
- β_1 is an EQUIJOIN on part number.
- β_2 is an EQUIJOIN operation on supplier number and a PROJECTION operation that eliminates the supplier number column.
- β_e is the operation that presents the query result to the query initiator.

The set of local operation groups for the query tree of Figure 14.12a is $\{\beta_1, \beta_2, \beta_1\beta_2, \beta_e, \beta_2\beta_e, \beta_1\beta_2\beta_e\}$. The set of query processing graphs that is constructed is shown in Figure 14.13a. The query processing graph for policy ψ_1 represents the policy of transmitting the files $f_1, f_2,$ and f_3 resulting from the initial operations $\beta_0^1, \beta_0^2,$ and β_0^3 to site 4 and processing them there by performing operations β_1 followed by β_2. The graph for policy ψ_2 represents performing the same sequence of operations, $\beta_1\beta_2$, at either site 1, 2, or 3 and then transmitting the query result to site 4. The graph for policy ψ_3 corresponds to performing operation β_1 at either site 1, 2, or 3, and then performing operation β_2 at site 4. The graph for

Table 14.2. Sample File Characteristics of a Distributed Data Base.

FILE	LOCATION	CONTENTS	LENGTH (IN BYTES)
F_1	1	(Part #, Part name)	10^5
F_2	2	(Supplier #, Part #, Quantity)	10^5
F_3	3	(Supplier #, Supplier name, City)	10^4

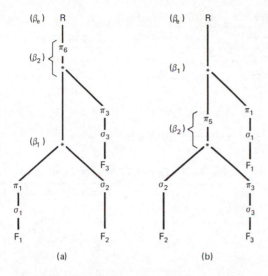

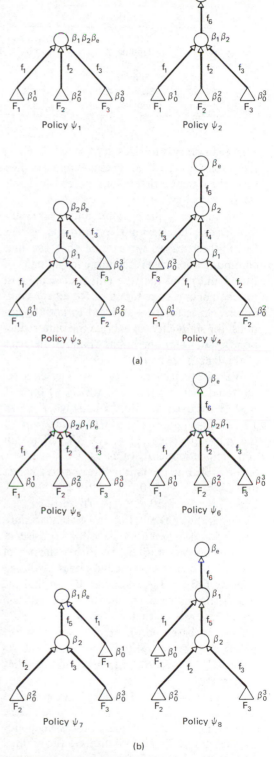

(a)

(b)

Figure 14.12. Feasible query trees for the example.

policy ψ_4 represents performing operation β_1 and β_2 separately at two of the sites 1, 2, and 3, by first performing operation β_1 at one site, then transmitting its result file to another site for processing by β_2, and then sending the final result to site 4.

In the same manner, the set of local operation groups for the query tree of Figure 14.12b is $\{\beta_2, \beta_1, \beta_2\beta_1, \beta_e, \beta_1\beta_e, \beta_2\beta_1\beta_e\}$. The set of query processing graphs constructed from this set is shown in Figure 14.13b. The query processing graph for policy ψ_5 represents the policy of transmitting the intermediate files f_1, f_2, and f_3 to site 4 for processing by operation β_2 followed by β_1. The graph for policy ψ_6 corresponds to performing operation β_2 followed by β_1 at one of the sites 1, 2, or 3, then transmitting the result of operation β_1 (the query result) to site 4. The graph for policy ψ_7 represents first performing operation β_2 at one of the sites 1, 2, or 3, then transmitting its result to site 4 for processing by operation β_1. Finally, the graph for policy ψ_8 corresponds to performing operations β_2 and β_1 at separate locations among sites 1, 2, and 3 by performing β_2 first, transmitting its result to the site for β_1, performing operation β_1, and finally transmitting its result to the site for β_1, performing operation β_1, and finally transmitting the query result to site 4.

The operations β_0^i, $i = 1, 2, 3$, reduce the files F_1, F_2, and F_3 to f_1, f_2, and f_3, respectively.

Figure 14.13. Query graphs for the example.
(a) Query graphs for the query tree of Figure 14.13a
(b) Query graphs for the query tree of Figure 14.13b

Table 14.3. Temporary File Characteristics.

f_i	CONTENTS	$\overline{\gamma}$ FOR β_0^i	$\alpha(\beta_0^i, F_i, \overline{\gamma})$	$\ell(f_i)$ IN BYTES
f_1	Part #	Part name is "calculators"	0.05	0.5×10^4
f_2	Supplier #, Part #, Quantity	Quantity $>$ 1,000	0.1	1×10^4
f_3	Supplier #, Supplier name	City is Los Angeles	0.3	0.3×10^4

The temporary file sizes $l(f_i) = \alpha(\beta_0^i, F_i, \overline{\gamma})$ $l(F_i)$ for $i = 1, 2, 3$. These temporary files have the characteristics summarized in Table 14.3.

We will study the example under three different cases by varying the parameter values. In all three cases, we assume that the unit communication cost is the same for all pairs of sites i and j and that the unit processing cost for each operation is the same for all the computers. Since file f_2 is an input to both operations, for simplicity we express the data reduction functions for operations β_1 and β_2 in terms of the length of file f_2.

We will first consider case A. The data reduction function values are $\alpha(\beta_0^i, F_i, \overline{\gamma})$ for $i = 1, 2, 3$ as given in Table 14.3, $\alpha(\beta_1, f_2, \overline{\gamma}) = 10^{-1}$, $\alpha(\beta_2, f_2, \overline{\gamma}) = 2 \times 10^{-1}$, and $\alpha(\beta_2 \mid \overline{\beta}, f_2, \overline{\gamma}) = (\beta_1 \mid \overline{\beta}, f_2, \overline{\gamma}) = 5 \times 10^{-2}$. The unit communication cost value is $C'_{ij} = C' = \$10^{-3}$/byte and the unit processing cost values are $C_0^i = C_0 = \$10^{-6}$/byte for $i = 1, 2, 3$, and $C_1 = C_2 = \$0.5 \times 10^{-3}$/byte.

The graph shown in Figure 14.8b has a multiple operation execution node that consists of a set of operation $\{\beta_1, \beta_2\}$ such that this set of operations can be executed in either of the sequences $\beta_1\beta_2$ or $\beta_2\beta_1$. It can be shown that the processing cost of the sequence of operations $\beta_1\beta_2$ is lower than that of the sequence $\beta_2\beta_1$. Therefore, based on Theorem 3, we chose the policy ψ_2 over ψ_6. Likewise, we chose the sequence $\beta_1\beta_2\beta_e$ over $\beta_2\beta_1\beta_e$, thus choosing policy ψ_1 over ψ_5.

Next we use Theorem 1 to select the sites of all the execution nodes in a given graph. This determines the optimal query processing policy for that graph. Table 14.4 displays the optimal sites selected for operations for all the query processing policies.

All the policies in the set $\{\psi_1, \psi_2, \psi_3, \psi_4\}$ have

Table 14.4. Optimal Sites for Operations.

POLICY	SITE FOR β_1	SITE FOR β_2	SITE FOR β_e
$\psi_{;1}$	4	4	4
ψ_2	2	2	4
ψ_3	2	4	4
ψ_4	2	3	4
ψ_7	4	2	4
ψ_8	1	2	4

the sequence of operations $\beta_0^1\beta_0^2\beta_0^3\beta_1\beta_2\beta_e$. Both of the policies in the set $\{\psi_7, \psi_8\}$ have the sequence of operations $\beta_0^1\beta_0^2\beta_0^3\beta_2\beta_1\beta_e$. In order to find the best policy within each of these sets, we need to compute the total communication cost $C'(\psi)$ for each policy in the set as follows.

$$C'(\psi_1) = C' \cdot [\ell(f_1) + \ell(f_2 + \ell(f_3)] = 18$$

$$
\begin{aligned}
C'(\psi_2) &= C' \cdot [\ell(f_1) + \ell(f_3) + \ell(f_6)] \\
&= C' \cdot [\ell(f_1) + \ell(f_3) \\
&\quad + \alpha(\beta_2 \mid \overline{\beta}, f_2, \overline{\gamma}) \cdot \ell(f_2)] = 8.5
\end{aligned}
$$

$$
\begin{aligned}
C'(\psi_3) &= C' \cdot [\ell(f_1) + \ell(f_3) + \ell(f_4)] \\
&= C' \cdot [\ell(f_1) + \ell(f_3) \\
&\quad + \alpha(\beta_1, f_2, \overline{\gamma}) \cdot \ell(f_2)] = 9
\end{aligned}
$$

$$
\begin{aligned}
C'(\psi_4) &= C' \cdot [\ell(f_1) + \ell(f_3) + \ell(f_5)] \\
&= C' \cdot [\ell(f_1) + \ell(f_3) \\
&\quad + \alpha(\beta_2, f_2, \overline{\gamma}) \cdot \ell(f_2)] = 10
\end{aligned}
$$

$$
\begin{aligned}
C'(\psi_7) &= C' \cdot [\ell(f_1) + \ell(f_4) + \ell(f_6)] \\
&= C' \cdot [\ell(f_1) + \alpha(\beta_1, f_2, \overline{\gamma}) \cdot \ell(f_2) \\
&\quad + \alpha(\beta_2 \mid \overline{\beta}, f_2, \overline{\gamma}) \cdot \ell(f_2)] = 6.5
\end{aligned}
$$

$$
\begin{aligned}
C'(\psi_8) &= C' \cdot [\ell(f_3) + \ell(f_5) + \ell(f_6)] \\
&= C' [\ell(f_3) + \alpha(\beta_2, f_2, \overline{\gamma}) \cdot \ell(f_2) \\
&\quad + \alpha(\beta_1 \mid \overline{\beta}, f_2, \overline{\gamma}) \cdot \ell(f_2)] = 5.5
\end{aligned}
$$

Since $C'(\psi_4) < C'(\psi_2) < C'(\psi_3) < C'(\psi_1)$, based on Theorem 4, ψ_4 is the optimal policy among the set of policies $\{\psi_1, \psi_2, \psi_3, \psi_4\}$. Likewise, ψ_8 is the optimal policy among the set of policies $\{\psi_7, \psi_8\}$.

Finally, we use Eq (15) to compute the operating cost of policies ψ_4 and ψ_8. Based on policy ψ_4 and the file allocation information in Table 14.2, we construct the following indicating functions:

$$Y(\psi_4) = \begin{vmatrix} 1 & 0 \\ 1 & 0 \\ 0 & 1 \\ 0 & 1 \\ 0 & 0 \\ 0 & 0 \end{vmatrix} \qquad Z(\psi_4) = \begin{vmatrix} 1 & 0 \\ 0 & 0 \\ 0 & 0 \\ 0 & 1 \\ 0 & 0 \\ 0 & 0 \end{vmatrix}$$

Substituting the parameters into Eq (15), we have

$$\begin{aligned} C(\psi_4) &= C_0 \cdot [\ell(F_1) + \ell(F_2) + \ell(F_3)] \\ &\quad + C_1 \cdot [\ell(f_1) + \ell(f_2)] + C_2 \\ &\quad \cdot [\ell(f_3) + \ell(f_4)] + C'(\pi_4) \\ &= 9.71 + 6.5 = 16.21 \end{aligned}$$

Likewise, for policy ψ_8, we have

$$Y(\psi_8) = \begin{vmatrix} 1 & 0 \\ 0 & 1 \\ 0 & 1 \\ 0 & 0 \\ 1 & 0 \\ 0 & 0 \end{vmatrix} \qquad Z(\psi_8) = \begin{vmatrix} 0 & 0 \\ 0 & 0 \\ 0 & 1 \\ 0 & 0 \\ 1 & 0 \\ 0 & 0 \end{vmatrix}$$

In the same manner, the operating cost of ψ_8 equals

$$\begin{aligned} C(\psi_8) &= C_0 \cdot [\ell(F_1) + \ell(F_2) + \ell(F_3)] \\ &\quad + C_1 \cdot [\ell(f_1) + \ell(f_5)] + C_2 \\ &\quad \cdot [\ell(f_2) + \ell(f_3)] + C'(\psi_8) \\ &= 10.21 + 5.5 = 15.71 \end{aligned}$$

We note that $C(\psi_8) < C(\psi_4)$; therefore, ψ_8 is the optimal query-processing policy for case A (see Table 14.5).

Let us now consider case B. All the parameter values remain the same as for case A except that the unit processing cost for operation β_1, C_1, has been reduced from 0.5×10^{-3}/byte to 0.25×10^{-3}/byte. The communication costs $C'(\psi_i)$ for $i = 0, 1, \ldots, 8$ of case A remain the same for case B. Therefore, based on Theorems 1, 3, and 4, policies ψ_4 and ψ_8 remain as the two local optimal policies for processing the query. The reduction in unit processing cost C_1 results in $C(\psi_4) < C(\psi_8)$. Therefore, ψ_4 becomes the optimal policy for processing the query as shown in Table 14.5.

Finally, let us consider case C. The unit processing costs C_0^i and C_j, $j = 1, 2$, the unit communication costs C_{ij}, and the data reduction functions for operations β_0^i, $\alpha(\beta_0^i, F_i, \overline{\gamma})$, remain the same as for case B. However, the data reduction functions for operations β_1 and β_2 have been increased. Their new values are: $\alpha(\beta_1, f_2, \overline{\gamma}) = 0.3$, $\alpha(\beta_2, f_2, \overline{\gamma}) = 0.45$, and $\alpha(\beta_2 \mid \overline{\beta}, f_2, \gamma) = \alpha(\beta_1 \mid \overline{\beta}, f_2, \gamma) = 0.4$. From Theorem 1, we know that site selections for the query execution nodes are independent of the data reduction functions for operations β_1 and β_2. Therefore, the sites for performing β_1 and β_2 remain the same as in cases A and B.

Because of the increase in the data reduction functions for operations β_1 and β_2, the output data volumes from these operations have increased. As a result, policy ψ_3 yields the lowest total communication cost among the set of policies $\{\psi_1, \psi_2, \psi_3, \psi_4\}$. Therefore, by Theorem

Table 14.5. Operating Costs of the Three Cases for the Example

CASE	POLICY	COMMUNICATIONS COST	PROCESSING COST	OPERATING COST
A	ψ_4	6.5	9.71	16.21
	$\underline{\psi_8}$	5.5	10.21	15.71
B	$\underline{\psi_4}$	6.5	5.96	12.46
	ψ_8	5.5	8.46	13.96
C	$\underline{\psi_3}$	11.0	6.96	17.96
	ψ_8	11.5	9.08	20.58

The optimal policy is shown underscored.

4, ψ_3 is the optimal policy among that set of policies. Likewise, policy ψ_8 is the optimal policy among the set of policies $\{\psi_7,\psi_8\}$. Comparing ψ_3 and ψ_8, we note that $C(\psi_3) < C(\psi_8)$. Thus the policy ψ_3 is the optimal policy for case C.

14.8. EXAMPLES OF DISTRIBUTED DATA BASE SYSTEMS

This section presents two different prototype distributed data base systems and how they were implemented. The first two parts give an overview of the two systems, distributed INGRES and SDD-1. The next part provides comparisons of key design issues between these two prototype systems. The last part discusses such issues as translation, site autonomy, etc. in implementing distributed data base systems under a given operating environment.

Distributed INGRES

Distributed INGRES [42,37] was developed at the University of California, Berkeley. It operates in a collection of DEC VAX II/780 and II/750s corrected by a 3MHz Ethernet Local Network. All the machines are running the Berkeley enhanced Unix Operating System (4.2BSD). The enhancement includes paging, support remote interprocess communication and remote execution of a process. Hence, one can spawn a process on a remote processor and do interprocess communication with that process as if it was on the same processor. Distributed INGRES uses relational data model and supports fragments of relations at different sites. Users interact with data through the use of non procedure Query Language (QUEL).

Several new user commands are added to the INGRES user language to carry out the distributed data base function. The command language is expanded to include a key word "LOCATION" by which a user can indicate his knowledge (or desire) concerning the physical location of a relation. A MOVE-RELATION command was added so that relations could be moved from one site to another in the network. A DIST. CREATE was added so that a relation could be created whereby the

distribution criteria of the system could be enforced automatically. The BACKUP command was added so that backup copies of relations was added to the system. A local relation is only visible at the machine where it resides, and a regular relation is visible through-out the entire system. By having local relations, the system does not have to spend as much time and overhead on local relations, since consistency with the global system does not have to be verified at every transaction.

To process distributed data base transaction, a master INGRES is generated by the application program which runs at the site where the application program resides. The master then calls on the slave INGRES at each site which have data involved in the command. The master INGRES does parsing, review resolution and creates an action plan to solve the command. The slave can be created by the master when appropriate. There are two types of commands that a master INGRES can give to a slave INGRES: 1)run the (local) query, 2) move the (local) fragment of a relation to a subset of the sites in the network. The slave process is essentially a single machine INGRES with minor extensions and the parser removed.

SDD-1 [31]

SDD-1 is a distributed data base system supported by DARPA and developed by Computer Corporation of America. SDD-1 supports homogeneous data bases and heterogeneous communication channels. The goals of SDD-1 are the following:

1. Reliability/survivability. The system must continue operation despite the failure or inaccessibility of one or more of its data base sites.
2. Tunable efficiency. It must be possible to distribute data in a manner such that portions that are heavily used in a given geographical region can be stored near that region.
3. Modular upward scaling. As data bases increase in size and usage, it must be possible to augment system capacity to ac-

commodate these increases by the incremental addition of new data base sites.

The key concepts of SDD-1 are the following:

1. It is implemented as a set of communicating processors that are dispersed worldwide and that are envisioned to have a large number.
2. The distributed implementation is invisible to users.
3. SDD-1 supports arbitrary redundancy. The physical storage of data items is defined in terms of logical subrelations called fragments.
4. Each processor is implemented as two communicating processes, called the transaction module and the data module. The partition of functions between these two components permits the eventual incorporation of existing data base management systems into a heterogeneous SDD-1.
5. Directory information is stored in SDD-1 as ordinary user data.
6. Controlling concurrency is a process that can represent an intolerable bottleneck in distributed systems. SDD-1 employs a transaction classification technique that avoids time-consuming intermodule synchronization for most concurrent transactions.

Each SDD-1 node is composed of three types of virtual machines: the *data module* (DM), the *transaction module* (TM), and the *reliable network* (RelNet). All data is stored and managed by data modules, which take commands from transaction modules. The four commands that a DM can perform on the data are: [26]

1. READ part of the DM's data base into a local workspace at that DM.
2. MOVE part of a local workspace from this DM to another DM.
3. MANIPULATE data in a local workspace at the DM.
4. WRITE part of the local workspace into the permanent data base stored at the DM.

Transaction modules do the following:

1. Control the execution of commands and distribute commands to DMs in the system.
2. Decide which copy of the data to access and find where it is stored.
3. Synchronize all transactions with other transactions in the system.
4. Plan the access to the data and decide whether parallel processing can be used.

The reliable network (RelNet) does the following:

1. Connects the TMs and DMs of the system.
2. Guarantees delivery of messages even if a node is down.
3. Sees that all or none of the copies of data are updated.
4. Monitors all sites in the network, and also keeps a virtual clock that is synchronized for all sites.

At run-time, there are three phases that a transaction goes through: the read phase, the execute phase, and the write phase.

1. Read phase. In the read phase, the TM decides which copy of the desired data is to be used. The TM then sends a command to the appropriate DM that instructs the DM to locate the desired data and set aside a private copy for the transaction to work with.
2. Execute phase. In the execute phase, the TM compiles the transaction into a program that takes the private copy of the data and manipulates it. The TM supervises this program at all times. When the program is completed, it will output any changes to the data.
3. Write phase. In the write phase, the data is either displayed at the user's terminal, or the updates are written onto the copies of the data base.

The data is distributed in SDD-1 in units called fragments. A *fragment* is a subset of a

324 HANDBOOK OF SOFTWARE ENGINEERING

relation defined as restrictions and projections of data base relations. A fragment is either totally present or totally absent at a node. The fragments are stored redundantly throughout the network. Since there are many copies of each fragment, the concept of a materialization is introduced. A materialization is a set of fragments that constitute a complete and nonredundant copy of a relation. A user working on a relation is assigned a materialization to work with. Tables in the system show how different materializations can be constructed.

Comparision of Distributed INGRES and SDD-1

Replication and Updating. Replicated copies of data items in a distributed data base system can be kept for two reasons. If copies are kept for reliability, then the system is only concerned with having at least two copies of the data so that if one site fails, the data will still be available to the system. If copies are kept for efficiency, then the system is concerned with keeping copies of the data at or near the sites that utilize the data most frequently.

Distributed INGRES keeps multiple copies of data items mainly for the purpose of reliability. SDD-1 keeps multiple copies of data items for reliability and efficiency. Overall, in a distributed system, both reliability and efficiency should be considered. Reliability is needed so that the data is available to all users at all times, whereas efficiency in storing the data near the location where it is used cuts down on the high cost of transferring data long distances over the network. If the distributed data base system were on a local network, then only reliability would have to be considered since usually the local network has a wide bandwidth (3–10 mHz); therefore, the delay and cost of transmitting data through a local network is insignificant.

When several copies of the data exist, it is desirable to do the updates such that the contents of all the copies are the same at all times. The ideal solution would be to have all updates done exactly at the same time on all copies; however, it is infeasible to require that all sites generate updates at exactly the same instance. There are several methods for achieving the same effect that are used by different distributed data base systems.

With INGRES, even though there are many copies of the data in the system for reliability, only one of the copies is the prime copy. Only the prime copy can be updated; therefore, there can be no inconsistency of the copies. Once the prime copy has been updated, the updates are generated throughout the rest of the copies.

A few problems exist, though, with this method. The first problem occurs when the prime copy site goes down. If this happens, then no updates can be done to the data; it can only be read. If a user wants to read the data, then any copy will do. However, if the user wishes to update the data, then the prime copy must be used. This causes an increase in the cost of accessing the data at a remote site, as well as the problem of providing access to the same copy of the data by several users.

A two phase commit protocol is implemented. Hence a "ready" message is sent from the slaves to the master when they are prepared to commit the update. If there are tuples which change sites, they are included with the ready message. The master can then process the tuples from all sites and redistribute them. This redistribution is accomplished by piggybacking the tuples onto the commit message when it is sent out.

SDD-1 employs a reliable writing technique that ensures the updating of either all or none of the copies of data at a given time. The RelNet of SDD-1 guarantees delivery of a message to a DM even if it is down. If a DM is up, then the techniques to ensure delivery are similar to those used in ARPANET protocols. If a DM is down, however, the messages are spooled in a secondary storage system until the DM is up again. In this method, the write messages are kept for the site so that when the DM is brought up it can bring its data up-to-date. A two phase commit-type method is used to ensure that all sites get the write message and execute it. In the first phase, the write messages are transmitted but not installed. In the second phase, commit messages are sent to all the DMs, and the updates are installed. This system protects against failures of the transmitting DM, but may not be as efficient in cases of multiple failures. A write rule ensures that the write commands are done in sequence. The write rule states that updates to data are done only in the order in which they were requested. A time stamp is put on each write request so that the order of the requests can be determined. If a write that is stamped earlier than the last update time stamp is received, then it is discarded. By employing this method, the system does not have to wait for all writes to arrive before executing them. Discarding old write commands does not hurt the consistency of the data since the data is in the same state it would be in had both writes been executed. More information on how updating is done is given in Section 14.5, in the paragraph on concurrency control entitled Variable Level of Synchronization Control.

Directory Management. A distributed system needs to store not only the local system catalogs for the data at each machine, but it also needs to have a global system directory that holds the relation name, parsing information, performance information, and consistency information for each item stored in the system that can be referenced globally. The means by which this global system directory is stored is a major design decision to be considered when implementing a distributed data base system.

Distributed INGRES directory consists of the following information: relation name, parsing information (domain name, format, etc.), performance information (number of tuples, storage requirements, etc.), and consistency information (protection, integrity constraints, etc.).

Distributed INGRES distinguishes between local relations (accessible from a single site) and regular relations (accessible from all sites). Each INGRES site maintains local directory entries for all the locally stored relations. However, at least the name of every regular relation is stored at every site. Further, complete parsing information exists on those sites where a relation has been used at that

site. This information is kept permanently and is kept up to date. In essence, the directory is partly redundant. INGRES uses a "cache" directory concept. Whenever a regular relation is used at a site, its information (for example, structure information) is appended to the local directory. To reduce update cost, certain appended information is not kept up-to-date. This information is discarded after a predetermined length of time. This out-of-date information can be detected at execution time. Creation of a regular relation involves broadcasting its name and location to all the sites of the network.

SDD-1 treats the global directory like regular data. Using this method, the directory is stored in fragments redundantly throughout the network. This method allows directory management to use existing functions in the system, such as security, integrity, and concurrency control. Having overhead costs for every directory access and executing a transaction for each access degrades the performance of the system. SDD-1 alleviates this problem by keeping a copy of the directory fragment it has just accessed for a period of time that is less than or equal to the time the next update to the directory is done. The part of the global system directory that cannot be treated as user data is the directory locator, which tells where all the fragments of the directory are kept. The directory locator is stored at each node since it is very small and is rarely updated.

Other methods of directory management include the centralized, distributed, and local directory systems discussed in Section 14.2. The best scheme seems to be to store the directory in fragments redundantly throughout the network. It saves overhead to store the accessed parts of the directory temporarily at each node. However, care must be taken that the copies are consistent when updates to the fragment occur. If the distributed data base system were on a local network, the transmission cost would be considerably less because of the low cost of bandwidth.

A directory locator stores the location of all the directory fragments. By having a directory locator at each node, the request for directory information would be sent directly to the desired node instead of contacting intermediate nodes. Since a directory locator is small and static, the cost incurred for storage and updating the locator would be less than the cost of searching for the directory fragment without the locator.

Query Processing with Distributed IN-GRES. The site where the transaction orig inated the query became the master site for the query. The master decomposes the query into a set of subqueries and uses a heuristic query optimization algorithm to generate the sequence and sites to perform these sub queries. The master communicates with the slave INGRES at each site that involves processing the query to carry out the necessary operations and return the desired information to the master site. The results are then compiled and given to the user.

A simple method for processing a distributed transaction is to move all the needed data to one site and process it there. This scheme, although simple, is costly since the cost of moving all the data could be very high. Also, the loss of efficiency, since there is no parallel processing, is not desirable. The SDD-1 technique for constructing a transaction processing strategy is to start with the above method and iteratively improve on it by adding operations to be performed at various nodes. Assuming that communication costs will dominate complex processing costs, the SDD-1 method tries to minimize first the communication costs and then the processing costs.

Each system uses an algorithm ultimately based on taking a query that involves data at multiple nodes and breaking it into a set of subqueries, each of which is executed at a single node. Both methods seek to minimize the volume of data transferred between sites and to utilize parallel processing whenever possible. They differ substantially, however, in their approach. The INGRES method appears to emphasize both goals equally, whereas the SDD-1 technique places much more emphasis on minimizing the volume of data transferred.

Both INGRES and SDD-1 query processing algorithm performed only limited search. Some experimental query processing experi-ments [43] reveal that limited search algorithms do not perform very well as compared to algorithms which exhaust all possible processing plans as discussed in Section 14.7.

Concurrency Control. In a distributed data base system, there must exist a concurrency control algorithm to make sure that there are no deadlocks in the system and that the concurrently running transactions do not cause inconsistencies to appear in the data base. INGRES prevents deadlocks by having all requests for resources declared before execution. If all the locks on the needed resources are obtained, then the transaction can be executed; otherwise, all the locks obtained must be released, and the system must try again until all the required locks can be secured. In case a deadlock still occurs, or a machine fails during the processing of a transaction, INGRES employs a backout scheme that chooses a victim (in the case of a crash, the victim is the process currently running), and backs out all commands executed by that victim for the current transaction. A graph is used to help with the backout scheme. The data base is recovered to the steady state it was in before the transaction was started. INGRES has a rule that a transaction is either all completed or not completed. Therefore, any changes incurred by a transaction are not permanent until the transaction is insured of completion. This rule makes backing out a very easy process in INGRES. The last steady state can be obtained easily, and any operations done on the data base are just not written out.

SDD-1 employs a unique and complicated concurrency control mechanism which is discussed in the section on variable level of synchronization control.

Discussions

SDD-1 and INGRES are compared in Table 14.6. Both were implemented with a relational data model; the question arises whether the systems could work for other data models, such as the network model and the hierarchical model. The main difference between these models is how the data is broken up, distributed, stored, and retrieved. Also, any routines that directly handle the data and are dependent on the structure of the data (such as user interface, query processing, or concurrency control) need to be modified.

One important consideration when designing a distributed data base system is to allow heterogeneous data base systems to exist. This is especially important when connecting many different data base systems. It could be very complex and costly to solve the problem under general cases. However, data translation can be handled inexpensively under special cases. For example, Digital Equipment Corporation defines a file transfer protocol called Data Access Protocol (DAP) for use with its DECNET product [46]. In the DAP system, all the computers in the network may be different; however, they are made by the same manufacturer, and the DEC Record Management Service (RMS) is able to translate the data format of one computer to that of another. Recently, several prototype systems for handling general heterogeneous distributed data base have been developed [47, 48]. Two key issues in data translation are correctness and cost. Much more research is needed to understand, quantify and improve the performance of data translation.

Transparency is one of the goals that a distributed data base management system should try to attain; that is, the user sees the entire data base as if it existed on the local machine. One of the issues in implementing distributed data base management system is the dual requirements of data sharing and autonomous operation of each site. To preserve each site's control over its own data is known as site autonomy. It has impact on authorization, query compilation and binding, catalog management and transaction management. R* is a prototype distributed data base system based on relation model of data that considered site autonomy in its architecture [49].

Although using centralized control for data base management is sometimes easier to implement, such strategies are usually highly costly and hinder the advantages of a distributed system. Further, a system should be able to recover from failures easily and allow for growth of the data base as well as enhancement of the implementation of the system.

There are intimate relationships among distributed operating system, distributed data base management, and data communication software. Such relationships effect the assigning task control responsibilities, parameter passing, features, and compatible interfaces. They should be carefully planned in implementing a distributed data base. Further, the distributed data code is more complex and difficult than that of the centralized data base. As a result, debugging is more complex. Therefore, better debugging tools are needed.

To improve performance of the distributed data base system, load balancing among different processors becomes an important problem. To improve response time of distributed transaction, one has to balance between the gain of decomposition of the transaction for parallel processing and the extra added interprocess communication cost.

The implementation of any of the key concepts of data base systems must take into account processing cost and communication cost. In some cases, a high storage cost is incurred

Table 14.6. Comparison of the Characteristics of Two Distributed Data Base Systems.

	DATA MODEL	GLOBAL DIRECTORY	CONCURRENCY CONTROL	QUERY OPTIMIZATION	OPTIMAL ALLOCATION	DATA TRANSLATION
INGRES	Relational	Partially redundant	Declare resource prior to execution	Yes	No	Not required
SDD-1	Relational	Distributed (in fragments)	Variable level of locking and serializability	Yes	No	Not required

*Without updating facility.
INGRES and SDD-1 both have a directory locator (relation names and their locations) that resides at each site.

to reduce an even higher communication cost. In the case of local network distributed data base systems, the concern about communication cost can be ignored, and an optimal strategy of implementation in such an environment is to use communication to reduce processing and storage cost.

Distributed data base system implementations are complicated and diverse. Choosing an implementation for a given network environment involves many trade-off issues. The goal in design is to get, for the least cost, the performance that the user requires and that clearly is environment dependent. Therefore, the optimal distributed data base system for one network may not be optimal for another, especially for the case in which one network is long haul and the other is local.

14.9. AREAS OF FURTHER INVESTIGATION

We have discussed the principles of distributed data base design with reference to areas of file allocation, directory design, deadlock prevention and detection, integrity and consistency in multiple copy data bases, fault tolerance, and query optimization, and have given examples of distributed data base systems that represent the past ten years of progress.

There are many areas that still need further investigation, such as data translation among heterogeneous data bases with different data structures, communication protocols for distributed data bases, joint optimization between file allocation and query optimization, fault tolerance and error recovery, performance monitoring and measurement, and security and privacy issues.

ACKNOWLEDGMENT

The author wishes to express his thanks to Prof. M. Stonebraker of the University of California, Berkeley, Dr. D. Reis of Computer Corporation of America, Cambridge, Mass., and Dr. Paul Hurley, Bell Telephone Laboratories, Holmdel, N.J. for their careful review of and comments on a draft of parts of this chapter.

REFERENCES

1. G. H. Sander, System Reliability Engineering, Prentice-Hall, Englewood Cliffs. N.J., 1963, pp. 112–144.
2. L. Kleinrock, "Computer Applications," *Queueing Systems*, vol. 2, Wiley-Interscience, 1976, pp. 320–323.
3. W. W. Chu, "Optimal Dile Allocation in a Multiple Computer System," *IEEE Trans. on Computers*, Oct. 1969, pp. 885–889.
4. R. Gomory, "All-Integer Integer Programming Algorithm," Mush and Thompson (eds.), *Industrial Scheduling*, Prentice-Hall, Englewood Cliffs, N.J., 1963, pp. 195–206.
5. P. L. Price and D. W. Smith, "Analysis and Use of an Integer Programming Model for Optimally Allocating Files in a Multiple Computer System," DTNSRDC-78/102, David W. Taylor Naval Ship Research and Development Center, Bethesda, Md., Nov. 1978.
6. V. K. M. Whitney, "A Study of Optimal File Assignment and Communication Network Configuration," Ph.D. dissertation, University of Michigan, 1970.
7. S. Mahmond and J. S. Riordon, "Optimal Allocation of Resources in Distributed Information Networks," *ACM Trans. on Database Systems*, vol. 1, no. 1, March 1976, pp. 66–68.
8. R. G. Casey, "Allocation of Copies of a File in an Information Network," *SJCC 1972*, AFIPS Press, vol. 40, 1972.
9. W. W. Chu, "Optimal File Allocation in a Computer Network," in N. Abramson and F. Kuo (eds.), *Computer Communication Networks*, Prentice-Hall, Englewood Cliffs, N.J., 1973.
10. H. L. Morgan and K. D. Levin, "Optimal Program and Data Locations in Computer Networks," *Communications of the ACM*, vol. 20, no. 5, pp. 315–322, May 1977.
11. W. W. Chu, "Performance of File Directory Systems for Databases in Star and Distributed Networks," *AFIPS Proc.*, vol. 45, 1976, pp. 577–587.
12. Frank W. Allen, Mary E. S. Loomis, and Michael V. Mannino, "The Integrated Dictionary/Directory system," *Computing Surveys*, 14(2), June 1982, pp. 245–286.
13. A. N. Haberman, "Prevention of System Deadlocks," *Communications of the ACM*, vol. 12, no. 7, July 1969, pp. 373–377, 385.
14. R. C. Holt, "Some Deadlock Properties of Computer Systems," *Computing Surveys*, vol. 4, no. 3, Sept. 1972, pp. 179–196.
15. P. F. King and A. J. Collmeyer, "Database Sharing—An Efficient Mechanism for Supporting Concurrent Processes," *Proc. of the 1973 National Computer Conference and Exposition*, vol. 42, June 1973, pp. 271–275.
16. W. W. Chu and G. Ohlmacher, "Avoiding Deadlocking in Distributed Databases," *Proc. of the ACM National Symposium*, vol. 1, March 1974, pp. 156–160.

17. P. A. Alsberg, and J. D. Day, "A Principle for Resilient Sharing of Distributed Resources," *Proc. of the 2d International Conference on Software Engineering,* 1976, pp. 562–570.

18. C. A. Ellis, "A Robust Algorithm for Updating Duplicate Databases," *Proc. of the 2d Berkeley Workshop on Distributed Data Management and Computer Networks,* May 1977, pp. 146–158.

19. M. Hammer and D. Shipman, "An Overview of Reliability Mechanism for a Distributed Database," *Proc. of COMPCON 78,* March 1978, pp. 63–65.

20. R. M. Shapiro and R. E. Millstein, "Failure Recovery in a Distributed Database System," *Proc. of COMPCON 78,* March 1978, pp. 66–70.

21. R. H. Thomas, "A Solution to the Concurrency Control Problem for Multiple Copy Databases," *Proc. of COMPCON 78,* March 1978, pp. 56–62.

22. E. Gelenbe and K. Sevick, "Analysis of Update Synchronization for Multiple Copy Databases," *Proc. of the 3d Berkeley Workshop on Distributed Data Management and Computer Networks,* Aug. 28–31, 1978, pp. 69–90.

23. D. A. Menasce and R. R. Muntz, "Locking and Deadlock Detection in Distributed Databases," *Proc. of the 3d Berkeley Workshop on Distributed Data Management and Computer Networks,* Aug. 28–31, 1978, pp. 215–234.

24. K. P. Eswarn, et al., "The Notions of Consistency and Predicate Locks in a Database System," *Commun. ACM,* Vol.19, No. 11, Nov. 1976, pp. 624–633.

25. J. N. Gary, "Notes on Database Operating Systems," in *Operating Systems: An Advanced Course, Lecture Notes in Computer Science 60,* (ed. Goos and Hartmanis), Springer-Verlag, 1978, pp. 393–481.

26. G. Gardarin, and W. W. Chu, "A Distributed Control Algorithm for Reliably and Consistently Updating Replicated Databases," *IEEE Transactions on Computers,* Dec. 1980, pp. 1060–1068.

27. M. Stonebraker, "Concurrency control and consistency of multiple copies of data in distributed INGRES," *IEEE Transactions on Software Engineering SE-5,* May 3, 1979, pp. 188–194.

28. Phillip A. Bernstein, and Nathan Goodman, "Concurrency Control in Distributed Database Systems," *Computing Surveys,* Vol. 13, No. 2, June 1981, pp. 185–221.

29. L. Lamport, "Time, Clocks, and the Ordering of Events in a Distributed System," *CACM,* vol. 21, no. 7, July 1978, pp. 558–564.

30. P. A. Berstein, D. W. Shipman, and J. B. Rothnie, "Concurrency Control in a System for Distributed Databases (SDD-1)," *ACM Trans. on Database Systems,* vol. 5, no. 1, March 1980, pp. 18–51.

31. J. B. Rothnie et al., "Introduction to a System for Distributed Databases (SDD-1)," *ACM Trans. on Database Systems,* vol. 5, no. 1, March 1980, pp. 1–17.

32. B. Lampson and H. Sturgis, "Crash Recovery in a Distributed Data Storage System," Internal Report, XEROX Palo Alto Research Center, 1976.

33. Wesley W. Chu, Joseph Hellerstein, and M. T. Lan, "The Exclusive-Writer Protocol: A Low Cost Approach for Updating Replicated Files in Distributed Real Time Systems." The *Proceedings of the 3rd International Conference on Distributed Computing Systems,* Oct. 1982, pp. 296–277.

34. M. L. Green, et al., "A Distributed Real Time Operating System," *Proceedings of the Symposium on Distributed Data Acquisition, Computing and Control,* Dec. 1980.

35. W. H. Kohler, "A Survey of Techniques for Synchronization and Recovery in Decentralized Computer Systems," *Computing Surveys,* Vo. 13, No. 2, June 1981, pp. 149–184.

36. E. Wong, "Retrieving Dispersed Data from SDD-1: A System for Distributed Databases," *Proc. of the 2d Berkeley Workshop on Distributed Data Management and Computer Networks,* May 1977, pp. 217–235.

37. R. Epstein, M. Stonebraker, and E. Wong, "Distributed Query Processing in a Relational Database System," *SIGMOD Proc.,* May 1978, pp. 169–180.

38. A. R. Hevner and S. B. Yao, "Query Processing on a Distributed Database," *Proc. of the 3d Berkeley Workshop on Distributed Data Management and Computer Networks,* Aug. 1978, pp. 91–107.

39. W. W. Chu and P. Hurley, "Optimal Query Processing for Distributed Databases systems," *IEEE Trans on Computers,* Vol. 6-31, No. 9, Sept. 1982. pp 835–850

40. D. Small and W. W. Chu, "A Distributed Database Architecture for Data Processing in a Dynamic Environment," *Proc. of COMPCON,* March 1979, pp. 123–127.

41. W. W. Chu, "Design Considerations of File Directory Systems for Distributed Databases," *Infotech, State-of-the-Art Report, Distributed Databases,* vol. II, invited papers, Infotech International Ltd., Maidenhead, Berkshire, England, 1979.

42. M. Stonebraker, and E. Nenhold, "A Distributed Data Base Version of INGRES," *Proceedings of the 2nd Berkeley Workshop on Distributed Data Management and Computer Network.* Lawrence Berkeley Laboratories, Berkeley, CA, May 1977, pp. 19–36.

43. R. Epstein, "Analysis of Distributed Data Base Processing Strategies," Technical Memorandum No. UCB/ERL M80/25. College of Engineering, University of California, Berkeley. April 14, 1980.

44. W. W. Chu, and Victor To, "A Hierarchical Conceptual Data Model for Data Translation in a Heterogeneous Database System," *Proceedings of the International Conference on Entity-Relational Approach to Systems Analysis and Design,* Los Angeles, Dec. 10-12, 1979, pp. 647–648.

45. A. F. Cardenas, and M. H. Pirahesh, "Data Base Communication in a Heterogeneous Data Base Management System Network," *Information Systems,* Vol. 5, Pergamon Press Ltd., 1980, pp. 55–79.

46. J. J. Passafiume, and S. Wecker, "Distributed File Access in DECNET", *Proc. 2nd Berkeley Workshop*

on Distributed Data Management and Computer Networks, Lawrence Berkeley Laboratory, Berkeley, CA, May 1977.

47. G. Gardarin, and J. LeBihan, "An Approach Towards a Virtual Data Base Protocol for Computer Network," *Proceedings AICA* 1977, Miliano, Italy. Also in *Tutorial: Centralized and Distributed Data Base Systems,* IEEE Computer Society. (Edited by W. W. Chu and P. P. Chen) 1979.

48. T. Landers, and R. L. Rosenberg, "An Overview of Multibase," in *Distributed Data Bases* (H. J. Schneider, editor), North-Holland Publishing Company, 1982, pp. 153–184.

49. B. Linsey, and P. G. Salinger, "Site Autonomy Issues in R*: A Distributed Data Base Management System," IBM Computer Science Research Report RJ2927 (36822), San Jose, CA, Sept. 15, 1980.

15

Concurrency Control and Reliability in Distributed Database Management Systems

Bharat Bhargava

Computer Science Department
University of Pittsburgh

15.1. INTRODUCTION

With the technological development in the field of communication systems, it has become feasible for computers to communicate at high speed with each other and share their resources. One such resource to be shared is the database of a given organization. A prime example of such sharing is the airline reservation information. Two passengers can make a reservation from two different cities at about the same time and be assured of knowing the correct status of the number of seats available on a particular flight. The canonical problem of selling the same seat twice gives rise to the research of concurrency control in distributed database systems.

When a set of computers are connected, the first problem faced by the system designer is how to organize and distribute the database. If all of the database is available at all the nodes (computers in a distributed system), the retrieval requests can be efficiently processed. But any update request cannot be completed unless all copies of the database are made identical. The other extreme choice is not to replicate the database at all and keep parts of the database at one node only. In such a case a retrieval or update request must migrate from one node to another until all the work is done. The third choice that many system designers prefer is a compromise to allow partially replicated databases across the computer nodes of a distributed database management system (DBMS). Though such design choices are meant to provide efficient access to the database by the user, they create interesting concurrency control problems for the system designer. The DBMS software must provide concurrent access to users and at the same time maintain control of the consistency of the database.

In a distributed database management system, many types of failures can occur. For example, a given computer node can become temporarily unavailable, the nodes of the system can be partitioned and cease communications with each other, the messages sent by a node may be either delayed or lost or delivered in a wrong order.

Some of these problems can also occur in a centralized database system where there is only one computer and one database, but they have new dimensions in the distributed case. One goal for the DBMS software should be to either complete a given user's request correctly or completely deny it within a certain time interval.

Thus the goal of DBMS software is to provide correct and integrated access to the database to all users. In effect, the DBMS software should provide the user interface complete transparency with respect to data location, data replication, concurrent access to the same data, and, finally, system failures. These transparencies have been defined in Reference 1.

Location transparency: Although data is geographically distributed and may move from place to place, the user can act as though all the data are at one node.

Replication transparency: Although the same data item may be replicated at several nodes of the network, the user may treat the item as though it were stored as a single item at a single node.

Concurrency transparency: Although the system executes many user requests concurrently, it appears to each request as though it is the only activity in the system. In other words, it appears as if there were no concurrency in the system.

Failure transparency: Either all the actions of a request occur or none of them occur. Once a request completes it execution, its effects survive hardware and software failures.

Concurrency control in distributed database management systems has been the focus of research in the past few years [1, 2, 3, 4]. Several prototype systems have been developed and are being tested. For example, the SDD-1 system was developed by Computer Corporation of America and has been reported in Reference 2, and SIRUS [5] is being developed, implemented, and tested. Many of these systems provide limited capabilities of protection against failure but the research in reliable distributed data base systems [6] is still in the preliminary stages.

15.2. BASIC CONCEPTS: CONCURRENCY AND CONSISTENCY

A good source of these concepts is the report by Jim Gray [7]. A *database* is a set of named items and one or more values associated with each item. Each ⟨name, value⟩ pair is called an *entity*. The system provides operations (e.g., read, write), each of which manipulates one or more entities. The execution of an operation on an entity is called an *action*.

A *distributed database* has *zero* or *one* copy of each entity stored at one or more nodes of a physically separated network of computers. If a copy of all entities is stored at all nodes, the distributed database is called *fully replicated*. If some of the entities are replicated while others are not, the database is considered *partially replicated*. If none of the entities are replicated, the database is considered *partitioned*.

A set of constraints or predicates is defined for the entities of the database. If these predicates are satisfied by a given database, the database is said to be *consistent*. If the database is replicated, a consistency constraint may require that all copies of an entity must be identical. Such constraints are called *mutual consistency* constraints. Similarly a consistency constraint may require that assets must equal the liabilities of an organization. The value of one entity must be less than the value of another entity and must be within a certain range. Such constraints are called *internal consistency* constraints.

The database is queried or updated by a mechanism called a transaction. Users request written as a computer program are actually a static description of a *transaction*. The execution of a program on a *database state* is called a transaction on the state. A transaction can be modeled as a fixed sequence of actions on entities. For example: $T = \langle \langle t, A_i, E_i \rangle \mid i = 1, \ldots, n \rangle$ where t is the transaction name, A_i are operations and E_i are entity names. A transaction can also be viewed as if it reads a set of entities, does some computation, and finally writes on a set of entities. The entities that are read and written may not be the same. The set of entities read by the transaction is called the *read set,* denoted by $S(R)$; and the set of entities on which the transaction writes is called the *write set,* denoted by $S(W)$. Two concurrent transactions conflict if the read set of one intersects with the write set of the other or the write sets of the two transactions overlap.

In general, it is difficult to study the computations carried out by a transaction in detail, and so only its effects on the write set are considered.

In addition to identifying the entities in the read and the write set, we can associate a *timestamp* based on the order in which read and write occur. For example if R_i and W_i are read and write operations of a transaction, we can say the timestamp of R_i is less than the timestamp of W_i if the order of the execution of action R_i is before that of action W_i.

In order to execute a transaction that updates an entity E_1 that has two copies on nodes N_1 and N_2, the system may initiate *sub-*

transactions that will be transparent to the user. For example: $\langle t_1, A_1, E_1, N_1 \rangle$ and $\langle t_1, A_1, E_1, N_2 \rangle$ are two subtransactions of a single transaction $\langle t_1, A_1, E_1 \rangle$.

To provide concurrent execution of operations of different transactions, the system may interleave the execution of such operations. The execution of a set of m transactions by the system starting from some database state is called a *history* and is denoted by the sequence:

$$H = \langle\ \langle t_i, A_j, E_j, \rangle\ \left|\ \begin{matrix} i = 1, \text{---}\ m; \\ j = 1, \text{---}\ n \end{matrix}\ \right\rangle$$

A history H is called *serial* if each transaction completes all its execution before the next one starts. In such a case no concurrent processing takes place.

If we give the responsibility of ensuring the correctness of a transaction to the user, we may assume that all transactions issued to the DBMS are correct. Thus a transaction will transform the data base from one consistent state to another. In effect, a serial history (or execution) will maintain consistency of the database.

A history H is *serializable* if there is some serial history (H_s) such that the effect of executing H is equivalent to H_s. The notion of serializable history (or serializability) is very fundamental to work in concurrency control.

It is also important to note that there may exist several serial histories equivalent to the actual interleaved execution history. The order of transactions in a serial history is of no concern to the system. It is considered the responsibility of the user to issue a transaction that must be executed after another transaction only when the earlier transaction has already completed, or else the user must inform the system of such a fact. Essentially the system considers all transactions as independently issued.

Transaction and System Failure

Redundancy is the key to achieving reliability. Since the redundant components can fail too, there is no way to design a completely reliable system. We can only increase the reliability to a point where catastrophic failures will be very unlikely.

In a distributed database system, we could have the following types of failures:

Transaction Failure: For some reason a transaction may need to be aborted or restarted. Deadlock is an example of such a failure.

Node Failure: A given computer node may stop processing transactions and may not respond to any requests, whether from users or from the system.

Communication System Failure: The communication network may partition and prohibit communication among various nodes. The communication media may also delay some messages beyond a certain time limit.

System Failure: There are two types of entities in a system: (1) *stable* entities, (2) *volatile* entities. When a failure occurs, the stable entities have values that will survive. The values of volatile entities are reset to null when the system restarts. For example, entities stored on secondary storage such as disks and tapes will be considered as stable entities while entities whose value exists in primary memory will be considered as volatile entities. There is one more type of entity called *real* entities which have initially null values and whose values cannot be changed once they are non-null.

Because a transaction may fail at anytime, we need a facility to *rollback* the actions of a transaction that did not complete. For example, for an action $\langle t, A, E \rangle$, we can have an *undo-action* $\neg \langle t, A, E \rangle$ that will cancel the effects of action A by t. Unfortunately, there are some entities that are real, and actions on them cannot be *undone*. For example $\langle t, drink, beer \rangle$ is an action of drinking beer that cannot be undone after it has taken place. As long as a transaction consists of actions that can be undone, the system has just to make a record of such action. But if the transaction completes an action for which there is no undo-action, the system must commit itself to completing the transaction. Thus a transaction can be partitioned into two parts delimited by a *commit action*. The first part consists of actions for which there are undo-actions and the second part for which there are no undo-actions. The commitment of a transaction is not undoable and in a good system design, the commitment action should be as late as possible.

For the system to be able to rollback a transaction, it is necessary for the system to keep a record in a transaction *undo log*. Thus when a transaction is to be rolled back, the actions in the *undo log* are applied (in last in/first out order) to reverse the effects of the transaction.

Prior to the commit action, any action on a real entity for which there is no undo action is deferred. Such actions are also called *intentions* and are recorded in a *redo log*. The undo log and the redo log are stored on stable storage.

The undo actions and redo actions must be *restartable*. That means that if an undo action and a redo action is repeated, the final effect is as if they were done only once. The repetition might be necessary because of repeated failures.

When a system fails, only the state of stable and real entities can be reconstructed. The state of volatile entities is lost. To minimize the cost of reconstruction, redo and undo work, the system can also employ *checkpoints*. A checkpoint is the time when a record of the volatile entity is made on a stable storage. Checkpoints are periodic.

Concurrency Control Approaches and Algorithms

Our main concern in designing a concurrency control algorithm is to correctly process transactions that are in conflict. As stated in the last section, each transaction has a read set and a write set. Two transactions *conflict* if the read set of one transaction intersects with the write set of the other transaction and/or the write set of one transaction conflicts with the write set of the other transaction. We illustrate this further in Figure 15.1.

If $S(R_1)$ and $S(W_2)$ have some database entities (or items) in common, then we say that the read set of T_1 conflicts with the write set of T_2. This is represented by the diagonal edge in the figure. Similarly if $S(R_2)$ and $S(W_1)$ have some database items in common, we draw the other diagonal edge.

If $S(W_1)$ and $S(W_2)$ have some database

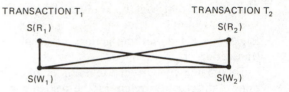

Figure 15.1. Types of conflicts for two transactions.

items in common, we say that the write set of T_1 conflicts with the write set of T_2. This situation is represented by the horizontal edge at the bottom.

We do not need to worry about the conflict between the read sets of the two transactions because read actions do not change the values of the database entities.

It must be noted that transactions T_1 and T_2 can conflict only if both are executing at the same time. If, for example, T_1 has finished before T_2 was submitted to the system, even if their read and write sets intersect, they are not considered to be in conflict.

If two transactions are in conflict, we have additional problems in a distributed database management system. Such a conflict is illustrated by the following example: Let the initial state of the database at two nodes N_1 and N_2 of a distributed database be as follows:

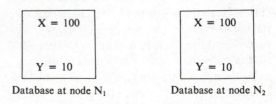

Database at node N_1 Database at node N_2

There are two items X and Y in the database, and their values on both nodes are 100 and 10, respectively. Suppose transaction T_1 arrives at node N_1. T_1 plans to increase the value of X by 10 and read the value of Y.

Suppose concurrent with the arrival of T_1, transaction T_2 arrives at node N_2. T_2 plans to increase the value of X by 20 and the value of Y by 10.

Let us assume that the system also requires transactions T_1 and T_2 to send the updated values of X and Y to the other nodes in the system.

Suppose a sequence of actions by the two

Table 15.1. Transactions at Nodes N_1 and N_2.

NODE N_1	NODE N_2
	T_2 arrives at N_2
	READ Y
	Y = Y + 10
	WRITE Y
	SEND Y to N_1
T_1 arrives at N_1	READ X
	X = X + 20
READ X	WRITE X
X = X + 10	SEND X to N_1
WRITE X	
SEND X to N_2	
RECEIVE X from N_2	RECEIVE X from N_1
WRITE X	
READ Y	WRITE X
T_1 FINISHES	T_2 FINISHES
RECEIVE Y from N_2	

transactions takes place at nodes N_1 and N_2, as shown in Table 15.1.

The final state of the database at nodes N_1 and N_2 is as follows:

X = 120		X = 110
Y = 20		Y = 20

If transaction T_1 and T_2 had arrived in the system one at a time, the values of X and Y would have been 130 and 20, respectively on each node. Unfortunately because of transmission delays of updated values to the other nodes, the values of X on the two nodes are wrong. The change of X by T_1 is reflected on node N_2 and has been lost on node N_1. Similarly, the change of X by T_2 is reflected on node N_1 and has been lost on node N_2. This problem is called *lost-update anomaly*. In addition, transaction T_1 read a value of Y to be

10 where it should have read the value 20. This problem is called *dirty read* or *retrieval anomaly*.

The task of a concurrency controller in a distributed database management system is to avoid the lost-update anomaly and the retrieval anomaly by synchronizing the execution of conflicting transactions. These problems become much worse in case of a crash of a particular node or any other types of failures, as mentioned earlier.

Generic Approaches to Synchronization

There are basically three generic approaches that can be used to design concurrency control algorithms. The synchronization can be accomplished by utilizing:

Wait: If two transactions conflict, conflicting actions of one transaction must wait until the actions of the other transaction are completed.

Timestamp: The order in which transactions are executed is selected a priori. Each transaction is assigned a unique timestamp by the system and conflicting actions of two transactions are processed in timestamp order.

Rollback: If two transactions conflict, some actions of a transaction are undone or rolled back or else one of the transactions is restarted. This approach is also called *optimistic* because it is expected that conflicts are rare and so only a few transactions would rollback.

In the following section, we give further details of each of these approaches and describe concurrency control algorithms that are based on them.

Algorithms Based on Wait Mechanism. When two transactions conflict, one solution is to make one transaction wait until the other transaction has released the entities common to them both. To implement this, the system can provide *locks* on the database entities. Transactions can get a lock on an entity from the system, keep it as long as the particular entity is being operated upon, and then give the lock back. If a transaction requests the system for a lock on an entity, and the lock has been given to some other transaction, the requesting transaction must wait. To reduce the waiting time when a transaction wants to read, there are two types of locks that can be employed, based on whether the transaction wants to do a read operation or a write operation on an entity.

Readlock: The transaction locks the entity in a shared mode. Any other transaction waiting to read the same entity can also obtain a readlock.

Writelock: the transaction locks the entity in an exclusive mode. If one transaction wants to write on an entity, no other transaction may get either a readlock or a writelock.

When we say lock, it means any of the above type of lock. After a transaction has finished operations on an entity, the transaction can do an *unlock* operation. After an unlock operation, either type of lock is released, and the entity is made available to other transactions that may be waiting.

It is important to note that lock and unlock operations can be embedded in a transaction by the user or be transparent to the transaction. In the later case, the system takes the responsibility of correctly granting and enforcing lock and unlock operations for each transaction.

Locking an entity gives rise to two new problems: *livelock* and *deadlock*. Livelock occurs when a transaction repeatedly fails to obtain a lock. For instance, suppose T_2 is waiting to get a lock on entity A currently held by T_1. When T_1 releases the lock on A, a new transaction T_3 arrives and gets the lock on A. Similarly, new transactions may keep getting the lock on A while T_2 finds it unavailable everytime it attempts to get the lock. The problem of livelock can easily be handled by implementing a first-come first-served strategy. Thus T_3 will get the lock only after T_2 has operated on the entity.

Deadlock occurs when various transactions attempt locks on several entities simultaneously; each transaction gets a lock on a different entity and waits for the other transactions to release the lock on the entities that they have succeeded in securing. As an example, suppose T_1 wants locks on entities A and B and gets a lock on entity A. Concurrently T_2 wants locks on entities B and A and gets a lock on entity B. Now T_1 waits for T_2 to unlock B, and T_2 waits for T_1 to unlock A. T_1 and T_2 can wait forever. The problem of deadlock can be resolved by the following approaches, among others:

Each transaction locks all entities at once. If some locks are held by some other transaction, then the transaction releases any locks that it was able to obtain.

Assign an arbitrary linear ordering to the items, and require all transaction to request locks in this order.

Since the correctness criterion for concurrently processing several transactions is serializability, locking must be done correctly to assure the above property. One simple protocol that all transactions can obey to ensure serializability is called *Two Phase Locking* (2PL). The protocol simply requires that in any transaction, all locks must precede all unlocks. A transaction operates in two phases: The first phase is the locking phase, and the second phase is the unlocking phase. The first phase can also be considered as the growing phase, in which a transaction obtains more and more locks without releasing any. By releasing a lock, the transaction is considered to have entered the shrinking phase. During the shrinking phase the transaction releases more and more locks and is prohibited from obtaining additional locks. When the transaction terminates, all remaining locks are automatically released. The instance just before the release of the first lock is called *lockpoint*. The two phase and lock point are illustrated in Figure 15.2.

The portion of the distributed database management system that is responsible for ensuring the serializability of concurrent transactions is called a *scheduler* or *concurrency controller*. The scheduler can be based on centralized control or distributed control. In the centralized control approach, the scheduler resides on a special node called the *central node*. All lock and unlock information is maintained at this node and all transactions must communicate with the central node to execute operations. In a distributed scheduler, there is no central node and all nodes share concurrency control functions.

We now discuss some centralized and dis-

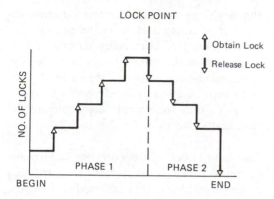

Figure 15.2. Two phase locking and lockpoint. ↑ Obtain lock. ↓ Release lock.

tributed control algorithms that utilize locking. For the sake of simplicity, we may assume that all transactions write into the database and the database is fully replicated. We must be aware of the fact that in real systems it might be very inefficient to have a fully replicated database. Moreover, the majority of the transactions will only read from the database. But since multiple copies of a given entity and the write operations of transactions are the major reason for studying concurrency control algorithms, we focus on these issues.

Centralized Locking Concurrency Control Algorithms.   A brief outline of a simple centralized locking algorithm is given below. When a transaction T_i arrives at node X, the following steps are performed:

1. Node X requests from the central node the locks for all the entities referenced by the transaction.
2. The central node checks all the requested locks. If some entity is already locked by another transaction, then the request is queued. There is a queue for each entity and the request waits in one queue at a time.
3. When the transaction gets all its locks, it is executed at the central node (the execution can also take place at node X, but that may require more messages). The values of read set are read from the database, necessary computations are carried out, and the values of the write set

are written in the database at the central node.
4. The values of the write set are transmitted by the central node to all other nodes (if the database is fully replicated).
5. Each node receives the new write set and updates the database; then an acknowledgment is sent back to the central node.
6. When the central node receives acknowledgments from all other nodes in the system, it knows that transaction T_i has been completed at all nodes. The central node releases the locks and starts processing the next transaction.

From this simple algorithm, we can immediately notice some problems for centralized control. First of all, if the central node crashes, then all transaction processing must cease until a new central node can be selected. Second, the central node is a performance bottleneck because all transactions must pass through this special node.

Some simple variations of the centralized locking algorithm are obvious.

Locking at Central Node, Execution at All Nodes.   Instead of executing the transaction at the central node, we can only assign the locks at the central node and send the transaction back to node X. The transaction T_i is executed at node X. The values of the read set are read, and the values of the write set are obtained at node X. Node X sends the values of the write set and obtains acknowledgments from all other nodes. It then knows that transaction T_i has been completed. The node X sends a message to unlock entities referenced by T_i. The central node after receiving this message releases the locks and starts assigning locks to waiting transactions.

Avoid Acknowledgments, Assign Sequence Numbers.   In the centralized control algorithm, the acknowledgments are needed by the central node (or node X in the above extension) to find out if the values of the write set have been written in the data base at every node. But it is not necessary for the central node to wait for this to happen; it is sufficient for the central node to guarantee that the write set values are written at every node in the same order as they were performed at the central node. To achieve this the central node can assign a monotonically increasing *sequence number* to each transaction. The sequence number is appended to the write set of the transaction and is used to order the update of the new values into the database at each node.

Now the central node does not have to wait for any acknowledgments, but the equivalent effect is achieved. This can make the centralized control algorithm more efficient.

Sequence numbers may cause additional problems. Suppose two transactions T_5 and T_6 are assigned sequence numbers 5 and 6, respectively, by the central node. Let us further suppose that T_5 and T_6 have no entities in common and so do not conflict. If transaction T_5 is very long, transaction T_6, which arrived at the central node after T_5, may be ready to write the values of its write set, but this operation for T_6 must wait at all nodes for T_5. A simple solution to this problem is to attach the sequence numbers of all lower-numbered transactions for which a given transaction must wait before writing in the data base. This list is called a *wait-for* list. In such a case, a transaction waits only for the transactions in its wait-for list. The wait-for list is attached to the write set of each transaction. In some cases the size of the wait-for list can grow very large, but transitivity among sequence numbers in wait-for lists can be used to reduce it. Moreover a complement of this wait-for list called *do not-wait-for* list can also be used.

Global Two Phase Locking. This is a simple variation of the centralized locking mechanisms. Instead of a transaction getting all locks in the beginning and releasing all locks in the end, the policy of two phase locking is employed. Each transaction obtains the necessary locks as they are needed, computes, and then releases locks on entities that are no longer needed. A transaction cannot get a lock after it has released any lock. So if more locks are needed in the future, it should hold on to all the present locks. The other parts of the algorithm remain the same as before.

Primary Copy Locking. In this variation, instead of selecting a node as the central controller, a copy of each entity on any node is designated as the primary copy of the entity. A transaction must obtain the lock on the primary copy of all entities referenced by it. At any given time the primary copy contains the most up-to-date value for that entity.

Distributed Locking Concurrency Control Algorithms. The ideas behind a distributed control algorithm is that each node is independent and capable of maintaining locks and executing transactions. Each node now needs to coordinate with other nodes to make sure that no two transactions concurrently hold a lock on the same item. Deadlocks are a real possibility in such a scheme and are hard to handle because locking information is distributed. Moreover, there are many more messages exchanged in deciding which transaction gets the lock and proceeds. The basic outline of a simple distributed locking algorithm is given below:

When a transaction T_j arrives at node X, the following steps are performed:

1. Node X requests from all nodes the locks for all entities referenced by the transaction.
2. If all nodes (or the majority of nodes) agree to grant locks to the transaction, the transaction may proceed to step 3. If the majority of nodes refuse to grant locks, the transaction must release all locks and restart again.
3. The transaction computes the new values of the write set and sends them to all nodes. When a node has updated the data base, it sends a message to node X.
4. Node X releases the locks for transaction T_i and requests all other nodes to do so, after receiving the update message from all other nodes.
5. All nodes release the locks on receipt of such an unlock request and may vote to grant locks to other transactions.

Once again some simple variations of this algorithm are given below:

Majority Voting. Instead of receiving acknowledgment of acceptance of lock requests from all the nodes, the system can execute a transaction whenever a majority of nodes have agreed to do so. Obviously, a majority of nodes will not grant a lock on the same entity to two different transactions.

Local Two Phase Locking. In this variation of the distributed locking algorithm, all transactions follow the policy of two phase locking. The local 2PL and global 2PL both provide correct synchronization but differ in an interesting way. We have defined the instance in the execution of a transaction when it decides to release the first lock as the *lockpoint* of the transaction. In local 2PL, the lockpoint of the transaction may be different on every node but is synchronized with respect to other conflicting transactions. Thus, the transaction may have flexibility in releasing a lock at different nodes while assuring two phase locking policy and equivalent serializable histories at all nodes. In global 2PL, there is a single lock point on all nodes for a given transaction. We have studied many locking algorithms for concurrency control and found that they follow the policy of global two phase locking. The difference between global 2PL and local 2PL is in the degree of concurrency provided. This has been discussed further in Reference 8.

As discussed earlier, deadlocks are a real possibility in algorithms based on a wait mechanism. In a distributed data base management system, this problem becomes worse. A mathematical construct called a *wait-for graph* is useful in characterizing dead lock situations. A wait-for graph is a directed graph that indicates which transactions are waiting for which other transactions. The nodes of the graph represent transactions. The edges represent the wait-for relationship. An edge is drawn from transaction T_i to T_j if T_i is waiting for an entity currently locked by T_j. There is a deadlock if and only if there is a cycle in the wait-for graph. Two deadlock avoidance procedures have been mentioned earlier. They were based on assigning all locks to the transaction at once or arbitrarily ordering the items. Another idea is to assign priorities to transactions. With this

every edge in the wait-for graph is guaranteed to be in priority order, that is, for all edges $\langle T_i, T_j \rangle$ T_i has lower priority than T_j. Since a cycle is a path from a node to itself and since it is impossible for T_i to have a lower priority than itself, a situation such as $\langle T_i, T_j, \cdots, T_k, T_i \rangle$ or a cycle in a wait-for graph is impossible. This solution leads to cyclic restarts or livelocks. To avoid this we mentioned the approach of first come, first served. A technique called *timestamps* has been proposed for assigning priorities and deciding who is considered to have arrived first. Intuitively, the timestamp of a transaction corresponds to the time at which it begins executing, and old transactions (ones that have been executing a long time) have higher priority than young transactions.

Timestamp-based deadlock prevention schemes have been proposed by Rosenkrantz, Sterns, and Lewis [9]. One is called the *wait-die* system. In this scheme if T_i waits for T_j and T_i is younger than T_j, then T_i is aborted (dies); otherwise T_i is allowed to wait. When T_i is restarted, it retains its old timestamp. Another scheme is called *wound-wait*. In this scheme if T_i has higher priority than T_j, then T_j waits; otherwise T_j is aborted. The wait-die and wound-die schemes behave quite differently. In the first, old transactions never start, whereas in the second an old transaction may have to be restarted many times but is assured of finishing.

The other alternative to deadlock avoidance is deadlock detection. Whenever a cycle is detected in the wait-for graph, one of the transactions in the cycle is aborted. The main difficulty in implementing deadlock detection in a distributed system is the construction of a global wait-for graph from partial information on different nodes. One can employ centralized deadlock detection proposed by Gray [10] and Stonebraker [11] or hierarchical deadlock detection proposed by Menasce and Muntz [12]. In the centralized approach, one site is designated the deadlock detector and the scheduler at each node periodically transmits its local wait-for graph to the deadlock detector. In the hierarchical approach, database nodes are organized into a hierarchy, and there is a deadlock detector for each node of the hierarchy. Deadlocks local to a node are detected at each node and deadlocks involving two or more nodes are detected by the parent deadlock detector.

Gray [7] has recently described experiments in which it was observed that deadlocks in database systems are very rare and it may be cheaper to detect and resolve them rather than to avoid them. Distributed database designers must decide this questions for themselves.

It is important to point out that locking approaches are in general *pessimistic*. For example, two phase locking is a sufficient condition rather than the necessary condition for serializability. As an example, if an entity is only used by a single transaction, it can be locked and unlocked freely. The question is, How can we know this? Since this information is not known to the individual transaction, it is usually not utilized. Thus locking that is based on prevention of access does not fully benefit from actual favorable conditions that may exist.

As we have noted, deadlock detection and resolution in systems utilizing distributed control is not a trivial task and generally requires additional message passing for coordination. A deadlock prevention algorithm reduces freedom of access to the database entity and the information made available to the concurrency controller. This restricts the level of concurrency that is achieved.

Finally, in hierarchically structured databases, such as B-trees, some entities such as roots are accessed by all transactions and can be a bottleneck in the mechanisms based on the wait approach.

Algorithms Based on Time-Stamp Mechanism. The notion of timestamp was introduced in the last section. Timestamp is a mechanism in which the serialization order is selected a priori; the transaction execution is obliged to obey this order. In timestamp ordering, each transaction is assigned a unique timestamp by the scheduler or concurrency controller. Obviously, to achieve unique timestamps for transactions arriving at different nodes of a distributed system, all clocks at all nodes must be synchronized or else two identical timestamps must be resolved.

Lamport [13] has described an algorithm to synchronize distributed clocks via message passing. If a message arrives at a local node from a remote node with a higher timestamp, it is assumed that the local clock is slow or behind. The local clock is incremented to the timestamp of the recently received message. In this way all clocks are advanced until they are synchronized. In the other scheme where two identical timestamps must not be assigned to two transactions, each node assigns a timestamp to only one transaction at each tick of the clock. In addition the local clock time is stored in higher-order bits and the node identifiers are stored in the lower-order bits. Because node identifiers are different, this procedure will ensure unique timestamps.

When the operations of two transactions conflict, they are required to be processed in timestamp order. It is easy to prove that timestamp ordering (TSO) produces serializable histories. Thomas has studied the correctness and implementation of this approach and described it in Reference 14. Essentially each node processes conflicting operations in timestamp order, each read-write conflict relation and write-write conflict relation is resolved by timestamp order. Consequently all paths in the relation are in timestamp order and, since all transactions have unique timestamps, it follows that no cycles are possible in a graph representing transaction histories.

Timestamp Ordering with Transaction Classes. In this approach, it is assumed that the read set and the write set of every transaction is known in advance. This information is used to group transactions into predefined classes. Class definitions are used to provide concurrency control. This mechanism was used in the development of a prototype distributed database management system called SDD-1, developed by the Computer Corporation of America.

A *transaction class* is defined by a read set and a write set. A transaction T is a member of a class C if the read set of T is a subset of the read set of class C and the write set of T is

A *class* is defined by a read set and a write set. For instance,

C_1: read set = $\{x_1\}$, write set = $\{y_1, y_2\}$
C_2: read set = $\{x_1, y_2\}$, write set = $\{y_1, y_2, z_2, z_3\}$
C_3: read set = $\{y_2, z_3\}$, write set = $\{x_1, z_2, z_3\}$

A transaction is a member of a class if its read set is a subset of the class read set and its write set is a subset of the class write set. For instance,

T_1: read set = $\{x_1\}$, write set = $\{y_1, y_2\}$
T_2: read set = $\{y_2\}$, write set = $\{z_2, z_3\}$
T_3: read set = $\{z_3\}$, write set = $\{x_1\}$

T_1 is a member of C_1 and C_2
T_2 is a member of C_2 and C_3
T_3 is a member of C_3

Figure 15.3. Transaction classes.

a subset of the write set of class C. Classes need not be disjoint; that is, T may be a member of several classes. The Figure 15.3 taken from Reference 15 illustrates these definitions.

Transaction classes are defined statically and do not change frequently during normal operations of the system. The concurrency controller utilizes the information about transaction classes as follows. Suppose a scheduler wanted to read an entity X with timestamp TS. Instead of waiting for the write sets of transactions with a smaller timestamp, the scheduler needs to wait only for the write sets of transactions whose classes contain the entity X in their write set. The conflicts of write sets of two transactions are handled similarly.

Timestamp Ordering with Conflict Graph Analysis. A *conflict graph* is an undirected graph that summarizes potential conflicts between transactions in different classes. If in Figure 15.1, we replace transactions by classes, we have a conflict graph between class C_1 and class C_2.

A conflict graph for classes defined in Figure 15.4 is similar to that of Figure 15.1.

Define C_1, C_2, C_3 as in Figure 15.3.

Conflict graph analysis identifies interclass conflicts that cannot cause nonserializable behavior. This corresponds to identifying horizontal and diagonal edges that do not require synchronization. Bernstein et al. have shown that concurrency control need only synchronize updating write sets from classes C_i and C_j if either:

- The horizontal edge between $S(W_i)$ and $S(W_j)$ is embedded in a cycle of the conflict graph; or
- Portions of the intersection of C_i's write set and C_j's write set are stored at two different nodes.

Similarly it is shown that reads from C_i and writes from C_j need to be processed in timestamp order if either:

- The diagonal edge between $S(R_i)$ and $S(W_j)$ is embedded in a cycle of the conflict graph; or
- Portions of the intersection of C_i's read set and C_j's write set are stored at two or more nodes.

Distributed Voting Algorithm. This algorithm uses distributed control to decide which transaction can be accepted and executed. The nodes of the distributed database system communicate among themselves and vote on each transaction. If a transaction gets a majority of *OK* votes, it is accepted for execution and completion. A transaction may also receive a *reject*

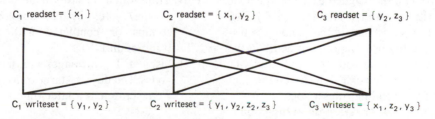

C_1 readset = $\{x_1\}$ C_2 readset = $\{x_1, y_2\}$ C_3 readset = $\{y_2, z_3\}$

C_1 writeset = $\{y_1, y_2\}$ C_2 writeset = $\{y_1, y_2, z_2, z_3\}$ C_3 writeset = $\{x_1, z_2, y_3\}$

Figure 15.4. Conflict graph. C_1 write set = $\{y_1, y_2\}$ C_2 write set = $\{y_1, y_2, z_2, z_3\}$ C_3 write set = $\{x_1, z_2, y_3\}$ C_1 read set = $\{x_1\}$ C_2 read set = $\{x_1, y_2\}$ C_3 read set = $\{y_2, z_3\}$.

vote, in which case it must be restarted. In addition to voting *OK* and *reject,* nodes can also defer or postpone voting on a particular transaction.

This approach is a result of the work of Thomas [14]. Interestingly the timestamps are maintained for the database entities. A timestamp on an entity represents the time when this entity was last updated. As before, we assume that all clocks can be synchronized to model a global clock.

When a transaction T_i arrives at a node, it immediately obtains the read set and its timestamps from the local database. The transaction is executed and the values for the write set are obtained. The transaction then enters the voting phase. If the distributed database system employs daisychain or ring architecture, the transaction visits the nodes along the chain. Between the time a node votes for a transaction and the transaction is resolved, the transaction is said to be pending at that node.

Each node checks if the timestamps of the read set of the transaction are the same as the timestamps on the read set in its local database. In otherwords, no other transaction has written in the local database after T_i has obtained its read set.

The node votes *reject* if any item in the read set has been changed (i.e., if we find a timestamp that is more recent than the one that was read at the transaction's originating node).

The node votes *OK* if the read set is current and the transaction does not conflict with a pending transaction (which got a vote from this node but has not been resolved because other nodes have not yet voted).

A node may also defer voting if T_i conflicts with a pending transaction with a higher priority (priority can be assigned based on the node at which the transaction originated, etc.). The reason for *defer* is that if the pending transaction is rejected by a majority of nodes in the future, the node may vote *OK* on T_i and vice versa. So the decision of T_i is based on the final decision of the pending transactions.

After voting *OK* or *reject,* the transaction is forwarded to the next node in the chain.

If a majority of nodes vote to reject or OK the transaction, the last node that voted sends the final reject or accept decision.

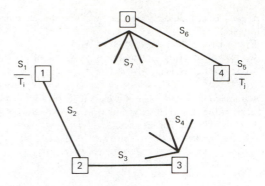

Figure 15.5. The DVA algorithm: An example.

On receipt of an "accept T_i" message, all nodes update the values of the entities in the write set of their database and take this transaction out of the pending list.

On receipt of a "reject T_i" message, all nodes take T_i out of the pending list and delete it. Then they start voting on deferred transactions that conflicted with T_i.

A simple example of this algorithm taken from Reference 16 is shown in Figure 15.5.

We illustrate the steps followed by update transactions in the DVA algorithm with the following two sample transactions T_i and T_j:

(s1) Transaction T_i arrives at node 1 and gets its first *OK* vote.

(s2) Transaction T_i visits node 2 where it gets its second *OK* vote.

(s3) Transaction T_i visits node 3 where it gets its third *OK* vote and is accepted. (Notice that 3 votes constitute a majority in this 5 node system.)

(s4) "Accept T_i" (or "perform update T_i") messages are sent to all nodes.

(s5) Transaction T_j arrives at node 4 and gets its first *OK* vote.

(s6) Transaction T_j visits node 0 and gets a *reject* vote. (T_j read obsolete timestamps or conflicted with another transaction.)

(s7) "Reject T_j" messages are sent to all nodes. (Node 4 restarts transaction T_j from scratch at a later time.)

Algorithms Based on Rollback Mechanisms. As we have seen in the last two sections, timestamp algorithms are a major departure from the locking or the wait mechanisms. In this section, a family of nonlocking or *optimistic* concurrency control algorithms are presented. In this approach, the idea is to validate a transaction against a set of previously committed transactions. If the validation fails, the read set of the transaction is updated and the transaction repeats its computation and again tries for validation. The validation phase will use conflicts among the read sets and the write sets along with certain timestamp information. The validation procedure starts when a transaction has completed its execution under the optimistic assumption that other transactions would not conflict with it. The optimistic approach maximizes the utilization of syntactic information and attempts to make use of some semantic information about each transaction. If no a priori information about an incoming transaction is available to the concurrency controller, it cannot preanalyze the transaction and try to guess potential effects on database entities. On the other hand, maximum information is available when a transaction has completed its processing. A concurrency controller can make decisions about which transaction must wait while other transactions may proceed at the time of arrival of a transaction, during the execution of a transaction, or at the end of processing. Decisions made at arrival time will tend to be pessimistic and at the end may invalidate the transaction processing and require rollback. If the transaction's effects are kept in a private space and are not made known to other transactions until the concurrency controller ensures their correctness, one can design concurrency control mechanisms that employ maximum information at the cost of restarting some transactions. The extent of this restart will be proportional to the degree of conflict among concurrent transactions. A similar approach was suggested by Kung and Robinson [17] for a centralized hierarchical data base system and was studied further by Bhargava [3, 18, 22, 27].

There are four phases of a transaction in the optimistic concurrency control approach.

Read: Since reading a value of an entity cannot cause a loss of integrity, reads are completely unrestricted. A transaction reads the values of a set of entities (called read set) and assigns them to a set of local variables. The names of local variables have one-to-one correspondence to the names of entities in the database, but the values of local variables are an instance of a past state of the database and are only known to the transaction. Of course since a value read by a transaction could be changed by a write of another transaction, making the read value incorrect, the read set is subject to validation. The read set is assigned a timestamp denoted by $\Pi(R_i)$.

Compute: The transaction computes a set of values for data entities called the write set. These values are assigned to a set of corresponding local variables. Thus all writes after computation take place on a transaction's copy of the entities of the database.

Validate: The transaction's local read set and write set are validated against a set of committed transactions. Details of this phase constitute a main part of this algorithm and are given in the next section.

Commit and Write (called *write* for short): If the transaction succeeds in validation, it is considered committed in the system and is assigned a timestamp denoted by $\Pi(W_i)$. Otherwise the transaction is rolled back or restarted at either the compute phase or the read phase. If a transaction succeeds in the validation phase, its write set is made global and the values of the write set become values of entities in the database at each node.

All four phases of concurrently processing transactions can be interleaved but the read phase should preceed the computation and validation phase.

The Validation Phase. The concurrency controller can utilize syntactic information, semantic information, or a combination of the two. First we discuss the use of syntactic information in the context of a validation at one node only. The extensions for the distributed case will be given later.

A. Syntactic Information. Kung and Papadimitriou [19] have shown that when only the syntactic information is available to the concurrency controller, serializability is the best achievable correctness criterion. We now describe the validation phase.

A transaction enters the validation phase

only after completing its computation phase. The transaction that enters the validation phase before any other transaction is automatically validated and committed. This is because initially the set of committed transactions is empty. This transaction writes updated values in the data base. Since this transaction may be required to validate against future transactions, a copy of its read and write sets is kept by the system. Any transaction that enters the validation phase validates against only the committed transactions. Of course the validation procedure could include validation against other transactions currently in the validation phase, but for the sake of keeping the discussion simple this aspect is discussed later.

Let T_j be a committed transaction when a transaction T_i arrives for validation. Let $S(R_i)$ and $S(R_j)$ be the read sets and $S(W_i)$ and $S(W_j)$ be the write sets of T_i and T_j, respectively. Let $\Pi(R_i)$ and $\Pi(R_j)$ denote the time when the last item of the read set $S(R_i)$ and $S(R_j)$ were read from the data base and let $\Pi(W_i)$ and $\Pi(W_j)$ denote the time when the first item of the write set $S(W_i)$ and $S(W_j)$ will be or were written in the data base.

Since T_j is already committed, we know read and write operations of T_j have already occurred. So $\Pi(W_i)$ will be greater than $\Pi(R_j)$ and $\Pi(W_j)$ is greater than $\Pi(R_i)$.

If T_i and T_j do not conflict, then T_i can be either before T_j or after T_j in any serial history.

If $S(R_i) \cap S(W_j) = \emptyset$ and $S(R_j) \cap S(W_i) \neq \emptyset$ and $\Pi(R_i) < \Pi(W_j)$, then T_i must precede T_j in any serial history. This situation is illustrated as follows:

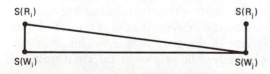

The edge between $S(W_i)$ and $S(W_j)$ does not matter because if $S(W_i)$ intersects with $S(W_j)$, then $S(W_i)$ can be replaced by $S(W_i) - [S(W_i) \cap S(W_j)]$. In other words, T_i will write values for only those entities that are not common with the write set of T_j. If we do so, we get the equivalent effect as if T_i were written before T_j.

If $S(R_i) \cap S(W_j) = \emptyset$
and $S(R_j) \cap S(W_i) \neq \emptyset$
and $\Pi(R_i) < \Pi(W_j)$
then T_i must follow T_j in any serial history.
This situation is illustrated as follows:

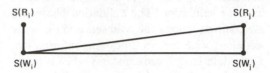

For each transaction that is validated and enters the list of committed transactions, we draw a directed edge according to the following rules:

- If T_i and T_j do not conflict, do not draw any edge
- If T_i must precede T_j, draw an edge from T_i to T_j, $T_i \rightarrow T_j$
- If T_i must follow T_j, draw an edge from T_j to T_i, $T_i \leftarrow T_j$

Thus a directed graph is created for all committed transactions with transactions as nodes and edges as explained above.

When a new transaction T_i arrives for validation, it is checked against each committed transaction to check if T_i should precede or follow, or if the order does not matter.

Condition for validation: There is never a cycle in the graph of committed transactions because they are serializable. If the *validating transaction creates a cycle* in the graph, it must *restart* or *rollback*. Otherwise, it is included in the set of committed transactions. We assume validation of a transaction to be in the critical section so that the set of committed transactions does not change while a transaction is actively validating.

In case a transaction fails in validation, the concurrency controller can restart the transaction from the beginning of the read phase. This is because the failure in the validation makes the read set of the failed transaction incorrect. The read set of such a transaction becomes incorrect because of some write sets of the committed transactions. Since the write sets of the committed transactions meet the read set of the failed transaction (during validation), it may be possible to update the values of the read set of the transaction at the time of validation. If this is possible, the failed transaction can start at the beginning of the compute phase rather than at the beginning of the read phase. This will save the I/O access required to update the read set of the failed transaction.

The validation can be implemented as follows. (For more ways, see Reference 18.)

Let T_i be the validating transaction and let T_j be a member of a set of committed transactions.

The read sets and write sets of the committed transactions are kept in the system. The transaction is validated against the committed transaction according to the above condition. The committed transactions are selected in the order of their commitment. The read set is updated by the conflicting write set at the time of each validation. If none of the transactions conflict with the validating transaction, it is considered to have succeeded in the validation and hence to have committed.

This obviously requires updating a given entity of the read set many times and thus is inefficient. But one nice property of this procedure is that the transaction does not have to restart from the beginning and does not have to read the database on secondary storage.

A practical question is whether the read sets and write sets can be stored in memory. The transactions T_j that must be stored in memory must satisfy the following condition: If T_j is a committed transaction, store T_j for future validation if $T_i \notin$ set of committed transaction such that

$$\{\Pi(R_i) < \Pi(W_j)\} \text{ AND}$$
$$\{S(R_i) \cap S(W_j) \neq \phi\}$$

It has been shown that the set of transactions to be stored for future validation will usually be small [27]. In general a maximum size of the number of committed transactions that can be stored in the memory can be determined at design time. In case the number of committed transactions exceed this limit, the earliest committed transaction T_j can be de-

leted from this list. But care should be taken to restart (or invalidate) all active transactions T_i for which $\Pi(R_i) < \Pi(W_j)$ before T_j is deleted.

B. Semantic Information. For a concurrency controller to utilize semantic information about a transaction, a new model of the transaction has to be used. This model is similar to the one used in Reference 20 and is described below.

A transaction operates on a set of entities. The granularity of entities is not a concern in the formalism, though they affect the cost of validation. The entities could represent bits, attributes (fields), tuples, or relations, as long as they are individually accessible. The value set X denotes the set of all possible values of the vector $\mathbf{X}$ of entities used by the transaction.

A transaction T_i is represented by a directed graph composed of two types of nodes shown in Figure 15.6, where $f_i : x \rightarrow x$ and $p_i : x \rightarrow \{\text{true,false}\}$ are multiple valued functions. At each assignment node k, a value of an entity x_{ik} is transformed according to the function f_{ik} based on the knowledge available to the transaction T_i.

In general computer programs, the interpretation of f_{ik} is arbitrary, but in a majority of data base transactions, the range of interpretation of f can be determined. Part of the semantics of the transaction is represented by the interpretation ϕ_{ik} of the function f_{ik}, for all k. These interpretations in general programs are arbitrary; nonetheless they have been used for proving program correctness. Fortunately in a majority of database transactions, the range of interpretations of function f is finite

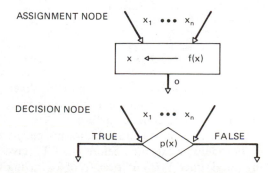

Figure 15.6. Two typical nodes in the transaction graph.

and determinable. For example, f_{ik} could be an identity function (representing a read). The interpretation of f_{ik} can be independent of the knowledge of values of data entities (representing a read). Moreover, f_{ik} may represent an arithmetic function (such as add or subtract) or could be a relational algebra operation (such as project, join, or select).

Several studies of application programs from which database transactions are usually derived have been done in the past. Knuth [28] studied a random sample of 440 production Fortran programs and found that 86% of assignment statements are of the form:

$$X_1 = X_2$$
$$X_1 = X_2 + X_3$$

or

$$X_1 = X_2 - X_3$$

Elshoff [20] examined 120 production PL/I programs and discovered that 97% of all arithmetic operators are $+$ or $-$. White and Cohen [21] studied 50 production Cobol programs and discovered that only 1 of 1,255 predicates in these programs was nonlinear. From these studies, it can be inferred that assignment functions f_i for a database transaction are not arbitrary and in most cases are linear arithmetic functions. One nice property of certain linear arithmetic functions is that they are commutable.

As an example, consider the assignment functions of two transactions T_1 and T_2 on a variable X, as follows.

T_1	T_2
$f_{11}: X \leftarrow X + 1$	$f_{21}: X \leftarrow X - 1$
$f_{12}: Y \leftarrow 3$	
$f_{13}: X \leftarrow X + 4$	

Naturally, f_{11} and f_{21} are commutable. Even though f_{11} and f_{21} compute on the same variable, they can be done in any order.

Considering only syntactic information, f_{21} of T_2 should be executed before f_{13} of T_1 (giving serial order T_2T_1) or after f_{13} of T_1 (giving

serial order T_1T_2). But utilizing interpretations and commutable properties of assignment functions, a concurrency controller can allow even nonserializable histories to be accepted as equivalent to serial history.

We agree that the analysis of such interpretation in general may not be efficiently doable. In hierarchically ordered databases, several concurrency controllers that allow nonserializability have been proposed. In our approach, we note that such interpretations for each transaction become available during its processing in its private space. The concurrency controller can decide to use the interpretations of the transaction during validation. If it is not possible to utilize them efficiently, it can employ only the syntactic information.

C. Partial Semantic Information. The complexity of considering the interpretation of different steps of several transactions may forbid their use. If this is the case, the concurrency controller can use information about the processing time required to execute each transaction, the size of its read set/write set, and so forth. This information can be weighted to estimate the cost of reexecuting a transaction if its validation fails.

Suppose a transaction is validating in the main processing unit and several transactions are waiting to enter the validation phase. If an additional processor is available, it can be used to validate the waiting transactions against each other and select the next transaction for validation such that the cost of restarting and executing the invalidated transactions is minimized. A simple algorithm is given below. Create a weighted directed graph where

1. Each node represents a transaction waiting for validation.
2. A directed edge from a transaction T_i to transaction T_j represents a read-write conflict (i.e., $S(R_i) \cap S(W_j) \neq \emptyset$ and $\Pi(R_i < \Pi(W_j))$).
3. The weight on the edge is some measure of the estimated cost of reexecuting T_i.

The weights of incident edges on a node represent the cost of reexecuting other transactions that become invalidated if the transaction

tions that become invalidated if the transaction representing this node is selected for validation. Similarly the weight on outgoing edges from a node represent the cost saving if the transaction is selected for validation. To reduce the cost of reexecuting invalidated transactions, the concurrency controller does the following:

Select a transaction among the waiting transactions to validate next against the committed transactions such that {sum of weights on incident edges on the node representing the transaction in the graph − sum of weights on outgoing edge from the node} is minimum.

Another type of partial semantic information is reflected through the size of the write set available after the execution of a transaction. This write set may be smaller than the write set that can be estimated at the start of a transaction. This is because some decision nodes are of the type IF THEN ELSE and some values of items in the write set may remain unchanged.

Centralized and Distributed Optimistic Concurrency Control Algorithms. The distributed database system may consist of a set of completely replicated databases, located at each node. We assume that the database is a set of entities. The concurrency control algorithm must ensure that all nodes in the system execute the same serial history.

Here we briefly present two types (centralized and distributed) of optimistic concurrency control algorithms for the distributed data base management system.

The Centralized Optimistic Algorithms. For this algorithm, one of the nodes is chosen as the *central node*. Let this be called *node C*.

Case 1: The validation takes place only at the central node. When a transaction T_i arrives at a node X, the following steps are performed.

1. The transaction reads a set of entities in its local variable space. Let us call this set $S(R_i)$.

2. The transaction goes to the central processing unit (CPU) of node X, and completes its execution. At this time an actual write set $S(W_i)$ based on $S(R_i)$ and computation function of T_i is known. In a sense the write set $S(W_i)$ is a semantic write set compared to the syntactic write set that could have been assumed before the computation phase. In general the semantic write set will be a subset or equivalent to the syntactic subset.

3. The transaction is sent to the central node C for validation. If validation succeeds, the transaction is committed. The central node assigns a sequence number to all committed transactions based on the order in which they are committed. If validation fails, the read set $S(R_i)$ of the transaction is updated and the transaction computes its new write set at the CPU of the central node. The transaction again enters the validation phase. The process is repeated until the validation succeeds.

4. The write set of the successful transaction is sent to all the nodes.

5. When the node X and other nodes of the system receive the write set of the transaction, they update their copy of the data base.

To avoid transmission delay problems, the nodes can execute transactions in the order of sequence numbers assigned at node C. They can also follow any of the approaches ("wait-for" list, "hole" list, etc.) as discussed in Reference 16.

Case 2: The validation takes place at the local node and then at the central node. When a transaction T_i arrives at node X, the following steps are performed.

Steps 1 and 2 are the same as in Case 1.

3. The transaction validates at node X. If validation succeeds, the transaction is considered semi-committed at node X. If validation fails, the read set $S(R_i)$ of the transaction is updated and the transac-

tion is sent for recomputation at node X. The transaction again tries for validation at node X. The process is repeated until validation succeeds.

4. The transaction is sent to the central node C for validation. The transaction is validated against
   a. The committed transactions from all other nodes and
   b. The transactions that were committed at node X, failed at the central node, and were later committed.

   If validation succeeds, the transaction is committed at the central node. If validation fails, the readset $S(R_i)$ is updated and the transaction is sent for recomputation at the central node. The process is repeated until validation succeeds.

   Steps 5 and 6 are the same as the steps 4 and 5 in case 1.

The Distributed Optimistic Algorithm. In this algorithm an identical concurrency control exists at all nodes of the system and the same validation procedure is followed. The algorithm is based on the assumption that a parameter MTD exits that represents the maximum transmission delay between any two nodes of the system.

When a transaction T_i arrives at a node X, the following steps are performed.

Steps 1 and 2 are the same as in the centralized optimistic algorithms.

3. The transaction is broadcast to all the nodes in the system at time $\Pi(V_i)$ (the time when transaction T_i completed its computation phase at node X).
4. At time $(V_i) + MDT$, transaction T_i enters the validation phase at all nodes. By this time, the transaction should have reached all nodes of the system.

If validation succeeds at the nodes, the transaction is considered committed. If validation fails, all nodes except node X ignore the transaction. At node X, the read set $S(R_i)$ of the transaction is updated and the transaction is submitted for recomputation. The process-

ing restarts from step 3 until validation succeeds.

We assume that clocks at all nodes are synchronized by using some mechanism [13]. If two transactions arrive at the same time at two nodes, they can be ordered in a fixed predefined manner (for example by assigning priorities to nodes). The assumption that each transaction reaches other nodes in the system within a fixed time interval MTD after its transmission ensures that all nodes have precisely the same set of transactions in the validation phase. Since the concurrency controller at each node is identical, the histories generated at each node will be identical. If each history satisifies the consistency criterion (say, serializability) then the distributed optimistic algorithm will produce correct and identical histories at each node. This leads to the following theorem.

Theorem: The distributed optimistic algorithm produces correct and identical histories at each node if each transaction arrives at other nodes within a fixed time interval MTD after its transmission and if no failures occur.

Proof: We give an information proof that is based on contradiction. The validation procedure ensures that the concurrency controller produces only correct histories. So we need to prove that histories at all nodes are identical. Suppose it is not true. Then there must be two histories in which the order of execution of some two transactions is different.

Case 1: Two transaction (say, T_i and T_j) arrive at the same node (say, N_1). In this case, the two transactions execute and become available for validation in some order (say, $\Pi(V_i)$ and $\Pi(V_j)$ and let $\Pi(V_i) < \Pi(V_j)$. Both of these transactions enter validation at times $\Pi(V_i) + MTD$ and $\Pi(V_j) + MTD$ at node N_1.

a. If both transactions are validated by concurrency controller, the history at node N_1, is T_iT_j.
b. If only T_i is restarted, the history at node N_1, will be T_jT_i.

c. If only T_j is restarted, the history at node N_1, will be T_iT_j.
d. If both are rejected $\Pi(V_i)$ and $\Pi(V_j)$ will get new values and there is no effect on the history.

Let us just consider in *a*, a history at another node (say, N_2). If the algorithm produces a history T_jT_i at node N_2, T_j must have entered the validation phase at node N_2 before T_i. This is possible only if $\Pi(V_i) + MTD > \Pi(V_j) + MTD$ but $\Pi(V_i) < \Pi(V_j)$. So MTD for T_i must be greater than MTD for T_j. But this is a contradiction to our assumption that MTD is constant. Thus history T_jT_i is not possible at node N_2. Hence histories at node N_1 and N_2 are identical. With the same argument, *b* and *c* will produce identical histories at nodes N_1 and N_2.

Case 2: Transaction T_i arrives at node N_1 and transaction T_j arrives at node N_2. Again suppose the two transactions execute and become available for validation at nodes N_1 and N_2 in some order (say, $\Pi(V_i)$ and $\Pi(V_j)$ and let $\Pi(V_i) < \Pi(V_j)$). We again consider the case when both transactions validate successfully. Note that the clocks are synchronized and the transactions can be ordered in a predefined fixed manner even if they arrive at the same time.

At node N_1, transaction T_i enters the validation phase at time $\Pi(V_i) + MTD$. The transaction T_j cannot arrive at node N_1 before $\Pi(V_j)$ and so before $\Pi(V_i)$. Thus T_j will enter the validation phase at time $\Pi(V_j + MTD$, which must be greater than $\Pi(V_i) + MTD$; otherwise we have a contradiction. Thus the history at node N_1 is T_iT_j.

Transaction T_i reaches node N_2 in the time interval $\{\Pi(V_i), \Pi(V_i) + MTD\}$ and becomes eligible for validation at time $\Pi(V_i) + MTD$. The transaction T_j become eligible for validation at time $\Pi(V_j) + MTD$. The history T_jT_i at node N_2 is different than at node N_1; that is, $\Pi(V_j) + MTD < \Pi(V_i) + MTD$. But as in case 1, $\Pi(V_i) < \Pi(V_j)$, so MTD for T_i must be greater than MTD for T_j, which is a contradiction of our assumption that MTD is fixed

and the same for all transactions. So the history of node N_2 cannot be T_jT_i and is T_iT_j.

Hence histories at node N_1 and N_2 are identical. The same can be shown to be true if either T_i or T_j is rejected. *Q.E.D.*

Let us now consider a system in which one cannot make the assumption that all transactions reach other nodes within the fixed time interval MTD.

In such a case a variety of mechanisms can be used. For example one can employ the principle of two phase commit [10]. A transaction is committed in two phases. In the first phase, all nodes are informed of the results of a validated transaction and are requested to inform the originating node if there is any conflict between this transaction and other transactions at their nodes. If the information at some other node requires invalidating the transaction, such nodes send a message to the originating node of the transaction, causing it to restart. If all nodes agree to validate the transaction, it is committed at the originating node and a message is sent to all nodes to commit the transaction. Otherwise a message is sent to all the nodes to ignore the transaction. Although this solution is workable, it requires several message transmissions before a transaction is committed.

Another suggested approach is based on the optimism that most transactions will reach other nodes within the time interval MTD and few transactions will be invalidated. The algorithm works as described earlier. But since it can no longer be guaranteed (due to variations in transmission delay) that the same information is available at each node at the time when a transaction enters the validation phase, it is possible that transactions commit in different order at each node. For this reason, we introduce a new phase in transaction processing called *semicommit*. All transactions validating according to the earlier algorithm are considered semicommitted rather than committed (effects of semicommit transactions can be nullified, but can be made available to read-only transactions with proper warning). To take the transition from semicommit to commit, it must be confirmed that all transactions that were committed at other nodes before its validation have also been considered in its validation. For this purpose an additional data structure is to be kept at each node. This contains (1) a monotonic sequence generator, (2) the sequence number of the last transaction committed at this node and, (3) the sequence number of the last committed transaction of every other node that was received at this node. No node validates a transaction from another node unless it has validated transactions with missing sequence numbers. Some transactions are in transmission if the sequence number of the transaction to be validated is not one more than the sequence number of the last transaction committed from the same node. The ideas of wait-for lists, hole lists, and so forth discussed in Reference 20 can also be used here.

When an originating node receives the information that a higher-sequence number transaction issued at the originating node has been validated at all other nodes, all transactions up to this sequence number make a transition from semicommit to commit. Such information can be attached to executed transactions and then transmitted from each node. Thus, we can avoid messages just for coordination at the cost of keeping some transactions in a semicommit state. If the transaction in the semicommit phase finds that no committed transaction from other nodes invalidate it, it is considered committed; otherwise it is removed from the semicommit phase and restarted. This restart may cause some other transactions in the semicommit phase to restart if they were affected by the result of the invalidated transaction. This approach is suitable in systems where only a few transactions will arrive too late and thus will conflict with transactions already in the semicommit phase. Details of this procedure and its correctness are discussed in Reference 3.

This procedure will ensure that all histories generated at each node of the distributed data base will become identical when all transmitted transactions have been received at all necessary nodes. One can also employ certain checkpoints at which time the concurrency controller at each node will transmit parts of the histories that were produced since the last checkpoint to all other nodes. Using this information the histories at all nodes can be synchronized and their effects on the data base made identical. These checkpoints can also be dynamically initiated, as for example when a node notices a lot of irregularity in transmission delays or when a node that failed or lost communication with other nodes is ready to join the system. The problem of node failure or communication line failures can be handled by mechanisms described in Reference 22.

Performance and Implementation

Even though a variety of concurrency control approaches have been studied, only a few of them have been implemented. It is essential to study the performance of these approaches in order to achieve efficient implementation.

There are two main areas where performance can be studied:

- The degree of concurrency provided by a concurrency control.
- The effort required to achieve mutual consistency on different modes.

We first present a theoretical treatment of the above two issues. It is known that the performance of a concurrency controller is dependent on the amount of information available to it. For example, the concurrency controller may use only syntactic information or may use semantics of transactions such as transaction classes. A concurrency controller must synchronize read-write and write-write conflicts among concurrent transactions and its performance can be judged on how well it does so.

The wait mechanism is pessimistic in nature because it must lock many more entities than is required (to avoid deadlocks, for example) and keep these entities locked longer than necessary.

For example, two phase locking is a sufficient condition rather than a necessary condition for serializability. As a case in point, if an entity is not needed by any other concurrent transaction, the concurrency controller can let the transaction unlock this entity and ask for more locks without violating serializability.

The rollback mechanism provides a higher degree of concurrency than the locking approach, as is illustrated in the following example.

Suppose we have two transactions T_i and T_j with read and write sets and conflicts as follows. Suppose T_i arrives before T_j.

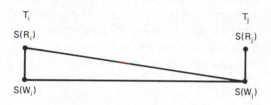

In the wait approach or the locking approach, T_i gets a readlock on R_i. T_j comes next and gets a readlock on R_j. Now T_j completes its computation and determines its write set. Since $S(R_i) \cap S(W_j) \neq \emptyset$, T_j cannot obtain writelocks and must wait for T_i to complete its computation and release its read set. Thus the only history possible will be $R_iR_jW_iW_j$.

Now let us look at the optimistic approach. T_i will read R_i and start its computation. T_j will arrive after T_i, read R_j, compute, and will determine its write set W_j. Since it arrives in the validation phase before T_i, which is still computing, T_j is validated (assume no other transactions before T_i and T_j) and the values of W_j are written in the database. When the write set of T_i becomes available, it is also written in the database. Thus a history such as $R_iR_jW_jW_i$ is allowed in addition to the history $R_iR_jW_iW_j$. Note that both of these histories are equivalent to the serial history (T_iT_j or $R_iW_iR_jW_j$).

Moreover, if $S(W_i) \cap (W_j) \neq \emptyset$, in locking, writing of W_j must wait until writelocks on W_i are released. On the other hand, in the optimistic approach W_i can be changed to $W_i - (W_i \cap W_j)$ and we may still allow both T_i and T_j to complete without either waiting for the other.

It should be pointed out that the work of T_i would have to be rolled back if $S(W_i) \cap S(R_j) \neq \emptyset$. But in such a case the only history possible would be $R_iW_iR_jW_j$. In case of rollback, T_i may not need to start from the beginning. If the readset R_i can be updated by the new values of W_j in the memory at the time of vali-

dation, then T_i can start computing again without making an I/O access to the database. In the locking approach the I/O access for T_i and T_j can only be started after the other transaction has finished. More discussion of this work is included in reports by Bhargava in References 18 and 27. The simulation of locking and optimistic approaches are discussed in these papers. The size of the database, the number of nodes, the size of the read sets and write sets of transactions, and the arrival rate of transactions were varied. It was found that in a centralized database system, the optimistic approach performs better than the locking approach for realistic transactions and data bases unless the arrival rate of transactions goes beyond six per second. In most commercial applications, except those of airlines and banks, the arrival rate seldom exceeds this rate. The results in the distributed case were much more supportive of the optimistic approach. It was noted that the optimistic approach will start to suffer as the percentage of conflicting transactions increased. In situations of up to 5% cycle conflicts, depending upon the choice of a restart mechanism, the optimistic approach performs better than the locking approach. In large databases with many users this conflict percentage is rare.

A similar simulation study was done by Garcia [16, 23] in which it was concluded that centralized locking performs better than the majority voting algorithm based on timestamps. This fact may be based on the number of messages required before a commit decision is made. Such studies imply that before we start implementing concurrency control algorithms, we must study their performance in detail. A simulation model is also being developed by Rosenkrantz [24] to compare concurrency control algorithms.

Several prototypes of distributed database systems have been developed. The most notable experimental work has been reported by Computer Corporation of America on SSD-1 [2], University of California, Berkeley on Distributed INGRES [11], Grenoble University and Cii Honeywell Bull on SCOT [25], and INRIA on SIRIUS-DELTA [5]. Some details of these systems have been given in previous chapters and we refer the reader to the detailed original reports.

15.3. RELIABILITY CONTROL APPROACHES AND ALGORITHMS

Types of Failures

Our main concern in reliability control is to provide recovery and continuity of operation in case a failure occurs in the distributed database system. A variety of failures can prevent a transaction from completing successfully. To provide continuity of operations in a distributed database management system, several copies of the entities are placed on different nodes. This replication increases the availability of databases in case of failures at the cost of increased concurrency control problems (see the discussion in the last section). A reliability controller (or recovery manager) should be able to deal with

- Transaction failure
- Node failure (local or remote)
- Communication system failure

Clearly, some of these failures will be visible to the end user, but we would like to design the system so that the application programmer or the user is insulated from many of them. Failure transparency relieves the user from the responsibility of restoring the database to a consistent state and terminating (either completing or aborting) unfinished transactions. The system will have the responsibility to detect failures and provide a certain level of continuity of operations until failures are corrected. Stopping the operations of the system by refusing to accept new transactions is not an attractive option unless it is the only choice.

Different failures are detected by the system in different ways. An *abort* request can be provided to allow the user to announce application failure. Local node crashes are detected when a node fails to respond to the messages from the communication system. Communication system and remote node failures are detected by timeouts as well as explicit messages from the failed component.

Research into the reliability and recovery of a distributed database management system is in the development stage and we can present only preliminary ideas. It should be evident that one cannot rely on the indefinite preservation of integrity and consistency of the database. For example, the states of computer registers or memory cannot be presumed to survive a power outage; data on magnetic devices such as tapes and disks are vulnerable to head crashes and fires; and finally no data is safe against undetected system software errors. So our objective in practice is to reduce damage to the database in case of failure, bring the database to a consistent state after recovery, and provide some level of transaction processing in parallel with recovery. In the following sections we discuss these failures and appropriate actions required to recover from them.

Transaction Failure

A variety of reasons can prevent a transaction from completion, including application-detected anomalies (e.g., insufficient funds), division by zero (program error), violation of security or integrity constraints, deadlock victim (system's decision) or unavailability of the entity that must be updated.

When a transaction fails, its effects must be undone. For example, if it has partially written in the database, the original database state must be restored. If some other transaction has already read the database state after a failed transaction has updated, this transaction must also be rolled back. Thus a cascade of rollbacks for several transactions can occur. To reduce the rollback, the system establishes checkpoints for concurrent transactions either at design-time or at run-time. All transaction processing since the checkpoint is rolled back, and all transactions except the failed transaction are reexecuted. In order to undo or redo the actions of a transaction, each node in the distributed system maintains an undo log or a redo log. It is important to note that certain actions cannot be undone. The system must ensure that the actions of a transaction that have no undo action are deferred until after the commit point. The definitions of undo and redo actions and logs were given earlier in the section on basic concepts.

Since the execution of undo actions and rollback is expensive, many systems keep the changes to be made in the database by a transaction in a private work space (or local variables). No other transaction is made aware of these changes. When the transaction has successfully executed, it is validated against other transactions and then committed. The commitment is immediately followed by changes in the database. This is the approach utilized in optimistic concurrency control algorithms [3, 22]. The optimistic algorithms have failure transparency with respect to transaction failures.

Node Failure

The system can find that the node at which the transaction is executing has failed or that some other node has failed. The node where the transaction is currently active is called the *local node,* and all other nodes are called *remote nodes.* The failure can occur because of a system failure in which the hardware and/or software may change the values of the volatile entities to null and refuse to respond to any transactions or messages. We will assume that a node failure or crash is immediately detected.

When a local node crashes, it is similar to a system failure in the centralized case. There are four kinds of transactions at the node restart (for further discussion see Reference 7).

1. Those that have all their committed actions reflected in real and stable entities
2. Those that were in the middle of a commitment phase
3. Those that have not made any changes to the database or any completed actions that can be undone
4. Those which have not begun

When the node recovers and restarts, it transforms transactions of type 3 to transactions of type 4 and transactions of type 2 to transactions of type 1.

In the optimistic approach, if the transaction is uncommitted and has not validated, all work done by the transaction is lost and the transaction can be resubmitted or restarted. If the transaction is committed, all its action can be redone using the redo log and the database can be updated. Sometimes, the transaction is validated at the local node and is sent to remote nodes for validation. If the node where the transaction has validated fails in the meantime, it may be possible to still commit the transaction by the other nodes of the system by using a commit protocol using majority votes.

If a remote node fails while a transaction is being committed at some other node, the communication system can take the responsibility of delivering the final decision to the failed node when it comes up. As an alternative we can use spoolers in each node which store messages that have been sent by other nodes. To avoid the failure of a spooler, multiple spoolers may be employed. This idea has also been used in the SDD-1 system and is described in Reference 6.

In case a transaction is requesting commitment from a failed remote node, the absence of a reply is considered a rejection. If a transaction is committed while a remote node is in a failed state, the commitment message is sent to the remote node and stored in its spooler. When the remote node recovers, it first executes and completes the updates of the committed transactions.

If a remote node fails after agreeing to commit a transaction and the rest of the system decides to reject the transaction, the rejection message is sent to the spooler of the failed node.

In case the node receives a transaction commitment from the system but fails before making a change in the database, the backup logs can be employed.

The above discussion leads us to many interesting protocols for terminating a transaction. These will be discussed in a later section.

Communication System Failure

The communication system fails when there are one or more of the following types of problems.

- Partition of the network: This occurs when the nodes of the distributed database are split into two or more groups, and the groups are unable to communicate with each other. The nodes in one group can communicate with other nodes in the same group. A group may have only one node.
- Messages are lost: This problem occurs when the message sent by one node does not reach a designated node.
- Messages are delivered in the wrong order: This can happen because of variable transmission delays.
- Network partition: When a partition occurs, we may have one of the following situations: One of the partitions has a majority of nodes. None of the partitions has a majority of nodes

Note that majority does not have to be decided by the number of nodes alone. It could be decided based on some other criterion, such as the importance of some nodes that must continue operating. In such cases weights can be assigned to nodes, and majority is defined by more than half of all weights.

To maintain mutual consistency among databases in different partitions, we have the following choices:

Do not allow any transactions to update the database. Allow read-only transactions.
This alternative is not very attractive because we like to continue to process as many transactions as possible
Allow transaction processing only in one partition. This partition can be the one with a majority of nodes.
This is a good alternative because many transactions can now be processed. Their results can be updated in databases of other partitions when the merger of the partitions takes place. There is one problem with this alternative. Read-only transaction can no longer be processed in other partitions because they may read old (or wrong) values.

The above two alternatives tend to be pessimistic but safe in nature. Our third choice is

based on an optimistic approach to concurrency control.

Allow transaction processing in all partitions but do not commit any transaction. Instead leave them in a semicommit *state that will be subject to validation when partitions merge.*
In this case, if the transactions processed in different partitions do not conflict or they can be serialized, we can immediately change their status from semicommit to commit. On the other hand, if transactions in different partitions conflict and produce a nonserializable effect, some transactions, based on the same approach as discussed in the Validation Phase section, can be rolled back. Note that the results of semicommitted transactions can be made available to users with proper warning. Since in a large distributed data base system, the probability of conflict for two transactions is usually small, very few transactions would need to *rollback*.

So far we have considered the granularity of database partition at the node level. We can also use partitions at the level of entities in the data base. We can designate one copy of the entity in the database as the primary copy (or the true copy). Each primary copy has a token that leads to the next alternative for transaction processing in a partitioned database.

Allow a transaction to be processed and committed in a partition if the partition has a primary copy token for all entities referenced by the transaction. This approach will allow transactions to be processed in different partitions. Since no transaction in different partitions operates on the same entities, the data base will remain consistent.

Finally, we may decide that the transaction processes only those operations that are not value dependent but that are commutative. For example, transactions can add and subtract values of entities but no values can be changed on the basis of the present values of entities (e.g., a 10% increase). When the partitions merge, all changes can be quickly merged without rollbacks.

We will not deal with the problem of lost

messages in detail here except to note that this problem can be detected by a time-out mechanism and lost messages can be reissued. The receiving node must ensure that identical messages are not processed twice.

The problem of messages being delivered in the wrong order can be handled by assigning sequence numbers at the source and utilizing wait-for lists at the receiver, an idea that was discussed earlier in this chapter.

Transaction Commitment in a Distributed Database Management System

In a distributed database management system, it is important to ensure that the transaction either succeeds or fails at every node. This requirement is also referred to as the *atomicity* of the transaction. Success means that all of the transaction's updates are completed at all nodes in the system. Failure means that there are no effects of the transaction on the database or other transactions. Transaction commitment ensures that all nodes make the same decision with respect to committing or aborting the transaction.

Transaction commitment may face the problem of an individual node's autonomous behavior. For example, a node may reject commitment of a transaction or the node itself may crash.

Two Phase Commit Protocol

A protocol that has been widely accepted for the transaction commitment is called *two phase commit protocol*. As the name implies, there are two phases in the commitment of a transaction.

Phase 1. All nodes are queried as to whether they can commit the transaction. All nodes agreeing to commit enter the *prepare state;* others send an *abort* message. If all nodes are willing to commit the transaction, a single node is selected as the commit coordinator. This decision can also be based on a majority of nodes willing to commit, in which case other nodes are forced to accept the decision of the majority. The majority of nodes may also decide to restart the transaction, in which case

the transaction is aborted by the system and there is no need for phase 2.

Phase 2. The commit coordinator records the update on stable storage to ensure recoverability against failures and commits the transaction on its node. Now all other nodes are notified to commit the transaction. Each node commits the transaction in the same way as the coordinator and acknowledges transaction commitment. It also changes its state from prepare to *initial state* and is ready to process other transactions. The coordinator broadcasts commit messages periodically to each participant until it acknowledges. When the coordinator has received all phase 2 acknowledgments, the transaction is considered committed in the system.

There are three implementations of a two phase commit protocol:

- Linear two phase commit protocol
- Centralized two phase commit protocol
- Decentralized two phase commit protocol

In each of these implementations, the coordination of polling and the decisions for commit or abort of a transaction are accomplished in a different way. A qualitative comparison will be given after we describe these protocols in the following section.

Linear Two Phase Commit Protocol.   In this protocol, all nodes of the distributed data base management system are ordered into a sequence and the messages travel from node to node in this sequence.

Phase 1 of the commit procedure begins when the transaction coordinator decides to initiate the commit. Each node willing to commit enters a prepare state and forwards the message to the next node. If any node does not agree to commit or is unavailable because of failure, it becomes the abort coordinator and supervises the abort of the transaction. It sends an abort message to all predecessors up to the node where the transaction's commit originated. All ready states are erased.

If every node in the sequence agrees to commit, then the last node becomes the commit coordinator. This site enters the *committing state* by recording the update in the log on stable storage. After committing, the last node sends the commit message to the predecessors who are in a prepare state. Upon receiving the commit response, each node enters the committing state by recording the update in stable storage. Once committed, the committing node acknowledges the commit from its successor. When a commit is acknowledged, the node is finished with the transaction and enters the initial state to handle other transactions. When the node of origin receives and completes the commit action, the transaction is committed in the system.

Centralized Two Phase Commit Protocol. In this protocol, a single node (the node where the transaction originated or completed) becomes the commit coordinator and sends all prepare and commit messages. The coordinator starts phase 1 in the *collecting state* and sends the updates of the transaction to all nodes and polls them. Each node determines whether to commit the transaction or reject it and sends this information to the coordinator. All nodes are considered in a prepare state. In phase 2, the coordinator makes the decision to commit or abort and enters this information on the stable storage to ensure recoverability. If all nodes agree to commit, the coordinator commits and asks all nodes to commit the transaction, then awaits acknowledgment. When the coordinator has received all phase 2 acknowledgments, it commits the transaction. If a certain node does not agree to commit or does not respond within a time limit, the transaction coordinator broadcasts the restart message to each participant. The broadcast message is periodically rebroadcast to each participant until it acknowledges that it has acted on the message.

Decentralized Two Phase Commit Protocol. In this protocol, no node acts as the coordinator and all nodes send prepare, commit, and abort messages to all nodes. Any node that receives the commit message from all nodes can commit and proceed with other transactions. In general, in the decentralized protocol, there could be several rounds of message inter-

changes. In each round a node sends an identical message to every other node. A simple decentralized commit protocol consists of a single message round and is described below.

When a node is ready to start commitment of a transaction, it sends a ready-to-commit message to all other nodes. It then waits to receive a commit message from all other nodes. It commits the transaction only if it has received a commit message from every node.

The major deficiency of this protocol is that it is not resilient to node failures. Some nodes may commit a transaction and fail, whereas other nodes must block the transaction or risk making an inconsistent commit decision.

By extending this simple protocol to require an extra message round when all sites agree to commit, we can take care of part of the above problem. So in effect we have a prepare phase and a commit phase, making it precisely a two phase commit protocol.

In order to terminate a transaction that requires either committing or aborting, successive rounds of message interchanges are needed. The maximum number of rounds required to terminate a transaction is equal to the initial number of operational nodes. Normally the protocol requires two rounds of message interchanges; however, additional node failures during the execution of the protocol cause additional rounds. The following is the list of rules followed in the resilient termination protocol.

- If a prepared-to-commit or commit message is received, a node may be able to commit the transaction; otherwise it may abort it.
- Once a node starts sending a prepared-to-commit, commit, or abort message, it is required to send the same message in subsequent rounds.
- A transaction is committed at a site only after the receipt of a round consisting entirely of committable messages.
- If a node receives two successive rounds of noncommitable messages (i.e., the state of the node is neither prepare, nor commit, nor abort) and it detects no node

failures between the rounds, it can safely abourt the transaction.

Details of centralized and linear protocol are given in Reference 4 and of decentralized protocols in Reference 26.

Brief Qualitative Comparison of Various Two Phase Commit Protocols. The linear protocol requires $3*(N-1)$ messages; the centralized protocol requires $4*(N-1)$ messages; and the decentralized protocol requires messages quadratic in the number of nodes. But the messages required up to the commit point in centralized protocol are 2, whereas in linear protocol the number is $N-1$. In the decentralized case it is proportional to the number of nodes. In another dimension of comparison, the read-only transactions can be processed much better in centralized protocol but get no help in linear and decentralized protocol. Finally, the decentralized protocol is very resilient and can handle node failures even during the commitment process, whereas the linear and centralized protocols block the transaction altogether.

15.4. CONCLUSIONS

Distributed database management systems have allowed access to large databases by many users who may be physically miles apart. To ensure that each user gets the same view of the database to read or update as if he or she were the only user in the whole system, we need the concurrency control component of the system. To ensure that a user request is done completely or not done at all and to avoid any partial effects in case of software or hardware failures, we need the recovery control component of the system.

The problem of concurrency control has been studied extensively in the past three to four years, and results have been applied to many prototype and commercial systems. Although we may be able to develop efficient distributed database systems, we must face the problems of hardware and software failures. Thus we need to focus on making systems reliable and robust. This direction is of interest

to many researchers, and new results and techniques are expected in the next two to three years.

In this chapter, we have discussed the concurrency control problem in detail but because of the lack of performance and implementation. We have discussed most major issues in the reliability problem and have presented current research results but see many open problems. For example, how to find algorithms that can minimize the number of messages or transaction rollbacks in case of multiple failures that occur while recovery is taking place. In addition, the problems of transaction commitment and node restart need to be investigated. At such time, we can classify recovery techniques and start studying performance and implementation issues.

ACKNOWLEDGMENT

This work has been influenced by the research of Dr. Jim Gray of Tandam Computers, Professor Phil Bernstein of Harvard University, Professor Mike Stonebraker of the University of California, Berkeley, and the contributers of the IEEE symposium on reliability in distributed software and database system, July 1981.

REFERENCES

1. I. L. Traiger, C. A. Galteri, J. N. Gray, and B. G. Lindsay, "Transactions and Consistency in Distributed Database Systems," *ACM Trans. on Database Systems.* vol.7, no. 3, 1902, pp. 323–342.
2. P. Bernstein, J. Rothine, and D. Shipman, "Concurrency Control in a System for Distributed Databases (SDD-1)," *ACM Trans. on Database Systems,* vol. 5, no. 1, 1980, pp. 8–52.
3. B. Bhargava, "Nonlocking (Optimistic) Concurrency Control in Distributed Database Systems," Technical report, University of Pittsburgh, submitted for publication.
4. B. G. Lindsay et al., "Notes on Distrubuted Databases," IBM Research Report, no. RJ2571, July 1979.
5. J. Bihan, C. Esculier, G. Lann, and L. Treille, "SIRIUS-DELTA: A Prototype Distributed Database Management System," in C. Delobel and W. Litwin (eds.), *Distributed Databases,* North Holland, 1980.
6. M. Hammer and D. Shipman, "Reliability Mechanisms for SDD-1: A System for Distributed Databases," *ACM Trans. on Database Systems,* Dec. 1980.

7. J. Gray, "A Transaction Model," IBM Research Report, no. RJ 2895, Aug. 1980.

8. C. Hua and B. Bhargava, "Classes of Serializable Histories and Synchronization Algorithms in Distributed Database Systems," *Proceedings of IEEE-CS Conference on Distributed Computing Systems,* Ft. Lauderdale, Oct. 1982, pp. 438–446.

9. D. J. Rosenkrantz, R. E. Sterns, and P. M. Lewis, "System Level Concurrency Control for Distributed Database Systems," *ACM Trans. on Database Systems,* vol. 3, no. 2, June 1978, pp. 178–198.

10. N. J. Gray, "Notes on Database Operating Systems," *Operating Systems: an Advanced Course,* Springer-Verlag, Berlin, Heidelberg, 1978, pp. 394–481.

11. M. Stonebraker, "Concurrency Control and Consistency of Multiple Copies in Distributed INGRES," *IEEE Trans. on Software Engineering,* May 1979.

12. D. Menasce and G. Popek, "Locking and Deadlock Detection in Distributed Databases," *IEEE Trans. on Software Engineering,* vol. SE-5, no. 3, May 1979, pp. 195–202.

13. L. Lamport, "Time Clocks, and the Ordering of Events in a Distributed System," *CACM,* vol. 21, no. 7, 1978, pp. 558–565.

14. R. H. Thomas, "A Majority Consensus Approach to Concurrency Control," *ACM TODS,* vol. 4, no. 2, 1979.

15. P. Bernstein and N. Goodman, "Fundamental Algorithms for Concurrency Control in Distributed Database Systems," ACM Computing Surveys, vol. 13, no. 2, 1981.

16. H. Garcia, "Performance of Update Algorithms for Replicated Data in a Distributed Database," Report STAN-CS-79-744, Department of Computer Science, Stanford University, Ph.D. Dissertation, 1979.

17. H. T. Kung and J. Robinson, "On Optimistic Methods for Concurrency Control," ACM Transactions on Database Systems vol. 6, no. 2, 1981, pp. 213–226.

18. B. Bharagava, "An Optimistic Concurrency Control Algorithm for Centralized Database Management Systems and Its Performance Evaluation Against Locking Algorithms," *Proc. International Computer Symposium,* Tiawan, Dec. 1980. (To appear in *International Journal of Computer and Information Science*)

19. H. T. Kung and C. H. Papadimitriou, "An Optimality Theory of Concurrency Control for Databases," *Proc. International Conference on Management Data,* May 1979, pp. 116–126.

20. J. L. Elshoff, "An Analysis of Some Commercial PL/T Programs," *IEEE Trans. Software Engineering,* vol. SE-2, June 1976, pp. 113–120.

21. L. J. White and El I. Cohen, "A Domain Strategy for Computer Program Testing," *IEEE Trans. Software Engineering,* vol. SE-6, May 1980, pp. 247–257.

22. B. Bhargava, "Resiliency Features of the Optimistic Concurrency Control Approach for Distributed Database Systems," *Proceedings of the IEEE-CS Symposium on Reliability in Distributed Software and Database System,* Pittsburgh, July, 1982, pp. 19–32.

23. H. Garcia, "Performance Comparison of Two Update Algorithms for Distributed Databases," *Proceedings of the Third Berkeley Workshop on Distributed Database Management and Computer Networks,* Aug. 29–31, 1978, pp. 108–119.

24. D. Rosenkrantz, Private Communication, 1980.

25. E. Andre and G. Bogo, "Ada Abstract Datatype, Distributed Database Transaction," *Proceedings of IEEE-COMPSAC,* Oct. 1980, Chicago.

26. D. Skeen, "Nonblocking Commit Protocols," *SIGMOD International Conference on Management of Data,* Ann Arbor, 1981.

27. B. Bhargava, "Performance Evaluation of the Optimistic Approach to Distributed Database Systems and its Comparison to Locking," *Proceedings of the IEEE-CS Conference on Distributed Computing Systems,* Ft. Lauderdale, Oct. 1982, pp. 508–517.

28. D. E. Knuth, "An Empirical Study of Fortran Programs," *Software Practice and Experience,* vol. 1, no. 2, 1971, pp. 105–137.

16

Software Testing Technology: An Overview

Edward F. Miller, Jr.
Software Research Associates

16.1. INTRODUCTION

This chapter provides a high-level overview and perspective on software testing technology as it is practiced today and as it may be practiced in the near future. Of all of the areas within computer science, none has received more attention in the past decade than the issue of software quality. Software quality lies at the foundation of many (or even all) of the problems facing the computing community; the issue of quality determines whether particular solutions to problems that involve a computer are, or are not, accepted. Certainly, there are sufficiently many examples of systems (i.e. software solutions) that have failed to meet minimum levels of acceptability; there are, in addition, a few instances of genuine success.

What is the difference between the successes and the failures? The answer is manifold: it not only involves the application of good software engineering techniques and the use of modern programming practices, software design methodologies, and more reliable high-level languages, but also must take into account the software engineering methods used (whatever they are) to assure the quality of the delivered software system. Quality is assured primarily through some form of software testing; a number of instances of formal program verification exist, but in relative terms the total amount of software that has been processed with this theoretically important but costly method is very small. Very often, what passes for software quality assurance with testing has not been called that at all: instead, it was termed advanced debugging, interface testing, or acceptance testing, and so forth.

Now, however, there is growing agreement on the role of testing as a software quality assurance discipline, as well as on the terminology, technology, and phenomenology of, and the expectations about testing. This chapter presents some intuitive descriptions of each of these categories.

16.2. HISTORY OF TESTING

Beginnings

The first formal technical conference devoted to software testing was held in June 1972 at the University of North Carolina. Although that certainly was not the first time a program was tested, it was the first time that researchers who were primarily concerned with the practicalities of software quality assembled to discuss the whole range of issues involved.

Subsequent to that meeting there have been seven International Software Engineering Conferences, and a spate of smaller workshops and symposia devoted either fully or in part to questions of program testing.

At the Oregon Conference on Computing in the 1980s [1], testing technology was considered as a formal part of software engineering technology, probably for the first time.

The history of testing goes back to the beginnings of the computing field; the programs that ran on the earliest machine were "tested." In fact, there is even an early paper by Turing indicating that "testing is the empirical form of software quality assurance, while proving is the theoretical way." Results of both approaches have varied widely. Some software has performed excellently, and other software has done quite badly. There are plenty of "doom and gloom" anecdotes such as the famous missing comma in the Venus probe software, the structural faults that led to the detection of our own moon as an incoming ICBM, and the like. Perhaps expectedly, many of the successes are not so well known or discussed.

The Direction for the Future

There is a steadily increasing need for effective software quality assurance at affordable prices. The need arises from various sectors of industry, all of which need practical methods for assuring quality (minimizing the chance of a latent error) without having the costs of doing so go off the scale. At the end of this chapter are some practical guidelines on what the costs to do this might actually be.

The one obstacle to the widespread adoption of software testing is its negative reward structure. The objective of a dedicated software tester is to find errors and report them to somebody, but that attitude and perspective may be at odds with the software implementors and/ or their managers. Hence, in many cases it is found necessary to consider special organizational setups both to isolate this negativity (or to turn it around as a positive force) and to maximize any benefits of synergy.

As more and more experience with testing is gained, an increasingly strong set of intuitions and guidelines on handling the software quality assurance problem is being developed as well as ideas on how to get the most out of what is currently known about the techniques for achieving software quality. Knowing how to choose among the many technical alternatives is the responsibility of the well-informed quality assurance manager.

16.3. MOTIVATING FORCES

This section describes the basics of testing (what is involved and how it is done). It suggests some of the primary motivating forces that push toward the use of formal testing methods and indicates in a general way what some of the benefits of testing are.

Basics of Testing

A quality analysis oriented test of a computer program consists of:

- Running the program with a controlled set of inputs
- Observing the run-time effect the inputs have on the program
- Examining the program outputs to determine their acceptability

One usually attends to these items informally during the program debugging process, whereas, during formal program testing, one thinks less in terms of *making* the program do something and more in terms of *showing* precisely what the program does. One way to distinguish between formal testing and a less formal debugging activity is to examine the tools used. Debugging relies on the program production tools (i.e., compilers, debugging packages that examine a program's internal operation), whereas testing may involve other kinds of tools.

In addition to the process of running programs under controlled and observable circumstances (a process called *dynamic testing*), a second stage called *static testing* is ordinarily included. Static testing may include manual code inspections, structured walkthroughs, or the use of automated tools that analyze software by looking for certain kinds of common errors (those not caught during the normal program production process). Contemporary testing technology advocates combinations of static and dynamic quality analysis processes.

The input data used to make a program demonstrate its own features are called a test case or test data. Individual programs can be tested, a process called unit testing.

Whole systems of software can also be tested in an activity called *system testing*. Normally, system testing is divided into a set of individual activities that are larger than unit testing but smaller than full system testing. Testing can be done from either the *black box* or the *white box* perspective, depending on whether the internal operation of the program is being observed during the testing process. Normally, black box testing is reserved only for the system level; most programs are fully unit tested using white box methods.

During white box testing, the tester observes the extent to which test cases exercise program structure. The resulting coverage is used as an indicator of the likelihoods of any remaining undiscovered errors. Note that input/output relationships still have to be examined in detail for appropriateness.

One of the more common strategies for testing involves declaring in a minimum level of testing coverage, ordinarily expressed as a percentage of the elemental segments that are exercised in aggregate during the testing process. This is called C1 coverage, where C1 denotes the minimum level of testing coverage so that every logically separate part of the program has been exercised at least once during the set of tests. Unit testing usually requires at least 85-90% C1 coverage.

At the system level it is possible to define similar measures of coverage that relate to the extent to which subroutines and invocations to them are exercised. Many different strategies exist for governing the process of multiple unit testing and/or system-level testing.

An underlying premise of structurally motivated and measured testing is that at a minimum, it is necessary to know that all of the functions in a software system have been exercised at least once. It is not reasonable to accept (or release, or approve) any software system unless it is known that every part of it has been exercised. Although this criterion cannot be guaranteed (in formally provable terms) to force discovery of all errors, it can be shown to be a practically effective method for systematically analyzing large and complex software systems (see below).

Typical Applications

Much of contemporary testing technology arises from the need to examine the quality of software that is embedded in products sold directly to consumers or that otherwise affects the public. This factor was not predicted as the

major motivating force in the past, perhaps because nobody expected that there would be such widespread use of software. It is valuable to take a look at some typical application areas and identify for each of them the primary areas of concern for software quality.

Instrumentation Systems. The use of computers, and especially microcomputers, in instrumentation has been increasing rapidly in the past five years. For example, many oscilloscope, data display, signal analysis, and communication link analyzers are more effective and can have more capabilities and flexibility with embedded microcomputers. The instrument manufacturers have found, however, that they are poorly equipped to deal with the software component in such instruments.

In a typical instrumentation system, the software is coded at the assembly language level, a choice usually dictated by economies of program storage space and execution time. It seems well understood now that the cost to repair or modify such systems is very large, particularly if it must be done after product introduction and/or if the production run is large.

As a consequence, the instrument manufacturers are generally providing fairly basic levels of software quality assurance through testing, with the effort level based on the relative cost to repair the software in the field.

Process Control Systems. Computers are finding increasing application in process control, particularly for those systems that have rapid real-time response requirements that cannot ordinarily be met by human controllers. Examples of systems that fall into this category range from nuclear reactors to petroleum plants to automated assembly lines. The cost of failure of such computer-based control systems ranges from politically unacceptable to economically undesirable.

Largely as a function of the potential impact of a failure caused by software, organizations responsible for these kinds of systems are "betting" on a number of techniques. In many cases, triple modular redundancy is provided at the hardware level to reduce the chances of a hardware failure to vanishingly small probability. Corresponding methods of multiple implementation of software control processes have also been used effectively, particularly in very critical applications.

Appliances. As with instrumentation systems, most appliance-based software is written at a very low level, sometimes even in direct machine code. The cost of failure, or the impact on the organization, as the result of a deficiency in software is ordinarily measured by a combination of direct and indirect costs. Direct costs include the costs of repair, as well as the cost to provide legal protection in the event of software failure. The indirect costs involve such factors as product image, organizational image, and reputation.

Automotive Computers. Everyone has been talking for some time about the forthcoming revolution in automotive electronics, in which many of the current mechanically implemented control functions are to be replaced by full digital control. While this has been slower to occur than many had thought, recent model cars do contain computers, even though they are used in only a peripheral fashion. Recently, announcements appeared for several retrofits based on dash computers, in many instances similar to previously available "rally-style" computers in function but not in technology. For this class of application, software reliability can affect the driver and passengers only in an indirect manner. An unanswered question, however, is extent of liability assumed by the supplier of the software/hardware combination.

Telephony. Computers are increasingly the central feature of complex telephone switching equipment, both for the public network and for privately maintained in-house systems. In addition to the switching function is the data transfer function represented by the new value-added data transmission networks. For all of these applications, the implications of software failure are generally less severe than those previously noted, being intrinsically restricted to the loss of communication and/or the effect of an errant call.

For value-added data switching networks, however, the implications of a failure are not so clear cut. While the telephone companies themselves have devoted substantial effort to systematically testing computerized switching systems and substantial experience has been gained in effectiveness evaluation of switched data networks, much quality assurance work remains to be done.

Military Systems. Because military systems typically involve the risk of human life, substantial emphasis has always been placed on the software quality issue. Modern concepts of third party verification and validation of software projects had their origin in the military community. Notwithstanding this head start, however, contemporary technology seems to be passing up military systems in favor of developing techniques more applicable to the popular languages and/or the popular computers. Much of research and development activity in the area of program verification has been focused on military applications software.

Full verification and validation for military-style software is a very expensive proposition. Estimates range from $10 to $25 per statement and higher for "the complete treatment." A number of companies have been active in this field for some time with measurable effectiveness. After all, strategic systems that employ computers have experienced no failures, although this may have been the result of luck.

Liability Questions

At a recent meeting of futurists, a scenario for the mid-1980s focused on the implications for software engineering of a hypothetical multimillion dollar malpractice claim against programmers responsible for a vehicle control package [1]. While the application in mind was somewhat facetious, indications are today that the issue of liability and, correspondingly, the issue of professional malpractice will be important ones in the future.

The noted columnist Allen Taylor has indicated the existence of "claims made" malpractice insurance available to software people (*ComputerWorld,* 26 June 1978). At least one underwriter in the United States, with the backing of Lloyds of London, is now writing this kind of policy. The key question to be answered is, What is the interaction between the cost of malpractice insurance and the kind and level of software testing that has been performed?

Benefits of Testing

Apart from all of these motivating forces, additional benefits may accrue as the result of instituting a systematic testing discipline. Some of these are:

- By focusing attention on the issues of software quality, programmers as well as program testers are made conscious of the need for error-free software.
- The processes involved in analyzing computer programs from the perspective of a program tester almost automatically ensure that the more flagrant kinds of errors will be detected.
- The systematic testing process, even if it does not identify significant errors, still acts as a backup to other techniques such as design reviews, structured walkthroughs, and so on.
- Instituting a systematic testing activity provides a framework in which new quality assurance technologies can be applied as soon as they become available.

As subsequent sections will show, contemporary technology does permit general kinds of statements about testing activity, how it should be organized, and what should be expected of it.

16.4. ORGANIZING FOR TESTING

If a testing activity is going to be instituted, some appropriate questions are:

- When should the program-testing methodology be applied?
- How should the testing group be organized?
- How much effort should be applied to the testing activity?
- What outcomes can be expected from the testing group?

Some answers to these and related questions are given in the paragraphs below.

When to Test

As already indicated, program testing is an activity that requires that the computer software be relatively stable. Testing as discussed here is a post-development process, or it could be interpreted as an "acceptance test" process. A software system can be considered reasonably stable:

- When the structure of the system is well determined, that is, all of the major subsystems and most of the modules are defined.
- At the time of first release of a working prototype.

It is important to delay the formal testing process until after the program is debugged because too many changes tend to complicate things by shifting the burden of testing to one of retesting.

Most typical applications of software-testing technology advocate testing at least at the following three levels (or stages) of software development:

- After individual modules have been completed and thoroughly tested by their programmers (unit testing)
- During integration of individual modules into subsystems or during integration of subsystems into the final system (development testing)
- During final integration (hardware/software integration) (system testing)

A tradeoff exists between the onset of formal testing and the quality ultimately achieved, although this relationship is not yet thoroughly documented. It appears necessary to plan for program testing fairly early in the software development process. By doing so the software engineer is thereby assured of a sufficiently good set of test cases with which to begin formal testing. Most of the time, programmers devise tests that exercise the working features of the program, rather than tests that identify errors. Hence, the testing process must concentrate on those features that were not exercised previously.

Organizational Schemes.   Precisely how the testing team is organized and how it fits into the software life cycle are important questions that need to be addressed early. As already suggested, current thinking advocates the beginning of formal test procedures immediately after module development. The question remains, however, whether the testing should be done by a programmer, by a separate group in the organization, by an independent group (either within the organization or outside), or by somebody else. Some of the factors to be investigated in choosing the organizational structure for the testing team are:

> To whom does the testing team report? If the test team reports to the ultimate buyer, then its independence is not in question. If software is supplied by a subcontractor, then the testing team should report to the prime contractor. In general, it is important that the testing team have adequate freedom to ensure that it can deliver its report without interference.

> How is the budgeting done? Testing budgets could be set as a function of total system implementation costs or as a fixed percentage of staff time, or be based on the size of the software system (e.g., a fixed dollar amount of testing per statement).

Note that a number of organizations offering quality assurance services are springing up all over the United States and elsewhere in the world. Only time will tell the extent to which such organizations can survive, and how effective they will be as independent entities.

16.5. THE PSYCHOLOGY OF TESTING

This section presents some basic information, both positive and negative, about the psychology of testing.

The Negative Side

As with many human-based methodologies, the overall effectiveness of program-testing activity can be influenced by the attitudes held about testing. The prevailing attitude, and one that should be resisted as much as possible, views testing in the following ways:

- Testing is a dirty business, involving cleaning up someone else's mess and not involving any of the fun of creating programs.
- Testing is unimaginative and lacks the sense of adventure and opportunity for self-expression ordinarily associated with software production.
- Testing is menial work and involves handling too many details.
- Testing is too difficult, because of the complexity of programs, because of the difficulty of the logic of programs, and because of deficiencies in technology.
- Testing is not important, is underfunded, and generally involves too much work in too little time.
- The tools associated with testing are primitive and difficult to use.
- The techniques of testing are not rigorous. Too much ad hoc thinking is required; there is too little systematic knowledge to rely upon; too often every new activity is another "special case"; and there are too few generally accepted principles with demonstrated value.
- Testing has a negative reward structure; finding mistakes requires a critic's mentality.

All of these factors, or any one of them in the extreme, can change a successful program-testing activity into a fiasco.

The Positive Side

It is possible to make the following claims about the psychology of testing:

- Testing is a challenge because it is a complicated problem that requires significant creativity at all times and because it rewards discipline.
- Testing is significant because software creators will appreciate having their oversights discovered, because managers will then feel more confident in the product, and because program testers can take pride in the software.
- Testing is interesting because the technology is imperfectly understood (and therefore represents an opportunity for innovation), because insights gained can be used in developing automated tools, and because many different approaches will be valued.

This positive view, unfortunately, has been apparent only in a few instances. Fortunately, this situation is changing in many areas of the computing community.

16.6. SOME MANAGEMENT GUIDELINES

This section presents general guidelines on the size, difficulty, cost, and expected outcomes of a formal software testing activity. Naturally, such estimates must be used carefully. Estimates are based on experience in testing software written in a high-order language (HOL) such as FORTRAN, PL/1, or COBOL, and so forth.

Size of Testing Budget

A common way to express the size of the testing activity is as a percentage of the total software development costs. For HOL-coded systems, experience suggests that budgets in the range of 25 to 45% of the total development cost for the software are appropriate. Here, total development cost is intended to include all of those costs up to the time when the first release of the software is made.

Naturally enough, the amount of effort devoted to the formal testing activity is a function of how critical the system is. The higher percentage figure is what appears to be minimally adequate for the highest-priority software system. Examples of systems that fall into this class are those that are man-rated and those that have a large production run (with value far exceeding the total software development cost).

A second rule-of-thumb that has been found useful in the past is to provide insurance based on the expected cost of failure. For a product with an embedded computer, for example, it would be reasonable to allocate 5 to 10% of the total cost to repair the first (set of?) software failure(s), in the field if necessary, solely with a well-organized search for errors through systematic testing. The attitude to have is that there are errors in the software and the only question is whether they are going to be found before or after issuance of the product! Note that this attitude allows for a product to be issued with a known error if the cost to repair it at the time it is found is too large (e.g., when the program is "burned" into ROM), or when the impact of it is judged too small to warrant changes until the "next model."

Size of the Testing Problem

It is possible to estimate the total difficulty of the testing activity for software systems written in an HOL from past experience in analyzing software. Naturally there is a rather wide variance in these properties, depending on both the kind of problem being solved and the style of programming.

To appreciate the numbers, it is important to understand the precise meanings of some testing-related terminology:

1. A *statement* in a program is either a declaration or an action statement, and may run to more than one line of text.

2. A *segment* is a logically independent piece of program text that corresponds to the actions the program takes as the consequence of a program decision (including the decision to make a subroutine invocation). Hence a program with no logic has one segment; each IF statement contributes two segments, and so forth.

3. A *test* is one transfer of control to the software system (regardless of the part being examined) and the consequential actions the system takes. This corresponds (in effect) to a single subroutine invocation.

Note that a subroutine with no logical statements—the so-called straight-line program—has one segment consisting of all the statements of the program, and at least one test would be required. Coverage is measured (in the C1 measure) by the percentage of segments that are exercised at least once in aggregate, that is, over all of the tests run.

Typical programs will have a number of segments approximately equal to between 5 and 25% of the number of statements. (That is, each segment corresponds typically to about 5 to 20 statements.) A good "middle" figure is 10%: Multiply the number of statements by 0.1 and you get the number of segments.

The number of tests required to achieve an 85% C1 coverage level also tends to be a constant. For typical HOL-coded programs, each test exercises between 5 and 50 statements. This figure should not be misinterpreted; achieving 85% C1 coverage may involve some tests that exercise only a few statements and others that exercise as much as 50% of the program.

The 85% C1 coverage figure was chosen because it represents a reasonably attainable goal in practice with a large software system. It is important to appreciate that, in most cases, bringing the figure to 100%, if it is possible at all, would increase the number of tests required substantially.

The Results of Testing

The most important questions is, Given 85% coverage of segments in a complex HOL-coded program, what is the likelihood of finding errors of varying severity? It is difficult to quote a precise figure, since the number of errors found is a function of the skill of the program testing team, the quality of the software (or lack of it), and the amount of prior testing that has been performed.

For a typical situation in which software has been fully unit-tested by the programmers, but which has not been systematically tested by a separate group, one can expect a latent defect count (see below) at a rate of 0.5 to 5.0% of the number of statements. This suggests that a 1000 statement program, when declared "finished" by the programmer, may have as many as 100 defects of varying levels of severity. Such defects fall into two classes: fatal and nonfatal defects. Approximately 15 to 20% of the defects are fatal. The implication is that the total number of fatal errors is as much as 1% of the total number of statements. (This may or may not be a comforting fact, depending on one's point of view!)

A Caveat

Some danger exists in stating estimates like those given in the previous sections. If one is too far wrong, then the credibility of all such estimating rules is cast in doubt. So it is important to point out the sources of these estimates:

- The author's experience with medium- and large-scale software systems
- Statistics from the literature (see below)
- Statistics from work by Software Research Associates
- Information from sources who need to remain nameless

16.7. QUALITY ASSURANCE AND TESTING TOOLS

This section addresses the functional characteristics needed in modern quality assurance support tools. Quality assurance is virtually dependent on the use of tools because of the highly complex nature of the analyses that must be done.

The section describes each general category of tool, the ways in which these functions can be integrated into a single automated testing system for use on complex software, and projections of tool development in the future.

Generic Descriptions of Tools

The two broad categories of software quality assurance support tools are: static and dynamic analysis tools. Most tool functions fall cleanly into one category or the other, but there are some exceptions like symbolic evaluation systems and mutation analysis systems (which actually run interpretively). The main tools used in quality assurance are:

- Static analyzers, which examine programs systematically and automatically
- Code inspectors, who inspect programs automatically to make sure they adhere to minimum quality standards
- Standards enforcers, which impose simple rules on the programmer
- Coverage analyzers, which measure the value of Cx, x = ?
- Output comparators, used to determine whether the output in a program is appropriate or not
- Test file/data generators, used to set up test inputs
- Test harnesses, used to simplify test operations
- Test archiving systems, used to provide documentation about programs

Each of these is discussed below. The discussion is organized into the two major divisions in the above list: static and dynamic. In all cases, tools that are mentioned are described in more detail in Reference 2.

Static Testing Tools

Static testing tools are those that perform analyses of the programs without executing them at all.

Static Analyzers. A static analyzer operates from a precomputed data base of descriptive information derived from the source text of the program. The idea of a static analyzer is to prove allegations, which are claims about the analyzed programs that can be demonstrated by systematic examination of all of the cases.

There is a close relation to code inspectors, but static analyzers are stronger. Typical cases include FACES, DAVE, RXVP, PL/1 Checkout Compiler, LINT on PWB/Unix, and so on [2]. All of these systems are language dependent in the sense that they apply to a particular language, and also often to a particular system.

Experience: Many applications using static analyzers find 0.1 to 2.0% NCSS (Noncomment Source Statements) deficiency reports. Some of these are real, and others are spurious in the sense that they are false warnings that are later ignored, after interpretation.

Possibility: Build a static analyzer for the language/machine being used; then apply it to all code produced.

Assessment: Probably a favorable benefit/cost ratio if the software analyzed is critical and the tool is well designed.

Problems: Dependence on language vagaries, variance between compilers, and high initial tool investment costs.

Code Inspectors. A code inspector does a simple job of enforcing standards in a uniform way for many programs. These can be single-statement or multiple-statement rules. Also, it is possible to build code inspector assistance programs that force the inspector to do a good job by linking him to the process through an interactive environment.

The AUDIT system is typical: It enforces some standards and also imposes some minimum conditions on the program. AUDIT, in use by the Navy for some time, is found effective in production coding [2].

Code inspection activity is found in some COBOL tools (like ADR's librarian system), and in some parts of tools like RXVP.

Experience: Found useful in many circumstances.

Possibility: Implement automated code inspector system for use in handling production coding, and possibly nonproduction codes.

Assessment: Used properly, it can be a big payoff.

Problems: Language dependence, programmer resistance, initial investment costs, and difficulty in constructing a good programmer interface.

Standards Enforcers. This tool is like a code inspector, except that the rules are generally simpler. The main distinction is that a full-blown static analyzer looks at whole programs, whereas a standard enforcer looks at only single statements.

Since only single statements are treated, the standards enforced tend to be cosmetic ones; even so, they are valuable because they enhance the readability of the programs. It seems well established that the readability of a program is an indirect indicator of its quality.

Experience: When used after initial programmer resistance, such tools are found helpful as a filter protecting against completely unreadable codes.

Possibility: Establish standards and support tools to enforce them and then have all suppliers use that standard.

Assessment: Indirect benefit on software quality, a factor difficult to justify quantitatively but one that has a certain palliative effect.

Problems: Programmer resistance and attitude of nonimportance of program format.

Other Tools. Related tools are used to catch bugs indirectly through listings of the program that highlight the mistakes.

One example is a program generator that is used (mostly in COBOL environments, but possibly also in others as well) to produce the pro forma parts of each source module. Use of such a method ensures that all programs look alike, which in itself enhances the readability of the programs.

Another example is using structured programming preprocessors that produce attractive print output. Such augmented program listings typically have automatic indentation, indexing features, and in some cases much more. (Ref. 2 mentions a number of such tools.)

Dynamic Testing Tools

Dynamic testing tools seek to support the dynamic testing process. Besides individual tools that accomplish these functions, a few integrated systems group the functions under a single implementation.

A test consists of a single invocation of the test object and all of the execution that ensues until the test object returns control to the point where the invocation was made. Subsidiary modules called by the test object can be real or they can be simulated by testing stubs.

A series of tests is normally required to test one module or to test a set of modules. Test support tools must perform these functions:

● Input setting: selecting of the test data that the test object reads when called
● Stub processing: handling outputs and selecting inputs when a stub is called
● Results display: providing the tester with the values that the test object produces so that they can be validated
● Test coverage measurement: determining the test effectiveness in terms of the structure of the program
● Test planning: helping the tester to plan tests so they are both efficient and also effective at forcing discovery of defects

Coverage Analyzers (Execution Verifiers). A coverage analyzer or execution verifier (or automated testing analyzer, or automated verification system, etc.) is the most common and important tool for testing. It is often relatively simple.

C1 is the most commonly used measure, but Cd is used sometimes (see below). Most often, C1 is measured by planting subroutine calls—called *software probes*—along each segment of the program. The test object is then executed and some kind of run-time system is used to collect the data, which are then reported to the user in fixed-format reports.

Experience: Use of coverage analysis can be incorporated into most quality assurance situations, although it is more difficult when there is too little space or when non-real-time operation is inequivalent to real-time operation (an artifact of the instrumentation process).

Possibility: Require use of Cl (at least) in all cases; 85% Cl is a practical, minimally acceptable value of testing coverage.

Assessment: Highest payoff in terms of quality achieved at the lowest possible cost through use of Cl measurement.

Problems: Programmer resistance, nonstandard system use, difficulty in interpreting Cl values for multiple tests (requires some kind of history analyzer).

Output Comparators. Output comparators are used in dynamic testing—both single-module and multiple-module (system level) varieties—to check that predicted and actual outputs are equivalent. This is also done during regression testing. The typical output comparator system objective is to identify differences between two files; the old and the new output from a program. Typical operating systems for the better minicomputers often have an output comparator, sometimes called a file comparator, built-in.

Experience: Basic utility, finds differences effectively and usually quite efficiently

Possibility: Equip the quality assurance facility with an output comparator for general use

Assessment: Needed tool for QA environment

Problems: May produce too much output if old and new files are lengthy and/or have many differences

Test File Generators. A test file generator creates a file of information that is used as input to the program and does so based on commands given by the user and/or from data descriptions (in a COBOL program's data definition section, for example). Mostly, this is a COBOL-oriented idea in which the file of test data is intended to simulate transaction inputs in a data base management situation. This idea can be adapted to other environments.

Experience: Good benefit when this kind of tool is used.

Possibility: Use test file generator, or adapt the concept, to create lengthy files of input transactions. The best use is to have the input data varied automatically to account for a range of cases.

Assessment: For a given software testing situation, it may be a good idea to include a test file generator system—either commercial or home brew—as a way to save valuable testing effort.

Problems: Difficulty of use.

Test Data Generators. The test data generation problem is a difficult one, and at least for the present is one for which no general solution exists (a known theoretical fact [2]). On the other hand, there is a practical need for methods to generate test data that meet a particular objective, normally to execute a previously unexercised segment in the program.

One of the practical difficulties with test data generation is that it requires generation of sets of inequalities that represent the conditions along a chosen path, and the reality is that:

- Paths are too long and produce very complex formulas.
- Formula sets are nonlinear.
- Many paths are illegal (not logically possible).

Practical approaches to automatic test data generation run into very difficult technical limits [2].

In practice, the techniques of variational test data generation are often quite effective. The test data are derived (rather than created) from an existing path that comes near the intended segment for which test data are to be found. This is often very easy to do, apparently because programs' structures tend to assist in the process.

Experience: Automatically generating test data is effectively impossible, but good R&D work is now being done on the problem.

Possibility: Use variational and machine-assisted methods only.

Assessment: Technical issues of this problem may be more formidable than the problem is in practice.

Problems: Recursive undecidability of test data generation problem, and difficulty in developing good interactive test data generation heuristics.

Test Harness Systems. A test harness system is one that is bound (i.e., link-edited and relocated) around the test object and that (1) permits the easy modification and control of test inputs and outputs and (2) provides for on-line measurement of Cl coverage values. Some test harnesses are batch oriented, but the high degree of interaction available in a full-interactive system makes it seem very attractive in practical use [3].

Modern thinking favors interactive test harness systems, which tend to be the focal point for installing many other kinds of analysis support.

Experience: Clear benefit/cost improvement, even with batch-oriented systems. (TESTMANAGER has nearly 300 installations, as a typical example of a batch system.)

Possibility: Current technology permits development of a test system for almost any system and for almost any language.

Assessment: Give strong consideration to building a test harness system for the candidate language and on the candidate machine, for both single-module and system testing.

Problems: Need an interactive environment and customizing on language/machine combination. Development cost.

Test-Archiving Systems. The goal of a test-archiving system is to keep track of series of

tests and to act as the basis for documenting that the tests have been done and that no defects were found during the process.

A typical design involves establishing both procedures for handling files of test information and procedures for documenting which tests were run when and with what effect.

Experience: Test archive systems are mainly developed on a system-specific/application-specific basis.

Possibility: Implement manual methods at least, and give consideration to automating test documentation processes.

Assessment: High potential value during regression testing (after maintenance phase is reached) because of automation.

Problems: Dependency on local environment, inadequate experience in automation.

Characteristics of Modern Tools

The characteristics of modern software quality assurance tools differ somewhat from previous systems. Modern tools are modular and highly adaptable to different environments. They also tend to make use of the facilities provided by most operating systems rather than provide those capabilities internally. The ingredients of an AVS package of modern design are:

1. Instrumentor: This component modifies source programs so that they emit subroutine calls to a RUNTIME package that reports to a COVERAGE analyzer.
2. Runtime package: This component receives data from programs that were processed by the INSTRUMENTOR and generates either an on-line trace file or a series of calls directly to the COVERAGE component.
3. Coverage analyzer: This component accepts information from the RUNTIME package and produces Cl coverage reports. This component also generates Sl (system level) coverage reports as an option.
4. Command processor: A unified component that interfaces between the user

and the remainder of the other components.

5. Test assistance component: This tool displays partial listings of program text for known-to-be-executable paths and provides input/output analysis that assists in employing the variational test data generation method.

6. Log processor: This component generates an archival log of all actions taken by the tester during processing of a system.

7. Test harness: This component provides standardized drivers and stub controllers for the test object (i.e., the program being tested).

8. Results analyzer: This component automatically compares the values produced by a program with the reference values recorded prior to the program's execution.

9. Archive controller: This unit manages a set of system-dependent files that keep permanent records of the effects of testing throughout the test process.

10. Report controller: This component monitors all the output produced by other components and guarantees that the total volume of information does not overwhelm the user.

Future Tool Prognosis

The future development of tools is dependent on at least two factors: (1) the level of use made of current tools—individual tools and integrated sets of tools, and (2) the degree of interest expressed by the software engineering community in having advanced tools.

Tools tend to lead the application of methodologies, at least in the sense that when a new methodology is conceived, it is normally necessary to construct (or at least envision) a set of tools to go along with the methodology. This means, in effect, that each new methodology invented by researchers in the field will have to be tried out first with prototypes of what may ultimately become integrated tool sets.

This happened in the early 1970s with such systems as JAVS and RXVP, among others, where early experimental prototypes of sys-

tems that are not in practical use were developed in most cases without complete information about their ultimate operational function. When translated into a projected trend, it is easy to conclude that, starting from the present, the phasing in of each new generic family of tool-type will mean that after 5 to 10 years, the third or fourth generation of tools will be in relatively widespread use.

It seems clear now that the central focus for the future will be on tools as interactive support facilities, connected to data base systems used to keep track of all of the detailed information, and effectively built in to the system and/or methodology that surrounds their use.

16.8. LEVELS OF UNIT TESTING TECHNOLOGY

Quality assurance is a set of disciplines that can be applied in a number of ways, and at varying levels of sophistication. The essential ingredients of typical quality assurance activities are three:

1. Systematic inspection and analysis, an activity that seeks to find discrepancies between requirements and the actual software

2. Dynamic test planning, an activity that defines a series of tests that will be run to demonstrate various functions of the software

3. Comprehensive test evaluation, an activity that occurs during dynamic testing and involves analysis of the test results after tests are run.

These three steps are included in one form or another in almost all testing processes—although not necessarily under precisely these names [4].

Note that the code inspection processes are fundamentally different from the other two—both of which involve execution of the program in some way. Hence, the technology for systematic inspection of the programs can be handled in a fully different fashion from the methods used to treat dynamic testing.

The following section describes a sequence of increasingly sophisticated levels of testing methodology, expressed in terms of *coverage measures* that indicate how thoroughly the process in steps 2 and 3 is actually accomplished.

The use of coverage measures for this purpose is intended as a basis for describing the methodologies that are associated with each of them. The measures are structural indicators of the thoroughness with which each portion of the software under examination is actually exercised. As Reference 2 points out, the relationship between the achieved coverage and the chance of an error remaining in the software is an indirect one at best, even though there is substantial evidence to indicate that the correlation is very high.

As a convenience to the reader, definitions of the various coverage measures are given at the beginning of each section.

Inspection Methods

The idea of code inspections was first described in full in Reference 5, in which Fagan describes IBM's internally developed procedures. They are an outgrowth of structured programming and as such may be naturally combined with regular structured programming methods.

The method of code inspection, when applied to critical software, can be expected to discover a number of problems with a software system. Code inspection is best performed, according to Fagan, with teams in which individuals have very well-defined roles:

- The moderator, the key person on the team, whose job it is to " . . . preserve objectivity and to increase the integrity of the inspection" [5]
- The designer, the expert responsible for doing the design for the system
- The coder/implementor who builds the software
- The tester, responsible for all software testing

This team applies a set of well-defined rules to the candidate software and seeks to find "errors" in the programs. Naturally, the errors are either fixed immediately, or they are held for later verification through dynamic testing.

Experience: Fagan's report seems to be the "bible" for this technique, and it quotes 80% or better error detection rates at costs that are quite low: between 650 and 900 NCSSs per team hour for preparation and inspection at two stages [5]. (This approximates 200 NCSSs per hour overall.)

Possibility: Application of code inspection generally increases overall final-product productivity by reducing error content early.

Assessment: Use code inspection methods as part of the quality assurance discipline, as software is delivered.

Problems: Rules to be followed are specific to each language/machine/application combination, so must be redone each time.

Testing Methods

The methods of testing always focus on execution characteristics of the programs being examined. A main theme of the testing literature is the trend to interpret the effect of tests in terms of the level of structural exercise the programs attain [2]. The levels of testedness then have a specific meaning in terms of testing coverage, described next at various levels.

Ad Hoc Testing (CO Coverage). The processing of programs assumes a constant structure viewed in a model called a "directed graph representation" of the program. In this model, nodes correspond to "places" in the program text, and edges correspond to actions (or segments).

Conventional programming methods normally involve only a limited amount of testing—sometimes called debugging—and typically result in less than full exercise of a program. Many writers during the 1970s advocated the following measure as a way to characterize the quality of a set of tests.

CO coverage measure: CO is the percentage of the total number of statements in a module that are ex-

ercised, divided by the total number of statements present in the module.

The intention of this measure is to ensure that the highest possible fraction of program statements are exercised at least once. The surprising thing about much of the work done by programmers is that most of the time they test programs very naively. CO is not normally considered an acceptable level of quality in the testing process but is generally felt to be better than nothing at all [6]. In other words, the CO measure decides what fraction of the total number of statements have been exercised.

Experience: Most programs when completed are about 50% tested in the Cl measure, and perhaps 75 to 90% tested in the CO measure.

Possibility: Use CO testing as the basic measure of programmer testing, but do not use it to measure actual quality assurance testing coverage.

Assessment: Use CO only if no other measure is possible; best to use Cl as the minimum (see below).

Problems: The main problem is that CO, even if achieved, would leave some segments unexercised.

Basic Testing (C1 Coverage). The next level in testing comprehensiveness is established by the first truly structure-based measure, called C1, and defined as follows:

C1 coverage measure: The percentage of segments exercised in a test relative to the total number of segments in a program.

The C1 measure has its origin in research work aimed at developing a strong measure for testing effectiveness that takes into account most, if not all, of the elementary features of a software system [2].

C1 measures the total number of segments exercised in each test, or when computed cumulatively, the total fraction of segments that are exercised in one or more tests in a series. The C1 goal is to have a set of tests that in aggregate exercise a high percentage of all of the segments it is possible to exercise.

Current thinking is that a value of C1 of 85% or greater is a practical level of testing coverage. Experience suggests that this level of C1 coverage is adequate to discover perhaps 90% (?) of the available errors, although there is no way of knowing that for certain. The 85% level arises from the fact that the JAVS system was purchased by the U.S. Air Force with an 85% self-test requirement (this percentage occurred in 1973 and 1974).

Even though 85% is not perfection, it is much stronger than the actual 25 to 50% achieved by most programmers—even the good ones. Even when coverage information is provided as part of the programming process, evidence suggests that unless prodded, programmers don't exceed the threshold levels for C1.

The methodology for getting C1 = 85% is quite well understood in general terms, and involves structured test planning, dynamic operation of the program, and a lot of study of the source text. This is discussed in more detail below.

Experience: 85% C1 or more means finding 2 to 5% NCSS defects, approximately 10 to 20% of which are probably fatal or dangerous.

Possibility: Apply C1-based measurement as soon as possible to critical applications.

Assessment: C1 is a good starting point for a systematic methodology for testing, a good minimum requirement.

Problems: No proof exists to back up the empirical evidence that software testing using the C1 measure has a predictable effect in forcing discovery of errors.

Intermediate Testing (C2 Coverage). The next most sophisticated level above C1 testing attempts to force exercise of some basic features of the program besides just trying all the segments. This is the C2 measure, which is defined as follows:

C2 coverage measure: This coverage measure assesses the quality of tests by requiring full Cl cov-

erage, plus one test for each iteration's interior and exterior.

C2 came about because a measure was needed to emulate the work of proof-of-correctness methods [2, 7]. The strength of C2 lies in the fact that achieving Cl forces all of the volume of the code, and C2 adds in the iteration. Note that C2 will normally require more tests than C1 alone would. In practice, although there is only a small amount of evidence, it is felt that C2 is significantly stronger than C1, in the sense that accomplishing it would more likely uncover looping errors in programs in much the same way a proof of correctness does.

Experience: Minimal, but much consideration given to use of this measure.
Possibility: Apply C2 in most important one-third of the application programs.
Assessment: Likely candidate for future use, if possible.
Problems: Tends to be structure dependent, so that if the program has a structural fault, there will be less chance of finding any defect easily (this is a common limitation of all structure-based measures).

Advanced Testing (Ct Coverage). Ct is a very strong test method. It designs tests in terms of the pure-structured representation of a program. The definition of Ct is as follows:

Ct coverage measure: The percentage of independent execution subtrees in the hierarchical decomposition tree of a program that have been exercised, relative to all of the possible subtrees that can be found for that program.

Ct for a pure-structured program is the same kind of testing that would be accomplished in a full-blown proof of the program. In other words, the set of tests indicated by this method is the same as the set that would be used if the set of verification conditions [8] for the program were each tested.

The way the Ct measure is computed is as follows: The hierarchical decomposition tree is generated from the directed graph (digraph) for the program, and the set of all possible sub-trees of this tree is found. Each subtree represents one distinct executional class for the program. Ct is measured as the percentage of all such subtrees that have been tried during testing. Another way to find the subtrees is to think of the program as if it were pure-structured, then choose the tests by inspection from that representation of the program. The use of decomposition methods is not necessary when the program is already pure-structured.

Experience: Primarily pencil and paper investigations, although some organizations have automated test planning methods based on this principle.
Possibility: Use Ct as the basis for very strong testing of modules of the application software.
Assessment: Use of Ct will probably represent the strongest of the dynamic testing disciplines.
Problems: Ct is highly dependent on program structure, so when there are structural faults, Ct may not be effective.

Symbolic Evaluation Methods. Besides proof of correctness, symbolic evaluation and symbolic execution are the strongest methods known for assuring quality through testing.

Actually, symbolic evaluation is a static-analysis-type method, because the program is never actually executed. Instead, a particular path through the program is evaluated in detail from the source-level version of the program. All the indicated computations are performed symbolically, subject to constraints that may exist along the path because of the kind and number of conditionals that specify whether the path is executable. The result is a set of formulas that tell what the path computes.

This is very close to proof of correctness, as Reference 8 points out. The relation is so close that the method is considered, along with test data generation systems and proof systems, as the partial basis for quality assurance systems of the future.

Most of the work in this area has been done quite recently. Reference 8 is typical of the approaches now considered as appropriate for mixed symbolic-evaluation systems and proving systems.

Experience: Primarily in academic-like environments, and for small (less than 2,000 NCSS) programs. Many errors are found during the symbolic evaluation process, but the method appears to depend on human interaction.

Possibility: Increased R&D work could lead to a user-interactive system that reduces the amount of work to be performed.

Assessment: Good prospects for this approach for the future.

Problems: Difficulties with combinatoric growth in the formula size, with complexity of the formulas and/or the path predicates, and difficulties in reducing the formulas to human-readable format.

Relation to Program Proving Methods. A proof of correctness is a mathematical demonstration of the consistency between a program and its specifications, relative to sets of statements about the environment and the semantic behavior of the program.

The largest program ever proved correct is about 1,700 statements, and that was done as part of a university research project [7]. As part of the proof process some 43 errors were found; it was later discovered that about 86 percent of these would have been detected through C1-based testing.

Some proofs that have been completed and even published in the technical literature have later been found to be proofs of programs that have easily visible errors present. This points out the fundamental dependence of proof methods on mathematically complete statements about the environment in which the programs are supposed to run [9].

The basic steps in a proof are: (1) establishing the assertions, (2) constructing the proof, (3) checking the result. These steps are only partially automatable. Finding the assertions is a process similar to that involved in setting up the plans for Ct-based testing. Constructing the proof can be done automatically, but most systems, when given a problem to work on that comes from a real-world example, require

human assistance. Lastly, the check process itself must be verified by running some actual tests of the program.

Experience: Much in the R&D community, little in the practical world. Largest program proved is about 2,000 statements or less.

Possibility: Scaling problems will limit proving methods to smaller systems.

Assessment: Use proofs for most important modules only.

Problems: What checks the proof? Known errors in proof-of-correctness exercises. Complexity of the method.

Future/Projected Techniques vs Current Methods. Prior sections have identified the basic methods of software testing, expressed in terms of the kind of coverage that must be achieved at each level for single-module analysis. The methodology for multiple-modules and for systems is similar, with the exception of the differences that result from the issue of complexity and size. Future methods of testing include at least domain testing and mutation analysis [2].

Domain testing [10] involves the analysis of the input space of each module to establish a set of domains that can be used as the basis for systematic demonstration of each module's behavior. The input domains' boundaries are analyzed in detail for their intersections; test data that push the behavior of the program close to the boundaries are deemed better than ad hoc test data.

Mutation analysis is the process of systematically constructing small variations, called mutants, to the given program and then determining if they can be distinguished by the existing test data. Each mutant that is distinguished is termed "retired"; the remaining mutants are either equivalent to the original program or inequivalent but undistinquished by the test data. In the latter case, one must add test data [11].

Although experimental, the mutation scheme is experiencing a great deal of interest because it provides a direct, quantitative measure of the quality of test data for a program.

The disadvantage of the method is that it may require rather large numbers of mutants, and the number of equivalent programs may be quite large.

Possibility: Methods like these will be used in the late 1980s as the basis of future quality assurance disciplines.

Assessment: Both domain testing and mutation analysis methods are too immature for real-world application.

Problems: Domain testing appears to be limited in effectiveness to linear-constraint (linear logic) applications. Mutation analysis is still in the experimental stages and needs extensive field validation prior to actual use in a practical situation.

16.9. TESTING METHODOLOGIES

This section describes some of the basics of two major classes of methodologies: single-module testing, and multiple-module testing (or system testing). The goal of the section is to establish a baseline of understanding about the processes that apply in typical quality assurance circumstances.

A way of determining how to work a testing methodology is to examine the characteristics of various methods against a backdrop of some typical situations. The four cases we can employ for this purpose are:

1. Case *a*: A high-criticality single module
2. Case *b*: A medium-sized, medium-criticality system
3. Case *c*: A large, medium-criticality system
4. Case *d*: A large, high-criticality system.

Case *a* is in a high-level language, it is maybe 250 to 500 statements long, and it has a very complicated control structure. It has many different things to do, and it must be error free.

Case *b* is a set of about 25 modules that support an on-line facility of some kind. If the software system fails, there is no serious loss because there is an automated backup system; however, it is expensive in terms of lost pro-

duction and associated waste. The system is written in a structured extension of FORTRAN and contains about 6,500 statements overall. The calling depth in the structure of the system is between 4 and 7—not complex and not flat.

Case *c* is a comprehensive system for control of a facility, and it is 80% in a high-level language like Pascal or Ada and 20% in an assembly language. The total volume of code is in the range of 175,000 NCSSs. If this system fails, there is a substantial loss of value, but no lives would be lost, and the damage would not normally be extensive and/or expensive to repair.

Case *d* is a geographically dispersed interactive control system where human life is at stake—like an advanced air traffic control system. The system approaches the limits of current complexity in the sense that the latest methods are employed in its design and implementation, perhaps 1,000,000 NCSSs overall.

Single-Module Test Methodology

Single-module testing puts maximum focus on each separately compilable and/or separately invokable software module. The process of handling exhaustive analysis of a single module has three stages.

First, there is an analysis and preprocessing stage during which the module is structurally analyzed and studied. If an automated test system is being used, this stage includes preparing the module to be the test object in the subsequent phases. Typically, there is some programmer-supplied test data that can be used to find an initial value for the testing coverage measure being used.

The coverage level obtained by these initial tests is normally quite low. In fact, there is reason to believe that a major reason for the presence of such high defect rates in software is that the programs are never tested very well by the programmers [2].

The next stage involves the middle game, during which tests are generated systematically to increase coverage. Only a few errors are likely to be found since even though the programmer may not have exercised the program thoroughly, many errors that can be found through the inspection process would have been removed.

The final stage involves the end of testing activity, during which it may be necessary to plan for a number of difficult tests so that all of the segments can be exercised. As an alternative to requiring exercise of a segment, the program tester can spell out the reasons why a segment was not exercised.

> *Experience:* Most errors are found near the end of the single module testing process, although the reasons why this is true are not clear [12].
> *Assessment:* At least every module should be tested to a high Cl level of structural coverage, and much more testing should be done if possible.
> *Problem:* Single-module testing is perhaps an order of magnitude easier with the right tool environment (i.e., an interactive test system); without good tools, the work is difficult.

System-Testing Methodology

System testing is analogous to single-module testing except that a segment corresponds to a whole module. The two modes of attack can be different—a fact that is highly dependent on the application software and its internal structure.

System testing is, typically, done either bottom up or top down. This means that the flow of attention during the entire testing process is from single modules at the bottom of a system to the topmost modules (driver modules) later on, if the bottom-up methodology is chosen.

If the top-down method is used, attention begins at the topmost module and continues until each module in the system is handled. Stubs are sometimes used to simulate subsidiary module behavior.

The choice of which method to use depends on many factors, but primarily on the structure of the software system itself. Large systems that are flat (in the sense they have a small maximum invocation chain length) tend to work better in a bottom-up mode, other factors being equal, than top down. Systems that are very narrow and deep tend to fall more easily into the top-down mode.

> *Experience:* Most experience is with single-module testing, but in some cases, there is extensive system-level experience. Early data seem to suggest that there is no effective difference between one level of testing and the other qualitatively, only quantitatively.
> *Possibility:* Direct extension of single-module testing to the system-level case, provided the right data are presented.
> *Assessment:* Proceed in all cases with system testing as if it were module testing, assuming that this option exists.
> *Problems:* Lack of experience in testing very large systems of software; unavailability of appropriate tools.

Application to Cases

The application of these methodologies to the cases described above should now be relatively straightforward.

- Case *a*: A high-criticality single module. In this case, the strongest methodology for single-module testing should be applied to the critical module. The Ct measure should be used if possible.
- Case *b*: A medium-sized, medium-criticality system. It is not possible to focus all the effort on each module, so a limited approach seeking to maximize the payoffs from rigorous single-module testing should be followed. This will tend to maximize the outcome in terms of numbers of errors found.
- Case *c*: A large, medium-criticality system. For a large system, there is presumably a somewhat larger budget, and so it is possible to consider building special-purpose tools that can be used to support the testing activity (see below). In addition, this level of effort can involve other features of quality assurance besides simple testing.
- Case *d*: A large, high-criticality system. This situation requires the use of the best

methodologies, thorough analysis of single modules throughout the software, and a good level of system testing.

Contemporary Results

As Reference 3 points out, it is possible to set up a systematic test factory or assembly line and have it work well. In the Software Research Associates' experimental test factory, the goal was to process a large amount of software at relatively low cost. In 24 man-months of work in the automated software test factory, some 60,881 statements of a PL/1-like language were processed. They had some 4,378 segments and required 1,544 tests to achieve 89.7% overall C1 coverage.

In the processing, some 1,486 discrepancies were found between the software as it existed and the specifications as they existed. About 190 of these were fatal program errors; the remainder were deficiencies that were accepted as such by the client organization.

The main lesson learned in this case was the necessity for a good tool environment, the costs of which are not reflected in the above figures.

In another activity, single-module and system-level testing were done on the Central Flow Control software [13]. Some 23,700 statements of JOVIAL/J2 were tested and 98+% C1 coverage was obtained. The results of the error detecting process were as follows:

- 3.57% NCSS defect rate in unit testing
- 0.25% NCSS defect rate in subsystem testing
- 0.08% NCSS defect rate in system testing
- 3.91% NCSS overall defect rate

The important feature of these values is that they were found by systematic examination of an existing software system.

A final example comes from the nuclear energy field [14]. In this experiment, C1- and C2-based testing were done on programs to determine whether multiple programming teams using different programming languages could produce significantly better software.

Using a coverage-analysis system based on RXVP, the team at the Kernforschungszentrum Karlsruhe was able to discover 100 errors in about 4,500 statements, for a 2.4% error rate. Most of these errors were "in the specification" in the sense that the programs had been written correctly even when the specification was faulty.

Experience: When done with good tools and a positive atmosphere, it is possible to find a significant number of errors (defects, deficiencies) in completed programs.

Possibility: Continued emphasis on this kind of technique can reduce the chances for errors to appear in programs.

Assessment: Costs for full C1-based methods are about 20 to 40% in addition to the programming costs (private-sector cost estimate).

Problems: Requires good tools; requires right QA management attitude; is far from a fully comprehensive methodology (C1 does not guarantee the discovery of errors); cost of right tool environment.

16.10. THE FUTURE

Predicting the future is difficult in a technical area and changeable as software quality assurance. Likely future events can be classified in three categories: methodology, supporting tools, and theory (which tends to lead methodological advances).

Theory Area

In the area of theory, it is reasonable to expect that most of the technical issues surrounding software testing will be fully resolved by the mid-1980s, but there is no guarantee of this. Progress seems to be good in most cases, but as with all theoretical work, there are some problems on which progress is slow.

Some of the unanswered questions deal with: What is the direct relationship between coverage analysis and testing? How will we know when errors can no longer be present in a program? What constitutes completely adequate and fully characterizing test data?

This is the most sensitive of the three technical areas to predict. Only time will tell for sure.

Tools Area

Contemporary tools, like those used to produce the results described in the preceding sections, are still far from being ready for full production use since they have the flavor of prototypes being evaluated for eventual use. Each new large-scale project leads to a new level of understanding of what the tools should be and how they should operate, but does not fully answer the question of what the ideal tool should be.

Certain required features of tools can be discerned from current experience, however. Among them are:

- Interaction level with the program tester is very important because it helps him or her to pay attention to more detail.
- Documentation backup systems are critical in tools to ensure that enough data are preserved.
- Structural test planning methods are crucial as a way to eliminate the burdens of test-planning computations.

These required features of tools overlay a second layer of needs and wants [6].

Methodology Area

Theoretical developments lead to the development of formal testing methodologies, so that when technical advances are made in the theory of testing, they can be applied to the practice. The current art of testing is based primarily on systematic structural and behavioral analysis of software, and this basis can be expected to continue for quite some time.

New standards for quality assurance may have a positive effect on the kinds of methodologies actually practiced. For example, if a minimum level-of-coverage criterion is adopted as the standard for acceptance testing of software systems, then one would anticipate the quick adoption of corresponding system-atic testing methodologies. In some cases, draft standards [12] have already been created, although not without some controversy.

Methodologies for system-level testing are less well developed than for single-module quality assurance; it is in this area where the greatest improvements can be made. One could expect that as more and more experience is gained, better methodologies will result.

REFERENCES

1. Software Research Associates, *Automated Tools for Software Engineering: Tool Index,* SRA TN-674, 15 Feb. 1980.
2. E. F. Miller and W. E. Howden, *Software Testing and Validation Techniques,* IEEE Computer Society, 1979.
3. E. F. Miller, "Some Statistics from the Software Test Factory," *Software Engineering Notes,* ACM/SIGSOFT, Jan. 1979.
4. G. J. Myers, *Software Reliability,* Wiley, New York, 1977.
5. M. E. Fagan, "Design and Code Inspections to Reduce Errors in Program Development," *IBM Systems Journal,* vol. 15, no. 3, 1976.
6. E. F. Miller, "Program Testing Technology in the 1980's," *Proc. 1978 Oregon Conference on Computing in the 1980's,* IEEE, 1978.
7. D. L. Patterson, Ph.D. thesis, University of California, Los Angeles, 1978.
8. S. L. Hantler and J. C. King, "An Introduction to Proving the Correctness of Programs," *ACM Computing Surveys,* Sept. 1976.
9. S. L. Gerhart and L. Yelowitz, "Observations of Fallibility in Applications of Modern Programming Methodologies," *IEEE Trans. Software Engineering,* Sept. 1976.
10. L. J. White and E. I. Cohen, "A Domain Strategy for Computer Program Testing," *Proc. IEEE/NBS Workshop on Software Testing and Test Documentation,* Ft. Lauderdale, Fla, Dec. 1978.
11. R. A. DeMillo, R. J. Lipton, and F. G. Sayward, "Hints on Test Data Selection: Help for the Practicing Programmer," *IEEE Computer Magazine,* Apr. 1978.
12. "Special Issue on Software Quality Assurance," *Computer Magazine,* Aug. 1979.
13. P. C. Belford, R. A. Berg, and T. L. Hannon, "Central Flow Control Software Development: A Case Study of the Effectiveness of Software Engineering Techniques," *Proc. 1979 International Conference on Software Engineering,* Munich, 1979.
14. H. Trauboth, et al., "Program Testing Techniques for Nuclear Reactor Protection Systems," *Infotech State of the Art Report,* 1979.

17

Formal Verification

General Research Corporation

17.1. INTRODUCTION

Motivation for Formal Verification

Formal verification comprises a set of techniques for showing that a program operates correctly for all possible combinations of input values. It is motivated by the fact that it is physically impossible to test most programs over all possible combinations of test data. Even programs that have been shown to work correctly for a large set of tests may not work correctly for a never-used combination of data values.

Formal verification is also motivated by the rising costs of software development. Since formal techniques can be applied early in the life cycle and do not require generating test data, errors may be corrected and programs validated sooner than with informal techniques.

Whereas formal verification seeks to demonstrate total correctness, present techniques have much more modest goals. Today it is possible to use formal verification to show that certain aspects of a program operate consistently for all combinations of data. This result is also called partial correctness. Although they are a long way from the eventual goal, present techniques permit certain errors to be eliminated without the need to execute the program with selected test cases.

Background

Formal verification has its basis in automatic theorem proving [1, 2] and in graph theory

[3]. Automatic theorem provers and theorem-proving techniques were first applied to problems stated in terms of the first-order predicate calculus. Typically the theorems that were proved automatically were problems from books on mathematical logic.

The first-known application of these techniques to computer software was proposed by Floyd [4] and implemented by King [5]. King developed a system designed to show the correct operation of a small set of programs written in ALGOL. The method he used is known as the inductive assertion technique. It continues to form a basis for modern formal verification systems and will be discussed in detail in the following sections.

Since King's system for formal verification, a number of other systems have been implemented. Notable among these are an interactive system by Deutsch [6], a Pascal system by Luckham [7], a JOVIAL system by Elspas [8], and LISP and FORTRAN systems by Boyer and Moore [9, 10]. Boyer and Moore have also written a book on formal verification [11].

Graph theory has also been used for formal verification. At first glance, one can see that a flow chart can be abstracted as a directed graph. Analysis of a program as graphs can be used to formally verify that all parts of a program are connected together and that it uses variables consistently, to discover loops in it, and to categorize certain of these as infinite. Applications of graph theory to formal verification have often been based on an algorithm by Tarjan [12] for the efficient analysis of graphs.

17.2. BASIC CONCEPTS

Assertions

The assertion is the basis of most formal verification systems. An assertion is a statement that is considered to be always true. It is this statement that is used as a check against the code to demonstrate program consistency. Examples of assertions that were used in a PASCAL verification system [13] are:

ASSERT TIME > 0.0;
ASSERT (−1.0 <= SIN__X) AND
(SIN__X <= 1.0);
ASSERT HEIGHT <
GLIDE__SLOPE * RANGE;

The first assertion states that the variable named TIME should always be greater than zero. This is an example of a one-sided bound on a variable. The second assertion is better, in that it places a two-sided bound on the variable SIN__X. This assertion gives the range of the variable as being

$$-1.0 \leq SIN\_X \leq 1.0$$

This is one of the easiest assertions for a programmer to write, and it can provide a very powerful check on the value that a variable takes. The third assertion is more powerful than the second in that it limits the value of the variable named HEIGHT with respect to other variables in a program.

To show the use of assertions in a formal verification system, we will use the following simple example: Let us assume that a programmer writes the statement

TIME := TIME − 1.0;

When the correct statement is

TIME := TIME + 1.0;

In other words, a subtraction is performed instead of an addition. Let us also assume that the assertion TIME > 0.0 was true before and after this statement. We can show this by writing

ASSERT TIME > 0.0;
TIME := TIME − 1.0;
ASSERT TIME > 0.0;

Since there is an assignment to the variable named TIME, the second assertion is rewritten with the new symbolic value substituted for the variable TIME. Thus, we have

ASSERT TIME > 0.0;
ASSERT TIME − 1.0 > 0.0;

A theorem is then formed that states

If TIME > 0.0 then TIME − 1.0 > 0.0.

or

If TIME > 0.0 then TIME > 1.0.

For the program to be consistent with its assertions, this theorem is to be true for all values of TIME. But, as can be seen, it is not true for all values; thus the program is said to be inconsistent with its assertion. If the correct statement had been used, the theorem would have read

If TIME > 0.0 then TIME + 1.0 > 0.0.

or

If TIME > 0.0 then TIME > −1.0.

Since this theorem is true for all values of TIME, the program is said to be consistent with its assertions.

The assertion, then, is an independent check on the code. It is a statement that is to be always true, and it can take on many different forms.

Two additional important forms of assertions deal with arrays in programming languages. The first form is used to state that a set of elements of the array satisfies the assertion. For example:

$$\text{ASSERT ALL I IN 1 TO N IS}$$
$$A[I] < B[I];$$

states that the I*th* element of array A is less than the I*th* element of array B for I between 1 and N. The second form is used to state that at least one element of an array satisfies the assertion. For example:

$$\text{ASSERT SOME I IN 1 TO N IS}$$
$$\text{CARD }[I] = \text{BLANK};$$

states at least one element of the array CARD contains the same value as the variable named BLANK.

For formal verification a program must contain assertions. A minimally asserted program has the minimum number of assertions. There are three types of these:

1. An *initial assertion* which is true on program entry
2. A *final assertion* which is true on program exit
3. An *inductive assertion* which is true each time a loop executes

Each separate loop requires an inductive assertion.

The initial assertion is the easiest to prepare. It usually states the legitimate ranges of the input variables to a program. Because it is a special type of assertion, several systems use a distinguishing keyword to differentiate it from the other assertions in the program. Also although one initial assertion that states the conditions on all input variables is sufficient, most systems provide separate assertions for each variable. For example, a program that takes, as its input, the variable X, which has a range 0 to PI/2, could have an initial assertion of the form

$$\text{INITIAL } (0.0 <= X) \text{ AND}$$
$$(X <= \text{PI}/2.0);$$

Where there are several input variables, each one will have an initial assertion.

The final assertion, which can take many forms, states the correct operation of the program for all data values that satisfy the initial assertion. The simplest form of the final assertion states the range of the output variables. For example,

$$\text{FINAL } (-1.0 <= \text{SIN\_X}) \text{ AND}$$
$$(\text{SIN\_X} <= 1.0);$$

The best form of the final assertion states a relation between the output and input variables. For example,

$$\text{FINAL } (X - \text{SQRT\_X} * \text{SQRT\_X}) <$$
$$X * 1.0 \, E-6;$$

where X is the input and SQRT_X is the output. In most cases it is desired to show not only that the outputs are within range, but to show that the outputs are the desired function of the inputs. It is often difficult to write an assertion that relates outputs to inputs, as was done in the last example. Therefore the final expression is sometimes written in terms of a function such as

$$\text{FINAL ANS} = F(X,Y,Z);$$

where ANS is the output, F is the function, and X, Y, and Z are the inputs. When this form is used, additional information to define F must be provided during the verification process. The method, however, is an acceptable means of simplifying the writing of final assertions.

The most difficult assertion to write is the inductive or loop assertion. It expresses the partial result that is computed each time a loop is executed. It also states the relation between control, local, and input and output variables. Although guidelines for writing loop assertions have been prepared [14], actually doing so remains very difficult. One approach to forming the loop assertion is to do them last and assume that they all take the form:

ASSERT TRUE;

Then proceed with the verification process by first determining what needs to be added in the way of conditions to show loop consistency, and then by demonstrating that these are valid conditions, to be substituted for the loop assertion.

Consider the following Pascal-like program which computes the length of a string contained in the array STR of length ARB. The string is terminated by the end of the array or by a special symbol named EOS:

```
(* COMPUTE LENGTH OF STRING *)
FUNCTION LENGTH (STR: ARRAY
[1..ARB] OF CHAR): INTEGER;
  VAR I: [1..ARB+1]; LEN: [0..ARB];
  BEGIN
    LEN:=0;
    I:=1;
    WHILE (I<=ARB) AND
          (STR[I]<> EOS) DO
      LEN:=LEN+1;
      I:=I+1;
    END WHILE;
    LENGTH:=LEN;
END (* LENGTH *);
```

At least three assertions are needed for this program which has as its inputs STR and ARB and as its output LENGTH. Possible assertions are

INITIAL ARB >= 1;
ASSERT TRUE;
FINAL (LENGTH >= 0) AND
      (LENGTH <= ARB);

The initial assertion states that the only constraint on the inputs is that ARB be at least one. A tighter input constraint could be

INITIAL (ARB >= 1) AND
(ARB <= HIGH_NO);
INITIAL ALL I IN 1 TO ARB IS
STR[I] IN LEGAL_CHAR;

Where the first assertion states that ARB is bounded on both sides and the second assertion states that each element of STR contains a legal character.

The loop assertion states that one is needed but does not give its form. It will be shown later how a proper loop assertion can be derived for this example.

The final assertion bounds the value of LENGTH but does not state the function of the program. A better assertion would be:

FINAL (LENGTH = ARB) AND
      (ALL I IN 1 TO ARB IS
      STR [I] <>EOS) OR
      (STR [LENGTH + 1] = EOS) AND
      (LENGTH < ARB) AND
      (ALL I IN 1 TO LENGTH IS
      STR [I] <> EOS);

This assertion states that LENGTH is ARB when no element of STR contains EOS, or that LENGTH is defined as one less than the array element that contains EOS. This is the type of assertion that is used in a formal verification. Another possibility for the final assertion is

FINAL LENGTH = LENGTH_F(STR);

In this form, it is stated that the actual functional relationship will be determined in the verification process.

Thus it is possible to add assertions to a program in many different ways; one can specify loose bounds or tight bounds, or defer the form of the assertion to a later stage. It is even possible to omit assertions by stating

INITIAL TRUE:

This means, however, that the program works on all possible values of input data, a rather unlikely situation.

The assertions discussed so far are also called logical assertions to differentiate them from additional assertions that can be used in formal verification. We will present two other types of assertions that have been used [15].

Other assertions may someday prove useful as well.

The two other assertions are:

1. Access rights assertions
2. Units assertions

Both add redundant information to the program that allows checks to be made over all paths in the program for all values of data without requiring the program to be executed.

Access rights assertions state what data is allowed to be accessed in a program and what rights are to be given to it. This assertion takes two forms: one listing the variables that can be input to the program and one listing the variables that can be output from it. Other variables in the program are then protected from alteration. An example of the assertion used to list the inputs to the program is:

> INPUTS TIME, SPEED,
> ACCELERATION;

And for outputs:

> OUTPUTS DISTANCE;

A formal verification system can check three things:

1. Only variables listed in an access rights assertion are accessed by the program or subprogram.
2. Variables listed as inputs are not set on any path of the program but are used on some path in the program.
3. Variables listed as outputs are not used on any path in the program but are set on some path of the program.

Stronger checks would be to check that variables are set or used on all instead of just some paths. This is particularly valuable for programs having many variables known to more than one subprogram. The assertion also provides valuable documentation on how variables are used in each subprogram.

The units assertions state each variable's physical units. When a program has been as-serted with units assertions, symbolic dimensional analysis can be performed on each statement. Examples of units assertions are:

> TIME: REAL UNITS SECOND;
> SPEED: REAL UNITS
>   METER/SECOND;
> ACCELERATION: REAL UNITS
>   METER/(SECOND * SECOND);
> DISTANCE: REAL UNITS METER;

When units assertions are used, errors such as

> DISTANCE: =
> ACCELERATION * TIME;

can be detected by a formal verifier.

Symbolic Execution

A valuable technique used by formal verifiers is symbolic execution. Using this technique, programs are executed with the *names* of the data instead of their *values*. Several symbolic execution systems have been built [16–19] to aid in program testing. As with any of the formal techniques, there are several approaches. There is forward symbolic execution, backward symbolic execution, symbolic execution over all variables, and symbolic execution over one variable or selected variables. Whereas interactive systems often choose forward symbolic execution over a single path for selected variables, batch systems use backward symbolic execution for all variables and all paths.

Assume the program shown below was executed by a symbolic execution system to obtain the value of SUM.

> SUM: = 0;
> FOR I: = 1 TO N DO
>   SUM: = SUM: +
>   A [I] * WEIGHT [I];
> END FOR;

An interactive forward symbolic executor would set SUM to "0" after the first statement.

It would then ask the user

$$\text{Is } 1 <= N?$$

to determine whether the loop construct should be entered. If the user answers no, the symbolic value of SUM would be "0". If the user answers yes, then SUM would be assigned the symbolic value

$$\text{SUM} = 0 + A\,[1] * \text{WEIGHT}\,[1]$$

That is, if the value of SUM were output at this point, the actual expression, $0 + A[1] * \text{WEIGHT}\,[1]$, would be printed.

If the system has a built-in simplifier it might recognize rules about zero and present the result as

$$\text{SUM} = A\,[1] * \text{WEIGHT}\,[1]$$

After this assignment, the user would be asked

$$\text{Is } 2 <= N?$$

On an affirmative answer the SUM variable will be reassigned to

$$\text{SUM} = A[1] * \text{WEIGHT}[1] \\ + A[2] * \text{WEIGHT}[2]$$

This process can then keep up as long as the user stays in the loop.

In every symbolic execution system there is some way to specify the paths over which the program is to execute. This must be done at every decision point in the program.

Symbolic execution can cause lengthy expressions to be generated unless restrictions are placed on its use. It has proved to be useful in analyzing units and loop control variables.

In the symbolic execution of units, the expressions do not grow large and the number of times a statement is executed is unimportant. Each statement need be analyzed only once, and paths need not be specified. Thus the analysis is valid for all paths and all data values. The units expression can grow when units are created via multiplication or division, but the growth is small compared to normal symbolic execution.

For example, with the assertions

$$\text{DISTANCE: REAL UNITS} \\ \text{METER;} \\ \text{SPEED: REAL UNITS} \\ \text{METER/SECOND;} \\ \text{ACCELERATION: REAL UNITS} \\ \text{METER/(SECOND} * \\ \text{SECOND);} \\ \text{TIME: REAL UNITS} \\ \text{SECOND;}$$

The statement

$$\text{DISTANCE:=} \\ 0.5 * \text{ACCELERATION} * \\ \text{TIME} * \text{TIME;}$$

when its units are executed symbolically will form

$$1 * \frac{\text{METER}}{\text{SECOND} * \text{SECOND}} * \\ \text{SECOND} * \text{SECOND}$$

The simplifier will cancel the units of SECOND to leave the units METER for the expression. Note that constants that are not given a name are considered dimensionless.

The units value of the expression will then be compared to the units used on the left side of the assignment statement. Since the units match in this case, the statement would be considered consistent.

The symbolic execution of control variables in loops can be done to demonstrate when loops terminate, to warn of possible infinite loops, and to provide conditions under which a loop will terminate.

Infinite loops can arise if WHILE or REPEAT statements are used. The best mechanism to avoid infinite loops is to forbid the use of logical conditions to exit loops and to forbid programmer alteration of control variables. That is, require the FOR statement to be the only loop statement used. In particular, the form

$$\text{FOR I:} = 1 \text{ TO N DO}$$

(where N is a constant and I is not altered in the loop) will protect against infinite loops.

However, there are some applications that seem to require the use of other loop constructs. For example, this loop which performs a binary search

```
WHILE M < N DO
    I: = (M + N)/2;
    IF X < TABLE [I] THEN
        N: = I
    OR IF X > TABLE [I] THEN
        M: = I
    ELSE
        ANS: = I
    END IF
END WHILE
```

will result in an infinite loop when X = TABLE [I] because the control variable is not altered on the path taken under this condition.

For the loop to terminate, each path should contribute to moving the control variables such that eventually M > = N. To be in the loop, the condition M < N must hold. By symbolically executing the exit condition M $\geq$ N backwards over each path and checking to see if it is implied by some case of M < N, one can show under what conditions the loop can be guaranteed to terminate. The three paths in the loop are

(1) I: = (M + N)/2;
    N: = I
(2) I: = (M + N)/2;
    M: = I
(3) I: = (M + N)/2;
    ANS: = I;

The backwards symbolic execution of M $\geq$ N over the three paths would be

(1) $M \geq \dfrac{M+N}{2}$

(2) $\dfrac{M+N}{2} \geq N$

(3) $M \geq N$

The conditions for termination are

(1) $M < N \Rightarrow M \geq \dfrac{M+N}{2}$

(2) $M < N \Rightarrow \dfrac{M+N}{2} \geq N$

(3) $M < N \Rightarrow M \geq N$

It is seen that the last condition is always false so that the loop will not terminate. The first and second conditions can be shown to hold true for some values of M and N.

Verification Conditions

A verification condition is a theorem in logic. If the theorem is shown to be valid, then the program is said to be consistent with its assertions. Since the assertions can be developed independently of the program, and since the theorem can be used to describe a condition that holds true for all values of inputs, the use of verification conditions is a very powerful means for verifying the operation of the program.

A verification condition is formed by stating, as the premise of the theorem, the initial assertion that is true on entry to the program.

The theorem may be stated as:

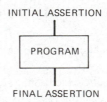

```
INITIAL ASSERTION
        |
   ┌─────────┐
   │ PROGRAM │
   └─────────┘
        |
 FINAL ASSERTION
```

If the initial assertion is true and the program is executed, then the final assertion is true.

Symbolically the theorem is written

INITIAL $\wedge$ {PROGRAM} $\Rightarrow$ FINAL

where
    INITIAL is the initial assertion.
      FINAL is the final assertion.
    PROGRAM is the program.
          $\wedge$ is the "and" operation.
          $\Rightarrow$ is the implies operation.

∧ OPERATION			⇒ OPERATION		
a	b	a ∧ b	a	b	a ⇒ b
0	0	0	0	0	1
0	1	0	0	1	1
1	0	0	1	0	0
1	1	1	1	1	1
0 is used for false					
1 is used for true					

Every term in a verification condition must be with respect to the same point in the program. Usually the point chosen is the origin of the path being verified. In order to achieve this common point, the assertions at the end of the path are symbolically executed back through the intervening code to the assertion at the start of the path.

For example, given the simple program

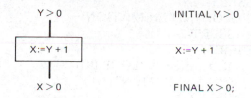

The verification condition could first be written as

$$Y>0 \; \wedge \; \{X:=Y+1\} \Rightarrow X>0$$

The symbolic execution of $X > 0$ back through the program would change X to be $Y + 1$ so the verification condition becomes

$$Y>0 \Rightarrow Y+1 > 0$$

Note that this is a valid verification condition since if $Y > 0$, then $Y + 1 > 0$.

Theoretically, a single verification condition could be written to describe the operation of a program. More practically, assertions are written for parts of a program, and then verification conditions are prepared for each part.

For example, a program that is split into two parts by an assertion would have as verification conditions:

INITIAL ∧ {PROGRAM-1} ⇒ ASSERT
ASSERT ∧ {PROGRAM-2} ⇒ FINAL

where the ASSERT is an assertion placed between the two parts of the program, PROGRAM-1 and PROGRAM-2.

In general, as many assertions as desired may be used to divide the program into small sections, each of which may be verified separately.

Assertions are usually placed in a program to divide up the paths in the program. For example, a decision point in a program can be represented by the test which is made at that point. This test is called the predicate.

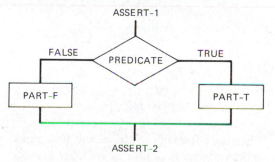

The predicate may be used to split the verification condition in two. One verification condition is written for the true side of the decision and one verification condition is written for the false side of the decision. The two verification conditions are written as

ASSERT-1 ∧   PREDICATE ∧ {PART-T}
  ⇒ ASSERT-2
ASSERT-1 ∧ ∼ PREDICATE ∧ {PART-F}
  ⇒ ASSERT-2

where ∼ is the "not" operation

∼	operation
a	∼ a
0	1
1	0

For example, in the program

```
INITIAL (Y>0) AND (Z>0);
IF Y > Z THEN
    X := Y/Z
ELSE
    X := Z/Y
END IF;
FINAL (X>1);
```

$(Y>0) \land (Z>O)$

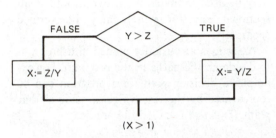

$(Y>0) \land (Z>0)$

the verification conditions would be

$$(Y>0) \land (Z>0) \land (Y>Z) \land$$
$$\{X := Y/Z\} \Rightarrow (X>1)$$
$$(Y>0) \land (Z>0) \land \sim (Y>Z) \land$$
$$\{X := Z/Y\} \Rightarrow (X>1)$$

When the effects of the assignment statements on the verification conditions are taken into account, the verification conditions become

$$(Y>0) \land (Z>0) \land (Y>Z) \Rightarrow Y/Z > 1$$
$$(Y>0) \land (Z>0) \land (Y \le Z) \Rightarrow Z/Y > 1$$

It can be shown that the first verification condition is valid. Since $Y > Z$, then $Y/Z > 1$. But the second verification condition is invalid. Since $Y \le Z$, then $1 \le Z/Y$. The assertion $X > 1$ must be replaced by $X \ge 1$ to show consistency between the assertions and the program.

A loop is a special form of a decision structure in which an assertion is held to be true every time the loop executes. A general loop structure, with the loop test at the head of the loop, is shown in the following figure.

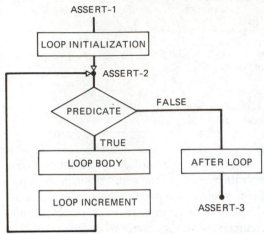

Three verification conditions are generated for this structure:

ASSERT-1 $\land$
   {LOOP INITIALIZATION} $\Rightarrow$
   ASSERT-2
ASSERT-2 $\land$
   PREDICATE $\land$ {LOOP BODY} $\land$
   {LOOP INCREMENT} $\Rightarrow$
   ASSERT-2
ASSERT-2 $\land$
   $\sim$ PREDICATE $\land$ {AFTER-LOOP} $\Rightarrow$
   ASSERT-3

The first verification condition represents the first entry into the loop. The second verification condition represents traversing the loop in general. The third verification condition represents exiting the loop.

Let us now take our Pascal example and show how it could be verified using verification conditions.

```
(*COMPUTE LENGTH OF STRING*)
FUNCTION LENGTH (STR:
ARRAY[1..ARB] OF CHAR): INTEGER;
VAR
    I: [1..ARB+1];
    LEN: [0..ARB];
BEGIN
    INITIAL (ARB >= 1) AND
        (ARB <= HIGH_NO);
    INITIAL ALL J IN 1 TO ARB IS
```

```
        STR[J] IN LEGAL__CHAR;
    LEN:=0;
    I:=1;
    WHILE (I <= ARB) AND
      (STR[I] <> EOS) DO
      ASSERT TRUE;
      LEN:=LEN+1;
    END WHILE;
    LENGTH:= LEN;
    FINAL (LENGTH = ARB) AND
      (ALL J IN 1 TO ARB IS
      STR [J] <> EOS) OR
      (LENGTH < ARB) AND
      (STR [LENGTH+1] = EOS) AND
      (ALL J IN 1 TO LENGTH IS
      STR [J] <> EOS);
    END; (*LENGTH*)
```

Note that the loop assertion has been stated as TRUE. This assertion will be derived to see if it is consistent with what the loop should do.

The verification conditions would be

```
    INITIAL ∧ {LEN:=0; I:= 1} ⇒
    ASSERT
    ASSERT ∧ (I≤ ARB) ∧
    (STR[I] ≠ EOS) ∧
    {LEN:=LEN+1;
    I:= I+1} ⇒
    ASSERT
    ASSERT ∧
    ((I>ARB) ∨ (STR[I] = EOS)) ∧
    {LENGTH:=LEN} ⇒ FINAL
```

The first verification condition takes the program into the loop. The next verification condition covers the loop traversal, and the last verification condition covers the exit from the program.

One approach to determining the loop assertion is to assume it to be TRUE and to write the verification condition that exits the loop. With this approach the last verification condition would be

(I>ARB) ∨ (STR[I]=EOS) ⇒
(LEN = ARB) ∧
∀ J(1≤ ARB) (STR[J] ≠ EOS) ∨

(LEN<ARB) ∧ (STR[LEN+1]=EOS) ∧
∀ J(1≤J≤LEN)(STR[J] ≠EOS)

Then the right side of the implies can be used as a first approximation to the loop assertion. The approximation is placed in the other verification conditions, and then modified so that they can all be verified.

A second approach is to consider the range of the loop variables

(1≤ I ≤ ARB+1) and
(0 ≤ LEN ≤ ARB),

and use these ranges as part of the loop assertion. For the remainder of the loop assertion, we ask questions about what is known so far in the loop. For example, it is known LEN = I − 1, so this is a good clause to add to the verification condition. Also while in the loop, instead of all elements STR[J] ≠ EOS, it is known that the last element examined and all preceeding elements are not EOS, so the assertion should state ∀J (1 ≤ J ≤ I −1) STR[J] ≠ EOS. This takes care of the case for I = 1 since there will be no value of J satisfying ∀ J(1 ≤ J ≤ 0).

Taking the loop assertion to be:

```
    (* LIMITS ON I *)
    ASSERT (1 <= I) AND
    (I <= ARB + 1);
    (* LIMITS ON I *)
    ASSERT (0 <= LEN) AND
    (LEN=I−1) ;
    ASSERT (ALL J IN 1 TO I−1 IS
    (STR [J] <> EOS ) );
```

The first verification condition would be

(ARB ≥ 1) ∧ (ARB ≤ HIGH__NO) ∧
∀ J(1≤J≤ARB)
(STR[J] IN LEGAL__CHAR) ⇒
(1≤1) ∧ (1 ≤ ARB+1) ∧ (0≤0) ∧
(0=0) ∧ ∀ J(1≤J≤0) (STR[J] ≠ EOS)

This is true since the right side is true under all conditions where ARB ≥ 1.

The second verification condition would be

$$(1 \leq I) \wedge (I \leq ARB+1) \wedge (0 \leq LEN) \wedge$$
$$(LEN = I-1) \wedge$$
$$(\forall J(1 \leq J \leq I-1)$$
$$(STR[J] \neq EOS)) \wedge$$
$$(I \leq ARB) \wedge$$
$$(STR[I] \neq EOS) \Rightarrow$$
$$(1 \leq I+1) \wedge$$
$$(I+1 \leq ARB+1) \wedge (0 \leq LEN+1) \wedge$$
$$(LEN+1 = I) \wedge$$
$$(\forall J(1 \leq J \leq I) (STR[J] \neq EOS))$$

since the following

1. If $1 \leq I$, then $1 \leq I + 1$
2. If $0 \leq LEN$, then $0 \leq LEN + 1$
3. If $LEN = I - 1$, then $LEN + 1 = I$
4. If $I \leq ARB$, then $I + 1 \leq ARB + 1$
5. If $(\forall J(1 \leq J \leq I - 1) STR[J] \neq EOS \wedge STR[I] \neq EOS$, then $\forall J(1 \leq J \leq I) STR[J] \neq EOS$

means all the clauses on the right side will be true if the clauses on the left side are true.

The last verification condition would be

$$(1 \leq I) \wedge (I \leq ARB+1) \wedge$$
$$(0 \leq LEN) \wedge (LEN = I-1) \wedge$$
$$\forall J (1 \leq J \leq I-1) (STR[J] \neq EOS) \wedge$$
$$\{(I > ARB) \vee STR[I] = EOS \}$$
$$\Rightarrow (LEN = ARB) \wedge$$
$$\forall J(1 \leq J \leq ARB) (STR[J] \neq EOS) \vee$$
$$(LEN < ARB) \wedge (STR[LEN+1] = EOS) \wedge$$
$$\forall J (1 \leq J \leq LEN) (STR[J] \neq EOS)$$

There are two cases, one when $I > ARB$ and one when $STR[I] = EOS$.

Case 1. $I > ARB$ means $I = ARB + 1$ since $I \leq ARB + 1$. It also means $LEN = ARB$ since $LEN = I - 1$ and $\forall J(1 \leq J \leq I - 1)$ is $\forall J(1 \leq J \leq ARB)$. So in this case, the first part of the conclusion will be true.

Case 2. $STR[I] = EOS$ means $STR[LEN + 1] = EOS$ since $LEN = I - 1$ or $I = LEN + 1$. Since $I \leq ARB + 1$, $LEN + 1 \leq ARB + 1$, or $LEN \leq ARB$ (Case 1 is covered when $LEN = ARB$), this case is for LEN

$< ARB$. Finally $\forall J(1 \leq J \leq I - 1)$ is $\forall J(1 \leq J \leq LEN)$, so the second part of the conclusion is true.

The process of verifying a program using verification conditions is tedious and error-prone. This is especially true when most of the work is done manually. Certain applications, however, have been verified in this manner, and it is hoped that mechanisms will be developed that will make the techniques easier to apply.

17.3. CURRENT APPLICATIONS

Three areas of current interest in the application of formal verification are microprocessor software, digital flight control software, and the kernel of secure operating systems. In all of them, the programs to be verified are small. The latter two application areas share the characteristic that a failure in the software can be costly in terms of human lives.

Microprocessor software has not in general been written in a high-level language. Formal verification systems that operate on the microcode itself have been developed by Patterson [20] and Crocker [21]. Crocker has applied his system to part of the software used in the ARPA network interface computer (IMP).

Digital flight control software, in the recent past, was not written in a high-level language. That trend, however, is changing. Digital flight control software has some interesting characteristics that will aid in applying formal verification:

1. The programs are small.
2. The programs have few paths.
3. Loops are not data dependent.
4. There are few data types.
5. Simple data structures are used.
6. There is no recursion.
7. Severe coding constraints may be applied if it will help verification.

Although no flight software has been formally verified to date, there is on-going work at Honeywell [22] to verify not only flight software but its requirements and design as well.

The kernel of operating systems is another

application area of current interest. The Mitre Corporation has prepared a secure operation system [23] and has verified it using a number of techniques. UCLA has also developed and verified a secure kernel [24].

17.4. FUTURE DIRECTIONS

Formal verification will have an impact on future verification systems. Techniques will be borrowed from these systems and incorporated in practical applications.

Formal verification will continue to be applied to critical software such as flight control, nuclear safety software, and secure operating systems. This will be done despite the cost of manpower and the tediousness of present tools and techniques. Eventually critical applications will support the development of formal verification systems that can be used by people other than their developers.

As more is learned about formal verification, constraints on software programs will be developed that will allow the software to be more easily developed.

REFERENCES

1. P. C. Gilmore, "A Procedure for the Production from Axioms of Proofs for Theories Derivable Within the First Order Predicate Calculus," *Proceedings International Federation of Information Processing Congress*, 1959.
2. J. McCarthy, "Computer Program for Checking Mathematical Proofs," *American Mathematical Society Symposium on Recursive Function Theory*, N.Y., 1969.
3. R. G. Busacker and T. L. Saaty, *"Finite Graphs and Networks, An Introduction with Applications*, McGraw Hill, N.Y., 1965.
4. R. W. Floyd, "Assigning Meaning to Programs," *Proceedings Symposium on Applied Mathematics*, Providence, 1967.
5. J. C. King, "Proving Programs to be Correct," *IEEE Transactions on Computers*, Nov. 1971.
6. L. P. Deutsch, "An Interactive Program Verifier," Ph.D. Dissertation, Department of Computer Science, University of California, Berkeley, 1973.
7. D. C. Luckham and N. Suzuki, "Verification of Array, Record and Pointer Operations in Pascal,"

ACM Transactions on Programming Languages, October 1979.
8. B. Elspas, R. E. Shostak, and J. M. Spitzen, *A Verification System for JOCIT/J3 Programs*, SRI International, Menlo Park, Calif., July 1977.
9. R. S. Boyer and J. S. Moore, "Proving Theorems about LISP Functions," *Journal of the ACM*, Jan. 1975.
10. R. S. Boyer and J. S. Moore, *A Verification Condition Generator for FORTRAN*, CSL Technical report 103, SRI International, Menlo Park, Calif., 1980.
11. R. S. Boyer and J. S. Moore, *A Computational Logic*, Academic Press, New York, 1979.
12. R. Tarjan, "Depth—First Search and Linear Graph Algorithms," *SIAM Journal of Computation*, June 1972.
13. N. B. Brooks and C. Gannon, *User Documentation for Verifiable Pascal*, General Research Corporation, CR-4-842, Oct. 1978.
14. B. Wegbreit and J. M. Spitzen, "The Synthesis of Loop Predicates," *Communications of the ACM*, Feb. 1974.
15. S. H. Saib et al., *Advanced Software Quality Assurance: Final Report*, General Research Corporation, CR-3-770, May 1978.
16. R. S. Boyer, B. Elspas, and K. N. Levitt, "SELECT—A Formal System for Testing and Debugging Programs by Symbolic Execution," *Proceedings of the International Conference on Reliable Software*, Los Angeles, 1975.
17. L. A. Clarke, "A System to Generate Test Data and Symbolically Execute Programs," *IEEE Transactions on Software Engineering*, Sept. 1976.
18. W. E. Howden, "DISSECT—A Symbolic Evaluation and Program Testing System," *IEEE Transactions on Software Engineering*, Jan. 1978.
19. J. C. King, "A New Approach to Program Testing," *Proceedings of the International Conference on Reliable Software*, New York, 1975.
20. D. A. Patterson, "STRUM: Structured Microprogram Development System for Correct Firmware," *IEEE Transactions on Computers*, Oct. 1976.
21. S. D. Crocker, "State Deltas: A Formalism for Representing Segments of Computation," Ph.D. Thesis, University of California, Los Angeles, 1977.
22. E. R. Rang, M. J. Gutmann, D. B. Mulcare, and W. G. Ness, *Digital Flight Control Software Validation Study*, Honeywell Systems and Research Center, 1979.
23. J. K. Millen, *Operating System Security Verification*, The MITRE Corporation, M79-223, 1979.
24. B. J. Walker, R. A. Kemmerer, and G. J. Popek, "Specification and Verification of the UCLA Unix Security Kernel," *Communications of the ACM*, Feb. 1980.

18
Software Reliability

John D. Musa
Bell Laboratories

18.1. INTRODUCTION

Use of Software Reliability Measures

At least four general areas of use for software reliability measures have been identified (this does not mean that others will not be added):

1. System engineering
2. Project management
3. Operational software change management
4. Software engineering technology evaluation

A software reliability measure is required for system engineering in order that the product attribute of reliability can be quantitatively characterized. Such a measure enables concrete tradeoffs to be made with other product characteristics such as program size, run or response time, maintainability, and so forth, and development process characteristics such as cost, resource requirements, and schedule. In some cases there may be an optimum value of reliability with respect to one of these other characteristics. For example, the total life cycle cost of a system is composed of development cost as well as operation and maintenance cost. Development cost increases with reliability, and operation and maintenance cost decreases. Hence, there will usually be a value of reliability that produces minimum life cycle cost. Another important function of system engineering is the allocation of reliability goals of a system to its component subsystems.

In the area of project management, software reliability provides a good measure for the evaluation of status and progress during test phases of the project. Reliability generally increases with the amount of testing. If a reliability goal is set for a software project, it is possible to estimate when that goal will be achieved during the system test period. Thus, software reliability theory provides a scheduling tool for managers. The time required to meet the goal is also a function of resources applied. This makes it possible to compute test and debugging costs (which can then be added to other costs to determine overall project costs) as a function of reliability. Tradeoffs among resources, cost, and schedules in the test period can be studied and alternative possibilities of action can be formulated for managerial decision in cases where some current process or product attribute is unsatisfactory.

A software reliability measure can be used to monitor software performance during the operational phase and control design changes to the program. Design changes usually involve a decrease in reliability, whereas reliability generally increases during periods of debugging. A reliability performance objective can be set for a system, based on user and other requirements. By continually comparing actual performance with the objective, management can determine when design changes can be allowed and perhaps even how large they can be.

Software reliability figures offer a useful quantitative means of evaluating the effect of software engineering technology. For example, one may run experiments to determine the increase in the mean time to failure (MTTF) of a delivered system (assuming the same amount of testing) that results from code reading.

Definitions. A few fundamental definitions, which appear to be reasonably well accepted in the software reliability field, must be introduced at this point for use in the sections that follow. *Software reliability* is the probability of failure-free operation of a software component or system in a specified environment for a specified time. A *failure* is defined as an unacceptable departure of program operation from program requirements. A *fault* is the software defect that causes a failure. An *error* is the programmer action or omission that results in a fault. The *hazard rate* is the failure rate (density with respect to time) given that the system or component has survived until now. *Software availability* will be defined as the expected fraction of time during which a software component or system functions acceptably.[1]

The user must determine the meaning of "acceptable" in terms of what is considered to be a failure. Thus the definition generally depends on the impact of the system on the user's operational cost and other factors. Often the situation is more complicated. The user may want to establish different classes of failures of different severities and establish reliability requirements for each class.

Hecht [2] defines three principal functions of software reliability: measurement, estimation, and prediction. Reliability *measurement* (used here in a specialized sense) uses failure interval data obtained by running a program in its actual operating environment. Reliability *estimation* uses failure interval data from a test environment. Estimation can be employed to determine present or future reliability. Reliability *prediction* uses program characteristics (not failure intervals) to determine software reliability. Prediction most commonly takes into account factors such as program size, complexity, and so forth. It is the only reliability function that can be performed during program phases prior to test.

In addition to the functions mentioned by Hecht, there are at least two other reliability activities with useful applications: combination and resource determination. Reliability combination is concerned with the methodologies that can be used for relating system and component reliabilities. One may either determine system reliability from component reliabilities or allocate the requirements for a system reliability level among planned component parts. Resource requirement determination provides the key for relating reliability with cost and schedules.

Relationship to Other Areas

Software reliability is closely linked to certain other product attributes of software, in particular, size and complexity. The number of faults inherent in a program and the program's MTTF at the start of testing are, of course, directly related to the previous program development process. Work to date indicates that size and complexity are perhaps the main factors that influence reliability [3]. In order to understand how these relationships arise, one needs to understand the nature of faults (fault taxonomy) and how they are generated. The methodologies of design (including software fault tolerance strategies) and development will have a major impact on software reliability. Contrariwise, software reliability measures will be a useful tool for comparing and evaluating methodologies, and pointing out where improvement is needed.

The field of software reliability is, of course, very closely allied to testing. It will be seen later that reliability estimates depend on testing being representative of the actual operational environment, which generally implies that careful test planning is essential. The way in which tests relate to the operational profile expected of the program determines one of the essential parameters involved in software reliability estimation.

Since software reliability is closely related to the amount of testing performed, and the effort in resources required for testing can be estimated, software reliability will be seen to be closely allied with the topics of software scheduling and software cost estimation. In fact, cost estimates made for test phases from an application of software reliability theory can

[1]This is an "interval" definition; one may also define availability in a "pointwise" fashion [1].

probably be used to refine some of the more general software cost models.

18.2. HISTORY OF FIELD

A paper by Hudson [4] in 1967 appears to have been the first significant one in the software reliability field. The correction of faults in software was viewed as a death process (a type of Markov process). The state of the process was characterized by the number of faults existing at any time, and transition probabilities were determined to describe fault correction. Hudson obtained a Weibull distribution of the time intervals between failures. The rate of fault correction was assumed to be proportional to the number of remaining faults and to some positive power of time.

In 1971, Jelinski and Moranda [5] developed a model that assumed a hazard rate for failures that was piecewise constant and proportional to the number of faults remaining. At each fault correction the hazard rate changed by a constant amount but remained unchanged between the corrections. Maximum likelihood estimation was used to determine the total number of faults existing in the software and the value of a proportionality constant between number of faults remaining and hazard rate. Moranda [6] has also proposed two variants of the initial model. In one variant, the hazard rate decreases at each correction as before but the step sizes form a geometric progression. In the second variant (the geometric Poisson model) the hazard rate decreases at fixed intervals rather than at each failure correction. The size of the decrements follows a geometric progression.

At about the same time as the Jelinski and Moranda work, Shooman [7] presented a similar model that introduced some new concepts. Although Shooman also assumed the hazard rate was proportional to the number of remaining faults, he postulated in addition that it was determined by the rate at which the remaining faults were passed in the execution of the program. Hence, the hazard rate depended on the instruction processing rate, the size of the program, and the number of faults remaining in the program. Shooman defined a bulk constant

to handle the fact that program structure (for example, loops) could result in repetitious executions in which new instructions and hence new faults were not accessed. Several different fault correction profiles (faults removed as a function of time) were proposed. One selected a profile depending on the nature of the project one was modeling and the variation of available personnel as a function of time. More complex models of the fault generation and correction process were also proposed by Shooman and Natarajan [8].

A somewhat different software reliability model was proposed by Schick and Wolverton [9]. It was assumed that the hazard rate was proportional to the product of the number of remaining faults *and* the time spent in debugging. The size of the changes in hazard rate at each fault correction increased with debugging time. The hazard rate itself typically increased with time to a peak and then decreased. The debugging time between failures had a Rayleigh distribution.

An empirical approach to software reliability modeling was taken by Schneidewind [10, 11]. He suggested that a selection be made among different reliability functions such as the exponential, normal, gamma, and Weibull functions in order to best fit the particular project. The best distribution was found to vary from project to project. Schneidewind emphasized the importance of establishing confidence intervals and not just relying on point estimates. He was the first to suggest that time be differentiated into operating time of the program and cumulative test time. He recommended [12] that the time lag between failure detection and correction be determined from the data and used to correct the time scale in forecasts.

Musa commenced work on an execution time model of software reliability in early 1973, leading to results that were published in 1975 [13]. The theory built on earlier contributions but also introduced a number of new concepts. Musa postulated that execution time (the actual processor time required to execute the program) was the best practical measure of the amount of failure-inducing stress placed on the program. He decided that software reliability theory should be based on execution time rather than calendar time. Varying usage of a program is not accounted for by most calendar time models. The execution time model is superior in simplicity and clarity of modeling, conceptual insight, and predictive validity.

The Musa model viewed execution time in two respects: the operating time of a product and the cumulative execution time that occurs during the test phases of development and post-delivery maintenance. The hazard rate was assumed to be constant with respect to operating time, but it varied as a function of the faults remaining and hence cumulative execution time. By using two kinds of time, Musa separated fault repair and growth phenomena from program operation, simplifying both conceptual thinking and analysis. If this were not done, it would be very difficult to obtain analytically manageable probability distributions and hard to relate the parameters of these distributions to meaningful software development variables.

The fault correction rate was assumed to be proportional to the hazard rate, making it unnecessary to consider fault correction profiles.

The execution time theory was tested on four development projects with excellent results [13]. The variation in models from project to project noted by Schneidewind and Shooman did not occur. Consequently, modeling became universal and much easier to apply. Hecht [14] has independently verified the simplification resulting from viewing software reliability as a function of execution time rather than calendar time.

A calendar time component was developed for the model that related execution time and calendar time, allowing execution time predictions to be converted to dates. This calendar time component was based on a model of the debugging process.

The execution time theory appears to have been tested more thoroughly and applied more extensively than any other software reliability model. The assumptions behind the model have been carefully stated and their validity has been examined with data from 16 software systems [15, 16]; good results have been obtained. In addition, Miyamoto [17] has presented evidence that corroborates the assumption that the hazard rate is proportional to the number of remaining faults. Applications of the model and discussions of the experience gained are presented in References 18, 19, 20, and 21.

Littlewood [22, 23, 24, 25] has taken a Bayesian approach to software reliability. He views software reliability as a measure of strength of belief that a program will operate successfully, as contrasted to the frequentist approach that he believes is taken by other modelers. The frequentist approach is the classical approach to probability that sees reliability as being determined by a (possibly hypothetical) experiment that would count the proportion of executions for which a program operates successfully.

Most software reliability researchers assume that failures occur randomly during the operation of a program. The hazard rate is assumed to be constant with respect to the program's operating time (in the sense defined by Musa). However, while other researchers postulate that the value of the hazard rate is a *function* of the number of faults remaining (and possibly other quantities), Littlewood models it as a *random process* in the failures experienced. He proposes different functional forms to describe the variation of the parameters of the random process with the number of failures experienced. One determines values of the parameters that produce the best fit for each functional form. Then the forms are compared at the optimal values of the parameters and the best-fitting form is selected.

Littlewood has also proposed a differential fault model [26]. This model assumes that faults make different contributions to the program failure rate from being accessed with different frequencies.

Littlewood views the hazard rate as a random process in order to take account of the uncertainty of repair involved in debugging. Musa handles imperfect debugging on an average basis, believing that the uncertainties that occur from failure to failure are second-order effects that do not justify the considerably greater complexity of the Littlewood model.

An imperfect debugging model that is intermediate in complexity between the Musa and Littlewood models has been presented by Goel and Okumoto [27]. This model views debugging as a Markov process with various transition probabilities between states. Several useful quantities can be analytically derived. An alternative model has also been formulated by Goel and Okumoto [28] that reasons from assumptions similar to those of Jelinski and Moranda. This model describes failure detection as a non-homogeneous Poisson process. With this model, both the cumulative number of failures detected and the distribution of the number of remaining failures are found to be Poisson.

Some researchers [29, 30] have recommended an input space approach to software reliability. All possible sets of input conditions for a program are enumerated and the proportion of these that result in successful operation is taken as the software reliability figure. There are two problems with this approach, however:

1. The enumeration is impractical because of the astronomical number of possible input sets for any program of usable size.
2. The proportion of input sets that execute successfully is not particularly meaningful for software engineers. Different input states execute for different periods of time and some input states are executed much more frequently than others. A MTTF figure is much more useful. It is relatable to cost and other effects of failure, and it allows software components to be combined with hardware components to determine overall system-reliability figures.

However, the input space approach is conceptually useful, and it may be helpful in obtaining a better understanding of the test compression factor (to be discussed later).

18.3. CURRENT STATUS

Two of the leading software reliability models, Musa's execution time model and Littlewood's Bayesian model, will be described in some detail. The main objective of software reliability modeling is the forecasting of the behavior that will be experienced when the program is operational or the measurement of the behavior when it is operational. This expected behavior changes during the period that the program is under test.

Both models make certain common assumptions (the first two are also implicit in hardware reliability measurement):

1. Testing is representative of the operational environment,
2. All failures are observed,
3. Failure intervals are mutually independent,
4. Failure intervals are exponentially distributed with respect to the operating time of the program.

Representativeness of testing and observation of failures require a well-planned and well-executed testing effort. Present evidence [15] indicates that the independence and exponential distribution assumptions are soundly based. Note that in the case of the Littlewood model, the exponential distribution is conditional on the failure rate, since the latter is assumed to be a random variable.

Both models assume complete integration of systems (all modules finished and connected together) prior to the collection of any failure data. Error is introduced when systems have been only partially integrated. However, current work is underway to remove this restriction and allow partially integrated systems to be reasonably acccurately modeled by means of a procedure for adjusting the failure intervals [31].

In actuality, one may deliberately wish to make the testing somewhat unrepresentative of the operating environment. One can remove the redundancy inherent in the operational environment and increase the efficiency of testing. Musa [18] proposed the use of a testing compression factor to account for this situation.

Musa's Execution Time Model

Musa's execution time model deals with two kinds of execution time. The first is the cumulative execution time, denoted τ. It measures development activity up to the reference point at which reliability is being evaluated. The second type is the program operating time, denoted τ', which is the execution time projected into the future from the reference point, on the basis that no additional fault correction is performed. The reference point can be viewed hypothetically as a point at which one stops testing and installs the program in the field.

There are two components of the model, the execution time component and the calendar time component. The former characterizes reliability as a function of cumulative execution time τ. The latter relates cumulative execution time τ to cumulative calendar time t.

Recall that reliability, denoted $R(\tau,\tau')$, represents the probability that failure will not occur in time τ' while

$$F(\tau,\tau') = 1 - R(\tau,\tau') \qquad (1)$$

represents the probability that failure will occur. The hazard rate, denoted $z(\tau, \tau')$, is the failure rate with respect to time τ' given that the system or component has survived until now. Hence

$$z(\tau, \tau') = \frac{f(\tau,\tau')}{R(\tau,\tau')} \qquad (2)$$

where $f(\tau, \tau')$ is the density function of $F(\tau, \tau')$ with respect to τ.

It is readily shown that

$$R(\tau,\tau') = \exp\left[- \int_0^\tau z(\tau, x) \, dx \right]. \qquad (3)$$

Mean-time-to-failure $T(\tau)$ is the expected value of the failure interval, which through integration by parts may be shown to be given by

$$T(\tau) = \int_0^\infty R(\tau,\tau') \, d\tau'. \qquad (4)$$

When the hazard rate is constant in τ' (the failure intervals are distributed exponentially), the MTTF is its reciprocal.

Execution Time Component

The execution time component of the model makes the following assumptions in addition to the ones common to it and the Littlewood Bayesian model noted above:

1. The hazard rate is proportional to the number of remaining faults.
2. The rate of change of the number of faults corrected with execution time τ is proportional to the hazard rate (the constant of proportionality that relates the rates will be designated the fault reduction factor B).

A number of relationships can be derived using the foregoing assumptions. The number of faults detected and corrected, n, is a function of the cumulative execution time,

$$n = N_0 \left[1 - \exp\left(- \frac{C\tau}{M_0 T_0} \right) \right] \qquad (5)$$

where N_0 is the number of inherent faults in the program, M_0 is the total number of failures occurring during the maintained life of the software, T_0 is the MTTF at the start of testing, and C is the test compression factor. "Maintained life" is the time period extending from the beginning of test to the discontinuance of program failure correction.

Since the hazard rate and fault change rate are proportional by assumption and the initial values of faults and failures experienced are zero, it follows that

$$N_0 = BM_0 \qquad (6)$$

and

$$n = Bm \qquad (7)$$

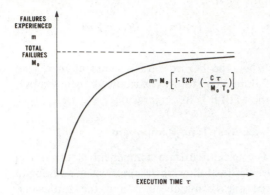

Figure 18.1. Failures experienced vs execution time.

where m is the number of failures experienced. The relationship of m to τ is similar to Eq. (5) and is shown in Figure 18.1. The fault reduction factor can account for

1. Fault growth resulting from new faults that are spawned in the process of correcting old ones
2. Faults found during code inspection that was stimulated by detection of a related fault during test
3. The inability to correct some proportion of failures because the causative faults cannot be determined

Note that the fault reduction factor B expresses the net faults removed per failure.

The present mean-time-to-failure T is also a function of the cumulative execution time,

$$T = T_0 \exp\left(\frac{C\tau}{M_0 T_0}\right), \qquad (8)$$

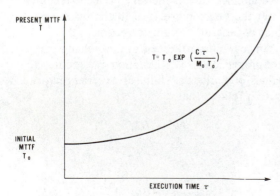

Figure 18.2. Present MTTF vs execution time.

illustrated in Figure 18.2. The MTTF increases as the test period proceeds. MTTFs are measured in execution time. One may find the reliability R for a period of operating time τ' from

$$R = \exp\left(-\frac{\tau'}{T}\right). \qquad (9)$$

Example. A time-sharing system is required to meet a reliability goal of 0.95 during the prime shift of 8 A.M. to 6 P.M. What is the equivalent MTTF?

With a 10 h prime shift, we have

$$R = \exp\left(-\frac{10}{T}\right) = 0.95.$$

Thus

$$T = \frac{10}{-\ln 0.95} = \frac{10}{0.0513} = 195 \text{ h}$$

One may set a MTTF objective, denoted T_F, for the program. The additional number of failures that must be experienced and the additional execution time required to meet this objective are

$$\Delta m = M_0 T_0 \left[\frac{1}{T} - \frac{1}{T_F}\right] \qquad (10)$$

and

$$\Delta\tau = \frac{M_0 T_0}{C} \ln\left(\frac{T_F}{T}\right). \qquad (11)$$

Example. A program has an initial MTTF of 0.2 h and 500 failures occurring during the maintained life of the software. The present MTTF is 1 h. Assume that the test compression factor is 1. How many failures must be detected to reach a MTTF objective of 10 h? How much additional execution time is required in each case?

Note that $M_0 T_0 = 100$.

We have

$$\Delta m = 100 \left[1 - \frac{1}{T_F} \right]$$

and

$$\Delta \tau = 100 \ln T_F$$

Hence:

T_F	Δm	$\Delta \tau$
10	90	230 h
100	99	461 h

It will be seen that extra time spent in testing produces a disproportionately good increase in MTTF.

Calendar Time Component

The calendar time component of the model determines the ratio between execution time and calendar time by examining the constraints that are involved in applying resources to the project. The rate of testing is constrained by failure identification or testing personnel, failure correction or debugging personnel, and available computer time. Although the quantities of these resources available may be more or less freely established in the early stages of a project, increases are usually not feasible during the system test phase because of the long lead times required for training and computer procurement. At any given point during testing, one of these resources will be limiting and will determine the rate at which execution time can be spent per unit calendar time. The test phase may have from one to three periods, each characterized by a different limiting resource. Figure 18.3 illustrates a typical plot of the calendar-time-to-execution-time ratio as a function of cumulative execution time τ.

The following scenario is reasonably typical. At the start of testing, large numbers of failures occur, separated by short time intervals. Testing has to be stopped from time to time in order to let the debugging team keep up. As testing progresses, intervals between failures become longer. Failure correction personnel are no longer fully loaded, and the test team

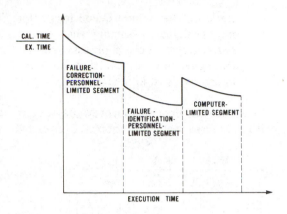

Figure 18.3. Calendar time/execution time ratio changes as testing proceeds.

becomes the bottleneck. They are fully occupied in running tests and analyzing the results. Finally, the failure intervals become very long and only the capacity of the computing facilities limits the rate at which testing can be accomplished.

The calendar time component of the model makes the following assumptions:

(1) Resource quantities available are constant for the remainder of the test period.
(2) Resource expenditures Δx_k associated with a change in MTTF can be approximated by

$$\Delta x_k = \theta_k \Delta \tau + \mu_k \Delta m \qquad (12)$$

where $\Delta \tau$ is the increment of execution time and Δm is the increment of failures experienced that are associated with the change in MTTF, θ_k is an execution time coefficient of resource expenditure, and μ_k is a failure coefficient of resource expenditure. Note that the subscript k is an index indicating the particular resource involved ($k = C$ for computer time, $k = F$ for failure correction personnel, and $k = I$ for failure identification personnel).
(3) Failure identification personnel can be fully utilized, computer utilization is constant, and utilization of failure correction personnel is established by lim-

itation of the failure queue length for any debugger, assuming that failure correction is a Poisson process and that debuggers are servers that are randomly assigned in time.

The calendar time increment Δt_k associated with each resource limited segment is given by

$$\Delta t_k = \frac{M_0 T_0}{P_k \rho_k} \left[\mu_k \left(\frac{1}{T_{k_1}} - \frac{1}{T_{k_2}} \right) + \frac{\theta_k}{C} \ln \left(\frac{T_{k_2}}{T_{k_1}} \right) \right]. \quad (13)$$

The quantity P_k is the amount of the resource available and ρ_k is its utilization factor. The values T_{k_1}, T_{k_2} are the limits of the segment and k is chosen among C, F, or I as the resource that yields the maximum derivative of calendar time with respect to execution time,

$$\frac{\theta_k T + C\mu_k}{P_k \rho_k T} \quad (14)$$

for any value of T in the segment. The segment limits are determined from the present mean-time-to-failure T, the MTTF objective T_F and the transition points $T_{kk'}$.

The transition points are given by

$$T_{kk'} = \frac{C(P_k \mu_{k'} \rho_k - P_{k'} \mu_k \rho_{k'})}{P_{k'} \rho_k \theta_k - P_k \rho_k \theta_{k'}}. \quad (15)$$

Any transition points outside the interval (T, T_F) are ignored.

Parameters

The number of parameters that must be known to apply the model depends on the purpose of the application. Most of the parameters are required for the estimation of the predicted completion dates (the dates on which the MTTF objective is reached). If the latter are not required, only three parameters need be evaluated.

The parameters are listed in Table 18.1. They may be grouped into four categories:

planned, debug environment, test environment, and program. Planned parameters are determined by project objectives and available resources. Debug environment parameters are concerned with the resources needed for failure identification and correction. It is hoped that the values of these parameters will be constant for all software projects or at least for large classes of projects. They are probably related to factors such as debugging aids available, computer used, language used, administrative and documentation overhead associated with corrections, batch debugging versus interactive debugging, and so forth. Some of these factors have been investigated by Herndon and Keenan [32]. The test environment parameter is the test compression factor that has been previously discussed. There are two program parameters, M_0 and T_0. Initially, they must be estimated from characteristics of the program itself (i.e., by reliability prediction). As soon as data is available on failure intervals, however, these parameters can be reestimated. The accuracy with which they are known generally increases with the size of the sample of failures.

Maximum likelihood estimation is used for reestimating the values of the program parameters, based on the execution time intervals between failures experienced in testing. The process is illustrated conceptually in Figure 18.4. The execution time model is characterized by a curve whose vertical axis intercept is T_0, the estimated initial MTTF, and that approaches the asymptote whose horizontal axis value is M_0, the estimated total failures. The values of these parameters are chosen to maximize the likelihood of occurrence of the set of failure intervals, which are plotted as dots in the figure. The failure interval is represented along the vertical axis and the sequential failure number on the horizontal axis. Several other quantities related to the model can be seen on the figure. In addition to maximum likelihood estimates, confidence intervals for the parameters can also be determined. The curve may now be viewed as a band, with its thickness increasing with the magnitude of the confidence interval (a 90% confidence interval will have a thicker band than a 75% one). The confidence interval

Table 18.1. Essential Parameters of Musa Execution Time Model.

Parameter	Definition	Category	Average Value Based on 4 Projects	Predictions Affected
P_C	available computer time (measured in terms of prescribed work periods)	planned	-	Δt
P_F	number of available failure correction personnel	planned	-	Δt
P_I	number of available failure identification personnel	planned	-	Δt
ρ_C	computer utilization factor	planned	-	Δt
ρ_F	failure correction personnel utilization factor	planned	-	Δt
T_F	objective MTTF	planned	-	$\Delta m, \Delta \tau, \Delta t$
θ_C	average computer time expended per unit execution time	debug environment	1.68	Δt
θ_I	average failure identification work expended per unit execution time	debug environment	2.86	Δt
μ_C	average computer time required per failure	debug environment	2.03 hr	Δt
μ_F	average failure correction work required per failure	debug environment	6.42 hr	Δt
μ_I	average failure identification work required per failure	debug environment	2.01 hr	Δt
C	testing compression factor	test environment		T, Δm, $\Delta \tau$, Δt
M_0	number of failures required to expose and remove all errors	program	-	T, Δm, $\Delta \tau$, Δt
T_0	initial MTTF at start of testing	program	-	T, Δm, $\Delta \tau$, Δt

for T_0 is given by the range of vertical axis intercepts and the confidence interval for M_0 by the range of asymptotes approached.

In order to estimate the parameter M_0 prior to test, one first determines the number of inherent faults N_0 and the fault reduction factor

B. The size of the program has the most impact on the number of faults [30, 33, 34, 35]. Some data have been taken on average fault rates per thousand delivered executable source instructions. A range of 3.36 to 7.98 faults per thousand delivered executable source instruc-

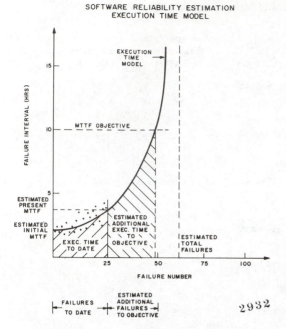

Figure 18.4. Program parameter reestimation.

tions for assembly language programs at the start of system test has been reported [13, 34, 36].

Knowledge of the fault reduction factor B is needed if one wishes to relate faults and failures, but it is otherwise not an essential parameter of the model. It is usually close to 1 for most development projects. In some cases one may have to compute it from

$$B = D(1 + A)(1 - G). \qquad (16)$$

Parameter D is the detectability ratio or proportion of failures whose faults can be found. It is usually 1 for the most developing projects. The quantity A is the associability ratio or the ratio of faults discovered by reading during test to faults discovered by testing proper. Discovery of faults during test by reading is usually stimulated by closely related faults found while testing. The number of faults discovered by reading during test for many projects is relatively small in amount; hence A is often close to 1. The parameter G is the fault growth ratio or the increase in faults per fault corrected. This factor can account for faults spawned in correcting other faults and faults added by design changes.

When fault growth occurs, N_0 must be interpreted as the initial inherent faults at the start of test. If growth is small, with the exception of faults spawned in correcting other faults, G will be close to 1 and will be determined principally by the spawning effect. Available data [17, 18] indicate that for spawning alone, G ranges from 0 to 0.09. Thus, under the foregoing circumstances, B can be expected to range from 0.91 to 1.

The parameter T_0 is predicted from

$$T_0 = \frac{1}{fKN_0}, \qquad (17)$$

where f is the linear execution frequency of the program. This is the average instruction execution rate divided by the number of object instructions in the program. The quantity K is a fault exposure ratio that relates "fault velocity" and failure rate. The fault velocity is the rate at which faults in the program would pass by if the program were linearly executed. Thus, the fault exposure ratio represents the fraction of time that the "passage" results in a failure. It accounts for the fact that

1. programs have many loops and branches, and
2. the machine state varies and hence the fault associated with an instruction may or may not be exposed at one particular execution of the instruction.

At present, K must be determined from a similar program. In the future it may be possible to relate K to program dynamic structure. On six projects for which data are available, K ranges from 1.54×10^{-7} to 3.33×10^{-7}. The small range of these values suggests that program dynamic structure may average out in some fashion for programs of any size; further investigation appears in order. Schneidewind [37] has proposed the use of simulation to relate program structure and failure characteristics—possibly a useful tool.

Example. A program with 50,000 source instructions and a source-to-object expansion ratio of 4 will be executed on a machine with a throughput of 333,333 instructions per second. On similar projects, a fault exposure ratio of $K = 1.67 \times 10^{-7}$ has been experienced, along with a fault rate of 6 faults per 1,000 source instructions. Estimate the initial MTTF at the start of system test.

Since there will be 200,000 object instructions, the linear execution frequency f of the program will be $333,333/200,000 = 1.67$ s^{-1} or 6,000 h^{-1}. Note that $N_0 = 300$. Hence from Eq. (17)

$$T_0 = \frac{1}{6000(1.67 \times 10^{-7})(300)} \qquad (18)$$
$$= 3.33 \text{ h}$$

Consider the above program after it has been executing for 100 h. Assume that the fault reduction and test compression factors are both 1. What is the present MTTF?

Since $B = 1$, $M_0 = 300$. Hence from Eq. (8) we have

$$T = 3.33 \exp\left(\frac{100}{300(3.33)}\right) = 3.33 \exp (0.1)$$
$$= 3.33 \ (1.11) = 3.70 \text{ h}$$

A program is available for the reestimation of M_0 and T_0 from failure interval data and the calculation of present MTTF, the number of additional failures that must be experienced to reach an MTTF objective, and the additional execution time and calendar time and associated completion dates [38, 39].

Application

Since the calendar time component of the model requires the estimation of various resource parameters, it is an easy step to the determination of relationships between reliability and system test cost. If other development costs can be considered constant with respect to reliability or the variation is known, total development costs as a function of reliability can be obtained. Since one can usually determine the impact of reliability on system operating costs, one may determine the total life cycle system cost as a function of reliability. Optimization may then be used to help establish a desired reliability objective [21].

Example. An online system is being planned to process orders received by a business, generate bills, break down the work involved into tasks and write work orders on those tasks, order materials, and so on. It is desired that a mean-time-to-failure (MTTF) objective for the system be established that will minimize total system cost over an estimated lifetime of 2 years. Faults are not to be corrected in the field for this system; they will be fixed at the next release. Assume for simplicity that the hardware components of the system are much more reliable than the software and hence may be neglected in this analysis. Also, for simplicity, assume that the entire system test period is failure-correction-personnel limited. All resources are profitably employed on some activity; that is, there will not be any charge for time during which this project cannot employ them. The system is expected to operate 250 days/yr, 8 h/day. The average total cost impact of a failure (in terms of reduced efficiency, extra supervisory time, and other work required to "straighten out the mess," etc.) is $10,000. Operational costs and development costs for other than the system test phase are independent of MTTF achieved.

The software consists of 100,000 source (400,000 object) instructions. Programmer loaded salary is $50/h and computer (CPU) time is $1000/h. There are 25 program designers available for debugging. The utilization factor for failure correction personnel will be 0.16. Average instruction execution rate is one million object instructions a second. On similar projects, a value of fault exposure ratio $K = 2.222 \times 10^{-7}$ has been experienced, and the average fault rate has been 5 faults per thousand source instructions. Assume that the fault reduction factor $B = 1$. Data taken in similar environments indicate that 5 person hours are required for failure correction per failure and that this effort is independent of amount of test execution time. Similarly, 4 person hours of system test team effort and 1 hour of chargeable computer time are required per hour of test execution time, and 2 person hours of system test team effort and ½ hour of computer time are required per failure; assume a testing compression factor C of 1.

404 HANDBOOK OF SOFTWARE ENGINEERING

What is the MTTF that minimizes total life cycle cost? What is the length of the system test period (in calendar time) for the minimum MTTF? What is the reliability of the optimum system for one day of operation?

We compute a value of $M_0 = N_0 = 500$, using the program size and average fault rate. The linear execution frequency, determined by dividing the object instruction execution rate by the number of object instructions, is 2.5 s^{-1} or 9000 h^{-1}. Hence, using Eq. (17),

$$T_0 = \frac{1}{9000(2.222 \times 10^{-7})(500)} = 1 \text{ h}$$

Now from Eq. (10)

$$\Delta m = 500(1)\left(1 - \frac{1}{T_F}\right)$$

$$= 500 - \frac{500}{T_F}$$

and from Eq. (11)

$$\Delta \tau = \frac{500(1)}{1} \ln\left(\frac{T_F}{1}\right)$$

$$= 500 \ln T_F.$$

The resource expenditures will be identical to the requirements. Applying Eq. (12), we have

$$\chi_C = \mu_C \Delta m + \theta_C \Delta \tau$$

$$= 0.5\left(500 - \frac{500}{T_F}\right) + 1\,(500 \ln T_F)$$

$$= 250 - \frac{250}{T_F} + 500 \ln T_F$$

$$\chi_F = \mu_F \Delta m = 5\left(500 - \frac{500}{T_F}\right)$$

$$= 2500 - \frac{2500}{T_F}$$

and

$$\chi_I = \mu_I \Delta m + \theta_I \Delta \tau$$

$$= 2\left(500 - \frac{500}{T_F}\right) + 4\,(500 \ln T_F)$$

$$= 1000 - \frac{1000}{T_F} + 2000 \ln T_F$$

The cost of system test will be

$$\$1000\,\chi_C + \$30(\chi_F + \chi_I)$$

$$= \$250,000 - \frac{\$250,000}{T_F} + \$500,000 \ln T_F$$

$$+ \$50\left(3500 - \frac{3500}{T_F} + 2000 \ln T_F\right)$$

$$= \$425,000 - \frac{\$425,000}{T_F} + \$600,000 \ln T_F$$

The number of failures during operation will be the total operating lifetime divided by MTTF or $4000/T_F$. Hence, the cost of failures will be $\$40,000,000/T_F$.

The expression for the sum of operational and system test costs,

$$\$425,000 + \frac{\$39,600,000}{T_F} + \$600,000 \ln T_F$$

is of the form

$$a + \frac{b}{T_F} + c \ln T_F$$

Because other life cycle costs do not vary with MTTF, we will ignore them. A simple minimization using calculus yields

$$T_{F\text{MIN}} = \frac{b}{c}$$

Thus, we obtain a value of 66 h for the MTTF objective that minimizes system life cycle costs. The cost of system test and operational failures for this value is $\$3,545,000$.

To determine the duration of system test, note that since there is only one limiting resource period and $\theta_F = 0$, Eq. (13) becomes

$$\Delta t_F = \frac{M_0 T_0 \mu_F}{P_F \rho_F}\left[\frac{1}{T_0} - \frac{1}{T_F}\right]$$

Hence

$$\Delta t = \frac{500(1)(5)}{25(0.16)}\left[\frac{1}{1} - \frac{1}{T_F}\right] = 625 - \frac{625}{T_F}$$

At the minimum cost point, the system test period will require 615 hours or 77 8-hour days.

The reliability of the software for one day (8 h) of operation, assuming the MTTF objective of 66 h is attained, is found from Eq. (9) as

$$R = \exp\left(-\frac{8}{66}\right) = 0.886$$

This figure can be combined with reliabilities of hardware components to give overall system reliability.

In order to evaluate the effects of software engineering technology (e.g., structured programming, better documentation, code reading, better test design, etc.), it is probably best to find the effects of these techniques on parameters of the execution time model first, using appropriate experiments. Then the parameters can be related to reliability. This two-stage approach is appropriate because it reduces the number of factors in effect at any given time.

By means of simulation, the execution time theory can help a manager reach tradeoff decisions among schedules, costs, resources and reliability in a continuing fashion. It can also assist in determining resource allocations. One selects several values of each parameter to be varied, then observes the effects on MTTF, project completion date, cost, and so forth [19].

Variations in the MTTF of operational software are highly correlated with periods of fault correction and introduction of new capabilities. MTTF tends to increase during fault correction and decrease during periods of addition of new capabilities. This behavior can be usefully applied by a manager who is responsible for the maintenance of operational software in determining when to schedule the addition of new capabilities and when to put a freeze on changes [20].

Users have indicated that the execution time model provides a good conceptual framework for understanding the process of software failure. The model is simple; its parameters are closely related to the physical world; and it is compatible with hardware reliability theory, so that hardware-software systems may be analyzed. The benefits of the model exceed the costs (which are basically data collection and computation). The process of defining just what constitutes a failure and the process of setting an MTTF objective have useful side benefits, in that they tend to open up communication between customer and developer. Most of the assumptions that were made in deriving the model have been validated [15] and experience has been gained with the model on more than 20 software systems to date. There is no evidence to indicate any class of software to which the model would not apply. This model has been tested and its validity examined much more thoroughly than any other proposed software reliability model.

Littlewood's Bayesian Model

Littlewood's Bayesian model [22, 23, 24, 25] is a more complex formulation for software reliability than the Musa execution time model. It is not known at the present time whether or not it justifies the extra complexity with greater accuracy.

The Bayesian model differs from the execution time model in that the failure rate parameter is assumed to be a random process with respect to the failures experienced, instead of a function of the faults remaining. The execution time model accounts for imperfect correction on an average basis by means of a fault reduction ratio. The possibility of imperfect correction is included in the Bayesian model's definition of the random process. Littlewood does not use a MTTF in describing his model. In fact, he objects to its use on the basis that a program might be perfect and therefore have an undefined or infinite MTTF [40]. The author believes that the simplicity promoted by the use of the MTTF concept is worth the very infrequent possibility of having to handle a perfect program in a different way as an exceptional case. The Littlewood approach is to estimate percentiles of the distribution of time to the next or to the kth failure from now.

Since the Bayesian model is subjective, periods of failure-free operation automatically cause the reliability to improve. The Musa model allows for such reliability improvement by using a continuous approximation to the detection and correction process. The Jelinski-Moranda model places a floor under the reliability improvement by assuming that a pseudofailure exists at the end of the failure-free period. The failure intervals τ_i' in the Littlewood model are assumed to have a conditional density function given by

$$f(\tau_i' \mid \lambda_i) = \lambda_i e^{-\lambda_i \tau_i'} \qquad (19)$$

The failure rate is postulated to be a random process with a gamma conditional density function:

$$
\begin{aligned}
&g[\lambda_i \mid \alpha, \Psi(i)] \\
&= \frac{\Psi(i)\{\Psi(i)\lambda_i\}^{\alpha-1} \exp[-\Psi(i)\lambda_i]}{\Gamma(\alpha)}.
\end{aligned} \qquad (20)
$$

The unconditional distribution of τ_i' is Pareto. The unknown quantities in the model are α and $\Psi(i)$. Reliability growth is reflected in the $\Psi(i)$ parameter.

Littlewood recommends that various types of growth functions be considered for any given project; the one that provides the best fit to the data should be chosen. The $\Psi(i)$ function reflects the repair activities (including their uncertainty). There are many possible families of functions; two that have been suggested by Littlewood are

$$\Psi(i) = \beta_1 + \beta_2 i \qquad (21)$$

and

$$\Psi(i) = \beta_1 + \beta_2 i^2 \qquad (22)$$

Musa [41] has suggested the use of a rational function for $\Psi(i)$, based on the concept that the parameter should be inversely related to the number of failures remaining. The suggested function was

$$\Psi(i) = \frac{M_0 T_0 \alpha}{M_0 - i} \qquad (23)$$

where M_0 is the number of failures expected during the maintained life of the software, T_0 is the initial MTTF, α is the parameter of the gamma distribution, and i is the index number of the failure.

Values of parameters for a given growth function and comparisons determining which growth function is best are established by testing goodness of fit to the data with the Cramér-von Mises statistic. This computation requires a sort of the data and minimization of the statistic over a multidimensional surface. These calculations are very expensive in computer time, several orders of magnitude greater than the computations required for the Musa model. Recent work by Iannino indicates that maximum likelihood estimation of parameters rather than a goodness-of-fit approach may reduce the difference in computation somewhat [42]. The Bayesian analysis assumes a uniform prior probability density function for alpha.

Littlewood's analysis leads to a hazard rate of the form

$$\lambda(\tau) = \frac{n}{\Psi(n)} \left[\log \prod_{i=1}^{n} \frac{\Psi(i) + \tau_i}{\Psi(i)} \right]^{-1} \qquad (24)$$

where $n - 1$ failures have previously occurred and τ_i represents the execution time since the $(i - 1)th$ failure [23]. The hazard rate changes discontinuously at each failure detection and correction and varies continuously with the cumulative execution time. Thus, the hazard rate changes in accordance with one's subjective ideas of how reliability should change in a failure-free environment.

Percentiles are derived for the probability distribution of the failure interval between the $(n + k - 1)th$ and the $(n + k)th$ failures, where $k \geq 0$. Note that n represents the next failure. The percentile $y_{q,n+k}$ is given by

$$y_{q,n+k} = \Psi(n + k)\{\theta^{[(1-q)^{-1/(n+1)}-1]} - 1\} \qquad (25)$$

for the 100q percentile [25], where θ is given by

$$\theta = \prod_{i=1}^{n} \frac{\tau_i + \Psi(i)}{\Psi(i)}. \qquad (26)$$

The general Littlewood model has been verified against one set of project data with essentially good results [43].

The Littlewood approach results in somewhat greater mathematical elegance than the

Musa model at the expense of greater complexity, which makes the model more difficult to understand and increases the computations required to apply it very substantially, as previously noted. It allows characterization of reliability decay as well as growth. The Musa model recognizes a situation of no growth or decay but it does not predict its future course. This is not a material disadvantage; prediction of decay is probably substantially poorer in quality than prediction of growth, the mechanisms being much less well known.

The Littlewood model usually leads more quickly to analytical difficulties than does the Musa model because of its more complex formulation. Hence, Littlewood has not developed (and probably cannot develop, because of analytical complexity) relationships for execution time required to reach a reliability objective in the general case (he has done this for the special case of the differential fault model, to be described). Musa considers the reliability or MTTF objective as a concept that is important and useful for software engineers and managers and determines the execution time required to reach it.

Unlike the Musa model, the Littlewood model does not include a calendar time component. Thus, the attainment of reliability objectives cannot be related to calendar dates. This is a capability of great interest to software managers and engineers.

The Musa model has parameters that have readily understood physical interpretations but the Littlewood model does not (although the growth function [41] suggested by Musa for the Littlewood model remedies this situation somewhat). Hence, it is not possible to apply current findings in software complexity research (discussed later) to the function of reliability prediction if the Littlewood model is used.

The differential fault model proposed by Littlewood may be viewed as an approximate particularization of the general Littlewood model, although it was not developed in this fashion. It is "approximate" because reliability growth is modeled through *both* parameters of the gamma distribution of the failure rate in the differential fault model. Littlewood hypothesizes that failures occur with different frequencies because of the variation in frequency with which different input states of the program are executed. The differential fault model thus postulates two sources of reliability growth; one is represented by each of the gamma distribution parameters. The first source is the detection and correction of faults. The second source follows from the hypothesis that failures occur with different frequencies; the most frequently occurring faults are detected and corrected first [26]. Littlewood considers that uncertainties in reliability growth probably result more from uncertainties in the relative frequencies of execution of different input states than the uncertainties in fault correction.

The random process representing the failure rate λ is assumed to be a sum of random processes ϕ_i, where each ϕ_i is associated with a particular fault:

$$\lambda = \sum_{i=1}^{N-n} \phi_i \qquad (27)$$

where N represents the total number of inherent faults in the software, and n represents the number of faults detected and corrected up to the present. The probability distributions associated with the individual faults prior to any debugging are assumed to be identical gamma distributions. The density function is given by

$$f(\phi) = \frac{\beta^\alpha \phi^{\alpha-1} e^{-\beta\phi}}{\Gamma(\alpha)} \ (\phi > 0) \qquad (28)$$

The distribution of each ϕ_i in Eq. (27) must be found from Bayes' Theorem; each will be a conditional distribution for ϕ_i, given that fault i has not been corrected up until the present. The overall hazard rate is given by

$$\lambda = \frac{(N-n)\alpha}{\beta + \tau} \qquad (29)$$

where τ represents the cumulative execution time at the point where the hazard rate is measured. The density function of the execution time to the next failure τ' is Pareto:

$$f(\tau') = \frac{(N - n)\alpha(\beta + \tau)^{(N-n)\alpha}}{(\beta + \tau + \tau')^{(N-n)\alpha+1}}. \quad (30)$$

It will be seen from Eq. (29) that:

(1) The failure rate drops by $\alpha/(\beta + \tau)$ for each failure that is detected and corrected. Hence, corrections in the early part of testing (small τ) result in greater reductions in failure rate than later ones.
(2) The failure rate decreases during periods of failure-free operation because of the presence of τ in the denominator.

If $\alpha \to \infty$, $\beta \to \infty$ such that α/β is constant, Eq. (30) reduces to an exponential distribution.

Littlewood's differential fault model has not yet been thoroughly tested against actual data. It is a more complicated model than a model in which all faults are assumed to be uncovered with equal frequency. Whether or not the model will provide enough additional accuracy to justify its added complexity is not known at the present time. The model appears plausible if one assumes that programmers generate faults at a constant rate with respect to the possible input states in the program. This is based on the concept that programmers devote approximately equal time to designing the actions for each input state. (A more naive view is that faults are distributed at a constant rate with respect to instructions. This model may represent the way programmers behave with respect to typographical errors, but the vast majority of errors are not typographical.) However, another hypothesis is possible. It may be that faults are distributed at a constant rate with respect to execution time. This would happen if programmers spent more time in designing the responses to input states that occur frequently, so that the fault rate for a particular input state would be (at least approximately) inversely proportional to its frequency of execution. This postulate is also plausible. The determination of which of these two postulates is in closer accord with reality (or is in close enough accord) will have to await evaluation with real data.

Combinatorics

The manner in which most software reliability models (including both the Musa and Littlewood models) have been developed results in a combinatorial compatibility with hardware reliability theory that permits determination of overall reliability of complete systems. The techniques of reliability budgeting or allocation commonly used in system engineering can therefore be applied to systems involving hardware and software components, provided that these components are concurrently functioning [18]. A system is considered to be composed of concurrently functioning components if the satisfactory operation of the system is dependent on continuous satisfactory operation of some combination of these components. This situation is analogous to the analysis of reliability for a hardware system. The system is analyzed by drawing a "failure logic" diagram of the system and applying the combinatoric rules for AND and OR combinations of components developed in hardware reliability theory [44, 45].

If a system is composed of sequentially functioning components (i.e., if only one component functions at a time and the satisfactory operation of the system is dependent on the satisfactory functioning of each component when it is active), then an approach developed by Littlewood may be used [46]. The system is assumed to consist of k components among which control is switched randomly according to a semi-Markov process; that is, the transition probabilities between components are dependent only on the identity of the immediately preceding component. The probability distributions of the sojourn times of the components in the active state are not restricted in any way. Failures for the ith component are assumed to occur in accordance with a Poisson process with rate λ_i. If the λ_i are small then the system process is Poisson with rate λ given by

$$\lambda = \frac{\sum_{i=1}^{k}\sum_{j=1}^{k} \rho_i p_{ij}\mu_{ij}\lambda_i}{\sum_{i=1}^{k}\sum_{j=1}^{k} \rho_i p_{ij}\mu_{ij}} \quad (31)$$

where the ρ_i are the equilibrium probabilities given by

$$\rho_i = \sum_{j=1}^{k} \rho_j p_{ji} \qquad (32)$$

The transition probability from component i to j is given by p_{ij}, and μ_{ij} is the mean duration spent in component i before switching to component j. The rate λ_i is the reciprocal of the MTTF T_i.

Availability

Availability may be computed for software as it is for hardware. Recall that availability was defined as the expected fraction of time during which a system will operate satisfactorily. If we let the time interval over which the measurement is made approach infinity, then the availability is given by the familiar ratio

$$A = \frac{T}{T + F} \qquad (33)$$

where A is the availability, T is the MTTF, and F is the mean time to repair (MTTR). It is assumed, of course, that these means exist. Usually the MTTF applied here is a figure computed for serious failures and not those that involve only minor degradation of the system. Since it is generally not practical to hold up operation of the system while performing fault determination and correction in the field, MTTR is ordinarily determined as the average time required to restore the data base for a program, to reload the program, and resume execution. Markov process theory has often proved to be useful in looking at the details of availability behavior [27, 47, 48].

Perspective for the Future

Software reliability measurement in the operational phase can at present be achieved with excellent accuracy. Therefore, use of MTTF as a means for controlling change in operational software and as a basis for evaluating different software engineering technologies is very feasible [49].

The quality of software reliability estimation (test phase) is most dependent on the representativeness of testing; it is essential to do a good job of test planning. Knowledge of the test compression factor is necessary if one wishes to know the absolute value of the MTTF or to make calculations dependent on it; it is not necessary when making relative comparisons (e.g., tracking progress on a project). At present one must estimate the test compression factor from measurement of a similar project in a similar test environment or be conservative and set it equal to 1. Research into the factors that influence the test compression factor might lead to ways of predicting it. The current quality of software reliability estimation could be characterized as good for present estimation and fair for future estimation. Present estimation (discussed in terms of the execution time model) requires the values of the test compression factor and the program parameters. Future estimation, in addition, depends on knowledge of the planned and debug environment parameters. Data collection is needed on a number of projects to determine the values of the debug environment parameters and the extent to which they vary between different projects or different classes of projects. If they do vary, a study of the factors that influence them should be undertaken. Given the current state of software reliability estimation, status monitoring and tracking of projects can be accomplished with a relatively good level of quality. Estimation of project completion dates can presently be characterized as fair [49].

The function of software reliability prediction needs the most work [49]. However, it also offers great promise in terms of ultimate potential benefits since it bears on how well system engineering and early planning decisions can be made. Such decisions often have the greatest impact on schedules and cost. All of the quantities required for software estimation (again, discussed in terms of the execution time model) are needed for software prediction as well. In addition, since one must predict the program parameters rather than estimate them from failure interval data, one requires the number of faults inherent in the software N_0, the fault reduction factor B, the fault exposure ratio K, and the linear execution frequency f.

One approach to determining the number of faults (already discussed) is based on the size of the program.

The question has been raised of the possibility of obtaining better predictions of the number of faults by developing and using expressions of program complexity in the predictions [3, 50, 51, 52]. Several different complexity measures have been proposed; they fall into the categories of structural complexity, textual complexity, and psychological complexity [53]. In some cases size is subsumed by the complexity measure. This field is an active area of research at the present time. It is not clear which complexity metrics will prove to be the best ones. It may turn out that the concept of complexity is a multidimensional one. Some workers [33, 54, 55] have taken a multidimensional approach, using regression analysis. However, there will be considerable pressure for simplification because the additional predictability that can be added by use of a complexity measure is limited. Since faults are introduced into software by human error, software psychology may have a great deal to contribute to unraveling this puzzle. Data on the relationships between faults and size and complexity is just beginning to accumulate, but much more is needed. Also, better ways of estimating size and complexity of a program in the requirements stage, before any code has been written, are required.

Some researchers have taken an empirical approach to predicting the number of faults in software. This approach variously goes by the names "error seeding" [56, 57, 58] or "debugging" [59]. One generates artificial faults in a program in some suitable random fashion, unknown to the people who will be testing and debugging the software. It is assumed that these "seeded" faults are equivalent to the natural or original faults occurring in the program in terms of difficulty of detection. Based on that hypothesis and measurement of the proportion of seeded faults that have been found

at any point in time, one can predict the number of natural faults, since it is assumed that the same proportion will have been discovered. For example, assume that 100 faults are seeded into a program containing an unknown number of natural faults. After one week of debugging (and the debugging may be either based on testing or on code reading), assume that 20 seeded faults and 10 natural faults have been discovered. Since the seeded faults discovered represent 20% of the total number it would be assumed that the natural faults discovered would be in the same proportion. Therefore, the total number of natural faults is 50. In actuality, the situation is a bit more complex than this since we are dealing with samples of random variables and we would be making probability statements about the number of natural faults falling into some interval. Unfortunately, it has proved to be very difficult to implement this simple concept because of the great difficulty involved in randomly generating artificial faults that are equivalent to natural faults in difficulty of discovery. It has proved much easier to find the seeded faults; therefore, the total number of natural faults is usually underestimated.

Initial data appears to indicate that the fault reduction factor B may be relatively stable across different projects, but more study is required. The fault exposure ratio K is expected to be dependent on the dynamic structure of the program and the degree to which faults are data dependent. Further investigation of the properties of this ratio and the factors upon which they depend is very important if we are to obtain good absolute software reliability predictions.

Although the present state of the art of software reliability prediction needs considerable improvement in terms of obtaining good absolute values, it is often possible to conduct studies involving relative comparisons with reasonable results [21].

The future will probably see more comparison of models since more and more data are becoming available to make this possible [16]. There is likely to be a weeding-out process among models as software reliability measurement comes into greater practical use. Application and the resulting feedback will probably lead to further refinement. Practical knowledge concerning application, already developing [18], will undoubtedly grow further.

REFERENCES

1. R. E. Barlow, F. Proschan. *Mathematical theory of reliability.* New York: Wiley, 1965, p. 7.

2. H. Hecht. Measurement, estimation, and prediction of software reliability. In *Software engineering technology,* vol. 2. Maidenhead, Berkshire, England: Infotech International, 1977, pp. 209–224; also in NASA Report CR145135, Jan. 1977.

3. L. M. Ottenstein. Quantitative estimates of debugging requirements. *IEEE Trans. Software Engineering* SE-5 (5)(Sept. 1979):504–514.

4. G. R. Hudson. *Program errors as a birth and death process.* System Development Corp. Report SP-3011, 4 Dec. 1967.

5. Z. Jelinski and P. B. Moranda. Software reliability research. In *Statistical computer performance evaluation,* ed. W. Freiberger, New York: Academic, 1972, pp. 465–484.

6. P. Moranda. Predictions of software reliability during debugging. *Proc. Annual Reliability and Maintainability Symposium.* Washington, D.C., Jan. 1975, pp. 327–332.

7. M. Shooman. Probabilistic models for software reliability prediction. In *Statistical computer performance evaluation,* ed. W. Freiberger, New York: Academic, 1972, pp. 485–502.

8. M. L. Shooman, S. Natarajan. Effect of manpower deployment and bug generation on software error models. *Proc. Symp. Computer Software Engineering.* New York, 1976, pp. 155–170.

9. G. J. Schick and R. W. Wolverton. Assessment of software reliability. Paper presented at 11th Annual Meeting of German Operations Research Society, Hamburg, Germany, 6–8 Sept. 1972. In *Proc. Operations Research,* Physica-Verlag, Wurzburg-Wien, 1973, pp. 396–422.

10. N. F. Schneidewind. An approach to software reliability prediction and quality control. *1972 Fall Joint Comput. Conf., AFIPS Conf. Proc,* vol. 41. Montvale, N.J.: AFIPS Press, 1972, pp. 837–847.

11. N. F. Schneidewind. *A Methodology for Software Reliability Prediction and Quality Control.* NTIS Report AD 754377, 1972.

12. Norman F. Schneidewind. Analysis of error processes in computer software. *Proceedings of 1975 International Conference on Reliable Software.* Los Angeles, Calif. April 21–23, 1975, pp. 337–346.

13. J. D. Musa. A theory of software reliability and its application. *IEEE Transactions on Software Engineering* SE1 (3)(Sept. 1975):312–327.

14. H. Hecht. Allocation of resources for software reliability. *Proc. COMPCON Fall 1981:*74–82.

15. J. D. Musa. Validity of the execution time theory of software reliability. *IEEE Transactions on Reliability* R-28 (3)(Aug. 1979):181–191.

16. J. D. Musa. *Software Reliability Data,* 1979. Report available from Data and Analysis Center for Software, Rome Air Development Center, Rome, N.Y.

17. I. Miyamoto. Software reliability in on-line real time environment. *Proceedings of 1975 International Conference on Reliable Software.* Los Angeles, Calif., 21–23 Apr. 1975, pp. 195–203.

18. J. D. Musa. Software reliability measurement. *Journal of Systems and Software,* 1(3)(1980):223–241.

19. J. D. Musa. The use of software reliability measures in project management. *Proceedings of COMPSAC '78.* Chicago, 13–16 Nov. 1978, pp. 493–498.

20. Patricia A. Hamilton and John D. Musa. Measuring reliability of computation center software. *Proc. 3rd Int. Conf. Soft. Eng.,* Atlanta, Geo., 10–12 May 1978, pp. 29–36.

21. J. D. Musa. Software reliability measures applied to system engineering. *1979 NCC Proceedings.* New York, 4–7 June 1979, pp. 941–946.

22. B. Littlewood. How to measure software reliability and how not to. *Proceedings of Third International Conference on Software Engineering.* Atlanta, Geo., 10–12 May 1978, pp. 39–45.

23. B. Littlewood and J. L. Verrall. A Bayesian reliability growth model for computer software. *Journal Royal Stat. Soc.—Series C* 22(3)(1973):332–346.

24. B. Littlewood and J. L. Verrall. A Bayesian reliability growth model for computer software. *1973 IEEE Symposium on Computer Software Reliability,* New York, 30 Apr.–2 May 1973, pp. 70–77.

25. B. Littlewood and J. L. Verrall. A Bayesian reliability model with a stochastically monotine failure rate. *IEEE Trans. Reliability* R-23 (2)(June 1974):108–114.

26. B. Littlewood. What makes a reliable program—few bugs, or a small failure rate? *1980 NCC Proceedings,* Anaheim, Calif., 19–22 May 1980, pp. 707–713.

27. A. L. Goel and K. Okumoto. *Bayesian Software Prediction Models.* Rome Air Development Center Report RADC-TR-78-155 (5 volumes), 1978.

28. A. L. Goel and K. Okumoto. Time-dependent error-detection rate model for software reliability and other performance measures. *IEEE Trans. Reliability,* R-28 (3)(Aug. 1979):206–211.

29. W. H. MacWilliams. Reliability of large, real time control software systems. *1973 IEEE Symposium on Computer Software Reliability.* New York City, 30 Apr.–2 May 1973, pp. 1–6.

30. T. A. Thayer. *Software Reliability Study.* RADC Report RADC-TR-76-238, 1976.

31. J. D. Musa and A. Iannino. Software reliability modeling-accounting for program size variation due to integration or design changes. *ACM SIGMETRICS Performance Evaluation Review* 10(2) (Spring 1981): 16–25.

32. Mary Anne Herndon and N. T. Keenan. Analysis of

error remediation expenditures during validation. *Proceedings of Third International Conference on Software Engineering.* Atlanta, Geo., 10–12 May 1978, pp. 202–206.

33. R. W. Motley and W. D. Brooks. *Statistical Prediction of Programming Errors.* RADC Report RADC-TR-77-175, 1977.

34. K. Akiyama. An example of software system debugging. *Proc. IFIPS Congress 1971.* Amsterdam: North-Holland, 1971, pp. 353–359.

35. A. R. Feuer and E. B. Fowlkes. Some results from an empirical study of computer software. *Proc. 4th. Int. Conf. on Software Engineering.* Munich, 17–19 Sept. 1979, pp. 351–353.

36. A. Endres. An analysis of errors and their causes in system programs. *Proceedings of 1975 International Conference on Reliable Software.* Los Angeles, Calif. 21–23 Apr. 1975, pp. 327–336.

37. N. F. Schneidewind. The use of simulation in the evaluation of software. *Computer* 10(4)(Apr. 1977):47–53.

38. J. D. Musa. *Program for software reliability and system test schedule estimation—User's guide,* 1977, available from the author.

39. J. D. Musa and P. A. Hamilton. *Program for software reliability and system test schedule estimation—Program documentation,* 1977, available from the authors.

40. B. Littlewood, MTBF is meaningless in software reliability. Correspondence in *IEEE Trans. Reliability* 24 (1)(Apr. 1975):82.

41. J. D. Musa. Private communication to B. Littlewood, 1979.

42. A. Iannino. Private communication to J. D. Musa and B. Littlewood, 1979.

43. B. Littlewood. Validation of a software reliability model. *Proc. Second Software Life Cycle Management Workshop.* Atlanta, Geo., 21–22 Aug. 1978, pp. 146–152.

44. D. K. Lloyd and M. Lipow. *Reliability: Management, methods, and mathematics,* 2d ed. Redondo Beach, Calif.: Published by the authors, 1977, chap. 9.

45. M. L. Shooman. *Probabilistic reliability: An engineering approach.* New York: McGraw-Hill, 1968, chap. 3.

46. B. Littlewood. A semi-Markov model for software

reliability with failure costs. *Proceedings of the Symposium on Computer Software Engineering.* New York, 1976, pp. 281–300.

47. A. K. Trivedi and M. L. Shooman. *Computer Software Reliability: Many-State Markov Modeling Techniques.* Polytechnic Institute of New York Report POLY-EE/EP-75-005/EER 116, March 1975.

48. A. Costes, C. Landrault, and J. C. LaPrie. Reliability and availability models for maintained systems featuring hardware failures and design faults. *IEEE Transactions on Computers* C-27 (6)(June 1978):548–560.

49. J. D. Musa. Software reliability modeling—Where are we and where should we be going? *Proceedings of 4th NASA Software Engineering Workshop.* Greenbelt, Md, 19 Nov. 1979.

50. Maurice H. Halstead. *Elements of software science.* New York: Elsevier North-Holland, 1977.

51. Y. Funami and M. H. Halstead. A software physics analysis of Akiyama's debugging data. *Proceedings of the Symposium on Computer Software Engineering.* New York, 1976, pp. 133–138.

52. N. F. Schneidewind and Heinz-Michael Hoffman. An experiment in software error data collection and analysis. *IEEE Trans. Software Engineering* SE-5 (3)(May 1979):276–286.

53. J. C. Rault. An approach towards reliable software. *Proc. 4th Int. Conf. on Software Engineering,* Munich, 17–19 Sept. 1979, pp. 220–230.

54. M. Lipow and T. A. Thayer. Prediction of software failures. *Symposium on Reliability and Maintainability, 1977,* pp. 489–494.

55. C. E. Martin. *A Model for Estimating the Number of Residual Errors in COBOL Programs.* Ph.D. thesis, Auburn University, June 1977.

56. H. D. Mills. *On the Statistical Validation of Computer Programs.* IBM Federal Systems Div. Report FSC-72-6015, Gaithersburg, Md., 1972.

57. S. L. Basin. *Estimation of software error rates via capture-recapture sampling: A critical review.* Science Applications, Inc.: Palo Alto, Calif., Sept. 1973.

58. B. Rudner. *Seeding/Tagging Estimation of Software Errors: Models and Estimates.* RADC Report RADC-TR-77-15, 1977.

59. T. Gibb. *Software metrics.* Cambridge, Mass.: Winthrop, 1977, p. 28.

19

Software Performance

Boris Beizer

Data Systems Analysis, Inc.

19.1. INTRODUCTION

System performance can be predicted by analytical models or by simulation, but only measurement can provide an accurate assessment of performance. The term *instrumentation* is used to denote hardware or software, or a combination thereof that is used to gather performance-related data. Performance measurements can be undertaken to determine the system's performance, to tune the system, or to determine the hardware and/or software elements that limit the system's performance.

Determining the factors that affect program execution time is of primary importance in batch-processing systems. Load-handling capacity is a more significant performance measure for on-line systems. In either kind of system, measurements are often undertaken in support of tuning. Tuning is defined as the achievement of an optimal balance of system resources. Because the application, the software, the load, and to a lesser extent, the hardware, undergo continual change over the system's life, tuning and the associated measurement activity are a continual, ongoing process rather than a singular event that takes place only once. Consequently, although considerable effort may be expended the first time measurements are attempted, there will be a continual payoff throughout the system's or the application's life.

Any effective measurement activity presupposes a working, debugged, stable system. Bugs induce uncertainties in measurement that can invalidate all analysis based on such measurements. Furthermore, bugs can induce symptoms that will mask the true causes of poor performance. Finally, there are bugs that do not affect the functions that a system does but that can affect its performance. Given a smoothly running, reliable, stable system of hardware and software, performance measurement has the following components:

1. A clear statement of performance objectives.
2. A source of transactions to drive the experiment.
3. A controlled experimental process.
4. A method for gathering data.
5. Analytical tools to process and interpret the data.

Each of these subjects is discussed in further detail in the sections below.

19.2. PERFORMANCE OBJECTIVES

General

Time is an implicit part of every notion of system performance. Other than memory size, the only fundamental difference between small and large computers is processing time. In principal, given sufficient memory, the smallest microcomputer can be programmed to do the work done by a supercomputer. What makes one system adequate and another inadequate is the time elapsed between the submission of a task and its completion. That elapsed time is called the *processing delay,* or *delay* alone when the context is clear. In primitive batch-processing systems that work on one task at a time, the processing delay is equal to the sum of the CPU execution time for the task, any overhead processing, and any time spent waiting for the completion of input or output operations. In a more typical multiprogramming, multitask, on-line system, the processing delay is longer than the CPU execution time because sharing the system's resources among many tasks induces queuing delays. The delay, then, is the sum of all actual execution times for the task and the time spent on all queues.

Processing delay depends on the total number of active tasks, which in turn depends on the rate at which those tasks are being submitted to the system for processing. In most multiprocessing systems, load is measured in terms of the simultaneous number of active tasks. Each active task can be looked upon as a source of internally generated transactions that occur at a statistically specifiable rate. The number of active users can therefore be translated into an equivalent job-submission/job-completion rate. The rate at which jobs are submitted and completed (they must on the average be the same) is called the *throughput* and is measured in transactions per second.

System performance can, for all systems, be reduced to establishing a relationship between throughput and delay. A system's performance is adequate if it does not reject or lose transactions when they are submitted at a rate lower than or equal to the design rate and when the delay at the rated throughput is within the margin deemed acceptable for that application. What constitutes an acceptable delay is application dependent. A few milliseconds may be intolerable in an aircraft's autopilot; several hours may be acceptable for a monthly payroll; and weeks may be reasonable for an annual inventory run.

Resources

A system consists of hardware resources, fixed characteristics of the system. Examples of resources are: computer instruction execution rates, memory access rates, bus and channel transfer rates, and processing rates for devices such as tapes, printers, card readers, communications channels, terminals, discs, and so forth. Each transaction makes a statistically

determinable demand on these rate resources. If a resource is available at, say, 100,000 units per second, and each task on an average requires 10,000 units of processing, it is clear that the system cannot handle a throughput of more than 10 tasks per second.

Memory resources are a second kind of resource. In principle, all memory must be included, that is, main memory, registers, cache memory, discs, tapes, and so on. In practice, only main memory and mass memory such as disc need be considered in the majority of cases. Memory can be distinguished as being static or dynamic. Static memory utilization does not depend on throughput. Static memory includes most operating system overhead and program space, fixed tables, fixed portions of a data base, and application program space. Dynamic memory is memory used in support of processing tasks. Dynamic memory is configured in pools of fixed or variable length blocks. Dynamic memory is allocated to a task when the task enters the system and returned to the pool when the task has been processed. What constitute static and dynamic memory can be subjective and is application dependent. For example, if the performance of a time-shared operating system is being considered, user program space and tables constitute "dynamic memory" because the space is continually being allocated and deallocated to support the several users. From the user's point of view, all space used may be "static." Given a fixed context for "dynamic" and "static" memory usage, performance measurements are also concerned with determining the amount of dynamic memory usage, whereas tuning may involve trades between dynamic and static memory.

Utilization of Resources

At any instant of time, a resource may be gainfully employed or unused. Dynamic memory in a pool, not allocated to any task, is not in use. If a period of time passes in which a disc transfer does not occur, then during that period, the resource represented by disc transfer rate is not in use. If a CPU is in an exerciser mode or in a supervisory wait state because there are no other tasks to process, that resource is not in use. It is clear that resource utilization will vary with throughput. If all resources are monitored (by some means, not important at the moment), they would all be seen to vary between *no useful work* and *fully occupied*. A resource that is fully occupied is said to be *saturated*. This is also a statistical concept, and there is an implied sample period. For example, a bus is used to transfer data. While the actual data transfer occurs, the bus is saturated because it transfers data at the maximum rate possible. This is followed by a hiatus, however, during which no transfers occur. If the transfer were to take an average of ten milliseconds, one would not draw conclusions on resource saturation based on a few milliseconds' worth of data generated when the bus was in use. Resource utilization should be measured and averaged over a period of time that is long compared to the typical duration of a task in the system. If the typical task enters and leaves the system in a few seconds, then the sample period over which utilization is averaged should be of the order of a minute. Similarly, in a batch-processing system with sojourn times measured in hours, the implied sample should be taken over a period of days.

Resource utilization is expressed as a percentage of what is available for each resource and is denoted by p_n for resource n. When $p = 1$ the resource is saturated.

Binding Resources

One can perform a simple but revealing conceptual experiment on which all measurement and tuning is based. Say that a program uses the CPU, a printer, and a moving-head disc to achieve some processing objective. Analyze the system three different ways (or n ways for n resources) under the assumption that all other resources are infinite. Each analysis would yield a different execution time for the transaction, and the system as a whole would exhibit a different processing delay at any given throughput. In this example, this conceptual analysis would yield three different processing times: for the CPU alone, the printer alone, and the disc alone. The resource for which the

system has the longest execution time under the conditions of this thought experiment is called the *binding resource*. In a hypothetical perfect system, all nonbinding resources would be fully overlapped with the binding resource and, therefore, only the binding resource would determine the delay. The binding resource, however, is not fixed and depends on throughput. Thus, at low throughput, disc transfer time may bind the system, whereas at high throughputs it is CPU execution that binds. As a first approximation, most systems behave at any given throughput as if the delay were determined by the resource that binds at that throughput.

Full overlap of the nonbinding resources with the binding resource is generally not achievable. Consequently, there must be periods during which a given resource is not gainfully employed, even though it is, for the most part, the binding resource. Whenever the execution time for a single task exceeds the execution time for the binding resource alone, full overlap is not achieved and the binding resource is to some extent wasted. The binding resource is said to have a *gap*. A major objective of performance measurement and tuning is the identification and elimination of gaps.

The achievement of these objectives is complicated because the identity of the binding resource is dynamic and can vary from task to task, in addition to varying with throughput. At best, one can only identify which resource is most often bound and which resources are most often gapped. That is, the entire approach must be statistical.

The Objectives of Tuning

Tuning is the identification of binding resources and the elimination of gaps therein. Gaps can be eliminated by several means:

1. Rearrange the order of processing.
2. Rearrange the priority of processing and/or resource allocation.
3. Make the binding resource faster, that is, less binding through more efficient code.
4. Trade between equivalent resources (e.g.,

main memory for disc, buffered channel for unbuffered channel, etc.).

5. Trade between inequivalent resources (e.g., increase program space to achieve faster code, tighten code to save space at the cost of time, etc.).

6. More or faster hardware—a faster CPU, more channels, a disc with a shorter seek time, more memory.

Corrective action without knowing what the binding factor is and the extent to which it is gapped may yield little or no improvement. Suppose that a system is disc-access bound and that it is well tuned—so well balanced, in fact, that memory utilization is almost always at maximum; furthermore, the CPU is gainfully employed 90% of the time. A new disc that is twice as fast as the old disc offers no noticeable improvement because now, memory has become the binding factor. Now add to the memory, but the system's load-handling capacity is not improved because the CPU binding has asserted itself. Improvements in nonbinding factors have little or no impact. Improvements in a gapped binding resource shift the binding resource to the cause of the gap, again with little improvement. Careful measurements and interpretation of those measurements are required to identify the binding resource, the gaps, if any, the relation to other resources, and the extent to which the alleviation of the binding resource or the reduction of the gaps will improve the system's performance rather than just bring another binding factor to light.

System Behavior

The measurement of resource utilization for a single program running under a uniprogramming environment is a special and simpler case of a multiprogramming or on-line system that is simultaneously handling transactions from many different sources. Therefore, most models of system behavior will deal with the more complex, general case. Figure 19.1 shows the typical behavior of a system when subjected to different steady-state transaction arrival rates. Only steady-state conditions are considered here. With few exceptions, the dy-

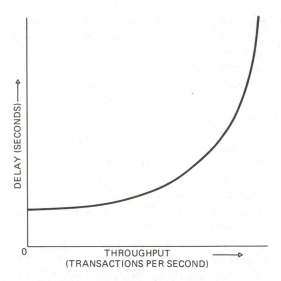

Figure 19.1. Typical throughput delay curve.

namic analysis systems subjected to time-varying loads are beyond the practical analytical state of the art and are experimentally difficult. The processing delay depicted in Figure 19.1 is small at low loads but increases nonlinearly with increasing loads—typically as $1/(1 - p)$. At some load, at least one resource becomes saturated and the delay becomes infinite. In practice, this does not happen because properly designed systems take preventive measures such as limiting the input rate, to forestall true saturation.

The same principal can be used to examine batch-processing systems, although the concept might not seem to apply at first. Let transactions be jobs submitted for processing and let the computer be considered the server of a single-server queueing system. If jobs are submitted at a steady rate, a queue will build up for the computing facility as a whole, even though a queue may not build up within the computer itself. The facility as a whole will experience a behavior like that of Figure 19.1.

Memory as a Resource

Memory utilization is one of the trickiest resources to analyze and interpret. It is tricky because the amount of dynamically allocated memory required to support a given transaction mix and arrival rate is affected by:

1. The amount of memory required to process the transaction.
2. The duration of time over which the blocks will be held for processing the transaction (called the holding time).

The number of memory blocks required to process a transaction is typically independent of the load. If a transaction requires an average of ten buffer blocks, it will require those blocks whether transactions arrive at one, ten, or a hundred per second. The holding time, however, is proportional to the processing delay rather than to the execution time for a single transaction. That is, the holding time is equal to the sum of the processing time and all the time spent waiting on queue for processing. Therefore, the amount of memory required to handle a steady-state load is, to a first-order approximation, proportional to the product of the transaction arrival rate and the delay. But the processing delay is proportional to $1/(1 - p_n)$ where n is the binding resource. Consequently, buffer utilization experiences an even faster increase with load than does processing delay. It is not unusual for buffer demand to follow a linear increase with increased load, and then to appear to zoom upwards discontinuously over an insignificant increase in load. It is this reason that makes memory depletion a sensitive indicator of binding in other resources. Unfortunately, although symptomatic of binding in other resources, memory is often erroneously thought to be the cause rather than the symptom. Additional memory (main, disc, etc.) is purchased, but because it is not the true binding factor, the result is an insignificant improvement in the system's performance. The correct identification of memory as the binding factor can only be done after other factors have been ruled out. For example, the system is channel bound, and the reason it is channel bound is that the channel is being used to swap between main memory and disc in order to compensate for inadequate memory. The key to determining memory binding is to separate its components—the amount of memory required (number of blocks) to process a transaction and the holding time for those blocks. The number of

blocks per transaction should be constant and the holding time should be proportional to processing delay. If a significant component of the delay is attributable to the alleviation of memory scarcity, then memory is probably the binding factor. If no such attribution can be made, then some other factor binds the system, and memory binding is only a symptom.

19.3. SIMPLE MODELS OF SYSTEM BEHAVIOR

General

Disentangling which resources are the true binding resources, how they affect one another, how to experimentally determine those effects, how to interpret the results of measurements, and how to best adjust the system to alleviate a binding resource, all require some notion of how the system behaves. Detailed analytical or simulation models can be constructed, but such models are rarely needed in support of an experimental determination of performance. Experimental performance models are simple and should be based on a black-box approach that is independent of the implementation details of the operating system or the application programs.

A Simple Model

Most practical models of system behavior can be reduced to a function of the form:

$$D = 1/(1 - f(p)) \qquad (1)$$

where:
  D is the expected processing delay.
  p is the utilization of the binding resource.
  f is a positive, nondecreasing function of the utilization.

The function is dominated by a linear term proportional to the transaction arrival rate R. Therefore, Eq. (1) can be restated as:

$$D = k_1/(1 - k_2R + \epsilon) \qquad (2)$$

Where k_1 and k_2 are constants (or nearly so) and ϵ represents the contribution of the nonlinear terms or higher-order terms in the resource utilization. Note that if we invert this expression and consider the reciprocal of the delay (call it S), the resulting expression becomes linear:

$$S = 1/D = (1 - k_2 R + \epsilon)/k_1$$
$$= S_0 - k_3 R \quad (3)$$

The right-hand side is obtained by renaming the constants and dropping negligible terms. Redefining the constants once again, we obtain:

$$\frac{S}{S_0} + \frac{R}{P} = 1 \quad (4)$$

where:

- S is the reciprocal of the delay and S_0 is the reciprocal of the delay at zero load, corresponding to the delay experienced by a single transaction in an otherwise empty system.
- R is the transaction arrival rate in transactions per unit time.
- P is the rate at which the system is capable of processing transactions.

Generally, P is a function of load and will shift as the binding factor shifts. Note that R/P is the utilization (p). S is called the *subjective rate* (in distinction to R, the *objective rate*) because it is the apparent rate at which the system appears to be capable of processing transactions when viewed by a single user who is ignorant of all other users. For example, if the system has a ten second delay, it appears to be able to process one-tenth of a transaction per second. A plot of S/S_0 versus R/P for an ideal system is a straight line sloping downwards at a 45° angle. Comparisons of systems can be made by normalizing the delay to the zero load delay and the transaction arrival rate to the maximum arrival rate; Figure 19.2 shows an ideal system (dotted line) and a real system. Figure 19.3 shows the same functions plotted from data taken from a real system.

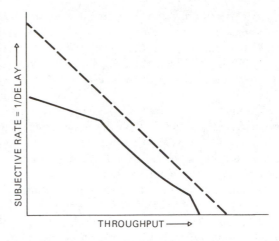

Figure 19.2. Real and ideal systems.

Interpretation of a Model

Consider a well-tuned system, without resource gaps but with several different binding resources. Under these assumptions, the system's processing delay is dominated by the resource that is most binding at any given throughput. We could plot a function like Eq. (4) for each resource separately, and obtain a figure like Figure 19.4. Delay is determined by resource 1 in the low-load region. As throughput increases, resource 2 becomes the binding factor. The system's ultimate load-handling capacity, however, is determined by resource 3. In each region, the system's behavior is linear (or almost so) and can be modeled by Eq. (4). Note the break in the points in the experimental data of Figure 19.3, which shows the shift in binding resource. Note also that be-

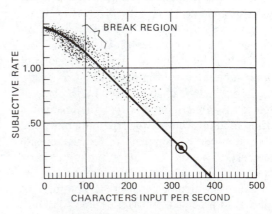

Figure 19.3. Subjective rate curve of actual system.

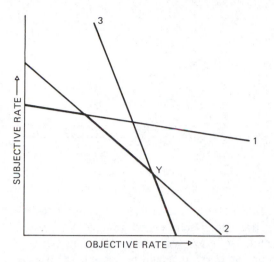

Figure 19.4. Several resources.

cause the binding factor shifts with load, experimental data taken at low load (resource 1 in Figure 19.4) may have no bearing on the system's capacity because it is resource 3 that limits the system. Therefore, a proper determination of the system's handling capacity can only be based on measurements taken over the entire range of loads from minimum to maximum so that the true binding factor, rather than low-load binding factors, can be determined.

Figure 19.2 can now be interpreted. It consists of three different behavior regions. The first region, with the gentle slope, is typical of disc latency binding. A transition occurs to a second region at point X. The curvature in this second region is typical of a resource that has a high initial overhead that is amortized over many more transactions as load increases, for example, program initialization, overlay overheads, and so on. A positive curvature indicates a process in which the processing time per unit transaction $(1/P)$ increases with increasing load. This might occur with a queue-scanning process, a sort, and similar processes with nonlinear increases in unit transaction processing time. The break at Y is indicative of the ultimate binding factor asserting itself.

Danger Points

Performance analysis based on experimental data consists of gathering the data, plotting the

values, fitting a curve to those values, and extrapolating the system's behavior to regions for which it is not possible to obtain data. Ideally, all experimentation should be based on a fixed test-bed in which all loads, from minimum to maximum, are measured so that no extrapolation is necessary. Unfortunately, a controlled test-bed for a system is often a luxury—most often, measurements must be taken on a live system in which it is not possible to explore the entire throughput range. There lies the fundamental danger to all extrapolations based on limited measurements. A prediction of load-handling capacity for Figure 19.4 based on extrapolating from data taken in the resource 1 region would be optimistic, as would be a prediction based on resource 2. The solution to this, when a controlled experiment is not possible, is to take data over a long period of time (hours, days, and weeks, if necessary) in the hope that the system will hit its peak or near saturating load for a few minutes.

Bugs and Tuning

With careful measurement of throughput and delays, we can occasionally see curves such as those shown in Figure 19.5. This kind of notch is typical of bugs or ill tuning. The slope of the subjective rate curve is a good indicator of the binding factor. Over a small range, the slope tends to be constant for any given factor. Therefore, regions with comparable slopes probably represent the same binding factor. There is a notch in Figure 19.5. The initial binding resource is A. The curve then shifts discontinuously to a new binding resource B.

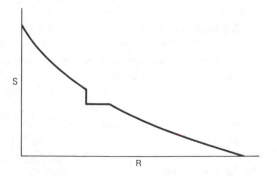

Figure 19.5. A notch.

The *A* slope then reasserts itself, indicating that the binding resource is once again *A*. This kind of notch is indicative of a bug in the processes that dominate the *A* binding factor. Typically, this occurs when there is a discontinuous increase in overhead that forces the entire curve down to a lower region. The overhead is consumed (i.e., the gaps are filled in) until the true binding factor is again asserted. Some examples are instructive:

1. A system has a hardware bug in the fixed-head disc. It should be capable of processing up to 64 read or write operations per revolution, but at approximately 50 transactions per revolution, transfers are missed, forcing an additional revolution. The increase of processing delay by one revolution at about 50 transactions per second shows up as a notch. Beyond that point, because more revolutions are committed to handling fewer transactions, the delay remains constant, until either the true binding factor dominates or until yet another superfluous spin is forced.
2. A system has many task queues. When load is low, the queues are examined by a sequential scan. At higher loads, in the interest of efficiency, the queues are sorted prior to examination. The sorting process is time-consuming. The shift to the sort routine is apparent as a notch. Note that if sort or scan time were not the binding factor, it would have been better to stick to the simpler, nonsorting approach. In either case, invoking the sort should have been delayed to a higher-load region to provide a continual and gradual change in the system's performance because discontinuous changes in the system's apparent behavior are always disturbing to users.

A definite indicator of bugs is a subjective rate curve that increases at any point, such as that shown in Figure 19.6. The delay at *B* is less than the delay at *A*, despite the fact that at *B*, the system has to handle *X* more transactions per second. This is contrary to common

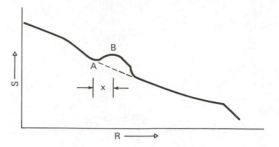

Figure 19.6. A bump.

sense because it tells us that in order to improve the system's performance we should pump in *X* extra useless transactions per second. At worst, it should be possible to improve the system by invoking whatever is happening at *B* earlier so that the system will follow the dotted curve in Figure 19.6. What usually happens is that the discovery and identification of the source of the anomalous behavior allows a redesign that extends the system's performance throughout the range and increases the ultimate throughput as well. Typical systems have simple subjective rate curves that consist of one, two, or three regions. Most systems have two regions, with the first region flat and corresponding to disc and other forms of I/O binding, followed by a sharp drop when processing binding takes over. The first region, or the central region, has a slight negative curvature caused by improved efficiency and increased amortization of overhead functions with increasing load.

Summary

A system's behavior is characterized by a simple subjective rate function. The objective of any experiment is to gather enough data to allow an accurate representation of the entire curve, and not just a segment thereof. Given the curve, the following must be done:

1. Identify the dominant factor in each segment of the curve.
2. Understand every break as a transition from one binding resource to another.
3. Identify negative curvature with a factor whose efficiency improves with increas-

ing load because of amortization of overhead functions.

4. Identify a positive curvature with a factor that increases with increasing load, such as queue-scanning operations, sorting, and interprocess interference.

5. Investigate notches as targets for improvements and indicators of potential bugs and/or ill tuning.

6. Investigate lumps in detail because they must be caused by bugs or ineffectual load management strategies.

19.4. TRANSACTION SOURCES

General

Performance measurement is an experimental process. This implies that as many variables as possible are under the experimenter's control. The primary control is over the load. Loads can be obtained in several different ways, each with advantages and disadvantages:

1. Load generators and simulators.
2. Cogeneration.
3. Self-generation.
4. Real loads.

These transaction sources are listed in order of increasing experimental complexity and instrumentation requirements.

Load Generators and Simulators

These can range from a simple predetermined set of transactions presented to the system under a job control language, to the entire real-time simulation of a complex environment. One of the most elaborate load generators is the FAA test facility at Pomona, New Jersey. This facility can provide realistic loads for an entire air-traffic control system, including pilots and air-traffic controllers. An air-traffic control program can be tested in this environment under a wide variety of situations. Different elements may be provided by other programs or by humans who act as pilots or controllers. Similarly elaborate test facilities and load generators are used in the space program and military applications.

Whether simple or elaborate, a load generator is a source of statistically specified transactions. The load may be generated on-line or various components may be produced off-line and run on-line. Because a load generator will often incorporate measurement hardware to measure the system's behavior under load, it can be as complex as the system for which it is generating a load. Furthermore, the resources required to support a load generator (i.e., the computer in which it is run) can be greater than the system under test. If not, the additional problems of load generator saturation and how to distinguish load generator saturation from system saturation will arise.

Elaborate load generators are effective when they are used to test many different systems, to simulate many different environments, or when no other approach is safe. For example, a product line process control system might make use of a load generator to simulate any of the many different processes to which that system might be applied. A telecommunications system might be tested with a load generator to simulate the different communications environment in which the system will be used.

Figure 19.7 is a block diagram of a typical load generator. It has three main components—an off-line scenario generator, an on-

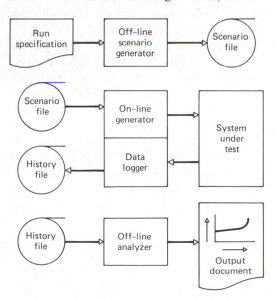

Figure 19.7. Load generator block diagram.

line system, and an off-line analyzer. The scenario generator accepts a statistical specification of the transactions to be generated, that is, transaction length and characteristics, and so forth, as well as a specification of the kinds of responses that will be accepted. The scenario generator then constructs a file of transactions for the scenario to be used in the test. The file contains the transactions themselves, the time at which the transactions are to be submitted (if possible) to the system under test, and the channel or communications line on which the transaction is to be presented. The logic of the generator and the details of transaction generation are application specific. For example, a generator for telephone systems would provide specification of numbers to be called, misdial percentages, waiting time between digits, wrong numbers, incomplete calls, and so on.

The on-line portion of the system is designed under the assumption that there is a response to every stimulus. For example, every inquiry has a response. If no such response exists, then additional instrumentation may have to be provided in the system under test to artificially create such a response. The on-line generator portion attempts to issue the transactions in accordance with the times scheduled for those transactions. If the system under test is not capable of accepting it because it is backlogged, then the on-line generator must provide a realistic reaction to that situation; for example, try again forever, try n times and then quit, and so on. That reaction may itself be part of the scenario. Whenever the generator issues or attempts to issue a transaction, it must log that fact for subsequent analysis. Similarly, it must measure (timestamp) the system's reaction and provide additional sufficient information to allow matching the stimulus to the response and to record the pertinent delays. The generator portion uses a scenario file to drive the experiment, but what happens is recorded on a history file.

Because much processing may be required to match stimulus to response, this is done off-line. The history file is analyzed and responses are matched to stimuli. Using the timestamp data provided, both the actual transaction ar-

rival rate and the processing delay can be determined, resulting in the throughput-delay function for the system. Additional instrumentation, as discussed in Section 19.5 may be incorporated into the system under test, or measured data may be transmitted to the simulator by the system under test.

Cogeneration

Cogeneration of load is using a system to provide load for another copy of the system. Cogeneration is called for when the requirements of a load simulator and the system being tested are almost identical, as is the case, for instance, in communications systems. It can also be used in process control systems, where the act of execution control and the software required to create control responses can be modified to provide the responses that the process itself would provide. Cogeneration is useful when it can be done by small modifications of the system under test. If major modifications are required, then one has built a simulator that happens to share software with the tested system.

An inherent difficulty in cogeneration is the problem of disentangling cause and effect—distinguishing between delays produced by the system being tested and delays internal to the generator itself (which result in timestamp errors). One solution is to bypass all processing in the generator that is not required for load generation or for data logging.

Self-Generation

This technique, used in communications systems, is applicable when input and output transactions are indistinguishable. Because an output message could be an input message coming in on some other communications line, one uses a combination of routing information in the data base and physical patches of lines in a loop to force messages to circulate in the system. Stable, controlled load can be generated in this way. And because communications systems are required to do extensive data logging, much of the data logging that would be required is done as a byproduct of normal message processing. A similar method can be used in process control systems; stability problems, however, at high, nearly saturated loads, can invalidate the results.

Real Loads

A real load is both the best and worst kind of load. Its best feature is that it does not compromise with reality. The load provides a proper measure of error conditions, anomalous cases, bursts, and so forth. It is difficult because far more data logging and instrumentation are required. A further difficulty is that it is hard to obtain reliable data over the entire range of load. However, because most systems once put into operation are not likely to be released for experimentation, the analysis of real loads becomes a part of most experimental programs and tuning efforts at some point in the system's life. To obtain data over the entire load range, it may be necessary to monitor the system around the clock (assuming it is in use 24 hours a day) and, furthermore, to monitor it for an entire week so that things like Friday afternoon rushes can be measured.

A further difficulty with real loads is that it is often impossible to force the system into saturation. The operators of a system used for credit card checking, say, would not tolerate artificially induced overloads in the interest of experimentation. Furthermore, because of the typical break at high loads, where the ultimate binding resource takes over, proper extrapolation of the system's capacity may not be possible. That is, it is dangerous to extrapolate linearly from the highest measured load if the binding resource has not been identified. One way out of this problem is to inject artificial load over-and-above the real load so that the system can be momentarily driven close to the limit.

The final difficulty with real loads is that the data are scattered. While data taken on test bed tend to follow subjective rate curves to within a fraction of a percent, real data tend to be scattered. The very realism of the load provides considerable variations in the statistical characteristics of the system's behavior, and only techniques like regression analysis

(see Section 19.7) can be used to determine what has happened. Breaks and gaps are represented by changes in regression coefficients, and the over-all scatter in the data may make this hard to see.

The ideal situation is to have the ability to run real loads, gather statistics on them, obtain crude indications of the system's behavior under real loads, and then to set up a controlled test bed in which to simulate that load.

19.5. INSTRUMENTATION

Purposes of Instrumentation

Instrumentation takes two principal forms: hardware and software. Hardware instrumentation is almost always augmented by some form of software instrumentation. Often, this combination is more effective than either of them alone. Either type of instrumentation may be used to measure or record:

1. Event logging.
2. Counts of events.
3. Duration of events and processes.
4. Sampling of events and states.

Event Logging.   An event is anything of interest in the context of system performance. Examples include interrupts, I/O operations, execution of specific programs or parts thereof, calls to subroutines, and so on. Assume for the moment that the occurrence of an event can be predetermined and recorded by means of software imbedded for the purpose. Logging an event consists of recording on some media, for subsequent analysis, all data pertinent to the event, including the time (to within a few milliseconds) the event occurred, and any other significant data—for example, register contents, system state, contents of memory locations, and so forth. An event log can be made as simple or as complex as one wishes. If software is used to log the event, then the processing time and resources required to do that recording must be considered. Any resource utilized to support instrumentation, be it processor execution of instructions, bus usage, I/O operations, or whatever, produces a distortion of the measurement process to the extent that resources are used. Such distortions are called *artifact*. The more elaborate the event log, the more artifacts are introduced by it. The extent of artifact is most noticeable in event logging because this tends to consume more resources than most other forms of instrumentation. Event logging highlights an instrumentation uncertainty principle: The more information you gather about an event, the more you distort the measurements.

Event Counting.   If an elaborate or simple event can be identified without much auxiliary data, then instead of logging the event, it may be sufficient to count the number of such events that occur in a predefined time period. For example, we are interested in keeping track of disc accesses. A copious log would contain the exact time at which an access occurred, whether it was a read or a write operation, the size of the transfer, and number of cylinders traversed. Alternatively, one could count the number of accesses to given cylinders or ranges of cylinders that occurred in a given time period. Much information is lost by this method, but artifact is reduced. Typically, event counts are accumulated either until specified counters fill up or until a specified time.

Duration of Events or Processes.   These can be measured directly, assuming that the system has either a hardware timer, software access to an external real-time clock, or a periodic clock interrupt. The event in question may be a program execution duration or the duration of disc accesses or other I/O activities. The start and stop of the event must be recognizable, and access to either an elapsed time counter or the clock can be used to determine the event's duration.

Sampling Events.   One powerful method for reducing artifact to an arbitrarily small level is to sample the data and events rather than to record them. Instead of recording the beginning and end of an event, one periodically (at a high-priority level triggered by a clock interrupt) examines hardware states or software states to see if the event is or is not in progress.

Artifact can be controlled by reducing the sample rate and by trading it for long elapsed time. For example, to determine the elapsed time of an event, say the execution of a specific routine, sample the program counter every 100 milliseconds and count the number of samples during which the program counter was within the memory location range appropriate to the routine being sampled. Knowing the sample rate and the percentage of hits allows one to deduce the percentage of time that the system was engaged in that program or subroutine. If furthermore, you know the execution time for the entire program, you can then determine the execution time for the sampled program. All sampling methods presume a predictable program that statistically repeats itself.

Software Instrumentation

The basic process of logging, counting, timing, and sampling can be accomplished by software means and is done by inserting code. Logging is the most artifact prone because many instructions may be needed to move the data to an output buffer for transfer to another media for off-line analysis and evaluation.

Controls.   Software instrumentation, because it is artifact inducing, cannot be inserted wholesale into a program lest the program spend most of its time processing artifact rather than doing "honest" work. As a result of this need to reduce artifact, it is necessary to provide means to limit it—to turn the software instrumentation probe on or off. Some examples follow:

1. Conditional Logic.   Instrumentation code is fitted with bypass control logic (e.g., flags), and control software is provided to turn the flags on or off. To obtain the measurements with minimum artifact, all but one probe, say, are turned off and the run repeated for each probe—as many times as necessary to obtain sufficient data. This method is relatively artifact-free, but caution must be used in systems with cache memories and instruction lookahead. Such systems may have different execution times with the probe active instead of inactive. Paged systems may also provide distorted measurements because the activation or deactivation of the probe may increase or decrease page boundary crossings or working set statistics.

2. Conditional Assembly or Compilation. Some compilers and assemblers permit tagging of statements or instructions for conditional assembly or compilation. The source code (in whatever language) contains the software instrumentation of interest, but only the specified part is assembled or compiled. The unused code is not included in the object program. The user must then prepare as many object versions of the program or system as there are cases to measure and must repeat the run as with conditional logic. As with conditional logic, there are possibilities of artifact that will not guarantee an artifact-free measurement. For example, an optimizing compiler may take a different strategy depending on whether the conditionally compiled probe is active or inactive. Cache memory operations may change; page boundaries may change, as may the working set.

3. Patching. Object code patching provides the greatest control for the most effort. It is possible, given an object level understanding of the program being instrumented to avoid the artifact induction possible in conditional logic or conditional compilation. A nonconditional branch to the next instruction in sequence is replaced by a nonconditional branch to a patch area where the instrumentation software is implemented. Because it is done by object-level patching, page boundary changes, register usage changes, working set changes, and so forth can be avoided (although cache memory artifact might not be avoided), and the additional processing time and resources consumed by the instrumentation software can be identified and analyzed.

Event-Logging Software. Events are logged by inserting code at those points in the program where events can be recognized. The logged information can be anything from a simple event count to an entire memory dump (as an extreme). Events are recorded in a buffer, which is written out to media when full. A time tag may be used for individual events or for the entire buffer. The buffer is used to minimize artifact by taking advantage of the efficiency of large block transfers to a disc, for instance. Fixed-length buffers are typical.

Elaborate logging is to be avoided in software instrumentation because it distorts the system's behavior. The best thing to do is to use normal by-product historical data in lieu of special logs. In many systems, accounting information (as in a time-shared system) can provide much of the data that would be obtained by elaborate special logs. Often, event logging is available as a by-product of the operating system's normal functioning. When logging is not inherent in the system's operation, it is best to keep logging as simple as possible even if this means extensive off-line processing. Binary information is kept in binary in the log. Superfluous data may be written into the log to avoid on-line extraction of that information.

Event-Counting Software. This instrumentation can be considered a simple form of log. Each time the event of interest occurs, the appropriate counter is incremented. If you are instrumenting a single program, then counter sizes can be set to allow for the worst case expected in a program run. A simple initialization routine (or equivalent declarations in the source code) initializes the counter values prior to the run. The counter's values are read out and recorded at the end of the run.

In on-line programs, the counters must either be periodically reset and recorded or the time at which the counter overflows must be recorded and logged as an event. In periodic resetting, all counter values are recorded in a buffer for logging and then reset to the appropriate initial value. This presumes access to a real-time clock. More elaborate systems will classify counters for different sample or reset rates. The overflow method requires logging the time at which the overflow occurs and is consequently more time- and resource-consuming for each individual counter. Also the off-line analysis is more complicated. If counters are maintained in a single block or array, then a single block transfer can be used to record the set of counters.

Event Duration Measurements. These measurements are a form of event logging for a pair of related events—the beginning and end of the event whose duration is measured. Event duration measurements presume access to an accurate time-of-day clock. Event duration can be measured more directly by modifying the clock interrupt handler. Say that the program operates at a low-priority level, while there is a clock interrupt routine (say every 10 milliseconds) that operates at a high-priority level. When the event is initiated at the low-priority level, a flag is set in a control array. When the event is concluded, the flag is reset. The clock interrupt routine now increments a corresponding counter for every flag that is active when the clock interrupt was being processed. The counters are then treated as event counters. When the event is concluded, the counter value is logged and the counter reset to await the next event. The more accurately one wants to time the event, the finer grained the clock interrupt will have to be and therefore the more artifact it will induce.

One of the inherent weaknesses of software event duration measurements is the uncertainty associated with such measurements. Most events occur at low-priority levels. There is no assurance (unless measures have been taken in the operating system or supervisory program) that the time recorded is the time at which the event took place. In event logging, this is not very important; but when a pair of event logs is used to measure the elapsed time of an event, the unknown time spent in higher-priority processing may induce additional uncertainties concerning the recorded time and the actual time at which the event started or ended. A method based on counting clock interrupts will typically not have an uncertainty greater than the interclock pulse duration.

Sampling Methods. Sampling methods, whether used for even counting, logging, or timing, can be the most accurate and can minimize artifact. Software instrumentation samples all events, counters, and so forth (although not all at the same rate). The probe point (i.e., the software instrumentation point) is used to set and reset event flags and increment and reset event counters. The sample is triggered by a periodic clock interrupt, and in accordance to coded instructions, all memory locations of interest are recorded. Efficiency is obtained by keeping such memory locations in a contiguous memory block.

Computers and operating systems with subroutines and/or priority stacks are particularly amenable to sampling methods. If the clock interrupt is operated at a high-priority level (the highest, say, except for hardware fault interrupts), the top of the stack can be sampled and the identity of the active routine (actually the routine that was active when the clock interrupt occurred) can be recorded. Typically, this is a program counter value. Subsequent off-line analysis, based on knowing the object level locations in which a subroutine lies, can then be used to determine which subroutine was executing when the interrupt occurred. Sufficient samples of this kind can be used to determine the effective elapsed time for all routines in the system. Depending on how much one wishes to incorporate of the program map, one can focus on individual routines, segments of programs, and the like. For example, three routines reside in locations 1776–2004, 2005–2151, and 2152–2200, respectively. After a specified period of time, 23% of the stack samples were in the first range, 54% in the second, and the rest in the third. Accuracy can be increased by increasing the number of accumulated counts. If means are provided to measure the execution time of the entire program, then the elapsed execution time for three routines can be accurately determined. Note that the artifact is constant and depends only on the processing done at the clock interrupt level. Because the program counter can only be in one location at the time the sample is made, the artifact is always the same, no matter what the system is doing—a constant amount for each clock interrupt. Note, however, that there is a considerable off-line software burden to map the recorded program counter ranges onto the identification of the routine. When software is relocatable or put into physical space by a re-locating loader, load information must be used to convert absolute stack values into program identities. Similarly, virtual memory systems complicate the issue if the stack contains physical, rather than virtual, addresses.

Sampling methods, then, provide the most accurate information and minimize artifact by repeated executions of the program. Sampling methods, however, require cooperation with utility software, operating systems, compilers, loaders, linkage editors, and complex off-line analytical packages to convert the sampled information into a useful form.

Hardware Instrumentation

Hardware Monitors.   A hardware monitor is typically a mini- or a microcomputer that has been fitted with high-impedance connectors that allow it to sample hardware elements within the computer that is being instrumented. For example, a probe connector placed on the system's bus allows one to monitor all events that are manifested on the bus. Connectors or probes are attached to the bus, I/O channels, memory data ports, memory address ports, interrupt lines, and so on. The connector or probe is a high-impedance device so that the hardware operation of the system being monitored is not affected. In principal, a hardware monitor is used in much the same way as software instrumentation is, the principal advantage being that the hardware monitor does not introduce artifact.

Event Detection.   Event detection in a software monitor is implicit. The programmer inserts instructions in the running program whose execution is dependent on the occurrence of the event. The logic associated with detection of the event can be, in the software monitor, as elaborate or as simple as circumstances require. Consequently, events detected by software monitors are meaningful from the point of view of application, but the price for this is that as the event becomes more meaningful, the artifact required to detect and record the event increases. This is the fundamental trade-off between hardware and software

monitors. Hardware monitors are free of artifact, but simplistic and limited.

Hardware monitors detect events by wired (plugboard) or programmed logic. Programmed logic in this context does not mean a normal computer's program, but the operation of a programmed logic device or microcode that can evaluate truth functions of a bit pattern. The idea behind a hardware monitor is to recognize events that occur at system bus speed or memory speed. Logic hardware detects the bit patterns traversing the probe lines and evaluates those patterns for a hit. The logic can range from simple masking, to ranges of values, to a combination of values or sequences of values. A list of examples follows:

1. Any memory address above 17777777.
2. A bus data line value between 234 and 236.
3. A memory data value of 12345671.
4. A bus sequence of Z C Z C.
5. A Boolean expression in line values.

Once detected, the event is logged and recorded. What happens subsequently depends on what the monitor has been programmed to do with that event, as discussed in subsequent sections.

The hardware-implemented logic is limited. Consequently, events with elaborate criteria must be recognized partially by the hardware and partially by software executed within the monitor. Often, this software is product line software and is provided with extensive "front-end" software to program the events to be detected. Although the execution of programs within the hardware monitor to extend the limited hardware logic is possible, such programs consume monitor resources. And even though the hardware monitor's operation does not create artifact in the program being measured, the hardware monitor is itself susceptible to saturation. For example, if it takes 20 microseconds of monitor CPU time to record an event, the monitor cannot record more than 50,000 events per second. If the hardware monitor is operated close to saturation, it, too, will run out of buffers, fall behind in time-tagging events, or otherwise fail to keep up with what it is recording. This is an indirect form of artifact which must be considered. As with software monitors, the answer may lie in splitting the measurements over several runs, with different probes activated in each run.

Event Logging. Event logging consists of detecting the event, time tagging it, and recording data for subsequent analysis. In the first two parts of this operation, the hardware monitor is superior. The event might be signalled by addressing a specific memory location, assuming that the monitor was monitoring the memory address bus. The artifact associated with time tagging the event that occurs in a software monitor does not exist. Typically, one attempts to get the memory address as a by-product of normal processing: that is, the event causes a jump to a specified location. The monitor detects the jump on the memory address lines. At worst, one has to insert a single instruction to write data to an arbitrary memory location reserved for the purpose.

If the data to be logged with the event is contiguous and appears on a channel, say, or will be transferred to specified (contiguous) memory locations without the monitor, then recording this data can be done with little or no artifact. If, however, it is necessary to move the data to get it recorded, then all the overhead that was associated with software data logging (except for event detection and time-tagging) remains. Hardware monitors are best suited to the detection and capture of data for simple events. Complex events are better handled by a software monitor scheme.

Event Counting. This is the region in which the hardware monitor's superiority is clear. Instead of time tagging the event, the monitor (under monitor software/hardware control) increments (decrements) specified counter(s) in the monitor's memory when the event is detected. Software in the monitor resets the counters in accordance to programmed schedules and criteria (e.g., periodic reset, reset on overflow, etc.).

Event Duration Measurement. Two events are required in event duration measurement.

An event must be detected that initiates a timer, and another that terminates the timer. The timer is updated at specified rates by the monitor software. For example, the first event is the detection of the I/O instruction that initiates the disc seek operation on the disc channel. The second event might be the detection of the seek-complete interrupt associated with the same channel. The first event is programmed to start the counter and the latter to stop the counter. Whereas most counters are programmed and implemented in monitor memory, some monitors use hardware counters and are consequently fast but limited. The completion of the time measurement causes the event, the time, and the completion time-tag to be recorded.

Internal Events. The typical monitor is a minicomputer. It can, therefore, detect and record internal events. For example, one can specify that event duration measurements be recorded in a set of counters that are used to record a distribution of, say, seek times. Monitor software, on-line, checks the range of the time interval and increments the associated counters. As with software monitors, there is no limit to sophistication other than monitor resources and monitor saturation.

Sampling Methods. Sophisticated monitors can be programmed to turn probes on and off and can therefore be used to sample events, thereby reducing the probability of monitor saturation. Just what can be sampled depends on the monitor's logic ability, and the architecture of the system it is monitoring. For example, microcomputers offer few opportunities to insert probes into the system. Conversely, large mainframe machines may be fitted with probes on ALUs, cache memory, and so forth, including hardware elements that are not directly monitorable by pure software techniques.

Monitor Data Processing. On-line processing and reduction of data gathered by a hardware monitor is minimized for the same reasons that such processing is avoided in software monitoring schemes—increased artifact and artificially low saturation. On-line data processing in hardware monitors is also avoided for another reason. Typically, the hardware monitor is based on a mini- or microcomputer. Consequently, its processing ability is limited (either on-line or off-line). The typical approach is to record the data on industry-compatible media and then to run all analytical software off-line in a machine that supports FORTRAN, say, whose power is considerably greater than that of the hardware monitor's computer. In this respect, the hardware monitor is the same as the software monitor. Data reduction is treated in Section 19.7.

19.6. THE EXPERIMENTAL PROCESS

Software performance measurement whether done by hardware or software monitors is an experimental process, and thus its success depends on the extent to which the experiment can be controlled. A controlled test-bed devoted to the experiment is ideal but almost never exists. The key to a successful measurement enterprise is control over variables, and barring that, full recording of all significant events.

Preparation

Measurement should be scheduled in advance. Most systems will require several thousand data points sampled over a period of a typical operational cycle. Because most systems operate on a weekly cycle, with low activity at night and peak activity toward the end of the week, it is necessary to arrange a full week's worth of data gathering to assure a statistically meaningful result. The measurements should be scheduled in advance. Unusual activities such as special runs, operating system changes, major data base changes, and so on should be avoided, similarly, for hardware changes and maintenance.

All hardware and software instrumentation used, recording techniques, data logging, and so forth should be debugged in advance of the measurement session. All such sessions tend to disrupt the on-going operations to some extent, and if an instrumentation bug invalidates the data gathered, a long time may pass before the

system is again available for experimentation. Short test runs of instrumentation and data-logging hardware and/or software should be attempted and carried through to final data reduction prior to the actual measurements. Immediately before the measurements are undertaken, the system's patch log should be examined to confirm that no changes have been made between the test run and the actual run that could affect the validity of the gathered data.

Conduct of Tests

The extent to which a test observer is required depends on the quality of the operations logs. If logs are copious, detailed, and explicit, and if all operator actions are logged, then it is not necessary to have an observer present during the data gathering. Attention to this kind of detail is important because in most instances, there will be some data points that must be discarded because of unusual circumstances that do not reflect the system's typical load.

A backup copy should be made of the source data even though considerable processing may follow. Errors may creep into the analysis and it may be necessary to go back to the raw data to validate it. If the data is being gathered for the first time, the raw data should be examined daily for reasonableness. Part of the analysis should be carried out to assure that what is gathered is what is wanted. A preliminary analysis of this kind may reveal gross problems that obviate further data gathering because conclusions regarding the system's performance or tuning may be obvious. Similarly, erratic behavior may indicate hardware or software problems that must be rectified before work can be done.

How Much Data and How Often

The instrumentation may gather data every few milliseconds or every second, but such detailed information is too fine-grained to be useful. Such measurements should be accumulated and averaged over a period of time (on-line) to yield a data point. Data points should be recorded at an interval which is long compared to the typical transaction's sojourn time (time-in to time-out). A recording interval of 10 to 20 times the length of a transaction's sojourn is a useful rule-of-thumb. For example, a data base inquiry system clears a typical transaction in 10 seconds—accumulates the data over a 2 minute interval and stores the summary every 2 minutes. The sojourn must be measured from the initiation of the transaction to its conclusion. If, for example, a terminal operates at 10 characters per second, and the typical input consists of 1,000 characters, then the sojourn time should include the 100 seconds it took to get the transaction in and the 100 seconds it took to get it out.

Long sample periods smooth the data out, making interpretation easier. Short periods of peak activity, however, will be smeared over, and valuable peak data will be lost. The long period also reduces the number of data points gathered, which can affect the conclusions drawn from the measurements. Very short sample periods do capture crucial peaks, but also a lot of noise. Furthermore, the resulting data are so scattered that it is difficult to draw "eyeball" conclusions on which to guide the subsequent analysis.

Enough data points (i.e., one minute samples) should be gathered to allow a statistically valid analysis whose results vary by not more than 10% at 90% confidence. That is, the probability that the real result is within 10% of the predicted result is 0.9. Typically, this requires from 500 to 1,000 points. For analytical reasons discussed below, more than half of these points will be discarded. Consequently, on the order of 2,000 data points will be needed. Conversely, in a controlled test-bed, valid results can be achieved with a few hundred points. Some systems have such regular behavior on the test-bed that it is possible to evaluate performance on the basis of a few dozen points.

Data Format and Transformation

Almost all analyses are based on the use of regression analysis and similar curve-fitting techniques. The computer used to do the analysis is often not the same as the computer being measured. For example, a telecommunications system cannot be interrupted, nor may it have the necessary software packages to support the analysis. If the computer used for analysis is the same as that which is being measured, compatibility problems do not exist. Unfortunately, because the analysis computer is often not the same, the data must be formatted, converted to another media, or otherwise transferred to the analysis computer. At worst, it might be necessary to manually key the data into the analysis computer. At best, media conversion and/or reformatting may be necessary to make the sojourn data compatible with the analysis computer. When a hardware monitor is used, the data gathered by it is invariably incompatible in format and media to the computer being measured and to the computer used for analysis.

19.7. DATA REDUCTION AND ANALYSIS

Tools

A small, technical computer is an indispensable tool. The computer should have the following capabilities:

1. Random access storage of at least 100k characters.
2. A scientific language and associated processors such as extended Basic, Fortran, or Pascal.
3. High-quality graphics with hard-copy printing.
4. The ability to store and operate (e.g., invert) at least a 10×10 matrix. At least two, possibly three, such arrays may have to be stored.
5. A minimum of 10 digits of floating-point arithmetic with a 2 digit mantissa.
6. A debugged library of statistical, regression analysis, and graphics packages.
7. Some means of inputting or translating the source data.

The importance of high-quality software cannot be overstated. In some cases, the data will lead to the inversion of near-singular matrices. If the software is not robust, the results of the analysis may be meaningless. If new software is constructed for the analysis, or if existing packages are modified for the purpose, the software should be debugged using old data that has been previously analyzed or by using well-constructed test cases.

Preliminary Analysis

A typical set of data consists of several hundred to a few thousand data points. Each data point consists of a dependent variable, such as the transaction delay or its reciprocal, and several independent variables such as the arrival rates for various transactions and resource utilization counts. The object of the analysis is to establish a relationship between throughput and delay. But throughput is usually the sum of several different transaction types, each of which makes different demands on the system's resources.

Are the Numbers Sensible? Add the throughput rates of the various transactions to get an over-all throughput for each data point. Plot the reciprocal of the delay (subjective rate) against the throughput for all data points. Plot the resource utilization levels for all important resources against throughput.

The purpose of this preliminary examination of the data is to assure that the data make sense. Gross computational errors will be caught at this stage. If the data exhibit several different populations that are isolated from one another, there may be problems with the data or the system may be ill-tuned. Any systematic grouping of points, such as repeating gaps in either the dependent or independent variable (sawtooth data), should be investigated for potential problems. The most important question to ask is, do the numbers make sense? Do the numbers represent physically realizable behavior? Look for outlying points, that is, data points that appear to stand out from the crowd. Check such points against the operations log to see if something unusual was going on at the time. If groupings of data correspond to different operational modes and that fact can be verified, then it will be necessary to split the analysis and evaluate the system's performance separately in each mode.

It may not be possible to answer such questions or to draw any conclusion from this preliminary evaluation because the data could be scattered. A lot of scatter does not mean that the data are poor, but that more than one factor influences the system's response to throughput. The scatter appears because a function of two or more variables is being forced onto a two dimensional plane.

Eyeballing. The throughput-delay curve, or better yet, the subjective rate curve can be extrapolated by drawing an "eyeball" regression line as in Figure 19.3. Unfortunately, this is often the point where some analyses stop. Such eyeball curves are unreliable. If, as is typical, there is a lot of scatter to the points, eyeball regression lines can lead to an extrapolation that is valid only over a 4 to 1 range. If the object of the analysis is to show that the system cannot, at best, reach a certain throughput with an adequate delay, or alternatively, to show that at worst a certain minimal performance will be met, then eyeballing, while dangerous, may be adequate.

The primary purpose of eyeballing the data is to achieve a qualitative understanding of the system's behavior and to establish working upper and lower bounds on the performance and/or the importance of various parameters. Eyeballing may show that additional data must be gathered, or that there are previously unsuspected behavioral anomalies or system bugs that must be investigated and corrected before further analysis is possible.

Data Transformation and Scaling

An initial processing pass is done to scale and/or transform the data to usable units. For example, a hardware monitor and an internal software monitor do not measure the data in the same way. The two sets of data must be merged and made compatible. Outlying points caused by abnormal system operation, as verified by the logs, must be removed. If data were input manually, keypunch errors must be corrected. Further transformation may be required to put the data into the format required by the regression analysis package. A transformation and extraction package is essential and should have the ability to:

1. Examine any source-point by point-number.
2. List all the data associated with a point or with a specified range of points.
3. Edit any point.
4. Do simple linear transformations of the form $Y = a + bX$. This may be needed to scale data to common units.
5. Extract data based on the values of any variable—that is, from the source data file, extract based on, say, variable number 1, all values within specified bounds.
6. Plot the results of the extraction.

If a typical analysis requires 1,000 points and each point consists of 10 numbers that require 8 characters of storage each, one such data set will require in excess of 80,000 characters of storage. A typical analysis may require 10 such files.

First-Cut Regression

Regression Analysis. A linear regression analysis fits a straight line through a set of data points. If the independent variable is a function of two dependent variables, then the linear regression analysis fits a plane through the set of points—similarly, for higher dimensions. Almost all regressions are based on the "least squares error" fit. That is, the line (plane, hyperplane, etc.) is chosen such that the sum of the squares of the differences between the plane and the actual values of the point is minimized. A linear regression analysis, therefore, expresses the value of the dependent variable (say, subjective rate) as a function of the various independent variables.

$$Y = a_0 + a_1X_1 + a_2X_2 \\ + a_3X_3 + \cdots + a_iX_i$$

The a_i are the regression coefficients that result from the analysis. A proper regression analysis package also provides a measure of how well the regression surface fits the data. Several such measures are in common use. Details can be found in the references.

First-Cut Analysis. The first-cut analysis is done by using a linear fit over all the data to establish which coefficients are most important. The coefficients, if properly scaled, define the apparent mean processing time per transaction for each transaction type. The constant term a_0 is a measure of the apparent overhead. The coefficients of the first-cut analysis should be examined and reconciled with what is known about the system's behavior. Remember that the value of these coefficients does not represent CPU time, but an agglomeration of CPU time, wait time, I/O time, and so forth. The purpose of this initial analysis is again qualitative. Does it make sense that transaction type 2 takes five times longer to process than transaction type 5? Often it is possible to identify the binding factor or factors on the basis of such a simple analysis.

In addition to the major regression of delay versus throughput, the following regression analyses should be done:

1. I/O time divided by throughput versus throughput.
2. Disc activity time versus throughput.
3. Resource utilizations versus throughput.

The objective of each of these additional analyses is to obtain a measure of what the per-transaction utilization of all factors is and how that utilization changes with increasing throughput. Generally, per-transaction resource utilizations should remain constant over a wide throughput range, with a slight tendency to decrease with increasing throughput as the system gains efficiency through amortizing the overhead over more transactions.

Data Culling

The ideal data consist of uniformly distributed points over the entire throughput range, that is, as many points taken at low loads as are taken at high loads. This is not achievable because most systems exhibit large diurnal load variations. Consequently, the data tend to be biased toward low throughput regions, which because of the typical system's behavior, will lead to an optimistic extrapolation of the system's capacity. The data should be culled to remove the surplus of low throughput points. This must not be done manually lest inadvertent bias creep in.

A data extraction program should be used to select points at random based on the distribution of values for the variable used as a selection key. Suppose that throughput is used as the selection criterion. Plot the probability frequency function for throughput—it will typically have an exponential distribution. Establish a cut-off probability and extract points using a random number generator. The random number generator produces a number between 0 and 1. Compare that random number (for each data point) to the cut-off probability divided by the distribution probability for that throughput value. If the random number is less than the specified ratio, the point is retained; if greater, the point is discarded. All points for which the distribution probability is less than the cut-off probability will be retained, while throughput values that have an excess of points will be cut down in a proportion that will make the distribution of values tend to a uniform distribution. A typical file of 2,000 points will be culled to 750 points by this method. Very low and high throughput values will not be lost. It may pay to do this culling several times and to carry the analysis through for several different files produced this way to assure the consistency of the results.

Piece-wise and Polynomial Fits

Piece-wise Fits.   Because systems tend to exhibit breaks as different binding resources assert themselves, a single linear fit is rarely adequate. The typical system should be fit with two or three straight-line segments. There are several ways to do this:

1. The break is evident in the plotted data. Note that the break may not be visible on a throughput-delay plot or even on a subjective rate versus throughput plot. It may, however, be visible on a plot of memory resource utilization versus throughput because of the multiplicative effect of the transaction arrival rate and holding time for memory resources. If such breaks are evident, subdivide the data file into regions bound by the breaks and analyze each separately.

2. Search for the break. The break may not be obvious because of excessive scatter. Split the file in half and analyze each separately. Note significant differences in the coefficients, particularly the constant term (a_0) because it is the most sensitive indicator of a slope change that the break represents. If a difference is found, split one side and try again. Continuing this way, you find the break by successive binary halving. Alternatively, there are packages that will do this kind of searching.

3. Use a polynomial regression (see below) and analytically determine the point of maximum curvature change to detect the presence of a break.

Polynomial Regression.   A regression analysis package can be used to do a nonlinear curve fit of a restricted kind. New variables are created that are a function of the original variables such that the resulting analysis is linear in the new variables. For example, if we want to fit a polynomial of the form:

$$Y = a_0 + a_1X + a_2X^2 + a_3X^3 \ldots$$

which is not linear, transform the problem to a new set of variables:

$$Y = a_0 + a_1Z_1 + a_2Z_2 + a_3Z_3 \ldots$$

where

$$Z_1 = X, Z_2 = X^2, Z_3 = X^3 \ldots$$

While Y is not a linear function of X, it is a linear function of the transformed variables Z_1, Z_2, Z_3. Similar transformations such as $Z = \ln(X)$, e^x, and so on can be used to linearize many nonlinear functions. Many regression packages contain facilities for making commonly used transformations. Polynomial regression programs contain additional capabilities that allow one to select that polynomial that best fits the data. Polynomial regressions are useful for finding breaks that would not otherwise be obvious. They can also be used to track nonlinear increases in resource utilizations or in processing that can result from bugs.

If one's analysis is based on the use of throughput versus delay, which is nonlinear, one will be forced to use polynomial regressions. The use of the subjective rate function (reciprocal of delay), then, is just a linearizing transformation. This is preferable to using a polynomial fit because it eliminates unnecessary variables, thereby leaving room in the analysis for additional variables.

If polynomial regressions are used, it is important to plot the entire polynomial over the range of throughput to assure that it is physically sensible. Polynomials are amoral and won't hesitate to produce physically meaningless coefficients that fit the data well. This danger increases with an increasing number of terms. Inherent nonlinearities in computer systems take the form of a square law (as in an inefficient sort or search routine), $N\ln N$, or $1/(1 - p)$. Cubic behavior of processing time per transaction, say, with increasing throughput, is rare. Generally, even-numbered exponents are better than odd, except for the first linear term. A good polynomial regression package will indicate which terms dominate and how much the fit is improved through incorporating yet higher-degree terms.

Nonlinear Fits. All nonlinear fits, such as $N\ln(N)$, $1/(1 - p)$, or e^x, should be based on a preliminary analysis of the system's behavior to serve as a guide to what functions are likely to work. Exponentials, while a favorite of the novice (because "it looks exponential") rarely have a basis in system behavior and consequently are not usually good candidates. Because the regression is done on linearized variables, the regression package can be used to select which of several alternative linearization functions will yield the best fit to the data. Therefore, a combination of direct linear, polynomial, and other forms of nonlinear transformations can be used to establish a model of the

system's behavior. Nonlinear regressions should be used sparingly because:

1. Each transformation, particularly polynomials, adds to the number of variables in the regression equations. Processing goes up as the second or third power of the number of variables. A simple analysis based on a half-dozen variables might take a few seconds of processing time, but the same analysis done on a fourth order polynomial for each variable could take days.
2. Increasing the number of variables increases the danger of round-off errors and meaningless, though precise, results. The typical regression analysis package, even with double precision arithmetic, is marginally accurate for more than 20 variables.
3. A sensible analysis is more useful than a good fit. The objective is not to get a good fit to the data points but to get a meaningful model. N data points can always be fit perfectly by an $N - 1$ order polynomial.

Finer-grained Analysis and Tuning

A good model is a prerequisite to tuning. A good model fits the known data to $\pm 15\%$ at 50% confidence. The initial analysis is done to obtain the relation between delay and resource utilization as a function of throughput. Tuning is based on determining, for each throughput, the resource utilization per unit transaction. Most tuning problems are exhibited by a nonsensible behavior in this unit resource utilization, for example, increasing and then decreasing processing time per transaction, discontinuous changes in resource utilization per transaction, and so forth.

Once overall behavior has been established, it is possible to bring in more detailed data. For example, processing time is measured for several of the more important processing routines. Overall processing time is then removed from the analysis and replaced by the several subsidiary processing components. Separate regressions can be done to determine how each component fares with increasing load; similarly, for I/O time and memory utilization. The possibilities are unlimited, however most tuning problems can be spotted without resort to complicated analyses.

Dangers of Extrapolation

Extrapolation is required when there is insufficient high-load data to determine the system's ultimate capacity. All extrapolation is an act of faith that expresses a belief in the status quo, that is, the belief that the system's behavior will continue linearly (after appropriate linearization of variables) out to the ultimate point. Because the binding factors at low throughput may mask the ultimate binding factor, we have no assurance that the system will not have yet another sharp break in the throughput region for which there is no data. There are statistical methods that can be used to establish the degree of confidence one can have on such extrapolations, but such means are also based on the assumption that there will be no sharp behavioral break, which is contrary to the observed behavior of systems. If extrapolation is the object of the analysis and of the data gathering, the following suggestions are helpful:

1. Be sure of the legal ramifications of the extrapolation and the possible direct and consequential damages associated with it.
2. Be copious with caveats regarding any conclusions drawn from the extrapolation. Being statistically meticulous is not enough.
3. Take additional data during peak period, if necessary.
4. Do additional runs with a shorter sample time. With the previous analysis as a base, it will be possible to see through the noise induced by the shorter sample.
5. Try to arrange to inject artificial loads during peak periods to force the system into saturation; this eliminates extrapolation altogether, but it is difficult to get users to agree to that kind of experiment.

BIBLIOGRAPHY

Organizations and Periodicals

1. Computer Measurement Group, Box 34578, Bethesda, Maryland, 20034.
   Professional society that sponsors annual conventions and symposia, local chapter meetings, and so on. The journal is devoted to performance analysis and measurement.
2. *Computer Performance*. IPC Science and Technology Press. Haywood Heath, Sussex, UK.
   Journal devoted to performance analysis, measurement, and modeling.
3. *EPD Performance Review*. Applied Computer Research, Phoenix, Arizona.
   Monthly journal that publishes abstracts, reviews, and short articles devoted to computer performance. Most valuable is an annual survey of performance-related hardware and software products. The survey lists several hundred products produced by more than a hundred vendors. This is probably the most easily accessible and complete guide to available products.
4. IEEE (Institute for Electrical and Electronic Engineers).
   Performance-related articles are published mostly under the aegis of the IEEE computer society in the IEEE Transactions on Computers and the IEEE Transactions on Software Engineering. Other related performance studies are often published in the IEEE Transactions on Communications and the IEEE Transactions on Reliability.
5. *Performance Evaluation*. North Holland Publishing, Amsterdam.
   Quarterly journal devoted to system and network performance.
6. *Performance Evaluation Review*. ACM Special Interest Group on Measurement and Evaluation (SIGMETRICS).
   Quarterly newsletter covering all aspects of performance analysis, simulation, and modeling. Announcement of pertinent conferences. Case studies.

Books

1. Beilner, H. and Gelenbe, E. eds. *Measuring Modeling and Performance Evaluation of Computer Systems*. Amsterdam: North Holland, 1977.
   Conference proceedings of an international workshop on performance evaluation, 1976. Statistical methods and many case studies.
2. Beizer, Boris. *Micro-Analysis of Computer System Performance*. New York: Van Nostrand Reinhold, 1978.
   General text on analytical modeling of systems with emphasis on models derived from program code. Treatment of cyclic systems, queuing network models, latency models, tuning, and measurement.

3. Benwell, Nicholas. *Benchmarking: Computer Evaluation and Measurement.* New York: John Wiley and Sons, 1975.
Conference proceedings all about benchmarking, instruction mixes, etc.

4. Borovits, Israel, and Neumann, Seev. *Computer System Performance Evaluation.* Lexington, Mass.: Lexington Books, 1979.
Readable introduction to performance measurement, analysis, organization of studies, and cost-benefit analyses.

5. Bunyan, C. J., ed. *Computer Systems Measurement: Infotech State of the Art Report No. 18.* Maidenhead, Berks., SL61LD, UK.: Infotech International Ltd., 1974.
A panel of experts discussing system performance, analysis, simulation, and tuning. An excellent overview.

6. Carnahan, B., Luther, H. A., and Wilkes, J. O. *Applied Numerical Methods.* New York: John Wiley and Sons, 1969.
A big book with lots of information on regression analysis methods. Programs, flowcharts, listings. A good source book.

7. Daniel, C., Wood, F. S., and Gorman, J. W. *Fitting Equations to Data.* New York: Wiley Interscience, 1971.
An excellent introduction to the subject of regression analysis with many examples worked out in detail. This book goes further than most performance studies are likely to need.

8. Draper, N., and Smith, H. *Applied Regression Analysis, Second Edition.* New York: John Wiley and Sons, 1981.
A very big book (more than 700 pages). A survey of the entire field of regression analysis covering theory and practice. A primary reference.

9. Drummand, M. E. Jr. *Evaluation and Measurement Techniques for Digital Computer Systems.* Englewood Cliffs, N.J.: Prentice-Hall, 1973.
Introduction to performance analysis and measurement. Use of benchmarks, simulation, and hardware and software instrumentation is discussed in detail.

10. Ferrari, D. *Computer System Performance Evaluation.* Englewood Cliffs, N.J.: Prentice-Hall, 1978.
Overview of the field including measurement, simulation, analytical models, computer selection, tuning, and design.

11. Freiberger, W., ed. *Statistical Computer Performance Evaluation.* New York: Academic Press, 1972.
Collection of articles from 1971 conference proceedings on statistical computer performance evaluation.

12. Gilb, T. *Software Metrics.* Cambridge, Mass.: Winthrop Publishers, 1977.
Measurement of software performance in the broad sense including reliability, and maintainability in addition to throughput-delay. Much philosophy and guidance related to the value of additional performance vis-a-vis its actual or potential cost.

13. Hellerman, H., and Conroy, T. F. *Computer System Performance.* New York: McGraw-Hill, 1975.
Survey of the field, strong statistical introduction, queuing theory, modeling, application to OS-360, time sharing, and virtual memory systems.

14. Kuo, S. S. *Numerical Methods and Computers.* Reading, Mass.: Addison-Wesley, 1965.
Source book on numerical analysis aimed at computer solutions. Flowcharts and listings.

15. Morris, M., and Roth, P. F. *Computer Performance Evaluation.* New York: Van Nostrand Reinhold, 1982.
Management of performance evaluation activity, monitors, benchmarking, with a commercial data processing orientation.

16. Spirn, J. R. *Program Behavior: Models and Measurement.* New York: Elsevier North-Holland, 1977.
Emphasis on analysis, measurement, and modeling of page-fault problems, thrashing, and other virtual memory system performance problems.

17. Svobodova, L. *Computer Performance Measurement and Evaluation Methods: Analysis and Application.* New York: American Elsevier, 1976.

20

Software Fault Tolerance

K. H. Kim

Computer Science Department
University of South Florida

20.1. INTRODUCTION

The insufficient reliability of computer systems employed in certain critical areas is becoming a major national concern. Serious incidents have occurred in defense, transportation, and financial management applications (e.g., see Ref. 1). There is no question about the attractiveness of the so-called *fault-tolerant computer systems* in many of those applications. Fault-tolerant computer systems are defined here as systems capable of recovering from failures of their hardware or software components to provide uninterrupted real-time service. In particular, fault-tolerant hardware, partly boosted by the continuously declining cost of hardware modules, has become a commonly accepted means of achieving the desired reliability in safety-critical applications [2-8].

It is the software reliability problem, though, that increasingly concerns computer system designers dealing with critical applications [9-13]. The advances in reliable software engineering technology are not keeping up with the steadily increasing size and complexity of the required software systems. The increasing popularity of distributed computing systems adds an additional dimension to the software reliability problem [14-16]. Spurred by the current infeasibility of complete validation of sizable software, the application of fault tolerance notions to software has become a subject of growing interest [6, 17-23].

It is important to understand that *software fault tolerance* is not meant to replace other reliable software engineering techniques such as formal specification, correctness proof, system-

atic testing, and so forth, but is meant to supplement them. In other words, software fault tolerance is aimed at containing the damaging effects of residual design errors that have gone undetected through all the rigorous design and validation stages. Error removal at design time is always preferable to error control at runtime. The software fault tolerance approach is based on the pessimistic but pragmatic view that large-scale programs, more often than not, will be put into operation with residual design errors.

The fundamental vehicle for realizing fault-tolerant computing is redundancy. Since software faults are all caused by design errors (unlike hardware faults, which may be caused by either physical material characteristics or design errors or both), extensive use of design redundancy is a basic means of achieving software fault tolerance. Extra design efforts result in a program containing redundancy that, in theory, would be useless if both the design process and the processing machine were guaranteed to be free of faults. Basically, a *fault-tolerant program* contains multiple routines that are produced from "independent" designs based on a common specification and thus aimed at computing the same objective function. If these routines use distinct algorithms, it is less likely that the same design error will exist in all of the routines that compute the function.

In the next section, useful types of program redundancy as well as the cost of using them are discussed. Section 20.3 deals with the issues involved in execution of fault-tolerant programs, in particular, the orderly interaction between hardware and software as well as the interaction among software components during error detection and recovery. Section 20.4 deals with the recovery block scheme, developed at the University of Newcastle upon Tyne, England [21, 24], for design and execution of fault-tolerant programs. Language constructs, supporting machine structures, and some design guidelines are reviewed. In Section 20.5 the relationship between software fault tolerance and exception handling is discussed. Section 20.6 then deals with the problems involved in providing fault tolerance capabilities in concurrent programs and reviews some proposed solutions.

20.2. PROGRAM REDUNDANCY

Types of Program Redundancy

Program redundancy can be used in many different forms to achieve fault tolerance. In Reference 24, Horning et al. identified three major types of program redundancy useful for achieving software fault tolerance: (1) *acceptance tests* or *error checks* [12, 22, 25] which check the reasonableness or acceptability of intermediate results during program execution, (2) *alternate try routines* which are invoked to compute the same objective function in different ways when the result produced by the primary try routine is rejected, and (3) *restoration routines* which, when invoked on rejection of a result by an acceptance test, restore the system to a "consistent" state where a retry or the execution of the rest of the program could start.

As a simple example, consider a program component SQRT that accepts positive real numbers and computes their square roots. SQRT contains two different algorithms for computing the function, one of which is designated as the primary try routine. SQRT also contains an acceptance test which consists essentially of squaring the result of the algorithm used and then comparing it to the operand input. Therefore, even if the primary try routine contains a residual design error, SQRT can successfully provide the service as long as

the alternate try routine is correct. Once the output of the primary try routine is rejected by the acceptance test, the computation state must be brought back to the state that existed at the beginning of the primary try so that the alternate try routine may be executed. This may include restoring some variables modified by the failed routine to the values that existed before modification. In many cases, this restoration action, also called a *program rollback,* can be handled automatically by the underlying machine [26–30]. This state restoration will be discussed in more detail in Section 20.4.

Cost of Program Redundancy

The use of program redundancy is not without cost, incurred largely in three different forms. First, program redundancy requires *design redundancy,* that is, the additional efforts required for designing redundant program components [31, 32]. Second, it requires *hardware redundancy,* primarily in the form of memory space (and possibly additional processors [28, 33]) for containing and executing redundant program components. Third, it requires *execution time redundancy,* that is, an increase in execution time because of incorporation of redundant program components.

Therefore, fault-tolerant programs generally have a high development cost and a higher execution cost than conventional programs. One way of reducing the development cost is to utilize methodologies and tools for systematic incorporation of redundancy in a well-structured form. Since the use of program redundancy increases the program size, good structure is particularly important in fault-tolerant programs.

The high execution cost of fault-tolerant programs is due to the increased processor time and increased storage space required for executing redundant program components. For example, to provide a restoration capability requires processor time and storage space for recording and retaining some histories of computation (i.e., saving of system states at various points in program execution) [27, 30, 34, 35]. Execution of error checks in fault-tolerant programs can also contribute to a large execution time. Some architectures aiming at the reduction of execution time and/or storage space have been proposed; they are reviewed in Section 20.4.

20.3. SYSTEM STRUCTURE FOR SOFTWARE FAULT TOLERANCE

Hardware-Software Interaction

The first step in fault tolerance is obviously error detection. One of the basic problems in implementing software fault tolerance is to distinguish between the errors caused by software faults and the errors caused by hardware faults. Distinguishability depends largely on the types of *error detection hardware* employed in the system. For example, the Fault-Tolerant Spaceborne Computer (FTSC) is equipped with a considerable amount of hardware redundancy that includes a CPU monitor, monitors for the codes carried on the buses, memory code checkers, watchdog timers, and other error detection hardware [3, 36, 37, 38]. The extensive set of error detection hardware is capable of detecting most of the hardware faults almost instantaneously so that the effects of the faults can not propagate to other parts of the system. Even so there are some hardware faults that escape the watch of the error detection hardware and lead to errors that have to be caught by *error detection software routines*. Such errors cannot be easily distinguished from software-caused errors.

Therefore, once an error is detected by an error detection software routine (i.e., an acceptance test), it is generally impossible to determine the source of the error without further diagnosis. Since software runs on hardware, the latter should be checked first to see if any of its components has failed. If a failed hardware component is found, a reconfiguration or a repair action should follow to bring the hardware to an operational state. Thereafter follows a program rollback, that is, a restoration of the program to the state that existed on initiation of the previously executed try routine, and then the same try routine can be reexecuted.

This is because the failed hardware component is suspected as the cause of the error detected by the acceptance test, and the hardware component is now operational. On the other hand, if no failed hardware component is found, then either software faults or transient hardware faults are suspected to be the cause of the detected error [37]. Determining which of the two is the exact source requires a retry with the previously executed try routine. If software faults are the cause, then a retry would again result in a rejection by the acceptance test. However, the attempt to distinguish between software faults and transient hardware faults that went undetected by error detection hardware may not always be worthwhile. Even when transient hardware faults are caught by error detection hardware, there is no harm done by simply carrying out a hardware checkout, a program rollback, and a retry with another try routine. In other words, both software faults and transient hardware faults, however detected, may be handled in the same way.

Sometimes errors caused by software faults may be caught by specialized error detection hardware in the machine, for instance, illegal operation-code detector, data type checker, illegal address detector, and so forth [29, 38, 39]. Again such error detection must be followed by a hardware checkout since in principle the same errors can be caused by some hardware faults. Thereafter, a program rollback takes place and a retry begins with another try routine.

In summary, a sequence of four major steps is involved in effecting software fault tolerance; *error detection, hardware checkout, program rollback,* and *retry* with a new try routine. The error detection may be performed by error detection hardware or software routines. Hardware fault tolerance requires the same sequence of steps, except that for the last step, retry, the previously used try routine may be used again. The second step, hardware checkout, is needed to facilitate recognition of the occurrences of permanent hardware faults as well as the occurrences of either software faults or transient hardware faults.

Interaction Among Fault-tolerant Virtual Machines

One of the better proven approaches to structuring large-scale software systems is that of hierarchical structuring [40, 41, 42]. In this approach a software system is structured in the form of multiple layers of virtual machines, $VM_0, VM_1, \ldots, VM_n$. The bottom-level virtual machine VM_0 is directly supported by the hardware machine and the top-level virtual machine VM_n provides facilities desired by the user (or environments). Each intermediate-level virtual machine VM_i provides computing services to the next higher-level virtual machine VM_{i+1} by utilizing the services of the next lower-level virtual machine VM_{i-1}. Virtual machine VM_i is called a *user* of VM_{i-1}, whereas the latter is called the *server* of the former. When program redundancy is embedded in each virtual machine to facilitate software fault tolerance, the pattern of interaction among such fault-tolerant virtual machines is a generalization of the hardware-software interaction discussed in the preceding section.

As an example, consider a hierarchically structured system that contains, among many components, component QUADRT that computes the roots of quadratic equations (Figure 20.1). Component QUADRT utilizes the service of component SQRT that computes the square roots of positive real numbers. Suppose that SQRT processes an input received from QUADRT and a residual program error causes an unreasonable result (i.e., the result is rejected by the acceptance test in SQRT). If SQRT possesses an alternate try routine that can compute the square-root in a different way, the alternate routine can be used for retry, and an acceptable result may be generated. If SQRT is unable to generate a reasonable output, SQRT returns a failure report to QUADRT. This failure report causes the immediate abandonment of the present try (execution) of QUADRT. In turn, if QUADRT possesses an alternate try routine (preferably a routine requiring no services of SQRT), retry with that alternate may lead to the successful completion of QUADRT. The alternate try

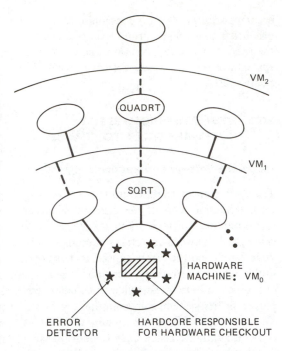

Figure 20.1. A hierarchically structured fault-tolerant software system.

routine in QUADRT provides a further chance for success when the primary try routine in QUADRT fails.

If the acceptance test in SQRT misjudges a bad result as an acceptable one and returns it to QUADRT, the subsequent execution of QUADRT using the bad data may produce a result that will be rejected by the acceptance test in QUADRT. If so, an alternate try routine in QUADRT attempts to retry the calculation. Thus, in a hierarchically structured system, program redundancy can be employed to establish multiple layers of safeguards that enhance total system reliability.

It is also possible for the user QUADRT to send an unacceptable input, for instance, a negative number, to the server SQRT. Upon detection of such an unacceptable input, component SQRT returns a failure report to component QUADRT. The current try routine in QUADRT that sent the rejected input to SQRT is then abandoned and a retry with another try routine follows. The fact that QUADRT passes an unacceptable input to

SQRT implies that the current try routine in QUADRT is in error. There is no real difference between this case and the case where QUADRT or SQRT sends an illegal operation code or address to the hardware machine. Therefore, in this case, component SQRT of a lower-level virtual machine detects an error in component QUADRT of a higher-level virtual machine.

In the above discussion, it was not explicitly stated but should be understood that each time an error is detected, a hardware checkout must follow to determine whether the error was caused by hardware faults or software faults, as discussed in the preceding section.

In summary, three types of errors can occur in interaction between a user and a server: (1) *input error,* passing of an unacceptable input to the server by the user, (2) *server failure,* failure of the server in producing an output that it can return to the user, and (3) *server-caused error,* returning of an erroneous result to the user by the server.

The input error represents the basic mechanism for downward propagation of errors, that is, propagation from a higher-level machine to a lower-level machine, whereas the server-caused error is the opposite, that is, the basic mechanism for upward error propagation. Once an input error is detected by the server, a hardware checkout is called for and then a rollback and a retry by the user follow. The previously executed try routine may or may not be used again, depending on the results of the hardware checkout. In the case where the server returns a failure report to the user, the user immediately carries out a rollback and a retry with another try routine. This is because the server tried every possible means available to it, including a hardware checkout, before it gave up and returned the failure report. The server-caused error can be detected by the acceptance test of the user (or higher-level users), but its exact source, the server, will never be known. A routine hardware checkout will follow that may not reveal any further information. Nevertheless, a program rollback and a retry with another try routine, preferably a try routine that does not rely on

the unreliable server, can result in a circumvention of the error.

20.4. RECOVERY BLOCK SCHEME

A practical scheme, based on the principles discussed in the preceding sections and aimed at cost-effective realization of software fault tolerance, has been developed by Randell and others at the University of Newcastle upon Tyne, England [21, 24, 26, 43]. The cornerstone of the scheme is a language construct called a *recovery block* (RB) [24]. In this section, implementation and use of recovery blocks will be discussed.

Recovery Block

A recovery block is a language construct supporting the incorporation of program redundancy into a fault-tolerant program in a concise and easily readable form. Its syntactic structure is shown in Figure 20.2. Here T denotes the *acceptance test,* B_1 the *primary try block* and B_k, $2 \leq k \leq n$, the *alternate try blocks.* All the try blocks are designed to produce the same or similar computational results. The acceptance test is a logical expression representing the criterion for determining the acceptability of the execution results of try blocks. It is evaluated when a try block has been executed. It may result in either accepting or rejecting the execution results of the try block. If accepted, control exits from the recovery block. If the result produced by a try block is rejected, the next alternate try block is entered. After the alternate try block finishes its computation, the acceptance test is repeated.

Before an alternate try block is entered, the system state is restored to the state that had

$$\begin{aligned} &\textit{ensure} \quad T \\ &\textit{by} \quad B_1 \\ &\textit{else by} \quad B_2 \\ &\quad \cdot \ \cdot \ \cdot \ \cdot \\ &\textit{else by} \quad B_n \\ &\textit{else error.} \end{aligned}$$

Figure 20.2. Recovery block.

existed immediately before the primary try block was entered. The underlying machine automatically performs this program rollback. To support program rollback, a state vector that contains the values of all the variables (that may be changed by the try blocks) is saved when a recovery block is about to be entered. If program rollback is later necessary, this state vector is used to restore the earlier variable values. Note that the programmer is relieved from specifying this "standard" restoration action.

In a sense, a recovery block defines a recoverable region of a software process consisting of three parts: (1) a *recovery point,* a saving of the process state, (2) a *try,* an execution of a try block, and (3) a *test point,* an execution of the acceptance test.

The abstracting power of recovery blocks becomes evident when a comparison is made between a fault-tolerant program written in a recovery block and an equivalent program written in simple statements. Figure 20.3a shows a recovery block containing an acceptance test and two different algorithms for computing the square roots of positive real numbers. In the figure, $prior(X)$ refers to the original value of variable X, that is, the value that existed at the initiation of the recovery block. Note that the acceptance test references both the original and the modified values of variable X nonlocal to the try blocks. The equivalent program in Figure 20.3b is written in simple statements and is several times longer than the program in Figure 20.3a. It is this abstracting power that makes the recovery block a promising tool for cost-effective use of program redundancy.

The following aspects of the recovery block scheme should also be noted: (1) The primary

```
XS := X; "saving of non-local variable"
X := SQRTA(X);
if |X² − XS| < TOLERABLE
then goto   CONTINUE;
X := XS; "restoration of changed non-local variable"
X := SQRTB(X);
if |X² − XS| < TOLERABLE
then goto   CONTINUE;
⟨send error message⟩
CONTINUE: ⟨purge saved variable values⟩
```

Figure 20.3b. A program equivalent to that in Figure 20.3a.

or alternate try blocks can contain, nested within themselves, further recovery blocks, and (2) it is not necessary that every block in a block-structured fault-tolerant program be a recovery block. This flexibility is important since it allows incorporation of program redundancy only where desired. It is not required that all the try blocks in a recovery block aim at exactly the same computational results. Instead, alternate try blocks can be designed to provide degraded service or less-desired results than the primary block does. The more degraded the service, the simpler the alternate try block may be and consequently the greater the hope that it does not contain any design errors [43]. An example of this type of a recovery block is borrowed from Reference 43 and shown in Figure 20.4. It is a program segment that enters a disk-to-core request into a queue of outstanding requests.

As mentioned earlier, program rollback following a rejection by the acceptance test is built into the definition of a recovery block and is thus carried out by the underlying machine

```
ensure   |X² − prior(X)| < TOLERABLE
by       X := SQRTA(X)
else by  X := SQRTB(X)
else error
```

Figure 20.3a. A recovery block for square-root evaluation.

```
ensure   ⟨consistency of disk transfer queue⟩
by       ⟨algorithm which enters request in
         optimal queue position⟩
else by  ⟨algorithm which enters request at
         end of queue⟩
else by  ⟨send warning 'request ignored'⟩
else error.
```

Figure 20-4. Alternate try blocks designed to provide degraded service [43].

supporting the recovery block. The machine performs it by saving a state vector at a recovery point and restoring it when a retry is needed. However, certain components of a system cannot be restored in such a manner. For example, operations involving file access, accounting operations, and operations dependent upon a real-time clock cannot be reversed by the method used for automatic reversal of assignments [24]. Therefore, recovery block alone cannot be used to safeguard a program segment involving such operations. Horning et al. proposed a language construct called *recoverable procedure* for specification of nonstandard restoration operations [24, 71]. A recoverable procedure allows the programmer to specify (1) the operations of saving information that may be required for nonstandard restoration, (2) the normal computation, and (3) the nonstandard restoration operations themselves. Details of the recoverable procedure are referred to in References 24 and 71. Shrivastava and Banatre developed another language construct called *port*-supporting specification of nonstandard restoration operations [44].

Efficient Execution of Recovery Blocks

Since the processing of fault-tolerant programs involves saving of state vectors and examination of saved state vectors (for validation and restoration), the processing cost can be reduced by saving state vectors in a compact form. It is useful to save only the differences between successive state vectors, rather than to save the entire state vector on entry to each recovery block. The processing cost can also be reduced by noting that the variables local to the try block being used are irrelevant to the restoration, and, in many cases, only a small subset of the nonlocal variables are modified by a try block. To exploit these properties, Horning et al. developed a scheme called *recovery cache* that saves state vectors in a compact form [24, 26]. The essence of this scheme is to record the original value *prior*(W) of each nonlocal variable W together with its logical address in a table immediately before the variable is modified for the first time in a new recovery block. The original values are thus saved in a compact table structure. For illustration, the fault-tolerant program in Figure 20.5a is used. Figure 20.5b shows a snapshot of the recovery cache taken when primary try block $B_{2.1}$ is in execution. As shown, there is a stack, called a *cache stack,* used for saving the original values of the variables modified by a try block. Similar to the *main stack,* the cache stack is also divided into regions, one region for each nested recovery block in the "active" state (i.e., a recovery block that has been entered but not exited). The top region of the cache stack in Figure 20.5b contains names (representing logical addresses) and previous values of the nonlocal variables that have been modified during execution of the current try block $B_{2.1}$ (i.e., Y2, X1, X2). Similarly, the bottom region of the cache stack contains the previous value of nonlocal variable X1, which had been modified by execution of try block $B_{1.1}$ before $B_{2.1}$ was entered. Figure 20.5b also shows a flag field in the main stack. The flag indicates whether the original value of the associated variable has already been saved since the current try block was entered. Thus the flags attached to Y2, X1, X2 in the main stack are currently set.

If the result produced by execution of $B_{2.1}$ is rejected by the acceptance test T_2, then the top region C_2 of the cache stack can be used to reset the main stack to the state that existed on entry to recovery block F_2. If it passes the test, execution of F_2 is complete and C_2 is merged into C_1 so that the result may contain previous values of those variables that are nonlocal to $B_{1.1}$ and have been modified since $B_{1.1}$ was entered. Thus the result will be a single region containing (X1, 9) and (X2, 2). Flags in the main stack are also adjusted so that only the flags of X1 and X2 are set. Therefore, creation of a region in the cache stack can be viewed as the *establishment of a recovery point (RP),* and the number of regions in the cache stack at any time is equal to the number of RPs existing at that time.

A detailed design of a recovery cache to be implemented in hardware and to be used in the PDP-11 family of machines is described in Reference 45.

Even with a recovery cache, the increase in

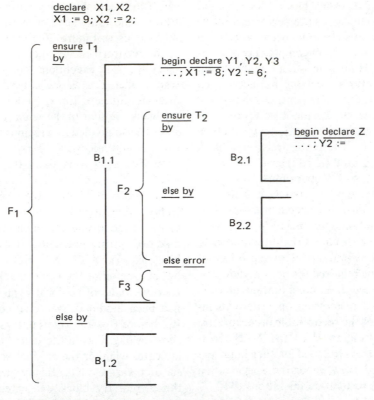

Figure 20.5a. A fault-tolerant program containing recovery blocks.

program execution time due to the execution of acceptance tests and saving of state vectors may be substantial. Often nontrivial acceptance tests may be employed. Also, large numbers of nonlocal variables may be modified during execution of some try blocks. Then program execution time even in the case of normal fault-free execution could be significantly larger than that for the irredundant program (that does not contain either acceptance tests or alternate try blocks). In order to minimize the execution time increase due to incorporation of program redundancy, an approach of overlapping try block execution with the validation and saving of state vectors was proposed in Reference 28. This parallel execution approach requires a multiprocessor system in which (1) histories of the mainstream compu-

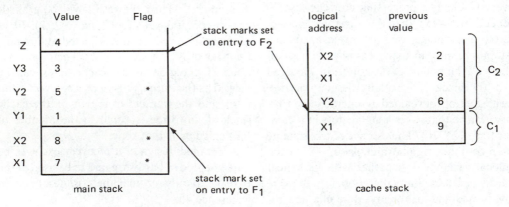

Figure 20.5b. Recovery cache during execution of the program in Figure 20.5a.

tation (i.e., try block execution) are kept in a compact form and (2) interference among processors, particularly storage conflicts, is negligible or absent. A multiprocessor system architecture that satisfactorily meets these requirements by employing a novel memory organization, named duplex memory, is described in Reference 28. However, implementation of the architecture is costly because it requires both random-access memory and content-addressable memory modules.

The programming language Pascal was extended to include recovery block, and then a compiler for the extended Pascal was developed by Shrivastava [46]. The compiler is a modification of that originally developed by Brinch Hansen for ordinary Pascal [47]. It produces an intermediate machine code that is interpreted by a software interpreter running on a PDP 11/45. Similarly, Concurrent Pascal [47] was also extended by Shrivastava [48] to include recovery block. (This extension does not handle erroneous process interactions, which are discussed in Section 20.6.) A preprocessor that accepts programs written in Pascal extended with both recovery block and recoverable procedure and translates them into equivalent ordinary Pascal programs was developed in Reference 71. This preprocessor written in ordinary Pascal was meant to be a research tool rather than a production aid. The machine code generated by the preprocessor used in conjunction with an ordinary Pascal compiler is often less efficient than the code generated by the extended compiler. However, the preprocessor is completely machine-independent and thus can be directly transported to different machines equipped with ordinary Pascal compilers.

Design of Acceptance Tests

The acceptance test is not necessarily aimed at complete validation of the execution results of try blocks, which is generally infeasible. It is rather aimed at checking a condition that is weaker than the correctness condition but that can be checked efficiently. There are some exceptions as discussed below.

One important case is where the objective computing function has an inverse function that can be computed in a reasonable amount of time. Many numeric computing problems have this property, for example, square root evaluation and finding the roots of a quadratic equation. In such cases, efficient and complete acceptance tests can be easily obtained. Another case that may be more specialized than the above case but yields an easily obtainable complete acceptance test is a sorting program. By definition, complete acceptance tests cannot be used together with alternate try blocks designed to provide degraded service.

In most cases, an acceptance test is designed to check if certain invariant relationships are maintained among nonlocal variables, including both old values (i.e., the values saved on entry to the recovery block) and current values. Such a test is aimed at a reasonableness check rather than complete validation. For example, in an aircraft control system, the variables representing acceleration and rate of change of acceleration are not expected to indicate that the pitch attitude has changed faster than at a certain rate, for example, from level to pointing straight down in $\frac{1}{60}$ of a second [49]. As another example of a reasonableness check, an acceptance test of a recovery block that manipulates a doubly linked list may be a test for connectivity of two-way linkages.

Another useful and widely applicable acceptance test is to check the execution time of a try block. The supporting hardware may take the form of a watchdog timer [18, 38]. It is set at the beginning of a try (block execution) and signals an error if the preset time is counted. It can be reset or turned off before the preset time is counted. This timing test is essential in detecting and resurrecting the program caught in an infinite loop.

Assessment of the quality of an acceptance test is beyond the reach of the state of the art. Future advances in requirements specification and module specification may shed some light on this important problem.

Simple Extensions of Recovery Block

Checking the validity of the input to a program module is a common programming practice especially in real-time applications. Two of the most reasonable approaches to incorporating an input check into a recovery block were discussed in References 19 and 50. One approach is to place before a recovery block F an "empty" recovery block F^e that contains nothing but an acceptance test T^e. Acceptance test T^e checks the validity of the input to F. If the input variables of F do not pass acceptance test T^e, F is not entered. A rollback and a retry may be attempted at the next higher level. However, the strong ties between the "empty" recovery block and the following recovery block are understood only by the programmer, not by the compiler. In other words, there is nothing illegal in making an empty recovery block F^e to check the validity of not only the input variables of F but also the input variables of successor blocks of F. Although this flexibility can be sometimes exploited to benefits, extensive use of such empty recovery blocks may result in degraded program readability.

The other approach is to extend the acceptance test to consist of two parts, the *input acceptance test* T^I and the *result acceptance test* T^R. The syntactic structure thus becomes:

$$
\begin{aligned}
&ensure\ on\ entry\quad T^I\\
&\qquad\quad on\ exit\quad T^R\\
&by\quad B_1\\
&else\ by\quad B_2\\
&\cdots\cdots\\
&else\ error.
\end{aligned}
$$

Figure 20.6. Recovery block with the input acceptance test.

The input acceptance test T^I is executed "before" the primary try block B_1. This approach has the advantage of yielding better, readable programs.

If a loop in a fault-tolerant program contains a recovery block as its body, then the acceptance test is entered at every iteration to confirm the result. Sometimes it is desirable to invoke the validation process less frequently than at every iteration. For flexible invocation of the acceptance test, an extension of the recovery block was proposed to include a predicate [19, 50]. When the predicate is "false" on entry to the recovery block, only the primary try block is executed without invoking the ex-

ecution of the acceptance test. The following example illustrates both the syntax and the semantics of the extended recovery block.

$$
\begin{aligned}
&for\ I := 1\ to\ 100\ do\\
&ensure\quad when\ I\ mod\ 10 = 0\ that\\
&\qquad\quad on\ exit\quad T^R\\
&by\qquad \langle\text{loop-body 1}\rangle\\
&else\ by\quad \langle\text{loop-body 2}\rangle\\
&else\ error.
\end{aligned}
$$

Figure 20.7. Recovery block with a predicate.

In this case, a full recovery-block execution cycle is carried out only at every tenth iteration. At other iterations only ⟨loop-body 1⟩ is executed. At the beginning of every tenth iteration, the state vector is saved and then the primary try block ⟨loop-body 1⟩ is executed. If the result is accepted by the result acceptance test T^R, then the recovery block is exited, the next iteration is initiated, and the saved state vector can be discarded. If rejected, the alternate try block ⟨loop-body 2⟩ is used for retry. If the result of ⟨loop-body 2⟩ is again rejected, the current execution of the recovery block fails and thus the entire loop fails.

Note the difference between the "ensure" clause augmented with a *"when"* subclause discussed above and the following "if" statement: *if* ⟨logical expression⟩ *then ensure . . . else error.* In the latter case, the entire recovery block is skipped if ⟨logical expression⟩ is "false."

It was mentioned earlier that a watchdog timer could be a useful tool for error detection. In order to support controlled use of the watchdog timer, the "ensure" clause of a recovery block can be extended with the subclause *"within . . . seconds."* Once execution of a try block is completed, the watchdog timer is turned off and then the acceptance test follows. If a rejection occurs, the timer is again set to the specified time limit at the beginning of the retry.

20.5. RELATIONSHIP BETWEEN SOFTWARE FAULT TOLERANCE AND EXCEPTION HANDLING

Exception handling is a generic term referring to detecting and responding to abnormal or undesired events [42, 51, 52, 53]. An example of an exception is an arithmetic overflow. Declaration of an exception is accompanied by a handler that is a routine executed whenever the exception occurs. Exception handling has been widely practiced by programmers and recognized as an important part of computer programming. For example, both PL/1, developed in the 1960s [54], and ADA, a new programming language recently developed by the U.S. Department of Defense [55], provide facilities for exception handling.

It is difficult to identify fundamental differences between an exception as defined above and an error. To make a point, failure in passing an acceptance test during execution of a fault-tolerant program can be viewed as an exception. Normally error detection occurs on completion of a try block in the recovery block scheme for software fault tolerance whereas exceptions are detected immediately as they occur in most exception-handling schemes. However, this distinction is often blurred since the recovery block scheme also deals with the errors detected in the middle of a try block execution.

The main difference between exception-handling schemes and the recovery block schemes seems to be in the ways response is made to the detected conditions. In the case of the recovery block scheme, response to the detected error follows a fixed pattern of rollback and retry. On the other hand, in exception-handling schemes, response to the detected exception is unrestricted. It could be an attempt to patch the system from an undesired state into a consistent state. For example, response to an overflow may be to turn the overflow indicator off, set the overflowed variable to a certain constant, print a message, and then skip several statements. This kind of patching is called *forward error recovery* whereas rollback and retry are called *backward error recovery*. Since there is no restriction, an exception handler can, in principle, be designed to perform rollback and retry. But then, the rollback operations must be explicitly specified, unlike in the recovery block scheme. Furthermore, saving a process state must be explicitly specified in an appropriate place.

In short, exception-handling schemes do not provide any useful support for incorporation of backward error recovery and encourage the use of forward error recovery. On the other hand, backward error recovery is a built-in feature of recovery block and thus the recovery block scheme relieves the programmer of the burden of explicitly specifying preparation and operation details of rollback. It should also be noted that meaningful forward error recovery cannot be attempted without full knowledge of the extent of the error. Such knowledge is rarely obtained in the case of software-caused errors because of the unpredictable and unidentifiable nature of software faults. Therefore, although exception handling is of value in dealing with foreseen undesirable events such as some hardware-caused errors, it is not appropriate for dealing with unforeseen software faults [53]. This also implies that exception-handling schemes and the recovery block scheme must be used for different purposes and they can complement each other. An example that illustrates such use is given in Reference 53.

20.6. FAULT-TOLERANT CONCURRENT PROGRAMMING AND DISTRIBUTED PROCESSING

A natural way of designing the software of a distributed processing system is to structure it in the form of a collection of cooperating asynchronous processes as described in Reference 41. Such *concurrent programming* is also an effective approach to designing multiprogramming and multiprocessing systems. The computation state of a concurrent program is a vector of the computation states of component processes. This concurrent programming introduces a new dimension to the problem of effecting software fault tolerance, that is, the possibility of erroneous interaction among processes [21, 56–62].

Domino Effect

A direct application of the recovery block scheme to a concurrent program would involve structuring each process with the aid of a recovery block. Figure 20.8 shows such a concurrent program in execution.

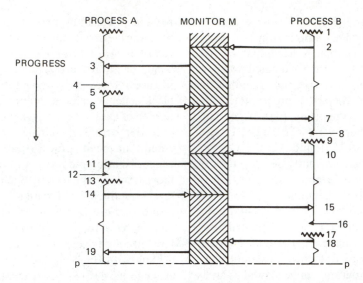

Figure 20.8. Two processes communicating through a monitor.

Two processes A and B progress downward and communicate through monitor M. *Monitor* is a shared data structure defined in References 47 and 63. A change in the direction of shading in the monitor represents a state change. A horizontal line directed toward the monitor represents a monitor update (e.g., B.2), whereas a line directed toward a process represents a monitor reference (e.g., A.3). A bracket represents a *recovery block execution* (RBE) and each wavy line represents a recovery point (RP). The bottom end of a bracket represents a test point (TP) (i.e., an execution of the associated acceptance test).

Suppose that process A successfully passes TP A.4. The RBE completed at A.4 has not yet been fully validated because the information received at A.3 through the monitor can be revoked later if process B does not succeed at TP B.8. This means that the RP established at A.1 must be maintained at least until process B reaches B.8. In fact, when process A reaches TP A.p, none of the RPs established by both processes will have been discarded.

On the other hand, suppose that process A fails at TP A.4. The error detected could have been caused by process A's own faults or process B's faults that occurred between B.1 and B.2. In the latter case, process A has detected undesirable behavior of process B. However, it is not feasible to distinguish between the two

possible causes and therefore, process A's failure at A.4 should be followed by rollbacks of both processes. Now, consider the case where process A fails at TP A.p. Process A rolls back to A.13 first, which in turn causes process B to roll back to B.9. Furthermore, this rollback propagation between processes continues until both processes reach their starting points (A.1 and B.1). This uncontrolled rollback propagation was called a *domino effect* by Randell [21].

The domino effect is a consequence of uncoordinated incorporation of recovery blocks into interacting processes or, to be more specific, uncoordinated establishment of RPs. It occurs because processes establish their RPs regardless of when others establish RPs. For example, a domino effect occurs in a system shown in Figure 20.8 even if an error is generated between A.14 and A.p or between B.17 and B.18; it occurs just because the RPs of processes A and B are not well coordinated. The domino effect could be a serious problem and does not yield to simple solutions [21,64,65,66]. Two proposed approaches to controlling the domino effect are briefly described in the following sections. One is a programmer-dependent approach, which is to provide a language tool aiding the programmer in coordinating the recovery block structures of interacting processes. The other is a programmer-transparent approach, which relies on an "intelligent" underlying machine.

Conversation Scheme

As an aid to designing fault-tolerant process interactions, a language construct called *conversation* was proposed by Randell [21]. Only the abstract semantics of conversation has been provided.

The conversation is a two dimensional recovery block, that is, a recovery block that spans two or more processes and creates a "boundary" that process interactions may not cross. The concept is depicted in Figure 20.9. As shown, the boundary of a conversation consists of a *recovery line,* a *test line,* and two *side walls.* A recovery line is a coordinated set of the RPs of interacting processes that are established (possibly at different times) before interactions begin. When all the processes roll back to the recovery line, there cannot be any further propagation of rollbacks among processes. A test line is a correlated set of the acceptance tests of the interacting processes. A conversation is successful only if all the interacting processes pass their acceptance tests at the test line. If any of the acceptance tests fail, all the processes roll back to the recovery line and retry with their alternate try blocks. (Whether a process that has passed its acceptance test must wait until other processes pass their acceptance tests or it can proceed without

discarding its RP belonging to the recovery line of the conversation is an implementation choice [50].) Conversations must be strictly nested in two dimensions [21, 67]. That is, when conversation X is nested within conversation Y, the set of processes that participate in nested conversation X must be a subset of the processes that participate in Y; the entire recovery line of X must be established after the entire recovery line of Y; and the entire test line of X must be set before the entire test line of Y. The conversation can thus be used to avoid the domino effect, but it must be used carefully. First, the strict two dimensional nesting requirement can be a nonnegligible burden on the program designer. The designer must also ensure that a deadlock situation will not occur where some processes enter a conversation, pass their acceptance tests at the test line, and then wait for the validation results from the processes that chose to bypass the conversation.

The conversation scheme dictates that processes act as a group in both rollback and retry. In other words, failure of any single process causes rollback of the entire group and switchover of all the processes to their alternate try blocks for retry. The try blocks of the processes interacting within a conversation can thus be grouped into one or more groups of communicating try blocks, each executed by a different process. Alternate groups of try blocks may specify different communication

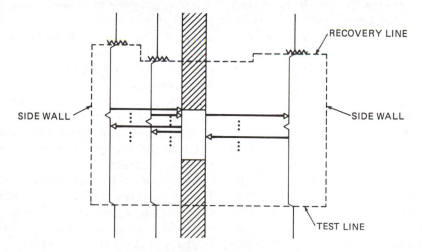

Figure 20.9. Conversation.

structures and thus, even if the execution of a group of try blocks generates unacceptable results because of the imperfectly designed interprocess communication structure, a try with another group of try blocks based on a different communication structure can result in passing the test line.

Efforts to produce a practical implementation of the conversation scheme began only recently [72,73]. Although the underlying principles of conversation can certainly be exploited in designing fault-tolerant process interactions with the aid of a recovery block, the design process might be much more cumbersome than it would be if conversation were provided as a concrete language construct. Obviously, the central problem in implementing the conversation scheme is to select a well-structured syntax and associated semantics for conversation. In reference 72, four different concrete language constructs meant to be mechanizations of the conversation scheme were explored. These language constructs have yet to be tested for their effectiveness in the field.

On the other hand, one can do without conversation in structuring fault-tolerant process interactions if some loss of parallelism can be tolerated. To be more specific, a recovery block can be used together with the facilities for dynamic process creation (see Figure 20.10). Acceptance test TL in the recovery block corresponds to the test line of an equivalent conversation, and the RP established on entry to the recovery block corresponds to the recovery line of the conversation. Each try block starts with creation of interacting child-processes and ends with their termination. Therefore, alternate try blocks may employ different communication structures within them. This recovery block structure is not a complete implementation of the rules of conversation because it loses some parallelism defined in the rules. The parallelism sacrificed in this scheme is that which processes preserve during entry into a conversation. That is, processes are allowed to enter a conversation at different times, whereas, like any other recovery block, the recovery block specifying fault-tolerant interaction among child-processes must be en-

```
ensure TL
by     begin
       initialize MONITOR.1(parameters);
       initialize PROCESS1.1(parameters);
       ............
       initialize PROCESSn.1(parameters)
       end
else by begin
       initialize MONITOR.2(parameters);
       initialize PROCESS1.2(parameters);
       ............
       initialize PROCESSn.2(parameters)
       end
............
else error
```

Figure 20.10. A recovery block specifying fault-tolerant interaction among child processes.

tered by a single process, which is an additional synchronization requirement that is not part of the semantics of conversation.

A major merit of the above recovery block structuring scheme is its simplicity. Under the scheme there is no possibility of creating the deadlock situation that can arise under the conversation scheme, that is, a situation where some processes wait for participation in a conversation of other processes which chose to bypass the conversation. However, the amount of parallelism sacrificed in this scheme may be intolerable in certain applications.

Programmer-transparent Coordination (PTC) Scheme

The *programmer-transparent coordination (PTC)* scheme proposed in Reference 64 is aimed at preventing the domino effect without burdening the program designer of the task of coordinating the RPs of interacting processes. This means that the program designer can structure error detection and recovery capability of a process independently of the recovery structures of other processes. The approach relies upon an "intelligent" underlying machine that runs processes.

The essence of the PTC scheme is two-fold. First, each process is held solely responsible for detecting and correcting errors that it originated. This means that processes cannot challenge the integrity of the information received from other processes. For example, if process

A in Figure 20.8 fails at TP A.4, it will roll back to RP A.1 to make a retry without asking process B to resupply information into monitor M. It is shown in Reference 64 that if a process that has failed in an acceptance test is allowed to "blame" another process and demands it to roll back, it is not generally possible to prevent a domino effect unless the program designer takes great care in coordinating the recovery block structures of the interacting processes.

Second, the intelligent machine establishes RPs immediately before some, but not all, monitor reference operations. These RPs are in addition to the RPs established on initiation of RBEs. The purpose of establishing additional RPs is to prevent a domino effect and enable processes to make minimum-distance rollbacks when the information that they received through a monitor is revoked. For example, if an RP is established immediately before monitor reference B.15 in Figure 20.8, then process B will make a minimum-distance rollback to the RP when process A fails at TP A.p and rolls back to RP A.13. Note that rollback propagation stops there. (If failure at TP A.p were caused by faults occurring between A.14 and A.p or between B.17 and B.18, the subsequent retry of the two processes from A.13 and B.15, respectively, can result in passing the acceptance test at A.p.)

Rules for establishing and maintaining a minimum number of RPs needed to preserve the minimum-distance rollback capability were obtained in Reference 64. When a process fails in an acceptance test and rolls back to an RP, the process should also be responsible for restoring monitors that have been updated during the rejected execution. For example, when process A in Figure 20.8 rolls back to RP A.13 from TP A.p, it should restore monitor M to a state that existed immediately before monitor update A.14. To prepare for this monitor restoration, a process must record the state of a monitor (into its own store area) before it updates the monitor. A rule is given in Reference 64 for making a minimum number of such monitor records.

Therefore, the PTC scheme simplifies the program designer's task at the cost of increased overhead in the underlying machine

and, more importantly, at the cost of nullifying the capability of a process for detecting erroneous behavior of others. Moreover, the PTC scheme does not provide an opportunity for the interacting processes to change to an alternate communication structure. Once interacting processes are created, their communication structure is fixed. If alternate communication structures need to be employed, then the structuring scheme depicted in Figure 20.10 should be used. That is, interacting processes based on each different communication structure should be created and terminated within a separate try block belonging to a recovery block. The logical structure of a practical implementation of the PTC scheme is described in References 36 and 68.

From the above discussion, it is quite clear that the PTC scheme and programmer-dependent schemes such as the conversation scheme or the recovery block structuring scheme depicted in Figure 20.10 are complimentary to each other. It should be useful in many situations to use conversations or recovery blocks to design macrolevel coordination of processes for RP establishment and validation while process coordination at a microscopic level (i.e., inside conversations or try blocks specifying interactions among child-processes) is left to an intelligent machine. The work in fault-tolerant concurrent programming is at a very early stage. Design aids supporting the schemes reviewed above have not been fully implemented yet. Also, more concrete demonstrations of the performance of the schemes have yet to be made.

20.7. SUMMARY

In spite of recent advances in program validation and automatic programming techniques, large-scale error-free programs are still very much a rarity. This situation is not likely to change drastically in the near future. Software fault tolerance is expected to continue as a feature desired by system designers in critical applications [8, 11, 15, 25, 49, 69, 70]. Techniques and tools have been developed for cost-effective use of program redundancy needed for software fault tolerance. The recovery block scheme developed at the University of

Newcastle upon Tyne, England, appears to be based on sound principles and warrants extensive experimentation. However, exception-handling schemes, for which substantial experience has been accumulated, appear to be inadequate for dealing with unforeseen software faults.

Employment of program redundancy for software fault tolerance has been a rarely exercised activity. This has been partly because of the high cost of designing redundant programs and partly because of the reluctance of software designers to admit that the software being put into operation is imperfect. With the recovery block and other high-level language tools, the design cost can be kept to an acceptable level in many critical applications. It was also conjectured by some people that system designers might be able to afford spending less testing efforts with fault-tolerant programs than they would do with irredundant programs. Although only limited experience with fault-tolerant programs has been obtained, optimistic projections have come out of the experience [18, 20, 25, 26, 32]. One of the basic problems that await further research in the area of software fault tolerance is that of validating fault-tolerant programs. The main difficulty stems from the nature of the faults that fault-tolerant programs are designed to deal with, namely, rarely occurring unforeseeable software faults.

Finally, software fault tolerance in concurrent programming and distributed processing applications is a new research subject. It has been learned that concurrent programming introduces a new fundamental problem in effecting fault tolerance, namely, possibly erroneous process interactions. Some promising approaches have been proposed but more concrete demonstrations of their effectiveness are needed.

REFERENCES

1. a, "The 20 sophisticated computers around the country used to help guide aircraft through the nation's crowded air corridors broke down 861 times in 1979 for a minute or longer." *Tampa Tribune,* August 1, 1980.

b, "Controllers at JFK International Airport charge a computer failure produced several possible 'near misses' in New York City Wednesday night, and sent one small plane in the path of a half dozen large jets." *Tampa Tribune,* July 1980.

c, "The temporary failure of a computer aboard the Columbia during a countdown Thursday caused at least a four-hour postponement in the oft-delayed simulated liftoff of the space shuttle." *Tampa Tribune,* January 11, 1980.

d, "Miscalculations at Manufacturers Hanover Trust Co., the nation's fifth-largest bank, caused the important tallies of the nation's cash and bank deposits to be overstated by billions of dollars recently. The bank attributed its error to a new computer program and to the use of a new form for Federal reports." *Evening Press,* Binghamton, NY, November 4, 1979.

e, "An apparent computer foul-up at the North American Air Defense Command (NORAD) caused a false missile alert and sent U.S. pilots scurrying to their nuclear bombers. There have been two other published false alarms at NORAD since November 1979." *Tampa Tribune,* June 1980.

2. A. Avizienis. Fault-tolerance: The survival attribute of digital systems. *Proc. IEEE,* Oct. 1978, pp. 1221–1268.

3. D. Burchby, L. W. Kerr, and W. A. Sturm. Specifications of the fault-tolerant spaceborne computer (FTSC). *Proc. IEEE Computer Society's International Symposium on Fault-Tolerant Computing,* 1976, pp. 129–133.

4. J. A. Katzman. A fault-tolerant computing system. *Proc. 11th Hawaii International Conference on System Science,* Honolulu, Jan. 1978, pp. 85–102.

5. S. M. Ornstein, W. R. Crowther, M. F. Kraley, R. D. Bressler, A. Michel, and F. E. Heart. Pluribus—A reliable multi-processor. *Proc. 1975 AFIPS National Computer Conference.,* pp. 551–559.

6. B. Randell, P. A. Lee, and P. C. Treleaven. Reliability issues in computing system design. *Computing Surveys,* June 1978, pp. 123–165.

7. J. Von Neumann. Probabilistic logics and the synthesis of reliable organisms from unreliable components. In C. E. Shannon and J. McCarthy, eds., *Automata Studies.* Ann. of Math Studies, no. 34. Princeton University Press, 1956, pp. 43–98.

8. J. H. Wensley. SIFT—Software implemented fault-tolerance. *Proc. AFIPS Fall Joint Computer Conference,* 1972, pp. 243–253.

9. B. W. Boehm. Software and its impact: A quantitative assessment. *Datamation,* May 1973, pp. 48–59.

10. J. J. Horning. A note on program reliability. *ACM Software Engineering Notes,* Oct. 1979, pp. 6–8.

11. A. B. Long, C. V. Ramamoorthy, S. F. Ho, H. H. So, H. L. Reeves, and E. A. Straker. A methodology for the development and validation of critical software for nuclear power plants. *Proc. IEEE Computer Society's 1st International Computer Soft-*

ware and Applications Conf. (COMPSAC), 1977, pp. 620–626.

12. C. V. Ramamoorthy, R. C. Cheung, and K. H. Kim. Reliability and integrity of large computer programs. *Lecture Notes in Computer Science*, vol. 12. Springer-Verlag, New York, 1974, pp. 86–161.

13. C. V. Ramamoorthy and S. F. Ho. Testing large software with automated software evaluation systems. *IEEE Trans. on Software Engineering*, March 1975, pp. 46–58.

14. J. Goldberg. Workshop on distributed fault-tolerant computers. *Computer*, March 1977, pp. 51–52.

15. C. R. Vick, J. E. Scalf, and W. C. McDonald. Distributed data processing for real-time applications. *Proc. 6th Texas Conference on Computing Systems*, Nov. 1977, available from IEEE Computer Society.

16. W. P. Warner. Navy interest in distributed computer systems. Technical Report NSWC/DL MP-31/78, Naval Surface Weapon Center, Dahlgren, Va., Nov. 1978.

17. T. Anderson and B. Randell, eds. Computing system reliability. Cambridge, England: Cambridge University Press, 1979.

18. H. Hecht. Fault-tolerant software for real-time applications. *Computing Surveys*, Dec. 1976, pp. 391–407.

19. K. H. Kim and C. V. Ramamoorthy. Recent development in software fault tolerance through program redundancy. *Proc. 10th Hawaii International Conference on System Science*, Honolulu, Jan. 1977, pp. 234–238.

20. H. Kopetz. *Software redundancy in real-time systems. Proc. IFIP Congress*, 1974, pp. 182–186.

21. B. Randell. System structure for software fault-tolerance. *IEEE Trans. on Software Engineering*, June 1975, pp. 220–232.

22. S. S. Yau and R. C. Cheung. Design of self-checking software. *Proc. 1975 International Conference on Reliable Software*, Los Angeles, pp. 450–457.

23. R. T. Yeh, ed. Special issue on fault-tolerant software. *Computing Surveys*, vol. 8, no. 4, Dec. 1976.

24. J. J. Horning, H. C. Lauer, P. M. Milliar-Smith, and B. Randell. Program structure for error detection and recovery. *Lecture Notes in Computer Science*, vol 16, Springer-Verlag, New York, 1974, pp. 171–187.

25. J. R. Connet, E. J. Pasternak, and B. D. Wagner. Software defenses in real-time control systems. *Digest of the IEEE Computer Society's International Symposium on Fault-Tolerant Computing*, 1972, pp. 94–99.

26. T. Anderson and R. Kerr. Recovery blocks in action: A system supporting high reliability. *Proc. IEEE Computer Society's 2nd International Conference on Software Engineering*, 1976, pp. 447–457.

27. K. M. Chandy and C. V. Ramamoorthy. Rollback and recovery strategies for computer programs. *IEEE Trans. on Computers*, June 1972, pp. 546–556.

28. K. H. Kim and C. V. Ramamoorthy. Structure of an efficient duplex memory for processing fault-tolerant programs. *Proc. ACM SIGARCH'S 5th Symposium on Computer Architecture*, Apr. 1978, pp. 131–138.

29. C. S. Repton. Reliability assurance for System 250: A reliable, real-time control system. *Proc. International Conference on Computer Communication*, Washington, D.C., 1972, pp. 297–305.

30. J. A. Rohr. STAREX self-repair routines: Software recovery in the JPL-STAR computer. *Digest of the IEEE Computer Society's International Symposium on Fault-Tolerant Computing*, 1973, pp. 11–16.

31. M. A. Fischler, O. Firnschein, and D. R. Drew. Distinct software: An approach to reliable computing. *Proc. 2nd USA-Japan Computer Conference*, pp. 573–579, available from AFIPS Press.

32. T. Gilb. Parallel programming. *Datamation*, Oct. 1974, pp. 160–161.

33. W. R. Elmendorf. Fault-tolerant programming. *Digest of the IEEE Computer Society's International Symposium on Fault-Tolerant Computing*, 1972, pp. 79–83.

34. K. M. Chandy. A survey of analytic models of rollback and recovery strategies. *Computer*, May 1975, pp. 40–47.

35. F. T. O'Brien. Rollback point insertion strategies. *Proc. the IEEE Computer Society's International Symposium on Fault-Tolerant Computing*, 1976, pp. 138–142.

36. K. H. Kim. Methodologies and Tools for Developing Robust FTSC Software. Final Report, U.S. Air Force—SAMSO Contract F04701-77-C-0120, August 1978. Also Tech. Report SAMSO-TR-78-142, available from the Defense Technical Information Center.

37. K. H. Kim, H. Hecht, J. P. Huang, and M. Naghibzadeh. Strategies for structured and fault-tolerant design of recovery programs. *Proc. IEEE Computer Society's 2nd International Computer Software and Applications Conference (COMPSAC)*, 1978, pp. 651–656.

38. U.S. Air Force SAMSO YAD. Development specification for the Fault-Tolerant Spaceborne Computer (FTSC). 1977.

39. P. J. Denning. Fault tolerant operating systems. *Computing Surveys*, Dec. 1976, pp. 359–389.

40. T. Anderson, P. A. Lee, and S. K. Shrivastava. A model of recoverability in multi-level systems. *IEEE Trans. on Software Engineering*, Nov. 1978, pp. 486–494.

41. E. W. Dijkstra. Hierarchical ordering of sequential processes. *Acta informatica*, vol. 1, no. 2, 1971, pp. 115–138.

42. D. L. Parnas and H. Wurges. Response to undesired events in software systems. *Proc. IEEE Computer Society's 2nd International Conference on Software Engineering*, 1976, pp. 437–446.

43. P. A. Lee. A reconsideration of the recovery block

scheme. Technical Report no. 119, Computing Lab., University of Newcastle upon Tyne, 1978.

44. S. K. Shrivastava and J. P. Banatre. Reliable resource allocation between unreliable processes. *IEEE Trans. on Software Engineering*, 1978, pp. 230–241.

45. P. A. Lee, N. Ghani, and K. Heron. A recovery cache for the PDP-11. *Proc. IEEE Computer Society's International Symposium on Fault-Tolerant Computing*, 1979, pp. 3–8.

46. S. K. Shrivastava. Sequential Pascal with recovery block. *Software—Practice and Experience*, Vol. 8, 1978, pp. 177–185.

47. P. Brinch Hanson. The architecture of concurrent programs. Englewood Cliffs, N.J.: Prentice-Hall, 1977.

48. S. K. Shrivastava. Concurrent Pascal with backward error recovery. *Software—Practice and Experience*, Dec. 1979, pp. 1001–1020.

49. H. Hecht. Issues in fault-tolerant software for real-time control applications. *Proc. IEEE Computer Society's 4th International Computer Software and Applications Conference (COMPSAC)*, Oct. 1980, pp. 603–607.

50. K. H. Kim, D. L. Russell, and M. J. Jenson. Language tools for fault-tolerant programming. Technical Memorandum PETP-1, Electronics Science Lab., University of Southern California, Nov. 1976.

51. J. B. Goodenough. Exception handling: Issues and a proposed notation. *Comm. ACM*, Dec. 1975, pp. 683–696.

52. R. Levin. Program structures for exceptional condition handling. Ph.D. diss., Department of Computer Science, Carnegie-Mellon University, June 1977.

53. P. M. Milliar-Smith and B. Randell. Software reliability: The role of programmed exception handling. *Proc. ACM Conference on Language Design for Reliable Software*, 1977, pp. 95–100.

54. IBM Corporation. IBM System/360 operating system PL/1 (F) language reference manual. Order no. GC28-8201-4, Dec. 1972.

55. U.S. Department of Defense. Preliminary ADA reference manual. ACM SIGPLAN Notices, June 1979, Part A.

56. L. A. Bjork. Recovery scenario for a DB/DC system. *Proc. 1973 National ACM Conference*, pp. 142–146.

57. N. Daouk. Optimal checkpointing in real-time multiprogramming systems. Ph.D. diss., Department of Electrical Engineering, University of Southern California, June 1979.

58. C. T. Davies. Recovery semantics for a DB/DC system. *Proc. 1973 National ACM Conference*, pp. 136–141.

59. C. T. Davies. Data processing spheres of control. *IBM Systems Journal*, 1978, pp. 179–198.

60. H. Gerstmann, H. Diel, and W. Witzel. The reliability of programming systems. *Lecture Notes in Computer Science*, vol. 23, Springer-Verlag, New York, 1974, pp. 87–113.

61. K. H. Kim. Error detection, reconfiguration and recovery in distributed processing systems. *Proc. IEEE Computer Society's 1st International Conference on Distributed Computer Systems*, Oct. 1979, pp. 284–295.

62. P. M. Merlin and B. Randell. State restoration in distributed systems. *Proc. IEEE Computer Society's International Symposium on Fault-Tolerant Computing*, 1978, pp. 129–134.

63. C. A. R. Hoare. Monitors: An operating system structuring concept. *Comm. of ACM*, Oct. 1974, pp. 549–557.

64. K. H. Kim. An approach to programmer-transparent coordination of recovering parallel processes and its efficient implementation rules. *Proc. IEEE Computer Society's International Conference on Parallel Processing*, Aug. 1978, pp. 58–68.

65. D. L. Russell. Process backup in producer-consumer systems. *Proc. 6th ACM Symposium on Operating Systems Principles*, Nov. 1977, pp. 151–157.

66. D. L. Russell. State restoration in systems of communicating processes. *IEEE Trans. on Software Engineering*, March 1980, pp. 183–194.

67. D. B. Lomet. Process structuring, synchronization and recovery using atomic actions. *Proc. ACM Conference on Language Design for Reliable Software* (also SIGPLAN Notices, March 1977), pp. 128–137.

68. K. H. Kim. An Implementation model for the programmer-transparent scheme for coordinating concurrent processes in recovery. *Proc. IEEE Computer Society's 4th International Computer Software and Applications Conference (COMPSAC)*, Oct. 1980.

69. J. C. Knight. Summary report of workshop on real-time programming for NASA flight projects. NASA Technical Memorandum 80236, Langley Research Center, Feb. 1980.

70. C. R. Vick and J. M. Williams. The requirements for a new generation of real-time data processing technology. Paper presented at the 10th Hawaii International Conference on System Science, Honolulu, Jan. 1977.

71. K. H. Kim, A. Arshi, and S. M. Yang. An approach to translation of Pascal augmented with recovery block and recoverable procedure. *Proc. IEEE Computer Society's Int'l Conf. on Parallel Processing*, Aug. 1978, pp. 58–68.

72. K. H. Kim. Approach to mechanization of the conversation scheme based on monitor. *IEEE Transaction on Software Engineering*, Vol. SE-8, NO. 3, May 1982, pp. 189–197.

73. D. L. Russell and M. J. Tiedeman. Multiprocess recovery using conversations. *Proc. IEEE Computer Society's International Symposium on Fault-Tolerant Computing*, 1979, pp. 106–109.

ACKNOWLEDGMENT Preparation of this chapter was supported in part by the National Science Foundation under Grant No. MCS-8012906 and in part by the U.S. Army Ballistic Missile Defense Advanced Technology Center under Contract No. DASG60-79-C-0074. The author wishes to thank Dr. Oscar Garcia for his helpful comments on the draft of this chapter.

21

Management of Software Development

R. D. Williams
TRW/DSSG

21.1. INTRODUCTION

The seven major development steps from creation of system requirements to the operation and maintenance of a system can be divided into three distinct phases of software development (Figure 21.1) [1]. The first phase, *setting the design baseline,* includes derivation of data processing requirements and preliminary design. The second phase is *production,* which includes detailed design and code and debug. The final step is the *test phase* followed by system operation and maintenance. The concerns of the program manager and, indeed, his or her management approach vary significantly between these three phases. This chapter will highlight both the definition of products from each phase and the tools available to speed and control the process.

Critical management concerns in the first phase are:

1. Understanding user requirements
2. Derivation of data processing requirements
3. Achieving customer/user concurrence on requirements
4. Mapping these requirements into a design
5. Validation of design—does it satisfy user requirements?
6. Identification of support tools required to create the DP system
7. Creation of development plans required

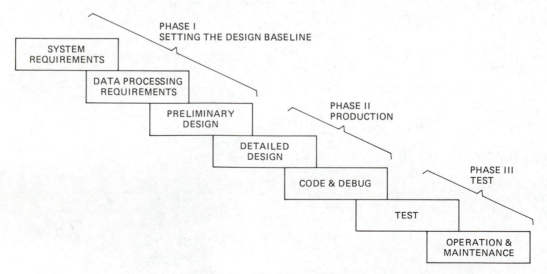

Figure 21.1. The development process.

to guide the program through subsequent phases

During this phase, a small, well-coordinated team is the optimum mode of operation. A sound design requires frequent detailed coordination between team members that is possible only with a small team. Dangers during this phase result when pressures to make progress (apparent—not real) cause staffing to be increased and the production phase to be initiated prior to completion of a sound preliminary design. Staffing in all phases, but especially in this phase, must be event- rather than schedule-driven if real progress is to be made and costs controlled. This simple concept is very difficult to apply as pressures to increase staffing grow if the project falls behind schedule. A project that is behind schedule, however, is enough of a problem; why trade it for a project that is behind schedule and also above cost?

In the production phase, the focus must be on:

1. Completing, documenting, and validating the design
2. Establishing the development approach—identifying and managing risk
3. Keeping visibility in the production status
4. Producing a quality product

In this phase, the program manager is much more distant from the daily tasks of detailed design and coding since, in general, a much larger team is now at work. Loss of program control, when interlocking software programs with dependent schedules are being produced, is a significant danger. The main focus of the program manager is to create the proper environment for high productivity without losing control of the design. This control is not possible without the solid baseline provided by the preliminary design.

In the test phase concerns are:

1. Selling the system to the customer
2. Choice of testing approach—bottom up

(unit level) versus top down (process level)
3. Configuration management
4. Documentation

If the first two phases have been performed precisely, this phase is easy. The greatest danger is that requirements were missed or misunderstood and, for at least part of the system, one must return to the requirements phase. Much can be done in previous phases to minimize this possibility, and succeeding sections will suggest some approaches. It must be remembered that neither quality nor performance can be "tested" into a system; they must be designed in at the outset.

21.2. SETTING THE DESIGN BASELINE

The initial steps of requirements definition and allocation to a design in the development process are clearly the most crucial. The leverage they can achieve in terms of cost and schedule of errors eliminated has been widely studied and reported. Figure 21.2 shows one set of results from IBM, GTE, and TRW [2]. In response to these data, many government agencies, universities, and a wide variety of companies have evolved approaches, techniques, and tools to improve the steps in the first phase of software development [2]. This chapter will describe some tools that are useful over a wide range of types of data processing systems and software systems; however, emphasis should focus on defining (1) the objectives for each step and (2) what the program manager must do to achieve those steps.

Starting with a set of reasonably defined system requirements, we first want to derive a set of data processing—subsequently software—requirements that satisfy the system requirements at acceptable cost and risk. The DP system functional requirements can be thought of as an input, followed by a processing requirement, followed by an output. The software requirements simply consist of:

1. What is to be processed—identification of functions

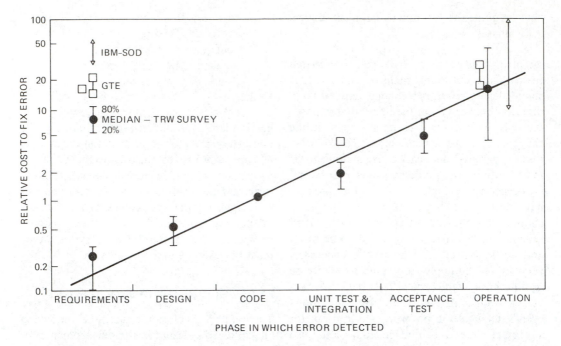

Figure 21.2. Software validation: the price of procrastination.

2. How well must the data be processed—accuracy
3. How fast must the data be processed—response timing
4. How many inputs there are—load
5. Where the inputs must be processed—the operational environment and interfaces

In deriving attributes to be used in judging the success of the requirements generation effort, the use of these requirements must be examined. First, the requirements will be used in generating a preliminary design for a DP system. Second, they will be used in final testing for acceptance of the product. To satisfy these needs, the requirements must be:

1. Complete
2. Consistent
3. Testable

These attributes must be met if the project is to succeed. Requirements generation is a difficult task, however, especially since system requirements are probably still undergoing change as software requirements are being generated. The key judgment made by the program manager and normally reviewed by the system's user is, Are the requirements mature enough to initiate the design activity? The most complete system to aid the process and to provide data to support this decision has been developed under the Software Requirements Engineering Program for the U.S. Army Ballistic Missile Advanced Technology Center (BMDATC) [3, 4, 5]. This effort derived many ideas from the pioneer work on ISDOS by Teichroew and his associates at the University of Michigan [6]. In using this set of tools, individual functional requirements are joined to show predecessor-successor relationships in a requirements network (R-NETs).

A typical R-NET representing the functional flow for processing a radar track return is shown in Figure 21.3. An important concept indicated on the figure is the inclusion of validation points for verifying the requirements and, indeed, the software after it is developed. SREM includes additional capabilities based on a formal structured *requirements statement language* (RSL) and *requirements engineering and validation system* (REVS) to automatically process the requirements statements and

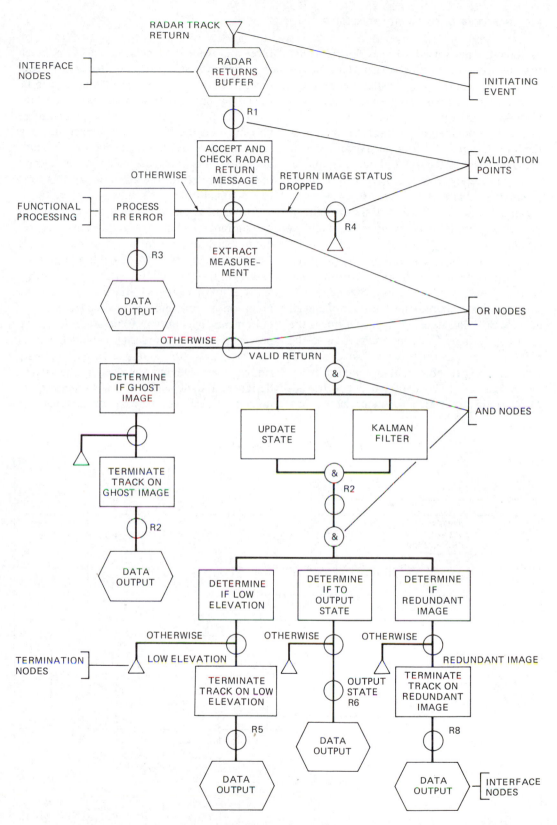

Figure 21.3. Processing-flow analysis confirms the logical consistency and completeness of the requirements.

to allow a wide variety of tests for completeness and consistency among requirements. Although this degree of sophistication may not be necessary in many programs, the use of a disciplined organized approach such as R-NETS is fundamental to an accurate derivation of software requirements. The creation of a complete set of R-NETS allows a completeness, consistency, and testability analysis to be conducted either manually or with machine assistance and with a degree of visibility difficult to obtain through the written words of a specification.

A second technique of great power [7] is the N^2 chart. Figure 21.4 shows the major functions required to guide an intercepting missile with a radar system along the main diagonal of a matrix. The signal path shown traces the total control loop from the interceptor to the radar to the data processor software and return. This representation allows interfaces between functions to be identified and portrayed. The visibility of which functions have inter-faces and what data must be passed is much improved over standard interface control documents. Progress in interface definition can be traced by checking off each active interface block. Response time requirements can also be portrayed on the N^2 chart. For example, if a requirement exists to update the missile guidance order within a specified time after receipt of the radar return, the allocation of this time to individual functions is easily displayed.

Although these techniques are valuable in maintaining visibility into the status of requirements, the key decision to be made is when to baseline the requirements and proceed to design. Early baselining of the requirements leads to many changes—waiting stretches the program and prevents design feedback to requirements generators. Experience in many programs shows that design should begin as soon as a reasonably stable set of requirements can be assembled and approved by the system designers and/or users. To guard against the impact of changes, several techniques are

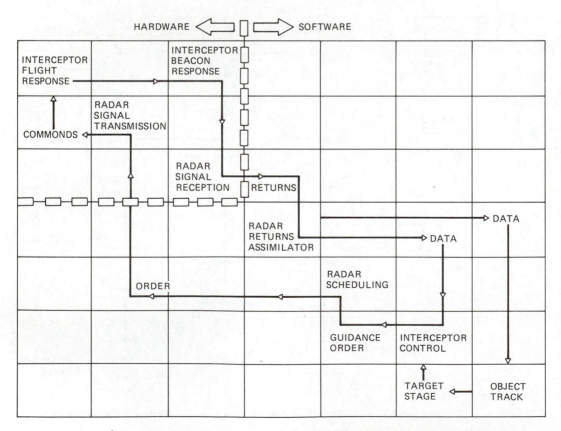

Figure 21.4. N^2 chart effective for understanding and minimizing data and execution control interfaces.

available. First, traceability from requirements to design must be maintained; that is, in which module of the design is each requirement satisfied. This allows easy identification of modules affected when changes occur. Modularity in the design will minimize the total impact of any changes, thereby, it is hoped, limiting the changes to a single module. Finally, use of structured programming techniques and automated construction techniques to assemble the modules into a process makes change less difficult and costly.

The preliminary design phase comprises the downward allocation of requirements to a data processing and software structure. It is a creative process where major changes occur almost daily until an acceptable design emerges. Preliminary design is complete when hardware has been selected and a software process (total set of software controlling DP at one time) has been defined. This definition must include the applications programs (real time if required), the operating system, and any support (off line) processing required to support the real-time program. For each program, the first step is to:

1. Define execution control concepts
2. Perform initial requirements allocation
3. Establish interfaces between programs
4. Identify critical algorithms
5. Set design guidelines, for example, modularity requirements, program structure, and so forth.

Second, the requirements and design concepts must be extended to a software structure. This normally consists of three parts:

1. *Software elements.* For each element there are allocated and derived requirements, budgets for execution time, storage usage, and, where applicable, accuracy. Data interfaces with all interfacing modules must be defined.
2. *Global data base.* Types and structures for all allowable data storage must be defined. Size must be estimated for all files and buffers.
3. *Process control structure.* Prioritization, interrupt structure, and events that drive

the process must be defined and all possible conflicts resolved.

Figure 21.5 shows an example of a software structure from the Ballistic Missile Defense Systems Technology Program conducted by MDAC/TRW for the U.S. Army BMD Systems Command. Of special note is the design guidelines established for the application program tasks (smallest unit recognized for scheduling by the operating system). First, all tasks were identically structured, the first routine in each task was to be a task control routine containing the basic logic (as opposed to algorithms) for task operation. This design guideline was intended to make the software easy to understand to minimize operation and maintenance personnel requirements and costs. In addition, a maximum routine size of 100 higher-order language statements was chosen (waiver required from program manager to exceed). Since the design was performed, much work has been accomplished by various authors on the choice of module size and functionality, possibly the most notable being that by Parnas [8].

A highly valuable method of representing the design is the data-flow diagram. Although it has limitations (e.g., it is incapable of representing a hierarchical control structure), it is easily understood by system designers and, therefore, a good communication tool. The thread analysis technique (a modified data-flow diagram), illustrated in Figure 21.6, allows analysis of critical software paths to verify completeness of the preliminary design. As the preliminary design work progresses, the program manager must concentrate on making sure the design will meet the requirements. As allocation of requirements to programs and modules proceeds, review must be accomplished to show that budgets for time and core are potentially achievable for all critical modules (large time or core users). This review can be based on experience or on actual prototyping of the hardware and software. For the design to meet deadlines in the presence of load, either analysis or functional simulation (where time and size estimates for code—not actual code—are used) can be employed.

The functional simulator [9] is a powerful

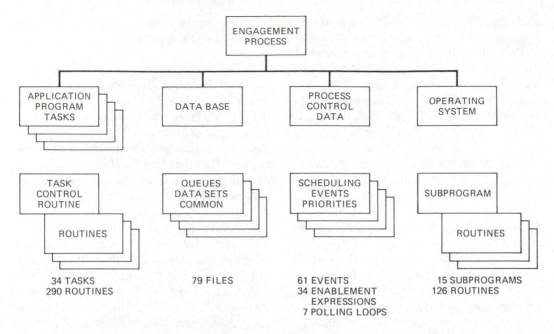

Figure 21.5. Preliminary design defines the development baseline: An example from BMD systems technology program.

tool for investigating total CPU load versus time or system load, memory use, and queue lengths for messages. As the design is developed alternate allocations of time and memory to units of code can be examined.

The completeness of the design is assessed as design work progresses. The intent of the preliminary design is to establish a valid complete structure and identify each module to be built, not to design completely each software module. The concentration must remain on definition and interface issues between program elements rather than on the design of each element. The pressures to have a design of very high confidence through forcing detail design will delay the completion of the preliminary design and make early baselining impossible. Only when program modules to be built are identified and assignments for their detail design and coding made, can management con-

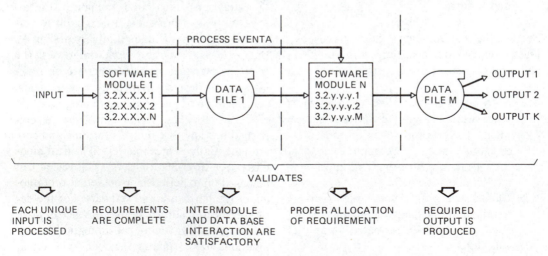

Figure 21.6. Threat analysis verifies completeness of preliminary design.

trol of the program be established. The identification of these elements, their hierarchical relationships, and the attendant data base allow design to proceed in an orderly fashion and integration and test sequences to be established. The preliminary design serves most importantly as a management tool, a management road map for the remainder of the program. The complete preliminary design, therefore, serves to force establishment of a sound design baseline for not only the product but for the development.

Establishing a design baseline is more than just requirements generation and preliminary design; planning for the remainder of the program must now be completed. These plans establish the environment and controls for the production and test phases. A minimum set of plans should include:

1. *Development plan.* This plan specifies the steps and schedules to be followed to complete the development. One approach, the *incremental development plan,* will be described later in this chapter.
2. *Software standards and procedures.* These procedures establish naming conventions, programming standards, and documentation conventions. The standards are a primary contributor to production of uniform code of high quality.
3. *Configuration management plan.* This plan establishes the level of management that controls the requirements, the design, and the code during each phase of the program.
4. *Management plan.* This plan specifies the project reporting and control structure. Success of the program depends on the establishment of routinized, accurate reports that keep the program manager informed as to performance, cost, and schedule status.
5. *Preliminary users guide.* Where man-machine interfaces exist, it is critical to communicate the capabilities of the design to support this interface to the users early in the program. The users guide provides a mechanism for forcing this

communication since it describes the interface in user language, not data processing language—how the system can be used.

21.3. PRODUCTION PHASE

Two key management actions are important to the success of the production phase. First is the choice of a low-risk development approach. Second is to maintain visibility into actual progress so that any problems will receive management attention.

Historically, the first time a process was totally assembled and testing initiated was quite late in the development cycle, that is, in the early part of the integration and test cycle. Under these conditions, any major risk that the process had basic flaws in the control structure or exceeded time or core available could be discovered only at a time when any problem would result in late delivery and attendant cost overruns. A strategy to allow visibility into these types of problems much earlier in the development cycle has been successfully used on a number of programs [10]. This approach, the incremental development approach, forces top down implementation of increments of total system capability. This is accomplished by building early in the cycle a basic process structure (or a network) with the majority of the software represented by dummies or stubs. The choice of this approach is one of the reasons that the previous section of this chapter stresses the development of a solid preliminary design, since that is where the process structure is developed. The choice and number of increments can be based on a number of factors, for instance, technical risk in estimating size of an important portion of the program, to support integration of the hardware of the system, or to minimize variations in manpower required over the life of the program. One additional factor to be considered is the system designer's point of view; if a significant increment of system capability can be provided early, it will raise confidence in the total system design. Figure 21.7 shows the development approach modified by the incremental concept.

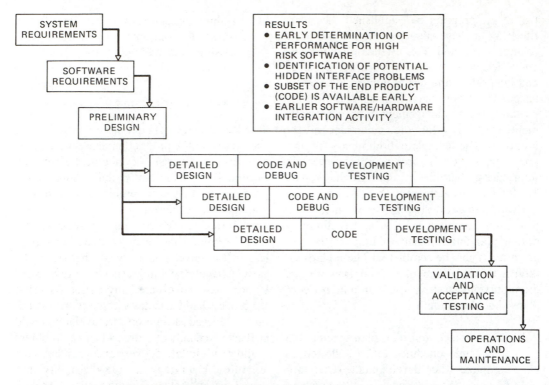

Figure 21.7. The incremental development of software to minimize risk.

During the preliminary design phase, it was emphasized that all modules to be developed should be identified and sized. The detailed design phase then begins with the assignment to appropriately sized groups the task of completing the design and coding. The next major problem faced by the program manager is to monitor and control the progress of these groups. The strategy we recommend for accomplishing this depends on use of what has been termed a *unit development folder* (UDF) [11]. A unit development folder is created for each routine or group of routines. The first item entered in the folder is the requirement for the software to be developed drawn from the preliminary design. This is normally documented in a specification, for instance, MIL STD 490 or equivalent. A set of mandatory milestones is provided to measure progress. Agreement must now be reached with the group leader as to completion date and cost to complete. All milestones must be measurable and, if estimates of the percentage completed are reported, they must be based on achievement of the selected milestones. A sample

cover sheet from a unit development folder used at TRW is shown in Figure 21.8. Although the majority of the milestones are obvious, two points need to be explained. First, the *functional capabilities list* is a minimum list of capabilities that must be demonstrated prior to software turnover to integration and test. This list should be generated by the integration and test team and is a protection for them against receiving partially tested code. Items 4 and 5 specify that unit test cases must be not only provided but separately reviewed for responsiveness to the functional capabilities list. This concentration on unit testing can be justified by experience and is consistent with the cost of error data presented in Figure 21.2. A review is required at each step and accomplishment of each step can be reported only after review. The use of the folder changes as the program progresses. In the early phase, it contains design data. Later the code, and finally test case results are included with a final documentation check. The UDF then serves as a common collection point for all data relating to a unit of code. It forces documentation as

UNIT DEVELOPMENT FOLDER COVER SHEET

MNEMONIC ____TFAST____   CUSTODIAN ____BRADLEY____

SECTION NO.	DESCRIPTION	DUE DATE	DATE COMPLETED	ORIGINATOR	REVIEWER/ DATE
1	REQUIREMENTS	14 Nov. 1975	12-23-75 RMB	Bradley	Norman GU 1/7/76
2	DESIGN INITIAL: DESCRIPTION CODE TO:	19 Dec. 1975	12-29-75 RMB	Bradley	Norman GU 1/7/76
3	FUNCTIONAL CAPABILITIES LIST	19 Dec. 1975	12-23-75 RMB	Bradley	Norman GU 1/7/76
4	DEVELOPMENT TEST DEFINITIONS	29 Dec. 1975	1-22-76 RMB	Norman 1-22-76	Bradley 1-22-76
5	DEVELOPMENT TEST CASE REVIEW	6 Jan. 1976	2-16-76	Bradley	Norman GU 2-16-76
6	UNIT CODE	9 Jan. 76 / 12 mar. 76	1-16-76 RMB / 3-1-76	Bradley / Bradley	Norman 1-23-76 GU 3-1-76 GU Norman
7	TEST CASE RESULTS	23 Feb. 1976	2-4-76 RMB	Judson	Norman 2-11-76 GU
8	AS BUILT DETAIL DESIGN DESCRIPTION	9 Feb. 1976	3-1-76 GU	Bradley	Norman 2-8-76 GU

Figure 21.8. Unit development folder cover sheet.

the design and coding progresses, by far the lowest-cost way to generate documentation. After initiation of unit development, it was suggested the end date had to be agreed to with the team leader responsible for the development; this is actually a negotiation. The team leader is then responsible for developing his intermediate milestones, which contributes to his personal commitment to the schedule, a commitment so necessary to assure high productivity. Finally, the UDF serves as a device for allowing upper management to assess progress by inspection of the project's status at any time.

The techniques that have been suggested have been successful in maintaining visibility and control of an ongoing software production process. In summary, we believe that the secret of visibility is to break the implementation into small, measurable, and meaningful steps. The creation of a realistic project schedule can now be accomplished through a series of logical steps.

1. Planning begins with the list of all modules to be produced that were identified in the preliminary design.
2. Integration sequences for these modules are chosen as a part of development planning, and increments are selected establishing the required delivery dates for each module.

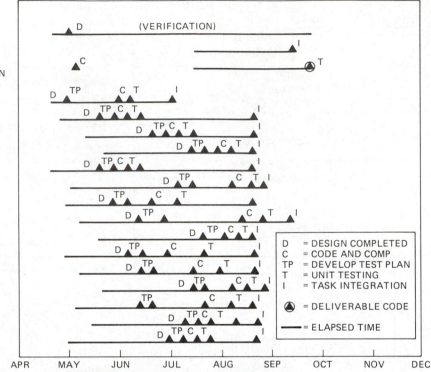

Figure 21.9. Object track task build 1 development schedule.

3. Intermediate milestones are selected by team leaders for each module and the integration team leader for the integration sequence.

4. A master project schedule has now been created from the top down but with the critical input from the module team leaders to assure realism.

An example schedule built in this way from the Systems Technology Program at TRW is shown in Figure 21.9. The very detailed schedules that result from this process allow precise tracking of program progress based solidly on the measurable milestones of the unit development folder.

21.4. TESTING

Estimates of the cost of the testing phase of a software program, based on historical data, range as high as 50% of total program cost. The majority of this cost is really due to having to rework the code, as was demonstrated in

Figure 21.2. The high leverage points to reduce testing cost are as we pointed out in the initial program phases; however, there are some important ways to organize and control the test process. First, it is important to establish test objectives early. The creation and validation of hardware and software needed to drive and monitor the software to be delivered may be as, or more, difficult and time-consuming than the deliverables. A test group should be established during the baselining phase to address this problem. Three types of testing must be considered: (1) bottom testing—unit test, normally performed by the developers, (2) thread testing—performed by developers or by the integration team depending on the extent of the thread, and (3) top-down testing—performed by the integration and formally by an independent test team (possibly a validation and verification contractor) using formal controlled test procedures and control. In the unit test, the objective is to execute all the code over the expected range of variables. A wide variety of tools from compilers to sophisticated programmers' workbench systems support this activity [12, 13]. Tools are also available to determine automatically the number of paths that have been executed by a set of test cases [14]. Finally, to force adherence to coding standards, code auditors have been developed [10].

The next level of testing is integration, where many modules are brought together and tested as a whole. Initial testing in this phase concentrates on nominal operability and compatibility (sanity) and verification of design interfaces. Final testing is normally against design goals. The incremental development approach reduces integration risk by allowing it to be initiated earlier with a smaller set of real software (stubs for other software) than in the conventional approach.

The final testing performed during development is a formal test to determine the degree to which the software of the data processing system meets its requirements. This testing is usually performed against a set of acceptance criteria approved by the system designers and/or users. It is important for the program manager to resolve the composition and extent of these tests as early in the program as possible, preferably prior to initiation of development. The user, however, normally wants to wait as long as possible so that he understands the system as well as possible before deciding on the test cases to be used. An approach to resolving this conflict, and indeed to provide excellent control and visibility into test program status, is the early creation of a *test evaluation matrix* [15], which defines the method chosen to validate the satisfaction of each requirement during the test program. The test evaluation matrix (TEM) shows traceability from detailed requirements to design allocations and to the test procedures chosen to verify the requirement. To initiate the planning, an initial allocation of each requirement is made to the unit or process (sometimes to a subprocess or increment) level. If the requirement is contained in a single unit, testing is performed at the task level. If the requirement is significantly affected by interfaces between tasks or is associated with a timing requirement it is allocated to the process level. A TEM report can be produced on a periodic basis summarizing the test status. An example from Reference 15 is shown in Table 21.1. During all test phases, much attention must be paid to configuration management. During the unit test phase, the group leader responsible for development should be responsible. When the final step of the UDF is complete, the responsibility shifts to the integration team leader. Problems and recommended solutions must be approved by the team leader prior to incorporation into the test process. Many copies of the test process can, of course, exist at the same time to support problem resolution, but the baseline process must remain under rigid control. Finally, in the formal test phase, the program manager, audited by his quality assurance support and/or the customer, is in control.

21.5. TRENDS

The present approach to improved software development clearly is to provide increased discipline during development together with im-

Table 21.1. STP Requirements Testing Summary.

	INCREMENT			
	1	2	3	TOTAL
1. No. of requirement entries	5,881	502	4,151	10,534
2. No. of testable requirements	3,603	477	2,089	6,169
3. No. of requirements referenced by more than one specification	847	9	82	938
4. No. of uniquely testable critical requirements	2,796	468	2,007	5,271
5. No. of completely tested requirements	2,277	406	1,603	4,286
6. No. of partially tested requirements	303	23	127	453
7. No. of requirements allocated but not yet tested	0	0	110	110
8. % tested (5 + 6 + 7)/4	92.3%	91.7%	91.7%	92.0%

proved tools to enhance programmer productivity. In applying the discipline, we must be careful to avoid stifling individual initiative and creativity. We are not ready to freeze out all but a single approach to data processing development. Major technological drives continue as the electronics industry continues to produce more computations per second and more storage per unit cost in smaller packages at a staggering rate. These developments have led to distributed systems with much promise, much of it so far unfulfilled.

We also are on the verge of a new generation of tools that support the development in all its phases. Can a new management approach employing all this be far behind?

REFERENCES

1. W. W. Royce, "Managing the Development of Large Software Systems: Concepts and Techniques," *TRW Software Series.*

2. B. W. Boehm, "Software Engineering," *TRW Software Series* TRW-SS-76-08.

3. C. G. Davis and C. R. Vick, "The Software Development System," *Proceedings IEEE/ACM Second International Conference on Software Engineering,* Oct. 1976.

4. M. Alford, "A Requirements Engineering Methodology for Real-Time Processing Requirements," *Proceedings IEEE/ACM Second International Conference on Software Engineering,* October 1976. This paper has also been published in the *TRW Software Series,* TRW-SS-76-07, Sept. 1976.

5. T. E. Bell, D. C. Bixler, and M. E. Dyer, "An Extendable Approach to Computer-Aided Software Requirements Engineering," *Proceedings IEEE/ACM Second International Conference on Software Engineering,* Oct. 1976. This paper has also been published in the *TRW Software Series,* TRW-SS-76-05, July 1976.

6. H. Sayani and D. Teichroew, "Automation of System Building," *Datamation,* August 15, 1971, pp. 25–30.

7. R. J. Lano, *A Technique for Software and Systems Design,* North Holland Publishing Company, 1979.

8. D. L. Parnas, "On the Criteria to Be Used in Decomposing Systems into Modules," *CACM,* Dec. 1972, pp. 1053–1058.

9. R. F. Jewett and E. D. Katz, "Functional Simulation of On-Line Computer Systems," *TRW Software Series,* TRW-SS-71-01, Feb. 1971.

10. R. D. Williams, "Managing the Development of Reliable Software," *Proceedings 1975 International Conference on Reliable Software* (available from IEEE), Apr. 1975, pp. 3–8. This paper has also been published in the *TRW Software Series,* TRW-SS-75-06, Apr. 1975.

11. F. S. Ingrassia, "Unit Development Folder (UDF): An Effective Management Tool for Software Development," *TRW Software Series,* TRW-SS-76-11, Oct. 1976.

12. S. B. F. Ho and C. V. Ramamoorthy, "Testing Large Software with Automated Software Evaluation Systems," *IEEE Transactions Software Engineering,* March 1975, pp. 46–58.

13. E. L. Ivie, "The Programmers Workbench—A Management Tool for Software Development," *ACM Communications,* Oct. 1977, pp. 746–753.

14. J. R. Brown and R. H. Hoffman, "Evaluating the Effectiveness of Software Verification—Practical Experience with An Automated Tool," *TRW Software Series,* TRW-SS-72-08, Dec. 1972.

15. L. W. Diamant and K. W. Krause, "A Management Methodology for Testing Software Requirements," *TRW Software Series,* TRW-SS-78-08, Nov. 1978.

22

Software Costing

R. W. Wolverton
TRW Systems

22.1. INTRODUCTION

It is safe to say that cause and effect relationships in software cost analysis and estimating have been investigated by every major aerospace firm since the landmark study in 1967 by the Systems Development Corporation [1]. Much of this cost information is proprietary because it is used in competitive bidding. However, certain underlying principles can be discussed based on experience in constructing cost models and their relationship to the structure of the software. This chapter takes the position that cost estimating is most important at the time of responding to a request for proposal (RFP). The RFP framework is used in this chapter, but the principles and procedures also apply to in-house software at the point of development budget commitment.

Problems of accuracy and generality in derived cost parameters arise from limited data sets, the inherent complexity of software development, ill-constructed historical data, and the organizational split between financial experts and software system experts. Reliable cost-estimating factors are difficult to derive for broad applicability because individual software development approaches reflect the custom of each software firm and the prior expectations of management [2].

Cost Estimating Approaches

Five additional approaches to software cost estimating are top-down estimating, similarities and differences estimating, ratio estimating, standards estimating, and bottom-up estimating, which—for cross-checking—are used in combinations of two or more (e.g., top-down versus bottom-up).

In *top-down estimating,* the estimator relies on the total cost of large portions of previously completed projects to estimate the cost of all or large portions of the current project. History, coupled with informed opinion, is used to prorate costs between packages. Among the pitfalls of this approach are the overlooking of special or difficult technical problems that may be buried in the project tasks and the problem of a lack of details needed for future cost justification. This approach should be used for a first estimate of the probable cost of a new acquisition.

Similarities and differences estimating breaks down the work units to be accomplished to a level at which the similarities to and differences from previous projects are most evident. Work units that cannot be compared are estimated by another method. Use this approach to refine—by further subdivision of work—the first top-down estimate or to make a bottom-up estimate.

In *ratio estimating,* the estimator relies on sensitivity coefficients or exchange ratios that are invariant (within limits) to the details of the design. If mission requirements can be mapped into software functions, then software functions can be transformed into software modules. The software analyst estimates the size of a module by its number of object (or source) instructions, classifies it by type, and evaluates its relative complexity.

With *standards estimating,* the estimator relies on standards of performance that have been systematically developed. These standards become stable reference points from which new tasks can be calibrated by ratio and/or by similarities, and different industries such as manufacturing and construction, which have records of repeated operations, use this method routinely. Standards estimating is accurate when the same operations have been performed repeatedly and good records are available. Obviously, custom software development is not suited to this approach. Most often this method should not be selected for estimating the cost of operational software.

In *bottom-up estimating,* the total job is broken down into relatively small work packages and work units. The work breakdown is continued until it is reasonably clear what steps and talents are required for completing each task. Each task is then estimated, and the costs are pyramided to form the total project costs. Use the bottom-up approach for pre-RFP cost estimating, and check it against the top-down estimating approach.

Note. Two approaches should always be used. It is necessary to cross-check one approach with the other and to provide a systematic basis that will account for any observed difference in the total cost.

The Importance of Estimating Size in Estimating Costs

Nearly all cost modeling relies, to a varying extent, on the number of steps taken by a sequential machine to complete the computation as measured in lines of source or object instructions. For instance:

1. Once the functions of a computer program have been visualized by the engineering staff, the length of each function should be estimated to improve the validity of the early design and the accuracy of the independent cost estimate.
2. Once the length of a computer program has been estimated by the engineering staff (e.g., lines of object code), work can begin on an independent cost estimate. The cost estimating team should consist of one experienced software designer and one financial analyst.

Table 22.1. Estimated Baseline F-111A/E Application.

FUNCTION	MEMORY REQUIREMENTS
Navigation	4,500
Navigation update	2,000
Steering	1,500
Target acquisition	2,000
Stores management	1,000
Weapon delivery	4,000
Mission planning	1,000
Controls/displays	4,000
Sensors control	1,000
System management	2,000
Utility routines	1,000
Total memory	24,000

3. An example of sizing the functions and memory requirements for the F-111 A/E avionics operational flight program is given in Table 22.1. The units of measure are object code based on J73/I source code, and 16 bit data words [3]. In practice, building this table would be one of the end products of the entire proposal design team.

Refinement of the Independent Estimate

Good engineering practice suggests that the functional estimates be made one level down and reported one level up, giving the practitioner a depth to his or her analytical work that can withstand challenge. Specifically:

1. This guideline means that whatever the level of internal reporting of planning results to the proposal manager from the engineering staff, the analytical work is refined one step below the level reported to upper management. For example, if results are reported at the subsystem level, the work is done at the module (or unit) level. Assume that the basic software hierarchy is system, subsystem, and module (or unit).
2. This guideline means that the proposal manager should allow time for questioning the internal estimate, particularly the basis of estimate at pre-RFP time. Various ways to implement this suggested

procedure are available to the manager: First, assign two cost teams to independently solve the same problem, or second, ask one cost team to use two different methods in solving the same problem. A cost team is assumed to consist of one software engineer and one cost analyst.

The proposal manager should schedule a day to review the internal cost estimates in response to the RFP. In his approach he should consider not only the development cost but also the operation and support cost. Together these constitute the life cycle cost of ownership to the government. A typical period to consider might be the first 10 years of ownership (e.g., a 2 year development time and an 8 year operation and support time). Many words have been used to describe the government's intention of turning to acquisition methods based on design-to-cost concepts. Sometimes this is the actual philosophy, and sometimes it is hypothetical. Still, if a particular design and its partitioning for ease of extensibility or transporting can be shown to reduce life cycle costs at essentially no increase in development cost, this is a valid point to be highlighted in the bidder's cost and technical volume.

The Statistical Meaning of a Cost Estimate

A statistical meaning must be defined for the software cost estimate regardless of what methodology is used to develop that estimate. For example, the proposal manager is given an estimate of 1,000 manmonths for the cost of a planned acquisition. It should be assumed that a given cost estimate is a 50% probability estimate. All levels of management should understand that, unless otherwise specified, any cost estimate is equally likely to be overrun as underrun.

Should the government want a 90% probability of not exceeding a given cost estimate, it would be specified in the RFP. The estimated cost would be expected to increase above the 50% probability estimate. This is where the government can choose the risk level: 50 (parity), 80, 90, or 95% probability of not exceeding that cost.

Only one level should be chosen and communicated to all bidders. Obviously, the source selection board cannot legitimately compare 50% probability costs with 90% probability costs.

22.2. SELECTING CHARACTERISTIC PARAMETERS

A major requirement for the cost analyst is access to auditable financial data and software engineering data from past projects. Cost data definitions for the present cost estimate should be made by the analyst and related to the statistical population comprising the costing data base.

Software Structural Parameters

Top-level characteristics parameters can be classified into software structural parameters and project financial parameters. The software cost model connects the structural and financial parameters. In this section, priority will be given to defining software structural parameters observed to be significant cost drivers. Where possible, the estimate should be made in units of manmonths from a well-defined beginning to an end point, (e.g., from contract go-ahead through analysis and design, code and debug, and integration, and test to operational demonstration and acceptance).

By convention, the operation and maintenance (O&M) phase begins at the time of operational demonstration and acceptance. Conversely, upon completion of this event, development is considered completed. Life cycle cost is the sum of development plus O&M phase costs. In principle, a clear distinction can be made between development and O&M costs and activities; in practice, the analyst should be mindful of the practical difficulty in separating these costs when looking at historical data.

Software structural parameters may be grouped into size, program attributes, hardware attributes, project attributes, and environmental attributes. Size factors ordinarily consist of the number of source instructions, object instructions, and routines, and the number of pages of documentation. Program attributes consist of software type, complexity, language, and fraction of reuse. Hardware attributes include time constraints, storage constraints, hardware configuration, and concurrent hardware/software development. Project attributes involve estimates of personnel quality, personnel continuity, hardware experience, application experience, language experience, and tools [4]. A more detailed discussion of the cost effect of these factors is given in Chapter 23.

Environmental attributes are expressed by measures associated with customer interface, requirements definition, requirements volatility, schedule constraint, security, computer access, rehosting, and required quality. Each cost model uses different combinations of these characteristics parameters as input (e.g., one cost model may use source statements and an-

other may use machine language instructions [MLI] as the measure of software size). An example of various input parameters to four cost models—Boeing [5], IBM [6], Putnam [7], and RCA PRICE [8]—is given in Table 22.2.

Project Financial Parameters

Project financial records, as used in this chapter, are grouped into direct labor charges, overhead, other direct charges, general and administrative, and fee. Embedded computer resource cost estimates generally do not include fee because this is subject to the outcome of bidding and negotiating strategy. By definition, the sum of cost plus fee is price. Fee is identical to profit. Whatever is assumed for fee, including zero, should be shown as a line item. The relationship between each of the fi-

Table 22.2. Characteristic Parameters Used as Input to Four Cost Models.

GROUP	FACTOR	BOEING	IBM	PUTNAM	RCA
Size	Source instructions	X	X	X	
	Object instructions				X
	Number routines				X
	Number data items		X		
	Documentation		X		
	Number personnel	X	X		
Program attributes	Type	X	X	X	X
	Complexity		X	X	X
	Language	X		X	X
	Reuse	X			X
Hardware attributes	Time constraints	X	X	X	X
	Storage constraints		X		X
	Hardware configuration				X
	Concurrent hardware and software development		X		X
Project attributes	Personnel quality		X	X	
	Personnel continuity		X		
	Hardware experience		X	X	
	Application experience	X	X	X	
	Language experience		X		
	Tools and techniques	X	X	X	X
Environmental attributes	Customer interface		X		
	Requirements definition		X		
	Requirements volatility		X		
	Schedule			X	X
	Security		X		
	Computer access	X	X		
	Rehosting				
	Required quality				X

Table 22.3. Authorized Cost Accounting Characteristic Parameters.

CATEGORY		COST (ACCOUNTING UNITS)
Direct labor charges		1,000*
By manhours ×		
approved rate		
10 labor categories		
Overhead		1,300
Employee benefits		
"Cost of doing		
business"		
	Subtotal	2,300
Other direct charges		
Computer time		100
Travel		50
Documentation		45
Other allowables		
	Subtotal	2,495
General and		
administrative		135
	Subtotal	2,630
Fee		270
	Total price	2,900

*For 1,000 *accounting units* worth of direct labor in this example, the cost is 2,630 accounting units when fully burdened through G&A. One accounting unit might equal $1,000.

nancial parameters is shown in Table 22.3. Working definitions of characteristic financial parameters are given in the following material in the sequence shown in Table 22.3.

Direct labor charges are developed by labor category and the labor rate approved by the resident *administrative contracting officer* (ACO) at each bidder's facility. In general, any software cost-estimating algorithm should take into account management, engineering, programming, clerical, and support hours. If the cost-estimated model provides its output in manmonths, the total manmonth figure must be converted to total hours. In turn, the total must reflect the labor mix. As a baseline case, the proposal manager can make an assumption about the number of manhours in a manmonth and a typical labor mix. This initial assumption can be improved upon later.

Assume that a standard manmonth consists of 152 manhours, unless otherwise specified.

For realistic planning, the basic manyear of 2,080 hours is reduced by nonproductive time* as follows:

Vacation		107 hr
Holidays		80 hr
Sick leave		64 hr
	Total	251 hr
Standard manyear		1,829 hr
Standard manmonth		152 hr

Assume that the typical labor mix for operational software development is distributed as shown below, unless otherwise specified:

Management	10
Engineering	40
Programming	40
Clerical/support	10
	100%

Suppose that a particular cost estimate gives a value of 500 manmonths for software development. As a first approximation, the functional distribution of manpower (according to the above definition of a developer's typical labor mix) would be further subdivided as: 50 manmonths of managerial effort, 200 manmonths of engineering work, 200 manmonths of programming work, and 50 manmonths of secretarial services. This functional distribution, of course, should be expected to vary from bidder to bidder for the same RFP. As a guideline, however, a baseline distribution of labor categories against which to compare each proposal estimate should be adopted. The proposal manager will then be in a better position to evaluate the overall understanding of the job and to ask questions of the proposal team as to why some labor category might seem out of line.

Overhead consists of costs incurred by organizations involved in the day-to-day support of operating tasks necessary for fulfillment of all contracts and includes management sup-

---

*This nonproductive time is not charged to the direct labor expense for a given project. Each aerospace bidder has other accounts as approved by the ACO to apportion these hours.

port, payroll expenses, and communications costs. Expenditures for overhead tasks are charged to one of the burden pools of the multiple burden pool system. Distribution of the pools to contracts is based on direct labor hours.

Other Direct Charges (ODC) are defined by a number of cost elements, of which only three are of immediate interest. These are computer time, travel, and documentation charges. All ODC bears G&A, but is not burdened by overhead.

ODC can be estimated as a ratio with respect to direct charges. If the proposal manager has cost accounting data for similar past projects, he can use this data to note the similarities and differences of the main ODC charges in his own independent cost estimate. A realistic baseline cost to allow for ODC in the absence of specific data is 20% of the direct labor charges.

Several ODC cost elements recognized by the ACO are excluded from the above definition because they are unique to each acquisition. The key guideline is to be aware of the ODC charges (what is included and excluded) in the independent cost estimate. For example, if computer time is furnished by the government to the software developer, it should not show up in the bidder's cost estimate. Instead the bidder may want to show his computer usage rate by month in terms of CPU hours. In some instances, travel expenses will be unusually high for a particular acquisition; a separate estimate might then be made for travel. Travel or computer cost should be accounted for once and only once.

General and Administrative (G&A) consists of expenditures for those functions that are identified with the overall management and sustenance of the software developer. The G&A rate is developed by dividing the G&A pool expenses by the cost of sales. The base for applying the G&A rate to the software developer's project is the total cost of the project, including all applicable direct and indirect costs.

Again, know what is and is not in the independent cost estimate. The simplest way to implement this guideline is to construct a table like Table 22.3.

Even if the cost algorithm gives only the number of manmonths as output, the proposal manager can assume a standard rate for burdened manmonth and separate the bottom line dollar cost into the separate cost elements of Table 22.3. Assume $5,000 (or an appropriate value) for a burdened manmonth in 1980 dollars, through G&A.

The Cost Model as Connection between Structural and Financial Parameters

The connection between software structural parameters and project financial parameters is accomplished by the software cost model. Achieving the right balance between accuracy and simplicity of a model depends on the model developer's judgment. Models form an important part of the developer's system-building process because economy, availability, and information must be related in a repeatable manner. Identical input parameters to a particular cost algorithm will produce identical outputs (i.e., any two people using the same model and same inputs will get the same output).

Typical classifications of models are descriptive and normative. A descriptive model describes a system by its characteristic parameters without making any assessment of the system's value or its performance. Normative models describe a system as it would be if it satisfied some criteria of optimality. The contractual design requirements for a system capability would represent a normative model of the system. Normative models provide goals for systems design and systems operation whether or not they are achievable. The general guidance to the proposal manager is to match his or her model of choice to the realism of the available inputs.

Mathematical optimization uses some model of the system plus a mathematical statement of the criteria for optimality. This statement is called a value function or an objective function. The optimization process may attempt to maximize value, a benefit-cost ratio, or reliability (error-freeness); or to minimize life cycle cost, time, or inputs. In practice, this degree of sophistication is beyond the current state of the art in software cost estimating and analysis technology.

Ideally, a top-level cost model would be a normative model with a cost-benefit side constraint for the total life cycle costs (i.e., recurrent and nonrecurrent costs for the development phase through the O&M phase). However, the functional form of most development phase cost models is descriptive and is not strongly influenced by O&M phase considerations [9].

22.3. MAINTAINING AND USING COST DATA AND RECORDS

Developing a Software Work Breakdown Structure

Before software cost data can be collected and records maintained, the proposal manager must set up a reporting mechanism at RFP time to fit present and future data collection needs. This reporting mechanism starts with a proper WBS. Personnel responsible for operational software must make software as prominent as a hardware end item in the WBS.

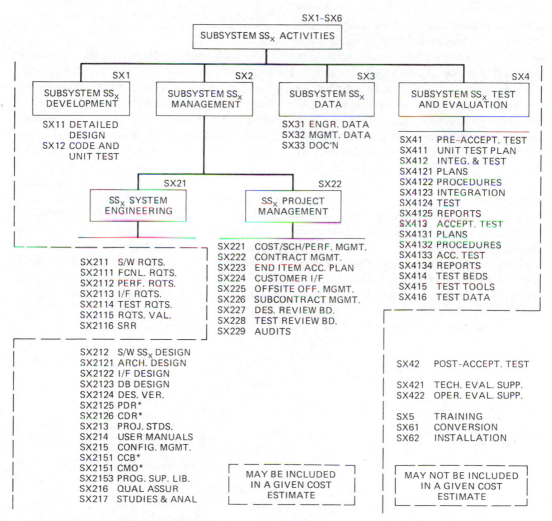

*SEE ACRONYMS AND ABBREVIATIONS

Figure 22.1. A process-oriented work breakdown structure (WBS).

The software's work breakdown structure must be process-oriented (e.g., analysis, design, code and unit test, integration, and test) at the cost entry level, and product-oriented (e.g., program, subprogram, module, and segment) at the work unit level, and must track back to milestone events in the software development plan. Unfortunately, the guidelines given in MIL-STD-881A are incomplete for the software development effort; workable guidelines, however, can be written within the framework of MIL-STD-881A, as done in Figure 22.1.

The proposal manager should set up the software WBS (see Figure 22.1) with the operational computer program directly supporting a prime mission end item in the language of MIL-STD-881A. This means operational software must be shown at all levels in the WBS needed to substantiate its proposed development cost and its actual cost during the period of performance. The software elements should be at the same organizational level as hardware elements (both are deliverable products), and should be controlled at the lowest entry level by a job number that is process-oriented. By tracking the labor costs for software building processes, the proposal manager can separate the costs for analysis, design, code and debug, and integration and test. Implementing this guideline will help solve a major cost accounting problem in software analysis and estimating practices.

Table 22.4. WBS Hierarchy and Related Product or Process.

WBS HIERARCHY	WBS PRODUCT OR PROCESS
Level 1	System
Level 2	Prime mission end item, training, support, . . .
Level 3	Software, hardware, . . .
Level 4 Software branch	Subsystem 1, subsystem N, . . .
Level 5 Software branch Subsystem 1	Subsystem requirements, subsystem design, subsystem implementation, subsystem test and integration, subsystem documentation
Level 6 Software branch Subsystem 1 Subsystem design	Subsystem preliminary design, subsystem preliminary design review, subsystem detailed design, subsystem critical design review

A WBS is a product-oriented, tree-structured representation of the hardware, software, services, and data that comprise an acquisition. Software development is labor-intensive and largely intangible until made concrete, especially by documentation and management tools like the *unit development folder* [10]. The connection between Figure 22.1, the activity hierarchy, and Figure 22.2, the product hierarchy, will be briefly explained.

The government requires that the WBS be divided into levels that subdivide the work into manageable units, as shown in Table 22.4.

At level 5 the character subdivision shifts from the product itself (e.g., level 4 subsystem 1) to the human processes that created the

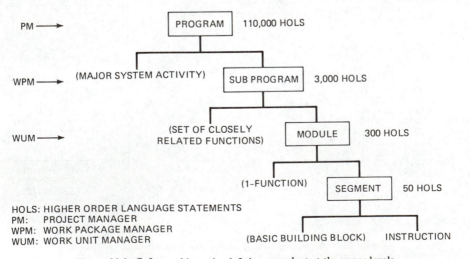

Figure 22.2. Software hierarchy defining a product at the upper levels.

product (e.g., requirements analysis, design, and implementation). At level 6, each constituent has still further subdivision (e.g., comprising design is preliminary design and PDR). Point-of-entry subdivision labor charges are at, say, level 6 for the work on subsystem 1, preliminary design, by means of the worker's weekly time card. Individual weekly time charges link into all higher levels; only one cost entry is made, however, from which all further cost records aggregate. This entry point is by the job number assigned by a project work authorization (or equivalent) in a way to be described in the section entitled Measuring Work Accomplished.

Figure 22.1 shows an abbreviated WBS that, as always, defines a product at the upper levels and is defined by a work procedure or process at the entry level. Figure 22.2 shows how a computer program might be subdivided into subprograms, modules, and segments down to the elemental instruction, the lowest identifiable element. Development of the computer program is managed by the software developer's *project manager* (PM). If subprogram and subsystem are equivalent terms, a *work package manager* (WPM) would be responsible for developing a set of subprograms that is representative of major software system activities. Likewise, a *work unit manager* (WUM) would be responsible for a set of modules (or set of closely related functions). Each manager supports objectives and aids in the collection of cost records suitable to his or her own level. The connection between Figures 22.1 and 22.2 will be further explained in the next sections.

Process Hierarchy and Product Hierarchy

Software is made up of a hierarchy of elements that aids in subdividing the work so that it can be done by separate groups of designers to meet schedule and other constraints. Programs are divided into successively smaller sections, herein called subprograms, modules, and segments (see Figure 22.2). This division into simpler parts allows a complex program to be defined, developed, implemented, and maintained. Statistical data gathered from software

projects amounting to 2,000,000 manhours supports the practicality of this general software hierarchy [11].

Theoretical work on how to modularize a software system so that the resulting modules are testable and maintainable has appeared in the literature [12, 13, 14]. Although the life cycle cost of software is strongly influenced by its modularity and complexity, the best practice developer is only now reducing some of the theory to practice.

Experience has shown that development resources are allocated approximately 40% for analysis and design, 20% for code and debug, and 40% for test and integration [15]. From life cycle analysis, we know that over a 10 year useful life about 39% of the total resources is spent for development and 61% is spent for operation and maintenance [16]. The objective is to cut the cost of testing and maintenance for the greatest leverage payoff.

Each software developer has some means of authorizing work among the various skill centers in the functional organization that supports his or her project manager. Normally, this project work authorization (PWA) specifies what measurable work is to be accomplished, by when, and at what maximum cost. Each work assignment supports its senior-level work objectives.

All cost data collected and reviewed by both the government and the software developer's PM originates as a planned expenditure by labor hours and dollars through the PWA (or an equivalent). An example of a particular project work authorization form is shown in Figure 22.3. Actual hours and costs incurred against this kind of PWA are generally reported to the software developer's PM weekly and to the government monthly. The government sees the aggregate of all PWAs.

Measuring Work Accomplished

The developer must not lose sight of the goal of having the lowest-level entry point (i.e., the job number or equivalent) be process-oriented. Process-oriented means work-oriented (e.g., analysis and design, code and debug, and integration and test). Labor expenditures are

XYZ,Inc.		PROJECT TITLE		REQUESTING		AUTHORIZING	
				LOG NO.	REV.	LOG NO.	REV.
PROJECT WORK AUTHORIZATION		PROJECT VAST				BBB 200	13

CONTRACT NO. F04704-76-C-0016	SALES NO. 30067	ORIGINATOR F. W. Hafermalz	SPONSOR ORG. SMD	DATE 3/19/78	PAGE 1	OF 1

FISCAL EFFECT

BUDGET INCREASE	X	PRELIM. BUDGET	☐
BUDGET DECREASE	☐	PERF. MEAS. BUDGET	☐
NO CHANGE	☐	FORECAST	☐

	DOLLARS	HOURS
AMOUNT THIS ISSUE	$150,000	

ECP·CCP/SSN #   CHANGE ORDER #

SCHEDULE EFFECT

| SCHEDULE | NO CHANGE ☐ | SEE TEXT X | ATTACH. ☐ | TO FOLLOW ☐ |

WORK IS DIRECTED TO:

BBB 200: Command and Control Subproject

REASON/AUTHORIZATION FOR CHANGE:

1. Contract Work Statement for Contract No. 123-456-789

2. IOC from F. W. Hafermalz to G. Wright, "Phase III System Analysis Software Support, AEP Development"

PROJECT APPROVAL X   DISAPPROVAL ☐   REASON:

SAMPLE

WBS ELEMENT OR JOB NO.	WORK DESCRIPTION & SPECIAL INSTRUCTIONS (Indicate Schedule Dates for each item, unless noted above)
	This PWA authorizes funds for all of the tasks required to analyze, design, code and test the Command Decoder which meets the requirements of the SAMSO Statement of Work. Detailed tasks required to accomplish this effort are:
2443-94	Command Decoder — $44,115
	1. Perform design analysis and support studies with the Vela Command Decoder.
	2. Evaluate approaches to LF filtering and display.
	3. Perform keyboard/printer utilization analysis.
	4. Test decoder for continuity.
	5. Analyze test results and develop requirements for flight OFP.
	Schedule
	This task is scheduled to start 1 January 1979 through 28 September 1979.
2443-95	OEP Software — $105,885
	1. Initiate Part I Specification.
	2. Initiate preliminary design activities.
	3. Support Part II Specification of OEP development.
	Schedule
	This task is scheduled to start 1 March 1979 through 23 October 1979.

USE CONTINUATION SHEET (SYSTEMS 4832) IF NEEDED

APPROVALS

AUTHORIZED BY			ACCEPTED BY		
PROJECT/SUBPROJECT MGR.	CCC	DATE	SUBPROJECT/OTHER MGR	CCC	DATE
			G. Wright *G. Wright*	6930	
			FUNCTIONAL MGR	CCC	DATE
F. W. Hafermalz	3621		D. Shepard *D. Shepard*	5900	

SYSTEMS 2332 REV. 6-76

Figure 22.3. Typical project work authorization (PWA) instrument.

charged against job numbers (JNs) by the individual worker every week. JN data can be automatically summed to all next-higher levels, eventually ending up with the cost of the computer program end item. Control of the JN allows control of the project and, simultaneously, control of the process.

Note. Cost data and records should be structured with the thought that the results will be used not only for ongoing cost reporting and control, but also for improving the accuracy of future cost estimates. Under present working conditions, it is usually impossible to reconstruct the distribution of resources as a function of the kinds of work accomplished. Accountants keep cost records, but the content of the records they keep should be determined by technical managers. The manager can plan the cost reporting activities to serve the dual purpose of present control and future cost estimating.

Once the groundwork for cost data and records is in place as the above guidelines suggest, the proposal manager should take advantage of cost records that enable him to measure work accomplished as a function of dollars expended. This is achieved by reporting earned value in accordance with a relatively new procedure that is being introduced by the government for all software projects whose face value is $2 million or more [17]. It can also be applied to smaller projects with discretion. Use the concepts of C/SSR in reporting and control requirements to the maximum extent possible. The general idea is this:

1. The government should ask the software developer to report on earned value, which is the central theme of C/SSR.
2. The formula for earned value is just the arithmetic product of the percentage of work completed and the authorized budget. The dollar value agreed to in the PWA is the authorized budget, which can be found by inspecting this record.
3. Cost reporting tasks should be subdivided into small enough increments (e.g., 4 to 6 months length of task and $10,000 to $60,000) so that reasonable accuracy is ensured. When work accomplished is reported as 100%, the earned value should equal the amount originally allocated by the PWA.
4. Monthly reports should be made to the government by the software developer for all costs, hours, and earned value according to the WBS level specified in the contract.
5. Conventional time-to-complete and cost-to-complete evaluations may or may not

be required. In conventional CPFF contracts, 60 days prior to reaching the 75% cost (including profit) the software developer must notify the government.

Central Collection Point

After the proper initial conditions are set up, the problem of maintaining cost data and records is much simpler. Two categories of cost data collection are important: cost records must be properly maintained on each new software project, and cost records are needed on a representative sample of software projects from which statistical inferences may be made. A completed data collection form for each project must be maintained. Then, as the data collection procedure itself becomes routine for new starts, some kind of on-line record storage and retrieval procedure can be considered.

Data items that comprise the inputs to the cost models should be maintained by a point contact within the developer's company and accessible to proposal-cost-estimating personnel. The principal requirement is for upper management to establish an enforceable cost data collection plan and a central collection point for maintaining the data so that it is readily accessible to any proposal manager.

Cost data entered into the central collection point records is largely determined by the input requirements of the developer's preferred cost model(s). It is assumed that the proposal manager will cross-check his results by adopting two or more cost models from the available state-of-the-art models and will not design his own. The proposal manager should be concerned with software acquisition problems, not with designing cost-estimating models.

The most important test of the validity of any cost model is to predict the manmonths required by a (completed) project from data in the data base and to plot the "predicted" versus the "actual" manmonths for all the projects in the repository (a minimum of 10, preferably 20, projects is needed). The guidelines are as follows:

1. Account for all direct labor manhours charged to the contract (i.e., management, engineering, programming, and

clerical support). Plot the estimated manmonths from the model (y axis) versus the measured manmonths from project cost (x axis).

2. Decide on the conversion factor for converting manhours to manmonths and document the rationale. Use a statistical procedure, such as least squares, to fit xy axis data.

3. Choose a goodness-of-fit parameter, such as the least-squares fit correlation coefficient or the coefficient of determination. The latter defines what decimal fraction of the variance is explained by the model.

4. Finally, use a simple criterion for evaluation of the goodness of fit: the cost model should be accurate to within 20% of the actuals, 80% of the time.

Few current software models demonstrate their accuracy in terms of the goodness of fit of "predicted" versus "actual" manmonths for a family of recently completed software projects. Some state-of-the-art cost models use current actuals to calibrate the model for a recently completed project. When used after self-calibration they appear to perform near-perfect in "estimating" the project used in the calibration. The analyst should be wary of this pitfall, especially if the new software to be estimated is not comparable to the single point calibration.

The crucial goodness-of-fit parameter test is often omitted because the functional form of the cost model is determined by the model developer, whereas the operational performance of the model is determined by the model user through the validity of his or her input data and the complexity of the application software. Each current cost model must be used with judgment. Criteria for evaluating the goodness of the cost model itself have been documented [4].

22.4. PROBLEMS IN COST ANALYSIS AND COMPARISON

Undefined Assumptions

Software engineering is a discipline founded on axioms and basic assumptions—often un-

defined. In dealing with the area of software cost analysis and comparison, the analyst should remember that only a handful of software structural parameters can be counted or measured from a hard copy of any computer program. Some measurable parameters of computer programs are length, volume, program level, language level, effort, and programming time [18]. From these tangible software parameters, model designers have developed relationships consistent with software structural parameters, financial records, development environment, and model fidelity [19]. From these a cost model is usually calibrated, using one or more past projects. Problems arise, however, from the lack of generality in most cost models.

In closed-form cost models, the population from which the sample is drawn should be representative of the new software. Representativeness is the main calibration tool in closed-form models. A set of undefined data points used in constructing a given closed-form model invalidates the model. Consequently, the analyst should insist on knowing the past projects from which the closed-form estimating algorithm was derived. For instance, if the set largely contains real-time software data points, *and* if the data are consistent with respect to endpoints, WBS elements included, lines of code counted, consistent indirect costs, and so forth, the analyst can be reasonably sure that the mode is suitable for a preliminary cost estimate. An example of a data set from which a closed-form cost-estimating model was derived is shown in the section Sparse Metrics. In general, the analyst should not expect the results of a least-squares fit to be as accurate as shown; the hypothesis is that these data points are samples of a homogeneous population.

Sparse Metrics

Given the guidelines in earlier sections of this chapter for identifying potential problems, several unanswered questions can be raised in looking at the closed-form model in Figures 22.4 and 22.5. Some of these problems can now be cleared up. Five characteristic prob-

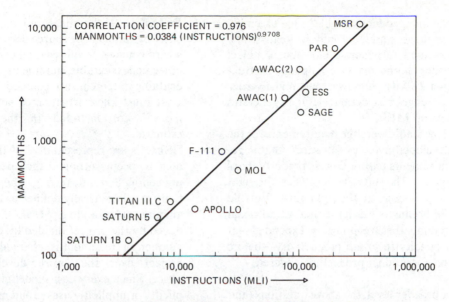

Figure 22.4. Real-time software cost-estimating relationship.

lems can be stated in the form of the following questions:

1. What was the development time for each project in the sample? This cannot be determined from looking at the data set in Figures 22.4 and 22.5.
2. How stressed was the real-time computer in each sample project? We have seen the extreme nonlinear effects of disproportionately using the available memory capacity. At delivery, at least 25%, and preferably 50%, spare core should be reserved for subsequent growth.
3. What was included in the resultant manmonth estimate: analysis and design, code and debug, test and integration? For example, did the sample point include the first several months of maintenance? Did it include requirements analysis? Was it made up of 40% new code and 60% off-the-shelf? This information is missing from Figures 22.4 and 22.5.
4. What were the exact units of measure of

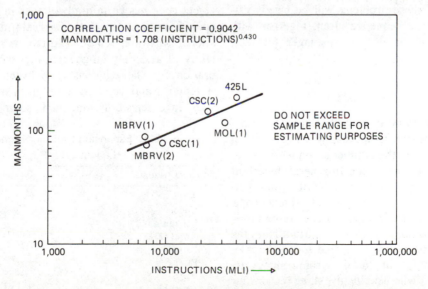

Figure 22.5. Nonreal-time software cost-estimating relationship.

the independent variable? One assembly language statement may be realistically assumed to generate one line of object code, or one machine language instruction (MLI); however, one higher-order language instruction (HOL) generates several MLIs.

5. How stable were the requirements for the developed avionics software? Stable requirements ensure that, if properly managed by the software developer, the right work is done at the right time. Volatile requirements mean that many additional manmonths are probably expended—at a penalty in group productivity—before the operational product is delivered.

On a broader level, the above questions (and there are many others) should be asked of any other model (e.g., assumptions about descriptive and normative models). A more complete list of problems can be defined for consideration by the proposal manager. Five top-level problems in cost analysis and comparison are:

1. Sizing units and rationale
2. Definition and comparability of terms
3. Breakage, requirements volatility effects, and incremental development effects
4. Disciplined data collection
5. Cost/quality tradeoffs

Each of these problems will be briefly discussed in the sequence given, together with guidance to the proposal manager for their solutions.

Sizing Units and Rationale

One of the important characteristic parameters in software cost estimating is the length of a program (i.e., the number of sequential steps taken by the computer). In general, length or size can be measured in units of source language statements or lines of object code. Source code is the input to the compiler-assembler and object code is the output from the compiler-assembler. Delivered source lines of code (DSLOC) are used by some model developers [6] who usually give three reasons for preferring DSLOCs:

1. DSLOCs can be measured unambiguously by running the source deck through a card counter. In this case all comments, other nonexecutable statements, and executable statements are counted. The analyst must know whether or not "comments" are included in the sizing estimate.
2. DSLOCs are representative of the work done by people sitting at their desks during coding and unit testing. The productivity rate is generally defined as the total amount of code (e.g., DSLOCs) produced by the project divided by the total number of manmonths charged to the project over the entire development phase. Since every cost model either explicitly or implicitly uses group measures of productivity, this attribute has intuitive appeal.
3. DSLOCs are useful when a relatively large data sample is accessible in the same source language. The projects analyzed by Walston and Felix were of mixed language: about 50% high-level language and 50% assembly level. If the real-time software is developed in assembly language, equations scaled for higher-order language source become invalid.

The measurement of program size in lines of object code has certain advantages in case of operational use, especially for real-time operational software, which is often written directly in assembly language. A general calibration for the relationship between source statements and object code is given in Table 22.5. In other words, one APL source state-

Table 22.5. Expansion Ratio for High-Level Languages.

SOURCE LANGUAGE	EXPANSION RATIO
APL	12:1
Cobol	5:1
Fortran	4–7:1
Jovial (J3)	4.5:1
Pascal	8:1
PL/I	3:1
PL/S	2.5:1
Assembly	1.05–1.1:1

ment may generate 12 lines of object code, and one assembly language statement may generate slightly more than one line of object code. The model user must clearly know what program-sizing units are required as input to his preferred cost model, particularly the difference between source statements and object code.

Three advantages to cost estimating in units of delivered executable machine instructions (DEMIs), along with a definition, are given below:

1. By running the source deck through a compiler-assembler, DEMIs can be measured unambiguously; the count that is automatically generated can then be used as a normal compiler output parameter. This excludes all nonexecutable lines, particularly comments. If assembly language is the "source," the compiler step is skipped and the production of object code begins with the assembler.
2. DEMIs are a measure of the useful work done by the target computer after the source code is compiled. They occupy main memory in the computer. When core-resident data are added to DEMIs, the ratio of memory used to memory available can be immediately calculated. As previously noted, this measure of stress on the computer can be a dominant cost driver, as shown in Table 22.6 [8].
3. DEMIs measure the size of the program to be tested in the computer. They are the lowest practical denominator for measuring work accomplished, even if the source deck is a mixture of one or more higher-order languages and assembly language for time-critical modules.

Table 22.6. Effect of Memory Stress.

STRESS FACTOR	NORMALIZED COST	NORMALIZED SCHEDULE
0.50	1.00	1.00
0.60	1.08	1.00
0.70	1.21	1.00
0.80	1.47	1.05
0.85	1.73	1.10
0.90	2.25	1.18
0.95	3.78	1.36

Also, if characteristic cost data are available from real-time software projects generated in various assembly languages, statistical analysis of the set is possible by using DEMIs and then combining the samples as if they were members of the same population.

Definition and Comparability of Terms

A major problem in software engineering is the definition and comparability of terms. One factor to which software cost analysis and estimating is sensitive is the comparison of similar measurable attributes, such as DEMIs, as the unit of size. By definition, the number of DEMIs means the number of deliverable executable machine instructions. In other words:

1. *Deliverable* is generally meant to exclude nondeliverable support software such as test drivers. However, if these are significant software development activities that require their own reviews, test plans, and documentation, they should be included in the size estimate and differentiated from the operational software. If the support software is core-resistant and is used, for example, in the self-test of the main program, it is a deliverable product anyway.
2. *Executable* is generally meant to exclude comments and data. If a portion of the operational software is table-driven and the table entries are used to control the execution sequence, these tables should be counted as executable instructions. Otherwise, data requirements should be covered in some other characteristic parameter.
3. *Machine instruction* is an elementary computer instruction as defined in the Principles of Operation or an equivalent manual for the target computer. For microcode, use the number of executable microinstructions.

Closely linked to the measure of computer program size as a cost driver is the problem of computer program complexity. Table 22.7 illustrates two problems facing the proposal

484 HANDBOOK OF SOFTWARE ENGINEERING

Table 22.7. Airborne Data-Processing Characteristics.

A/C SYSTEM	ONBOARD, WORK-ORIENTED DIGITAL COMPUTERS	NUMBER OF COMPUTERS/ AIRCRAFT	PRIMARY FUNCTIONS OF OFP
F-106	Hughes, 2K RWM, 32K drum	1	Fire control
	Total: Memory = 2K RWM 32K drum	1	
C-141	General precision, 4K by 25 bit RWM	1	General navigation
	Total: Memory = 4K	1	
A-7D/E	IBM 4PI/TC-2, 16K by 16 bit RWM	1	Navigation, weapons delivery, delivery controls, and situation displays
	Elliotson, 2K by 12 bit ROM	1	Display generation for HUD
	Total: Memory = 18K	2	
C-5	Northrop NDC-1051A, 12K by 28 bit RWM	1	Primary navigation
	Northrop NDC-1051A, 8K by 28 bit RWM	1	Auxiliary navigation
	Northrop NDC-1060, 8K by 28 bit RWM	1	Malfunction detecting analysis/ recording.
	Total: Memory = 28K	3	
F-111	IBM 4PI/CP-2, 16K by 16 bit RWM	2	Navigation, weapons delivery, controls and displays
	Autonetics D26J-41, 4K by 12 bit RWM	1	Inertial navigation controls
	Autonetics D26J-103J, 16K by 24 bit RWM (Added post-1971)	1	Prelaunch control
	Total: (Pre-1971) Memory = 36K	2	
	(Post-1971) Memory = 52K	3	
F-15	IBM 4PI/AP-1, 16K by 32 bit RWM	1	Navigation, controls and displays, weapon delivery, mission eval.
	TI 2520-2, 16K by 16 bit RWM	1	Electronic warfare
	Hughes 081, 24K by 24 bit RWM	1	Radar processing, fire control
	Sperry, 2.8K by 16 bit ROM	1	Air data processing
	Hamilton std., 1K by 16 bit ROM	1	Engine inlet control
	Total: Memory = 60K	5	
B-1	Singer SKO-2000, 16K by 32 bit RWM	2	Navigation, controls and displays, weapons delivery, flight director
	IBM 4PI/AP-2, 16K by 32 bit RWM	1	Central integrated test
	Rockwell, 11K by 20 bit ROM	4	Electrical power multiplexer control
	Airesearch, 2K by 20 bit ROM	2	Air data computations
	Sundstrand, 2K by 8 bit ROM	2	Rotate-go-around, angle-of-attack air vehicle limit functions
	Autonetics D216, 8K by 16 bit ROM	2	Fuel/center of gravity functions
	Bendix BDX-900, 3K by 16 bit ROM	8	Air induction control
	Unknown, 32K by 16 bit RWM	1	Threat-warning and ECM
	Total: Memory 204K	22	

manager: First, what is the size of the operational software resident in each computer configuration specified, and second, what is the complexity of each program in some realistic measure [20]? Guidelines on complexity measures will be given for the analyst.

Studies of complexity metrics have recently been published in which three measures were examined: Halstead's E, McCabe's $v(G)$, and program length in FORTRAN statements. Correlations are reported in Table 22.8 for measures computed on modified programs. For

Table 22.8. Correlations between Complexity
and Performance Measures.

COMPLEXITY METRIC	PERCENTAGE RECALLED (EXP. 1)	ACCURACY (EXP. 2)	TIME (EXP. 2)
Halstead's E	−0.13	−0.29	0.44**
McCabe's			
$v(G)$	−0.35*	−0.36*	0.38*
Length	−0.53**	−0.34*	0.46**

Note: n = 27 − number of data points
*p ≤ 0.05
**p ≤ 0.01

example, in Experiment 1 the correlations between performance (i.e., functional correctness of each program statement reconstructed from memory) were all negative, indicating that fewer lines were recalled as the level of complexity represented by the three metrics increased. All three measures were moderately correlated with time to complete the modification, whereas only length and McCabe's $v(G)$ were significantly related to accuracy. Analyses of relationships among Halstead's E, McCabe's $CSB(G)$, number of statements, and performance were conducted with Pearson product-moment correlation coefficients [21].

The proposal manager would need an extremely complete cost data base—an almost impossible prerequisite—to use Halstead's E metric at RFP time. Halstead's E formula is:

$$E = \frac{\eta_1 N_2 (N_1 + N_2) \log_2(\eta_1 + \eta_2)}{2\eta_2}$$

where

η_1 = Number of unique operators
η_2 = Number of unique operands
N_1 = Total frequency of operators
N_2 = Total frequency of operands

High degrees of correlation have been reported between Halstead's measure of complexity and the number of errors in a program, the length of programming time, and the quality of programs [22]. Useful research results have been observed in completed computer programs for which the independent variables can be measured. Properly used and understood, this metric may be of some value in the future. At present, Halstead's E measure of

complexity is considered too advanced to be of any practical use at RFP time.

McCabe developed a definition of complexity based on the decision structure of a computer program. His metric is based on the graph theoretic cyclomatic number that represents the number of linearly independent control paths comprising a program [12]. His metric is defined as:

$$v(G) = \# \text{ edges} - \# \text{ nodes} + 2 (\# \text{ connected components})$$

Again, the software data base accessible to the proposal manager is not considered of sufficient clarity to enable him to use the McCabe complexity metric in response to an RFP. However, availability of needed information is not the only problem. Some technical problems have been experienced such as a higher McCabe complexity number associated with structured programs rather than with unstructured programs. This finding is counterintuitive and raises a question about the broader applicability of McCabe's metric [23].

Requirements Volatility Effects

Generally, requirements volatility refers to the degree to which software requirements are subject to change during the course of performance. Although requirements volatility is not a commonly used characteristic parameter for cost estimates based on a fixed *statement of work* (SOW), it should be evident, at this point, that changes in software requirements after contract award can adversely affect cost and schedule performance.

Problems within an initial SOW often reach back to individual requirements that were uncertain or ambiguous; invariably these ill-defined initial requirements require clarification and corrective action at a later time. Such corrective action may obligate the contractor to spend more time and money than he had originally anticipated. The government can avoid these problems altogether by precisely and clearly stating what results are required in the initial SOW. However, there are acquisitions in which the nature of the software development is embryonic or tentative. In these cases, it is more to the government's advantage to state in the RFP that it is unsure of, or flexible with respect to, some of the software requirements than it is to remain silent at the issuance of the RFP. If the bidder can make an early and reasonable assessment of the inherent requirements volatility, he can make a more realistic cost analysis. This frankness on the part of the government reduces the risk of cost and schedule overruns for both the government and the contractor.

The government must remember that the bidder prepared his or her bid on the premise that it would provide what the contract required. By accepting the contractor's bid, the government bought only what was described in the contract documents. Anything more is outside the scope of the contract. In light of this caveat, eight manageable problems are shown in Table 22.9. Experience suggests that these are the leading problem areas and that they can be reduced to manageable size by program office restraint and pragmatism.

Disciplined Data Collection

Two kinds of cost-related data collection are important to the proposal manager: cost data from past operational software projects and cost data from a single current software project at key milestone events (e.g., PDR, CDR, TRR). An example of data collection from past projects is given in Figure 22.4, in which the 12 plotted points represent 12 completed real-time projects in terms of total man-months versus total size (machine language instructions).

Data collection from past projects is of most benefit to the model builder; however, the proposal manager and his or her staff, the real users of a model, determine its validity. Therefore, it is in their best interest to know the general strengths and weaknesses of various models, beginning with the data-gathering and model-building process. The proposal manager and his or her staff should collect data from a selected project and overlay the new point with the other data points that are presumed to be representative samples of a common population (e.g., real-time operational software).

Table 22.9. Some Manageable Causes of Cost and Schedule Overruns.

• Simultaneously unattainable requirements	• Increased design risk
• Defective specifications	• Air Force Program Office delay/ acceleration
• Over-inspection and over-testing	• Disputed interpretations
• Contract ambiguities	• Stated preference

Should a mismatch occur, an effort to reconcile the difference is needed.

Collecting data from a current project is probably of most benefit to the proposal manager during proposal preparation and subsequent cost control. The analyst should select one or two cost algorithms to use with data from his or her own ongoing project and run the model(s) at different intervals or at the completion of key milestones. Again, the analyst should gather only the data needed as input to the model(s). At some point in time, however, development cycle time-dynamics enter in because each model is run with improved estimates of the data at each major milestone.

A more sophisticated problem, which requires cost data collection and analysis, is associated with relating development cost to language level. Sometimes an experienced manager will ask, Why does it cost more to develop a program in high-level language than in assembly language? This is a misconception based on comparing seemingly similar parameters. One situation leading to this error in reasoning is shown by the data in Table 22.10. The fallacy in data interpretation is easily explained:

1. Basic Assembly Language (BAL) appears to cost $22.50 per line in comparison to a cost of $35.00 per line for high-level language. At this point it does appear to cost more to develop a program in high-level language than in assembly language.
2. In the middle of Table 22.10 is a row labeled "Lines of Source Code." The real

Table 22.10. Some Cost Attributes (and Pitfalls) Associated with Language Level.

	BAL	HIGH LEVEL
Design, manmonth (MM)	1	1
Code, MM	1	0.5
Test, MM	1	0.5
Documentation, MM	0.5	0.5
Management and staff, MM	1	1
Total manmonths	4.5	3.5
Lines of source code	1,000	500
Lines per MM	222	143
MM per 1000 lines	4.5	6.9
$5,000 per MM	$22,500	$17,500
Unit cost	$22.50 per line	$35.00 per line

problem associated with comparability of terms begins here, although it is not obvious. BAL is a "source" language, but not in the same sense as high-level languages (e.g., FORTRAN or JOVIAL).

3. As shown previously in Table 22.5, the expansion ratio from source statements to object code for a true high-level language varies from 3:1 to 12:1, whereas the expansion ratio for assembly language is approximately 1:1. Therefore, to directly compare BAL, an assembly source language, with a high-level source language is deceptive and can cause gross cost estimating errors if misinterpreted.

4. Finally, the bottom line cost in dollars is higher for assembly language, BAL, than for the high-level language—$22,500 versus $17,500 in this example.

Cost/Quality Tradeoffs

At least 40% of software development costs are traceable to software testing costs. The need for testing is related to the characteristic quality of software as it is designed and coded. Modular construction, top-down design, program design language, desk check, structured walk-through, and test tools are among a variety of useful design methodologies and techniques that result in higher-quality software.

Testing can reveal the presence of bugs, but it cannot prove their absence. The approach in this section is to present methods, especially the use of test tools and analytical models, that may reduce the cost of testing and aid the developer in answering the questions: How much testing is enough? How do we know when we are through? How much more calendar time is required based on the evidence to date?

To narrow the problem, we should view quality in the more limited sense of software reliability or the degree of freeness from error. Software reliability can be defined as the probability of correct operation over a specified increment of exposure. This definition applies to either the time domain or the data domain.

In the time domain, reliability is expressed as the likelihood that the unit of software will not experience a failure for a stated interval of time. (Or conversely, that the interval of time until the next probable error is a certain estimated value.) The measure of "exposure" is best made in seconds of computer execution time, which can be related to calendar time.

In the data domain, the measure of exposure is the "run." Reliability in the data domain is expressed as the probability that the software will not experience a failure (e.g., construct an incorrect function value) when exposed to all run conditions in the operational profile. This leads to a very large, but finite, number of runs to be chosen from the data sets that are representative of the operational profile.

A cost payoff is realizable if both the amount of testing can be reduced and the indigenous errors can be kept acceptably low. A reliability model can aid the manager in making a statistical evaluation of the number of remaining errors, and an approximation of the probable time until the next error, based on the frequency of error occurrence up to the present time.

An evaluation of several state-of-the-art software reliability models is available to the interested reader [24]. The Hughes report analyzes the performance of several reliability models when subjected to 10 sets of actual software error data. Two principal conclusions are drawn in the report:

1. Software error data collection practices are generally incompatible with the sophisticated reliability models they examined.
2. Based on the 10 data sets, Hughes can recommend the Generalized Poisson Model and to a lesser extent the Jelinski-Moranda Model and the Schick-Wolverton Model.

A basic problem with most reliability models is their lack of sensitivity to the level of effort and error reduction. One reliability model now solves this problem for one data set.

Tausworthe of JPL calculated various statistical estimates as a function of the observed software errors to find the cumulative error discovery distribution for the JPL Deep Space Network (DSN) computer software project

and used it as a management tool in predicting when all anomalies would be discovered (See Figure 22.6). His statistical analysis was successful in estimating the time to discover all remaining errors in terms of the predicted number of errors and the predicted calendar time [25]. The theory allowed him to compute a confidence interval for each estimate; for example, the DSN software consisted of 300,000 lines of minicomputer assembly language code and the theoretical estimate was 306 ± 2 predicted anomalies and 263 ± 54 days to discover them. The theoretical estimate, after adjustment for a step-wise varying level of effort, was almost exactly equal to the actual experience (denoted by xs in Figure 22.6).

These estimates were obtained by fitting a piece-wise continuous function to the observed anomalies using least-squares methods. The fit was reinitialized each time the DSN software entered a new operating environment (justified by capture-recapture rationale). Error-reduction modeling provided a tool for economic and strategic tradeoffs in test policy.

The cost of latent error correction for a large real-time system has been studied as a function of its development phases [26]. One of the main conclusions is that nearly two-thirds of all changes during test and integration resulted from latent requirement and design errors.

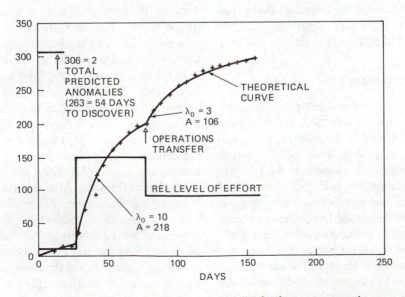

Figure 22.6. Prediction of software anomalies for deep-space network.

More than 85% of these errors fall into 5 of 25 error types:

1. Performance criteria inadequate
2. Requirement incompatibility
3. Environmental data incomplete
4. Mission information partially missing
5. Operating rules inadequate or missing

On the average, 27 lines of code were patched per change. Approximately 5,100 changes were incorporated during the project's development phase, or 137,000 lines of code. The average cost of a change is shown below (see Figure 22.7):

During code and unit test	$ 977	$ 36 PLC
During test and integration	$7,136	$264 PLC
Weighted average		$186 PLC
Note: PLC = Per line of code		

The cost of correcting a software fault during code and unit test was 5 times greater than the cost of finding it during requirements analysis, and during test and integration the cost was 36 times greater. Look for ways to catch these types of errors early and thereby hold down the cost of development. One way suggested by experience is a balanced use of software tools by the software developer.

Table 22.11 shows a few up-to-date software tools for verification and certification [27]. If one views maintenance, especially enhancement maintenance, as a series of minidevelopment cycles, one can apply the same tools to the planned enhancements during maintenance. Under these conditions, a tool may have a useful lifetime of 10 or more years. Barriers to tool usage is one of the top problems facing software managers today [28]. As viewed by the manager, the payoff for the investment of time to educate and train the practitioner in the use of unfamiliar tools is not clear and not well documented.

Product design tools may be categorized as existing or advanced tools. Existing or availa-

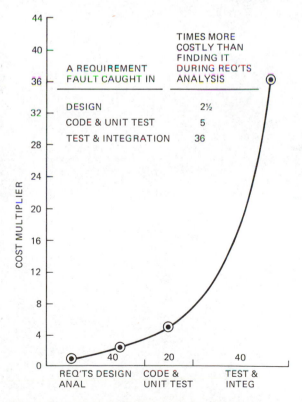

Figure 22.7. Cost of latent error correction for language real-time system.

Table 22.11. Verification, Validation, and Certification Relationships.

| | VERIFICATION | | | | | |
TOOL AND TECHNIQUE	SYSTEM REQUIREMENTS VERIFICATION	REQUIREMENTS VERIFICATION	DESIGN VERIFICATION	CODE VERIFICATION	VALIDA- TION	CERTIFICA- TION
1. Accuracy study analyzer				x		
2. Algorithm evaluation test			x			
3. Analytical modeling		x	x			
4. Assembler				x	x	
5. Automated test generator				x	x	
6. Capability matrices	x	x				
7. Code inspection				x		
8. Comparator				x	x	
9. Compiler				x	x	
10. Compiler validation system					x	
11. Consistency checker	x	x	x			
12. Correctness proofs			x	x		
13. Cross-assembler				x	x	
14. Cross-reference program				x		
15. Data analyzer				x		
16. Decision tables		x	x			
17. Decompiler				x		
18. Design inspection			x			
19. Design language processor			x			
20. Diagnostics/debug aids				x	x	
21. Driver				x	x	
22. Dynamic analyzer				x		
23. Dynamic simulator				x	x	
24. Editor				x		
25. Emulation				x	x	
26. Engineering simulations	x	x	x			
27. Environment simulator				x	x	
28. Equivalence classes				x	x	
29. Error-prone analysis				x		
30. Execution analysis				x	x	x
31. Flight tests						x
32. Functional testing				x	x	x
33. Flowcharter			x	x	x	
34. Hardware monitor				x	x	
35. Instruction simulator				x	x	
36. Instruction trace				x		
37. Interface checker				x		
38. Interrupt analyzer				x		
39. Logical testing				x	x	
40. Logic/equation generator				x		
41. Modular programming				x	x	
42. Overlay program				x		
43. Path analyzer				x		
44. Path testing				x		
45. Performance evaluation	x	x	x	x	x	x
46. Post-functional analysis				x		
47. Process construction			x			

Table 22.11. Verification, Validation, and Certification Relationships. (*continued*)

| | VERIFICATION | | | | | |
TOOL AND TECHNIQUE	SYSTEM REQUIREMENTS VERIFICATION	REQUIREMENTS VERIFICATION	DESIGN VERIFICATION	CODE VERIFICATION	VALIDA- TION	CERTIFICA- TION
48. Production libraries			x	x	x	
49. Program sequencer				x		
50. Prototyping	x	x	x			
51. Relocatable loader				x		
52. Requirements processor	x	x				
53. Requirements tracer		x	x			
54. Restructuring program				x		
55. Simulation	x	x	x	x	x	x
56. SNAP generator				x		
57. Software monitor				x	x	
58. Standardization		x	x	x	x	x
59. Standards enforcer				x		
60. Statement simulator				x		
61. Static analysis				x		
62. Static analyzer				x		
63. Stress testing				x	x	
64. Structured programming				x	x	
65. Symbolic execution				x		
66. System simulations	x	x				
67. Test beds				x	x	x
68. Test drivers, scripts, generators				x	x	x
69. Test-result processor				x	x	
70. Timing analyzer				x		
71. Top-down programming		x	x			
72. Trace				x		
73. Units consistency analyzer				x		
74. Walk-throughs			x	x		
75. Workload aids	x	x				

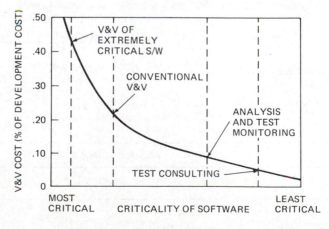

Figure 22.8. Spectrum of V&V levels.

ble tools customarily include assemblers, linkers, program preparation aids (editors, etc.), debug assist tools (path tracers, etc.), and high-level language manipulators (compilers, etc.). Advanced tools are defined to cover very high-level languages (automatic-program generators, etc.), products to assist in creating and debugging executive and real-time programs, products to assist in performance analysis, and products to assist in verifying operational software readiness.

Tool selection criteria are needed by the developer. The proposed tool should automate any repetitive part of the programming or design task, increase productivity and accuracy, and improve morale. The proposed tool should automate the extraction and correlation of various data files containing management or technical information about the program.

The greater the criticality of software, the greater the payoff for tools. Critical software is defined as any operational software module that, if a failure is encountered, might cause an aircraft to crash, a thermonuclear device to prearm, or a catastrophic event to occur. In addition to tools, independent verification and validation (IV&V) is often needed. IV&V is an activity in which a separate contractor independently performs V&V actions on software being developed by another contractor. It is generally used only to guarantee higher levels of fault-freedom than the nominal level. The relative cost of IV&V for critical software applications is shown in Figure 22.8, together with a rectilinear resource allocation in Figure 22.9 [29]. The government usually decides

whether or not an independent V&V contractor will be employed for the testing of critical software.

To sum up, this chapter defines software structural parameters and project financial parameters in enough detail to remove critical ambiguities persistent in the field. The primary conclusion is that these properties are brought together by the software cost model developer and must be understood by the software engineer to aid him or her in avoiding budget and schedule overruns and unsatisfactory performance.

ACKNOWLEDGMENTS

The author is grateful to Mel Hoeferlin, L. D. Parriott, Jr., and B. W. Boehm for many helpful suggestions. Material was heavily adapted from the "ASD Acquisition Guidebook for System Cost Analysis and Estimating" in preparing this chapter, which is gratefully acknowledged.

REFERENCES

1. E. A. Nelson, *Management Handbook for the Estimation of Computer Programming Costs,* System Development Corp., Santa Monica, Calif., March 30, 1967, 141 pp., 68 refs.
2. V. R. Basili and R. W. Reiter, Jr., "An Investigation of Human Factors in Software Development," *Computer,* vol. 12, no. 12, Dec. 1979, pp. 21–38.
3. E. F. Hitt, *F111A/E Digital Bomb-Nav System Software Analysis,* Battelle, Columbus Laboratories, Columbus, Ohio, November 17, 1978, 310 pp., 136 refs.
4. B. W. Boehm and R. W. Wolverton, "Software Cost Modeling: Some Lessons Learned," presented at

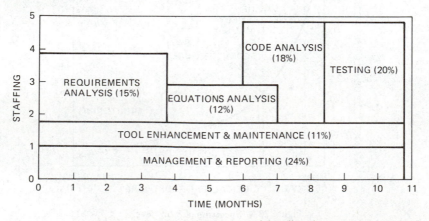

Figure 22.9. Sample V&V case-activity allocation.

Second Software Life Cycle Management Workshop (AIRMICS), IEEE Computer Society No. 78CH1390-4C, Atlanta, Ga., August 21–23, 1978, pp. 129–132.

5. R. K. E. Black and R. Katz, "Effects of Modern Programming Practices on Software Development Costs," Space Energy and Military Applications Group, Boeing Computer Services, Seattle, WA, in *IEEE Proceedings of Fall COMPCON:* Sept. 1977, pp. 250–253; R. K. E. Black, R. Katz, M. D. Gray, and R. P. Curnow, "BCS Software Production Data Final Technical Report," Contract No. F30602-76-C-0174, Report No. RADS-TR-77-116, March 1977.

6. C. E. Walston and C. P. Felix, "A Method of Programming Measurement and Estimation," *IBM Systems Journal,* vol. 16, no. 1, pp. 54–73.

7. L. H. Putnam and A. Fitzsimmons, "Estimating Software Costs," *Datamation:* Part I, Sept. 1979, pp. 189–198; Part II, Oct. 1979, pp. 171–178; Part III, Nov. 1979, pp. 137–140.

8. F. R. Freiman and R. E. Park, *PRICE Software Model—Version 3,* PRICE Systems, RCA Corp., Cherry Hill, N.J. National Aerospace Conference (NAECON 79), Dayton, Ohio, Apr. 1979; *IEEE Reliability Society,* Polytechnic Institute of New York, Workshop on Quantitative Software Models for Reliability, Complexity and Cost, Kiamesha Lake, N.Y., October 9–11, 1979.

9. R. E. O'Donahue Jr., "Summary of Design to Cost Experience," address by Asst. Director (Planning), Office of the Director of Defense Research and Engineering," AIAA and EIA/TMSA Conference Proceedings, June 20, 1975.

10. F. S. Ingrassia, "The Unit Development Folder (UDF): An Effective Management Tool for Software Development," TRW Software Series, TRW-SS-76-11, Oct. 1976; see also, idem, "Combating the '90 Percent Complete' Syndrome," *Datamation,* Jan. 1978, pp. 171–176.

11. E. B. Daly, "Management of Software Development," GTE Automatic Electric Laboratories, in *IEEE Trans. on Software Engineering,* vol. SE-3, no. 3, May 1977.

12. T. J. McCabe, "A Complexity Measure," *IEEE Trans. on Software Engineering,* vol. SE-2. no. 4, Dec. 1976, pp. 308–320.

13. D. L. Parnas, "Designing Software for Ease of Extension and Contraction," *Proc. ICSE3,* May 1978, pp. 264–277; ibid., *IEEE Trans. Software Engineering,* March 1979, pp. 128–137.

14. E. Yourdon and L. L. Constantine, *Structured Design,* 2d ed., Yourdon Press, New York, 1978.

15. R. W. Wolverton, "The Cost of Developing Large-Scale Software," *IEEE Trans. on Computers,* June 1974; R. W. Wolverton, "ASD Acquisition Guidebook for Software Cost Analysis and Estimating," ASD-TR-80-5025, Aug. 1980, 164 pp.

16. L. H. Putnam and R. W. Wolverton, "Quantitative Management: Software Cost Estimating," tutorial presented at *IEEE Computer Society COMPSAC 77,* IEEE catalog no. EHO 129-7, Chicago, November 8–11, 1977, 326 pp.

17. Air Force Systems Command, et al., "Cost/Schedule Management of Non-Major Contracts (C/SSR Joint Guide)," AFSCP 173-3, Washington, D.C., November 1, 1978, 55 pp.

18. A. B. Fitzsimmons and T. L. Love, "A Review and Evaluation of Software Science," *ACM Computing Surveys,* vol. 10, 1978, pp. 3–18.

19. M. G. Roach, "A Comparison of Cost Estimation Techniques for Software Development Projects," *19th Symposium, System Integrity,* WDC, Chapter ACM, NBS/DOC, 1979.

20. W. L. Trainor, "Software—From Satan to Saviour," prepared for the National Aerospace Electronics Conference, U.S. Air Force Avionics Lab, WPAFB, Ohio, May 1973, 8 pp.

21. S. B. Sheppard, B. Curtis, P. Milliman, M. A. Borst, and T. Love, "First-Year Results from a Research Program on Human Factors in Software Engineering," General Electric Company, in *National Computer Conference: Human Factors in Software Engineering,* 1979, pp. 1021–1027.

22. Data and Analysis Center for Software, "Quantitative Software Models," Report no. SRR-1 prepared by ITT Research Institute under contract to RADC, Griffiss AFB, NY, March 1979.

23. J. L. Elshoff, "On the Use of the Cyclomatic Number to Measure Program Complexity," *SIGPLAN Notices,* vol. 13, no. 12, Dec. 1978, pp. 29–40.

24. R. E. Schafer, J. E. Angus, J. F. Alter, and S. E. Emoto, "Validation of Software Reliability Models," Hughes Aircraft Co. under contract to Rome Air Development Center, Final Technical Report, RADC-TR-79-147, June 1979.

25. R. C. Tausworthe, "Software Engineering Workshop: Models, Measures and Metrics," *Proceedings of Second Summer Software Engineering Workshop,* Goddard Space Flight Center: Greenbelt, Md., September 19, 1977, pp. 22–24; R. C. Tausworthe, "Discovery and Repair of Software Anomalies," JPL Deep Space Network Progress Report 42–37, June 1977, pp. 49–59.

26. R. O. Lewis, *The Cost of an Error: A Retrospective Look at Safeguard Software,* Science Applications, Inc., prepared under Contract DA660-76-C-0011, Huntsville, Ala., March 1977.

27. D. J. Reifer, "Verification, Validation and Certification: A Software Acquisition Guidebook," TRW-SS-78-05, Sept. 1978, 120 pp.

28. C. Giese, "Second Software Life Cycle Management Workshop," U.S. Army Institute for Research in Management Information and Computer Science, Atlanta, Ga., August 20–22, 1978; proceedings available through *IEEE Computer Society,* No. 78CH1390-4C, 1978, pp. 21–29.

29. R. D. Hartwick, "Software Verification and Validation," *Proceedings, AIAA Third Software Management Conference,* Washington, D.C., 1977.

23

Software Life Cycle Factors

B. W. Boehm
TRW Systems

23.1. INTRODUCTION

This chapter serves as an extension of Chapter 22, which covers recommended techniques for software cost estimation. It provides definitions of the various software life cycle phases, discusses the economic implications of various software development strategies, and presents tradeoff relations between the various software product and project attributes that primarily determine software development and maintenance costs. This section presents the software life cycle and its phases from the perspective of the familiar "waterfall" model.

The Waterfall Model

The waterfall model of the software life cycle is illustrated in Figure 23.1. The original version was presented in Reference 1 and was foreshadowed in various U.S. Air Force and System Development Corporation publications such as References 2 and 3. The major overall features of the waterfall chart in its current form are:

- Each phase is culminated by a verification and validation of (V + V) activity whose objective is to eliminate as many problems as possible in the products of that phase.
- As much as possible, iterations of earlier phase products are performed in the next succeeding phase.

The waterfall model is most effective when used with the baseline-milestone method of software configuration management. In this method, the completion of a phase in the waterfall diagram (a *milestone*) is established by successfully passing an end-of-phase review and by formalizing the phase products as *baselines* for subsequent development. This provides a vital unifying link between the management and control of the software *process,* and the management and control of the software *product*. The milestone-baseline process generally works in the following way [4]:

1. An initial version of the intermediate or final software product is developed.
2. This initial version is verified and validated, and iterated as necessary.
3. A formal product review (e.g., a *software requirements review*) determines whether or not the product is in satisfactory shape to proceed to the next phase (i.e., whether or not the milestone has been reached). If not, the process reverts to step 1.
4. If the product is satisfactory, it is baselined (i.e., put under a formal change control process).

The baselining of the product has the following three main advantages:

- No changes are made thereafter without the agreement of all interested parties.
- The higher threshold for change tends to stabilize the product.
- The controller of the configuration management process (e.g., the *project librarian*) achieves the goal of having at any time a definitive version of the product.

494

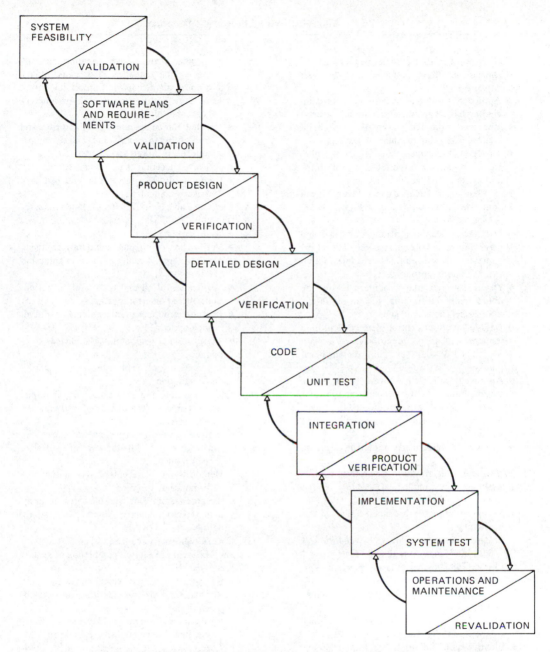

Figure 23.1. The "waterfall" model of the software life cycle.

Table 23.1 provides definitions of the major life cycle milestones corresponding to the phases shown in Figure 23.1.

Economic Rationale for the Waterfall Model

The waterfall model presents the software life cycle as a set of sequential subgoals to be achieved in pursuit of the overall goal of a successful software product. In fact, to say that these goals are approached in pure sequence for the entire project is a convenient oversimplification. There are several situations in which it is cost-effective to modify the sequence, including prototyping, incremental development, and advancemanship.

Table 23.1. Major Software Life Cycle Milestones.

I. End System Feasibility Phase. Begin Plans and Requirements Phase. (completion of *life cycle concept review*)
- Approved, validated system architecture, including basic hardware-software allocations
- Approved, validated concept of operation, including basic man-machine allocations
- Top-level life-cycle plan, including milestones, resources, responsibilities, schedules, and major activities

II. End Plans and Requirements Phase. Begin Product Design Phase. (completion of *software requirements review*)
- Detailed development plan: detailed development milestone criteria, resource budgets, organization, responsibilities, schedules, activities, techniques, products
- Detailed usage plan: counterparts of the above items for training, conversion, installation, operations, and support
- Detailed product control plan: configuration management plan, quality assurance plan, overall V+V plan (excluding detailed test plans)
- Approved, validated software requirements specification: functional, performance, and interface specifications validated for completeness, consistency, testability, and feasibility.
- Approved development contract: based on the above items.

III. End Product Design Phase. Begin Detailed Design Phase. (completion of *product design review*)
- Verified software product design specification:
  Program component hierarchy, control and data interfaces through unit* level
  Physical and logical data structure through field level
  Data processing resource budgets (timing, storage, accuracy)
  Verified for completeness, consistency, feasibility, and traceability to requirements
- Identification and resolution of all high-risk development issues
- Preliminary integration and test plan, acceptance test plan, and user's manual

IV. End Detailed Design Phase. Begin Code and Unit Test Phase. (completion of *critical design review* for unit)
- Verified detailed design specification for each unit.
  For each routine (≤ 100 source instructions),

specifies name, purpose, assumptions, sizing, calling sequence, error exits, inputs, outputs, algorithms, and processing flow
  Data base description through parameter/character/bit level
  Verified for completeness, consistency, and traceability to requirements and system design specifications and budgets
- Approved acceptance test plan
- Complete draft of integration and test plan and user's manual

V. End Code and Unit Test Phase. Begin Integration and Test Phase. (satisfaction of *unit test criteria* for unit)
- Verification of all unit computations, using not only nominal values but also singular and extreme values
- Verification of all unit input and output options, including error messages
- Exercise of all executable statements and all branch options
- Verification of programming standards compliance
- Completion of unit-level "as built" documentation

VI. End Integration and Test Phase. Begin Implementation Phase. (completion of *software acceptance review*)
- Satisfaction of software acceptance test
  Verification of satisfaction of software requirements
  Demonstration of acceptable off-nominal performance as specified
- Acceptance of all deliverable software products: reports, manuals, asbuilt specifications, data bases.

VII. End Implementation Phase. Begin Operations and Maintenance Phase. (completion of *system acceptance review*
- Satisfaction of system acceptance test
  Verification of satisfaction of system requirements
  Verification of operational readiness of software, hardware, facilities, personnel
- Acceptance of all deliverable system products: hardware, software, documentation, training, facilities
- Completion of all specified conversion and installation activities

VIII. End Operations and Maintenance Phase (via Phaseout).
- Completion of all items in phaseout plan: conversion, documentation, archiving, transition to new system(s)

---

*A software unit performs a single well-defined function, can be developed by one person, and is typically 200 to 600 source instructions in size.

The next two sections discuss a basic economic rationale for the waterfall model, and some of its refinements as indicated above.

The economic rationale for the subgoal-at-a-time waterfall model is based on two major premises:

1. In order to achieve a successful software product, we must achieve all of the subgoals at some stage anyway.
2. Any different ordering of the subgoals will produce a less successful software product.

Premise A: Necessity for All Process Subgoals.

For premise *A,* clearly subgoal V (code and unit test) and all the later subgoals (except phaseout) are necesary to achieve any sort of functioning product. The key question is whether the earlier subgoals (feasibility, plans and requirements, product design, and detailed design) are necessary. For many small, simple software products, it is possible to achieve an acceptable result with relatively little formal attention to the earlier subgoals because the developer already has a clear understanding of what the user needs and because the consequences of each of his programming decisions are easy to foresee. However, this sort of informal approach often leads to highly unacceptable results that can often be anticipated if the earliest subgoals have been thoroughly satisfied.

On larger, more complex projects, the lack of thorough attention to the earlier subgoals has almost always led to serious deficiencies in the success of the software product and process:

- In two large command-control systems, the software had to be rewritten 67% and 95% after delivery because of mismatches with user requirements [5].
- Lack of appropriate requirements and early feasibility analyses have led to total cancellation of many projects whose successful completion was found to be totally infeasible. Some of the more expensive examples are the $56 million Univac-United Airlines reservation system [6]

and the $217 million Advanced Logistics System [7].*

Premise B: Sequential Approach to Process Subgoals.

The economic rationale behind premise *B* is given primarily by Figure 23.2 [8]. The solid line in this figure shows a summary of current experience on larger projects at IBM [9], GTE [10], the Safeguard software project [11], and several TRW projects on the relative cost of correcting software errors (or making other software changes) as a function of the phase in which the corrections or changes are made. If a software requirements error is detected and corrected during the plans and requirements phase, its correction is a relatively simple matter of updating the requirements specification. If the same error is not corrected until the maintenance phase, the correction involves a much larger inventory of specifications, code, user and maintenance manuals, and training material.

Further, it involves a much more formal change approval and control process, and a much more extensive activity to revalidate the correction. These factors combine to make the error typically 100 times more expensive to correct in the maintenance phase on large projects than in the requirements phase.†

The dotted line in Figure 23.2 shows the escalation in cost-to-fix versus phase for two smaller, less formal software projects analyzed in Reference 13. It indicates that the degree of support for premise *B* is less for such projects than it is for larger, more formal projects. There were two main reasons for this reduced effect in the projects studied:

---

*On the Univac-United system, the initial unvalidated estimate for the number of instructions executed per transaction was 9,000. By the time the project was cancelled, the number was 146,000. On the Advanced Logistics System, the initial unvalidated specification required 90% of the transactions to be performed in real time. During the review leading to project cancellation the actual percentage of transactions for which users needed real-time response was determined to be about 10%.

†The total economic impact of leaving errors to be found after the software has become operational is actually much larger because of the added operational costs incurred by the error. See References 5 and 12 for examples.

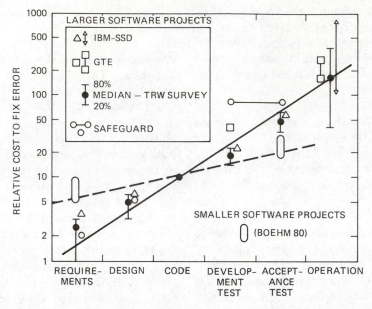

Figure 23.2. Increase in cost to fix or change software throughout life cycle.

- The smaller size meant that there was a relatively smaller inventory of items to fix in the later phases.
- The reduced formality meant that if a fix appeared to be very time-consuming, the project could generally decide to implement a simpler fix, an option not as easily available on more formal projects.

Although the effect for such smaller projects is less pronounced, the 4-to-1 escalation in cost-to-fix between the requirements phase and the integration and test phase still supports premise *B* and places a considerable premium on the value of early requirements and design specification and validation, even for small projects.

Premise *B* thus says that if we proceed to write code without having performed the earlier requirements and design activities, there will be many more requirements and design errors in the resulting product. In Figure 23.2, these errors are shown to be much more expensive to correct in the later phases, which thus leads to a less successful software project and product.

Deviations from the Sequential Approach: Prototyping Tradeoffs. It is important to note that Figure 23.2 provides a *relative* rather than an absolute rationale for the purely sequential approach to the successive software process subgoals. In fact, it provides a tradeoff curve that indicates when it may be more cost-effective to proceed with development of a first-cut prototype product rather than spend more effort pinning down requirements in full detail.

For example, consider an interactive user-application system (e.g., a decision support system for command and control or medical diagnosis). Here, the analysis of just what information processing is required may consume much more than 100 times the cost of fixing the requirements specification once the analysis is complete. If the same result could be obtained (often more reliably) by the option of developing a first-cut prototype system and letting the users try it, even the 100-to-1 increase in software correction cost would not keep this option from being preferable to the pure-sequential approach. (An even stronger case for the prototype approach can be made for small, informal projects with the 4–6-to-1 cost-to-fix increase, and for problem domains with rapid-prototyping capabilities.) These tradeoff curves thus provide us with a more quantitative approach to resolving the "when to prototype" issue.

Refinements of the Waterfall Model

Two refinements of the idealized waterfall model must be presented here, both because of their intrinsic importance to software engineering and their impact on the time and phase distribution of software cost and effort. These refinements are *incremental development* and what we shall call *advancemanship*.

Incremental Development. Incremental development [see Refs. 15 and 16 for guidelines] is a refinement of both the "do it twice" full prototype approach and of the level-by-level, top-down approach discussed in a number of structured programming textbooks. It holds that, rather than the two approaches above, we should develop the software in *increments of functional capability*.

Incremental development has been used successively as a refinement of the waterfall approach on extremely large software products such as the $100 million Site Defense System [14] and on small software products as well.

Figure 23.3 shows how the development of one such small software product, an interactive software cost estimation model, was broken

down into three successive increments. Increment 1 (the rectangles) provided a basic capability to operate and gain experience with the model: a bulk input option, the basic algorithms required to compute cost estimates, and a basic printout of the results. Increment 2 added some valuable production-mode capabilities such as the ability to file and retrieve previous runs and an input-by-address mode for selective modification of inputs. Increment 3 added various "nice to have" features such as query-directed input for new users and added computational features such as schedule calculations and activity breakdowns.

The main advantages of incremental development over the total "do it twice" approach and the pure level-by-level, top-down approach are the following:

- The increments of functional capability are much more helpful and easy to test than the intermediate-level products in top-down development.
- The use of the successive increments provides a way to incorporate user experience into a refined product in a much less ex-

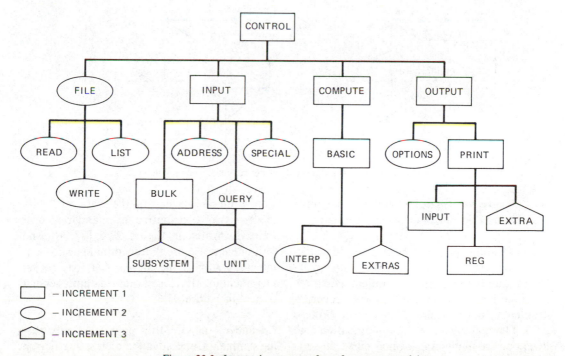

Figure 23.3. Integration strategy for software cost model.

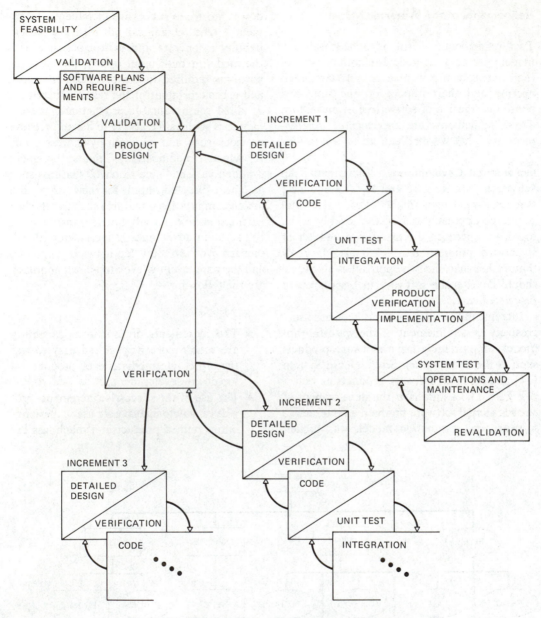

Figure 23.4. The waterfall model using incremental development.

pensive way than the total redevelopment involved in the "do it twice" approach.

The implications of incremental development for software cost estimation are primarily in the time-phasing of project effort. A modification of the waterfall chart to cover incremental development is shown in Figure 23.4. The main result of this modification is to level out the manpower-loading curve on soft-ware projects. Instead of the classical "Rayleigh curve" distribution of manpower over time, illustrated in Figure 23.5 [17, 18, and 19], one has a more flattened manpower loading curve, such as the curve shown for a recent incrementally developed radar data-processing project in Figure 23.6.

Advancemanship. In a political or advertising campaign, the advance man is the person

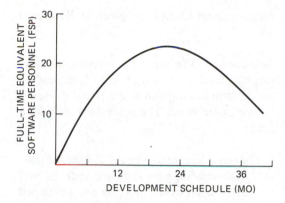

Figure 23.5. Rayleigh-curve manpower distribution.

who gets everything ready before the main body of people arrive in town. He makes sure that, by the time they arrive, all the potential logistical, political, and support problems have been smoothed out so that the main body of people can achieve their objectives efficiently and successfully. The same sort of "advance-manship" is essential to a software development project or campaign. For a software project, it takes two main forms, which we call anticipatory documentation and software scaffolding.

Anticipatory Documentation. Anticipatory documentation is advance documentation prepared for two main reasons:

1. To define detailed objectives and plans for future software development activities (e.g., development plans, test plans, conversion plans).
2. To produce early versions of user documentation (e.g., a draft users' manual to

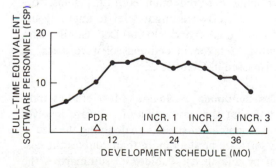

Figure 23.6. Incremental development manpower distribution.

be available for review by the end of the product design phase). This has the powerful advantage of giving the user a chance to look at how the system will affect him, *in his own terms,* and to negotiate necessary changes before the changes become expensive—as they will later on, as shown by Figure 23.2. (It also has the advantage of a better guarantee that adequate user documentation will be produced along with the code.)

Scaffolding. Scaffolding refers to the extra products that must be developed to make the main job of software development and V+V go as smoothly and efficiently as possible. As indicated in Reference 20, it includes dummy software components or stubs, miniature files or other simulated portions of the future operational environment, and auxiliary programs such as test data generators, post processors, cross-reference generators, conversion aids, standards checkers, or requirements and design language processors.

Software Economics Implications. Anticipatory documentation and scaffolding tend to have two major economic implications for the software life cycle:

1. They reduce overall costs, primarily by reducing the entropy [21] involved in the software life cycle: the activities that consume people's energy and talent with no constructive result.
2. They tend to front-load the software manpower distribution. Acquiring test tools or writing test plans and draft users' manuals tends to increase the costs of the requirements and design phases and significantly decrease the costs of the testing and maintenance phases.

22.2. FACTORS INFLUENCING SOFTWARE LIFE CYCLE COSTS

This section's discussion of the major factors influencing software life cycle costs is useful both as an aid in software cost estimation, as discussed in Chapter 22, and in software management decision making, in providing insight into the economic consequences of decisions on software project staffing, hardware acquisition, software support facilities, software reuse, and so forth.

The major factors influencing software life-cycle costs can be organized into five primary categories:

1. Size attributes (number of instructions, data elements, inputs, outputs, etc.)
2. Product attributes (required reliability, complexity, language, etc.)
3. Computer attributes (speed and storage constraints, turnaround time, etc.)
4. Personnel attributes (experience, capability, teamwork, etc.)
5. Project attributes (use of tools, modern programming practices, schedule constraints, etc.)

Each of these categories is discussed in more detail below, followed by a discussion of software maintenance cost factors.

Size Attributes

At this time, software life cycle costs are better explained in terms of *delivered source instructions* (DSI's) than in terms of other software product size attributes. More highly aggregated size measures such as number of modules, inputs, outputs, functional requirements, or lines of program design language have generally not worked too well because of the large uncertainty in the amount of software corresponding to each module, input, and so forth. (Some success has been reported in correlating software costs for one application domain with "function points," a linear combination of some of the above quantities [22].) Using object instructions as a base entails the additional resolution of issues involving higher-order-language expansion ratios, compiler optimization, and so on. Using more detailed size measures such as Halstead volume [23], control-graph complexity [24], and so forth, shows some promise, but to date has not produced better correlations with software cost than have DSIs. More detailed discussions of these candidate size attributes are given in Reference 25.

Definitions. The size of a software product can vary by factors of up to 5 to 1, depending on the definitions given to the terms *delivered source instructions*. The definitions used here are:

Delivered. Generally meant to exclude non-delivered support software such as test drivers. However, if these are developed with the same care as delivered software, with their own reviews, test plans, documentation, and so on, then they should be counted.

Source instructions. Includes all program instructions created by project personnel and processed into machine code by some combination of preprocessors, compilers, and assemblers. *Excludes* comment cards and unmodified "utility" software. *Includes* job control language, format statements, and data declarations. *Instructions* is defined as *lines of code* or *card images*. Thus, a line containing two or more source statements counts as one instruction; a five-line data declaration counts as five instructions.

As an example of the influence of software-sizing definitions, a typical 100,000 DSI operational software product is likely to have an additional 100,000 DSI in maintenance and diagnostic software, 150,000 DSI in development support software, and 150,000 DSI in application support software (simulation, training, data reduction, etc.) [25]. Thus, "delivered" software might refer to anything between 100,000 and 500,000 DSI. Similar care must be taken in defining software costs, as discussed in Chapter 22.

Diseconomies of Scale. Most studies indicate that the production of software involves diseconomies of scale (i.e., doubling the size of a software product more than doubles the cost of producing it). Table 23.2 summarizes the results of a number of studies producing software scaling equations of the form

Table 23.2. Comparison of Effort Equations.

REFERENCE	EFFORT EQUATION
[26]	$MM = 5.2 (KDSI)^{0.91}$
[27]	$MM = 4.9 (KDSI)^{0.98}$
[28]	$MM = 1.48 (KDSI)^{1.02}$
[25]: Organic mode	$MM = 2.4 (KDSI)^{1.05}$
[29]	$MM = 5.3 (KDSI)^{1.06}$
[25]: Semidetached mode	$MM = 3.0 (KDSI)^{1.12}$
[30]	$MM = 2.43 (KDSI)^{1.18}$
[25]: Embedded mode	$MM = 3.6 (KDSI)^{1.20}$
[31]	$MM = 0.99 (KDSI)^{1.275}$
[32]	$MM = 1.0 (KDSI)^{1.40}$
[33]	$MM = 1.12 (KDSI)^{1.43}$
[23]	$MM = 0.70 (KDSI)^{1.50}$
[34]	$MM = 28 (KDSI)^{1.83}$

$$MM = a(KDSI)^b$$

where MM is the number of man-months required to develop the software product and b is the scaling factor indicating the magnitude of the diseconomy of scale (for $b = 1.0$, increasing KDSI by a factor of 2 increases MM by a factor of 2. For $b = 1.20$, MM increases by a factor of 2.30; for $b = 1.40$, MM increases by a factor of 2.64). The scaling factors of 1.05 to 1.20(25) appear to be reasonably well bracketed by those of other studies, but note the wide range of variation.

Product Attributes

The Productivity Range. The effect on software costs of other attributes discussed in this chapter are expressed in terms of the

$$\text{Productivity Range} = \frac{(DSI/MM)_{\text{very good}}}{(DSI/MM)_{\text{very poor}}}$$

where $(DSI/MM)_{\text{very good}}$ is the productivity of a project with a very good rating with respect to the attribute in question, with $(DSI/MM)_{\text{very poor}}$ being defined similarly, and assuming that all other factors are equal for the two projects.

The productivity ranges of the most significant software cost driver attributes determined in the analysis of 63 software projects [25] that were used to develop a software cost estimation model called COCOMO (COnstruc-

tive COst MOdel) are shown in Figure 23.7. Each of these attributes and productivity ranges is discussed below, with comparative results from other studies of the attribute's cost impact published to date.

Required Software Reliability. A software product possesses *reliability* to the extent that it can be expected to perform its intended functions satisfactorily. Several levels of required software reliability can be defined for a software product:

Very low: The effect of a software failure is simply the inconvenience incumbent on the developers to fix the fault. Typical examples are a demonstration prototype of a voice typewriter or an early feasibility phase software simulation model.

Low: The effect of a software failure is a low-level, easily recoverable loss to users. Typical examples are a long-range planning model or a climate forecasting model.

Nominal: The effect of a software failure is a moderate loss to users, but a situation from which one can recover without extreme penalty. Typical examples are management information systems or inventory control systems.

High: The effect of a software failure can be a major financial loss or a massive human inconvenience. Typical examples are banking systems and electric power distribution systems.

Very high: The effect of a software failure can be the loss of human life. Examples are military command and control systems or nuclear reactor control systems.

Table 23.3 [25] shows some of the reasons why software products with lower required reliability ratings will take fewer man-months to complete. This table indicates the differences in project activities that will result from having a higher or lower required reliability, and that in turn result in the higher or lower costs experienced on the project.

As indicated in Figure 23.7, the analysis in Reference 25 indicates a relatively high pro-

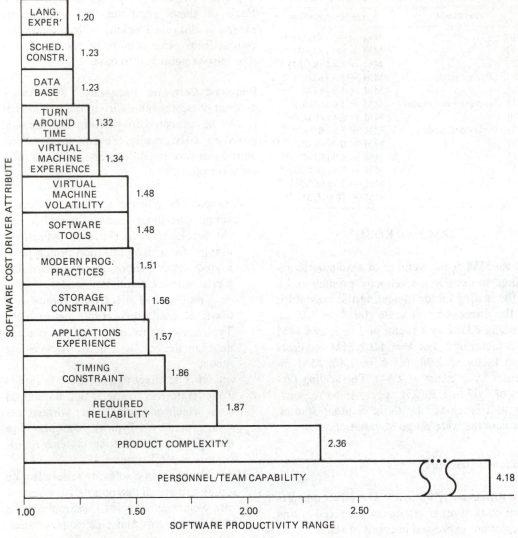

Figure 23.7. Comparative software productivity ranges [25].

ductivity range of 1.87 between projects with very low and very high reliability ratings and all other factors held constant. Somewhat surprisingly, very few other studies and models have included such a factor. The RCA PRICE S model [35] has a productivity range of about 6 to 9 for a "Platform" variable, whose ratings go from "Internal Computer-Center Software" to "Manned Spaceflight" software, a factor that includes some additional effects besides required reliability.

Data Base Size. This factor is meant to account simply for the overall size of the data base to be designed, assembled, and validated prior to acceptance. Considerations of the complexity of data structures are accommodated via the inclusion of data statements as source instructions and via the "data management operations" scale in the complexity factor (see below).

Relatively little has been determined about the effect of this factor. The Doty study [32] indicated it had a "minor" effect, but no quantitative data were given. The Air Force-Industry Software Cost Estimation Workshop [36] considered it an important factor but provided no estimates on the magnitude of its effect.

Table 23.3. Project Activity Differences Caused by Required Software Reliability.

FACTOR	RATING	REQUIREMENTS AND PRODUCT DESIGN	DETAILED DESIGN	CODE AND UNIT TEST	INTEGRATION AND TEST
Required software reliability	Very low	Little detail Many TBDs Little verification Minimal QA, CM, draft user manual, test plans Minimal PDR	Basic design information Minimal QA, CM, draft user manual, test plans Informal design inspections	No test procedures Minimal path test, standards check Minimal QA, CM Minimal I/O and off-nominal tests Minimal user manual	No test procedures Many requirements untested Minimal QA, CM Minimal stress, off-nominal tests Minimal as-built documentation
	Low	Basic information, verification Frequent TBDs Basic QA, CM, standards, draft user manual test plans	Moderate detail Basic QA, CM, draft user manual, test plans	Minimal test procedures Partial path test, standards check Basic QA, CM, user manual Partial I/O and off-nominal tests	Minimal test procedures Frequent requirements untested Basic QA, CM, user manual Partial stress, off-nominal tests
	Nominal	Nominal project V+V	⟶		
	High	Detailed verification, QA, CM, standards, PDR, documentation Detailed test plans, procedures	Detailed verification, QA, CM, standards, CDR, documentation Detailed test plans, procedures	Detailed test procedures, QA, CM, documentation Extensive off-nominal tests	Detailed test procedures, QA, CM, documentation Extensive stress, off-nominal tests
	Very high	Detailed verification, QA, CM, standards, PDR, documentation IV&V interface Very detailed test plans, procedures	Detailed verification, QA, CM, standards, CDR, documentation Very thorough design inspections Very detailed test plans, procedures IV&V interface	Detailed test procedures, QA, CM, documentation Very thorough code inspections Very extensive off-nominal tests IV&V interface	Very detailed test procedures, QA, CM, documentation Very extensive stress, off-nominal tests IV&V interface

The IBM [26] study indicates a productivity range of 1.73 for the factor "Number of classes of items in the data base per 1,000 lines of code." The COCOMO [25] productivity range is 1.23.

Software Product Complexity. Some studies have lumped a wide variety of effects into the "complexity" attribute and obtained relatively high productivity ranges as a result, for example, the productivity ranges of 4 to 6.67 in the Aron [18] model and 6 to 7 in the RCA PRICE S model [27]. The later Aron model [37] has productivity ranges of 2 to 4 for assembly language and 4 to 6 for higher-order languages, depending on the type of function being developed. The Wolverton [38] model

had a relatively small productivity range because of a complexity of 1.42 to 1.53; this was most likely because of its being based on a highly uniform project sample. The NAR-DAC model [39] has a productivity range due to a complexity of 12, but as it is a module-level rating, its range of variability across an entire product is less pronounced. The Delphi survey of productivity determinants [40] surprisingly gave "Complexity of Application" a slight *positive* correlation with increased productivity (+1 on a scale of −7 to +7).

In the COCOMO [25] analysis, complexity was defined as the intrinsic complexity of the software product, using the rating scales shown for various types of software in Table 23.4. The resulting productivity range between

Table 23.4. Module Complexity Ratings vs Type of Module.

RATING	CONTROL OPERATIONS	COMPUTATIONAL OPERATIONS	DEVICE-DEPENDENT OPERATIONS	DATA MANAGEMENT OPERATIONS
Very low	Straightline code with a few non-nested SP* operators: DO's, CASE's, IFTHENELSE's. Simple predicates	Evaluation of simple expressions: e.g., $A = B + C * (D - E)$	Simple read, write statements with simple formats	Single arrays in main memory
Low	Straightforward nesting of SP operators. Mostly simple predicates	Evaluation of moderate-level expressions, e.g., $D = SQRT (B**2 - 4.*A*C)$	No cognizance needed of particular processor or I/O device characteristics. I/O done at get/put level. No cognizance of overlap	Single file subsetting with no data structure changes, no edits, no intermediate files
Nominal	Mostly simple nesting. Some intermodule control decision tables	Use of standard math and statistical routines, basic matrix/vector operations	I/O processing includes device selection, status checking and error processing	Multifile input and single file output. Simple structural changes, simple edits
High	Highly nested SP operations with many compound predicates. Queue and stack control. Considerable intermodule control.	Basic numerical analysis: multivariate interpolation, ordinary differential equations. Basic truncation, roundoff concerns	Operations at physical I/O level (physical storage address translations; seeks, reads, etc.). Optimized I/O overlap	Special purpose subroutines activated by data stream contents. complex data restructuring at record level.
Very high	Reentrant and recursive coding. Fixed-priority interrupt handling	Difficult but structured N.A.: Near-singular matrix equations, partial differential equations	Routines for interrupt diagnosis, servicing, masking. Communication line handling	A generalized, parameter-driven file structuring routine. File building, command processing, search optimization
Extra high	Multiple resource scheduling with dynamically changing priorities. Microcode-level control	Difficult and unstructured N.A.: highly accurate analysis of noisy, stochastic data	Device timing-dependent coding, microprogrammed operations	Highly coupled, dynamic relational structures, natural language data management

*SP: structured programming

the "very low" rating and the "extra high" rating was 2.36.

Programming Language. Most recent software cost estimation and productivity studies, such as the COCOMO [25] studies and the IBM [26] studies have found that software productivity per source statement is relatively independent of the level of the source language (HOL vs MOL), as long as a project has used an MOL only where necessary. That is, the project follows the guidelines:

- Whenever a software function can be conveniently expressed in HOL, use HOL.
- Use MOL for reasons of efficiency only after programming the function in HOL, determining the sources of inefficiency, and then selectively reprogramming these in MOL.

By using these guidelines, organizations which had previously been using MOL for many HOL-expressable functions have experienced significant productivity gains. Some recent German studies comparing projects using MOL versus the HOL PEARL report savings of 25 to 37% (or productivity gains of 33–59%) across the overall development cycle due to the use of HOL [41]; these figures are consistent with most previous studies.

Even larger productivity gains are achieved during the maintenance phase by using HOLs, as evidenced by the study results [42] that typically four times as many people were required to maintain a given number of object instructions on MOL products as compared to HOL products.

Assessing the relative effects on software productivity of different HOLs (e.g., Fortran vs Pascal) is a much more difficult task. The results of the Reference 13 experiment, in which two teams used Fortran and Pascal to develop the same small-applications software product, indicate that the choice of programming language was not a major determinant of the projects' outcome or of their productivity. However, the study also concluded that:

- The choice of programming language would be a more significant factor in developing more complex and ambitious software products.
- The choice of programming language is a more significant factor to an organization with many products to develop than it is for a single standalone product.

Further, the choice of HOL is likely to have a significant influence on the maintenance productivity of an entire organization. In general, an HOL that facilitates the use of modern programming practices (such as Pascal and Ada), and that is strongly supported by software tools, is the strongest choice for enhancing productivity in the long run.

Computer Attributes

Execution Time and Main Storage Constraints. The cost of software increases significantly if it is necessary to "shoehorn" the software into a computer with barely adequate execution speed and memory capacity. Figure 23.8, based on avionics software data [43] and command-control software data [5], shows the magnitude of the combined increase in cost per instruction. Some more recent studies have developed separate productivity ranges for execution time constraints and for main storage constraints; these are summarized in Table 23.5.

Virtual Machine Volatility. For a given software subsystem, the underlying virtual machine is the complex of hardware and software that the subsystem calls on to accomplish its tasks. For example:

- If the subsystem to be developed is an operating system, the underlying virtual machine is the computer hardware.

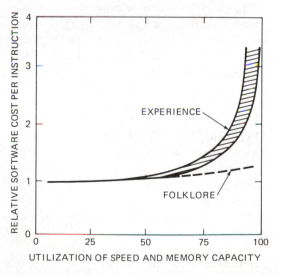

Figure 23.8. Correlation of hardware constraints and increases in software costs.

Table 23.5. Hardware Constraint Productivity Ranges.

SOURCE	TIME CONSTRAINT PRODUCTIVITY RANGE	STORAGE CONSTRAINT PRODUCTIVITY RANGE
TRW, 1972 [38]	3.00	—
Boeing, 1977 [44]	3.33–6.67	—
Doty, 1977 [29]	1.33–1.77	1.43
GRC, 1979 [45]	1.60	7.00
GTE, 1979 [46]	1.25	1.25
IBM, 1977 [26]	1.37–1.77	2.03
COCOMO [25]	1.66	1.56

- If the subsystem to be developed is a data base management system (DBMS), the underlying virtual machine generally consists of the computer hardware plus an operating system.
- If the subsystem to be developed is a data base oriented user-application subsystem, the underlying virtual machine often consists of the computer hardware, an operating system, and a DBMS.
- Further, the underlying virtual machine includes any compilers or assemblers supporting the languages in which the software subsystem is written.

Clearly, the development of a software subsystem will take more effort if its underlying virtual machine is concurrently undergoing change.

The overall productivity range due to virtual machine volatility in COCOMO [25] is 1.49. An IBM study [26] indicates a productivity range of 1.62 for the factor "hardware under concurrent development" (again, possibly including the effects of correlated factors). The Doty Model [29] has a productivity range of 1.82 for the factor "first software developed on CPU." The RCA PRICE S model [35] has a complexity adjustment factor of +0.3 for the attribute "hardware developed in parallel," which generally corresponds to a productivity range of about 1.4. None of the other published models and studies includes a virtual machine volatility factor.

Computer Turnaround Time. The effect of interactive programming on software productivity has been the subject of considerable study. Early studies summarized by Sackman [47] indicated an average of 20% improvement in productivity in code and unit test tasks. Since 1970, improved interactive systems have been developed that provide a more powerful range of conversational programming capabilities. Several more recent controlled studies have been summarized in Reference 48. The equivalent effort multipliers (interactive programming effort as a fraction of batch programming effort), determined, generally, for code and unit test tasks, are as follows:

U.S. Army	0.47
Royal Globe	0.50
Rolls Royce	0.56
AT&T	0.62

Several difficulties arise in evaluating the meaning of the above figures. For the later studies, the turnaround time effects are mixed in with effects of improved software tool capabilities. Also, it is difficult to tell how much of the programmer time used in waiting for batch results (about 16% in the U.S. Army Study [49]) could be productively used on other tasks, such as documentation or work on other portions of the code, particularly on larger projects. Further, there are a number of nonprogrammer activities (management, integration and test planning, quality assurance) going on during even the code and unit test phase that are not strongly affected by interactive programming. Thus, it is not too surprising that current cost estimation models incorporate smaller effort multipliers for interactive programming effects than those summarized above. Below is a summary of effort multipliers used in current models:

| MODEL | EFFORT MULTIPLIERS | |
	CODE & UNIT TEST	OVERALL PROJECT
Boeing [44]	.54	.875
Doty [29]	—	.83
GTE [46]	—	.80
NARDAC [39]	—	.75
COCOMO [25]	.70	.87

Studies on the effect of longer response times are scarce. The IBM study [26] reports effort multipliers in the range of 1.58 to 1.78 for two factors reflecting restrictions in computer access. The Doty model contains three multiplicative factors covering related effects:

Developer using computer at another facility   1.43
Development at operational site   1.39
Development computer different from target computer   1.25
Combined effect of all three factors   2.48

The combined effect of these factors appears extremely high.

The NARDAC model [39] contained the following effort multipliers for batch turnaround times:

More than one per day   0.8
One per day   1.0
Less than one per day   1.2

The Daly model [46] has an effort multiplier of 1.1 for batch turnaround greater than four hours.

Personnel Attributes

As indicated in Figure 23.7, personnel attributes have a much larger impact on software costs than do the other attributes. Some of the major individual factors discussed below are personnel/team capability, applications experience, virtual machine experience, programming language experience, and management quality.

Personnel/Team Capability.

The productivity range of 4.18 for personnel/team capability in the COCOMO model [25] reflects the difference between a 90th-percentile team of programmers and analysts and a 15th-percentile team. Some related observational findings are:

A productivity range of 26 between experienced programmers participating in the Sackman-Grant batch-vs-time sharing experiments [47].

A productivity range of 3.11 between IBM projects characterized as "low" versus "high" with respect to "overall personnel experience and qualifications" [26].

A typical productivity range of 5.0 attributable to personnel reported at the U.S. Air Force-Industry Software Costing Workshop [36].

The percentile ratings above of personnel/team capability are given in terms of some hypothetical percentile distribution with respect to the overall population of software analysts and programmers. Actually:

There is no such one dimensional scale. Analyst capability and programmer capability are highly multidimensional attributes, and ratings must be made with respect to the particular combination of skills needed for the job. An indication of the complexity of the situation is given by the AFIPS Programmer Job Description Survey [50].

There are no objective measurement instruments whose results correlate reliably with analyst capability or programmer capability. Instruments such as the IBM Programmer Aptitude Test (PAT) or the Test on Sequential Instructions (TSI) for measuring programming ability and the Strong Vocational Interest Blank (SVIB) for measuring interest or motivational level have at best produced very weak correlations with analyst capability or programmer capability. See References 51, 52, or 53.

The important attribute to rate is not averaged individual analyst or programmer capability, but the effective analyst or programmer *team* capability. This means including factors such as the team's cohesiveness, communicativeness, and motivation toward group versus individual achievement. Weinberg [52] is a gold mine of good examples and principles on effective versus ineffective software team performance.

Underlying a software team's capability—its analysis and programming ability, efficiency, and thoroughness. and its ability to communicate or cooperate—is the fundamental driving force of personal motivation. Here again, there is no good rating scale with which to evaluate motivation, but it is extremely important to factor it into the capability ratings used to predict productivity.

Applications Experience. Below is a summary of applications experience productivity ranges reported in recent software cost estimation studies and models.

SOURCE	APPLICATIONS EXPERIENCE PRODUCTIVITY RANGE
TRW, 1972 [38]	1.46–1.65
Boeing, 1977 [44]	2.05
NARDAC [39]	3.00
IBM, 1977 [26]	2.81
RCA PRICE S [35]	1.70
COCOMO [25]	1.57

It should be noted that the productivity ranges for factors in the IBM Walston-Felix study are not generally independent. They tend to be larger than the other ranges, since they often include the effects of other correlated factors. In the Delphi survey [40], the factor "programmer experience in functional area" was one of the highest-ranked correlates of programmer productivity, being rated +5 on a scale of −7 to +7. On the other hand, the Reference 54 study found very little correlation between experience and productivity.

Virtual Machine Experience. Many models do not have a factor for virtual machine experience. The Doty model [29] gives a productivity range of 1.92 (the highest of all the factors in the model) for the factor "first software developed on CPU." The IBM study [26] gives a productivity range of 2.14 for the factor "previous experience with operational computer"; again, this may be partly the effect of other correlated factors. The RCA PRICE S Model [35] assigns a complexity adjustment factor to the item "new hardware," producing a corresponding effort multiplier of roughly 1.2. The COCOMO productivity range is 1.34 [25].

Programming Language Experience. Although some papers indicate that language experience is a significant cost driver, most models do not include it as a factor. The IBM study [26] gives the factor a productivity range of 3.14; again, this is likely to be partly the effect of other correlated factors. The RCA PRICE S model [35] assigns a complexity adjustment factor of +0.1 to the item "new language," producing a corresponding effort multiplier of roughly 1.2. The COCOMO [25] productivity range for this factor is 1.20.

Management Quality. Poor management can increase software costs more rapidly than any other factor. Particularly on large projects, each of the following mismanagement actions has often been responsible for doubling software development costs:

- Assigning the wrong (combination of) people to project jobs
- Creating task overlaps and underlaps through poor organization, delegation, and task monitoring
- Demotivating people by unnecessarily poor working conditions and failure to reward good performance
- Bringing large numbers of people onto the project before there is a clear understanding of their responsibilities
- Failing to prepare needed resources: computer time, terminals, communications, test data, support software
- Failing to validate software requirements and design specifications, and to identify and resolve high-risk elements early

Despite this cost variation, there have been no studies establishing a well-defined productivity range for management quality. One reason for this is that poorly managed projects rarely collect much data on their experiences.

Project Attributes

Modern Programming Practices. The specific modern programming practices included here are the following:

1. *Top-down requirements analysis and design.* Developing the software requirements and design as a sequence of hierarchical elaborations of the user's information processing needs and objectives.
2. *Structured design notation.* Use of a modular, hierarchical design notation (Program Design Language, Structure Charts, HIPO) consistent with the structured code constructs in item 5, below.
3. *Top-down incremental development.* Performing detailed design, code, and integration as a sequence of hierarchical elaborations of the software control structure.
4. *Design and code walk-throughs or inspections.* Performing preplanned peer reviews of the detailed design and of the code of each software unit.
5. *Structured code.* Use of modular, hierarchical control structures based on a small number of elementary control structures, each having only one flow of control in and out.
6. *Program librarian:* A project participant responsible for operating an organized repository and control system for software components.

These concepts are described in detail in a number of books and articles [55, 56, and 57]. One resource often associated with the above list but not included here, is the *program support library,* which is included under *software tools* (see below). Another not included here is the *chief programmer team.* This practice has had highly mixed results: With a first-class chief programmer, productivity can be very high; with a poor chief programmer, productivity can be very low.

There have been quite a number of papers written that cite impressive productivity gains because of the adoption of modern programming practices. Even more so than with the other factors, it has been difficult to distinguish the gains due to MPPs from the effects of possibly correlated factors: use of better people, better software tools, higher management visibility, concurrent improvements in management, and so forth.

For example, an extensive analysis of the IBM data base was performed in the Walston-Felix [26] study. The productivity ranges below represent the ranges between projects using an MPP greater than 66% of the time and projects using an MPP less than 33% of the time.

Structured programming	1.78
Design and code inspections	1.54
Top-down development	1.64
Chief programmer teams	1.86

However, these figures may include the effects of correlated factors, and certainly include a high degree of correlation between the individual factors above. That is, the ranges above largely represent the joint effect of all four MPPs, since they were usually used together.

More recently, an MPP productivity improvement factor of 1.44 has been cited at the Bank of Montreal [58], a factor of 1.48 at SNETCo [59], and a factor of 1.58 in a French software organization [60].

The COCOMO productivity range [25] is 1.51. Two extensive and valuable MPP surveys [61, 62] provide similar results among their many findings.

Use of Software Tools. Although investments in software tools are generally considered to pay off in improved productivity, there have been very few quantitative studies of this attribute. Informally, various software development teams recently coming from well-tooled maxicomputer environments onto poorly tooled microprocessor software projects have estimated typical productivity losses of 33% as a result of such investments.

A curve relating software productivity to percentage of support software available was developed by System Development Corporation (SDC) for the U.S. Army Military Computer Family studies [63, 64]. The curve has a productivity range of 1.93 between its 30th and 70th percentiles, and a range of 2.66 between its 20th and 80th percentiles. The COCOMO productivity range is 1.49 [25].

Schedule Constraint. Trading software effort and schedule can be done to some extent if the project manager knows about the required schedule acceleration or stretchout in advance and is able to plan and control the project in the most cost-effective way with respect to the off-nominal schedule. For a stretchout, this primarily implies spending a longer time with a smaller front-end team to thoroughly develop and validate the software requirements, and design specifications, test plans, and draft user's manuals.

For a schedule acceleration, there are a number of ways that the manager can buy some schedule reduction at an increased cost in effort or dollars*:

- Providing extra advance training for programmers and test personnel in the application area and in the use of the computer and support software
- Buying added computer hardware resources (terminals, computers) to support faster coding, checkout, and test
- Providing extra clerical personnel
- Acquiring automated aids, and training personnel in their use
- Developing extradetailed unit-level and interface design specifications for maximum parallel programmer effort
- Deferring all nonessential documentation and testing

However, there is a limit beyond which a software project cannot reduce its schedule by buying more manpower and equipment. This limit occurs at roughly 75% of the nominal schedule.

The nominal schedule T_{NOM} for a software development project is approximated fairly well by the simple equation

$$T_{\text{NOM}} = 2.5 \sqrt[3]{\text{MM}},$$

---

*This is only true at the beginning of the project. Projects attempting to compress schedule by adding more people in the middle of the project will run afoul of Brooks' law [20]: "Adding manpower to a late software project makes it later."

where MM is the number of man-months required for development. Very similar equations have been determined in References 19, 25, and 26.

Analysis of TRW and other project data bases appears to corroborate the figure of 75% as a schedule compression limit (see Figure 23.9). Of Putnam's 19 project data points [19], only one falls below the 75% limit, and that one has a compression of 68.4%. Of the 37 data points in Reference 65 (which appear to be a subset of the IBM data analyzed by Walston and Felix), only two clearly show a compression below 75%; these two have compression factors of 59% and 46%. One would like to know more about how these projects achieved such impressive schedule compressions.

The cost effect of a schedule compression or stretchout has been represented in a variety of functional forms, as indicated in Figure 23.10. The results of a U.S. Air Force workshop [36] indicate that an $x\%$ compression or stretchout produces an $x\%$ increase in cost. The CO-COMO relationship [25] is flatter around the nominal schedule and in the stretchout direction, and reaches a maximum of 23% added effort to achieve the maximum schedule compression of 75% of nominal. The Putnam [19] effort-schedule tradeoff equation

$$\text{Effort} = c/t_d^4$$

where t_d represents development time or schedule, produces an extremely steep penalty for compression and an extremely steep effort reduction for a stretchout: by the equation, for example, doubling the schedule of a nominal 100 man-month project would reduce the required effort to $100/2^4 = 6.25$ man-months.

Software Maintenance

Software maintenance is defined as *the process of modifying existing operational software while leaving its primary functions intact*. This definition *excludes* the following types of activity from the category of software maintenance:

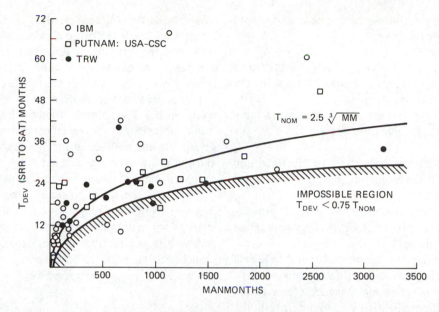

Figure 23.9. Software development schedule experience.

Major redesign and redevelopment (more than 50% new code) of a new software product performing substantially the same functions

Design and development of a sizable (more than 20% of the source instructions comprising the existing product) interfacing software package that requires relatively little redesign of the existing product

Data processing system operations, data entry, and modification of values in the data base

The definition *includes* the following types of activity within the category of software maintenance:

Redesign and redevelopment of smaller portions of an existing software product

Design and development of smaller interfacing software packages that require some redesign of the existing software product

Modification of the software product's code, documentation, or data base structure

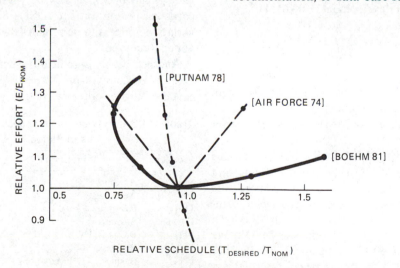

Figure 23.10. Relative effort required for off-nominal schedules.

Software maintenance can be classified into two main categories:

1. Software *update,* which results in a changed functional specification for the software product
2. Software *repair,* which leaves the functional specification intact

In turn, software repair can be classified into three main subcategories [66]:

    a. Corrective maintenance (of processing, performance, or implementation failures)
    b. Adaptive maintenance (changes in the processing or data environment)
    c. Perfective maintenance (for enhancing performance or maintainability)

Software Maintenance Cost Factors. Software maintenance cost estimation models have largely been based on simple linear ratios. Three primary bases have been used for these ratios: development cost, product size, and number of instructions changed.

The Maintenance/Development Cost Ratio. The maintenance/development cost ratio (M/D) is used to estimate the overall life cycle maintenance cost $(MM)_M$, from acceptance test through phaseout, as a function of actual or estimated development cost $(MM)_{DEVEL}$:

$$(MM)_M = (M/D)(MM)_{DEVEL}$$

Thus, for example, a 32 KDSI product requiring 100 MM to develop, with an M/D ratio of 2.0 (67% maintenance) would require an estimated (2.0)(100MM) = 200MM for maintenance.

The Putnam SLIM model [67] uses a value of 1.5 for the M/D ratio (corresponding to a 60% maintenance, 40% development life cycle), and calculates the distribution of maintenance effort using the tail of the Rayleigh distribution. Other cited values of M/D range from 0.67 (or 40% maintenance) in Reference 20 to 4.5 (or 82% maintenance), used for application software in Reference 64.

The Cards-Per-Person Ratio. This ratio stems from early software folklore often expressed in the form "Each maintenance person can maintain four boxes of cards." (A box of cards held 2,000 cards, or roughly 2,000 source instructions in those days of few comment cards.) The number four in the saying would occasionally be replaced by three, or seven, or some number in that general region, and the result served as a handy way to get a rough estimate of maintenance staffing needs.

Currently, the ratio is usually expressed in terms of $(KDSI/FSP)_M$, thousands of source instructions maintained per full-time software person, and the number of maintenance personnel $(FSP)_M$ required to support a product of size $(KDSI)_{DEVEL}$ estimated as:

$$(FSP)_M = \frac{(KDSI)_{DEVEL}}{(KDSI/FSP)_M}$$

The annual maintenance effort $(MM)_{AM}$ is then simply

$$(MM)_{AM} = 12(FSP)_M$$

Thus, a 32 KDSI product with a cards-per-person ratio of $(KDSI/FSP)_M = 16$ would require an estimated $^{32}/_{16} = 2$ person staff for maintenance, or an annual maintenance effort of 12(2) = 24 MM. As seen in Table 23.6, a wide range of values has been given for the cards-per-person ratio $(KDSI/FSP)_M$. Their variation appears to be primarily a function of application type.

Another highly significant aspect of Table 23.6 is the comparison [42] between maintenance of higher-order language (HOL) soft-

Table 23.6. Software Maintenance Cards-per-Person Ratios.

SOURCE	APPLICATION TYPE	$(KDSI/FSP)_M$
[68]	Aerospace	8
[69, 79]	Aerospace	10
[10]	Real-time	10–30
[70]	Business	20
[42]	Business, HOL	20
[42]	Business, MOL	22
[71]	Business, 487 installations	32
[10]	Support software	30–120

Table 23.7. Maintenance-Productivity Ratios (Boeing [79])

RATING	TYPES OF SOFTWARE	TYPICAL $(DSI/MM)_{MOD}$	TYPICAL ACT
Easy	Non-real-time input-output	500	0.15
Medium	Mathematical and logic operations, signal processing	250	0.05
Hard	File, data base manipulation, real-time control, input-output	100	0.01

ware and maintenance of machine-oriented language (MOL) software. The fact that their $(KDSI/FSP)_M$ ratios are roughly the same *per source instruction* means that there is a large benefit in maintenance costs per object instruction to be gained by programming in a HOL. The HOL program typically compiles into a much larger number of assembly language instructions that would have to be individually maintained if the job had been written in MOL.

The Maintenance-Productivity Ratio. The maintenance-productivity ratio $(DSI/MM)_{MOD}$ is the average number of instructions that can be modified per man-month of maintenance effort. It can be used to estimate the annual maintenance effort required for a product of size $(DSI)_{DEVEL}$ by means of the *annual change traffic* parameter ACT*:

$$(DSI)_{MOD/YR} = (ACT)(DSI)_{DEVEL}$$

$$(MM)_{AM} = \frac{(DSI)_{MOD/YR}}{(DSI/MM)_{MOD}}.$$

Thus, a 32 KDSI product with an ACT of 0.10 and a maintenance productivity of $(DSI/MM)_{MOD} = 200$ would have $(DSI)_{MOD/YR} = (0.10)(32,000) = 3200$ and an annual maintenance effort of $(MM)_{AM} = \frac{32}{200} = 16$ MM.

One set of values for ACT and $(DSI/MM)_{MOD}$ is given in Reference 72 in terms of a categorization of software maintenance into easy, medium, and hard ratings. These values are summarized in Table 23.7.

The estimator can then determine how much of his software product is easy, medium,

---

*Annual Change Traffic (ACT): The fraction of the software product's source instructions that undergo change during a (typical) year, either through additional or modification.

or hard, and apply the above equations with the appropriate values of ACT and $(DSI/MM)_{MOD}$ to obtain his overall annual maintenance estimates $(MM)_{AM}$.

More Detailed Maintenance Cost Estimation. The simple linear ratios above provide a basic capability for estimating software maintenance costs. However, they are insensitive to a number of factors that may be critical (e.g., personnel experience and capability, main storage constraints). One model which accommodates these factors is the COCOMO model [25]. It uses the productivity ranges discussed above for development as a means to estimate maintenance costs, with two exceptions:

- Use of modern programming practices has a greater benefit in maintenance than in development.
- A low required software reliability reduces development costs, but incurs a penalty in maintenance.

23.3. IMPROVING SOFTWARE PRODUCTIVITY

A sound understanding of the factors influencing software costs has two major benefits. One is an improved capability to perform accurate software cost estimation, and thereby provide a more solid foundation for the planning and control of software projects.

The other is a valuable set of insights into improving software productivity. Many of the software cost driver attributes discussed above are project "controllables," figuratively, control knobs that can be set to positions that improve software productivity. Clearly, some cost driver attributes, such as the type of software being developed, are uncontrollable, but most are at least partly controllable in ways that increase software productivity.

Thus, for example, even the size of the software to be developed is a major controllable that may yield impressive savings in software costs through a choice of options that reduces the number of instructions we need to develop, and that in some cases avoids the requirement to develop software at all. For example, we may choose instead to purchase a software product or to adapt a number of existing software routines or subsystems as part of our software product.

In doing so, we provide the required software functions but do not create many new software instructions. Thus, we need once more to keep our concepts of software "productivity" in perspective: producing a great many new delivered source instructions per MM may be much less productive in terms of needed software functions per MM than an alternate strategy of buying a software product that already furnishes the needed functions.* On the other hand, we cannot simply use the number of DSI in a purchased software product as an index of productivity: For one thing, we will often find that many of the functions provided in the software product are not needed for our application.

Development versus Life Cycle Productivity. Another valuable perspective on software productivity provided by software cost estimation technology is the distinction between software development productivity and software life cycle productivity. The tradeoffs between lower development costs and lower life cycle costs are characterized by the modern programming practices and required reliability cost estimating relationships for software development and maintenance. These emphasize the reduction in maintenance costs it is possible to achieve through better structured and documented software, program support library procedures, and reliability-ori-

ented aids such as diagnostics, environmental simulators, and test data management systems. Even though some of these latter steps may increase development costs, they will pay off in reduced maintenance costs, particularly for software products with long lifetimes.

Software Productivity and Human Economics. Another perspective we need to consider in improving software productivity is that our concern for the life cycle of the software *product* needs to be balanced by our concern for the life cycle of the software *people* involved. Thus, we need to balance the material-economic concepts of work as an activity that adds monetary value to a product with such human-economic concepts of work as an activity that helps people develop character [73]. We can't allow ourselves to "routinize" software development along the lines of the scenario developed in Reference 74 by fragmenting software jobs into small, meaningless pieces or by binding a programmer in perpetuity to a boring maintenance job. Fortunately, a good manager can avoid this pitfall, as the objectives of effective software development and effective software career development are not necessarily in conflict.

REFERENCES

1. W. W. Royce, "Managing the Development of Large Software Systems: Concepts and Techniques," *Proc. WESCON,* Aug. 1970.
2. Air Force Space and Missile Systems Organization, "Computer Program Subsystem Development Milestones," SSD Exhibit 61-47B, April 1, 1966.
3. P. E. Rosove, *Developing Computer-Based Information Systems,* Wiley and Sons, New York, 1967.
4. TRW, Inc., "Software Development and Configuration Management Manual," TRW-SS-73-07, Dec. 1973.
5. B. W. Boehm, "Software and Its Impact: A Quantitative Assessment," *Datamation,* May 1973.
6. "United Drops Univac Contract for $56 Million Data System," *Aviation Week,* February 9, 1970, p. 31.
7. U.S. Congress, House of Representatives, *Advanced Logistic (ADP) System,* Dept. of Defense Appropriation Bill, 1976, Report No. 94-517, September 25, 1975, pp. 163–165.
8. B. W. Boehm, "Software Engineering," *IEEE Trans. Computers,* Dec. 1976.

---

*It would be highly valuable for the software field if we could develop a software productivity metric in terms of desired product functionality rather than in terms of DSI. Unfortunately, this ideal has been and will be very difficult to achieve.

9. M. E. Fagan, "Design and Code Inspections to Reduce Errors in Program Development," *IBM Systems Journal*, vol. 15. no. 3, 1976, pp. 182–211.

10. E. B. Daly, "Management of Software Engineering," *IEEE Trans. Software Engineering*, May 1977, pp. 229–242.

11. W. E. Stephenson, "An Analysis of the Resources Used in Safeguard System Software Development," Bell Labs, draft paper, Aug. 1976.

12. G. J. Myers, *Software Reliability*, Wiley and Sons, New York, 1976.

13. B. W. Boehm, "An Experiment in Small Scale Application Software Engineering," *Proc. IFIP 8th World Computer Congress*, Oct. 1980.

14. R. D. Williams, "Managing the Development of Reliable Software," *Proc. International Conference of Reliable Software, IEEE/ACM*, Apr. 1975, pp. 3–8.

15. V. Basili and A. Turner, "Iterative Enhancement: A Practical Technique for Software Engineering," *IEEE Trans. Software Engineering*, Dec. 1975, pp. 390–396.

16. D. L. Parnas, "On the Design and Development of Program Families," *IEEE Trans. Software Engineering*, March 1979, pp. 128–137.

17. P. V. Norden, "Curve Fitting for a Model of Applied Research and Development Scheduling," *IBM Journal of Research and Development*, July 1958.

18. J. D. Aron, *Estimating Resources for Large Programming Systems*, NATO Science Committee, Rome, Oct. 1969.

19. L. H. Putnam, "A General Empirical Solution to the Macro Software Sizing and Estimating Problem," *IEEE Trans. Software Engineering*, July 1978, pp. 345–361.

20. F. P. Brooks, Jr., *The Mythical Man-Month*, Addison-Wesley, Reading, Mass., 1975.

21. R. W. Jensen and C. C. Tonies, *Software Engineering*, Prentice-Hall, Englewood Cliffs, N.J., 1979.

22. A. J. Albrecht, "Measuring Application Development Productivity," SHARE-GUIDE '79, pp. 83–92.

23. M. H. Halstead, *Elements of Software Science*, Elsevier, New York, 1977.

24. T. J. McCabe, "A Complexity Measure," *IEEE Trans. Software Engineering*, Dec. 1976.

25. B. W. Boehm, *Software Engineering Economics*, Prentice-Hall, Englewood Cliffs, N.J., 1981.

26. C. E. Walston and C. P. Felix, "A Method of Programming Measurement and Estimation," *IBM Systems Journal*, vol. 16, no. 1, 1977, pp. 54–73.

27. R. Nelson, "Software Data Collection and Analysis at RDAC," Rome Air Development Center, Rome, N.Y. 1978.

28. K. Freburger and V. R. Basili, "The Software Engineering Laboratory: Relationship Equations," University of Maryland Report TR-764, May 1979.

29. J. R. Herd, J. N. Postak, W. E. Russell, and K. R. Stewart, "Software Cost Estimation Study—Study Results," Doty Associates, Inc. Final Technical Report (in 2 vols.), RADC-TR-77-220, vol. 1, June 1977, NTIS No. Ad-A042264.

30. B. C. Frederic, "A Provisional Model for Estimating Computer Program Development Costs," Tecolote Research, Inc., Dec. 1974.

31. M. Phister, Jr., *Data Processing Technology and Economics*, Digital Press, Bedford, Mass., 1979.

32. T. C. Jones, "Program Quality and Programmer Productivity," IBM TR 02.764, January 28, 1977.

33. C. E. Walston and C. P. Felix, "Authors' Response," *IBM Systems Journal* no. 4, 1977, pp. 422–423.

34. V. Schneider, "Prediction of Software Effort and Project Duration: Four New Formulas," *ACM SIGPLAN Notices*, June 1978, pp. 49–59.

35. F. R. Freiman and R. E. Park, "PRICE Software Model—Version 3: An Overview," *Proc. IEEE-PINY Workshop on Quantitative Software Models*, IEEE catalog no. TH0067-9, Oct. 1979, pp. 32–41.

36. *Proc., Government/Industry Software Sizing and Costing Workshop*, U.S. Air Force Electronic Systems Div., Bedford, Mass., Oct. 1974.

37. J. D. Aron, *The Program Development Process: The Individual Programmer*, Addison-Wesley, Reading, Mass., 1974.

38. R. W. Wolverton, "The Cost of Developing Large-Scale Software," *IEEE Trans. on Computers*, June 1974, pp. 615–636.

39. I. M. Williamson, "NARDAC Model," NRL Technical Memorandum 7503-XXX, July 16, 1979.

40. R. F. Scott and D. B. Simmons, "Programmer Productivity and the Delphi Technique," *Datamation*, May 1974, pp. 71–73.

41. T. Martin, "PEARL at the Age of Three," *Proc., Fourth International Conference on Software Engineering*, IEEE catalog no. 79CH 1479-5C, Sept. 1979, pp. 100–109.

42. C. A. Graver, et al., "Cost Reporting Elements and Activity Cost Tradeoffs for Defense System Software," General Research Corp., Santa Barbara, Calif., March 1977.

43. A. O. Williman and C. O'Donnell, "Through the Central 'Multiprocessor' Avionics Enters the Computer Era," *Astronautics and Aeronautics*, July 1970.

44. R. K. D. Black, R. P. Curnow, R. Katz, and M. D. Gray, "BCS Software Production Data," Boeing Computer Services, Inc., Final Technical Report, RADC-TR-77-116, March 1977, NTIS no. AD-A039852.

45. W. M. Carriere and R. Thibodeau, "Development of a Logistics Software Cost Estimating Technique for Foreign Military Sales," General Research Corp., Report CR-3-839, June 1979.

46. E. B. Daly, "Organizing for Successful Software Development," *Datamation*, Dec. 1979, pp. 107–120.

47. H. Sackman, *Man-Computer Problem Solving*, Auerbach, Philadelphia, Pa., 1970.

48. L. C. Jones and D. A. Nelson, "A Quantitative Assessment of IBM's Programming Productivity Techniques," *Proc., ACM/IEEE 13th Design Automation Conference*, June 1976.

49. J. M. Reaser and J. C. Carrow, "Interactive Programming: Summary of an Evaluation and Some

Management Considerations," U.S. Army Computer Systems Command Report USACSC-AT-74-03, March 1975.

50. "AFIPS Programmer Job Description Survey Booklet," *AFIPS*, 1973.

51. D. B. Mayer and A. W. Stalnaker, "Selection and Evaluation of Computer Personnel," *Proc., ACM National Conference 1968*, ACM, 1968, pp. 657–670. Also in (Weinwurm 70), pp. 133–157.

52. G. M. Weinberg, *The Psychology of Computer Programming*, Van Nostrand Reinhold, New York, 1971.

53. B. Schneiderman, *Software Psychology: Human Factors in Computer and Information Systems*, Winthrop Press, Cambridge, Mass., 1980.

54. D. R. Jeffery and M. J. Lawrence, "An Inter-Organizational Comparison of Programming Productivity," *Proc., Fourth International Conference on Software Engineering*, IEEE catalog no. 79 CH 1479-5C, Sept. 1979, pp. 369–377.

55. C. L. McGowan and J. R. Kelly, *Top-Down Structured Programming Techniques*, Petrocelli-Charter, 1975.

56. H. D. Mills, "Structured Programming in Large Systems," IBM-FSD, 1970.

57. E. Yourdon, *Techniques of Program Structure and Design*, Prentice-Hall, Englewood Cliffs, N.J., 1975.

58. F. A. Comper, *Project Management for System Quality and Development Productivity*, Bank of Montreal, Quebec, 1979.

59. R. Pitchell, "The GUIDE Productivity Program," *GUIDE Proc.*, 1979, pp. 783–794.

60. Personal communication from M. Galinier, University of Toulouse. 1978.

61. *Structured Programming: Practice and Experience*, Infotech International Ltd., Maidenhead, England, 1978.

62. "GUIDE Survey of New Programming Technologies," *GUIDE Proc.*, 1979, pp. 306–308.

63. H. S. Stone, "Final Report: Life-Cycle Cost Analysis of Instruction Set Architecture Standardization for Military Computer-Based Systems," U.S. Army Research Office, Jan. 1978.

64. H. S. Stone and A. Coleman, "Life-Cycle Cost Analysis of Instruction Set Architecture Standardization for Military Computer-Based Systems," *IEEE Computer*, 1979.

65. L. A. Belady and M. M. Lehman, "Characteristics of Large Systems," in P. Wegner (ed.), *Research Directions in Software Technology*, M.I.T. Press, Cambridge, Mass., 1979.

66. E. B. Swanson, "The Dimensions of Maintenance," *Proc., IEEE/ACM Second International Conference on Software Engineering*, Oct. 1976.

67. L. H. Putnam and A. Fitzsimmons, "Estimating Software Costs," *Datamation*, Sept. 1979, pp. 189–198. Continued in *Datamation*, Oct. 1979, pp. 171–178, and Nov. 1979, pp. 137–140.

68. R. W. Wolverton, "Airborne Systems Software Acquisition Engineering Guidebook: Software Cost Analysis and Estimating," U.S. Air Force ASD/EN, Wright-Patterson AFB, Ohio, Feb. 1980.

69. D. V. Ferens and R. L. Harris, "Avionics Computer Software Operation and Support Cost of Estimation," *Proc., NAECON 79*, Dayton, Ohio, May 1979.

70. I. R. Elliott, "Life-Cycle Planning for a Large Mix of Commercial Systems," *Proc., U.S. Army ISRAD Software Phenomenology Workshop*, Aug. 1977, pp. 203–216.

71. B. P. Lientz and E. B. Swanson, *Software Maintenance Management: A Study of the Maintenance of Computer Application Software in 487 Data Processing Organizations*, Addison-Wesley, Reading, Mass., 1980.

72. Boeing Co., "Software Cost Measuring and Reporting," U.S. Air Force-ASD Document D180-22813-1, Jan. 1979.

73. E. F. Schumacher, *Small is Beautiful: Economics as if People Mattered*, Harper and Row, New York, 1973.

74. P. Kraft, *Programmers and Managers: The Routinization of Computer Programming in the United States*, Springer-Verlag, New York, 1977.

24

Software Requirements:
New Directions and Perspectives

Raymond T. Yeh
University of Maryland

Pamela Zave
Bell Laboratories

Alex Paul Conn
Digital Equipment Corporation

George E. Cole, Jr.
Johns Hopkins Hospital

24.1. INTRODUCTION

Statistics gathered during the past few years have produced an awareness of the enormous and alarming cost of maintaining large software systems. If the trend continues, the data-processing industry not only will become the most labor-intensive industry, but also will devote most of its productivity to maintaining old, ill-structured, and difficult-to-modify software.

Furthermore, it has been shown [1] that as the complexity (and entropy) of a system grow, the probability increases that any change will introduce additional errors. The result in each case is an increasingly unreliable system. Real danger is involved in the dependence of our society on such systems, as illustrated recently by false alarms triggered by software errors at the Strategic Command Center (reported in the *Washington Post*).

Although there are many reasons for the difficulty of maintaining software, lack of thorough attention to requirements analysis and specification, the earliest phase of software development, is a major one. For example, in two large command/control systems, 67 and 95%, respectively, of the software had to be rewritten after delivery because of mismatches with user requirements [2]. There are also many examples of total cancellation of projects because of lack of appropriate requirements and feasibility analyses. Some of the more expensive cases are the $56 million Univac-United Airlines reservation system and the $217 million Advanced Logistic System [3]. In general, it has been found that "design errors" (all errors made before implementation) range from 36 to 74% of the total error count [4]. These numbers are not the whole story, however; a design error takes from 1.5 to 3 times the effort of an implementation error to correct.

We have illustrated the importance of developing a good requirements methodology to control maintenance costs, but there are other equally pressing reasons. The requirements document has a unique role in the development of a software system: It is the basis for communication among customers, users, designers, and implementers of the system, and unless it represents an informed consensus of these groups, the project is not likely to be a success.

It must also carry the weight of contractual relationships between parties that sometimes become adversaries. In particular, the design and implementation must be validated against it.

The costs of neglecting these functions include lack of management control, inability to use top-down design or other software engineering techniques, user hostility, and lawsuits. In short, because the requirements phase comes so early in development, it has a tremendous impact on the quality (or lack thereof) of the development effort and the final product.

Current approaches to requirements engineering, unfortunately, are inadequate. Most of the available techniques concentrate on functional requirements and provide relatively weak structures for expressing them. They offer basically tools (primarily languages), rather than guidelines for analysis *or* specification.

In this paper, we suggest a systematic approach to obtaining software requirements, and point out the existence of available results from other fields such as data base management, artificial intelligence, and psychology that are of great relevance to the development of a good requirements document. We deal with all aspects of requirements documents and illustrate them with examples taken from an existing requirements document (see below). Because of space limitations, our discussion will be largely informal, but will guide the interested reader to more thorough presentations elsewhere.

The AFWET system (*Air Force Weapons Effectiveness Testing*, ultimately realized under the name *WESTE*) was an early real-time system that supported quantitative testing of U.S. military (conventional warfare) capability (see Figure 24.1). We describe it briefly here because its requirements document [5] is a plentiful source of bad examples and unsolved problems.

Weapons tests were military exercises involving such "test elements" as airplanes, ships, tanks, and ground defense positions (some playing the role of enemy forces) confined to a circle centered on Eglin Air Force Base in Florida. Test elements communicated

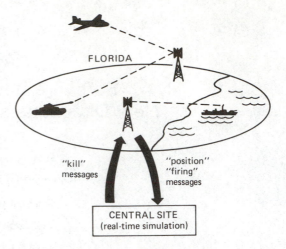

Figure 24.1. The AFWET system.

with a central site through standard military radio equipment, plus a contractor-supplied communications network.

During the test, moving elements would send periodic notifications of their positions to the central site. Mock firings of weapons would also cause messages to be sent, supplying all relevant parameters such as the direction of aim and so forth. The central system would simulate the battle in real time, determining which of the mock firings would have resulted in "kills." The results of the simulation were (1) used to display the course of the battle on graphics scopes for the benefit of officers in a control room, (2) dumped onto archival storage for later analysis, and (3) used to send "kill" notifications to "killed" test elements in the field. They would then react with a flashing light or loud noise and cease to participate in the battle.

24.2. CONCEPTUAL MODELING

In the early days of software development, machines were relatively small and so were systems. A program served in a well-understood, well-specified scientific domain, and thus could be written directly from a statement of need.

As we have moved to much larger systems and a variety of application domains, the need for precise specification of a system before implementation has increased. But the complexity of these systems demands an additional layer of understanding, a "buffer," between the real world and the requirements specification. This buffer allows an analyst to understand the problem before proposing a system to solve it—an understanding that can be achieved with an unassisted mental model if the problem is simple enough. For complex problems, a model must be constructed that is explicit and formal enough to be shared by a group of people. We call such problem models *conceptual models* because they are constructed at the level of human concept formulation.

One possible consequence of the lack of a conceptual model appears in the AFWET requirements:

Choice of major subsystems shall be the responsibility of the contractor; however, a typical range configuration may consist of the following subsystems. . . . Space Position Subsystem . . . Data Subsystem . . . Timing Subsystem . . . Communication Subsystem . . . Processor Subsystem . . . Kill and Display Subsystem. . . .

For lack of an approach to providing an introduction to, or overview of, the AFWET problem, the requirements writers had to present part of a design for the system!

If we accept the assumption that constructing a conceptual model is a necessary step in gaining understanding of large, complex problems, what do we model and how do we construct it?

We believe that conceptual modeling should be done "outside-in," beginning with the proposed system's environment and working inward toward the system. In many cases this will lead the analyst directly to the requirements, since the purpose of the system is to support a desirable mode of operation in the environment. This is particularly true when the project is to automate existing manual procedures, because then the computer system is a direct reflection of the current operations.

Other reasons for stressing understanding of the environment are that it will improve communication with customers and users (who are much more interested in their environment than your system) and because large applica-

tion programs are parts of their own environments [6]. But perhaps the most important reason of all, given the intrinsically evolutionary nature of large software systems [1], is that change in a system originates with change in the environment. By modeling the environment, the analyst can study potential changes, and possibly even provide a designer information that can be used during design so as to achieve modularity—the property whereby small changes in the environment cause correspondingly small changes in the system.

The overall structure of a conceptual model is shown in Figure 24.2. The environment consists of identifiable objects such as people, airplanes, terminals, forms and other types of data, and so forth. The states of these environment entities must be represented, as must the events (an agent makes a flight reservation, a machine overheats) that cause state changes. The target system can be similarly divided into states, and activities that interact with environmental events so as (ultimately) to influence them.

The model is structured by relationships and constraints on all these objects. "A is a subnet of B," "Helen and Bob are married," "faucet must be opened before water can flow," and so on, are simple examples of constraints and relationships, but new government regulations, hardware configuration changes, and a wide variety of other facts can be relevant.

To collect information on the environment, personal interviews and questionnaires are most often used. The actual modeling process can begin with either entities or events. When starting from an event, the information change

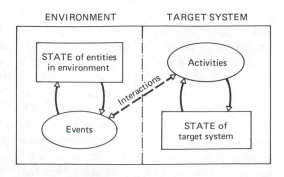

Figure 24.2. A conceptual model.

due to occurrence of that event must be reflected into the structure of the model. For example, a transaction "reservation request" from a remote terminal linked to an airline reservation system will change the available seats on a particular flight. Assuming such information is stored in a target system data base, this event will also trigger a system activity to change the data base. The state information is thus transmitted through the interaction between the system and its environment. Similarly, an analyst may start with entities from the environment to build up state information, and then consider changes to these entities so as to develop the structure of processes within the system. Interested readers are referred to Reference 7 for more details about information collection and to Reference 8 for more examples of conceptual modeling.

Note that the *outside-in* approach is neither *top-down* nor *bottom-up*—the model structure must be evolved in both directions. Top-down analysis is employed when an analyst asks an interviewee to elaborate on some previously identified feature of the environment, but a bottom-up approach is required to collect and integrate views of users in different parts of an organization.

The conceptual model is an important tool for understanding the requirements of a system, but it is *not* a requirements document. The latter, though derived from the model, has somewhat different properties, which will be the subject of the next section.

24.3. REQUIREMENTS DERIVATION

The conceptual model should be a rich, complex information structure—probably too rich and complex for the purposes of the software requirements document (SRD). For instance, a conceptual model of AFWET might include views of the system as seen by soldiers, officers, computer operators, and hardware maintenance personnel, and thus be highly redundant. It might also model more of the environment than is needed just to define the proposed system. This would be the case if the AFWET analysts were to decide (quite correctly!) that they need to understand the military background and purpose of the tests they are to in-

strument to assure themselves that the data they gather and display will be useful.

Thus the SRD is derived from the conceptual model by filtering and organizing, constantly aiming toward the "best-engineered" specification. Explicit goals for the SRD can be found by considering the thing it will be used for:

Many groups of people must communicate with each other through and about the SRD. Therefore it must be *understandable*.

In order to accommodate the evolutionary nature of large systems, the organization of SRD must be structured so that changes can be made with minimum effort. In a word, it must be *modifiable*.

Last but not least, the SRD is used to define the target system. To do this properly it should be *precise* (preferably formal), *unambiguous*, *complete* (a particularly important aspect of completeness being the role of the SRD in contractual obligations), *internally consistent,* and *minimal*. A minimal specification does not overconstrain the design of the system, which might exclude the best solutions to design problems.

As in most engineering situations involving multiple goals, the above properties cannot all be achieved in most situations. However, there does exist a set of mental tools and principles that can help the analyst to meet many of them.

The crucial issue here is the *decomposition of complexity,* also referred to as "separation of concerns," "divide and conquer" strategy, and so forth. For software development we can describe the goal of this method via two subgoals, namely, the *process goal* and the *product goal*. The process goal is to keep the process under our intellectual control at all times. The product goal is to organize the product in a fashion that allows others to comprehend the product by an amount of effort which is proportional to the size of the product. There are three powerful tools for decomposing complexity so as to achieve these goals (see Figure 24.3).

The first tool is the notion of *abstraction*. The use of abstraction allows us to suppress details and concentrate on essential properties. Thus, we refer to something as an abstraction

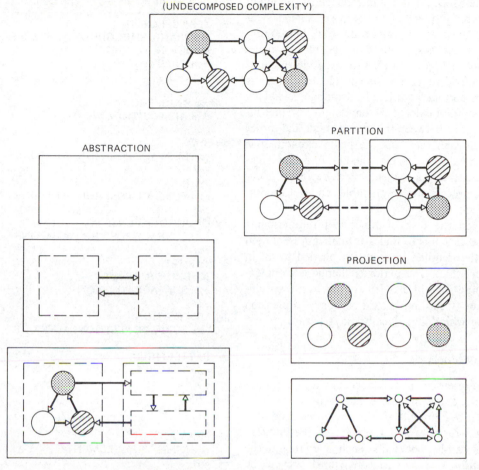

Figure 24.3. Three ways to decompose complexity.

if it represents several actual objects but is disassociated from any specific object. The use of abstraction forms natural hierarchies, allowing elaboration of more and more detail and hence providing intellectual control of the process.

The second tool is *partition,* that is, representing the whole as the sum of its parts. This tool allows us to concentrate on components or subsystems of the system one at a time. Partitioning makes systems modular. Note that if each partitioned component also has an abstraction hierarchy, then we have both a horizontal and a vertical decomposition of the system.

The third tool is *projection,* which enables us to understand a system from different viewpoints. A projection of a system represents the entire system, but with respect to only a subset of its properties; the perfect physical analogy

is an architectural drawing, which is a two-dimensional view of a three-dimensional building. The notion of a "view" of a data base [9] is another such example. Again, this tool allows us to separate particular facets of a system from the rest and therefore retain intellectual control.

Of course, any tool can be abused. In using the three structuring principles above, one must be guided by the principle of "information hiding" [10] and other observations about how specifications can be made coherent and flexible [11]. Arbitrary decompositions forced on system aspects that are too interdependent will cause more problems than they solve.

24.4. FUNCTIONAL REQUIREMENTS

Functional requirements describe what the target system *does,* and are clearly the heart of the SRD. Section 2 introduced the notion of an explicit model of the proposed system's environment as an important tool in requirements analysis (leading to the global model shown in Figure 24.2). From the viewpoint of functional requirements specification, there is an important additional advantage to having an explicit model of the environment: Since interactions between the environment and target system can then also be made explicit, it is much easier to specify the all-important environment/target system interface in an accurate, precise, understandable, and yet modifiable manner.

Thus the task of functional requirements specification is to find a formal representation for the detailed information needed to fill in Figure 24.2. The major challenge is complexity, and we will classify approaches to specification according to the primary dimension along which they decompose structure.

Data Models

Data-oriented models concentrate on specifying the *states* of Figure 24.2—the state of the target system will always be represented as a data structure, and the state of the environment can be modeled as such, even though the resulting data structure need never be implemented.

Research on data base problems has led to the recognition of abstract concepts that can be fruitfully used in data-oriented specifications of software systems of all kinds. We shall use the notation presented in Reference 12, a survey aimed at non-data-base specialists, to explain the most prominent data-structuring concepts.

At any moment, a data base or "data space" consists of a population of "individuals" or items. A data base modeling the environment of the AFWET system ("STATE of entities in environment" in Figure 24.2) could contain individuals representing test elements.

Individuals belong to (are instances of) types, and types can be subtypes of other types (obviously, an instance of a type is also an instance of all its supertypes). The type hierarchy for a data base is specified as part of the

Table 24.1. AFWET-Type Definition.

def TEST-ELEMENT:
  sub PLANE, SHIP, GROUND-DEFENSE-
  POSITION, TARGET
  com ROLE
  end
def PLANE:
  sub B-52G, F-4C
  com AIR-POSITION, WEAPONS
  end
def SHIP:
  com SURFACE-POSITION, WEAPONS
  end
def TANK:
  com SURFACE-POSITION, WEAPONS
  end
def GROUND-DEFENSE-POSITION:
  com SURFACE-POSITION, WEAPONS
  end
def TARGET:
  sub BRIDGE, DEPOT
  com SURFACE-POSITION
  end
def AIR-POSITION:
  com SURFACE-POSITION, ALTITUDE
  end
def BATTLEFIELD:
  com TEST-ELEMENT*
  end
def TEST:
  com FRAME*
  end
def FRAME:
  com TIME, TEST-ELEMENT*
  end

*The individual can have multiple components.

data base's *type definition*. Table 24.1, for instance, is a type definition for the real-time simulation portion of the AFWET system. It defines types using the syntax:

$$def \quad \text{TYPE-NAME:}$$

.

.

.

$$end,$$

and the types listed after the keyword *sub* are its subtypes. Thus an individual plane may be a member of types B-52G, PLANE, and TEST-ELEMENT. The use of types to structure data is referred to as *generalization*.

Individuals also have components that are

needed to describe them fully. Each component is identified with a type to which it must belong, and the proper components of individuals of certain types are listed after *com* in that type's definition. Thus a full description of an air position (an instance of type AIR-POSITION) requires a surface position and an altitude. Full description of a plane requires its air position and the weapons it is carrying. It also requires a role (friend or foe), a component that the PLANE type inherits from its supertype TEST-ELEMENT. It is clear that the component relation is also hierarchical, and its use to structure data is referred to as *aggregation.*

The state of the AFWET system (real-time simulation portion only) and its environment at any given time, is a data base consistent with this type definition (plus a great deal of read-only information, such as models of test-element motion and weapons threats, needed for simulation). There should be only one instance of type BATTLEFIELD, and its components represent the currently active test-elements (for elements marked by *, the individual can have multiple components of the designated type). Within the system, the state of the battlefield at a given time is represented by an instance of type FRAME, having as components a time and the test-elements that were active at that time. A full test is recorded in multiple frames. This is a particularly good example of what it means to reflect the structure of the environment within the system!

A data model must be interfaced with processing aspects of the system. At the very least, a set of primitive data manipulation operations should be enumerated, and these operations should be defined in terms of a first-order predicate language and the operations *create, destroy,* and *modify* applied to individuals in the data base. For instance, in the AFWET data base a simulated kill should *destroy* a test-element that is a component of the current battlefield. Once defined, these operations can be used as the interface between the data model and whatever higher-level processing model is preferred.

Data-oriented models, as the heart of requirements analysis and specification, have been very successful—especially in the domains of data processing and business information systems. Some good examples can be found in References 7, 13, and 14. The primary notion used there is the semantic net, a graphical formalism that was originally developed by artificial intelligence researchers for representing knowledge structures.

Data-Flow Processing Models

The most common model of processing used in conjunction with data-oriented models is the data-flow diagram, which simply names the major processing activities of the system and indicates which parts of the data model are inputs and outputs to each activity. If iterative refinement of the data-flow diagram is supported, and activities are defined (usually informally) in terms of data manipulation operations, a level of expressive power sufficient for many data-processing systems may be achieved.

The dataflow approach is central to SADT [15, 16], although there is additional emphasis on a methodology for team cooperation. The data-flow approach is supported with automated tools in PSL/PSA [17]. It can be extended with control information via Petri nets [18] or with resource synchronization [19].

The deficiencies of the data-flow model for specifying embedded (real-time) systems are apparent in the dataflow diagram for the AFWET system shown in Figure 24.4 (the "fight" function has been added to provide the "processing" that modifies the state of the environment). The global events and activities in this system are continuous, and are not activated by the appearance of a single input or any simple combination of inputs. At a lower level, they consist of complex combinations of pieces of computation that must occur asynchronously and in parallel. Data flow as a concept is simply not powerful enough to permit precise specification or effective decomposition of systems, such as embedded ones, in which concurrent and asynchronous operations occur at the requirements level.

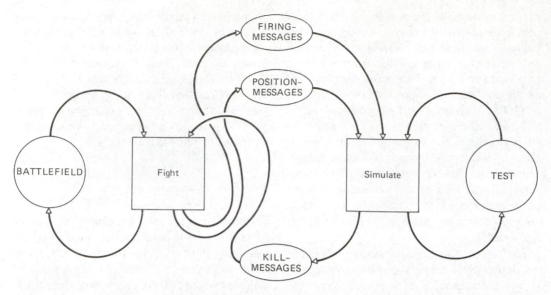

Figure 24.4. AFWET dataflow.

The Process Model

An approach that is better suited to specification of embedded systems emphasizes the "events" and "activities" portions of Figure 24.2. The central concept is the *process,* an autonomous computational unit that is understood to operate in parallel with, and interact asynchronously with, other processes. Processes have long been used as abstractions of concurrent activity within multiprogramming systems [20] and many recent articles have shown that they can be used to model data bases, monitors, functional modules, I/O devices, and presumably any other identifiable structure within a computing system [21, 22].

Formally, a process is just a "state space" (set of possible states) and a "successor relation" that maps predecessor states onto their possible successors. This simple concept is easily adapted to being a digital simulation of an object (person, machine, sensor, etc.) in the environment of a computer system.

The result of the generality of processes is that the requirements for a system can be specified by a set of asynchronously interacting processes, some of which represent objects in the environment and some of which represent objects in the target system. The environment of AFWET, for instance, becomes a set of processes, each one simulating a test element. All processes respond to kill messages by becoming inactive. All processes representing test elements with weapons send firing messages whenever their internal, cyclic simulation algorithms decree that they have fired a weapon. All processes representing moving test elements periodically update their positions and send position messages to the central system. The result is an easily constructed, easily understood model with highly complex overall behavior; it is understandable simply because it is naturalistic, being made up of semiautonomous objects acting in parallel, just as the real world is.

Figure 24.5 shows an overall process-and-communication structure for the simulation portion of the AFWET system. The *test-element* processes are as described above. Processes representing radio towers put timestamps on the input messages and relay them to an *input-buffer* process. The *input-buffer* process collects into a batch all the messages relating to the period covered by a particular simulation step, waits until all messages from that period can reasonably be expected to have arrived, and then passes the batch to the *simulation* process. This simulator computes a new frame (and kill messages) from the old frame, the batch of messages, and its various mathematical models. Frames are passed on

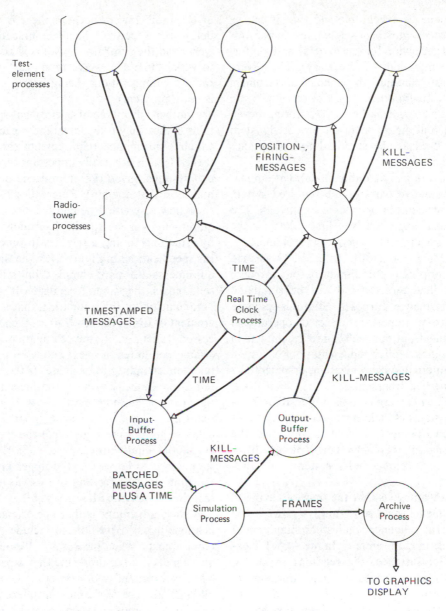

Figure 24.5. Processes of the AFWET system.

one by one to the rest of the system, where they are stored and otherwise used. Kill messages are relayed to the *test-element* processes via an *output-buffer* process and the *radio-tower* processes.

This has been an informal description of a formal requirements specification in PAISLey (Process-oriented, Applicative, Interpretable Specification Language [23–26]. PAISLey is a process-oriented language aimed at embedded systems. As the acronym indicates, its

other major characteristics are that it is applicative and interpretable. The advantages of applicative languages are currently receiving well-deserved attention; recent results and trends are surveyed in Reference 27. The most important properties of applicative languages (for our purposes) are that they are precise and convenient vehicles for abstraction and that they are interpretable.

Interpretability carries with it many advantages. It means that the system-plus-environment model is executable and that it can be validated by testing—including demonstrations of behavior for customers, and performance simulations (if necessary). The advantages also continue throughout development since the environmental part of the model can be used as a *test bed* or *driver* during development, and the model of the proposed system can be used as the standard for acceptance testing.

The use of an excutable model that emphasizes the active parts of the required system can be termed the *operational* approach. The operational approach was first taken by the SREM system and its requirements language RSL [28, 29, and 30]. In RSL, processing paths from input stimulus to output response are specified directly and can be simulated for performance purposes. Stimulus-response paths are an important aspect of operational requirements, of course, but are incomplete in not including explicit representations of system states, internal synchronization, or potentially distributed environments.

PAISLey is more complete than RSL in including states, synchronization, and the system's environment, and it shows that the operational approach has some striking advantages for embedded system requirements.

One advantage is that the rigor of having to make a model that "runs" always proves to be a powerful influence against ambiguity and vagueness in requirements. In the AFWET example, for instance, the relationship among frames, input messages, and real time was arrived at after a great deal of confusion. It finally became clear that (1) simulation had to be oriented toward increments of time rather than toward events because the effect of a firing event may occur at any point during the entire interval that the bullet is still in the air, (2) the cost of backtracking would be prohibitive—once a computation was done it could not be undone by a late-arriving message, and (3) this meant that simulation time had to be enough behind real time so that all messages relating to a new frame could be assumed to have arrived when computation of the new frame began. Timestamps are put on messages

at the radio towers because there is variable delay in the rest of the communication network, and the simulator must know accurately to which time a message refers (delay in the radio communications, being nearly constant, is not a problem).

Another advantage of operational specifications is that they provide natural structures to which performance requirements can be attached (this is especially important for embedded systems, given the prominence of performance in that domain). References 24 and 26 show how response time and feedback loop requirements can be specified formally, simply by attaching timing attributes to functions in the specification. In Figure 24.5, the timing requirements are more complex, but still representable in the same formalism. If g is the "granularity" of the simulation, that is, the increment of time between frames, then the successor function of the simulation process (which computes the next frame) must never take longer than g to evaluate. If the delay in radio communications is r, and the simulation time is to be no more than $r + d + g$ behind real time, then d must be the upper bound on delay in getting messages from the radio towers to the input buffer. Finally, if the timestamps are to be useful, the upper bound on the time it takes for any process to read the real-time clock must be very small.

A third advantage is that operational specifications make it possible to include resource requirements when necessary. Resource requirements are requirements that a particular resource or quantity of a resource be used. In AFWET the use of a time-multiplexed, fixed-delay radio communication link was a resource requirement,* imposed because that equipment was already owned and installed. PAISLey offers the generality of a complete model of computation, *including* asynchronous distributed computation. This means that no new system problem will surprise us with concepts unexpressible in the language.

Observations about performance and resources bring us to everyone's major reserva-

---

*Actually this is an inference from the requirements document, which is by no means clear on this point.

tion about operational requirements: Aren't these actually *design* specifications? Don't they say much more than should be said in the requirements? We believe that the answer is no, for the following reasons.

Extensive experience with requirements examples shows clearly that the essence of true design is *managing scarce resources to meet performance goals*. As long as a formalism does not force the specifier to make unnecessary decisions about performance and resources, then it is not forcing him to specify design rather than requirements. Fortunately, both applicative languages and the process model are excellent in this respect. For the "design-independence" of applicative languages, see References 31, 32; for the "design-independence" of processes, consider this very basic example: In Figure 24.5, we used as many processes to describe the central site as were logical and convenient. The design for this system will look quite different since it will probably have to deal with a scarce resource problem—only one processor. The designer will have to determine how a single processor can be multiplexed so as to implement, and meet the performance requirements of, all processes at the central site.

Another example of how the specification described by Figure 24.5 differs from a design

involves the real-time clock process, which "ticks" at regular intervals and can be read by other processes. It is not technically feasible to build a single global clock that can be read fast enough by a collection of remote sites. The design to meet this performance requirement will probably entail local clocks (which *can* be read fast enough) and a global synchronization protocol executed before each test begins.

The existence of resource requirements forces us to recognize two distinct meanings of design: from the "technical" viewpoint, it is managing resources to meet performance goals, but from the "administrative" (economic, political) viewpoint it is any property of the system that is not required to satisfy whoever is paying for it. From the technical viewpoint resource requirements are premature design decisions, but from the administrative viewpoint they are common and entirely legitimate requirements. They should be minimized, but can never be eliminated, and any requirements language that cannot handle them will be inadequate in many situations.

To summarize, operational structures do not overconstrain design unless they select a particular solution to a problem that has other feasible solutions. The AFWET example is rather extreme in that it involves quite a bit of what is technically design detail, but all the

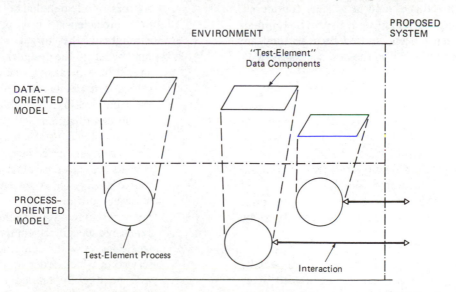

Figure 24.6. The AFWET environment model, projected onto process-oriented and data-oriented views.

"design" decisions were forced into requirements analysis by the customer's wishes or the technical infeasibility of other approaches.

A final, but important, property of any activity-oriented requirements language is its interface with data-oriented specifications. Different as Figure 24.5 may seem from the data model of Table 24.1, the two are actually quite compatible. The components of a test-element in the data model are exactly the same as the components of the state of a *test-element* process in the process model (see Figure 24.6)! This means that the process model and the data model can be viewed as *projections* of the same underlying model, which contains both, and the proposed system model supports a similar decomposition. Given the data *and* process complexity found in most large systems, compatibility between appropriate models for them cannot receive too much attention.

24.5. NONFUNCTIONAL REQUIREMENTS

Requirements other than functional ones have received very little attention, but may be an equally important part of the SRD. Since the state of the art is very far from having a comprehensive theory or methodology for these requirements, we present an annotated outline, intended to be used as a checklist of the various topics that should be at least considered, if not actually included, in the SRD. (Human factors have been omitted because they are discussed at length in the next section.)

   I. Target System Constraints
     A. *Performance*
       Performance is defined here to include all factors that describe both the subjective and objective qualities of the target system. It is thus a measurement of the "success" of the target system, a constraint below which the system must not be allowed to fall.
       1. Real time
         In many systems, especially those that are embedded in or connected to specialized equipment, the real-time performance

is essentially a measurement of the success of the system. For example, in AFWET, if the system is not designed in some way to accept weapons firings in real time, then it is likely that some of the firings will be entirely missed and the validity of the mission compromised.
       2. Other time constraints
         Other time constraints refers to important relative timing considerations within the target system, which relate events to each other rather than to real time. These relationships would normally involve precedence but might also include information for choosing between competing activities based on some kind of priority system. In AFWET, for example, the computation of the lethality of a missile might not be carried out until the trajectory has been determined, and both the computations may be considered more important (of higher priority) than the movement of an unrelated tank, given a scarcity of computational resources. While detailed decisions on precedence or priority throughout the target system may be left to the designer, there should be a means for including critical constraints in this area in the requirements.
       3. Resource utilization
         Closely related to the rationale for assigning precedence constraints are the constraints on resource utilization. A system will often be built in which the computer resources are attached to expensive specialized equipment. Decisions on which equipment to service in which order may very well be directly related to the cost or importance of each item of specialized equipment, and

the performance of the system may very well be assessed in terms of the response to the needs of this equipment. The requirements thus should provide a means for specifying the handling of critical equipment and also for placing a constraint on the balanced or optimal use of the remaining resources in the system.

4. Accuracy, quality, comprehensiveness

Although timing and resource utilization are fundamental aspects of performance, other factors also characterize the target system performance. The accuracy of the detection and computation of data can be critical. In AFWET, two elements in combat must be accurately tracked for position, both by information that might be transmitted by the elements themselves or by appropriate external equipment, such as radar. This position information must be maintained at the same degree of precision during computations or the determination of a kill condition might be erroneous.

The quality of the target system can be an important requirement. For example, if a CRT display is fuzzy or distorted, then the relationships between elements might be incorrectly interpreted by viewing personnel. Akin to quality is the idea of comprehensiveness. If important data that could be displayed is never made available, or not presented when it could be a determining factor in a mission, the target system is performing at a less-than-optimal level. The requirements constrain the eventual design by identifying, at least in general terms, the degree of comprehensiveness desired. Designers can later figure out how to manipulate the data within the quality and human factors constraints.

B. *Reliability*

The relaibility portion of the requirements outline has been adapted from the presentation in Reference 33, a study of multiprocessor systems. Reliability can be divided into two basic categories: availability of the physical equipment and integrity of the information. For requirements, the concern is about *failures* (noticeable events where the system violates its specifications) rather than *faults* (mechanical or algorithmic defects that will generate an error) [34] since the means by which the system maintains its specified level of reliability is a concern of the system developers, not those who write requirements. The purpose of defining and classifying the failures is so that constraints can be placed on the likelihood of such failures.

1. Availability

Failures that affect the availability of the system are, in general, ones that cause one or more devices to cease to function. Occasionally, a device will continue to operate, but at a reduced speed. If equipment ceases to function, we are not only interested in the duration of such failures, but also in their actual impact on the system. Today, it is much more common for critical components to be replicated and interconnected in such a manner that the target system continues to operate under a wide variety of failures. The requirements will have to be able to address the extent of degradation permissible under specified failures and the means with which the system copes with these problems (e.g., manual versus automatic reconfiguration). In a system such as AFWET, the ability to transmit critical information over more than one communication channel might be a requirement for dealing with a failure of one of those channels.

a. Definition and classification of failures that cause degraded functioning
b. Probability of each failure
c. Extent of degradation due to each failure (e.g., graceful degradation, reconfiguration, and self-repair)
d. Duration of each degradation

2. Integrity

Failures that affect the integrity of the system are those in which the computer is prevented from proceeding because loss of information precludes the computation of a valid result. When a failure does occur, the nature of the mission dictates the necessity of recovering outstanding requests or computations in progress. A requirement may specify the degree to which efforts should be taken to assure data integrity. In AFWET, trajectory and lethality computations should be completed without loss of information. On the other hand, an element that is not engaged in combat with another element might sustain a temporary loss of position without affecting the mission. The cost of recovering from every possible loss of state can be enormous with frequent rollback points causing a significant degradation in performance. The requirements might wisely place a limit on the cost of recovery by identifying states that are not critical

enough to warrant a full roll-back-and-recovery exercise.

a. Definition and classification of failures that cause loss of state
b. Probability of each failure
c. Cost of recovery of state

C. *Security*

Most of security is arguably in the realm of design since it pertains to specific means by which the reliability of the system may be enhanced. However, there appear to be two areas in which security may be an appropriate requirement. The first is physical security, which may include, for example, all military standards for pressurized cable, disconnectable terminals, safes for storing classified tapes and disks, and even the criteria for destroying or reusing such storage media. The operational category includes any method that must be used to cipher, modularize, limit transmission or otherwise affect how or where sensitive information will be available. Note that the above physical considerations for reuse of tapes are in some ways part of the operational category since it is well known that disks, for example, even when erased or overwritten a dozen times, can be made to reveal their original (e.g., classified) information with specialized signal differentiating equipment.

1. Physical (e.g., gates, locks, safes, etc.)
2. Operational—protection of integrity of information

D. *Operating constraints*

1. Frequency and duration of use

Both the frequency and duration of use are not only important to know from a staffing and maintenance point of view, but also from the standpoint of available resources. If the computer equipment is, for example, only used as part of the target system for a limited time period, it might be provided as a general facility at other times. Conversely, an already-existing facility may be adequate for supporting the needs of the target system. In a satellite probe, it might be very important to know that a computer module could be connected to some network and used for computational assistance when not operating in its primary capacity.

2. Control (e.g., remote, local, or not at all)

Control is another important operating constraint in many systems. An unmanned remote facility cannot be restarted by personnel if a failure occurs. Depending on the ability of personnel to reach the remote site, the equipment may need sophisticated automatic restart and even reconfiguration capabilities. Preventive maintenance may also not be possible in inaccessible locations such as in satellite or deep-sea probes. In addition, the proximity of the remote facility may affect the nature of interaction required since distant space probes experience significant transmission delays because of speed-of-light limitations.

3. Staffing requirements

E. *Physical constraints (e.g., size, weight, power requirements, temperature, humidity, portability, ruggedness)*

The physical constraints requirements are intended to include all factors relating to the physical placement of the equipment in the field. In the AFWET system, the nature of the pods connected to the wings of the aircraft placed lim-

its on the size, weight, power requirements, and ruggedness of the equipment that could be placed onto the pods. In some applications, even the camouflaging of the cabinets might be an important physical constraint.

II. System Development, Evolution and Maintenance

In many organizations, the plan for the development, evolution, and maintenance of the target is a separate document from the requirements since a development plan is considered to be a statement of how the requirements will be carried out. On the other hand, in many instances, large computer systems are requested and paid for by one group and developed and delivered by another. Constraints on the magnitude and cost of the development effort may very well be considered requirements to the group paying the bill. In this section, we discuss various categories relating to the life cycle plan for the target system.

A. *Kind of development*

The development of target systems can be divided into two gross categories: those efforts that are directed toward a single delivery date at which time the completed operational system will be furnished, and those efforts that plan to deliver working subsets of the requirements for evaluation in the field before embarking on a more complete version. The single full-scale effort is often itself iterative [35], but the early versions of such a system are not intended for use by the customer. Prototyping may be required in time-critical situations where delivering any kind of working system will fulfill an immediate need. Similarly, in state-of-the-art projects, careful analysis of a system shell may be needed to evaluate human factors and to clarify the require-

ments. Many software systems are almost always iterative. For example, operating systems are usually updated on a regular basis throughout their useful lives.
1. Single full-scale development
2. Iterative with prototyping

B. *Scale of effort*
The scale of effort is an essential factor in establishing requirements for the development of a target system. In iterative efforts, in which many prototypes or versions are envisioned, resources should be allocated for personnel, equipment, and overhead associated with the development of each version. When development time is included as a requirement, then an evaluation can be made assessing the feasibility of completing the stated goals within the proposed time frame. If an extended or advanced development is foreseen for one or more iterations, this information should also be incorporated into the requirements. Finally, each version should have a plan for delivery and installation. When equipment is to be installed in aircraft or naval vessels, delivery and installation may be a complex technical endeavor. And when numerous installations are already in the field, the requirements may need to call for special procedures for handling the complicated logistics of updating each installation.
For each iteration:
1. Development time
2. Development resources
   a. Personnel
   b. Equipment
   c. Cost
3. Delivery and installation (e.g., packaging, shipment, assembly and test equipment)

C. *Methodology*
1. Quality control standards
   Methodology includes all the management techniques and procedures that assure the success of the project. Quality control is meant to address software as well as hardware, including the current ideas on top-down, structured, provable, modularized (and so on) software. Many organizations now include standardization enforcement software in their compilers and assemblers.
2. Milestones and review procedures (including feasibility studies)
   Milestones and review procedures track and evaluate partially completed systems. The milestone is an identifiable stage of completion, which can be used to determine whether parallel efforts are progressing on time with respect to one another. Review procedures are used by the developers themselves to assess the current progress of an effort. The contracting agency may request a feasibility study for implementing all or a portion of the entire system. In this case, a milestone might reflect the point at which the feasibility has been proven, thus enabling the initiation of serious subsystem design efforts.
3. Acceptance criteria (e.g., benchmarks)
   While a completed system is supposed to in all ways fulfill the requirements, the acceptance criteria identify specific tests and evaluation factors by which the developed system can be judged. Traditionally, the acceptance criteria are the "teeth" in the contract, against which disputes are settled. Since a target system can almost never be exhaustively tested, it is critical that the acceptance tests cover every significant combination of functions or

activities that the system is supposed to carry out successfully.

D. *Priority and changeability*

The priority and changeability category recognizes that requirements writers may need some way to incorporate flexibility into the requirements. It may be very important that some requirements be carried out, whereas others may represent "gold plating." When other constraints are considered, such as cost, size, training, development time, and so on, it may be necessary to drop some of the less critical requirements. A means for ranking requirements or associating some weighting factor to particular facets of a target system would be very useful. This ranking can follow Parnas's modularization based on the likelihood of change [36]. If a designer is to be expected to hide, in some modular organization, system decisions that could easily change, the information about what might change must be represented in the requirements. Along the same lines, if a general requirement could be satisfied by more than one entirely different solution, it might be necessary to be able to include detailed requirements for each of the solutions. For example, in AFWET, if the transmission of certain information could be satisfied either by ground cables or by microwave communication, the military specifications for each form of transmission would have to be included in the requirements.

1. Establishing relative importance of requirements
2. Identifying factors likely to change
   a. Ordering by changeability
   b. Identification of alternative requirements

E. *Maintenance*

The maintenance category here is specifically meant to exclude the evolutionary software activities that are often classified under "maintenance." The requirements are concerned with the system's breaking down and having to be brought back to working condition. For the software, the requirements might specify the staffing needed or a contractual agreement for fixing bugs. The document might list the kinds of programs or packages that will be supplied to fix bugs, and, in addition, what kinds of software will be embedded in the system (such as error logging or path counters) to aid in the discovery and tracing of errors. For hardware, it is necessary to know who will carry out both the preventive and repair-oriented maintenance. The requirements might need to spell out standards for a minimal set of test points at which the repairing individual can probe and assess the operation of the circuit.

1. Software
   a. Responsibility for fixing bugs
   b. Instrumentation (e.g., check points, audit trails, driver programs, simulators)
2. Hardware
   a. Frequency and duration of preventive maintenance
   b. Responsibility for repair of faults
   c. Test equipment and procedures (e.g., test points)

III. Economic Context of System Development

Very few projects are undertaken in which cost is no object. Even in extravagant programs, cost tradeoffs are seriously considered. However, satisfactory economic decisions are much more likely to be made if the cost goals and guidelines are spelled out in the requirements document.

A. *Cost tradeoffs*

Requirements for cost tradeoffs establish guidelines for determining whether existing equipment and software can be satisfactorily incorporated into the target system or whether a new effort is required. Very often this off-the-shelf equipment is not ideal and does not entirely satisfy the requirements in every respect. However, these cost-tradeoff requirements can be used effectively to overrule other requirements if the sacrifice is not too great. Some criteria are needed to indicate just how important the ready-made requirement is and what might be given up to fulfill it. It is important that the requirements convey the intended principles of cost tradeoffs. The military is, in many projects, using an approach that identifies a minimal set of capabilities to which desired features are added until a certain cost level is exceeded. The requirements must be able to convey just which functions are needed at any cost and which are add-ons. Note that some projects (e.g., computer toys or games) may be almost entirely a design-to-cost consideration. Even the nature of the functions may be relatively unimportant compared to the price at which it can be sold. Most projects fall between the two extremes, and the requirements must be able to indicate where the tradeoffs are to be made.

1. Utilization of existing technology versus development of new
   a. Hardware (e.g., CPUs, interfaces, peripheral equipment)
   b. Software (e.g., operating systems, compilers)
2. Primary objectives: design-to-cost versus design-to-function
   a. Established minimal requirements for designated levels of cost
   b. Relating alternate requirements with costs

B. *Cost of iterative system development*
   Many projects are developed iteratively, whether or not the customer sees the intervening stages or prototypes. And almost all projects have milestones or baselines that indicate the achievement of some level of operation or functionality. Without cost limitations placed on these stages by the requirements, funds could be allocated to project phases in an unbalanced manner, starving, for example, later efforts due to disproportionate expenditures at the beginning of the project. In addition, if prototypes are to be delivered to the customer for interim use or evaluation, these costs should be addressed in the requirements.
   1. Development cost of each prototype or milestone
   2. Cost of delivery of prototype
C. *Cost of each instance of target system*
   The development effort may be directed at producing many similar or identical target systems. Under these circumstances, the development costs will usually be amortized over the entire projected production run. Each instance of the target system in this case will have costs both from materials and from the applicable fraction of the development expenses. Any proposed evolutionary change to the target system after delivery will have to take into account the costs of updating each installation.

24.6. HUMAN FACTORS

Introduction

The psychological factors involved in software engineering are certainly one of the most neglected aspects of the entire discipline. Omission of such considerations from requirements analysis and specification may be a major reason for eventual user dissatisfaction with the delivered product. We conjecture that many of the human factors are of as much importance to the user as the so-called functional requirements. Thus, consideration of the psychological impacts, both of and on the user, in the requirements phase should have a substantial effect in helping to deliver software products that truly meet the needs of the user. Furthermore, an aggressive view of this facet of requirements should have an important impact on the lifetime cost of the entire project.

In the following sections we explore the nature and importance of human factors as related to the requirements of a project. We shall discuss the problems of communication between members of the user organization and software engineers, followed by specific human factors problems dealing with the target system's user interface. We then review some tools from psychology that may be used in attempting to solve some of these problems.

The Communication Problem

Many of the problems that originate early in requirements analysis can be attributed to lack of communication between the user community and the software engineers. There are several well-known communication problems. Ideas may be expressed in a vague or ambiguous manner, goals may be contradictory or incompletely formulated, and various users may have differing views of the desired system. Realization that these difficulties exist leads to the conclusion that good requirements analysis must depend upon intensive interaction with the user community at all authority levels, as well as feedback from the software engineers concerning their understanding of the desired system.

There are communication problems that cannot be solved simply by verbal communication, however, regardless of the amount of interaction and feedback involved. In this section we shall discuss the problem of novice versus expert knowledge, and the problem of tacit knowledge. These as-yet-unresearched prob-

lems may hold the key to developing systems that are well-engineered for humans.

When considering the members of the user community, we shall continue to use the word *user* in its broadest sense, including all of the members of a user organization who will have any degree of contact with the system at any time during its lifetime. This is certainly a broad class of users, with varying degrees of interest in the project, but we need not distinguish between them at this time.

Kaplan cites a rather disturbing example wherein the designer asks, "What do you want?", to which the user responds, "What have you got?" [37]. Although this is, or should be, an extreme example of initial interaction, it does point out some of the inherent difficulties in user/analyst dialogues. It also makes a strong case for the need to know the user [38]. This one principle is of major importance, for when the analyst truly knows the user (actually, users at all authority levels), then "What do you want?" will be be replaced with a whole series of ideas and questions with which meaningful discussion can begin.

It would be naive to think, however, that the analyst will find it easy to "get to know" the user. One major problem is that experts "see" quite differently from novices [37], as has been demonstrated in such famous studies as the one involving chess masters and novices [39]. In requirements analysis, the user is an expert in the application domain, the analyst is an expert in software engineering, and each is a novice in the domain of the other!

This phenomenon of seeing differently is partially explained by the compact and complex structure of the experts' knowledge. Experts have more points of entry into their semantic structures, and they form abstractions at a higher level than novices. This means that they have the ability to make use of a number of different representation schemes for mentally working with the same information. Thus, an expert might be able to make use of a picture, a sketch, a map, or even a cardboard model, whereas a novice might find the picture to be the only meaningful representation [40]. So we must conclude that the choice of model presentation is a critical factor to be considered when dealing with novice users. In general, the process of establishing a common domain of discourse should be the first matter of attention in a user/analyst dialogue. Also, this has to take place at all levels within the user organization because of the different views of the users.

We know that people, whatever their organizational status, have detailed and highly developed internal models of their working environments [37]. They understand what they do, how they accomplish their duties, and with whom or what they interact in their performance of daily tasks (we speak, of course, of people with a general level of work-related competence.) Regardless of their level of expertise, however, people know more than they can ever tell [41]. When this "tacit knowledge" concerns a desired software product, we are often at a loss as to how to bring forth this information. The problem is more than just a vagueness on the part of the user concerning desired functions for a proposed system because tacit knowledge is not describable by the user. Some tacit knowledge will always exist, but much can be brought out and made explicit.

Polanyi illustrates the existence of tacit knowledge with this example: We are all experts at recognizing familiar faces, yet how many features of a familiar face can you give specific details about? This is very difficult, even for faces with which you may be intimately familiar. Police artists, however, have developed methods that allow them to produce composite sketches of remarkable quality.

The idea of tacit knowledge is certainly not new. William James, in discussing what he called the "fringe" [42], said that

Every definite image in the mind is steeped and dyed in the free water that flows round it. With it goes the sense of its relations, near and remote, the dying echo of whence it came to us, the dawning sense of whither it is to lead. The significance, the value, of the image is all in the halo or the penumbra that surrounds and escorts it. . . .

Thus, we must probe, define, and refine this fringe in order to discover some of the tacit knowledge contained therein.

Since users are incapable of expressing their tacit knowledge, we should consider experimental techniques for revealing some of it. For now we simply note that people have an innate ability for nonverbal communication, primarily with themselves. People have the capacity to assume an "as if" stance [37]—they have the ability to assume roles and pretend. This means that one should expect to be able to produce worthwhile results from studies and experiments concerning human factors engineering. This has certainly proved to be the case in scientific investigations of programming languages [38, 43, 44, and 45]. We will have more to say on the subject of experimentation in the section on psychological tools.

In summary then, the apparent requirements will vary depending upon the view of the user. Regardless of his status within an organization, each user will have a well-developed internal model of the environment and his functions within it. Some of this information is readily available in the form of immediate needs (however vaguely they may be expressed), but some is tacit knowledge and may have to be determined experimentally.

The Target System's User Interface

In discussing the user interface requirements for a system, it is essential to differentiate between upper-echelon management and the end-user [14, 46]. Their views of the system are sure to be different. Management will be primarily concerned with the system's functional requirements, constraints, development schedule, and cost. The end-user, however, may take such factors as "correctness" for granted; he or she must work with the final product, and wants a system that provides a comfortable environment, not a hostile one.

The AFWET system requires displays, and so we will concentrate on displays as a good example of various user-interface issues. Luxenberg and Kuehn [47] note that

It is essential to display design that standard human factors requirements be satisfied. This covers a broad range of topics such as perception, comprehension, viewing environment, psychological factors, and operator comfort.

These issues are of great importance if the system is to be acceptable to the user community. Thus, in a requirements document it is not enough to simply specify that the display equipment will consist of certain kinds of devices, which is all that was done in the AFWET document. The details that seem to be most needed are given by Luxenberg and Kuehn and are shown in Table 24.2.

The information required in each of the table's categories and subcategories, however, is much more than just specifications in terms of certain absolutes or generalities—for instance, response time must be 3 seconds, or response must be real time. The requirements document should have proposals for testing the acceptability of various factors with the end-users. Thus, we are immediately led into the general area of testability and to the questions that naturally arise about what is or is not a testable requirement. If there is to be a display that queries a data base, for example, then the requirements for response time should also include either solid reasons for specifying a certain value or proposed experiments to determine what the needs of the end-user

really are and how the determination can be validated. It is necessary not only to verify what the needs are, but also to check that the final product meets them. This practice should be applied liberally to any parts of the specification that deal with the broad area of human factors.

Thus, requirements for AFWET should contain proposals for pilot studies of (1) the best symbology to use for the displays, (2) the qualities desired in such device specifics as contrast, resolution, and flicker, (3) the best means to display a kill. There should also be proposals to study whether or not the display needs to run "in real time," as stated in the AFWET document. Even a small difference in the amount of acceptable delay can make a tremendous difference to the system's designers, and it is all too easy to accept serious constraints on a user's word, without questioning the real need for them. It certainly seems plausible that observers could get as much information from delayed or replayed tests as from those seen in real time. In the AFWET case, probably the crucial factor is the extent to which the observers of the displays participate in the test as commanders, but this is nowhere mentioned in the requirements document.

Table 24.2. A Major Step in Display Design: Determination of Specifications.

A. Data Rates and Response Times
  1. Updating response time
  2. Rates of change of display data
  3. Display access time
  4. Display request rates
B. Amount of Data
  1. Amount of display information
  2. Number of display units
  3. Display sizes
  4. Audience size
C. Types of Display
  1. Coding
  2. Symbology
  3. Display formats
D. Visibility
  1. Luminance
  2. Ambient lighting
  3. Contrast
  4. Resolution
E. Quality
  1. Accuracy
  2. Distortion
  3. Flicker

Psychological Tools

Some of the problems of user/analyst interaction have been highlighted in the previous sections. We believe that aggressive work on the human factors of a project will not only help alleviate some of the inherent communication problems, but also provide a sound basis for a project that is manageable in terms of schedule, cost functionality, and human acceptability.

Besides the obvious need for much interaction and discussion in order for users and designers to speak a common language, what else can be done to help alleviate the communication problem? Winograd discusses three different domains of discourse and suggests that the terms used in the subject domain be those familiar to the user [48]. Other ideas presented by Kaplan [37] suggest that we can take advantage of users' abilities to assume roles, to mentally validate or reject "what if" conditions, and to become involved in the entire process of design. He suggests that simple models work better from the viewpoint of the user than do complicated or elaborate models. This confirms what we already know about expert versus novice knowledge structures. So, once a dialect has been established, the software engineer may begin planning experiments, pilot tests, and other interactions with actual end-users in an attempt to bring forth tacit knowledge that may play an integral role in the functioning of the desired product.

The early phases of requirements analysis should concentrate on dissolving the differences in the ways in which experts and novices see. Definitions (based upon the users' perspectives), intensive discussions, and notations should help make problem areas explicit, remove bias, and thus add to the understandings of both user and analyst. The use of models, quick prototypes, graphic aids, and other forms of nonverbal communication should be encouraged, since these give the user something that can be "indwelled" [41], that is, internalized. This process of indwelling is most important, for it is the only way to really know something. The "one picture is worth ten thousand words" idea may sound too simple, but the replacement of words by actions can give the user a better understanding of what is being developed. Thus, by having something to indwell, the user will have the ability to make a comparison with his internal model, which already exists. This could not be done, and certainly is not done, with any of the static, formal notations currently in use for the specification of requirements.

The use of models, and their associated tests with actual end-users, should become a part of the planned system development from the very beginning. These pilot tests must be used for a sufficient period of time to allow the user to get beyond any difficulties of novelty. They must also be repeated many times after there are no more learning problems, because the nature of "participant behavior" is characterized by the fact that the participant considers a number of hypotheses on each trial and can only reject some, but not all, of those that are not consistent with his internal models [49]. Further-more, users can more readily reject undesirable qualities than affirm desirable ones, probably because many of the desirable properties are part of their tacit knowledge.

Finally, studies should be planned to further define and refine human needs. Brooks [50] states the advantages of behavioral/psychological studies, which are important here for two reasons. First, we can affirm or refute any behavioral assumptions that have been made. Second, such studies give quantitative information on the relative effectiveness of various techniques, thus giving us a solid basis for the selection of new tools, new features, and new areas of concern. Careful selection of the studies to be made can help reduce costs for the entire project by confirming at an early stage that any of a number of quality-control attempts are, or are not, successful. We should be most concerned with the ideas of simplicity, psychological acceptability, the "engineering out" of errors, and the bounds on human performance [38, 45, 51]. Scientific experimentation during the requirements phase can help assure that the developing product will meet any of a number of such goals, and at a lesser cost than if they are ignored until later in the project lifetime.

There may certainly be economic considerations and developmental time limitations to restrict the amount of experimentation involved in a particular project. Time constraints on the end-users may also be a factor. However, the nature of human factors is such that they are very amenable to a requirement that specifies that a study or experiment be used to further define some quality of the end-users' environment. The life-cycle of a project may easily be long enough so that, with good modularization of requirements, such studies can proceed in parallel with some of the other work.

Our section on human factors is intended, like the rest of this chapter, to serve as a checklist for topic inclusion. Many of the suggested areas should be cross-referenced with proposals, milestones, and experiments, as in the section on system development. Note that the issues raised in this section should follow from the broadest possible interpretation of human factors—we intend for the requirements to consider a wide range of psychological and physical factors, for instance, user acceptability, motivation, and the work environment.

We have been deliberately vague about the types of pilot tests, models, and other nonverbal communication tools the engineer may find of value. Much research needs to be done to discover what prototypes work best for the desired interaction between user and designer. Kaplan has performed some studies with architects and users, and his results indicate that simplicity helps avoid much confusion on the part of the user [37].

Another example concerns the use of the "operational" requirements specifications mentioned in Section 4. The requirements consist of an executable model of the proposed system interacting with its environment; this model could be exercised interactively to provide demonstrations to users. This is a promising direction since functional and performance requirements at all levels can be incorporated into the formal specification [23, 24]. The model could provide a basis for conducting many of the experiments proposed in the requirements document. The next question, however, is: How can system behaviors be communicated to the user? What tests of the system should be performed? How can the information be made suitable for indwelling by the user? These are issues relating to nonverbal communication that deserve immediate attention.

24.7. CONCLUSION

This report is by no means a complete survey of current knowledge on requirements. Some of the best-known approaches have been given short shrift (although they have already been widely reviewed). We have made no attempt to survey tools, even though it is apparent that automated data base facilities for requirements information, however primitive, may be tremendously helpful.

The significance of this chapter, in our view, is that we have included the "forgotten" areas of requirements: process-oriented as well as data-oriented requirements, nonfunctional as

well as functional requirements, and human factors. We have stressed the newest and (to us) most promising approaches, over the familiar and (to us) inadequate ones.

We believe that the problem of deriving good requirements can be solved in three stages. The first concerns discovering, understanding, and describing informally the users' requirements (interpreting *user* in its broadest sense). The second involves constructing a conceptual model that integrates and consolidates different user views. The third consists of specifying a system to meet the requirements in an executable language, and validating that specification.

Specification languages, categorized on the basis of system types, fit some of these stages better than others. PAISLey is a good candidate for an executable specification language, but a structured data model expressed in terms of semantic nets many make the best all-around conceptual model. And for first-stage description of users' needs, application-specific, user-oriented languages are clearly called for. It is our belief that a general framework for such languages can be developed on the basis of a case-structured syntax. These are the directions which researchers will be pursuing in the near future.

ACKNOWLEDGMENTS

The research reported on here is partially supported by the U.S. Air Force under Contract AFOSR-77-3181B, and by the U.S. Army under Contract DASG60-80-C-0024.

REFERENCES

1. L. A. Belady and M. M. Lehman, "The Characteristics of Large Systems," in Peter Wegner (ed.), *Research Directions in Software Technology*, M.I.T. Press, Cambridge, Mass., 1979, pp. 106–138.
2. Barry W. Boehm, "Software and Its Impact: A Quantative Assessment," *Datamation* 19(May 1973):48–60.
3. Barry W. Boehm, *Software Engineering Economics*, Prentice Hall, Englewood Cliffs, N.J., 1981.
4. T. A. Thayer, "Understanding Software through Analysis of Empirical Data," TRW Software Series, TRW-SS-75-04, May 1975.
5. U.S. Air Force, "Air Force Weapons Effectiveness

Testing (AFWET) Instrumentation System," R&D Exhibit No. PGVE 64-40, Air Proving Ground Center, Eglin Air Force Base, Florida, 1965.

6. M. M. Lehman, "Programs, Life Cycles, and Laws of Software Evolution," *Proceedings of the IEEE 68*, (Sept. 1980):1060-1076.

7. Raymond T. Yeh, "Systematic Derivation of Software Requirements through Structured Analysis," *Computer Science SDBEG-15*, University of Texas at Austin, Sept. 1979.

8. Raymond T. Yeh and Pamela Zave, "Specifying Software Requirements," *Proceedings of the IEEE 68*, (Sept. 1980):1077-1085.

9. M. M. Astrahan, *et al.*, "System R: Relational Approach to Database Management," *ACM Transactions on Database Systems* 1(June 1976):97-137.

10. D. L. Parnas, "A Technique for Software Module Specification with Examples," *Communications of the ACM* 15(May 1972):330-336.

11. D. L. Parnas, "Designing Software for Ease of Extension and Contraction," *IEEE Transactions on Software Engineering* 5(March 1977):128-137.

12. John Miles Smith and Diane C. P. Smith, "A Data Base Approach to Software Specification," in W. E. Riddle and R. E. Fairley (eds.), *Software Development Tools*, Springer-Verlag, New York, 1980.

13. Nicholas Roussopoulous, "CSDL: A Conceptual Schema Definition Language for the Design of Data Base Applications," *IEEE Transactions on Software Engineering* 5(Sept. 1979):481-496.

14. Roland Mittermeir, "Requirements Analysis: Top Down or Bottom Up," TR DA 80/02/02, Institut Für Digitale Anlagen, Technische Universität Wien, Wien, Federal Republic of Germany, 1980.

15. Douglas Ross and Kenneth E. Schoman, Jr., "Structured Analysis for Requirements Definition," *IEEE Transactions on Software Engineering* 3(Jan. 1977):6-15.

16. Douglas Ross, "Structured Analysis (SA): A Language for Communicating Ideas," *IEEE Transactions on Software Engineering* 3(Jan. 1977):15-34.

17. D. Teichroew and E. A. Hershey III, "PSL/PSA: A Computer-Aided Technique for Structured Documentation and Analysis of Information Systems," *IEEE Transactions on Software Engineering* 3(Jan. 1977):41-43.

18. James L. Peterson, "Petri Nets," *Computing Surveys* 9(Sept. 1977):223-252.

19. M. Conner, "Process Synchronization by Behavior Controllers," Ph.D. thesis, Computer Science Department, University of Texas at Austin, 1979.

20. J. J. Horning and B. Randell, "Process Structuring," *Computing Surveys* 5(Jan. 1973):5-29.

21. C. A. R. Hoare, "Communicating Sequential Processes," *Communications of the ACM* 2(Aug. 1978):666-677.

22. Per Brinch Hansen, "Distributed Processes: A Concurrent Programming Concept," *Communications of the ACM* 21(Nov. 1978):934-941.

23. Pamela Zave, "A Comprehensive Approach to Requirements Problems," *Proceedings COMPSAC*, Chicago, Nov. 1979, pp. 117-122.

24. Pamela Zave, "Formal Specification of Complete and Consistent Performance Requirements," *Proceedings Texas Conference on Computing Systems*, Dallas, Tex., Nov. 1979, pp. 4B-18-4B-25.

25. Pamela Zave, "An Operational Approach to Requirements Specification for Embedded Systems," *IEEE Transactions on Software Engineering* 8(May 1982):250-269.

26. Pamela Zave and Raymond T. Yeh, "Executable Requirements for Embedded Systems." *Proceedings 5th Intl. Conf. on Software Engineering*, San Diego, Cal. (Mar. 1981): pp. 295-304.

27. Stephen W. Smoliar, "Applicative and Functional Programming," in C. R. Vick and C. V. Ramamoorthy (eds.), *Handbook of Software Engineering*, Van Nostrand Reinhold, New York, N. Y., this volume.

28. Mack Alford, "A Requirements Engineering Methodology for Real-Time Processing Requirements," *IEEE Transactions on Software Engineering* 3(Jan. 1977):60-69.

29. Thomas Bell, David Bixler, and Margaret Dyer, "An Extensible Approach to Computer-Aided Software Requirements Engineering," *IEEE Transactions on Software Engineering* 3(Jan. 1977):40-69.

30. Carl G. Davis and Charles R. Vick, "The Software Development System," *IEEE Transactions on Software Engineering* 3(Jan. 1977):69-84.

31. John Backus, "Can Programming Be Liberated From the von Neumann Style? A Functional Style and its Algebra of Programs," *Communications of the ACM* 21(Aug. 1978):613-641.

32. Stephen W. Smoliar, "Using Applicative Techniques to Design Distributed Systems," *Proceedings Specifications of Reliable Software Conference*, Cambridge, Mass., Apr. 1979, pp. 150-161.

33. A. K. Jones and P. Schwarz, "Experience Using Multiprocessor Systems—A Status Report," *Computing Surveys* 12(June 1980):121-165.

34. M. V. Zelkowitz, A. C. Shaw, and J. D. Gannon, *Principles of Software Engineering and Design*, Prentice-Hall, Englewood Cliffs, N.J., 1979, p. 8.

35. Alex Paul Conn, "Maintenance: A Key Element in Computer Requirements Definition," *Proceedings COMPSAC*, Chicago, Ill., Nov. 1980.

36. D. L. Parnas, "On the Criteria to be Used in Decomposing Systems into Modules," *Communications of the ACM* 15(Dec. 1972):1053-1058.

37. Stephen Kaplan, "Participation in the Design Process," in D. Stokes (ed.), *Psychological Perspectives on Environment and Behavior: Conceptual and Empirical Trends*, Plenum, New York, 1976.

38. Ben Schneiderman, "Human Factors Experiments in Designing Interactive Systems," *Computer* 12(Dec. 1979):9-20.

39. Herbert Simon, *The Sciences of the Artificial*, M.I.T. Press, Cambridge, Mass., 1970.

40. Mark David Weiser, "Program Slices: Formal, Psychological, and Practical Investigations of an Automatic Program Abstraction Model," Ph.D. thesis, University of Michigan, 1979.

41. Michael Polanyi, *The Tacit Dimension,* Anchor Books (Doubleday), New York, 1967, pp. 3–25.

42. William James, *Psychology: The Briefer Course,* Harper, 1892, pp. 30–37, 106–110.

43. Victor R. Basili and Robert Reiter, Jr., "An Investigation of Human Factors in Software Engineering," *Computer* 12(Dec. 1979):21–40.

44. H. E. Dunsmore and J. D. Gannon, "Data Referencing: An Empirical Investigation," *Computer* 12(Dec. 1979):50–59.

45. Ben Schneiderman, *Software Psychology: Human Factors in Computer and Information Systems,* Winthrop Publishers, Inc., 1980.

46. Roland Mittermeir, "Application of Database Design Concepts to Software Requirements Analysis," TR DA 79-11-01, Institute Für Digitale Anlagen, Technische Universität Wien, Wien, Federal Republic of Germany, 1979.

47. H. R. Luxenburg and R. L. Kuehn, *Display Systems Engineering,* McGraw-Hill, New York, 1968.

48. Terry Winograd, "Beyond Programming Languages," *Communications of the ACM* 12(July 1979):391–401.

49. Michael T. Rosner, *Cognition: An Introduction,* Scott, Foresman and Company, Glenview, 1975, pp. 61–92.

50. Ruven E. Brooks, "Studying Programmer Behavior Experimentally: The Problem of Proper Methodology," *Communications of the ACM* 23(Apr. 1980):207–213.

51. Ben Schneiderman and Richard Mayers, "Syntactics/Semantic Interactions in Programmer Behavior: A Model and Experimental Results," *Int. Journal of Computer and Information Sciences* 8(March 1979):219–238.

25

Process Design

N. A. Vosbury
System Development Corporation

25.1. INTRODUCTION

The Design Problem

Although the following quotation is over a decade old, the situation it describes is little improved today. "Programming management will continue to deserve its current poor reputation for cost and schedule effectiveness until such time as a more complete understanding of the program design process is achieved" [1].

Poor design causes bugs directly because of specific errors and omissions and indirectly because of the confusion created by ambiguity. This confusion often continues when attempts are made to fix the bugs. Costs can be very high. In Reference 2 the author states that a programmer has a 50% chance of successfully fixing a bug on the first attempt if the work involves only 5 to 10 lines of code, and only a 20% chance of success if 40 to 50 lines are involved.

Poor design arises from a variety of factors: One is not doing a design at all. But assuming a design effort is made, we find the following problems. Requirements may be inconsistent, incomplete, and ambiguous. The designer may include technical errors. Probably the biggest source of error is poor organization, which, in turn, arises from poor technique and from system complexity so great that the designer cannot comprehend the scope of the whole process.

This chapter looks briefly at a nonexhaustive list of design systems that have been developed, gives some opinions on the current status of design systems, suggests some views of the future, and presents a guide to aid designers in organizing their design efforts.

Learning Software Design. "The mastery of software design and development is similar to learning how to ride a bicycle. Although the laws of physics fully describe the process, almost no one learns to ride a bicycle merely by reading a book. A balance is needed . . ." [3]. If it were possible for this chapter to describe everything there is to know about process design, that alone would not teach you to do a good job of process design. You must get involved.

Design: Building on Requirements. An apocryphal anecdote in a recent periodical describes a project manager who rushes into his office, announces the company has won a contract, sends two men to see just what the customer wants, and orders the rest to start coding immediately (since a demonstration is required in 2 months). This comes all too close to home for many software projects. Poor or missing requirements result in an inadequate design or in no design at all. The coding becomes the design, with disorder increasing as the number of programmers increases. Documentation is not done at first because the problem is not understood. Interfaces and modules are produced almost by accident. Documentation after the fact is incomplete because the interactions [of parts] of the system, never having had criteria to measure up to, are not understood and because of human factors, for instance, people's readiness to leave the project.

A good design must be done to ensure reasonable expectation of a successful project. The design must build on the requirements, just as implementation builds on the design. Each stage of the software development process forms specifications for the next stage. It would be nice if all designs had a consistent, complete, and unambiguous set of requirements to build on, but we cannot count on it. The designer must analyze the requirements to obtain the knowledge he or she needs. Reference 4 gives a good example of the thought processes involved in analyzing requirements. The specific analysis of requirements will depend on the situation, but the following items suggest some typical questions:

- Is every item of input data specified?
- Is every item of output data specified?
- What are the criteria for the validity of data?
- What action should be taken if a source ceases to provide data?
- What should be done if a destination ceases to accept its respective data?
- What should be done with invalid data?
- Are constraints arbitrary or inherent in the process?
- What factors may change in the future?

The author observed a recent software development in which every significant problem that arose had to do with the lack of requirements in the beginning and the failure to consider the above questions. For instance, one module ceased to accept messages when a buffer was full. Another module assumed a message had been received. A whole multiprocessor network collapsed. Always determine what will happen at the boundaries of data domains. Do not forget to look for singular points—not only the obvious ones, like implied division by zero, but the hidden singularities that may involve the interaction of several domains.

We need rigorous discipline in program design and implementation. Mills points out the difference between heuristic and rigorous design [5]. A program developed heuristically "almost always works. When it fails it must be fixed.... After a succession of such failures and fixes the design will become highly idiosyncratic.... If designers mentally test and fix, ... then the design becomes idiosyncratic...." even before implementation. Mills [6] quotes: "A program which does not work is undoubtedly wrong; but a program which does work is not necessarily right."

This point reminds us that the requirements and the design should be stated in such a way that system testing is supported. The valid and the invalid system states should be clearly identified, and the system should respond positively in all cases.

Weaknesses in the requirements are usually found by analyzing them and attempting to express them in the design, which causes an iteration back to the requirements development phase. This is normal and forms a first-order check on the requirements. No software development system, automated or not, is currently available that will avoid this occurrence.

Design as Specification for Implementation and Testing. A set of requirements forms a specification for design. In the same way, design forms a specification for implementation and testing. (The implementation adds to the specification for testing by determining the specifics of how to use the system.)

Characteristics of a Design Methodology.

- A two-stage design consists of parts A and B, where
  A is machine and language independent
  B is machine and language dependent
- Basic functions must be described. Functions are described in a top-down manner so that at the highest level one person can comprehend the complete process.
- Design tells what to do, not how to do it.
- In Stage A, relationships between functions are given; in Stage B, specific interfaces are given.
- Basic data structures from external sources that are independent of the software must be exactly described.

- Main internally generated data structures should be described by contents. Specific structures may be suggested in the second stage of design.
- Design should be fully documented not only in final decisions but in Stage A. The reasons for decisions should be documented.
- The criteria for testing should be explicitly given.
- Requirements should be mapped onto elements of the design that satisfy them. In turn, these parts of the design should be mapped to the implementation and to corresponding elements of the test plan.
- The implementation process produces a deeper understanding of the design, and feedback from implementation may cause changes in the design. This iteration is normal and just as inevitable as that between requirements and design.

Several Existing Design Tools. For the past several years, researchers have been working on methodologies and systems to improve the software development process. Some of these are basic philosophies of design, embodying step-by-step instructions to be performed manually. Use of such a system requires a clear understanding of the design philosophy and strict adherence to the spirit of the rules. Other systems implement their method with a semiautomated system that provides a language for expressing the design and/or a way of prompting the user interactively. A semiautomated system checks for errors, keeps track of components of the design, provides various types of analysis and listings, and so on. Of course, a system that is primarily manual may be implemented later in an automated system.

Some of the systems emphasizing methodology and not necessarily automation are the various top-down design [7] systems, structured design [8, 9], the Jackson method [6, 10], SADT [11–14], and composite/structured design [15]. Some extensions have been made to SADT to add some automated graphics (at Brown University, for instance). Some systems that have varying degrees of automation are PSL/PSA [16], SSL [17], PDS [18, 19], HOS [20, 21], and designer/verifier assistant [22]. A thumbnail sketch of these systems is given below.

Other systems in various stages of development are not in the strictest sense design systems but may have an impact on design because of the kind of programming language they employ. Examples are ALPHARD [23], KLR (referred to in Reference 24), and Backus' functional programming [25].

From Past Language Development to Future Design Language. In the early days of computing, programming was done essentially in binary. Program design in some cases was done in a language with the basic characteristic of assembly, which had the advantage of describing the program in a form that involved a great reduction in decision points. It was natural for assembly, representing an abstraction of the basic program, quickly to become the normal programming language. Of course, someone programming in assembly might often design a program in a higher-level language (using algebraic forms, for example). The resulting abstraction achieved another great reduction in decision points (as large as one full order of magnitude). In time, the normal programming languages became FORTRAN, ALGOL, COBOL, or some other higher-level procedural language. Software development quickly moved up through two generations of design and implementation language early in its history. The reduction in decision points enabled designers to comprehend more complex processes.

The move from binary to assembly was easy. The correspondence of sequences of bits to an assembly instruction is easy to comprehend. For the most part, for one assembly instruction there is just one bit pattern. The move from assembly to languages such as FORTRAN was a little harder, but the correspondence of a given higher-level statement to a sequence of assembly instructions is comprehensible. Of course, one FORTRAN statement can be represented by several sequences of machine instructions, which gave rise to arguments over the efficiency of the resultant program but gave no problem in understanding the basic meaning of the FORTRAN statements. What we would like to have now is a very high-level language (VHLL) that would allow program description with another great reduction in decision points. The reduction in decision points would be most dramatic if the language allows the programmer to specify *what* is to be done but does not require the *how*. This would require the compiler to decide on which of a class of algorithms to use. It might require a capability for automatic composition and/or sequencing, which involves unsolved problems. In the author's opinion, this level of compiler performance is not possible in general since some functions to be performed might involve algorithms that have not been discovered. However, in many environments in which software development is done, many processes are similar in terms of the specific tasks they involve. So it may be possible to achieve a VHLL that fills in the *how* automatically in some cases and leaves it to the user in others.* In any case, the VHLL compiler should check interfaces, trace requirements, and so forth. Production of executable code is not required in the VHLL compiler, but could be done at a lower level. We can also note that a VHLL could be used manually to form an organizing tool for a design.

Design features in some programming languages, such as the class concept, improved iteration, and array manipulators, have moved to higher levels of abstraction. The increments have been relatively small, not an overall order of magnitude reduction in decision points. A good discussion of the philosophy and difficulties involved in the development of such a higher-level language is in Reference 24.

A Design Methodology with or without Automated Tools. When one analyzes many of the existing design methodologies or thinks through one's own system, one discovers at least six helpful features in common:

1. Organizing
2. Functional decomposing

3. Data-flow analyzing and decomposing
4. Documenting
5. Requirements tracing
6. Interface checking

Any good design approach will do an acceptable job in the above areas if the system is properly applied. If the designer does not have an automated system at his disposal, he can use one of the several nonautomated methods, some of which may seem quite complex. For a design requiring a simple system, the one described in Section 25.3 provides help in the above areas. It has been automated using a macroprocessor [26].

Future Developments. The history of programming languages shows that a higher level of abstraction is needed in a design language. It should have the following characteristics:

- The number of detailed decision points in the design language should be an order of magnitude less than in the implementation language.
- The level of desirable *transparency*—that is, features hidden to the user—should rise.
- Complex data structures should be handled as entities.
- Data and associated operations should be handled as entities.
- Functions may be generalized and manipulated.
- Documentation should be enforced.
- The language should enable incremental design verification.
- Organization and management visibility should be emphasized.
- The transition from requirements to design to implementation should be smooth, with automated evaluation.

The work of the designer will not be made easy by automated systems; they should, however, enable the designer to do what he does best while the computer does what it does best. As a result, the designer will be able to design more complex systems.

---

*Perhaps VHLL could be used in an environment where operating systems are constructed. Compiler-compilers are a step in this direction, also.

25.2. PAST DEVELOPMENT

History of Software Design

The design techniques used in the early years of programming derived from techniques already in use in other fields, including flowcharts, parts lists, and decision tables. As computer systems became more complex, various forms of finite state automata and algorithmic notations were developed. These tend to be satisfactory for describing individual modules but become unwieldy when applied to large systems.

In the methodology of design, ideas of abstraction developed to simplify system conception. The characteristics of modularity were analyzed as applied to software, and the concept of top-down design and programming was formalized. Much of this development was speeded up by the open admission in the late 1960s that there was a software crisis and by the acceptance of the ideas of structured programming [1].

Structured programming viewed narrowly and naively was considered to be simply a better way of coding (some only thought of go-to-less coding). But since the full implication of those ideas applies to design, soon structured design and languages began to reflect structured concepts both in statements and data, as for instance in References 8 and 15.

In the 1970s, more sophisticated approaches were developed by which a computer system could help the design process by interaction, consistency checks, data base management, graphics, and so forth. Attempts have been made at design and program proof after the fact and, lately, languages have developed in which the form of the language ensures the proof as the design develops.

Top-Down, Structured Design. References 2, 6, 22, and 23 contain helpful material about structured design. It is automatic that structured design should be top-down because it involves analysis of the functions of a process and their refinement to modules small enough to be easily worked with. At the same time, the data to be used in the process is represented at a high level of abstraction and then filled in with more detail in the representations used at lower levels. It is reasonable that this process begin at the top.

Design is a creative process. In some situations the refinement of functions will lead to the appropriate detailed representation of abstract data. In other cases, it will be the refinement of the data that suggests the functional refinement.

A key concept in structured design is the module. The goal of design work is to define a set of cooperating modules exhibiting a high level of strength and a low level of coupling. The following description of these ideas and the decomposition techniques used in developing modules are adapted from Reference 22.

Module strength has to do with singleness of purpose. A module is weak if it does several unrelated things. It is strong if it does one thing. Stronger modules are likely to be easier to understand and less likely to have surprising effects. The recommendation in structured programming that a block of code have just one entrance and one exit has a similar effect. Table 25.1 describes levels of module strength.

Module coupling has to do with the amount of interaction or secondary effects occurring between different modules. The more one module depends on another, the greater the coupling. When the coupling of modules is high, development and maintenance usually take longer because the effect of errors spreads wider, and changes in one module will be likely to require changes in another. Table 25.1 describes levels of coupling.

It is helpful to have a few strategies in mind to use in decomposing processes into subordinate parts. Here we briefly describe three: *source-transform-sink* (STS), *transactional,* and *functional.* Transactional is emphasized in the Jackson method discussed later. Structured design normally emphasizes functional.

STS iterates on a sequence of four steps: It

1. Outlines the problem structure; loosely identifies data and operations.
2. Identifies the streams of data, sequencing the operations on them.
3. Finds points in a data stream where it

Table 25.1. Coupling Levels.

MODULE STRENGTH*		
	LEVEL	CHARACTERISTICS
Strong	1	Informational: Multiple entry points. Each entry has single function. Functions related by an entity hidden in module
	2	Functional: Single function.
	3	Communicational: Sequence of functions closely related by data.
	4	Procedural: Sequence of functions closely related by implication.
	5	Classical: Sequence of weakly related functions (e.g., initialization).
	6	Logical: Performs one of a set of related functions. May have different argument interpretations. Needs function code.
Weak	7	Coincidental: Several unrelated functions or undefinable functions.

MODULE COUPLING*		
	LEVEL	CHARACTERISTICS
High	1	Content: Direct reference to other module's data.
	2	Common: Heterogeneous global data.
	3	External: Homogeneous global data.
	4	Control: Control codes are passed.
	5	Stamp: Modules being passed the same data structure. Modules using the same interpretation of it are stamp coupled.
	6	Data: Passing scalar arguments only.
Low	7	No direct coupling: None of the above.

*Adapted from Reference 15

ceases to exist or becomes useless (data sinks).

4. Uses these points to divide the problem into functions.

These steps are repeated for each function until the functions exhibit as high a degree of strength as seems practical.

The transactional approach determines the set of functions by the needs of the various data types. This works well in processes that are data driven. In a payroll process, for example, the transformation and accumulations can be completely determined by the types of input records. There will probably be little secondary transformation of the data after the initial processing.

The functional approach isolates single functions to become immediate subordinate functions in a hierarchy or makes the entries in an information strength module. This is generally the approach for processes that are specific cases of a general class of processes in which similar things are done regardless of the input data, for example, data base management systems and compilers.

Jackson Method. References 8 and 12 describe the Jackson method. The assumption of this method is that the nature of the data determines the characteristics of the functions. Therefore, it is concluded that functional decomposition tends to be intuitional; beginning with the data is objective.

First, design the structure of the input data. Second, design the structure of the output data. Third, show the correlation between the input and output, that is, which input produces which output. Last, design the program to produce the output. The design will follow the data structure; sequencing and parallelism will arise naturally.

Commonly cited uses of the Jackson method are based on data that are similar to the structure in Figure 25.1, where each line represents a record. The figure could represent census data with categories corresponding to states, sections to counties, and items to townships. The data could be student grade records, with each category being a department, each section a class, and each item a student grade report. Similar examples could be given using pay records, inventory data, and so forth. Data not sorted into a convenient order entail a preprocessing phase to sort the data or a slight additional complexity in determining what actions to take when a given record is encountered. Basically, if items are encountered in random order, the action is the same as if three ordered records of category, section,

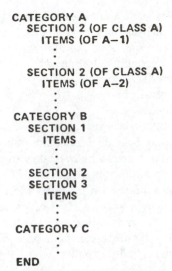

```
CATEGORY A
    SECTION 2 (OF CLASS A)
        ITEMS (OF A−1)
            ⋮

    SECTION 2 (OF CLASS A)
        ITEMS (OF A−2)
            ⋮

CATEGORY B
    SECTION 1
        ITEMS
            ⋮

    SECTION 2
    SECTION 3
        ITEMS
            ⋮

CATEGORY C
            ⋮

END
```

Figure 25.1. Typical data set structure.

item were encountered. Of course, this assumes that category and section data are on the item record. Generally speaking, the actions taken will tend to be the same for a given item regardless of the data on other items.

As stated earlier the Jackson method will work out best in processes that are obviously data driven. That is, the state of the system corresponds to the input data. In more complex systems, the state may depend on complex interactions of several input streams, past history, exceptional conditions, and even on implicit inputs such as the time of day.

Functional decomposition without consideration of the data is out of the question since the existence of a function without data is a paradox. In practice, most analyses of data and functions will proceed in parallel.

SADT. The structured analysis and design technique (SADT) was developed by Douglas Ross and Associates of Softech, Inc. References 9, 10, 13 and 14 may be consulted for more detail.

SADT models a process by a top-down decomposition of functions and data, resulting in two models that are expressed through a graphic language. Functions and data sets are represented by boxes. Relationships between them are represented by connecting arrows.

The boxes and arrows are labeled with their meanings. As the decomposition proceeds, each box is broken down to several subordinate boxes (Figure 25.2). As a general rule, function boxes are decomposed into no more than six parts. This is in agreement with the structured design and programming ideas that modules should always be small.

Another important part of the SADT approach is a disciplined team structure. A highly sophisticated form of the chief programmer team is used for the design team. Each member of the team has his or her job. Design moves through a careful process of checking. Some of the activities allocated to specific members of a team are to:

- Study requirements. Express them in SADT models.
- Review the work of others.
- Maintain the library.
- Advise others on the use of SADT.
- Interview "experts" about the characteristics of the physical process involved.

Table 25.2 indicates the specific titles and functions of personnel in an SADT team.

SADT is primarily a manual methodology, although the graphic language has been automated. This should ease the labor involved in keeping up with the design data base. The SADT data base has been fed into the PSL/

MORE GENERAL
↕
MORE DETAILED

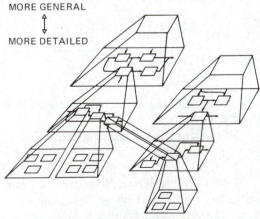

SHARED DETAIL INTERLOCKS MODELS

Figure 25.2. The decomposition of SADT-1.

Table 25.2. SADT Team.

NAME	FUNCTION
Authors	Personnel who study requirements and constraints, analyze system fuctions and represent them by models based on SADT diagrams.
Commenters	Usually authors, who must review and comment in writing on the work of other authors.
Readers	Personnel who read SADT diagrams for information but are not expected to make written comments.
Experts	Persons from whom authors obtain specialized information about requirements and constraints by means of interviews.
Technical committee	A group of senior technical personnel assigned to review the analysis at every major level of decomposition. They either resolve technical issues or recommend a decision to the project management.
Project librarian	A person assigned the responsibility of maintaining a centralized file of all project documents, making copies, distributing reader kits, keeping records, etc.
Project manager	The member of the project who has the final technical responsibility for carrying out the system analysis and and design.
Monitor (or chief analyst)	A person fluent in SADT who assists and advises project personnel in the use and application of SADT.
Instructor	A person fluent in SADT, who trains authors and commenters using SADT for the first time.

PSA system. The application of SADT by Softech is primarily for large companies in large projects.

PSL/PSA. The problem statement language and problem statement analyzer (PSL/PSA) was developed at the University of Michigan as part of the ISDOS project. It is a computer-aided tool for expressing the design of a data processing system, storing the description in a data base, and providing access to and analysis of that description. The benefits of PSL/PSA use are that costs remain about the same and the quality of software design improves.

PSL/PSA assists in process design in five main areas:

1. Providing a language, PSL, in which the design can be stated and related to requirements.
2. Maintaining a data base of design specifications and documentation
3. Maintaining a history of modifications
4. Performing analysis of the design for such things as use of data, consistency, work measures, and so on.
5. Reducing clerical work.

Some other systems, such as SADT, have interfaced with PSL/PSA to make use of its data base and analysis capabilities.

PSL/PSA is available currently on many common computers including IBM (MVS/ TSO, VM/CMS), DEC VAX 11/780 (VMS), UNIVAC (EXEC8), Honeywell (GCOS), Burroughs 6700 (MCP), SEL (RTM6.0), CDC (NOS), Perkins-Elmer, and Siemans.

ISDOS has under development an upward compatible replacement for PSL, *system definition language* (SDL). SDL is designed to have an enlarged viewpoint of system design and to support automatic simulation generation. The system will generate SIMSCRIPT programs from the SDL data base.

Process Design Methodology (PDM). PDM [27] is a broad system developed at the Ballistic Missile Defense Advanced Technology Center, Huntsville, Alabama, by Texas Instruments, Inc. It includes both automated tools, the process design system (PDS), and a philosophy of how design should be done and implemented.

PDS assumes an acceptable set of requirements as a beginning. The design is done top-down. The design statements are written in the process design language (PDL), and a PDL compiler can check the process statements even at the early design stage. The language, PDL, is Pascal derived with many advanced features. As the process is decomposed some functions become stubs. Data are at first generally defined, then refined later. Many functions evolve through three stages: a design stub, functional or simulated modules, and production code.

The configuration of the process is managed by the system so that recompilation of modules is automatic if the module is changed or if its environment is changed. The organization of the process is enhanced by the system's management of libraries, documentation, and module status.

The PDL compiler checks interfaces, usage of data types, and program structure. This helps to keep the top-down development organized. The design of the process then evolves into the implementation, implying that the implementation needs to be in PDL.

Simulation capabilities were built in PDM so that its concurrent capabilities could be tested on a single processor. The addition of random number utilities resulted in a complete simulation system.

PDM's approach to design was evolutionary. Incomplete code became functional code, which became analytic. This description applies more to implementation in today's systems. A design system can be more generally applied if it is independent of the implementation at the higher level of the design.

HOS/AXES. Higher Order Software, Inc., has developed a sophisticated methodology called HOS. A language, AXES, based on HOS, is used to describe processes axiomatically. The method, which builds upward from a set of primitives, is described in References 4 and 28.

INA JO. INA JO* is a methodology being developed at System Development Corpora-

tion. It is a highly coordinated method that enforces rigorous connections between successive stages of development. These stages include requirements and modeling of requirements, design specifications, verification of specifications, program design specifications, and verification of implementation. A small example of INA JO is given in Reference 29.

Interactive Design. A number of experiments have been made to design interactively. Reference 30 describes a system in which a computer program keeps track of a data base describing a developing process and asks questions of the designers. It may suggest what might be done next, makes incremental verifications, and generally keeps things organized. The system acts as the "designer's assistant."

Incremental Modeling. Reference 17 introduces the *design realization evaluation and modeling* [DREAM] system. It helps a designer build confidence in a design by modeling its behavior as it is developed incrementally.

Layered Approach. The software design activity involves a problem P and a machine M to solve the problem. A process C must be written to execute on M to solve P. A great gap may exist between P and C. Reference 1 describes an approach for bridging that gap. We postulate a set of capabilities for a machine M_1, which makes it easy to solve P. Now the problem P is changed to the problem of implementing the machine M_1. We iterate, generating a series of virtual machines, $M_1, M_2, \ldots, M_n$, until a virtual machine is seen that is easily implemented on M. This should provide an understanding of how to decompose P to be solved on M.

Reference 31 describes a system that also describes a sequence of virtual machines. This system is the *software specification language* (SSL). SSL goes much further than just methodology. It provides a language and translator that perform several consistency checks. It was developed by Science Applications, Inc., Huntsville, Alabama for Marshall Space Flight Center.

---

*INA JO is a trademark of the System Development Corporation.

Other Design Tools.   Sophisticated tools are fine, but one shouldn't underestimate the value of some of the more common general-purpose tools, such as libraries of modules, editors, and macroprocessors.

A good software library is seldom found. Designers and implementers should be able to put together building blocks for many parts of processes. The value to be gained is very high—greater reliability, less time, and less cost. But, unfortunately, in most environments—even where the virtues of advanced software design are extolled—the effort to maintain such a library is not made. There are a few sources such as the *Collected Algorithms of ACM,* the algorithms in Knuth's books [32], and the International Mathematical and Statistical Library. However, these sources will not cover the types of algorithms that may be peculiar to a given design group's work. In many groups, designs are often similar and should not always start from scratch. Isaac Newton is said to have replied to a question about his achievements, "I stood on the shoulders of giants." We need to follow his example.

The use of editors, especially on line, can help to organize and speed up design as well as implementation. Organization is a key to good design. With an editor you can usually save old versions while making changes and be able to recover if the changes prove undesirable.

Macroprocessors of a general nature can be of great use. One can implement one's own design language; notations can be standardized. For example, the simple design system described below was implemented quickly using the macroprocessor STAGE2 (which is described in Ref. 33).

25.3. A DESIGN SYSTEM (ADS)

Regardless of what has been written about process design systems in the many papers published in recent years, the following characterizes design activities: Few designers have any kind of automated system, although they may have some tools, such as libraries, editors, and simulators. Many software projects are designed with ad hoc, hurried, fragmented approaches. The academic background of our practicing computer people does not often include software design, and they often observe it more in the breach. ADS is suggested here as an approach that can be used without automation, that can be automated easily, and that can help provide the organization essential to a design effort. Various other design methodologies can be used with ADS to aid in analyzing a process. ADS is not a complete, mature system, and there is no reason a user cannot add his or her own touches to it.

Conventional Tools

We suggest the use of the on-line capabilities of a computer if possible. Use a text editor to develop the skeletal structure of the design. Use formatting tools for producing documentation. It takes time to become familiar with some of these tools, but the effort will save time in the long run. As illustrated by an implementation of the little design language shown in the appendix to this chapter, a macroprocessor can be of great use in standardizing your design forms. As the design evolves, it may be desirable to use simulation tools to try out the design. Don't neglect the use of these tools and hurry into implementation.

We can put conventional tools together, add interfaces, and put in additional features to get more sophisticated tools. We must avoid the trap, however, of developing a system top heavy with new vocabulary and techniques. A system that, on a scale of 1 to 10 for complexity, ranks 1 or 2 and achieves 90% of what we intended is better than one ranking 9 or 10 and achieving 100%. The reason is that the simpler system is more likely to be used. Substituting one complexity for another is a poor trade.

Sometimes in our computer zeal and enthusiasm we design our automated systems to do a job that might be more suitable for humans. For instance, at this point, it is more efficient to let a human determine if a photograph of a man matches a particular individual. A human being can quickly "gestalt" a remarkable amount of data that a computer would work very hard on. Similarly, parts of process design are more suitable for human beings. If we automate those parts, we create a poor system.

Ads Overview

The ADS step-by-step approach to design involves requirements refinement as the basis of the design. When all requirements have been broken down to "atomic" parts, each being unambiguous and measurable, they are given identifying labels. We might call them R_1, R_2, ..., R_n. The requirements must describe the environment of the process to be designed. That is, all the data to be input to the process must be specified. The data to be produced and output by the process must be specified. Any constraints on the input and output must be given. Additional constraints on the performance of the process may be given, such as memory size and execution times.

Some characteristics of the environment of the process may be implied only by the requirements, especially features of the hardware, such as internally and externally generated interrupts. Requirements may not even specify hardware, but before final design can take place, it usually must be known.

The process is described by building a *tree*. At the conclusion of the first phase of design, all the terminal nodes of the tree represent "atomic" functions that should not be further divided. Each node is described by specifying the data, events, constraints, and functions associated with it. The requirements of the process are linked to corresponding data, events, or constraints of the root node that represents the whole process. The data, events, and constraints of each node are linked to their corresponding parts in subordinate nodes. In this way, requirements can be traced to the process components that satisfy them.

The design itself begins by describing the root node in a multiply threaded tree. The root, of course, represents the whole process and is broken down by data or function into subnodes. These data or function refinements are continued until each node represents a single, well-defined block. This does not necessarily represent an implementation hierarchy. It is simply a way of organizing our view of the process components. Each node will be given a name for reference. We will call them N1, N2, ... We might use short names like Ni for

some references but also give each node a descriptive name. It is not important whether one thinks of refining data or functions first. In practice, one usually thinks of both since they go together. Our approach to node description is to determine:

1. The data provided as input
2. The data desired as output
3. The function necessary to get from 1 to 2.

To subdivide a node, we break up the function into components.

Data can be divided into two classes: voluntary or involuntary. By voluntary we mean data that a process gets by explicitly asking for it, as would be done in many languages with a READ, or data that is generated internally. Involuntary data is that which is entered into the scope of the process by outside forces or by a reaction to unusual system states. We might think of involuntary data as active or passive. The passive case is illustrated by the entry of data into processor A's memory by a direct memory access from another processor. The data quietly enters and sits there in memory unknown to A unless A looks at it. The active case is illustrated by interrupts either imposed from the outside or caused by internal conditions. We call it active because an automatic action occurs in response to the data. The data itself is fleeting; in fact, the only trace left of it is the effect of the action taken. We will refer to these kinds of data as an event. We will also consider as events special system states defined by the designer.

Data are described by specifying their source, destination, and meaning. The source is either input, which means it comes from outside the process (passed from another function) or internal generation. The destination is output, which means it is presented to the outside as a result (passed to another function) or processing, in which case it is used to form some new data, or both. The meaning is a text description of what the data represents. Data may represent a scalar, a sequence of scalars, or the most complicated structure, but it will be simply referred to as one item at this level.

Setting an exact form for the data is a step of detailed design or implementation.

Events are described by giving their source, related action, and meaning. The source is either input or internal generation. The related action is the name of a node that represents the function to be executed in response to the event. The meaning is the text description of what causes the event.

Constraints are bounds placed on some aspect of the process. It may be an assertion on the value range of a scalar, the size of a structure, or the time to produce a result. To aid in expressing performance constraints, two system functions are assumed, $SIZE and $TIME. $SIZE(X), where X is a data item, means the size of the data. At this point, we leave the units of size to the user. $SIZE(N), where N is a node, means the size of the code for N. $TIME(N), where N is a node, represents the execution time of that node. $TIME(IN.X) or $TIME(OUT.X) means the time that data item X was input or output. Using these functions, we can express per-

formance constraints. For instance, $TIME(OUT.Y) − $TIME(IN.X) < 100 means that the time interval from the input of X to the output of Y is less than 100 time units.

Functions of terminal nodes are described by plain text. When a node is decomposed, the parent function must be refined and allocated to the offspring. It is useful to describe the relationships of the new functions through a concept borrowed from HOS/AXES. Three primitive relationships are used: composition, set, and conditional. They are described in the language description for ADS. The function of the parent is replaced by the relationships of the offspring nodes. Pictorially, the process design tree (without details) might look like Figure 25.3.

N1 AND N2 AND N3 means the output of ABCROOT is made up of the set of outputs from N1, N2, and N3, independent of order. N4(N5) means the output of N5 is used by N4 to produce the output for node N1. N8/C1 OR N9/C2 means the output of N3 is the out-

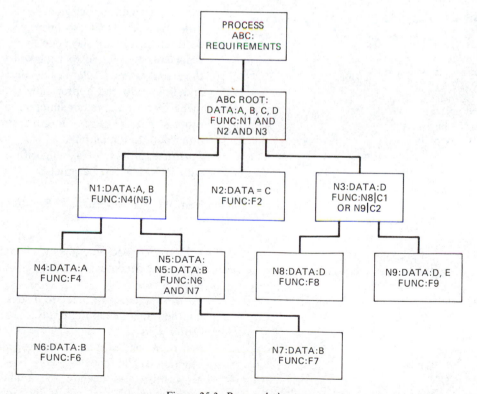

Figure 25.3. Process design tree.

put of N8 if condition C1 is true or else N9 if C2 is true. C1 and C2 must be disjoint conditions. These conditions might be data constraints, such as $A < 10$, events and so on.

In tabular form the same process would look like Table 25.3.

Each node is either a terminal node representing a basic function, or it is a parent node of two or more offspring. All the data, constraints, events (if any), and functions in a parent must map to those in one or more of the sons.

These representations should not be thought of as actual program implementation structure. They represent a functional and data partitioning only. The finer detail of program structure develops later and depends on the nature of the functions, data dependencies, and the implementation language.

This breakdown does tell us something, in addition to organizing the parts of the process. The logical scope of certain data can be observed. For instance, we see that node N5 has data B, which maps into both N6 and N7.

Table 25.3.   Parent and Offspring Relationships in Tabular Form.

ABC
  Requirements (not shown)
ABCROOT
    DATA: A,B,C,D
    FUNC: N1 AND N2 AND N3
    Sons of ABCROOT
      N1 Data: A,B
        Func: N4(N5)
        Sons of N1
          N4 Data: A
            Func : F4
          N5 Data: B
            Func : N6 AND N7
            Sons of N5
              N6 Data: B
                Func: F6
              N7 Data: B
                Func: F7
      N2 Data: C
        Func: F2
      N3 Data: D
        Func: N8/C1 OR N9/C2
        Sons of N3
          N8 Data: D
            Func: F8
          N9 Data: D, E
            Func: F9

Thus, the scope of B must include both N6 and N7. The exact nature of implementing this relationship will depend on language factors. It may involve a Pascal scope, a FORTRAN common, or a passing of arguments. We observe this scope of a data item X by finding the highest node that maps X into two or more sons.

The following algorithm can be used to develop the process tree:

Algorithm D

1. *Refine requirements.* Break all requirements down to "atomic parts." Each refined requirement must express an explicit numeric relation, describe a part of the process environment, or describe a result to be produced. Give each requirement an identifying name.
2. *Define node ROOT.* Identify all data in the requirements, declare each item by name, give its source (input or generated), give its destination (output or processing), give its meaning, and link it to the requirement specifying it. Do the same for each event except instead of a destination, specify the node name that represents the action to be taken when the event occurs. Declare each constraint and link it to the appropriate requirement. Declare the major functions of the process that are needed to get from the input data to the output.
3. *Partition process.* Call algorithm D1 with ROOT as the parameter.

Algorithm D1   (F: nodename). Partition and build

1. If F has only one function and should not be further decomposed, quit.
2. *Declare sons*
   For *n* functions of F declare *n* sons, giving them unique names, S1, S2, . . . , S*n*.
3. *Define sons*
   For each son, S*i*, and its corresponding function do the following:
   a. Identify and declare the applicable data, events, and constraints for the function of this node. Link those that

are inherited to the corresponding element in F. All others are generated internally. Partition the function of this node into subfunctions and declare them.

   b. Call algorithm D1 with Si as parameter.

4. When all sons are processed, replace the function of F with a description of the relationship of S1, S2, . . . , Sn. A notation for describing the functional relationship of sons is given in the appendix. Quit.

The results of this algorithm could be entered on a form something like the following illustration. The underlined words are form. The rest is user entered.

Consistency of the design can be checked by the following:

1. At the conclusion of the first phase design activity, each requirement should be mapped (via the links given at each node) to one or more data items, events, or constraints that satisfy it. Tracing those links should end at a terminal node.
2. At each nonterminal node, the elements in the function list should include all the sons.
3. Each node contains entries for function, data, constraints, and, optionally, events.
4. All data, events, and constraints at a nonterminal node map to corresponding elements in son nodes.

Sample Form for Process Design
Process name ABC

Requirements
  R1 links to ROOT.A
  R2 links to ROOT.B
  R3 links to ROOT.C
  R4 links to ROOT.A < 50.0
Node ABCROOT

DATA	Src	Dest	Meaning	Back Link	Forward Link
A	Input	Proc	Acceleration	ABC.R1	N1.A
B	Input	Proc	Bulk	ABC.R2	N2.B
C	Gen	Output	Cost	ABC.R3	N3.C

Constraints

	Back Link	Forward Link
		N1.A <
A < 50.0	ABC.R4	50.0
Functions		Call List
N3(N1,N2)		
PRINT		

Sons of ABCROOT: N1, N2, N3
  NODE N1

DATA	Src	Dest	Meaning	Back Link	Forward Link
A	input	proc		ROOT.A	—

  Constraints

	Back Link	Forward Link
A < 50.0	ROOT.A < 50.0	
Function		Call List
COMPUTE TIME		

5. All data, events, and constraints that are not internally generated map back to the father node or to requirements if in the ROOT node.

Size and time constraints cannot be completely checked until the process is implemented. The functions, such as $SIZE, can be included in the implementation. Including them in the process code, however, will affect their measurement. Measurement for size can usually be done manually. If the code for measuring is included in process code and the constraints are met, they will be met if the code is removed after testing.

The foregoing is not sophisticated. Its value lies in having a form to follow that provides organization. It becomes easier to see the relationships between parts of the process. Also, one can easily adapt the system to suit one's own needs.

ADS can easily be automated. In fact, the author has automated ADS by using the macroprocessor STAGE2 [33]. The language used is described in an appendix to this chapter.

Detailed Design

We recognize five things to do in transforming a first-level design to a detailed design: (1) detail the data, (2) specify algorithms, (3) merge common functions, (4) specify interfaces, and (5) answer questions about the design.

Detailing the data means to add specific structure to the description of data that previously was described by telling what it means. This will add the knowledge of how the data is referenced. For input data, specify what part of the environment it comes from.

Specifying algorithms may be done by adding to the function description of a node. Either a reference by name for well-known algorithms, reference to a document, or a thumbnail description can be given.

Merging common functions is done when two or more terminal nodes are found to have the same function (or nearly so), though perhaps performed on different data. Those nodes can be deleted from their parents and a new node added as a son to the lowest common ancestor of the merged nodes. The original

parent nodes have the new node and the data from the appropriate merged node added to a call list. The new node is defined with its data having Source = Pass. A call list is simply a node used that is not a son.

Specifying interfaces involves identifying arguments passed, the scope of data, and message protocols. Arguments passed are indicated in nodes by data with Source = Pass. Nodes that will call other nodes have the called nodes on a call list with the list of data to be passed. The scope of the data is determined by finding the highest node at which the data maps to two or more offspring nodes. Message protocols include the medium of message transmittal as well as the structure of the data in the message. It may be indicated in the meaning of the data by a reference to a document.

The following list of questions should be asked of every design:

1. *Is every item of input and output data specified?* If all requirements that specify data trace to data descriptions satisfying them, this answer should be *yes*. If not, something was left out. If there is input data not traced back to a requirement, find out why.

2. *For any data item D, where D.SOURCE = x, what happens if x ceases to send data?* For example, what action is taken if no response from a customer at a terminal occurs, of if an input buffer remains empty.

3. *For any data item D, where D.DEST = x, what happens if x ceases to receive?* For example, what if the output buffer fills up?

4. *For any data item D, with the constraint $a < D < b$, what happens if $D < a$ or $D > b$?* Murphy's law holds that even data that can never go out of bounds, will.

5. *In general, what action is taken if any constraint is violated?*

6. *Have you looked for the existence of singular points?* A singular point is a set of data that for some reason would produce an invalid result. Division by zero is an example. Often the situation is covered by the bounds placed on the data by the

constraints. However, it can occur that data that individually are valid may be invalid when combined—a condition that is hard to find. This question should be asked all the way through implementation. It may be that the order of certain operations will be the factor that causes the invalid condition.

7. *For a node X containing a data item D, where D.SOURCE = input, what conditions might require that X stop accepting the input of D?* (Forethought) What changes are likely to be made in the future? What facilities can be provided to ease those changes? Do not believe that nothing will change. Parameterize, modularize, and thoroughly document the design so that changes can be made intelligently. Use of a macroprocessor can allow parameterization of large blocks of a system.

8. *Is a data representation arbitrary and subject to change?* If so, localize its explicit representation and represent its essential nature mnemonically.

Distributed Design

Complex systems must be designed by many people. It may be that no single person will comprehend the whole process in detail. At some higher level, however, the process must be expressed in a way that is comprehensible to one person. Below that level, the designs of subsystems of the process are distributed among several people. In many of today's systems, the process may be physically implemented on several processors. A distributed system is designed in basically the same way. The process function is decomposed to a level in which the terminal subfunctions are relatively independent. These will be the subprocesses that may be distributed on separate processors. These will, in turn, be decomposed further to design the individual processes in the distributed system.

A necessary addition to the design methodology for a distributed system is an analysis of the intercommunication needed between subprocesses. When subprocesses are allocated to processors, the data traffic on the communication network must be estimated to determine if the allocation is feasible. Better estimates from each stage of design and implementation must be fed back to ensure that the allocation of processes to processors continues to be valid.

25.4. PERSPECTIVE FOR THE FUTURE

Earlier we showed that design languages have become implementation languages. We also traced concepts from design usage to implementation languages. We can expect to see more of this development. We will see a higher level of abstraction possible in the implementation languages, and we will see design languages with a higher level of asbtraction come into use that will build on requirements that in turn make use of a formal language for requirements. Since the abstractions must apply not only to data but also to the applicable functions, some approach such as suggested by Backus [25] is likely, to allow the expression of functional forms and the power to combine existing forms to make new ones.

In the design language, the "level of invisibility" will rise. More powerful abstraction mechanisms will evolve which will allow representation of complex data structures as entities. The data and its associated functions may be combined into entities to allow a better mapping into implementation languages.

Most important will be the organization provided by the system. Ultimately, good design requires a high degree of organization of data. The design system will provide a data base system to handle the design description.

25.5. BENEFITS OF USING A FORMAL DESIGN SYSTEM

What do you get out of using a formal design system? Just as we often see program developers in a hurry and designing on the fly as they program, so we also see designers trying to short cut the system and do the design on the back of an envelope. Whatever system you use, use it as it is meant to be used. Otherwise, you will not get the anticipated benefits, such as:

Organization. This is the key to everything in process design. The particular form of the organization may be less important than the fact that you have it.

Documentation. Every system should aid in setting up the documentation. It is essential to have a design document before implementation begins. Following the system will produce documents at the right time instead of after the fact, and they will be of better quality because they will be produced at a time when the designers are most familiar with their decisions and more enthusiastic.

Testing. Use your system to plan for testing. Make sure that for each requirement all related constraints are tested. Then the test phase will proceed smoothly, be more complete, and have a criterion to test against.

Implementation Foundation. Implementation will begin with a more complete and consistent set of specifications. Debugging the developing code will be easier because it will be more likely that the developers will know where certain effects take place. There will be less confusion for the programmers.

Maintenance Made Easier. For the same reasons as above, maintenance will be easier both for correcting bugs and for modifications. Since any design system will encourage one to develop a good module structure, it will be easier to know where to make changes and what effects the changes will have.

Forecast Development Time. With experience, the use of a design system will enable forecasts of development time to be made more accurately because of the above benefits and because all projects will follow similar paths.

APPENDIX: SUMMARY OF A DESIGN LANGUAGE (ADL)

This appendix describes the system implemented in STAGE2. In ADL we are manipulating strings. For any string X, there is the string X itself and the string that X contains, that is, the value of X. In the following, ⟨xxx⟩ means the string used for xxx. Capitalized strings are used for exact literal strings. A list is a set of strings separated by commas.

Entities in ADL Process

- $PN contains the process name.
- ⟨process name⟩ contains a list of requirement names. A list is a series of character strings separated by commas.

Requirements

- ⟨process name⟩ contains a list of requirement names.
- ⟨req. name⟩. FW contains a list of first-level constraints or data that satisfy the requirement.
- ⟨req. name⟩ contains abbreviated text of requirements (optional).

Node

- Node name is ⟨process name⟩ ROOT for the first node and the name used in the ADD SONS command for others.
- Each node name contains a list of: ⟨define flag⟩, ⟨name of father⟩.
- For each node XX, there exists:
  XX.DAT containing a list of XX's data
  XX.CON containing a list of XX's constraints
  XX.EVT containing a list of XX's events
  XX.FUN containing a list of XX's functions
  XX.SONS containing a list of XX's sons
  XX.CAL containing a list of XX's called nodes

Data

- Names of data for node XX are in a list contained in XX.DAT.
- For each data item DD in XX, there exists:
  XX.DD.FW containing forward links to uses of DD in offspring nodes
  XX.DD.BK containing backward link to DD in the parent node
  XX.DD containing a list composed of source, destination, and meaning
  Source can be INPUT, GEN, or PASS.
  Destination can be OUTPUT, PROC, or PASS.
  INPUT means the data come from the outside world.
  GEN means the data is generated internally.
  PASS means the data is passed from a calling node, if source, or passed to a node if destination.
  OUTPUT means the data goes to the outside world.

PROC means the data is used in processing.

Meaning is plain text.

Constraints

- Constraints for node XX are in a list contained in XX.CON.
- For each constraint YYY, in XX there exists:
  XX.YYY.FW containing forward links to associated constraints in son node
  XX.YYY.BK containing back links to associated constraints in parent node

Events

- Events are occurrences of instantaneous data. An action is associated with each event. An example of an event is an interrupt or a specific state of a system.
- Names of all events for node XX are in a list contained in XX.EVT.
- For each event EE, in XX there exists:
  XX.EE.FW containing forward links
  XX.EE.BK containing backward links
  XX.EE contains a list composed of source, action, and meaning.
    The source of an event is either input or internally generated.
    The action is text describing what happens or a node name.
    The meaning is descriptive text.

Calls. As more-detailed design proceeds, nodes with similar functions will be merged. These nodes will then represent a call to a new node setup as an offspring of their lowest common ancestor. Since the original parents need the new node's function, the new node, with the original node's data, is put on the parent's call list. For example, suppose the following:

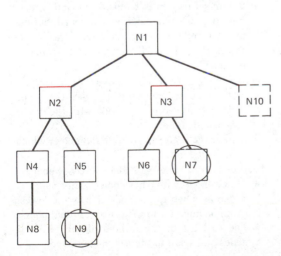

Nodes N9 and N7 are to be merged to a new node, say N10, as a son of N1. The parent of N9 is N4. After the merge, the list contained in N4.CAL will include N10.N9.DAT. This shows that N4 will call N10, passing the data of N9 (which was inherited from N4).

Operations of the Language

In the following commands, the italic letters are all that are required in the command word.

PROCESS ⟨name⟩;

- Initializes for a description of a new process with the given name.
- Requests requirement names.

REQUIREMENTS ⟨list of names⟩;
  or
REQUIREMENTS ⟨number⟩;

- A list of requirement names is appended to the current list (possibly empty) contained in the process name.
- If the first form of the command is used, the list of requirement names is as given. If the second form is used, the list R1, R2, ... Rn (where n is ⟨number⟩) is generated.
- A request to define the root node is given.

DATA ⟨list of names⟩;

- Assuming the current node is Ni, the list of data names is appended to the contents of Ni.DAT.
- If an element of the list is already declared for Ni, a message is given, and it is ignored.
- If the data element is not in the father node, its meaning is requested.
- If the current node is the root, a request to link the data elements to requirements is given.
- If a data element is "inherited" from the father node, it is automatically linked.

⟨data name⟩ MEANS ⟨text⟩;

- The text describes what ⟨data name⟩ represents. It is entered in the current node.

SOURCE OF ⟨dataname⟩ IS {INPUT, PASS, GEN};

- The indicated source is entered.
- INPUT means the data comes from outside the process.
- GEN means the data is generated internally.
- PASS means the data is passed from a calling node.

DESTINATION OF ⟨dataname⟩ IS {OUTPUT, PASS, PROC};

- The indicated destination is entered.

- OUTPUT means the data is presented to the environment.
- PROC means the data is used in processing.
- PASS means the data is passed to a called node.

CONSTRAINTS ⟨list of constraints⟩;
- Each constraint is entered for the node. A constraint is concise text, such as A < 50.
- For the root node, a request to link the constraint to a requirement is given.
- For other nodes, the constraint is automatically linked to the corresponding constraint in the father. A constraint on internally generated data must be explicitly linked.

LINK xx TO yy;
- If xx is a data name, yy must be a requirement name, if in the root node, or else the corresponding data name in the father node.
- If xx is a constraint, yy must be a requirement name, if in the root node, or else the corresponding constraint in the father node.
- Similarly, for events.

FUNCTION ⟨list of function text⟩;
- The functions of the current node Ni, are entered as the value of Ni.FUN. For a terminal node, this will be plain text descriptions.
- Function relations: When sons are added to a node Ni, then it is no longer a terminal node. ADS will request that Ni's functions be reallocated to the offspring. Ni's function entry will be blanked out. ADS will request that the functional relationships of the offspring be described. The user would reenter the definition of Ni and enter the new function as follows. There are three basic relationships.
  1. Composition: an input of Ni, x, is to produce an output, y, i.e., $y = Ni(x)$. A functional decomposition of Ni into Nj and Nk has $w = Nk(x)$ and $y = Nj(w)$ or $y = Nj(Nk(x))$. The notation for the parent node is Nj(Nk). There could be Nj(Nk,Nm).
  2. Union: multiple outputs are produced by Ni, e.g., $y1, y2 = Ni(x1,x2)$. Decomposition of Ni into Nj and Nk produces $y1 = Nj(x1)$ and $y2 = Nj(x2)$. The notation used is: Nj AND Nk.
  3. Conditional: output for Ni is produced differently under varying conditions. For $y = Ni(x)$ there could be decomposition of Ni into Nj and Nk such that

$$y = \begin{cases} Nj(x) \text{ given condition C} \\ Nk(x) \text{ given condition not C} \end{cases}$$

Of course, there may be any number of conditional functions. The conditions must cover all possibilities. The notation to be used is: Nj|⟨condition⟩ OR Nk|⟨condition⟩.
Example:
    NODE Ni;
    FUNCTION (Nj AND
      Nk(Nm))|A⟨10
      OR Np|A⟩ = 10;
    END NODE;

WRITE FUNC;
- The functions of the current node are listed.

NODE ⟨nodename⟩;
- The current node is set to ⟨nodename⟩. Subsequent node definition commands will apply to it until an END NODE or another NODE command is given.
- The definition flag is reset for ⟨nodename⟩.
- CUR$NOD contains the name of the current node. The command $WRITE CUR$NOD; will display it.

END NODE;
- The current node's definition flag is set.
- The current node is set to null.

DELETE NODE ⟨nodename⟩;
- Deletes the given node (and its whole subtree). Links to its data and constraints are removed from the father node.

ADD SONS ⟨list of node names⟩ TO ⟨father nodename⟩;
- Each son node name is appended to the list contained in ⟨father nodename⟩.SONS.
- The initial state of the son nodes is set indicating the father and the define flag is reset.
- A message requests definition of each son.
- Parent's function is blanked out and a message requests reallocation of parent functions to offspring and functional relationship description put into parent (see function relations).

UNDEF NODE IN ⟨NODENAME⟩:
- The whole subtree starting with the given node is searched until a node with the define flag reset is found.
- A message is given: either all defined or which node is undefined.

MERGE ⟨list of terminal nodes⟩ IN ⟨newnode⟩;
- A new node with ⟨newnode⟩ as its name is added as a son to the node that is the lowest common ancestor to the list of terminal nodes.
- The call list of the fathers of the terminal nodes has a call to the new node added.

- The terminal nodes are deleted.
- A message is given to define the new node.

DISPLAY PROC;
- An indented listing of the whole process tree is given.

DISPLAY SUB 〈nodename〉;
- The subtree beginning with the given node is listed.

DISPLAY NODE 〈nodename〉;
- The description for the given node is listed.

HELP;
- An explanation of the commands is given. The explanation of this list is made available.

DELETE CONSTRAINT 〈nodename〉.〈constraint〉;
- The given constraint is deleted from the specified node and all nodes lower in the subtree.

DELETE DATA 〈nodename〉.〈dataname〉;
- The given data element is deleted from the given node and all nodes lower in the subtree.

DELETE FUNCTION 〈nodename.〉.〈function text〉;
- The one specified function is deleted at the given node. 〈function text〉 must be the exact string used in the function to be deleted from the list.

EVENT 〈event list〉;
- Each event is added to the events for the current node. Inherited events are linked to the higher level. If the event is not inherited, the user is asked for meaning and action.

EVENT 〈event name〉 CAUSES ACTION 〈nodename〉;
- The event is linked to the node.

$STORE;
- The ADS memory is saved in a file. The name of the file is FOR090.DAT. Memory is not affected, and processing can be continued.

$RESTORE;
- The ADS memory is restored from the latest version of file FOR090.DAT. Previous contents of memory are lost. Processing can continue at the point at which the file was stored.

CMPROC 〈process name〉;
- A file of commands and text to a configuration manager is built. The commands will set up the skeleton structure of the process for implementation. The file name is FOR097.DAT.

$WRITE 〈string〉;
- The value of 〈string〉 will be printed. For instance,

  $WRITE $PN;

  will cause the output:

$PN = 〈process name〉.

$WRITE $CURNOD;

will produce:

$CURNOD = 〈name of node being defined〉.

$WRITE 〈process name〉;

will output the list of requirement names that are the value of 〈process name〉.

This command enables detailed examination of every part of the process structure.

〈string1〉 $EQT 〈string2〉;
- 〈string2〉 is made the value of 〈string1〉. This command will allow any part of the tree structure to be patched.

In addition, any STAGE2 utility is available for use, including defining new macros.

REFERENCES

1. P. Naur and B. Randell (eds), *Software Engineering,* NATO Scientific Affairs Division, Brussels 39, Belgium, Jan. 1969.
2. B. Boehm, "Software and Its Impact: A Quantitative Study," *Datamation,* May 1973.
3. J. Donovan, "Tools and Philosophy for Software Education," *CACM,* Aug. 1976, pp. 430–436.
4. K. L. Heninger, "Specifying Software Requirements for Complex Systems: New Techniques and Their Applications," *IEEE Transactions on Software Engineering,* Jan. 1980, pp. 2–13.
5. H. D. Mills, "Software Development," *IEEE Transactions on Software Engineering,* Dec. 1976, pp. 265–273.
6. M. A. Jackson, *Principles of Program Design,* Academic Press, New York, 1975.
7. R. C. Tausworthe, *Standardized Development of Computer Software,* Prentice-Hall, Englewood Cliffs, N.J., 1977.
8. E. Yourdon and L. L. Constantine, *Structured Design,* Yourdon Press, New York, 1975.
9. E. Yourdon, *Techniques of Program Structure and Design,* Prentice-Hall, Englewood Cliffs, N.J., 1975.
10. K. T. de Lavigne, "Basic Program Design—The Jackson Way: An Example," *Proceedings 1977 Annual Conference ACM,* pp. 115–124.
11. M. E. Dickover, C. L. McGowan, and D. T. Ross, "Software Design Using SADT," *Proceedings 1977 Annual Conference ACM,* pp. 125–133.
12. D. T. Ross and J. W. Brackett, "An Approach to Structured Analysis," *Computer Decisions,* Sept. 1976, pp. 40–44.
13. D. T. Ross and K. E. Schuman, "Structured Analysis for Requirements Definition," *IEEE Transactions on Software Engineering,* Jan. 1977, pp. 2–15.
14. D. T. Ross, "Structured Analysis (SA): A Language for Communicating Ideas," *IEEE Transactions on Software Engineering,* Jan 1977, pp. 16–33.

15. G. Myers, *Composite/Structured Design,* Van Nostrand Reinhold, New York, 1978.

16. D. Teicherow and E. A. Hershey, "PSL/PSA: A Computer Aided Technique for Structured Documentation and Analysis of Information Processing Systems," *IEEE Transactions on Software Engineering,* Jan. 1977, pp. 34–40.

17. B. P. Buckles, "Formal Module Specifications," *Proceedings 1977 Annual Conference of ACM,* New York, 1977.

18. C. G. Davis and C. R. Vick, "The Software Development System," *IEEE Transactions on Software Engineering,* Jan. 1977, pp. 69–84.

19. *Process Design Methodology Design Specification;* vol. 1, vol. 5, Texas Instruments, Inc., 1976.

20. J. Schied, "KVM/320 Verification Methodology: A 'Toy' Example," System Development Corporation, TM-5855/100/00, 1977.

21. M. Hamilton and S. Zeldin, "Higher Order Software—A Methodology for Defining Software," *IEEE Transactions on Software Engineering,* March 1977, pp. 9–32.

22. M. Moriconi, "A Designer/Verifier's Assistant," *IEEE Transactions on Software Engineering,* July 1979, pp. 387–401.

23. W. Wulf, "ALPHARD: Toward a Language to Support Structured Programs," Computer Science Department, Carnegie-Mellon University, Pittsburgh, Pa., Apr. 1974.

24. T. Winograd, "Beyond Programming Languages," *CACM,* July 1979, pp. 391–401.

25. J. Backus, "Can Programming Be Liberated From the Von Neumann Style? A Functional Style and Its Algebra of Programs," *CACM 21, 8* (Aug. 1978) pp. 613–641.

26. N. A. Vosbury, "A Design System," System Development Corporation, TM-HU-288/000/00, 1980.

27. "Process Design Methodology Specification," vols. I–V, Texas Instruments, Inc., prepared for the U.S. Army Ballistic Missile Defense Advanced Technology Center, Huntsville, Ala., 1976.

28. M. Hamilton and S. Zeldin, "The Relationship Between Design and Verification," *The Journal of Systems and Software,* 1(1979):29–56, Elsevier North Holland Inc.

29. J. M. Spitzer, K. N. Levit, and L. Robinson, "An Example of Hierarchical Design and Proof," *CACM 20, 12* (Dec. 1978): 1064–1075.

30. W. E. Riddle, J. C. Wileden, J. H. Saylor, A. R. Segal, A. M. Stavely, "Behavior Modeling During Software Design," *IEEE Transactions on Software Engineering,* July 1978, pp. 283–292.

31. W. Wulf, "Trends in the Design and Implementation of Programming Languages," *Computer,* Jan. 1980, pp. 14–25.

32. D. Knuth, *The Art of Computer Programming,* vols. 1–3, Addison Wesley, Reading, Mass., 1969.

33. W. Waite, *Implementing Software for Non-Numeric Applications,* Prentice-Hall, Englewood Cliffs, N.J., 1973.

26

Applicative and Functional Programming

S. W. Smoliar
General Research Corporation

26.1. INTRODUCTION

Motivating Factors

Problems with Conventional Programming Languages.

Conventional programming languages are growing ever more enormous, but not stronger. Inherent defects at the most basic level cause them to be both fat and weak: their primitive word-at-a-time style of programming inherited from their common ancestor—the von Neumann computer, their close coupling of semantics to state transitions, their division of programming into a world of expressions and a world of statements, their inability to effectively use powerful combining forms for building new programs from existing ones, and their lack of useful mathematical properties for reasoning about programs. *John Backus* [1]

The evolution of programming practices has always appeared to respect some implicit connection between a programming language and the architecture of the computer which supports that language. Since the initial development of FORTRAN, a variety of programming languages has engendered a plethora of constructs that purport to deal with the many new problem domains that have come into the purview of data processing; but all of these constructs turn out to be new syntactic conventions for operational techniques that have been with us since the very first computers.

The weakness of these conventions stems from von Neumann's initial conception of architecture: A computer essentially consists of two relatively "large" boxes, a CPU, and a memory, connected by a relatively "thin" wire,

generally, a bus that supports an address register and a data register. The size of this data register generally dictates the size of a "word," the basic unit of storage; and programming ultimately reduces to the rather tedious activity of fetching words, one at a time, from memory, manipulating them in the CPU, and occasionally sending some of those words back into memory in an updated form. We would like to believe that the so-called higher-level languages developed over the past twenty years have helped to transcend this rather grueling view. However, the basic constructs of most of these languages, variables, and assignment statements tend to reinforce the belief that programming is ultimately little more than retrieving values from some collection of words (variables), manipulating them, and putting (i.e., assigning) the results of those manipulations into another collection of words. If we can recognize the manipulations in the midst of all the assignment statements, we discover that they generally look very much like mathematical expressions (such as the expressions in FORTRAN); but they are inevitably so outnumbered by the assignment statements that it is no wonder that many programs are so hard to read.

Possibilities for Improvement.

The commonplace expressions of arithmetic and algebra have a certain simplicity that most communications to computers lack. In particular, (a) each expression has a nesting subexpression structure, (b) each subexpression denotes something (usually a number, truth value or numerical function), (c) the thing an expression denotes, i.e., its "value", depends only on the *values* of its subexpressions, not on other properties of them. *P. J. Landin* [2]

The heart of most software modules is almost always some *expression,* quite mathematical in nature, that embodies the basic input-output relation of the module. This expression may be stated explicitly, but, more often than not, it is manifest as many little subexpressions tied together by a large number of *statements* that are responsible for assigning the appropriate values to variables used in each subexpression and then picking up the output and putting it in some proper location. In other words, the statements do little more than bookkeeping—processing that bears no direct relation to the functionality of the module but that is required, by virtue of the presence of variables, to "set up" each subexpression for evaluation and to recover the corresponding results [3].

The alternative to succumbing to the debilitating properties of statements is to do away with them altogether. The many arguments for the viability of an expression-based, statement-free language set forth above have been substantiated, perhaps most noticeably, by the computational power of "pure" LISP [4]. The design of LISP, however, did not sufficiently recognize the possibilities for incorporating powerful combining forms for synthesizing expressions from subexpressions. These combining forms are called *functionals,* and they will be discussed below in greater detail. Expression-based languages also provide a convenient *mathematical* formalism for describing programs, to the extent that Backus [1] has demonstrated that problems of program description, analysis, and synthesis may all benefit from the basic tools of algebra.

Basic Definitions

Applicative Programming.

The characteristic semantic feature of expressions is that they are "evaluated"; that is, the semantic interpretation of an expression ultimately defines its "value." Furthermore, for "pure"

expressions, it is *exclusively* the value that has semantic importance. This linguistic property is termed *referential transparency* [5], for it allows a subexpression to be replaced by any other expression having the same value without any effect on the value of the whole. Languages or language subsets having the property of referential transparency are termed *applicative;* other adjectives that have been used include declarative, denotative, descriptive, and functional. *R. D. Tennent* [6]

The reader can deduce from the title of this chapter an attempt to draw a distinction between *applicative* and *functional* programming. The above remarks, on the other hand, might lead one to believe that such a distinction is rather artificial. Nevertheless, there is now arising a sufficient proliferation of expression-based languages to justify some attempt at finer classification.

In its most general sense, the term *applicative* may refer to any expression-based language. In more restrictive contexts, however, the term may apply to those languages whose structures are based on the lambda calculus of Alonzo Church [7]. (The most established of these languages is pure LISP, which is discussed in greater detail in Section 26.2) These languages all share an abstract syntax that classifies all expressions according to the following taxonomy [6]:

1. Atomic constituents—These are symbolic entities that may denote either constants or "local variables."
2. Operator-operand combinations—These denote the application of a function to an argument. All functions take exactly one argument, but that argument need not be an atomic constituent.
3. Identifier-binding constructions—These are also known as *abstractions* or *lambda expressions.* They establish the binding of values to local variables.

Functional Programming.

If one constantly invents new combining forms to suit the occasion, as one can in the lambda calculus, one will not become familiar with the style or useful properties of the few combining forms that are adequate for all purposes. Just as structured programming eschews many control statements to obtain programs with simpler structure, better properties, and uniform methods of understanding their behavior, so functional programming eschews the lambda expression, substitution, and multiple function types. It thereby achieves programs built with familiar functional forms with known useful properties. These programs are so structured that their behavior can often be understood and proven by mechanical use of algebraic techniques similar to those used in solving high school algebra problems. *John Backus* [1]

Functional programming is distinguished from applicative programming by its elimination of the need for identifier-binding constructions. A functional programming expression is always an operator-operand combination. The operator may be a primitive function, or it may be synthesized through the use of *combining forms,* also known as *higher-order functions, functional forms, functionals,* or *operators.* These are simply functions that yield functions as their values; but, as is shown later on, if used properly, they eliminate the need for any representation of local variables (or any other variables, for that matter) and provide what may well be the cleanest mathematical representation of a program.

Applicability

Requirements Specification.

Requirements analysis often yields a poor description of the required system. Specifications of requirements can be informal, ambiguous, incomplete, inconsistent, and difficult to understand. This leads to situations in which either (a) inconsistencies and ambiguities are not found until the detailed-design or implementation phases, necessitating costly revisions, or (b) the final product does not meet the customer's needs. This could happen because of poor communication between the designers and the customer, or because the customer did not understand his own needs (and the designers could not help him). *Pamela Zave* [8]

Any system development process must begin with a statement of some problem to be solved.

This initial description is known as *requirements specification,* an undertaking whose ultimate mission is to make sure that the finished product will satisfy the customer's needs. It is now almost taken for granted that any elaboration of a system's tasks should involve some elementary level of functional decomposition. This does not necessarily involve a full-blown top-down stepwise refinement of the entire system in one's favorite structured programming language. In fact, this is precisely what should be avoided at this stage of the development. Anything that elaborate will never get more than a cursory glance from the customer. Nevertheless, it would be desirable to be able to state the overall task of the system in terms of some sort of *transducer* that transforms inputs into outputs. This, in turn, will involve some elaboration regarding what the inputs and outputs look like. This description may then lead to a decomposition of the transducer into subtransducers, interconnected in some fashion [9]. Needless to say, any description based on such transducers will have referential transparency, and, in fact, any information concerning the interconnection of transducers may be expressed in terms of the combining forms of functional programming.

Thus, functional programming is powerful enough to allow for the representation of a system's functionality as a *single* mathematical expression. The compactness of such a representation, together with its referential transparency, should encourage easy communication with the customer. (This is not to imply that the customer should be expected to understand such expressions. Rather, the structure of the expression will clearly indicate to the designer *what* information should be communicated to the customer in any language he happens to be comfortable with.) Furthermore, these expressions tend to avoid any premature biases regarding implementation. Because they preclude any manipulation of variables, their implementation may be "liberated" from any particular storage medium. Similarly, the referential transparency of an expression implies that its component subexpressions may be processed concurrently and asynchronously, which "liberates" the implementation from any specific processing architecture.

Design.

Everything worth saying
about anything worth saying something about
must be expressed in six or fewer pieces.
Douglas T. Ross [10]

The varieties of approaches to software design are as wide as the varieties of programming languages, as evidenced by the considerable attention this topic receives in other chapters in this book. Quite often, in fact, a particular design methodology arises because of its compatibility with a given representation language. If an expression-based language is used for requirements specification, then one may view the subsequent design task as incorporating four activities: abstraction, elaboration, transformation, and evaluation. These do *not* constitute a four-step design process; rather, they should be regarded as four aspects of analysis that should be applied to the expression that is formulated during requirements specification.

Indeed, the activities of abstraction and elaboration are very closely intertwined. The first actually has its roots in requirements specification: it entails the ability to postulate the existence of a function before the definition of that function is actually formulated as an expression. In fact, the formulation of that definition is the activity of elaboration. This will generally involve postulating new functions, a further act of abstraction, which will, in turn, require the elaboration of further definitions. The purview of both of these activities is determined, once again, by the principles of referential transparency: The elaboration of a function's definition should depend strictly on a set of side-effect-free properties provided by the abstraction of that function; and, conversely, an abstraction of a function should provide sufficient information for the representation of that function as a side-effect-free expression.

Given an expression that represents a system, the mathematical nature of the expression allows for its transformation into a variety of equivalent expressions through the manipulation of simple algebraic identities. This collection of expressions represents several *alternative* approaches to the construction of a given system. Only an expression-based representation allows such alternatives to be investigated with only the most basic tools of algebra.

Finally, given the need to choose between alternatives, one must have some means of comparative evaluation. A functional or applicative representation can readily be subjected to interpretation, and this interpretive process can serve as a basis for either simulation or implementation. These issues will now be addressed in greater detail.

Simulation and Implementation.

When I found so astonishing a power placed within my hands, I hesitated a long time concerning the manner in which I should employ it. Although I possessed the capacity of bestowing animation, yet to prepare a frame for the reception of it, with all its intricacies of fibres, muscles, and veins, still remained a work of inconceivable difficulty and labour. I doubted at first whether I should attempt the creation of a being like myself, or one of simpler organization; but my imagination was too much exalted by my first success to permit me to doubt of my ability to give life to an animal as complex and wonderful as man. The materials at present within my command hardly appeared adequate to so arduous an undertaking, but I doubted not that I should ultimately succeed. I prepared myself for a multitude of reverses; my operations might be incessantly baffled, and at last my work be imperfect, yet when I considered the improvement which every day takes place in science and mechanics, I was encouraged to hope my present attempts would at least lay the foundations of future success. Nor could I consider the magnitude and complexity of my plan as any argument of its impracticability. *Mary W. Shelley* [11]

All issues of systems analysis may be categorized according to whether they address the *what* or the *how* of a system's behavior. The preceding discussion has focused on the use of expressions concerned with the *what*. It is also possible to base an operational model upon a given expression that will deal with the *how*. The problem is actually twofold. First, there is the issue of behavior: associating the evaluation of the expression with the actual functionality of the system under analysis. Second, there is the issue of performance: translating the specifics of expression evaluation into specific attributes of system performance. There is also the question as to whether the evaluation process, once it is formulated, can be realized in real time with available facilities. If this is possible, then the evaluation will describe an actual implementation. Whether or not this is the case, the evaluation may always serve as the basis for a simulation.

From an operational point of view, the most important attribute of an expression is that its evaluation is essentially an interpretive process. The basic interpretation mechanism must be capable of replacing any instance of a functional with the function it synthesizes, replacing the name of a defined function with the body of the definition, and replacing any operator-operand combination with its associated value. Once again, referential transparency reveals itself as an important issue. With respect to interpretation, it allows for a great deal of flexibility regarding the *order* in which replacements may be performed. Thus, expression evaluation may be achieved by operational configurations ranging from a single task residing on a single processor through a distributed multitasking system and even to a network of special-purpose hardware modules. The design of a specific interpreter entails a mapping of the process of expression interpretation onto a particular implementation environment, which permits access to some predetermined collection of computational resources.

The most straightforward use of the interpreter is the verification that the behavior of expression evaluation reflects the functionality of the system under study. However, one must also consider the ability to observe specific aspects of system *performance*. This necessitates extending the interpreter with the ability to model the specific resources of space and time, which are associated with the entire domain of elements constituting a functional programming expression. (This issue is discussed in greater detail in Section 26.4.)

26.2. BACKGROUND

LISP has jokingly been described as "the most intelligent way to misuse a computer." I think that description a great compliment because it transmits the full flavor of liberation: it has assisted a number of our most gifted fellow humans in thinking previously impossible thoughts. *Edsger W. Dijkstra* [12]

As observed in Section 26.1, the principles of applicative and functional programming have a variety of foundations that encompass both mathematics and the theory of programming languages. This section surveys the contributions of these foundations, as well as those of some more recent research projects. Since LISP was the first major programming language to incorporate the foundations of applicative programming, it is in terms of LISP that these foundations are discussed. The implications of these foundations for the denotational theory of programming language semantics are then considered. The algebraic view of applicative and functional programming is based on the research of John Backus, which is summarized next. There follows a presentation of the innovative work of Daniel P. Friedman and David S. Wise, who have devoted considerable effort to extending the computational power of pure LISP. There is also a look at how the power of functional programming has been investigated and extended by Robert E. Frankel and Thomas Myers. Finally, the current state of data-flow research in terms of its relation to applicative and functional programming is summarized.

Basic Principles of LISP

Lambda Conversion.

... "(LAMBDA" is a necessary part of the scenery, but for our purposes, it is as useful as a screen door on a submarine sandwich. *Daniel P. Friedman* [13]

LISP is a programming language based on the abstract syntax of the lambda calculus. It has a single data structure, which is called the *S-expression.* (The *S* stands for *symbolic.*) An S-expression is either an atomic constituent (which may be either symbolic or numeric) or a *list,* which is an ordered sequence of S-expressions enclosed in a pair of matching parentheses. For example,

(YOU (WALRUS) (HURT THE (1 YOU LOVE)))

is a list of *three* S-expressions: the atomic constituent YOU, the list (WALRUS), and the list (HURT THE (1 YOU LOVE)), which also happens to be a list of three S-expressions. It is also possible to have a list with *no* S-expressions between the matching parentheses: (). This is known as the *empty list;* and it is distinguished by being identified with the atomic constituent NIL [14].

Both operator-operand combinations and identifier-binding constructions are represented by lists. An instance of the latter is always a list of three elements. The first of these elements is the atomic constituent LAMBDA, the second is a list of atoms, and the third may be any S-expression. The elements of the list of atoms are called the *local variables* of the lambda expression, while the general S-expression is called the *body.*

Any other list represents an operator-operand combination. The first element of the list always represents the operator. The remainder of the list constitutes the operand. If the operator is an identifier-binding construction, then there must be a one-to-one correspondence between the elements of the operand and the local variables of the lambda expression; this correspondence is known as the *variable binding.*

Lambda conversion is simply the process of interpreting an expression in the lambda calculus. It is best demonstrated by an example.

Consider the problem of solving the equation $Ax^2 + Bx + C = 0$. If $A = 0$, this is equivalent to solving the linear equation $Bx + C = 0$; otherwise, it is a genuine quadratic equation, whose solutions will be real or imaginary, depending upon the sign of the expression $B^2 - 4AC$. This may be expressed in LISP by defining the atomic constituent SOLVE to be an operator whose operation is given by an identifier-binding construction as shown in Example 26.1. (DEFINE is an operator that takes an arbitrary number of operands, each of which is a *definition.* A definition, in turn, is always a list of two elements: an atomic constituent, which is the *name* of the operator being defined, and an S-expression, which is the *body* of the definition.)

The body of the definition of SOLVE is a lambda expression with three local variables, A, B, and C, corresponding to the coefficients of the equation to be solved. The body of the lambda expression, in turn, is a *conditional expression.* It is a list whose first element is the atom COND and whose remaining elements are all two-element lists. These lists are scanned in order, the first element being evaluated. If the value of this element is T (true), the conditional expression evaluates the second element of the pair. If it is NIL (false), the next pair is tested. In this example the first test determines whether or not the value bound to the local variable A is equal to 0. If it is, then the value of the conditional expression (and, hence, the value of SOLVE) is the value of (LINSOLVE B C), where LINSOLVE is an operator that solves linear equations given their coefficients. Otherwise, the T forces SOLVE to evaluate to the combination:

(QUADSOLVE A
B
(DIFFERENCE (TIMES B B)
(TIMES 4 A C)))

Example 26.1

```
(DEFINE
  (SOLVE (LAMBDA (A B C)
    (COND
      ((EQUAL A 0) (LINSOLVE B C))
      (T (QUADSOLVE A B (DIFFERENCE (TIMES B B) (TIMES 4 A C)))))))))
```

Rather than taking A, B, and C as inputs, QUADSOLVE will be assumed to take as inputs A, B, and the expression $B^2 - 4AC$, which will be used to determine if the solutions are real or imaginary.

While this example is not a strict description of the operation of most LISP systems, it essentially covers the basic principles of lambda conversion, as utilized by LISP. LINSOLVE and QUADSOLVE may be defined similarly. Their definitions are as in Example 26.2. (ERROR is an operator that takes no operands.)

takes a nonempty list as its input and yields the first S-expression in that list as its output. Thus, if we assume that the atom X has the value (YOU (WALRUS) (HURT THE (1 YOU LOVE))), then the value of (CAR X) is the atomic constituent YOU. The function CDR also takes a nonempty list as its input and yields the list that remains when the first S-expression is deleted. Thus, (CDR X) is evaluated as ((WALRUS) (HURT THE (1 YOU LOVE))). Lists are *constructed* by

---

Example 26.2
```
(DEFINE
  (LINSOLVE (LAMBDA (B C)
    (COND
      ((EQUAL B 0) (ERROR))
      (T (MINUS (QUOTIENT C B))))))
  (QUADSOLVE (LAMBDA (A B DISC)
    (COND
      ((MINUSP DISC)
        (LIST (IMAG (QUOTIENT (DIFFERENCE (SQRT (MINUS DISC)) B)
                    (TIMES 2 A)))
              (IMAG (QUOTIENT (MINUS (PLUS (SQRT (MINUS DISC)) B))
                    (TIMES 2 A)))))
      (T (LIST (QUOTIENT (DIFFERENCE (SQRT DISC) B) (TIMES 2 A))
               (QUOTIENT (MINUS (PLUS (SQRT DISC) B)) (TIMES 2 A)))))))))
```

Recursion.

Thou shalt always realize when building a list, thou need only describe the first typical element, and then CONS it onto the natural recursion. *Daniel P. Friedman* [13]

Solving a quadratic equation has very little to do with manipulating S-expressions that are lists. Such manipulations require the ability to define recursive functions. This is because the abstract syntax of a list admits of a recursive formulation:

A *list* is either *empty*
 or it has a *first* element that is an
  S-expression
 and a *rest* element that is a *list*.

The basic list manipulation functions of LISP are based on this abstract syntax.

There are two primitive functions concerned with decomposing lists. The function CAR

the function CONS, which takes two inputs, an S-expression, and a list. Its output is a list whose first element is the same as its expression input and whose remaining elements are the elements of its list input. For example, the value of (CONS 1984 X) would be (1984 YOU (WALRUS) (HURT THE (1 YOU LOVE))). These functions may also be composed in any way that provides them with valid inputs. For example, (CONS (CAR X) (CDR (CDR X))) evaluates to (YOU (HURT THE (1 YOU LOVE))) [14].

These functions enable fairly sophisticated operations to be performed on lists by recursive functions. For example, the function shown in Example 26.3 will take as input two lists of numbers in ascending order and merge them into a single list of numbers in ascending order. The strategy of the conditional expression is very simple: The first two pairs state that if either input is an empty list, the result of the

Example 26.3
```
(DEFINE
 (MERGE (LAMBDA (A B)
  (COND
   ((NULL A) B)
   ((NULL B) A)
   ((LESSP (CAR A) (CAR B)) (CONS (CAR A) (MERGE (CDR A) B)))
   (T (CONS (CAR B) (MERGE A (CDR B))))))))
```

MERGE is the other input. If neither input is empty, then it is possible to arithmetically compare the first elements of the two lists. If the first element of the first list is the smaller number, then the merged list will have that number as *its* first element; the remaining elements of the merged list will then consist of the list obtained by merging the remainder of that first list with all of the second list. Otherwise, the merged list will have the first element of the second list as its first element, and its remaining elements will be the result of merging all of the first list with the CDR of the second list. The recursive structure of the lists has allowed for a convenient recursive formulation of their merging.

Self-Definition. Since all LISP functions may be represented as S-expressions, it follows that it should be possible to define a LISP function that takes such an expression as its input and yields as output the value of that expression. This is the function APPLY. As originally formulated by McCarthy [4], it takes two inputs, corresponding to the two parts of an operator-operand combination; the first argument is the operator, and the second is the list of inputs to that function, as given in Example 26.4.

A full discussion of these definitions is beyond the scope of this chapter, and the reader is referred to the original discussion in Reference 4. However, it is worthwhile to mention a few constructs that are new to this definition. The quote sign (') is used to signify *constant expressions,* that is, expressions that are their own value. Thus, when EVAL is processing an S-expression bound to the local variable E, if the first element of E is known to be an atomic constituent, then (EQ (CAR E) 'QUOTE)

checks if that first element of E is equal to the atom QUOTE. (Actually, 'QUOTE is an abbreviation for the S-expression (QUOTE QUOTE); in other words, any quoted S-expression is actually a two-element list whose first element is QUOTE and whose second element is the S-expression.)

Most of the work of this interpreter is actually done by EVAL, whose first argument is the expression to be evaluated and whose second argument is an (initially empty) *association list.* This list keeps track of all bindings of lambda variables. The processing of a lambda expression causes the lambda variables to be paired together with the input parameters, and these pairs are then saved on the association list while that lambda expression is evaluated. In a similar manner, LABEL allows for a function definition to be saved on the association list, thus allowing for the processing of recursive function definitions.

Denotational Semantics

Despite the distinctions between them, [these different] sorts of semantics ... have one crucial feature in common: the values that they associate with constructs like labels and procedures have "abstract" constituents that are functions mapping one domain into another. Valuations possessing this feature are styled 'denotational', as they give any piece of program a meaning that involves the constituents of the piece only through the meanings of those constituents. However, this feature is absent from implementations, for computers work with finite representations in which the values associated with labels and procedures include not functions but parts of programs or pointers to programs. To connect values of these various kinds by nothing stronger than a pious hope would be unhelpful, for there is no point in showing that pro-

Example 26.4

```
(DEFINE
  (APPLY (LAMBDA (F ARGS)
    (EVAL (CONS F (APPQ ARGS)) NIL)))
  (APPQ (LAMBDA (M)
    (COND
      ((NULL M) NIL)
      (T (CONS (LIST 'QUOTE (CAR M)) (APPQ (CDR M)))))))
  (EVAL (LAMBDA (E A)
    (COND
      ((ATOM E) (ASSOC E A))
      ((ATOM (CAR E))
        (COND
          ((EQ (CAR E) 'QUOTE) (CADR E))
          ((EQ (CAR E) 'ATOM) (ATOM (EVAL (CADR E) A)))
          ((EQ (CAR E) 'EQ) (EQ (EVAL (CADR E) A) (EVAL (CADDR E) A)))
          ((EQ (CAR E) 'COND) (EVCON (CDR E) A))
          ((EQ (CAR E) 'CAR) (CAR (EVAL (CADR E) A)))
          ((EQ (CAR E) 'CDR) (CDR (EVAL (CADR E) A)))
          ((EQ (CAR E) 'CONS) (CONS (EVAL (CADR E) A) (EVAL (CADDR E) A)))
          (T (EVAL (CONS (ASSOC (CAR E) A) (EVLIS (CDR E) A)) A))))
      ((EQ (CAAR E) 'LABEL)
        (EVAL (CONS (CADDAR E) (CDR E)) (CONS (LIST (CADAR E) (CAR E)) A)))
      ((EQ (CAAR E) 'LAMBDA)
        (EVAL (CADDAR E) (APPEND (PAIR (CADAR E) (EVLIS (CDR E) A)) A))))))
  (EVCON (LAMBDA (C A)
    (COND
      ((EVAL (CAAR C) A) (EVAL (CADAR C) A))
      (T (EVCON (CDR C) A)))))
  (EVLIS (LAMBDA (M A)
    (COND
      ((NULL M) NIL)
      (T (CONS (EVAL (CAR M) A) (EVLIS (CDR M) A)))))))
```

grams have certain properties if implementations never reflect these properties. Thus we feel obliged to relate denotational valuations to valuations which are 'operational', in that they model particular implementations by providing finite representations of the values associated with labels and procedures. *Robert Milne and Christopher Strachey* [15]

The discussion of the role of expression-based languages in the system development cycle, as presented in Section 26.1, was based on the concept that an expression-based representation described *what* a system would do, whereas an interpreter for that expression

would describe *how* that activity would be achieved. This distinction has recently been recognized in the more general discipline of programming language semantics. Initial attempts at semantics tended to be purely *operational*. The semantics of a language was essentially some abstraction of a definition of a compiler for that language. (This was the general approach of the Vienna Definition Language [16].) More recently, the *denotational* approach to semantics has attempted to relate the meaning of a program to its constituent structure, attempting to maintain referential transparency in the program structure.

The best way to demonstrate the denota-

SYNTACTIC DOMAINS:

Ξ:*Var*	VARIABLES
E:*Exp*	EXPRESSIONS
Γ:*Cmd*	COMMANDS
Ψ:*Prog*	PROGRAM

PRODUCTIONS:

E ::= "0"	CONSTANT
|Ξ	VARIABLE
| *Succ* E	OPERATION
Γ ::= Γ_1; Γ_2	SEQUENCING
|Ξ := E	ASSIGNMENT
| *To* E *Do* Γ	REPETITION
|(Γ)	PARENTHESIZATION

Ψ ::= *Read* Ξ; Γ; *Write* E

Figure 26.1. Abstract syntax of the LOOP language.

tional approach is with an example. R. D. Tennent [6] prepared such an example for the extremely simple LOOP language. The abstract syntax for this language is given in Figure 26.1.

The basic task of denotational semantics is to define interpretation functions for the individual syntactic domains of the language. Thus, for each syntactic domain it is necessary to postulate a function and determine both its range and its action. In this example, it will be assumed that LOOP operates only on N, the set of non-negative integers.

Under this assumption, an interpretation function for *Prog* may be given as follows:

$$\mathcal{M}:Prog \to (N \to N)$$

In words, this means that the interpretation function $\mathcal{M}$ maps every program into a function over the non-negative integers. Thus, every program has as its "meaning" a function that maps a non-negative integer to a non-negative integer.

Variables are interpreted in terms of the existence of *states*. S will stand for the set of all possible states that associate values with variables. Symbolically:

$$S = Var \to N$$

Thus, S is actually a set of interpretation functions for *Var*.

Given the set S, the interpretation function for expressions may be given as follows:

$$\mathcal{E}:Exp \to (S \to N)$$

Thus, the meaning of an expression is a function that maps a state into a non-negative integer. Finally, the interpretation function for commands is simply a state transition function:

$$\mathcal{C}:Cmd \to (S \to S)$$

All that remains now is to stipulate the actual behavior of these interpretation functions. For expressions, commands, and programs, these descriptions will be based on the productions of the abstract syntax. For variables, it will be necessary to notate the updating of a state. Thus, if $\sigma \in S$ is a state, the notation $\sigma[\nu/\Xi]$ will stand for the alteration of that state in which the variable Ξ is now mapped to the non-negative integer ν. More formally, $\sigma[\nu/\Xi]$ is the state σ' whose functional definition is as follows:

$$\sigma'(\Xi) = \nu$$
$$\sigma'(\Xi') = \sigma(\Xi') \text{ for all } \Xi' \neq \Xi$$

Since there is only one production for programs, $\mathcal{M}$ need only be defined for any input of the form:

$$read\ \Xi;\ \Gamma;\ write\ E$$

for any variable Ξ, command Γ, and expression E. Since $\mathcal{M}$ will map this program into a function over the integers, the definition of $\mathcal{M}$ may be defined in terms of an integer input ν as follows:

$$\mathcal{M}(read\ \Xi;\ \Gamma;\ write\ \text{E})\nu = \mathcal{E}(\text{E})\sigma_f$$
$$\text{where } \sigma_f = \mathcal{C}(\Gamma)(\sigma_i[\nu/\Xi])$$
$$\text{where } \sigma_i(\Xi') = 0 \text{ for all } \Xi' \in Var$$

This may be interpreted in words as the following sequential process:

1. σ_i is defined to be the *initial state* that maps all variables to 0.

2. An integer ν is read as input and assigned to the variable Ξ; this causes σ_i to be updated to the new state $\sigma_i[\nu/\Xi]$.
3. This new state is passed as input to the state transition function $\mathcal{C}(\Gamma)$, which interprets the body of the program Γ. The result of this transition is the state σ_f.
4. The integer output is the result of interpreting the expression E given the state σ_f.

The definition for $\mathcal{E}$ can be stated in terms of the three productions for expressions. It is much more straightforward:

$$\mathcal{E}(\text{``0''})\sigma = 0$$
$$\mathcal{E}(\Xi)\sigma = \sigma(\Xi)$$
$$\mathcal{E}(succ\ \text{E})\sigma = \mathcal{E}(\text{E})\sigma + 1$$

(Note that the quotation marks distinguish the syntactic construct for the constant zero from the numerical quantity $0 \in N$.)

The definition of $\mathcal{C}$ may be given in a similar manner:

$$\mathcal{C}((\Gamma)) = \mathcal{C}(\Gamma)$$
$$\mathcal{C}(\Gamma_1; \Gamma_2) = \mathcal{C}(\Gamma_2)(\mathcal{C}(\Gamma_1))$$
$$\mathcal{C}(\Xi := \text{E})\sigma = \sigma[\mathcal{E}(\text{E})\sigma/\Xi]$$
$$\mathcal{C}(to\ \text{E}\ do\ \Gamma)\sigma = ((\mathcal{C}(\Gamma)^\nu)\sigma$$
$$\text{where } \nu = \mathcal{E}(\text{E})\sigma$$

(This last line defines iteration as a ν-fold composition, where $(\mathcal{C}(\Gamma)^0)$ is simply the identity function.)

This completes the denotational semantic definition of LOOP. Note that this definition has made no commitment to any operational implementation. It is also worth noting that almost all of the complexity of the definition stems from the necessity to interpret commands in terms of states. Thus, while the definition of LOOP is relatively simple, simplicity of definition is even more evident in languages whose syntactic domains are restricted to expressions.

Contributions of Backus

Closed Applicative Languages.

Up to this point, everything is static; the elements of E do not move; they do not light up, make noise,

or otherwise show signs of life. We have sketched many pictures of elements of E and *on the paper,* on these diagrams, we can move *our* fingers or shift *our* eyes back and forth. The abstract elements of E remain impassive, however, and must remain so, frozen in the eternal realm of ideas. But they neither expect or want our pity. And, we are free to study them, to talk about them as we do of works of art.   *Dana Scott* [17]

The work of John Backus has primarily been concerned with a view of programs as static mathematical objects whose properties may be determined by elementary algebraic methods. His initial efforts concentrated on a restricted class of programming languages that he called "closed applicative languages," This class may be defined as follows [18]:

One begins with the general definition of a *language* (or *programming language*). This is a triple (E, D, σ) where E is a set of *expressions,* D is a *domain of discourse,* and σ is a *semantic relation* with domain E and range D. The language is said to be *complete* if it satisfies three properties:

1. The domain of discourse is a subset of the set of expressions.
2. The semantic relation is a partial function from E onto D.
3. The domain of discourse is the set of fixed points of the semantic relation.

In this case, the domain of discourse is called the set of *constants* and is generally represented by C. Similarly, the semantic relation may be called the *semantic function* and is generally designated by μ.

Every complete language may have a *constructor syntax.* This is a pair (A, K) that satisfies the following three properties:

1. $A \subseteq E$.
2. Each $k \in K$ is a function from a subset Sk of E^n (for some non-negative integer n) into E.
3. Every $e \in E$ is either an element of A or is equal to $k[e1, \ldots, en]$ for some unique $k \in K$ and unique $e1, \ldots, en \in E$.

An *applicative language* is a complete language (E, C, μ) with constructor syntax (A, K) such that:

1. $A \subset C$.
2. There is a two-place constructor $ap \in K$ such that for all $e, f \in E$: $\mu(ap[e, f]) = \mu(ap[\mu(e), \mu(f)])$.
3. $\mu(kn[e1, \ldots, en]) = kn[\mu(e1), \ldots, \mu(en)]$
   for every other $kn \in K$.

Finally, an applicative language is *closed* if there exists a *representation function* ρ for it. This function has the following properties:

1. It is total over C.
2. It maps every constant $c \in C$ into a partial function $\rho c \in [C \to E]$.
3. For all $c, d \in C$: $\mu(ap[c, d]) = \mu([\rho c](d))$.

For a trivial example of a closed applicative language, let $C = A = N \cup \{succ\}$, where N is the set of non-negative integers as in the semantics of LOOP. Suppose ap is the only element of K. This is an applicative language, and an appropriate representation function ρ may be defined as follows:

1. For all $x \in N$, ρx is the constant function that maps all $y \in C$ to x.
2. $\rho succ$ is the successor function g. g maps every $y \in N$ to $y + 1$ and maps *succ* to itself.

Reduction Languages.

The ability to define an unlimited number of powerful modifiers of various types is one of the most interesting features of Red languages. They offer the chance to provide almost any conceivable semantic ability without the slightest change in the simple syntax of Red languages. Contrast this ability with that of Algol, for example. If Algol lacked its *for* statement, it would be impossible to introduce a procedure within Algol which would provide the facilities of *for* without first introducing new syntactic structures.   *John Backus* [19]

Reduction languages (also called "Red languages") provide a bridge from the formal properties of closed applicative languages to the operational capabilities of functional programming. Historically speaking, their development preceded that of functional program-

ming, and they essentially evolved as a special class of closed applicative languages. However, rather than reconstruct this development, it will be sufficient for this exposition to demonstrate the means by which closed applicative languages provide a formal view of functional programming.

The crux of this approach lies in the proper selection of a constructor syntax. Clearly, the ap constructor is used to designate operator-operand combinations. In addition, functional programming expressions will involve not only atomic constituents but also sequences of finite length, whose elements may be either atomic constituents or other sequences. In terms of a constructor syntax, every sequence of length n, $\langle x_1, \ldots, x_n \rangle$, arises through the constructor σn, i.e., $\langle x_1, \ldots, x_n \rangle = \sigma n[x_1, \ldots, x_n]$. There is also a zero-place constructor ω that stands for the "undefined" object $\perp$.

The primary purpose of the representation function ρ is to represent semantics strictly in terms of functional composition. All operators are classified according to a *meta predicate,* which serves to distinguish functions from functionals. The former are composed by regular composition; the latter are composed by *meta composition,* which provides the machinery for synthesizing new functions. Finally, a *definition function* Γ allows for the synthesis of a set of definitions. This provides all the necessary components for a functional programming language.

Variable-Free Programming.

This program . . . does not name its arguments or any intermediate results; contains no variables, no loops, no control statements nor procedure declarations; has no initialization instructions; is not word-at-a-time in nature; is hierarchically constructed from simpler components; uses generally applicable housekeeping forms and operators . . . ; is perfectly general; yields $\perp$ whenever its argument is inappropriate in any way; does not constrain the order of evaluation unnecessarily . . . ; and, using algebraic laws . . . , can be transformed into more "efficient" or into more "explanatory" programs. . . . None of these properties hold for the typical von Neuman . . . program.   *John Backus* [1]

Functional programming expressions are composed from the elements of a Backus FP (functional programming) system [1]. Such a system comprises the following:

1. A set O of *objects*
2. A set F of *functions* that map objects into objects
3. An operation, *application*
4. A set of *functionals,* used to combine existing functions and objects to form new functions in F
5. A set D of *definitions* that define some functions in F and assign a name to each

The programming capabilities of such a system may be demonstrated through the simple example of a program that computes the inner product of two vectors. The FP system will include functions that perform addition and multiplication. In addition, it will be assumed that a single vector will be represented as a sequence of numbers; so the input to the inner product function will be a pair (i.e., sequence of length two) of vectors. Consequently, the existence of a *transposition* function will also be assumed. Thus, for example, an input such as $\langle\langle 1, 2, 3\rangle, \langle 6, 5, 4\rangle\rangle$ will be mapped by Trans, the transposition function. to $\langle\langle 1, 6\rangle, \langle 2, 5\rangle, \langle 3, 4\rangle\rangle$.

The definition of inner product will require three functionals. The simplest of the three is composition, represented by the symbol ○. This is simply composition in the ordinary mathematical sense; if f and g are functions, then $f○g$ is the function that consists of first applying g and then applying f to the intermediate result. The second functional, called Insert, is represented by the symbol /. It applies a function pairwise to successive elements of a vector. accumulating the result; for example, $/+$ will add up all the elements in a vector of numbers. The third functional, ApplyToAll (α), extends a function by applying it to every element of a vector.

This defines enough of an FP system to present an expression defining the inner product function:

$$Def\ IP \equiv (/+)○(\alpha\times)○Trans$$

At the top level, this is a composition of three functions, the first of which is simple transposition. This has already been demonstrated for a typical input, and the result will be a sequence of pairs. Each of these pairs will be multiplied, according to the operation of the ApplyToAll functional. If the original input, as above, is $\langle\langle 1, 2, 3\rangle, \langle 6, 5, 4\rangle\rangle$ then the intermediate result at this stage would be $\langle 6, 10, 12\rangle$. Finally, $/+$ will cause the numbers in this vector to be added up, giving the inner product, 28, as the final result.

Contributions of Friedman and Wise

In the past several years I have had periodic contacts with the APL people and I find that they are very much like both ardent catholics and communists in that, when they get to certain topics, all discussions must be in their framework, otherwise no contact can be made.... I have also observed this in the past with LISP programmers and it has been very important for them.   *A. J. Perlis* [20]

The research of Daniel Friedman and David Wise at Indiana University beginning in 1976 has been primarily concerned with extending the power of pure LISP. Much of the LISP community has tended to devote considerable attention to enhancing LISP with a number of FORTRAN-like constructs in the interests of improving the efficiency of the programs. Pursuing a philosophy analogous to that of limiting control structures in structured programming, Friedman and Wise argued in favor of the original recursive style of pure LISP and posed a variety of constructs to accommodate the need for efficiency. Two of these constructs, a constructor for vector-valued functions and a replicator, are essentially functionals. The third, a suspended constructor, has demonstrated the applicability of LISP to real-time processing; and the fourth, a multiset constructor, is applicable to multiprocessing concerns. These constructs will now be summarized.

Vector-Valued Functions.   Consider the following problem: given S, a list of integers, and N, a singer integer, construct a list of three lists: the first consisting of those elements of S that are less than N, the second the elements of S that are equal to N, and the third the elements of S that are greater than N. (This function is particularly useful for certain sorting algorithms [21].) The most straightforward solution to this problem in LISP would be the that given in Example 26.5. (The definitions of EQ and GT have the same form as that of LT.)

The easiest way to understand this example is to work through it line by line. The square brackets are *vector constructors*. Vectors are essentially the same as lists; they are generally used in contexts in which the list in question is of a known length. Thus, if S is empty, the result will be a vector of three empty vectors (lists). Now, using the general strategy of recursive programming, assume a vector that is the result of sorting (CDR S); how would

---

Example 26.5

```
(DEFINE
  (LT-EQ-GT (LAMBDA (N S)
    (LIST (LT N S) (EQ N S) (GT N S))))
  (LT (LAMBDA (N S)
    (COND
      ((NULL S) ())
      ((LESSP (CAR S) N) (CONS (CAR S) (LT N (CDR S))))
      (T (LT N (CDR S))))))
  ... )
```

The problem with this solution is that it requires that the list S be scanned three times, once for each of the three lists to be constructed. On the other hand, almost any conventional FORTRAN program would be able to construct all three lists in a single pass through S. Consequently, Friedman and Wise posed a means of expressing vector-valued functions, where each element of the vector may be determined by a distinct subfunction. Their solution to the problem is in Example 26.6

(CAR S) be incorporated into this vector? Clearly, it will be added to one of the three lists in the vector, depending upon its arithmetic relation to N. This is expressed by the remainder of the definition. Suppose (CAR S) is greater than N. The result is given by the following expression:

```
([1   1   CONS ]
 [#   # (CAR S)]
 (LT-EQ-GT N (CDR S)))
```

Example 26.6

```
(DEFINE
  (LT-EQ-GT (LAMBDA (N S)
    (COND
      ((NULL S) [[] [] []])
      ((GREATERP (CAR S) N) ([1    1    CONS ]
                             [#    #    (CAR S)]
                             (LT-EQ-GT N (CDR S))))
      ((LESSP (CAR S) N) ([CONS    1    1       ]
                          [CAR S)  #    #       ]
                          (LT-EQ-GT N (CDR S))))
      (T ([1    CONS    1     ]
          [#    (CAR S) #     ]
          (LT-EQ-GT N (CDR S))))))))
```

This construction represents the application of three distinct functions to the three elements of the vector resulting from (LT-EQ-GT N (CDR S)). The third of these functions is CONS, whose first argument is (CAR S) and whose second element is the third component of the result vector. The other two functions are identity functions; the fact that their only argument is retrieved from the result is indicated by the # in the second list. Thus, each "column" of this expression represents an element of the result vector. In this manner, the entire sorting operation will be performed by a single pass through the list S. More recently, Friedman and Wise have turned to a less LISP-like notation; their current notation of this solution is as follows:

lt-eq-gt:⟨n s⟩ ≡
    if null:⟨s⟩ *then* ⟨⟨⟩ ⟨⟩ ⟨⟩⟩
    elseif greater:⟨first:⟨s⟩ n⟩
        then⟨1 1 cons⟩:⟨
            ⟨# # first:⟨s⟩⟩
            lt-eq-gt:⟨n rest:⟨s⟩⟩⟩
    elseif less:⟨first:⟨s⟩ n⟩
        then⟨cons   1 1⟩:⟨
            ⟨first:⟨s⟩ # #⟩
            lt-eq-gt:⟨n rest:⟨s⟩⟩⟩
    else⟨1   cons   1⟩:⟨
        ⟨# first:⟨s⟩ #⟩
        lt-eq-gt:⟨n rest:⟨s⟩⟩⟩

The Star Operator. Given the ability to represent a vector of functions, it would also be desirable to represent a vector of replications of the *same* function. This is essentially the role of ApplyToAll, where it was necessary to construct pairwise products from the numbers in two vectors. Friedman and Wise represent the replication of a function within a vector by the Kleene star (*). Thus, they define the inner product function as follows [21]:

dotproduct:⟨v1 v2⟩ ≡ sum:⟨product*⟩:⟨
                    v1
                    v2   ⟩

Thus, the input to *sum* is the result of a vector-valued function with as many replications of *product* as there are elements in the input vec-

tors. The star operator may also be applied to data. For example, the following expression yields the result of adding 1 to every element of the vector x:

⟨sum*⟩:⟨
⟨ 1* ⟩
   x   ⟩

Suspended Evaluation.

If it were done, when 'tis done, then 'twere well It were done quickly. *William Shakespeare* [22]

Suspended evaluation is concerned with a reinterpretation of the primitive functions *first, rest* (formerly CAR and CDR), and *cons*. The basic operation of the LISP interpreter is based on a protocol that in every operator-operand combination, the operator cannot "take action" until after the operand is evaluated. Friedman and Wise have proposed to relieve the function *cons* of this protocol, with particularly fruitful results for multiprogramming and real-time systems [21, 23]. (The lazy evaluator of Peter Henderson and James Morris [24] embodies a similar proposal.)

The term *manifest* [25] is used to describe the sort of data structure that is actually formed by *cons* after its arguments have been evaluated. This structure, called a *cons-cell*, consists of two fields that are extracted by the selector functions *first* and *rest*. Alternatively, it is possible to consider a data structure that is not completely manifest; such a data structure is said to be *promised*. Promised structures may be implemented by *suspended references,* references to all information necessary to evaluate a given argument at a given point in time. That information is sufficient to *coerce* the reference to its ultimate value whenever appropriate. A manifest structure has had all its suspended references coerced, but coercion never has to take place until a selector function actually accesses a field containing a suspended reference.

Consider the simple LISP examples discussed earlier in this section, under the assumption that the atom X has the value

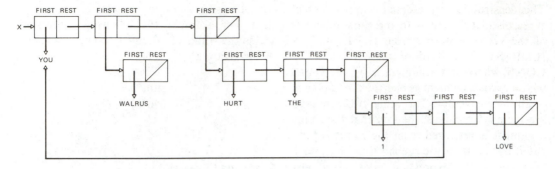

Figure 26.2. A totally manifest data structure.

(YOU (WALRUS) (HURT THE (1 YOU LOVE))). If the data structure corresponding to this value is entirely manifest, then it may be illustrated as in Figure 26.2 [14]. The fact that X has a value is depicted by the arrow emanating from X. The cons-cells are illustrated as double-chambered rectangles, the left and right chambers corresponding to the "first" and "rest" fields, respectively. These chambers are all sources of arrows that point to their corresponding values. Now consider evaluation of the expression:

cons:⟨first:⟨X⟩   rest:⟨rest:⟨X⟩⟩⟩.

If all data structures are manifest, then the result of this evaluation is YOU (HURT THE (1 YOU LOVE))), as illustrated in Figure 26.3. If, on the other hand, all data structures are not necessarily manifest, Figure 26.4 illustrates the result of evaluating the same expression using suspended references. The arrows emanating from the "first" and "rest" fields of the new cons-cell now point to suspended references, represented by "clouds," each one of which contains an expression to be evaluated

and an *environment* specifying the variable bindings to be assumed when that evaluation takes place.

Because *first* requires a list as its input, we know that this input must take the form of a data structure generated by *cons*. The "action" of *first* will be to inspect the "first" field of the corresponding cons-cell to see if it contains a value or a suspended reference. If it contains a suspended reference, the promised evaluation is performed; the result overwrites the promise and is returned as output. Thus, evaluating the expression:

first:⟨cons:⟨first:⟨X⟩   rest:⟨rest:⟨X⟩⟩⟩⟩

yields the atom YOU as output, but it also updates the associated data structure, as in Figure 26.5; rest operates in a similar manner.

The applicability of suspended evaluation to real-time processing may be demonstrated by the MERGE function. This function was defined to operate on two predefined (i.e., manifest) lists of numbers. However, these lists could just as easily have been constructed by a suspended CONS. They could be located on

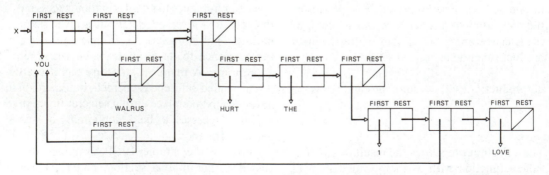

Figure 26.3. Manifestation of cons:⟨first:⟨x⟩rest:⟨rest:⟨x⟩⟩⟩.

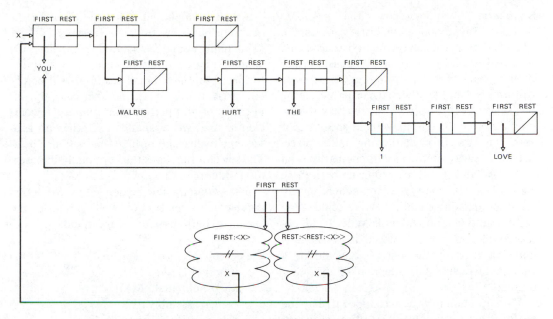

Figure 26.4. Evaluation of cons:⟨first:⟨x⟩rest:⟨rest: ⟨x⟩⟩⟩ using suspended references.

disk files, in which case the suspension essentially corresponds to the action of the disk controller. They could even be lists typed in realtime at two separate terminals. However, the definition is formulated in such a way as to specify how much of the list must be manifest in order for the merge operation to proceed. If more of one of the lists is manifest, that amounts to buffering information before it is needed. If a required element is not yet manifest, it means that the merge operation will have to wait until it is available.

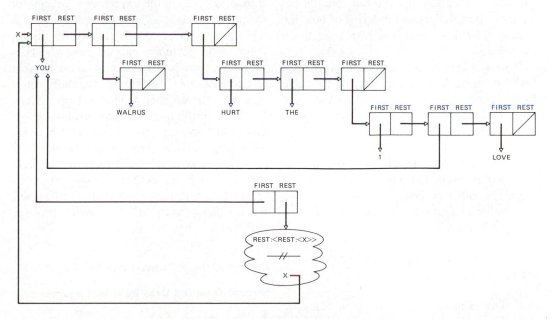

Figure 26.5. Evaluation of first:⟨cons:⟨first:⟨x⟩rest:⟨rest:⟨x⟩⟩⟩⟩ coerces a suspended reference.

Multisets. Consider, now, the *assembly* function [14], a nondeterministic variation on MERGE. Suppose the two input lists are being provided in real time from terminals. Rather than merging these inputs, however, *assembly* will simply "shuffle" them: the orderings of the two sources will be preserved; but they will be interleaved in the output, without specific concern for how this interleaving takes place. MERGE always performed its comparisons on (CAR A) and (CAR B), requiring both these elements to be manifest. Consequently, any real-time delay from either source could delay the merging operation. On the other hand, *assembly* should not be delayed if no input is manifest at one of the sources; it should know enough to devote full attention to the other source.

This situation may be accommodated by the *multiset* data structure. A multiset is distinguished from a list in that no order is imposed on its elements. (The term *multiset* is used because there may be multiple elements of a multiset that are identical, a situation that does not obtain for sets [26].) Multisets are constructed by the function *frons,* which, analogous to *cons,* takes two arguments, an expression and a multiset. (The etymology of *frons* is given in Reference 27.) Also, like *cons, frons* suspends evaluation of its arguments; its behavior is best understood in terms of how the selector functions, *first* and *rest,* operate on multisets.

If *first* is applied to some multiset m, then that m must have been created by some frons: $\langle o\ M \rangle$, for some expression o and some other multiset M. The value of first:$\langle m \rangle$ may now be determined by one of two cases:

1. The value of first:$\langle m \rangle$ *can* be the value of o if evaluation of o is not undefined.
2. The value of first:$\langle m \rangle$ *can also* be the value of first:$\langle M \rangle$ if evaluation of first:$\langle M \rangle$ is not undefined.

For each of these cases, there is a corresponding interpretation of *rest:*

1. The value of rest:$\langle m \rangle$ is the multiset M.
2. The value of rest:$\langle m \rangle$ is the value of frons:$\langle o$ rest:$\langle M \rangle \rangle$.

As an example, let the value of m be the multiset built by frons:$\langle 1$ frons:$\langle 2$ NIL$\rangle \rangle$. (This multiset may be notated {1 2}.) Then the value of first:$\langle m \rangle$ may be either 1 or 2. In the former case, the value of rest:$\langle m \rangle$ will be {2}; otherwise, it will be {1}. In either case, the application of *first* performs an *immutable* coercion; if first:$\langle m \rangle$ evaluates to 2, then all subsequent evaluations of first:$\langle m \rangle$ will also be 2. The selector functions thus gradually impose a total order on an unordered set.

assembly may now be defined as a function that expects a multiset of two lists built by the terminal controllers for its argument:

assembly:M ≡
  if null:$\langle$M$\rangle$ *then* NIL
  elseif null:$\langle$first:$\langle$M$\rangle \rangle$
    then assembly:rest:$\langle$M$\rangle$
  else cons:$\langle$first:$\langle$first:$\langle$M$\rangle \rangle$
      assembly:frons:$\langle$rest:$\langle$first:$\langle$M$\rangle \rangle$
      rest:$\langle$M$\rangle \rangle \rangle$

Several explanatory comments are in order. First of all, no structural commitment is made regarding the input to *assembly;* according to the body of the definition, if M is not NIL, then all that is required is that it have "first" and "rest" components, which happens to be true of all values of expressions except for atomic constituents. The assumption that M is a multiset is merely consistent with the use of *frons* in the recursive call of *assembly.* Furthermore, there is no constraint on the number of elements in M. The size is essentially determined by the number of terminal controllers. What is important is that evaluation of first: $\langle$M$\rangle$ implies that *some* terminal has something ready for processing. One final observation: *cons* is still building suspended references, but if the output of *assembly* is directed to a terminal, then that terminal will reflect the activity of the input pool of terminals.

Contributions of Frankel and Myers

Stream-Oriented Data Base Management.

The value of infinite sequences in programming is essentially that of saving on bookkeeping; one can write programs without worrying about boundary conditions or synchronization between parts of the code. Even if it is necessary to put these in later, an uncluttered design is easier to work with. *Thomas Myers* [28]

FP systems, as defined in Reference 1, limit the domain of structured objects to finite sequences. An alternative approach is to regard all sequences as potentially infinite, so that they are actually *streams* [29]. It was possible to interpret MERGE as a real-time program because suspended evaluation allowed the processing of stream input. In fact, all real-time processing may be regarded as the manipulation of streams of values that are received on sensors and the generation of streams of values that are dispatched to effectors. This ability of expressions to accommodate stream processing has proven particularly fruitful in the area of data base management [30].

The primary result of this approach is FQL, a *functional query language*. This query language is supported by a *functional data model,* which regards a data base as a collection of *functions* over various sets of *objects* (using the terminology of FP systems). A simple example is illustrated in Figure 26.6. The object sets include employees and departments, as well as the more conventional data types of numbers, character strings, and truth values. All objects are related by functions: WORKS-IN maps every employee to a department, while ENAME maps that employee to the character string that gives his name. Every function has an *inverse,* which maps a range object into the *stream* of domain objects mapped to it by the function. Thus, the inverse of WORKS-IN, denoted !WORKS-IN, maps a single department to a stream of employees. In addition, each object set in the data base has a generating function that yields a stream of all the elements of that set; for example, *!EMPLOYEE* is a function of no inputs whose output is a stream of all employees.

Given this data model, queries may be formulated by applying functionals to the functions and objects of the data base. For example, a request for the department name and salary of all married employees may be formulated as as Example 26.7. Because this no-

Example 26.7

!EMPLOYEE . |MARRIED . *[WORKS-IN . DNAME, SAL]

A SIMPLE DATABASE

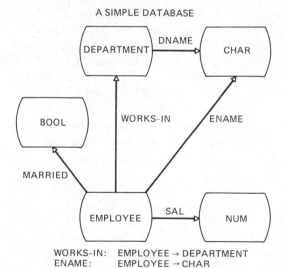

WORKS-IN: EMPLOYEE → DEPARTMENT
ENAME: EMPLOYEE → CHAR

!WORKS-IN: DEPARTMENT → *EMPLOYEE
!ENAME: CHAR → *EMPLOYEE

!EMPLOYEE: → *EMPLOYEE

Figure 26.6. A simple data base.

tation differs from Backus's it will be discussed in sufficient detail to observe the power of the functionals. Composition is represented by a period (.); but the composition of functions is now read from left to right. Thus, the expression indicates that !EMPLOYEE will first generate the stream of all employees, this stream will then be processed by the function |MARRIED, after which the output of that processing will serve as input to the function *[WORKS-IN . DNAME, SAL]. The vertical bar designates the *restriction* functional; it operates on a predicate and yields a function that *filters* a stream. In this particular example, |MARRIED takes the stream of all employees as input and yields as output a stream of those employees for which the predicate MARRIED is true. The star is again an instance of the ApplyToAll functional, and it operates on an instance of the *construction* functional. This is similar to the notation of vector-valued functions by Friedman and Wise; the square brackets enclose a tuple of functions, all of which are applied to the same input to yield a tuple of values. Thus, for each employee passed as input,

[WORKS-IN . DNAME, SAL]

will yield the pair of his or her department name and salary; and the * functional will cause this function to be applied to each member of the stream of married employees.

Transitive Closure. The streams manipulated in data base management all arise from subsets of data types and are therefore finite in most practical cases. However, the idea of a function that *generates* a stream by enumeration can be extended beyond simple set member enumeration. Truly infinite streams may be obtained through use of the *transitive closure* functional. Given a function f whose domain and range are the same set α, this function can be applied repeatedly to the results of previous applications. The transitive closure of f thus maps elements of α to streams of elements of α. Such a stream is constructed according to the "classical" definition of transitive closure. For example, letting & stand for transitive closure, $\&f$ is the function that maps $x \in \alpha$ to the stream whose first element is x. whose second element is $f(x)$, whose third element is $f(f(x))$, and, in general, whose ith element is $f^{i-1}(x)$.

Perhaps the most interesting feature of transitive closure is that it transcends a need for recursion in the formulation of many algorithms. Consider a typical recursive algorithm for computing the greatest common divisor of two positive integers (given in Example 26.8 in LISP). This definition is straightforward

&[[MAX, MIN] . DIFFERENCE, MIN]
|EQUAL . FIRST . MAX

The recursion step of the LISP program has now been transformed into a function that generates successive stream elements through transitive closure. The first time a pair of equal integers appears in this stream. it will correspond to the greatest common divisor. The restriction function will extract elements with this property, and FIRST will extract the first of them. MAX then extracts a single integer from the pair.

Combinatory Programming.

One soon learns to appreciate equations. And, the equations are more precise as well as being more perspicuous—though sometimes they become so involved as to be unreadable. *Dana Scott* [17]

Up to this point, the exposition has been heading toward more and more generality regarding the nature of expressions. At this stage, an expression may be regarded simply as a *combination* of objects, functions, and functionals, a view that essentially has its "roots" in combinatory logic [32]. The actual *structure* of these combinations is not germane. What is important, however, is that certain combinations may be *reduced* to other combinations: combinations of functions and objects will yield objects, whereas combinations of functionals, functions, and objects will yield functions (which, if combined with objects, will then yield objects). This basic mechanism of *combination reduction* embodies the traditional view of *expression evaluation*.

Example 26.8

```
(DEFINE
  (GCD (LAMBDA (A B)
    (COND
      ((EQUAL A B) A)
      (T (GCD (DIFFERENCE (MAX A B) (MIN A B)) (MIN A B)))))))
```

---

enough, but it is also possible to represent the computation through the generation of a stream of integer pairs that give the intermediate results [31]:

The "state of the art" of combinatory programming is currently undergoing considerable development. The major contribution is the design of the ASTRAL language at the University of Pennsylvania [31]. This language combines the spirit of FP systems, the basic structure of FQL, and the facility for defining functionals, as well as functions, based on a technique introduced in APL [33].

Relation to Data-Flow Research

We thus do not teach you how to swim through the channels of the flow diagram, but content ourselves with telling you what you look like when you come out as a function of what you looked like when you jumped in. Dana Scott [17]

Recent research in computer architecture has become involved with alternatives to the configuration of a single, centralized processor connected to a single, centralized memory. A data-flow computer is a loosely coupled configuration of special-purpose functions that receive their inputs and return their outputs through special-purpose communication channels. There is no common memory; each function is totally encapsulated. Furthermore, because all the functions are disjoint, they may

operate asynchronously, depending upon whether or not there is input waiting to be processed.

Considerable attention has been devoted to the design of languages to specify the configurations and behaviors of data-flow computers. The nature of the structure of such architectures tends to favor languages with referential transparency. An excellent example is Flow Graph LISP [34], which is essentially a data-flow interpretation of LISP expressions. As an example, the above *assembly* example is shown in FGL in Figure 26.7. Since data flow through this graph according to a demand-driven protocol, its behavior is very similar to that of LISP with suspended evaluation.

A similar project has been undertaken at the University of California at Irvine [35]. In this case, however, the language has a syntax that is more traditional. Expressions have local variables corresponding to input lines, as well as labels for intermediate connections. However, to maintain a data-flow protocol the language is constrained in such a way that a value may be assigned to a variable at most once in

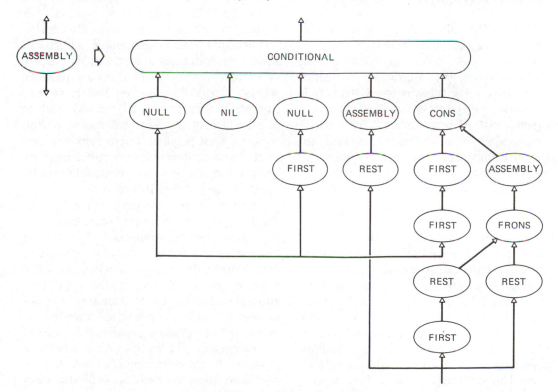

Figure 26.7. FGL definition of *assembly*.

an expression. Thus, there is always a straight-forward interpretation of every expression as a data-flow graph.

This concern for the single-assignment rule has all but overwhelmed the initial motivation for data-flow computation in the development of the VAL language at MIT [36]. All of the traditional concerns for variables are present here. The language is "applicative" by virtue of the single-assignment rule, but it has drifted far from the relation of data flow to referential transparency.

10.3. CURRENT STATUS

Techniques and Tools

Applicative and Functional Thinking.

. . . there is a desperate need for a powerful methodology to help us think about programs, and no conventional language even begins to meet that need. In fact, conventional languages create unnecessary confusion in the way we think about programs.   *John Backus* [1]

Methodologically speaking, the primary objective of the functional style is to make programming look more like mathematics. Expressions are, after all, clean mathematical objects, and if the behavior of a system can be expressed as a system of equations, then these equations should pretty much define the associated program in an expression-based language. Unfortunately, so many programmers become so wrapped up in the minutiae of accommodating the von Neumann architecture that this relatively elementary observation tends to escape them.

Applicative and functional languages have had to live with a reputation of being hard to learn. Nevertheless, at several academic institutions, these languages have thrived when they are taught as first languages. The learning difficulty seems to be one of shaking off the bad habits of the von Neumann tradition. There is too much of a tendency to regard programming as the skillful manipulation of variables. This is a tragic injustice: Programming is no more concerned with variables than mathematics is with numbers. Anyone com-fortable with the mathematical notion of a function will be just as comfortable with the machinery of the functional style of programming.

There is, however, a potential shortcoming. The popularity of personal computing may bring about an age where children will learn about BASIC before they learn about mathematical functions. This may yet be the final triumph of the von Neumann style. There is a clear and present danger that our very view of mathematics will be eroded by our approach to computing, whereas the influence really ought to be the other way around.

Language Support.

If you are convinced of the usefulness of the procedure concept and are surrounded by implementations in which the overhead of the procedure mechanism imposes too great a penalty, then blame these inadequate implementations instead of raising them to the level of standards!   *Edsger W. Dijkstra* [37]

As should be evident from Section 26.2, there is no shortage of languages for applicative and functional programming; and most of these languages enjoy at least a modest degree of support. Almost all of them are provided with some sort of *interpreter*. The tradition of interpreter support goes all the way back to LISP, which, in its original batch environment, was not very popular. Interpreters are certainly more conducive to interactive programming, a fact that has now been established by the popularity of BASIC and APL.

There has been some work on the development of compilers for some of these languages. Several impressive compilers for LISP have been developed, and the work of Friedman and Wise began with an attempt to design a LISP compiler based strictly on the applicative structure of pure LISP. However, the increased availability of powerful processing circuitry and the growing popularity of interactive computing have led to a greater interest in powerful interpreters, some of which may eventually form the basis for dedicated computer architectures.

As Backus has observed, programs that are

clean mathematical objects are readily susceptible to mathematical manipulation. This is particularly important in the area of verification. Research in both denotational and axiomatic semantics, though extremely impressive, has done much to reveal just how unwieldy von Neumann languages can be. Therefore, it should come as no surprise that one of the best performing verification systems has been built around pure LISP [38]. Equally impressive is Backus's proof of a matrix multiplication function [1]. This proof is based entirely on the manipulation of equations that serve as theorems describing the behavior of functions in an FP system.

Finally, there is the somewhat unpleasant issue of debugging. In the best of all possible worlds, of course, one's programs never *need* debugging. However, several systems built around interpreters have extended the capabilities of their interpreters to aid the user in the event of a run-time error. The most impressive of these systems is the interpreter for INTER-LISP [39]. This system includes a thorough "break package" that is essentially capable of recovering all intermediate results accumulated by the interpreter to inform the user as to the progress of his or her program. In addition, the interpreter is provided with a tracing facility that can determine the input-output behavior of any specified set of functions.

Specific Applications

We have encapsulated all indeterminism in data structures ... where the programmer may ignore it after he has specified his multiset. A significant contribution of the applicative style to this development is the experience with an applicative regimen which allows the *simple* introduction of indeterminate behavior as a trivial twist in programming style. *Daniel P. Friedman and David S. Wise* [27]

So far the only specific example of a working system defined in the functional style has been the discussion of FQL. Two examples of system *designs* are given here: an airline reservation system and a radar detection and designation system. Neither constitutes an implementation. Rather, these examples serve to demonstrate specific aspects of the functional style that are conducive to describing real-time systems.

An Airline Reservation System. This somewhat simplified example illustrates the basic approach to applicative multiprogramming advocated by Friedman and Wise [40]. Assume a single plane with a fixed capacity and an arbitrary number of terminals receiving reservation and cancellation messages. Reservations are either acknowledged or rejected with a message that the plane is full. The input is thus a multiset of "files" corresponding to the commands from the different terminals and a constant value specifying the capacity. The top-level structure is as follows:

airlinereservationsystem:⟨files capacity⟩ ≡
fanout:genresponses:⟨fanin:⟨files naturals⟩ capacity⟩

fanin is an extension of the *assembly* function given earlier. It not only assembles the messages from the multiple terminals into a single list but also marks each message with a natural number corresponding to the source of the message. This number is then used by *fanout* to route the response back to the appropriate terminal. *genresponses* thus takes as its input a list of command-source pairs and produces a list of response-source pairs to be routed by *fanout*.

genresponses is defined as given in Example 26.9. *gen* keeps track of both vacancies and capacity, checking for erroneous commands and updating the vacancies for valid commands. Also, any command that is not recognized will return the current number of vacancies.

A Ballistic Missile Defense Construct. Figure 26.8 illustrates another example, both as a flow graph and as an FQL expression. This is a component of a "typical" construct for ballistic missile defense (BMD). The construct may best be defined in terms of an environment consisting of three radar devices— a *search radar,* a *designation radar,* and a *tracking radar.* These three devices are capable of progressively finer resolution in their scanning power. The search radar performs a "coarse" scan of its field of view for an initial

Example 26.9

genresponses:⟨pairs capacity⟩ ≡
   gen:⟨first:⟨pairs⟩ rest:⟨pairs⟩ capacity capacity⟩

Gen is an auxiliary function that processes one pair at a time, creating the next pair to be routed by *fanout:*

gen:⟨⟨command index⟩ pairs vacancies capacity⟩ ≡
  if isrequest:⟨command⟩ *then*
    if iszero:⟨vacancies⟩ *then* cons:⟨⟨"full" index⟩ gen:⟨first:⟨pairs⟩
                                rest:⟨pairs⟩
                                vacancies
                                capacity⟩⟩
       else cons:⟨⟨"ok" index⟩ gen:⟨ first:⟨pairs⟩
                            rest:⟨pairs⟩
                            pred:⟨vacancies⟩
                            capacity⟩⟩
  elseif iscancellation:⟨request⟩ *then*
    if equal:⟨vacancies capacity⟩ *then* cons:⟨⟨"empty" index⟩ gen:⟨first:⟨pairs⟩
                                      rest:⟨pairs⟩
                                      vacancies
                                      capacity⟩⟩
       else cons:⟨⟨"cancelled" index⟩ gen:⟨first:⟨pairs⟩
                                rest:⟨pairs⟩
                                succ:⟨vacancies⟩
                                capacity⟩⟩
  else cons:⟨⟨vacancies index⟩ gen:⟨first:⟨pairs⟩
                            rest:⟨pairs⟩
                            vacancies
                            capacity⟩⟩

detection of potentially threatening objects. The designation radar is capable of observing more sharply defined volumes within its field of view and collecting a sequence of data points for deciding whether or not the observed object is actually a threatening reentry vehicle (RV). Finally, the tracking radar is capable of tracking the path of the RV well enough to predict its trajectory, information which may then be provided to the system responsible for intercepting the RV.

The construct under consideration assumes

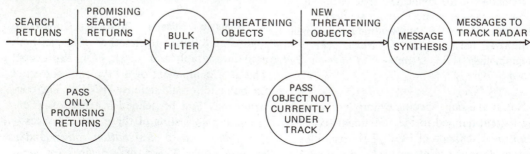

│VALID.*BULK-FILTER.│NEW.*MESSAGE-SYNTHESIS

Figure 26.8. A ballistic missile defense construct.

that the search radar and designation radar are actually the same device, while the tracking radar is a separate device that may even be geographically removed from the search/designation radar. It is thus necessary for the search/designation system to prepare *handover messages* for the tracking system. In addition, it is desired to avoid sending redundant handover messages; that is. one should not tell the tracking system about an RV it is already following. Consequently, it is assumed that the tracking system maintains a record of its progress which the search/designation system may consult before preparing a handover message.

The solution is structured as an expression that processes a stream of search returns. This stream is first restricted by the VALID predicate, which only passes those returns that are to be subjected to designation processing. This processing is performed by the BULK-FILTER function, applied to every element of the stream of promising search returns. This function is rather complicated, in that it encompasses all the activity of the designation radar; but this activity can be defined at a later level of refinement. The result is a stream of threatening objects, restricted by the predicate NEW, which only accepts objects that are not currently being tracked. The stream of objects that pass are then restructured as messages to the track radar by MESSAGE-SYNTHESIS.

Limitations

Human Engineering.

Up to this very day there is among the more theoretically inclined computing scientists still a widespread feeling that recursive programs "come more naturally" than repetitive ones. *Edsger W. Dijkstra* [37]

Claims of the "unteachability" of applicative and functional languages are generally supported by claims of the unreadability of their respective programs. There is no doubt that FP systems and FQL are inclined toward a singularly terse notation that is sometimes intimidating at first sight. Nevertheless, it is hard to understand why that which is accurate and compact should be rejected in favor of that which is obscure and verbose. The cynical observer might be inclined to believe that people reject solutions that ultimately reveal how simple the problem was in the first place.

Nevertheless, applicative and functional languages are sufficiently well structured to be able to aid any user readily intimidated by notation. Because such languages are readily interpreted, they also tend to be conducive to incremental formulation. Thus, for example, an activity known to consist of three consecutive phases will obviously involve the composition functional, after which each phase may be handled independently. There thus appears to be a wealth of opportunities for automated assistance in the formulation of applicative and functional programs, which will doubtless improve the popularity of their associated languages.

Incompatibilities with Existing Hardware. Difficulties will also arise in trying to use a von Neumann architecture to support languages based on alternative architectures. Fortunately, the highly encapsulated nature of many of these languages allows for realizations that may take advantage of a variety of multiprocessing constructs. The most powerful aspect of expression manipulation is that fairly powerful amounts of computation may be performed in isolation with relatively little excess information. Thus, such languages may be supported either by multiprocessing systems on conventional computers or by more unorthodox systems, such as microprocessor-memory arrays. Proper architectures for expression evaluation are still being evaluated and will be discussed in somewhat greater detail in the following section.

10.4. PERSPECTIVE FOR THE FUTURE

Architectures to Support Applicative and Functional Programming

If applicative and functional languages are best suited to describe the activities of dataflow computers, then, conversely, data-flow architectures seem to have the best properties for implementing these languages. Such architectures lend themselves best to the highly encapsulated nature of the primitives of the languages. Functions are simple transducers, whose only knowledge of other functions need be maintained by input and output message buffers. Objects may be manifest strictly as messages, without any concern for uniquely assigned storage locations.

The architectural implementation of functionals, however, may be a more problematic issue. It may, in fact, be possible to regard functionals as encapsulated modules that behave in an analogous manner to functions. However, this would be the case only if some sort of function description can be passed as a message to such a model. This is the situation in the Irvine data-flow computer, which actually has an explicit APPLY module [35].

Nevertheless, the proper concern of functionals is actually with the *connectivity* of the functions. Functionals say more about the protocols regarding how functions exchange messages than they do about specific modules that transform inputs into outputs. Thus, functionals should be regarded either as a specification for how a particular architecture should be "hard-wired" to realize a given expression, or they should be realized through a programmable switching mechanism, such as a crossbar, to allow for the dynamic implementation of interconnections among function modules.

Application to Hardware Description

Complementing the issue of architectures to support expression-based languages is the realization that expression-based languages may be used to *describe* architectures. The techniques applied above to real-time systems are just as applicable to digital systems, which are, after all, a special class of real-time systems. Combinational circuits are already expressed, as a matter of course, using the formulae of Boolean algebra. The primary issue involves the introduction of the flip-flop—the basic element of memory.

The information that constitutes memory is generally referred to as *state*. The combina-

tional logic of a sequential circuit embodies a *state transition function*. This function will be purely combinational if its input includes the *current state*. In other words, the state transition function is a side-effect-free transformation of the current state and some collection of external inputs. Since combinational logic is asynchronous, the question of *when* the actual state transition takes place is a crucial one. It is generally assumed that all registers will be connected to a common *clock* signal in such a way that a pulse on this signal will cause their "memories" to assume the information that has been collected on their input lines.

A sequential circuit may thus be viewed as a *stream of states*. This stream will be generated by applying the transitive closure functional to a function that embodies the combinational logic component. Each element of this stream will thus correspond to a single "tick" of the clock, or, from the opposite point of view, each clock pulse may be regarded as a request for transitive closure to generate the next element of the stream. The external inputs may be regarded as streams of digital signals whose generation does not concern the behavior of the sequential circuit itself. Sequential circuit design may thus be regarded as a three-stage process:

1. Characterize the information that constitutes *state*.
2. Extend this characterization to include a representation of external inputs.
3. Using this extended characterization as the assumed domain and range space, define a transition function that may be used as argument to the transitive closure functional.

Consider, as an example, a simple four-bit shift register whose state is given by four parallel outputs. A stream of inputs will enter "from the left," causing a right shift with every clock pulse. The first step is to represent the state of this device by a 4-tuple of logical values (0 and 1). The next step involves incorporating external inputs. In this case, there is only one external input (excluding the clock): the serial input "on the left." This will be represented by a stream of logical values. Consequently, the extended data representation will consist of a 2-tuple, whose first element is a stream of logical values corresponding to the serial input and whose second element is a 4-tuple of logical values corresponding to the state of the shift register.

The "function" of the shift register may now be easily defined in FQL. The heart of this definition will be construction functionals that construct both the 2-tuple and the 4-tuple for each element of the stream of states. These are constructed using *selector functions* represented by integers. That is, given a tuple as input, the function represented by the integer n will extract the nth element of that tuple. Thus, the FQL definition is as follows:

SHIFT = [1 . REST, [1 . 1, 2 . 1, 2 . 2, 2 . 3]]

This definition says that the function SHIFT is constructing a 2-tuple (as transitive closure demands). The first element is obtained by selecting the serial input and "advancing" it with REST. This reflects the fact that one element of serial input is "consumed" with each clock pulse. The second element of the 2-tuple is the "next state" of the shift register, which is a constructed 4-tuple. The first element of this 4-tuple is the first element of the serial input, while the remaining three elements are the first, second, and third elements of the "current state." Thus, the behavior of the shift register may be described as the transitive closure of SHIFT with the extension of the selection of the state component of the 2-tuple:

&SHIFT . *2

This composition yields a function that generates the stream of states of the shift register.

Application to Simulation

So they rolled up their sleeves and sat down to experiment—by simulation, that is, mathematically and all on paper. And the mathematical models of King Krool and the beast did such fierce battle across the equation-covered table, that the

constructors' pencils kept snapping. *Stanislaw Lem* [41]

Section 26.1 covered the use of interpreters for expression-based languages as simulation tools, with the discussion concentrated primarily on issues of functionality. Given the basic structure of an FP system, it is now possible to consider issues of performance in greater detail. In particular, any simulation based on an expression in an FP system should be capable of modeling the elements of that system in terms of the space and time resources they consume.

In modeling each object in the set O, one must consider the storage it requires (space) and the time consumed in accessing it. Two observations are necessary to clarify this remark. First of all, access time will always apply to the *entire* object. Structured objects may always be decomposed into component parts, each of which is an object unto itself. Secondly, an object will be regarded as having some *fixed* instantiation. Consequently, a data item that resides in main memory and a copy of that data item residing on a disk will always be regarded as distinct objects, which, necessarily, will have different access times.

All functions will behave operationally as transducers, transforming values received at their input ports into values placed on their output ports. Consequently, a model of time resources consumed by a function may be based on a direct port-to-port response: the time between receipt of inputs and creation of outputs. Space resources must include storage requirements for the "body" of the function (if it is an element of the definition set D or if it is a primitive module manifest as software) and for the input and output ports (which may or may not be necessary, depending upon the nature of the data themselves).

Time resources for a functional will probably best be modeled as a function of the time resources of the functions and objects that are transformed by that functional. Modeling of space resources, however, will again depend on the specific *manifestation* of the functional. This manifestation may range from a specific software driver to an interconnection of hardware components. Once again, the actual model will have to depend upon the models of the functions and objects processed by the functional.

This approach allows a variety of modeling problems to be addressed by a common methodology:

1. Classify the objects in the system under study, identifying all constants, functions, and functionals.
2. Formulate a representation of the system's functionality as an expression.
3. Define an expression interpreter corresponding to the available operational resources.
4. Define performance models for all of the objects enumerated in Step 1.
5. Run the interpreter defined in Step 3 in conjunction with the models defined in Step 4 to prepare a performance profile of the system.

The first step, that of recognizing the objects, functions, and functionals, is probably the most crucial and may demand the most creativity on the part of the systems analyst. Nevertheless, the examples presented in this chapter should be sufficient to demonstrate that this step is always *feasible* for any modeling problem.

REFERENCES

1. J. Backus, "Can Programming Be Liberated from the von Neumann Style? A Functional Style and Its Algebra of Programs," *Comm. ACM* 21(8)(Aug. 1978):613–641.
2. P. J. Landin, "The Next 700 Programming Languages," *Comm ACM* 9(3)(March 1966):157–166.
3. R. E. Frankel and S. W. Smoliar, "Beyond Register Transfer: An Algebraic Approach for Architectural Description," *Proc. 4th International Symposium on Computer Hardware Description Languages,* Palo Alto, Calif., Oct. 1979, pp. 1–5.
4. J. McCarthy, "Recursive Functions or Symbolic Expressions and Their Computation by Machine, Part I," *Comm. ACM* 3(4)(Apr. 1960):184–195.
5. W. V. Quine, *Word and Object,* Technology Press, Cambridge, Mass., 1960.
6. R. D. Tennent, "The Denotational Semantics of Programming Languages," *Comm. ACM* 19(8)(Aug., 1976):437–453.
7. A. Church, *The Calculi of Lambda-Conversion,* Kraus Reprint Corp., New York, 1965.

8. P. Zave, "Functional Specification of Asychronous Processes and Its Application to the Early Phases of System Development," Technical Report TR-775, Department of Computer Science, University of Maryland, College Park, 1979.
9. J. F. Stay, "HIPO and Integrated Program Design," in P. Freeman and A. I. Wasserman (eds.), *Tutorial on Software Design Techniques,* 2d ed., IEEE, Long Beach, Calif., 1977, pp. 174–178.
10. D. T. Ross, "Structured Analysis (SA): A Language for Communicating Ideas," ibid., pp. 149–167.
11. M. W. Shelley, *Frankenstein,* New American Library, New York, 1978, p. 52.
12. E. W. Dijkstra, "The Humble Programmer," *Comm. ACM* 15(10)(Oct. 1972):859–866.
13. D. P. Freidman, *The Little LISPer,* Science Research Associates, 1974.
14. S. W. Smoliar, "Using Applicative Techniques to Design Distributed Systems," *Proc. Specifications of Reliable Software,* Cambridge, Mass., Apr. 1979, pp. 150–161.
15. R. Milne and C. Strachey, *A Theory of Programming Language Semantics,* Halsted Press, New York, 1976.
16. P. Wegner, "The Vienna Definition Language," *Computing Surveys* 4(1)(March 1972):5–63.
17. D. S. Scott, "The Lattice of Flow Diagrams," in E. Engelar (ed.), *Symposium on the Semantics of Algorithmic Languages,* Springer-Verlag, Berlin, 1971, pp. 311–366.
18. J. Backus, "Programming Language Semantics and Closed Applicative Languages," *Conference Record, ACM Symposium on Principles of Programming Languages,* Boston, Oct. 1973, pp. 71–86.
19. J. Backus, "Reduction Languages and Variable-Free Programming," Technical Report RJ 1010, Computer Sciences, IBM Research, San Jose, Calif., 1971.
20. J. M. Buxton, P. Naur, and B. Randell, *Software Engineering: Concepts and Techniques,* Petrocelli/Charter, New York, 1976.
21. D. P. Freidman and D. S. Wise, "Aspects of Applicative Programming for Parallel Processing," *IEEE Trans. on Computers* C-27(4)(Apr. 1978):289–296.
22. W. Shakesphere, *The Riverside Shakesphere,* Houghton Mifflin, Boston, 1974, p. 1317.
23. D. P. Friedman and D. S. Wise, "Aspects of Applicative Programming for File Systems," *SIGPLAN Notices* 12(3)(March 1977) pp. 41–55. Also in *Operating Systems Review* 11(2)(Apr. 1977), and *Software Engineering* Notes 2(2)(March 1977).
24. P. Henderson and J. H. Morris, Jr., "A Lazy Evaluator," *Conf. Record 3d ACM Symposium on Principles of Programming Languages,* Atlanta, Ga., Jan. 1976, pp. 95–103.
25. D. P. Friedman and D. S. Wise, "Output Driven Interpretation of Recursive Programs, or Writing Creates and Destroys Data Structures," *Information Processing Letters* 5(6)(Dec. 1976):155–160.
26. D. E. Knuth, *The Art of Computer Programming,*

vol. 2: *Seminumerical Algorithms,* Addison-Wesley, Reading, Mass., 1969.

27. D. P. Friedman and D. S. Wise, "An Inderterminate Constructor for Applicative Programming," *Conference Record, 7th ACM Symposium on Principles of Programming Languages,* Las Vegas, Jan. 1980, pp. 245–250.

28. T. Myers, "Proposal for A Dissertation on Infinite Structures in Programming Languages," Unpublished report, Department of Computer and Information Science, University of Pennsylvania, Philadelphia, 1979.

29. W. H. Burge, *Recursive Programming Techniques,* Addison-Wesley, Reading, Mass., 1975.

30. R. E. Frankel, "FQL—The Design and Implementation of a Functional Database Query Language," Technical Report 79-05-13, Department of Decision Sciences, University of Pennsylvania, Philadelphia, 1979.

31. T. Myers, "An Algebraic Programming Language for Non-Terminating Computations," Unpublished report, Department of Computer and Information Science, University of Pennsylvania, Philadelphia, 1979.

32. H. B. Curry and R. Feys, *Combinatory Logic,* vol. I, North-Holland, Amsterdam, 1974.

33. K. E. Iverson, "Operators," *ACM Trans. on Programming Languages and Systems* 1(2)(Oct. 1979):161–176.

34. R. M. Keller. G. Lindstrom, and S. Patil, "A Loosely-Coupled Applicative Multiprocessing System," *Proc. NCC,* vol. 48, New York, 1979, pp. 861–870.

35. Arvind, K. P. Gostelow, and W. Plouffe, "The (Preliminary) Id Report: An Asynchronous Language and Computing Machine," Technical Report #114, Department of Information and Computer Science, University of California, Irvine, 1978.

36. W. B. Ackerman and J. B. Dennis, "VAL–A Value-Oriented Algorithmic Language," Unpublished report, Laboratory for Computer Science, Massachusetts Institute of Technology, Cambridge, 1978.

37. E. W. Dijkstra, *A Discipline of Programming,* Prentice-Hall, Englewood Cliffs, N.J., 1976.

38. R. S. Boyer and J. S. Moore, "Proving Theorems About LISP Functions," *Journal of the ACM* 22(1)(Jan. 1975):129–144.

39. W. Teitelman, "INTERLISP Reference Manual," XEROX, Palo Alto, Calif., 1975.

40. D. P. Friedman and D. S. Wise, "Applicative Multiprogramming," Technical Report No. 72, Computer Science Department, Indiana University, Bloomington, 1979.

41. S. Lem, *The Cyberiad: Fables for the Cybernetic Age,* Translated by M. Kandel, Seabury, New York, 1974.

BIBLIOGRAPHY

The following references were compiled by Jack Dennis and his colleagues and students in the Computation Structures Group of the MIT Laboratory for Computer Science. The list was distributed to participants in the Workshop on Applicative Languages and Parallel Computation, held at the MIT Endicott House in July 1980. References cited in this chapter have been deleted. All other modifications are of a minor, editorial nature, although the reference to the paper by Wand has been updated to reflect its presentation at the 1980 LISP Conference.

Ackerman, W. B., "A Structure Memory for Data Flow Computers," Technical Report TR/186, Laboratory for Computer Science, MIT, Cambridge, Mass., 1977.

———,"A Structure Processing Facility for Data Flow Computers," *Proceedings of the 1978 International Conference on Parallel Processing,* Aug. 1978, pp. 166–172.

———, "Data Flow Languages," *Proceedings of the 1979 National Computer Conference, AFIPS Conference Proceedings 48,* June 1979, pp. 1087–1095.

Adams, D. A., "A Model for Parallel Computations," in L. C. Hobbs, D. J. Theis, J. Trimble, H. Titus, and I. Highberg (eds.), *Parallel Processor Systems, Technologies, and Applications,* Spartan Books, New York, 1970, pp. 311–333.

Allan, S. J., and A. E. Oldhoeft, "A Flow Analysis Procedure for the Translation of High Level Languages to a Data Flow Language," *Proceedings of the 1979 International Conference on Parallel Processing,* Aug. 1979, pp. 26–34.

Arvind, and R. E. Bryant, "Design Considerations for a Partial Differential Equation Machine," *Scientific Computer Information Exchange Meeting,* Sept. 1979, pp. 94–102.

Arvind, and K. P. Gostelow, "Some Relationships Between Asynchronous Interpreters of a Dataflow Language," in E. J. Neuhold (ed.), *Formal Description of Programming Concepts,* North/Holland Publishing Company, New York, 1977, pp. 95–119.

——— "A Computer Capable of Exchanging Processors for Time," *Information Processing 77: Proceedings of IFIP Congress 77,* Aug. 1977, pp. 849–853.

Arvind, K. P. Gostelow, and W. Plouffe, "Indeterminacy, Monitors and Dataflow," *Operating Systems Review* 11(5)(Nov. 1977):159–169.

Ashcroft, E. A., and W. W. Wadge, "LUCID—A Formal System for Writing and Proving Programs," *SIAM Journal of Computing* 5(3)(Sept. 1978):336–354.

——— "Lucid, a Nonprocedural Language with Iteration," *Communications of the ACM* 20(7)(July 1977):519–526.

——— "Clauses: Scope Structures and Defined Functions in Lucid," *Conf. Record 5th ACM Symp. on Principles of Programming Languages,* Jan. 1978, pp. 12–22.

Atkinson, R. R., and C. E. Hewitt, "Synchronization in

Actor Systems," *Conf. Record 4th ACM Symp. on Principles of Programming Languages,* Jan. 1977, pp. 267–280.

Bahrs, A., "Operation Patterns," in A. Ershov and V. A. Nepomniashy (eds.), *International Symposium on Theoretical Programming,* Springer-Verlag, Berlin, 1972, pp. 217–246.

Berkling, K. J., "Reduction Languages for Reduction Machines," *The Second Annual Meeting on Computer Architecture,* 1975, pp. 133–138.

Bic, L., "Protection and Security in a Dataflow System," Technical Report #126, Department of Information and Computer Science, University of California, Irvine, 1978.

Brinton, J. B., "New Architecture Goes with Flow," *Electronics* 52(9)(April 26, 1979):92–94.

Brock, J. D., "Operational Semantics of a Data Flow Language," Technical Report TM-120, Laboratory for Computer Science, MIT, Cambridge, Mass., 1978.

——— "Consistent Semantics for a Data Flow Language," To appear in *Proceedings of the Ninth International Symposium on Mathematical Foundations of Computer Science,* Sept. 1980.

Brock, J. D., and W. B. Ackerman, "An Anomaly in the Specifications of Nondeterminate Packet Systems," Computation Structures Group Note 33-1, Laboratory for Computer Science, MIT, Cambridge, Mass., 1978.

Brock, J. D., and L. B. Montz, "Translation and Optimization of Data Flow Programs," *Proceedings of the 1979 International Conference on Parallel Processing,* Aug. 1979, pp. 46–54.

Bryant, R. E., "Simulation of Packet Communication Architecture Computer Systems," Technical Report TR-188, Laboratory for Computer Science, MIT, Cambridge, Mass., 1977.

———, "Simulation on a Distributed System," *Proc. The 1st International Conference on Distributed Computing Systems,* Huntsville, Ala., Oct. 1979, pp. 544–552.

Bryant, R. E., and J. B. Dennis, "Concurrent Programming," in P. Wegner (ed.), *Research Directions in Software Technology,* MIT Press, Cambridge, Mass., 1979, pp. 584–610.

Burge, W. H., "Combinatory Programming and Combinatorial Analysis," *IBM Journal of Research and Development* 16(5)(Sept. 1972):450–461.

———, "Stream Processing Functions," *IBM Journal of Research and Development* 19(1)(January. 1975):12–25.

Burton, F. W., and M. R. Sleep, "A Network for the Rapid Distribution of Work," Report CS/80/018/E, School of Computing Studies, University of East Anglia, Norwich, England, 1980.

Burstall, R. M., J. S. Collins, and R. J. Popplestone, *Programming in POP/2,* Edinburgh University Press, Edinburgh, 1971.

Comte, D., G. Durrieu, O. Gelly, A. Plas, and J. C. Syre, "Parallelism, Control and Synchronization Expressions in a Single Assignment Language," *SIGPLAN Notices* 13(1)(Jan. 1978):25–33.

Comte, D., and N. Nifdi, "LAU Miltiprocessor: Micro-

functional Description and Technological Choices," *Proceedings of the First European Conference on Parallel and Distributed Processing,* Toulouse, Feb. 1979, pp. 8–15.

Davis, A. L., "The Architecture and System Method of DDM1: A Recursively Structured Data Driven Machine," *SIGARCH Newsletter* 6(7)(Apr. 1978):210–215.

———, "A Data Flow Evaluation System Based on the Concept of Recursive Locality," *Proceedings of the 1979 National Computer Conference, AFIPS Conference Proceedings* 48(June 1979):1079–1086.

Dennis, J. B., "Programming Generality, Parallelism and Computer Architecture," *Information Processing 68: Proceedings of IFIP Congress 1968,* pp. 484–492.

———, "First Version of a Data Flow Procedure Language," in B. Robinet (ed.), *Programming Symposium: Proceedings, Colloque sur la Programmation,* Springer/Verlag, Berlin, 1974, pp. 362–376.

———, "Packet Communication Architecture," *Proceedings of the 1975 Sagamore Computer Conference on Parallel Processing,* Aug. 1975, pp. 224–229.

———, "A Language Design for Structured Concurrency," in J. H. Williams and D. A. Fisher (eds.), *Design and Implementation of Programming Languages: Proceedings of a DoD Sponsored Workshop,* Springer-Verlag, Berlin, 1976.

———, "The Varieties of Data Flow Computers," *Proc. The 1st. International Conference on Distributed Computing Systems,* Huntsville, Oct. 1979, pp. 430–439.

Dennis, J. B., G. A. Boughton, and C. K. C. Leung, "Building Blocks for Data Flow Prototypes," *The Seventh Annual Symposium on Computer Architecture,* May 1980, pp. 1–8.

Dennis, J. B., C. K. C. Leung, and D. P. Misunas, "A Highly Parallel Processor Using a Data Flow Machine Language," Computation Structures Group Memo 134-2, Laboratory for Computer Science, MIT, Cambridge. Mass., 1980.

Dennis, J. B., and D. P. Misunas, "A Preliminary Architecture for a Basic Data-Flow Processor," *The Second Annual Symposium on Computer Architecture,* Jan. 1975, pp. 126–132.

Dennis, J. B., and D. P. Misunas, "A Computer Architecture for Highly Parallel Signal Processing," *Proceedings of the ACM 1974 National Conference,* Nov. 1974, pp. 402–409.

Dennis, J. B., and K.-S. Weng, "Application of Data Flow Computation to the Weather Problem," in D. J. Kuck, D. H. Lawrie, and A. H. Sameh (eds.), *High Speed Computer and Algorithm Organization,* 1977, pp. 143–157.

———, "An Abstract Implementation for Concurrent Computation with Streams," *Proceedings of the 1979 International Conference on Parallel Processing,* Aug. 1979, pp. 35–45.

Dhas, C. R., "Performance Evaluation of a Feedback Data Flow Processor Using Simulation," *ACM SIGMETRICS* 9(2)(May 1980):191–197.

Ellis, D. J., "Formal Specifications for Packet Communication Systems," Technical Report TR-189, Laboratory for Computer Science, MIT, Cambridge. Mass., 1977.

Frank, G. A., *Virtual Memory Systems for Closed Applicative Language Interpreters,* Ph.D. dissertation, University of North Carolina at Chapel Hill, Chapel Hill, 1979.

DeFrancesco, N., G. Perego, A. Tomasi, G. Vaglini, and M. Vanneschi, "On the Feasibility of Nondeterministic and Interprocess Communication Constructs in Data-Flow Computing Systems," *Proceedings of the First European Conference on Parallel and Distributed Processing,* Toulouse, Feb. 1979, pp. 93–100.

Friedman, D. P., and D. S. Wise, "CONS Should Not Evaluate its Arguments," in S. Michaelson and R. Milner (eds.), *Automata, Languages, and Programming,* Edinburgh University Press, Edinburgh, 1976, pp. 257–284.

————, "An Approach to Fair Applicative Multiprogramming," in G. Kahn (ed.), *Semantics of Concurrent Computation,* Springer-Verlag, Berlin, 1979, pp. 203–225.

Gavish, B., and H. Koch, "An Extensible Architecture for Data Flow Processing," *SIGIR* 13(2)(Aug. 1978):71–76. Also in *SIGARCH* 7(2) and *SIGMOD* 10(1).

Gelly, O.. et al., "LAU System Software: A High Level Data Driven Language for Parallel Programming," *Proceedings of the 1976 International Conference on Parallel Processing,* Aug. 1976, p. 255.

Glauert, J., "A Single Assignment Language for Data Flow Computing," M.Sc. dissertation, Department of Computer Science, University of Manchester, Manchester, England, 1978.

Gostelow, K. P., and R. E. Thomas, "A View of Dataflow," *Proceedings of the 1979 National Computer Conference, AFIPS Conference Proceedings* 48(June 1979):629–636.

Gostelow, K. P., and R. E. Thomas, "Performance of a Simulated Dataflow Computer," *IEEE Transactions on Computers* C-29(10)(Oct. 1980):905–919.

Grit, D. H., and R. L. Page, "A Multiprocessor Computer System for Parallel Evaluation of Recursive Programs," *Proceedings of the First Annual Rocky Mountain Symposium on Microcomputers,* Aug. 1977, pp. 142–160.

————, "Performance of a Multiprocessor for Applicative Programs," *ACM SIGMETRICS* 9(2)(May 1980):181–189.

Gurd, J., and I. Watson, "A Multilayered Data Flow Computer Architecture," *Proceedings of the 1977 International Conference on Parallel Processing,* Aug. 1977, p. 94.

————, "Data Driven System for High Speed Parallel Computing—Part 1: Structuring Software for Parallel Execution," *Computer Design* 19(6)(June 1980):91–100.

Glushkov, V. M., M. B. Ignatyev, V. A. Myasnikov, and V. A. Torgashev, "Recursive Machines and Computing Technology," *Information Processing 74: Proceedings of the IFIP Congress 74,* Aug. 1974, pp. 65–70.

Hopkins, R. P., P. W. Rautenbach, and P. C. Treleaven, "A Computer Supporting Data Flow, Control Flow, and Updateable Memory," Technical Report TR # 144, Computing Laboratory, University of Newcastle upon Tyne, Newcastle upon Tyne, England, 1979.

Henderson, P., *Functional Programming: Application and Implementation,* Prentice/Hall International, Englewood Cliffs, N.J., 1980.

Hewitt, C. E., "Viewing Control Structures as Patterns of Passing Messages," *Artificial Intelligence* 8(3)(June 1977):323–364.

Hewitt, C. E., G. Attardi, and H. Lieberman, "Specifying and Proving Properties of Guardians for Distributed Systems," in G. Kahn (ed.). *Semantics of Concurrent Computation,* Springer-Verlag, Berlin, 1979, pp. 316–336.

Hewitt, C. E., and H. Baker, "Actors and Continuous Functionals," in E. J. Neuhold (ed.), *Formal Description of Programming Concepts,* North-Holland Publishing Company, New York, 1977, pp. 367–390.

Jacobsen, R. G., *Analysis of Structures for Packet Sorting Networks,* Computation Structures Group Memo 163, Laboratory for Computer Science, MIT, Cambridge, Mass., 1978.

Jacobsen, R. G., and D. P. Misunas, "Analysis of Structures for Packet Communication," *Proceedings of the 1977 International Conference on Parallel Processing,* Aug. 1977, pp. 38–43.

Johnson, D., et al., "Automatic Partitioning of Programs in Multiprocessor Systems," *COMPCON Spring 80,* San Francisco, Feb. 1980, pp. 175–178.

Kahn, G., "The Semantics of a Simple Language for Parallel Programming," *Information Processing 74: Proceeding of the IFIP Congress 74,* Aug. 1974, pp. 471–475.

Kahn, G., and D. MacQueen, "Coroutines and Networks of Parallel Processes," *Information Processing 77: Proceedings of IFIP Congress 77,* Aug. 1977, pp. 993–998.

Keller, R. M., "Formal Verification of Parallel Programs," *Communications of the ACM* 19(7)(July 1976):371–384.

————, "Denotational Models for Parallel Programs with Indeterminate Operators," in E. J. Newhold (ed.), *Formal Description of Programming Concepts,* North-Holland Publishing Company, New York, 1977, pp. 337–366.

Keller, R. M., G. Lindstrom, and S. S. Patil, "Data-Flow Concepts for Hardware Design," *COMPCON Spring 80,* San Francisco, Feb. 1980, pp. 105–111.

Kessels, J. L. W., "A Conceptual Framework for a Nonprocedural Programming Language," *Communications of the ACM* 20(12)(Dec. 1977):906–913.

Kornfeld, W. A., "Using Parallel Processing for Problem Solving," Memo 561, Artificial Intelligence Laboratory, MIT, Cambridge, Mass., 1979.

P. R. Kosinski, "A Data Flow Language for Operating Systems Programming," *SIGPLAN Notices* 8(9) (Sept. 1973):89–94.

————, "Mathematical Semantics and Data Flow Programming," *Conference Record of the Third ACM*

Symposium on Principles of Programming Languages, Atlanta, Ga., Jan. 1976, pp. 175–184.

———, "A Straightforward Denotational Semantics for Non-Determinate Data Flow Programs," *Conference Record of the Fifth ACM Symposium on Principles of Programming Languages,* Jan. 1978, pp. 214–221.

———, "Denotational Semantics of Determinate and Non-Determinate Data Flow Programs," Technical Report TR-220, Laboratory for Computer Science, MIT, Cambridge, Mass., 1979.

Landin, P. J., "A Correspondence between ALGOL 60 and Church's Lambda Notation: Part I," *Communications of the ACM* 8(2)(Feb. 1965):89–101.

Leung, C. K. C., "ADL: An Architecture Description Language for Packet Communication Systems," *Proceedings of the 4th International Symposium on Computer Hardware Description Languages,* Palo Alto, Calif., Oct. 1979, pp. 6–13.

———, *Fault Tolerance in Packet Communication Computer Architecture,* Ph.D. thesis, Department of Electrical Engineering and Computer Science, MIT, Cambridge, Mass., 1980.

Lieberman, H., "A Preview of Act 1," to appear in L. Steels (ed.), *Society Models of Intelligence.*

MacQueen, D. B., "Models for Distributed Computing," Rapport de Recherche No. 351, Institut de Recherche d'Informatique et d'Automatique, Le Chesnay, France, 1979.

Magó, G. A., "A Network of Microprocessors to Execute Reduction Languages," *Part I, International Journal of Computer and Information Sciences* 8(5)(1979):349–385; *Part II, International Journal of Computer and Information Sciences* 8(6)(1979):435–471.

———, "A Cellular Computer Architecture for Functional Programming." *COMPCON Spring 80,* San Francisco, Feb. 1980, pp. 179–187.

McCarthy, J. P., P. W. Abrahams, D. J. Edwards, T. P. Hart, and M. I. Levin, *LISP 1.5 Programmer's Manual,* MIT Press, Cambridge, Mass., 1965.

McGraw, J. R., "Data Flow Computing: Software Development," *Proc., The 1st International Conference on Distributed Computing Systems,* Huntsville, Oct. 1979, pp. 242–251.

———, "Data Flow Computing—The VAL Language," Computation Structures Group Memo 188, Laboratory for Computer Science, MIT, Cambridge, Mass., 1980.

Miller, R. E., and J. Cocke, "Configurable Computers: A New Class of General Purpose Machines," in A. Ershov and V. A. Nepomniashy (ed.), *International Symposium on Theoretical Programming,* Springer-Verlag, Berlin, 1972, pp. 285–298.

Miranker, G. S., "Implementation of Procedures on a Class of Data Flow Procedures," *Proceedings of the 1977 International Conference on Parallel Processing,* Aug. 1977, pp. 77–86.

Misunas, D. P., "Deadlock Avoidance in Data-Flow Architectures," *Proceedings of the Third Milwaukee Symposium on Automatic Computation and Control,* Apr. 1975.

———, "Performance Analysis of a Data-Flow Processor," *Proceedings of the 1976 International Conference of Parallel Processing,* Aug. 1976, pp. 100–105.

———, "Error Detection and Recovery in a Data-Flow Computer," *Proceedings of the 1976 International Conference of Parallel Processing,* Aug. 1976, pp. 117–122.

——— "Workshop on Data Flow Computer and Program Organization," *Computer Architecture News* 6(4)(Oct. 1977):6–22.

———, *A Computer Architecture for Data-Flow Computation,* Technical Report TM-100, Laboratory for Computer Science, MIT, Cambridge, Mass., 1978.

———, *Report on the Second Workshop on Data Flow Computer and Program Organization,* Technical Report TM-136, Laboratory for Computer Science, MIT, Cambridge, Mass., 1979.

Montz, L., *Safety and Optimization Transformations for Data Flow Programs,* S. M. thesis, Department of Electrical Engineering and Computer Science, MIT, Cambridge, Mass., 1980.

Oldehoeft, A. E., S. Allan, S. A. Thoreson, C. Retnadhas, and R. J. Zingg, "Translation of High Level Programs to Data Flow and Their Simulated Execution on a Feedback Interpreter," Technical Report 78-2, Department of Computer Science, Iowa State University, Ames, Iowa, 1978.

Patil, S. S., "Closure Properties of Interconnections of Determinate Systems," *Record of the Project MAC Conference on Concurrent Systems and Parallel Computation,* Woods Hole, Mass., June 1970, pp. 107–116.

Peterson, J. C., and W. D. Murray, "Parallel Computer Architecture Employing Functional Programming Systems," *Proceedings of the International Workshop on High-Level Language Computer Architecture,* May 1980, pp. 190–195.

Plas, A., D. Comte, O. Gelly, and J. C. Syre, "LAU System Architecture: A Parallel Data Driven Processor Based on Single Assignment," *Proceedings of the 1976 International Conference on Parallel Processing,* Aug. 1976, pp. 293–302.

Pozefsky, M., "Programming in Reduction Languages," Technical Report 77-009, Department of Computer Science, University of North Carolina at Chapel Hill, Chapel Hill, 1977.

Rodriguez, J. E., "A Graph Model for Parallel Computation," Technical Report TR-64, Laboratory for Computer Science, MIT, Cambridge, Mass., 1969.

Rumbaugh, J. E., "Data Flow Language," *Proceedings of the 1975 Sagamore Computer Conference on Parallel Processing,* Aug. 1975, pp. 217–219.

———, "A Data Flow Multiprocessor," *IEEE Transactions in Computers* C-26(2)(Feb. 1977):138–146.

———, "A Parallel, Asynchronous Computer Architecture for Data Flow Programs," Technical Report TR-150, Laboratory for Computer Science, MIT, Cambridge, Mass., 1975.

Seeber, R. R., and A. B. Lindquist, "Associative Logic for Highly Parallel Systems," *Proceedings of the AFIPS Conference* 24(1963):489–493.

Shapiro, R. M., H. Saint, and D. L. Presberg, "Representation of Algorithms as Cyclic Partial Orderings," Report CA-7112-2711, Applied Data Research, Wakefield, Mass., 1971.

Sleep, M. R., "Instruction Sets for Dataflow Architectures," Report CS/79/017/E, School of Computing Studies, University of East Anglia, Norwich, England, 1979.

———, "Applicative Languages, Dataflow, and Pure Combinatory Code," *COMPCON Spring 80,* San Francisco, Feb. 1980, pp. 112–115.

Stoy, J. E., "Proof of Correctness of Dataflow Programs," Computation Structures Group Memo 110, Laboratory for Computer Science, MIT, Cambridge, Mass., 1974.

Sussman, G. J., and G. L. Steele, "SCHEME: An Interpreter for Extended Lambda Calculus," Memo 349, Artificial Intelligence Laboratory, MIT, Cambridge, Mass., 1975.

Syre, J. C., D. Comte, and N. Hifdi, "Pipelining, Parallelism and Asynchronism in the LAU System," *Proceedings of the 1977 International Conference on Parallel Processing,* Aug. 1977, pp. 87–92.

Tesler, L. G., and H. J. Enea, "A Language Design for Concurrent Processes," *Proceedings of the 1968 Spring Joint Computer Conference, AFIPS Conference Proceedings 32,* Apr. 1968, pp. 403–408.

Thomas, R. E., "Performance Analysis of Two Classes of Dataflow Computing Systems," Technical Report # 120, Department of Information and Computer Science, University of California, Irvine, 1978.

Treleaven, P. C., "Principal Components of Data Flow Computers," *Proceedings of the 1978 Euromicro Symposium,* Oct. 1978, pp. 366–374.

———, "Exploiting Program Concurrency in Computing Systems," *Computer* 12(1)(Jan. 1979):42–50.

Treleaven, P. C., and G. F. Mole. "A Multi-Processor Reduction Machine for User-Defined Reduction Languages," *The Seventh Annual Symposium on Computer Architecture,* May 1980, pp. 121–130.

Turner, D. A., *SASL Language Manual,* University of St. Andrews, St. Andrews, Scotland, 1976.

———, "An Implementation of SASL," Technical Report TR/75/4, Department of Computer Science, University of St. Andrews, St. Andrews, Scotland, 1975.

———, "A New Implementation Technique for Applicative Languages," *Software—Practice and Experience* 9(1)(Jan 1979):31–49.

Wadge, W. W., "An Extensional Treatment of Dataflow Deadlock," in G. Kahn (ed.), *Semantics of Concurrent Computation,* Springer-Verlag, Berlin, 1979, pp. 285–299.

Wand, M., "Continuation-Based Multiprocessing," *Conference Record of the 1980 LISP Conference,* Stanford, Aug. 1980, pp. 19–28.

Watson, I., and J. Gurd, "A Prototype Data Flow Computer with Token Labelling," *Proceedings of the 1979 National Computer Conference, AFIPS Conference Proceedings* 48(June 1979):623–628.

Weng, K.-S., *Stream-Oriented Computation in Recursive Data Flow Schemas,* Technical Report TM-68, Laboratory for Computer Science, MIT, Cambridge, 1975.

———, "An Abstract Implementation for a Generalized Data Flow Language," Technical Report TR-228, Laboratory for Computer Science, MIT, Cambridge, Mass., 1979.

Whitelock, P. J., *A Conventional Language for Data Flow Computation,* M.Sc. dissertation, Department of Computer Science, University of Manchester, England, 1978.

27

Software Development for Micro/Mini Machines

Robert Glaser
Telesaver

27.1. INTRODUCTION

Microprocessors and minicomputers continue to become more powerful every year. As a result, each has found growing application in areas where larger computers had previously been used and new uses that had earlier been impractical. With rapidly changing technology, the classifying distinctions between microcomputers, minicomputers, and conventional computers have become less clear. Because minicomputers fall between microprocessors and large computers, emphasis in this chapter is placed upon microprocessors. Generalizations about microcomputers apply to low-end minicomputers, whereas high-end minicomputers bear a closer relationship with large mainframe computers.

A multitude of microprocessor chips are available, each of which has its own peculiarities. This chapter, however, will focus on the features the various chips have in common.

A major difference between software for micros and larger computers is that the micro software is highly dependent upon the microcomputer hardware. Micro software is nearly always concerned with low-level input/output tasks. Communication with peripheral chips is of major concern. When dealing with microprocessors, it is not possible to effectively discuss software independent of hardware, and thus this chapter includes microprocessor-hardware-oriented material.

A microprocessor, as discussed in this chapter, is a central processing unit (CPU) contained within a single integrated circuit package. The CPU provides logical, arithmetic, and control functions. The instruction set is predefined. The control functions include instruction decoding, and memory address, data, read/write, and selection signals. This type of microprocessor is different from a microprogrammable processor, which is also sometimes called a microprocessor. This device requires a number of integrated circuits to implement the central processing section alone. User-written microcode defines the instruction set of this type of processor system. These microprogrammable processors find their chief use in specialized applications requiring high speed.

A microcomputer consists of a microprocessor CPU, program memory, data memory, input/output (I/O) devices, and supplementary control logic. This may require several chips on a single circuit board, or several boards. The program memory is often nonvolatile read-only memory (ROM). Data memory is read/write random-access memory (RAM), and I/O can be through a variety of peripheral chips.

Minicomputers generally have higher speeds and larger word sizes than microcomputers. They contain the same elements as microcomputers, though implemented from a larger number of integrated circuits. At one time minicomputers consisted largely of TTL logic gates, though now many are constructed with fast microprogrammable processor chip sets. The circuitry typically requires several circuit boards.

27.2. APPLICATIONS OF MICRO/ MINICOMPUTERS

The applications of micro/minicomputers fall into two distinct categories: equipment controllers and general purpose computers. The software for equipment controllers is somewhat different from that for large computers; hence, equipment controller applications are stressed here. The more general purpose uses of micro- and minicomputers, which can be different from those of larger computers, are included as well.

Equipment Controllers

There are several advantages of implementing controllers from microcomputers. Random-logic designs require different parts for each system. Low-quantity products do not justify the large capital outlay required to design, lay out, and manufacture specialized integrated circuits. Available parts must be used, and several circuit boards filled with logic gates are the usual result. The cost of design, layout, board manufacture, and testing must all be covered by a single controller product. Microcomputer implementation of the product permits much of the work to be useful for a variety of similar products. Off-the-shelf microprocessor parts that are mass produced provide low-cost alternatives to special-purpose integrated circuits. Several controller products can use a standardized microcomputer circuit board. The development cost of a controller is then reduced to that of the controller program. A smaller number of circuit boards is also possible because of the use of a cost-effective sophisticated microprocessor part. Product modifications are program changes requiring only a ROM change, whereas with a random-logic design, circuit board modifications and additions are necessary. The scope of possible product modification is greatly limited for random-logic designs as compared with microprocessor implementations. Through the use of microprocessor-based design, the special-purpose functions of an equipment controller are supplied by a special-purpose controlling program, and other aspects of the product can be used for a multitude of other products.

Computerizing an equipment controller imposes certain limitations on the microcomputer. The physical size, power drain, and cost of the computer must be no larger than that of the random-logic design being replaced. These restrictions become more important when new applications rather than replacement applications are considered. Intelligent products are possible that cannot be contructed without microprocessors because of limitations of size, power, and cost. The low size, power, and cost of microprocessor-based controller designs are precisely what create the new applications.

Microprocessor-based controller applications can be found in a variety of areas. Consumer-oriented devices show a large number of examples. Uses in radio receivers and home entertainment equipment proliferate and are but a sample of what can be done in consumer electronics. The Ahwatukee House is perhaps the ultimate in computerizing a home [1–3]; the possibilities for improving everyday living are immense [4]. The automotive controller [5] is a particularly high-volume application. Uses in traffic control [6] are growing. Very human-oriented applications include aid for the handicapped [7] and medical uses as common as aid in childbirth [8]. Commercial and industrial applications include controlling satellites [9], astronomical telescopes [10], and gas turbine generators [11]. Applications in the field of test equipment [12, 13] are enormous.

Many consumer, commercial, industrial, and research devices can be enhanced with intelligent controllers. The wide spectrum and sheer number of applications is limited only by the creativity of equipment designers. Other applications can be found in References 14 to 19.

General Purpose Computers

The microprocessor revolution has made it possible for micro- and minicomputers to be used in much the same ways as larger conventional computers. Standard business applications of payroll computation, inventory maintenance, general ledger, and address label sorting and printing have become feasible for small businesses utilizing micro- or minicomputers. Development systems for controller development and support are often implemented with micro- or minicomputers. Section 27.8 deals with these systems. Small computer systems for educational uses have improved computer science educational programs. Small stand alone-systems can give students a better learning opportunity than punched card/batch submission methods. The introduction of microprocessor-based low-cost general-purpose computers spurred the entrance of the computer into the home. Home computing, which has grown to significant levels, includes games, computer-aided instruction, and text processing. As the hobby has grown, so has the number of magazines to serve it [20–24]. Personal computing equipment has proliferated to the point where some of it has been called into professional service [25].

27.3. MICROCOMPUTERS, MINICOMPUTERS, AND LARGER COMPUTERS

The classification of computer systems as micro, mini, or large can be based at best only on general characteristics. The dividing lines between each category are difficult to draw and keep changing.

Word Size

The more bits per word a processor has, the more powerful each instruction is. This is particularly noticeable in arithmetic computation. The number of operation codes is limited when dealing with small word sizes, so machines with small word sizes have a correspondingly greater number of multiple word instructions. Microcomputers generally have 4- or 8-bit words, although 16 bit microprocessors are available, and 32 bit chips are not far off. Minicomputers have between 12- and 24-bit words, with 16 bit being the most prevalent. Large computers have 32 bit words and up. Processor word size is not as reliable an indicator as it once was, although 4- or 8-bit processors would almost always be classified as microprocessors, geared to control applications and low-complexity processing problems.

Architecture

Processor architectures vary considerably within each category. Microprocessors tend to have more restrictive architectures than the others; data paths can be quite specialized, with one or more memory registers required to access general data memory. Larger word sizes facilitate easier memory access by supplying a greater number of bits for address specification. Separate program memory and data memory paths are more often encountered in microprocessors than larger machines. This is more natural for controllers because there are normally different types of memory for each function. These architectures usually require memory address pointers for data storage.

The simplest architectures provide a single accumulator for arithmetic, logical, and move operations. More sophisticated arrangements provide several accumulators, or general-purpose registers for these operations. Microprocessor chips tend to have single or double accumulators, since the small word size makes it difficult to have enough instruction code space to reserve register fields. This limitation creates data bottlenecks, which require data moves to achieve proper positioning for subsequent operations. Minicomputers tend to have a number of general-purpose registers, permitting operation code specification of register operands.

Instruction Set

The larger the word size, the greater number of instructions that can be specified in single word instructions. Consequently, in addition to the fact that larger machines have greater capabilities otherwise, microprocessors have much sparser instruction sets than minicomputers and larger computers. Internal stack space is sometimes found in microprocessors, a useful hardware feature but a software-limiting situation. Paged addressing, instead of relative or even absolute addressing, is often found in microprocessors. A bare minimum instruction set includes data moves, logical shifts, AND, OR, exclusive OR, and addition. Some microprocessor sets include little more than this minimum, whereas others include a respectable number of additional operation codes (op-codes). Small machines use subroutines to replace missing op-codes. Codes such as multiply and divide are typically missing from microprocessors, and floating point instructions are often missing from minicomputers.

Speed

Naturally, the operation speed increases from micro- to mini- to large computer. This is partly inherent in the type of technology from which the devices are constructed, and partly because of the greater number of instructions that must be performed to provide the same throughput for smaller processors. Dealing with 32 bit integers on a 4 bit machine clearly requires over 8 times the execution time of a 32 bit machine. Accumulator and memory address register bottlenecks result in even more operations being necessary. Limited instruction sets call for greater use of subroutines. All of these restrictions produce the same result: a slower machine. Even if the instruction execution times of micro-, mini-, and large computers were equal, there would still be a speed contrast. Additionally, there usually is an inherent speed differential. Microcomputers can have execution times of several microseconds, with minicomputers slightly less, and large computers well into the submicrosecond range.

Hardware Interfaces

Microprocessors have simple interface requirements when compared with mini- and large computers. Input/output devices and general hardware can be added more easily to micros because the interfaces are less restrictive. Sophisticated handshaking and bus-driving requirements are necessary to obtain the higher operating speeds of mini- and large computers. Additional peripheral chips may be placed right on the bus on controller-size micros, where separate boards and bus extenders and terminators may be required for larger systems.

27.4. A MICROPROCESSOR SURVEY

There are scores of microprocessor chips available. A history of microprocessor development can be found in References 26 to 28. A brief description is given for some of the more popular ones.

Four Bit

These micros are intended chiefly for use in control applications, particularly when tasks are I/O intensive. Computations are often done in binary coded decimal form (BCD).

Intel's MCS-4 chip set [29], announced in 1971, is notable for opening the microprocessor era. Each member of the chip set is packaged in a 16 pin dual in-line package (DIP), made possible through the use of a multiplexed 4 line bus for address and data. This set consists of the 4004-CPU, 4001-ROM, 4002-RAM, and 4003-shift register. The system utilizes 12-bit addresses and 4-bit data words. The ROM, RAM, and shift register each provide I/O lines. The pMOS CPU supplies 46 instructions, contains a 3-level internal stack, and the minimum instruction time is 10.8 microseconds. An external clock and driver are required, and no interrupts are provided. Sixteen 4 bit general-purpose registers may also be used as eight 8 bit index registers. I/O addressing is set up by special control commands.

Eight Bit

There are more micros in the 8 bit category than any other. These are suited to character manipulation as well as I/O control and moderate arithmetic computation.

The 8008 CPU [30] was the first 8 bit CPU. Housed in an 18 pin DIP, an 8 line bus is multiplexed to supply 14-bit addresses and 8-bit data words. This pMOS-fabricated CPU supplies 48 instructions, contains a 7-level internal stack, and has a minimum instruction time of 20 microseconds. An external clock and driver are needed, and a single interrupt input is provided. Seven 8-bit scratch-pad registers are available. The 8008's architecture, less limiting than the 4004's, opened up many applications for microprocessors.

A step up from the 8008, Intel's 8080 CPU [31] has a 2 microsecond minimum instruction time because of nMOS fabrication. The 8080 has separate address and data lines, requiring the larger 40 pin package. There are 16 address lines, permitting up to 64K memory bytes to be accessed. The register set is the same as that of the 8008, and the instruction set is an expanded set of the 8008, with 72 instructions. Several stack instructions and one register indirect branch instruction are added. The processor uses an external stack, has a single interrupt input, and requires an external clock. A hold mode is incorporated that permits direct memory access (DMA).

The Intel 8085 CPU [32] incorporates all of the features of the 8080. It has five interrupt inputs and an on-chip clock oscillator, and requires only a single power supply voltage. To retain the 40 pin package, a multiplexed address/data bus is utilized. The minimum instruction time is 1.3 microseconds. The chief advantage of the 8085 over the 8080 is a reduction in system support components.

Software-compatible with the 8080/8085, Zilog's Z-80 CPU [33] adds relative and indexed addressing modes to the base instruction set. Block transfer and search instructions are also provided, and the Z-80 executes 158 instructions. Seven alternate general-purpose registers and two index registers are included in addition to those of the 8080/8085 set. Hardware features include a single power supply requirement, dynamic memory refreshing, two interrupt inputs, and provision for DMA.

The 8080 processor series may be considered to be register oriented; instructions permit operations with the general-purpose registers. Motorola's 6800 CPU [34] has two accumulators and a 16 bit index register; the instruction set includes operations with memory locations. This CPU can be considered to be memory oriented. Accumulator, immediate, direct, extended, indexed, implied, and relative addressing modes are available. The minimum instruction time is 2 microseconds, and there are 72 instructions. Housed in a 40 pin package, the 6800's 16 bit address bus is separate from the data bus. An external clock generator is required, and only a single power supply voltage is needed. There are two interrupt inputs, and the chip is capable of DMA. No special I/O control lines or instructions are provided, mandating memory-mapped I/O.

The Motorola 6802 CPU [35] is virtually identical with the 6800 except that it has a built-in clock generator, and 128 bytes of internal RAM. The chief advantage of the 6802 is a reduction in system components.

MOS Technology's MCS6502 CPU [36] is also a memory-oriented device, with an accumulator and two 8 bit index registers. A number of addressing modes are available: accumulator, immediate, absolute, zero page, indexed zero page, indexed absolute, implied, relative, indexed indirect, indirect indexed, and absolute indirect. There are two interrupt inputs, and the only active devices required for clock generation are two inverters. A single supply voltage powers the chip, and the minimum instruction time is 2 microseconds. The 6502 has a 64K address space, but 28-pin package variants of this CPU have 4K or 8K addressing.

The RCA CDP1802 COSMAC CPU [37] operates over the wide temperature range of -55 to $+125\,^{\circ}C$ and can draw very little current at slow clock rates. The 1802 is powered from a single voltage, has one interrupt input, a built-in clock, and excellent DMA provision. The 40 pin COSMAC includes four input lines and one output line. There are I/O instructions and control lines. The instruction set is centered about its sixteen 16 bit registers. The COSMAC's architecture is uncommon; manipulation of the registers produces results that with most other processors are handled in a different fashion. Register, register-indirect, immediate, and stack addressing modes are available.

Intel's MCS-48 [38] series of CPUs finds utilization in physically small control applications. The 8048 contains 1K bytes of ROM program memory, 64 bytes of RAM data memory, an 8-level stack, 27 I/O lines, a programmable timer counter, an interrupt input, and a clock oscillator. There are 96 instructions and the minimum instruction time is 2.5 microseconds. The CPU operates from a single power voltage and the 40 pin package can be used with no support devices. Other members of the MCS-48 family contain twice as much RAM or ROM, erasable, programmable ROM (EPROM), no ROM, or are housed in a 28 pin DIP.

Sixteen Bit

Microprocessors with large word size can challenge the power of minicomputers. These processors are suited for high-throughput control systems, and relatively complex computations.

Texas Instruments' TMS9900 CPU [39] features a memory-to-memory architecture. A workspace pointer points to 16 workspace registers in memory. The register file can be changed by altering the workspace pointer. The 15-line address bus accommodates 32K words (64K bytes). A single interrupt input, operating in conjunction with 4 interrupt code inputs, provides 16 vectored interrupts with the addition of an external priority encoder. Housed in a 64 pin package, the 9900 requires 3 power supply voltages and an external 4-phase clock. The instruction set includes multiply and divide, and 8 addressing modes. The minimum instruction time is 2.7 microseconds.

Intel's 8086 CPU [40] can address 1M byte of memory with a 20 bit address bus, and has fourteen 16 bit registers. Housed in a 40 pin package, a single power supply voltage is required. There are two interrupt inputs and an external clock generator is needed. The instruction set includes multiply and divide, and has 24 addressing modes. The minimum instruction time is 400 nanoseconds.

Zilog's Z-8000 CPU [33] can address 8 megabytes of memory, and has sixteen 16-bit general-purpose registers. The Z-8000 operates from a single power supply voltage and is housed in a 48 pin package. The instruction set includes multiply and divide, and 8 addressing modes are available. The minimum instruction time is 750 nanoseconds.

Motorola's 68000 CPU [41] can address 16 megabytes and contains 17 32-bit registers. The instruction set includes multiply and divide, and has available 14 addressing modes. Data types associated with the 68000 are bits, BCD digits, bytes, words, and long words. Because of the 32 bit word option, this microprocessor can be considered a 32 bit machine with 16 bit memory access.

27.5. HARDWARE FEATURES

The microprocessor hardware knowledge that is most frequently required deals with interfacing: how to interface a CPU with memory and peripheral devices; how to interface support chips with the external environment; and how to interface several processors together to produce a larger system. The hardware interface method chosen determines the type of software driver that is necessary. Interchip interfacing problems are alleviated by manufacturer's chip sets. Understanding the processor buses is mandatory for peripheral connections, and various communication methods may be utilized between devices.

Chip Sets

Most manufacturers produce support chips for their microprocessors [42]. These include clock generators, ROM, RAM, bus drivers, and I/O. This permits an entire microcomputer system to be constructed from components that are guaranteed compatible. This can sometimes offer the advantage of multiple functions in support chips that are matched to the CPU's needs.

An Intel MCS-80 family [31] processor system could consist of the following: 8080, 8224, 8228, 8205, 8255, 8708, and two 8111s. The 8224 generates the clock and produces a reset signal. A data bus buffer, control signal demultiplexer, and single interrupt handler are combined in the 8228 system controller. The 8205 address decoder supplies chip selects. The 8708 gives 1K bytes of program memory, and the 8111s together provide 256 bytes of data memory. Three ports of I/O are handled by the 8255. This set of chips comprises a complete microcomputer package.

A similar Motorola 6800 system [34] would consist of the following: 6800 CPU, 6870 clock, 6830 ROM, 6810 RAM, and 6820 peripheral interface adapter. This combination gives 1K bytes of program memory, 128 bytes of data storage, and 20 I/O lines.

Combination support chips can reduce the component count greatly. An Intel MCS-85 system [32] could consist entirely of three chips: 8085, 8755, and 8155. The 8085 CPU contains the clock, the 8755 gives 2K bytes of EPROM program storage and 16 bits of I/O, and the 8155 supplies 256 bytes of RAM data memory, 22 bits of I/O, and a programmable timer/counter. The 8755 and 8155 support chips contain the demultiplexing circuitry required to interface with the 8085 bus. Because of the importance of matching chip sets, the choice of a microprocessor often is more dependent upon the availability of suitable support components for a particular application than characteristics of the CPU itself.

Processor Buses

Most microprocessors share bus characteristics. Figure 27.1 shows a typical CPU. The address bus is a set of output lines that is used to select a single word of memory or I/O. To permit DMA operations, this bus may have a high-impedance state to allow another device to generate a system address. The data bus is bidirectional, and the width sets the processor word size. This bus inputs data returning from memory or I/O during a read cycle, and outputs data going to memory or I/O during a write cycle. Data bus direction and access timing are set by the control bus. The control bus consists of the signals necessary to access memory and I/O, to distinguish memory from I/O, and other controls that may be processor dependent.

In an MCS-80 system, the 8228 provides four control signals: memory read, memory write, I/O read, and I/O write. With this set of controls, only one is active at any time. The appropriate line is gated with an address decoder output to activate the desired component. A ROM should only be activated during a memory read cycle, so that signal need only

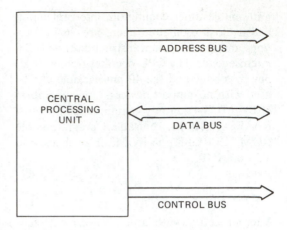

Figure 27.1. Processor buses.

be used for ROM. RAM chip selects must be gated with the memory-read and memory-write lines to allow both operations. I/O device selects are gated with one or both of the I/O control signals. Devices gated with I/O control signals will only be activated during I/O commands; for the 8080 these are but two instructions: IN and OUT. Alternatively, I/O devices may be gated with the memory control signals. Naturally, addressing is required to distinguish these devices from memory locations. This is called memory-mapped I/O; I/O devices are treated the same as memory, and therefore can be addressed through any memory-accessing instruction. Processors that have separate I/O channels supply the option of using the separate I/O address space or using a portion of the memory address space via memory-mapped I/O. For those processors that have no special I/O address space, memory-mapped I/O must be used.

On the 6800, there are three control lines: R/W, VMA, and Ø2. The R/W line distinguishes between read and write operations. A valid memory address is on the address bus only when the VMA line is active. In addition, the clock phase two is reserved for memory accesses. Chip selects should be gated with all three signals and an address decoder. There are no I/O signals or instructions on the 6800, so memory mapped I/O is used exclusively.

The control bus emanating from the CPU may be converted into a different set of control signals used throughout the microcomputer;

the three 6800 signals can be converted into two control signals (memory read and memory write) if desired. Which set of control signals is preferable in any system is wholly dependent upon the accessing organization of the peripheral chips.

I/O Peripherals

Peripheral chips range from the very simple to the quite complex. The simplest output port is just a latch; the latch inputs go to the data bus, the gate is the chip select, and the outputs comprise the peripheral lines. The simplest input port is a tristate buffer; the processor reads the peripheral lines when the control signals activate the buffer. Several of these I/O ports can be combined into a single chip with additional steering logic, and are called peripheral interface adapters (PIA), or programmable peripheral interfaces (PPI). (For example, the 6820 and the 8255.) More sophisticated logic functions realized on a single chip can be used as peripheral devices, such as a universal asynchronous receiver/transmitter (UART). Most processor families contain at a minimum PIA and UART chips.

Complex peripheral functions are implemented with single chip microprocessors. Intel's UPI-41 [43, 44] is a universal peripheral interface chip that is a complete processor with controls configured as a slave device. The UPI-41 can be used to preprocess information to conform with any number of external devices, removing this burden from the main processor and permitting more time to be allocated to higher-level processing. There are other specialized peripheral chips that are actually single chip processors programmed by the manufacturer for a specific function; this is transparent to the user.

The most sophisticated peripherals can be coprocessors. These devices monitor CPU operation and perform functions as needed without specifically being requested by the main CPU; the effect is to extend the instruction set of the CPU. Intel's 8087 [45–47] floating-point processor and 8089 [40] I/O processor are in this category.

Communication Methods

The CPU must know when a peripheral is ready to receive data, and then have a method to send the data. Alternatively, when a device needs servicing a method must be provided for it to inform the CPU. Communication between peripheral chips and the CPU is usually through registers in the peripheral. A control register permits the CPU to configure the peripheral as required. A status register is read by the CPU to determine current device conditions. Data registers are used to transfer the actual information.

In the simplest control environment, the CPU constantly polls the peripherals to determine if any require servicing. Polling stops to permit peripheral handling when servicing is required, and continues when the request is met. A disadvantage of this polling method is that the CPU can spend a large portion of its processing time just checking service request bits of each device. During the servicing of a device, it may be desirable for higher-priority peripherals to have the ability to request servicing. Polling during device servicing can become complicated when a number of peripherals exist. There also can be a high or unpredictable latency period between when the request occurs and when the servicing is granted. These problems can often be eliminated by using interrupt-driven peripherals.

With an interrupt-driven system [48, 49], in addition to the device register communications, a peripheral output line is fed to a CPU interrupt input. When the device requires servicing, the processor is interrupted, and the service routine can communicate through the peripheral registers. Through proper handling of interrupt enables, masks, and priorities, all devices can be serviced optimally with interrupts.

Some peripheral devices require data rates that are too high to be handled through CPU/data register communications. An example is that of a floppy disk controller peripheral. These peripherals may achieve the necessary data rate through direct memory access (DMA). The peripheral activates an output line when data are either available or required.

This output feeds an input on the CPU which requests a DMA cycle. When the current instruction is completed, the CPU grants the DMA cycle and notifies the peripheral by activating a DMA-granted output line. This tells the peripheral that the CPU has freed the buses, and the peripheral can seize the buses and communicate with memory directly, instead of going through the processor. When the data transfer is complete, the peripheral lowers the DMA request line, and the CPU regains control of the buses. This method permits data rates as high as the memory bandwidth is capable. DMA may be handled completely by the peripheral device, or there may be a special DMA controller peripheral chip that provides the addresses and control signals for the data-requesting peripheral.

27.6. LANGUAGE FEATURES

Microprocessor instruction sets vary between processors, and machine language is greatly affected by architecture. The operations available are generally similar for many CPUs. Special architecture-related instructions are usually provided. A microprocessor language can be best understood through knowledge of the machine's architecture, the various addressing modes, how flags are affected and tests are made, and familiarity with the available instructions. The 8080 and 6800 are used in this section for illustration.

Addressing Modes

Machine operations must specify an operand or operands. The allowable addressing modes designate the operands that may be selected.

Register addressing is used when operands are general-purpose registers. The 8080 instruction "INR r" increments the contents of register r, where r is any of the seven 8080 registers. With other processors, register addressing is called accumulator addressing. The 6800 instructions "INC A" and "INC B" increment accumulator A and B, respectively. The register- (or accumulator-) addressing mode tends to be the fastest because the operands are internal to the CPU, and additional memory ac-

cesses are not required beyond the instruction fetch. Register addressing produces compact code because these are single byte instructions.

The immediate addressing mode is used when an operand is constant data. The 8080 instruction "ADI data" adds the data in the memory location following the op-code to the accumulator and stores the result in the accumulator. The 6800 instruction "ADD A,#data" does likewise with accumulator A. Immediate addressing can refer to single- or double-byte data, resulting in either 2- or 3-byte instructions.

Direct, absolute, or extended addressing specifies an exact memory location for use as an operand. The 8080 instruction "LDA addr" is a 3 byte instruction where the address of the memory location containing the data to be loaded into the accumulator is given. This is similar to the 6800 instruction "LDA A addr" when extended addressing is used—this 3 byte instruction performs the same action with accumulator A as the 8080 instruction does. A variant of extended addressing on the 6800 is direct addressing. This mode implies operands located at addresses within the first page of memory (addresses 0 through 255). Only a single byte is needed to specify the operand; hence these instructions are 2 bytes long.

Register indirect addressing specifies a register pair that contains the memory address where the data are located. The 8080 instruction "LDAX rp", where rp is a register pair, loads the accumulator from the memory location whose address is the contents of the specified 16 bit register. Indexed addressing takes this method a step further. An index register specifies a base address to which a single byte offset given in the second byte of the instruction is added, supplying the address of the data. The 6800 instruction "LDA A offset,X" takes the 8 bit quantity offset, adds it to the 16 bit index register, and uses the resultant 16 bit address to locate the data to be placed into accumulator A. Register indirect and indexed addressing are powerful addressing modes because the data address can be changed dynamically during program execution. These addressing modes are essential for efficient table lookup routines.

There are instructions for which an addressing mode need not be given, either because one is implied by the instruction, or because an addressing mode is not applicable. An example of the former is the 6800 instruction "ABA" which adds accumulators A and B and stores the result in A; an example of the latter is the 8080 instruction "STC" which sets the carry flag. These instructions are referred to as having either implied or inherent addressing.

Relative addressing references data or addresses to the program counter. The 6800 branch instructions use the second byte of the instruction as a signed 8 bit offset to the address, which the program counter would contain were a branch not encountered. There are two advantages to the relative addressing mode: 2-byte instructions result instead of 3-byte instructions, and the reference to the program counter produces machine code blocks that are not dependent upon memory location.

Flags and Tests

Flags are single bit flip-flops that are set and reset by processor operations and can be subsequently tested for the purpose of conditional branching. Flag bits are collected into a register called the processor status word (PSW) or the condition code register (CCR). Most of these flags are defined by Boolean arithmetic: overflow, carry/borrow, sign bit, auxillary or half carry, zero, or parity. Arithmetic and logical operations affect these flags in the usual sense.

The operations that do and do not set flags differ greatly from processor to processor. This can easily confuse the programmer familiar with one processor who is learning to use another. The instructions can perform the same operations on different processors yet affect flags quite dissimilarly. On the 8080, "MOV" operations affect no flags; on the 6800, the equivalent "LDA" instructions clear the overflow flag, and set or reset the sign and zero flags in accordance with the data. When flags have not been affected, and it is desired to make a test concerned with data from a previous operation, an additional flag-setting operation is required. The 8080 input instruction

affects no flags. To use the zero or sign bit flags after inputting data with the "IN port" instruction, a flag-setting operation such as "ORA A" must follow the input instruction. Conversely, sometimes instructions will affect flags when it is not desired, and in these cases it is necessary to save them prior to the operation for later retrieval.

Flags can be used for simple parameter passing between routines. For example, a subroutine can be defined that exits with the carry set if an invalid condition is encountered, and exits with the carry clear otherwise. Software that called the routine can then easily branch to handle the different cases by performing a simple carry flag test upon return from the subroutine. Care must be taken to ensure that flags are not inadvertently modified in such instances.

Included in processor instruction sets are special flag-testing operations. The 6800 bit test instructions permit testing of particular bits without modifying data. Compare instructions are essentially subtract operations that modify only flags, not data. Conditional branch, jump, and return instructions test the flags in various combinations.

Other flags may be included in the CCR. The 6800 has an interrupt status flag, which signifies whether the interrupt mask is set or reset. The 8048 has two general purpose flags that can be used as the programmer desires. Both flags can be cleared and complemented, and tested by conditional jump instructions. The 8048 also has eight conditional jump instructions that test the individual bits of the accumulator; these are not flag bits but can be tested just as easily as flags.

Flags and tests permit conditional branching, which is the greatest source of program complexity. Great care must be taken so that flags are modified correctly to ensure proper branching.

Instructions

The specific instructions with which processors are equipped varies, but a certain number are shared by most, and fit into categories.

Data transfer instructions include move,

load, store, and exchange operations. A large part of controller software consists of data transfer, and this instruction block is heavily utilized.

Arithmetic instructions are add, subtract, increment, decrement, and decimal adjust. Logical instructions consist of AND, OR, exclusive OR, rotate and shift, clear, complement, negate, compare, and test instructions. Branch instructions are jump, conditional jump, subroutine call, conditional subroutine call, return from subroutine, return from interrupt, conditional return from subroutine, software interrupt, and wait for interrupt instructions.

Stack instructions are push, and pop or pull operations on registers. Machine control instructions include interrupt handling, halt, no operation, and I/O instructions.

The instruction set differences between processors will cause different software techniques to be employed for different processors. Registers or memory for parameter storage, stack or reserved memory for temporary data save, and methods for parameter passing [50] between routines are choices that are processor dependent.

27.7. CONTROL PROGRAMS

Controllers require programs that are typically several thousand bytes long. Sufficient hardware is provided for the controller to satisfy the needs of the specific application. The resulting small size serves to keep the cost down. The size and execution speed of controller software have a direct effect on the amount of hardware required for a particular function. Control programs should not be viewed in the same fashion as large system software. This section discusses choice of language, software interfaces with peripherals, and some programming techniques and concludes with a controller example.

Language

Control programs are often written in assembly language, partly because of the fact that in the early microprocessor years flexible software packages were not available. This left the engineer with little alternative than to write an entire control program in assembly language. There are a number of advantages of assembly code for control applications.

Much of the software is at a very low level, consisting of software interfaces with peripherals. This is easily handled with assembly language, and little advantage can be found in other languages for this type of software—indeed, higher-level languages are often unwieldy when dealing with very low-level tasks. Assembly language lets the programmer utilize the full power of a processor's instruction set, with no other limitations imposed. Assembly code can be shorter and execute faster than higher-level languages, a particularly important feature for microprocessor controllers because shorter programs require less ROM, and the relatively slow microprocessor can be used in some applications only by optimizing software for speed. Control programs are short enough so that it is reasonable to code with assembly language, whereas for much larger programs it is generally recognized that a higher-level language would be preferable. For these reasons, assembly language has maintained a strong hold on controller software.

However, assembly language has its disadvantages. There are a large number of instructions required to perform a complicated task. If an equivalent program can be written with fewer instructions in a higher-level language, the software cost will be reduced. Following program flow in assembly coding can be difficult. Higher-level languages can be understood more easily. Although effort has been made to standardize assembly code [51, 52], more often than not a new assembly language must be learned for every CPU that is used. Structured programming can be enforced or encouraged with a high-level language.

High-level languages that permit low-level functions and assembly-level subroutine calls can remove the disadvantages of completely assembly-coded programs, while retaining much of the advantages of assembly coding. Some increase in program size must be granted, and time-critical routines can still be optimized in assembly code [53]. Software portability can be obtained through languages that exist for several processors. Even interpretive languages may be suitable for some tasks [54]. Compiled languages can execute at respectable speeds and do not require a large run-time software package for execution. A number of high-level languages are available for microprocessors [55–64].

Some applications can be met through the development of a specific pseudocode. A set of subroutines may need to be called in varying order, and a list of addresses that point to subroutines can be formed into a pseudocode program. A small interpreter can be used to call the appropriate routines from the pseudocode program. Pseudointerpreters can range from the very simple to complete high-level, user-defined languages [65–68].

For complex control applications, control software can be simplified by utilizing a real-time operating system (RTOS) [69]. This permits multitasking software to be written for an application without the programmer becoming involved with the complexity of the multitasking software—only the application-dependent software. A prepackaged RTOS can be used to advantage in these instances.

Software Interface with Peripherals

A representative peripheral device communicates with the CPU through several peripheral registers. These registers are part of the peripheral chip and are accessed through proper manipulation of the address and control lines. Data are transferred through a data register. The CPU can determine the state of the peripheral by reading its status register. Status register bits are reserved to indicate that the device is ready to receive data, or that the device has received external data and that data are available to be read by the CPU. Through interrogation of the status register, the processor can send or receive information through the data register in a controlled fashion.

Many peripheral devices can be configured in different ways. The CPU can configure the peripheral by writing to its control register. This permits a single hardware device to serve different functions under software control.

Complex peripherals may have additional parameter registers for storage of control parameters.

A processor can service several peripherals by polling their status registers and handling the devices as required. Interrupt-driven devices need the appropriate handling software. A peripheral requiring service raises its interrupt request line. If the processor has interrupts enabled and unmasked, the CPU executes an interrupt acknowledge cycle, and control is transferred to the interrupt service routine. If more than one device can cause the same interrupt, the relevant status registers are read to ascertain which is the interrupting device. The necessary servicing software is then executed, followed by a return from the interrupt routine.

When the interrupt is acknowledged, the processor interrupts are usually disabled, which prevents multiple interrupts from level sensitive interrupt inputs. If interrupts are to be permitted during the execution of the interrupt service routine, then the processor interrupts should be reenabled or unmasked near the beginning of the service routine. Otherwise, steps should be taken to ensure that interrupts are reactivated after the completion of the service routine. Some processors will automatically do this via a return from interrupt instruction. Others require interrupt-enabling instructions before the return instruction. If some means is not taken to restore the interrupt status after the completion of the interrupt-handling software, no further interrupts will be possible.

A controller may have several interrupt-driven peripherals utilizing different interrupt inputs. Sophisticated interrupt-handling software can be devised by selectively masking the interrupts. One device may have priority over the others; its interrupt service routine should not reactivate interrupts until after completion of its task. The other interrupt service routines, upon entry, should reactivate interrupts after masking all but the one priority device. Proper manipulation of interrupt enables and masks can produce any desired relationship between peripherals and the CPU. Minicomputers and some 16 bit micros support prioritized vectored interrupts. This hardware function reduces software interrupt controls to modification of priority registers.

Programming Techniques

Control processors lack the high-powered instructions and high speed of large computers. This weakness can often be combatted with the extensive use of lookup tables. Values that can be determined by complex calculation are instead placed into a table in ROM. The advantage is that the complex calculation, which is difficult to implement in the restricted instruction set and requires a long execution time, is avoided. A properly indexed table lookup routine can execute rapidly. An example of a lookup table replacing a conventional gravity calculation is found in Reference 70. An additional advantage is that should the control equation require substitution with another in a program revision, instead of requiring a new complex calculation routine, table value changes are simply needed. Table data can be trimmed to match true specifications versus approximation by a mathematical formula. The disadvantage of this type of lookup table is that much ROM space can be occupied, particularly when small step sizes are utilized. Linear interpolation and clever methods for finding values through multiple tables can reduce table lengths to manageable sizes.

The proper use of interrupts can simplify software beyond the needs of peripheral interfacing. The segmentation of software between several interrupt routines and the main program serves to make the software structure more comprehensible. Placement of interrupt-driven peripheral data into a queue permits other routines to directly work with the data queue instead of the I/O details. A real-time clock interrupt may be desirable as a programming tool even if a clock function is not required in the controller. Multiple functions can be handled by a single controller almost as simply as dedicating a separate processor to each function if clock interrupts are used to allocate time to each task. The alternative is to write one integrated control program that performs each function; this is certainly more complex than writing separate, individual control programs and allocating CPU time to each through a clock interrupt routine.

Care must be taken to check the execution times of interrupt routines to ensure adequate time before another interrupt service is required. Perishable peripheral data must be handled before being overwritten and lost. It should be seen that the use of interrupts falls into two distinct categories: efficient peripheral communication and desirable software segmentation.

Special programming techniques are usually not required for DMA processing since DMA is inherently a hardware procedure. This can be limited to programming a special purpose DMA-handling peripheral chip. An example of this can be found in [71].

Control programs can have need for standard computations as do larger machines, but these must be written with the imposed restrictions of the less powerful CPU. Examples of pseudorandom sequence generation [72–74], multiply routines [75, 76], and fast Fourier transforms [77] can be found. Programming techniques can be found in References 78, 79.

A Controller Example

The software structure of a microprocessor based CRT terminal will be described. Before writing the control software, the programmer must first have knowledge of the hardware structure: which chips perform peripheral functions, and how communication is established between the CPU and peripheral devices. The terminal accepts serial data and displays the ASCII character on a CRT monitor connected to the video output of the terminal. Characters entered on a keyboard are translated into ASCII and transmitted over the serial line. Keyboard characters may optionally be echoed on the display. Activating a *mode key* temporarily replaces the displayed screen with a menu of available terminal options, such as baud rate, parity modes, tabs, scrolling, and cursor type. Keyboard entries change the options and modify the menu accordingly. A second depression of the mode key restores the original display screen and returns operation to that of a standard CRT terminal.

Figure 27.2 shows a block diagram of the

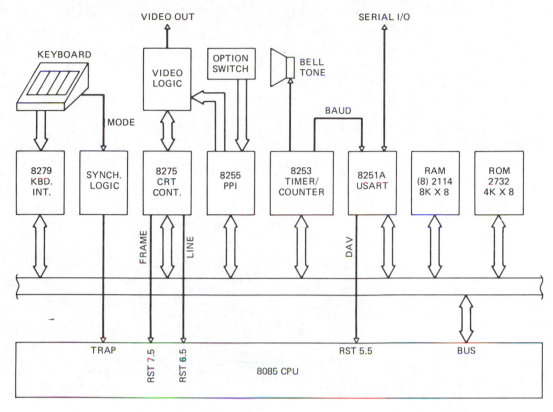

Figure 27.2. Sample CRT terminal controller.

CRT terminal. A similar system can be found in References 71 and 80. An 8085 CPU with 8K of RAM and 4K of ROM forms the basis of the controller. Most of the RAM is used for screen memory and is large enough to permit off-page scrolling. The control program and its associated tables are contained in the ROM. Serial interface is handled by an 8251A USART (universal synchronous asynchronous receiver/transmitter). An 8253 timer/counter is used as a programmable divider operating from the CPU master clock to provide two signals: the baud rate clock for the USART, giving software-controllable baud rates, and an audio output tone to produce a bell signal. An 8275 CRT controller operates in conjunction with video circuitry to generate the video output. Power-on options are set by an internal switch and read by an input port of an 8255 PPI, which also has output ports to control the video circuitry. The keyboard is scanned by an 8279 keyboard interface device.

The controller operates with four interrupts. The mode switch signal is passed through synchronizing logic to the TRAP input. This is a nonmaskable interrupt input. When a character is received on the serial line, the USART raises the data available (DAV) output, requesting an RST5.5 interrupt.

The remaining two interrupts are used for communication with the CRT controller chip. The 8275 is designed to obtain display characters through DMA. One line of characters is loaded at a time, and video timing requirements are such that 80 characters must be loaded in less than 600 microseconds. This high-speed data transfer is best accomplished with DMA logic, a procedure that is shown in Reference 71 and that requires a DMA controller chip. A different method, using interrupts instead of DMA, is found in Reference 80. Hardware transforms the 8275 DMA control signals into signals that permit data transfer via a sequence of memory reads, initiated by an interrupt. The end of a display line interrupts the RST6.5 line. This interrupt service routine must send the appropriate characters to the 8275, which then converts them

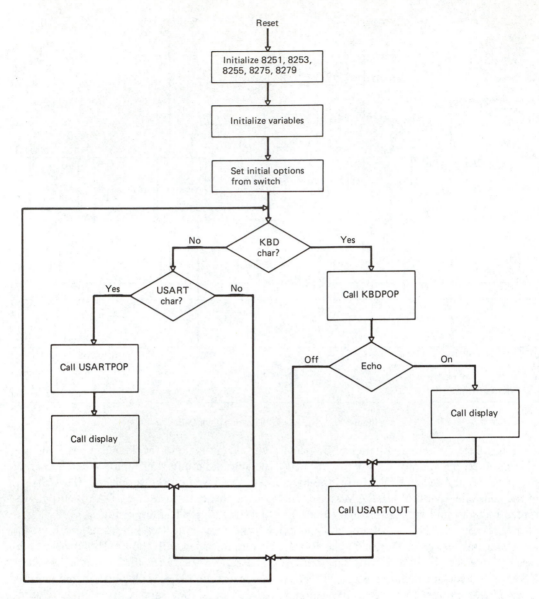

Figure 27.3. Main program.

into video signals with the external logic. When the display page is complete, the 8275 signals the CPU through the RST7.5 interrupt that the frame is complete. The CPU must then reset the display pointer to the top display line in preparation for the next RST6.5 interrupt. Video conventions cause the RST7.5 interrupt to be activated 60 times per second. This accurate interrupt is also used as a real-time clock interrupt.

Figure 27.3 shows the main program, and

Figure 27.4 shows the interrupt routines. Upon power-up, variables are initialized. The peripheral devices are then initialized through their control registers. This device initialization must set the operating modes and the starting data. Figure 27.5a gives the software necessary to initialize the PPI.

The RST7.5 interrupt routine sets the display line pointer (used in the RST6.5 routine) to the top display line of the screen. The keyboard peripheral is checked for key depres-

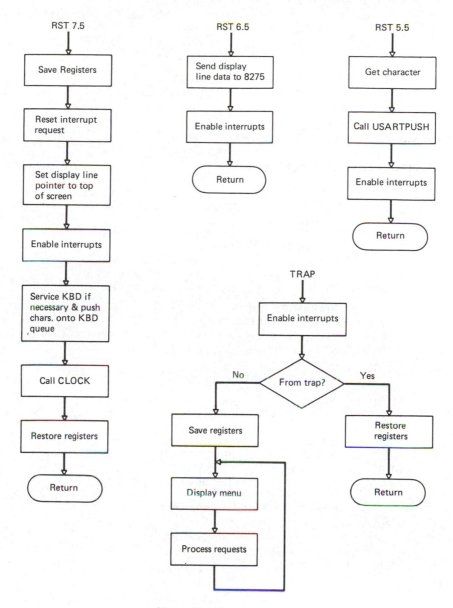

Figure 27.4. Interrupt routines.

sions; if any are found, the character is translated into ASCII and pushed into a keyboard queue. A real-time clock updating routine is called, and the interrupt routine exits. Interrupts are reenabled during the servicing of the RST7.5, permitting the much faster RST6.5 interrupts to occur during the clock and keyboard processing.

The RST6.5 interrupt routine sends the display line of data specified by the display pointer to the 8275. Because this occurs at ap-

proximately 600 microsecond intervals, this consumes a large portion of the available CPU time, and this interrupt service routine must be trimmed for rapid execution.

The RST5.5 interrupt is straightforward—the status register need not be checked since a character must be available (it caused the interrupt). The character, therefore, is read from the USART data register and pushed into a received character queue. This software is shown in Figure 27.5b.

A. 8255 PPI Initialization

```
MVI        A,90H             ;SET PORT A TO INPUT,
OUT        PPICONTROL        ;PORTS B & C TO OUTPUT
MVI        A,BYTEB           ;INITIALIZE
OUT        PPIPORTB          ;PORT B
MVI        A,BYTEC           ;INITIALIZE
OUT        PPIPORTC          ;PORT C
```

B. USART Interrupt Routine

```
;RST 5.5 INTERRUPT SERVICE ROUTINE
;
; CHARACTER AVAILABLE FROM USART
;
RST55: PUSH  PSW             ;SAVE ACCUMULATOR & FLAGS
       IN                    ;READ CHARACTER FROM
             USARTDATA       USART
                             ;PUSH CHARACTER ONTO
       CALL  USARTPUSH       QUEUE
       POP   PSW             ;RESTORE ACC. & FLAGS
       EI                    ;REENABLE INTERRUPTS
       RET                   ;RETURN FROM INTERRUPT
```

C. OUTPUT CHARACTER ROUTINE

```
; OUTPUT A CHARACTER FROM REGISTER A
TO THE USART.
; WAIT UNTIL USART IS READY IF
NECESSARY.
;
USARTOUT:
WAIT: PUSH   PSW             ;SAVE CHARACTER TO BE SENT
      IN     USARTSTATUS     ;READ USART STATUS REGISTER
      RAR                    ;CHECK BUSY BIT
      JNC    WAIT            ;LOOP IF BUSY
      POP    PSW             ;RETRIEVE CHARACTER
      OUT    USARTDATA       ;TRANSMIT IT
      RET                    ;RETURN FROM ROUTINE
```

Figure 27.5. CRT terminal controller software.

After main program initialization, a simple loop program is executed to perform the CRT terminal function. The keyboard queue is checked; if it is not empty, a keyboard pop routine retrieves a character in a first in, first out (FIFO) order. If the echo is enabled, the display routine is called, placing the character on the screen. The character is then transmitted with the USART output routine (shown in Figure 27.5c). When all keyboard characters are sent, the received character queue is checked. If a character is found, a character is retrieved from this FIFO queue by the USART pop routine, and the character displayed.

Depression of the mode switch takes control from the main terminal loop and transfers it to the TRAP routine. Interrupts are reenabled, permitting video functions to continue. A program loop is entered that displays terminal options and permits changes via the keyboard. Any serial characters arriving during execution of this function continue to be placed into the received character queue, and will be displayed when the options-setting mode is departed. The various terminal options are stored in lookup tables, and one table-accessing routine serves for many options. Rather than calculating the required divider ratio to supply specified baud rates from a fixed master clock, these ratios are precalculated and stored in the same table that supplies the baud rate menu. A second mode switch depression interrupts the TRAP interrupt routine itself, this is detected, and a return from the original interrupt is performed, returning normal CRT terminal operation.

This microprocessor controller example shows how control, status, and data registers and interrupts are used for communication with peripherals. A typical use of lookup tables is also given.

27.8. DEVELOPMENT AIDS

Software production requires much time. Methods that can reduce the required time to write, test, debug, and finalize programs are valuable.

Assemblers

CPU manufacturers assign mnemonics to the binary machine language instructions. An assembler is a program that accepts as input an assembly language source program written with mnemonics, and that outputs the corresponding machine language object code. A minimal assembler performs other functions: address calculation, symbol substitution for data and addresses, offset calculation, binary, octal, decimal, and hexadecimal conversions, addition, subtraction, multiplication, and division of data and addresses, error flagging, and formatted listing and symbol table preparation. A discussion of assemblers can be found in Reference 81.

An assembler program may execute on the same processor for which it is written, in which case it is called a resident assembler, or on a different host processor, where it is called a cross assembler. Controller software will always be assembled on a host machine, not on the controller itself; the host may be of the same type CPU as the controller or completely different. This is in contrast with software for large computers, which is usually assembled on the machine for which it is being written.

Cross assemblers are often more powerful than resident assemblers for micros because of the greater size and speed of the computer on which the cross assembler is being run, compared with even a large size micro hosting a resident assembler.

A standard assembler operates on a one-for-one basis between mnemonics and object code. A macro assembler permits a set of instructions to be defined as a macro command. Commonly used instruction sequences can be simplified with macros. Caution should be exercised not to use macros when subroutines are more appropriate; the use of macros can increase speed while sacrificing program shortness. Discussions of macro assemblers can be found in References 78 and 82.

Development Board

A controller prototype may be constructed from a standard development board for a specific CPU. The board contains the CPU, ROM, RAM, and I/O. A monitor program located in ROM permits loading programs into RAM for test execution. The prototype is not identical to the dedicated, special-purpose final product, but contains enough devices to substitute for the actual controller. Most development boards contain an area where specialized circuitry can be quickly added with wire-wrapped or point-to-point connections. The advantage of the development board is that software can quickly be loaded into RAM for execution, and the debug features of the development board can be exercised to decrease the time between program iterations. Development boards have a keyboard for program entry and control, and display readouts for memory interrogation and status checking. Down-line loading—the capability to directly load software from a host system to the board—greatly reduces turn-around time. Development boards are available for most microprocessors.

Debug Capabilities

The low-level ROM monitor resident on a development board permits the power of the CPU to be utilized for debugging purposes. At a minimum, after execution of test software, memory locations can be examined to determine the effect of the test program. Data values can be changed through the monitor and the test program again executed. Subroutines for I/O and other functions located in the monitor can be called by test programs to simplify testing. An example of a low-level monitor that can be used on a development board is found in Reference 83.

When all else fails, if the development board has the capability, single stepping through a program will usually locate a problem, although patience is advised with this method. Single stepping can be performed either with hardware or monitor software. The effect is to permit only a single instruction of the test program to be executed at a time. A more effective debug method consists of placing breakpoints at critical spots in the test program. When execution reaches a breakpoint, control is transferred from the test program to the ROM monitor, from which additional tests can be performed. Multiple breakpoint setting can permit zeroing in on a problem in short order. Sophisticated breakpoint capabilities allow a breakpoint to be passed a specific number of times before transfer of control takes place. This is useful in testing program loops.

Development Systems

Because of the inherent nature of a controller, software development must be done on a different system or on a host processor. Although general-purpose computers can be used to this end, development systems are produced specifically for this purpose [84–86]. The development system includes assemblers and high-level language compilers. Test program execution can be done to a limited extent directly on the system.

Simulation can be used to provide debug features that are not available on a development board or test controller. A simulator is a program that creates a virtual machine patterned after the CPU of interest, and the test software is supplied to the simulator as input. Simulation runs much slower than direct execution, and timing relationships may not hold. As a result, simulation may not be effective in testing software interfacing between devices that are time critical.

The most sophisticated of debug techniques is emulation. With this method the development system controls a special hardware package that behaves the same as an actual CPU. A plug from the emulator replaces the processor chip from a test controller. Timing remains the same as with the actual CPU, and the development system can track the behavior of the test controller to provide advanced debugging capabilities at actual operating speed in the actual controller. Descriptions of emulators can be found in References 87 to 91.

After debugging, the program must be placed, or burned, into EPROM. The development system must have the capability to burn the EPROM. A large number of EPROMs are available, and EPROM programmers generally have personality modules that are selected for individual EPROMs. This capability is most important when the debug features of a sophisticated development board or system are not available: in this case, the test programs must be placed into EPROM and tested on the actual controller for each program iteration.

It can be seen that the development aids for small microprocessor controllers can be very powerful computers when compared with the small controller for which they are created.

27.9. HARDWARE/SOFTWARE TRADEOFFS

There are many controller functions that can be realized through either hardware or software. A choice must be made between hardware peripheral devices and additional software for hardware replacement. A common example is that of a serial interface. Hardware implementation can be done with a UART, satisfying both sending and receiving functions. A program, called a software UART, may instead by written that, in conjunction with two bits of parallel I/O, performs the UART task.

The advantage of the software UART is clear—one integrated circuit package is eliminated (if two I/O bits are otherwise available). There are several disadvantages. Unless complicated software is used, it is not possible to send and receive a character at the same time. The CPU is occupied with the actual timing of the serial data, and this time is generally wasted in software UARTs. An input character may be missed or received incorrectly if it arrives while the processor is not ready for it. With clever software these drawbacks can be removed. The complexity of the software must be contrasted with the almost trivial software interface that a hardware UART requires.

The decision to implement a function in software or hardware depends upon the demands on the CPU and the relative cost of either approach. If spare processor time is available, and a large number of controller units are to be produced, the additional software cost will be overshadowed by the reduction in hardware in production quantities. For low-quantity products, depending upon the additional software complexity, it may be preferable to use a hardware implementation simply to save on software cost. Software implementations may require an additional ROM for greater program storage, cancelling the advantage of eliminating peripheral chips.

Software implementation of several hardware functions may bog the processor down such that it barely has enough time to perform its task. Costs may indicate that the software approach is preferable, but if product updates are expected, it might not be possible to handle additional software because it could overextend the processor power. Eliminating hardware peripherals from a controller design may result in a compact, several-chip design. As a byproduct, address decoders for peripheral device selection may not be needed and may be left out. If the time comes when a peripheral needs to be added, the bus structure of the mostly software approach may preclude additional devices without extensive redesign. This tradeoff is clear: structuring a controller so that it has good capability for hardware expansion increases costs. This fact must be weighed against the lower flexibility of a wholly software implementation.

The major distinction between hardware and software function implementations is speed. Floating-point operations can certainly be handled in software—but the speed can be increased tremendously with the addition of a floating-point processor chip. The chip versus subroutine question will usually be answered in terms of the performance requirements.

27.10. FAULT TOLERANCE

The subject of fault-tolerant computing encompasses a large area. Considering microprocessor-based controllers instead of general-purpose computers causes a shift in fault-tolerant perspectives.

High Reliability Requirements

Processor-based devices often control critical mechanisms. The results of many microprocessor applications would be disastrous, were the processor system to fail in a particular fashion [92]. Automotive controllers, power plant controls, industrial process control, and air- and space-borne systems provide examples where reliability considerations must seriously be explored. Greater concern must be given to reliability in computer control applications than general-purpose computing applications.

There are two types of faults: permanent and intermittent or transient (I/T). Permanent faults cause physical damage and the malfunctioning device must be replaced. I/T faults can be due to many causes, some of which are the effects of a hostile environment. Electromagnetic interference from various sources can disturb processor systems, not physically damaging any circuit element, but nevertheless causing a system upset. ROM program storage in microprocessor controllers prevents I/T faults from modifying the program store, improving recovery chances. Depending upon the I/T fault severity and hardware and software configurations, the system may or may not be able to recover from an upset. A number of approaches can be used to increase the likelihood of system recovery.

Hardware Modifications

Additional hardware can be used to improve a controller's reliability. Checkbits increasing the number of bits per word can augment processor memory with error-correcting codes. This approach safeguards a portion of a controller but does not guard the entire system.

Traps of several sorts can flag system errors. Invalid memory access is often a result of a program crash, and invalid address traps can be used to interrupt or reset the CPU. Invalid op-code fetch traps will catch system upsets that result in data being incorrectly interpreted as instructions. Special monitoring circuitry can detect undesirable states such as halts or interrupt disable modes. The primary concern of reliability constraints in controllers is to prevent a total program crash, in which

event the control function is terminated. The secondary concern is to then preserve data integrity. If a system crash is aborted, the power of the processor can be used to determine the best place to resume control—once a fault causes a crash, unless the system is somehow restarted, all is lost.

Software Modifications

Internal state variables can be encoded in a fashion such that faults causing variable changes can be caught later as data inconsistencies. Proper segmentation of software modules permits subprograms to check one an-

A. Routine Correct for Defined Inputs, But an
Undefined Input Causes Endless Loop

```
;BIT POSITION TO BINARY CONVERTER
ROUTINE
;
;ENTER WITH A SINGLE BIT SET IN REGISTER
A
;EXIT WITH REGISTER B CONTAINING THE
BINARY
;POSITION OF THE SINGLE SET BIT.
;DESTROYS REGISTER A.
;

           MVI    B,-1      ;INITIALIZE REGISTER B
LOOP:      INR    B         ;BUMP COUNTER
           RRC              ;ROTATE REGISTER A RIGHT
           JNC    LOOP      ;CHECK FOR CARRY SET
           RET              ;RETURN FROM SUBROUTINE
```

B. Corrected Subroutine

```
;BIT POSITION TO BINARY CONVERTER
ROUTINE
;
;ENTER WITH A SINGLE BIT SET IN REGISTER
A
;EXIT WITH REGISTER B CONTAINING THE
BINARY
;POSITION OF THE SINGLE SET BIT.
;DESTROYS REGISTER A.
;
;NOW WITH GUARANTEED EXIT.

           MVI    B,-1      ;INITIALIZE REGISTER B
LOOP:      INR    B         ;BUMP COUNTER
           ORA    A         ;SEE IF REGISTER A=0
           RZ               ;YES, ABORT AND RETURN
           RRC              ;ROTATE REGISTER A RIGHT
           JNC    LOOP      ;CHECK FOR CARRY SET
           RET              ;RETURN FROM SUBROUTINE
```

Figure 27.6. Effects of out-of-range input variables.

other. Obvious checks—such as verifying that the stack pointer and other data pointers are within the proper boundaries—can be made to permit a software reset.

A fairly simple, yet important constraint can be added to program modules to improve survivability, which may not be addressed other than in the context of upset phenomena. Program modules often execute on the assumption that some conditions hold on input variables. If no faults appear, these assumptions will be correct. A fault arrival can change a variable, either directly or indirectly, and the effect on the subsequent program module must be considered. Correct results must be guaranteed from a module if entry is with uncorrupted variables; module exit must be guaranteed under all input possibilities. An endless loop created by invalid input conditions causes a program crash. Figure 27.6a shows how this can occur. This module works on the assumption that upon entry, register A contains a single set bit. If this subroutine is called with register A erroneously containing all zeroes, an endless loop results. A simple test shown in Figure 27.6b can correct this problem.

Totally software checks can be made by performing calculations several times and checking to see if the results agree. This method can be effective by spreading the computations out over time so that environmentally induced faults will only affect some computations and not others. The byproduct of this fault tolerance method is lowered throughput, since one processor is repeating its calculations many times, where only once is required in the absence of faults.

Combined Hardware and Software Modifications

A commonly used procedure to guard against program crashes is that of a watchdog timer. A hardware timer is appended to the system, and the software is modified so that it periodically activates it. The timer is connected so that if the processor fails to activate it within a specified period of time, the system is interrupted or reset. This method works on the assumption that when the system crashes, it will fail to periodically activate the external timer.

Very elaborate fault-tolerant schemes are possible with microprocessor controllers. The use of voters and triple modular redundancy techniques [93], with appropriate system software exercising, can be used to achieve high reliability.

Much can be done with both hardware and software to improve controller reliability [94]. It is very difficult to be able to evaluate general systems for proper validation.

27.11. PERSPECTIVE FOR THE FUTURE

Microprocessor-based controllers will surely continue to replace a greater number of random-logic designs, and applications will place such controllers in almost all electronic equipment, providing intelligent interfaces with humans. This expanded controller usage will expedite the concern of fault tolerance in such devices. If chips become available that are designed for use with high-reliability measures, then built-in fault tolerance should be addressed.

The semiconductor industry is preparing itself for designs that can intelligently utilize a million transistors per integrated circuit. Design considerations for single-chip processors of the future can be found in Reference 95. Microprocessors that can challenge the power of current mainframe computers are appearing now. Intel's iAPX 432 micromainframe [96] is an indication of the future of sophisticated microprocessors.

The predicted software catastrophe resulting from transferring system design from hardware to software will be combatted with built-in operating systems [97]. This could alleviate software design problems in much the same way as standard digital logic packages aided random-logic synthesis.

Powerful computing systems constructed from many inexpensive microprocessor elements promise to be the way of the future. These distributed intelligence designs will depend upon much microprocessor software development.

REFERENCES

1. L. Waller, "Microcomputers to Run Test House," *Electronics,* vol. 52, no. 15, July 19, 1979, pp. 92–93.

2. P. J. O'Malley, "The Ahwatukee House," Motorola Semiconductor Group, Motorola Inc.
3. W. D. Pierce, "Microprocessor-Controlled Home Environment," Motorola Semiconductor Division, Motorola Inc.
4. "Microcomputer Net is Ultimate Thermostat," *Electronics,* vol. 53, no. 15, July 3, 1980, pp. 88–90.
5. J. G. Rivard, "Microcomputers Hit the Road," *IEEE Spectrum,* vol. 17, no. 11, Nov. 1980, pp. 44–47.
6. L. B. Sanderson and J. C. Lord, "Microcomputers Promise Less Stop, More Go," *IEEE Spectrum,* vol. 15, no. 11, Nov. 1976, pp. 30–32.
7. R. L. Ramey, J. H. Aylor, and R. D. Williams, "Microcomputer-Aided Eating for the Severely Handicapped," *Computer,* vol. 12, no. 1, Jan. 1979, pp. 54–61.
8. "Computerizing Human Birth," *IEEE Spectrum,* vol. 17, no. 5, May 1980, p. 26.
9. "C-MOS Processor to Control Attitude," *Electronics,* vol. 52, no. 18, August 30, 1979, pp. 42–44.
10. M. J. Ellis, G. R. Hovey, and T. E. Stapinski, "MTEC: A Microprocessor System for Astronomical Telescope and Instrument Control," *IEEE Transactions on Computers,* vol. C-29, no. 2, Feb. 1980, pp. 208–211.
11. C. Ringel and J. Tamburri, "Use of Microprocessors to Control and Monitor Operations of Gas Turbine Generators," *IEEE Transactions on Industrial Electronics and Control Instrumentation,* vol. IECI-23, no. 3, Aug. 1976, pp. 238–248.
12. V. Garuts and J. Tallman, "On-board Digital Processing Refines Scope Measurements," *Electronics,* vol. 53, no. 6, March 13, 1980, pp. 105–114.
13. L. Meyer, "Calculatorlike Controller Teaches Precision Multimeter New Steps," *Electronics,* vol. 53, no. 8, April 10, 1980, pp. 105–112.
14. A. J. Nichols, "An Overview of Microprocessor Applications," *Proceedings of the IEEE,* vol. 64, no. 6, June 1976, pp. 951–953.
15. "Smart Gamma Unit Forms Images Faster," *Electronics,* vol. 53, no. 17, July 31, 1980, pp. 44–46.
16. "6800 Varies Speed of Synchronous Motor," *Electronics,* vol. 53, no. 5, February 28, 1980, pp. 42–44.
17. L. Lowe, "Roundup: Smart Controllers Take Over," *Electronics,* vol. 53, no. 5, February 28, 1980, pp. 171–178.
18. "Control System Uses Multiple 8048s," *Electronics,* vol. 52, no. 25, December 6, 1979, pp. 43–44.
19. K. Karstad, "Microprocessor Adds Flexibility to Television Control System," *Electronics,* vol. 52, no. 24, November 22, 1979, pp. 132–138.
20. *Byte,* 70 Main St., Peterborough, N.H. 03458.
21. *Kilobaud Microcomputing,* 80 Pine St., Peterborough, N.H. 03458.
22. *Dr. Dobb's Journal of Computer Calisthenics and Orthodontia,* Box E, 1263 El Camino Real, Menlo Park, Calif. 94025.
23. *Creative Computing,* P.O. Box 789-M, Morristown, N.H. 07960.
24. *Interface Age,* 13913 Artesia Blvd., Cerritos, Calif. 90701.
25. "Apple Turns Pro to Aid Professionals," *Electronics,* vol. 53, no. 12, May 22, 1980, pp. 44–45.
26. "Fifty Years of Achievement: A History," *Electronics,* vol. 53, no. 9, April 17, 1980, pp. 375–381.
27. R. N. Noyce and M. E. Hoff, Jr., "A History of Microprocessor Development at Intel," *IEEE Micro,* vol. 1, no. 1, Feb. 1981, pp. 8–21.
28. S. P. Morse, B. W. Ravenel, S. Mazor, and W. B. Pohlman, "Intel Microprocessors—8008 to 8086," *Computer,* vol. 13, no. 10, Oct. 1980, pp. 42–60.
29. *MCS-4 Microcomputer Set—User's Manual,* Intel Corporation, Feb. 1973.
30. *MCS-8 Microcomputer Set—8008 User's Manual,* Intel Corporation, Nov. 1973.
31. *8080 Microcomputer Systems User's Manual,* Intel Corporation, 1976.
32. *MCS-85 User's Manual,* Intel Corporation, 1978.
33. *Microcomputer Components Data Book,* Zilog Inc.
34. "M6800 Microcomputer System Design Data," Motorola Inc., 1976.
35. "MC6802—Microprocessor with Clock and RAM," Motorola Inc., 1979.
36. "MCS6500 Microprocessors," MOS Technology Inc., May 1976.
37. *User Manual for the CDP1802 COSMAC Microprocessor,* RCA Solid State Division, 1976.
38. *MCS-48 Family of Single Chip Microcomputers User's Manual,* Intel Corporation, July 1978.
39. *TMS9900 Microprocessor Data Manual,* Texas Instruments Inc., Nov. 1975.
40. *The 8086 Family User's Manual,* Intel Corporation, Oct. 1979.
41. B. Hartman, "16-bit 68000 Microprocessor Camps on 32-bit Frontier," *Electronics,* vol. 52, no. 21, October 11, 1979, pp. 118–125.
42. J. G. Posa, "Peripheral Chips Shift Microprocessor Systems Into High Gear," *Electronics,* vol. 52, no. 17, August 19, 1979, pp. 93–106.
43. "Control System Fits on Chip," *Electronics,* vol. 53, no. 4, February 14, 1980, p. 198.
44. *UPI-41A User's Manual,* Intel Corporation, Apr. 1980.
45. *The 8086 Family User's Manual—Numerics Supplement,* Intel Corporation, July 1980.
46. J. Palmer, R. Nave, C. Wymore, R. Koehler, and C. McMinn, "Making Mainframe Mathematics Accessible to Microcomputers," *Electronics,* vol. 53, no. 11, May 8, 1980, pp. 114–121.
47. K. Rallapalli and J. Kroeger, "Chips Make Fast Math a Snap for Microprocessors," *Electronics,* vol. 53, no. 10, April 24, 1980, pp. 153–157.
48. R. T. Atkins, "What Is an Interrupt?", *Byte,* vol. 4, no. 3, March 1979, pp. 230–236.
49. T. A. Harr, Jr. and R. Phillips, "Interrupts Call the Shots in Scheme Using Two Microprocessors," *Electronics,* vol. 53, no. 4, February 14, 1980, pp. 166–170.
50. W. D. Maurer, "Subroutine Parameters," *Byte,* vol. 4, no. 7, July 1974, pp. 226–230.

51. W. P. Fischer, "Microprocessor Assembly Language Draft Standard," *Computer,* vol. 12, no. 12, Dec. 1979, pp. 96–109.

52. M. Marshall, "Assembly Language Plan Raises Dust," *Electronics,* vol. 53, no. 2, January 17, 1980, pp. 98–100.

53. P. Caudill, "Using Assembly Coding to Optimize High-Level Language Programs," *Electronics,* vol. 52, no. 3, February 1, 1979, pp. 121–124.

54. M. Maples and E. R. Fisher, "Real-Time Microcomputer Applications Using LLL Basic," *Computer,* vol. 10, no. 9, Sept. 1977, pp. 14–21.

55. S. Crespi-Reghizzi, P. Corti, and A. Dapra, "A Survey of Microprocessor Languages," *Computer,* vol. 13, no. 1, Jan. 1980, pp. 48–66.

56. J. G. Posa, "Programming Microcomputer Systems with High-Level Languages," *Electronics,* vol. 52, no. 2, January 18, 1979, pp. 105–112.

57. M. Krieger, "Structured Assembly Language Suits Programmers and Microprocessors," *Electronics,* vol. 53, no. 2, January 17, 1980, pp. 118–122.

58. L. Waller, "High-Level Language Will Run on All Microprocessors," *Electronics,* vol. 52, no. 26, December 20, 1979, pp. 39–40.

59. "Pascal Resides in PROM," *Electronics,* vol. 52, no. 9, April 26, 1979, p. 212.

60. "C Language Befriends Microprocessors," *Electronics,* vol. 52, no. 4, February 15, 1979, pp. 41–42.

61. "PL/1 Shrinks to fit Microprocessors," *Electronics,* vol. 53, no. 10, April 24, 1980, pp. 41–42.

62. "CAP-CPP Writes Microcobol Software for Small-Business Applications," *Electronics,* vol. 52, no. 13, June 21, 1979, pp. 71–72.

63. R. R. Bate and D. S. Johnson, "Pascal Software Supports Real-Time Multiprogramming on Small Systems," *Electronics,* vol. 52, no. 12, June 7, 1979, pp. 117–121.

65. *8008 and 8080 PL/M Programming Manual,* Intel Corporation, 1975.

65. J. Brakefield, "A Coding Discipline for Microprocessors," *Computer,* vol. 13, no. 5, May 1980, pp. 120–121.

66. S. M. Hicks, "Forth's Forte is Tighter Programming," *Electronics,* vol. 52, no. 6, March 15, 1979, pp. 114–118.

67. T. Ritter and G. Walker, "Varieties of Threaded Code for Language Implementation," *Byte,* vol. 5, no. 9, Sept. 1980, pp. 206–227.

68. K. Meinzer, "IPS, An Unorthodox High Level Language," *Byte,* vol. 4, no. 1, Jan. 1979, pp. 146–159.

69. *iRMX 80 User's Guide,* Intel Corporation, 1980.

70. D. Kruglinski, "How to Implement Space War," *Byte,* vol. 2, no. 10, Oct. 1977, pp. 86–111.

71. J. Murray and G. Alexy, "CRT Terminal Design Using The Intel 8275 and 8279," *Peripheral Design Handbook,* Intel Corporation, Apr. 1978, pp. 2-119 to 2-176.

72. R. L. Harding, "Fractional-binary Program Creates Pseudorandom Integers," *Electronics,* vol. 52, no. 6, March 15, 1979, pp. 129–131.

73. C. B. Honess, "Three Types of Pseudorandom Sequences," *Byte,* vol. 4, no. 6, June 1979, pp. 234–246.

74. R. Grappel, "Randomize Your Programming," *Byte,* vol. 2, no. 1, Sept. 1976, pp. 36–38.

75. G. Sitton, "8085 Program Rapidly Computes 8- by 16-bit Product," *Electronics,* vol. 52, no. 6, March 15, 1979, p. 129.

76. J. Bryant and M. Swasdee, "How to Multiply in a Wet Climate," *Byte,* vol. 3, no. 4, Apr. 1978, pp. 28–35, 100–110.

77. R. H. Lord, "Fast Fourier for the 6800," *Byte,* vol. 4, no. 2, Feb. 1979, pp. 108–119.

78. "8080/8085 Assembly Language Programming," Intel Corporation, 1977.

79. "Chapter 2: Programming Techniques," *M6800 Microprocessor Applications Manual,* Motorola Inc., 1975.

80. "A Low Cost CRT Terminal Using the 8275," Intel Corporation, Nov. 1979.

81. I. Watson, "Comparison of Commercially Available Software Tools for Microprocessor Programming," *Proceedings of the IEEE,* vol. 64, no. 6, June 1976, pp. 910–920.

82. H. A. Cohen and R. S. Francis, "Macro-Assemblers and Macro-Based Languages in Microprocessor Software Development," *Computer,* vol. 12, no. 2, Feb. 1979, pp. 53–64.

83. R. C. Allen and J. Kasser, "Amsat 8080 Standard Debug Monitor: AMS80 Version 2," *Byte,* vol. 2, no. 1, Sept. 1976, pp. 36–38.

84. "Development Systems Thrive," *Electronics,* vol. 53, no. 8, April 10, 1980, pp. 164–165.

85. C. Bailey and T. Kahl, "Evaluation Delay Cut by Low-Cost Microprocessor Development Tool," *Electronics,* vol. 52, no. 18, August 30, 1979, pp. 121–125.

86. J. Kister and I. Robinson, "Development System Supports Today's Processors—and Tomorrow's," *Electronics,* vol. 53, no. 3, January 31, 1980, pp. 81–88.

87. B. Kline, M. Maerz, and P. Rosenfeld, "The In-Circuit Approach to the Development of Microcomputer-Based Products," *Proceedings of the IEEE,* vol. 64, no. 6, June 1976, pp. 937–942.

88. "Emulator Uses Multiprocessor, Multiple Bus Approach," *Electronics,* vol. 52, no. 18, August 30, 1979, pp. 192–193.

89. C. Zing, "Development System Puts Two Processors on Speaking Terms," *Electronics,* vol. 53, no. 17, July 31, 1980, pp. 93–97.

90. J. Moon, "Microcomputer for Emulation Bares Hidden Buses, Functions," *Electronics,* vol. 53, no. 16, July 17, 1980, pp. 126–129.

91. "Compact Emulator Simulates I/O," *Electronics,* vol. 53, no. 6, March 13, 1980, pp. 168–170.

92. D. R. Ballard, "Designing Fail-Safe Microprocessor Systems," *Electronics,* vol. 52, no. 1, January 4, 1979, pp. 139–143.

93. J. F. Wakerly, "Microcomputer Reliability Improvement Using Triple-Modular Redundancy," *Proceed-*

ings of the IEEE, vol. 64, no. 6, June 1976, pp. 889–895.

94. R. E. Glaser, *Upsets in Microprocessor Controllers,* Ph.D. Dissertation, Dept. of Electrical Engineering, Johns Hopkins University, Baltimore Md., 1981 (University Microfilms No. DA8205099).

95. D. A. Patterson and C. H. Sequin, "Design Consid-erations for Single-Chip Computers of the Future," *IEEE Transactions on Computers,* vol. C-29, no. 2, Feb. 1980.

96. "Microsystem 80 Advance Information," Intel Cor-poration, 1980.

97. J. Posa, "Intel Takes Aim at the '80s," *Electronics,* vol. 53, no. 5, February 28, 1980, pp. 89–95.

28

Software Development for Array Machines

Howard O. Welch
System Development Corporation

28.1. INTRODUCTION: PROBLEM DEFINITION

Three fundamental methods for improving computation speed are faster digital logic circuitry, addition of logic arranged so that concurrent computations may be performed, and improvement of computational algorithms. A conventional uniprocessor architecture is essentially limited to improvement in circuitry and, for any given problem, to improvements in algorithms to achieve greater speed. Powerful uniprocessor architectures such as the CDC 7600 have logic to perform concurrent operations at the lowest level, for instance, simultaneous adds and multiplies are performed using an instruction look-ahead and separate hardware for the two operations. Algorithm improvements such as the Fast Fourier Transform have provided dramatic increases in computing speed through clever storage and retrieval of data elements. These methods are constrained by physical and practical limits without dramatic extraordinary effort, cost, and difficulty.

An alternative approach is to arrange a large amount of not necessarily fast circuitry so that if the problem is properly structured, a number of problem elements are simultaneously computed. The architecture may be parallel in space and time as are the various forms of parallel array processors such as ILLIAC IV [1], PEPE [2], and STARAN [3], or may be parallel in time as are pipelined processors such as the STAR and TI ASC machines [4]. In any case, the parallel processing of data opens the way for large increases in computational capacity without concomitant technological advances in circuitry.

Although the real world is made up of a large number of problems suitable for concurrent processing, our computational perception of the world is constrained by the historical foundation of von Nuemann machines, sequential mathematics, as well as the sequential data collection capability of most systems. Parallel processing systems, therefore, have largely been designed for particular applications and have not been produced in large production runs for general use. Certain applications such as ballistic missile defense, air traffic control, and signal processing have availability and response requirements that not only lend themselves to parallel processing but make its use mandatory, whereas others such as fluid flow modeling, numerical weather prediction, and nuclear effects modeling have computational data structures suited for concurrent processing and require huge computational resources available through parallel processing. The challenge of parallel processing is to devise architectures and parallel algorithms general enough for some range of problems yet powerful enough to provide a cost-effective reduction of computation time.

Flynn [5] categorized machine organizations into a generally accepted and useful set based on instruction and data stream multiplicity. Flynn allows for both single and multiple data and instruction streams giving rise to four categories of architectures:

	SINGLE DATA STREAM (SD)	MULTIPLE DATA STREAM (MD)
Single Instruction (SI)	SISD Uniprocessor	SIMD Array Processor
Multiple Instruction (MI)	MISD Pipeline Machine	MIMD Multiprocessor

The SIMD or single instruction, multiple data stream architecture is characterized by a set of limited capability processors attached to a bus that routes instructions from a central controller containing the instruction sequencing and decoding logic for the machine. This architecture operates the same instruction in all active processors simultaneously to achieve parallelism.

An architecture composed of a set of complete processors and their memories interconnected in some manner but capable of independent activity is termed an MIMD or multiple instruction, multiple data stream architecture. The MIMD structure is theoretically capable of fully exploiting the inherent parallelism in a program although a large number of yet unsolved control and data access problems currently limit the full effectiveness of the architecture.

This chapter is concerned with software engineering of SIMD machines—primarily array processors.

SIMD processors have the general configuration shown in Figure 28.1: A single control unit accesses a unique program memory, distinct from the parallel operand memory, to fetch and decode the single instruction stream. Decoded instructions are passed down a common instruction bus to a set of *n* identical parallel processing elements (PE), where the instruction stream acts simultaneously on the *n* operands in the PEs. The data memories may be directly connected to a PE, connected to the other PEs through an interconnection network or, in the most general case, to both.

The interconnection network is not mandatory; if it is not present, the parallel array is called an ensemble of PEs. PEPE is an example of such an architecture.

All processing elements execute the same instruction simultaneously, so provision is made to deactivate PEs or otherwise disassociate them from the instruction stream. PEs may be programmed actively or inactively by address mask, by PE register status, memory word status, or by any other programmable means. An instruction received at a PE may be executed or may be ignored; however, an inactive PE cannot perform any other function while that instruction is being ignored. It is apparent, therefore, that the efficiency and power of a

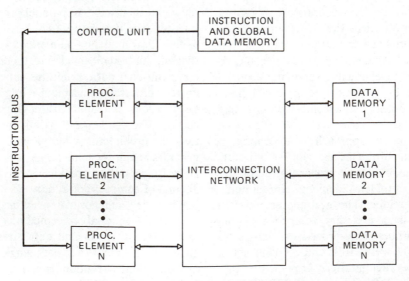

Figure 28.1. Generic SIMD parallel processor.

SIMD machine is dependent on problems and data structures that maximize the number of active PEs.

The following section presents an overview description of two SIMD machines that were built and for which a body of operating experience exists.

28.2. CURRENT DEVELOPMENT

ILLIAC IV Architecture

The ILLIAC IV was designed expressly for integrating the partial differential equations encountered in numerical weather forecasting, fluid dynamics, and nuclear effects data processing. These problems require a high degree of connectivity between neighboring processors to process a finite difference lattice in an efficient manner. An ILLIAC quadrant consists of 64 processing elements (PEs) arranged in an 8 x 8 array (Figure 28.2). Although designed for four quadrants, ILLIAC was constructed with a single quadrant for cost reasons. A 64 PE quadrant is governed by a *control unit* that breaks down the instructions to the point where a microcode sequence is generated to execute the instruction in the PEs. Instructions are of two types: those executed in the CU and those executed in the PEs. These two instruction streams are interlaced but are executed separately and independently. The PE microcode sequence is bussed

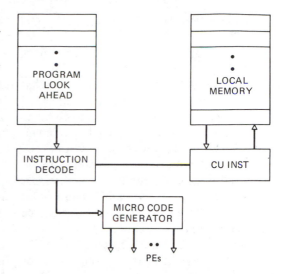

Figure 28.3. ILLIAC IV control unit.

to all PEs in the quadrant simultaneously. Figure 28.3 is a functional description of the CU.

The processing unit (PU) contains the memory logic unit, processing element memory (PEM), and PE. The PE executes a full repertory of instructions on 64 and 32 bit integers and floating-point operands. Operands may be accessed from array memory, PE registers, data bus, or four nearest neighbor arrays.

A PE is addressed by an indexable 16 bit adder. Instructions may be globally indexed in the CU and further indexed locally in PEs. The memory logic unit interfaces a PE to the processing element memory.

Each processing element is basically a four register arithmetic unit with an A register and a B register to hold operands, an S register for temporary storage, and an R register used to transfer information among the PEs in the routing operation. The 64 bit R register of every PE is wired to the R register of four other PEs so that PE_i connects to PE_{i+1}, PE_{i-1}, PE_{i+8}, and PE_{i-8}. The routing operation acts as if the 64 R registers were a 4096 register with an end around shift capability. A route 1 right command causes every R register to be shifted 64 bits to the right. The connection to PE_{i+8} allows rapid movement of data over a longer distance.

PEs may be disabled from the microcode sequence by command from the CU or as a result of a local PE test of some condition in the

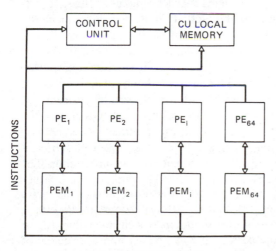

Figure 28.2. ILLIAC IV Quadrant.

registers. A PE must be reenabled by CU control.

Operands and control information can be transferred in several ways. The CU can broadcast a 64 bit word to all PEs simultaneously. The word can originate in CU local memory or a CU register and can be sent to any PE operating register. The CU can broadcast a 64 bit word with one bit going to each PE. This is the method by which PEs are enabled and disabled; it can be reversed so that one bit from each PE is assembled into a 64 bit word in the CU. PE activity status can thus be sampled for program control.

Finally, the CU can fetch words from PEM of any PE. This fetch can be a single word or an 8 word block.

PEPE Architecture

The PEPE parallel processor was designed expressly for the enormous real-time data-processing loads of the types encountered in ballistic missile defense applications. It was designed as an augmentation of a commercial serial computer to assume that part of the ballistic missile algorithm having the following characteristics:

- Correlation of input data with existing data base using one or more attributes
- Repetitive arithmetic operations on a large number of independent data sets
- Multilevel ordering and search of a large data base

Radar return correlation, digital noise filtering and tracking, and radar resource allocation and scheduling have those characteristics and provide the driving requirements of the PEPE design.

PEPE consists of an ensemble of independent digital processing elements, indefinite in number, that operate in parallel under global control. The design incorporates three independent global control units each driving an associated processing unit. The three processors in the element share a common element memory for parallel operand storage. The three modules are each optimized for a specific function: (1) correlative data base search and data input, (2) floating-point arithmetic, and (3) associative data search and output.

Each global control unit has data memory and program memory independent of the other control units to allow independent conflict-free global operand and program instruction fetch. The global control units have limited data processing capability, the instruction repertory being limited to logical test, branch, index register, and input/output control plus enough integer arithmetic to compute indexes and addresses. This instruction set serves mainly to control the parallel instruction sequence. Both parallel and control unit instructions are stored in the program memory associated with the control unit.

Parallel instructions are decoded in the global control units to cause a microinstruction sequence of control pulses to move from a wide bandwidth read-only memory to a parallel instruction bus for execution in the processing elements. The control pulses cause simultaneous and identical operations in the set of active processing elements.

Each processing element has three units, corresponding to and identically controlled by the three control units. Each processing element is constructed with (but not architecturally limited to) 2,048 words of 32 bit memory shared by the three-element units for operand storage. This memory is the primary interunit connection at the element level.

The element-processing units have a programmable activity indicator that can be dynamically set active or inactive according to the content of the unit's accumulator or other condition register. The instruction stream from a control unit is routed only to active processing units. A full set of parallel instructions, analogous to logical test and branch instructions, allows the programmer to set activity and, therefore, to control the set or subset of elements that participate in processing. The subset can be selected by data attribute rather than data location address; hence, the claim for associative memory access in PEPE. A hardware extremum search algorithm [6] in the parallel instruction set allows selection of the processing element with the largest (or smallest) accumulator value in the active subset. This feature provides a fast data-ordering capability in the PEPE hardware.

Consider the aggregate of element memory as a two-dimensional $m \times n$ memory array with columns formed by the m words of a single element memory and the rows formed by the n PEPE processing elements. Rows are addressed conventionally by parallel instruction operand address; each row consists of a vector whose elements are defined by the set of active processing elements, where activity is defined by the activity selection instructions described above. Arithmetic and logical operations are performed simultaneously on all vector elements so that data access and manipulation in the row dimension uses the same processing time for n vector elements as for one or none. The PEPE instruction format has no provision for direct addressing of any specific physical element and no provision for specifying any set size (except for isolation of a single element).

Output from elements requires that a single processing element be selected, either by extremum search on some element memory value or by selecting the physically first PE from a set of active elements. A read instruction causes the element accumulator contents to be transferred to the control unit accumulator for storage in global data memory. An inner loop on successive element accumulator loads inside a loop of successive element extrema selection can be used to output a set of values ordered by selected parallel vector elements. The extremum search implies that the PEPE parallel data base is simultaneously ordered within any vector in element memory.

The ballistic missile tracking application that drove PEPE design did not require extensive interelement data access. Hence, PEPE has no capability for an element processor to access any element memory except that directly connected to it. This feature limits PEPE potential as a general-purpose parallel processor, although mapping of a problem to the architecture can emphasize PEPE strengths and minimize its weaknesses.

It is possible to transfer data from one element memory to another by moving data from source to memory to global control unit and then back to one or more target element memories. The process reduces PEPE to a serial machine during the operation, which reduces the total leverage that can be applied to the problem. I/O is a traditional problem in parallel processors because of the essentially serial nature of mass storage data access. PEPE's independent associative input and output units can load parallel memory fully time overlapped with processing in the floating-point arithmetic control unit. This lessens the need for the large amounts of parallel hardware to idle while loading input from and moving results to the host.

Parallel Array Compiler

Higher-order language compilers for parallel array processors are usually written for execution on a conventional uniprocessor that acts as a host or ancillary to the parallel machine. There are several reasons for this. Compiler theory, design, and implementation methods are well known for conventional machines. The construction of compilers that generate code for parallel processors does not differ greatly from those whose target code is for a sequential machine. Parsing, syntax analysis, and grammar checking are fundamental compiler operations independent of the target machine architecture.

The power of the parallel array should be dedicated to applications rather than to support overhead such as compilation and linking. Compilation is an inherently serial process devoid of the long vectors necessary for parallel array efficiency.

A host machine is usually closely associated with the parallel machine to perform I/O control, parallel array program loading, interface mass storage peripherals, and other overhead tasks not normally performable by the parallel array processor. Compilation and link editing are natural extensions of these host tasks.

The host cross-compiler generates code in binary relocatable machine language format and stores the program in host mass storage files. The set of compiled programs, subroutines, and functions are linked into absolute binary form by a conventional link loader utility that either writes the execution file to mass storage or passes it to a loader that transfers it to the parallel processor. A parallel load utility moves the program to memory and initiates program execution. This technique is conventional and familiar with only the cross-compilation and load processes unique to parallel array computers.

Parallel Languages

A valid commercial and practical argument exists that a parallel processor (or its host) should have the ability to compile programs written in languages originally intended for serial machines. A vectorizing FORTRAN compiler that would generate reasonably efficient parallel data structures and parallel code would conserve the vast amount of effort expended in code development through the years and would allow transfer of codes from a serial machine to the parallel machine with minimal effort. The acceptance of the parallel machine would be more immediate, and commercial sales potential could more readily be exploited.

The full potential of a parallel machine would probably be better exploited, however, if there were a compiler available that inherently contained the architectural features of the machine such as most higher-order languages now exploit the conventional von Neuman architecture. PEPE was programmed using PFOR, a FORTRAN augmented with language forms to exploit the PEPE associative memory and extremum search hardware capabilities. ILLIAC IV uses several parallel languages including IVTRAN and GLYPNIR. GLYPNIR is an ALGOL-based language that includes forms embodying ILLIAC IV architectural features. The following short descriptions of PFOR and GLYPNIR serve as examples of how the parallel architecture may be both explicitly and implicitly contained in the language.

PEPE PFOR

PFOR is ANSI FORTRAN IV extended to include parallel data types, subsetting, and ordering forms. Parallel data types are declared explicitly similar to FORTRAN practice:

PAR INTEGER
PAR REAL
PAR LOGICAL

No implicit typing of parallel variables is allowed but implicit typing of sequential variables (operands stored in control unit data memory) follows FORTRAN practice.

PEPE elements are selected into active subsets of the ensemble by subsetting language forms.

WHERE (Parallel Logical Expression) S# (NONE)

.

.

.

S# CONTINUE

The parallel logical expression is any Boolean expression on parallel variables. The PEs in which the expression is true remain active; the PEs in which the expression is false are made inactive within the bounds of the statement number.

The optional form NONE causes a branch around the code delimited by the statement number if the active subset is empty after evaluation of the parallel logical expression. A subset may be further subsetted by another nested WHERE subject to the rule that a nested WHERE must be fully contained within the next outer subset. The nesting form

WHERE NOT S#

causes the complement subset to be acted on so that a bifurcated path acting on two disjoint subsets may be taken with a single evaluation of the logical expression.

PEPE requires one and only one element to be active when transmitting data to the control unit from the PEs. The subsetting form

WHERE FIRST S#
.
.
.
S# ·

causes the physically first element to be selected and remain active from the active subset and allows unambiguous output to the control unit.

Two language forms allow use of the PEPE hardware extremum search capability:

WHERE MAX (Parallel Arithmetic Expression) S#

and

WHERE MIN (Parallel Arithmetic Expression) S#.

The parallel arithmetic expression is any expression (including a single variable) evaluated in the parallel elements. The one or more elements in the active set with the maximum (minimum) value are selected and remain active while all other elements are inactive through the range of the statement number.

A set of logical program control language forms are available based on the active subset size.

IF ANY (Parallel Logical Expression) GO TO S#
IF ALL (Parallel Logical Expression) GO TO S#
IF NONE (Parallel Logical Expression) GO TO S#.

PEPE control unit hardware can determine if at least one, all, or no elements remain active as a result of evaluation of the Parallel Logical Expression. The statement on the same line is executed or skipped depending on whether the Parallel Logical Expression is true or false, in a manner analogous to FORTRAN IF forms.

The PEPE extremum search algorithm may be used sequentially to order the elements using the following form.

DO SEQ S# (Parallel Logical Expression) m,n
DO ASC S# (Parallel Arithmetic Expression) m,n
DO DESC S# (Parallel Arithmetic Expression) m,n.

DO SEQ sequentially selects PEs for which the parallel logical expression is true and performs the code delimited by the statement number on at least the number of elements specified by n. This loop variable m is left with the actual number of iterations if n is greater than the active set.

DO ASC (DESC) sequentially selects the PE with a minimum (maximum) value of the PAE and executes the code delimited by the statement number in the same manner as the DO SEQ. These forms provide an ordering of the parallel data base on any arithmetic variable.

All other arithmetic and logical forms are exactly as in ANSI FORTRAN. Parallel versus serial operations are determined by context so that parallel variables are always operated on in the PEs. If the result of a parallel operation is stored in a sequential variable, the compiler provides for output to the control unit but does not guarantee a single PE subset; hence, it is the programmer's responsibility to prevent ambiguous output to the control unit with the resulting hardware error alarm condition.

PFOR embodies the basic architectural features of PEPE by using the associative addressing (subsetting), extremum search, and subset counting hardware. While the basic concept of vector operations on subsets tends to force a structured approach to PEPE programming, PFOR could be modernized to include structured FORTRAN constructs from FORTRAN 77. A more modern language base such as Pascal could make profitable use of the associative memory capabilities of the hardware. PFOR has no language form to allow an element to access data from another element nor has it any other form of interelement data movement, which reflects the lack of connectivity of PEPE PEs.

ILLIAC IV GLYPNIR

GLYPNIR is a block-structured derivative of ALGOL designed to provide visibility into ILLIAC IV capabilities. The block structure allows a single statement to be replaced with a block of statements delimited by BEGIN and END.

Data types in GLYPNIR are: real, integer, alpha, pointer, Boolean. All types are generally familiar except pointer types that at execution time are machine addresses containing a link to a block of data. A PE may have a confined pointer which has an address value that is a row of PE memory while the control unit has unconfined pointers that address any word in the processing element memory.

Vectors are arrays of memory elements that must be declared, for example,

PE REAL VECTOR V[10].
CU REAL VECTOR S[10].

This form declares **V** to be a real vector with 10 rows of 64 words per row. The vector **V** may be accessed as a subscripted quantity starting from 0 as per ALGOL practice. A CU vector has one word per row so that **S** is a real CU vector of 10 rows of 1 word per row.

Three types of data referencing may be used in GLYPNIR. A simple variable has one identifier that refers to either a PE or CE variable. A vector references an array whose location is fixed at compile time. Finally, a pointer reference is an indexed reference to either a PE or CU vector, where the index may be either static or dynamic.

GLYPNIR allows dynamic storage allocation through the GETPEB and GETCUB constructs used in pointer procedures to allocate storage in the PE and UCs, respectively. FREEPEB and FREECUB release allocated storage for reallocation. Static storage allocation is made at compile time by means of data declarations.

GLYPNIR is block structured in that a block of statements delimited by BEGIN and END are considered a single statement. Block size can vary from one statement to a complete program, and a block may have its own data declarations, subroutines, and subblocks. Variables declared in a block are valid only in that block.

Assignment statements transfer values, either PE or CU variables, from one memory location to another. The general form of an assignment statement is an identifier followed by := followed by a routing index, followed by an expression. Statements are terminated by a semicolon. Data-type conversions are automatic and conform to ALGOL convention. If the right side of an assignment statement is a PE variable and the left side is a CU variable,

the values in all enabled PEs are OR'd together and the result is assigned to the CU variables; hence, a meaningful statement of this type generally implies a singled PE being enabled. If the left side of an assignment statement is a CU variable and the right side is a PE variable, the CU variable is broadcast to enabled PEs. Consider the general form of the assignment statement

$$C := [R]A + B$$

In this expression R is the routing index and may be a general arithmetic expression whose result is a positive or negative integer, where positive values specify a right- and negative a left-routing procedure. The quantity $A + B$ is computed in the enabled PE R to the right (or left if negative) of the PE currently being addressed. The result $A + B$ is then routed back to the addressed PE.

Assignment statements are classed into four types: arithmetic, alphanumeric, Boolean, and pointer. A pointer expression is a field designator or a type pointer identifier, either confined or nonconfined. Boolean expressions are 64 bit patterns with false assigned to all zeros and true to all ones. Alphanumeric operators are Boolean operators that use the ILLIAC IV logical instructions such as AND, OR, and so forth.

This brief overview of GLYPNIR shows how the interconnecting PE architecture is embodied in the higher-order language to exploit the machine capability.

SIMD Operating Characteristics

The SIMD machine is inherently most powerful when operating on vectors of numbers such that each element of a vector is serviced in a processor of the parallel array. However, most problems are a mix of vector and scalar operation, so that a primary problem of any SIMD is to maximize vector and minimize scalar operations.

Consider a data set $S = \{e_1, e_2, \ldots, e_n\}$ partitioned into r subsets, not necessarily disjoint and let the cardinality of each of the r subsets be given by the set $C = c_1, c_2, \ldots, c_r$. Let S be acted on by a set of code sequences or algorithms $A_i(S_i)$ where the ith algorithm acts on the data set S_i.

The parallel machine utilization of an SIMD machine executing the total algorithm A is

$$U = \frac{C_1 + C_2 + \cdots + C_r}{nr}$$

Figure 28.4 illustrates a utilization profile for an algorithm of this type. The swept area under the curve represents the machine utilization for the machine. It is obvious that problem vector size should be matched to the number of parallel elements. The SIMD machine sized to some peak load in terms of vector size has a potential for considerable underutilization of the hardware but this must be balanced by the processing time used by the parallel processor when compared to a comparable serial machine.

In the above example, let $\pi_1, \pi_2, \ldots, \pi_r$ be the parallel processors times to execute each of the code segments $A_1, \ldots, A_r$. Also let $\sigma_1, \sigma_2, \ldots, \sigma_r$ be the serial processor time for a single execution of $A_1, \ldots, A_r$, respectively. Then the time required for the serial processor to complete the algorithm set S is:

$$T_s = C_1\sigma_1 + C_2\sigma_2 + \cdots + C_r\sigma_r$$

and the time required by the parallel machine is $T_p = \pi_1 + \pi_2 + \cdots + \pi_r$. Aside from small differences in instruction set and code overhead, the ratio σ_i/π_i is constant and is the raw execution speed ratio of the two machines. The data processing leverage of the parallel machine compared with a serial processor is, therefore, approximately

$$\frac{T_s}{T_p} = \frac{\sigma}{\pi}\left(\sum^r C_i\right)$$

for any given algorithm. For most real-time applications, the ability to handle real-time peak loads is of more concern than raw hardware utilization or average utilization. Many batch processes, such as the integration of partial differential equations, are beyond the capability of conventional processors but are solvable with the data-processing leverage provided by SIMD machines even though vector sizes may be imperfectly matched to processing array size.

A characteristic of all parallel architectures is that global data accessibility degrades as parallelism is increased. Row vectors of a matrix may be stored in parallel memory as vectors; however, if it is necessary to act on the matrix in transpose form, the machine suffers severe performance degradation because of the separation of column elements in physical memory.

SIMD machines have generally been designed with an interconnection network between processors and memories to alleviate the data access problem.

Switching Networks

A fundamental problem with all parallel processing configurations is the accessibility of data. Data vectors are arranged for maximum accessibility in a single direction when the data base is considered as a multidimensional array. Vectors may be arranged in contiguous memory locations in a pipeline machine or in the same element memory location in each processing element memory in a parallel array processor to effectively access data. Should the

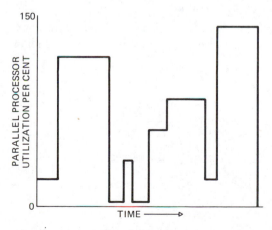

Figure 28.4. Typical SIMD parallel processor utilization profile.

process vector be in transpose form, however, then processing effectiveness degrades. A pipeline machine must operate with a sparse pipeline or must treat the transform vector as a set of scalars. A parallel array processor must have some form of bidirectional element to memory interconnection to access the jth vector element from the ith processor. The design of SIMD interconnection networks is a major consideration of the parallel computer architect, not only for machine cost and complexity reasons but also for algorithm performance reasons.

The possibilities for interconnection networks are many (Figure 28.5) and range from full crossbar networks connecting every processor to every memory to the extreme used in PEPE in which no direct interelement connection was employed.

The crossbar network is a nonblocking, minimum time interconnection that has the characteristics that n^2 interconnections are required to connect n processors to n memories. This complexity growth characteristic tends to eliminate the crossbar as a viable design in all but the simplest configuration option, not only because of the complexity but because of pinout, power, and size considerations.

At the other end of the complexity spectrum is the ring interconnection—the simplest network that provides full connection between n processors and n memories. The complexity of the ring increases as n rather than n^2. Consider the ring as a series of m bit registers with the output of the ith register connected to the ith register inputs (modulo n). During operation, all the individual registers are clocked simultaneously and continuously, forcing the contents of each register to the next successive register. A fetch from the jth memory is made by the ith processor by composing a fetch request packet that specifies both memory ident and processor ident. The processor/ring interface interrogates its ring register and, if empty, places the packet in the register, or waits until an empty ring slot passes the processor. The packet is then clocked sequentially around the ring until the jth processor is reached where the packet is removed from the ring and a memory fetch is made. A return packet is then composed to return the fetch operand to the originating processor in a manner similar to the outward packet.

Response time T in the ring is a function of the number of slots on the ring n, the average time for any process between ring operations f, and the memory access time. If $f = 2n$, then blockage causes doubling of the fetch response time; hence, the circuit speed of the ring switch must be quite fast with respect to processor speed for successful ring operation in high-load environments.

A number of switching networks fall between the crossbar and the ring in complexity and performance. These may be characterized as permutation networks because the transition through the switch to connect any processor to any memory is a sequence of permutations on the source address leading to the destination address (Figure 28.5).

The interconnection problem is important to the software engineer because of its impact on

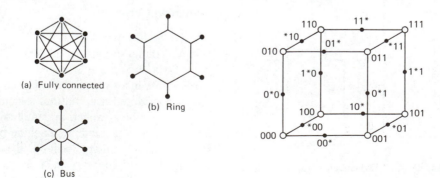

Figure 28.5. Processor interconnections.

processing speed if the major algorithm requires considerable access by PEs of other PE memories. Most problems of interest except real-time radar tracking fall into this category.

A vectorizing compiler should assign PEs so that algorithm topology is mapped to minimize element memory access time—an unsolved problem at this time. Manual methods have been developed such as skewed storage in IL-LIAC IV to optimize accesses in matrix operations but little general work has been done in this field.

Parallel Algorithm Design

Problem computational complexity is primarily a function of running time in that problem size can be mapped into the time required to solve the problem. A device such as the SIMD parallel processors computer increases the computational time density by increases in concurrently operational functional hardware. The mapping of problem computational complexity to parallel hardware is a way to effectively reduce absolute computational complexity and to reduce problem running time.

A primary problem of the parallel algorithm designer is to recognize the realizable parallelism inherent in the problem, to define the problem data structure for maximum parallel data manipulation, and to order the sequence of operations for maximum parallel functional operation. Parallel compilers can perform at least some of these functions to transform a given algorithm from serial to parallel implementation, but parallel software designers must know both the strengths and weaknesses of their parallel processor to effectively capitalize on its full potential.

Architectural considerations that require primary consideration in algorithm design are:

- *Data access.* Data access is data access out of local memory; it may be constant or may be a function of spatial proximity. Memory interconnections may be clustered so that data access out of the local cluster is much slower than within. Algorithms may be designed for this characteristic to minimize memory access

time. For example, the Fast Fourier Transform butterfly maps into an interconnection network made of 2×2 crossbar nodes with great efficiency.

- *Maximum/optimum vector length.* SIMD efficiency is always inherently sensitive to vector size. It is generally true that effective use of MIMD systems depends on the parallelism inherent in large vectors rather than the parallelism to be found in computation of nondependent scalar functions. A parallel processor is seldom designed for a single problem that would allow the PE population to be optimized to the problem. Parallel algorithm design must be concerned with maximizing vector lengths through the majority of problems, while reflecting the constraints imposed by minimum bounds to a solution.

Extensive work has been performed [7, 8] investigating execution time bounds for rational expressions. The following discussion shows a number of the results that are valid for SIMD architectures.

Rational Expressions

It can be proven [9] that if division is not used, $M(\log_2 n)$ is a lower bound for the evaluation of x^n, where M is vector multiplication time and $M > A$, where A is vector add time. This relation holds for extensions of this problem such as evaluation of: $x^2, x^3, \ldots, x^n, \pi^n (x + a_i)$, $\Sigma^n a_i x^i$, and so on. Kung [9] proves that if the number of processors is greater than n, then x^n can be evaluated in less than $A \log_2 n + 2A_s + 2D_s$, where A_s and D_s are scalar add and scalar divide times. For large n (and hence for large array sizes), the speed-up is on the order of M/A.

Nonlinear recurrence relationships are frequently encountered in applied mathematics where it is necessary to compute y_n from $y_0, y_1, \ldots, y_m$ where y_m is defined by:

$$y_{i+1} = \phi(y_i, \ldots, y_{i-m})$$
$$\text{for some function } \phi(x_1, \ldots, x_{m+1}).$$

This is a relation such as $y_{i+1} = \frac{1}{2}(y_i + a/y_i)$ used for evaluating $a^{1/2}$. Kung shows that any parallel algorithm using any number of processors is not essentially faster than the sequential algorithm for any first-order rational recurrence of degree greater than 1.

This theorem is important in that it identifies a class of problems not suitable for parallel solution and that early recognition of lower time bounds to a solution should be investigated before considering the parallel machine as a computational vehicle.

The above classes of problems are more local in nature than the more general class of problems suitable for SIMD machines and are probably much more amenable to parallel solutions in MIMD processors such as data-flow machines where low-level parallelism can be exploited.

Partial Differential Equations

The physics problems that can be expressed as partial differential equations (PDE) are large, interesting, and important. These problems require huge numbers of computations and exhibit both spatial and temporal regularity that is applicable to parallel computation. Data dependencies are generally localized around any data point that minimizes the parallel data access problem.

A typical PDE problem goes through the steps shown in Figure 28.6. A problem is first described as a set of partial differential equations

$$(au_x)_x + (cu_y)y + fu = g$$

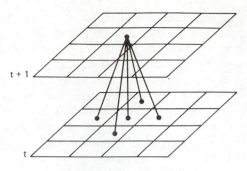

Figure 28.7. PDE 2 explicit PDE technique.

in some region R bounded by some curve C, subject to the condition that $u = h$ on the boundary C. Next a mesh is superimposed on a plane section of the region, and a set of difference equations are derived from the PDE and superimposed on the mesh. The finite difference equations take the form

$$u_{ij}^{t+1} = f(u_{ij}^t, u_{i\pm1\ j\pm1}^i)$$

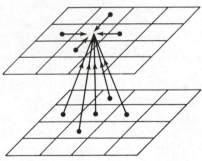

Figure 28.8. PDE 3 implicit PDE solution.

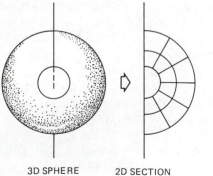

| 3D SPHERE | 2D SECTION | DISCRETE FINITE DIFFERENCE APPROXIMATION | LOGICAL REPRESENTATION |

Figure 28.6. PDE Formulation.

for explicit PDE methods as shown in Figure 28.7. Alternatively, implicit PDE solution methods are of the form

$$u_{ij}^{t+1} = f(u_{ij}^t,\ u_{i+1\ j\pm1}^t,\ u_{i\pm1\ j\pm1}^{t+1})\quad \text{(Figure 28.8)}.$$

Implicit methods require the solution of a set of homogenous linear equations that, in general, require solution of a banded matrix (bidiagonal or tridiagonal).

Explicit methods perform direct calculation of a time step from the previous step and lend themselves to use of long vectors; thus, they are well suited to SIMD architectures. Implicit methods impose limitations on vector lengths in the inversion of the banded matrix, hence, they are relatively unsuited to SIMD machines (or any other parallel machines). The choice of method is constrained by the physics of the problem, the stability of the solution, and time step and mesh sizes; therefore, the parallel software engineer should keep in mind the computational efficiencies of the two solutions.

Some problems such as global weather predictions may be partitioned so that nodal quantities such as wind velocity are predicted forward using explicit methods while zonal quantities such as energy, density, and viscosity are predicted using an explicit method.

Another method that can potentially use the full resources of a parallel machine is the Monte Carlo method for the solution of elliptic partial differential equations [10].

Consider a problem that can be represented by Poisson's equation

$$\nabla^2 V(\mathbf{r})\ =\ F(\mathbf{r})$$

where the potential V is a function of the position vector $\mathbf{r}$. A Monte Carlo method allows the solution $V(P)$ at a single point P to be obtained without obtaining the solution of any other point. This method has applicability where interelement communication is a limiting factor on data access and where a part of the data base describing the region can be made accessible to a single processor.

The steps in the solution by Monte Carlo method are as follows:

1. The region enclosed by the boundary C is replaced by a rectangular mesh of lattice points as described above for explicit and implicit methods. The boundary curve C is replaced by points C_h, which are nearest neighbors to points within C.

2. Poisson's equation is rewritten as a difference equation that relates values of potential at adjacent points in the lattice. The coefficients at the difference equation are the transition probabilities from one point to another in the lattice. The value $\phi(\mathbf{r})$ of the potential at the boundary is assumed given.

3. To find the solution at any point P within C, construct a set of random walks starting at P and terminating at the boundary points C_h. Steps in the walk from any lattice point to an adjacent point are taken by random sampling techniques using the transition probabilities derived from the difference equation. A talley is made for each walk from which $V(P)$ is estimated. The talley depends on the transition probabilities between successive points visited, the value of $F(x,y)$ at the points, and the values $\phi(\mathbf{r})$ at the boundary point terminating the walk.

For details of the formulation of such a technique see Reference 10.

This method has several appealing features for parallel processing. The walks within a processor are independent of any others; hence, the talleys may be made in a processor without the lockstep normally found in SIMD processes. Also, the walks are determined only by that lattice and transition probabilities.

Depending on storage, the grid may be allocated repetitively in the local memories of the array to minimize distant memory fetches in the interconnection network. This feature could be useful in clustered interconnects where fetch time is a nonlinear function of memory/processor distance.

The method also allows essentially full use of the processors in the system because the walks are not lockstepped.

Ordinary Differential Equations

Sequential block implicit methods have been found useful in the numerical solution of ordinary differential equations of the form

$$y' = f(x, g), \; y(x_0) = y_0$$

The term block refers to a set of new values that are produced by each application of the algorithm. For a K point block, each pass through the algorithm produces K new equally speed solution values. These methods have been studied for sequential machines in Reference 11 and applied to parallel architectures in References 7, 12, and 13.

A block one-step approach is typical of block methods although they may be applied equally effectively to predictor-corrector methods. In the sequential one-step approach, a sequence of open and closed Newton-Cotes formulas is used to generate initial approximations to the solution $y(x)$ at each point in the current block. The implicit formulas are applied iteratively until convergence is obtained to the maximum order of accuracy obtainable. Only the solution to the last point in the block is used to start the next block.

These algorithms may be modified for parallel machines in a straightforward manner. Let k be the number of points in a block and $N \geq k$ be the number of processors in the parallel machine. Let y_n represent the approximate solution and $y(x_n)$ the exact solution to the differential equation of x_n, the initial node of the current block. Assume equally spaced nodes within the block so that $x_{n+r} = x_n + rh$ for $r = 1, 2, \ldots, k$ where h is stepsize and kh is the blocklength. Also let f_y be the partial derivative of f with respect to y.

The formulation of the sequential two-point block scheme is

$$y_{n+1} = y_n + hy'_n$$
$$y_{n+1,1} = y_n + \frac{h}{2}(y'_n + y_{n+1,0})$$
$$y_{n+2,1} = y_n + 2hy_{n+1,1}$$
$$y_{n+1,2} = y_n + \frac{h}{12}(5y'_n + 8y_{n+1,1} - y'_{n+2,1})$$

$$y_{n+2,S+1} = y_n + \frac{h}{3}(y'_n + 4y'_{n+1,2} + y'_{n+2,S})$$
$$S = 1, \; (y2)$$

The formulas are applied in this sequence.

The corresponding formulas for the parallel process are:

$$y_{n+r,0} = y_n + rhy_n \qquad\qquad r = 1,2$$

$$y_{n+1,S+1} = y_n + \frac{h}{12}(5y'_n + 8y'_{n+1,S} - y'_{n+2,S})$$

$$y_{n+2,S+1} = y_n + \frac{h}{3}(y'_n + 4y'_{n+1,S} + y'_{n+2,S}) \; S$$
$$S = 0, 1, 2, \; (3)$$

On the parallel machine $y_{n+1,S+1}$ and $y_{n+2,S+1}$ are obtained simultaneously for each S.

The value of S is selected to reduce the order of error in the last node in the block.

In general, on the parallel machine, y_{n+r} and y'_{n+r} are computed on the rth processor. The process of increasing the block points k or changing stepsize h is given in detail in Reference 12.

The serial versus parallel times may be compared by comparing the number of derivative evaluations required by the serial algorithm with the number required by its parallel counterpart.

The serial time for the maximum number of iterations is:

$$E_s = \tfrac{1}{2}(k + 5)$$

and the parallel

$$E_p = (1 + 2/k)$$

This equation shows that larger block sizes k favor the parallel process. Consequently, parallel processors may be used to advantage for solution of ordinary differential equations.

Real-Time Processes

A real-time closed loop control process with repetitive operations on similar data inputs lends itself to implementation on a SIMD machine. A classic example of this case is the phased array radar target-tracking and radar-scheduling process as shown in Figure 28.9.

A phased array radar consists of a static array of antenna elements that radiates coherent beams differing slightly in phase in such a way that they add to a large amplitude beam directed to an angle off of the normal to the antenna array plane. A radar operated in this way uses a electronically steered beam that replaces the need to physically move the antenna focus, thus improving the directional agility of the radar. Electronic beam steering requires that there be a digital computer to command the radar using a preselected set of search angles and distances and the positions of known objects. A computer program generates a time sequence of commands, each giving angle and range parameters of known objects or a volume of space to be searched. The radar returns are then used to establish or update a target state vector consisting of position and velocity data that is then used to predict the target position for the next radar pulse directed to that object. A digital filter, usually some form of Bayesian or polynomial filter, is used to estimate and correct for random noise effects and to update the target's position, velocity, and acceleration file in the computer data base. The update rate is dictated by the equations of motion, maneuver characteristics, and general requirements of the application but can be short enough to impose severe data processing loads onto the control computer. It is necessary to execute the filter, update the track state, and schedule the next pulse within the period between successive pulses for any object in track.

Task-scheduling strategy in a serial processor is to execute the filter algorithm and schedule the next pulse as early as possible in the update cycle because the future demand for CPU resources is an uncertain linear function of total track load and search detection probability.

The parallel processor's weak dependence of CPU loading on track load suggests that the best scheduling strategy is to wait as long as possible in the update cycle to accumulate the maximum data set size. The parallel processor then operates with a large number of active PEs and machine efficiency is optimized.

The finite algorithm execution time requires the filter (and scheduler) to run at a frequency greater than the nominal update frequency.

For example, if the nominal track update is 50 ms (20 Hz) and the filter/scheduler sequence uses 15 ms of processing time, then the sequence must be scheduled every 35 ms or a 28.5 Hz rate. The maximum efficiency of the parallel processor is 70% if all available PEs are loaded with a track. One must therefore add about 10 PEs to gain 7 in track capacity.

The operating characteristics of a parallel machine performing the radar control task are quite predictable because of the relative independence of filter execution time from track load. This allows the system designer to confidently predict performance under stressing loads. The parallel machine usually runs very predictably until PE capacity is reached. Several options are available at this point including stopping of the search task and dropping tracks of lesser interest to the system purpose. This choice can be made only during system design and is a function of system purpose.

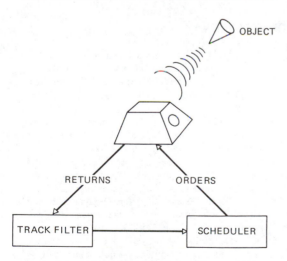

Figure 28.9. Generic BMD construct.

The inherent modularity of SIMD generally allows addition of PEs as system growth dictates. PEPE, designed for this task, is an ensemble of associatively rather than directly addressed elements and hence is optimized for this sort of modular growth.

28.3. FUTURE REQUIREMENTS AND PROSPECTS

The computationally intensive problems driving past developments in parallel processing technology are still essentially unsolved. Computational physics can be employed for engineering design purposes if two conditions are met: The physics of the problem must be well enough understood to be represented by an accurate mathematical model, and a sufficiently large computer must be available to solve the equations within practical cost and time constraints. The partial differential equations of fluid flow, neutron diffusion, and atmospheric energy transport are well known and can be expressed to a level of detail that accurately reflects the physical process, yet the available computational resource does not permit solution. Practical solutions require the use of approximations to reduce the computational load to practical limits.

The problems of computational physics have traditionally been solved by means of some physical modeling techniques such as a wind tunnel or wave tank, which replace theory with direct measurement that can be extrapolated to a full-scale system. These devices serve as analog computers to integrate the system partial differential equations. This method has some inherent limitations including model size, control of ambient conditions such as temperature, velocity, wall and support interference, and measurement interference. A physical model is not always possible on a small enough scale to be cost effective, and extrapolation errors make the results uncertain.

The cost curves for physical modeling have been accelerating during the period that digital computation size, speed, and cost are becoming more favorable so that computational modeling is becoming a cost-effective replacement for physical modeling. The immense

computational requirements of computational physics still preclude conventional uniprocessor solutions, and the data characteristics of the partial differential equation provide the vector lengths compatible with parallel processor efficiency. It is reasonable to assume, therefore, that there will be a demand for parallel machines. SIMD parallel processors are not suitable for general-purpose applications so that their use will be restricted to the relatively few centers where the digital modeling comprises the major computational activity. Thus, limited production machines tailored to a specific application and funded by the government will predominate. The SIMD architecture may well predominate this market even though there is less generality in its spectrum of applications. The small production run of such machines will continue to make the engineering and hardware savings gained with central instruction stream control an important consideration.

Real-time control applications such as phased array radar control are ideally suited to SIMD machines. The majority of circuitry in a SIMD machine is in the replicated elements; hence, there are fail soft characteristics inherent in the architecture that are appealing. As the cost of replicated logic is reduced by VLSI technology, the SIMD machine can be expected to be applied to these problems.

REFERENCES

1. D. E. McIntyre, "An Introduction to the ILLIAC-IV Computer," *Datamation,* Apr. 1970, pp. 60–67.
2. J. A. Cornell, "Parallel Processing of Ballistic Missile Defense Radar Data," Compcon 72, 1972 pp. 69–72.
3. K. E. Batcher, "The Multi-Dimensional Access Memory in STARAN," *IEEE Transactions in Computers,* Feb. 1977, pp. 174, 177.
4. D. J. Kuck, "Parallel Processor Architecture—A Survey," *Proceedings of the 1975 Sagamore Computer Conference on Parallel Processing,* pp. 15–37.
5. M. J. Flynn, "Some Computer Organizations and Their Effectiveness," *IEEE Transactions on Computers,* Sept. 1972, pp. 248–260.
6. M. C. DiVecchio, "The Design and Implementation of a High/Low Magnitude Search Instruction on PEPE," *Proceedings of the 1975 Sagamore Conference on Parallel Processing,* p. 122.
7. J. F. Traub (ed.), *Complexity of Sequential and*

Parallel Numerical Algorithms, Academic Press, New York, 1973.

8. R. P. Brent, "The Parallel Evaluation of General Arithmetic Expressions," *Journal of ACM,* Apr. 1979, pp. 201–206.

9. H. T. Kung, "New Algorithms and Lower Bounds for the Parallel Evaluation of Certain Rational Expressions and Recurrences," *Journal of ACM,* Apr. 1976.

10. A. Ralston and H. S. Wilf (eds.), *Mathematical Methods for Digital Computers,* Wiley, New York, 1967, Chapter 14.

11. L. F. Shampiac and H. A. Watts, "Block Implicit One-Step Methods," *Mathematical Computers,* vol. 23, 1969, pp. 731–740.

12. P. B. Worland, "Parallel Methods for the Numerical Solution of Ordinary Differential Equations," *IEEE Transactions on Computers,* Oct. 1976, pp. 1045–1048.

13. J. Nievergelt, "Parallel Methods for Integrating Ordinary Differential Equations," *Communications of ACM,* vol. 7, 1964, pp. 731, 733.

ADDITIONAL REFERENCES

Banerjee, U., Shyh-Ching Cheu, David J. Kuck, and Ross A. Towle, "Time and Parallel Processor Bounds for FORTRAN-Like Loops," *IEEE Transactions on Computers,* Sept. 1979, pp. 660–670.

Batcher, K. E., "STARAN Series E," *Proceedings of the 1977 International Conference on Parallel Processing.*

Blakely, C., "PEPE Application to BMD Systems," *Proceedings of the 1977 International Conference on Parallel Processing,* pp. 183–198.

Chapman, H. M., and M. W. Pirtle, "Computers vs. Wind Tunnels for Aerodynamics Flow Simulations," *Astronautics and Aeronautics,* Apr. 1975.

Cornell, J. A., "PEPE Application and Support Software," *WESCON'72,* Sept. 1972.

Davis, R. L., "The ILLIAC-IV Processing Element," *IEEE Transactions on Computers,* Sept. 1969, pp. 800–816.

Dingeldine, J. R., H. G. Martin, and W. M. Patterson, "Operating Systems and Support Software for PEPE," *Proceedings of 1973 Sagamore Conference on Parallel Processing.*

Enslow, P. E., *Multiprocessing and Parallel Processing,* Wiley, New York, 1974.

Evensen, A., "PEPE Hardware and System Overview," *Proceedings of 1977 International Conference on Parallel Processing,* p. 185.

Evensen, A. J., and J. L. Troy, "Introduction to the Architecture of a 288 Element PEPE," *Proceedings of 1973 Sagamore Conference on Parallel Processing.*

Finnela, Charles A., and H. H. Love, "The Associative Linear Array Processor," *IEEE Transactions on Computers,* Feb. 1977, pp. 112–125.

Gilmore, P. R., "Numerical Solution of Partial Differential Equations by Associative Processing," *Proceedings at Fall Joint Computer Conferences,* 1971.

Kogge, P. M., "Parallel Solution of Recurrence Problems," *IBM Journal of Research and Development,* March 1974, pp. 138–148.

Lloyd, Gregory R., and Richard E. Merwin, "Evaluation of Performance of Parallel Processors in a Real Time Environment," *Proceedings of National Computer Conference,* 1973.

Lowrie, D. H., "GLYPNIR—A Programming Language for ILLIAC-IV," *Communications of the ACM,* March 1975, pp. 157–164.

Marshall, D. D., "A Parallel Processor Approach for Searching Binary Decision Trees," *Proceedings of 1977 International Conference on Parallel Processing,* pp. 191–201.

Shapiro, Henry D., "Storage Schemes in Parallel Memories," *Proceedings of the 1975 Sagamore Conference on Parallel Processing.*

Siegel, H. J., "A Model of SIMD Machines and a Comparison of Various Interconnection Networks," *IEEE Transactions on Computers,* Dec. 1979, pp. 907–917.

Stone, H., "An Efficient Parallel Algorithm for the Solution of a Tridiagonal Linear System of Equations," *Journal of the ACM,* vol. 20, Jan. 1973, pp. 27–38.

Stone, H. S., "Parallel Processing with Perfect Shuffle," *IEEE Transactions on Computers,* Feb. 1971.

Thurber, K. J., and L. D. Wald, "Associative and Parallel Processors," *Computer Surveys,* December 1975.

Thurber, K. J., *Large Scale Computer Architecture,* Hayden Book Company, Inc., New Jersey, 1976.

Chi Chen Tien, "Unconventional Superspeed Computer Systems," *Proceedings of Spring Joint Computer Conference,* 1971.

Vick, C. R., "Research and Development in Computer Technology, How Do We Follow the Last Act?" Keynote Address, *Proceedings of 1978 International Conference on Parallel Processing.*

Weide, Bruce, "A Survey of Analysis Techniques for Discrete Algorithms," *Computer Surveys,* vol. 9, no. 4, Dec. 1977, pp. 291–313.

Welch, H. O., "Numerical Weather Prediction in the PEPE Parallel Processor," *Proceedings of the 1977 International Conference on Parallel Processing,* pp. 186–192.

29

Software Development for Data-Flow Machines

Don Oxley

Bill Sauber

Merrill Cornish

Texas Instruments, Inc.

29.1. INTRODUCTION

Because of a need for increased performance in solving many computation problems, considerable interest has developed in computer architectures capable of exploiting parallelism. One important parallel architecture is based on the concepts of data flow [1, 2, 3, 4].

The exploitation of parallelism is necessary because the advances in improved circuit technology are approaching physical limits and are not sufficient to meet the need for increased performance [5]. The goal is to develop a flexible multiprocessor system, not to develop fast special-purpose systems (such as FFT boxes). Such a system is required to reduce the costs of application development while still achieving the maximum computing power.

Development of data-flow systems began seriously in the late sixties and continues in the work of many groups around the world. Additional details on the various approaches are given below and are described in Reference 6. The descriptions and approach taken in this chapter are strongly influenced by the authors' work at Texas Instruments. Two assumptions are made in the majority of research that are not true of the TI effort:

1. Data-flow graphs are purely applicative in nature.
2. Data-flow systems require special languages (single assignment languages) for their implementation.

The fundamental problem that data-flow systems attack is the representation of the problem. Classical computers represent a problem (computation) as a serial list of instructions that is executed by following the sequence with a hardware program counter. A data-flow system represents the problem as a directed graph that shows explicitly the serial/parallel relationships within the program. The program counter is replaced by a data-flow sequencer that implements the data-flow sequencing rules [7].

There are many sources of parallelism in a program [8], and it is important to provide mechanisms that exploit as many different classes of parallelism as possible. These classes include:

1. Operation level. Independent operations within an expression may proceed in parallel.
2. Structure level. Loop iterations, independent serial sequences, and other low-level structures may be executed in parallel.
3. Functional. Independent functions of arbitrary complexity (including parallel recursions) may be executed in parallel.
4. Tasks. Programmer specified divisions of a program may be executed in parallel.
5. Programs. Independent programs in a multiprogramming environment may be executed in parallel.

The design goals for a data-flow system include:

1. Flexibility. The ability to effectively exploit many different forms of parallelism.
2. Ease of use (transparency). The parallel nature of the system should be minimally apparent to the user.
3. Replication of parts. The system should be easily expandable by the addition of processors. These processors may be identical; however, this is not a requirement.
4. Standard languages. The system should be accessible to programmers without using new or special languages. This requirement differs from those of most researchers [5, 9, 10, 11].

29.2. BACKGROUND AND RESEARCH SUMMARY

The original papers that led to today's data-flow techniques were published over 15 years ago and numerous proposed data-flow implementations have been presented since then. The common thread of data-flow sequencing that runs through all of these designs is often hard to follow. It is a case of not seeing the trees for the forest: The various unique data-flow ideas (the trees) are invariably packaged in theoretical graph schemas or comprehensive design proposals (the forest). Too often real or imagined imperfections in the packaging misdirect attention from appreciation of the underlying data-flow idea.

This section will introduce data-flow research by comparing and contrasting the variation in data-flow sequencing techniques rather than exploring each "package" in detail or assigning precedence to the development of new ideas.

Karp and Miller

Karp and Miller's paper written in 1964 [7] is a convenient starting point. The paper's main purpose was to prove determinacy and termination in a graph theoretic model, but the authors also observed that a directed graph is "one natural way to depict the sequencing of a parallel computation. . . ."

They described what has become the standard data-flow program representation of directed arcs carrying operand tokens between operational nodes. For this representation, they proposed a straightforward set of data-flow firing rules:

- All arcs between nodes are FIFO queues;
- A node becomes eligible for execution when each of its input arcs contains a number of tokens equal to the threshold for that arc;
- When a node finally executes, it reads and then removes a specified number of tokens from each input arc and performs its operation; and finally
- The node completes execution by outputting some number of result tokens on its output arcs.

This schema covers the simple arithmetic operator case of a threshold of one token per input which is consumed producing the single token on the output (e.g., A + B = C).

A Signal-Processing Extension

The "signal-flow graphs" traditionally used to describe digital signal processes are an obvious instance of data flowing thru directed graphs. Almost 15 years after Karp and Miller's paper, and after hundreds of alternative proposals in other papers, the Navy incorporated Karp and Miller's original model—with one extra feature—in a Request For Proposal for a new signal processor [12].

The extra feature is that the number of tokens read from an input arc does not have to be the same as the number of tokens consumed. For example, a node that must calculate the first-order derivative of an input stream would read two (to take their difference), but would only remove one (leaving the second one for the next difference).

Unordered Queues

Arvind and Gostelow of the University of California at Irvine kept the arc queues, but removed the FIFO constraint [10]. Each token carries a tag identifying its iteration number or recursion level. Threshold detection is now more complicated. A node must compare tags across all entries in all queues to determine if an input *set* is available.

Unqueued Operations

In Britian, Watson and Gurd at the University of Manchester [13] and Treleaven and others at the University of Newcastle upon Tyne [14] removed the queuing constraint altogether. All tokens in the system are kept in a heap with each token not only tagged with its iteration number, but also its destination node name.

The net effect of removing the ordering constraints is to allow unrolled loops or recursions. For example, all inputs to all iterations of a loop can be turned loose on one loop body and still produce the same output as serial execution.

Forwarding on Availability

Jack Dennis at MIT has been responsible for popularizing data flow in the U.S. through his numerous papers and presentations. Dennis's design introduced the powerful implementation concept of forwarding on availability. His schema uses single entry input queues, which amounts to reserving locations in each instruction for one set of incoming operands. Instead of handing a result off to a third party heap or queue manager, a copy of each result is sent to each instruction that needs it. This implementation causes the operand values to be automatically cached along with their instructions for simple fast access once the instruction is enabled.

Null Tokens

In most schemata, tokens represent only operand values, but in the Texas Instrument data-flow design [3] and the French LAU design at CERT [15] tokens may also represent a simple valueless completion signal. That is, a node must not only wait for all of its input operands but also wait for all necessary "go ahead" signals. These null tokens provide a way of regulating the execution by adding synchronization

tokens beyond those required by the *data-flow criteria*.

A graph may be able to prove that a program's queues never become infinite, but million entry queues are infinite, as far as dedicated data-flow hardware is concerned. If execution can be constrained beyond the minimum requirements of the data-flow criteria, then the size of the instantaneous program state can be limited to whatever the hardware can accommodate. If the data-flow schema does not contain some way of "throttling" execution, then "the compiler must ensure that the maximum concurrency of an activation does not exceed the pipeline capacity $\cdots$," as James Rumbaugh suggested for avoiding data-flow processor deadlock [16].

29.3. BASIC DATA-FLOW CONCEPTS

This section will attempt to take the fundamental ideas of a data-flow system and show how they can be used as the basis of a computer architecture. The fundamental concepts are in themselves very simple; however, as they are expanded and combined into the basis for a computing system, their effect may be much more complex. This section will in general attempt to develop a data-flow system along intuitive lines that correspond to similar notions in classical sequential systems.

Conceptual Foundation of a Data-Flow System

Data flow as a system concept is intended to support the development and use of multiprocessor systems that cooperate very closely to solve a common problem (single application). Although data-flow systems are useful in a multiprogramming environment, it is the ability to use MULTIprocessing in a MONOprogramming environment that is the main advantage of a data-flow system.

There are three basic cornerstones of a data-flow system (Cornish [17] calls them multiprocessor design criteria):

- Directed graph program representation
- Data-flow program sequencing

- Forwarding-on-availability data movement

These three concepts permeate the entire system philosophy, although none are dogmatically used to the exclusion of other ideas. As discussed below, it would appear that an "optimal" solution to the multiprocessor problem may well involve a combination of ideas from classical sequential systems and ideas from data-flow systems.

In the execution of the user program, these concepts are directly realized in the hardware. It is important to note, however, that these same ideas have contributed at least as significantly to the entire process of compiling a program, debugging it, and measuring its performance.

Directed Graph Problem Representation. Representing a problem as a directed graph makes explicit the serial/parallel relationship among the parts of the problem. Figure 29.1 is an example of a simple directed graph that orders a set of three values and computes their mean. The nodes of the graph correspond to the operations to be performed on the data values of the program. The arcs represent the "flow" of data between the operations. An arc from node i to node j represents a value that is a result of the computation in node i and is an input to the computation in node j. In the example, the eXCHange node is an operator that accepts two inputs and sends the larger out on one output arc and the smaller out on the other.

There are some additional features of a data-flow graph that are useful in constructing programs:

Null Synchronization Arcs. It is normal for each arc in a data-flow graph to correspond to the transmission of a data value from one operation to another. It is also convenient to be able to cause two computations to be ordered with respect to one another even though no data are transmitted between them. For example, two computations that cause output to a single device must be serially constrained even though they do not exchange data. The synchronization is accomplished by an arc that can be thought of as transmitting a special "null" value, which indicates that an event has occurred but which is not itself used in any subsequent computation.

Conditional Operations. In Figure 29.1, all the nodes perform a fixed computation and feed values forward on all output arcs. By allowing an arc to forward values on some of its output arcs but not all of them for any given execution, subsequent parts of the directed graph can be caused to conditionally execute. These conditional operations can be used to implement IF..THEN..ELSE and similar programming structures.

Data Referencing. No restrictions are placed on the computation that is performed by a single node. In particular, a node may use data that it can access without receiving them on an input arc. If two or more nodes can access the same data item, then this allows the creation of side effects or "non-applicative" programs. It also allows a more realistic solution to many problems of managing and accessing data in a multiprocessor computer system.

Data-Flow Sequencing. The directed graph shown above is a static representation of a problem. Although there is an intuitive feel for how to use the graph to perform a computation, it is necessary to specify exactly what must happen in order for a directed graph to be "executed" to perform some computation. This procedure for executing a program specified as a directed graph is known as data-flow

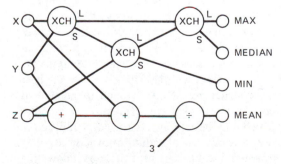

Figure 29.1. A directed graph.

sequencing. The requirements for performing any operation in the graph are:

1. All required inputs (including null synchronization inputs) must be available.
2. There must be a place to put the outputs.

The first criterion is obvious and intuitive. The second is also intuitive but less obvious. Some data-flow systems achieve the second by allowing multiple values to be associated with a single arc of the graph [13, 15]. Others explicitly (in the hardware) or implicitly (with the compiler) guarantee that the output arc is available.

A critical characteristic of a data-flow sequencer is its distributed nature. The information necessary to determine if an operation may be performed can be found by examining only a node of the graph and its input and output arcs. There is no need for a centralized control to decide which operations may proceed at any time. This of course is the key to creating a distributed system.

This sequencing operation is implemented by different researchers in many different ways. In the Texas Instruments system, each operation has an associated count of the number of inputs that are required in order for the operation to be enabled. As inputs to an operation arrive, the local memory which contains the operation decrements the operand count and tests it for zero. When a count reaches zero, then the operation has all its inputs and may proceed (the compiler uses null synchronization arcs in the construction of the graph to guarantee that the output arc is available).

The data-flow sequencing requirements specify when an operation *may* be performed. They do not require that it be performed at that time. One of the implementation problems in building a data-flow system occurs because more operations may be available for execution than there are hardware resources to execute them. Thus the hardware must be able to keep track of those operations that have been enabled (are ready for execution) but have not been fired (assigned to a hardware resource for execution). Again, there are many schemes in use, the TI system links instruc-

tions on a hardware-maintained list as they are enabled. The processors take instructions from the head of a list (there may be multiple lists) for execution while the memories attach newly enabled instructions to the tail of a list. The combination of the operand count scheme and the ready instruction list in the TI system replaces the program counter in a sequential machine.

Forwarding on Availability. *Forwarding on availability* is a new term for an obvious, but little appreciated, concept. Forwarding on availability simply means that an operation (instruction, block, subroutine, task, program, etc.) sends (or forwards) copies of its result as soon as it is calculated to every other operation that needs it. By implication, when an operation begins execution, all of its inputs have been collected in one place.

The value of *forwarding on availability* is clearer when it is contrasted with the more common alternative—*fetching on demand*. When data is fetched, the unit needing the data issues a request to the unit containing the data. The requestor is usually delayed until the data is returned. In a conventional uniprocessor, the requestor might be a processor and the responder might be a fast memory. Fetching in a multiprocessor environment, however, introduces bus and communication delays as well as memory interference which causes the turnaround time for fetch requests to become intolerable.

Data-Flow Programs

The basic data-flow ideas above provide a good foundation for the development of a computer system, but they are not yet sufficient to represent actual programs. In particular, key notions such as iteration, conditionals, subroutines, and arrays have not been presented.

This section will describe one form of these basic structures. The approach taken here is not "pure" in that the concept of a memory which may be referenced is used in addition to the transmission of values between data-flow instructions. The use of a memory allows the maintenance of "state information" which is viewed as inconsistent with the notions of applicative programming. In many cases, it does allow a considerable reduction in the number of values which must be transmitted. For other examples of the construction of data-flow programs, see References 1, 13, and 18.

One important point concerning the use of a data memory is that a processor that stores a value into memory knows that the store has actually taken place. It does not simply "forward" the value to the memory and continue on. In general, it is important to minimize and localize as much as possible the use of variables in a memory.

Looping Structures. There are four considerations in implementing a loop as a data-flow graph:

1. Loop initiation. Loop initiation is the process of passing the initial values of variables into the loop and starting the first iteration. This includes both the loop control variables such as increments or limit conditions and the values of variables used in the loop body for computation.
2. Loop control. The loop control is responsible for initiating each pass through the body of the loop. It will determine when the loop termination condition has been satisfied and pass control to statements outside the loop itself.
3. Loop body. The loop body carries out the computation of the loop. It is initiated by the loop driver once for each iteration of the loop.
4. Loop completion. Loop completion refers to the specific process of passing results out of the loop after the termination condition has been satisfied. In most cases, the loop body does not pass a result outside of the loop on each pass. When the loop completes, the result must be forwarded to subsequent portions of the graph. In the case of an array operation where a different element of the array is computed on each pass through the loop, the result is stored in the array. However, no result values are passed to a portion of

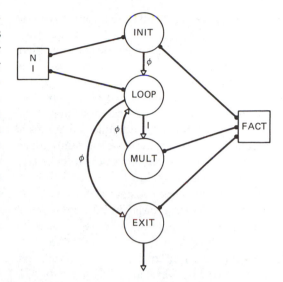

Figure 29.2. A data-flow loop.

the graph outside the body of the loop. When the loop is complete, a signal is passed outside the loop indicating that the entire array is available for use.

Figure 29.2 shows a loop that will compute the factorial of a number. The INIT node is responsible for setting the value of N (the termination condition), I (the index variable), and FACT (the accumulated result). LOOP increments I and tests for completion. The MULT node multiplies the variable FACT times the index and saves the result. EXIT is responsible for retrieving the result of the computation (FACT) and forwarding it to subsequent portions of the graph.

Conditionals. Conditionals or decisions may be handled in two different ways in a data-flow graph. The first, conditional flow of control, is similar to a classical program in that one of a set of mutually exclusive subgraphs is executed. The processing of the conditional then consists of directing control and inputs to the selected subgraph. The second, conditional gating of result, may be thought of as executing all subgraphs and selecting only one of the results.

From an analysis point of view, the second approach reduces a conditional graph (there are subgraphs that may not be executed) to an unconditional one (all subgraphs are executed). It may also allow parts of the computation to occur at a much earlier time than would otherwise be possible because they would no longer be constrained by the execution of the control function itself. In a parallel machine, it may in some cases be more productive to evaluate the additional subgraphs in parallel than to constrain their execution and potentially cause some processors to be idle.

Another advantage of the conditional selection of result occurs in simplifications that may be made in passing variables into the scope of the condition. In general, no values required by either subgraph may be forwarded to that subgraph until after it is known that the subgraph will be executed. With conditional selection of result, it is known that the subgraph within the scope of the conditional will be executed; and thus, it may receive its input values as soon as they are available.

Figure 29.3 is an example of a conditional graph. Figure 29.3a shows conditional flow of control, Figure 29.3b shows conditional selection of result.

Subroutines. The use of subroutines in a data-flow graph implements the notion of a single instruction or node in a graph that is replaced at execution time by a complete subgraph. This is exactly analogous to the classical idea in which a subroutine CALL instruction can be considered to be replaced by the module it calls. However, in a data-flow graph, a number of additional considerations exist. There may be multiple concurrent invocations of a single subroutine body that must be shared among the different invocations. This requires that the independent accesses be synchronized. There may be more than one copy of the subroutine body, in which case some mechanism must exist for associating a copy of the subroutine with the execution of a subroutine call.

The possibility of parallel access to a single subroutine body means that the notion of forwarding values to the instructions that use them must also be handled carefully for subroutines. The storage location in the subroutine instruction may not be available when the instruction supplying the value wishes to execute because of a simultaneous use by another call to the subroutine.

In classical programming, a subroutine call or return can be considered to occur at a single place or instant as an indivisible operation. This is not true in data flow. Since the first argument may be passed to a subroutine as soon as it is available and the subroutine may begin operating with it, a subroutine may be consid-

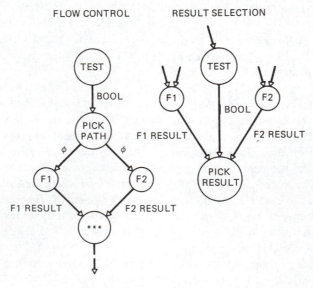

Figure 29.3. Data-flow conditionals.

ered to be "called" when it receives its first argument. There may be substantial delay before additional arguments are available. Similarly, the first result may be returned long before the subroutine actually completes execution. For control purposes, subroutine completion is considered to occur when the last argument is returned.

There are a number of cases of subroutine bodies and subroutine calls to be considered:

1. *Serial subroutine calls with a single subroutine body.* The calls to the subroutine occur serially (there is a serial order required by the nature of the computation, and all results from one call will be returned from the subroutine before any of the inputs for another call arrive). There is no additional synchronization required and a single copy of the subroutine is sufficient. It is only necessary to establish a convention for passing arguments and returning results.

2. *Parallel subroutine calls with a single subroutine body.* In this case, there may be multiple concurrent attempts to call the subroutine (at least one result has not been returned from one call before a conflicting argument arrives for a second call). Since the subroutine is effectively a serially reusable resource, each call must reserve the resource before it attempts to use it. This can be accomplished by associating a semaphore with the subroutine and requiring a standard protocol be used to access the subroutine.

3. *Parallel calls with multiple subroutine bodies.* If there is more than one subroutine body, then different copies of the subroutine may execute in parallel. There are three distinct cases:
   a. *Number of subroutine copies equals maximum number of parallel calls.* Each call may be assigned at compile time to a specific copy of the subroutine body. The operation is then identical to the case of serial calls.
   b. *Number of subroutine copies less than number of parallel calls.* Access to the subroutine must be queued as in the

parallel call case. Efficient execution may also require that the subroutine bodies need to be dynamically assigned to subroutine calls. This is particularly useful when the execution time of a subroutine is data dependent.
   c. *Separate subroutine body for each call.* If each node in the graph that invokes a subroutine has its own copy of the subroutine body, the linkage may be completed at compile time (the subroutine is expanded in-line) and the subroutine becomes a part of the calling routine. This may allow additional optimization to be performed by the compiler.

4. *Parallel calls with dynamic copies.* If a copy of the subroutine body is made at execution time, the problem is reduced to that of a separate copy of the subroutine for each call; thus there is no conflict. There are, however, a number of implementation issues such as allocation of space for the copy and the tradeoff between the execution time of the subroutine and the time required to make the copy.

Use of Data Arrays. As mentioned earlier, nodes of the graph may reference data values or variables that have not been passed along arcs of the graph. In particular, aggregates of data such as arrays or records use this capability. An array is stored in a memory as a sequence of individual elements. When an element of an array is required in a computation, the node of the graph can fetch it directly from the memory.

The process of allocating data items in physical memories and of allowing the individual processors to access those items involves many difficult design decisions and is one of the most difficult issues. It is also one of the least well understood problems. The process of assigning code and data to processors is called (in the TI system) allocation and involves analyzing the code to determine reference patterns for nodes of the graph. From the reference patterns and other constraints, various heuristics are used to develop an assignment strategy for data and code. A good job of allocation will result in significantly better performance (because of locality of reference).

The reading and writing of data arrays allow the notion of a memory "state" and therefore introduce side effects into the computation. To achieve the result specified by the programmer, it is necessary to maintain the same access order to variables that was specified in the source code. This order is maintained by adding additional arcs to the graph (null synchronization arcs) that may cause otherwise parallel portions of a graph to be serialized for access to the variable. Finding and minimizing these constraints are handled through read/write variable analysis in the compiler and are an important part of optimization. Note that a single assignment language does not have the problem of side effects.

Static versus Dynamic Systems

The allocator mentioned earlier and the general use of memory local to a node imply a binding of code and data to specific physical processors for execution. This is a "static" view of the world in which the graph has been partitioned among a set of processors based on its static characteristics. TI uses this approach to static binding.

The alternate approach is to assign instructions to physical processors dynamically during execution. This is the approach taken in most research [1, 13, 18].

The motivations for using a static approach to allocation include:

1. *Communication delays.* It takes longer for signals to move between processors than to remain local. When two instructions are serially constrained by an arc of the graph, the second could potentially be executed sooner if it is in the same processor as its predecessor(s). This becomes particularly important during portions of the graph that exhibit little parallelism.
2. *Interconnect bandwidth.* The interconnect between processors can be much simpler and cheaper if the required bandwidth can be reduced.
3. *Simplified data management.* Access to data arrays is much faster when the accessing code is physically near the containing memory.
4. *Dynamic load balancing.* A strong argument for dynamic assignment is that a ready-to-execute instruction may execute in ANY available processor. With some specific exceptions, if there is sufficient parallelism to support a certain number of processors, then a reasonable allocation strategy will have a high probability of some instruction being available for each processor at all times. Note that the number of parallel instructions needed to support a certain number of processors exceeds the number of processors by a significant multiple.
5. *Reduced hardware complexity.* The process of dynamically assigning instructions requires decisions to be made at execution time. Making the same decisions at compile time will reduce the amount of work that must be done at execution time, with the result that the complexity of the hardware is reduced. It will also allow decisions to be made once at compile time rather than every time an instruction executes at run time. Rules embedded in hardware are inflexible and must be designed for the typical case. All other cases will suffer.

On the other hand, the use of static allocation causes significantly greater work for the supporting software system. The allocator is that portion of the software system that is responsible for deciding how to partition code and data among a set of processors. The basic approach taken at TI is to use a set of heuristics based on PERT/CPM and bin-packing techniques.

A Two-Level Architecture

The notion that a single node may perform an arbitrary computation has been used in describing the behavior of the nodes of a data-flow graph. In the TI system, this is formalized in the notion of a two-level architecture.

The system is viewed as a combination of a data-flow-based architecture between the nodes of the graph in which the nodes are implemented as classical von Neumann instruction sequences. This allows the software system to construct nodes that perform functions directly relevant to the problem being solved (there is no fixed instruction repertoire that defines the available functions of the graph nodes).

The data-flow control is responsible for receiving operands, determining when nodes are ready to execute, and scheduling the execution of the nodes. The sequential level (intranode) is responsible for carrying out the actual computation. Communication between the sequential machine and the data-flow control is accomplished with a set of primitive instructions that allow the sequential machine to send operands to other data-flow nodes, signal its own completion, call subroutines, and so forth.

The general model assumes that each node of the graph is a set of instructions that perform a small part of the overall computation. The minimum size (number of instructions or execution time) of a node is determined by the time required to prepare it for execution and the time required to physically context switch the sequential machine to the node.

29.4. ENHANCEMENT OF A PARALLELISM

With the exception of some general guidelines and cases of explicit parallelism such as multitasking in Ada, the programmer is not overly concerned with writing the program in a parallel fashion. The compiler and system software take the source program (possibly along with additional information) and construct the graph to exploit as much parallelism as possible.

The extraction of parallelism may involve additional interaction with the programmer in the form of requests for advisories or recoding of some sections of code where some construct inhibits parallel execution. The compiler is responsible for informing the programmer of problems it encounters. The programmer may then provide an advisory or code modification to get around the problem.

The compiler (and supporting software) carries out a series of optimizations and transformations on the graph to prepare it for execution. This approach allows the programmer to write in a notation (language) that is most convenient to his or her problem. In general, all the optimizations required are forms of well-known compiling techniques, although some are applied in a much wider scope.

Improving Compiler Analysis

The presence of global variables or side effects within subroutines requires that serial constraints be added to the graph to ensure correct execution. This often occurs because the compiler has a limited visibility for the reference or definition of variables that are available in other modules. Since its visibility is limited, it must make worst-case assumptions about what could happen.

One approach to this problem is to use a single-assignment language that is free of such side effects. An alternate mechanism that allows programmers to use conventional languages is to increase the visibility of the compiler across module boundaries. This can be done by linking individual modules together before carrying out optimization. The compiler can then determine the exact use of a global variable, or it can see what is really happening within a subroutine. This will allow it to provide only those constraints actually needed by the program.

In addition to standard compiler analysis techniques, the useable parallelism in a program may be increased by various transformations on the program graph—particularly on the loops. The transformations are semantically equivalent to the original program but allow the exploitation of more parallelism than the original input. These transformations include:

Static or Textual Unrolling. The body of the loop is duplicated in the internal text of the program and the loop indices are changed accordingly. This is done on classical machines to minimize the loop control overhead. In a parallel machine, it may allow the operations in multiple iterations of the loop to proceed simultaneously.

From a performance point of view, static unrolling *tends* to maintain a constant memory time product (the memory required for the loop times the total execution time). This implies that such unrolling will allow the programmer to trade storage for speed.

Loop Pipelining. Loop pipelining is a data-flow technique that corresponds to vectorization. By viewing the code in a loop body as a pipeline, it is possible to initiate new iterations for the loop before previous iterations complete. Pipelining allows an increase in speed for a relatively small increase in space—thus providing an improved memory time product. Pipelining also introduces a number of additional constraints analogous to those found in vector-processing computers.

Dynamic Loop Unrolling. Dynamic loop unrolling is similar to static loop unrolling except that the loop body is created at run time. This allows the total memory requirements to be reduced. If a new iteration is started in each unrolled loop body as soon as a previous iteration completes in that body without regard to the order of completion of loop iterations, then dynamic unrolling can be a very effective tool when individual iterations of the loop exhibit large variations in execution time.

Static unrolling, pipelining, and dynamic unrolling can also be combined in many hybrid forms to accomplish specific execution time goals.

The various combinations of subroutine bodies and subroutine calls discussed earlier also provide many opportunities to increase the effective parallelism. As an aid to understanding, it is often useful to consider the similarity between loop bodies and subroutine bodies and between loop initiations and subroutine calls.

Interactions with the User

Other sources of parallelism are more closely associated with the programmer. The use of such features as multitasking in Ada or Concurrent Pascal provides explicit parallelism that may be used.

The user may also provide advisories (Ada PRAGMAs) to assist the compiler. The information can be used to improve code generation or may provide information about a program that cannot be proven from the source code (such as the disjointness of different sets of indices to an array).

A third type of user interaction is compiler directed. If the compiler can indicate to the programmer why it cannot execute some parts of a program in parallel, the programmer may be able to add an advisory or modify the code to remove the constraint.

29.5. USER'S PERSPECTIVE

From the perspective of the user who must write software for a data-flow system, the system should impose no unreasonable coding constraints and should in fact simplify the process. There are three areas of interest or concern.

Structured Programming

Structured programming is an important concept for improving the software development process. Interestingly, the use of structured programming simplifies the job of the compiler. A well-structured program does for the compiler exactly what it does for the programmer: It clearly shows what is being done. A compiler can correctly optimize only what it can unambiguously understand; therefore, structured programming is the *preferred* coding technique for optimization by compilers. Since a data flow system depends on compiler optimization in order to exploit parallelism, structured programming contributes significantly to the development of a high-quality data-flow program.

Choosing Parallel Representations

In designing a program for a specific application, the programmer should consider the parallelism in the algorithm. If a serial algorithm is chosen, then no amount of analysis can convert it to a parallel implementation.

Debugging

Some additional complexity is introduced into the development process because the programmer must realize that the order of actual execution is not necessarily the same as the textual order of the program. On the other hand, the representation of the problem as a directed graph tends to assist in the development of tools for debugging. The directed graph also carries a great deal of temporary information that can be used in a debugging process to assist in the traceback of errors.

On the whole, our experience indicates that debugging a program on a data-flow system is no worse than on a conventional system and that with proper tools it is somewhat easier.

Hardware Considerations

Certain data-flow hardware design decisions are critical to maximizing the benefit of data-flow architectures. Proper decisions will insure better performance over a wider range of applications and better productivity to the software designers targeting their work for data-flow systems.

Characteristic Overhead. Conventional computer system sequencing techniques assume an order in which instructions are to be executed, and are capable of overlapping sequencing and instruction execution functions. In general, a program executes through repetition of the following steps:

- Determining the location of the next instruction
- Fetching the next instruction
- Executing the next instruction

Conventional computer systems use a program counter to determine the location of the next instruction. In these systems, there is an assumed sequencing order: The location of the next instruction is the next location in memory. Thus, sequencing, fetching, and execution

functions can proceed in parallel (given sufficient hardware support). This implied order is normally interrupted only by branches.

Data-flow sequencing has no implied order and can not overlap sequencing and execution functions for *serial* instruction sequences. In conventional systems, a program counter controls sequencing, but in data-flow systems, the *instructions* perform the sequencing function. They activate new instructions by sending their results to all instructions requiring those results as operands. A program executes through repetition of the following steps:

- Sending results to the instructions requiring them
- Fetching an instruction with all of its operands available
- Executing a fetched instruction

In the case of a series of instructions with dependencies (the results of one instruction are used as inputs to another), data flow does not allow overlap of sequencing and fetch functions with execution functions. Thus, in cases of code that *must* be executed a serial order (code with dependencies), program counter sequencing allows overlap of functions that could not be overlapped using data-flow sequencing. Note that the data-flow approach allows overlap of these functions for *all* independent instructions, and the issue may be summarized in the following statements:

- The program counter allows overlap of some functions required to execute operations with dependencies, and
- Data flow allows overlap of all functions required to execute any independent operations.

The above discussion suggests that serial programs should be executed on a program counter machine and parallel programs should be executed on a data-flow machine. Rather than require the programmer to make decisions based on the characteristics of his or her code, data-flow systems should be structured to provide acceptable performance for serial as well as parallel code sequences.

Providing acceptable performance for serial sequences can be achieved through hybrid (also referred to as two-level) architectures: architectures that use both program counter and data-flow sequencing. The ideal way to structure a program for execution on an architecture of this type is by forming blocks of code that must be executed serially because of dependencies. (Note that this would be done by a compiler, not a programmer.) The execution of the blocks is controlled by data flow and the execution within a block is controlled by a program counter. Thus, both the implied order of the program counter and the potential for concurrency of data flow are exploited.

Practical considerations may cause deviations from the ideal serial/parallel split. Physical or economic constraints may dictate that hardware can not be provided to execute sequencing functions in parallel with execution functions. Practical limits may be imposed on the minimum or maximum lengths of serial sequences. In any case, the goal should be to execute that which is serial under control of a program counter and to allow execution of that which is parallel under control of data flow.

It should be noted that hybrid approaches without constraints (no minimum or maximum code block lengths) allow compilers to function in a more efficient manner. The compiler translates a high-level language representation of a program into a serial/parallel representation (such as a directed graph). If operations that are serial must use data-flow sequencing or operations that are parallel must be constrained to program counter control, the compiler must do extra work. It must determine the optimum way to apply the constraints (minimum or maximum block length) as well as physically change the program representation (e.g., modify the directed graph).

Sequencing Support. Hardware dedicated to sequencing functions improves processor performance. For program counter sequencing, sufficient hardware support can be provided to allow incrementing of the program counter and fetching of the next instruction while the current instruction is executing. In a data-flow system, hardware dedicated to transmission of results, notification of the arrival of results, detection of ready instructions, and fetch of instructions will allow overlap of these functions with instruction execution.

For pure data-flow and for program counter sequencing, a decision to include hardware support for sequencing is based on a cost/performance tradeoff. Addition of sequencing support will provide uniform performance improvements over all applications. This is not the case in hybrid data-flow systems.

The importance of hardware support for data-flow sequencing is dependent on the application in hybrid systems. If the application contains long serial sequences, the improvement provided by hardware support for data-flow sequencing is minimal. If many short serial sequences dominate the application, the absence of dedicated data-flow sequencing hardware seriously degrades system performance. Systems dedicated to particular applications may be designed without hardware support for data-flow sequencing; however, any general-purpose hybrid data-flow processor should contain data-flow sequencing support.

There are two general approaches to providing sequencing support in hybrid architectures: hardware shared between program counter and data-flow sequencing operations and hardware dedicated to each type of sequencing. Since the hardware structures required to support program counter and data-flow sequencing are similar (incrementers, adders, registers, etc.), the data-flow and program counter sequencing functions may share hardware resources. The advantage of dedicated resources for each type of sequencing is the elimination of potential conflicts over the use of the shared hardware. Whether these conflicts would significantly impair performance would depend on other architecture characteristics such as the ratio of the time required to perform sequencing functions to the average time required to execute the operations.

Interconnect. Order of delivery is an issue in the design of multiprocessor data-flow system interconnects. The data must arrive at its destination not later than the *notification* of the arrival of data reaches the receiver. (If this could not be assured, then an instruction might begin execution before its inputs arrived.) If the interconnect preserves the order of operations, primitive functions that separate the data transmission and notification functions can be made available to the programmer. If the interconnect generally allows delivery of information out of order, it must provide at least one mechanism for preserving order. This could be accomplished by providing an indivisible operation that transmits data and notifications as a unit. The programmer would be required to use this operation for data-flow sequencing.

The level of communication that the interconnect must support depends on the language processors and the applications. Ideally, language processors will partition programs among processors such that interprocessor communication is kept at a low level. However, there are some applications for which any partition will require a high interconnect bandwidth. Although data-flow systems can do little to reduce bandwidth requirements, a natural companion of data-flow sequencing, forwarding on availability, can relax response time requirements.

When a data-flow instruction completes, it must notify all instructions requiring its results that those results are available. If the data are transmitted together with the notification, forwarding on availability has been implemented. That is, operands are forwarded to their destinations when the results become available rather than when the receiver needs them. Thus, the data-flow processor can be structured to perform processor to processor data transfers (equivalent to operand fetch in conventional architectures) on availability rather than on demand. Without fetch on demand, a processor may operate efficiently with relaxed interconnect response time requirements.

Forwarding on availability decreases the required interaction between processor and interconnect. Information can be routed to the interconnect for later delivery without interaction with the receiver. Once the information is accepted by the interconnect, the sender may proceed with other functions.

If the data-flow multiprocessor is structured such that the data and the notification traverse the interconnect in a single packet, the order of arrival of packets is not critical. Thus, buffering and routing techniques that are not required to deliver packets in the order in which they are sent may be used to achieve higher bandwidth.

Debug Support. There are many features that could be included in data-flow systems to facilitate program debug. Two features are of particular interest where data flow is concerned and hardware support for those features may be important: detection of overrun and breakpoint.

Detection of overrun conditions should be supported by hardware in data-flow systems. Instructions in data-flow systems may be in any one of the following states:

- Waiting for inputs
- Ready to execute (all inputs have arrived)
- Executing

Assuming that only enough space for one set of inputs is available for each data-flow controlled operation, the arrival of any inputs during the "ready to execute" or the "executing" states is an error. By making space available for a copy of the executing instruction and providing a queue for multiple sets of inputs, an error does not occur unless the queue overflows. In any case, an error ("called overrun") occurs when new inputs arrive in locations where data which have not yet been used resides. Normally the program is structured such that this condition does not occur; however, compiler bugs or hardware malfunctions could result in overrun conditions. Without hardware detection of these conditions, the program could run beyond the point of error and further conceal the source of the problem.

A conventional feature that allows a programmer to set a breakpoint on a particular instruction is especially useful in data-flow systems. This feature would allow the programmer to stop program execution prior to the execution of a specific instruction. At this point it would be possible to examine any information in the system related to the state of the program. Execution would be restartable after the breakpoint. Parallel execution (which is characteristic of data flow) allows many instructions to proceed in parallel. In many cases, it is difficult to determine which of the concurrently executing functions caused an error. The break point provides a mechanism for interrupting execution and examining the progress of all parallel activity.

29.6. FUTURE PROSPECTS

Data flow is not a parallel processing panacea but rather one of several parallel control strategies. So, where does data flow fit in?

A Common Purpose

All parallel control strategies have the same purpose: to enforce the data-flow criteria that no operation executes unless its inputs are available and there is a place to put its outputs. These "different" strategies differ only in the programming abstraction they present to the programmer to allow him or her to enforce the data-flow criteria.

Levels of Control

The main difference between data flow and all the other alternatives is the intended level of control. Data flow is intended to provide parallel control at the individual structure or instruction level while the others are intended for the subroutine or subtask level.

The intended level of control translates into a level of efficiency. A high level of control implies relatively few control points so that even an inefficient control strategy adds relatively little overhead. On the other hand, a low level of control implies many control points so that only an efficient strategy can limit the overhead.

Furthermore, the level of control relates to the amount of exploitable parallelism: the lower the level of control, the more the exploitable parallelism. Therefore, as a rule of thumb,

The traditional parallel control software can efficiently control a system limited to high-level parallelism only;

The data flow hardware, however, can efficiently control any system, including low-level parallelism.

But as an unobvious corollary, notice that,

The data flow hardware cannot cost effectively replace the traditional strategies in a system with strictly high-level parallelism.

The Compiler Interface

Data flow does have one other advantage that should be considered when choosing a system's parallel control strategy. The traditional strategies were designed as abstractions convenient to a programmer while data flow is an abstraction that is also convenient to a compiler.

If the system designer intends that the main source of parallelism is to be based on the programmer's understanding of the program's functional structure, then the traditional strategies tailored to high level parallelism are adequate. If the designer intends that the principal source of parallelism is the compiler's analysis of the program, then data flow is a prime requirement.

Data-flow techniques match the compiler's internal directed graph data structure. A program level, directed graph simultaneously describes parallelism at both high and low levels. A compiler option could be used to ignore low-level parallelism and only exploit high-level parallelism. But even so, the compiler would still use data flow to control this high level since it is the abstraction that fits the compiler's "world view" of the program.

Therefore, the corollary mentioned above can be expanded to say that if data flow must be used to control high-level parallelism, then it may as well be implemented in firmware or even software. In this case, it is the data-flow abstraction that the compiler needs, not the efficiency of data-flow hardware.

REFERENCES

1. J. B. Dennis, D. P. Misunas, and C. K. C. Leung, "A High Parallel Processor Using a Data Flow Machine Language." Computation Structures Group Memo 134, Laboratory for Computer Science, MIT, Cambridge, Mass., Jan. 1977.
2. J. B. Dennis, "Data Flow Supercomputers," *Computer,* Nov. 1980.
3. W. F. Sauber and M. A. Cornish, "A Computer Without a Program Counter," *Equipment Group Engineering Journal,* Texas Instruments Inc., Dec. 1980.
4. J. C. Syre, "From the Single Assignment Software Concept to a New Class of Multiprocessor Architectures," R-75-105, IEEE Computer Society Repository, May 1975.
5. J. R. McGraw, "Data Flow Computing: The VAL Language," Preprint UCRL-83251, submitted to ACM Transactions on Programming Languages and Systems.
6. P. C. Treleaven, D. R. Brownbridge, and R. P. Hopkins, "Data Driven and Demand Driven Computer Architecture," Computing Laboratory, University of Newcastle upon Tyne, July 1980, to be published.
7. R. M. Karp and R. E. Miller, "Properties of a Model for Parallel Computations: Determinancy, Termination, Queueing," *SIAM Journal of (Applied) Mathematics,* Nov. 1966.
8. M. J. Flynn and J. L. Hennesey, "Parallelism and Representation of Problems in Distributed Systems," *IEEE Transactions on Computers,* Dec. 1980.
9. W. B. Ackerman and J. B. Dennis, "VAL—A Value-Oriented Algorithmic Language: Preliminary Reference Manual," Computation Structures Group, TR-218, Laboratory for Computer Science, MIT, Cambridge, Mass., June 1979.
10. X. X. Arvind, K. P. Gostelow, and W. Plouffe, "The (Preliminary) Id Report," Department of Information and Computer Science (Tr114a), University of California at Irvine, Irvine, California, May 1978.
11. O. Gelly, et al., "LAU System Software: A High Level Data Driven Language for Parallel Programming," *Proceedings of the 1976 International Conference on Parallel Processing,* Aug. 1976.
12. U.S. Navy Shipboard Tactical Embedded Computer Systems Project Office, "Extended Modular Signal Processor Request for Proposal," Oct. 1980.
13. J. R. Gurd and I. Watson, "A Multilayered Data Flow Computer Architecture," Department of Computer Science, University of Manchester, Manchester, England, draft, March 1980.
14. R. P. Hopkins, P. W. Rautenbach, and P. C. Treleaven, "A Computer Supporting Data Flow, Control Flow and Updateable Memory," Computing Laboratory Technical Report No. 114, University of Newcastle upon Tyne, Sept. 1979.
15. A. Plas, et al., "LAU System Architecture: A Parallel Data-Driven Processor Based on Single Assignment," *Proceedings of the 1976 International Conference on Parallel Processing,* Aug. 1976.
16. J. E. Rumbaugh, "A Data Flow Multiprocessor," *IEEE Transactions on Computers,* Feb. 1977.
17. M. A. Cornish, "Data Flow Control: a 'Motherboard' for VHSIC Architecture," *Proceedings of the IEEE Workshop on Microprocessors in Military and Industrial Systems,* Jan. 1980.
18. X. X. Arvind, K. P. Gostelow, and W. Plouffe, "An Asynchronous Programming Language and Computing Machine," Department of Information and Computer Science, University of California at Irvine, Irvine, Calif., Dec. 1978.

30

Software Development for Distributed Computing Systems

M. P. Mariani
TRW Systems

D. F. Palmer
General Research Corporation

30.1. INTRODUCTION

Problem Definition

Distributed system software development should not be developed alone but instead should be an integrated software/hardware (SW/HW) design and development approach. Therefore, the topic of this chapter might be more accurately stated as distributed computing system SW/HW design and development.

A distributed computing system has many meanings to many people. To some, a distributed system is one that allows various users to share resources. To others, the processing components must be engaged in a common application.

The major characterizations of distributed systems are their degrees of distribution and their intended application. The development context with respect to these characterizations is defined below.

Distribution Characterizations. Probably the most notable characteristic of a distributed computing system is the distribution of processing hardware. In general, hardware may be distributed at a number of levels (Figure 30.1). Here a distributed computing system may be composed of a global (geographically dispersed) network of computing facilities, or nodes. Each node may contain a set of inter-

connected computing systems; each computing system may be an interconnection of computers; each computer may be an interconnection of elements; and each element may contain interconnected modules.

The distribution of hardware alone does not adequately categorize distributed systems. This chapter is also interested in control and data interaction characteristics. At the computer level, Flynn [1] presents the classical categories based on control and data stream parallelism: single instruction, single data stream (SISD); single instruction, multiple data stream (SIMD); multiple instruction, single data stream (MISD); and multiple instruction, multiple data stream (MIMD).

The categorization of distributed systems at other levels requires additional descriptors to present potential variations. For example in a system of multiple computers, the degree of autonomy of the computers is important; a system with one master control computer generally differs in reliability, performance, and complexity from a system in which all computers share the control. Enslow [2] categorizes multicomputer systems in terms of three distribution dimensions, shown in Figure 30.2. The axes in the figure correspond to:

1. Degree of data base distribution—distribution may range from a single file or file system with a file directory maintained

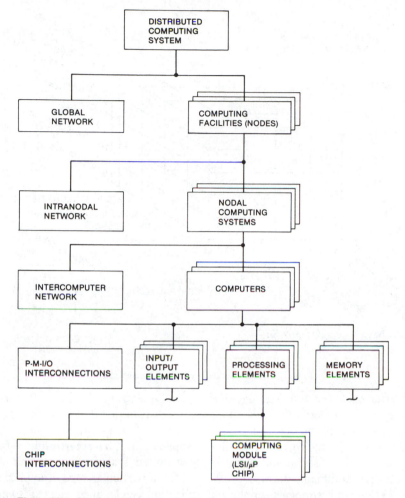

Figure 30.1. Hardware hierarchy for distributed computer systems.

as a single copy in a central storage medium (totally centralized data base), to a multiple file system with replication of both files and directory maintained across several storage mediums.

2. Degree of hardware/software distribution—distribution may range from a single uniprocessor computer (totally centralized) to a network of multiple general-purpose computers each with identical capability.

3. Degree of control distribution—distribution may range from a single fixed control point that makes all operational decisions based on continual observation of the system performance (centralized control) to a fully distributed set of identical control centers cooperating in the decision process governing the operation of the system.

In Figure 30.2, distribution can occur along any axis. Each axis has varying degrees of distribution. The distributed systems represented by the shaded cells of this figure are the most fully distributed and offer the greatest potential advantages.

The degree of distribution implies a great deal about the inherent design and control complexity of the system. At one extreme, systems can be composed of multiple components, each of which operates autonomously. At the other extreme, component-level decisions can be made cooperatively. The degree of cooperation among components may vary from occasional information exchange to exchange of

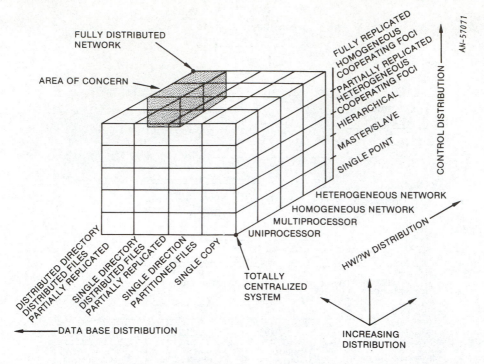

AN-57071

Figure 30.2. Distributed system characterization.

information after each decision. The decision to employ a system composed of cooperating components, regardless of the degree of cooperation, immediately complicates the design process—including the distribution of functions and data, the communications network architecture design and protocols employed, and the tradeoff between excess hardware and control software. The higher the degree of cooperation (i.e., frequency of cooperative decisions), the higher the frequency of information exchange and the intercomponent message rate. Both the complexity of control and data base are affected by the degree of cooperation.

This chapter concentrates on the most fully distributed systems, those in the shaded area of Figure 30.2. The lesser distributed systems can be considered as simplifications. In summary, the concern here is with systems having the following distribution characteristics:

1. Networks of homogeneous or heterogeneous computers
2. Decentralized data base (distributed files and directory, with partial replication of files)

3. Decentralized control (nearly uniform distribution of controlling logic)

Application Characterization. Most often, distributed systems are custom designed to match a particular type of application; an application is classified as: (1) single function versus multiple functions and (2) real time versus nonreal time.

Single function problems (e.g., a satellite control system or a bank transaction system) permit architectural tuning to optimize hardware utilization efficiency. Frequently, some parts of the processing are implemented in hardware rather than software. Multifunction problems (e.g., dual purpose processing center: a military command and control center that also serves as a batch-oriented data processing center during peacetime) lead to more global optimizations so that each function is implemented suboptimally resulting in less efficient hardware utilization. Built-in changeability usually is more important here.

The system may be required to operate in real time or nonreal time as measured by the degree of system responsiveness to external stimulus. Typically, the system responsiveness is measured in terms of the data arrival rate. For example, systems involving man-machine interfaces such as air line reservations systems may require real-time operation on the order of seconds to minutes, whereas radar systems often require much shorter response times on the order of fractions of a second. Systems that must operate at response times of substantially less than a second require automation of much of the complex control operations that normally are handled manually. As a result, such systems can be much more expensive to develop because of the complexity of automated control. Systems that involve nonreal-time response often employ manual control techniques, and as a result, they can usually be developed at much less cost.

Here the concern is directed toward developing single rather than multiple function systems with a concentration on techniques applicable to real-time systems. To obtain real-time performance in specialized systems, emphasis is placed on the requirements engineering aspects of development. A good requirements engineering phase enables better matching of the system to the application requirements, and hence, better potential performance.

Development Goals

The development of any computing system, distributed or centralized, should concentrate on satisfying the intended user. During the design process, the user's immediate concern often is to acquire a system that performs required functions at an acceptable design cost and within an acceptable time. More sophisticated users have learned, however, that designs should be evaluated with respect to the total cost of the system, including: the cost of a system not being entirely useful (not fulfilling its functional requirement); the cost of testing and documentation during development; and the cost of maintenance (continued debugging) and modification. These costs are mostly personnel costs, and they usually overwhelm hardware costs in medium to large systems [3]. In distributed systems, with lower-cost hardware and potentially greater testing costs,

personnel costs are expected to be even more of a driving factor than in conventional systems.

Figure 30.3 shows the major cost trends for contemporary processing systems. The rapidly decreasing costs of processor and memory logic (25 and 40% per year) will permit decreased emphasis of hardware utilization efficiency. The increased personnel costs (10 to 15% per year) will result in the continued increase of system development and maintenance costs.

Conventional system software designers have concluded that personnel costs are a function of the apparent complexity of a system; a system that is easy to understand requires much less effort to develop, test, maintain, modify, and use. Also, simple systems invite fewer errors. Since some problems are inherently large and complex, techniques for reducing the complexity of system solutions have received much attention. The currently most powerful method of reducing complexity is by structured design [4]. The goal of structured design is to divide a system into individually understandable modules, which involves the following considerations:

- Size—computing modules must be small enough to be fully comprehended by one person (usually corresponding to 50 to 100 lines of high-level code).
- Functional cohesiveness—a module should address a single function or purpose with respect to the problem being solved by the system.
- Visibility—the functions and structure within a module should be clear to an examiner, without requiring review of other modules and external documentation.
- Clear interfaces—interactions between modules must be restricted to clearly defined "ports"; modules must not be allowed to "reach" into one another's inner data areas and control sequences.

When structured design approaches are applied in conventional systems, the application designer usually has a good notion of the type of target system hardware and operating sys-

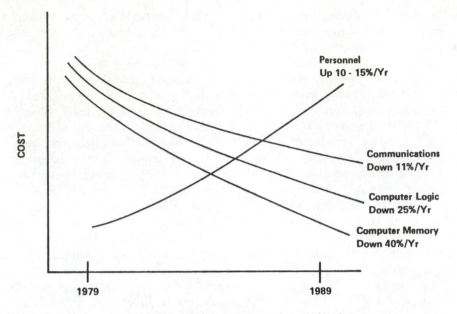

Figure 30.3. Changing costs over the next decade.

tem cabability he will have available. He has to structure only the application software and map it onto a potential system. This early commitment to hardware often occurs because of the relatively high cost and long procurement times of medium-to-large scale centralized processors, or it may be dictated because of the desire to use currently available system hardware. The commitment usually is based on preliminary sizing estimates, which always seem to be too low. The resulting space and response constraints frequently force abandonment of structured software design approaches and high-level languages for improved efficiency, with greatly increased complexity as a result. Furthermore, the high hardware utilization efficiency necessitated by undersizing the required computer capacities tends to increase software programming costs, as illustrated in Figure 30.4. As hardware utilization approaches system capacity, software must be developed more efficiently (and more complexly), which generally increases errors and lowers programmer productivity. The operating system also becomes an object of modification to obtain better efficiency. The overall results of this early hardware commitment are increased costs and errors.

Hardware commitment can be postponed in distributed system design; instead, hardware

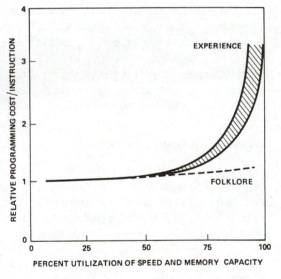

Figure 30.4. Hardware utilization/software cost relationship.

and software requirements can be evolved together. The use of smaller, less complex components makes such hardware postponement technically more viable because the long lead times will not be necessary; the components may well be readily available from many sources. The cost of late commitment is that the developer must now define requirements for hardware, software, and portions of operating systems. Furthermore, tradeoffs between hardware and software and between algorithms and architectures make decisions very complex. This decision complexity must be handled efficiently.

In summary, the specific goals of distributed system development are: (1) low complexity to minimize personnel costs, (2) integrated hardware/software development (late hardware commitment) for lower overall costs and better performance, and (3) efficiency in hardware/software decisions for lower development costs and time.

Related Work

Distributed processing recently has received much attention. Tutorials have been published on the general development problem [5] and specific issues of distributing control [6], distributing the data base [7], and communications [8]. The concepts represented in this work are still evolving, however, and supporting computer aids and languages are mostly lacking. The highlights of this work and the status of supporting technologies are discussed in Section 30.2. This section describes related work that is not usually labeled as distributed system design, so that the readers will have a better understanding of the issues and, perhaps, a starting point for developing alternate approaches, computer aids, and languages. (The remainder of this section is taken from Ref. 5, pp. 7–10.)

Many design technologies exist in varying degrees for large, complex systems in general; references abound in the areas of systems theory, architecture, and general engineering [9, 10, 11, 12]. In areas more directly related to computing system design, applicable work is found in: (1) software engineering, (2) multiprocessor scheduling, (3) optimizing compilers, and (4) circuit board layout and (MSI, LSI, VLSI) chip design. The applicability of work in these four areas for establishing a foundation for the development of a distributed system is discussed below.

Software Engineering.

Software engineering [3, 13] has become an area of ever-increasing interest, particularly as the cost of software has increased to a point where it, not the hardware, is becoming the major cost factor of data processing systems. The complexity associated with the software design for centralized systems has resulted in a great deal of emphasis on the development of software design techniques that promote such features as reduced development time, improved reliability, and reduced maintainability. All of these attributes must be traded off against higher storage and instruction costs, which result in higher computer resource costs. In the current hardware economic environment, however, such additional hardware resource requirements are becoming of less concern when compared to the associated reduction in software costs.

Much of the software engineering emphasis is on principles for structuring the software into modules (often referred to as partitioning), which collectively produce an effective software design. Several methodologies, concepts, and principles for software design currently exist. Collectively, they acknowledge several factors as being of importance to the design process: control flow [14], intramodule cohesion [15, 16], module coupling [4, 17], intermodule balance, data structure [18], data flow, data transformation, and data usage. Depending on the methodology, concept, or principle, the factors that are emphasized will vary.

Multiprocessor Scheduling.

Techniques and algorithms for multiprocessor scheduling require design methods parallel to those for real-time design of a distributed computer. Resource management algorithms used for multicomputer nodal architectures, such as the bidding scheme used by the UC Irvine Distributed Computer System for program to computer assignment [19], can also be viewed as a real-time distributed design problem. Such scheduling of algorithms can, in general, be classified as to whether the scheduling is of independent job streams (e.g., batch processing) or interdependent job networks (e.g., task networks with predecessor-successor relationships). Examining the formulation of the scheduling problem for interdependent job networks can provide valuable insight into the distributed system design problem.

Optimal scheduling for such job networks

has been widely studied, and methods are available for finding the minimum number of processors required to execute the job network within a critical path time, and to find the lower bound on the minimum execution time for a fixed number of computational resources. In most cases, the job network is described by an acyclic-directed graph, with the nodes representing the jobs/tasks and the arcs the predecessor-successor constraints. The jobs are characterized in terms of performance and resource-oriented parameters (e.g., task execution times, storage requirements, special resource requirements). A technique for optimal solutions for cases where the task times are equal has been defined by Ramamoorthy, Chandy, and Gonzales [20], who have suggested methods for handling unequal task times. Fernandez and Bussell [21] have defined an optimal algorithm that handles unequal task times with equal processor speeds.

A major drawback of using optimal scheduling techniques is the computational complexity and the run time necessary to support them. An alternative to such optimal algorithmic techniques is suboptimal heuristic approaches that can be substantially less complex and can execute in significantly less time. Chandy and Dickson [22] studied heuristic algorithms for scheduling task networks in which the predecessor-successor task interrelationships were dynamic and not known a priori. For their model, the task interrelationships were modeled as stochastic processes. The algorithm developed was based on establishing levels of execution times for each node of the acyclic graph. The algorithm was not considered optimal but was very efficient in both run time and average deviation from the optimal solution.

Optimizing Compilers.   Many contemporary supercomputers must employ sophisticated compiler algorithms to ensure optimal use of their internal resources—resources that include concurrently executable functional units (e.g., CDC 7600), special functions such as vector multiplication, or matrix operations (e.g., TI ASC, Cray-1). Many of these compiler design techniques are approached in the

same manner as the multiprocessor scheduling problem. The high-level language user program is represented as a directed graph with each node in the graph representing an instruction. The optimizing compiler must scan the graphic representation of the user's program to look ahead for parallelisms that may exist within the machine-language translation of the user program.

The scanning process often is based on heuristics for speed and may involve multiple passes (i.e., scans of the object code) of increasing complexity. For example, the first pass may look only for obvious parallelisms, such as DO loops, whereas later scans may examine details of the machine-code equivalent of the input user-language code. Such detailed consideration could result in different, but equivalent, machine translations of code being generated. For example, a secondary instruction stream translation could represent more distinct machine operations but a shorter execution time if the principal functional units are tied up by previous instructions. One possible condition could lead to using a series of scalar multiplications to solve a vector multiplication operation because the vector multiply functional unit is active.

Unlike multiprocessor scheduling, no execution timing requirements serve as scheduling constraints. Instead, the compiler objective is typically maximizing the utilization of the computer's internal functional resources. In general, maximizing resource utilization leads to improved performance. Depending on the computer's sophistication, its internal architecture may be based on extensive use of special-purpose functional units, matrix, operations, vector operations, and data manipulation functions. The compilation of such complex computer architectures is typically based on multiple passes in which the initial passes are based on optimizing the use of the most complex of the computer's special-purpose functional units.

Circuit Board Layout and Chip Design.   The design of circuit boards and chips is becoming increasingly complex as new technology leads to ever smaller-scale component technology.

Potential breakthroughs to molecular-level and optical components will further reduce the component size and increase complexity. Such reduced size will require additional improvements in LSI/VLSI fabrication techniques to combat its inherent design complexity.

The automated design tools must solve a mapping problem quite similar to that faced by the multiprocessor scheduler of the optimizing compiler. However, the dimensionality of the LSI/VLSI design problem can involve the mapping of 10^5 to 10^6 chips onto a single circuit board. Instead of mapping to meet a timing objective (e.g., multiprocessor scheduling), automated design tools map chips onto circuit boards so that the line widths (between components) are minimized for increasing speed, and the line crossings are minimized for reduced board depth. Multilayered boards of between five to seven layers are typically used to handle the line crossings for MSI fabrication technology. As the number of board layers increases, however, the typical yield will decrease and the cost will increase. The orders-of-magnitude increase in chip density with LSI/VLSI fabrication can significantly increase the board depth if inefficient mapping algorithms cannot be found.

Summary of Related Work. Common approaches in related work involve top-down or iterative evolution of the design and deal with levels of abstraction and rules of modularity. Computer aids involve an assortment of design languages and supporting computer programs to catalog, test, and display the evolving design. Various management and documentation guidelines are available.

Each of the four computer design areas provides some help in developing various elements of an overall approach to the design of distributed systems. The work in software engineering—especially requirements specification, identification of inherent parallelisms, and software structuring—can be of great help in evolving the structure of the distributed architecture. Top-down design approaches are particularly applicable to tailoring architectures to application structures. Similarities currently exist between mapping applications across multiple resources of a distributed system and the multiprocessor scheduling problem, the optimizing compilers used for contemporary supercomputers, and the circuit board layout problems of LSI/VLSI fabrication technology. Even though the design objectives may vary among such abstractions of the design problem, the techniques and solution concepts are helpful in formulating an approach to the design of distributed systems.

30.2. CURRENT DEVELOPMENT TECHNOLOGIES

It is reasonable to expect that many conventional design principles are applicable to distributed design, but at some point the designer approaches must depart. This section presents a brief overview of conventional structured design with deviations and additions when designing for implementation on a network of computers. Generalizations are given for multilevel distributions, that is, geographical distribution of facilities that contain distributed computer systems, which in turn contain computers that are internally distributed.

Conventional Software Development

When computers started being used for more complex problems, early software designers recognized the need to stop-and-think before coding. Alternate forms of representing software were found necessary to communicate design information; code, alone, was found incomprehensible except for simple problems.

The conventional flow chart came into wide use for designing and communicating designs. Use of conventional (sequential) flow charts is considered to be the first attempt at reducing personnel costs, although at the time hardware costs were dominant. Flow charts are still useful for relatively small designs that will be implemented on sequential computers [23].

The tendency in modern structured design is to continue using graphical representations during initial design steps, but to concentrate on representing data flow rather than control flow [24]. (Conventional flow charts define sequential control flow, which often obscures basic structural relationships of design components. Also, when applied to distributed systems, conventional flow charts obscure ways of employing concurrency.) Later in design, graphs tend to become cluttered with detail, and a language form of representation is recommended [25].

The outline presented here of modern structured design in conventional systems begins with a form of a data-flow graph and then derives a structure chart. Figure 30.5a is a simple example of a data-flow graph for a problem where data (D1) are input to function (F), which outputs data (D2). Figure 30.5a represents the design at its top level of abstraction. In subsequent structured design steps, the solution is repeatedly decomposed (refined in detail, lowered in abstraction). Figures 30.5b and 30.5c illustrate typical steps of decomposition. The asterisk (*) in Figure 30.5c indicates that both outputs of D3 are required to execute F2.1 and F2.2. The symbol $\oplus$ would be used to indicate that either one or the other output of D3 is required because either/or F2.1 or F2.2 will be executed, but not both. Note that no control flow is indicated. Data are implied to flow when available.

After decomposition, the next step is to form a hierarchical structure chart. For example, Figure 30.6 charts the lineage of functions in Figure 30.5. In Figure 30.6, the root function F is the "parent" of functions F1, F2, and F3. Likewise, function F2 is the parent of F2.1, F2.2, and F2.3.

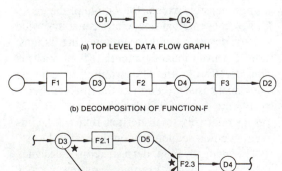

(a) TOP LEVEL DATA FLOW GRAPH

(b) DECOMPOSITION OF FUNCTION-F

(c) DECOMPOSITION OF FUNCTION-F2

Figure 30.5. Typical decompositions of data-flow graphs.

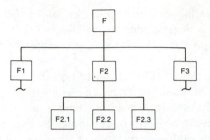

Figure 30.6. Typical hierarchical structure chart.

The structure chart is used to guide the development of software modules. If the structured design of Figure 30.6 on an adequate-size conventional computer were realized, a hierarchy of software modules matching the components shown would be produced. A main program F would call routines F1, F2, and F3. Routine F2, when called, would call routines F2.1, F2.2, and F2.3. Typically, only the most subordinate modules would do any significant computation. The higher modules would mainly handle external interfaces and make control decisions.

If the sample problem had to run on a computer too small for the entire program F, there would be a packaging problem. The components of F would have to be packaged into separate load modules (or overlays or tasks) that could execute separately. In packaging, the frequencies of control transfers and data flows between components would need to be considered to minimize swapping of load modules and data transfer between modules to minimize the associated overhead. Note that packaging software in separate load modules normally requires additional operating system interactions for control and communications.

At this point, structured design ends and code may be implemented. The status of technologies supporting the steps described above is now considered:

1. Decomposition approach—although guidelines exist [24], decomposition is a creative act. The designer must extract necessary functions and data from experience and/or user interaction. The stopping point of decomposition also is not well defined.

2. Packaging approach—packaging also is largely a matter of experience [25], but simulation data could be very helpful.

3. Supporting tools and languages—a variety of tools and languages have been developed to catalog, check, simulate, and test designs [26]. However, no existing tool and language are completely satisfactory with respect to all of the following criteria: (1) automated and readily available and transportable; (2) interactive; (3) facilitates decomposition and tracing of component relationships; (4) automatic simulation generation from design data; and (5) having data gathering and decision aids for structuring and packaging.

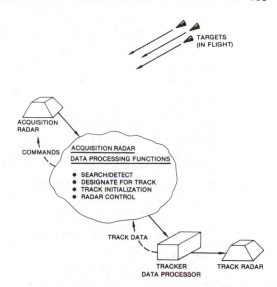

Figure 30.7. Example of acquisition radar system.

Multicomputer System Development

This section discusses the applicability of conventional structured design technologies to distributed systems. In designing a multicomputer system to satisfy a given application, it is assumed that the implementing hardware and operating system are largely undefined at the beginning of design. It is also assumed that the inputs to design are: (1) the computing requirements for a specific type of application, such as processing the outputs and control of the operations of a given type of radar and (2) guidelines and constraints with respect to the types of computers and interconnecting networks that may be used. The goal here is to design a distributed computing system that best satisfies the problem requirements and implementation constraints. (*Best* means *nearly optimal* with respect to total life cycle costs). The design is to include specifying of the numbers and types of computers, the computer interconnection network, requirements for the application software modules to be implemented on each computer, and requirements for (hardware/firmware/software) logic for system control, data base handling, and communications. The design is outlined only in sufficient detail to emphasize required differences and extensions to conventional design.

To illustrate the distributed design approach, consider the acquisition radar system shown in Figure 30.7. The basic operation of this system is to search the sky with an acquisition radar, detect the presence of targets, designate which targets are to be tracked (on the basis of observed target characteristics and trajectory), obtain initial tracking data, and hand over the track initialization data to a tracking radar system. The acquisition system is to ensure that targets are not handed over redundantly. Performance and operational requirements (reliability, change flexibility, etc.) are also given.

To initiate design in conventional structured design, data-flow requirements are identified and represented in graphical form—using data-access rather than data-flow graphs. Data-access graphs look like the data-flow graphs of Figure 30.5, except that the AND and OR conditions on data are not indicated (asterisks and zero signs are not used). Every function and data node in the graph potentially can exist in multiple copies simultaneously, and all nodes may be simultaneously active (since there are to be multiple computers). For instance in Figure 30.5c, one copy of function F2.2 might be receiving data D3 while another copy of F2.2 is sending data D6, where the output data D6 were calculated from prior inputs. Since all of a data-access graph can be active simultaneously when multiple instances

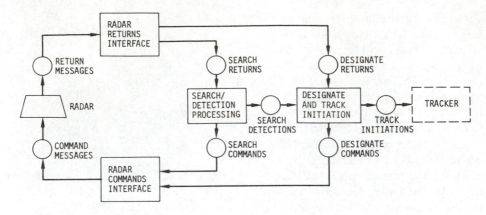

Figure 30.8. Top-level data-access graph for the acquisition radar system (Fig. 30.7).

of data are present, data do not appear to flow in the same sense as in a conventional data-flow graph. (Note that the nodes of data-access graphs are often called functional and data entities as a reminder that the subject is dealing with conceptual function and data relationships.)

Figure 30.8 is a top-level data-access graph for the acquisition radar system shown in Figure 30.7. The functions shown correspond to the basic functions indicated in Figure 30.7, with radar control subsumed in other functions. Abstract interfunctions [27] have been added to isolate the design from external (radar) changes during or after development.

The data entities are abstract representations of basic data flows deemed necessary to support the functions.

The top-level diagram is next elaborated through a number of levels of abstraction. One form of elaboration is decomposition, previously illustrated in Figure 30.5. Figure 30.9 shows a decomposition of the two major application functions of the radar system example. A data entity also has been decomposed: designate commands in Figure 30.8 became first designate commands and designate update commands in Figure 30.9.

The search-returns processing and designate-initiation functions of Figure 30.9 are

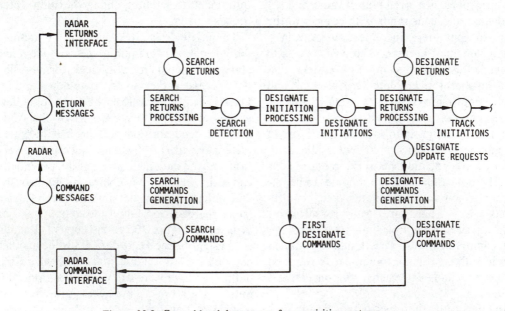

Figure 30.9. Second-level data-access for acquisition system.

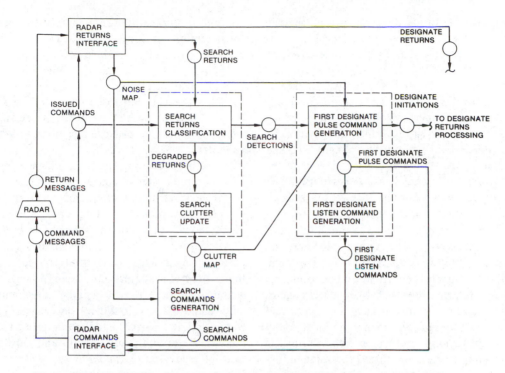

Figure 30.10. First elaboration of search returns processing and designate initiation processing.

further elaborated in Figure 30.10; here is seen an adding of detail (the data entities issued commands, noise map, and clutter map) that is not truly a decomposition of previous entities. Note also that the clutter map forms a new link between search-returns processing and search-commands generation not shown in Figure 30.9. Although this may be contrary to true top-down design, two situations are found where the introduction of new entities is ap-

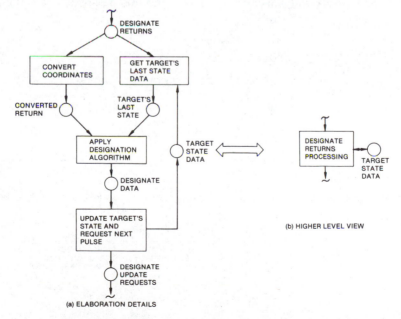

Figure 30.11. Elaboration of designate returns processing.

propriate: (1) in some cases, new requirements are discovered as complicated problems are being decomposed; and (2) in some cases, requirements having different purposes or importance are treated separately. In Figure 30.10, the new data entities were discovered to be necessary to perform the required functions. A secondary requirement to be added later, for example, would be data recording. Of course, earlier figures (Figures 30.8 and 30.9 in the radar example) can always be retrofitted with newly developed entities to give the appearance of pure decomposition.

Elaboration is continued in much the same way as in conventional design. However, increased attention is required to identify potentially concurrent operations and to represent all data relationships that would affect concurrency. An important consideration is data that must be retained within a functional entity from activation to activation. For example, in examining designate-returns processing in Figure 30.11a, the target state data must be retained to properly process designate returns from the radar. Figure 30.11b shows designate-returns processing at a higher level of abstraction. Here the retained data are explicitly shown to enable proper evaluation of concurrent implementations. Retained data must be represented because they are major factors in

computing storage requirements and overhead for potential run-time relocation of functional entities. Secondly, retained data must be shared by multiple copies of a functional entity. For example, if different designate returns for a given target are to be processed by different copies of designate-returns processing, every copy must have knowledge of the target's state data.

Now the packaging problem is considered. In structured design of conventional systems, a hierarchical structure chart showing the results of elaboration is usually prepared. Figure 30.12 shows results for the radar example. If this design were to be implemented as a single program on a single sequential computer, a main program acquisition radar processing would likely be written to handle data input/output and call the four next lower modules. Similarly, the search/detection-processing module would input/output data and call the next lower-level modules.

Suppose the example design were to be mapped onto two computers. One reasonable partitioning of functionality for two computers is indicated by the dashed lines in Figure 30.12. The question arises as to where to locate the remaining elements of the structure: acquisition radar processing, search/detection processing, and designate and track initiation.

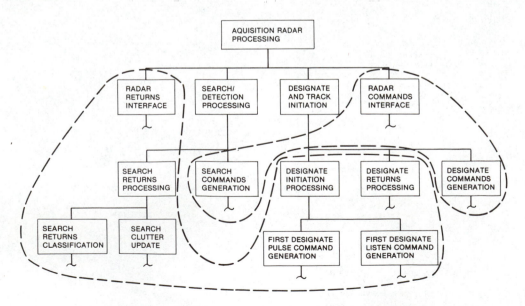

Figure 30.12. Partial structure chart for radar system example.

Placing these modules on either computer would mean that they must control modules on the other computer. This would cause additional communications between computers, make control more complex, and reduce achievable concurrency.

If hierarchical structures must be implemented in modular computer systems to gain structuring advantages, the normal transfer of control and data that would otherwise be necessary must be avoided. One approach is to restrict high-level modules to execute only during initiation and termination phases. Thus upon initiation, the acquisition-radar-processing program would initiate execution of lower-level modules and then become inactive until termination. Such high-level modules would not contain their subordinates as in conventional structured systems. This difference in implementing structures is an important departure from conventional design.

Usually, data-driven control is most advantageous for distributed systems. In data-driven control, each module executes upon arrival of required input data. This approach allows the modules to operate asynchronously with maximum concurrency. The control system is very simple if the computers' native operating systems have message control operations [28, 29].

Ordinarily, a processing structure would be partitioned into many modules, and more than two computers would be used. The modules must be identified, the number of computers determined, and the mapping of modules to computers defined. Generally this is a very complex task. For example, a typical problem of 15 modules presents about 7×10^8 alternatives for partitioning and allocation to N identical computers, $N = 1, 2, \ldots, 15$. If the number of computers were constrained to $N = 8$, there would still be some 2×10^8 different alternatives for mapping 15 modules onto 8 computers.* An automated, efficient decision algorithm obviously is necessary to solve typical problems.

Because of the complexity of computer selection and functional mapping, the tasks are

---

*The numbers of combinations are tabulated as Stirling Numbers of the second kind [30].

usually accomplished as shown in Figure 30.13. The first major step, partitioning, lowers the complexity of following steps by grouping functions according to intrinsic commonalities, for example, common data-accessing patterns. Computer characteristics are mostly ignored during partitioning, except that sizes of partitions may be constrained in terms of instructional rates and data storage requirements.

The selection of candidate resources (computers in this case) in Figure 30.13 is usually done by exhaustive enumeration; that is, try every feasible and reasonable alternative. In this example, select N identical computers, letting N range from one to the number of partitions, and then determine a specific value for N based on evaluation of the ensuing allocation. Some characteristics (throughput, storage, etc.) of the computers might be optimized in the process.

Allocation is similar to partitioning. The main difference is that allocation relates characteristics of partitions to characteristics of resources, whereas partitioning looks at commonalities of processing entities with only incidental concern for potential resource characteristics. Allocation binds partitions to physical resources. In general, a partition may be

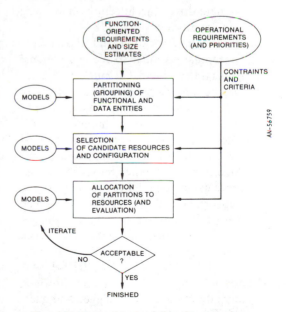

Figure 30.13. Partitioning/allocation procedures.

bound dynamically to different resources at different times. The results of the allocation are evaluated with respect to given constraints and criteria, and iterations of alternative resource selections and/or partitionings are possibly made.

The partitioning-selection-allocation procedure is a problem in constrained discrete optimization. The difficulties in achieving an analytic solution have been noted [31]. Numerical techniques have been successful. A fuzzy clustering approach to partitioning [32] and an implicit enumeration (or branch and bound) approach to allocation [33] are recommended. Variations in techniques and decision-guiding algorithms are described by Morgan and Levin [34, 35] and Boorstyn and Frank [36]. Another important approach uses network-flow algorithms [37].

The status of technologies for the multicomputer design steps described above is:

1. Elaboration approach—uses essentially the same technologies as conventional decomposition.
2. Control structure definition—often used in conventional design but avoided because it requires high communication and control overheads; data-driven control is recommended. A body of literature on data-driven architectures and some prototype systems exist [38–43].
3. Partitioning, selection, and allocation—conceptually similar to the conventional packaging problem, but much more complex because more variables are involved. Algorithms exist that give good or optimal solutions when the number of variables is less than 50 and when the goal and constraint models have simple forms. Algorithms for other situations sometimes can be tailored to the problem.
4. Supporting tools and languages—some conventional design tools and languages can be extended to catalog and check multicomputer designs. For example, PSL/PSA [44] and RSL/REVS [45] are basically data base systems in which any information can be logged and queried. The greatest shortcoming of existing

tools is in automated generation of simulations that properly depict and evaluate concurrency. Simulations need to contain capabilities for making processes wait for data accessing and restart appropriately; existing concurrent programming languages contain primitives for expressing such operations [28, 29, 46].

Multilevel Distributions

Systems may have multiple levels of distribution (Figure 30.1). For instance, each of the computers of the multicomputer design in Section 30.2 may be composed of a distributed set of hardware and software components. Similarly, groups of computers (and software) may be connected to form a distributed computing system, groups of computing systems may form a computing facility (or node), and a network of nodes forms a geographically distributed system.

Multilevel systems are designed by treating each level of distribution in sequence, as illustrated in Figure 30.14. The same four activities as for multicomputer design are applied at each level: analysis, partitioning, allocation, and synthesis. Figure 30.15 represents the overall approach.

Usually the analysis activity is given most effort at the highest level of design because it provides the initial description of processing requirements. The other activities are much the same at different levels except for detailed criteria used for decisions. For example, criteria for partitioning and allocation between nodes would more likely concern communication distances, message rates, and link reliability, whereas within a node, criteria would more likely concern throughput, storage, and types of algorithms.

Once requirements have been mapped across all distribution levels, implementation may begin. In conventional design, there are good reasons for both top-down and bottom-up implementation approaches [47]. In a top-down software implementation, intermediate testing requires an overall test driver and stubbing off lower-level functions that have not yet

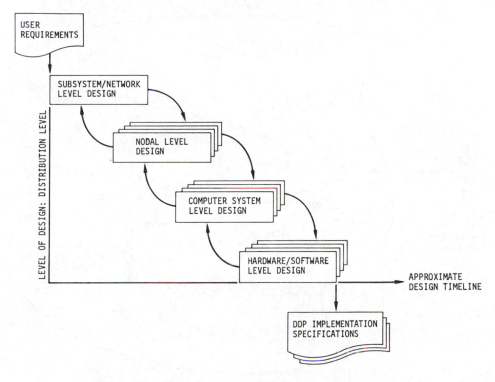

Figure 30.14. Vertical structure of baseline design approach.

been implemented. Bottom-up software implementation requires test drivers for each function. In distributed systems, where both hardware and software are being implemented, a bottom-up implementation may be necessary because of difficulties in stubbing off hardware.

The status of technologies for multilevel systems is nearly the same as for multicomputer design (Section 30.2). The main difference is that multilevel design requires representation and simulation of additional elements: nodes, internodal network, and processing elements.

30.3. FUTURE REQUIREMENTS AND PROSPECTS

Although distributed computing systems potentially satisfy application requirements much better than centralized systems, they

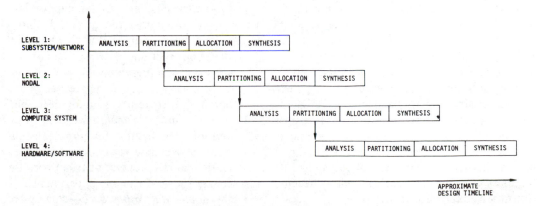

Figure 30.15. Baseline design approach overall framework.

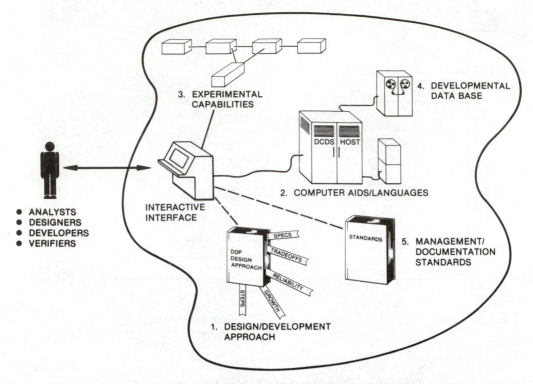

Figure 30.16. Technology requirements for distributed system development. A distributed computing design system.

make design more difficult. Design of distributed systems is more difficult because more variables and complexities are involved. Distributed systems contain concurrent processes that must share resources and data, often without centralized control. Processes and data are distributed and sometimes replicated at different locations, in different computers at a location, and in different processing components of a computer. Communications and data management are major problems. The explicit treatment of reliability, changeability, testability, and other operational requirements increases design complexity significantly.

Early attempts to develop fully distributed designs for stressing applications have revealed that no existing design technology is completely adequate for treating the extremely complex and varied requirements. For example, methods for partitioning of functionality for most efficient distribution, control decentralization, data base distribution and access sharing, fault tolerance, and so on, involve more art than science. The technology required for efficient, effective distributed system development is embodied in five tangible products, illustrated in Figure 30.16:

1. *A design development approach*—sequence of steps to be taken, guidelines for decisions and tradeoffs at each step, and methods of evaluating results.
2. *Computer aids language*—computer languages, programs, and display facilities to help create, catalog, and check the design; construct and exercise simulations; standardize representations; control configurations; and communicate results. An interactive capability is highly desirable.
3. *Experimental capabilities*—hardware and software facilities for empirical studies to develop and verify design and simulation models; operational support for configuring and running experiments.
4. *Developmental data base*—catalog of implementation component characteris-

tics to enable the effects of design decisions to be anticipated; coded models for simulations, and so forth.

5. *Management/documentation standards*—guidelines for design team structures, program milestones, reviews, and specification publications.

A considerable investment will be necessary to obtain this technology. Only relatively small steps are being taken at present. Hopefully, larger investments will be made as distributed designs become more common.

REFERENCES

1. M. J. Flynn, "Some Computer Organizations and Their Effectiveness," *IEEE Transactions on Computers*, vol. C-21, no. 9, Sept. 1972.
2. P. H. Enslow, Jr., "What is a Distributed Data Processing System?" *Computer*, Jan. 1978.
3. B. W. Boehm, "Software Engineering," *IEEE Trans. on Computers*, C-25, no. 12, Dec. 1976, pp. 1226–1241.
4. E. Yourdon and L. L. Constantine, *Structured Design; Fundamentals of a Discipline of Computer Program and Systems Design*, Prentice-Hall, Inc., Englewood Cliffs, 1979.
5. M. P. Mariani and D. F. Palmer (eds.), *Tutorial: Distributed System Design*, EHO 151-1, IEEE Computer Society, 1979.
6. R. E. Larson, *Tutorial: Distributed Control*, EHO 153-7, IEEE Computer Society, 1979.
7. W. W. Chu and P. P. Chen, *Tutorial: Centralized and Distributed Data Base Systems*, EHO 154-5, IEEE Computer Society, 1979.
8. K. J. Thurber, *Tutorial: Distributed Processor Communication Architecture*, EHO 152-9, IEEE Computer Society, 1979.
9. G. J. Klir (ed.), *Trends in General Systems Theory*, Wiley-Interscience, New York, 1972.
10. W. R. Spillers (ed.), *Basic Questions of Design Theory*, North-Holland Co., New York, 1974.
11. J. C. Jones, *Design Methods: Seeds of Human Futures*, Wiley-Interscience, New York, 1970.
12. J. D. Couger and R. W. Knapp (eds.), *System Analysis Techniques*, Wiley & Sons, New York, 1974.
13. C. V. Ramamoorthy and R. T. Yeh, *Tutorial: Software Methodology*, EHO 142-0, IEEE Computer Society, Nov. 1978.
14. M. Hamilton and S. Zeldin, "Higher Order Software—A Methodology for Defining Software," *IEEE Transactions on Software Engineering*, vol. SE-2, no. 1, March 1976, pp. 9–31.
15. D. L. Parnas, "On the Criteria Used for Decomposing Systems into Modules," *Communications of ACM*, vol. 15, Dec. 1972, pp. 1053–1059.
16. D. L. Parnas, "Designing Software for Ease of Extension and Contraction," 19XX.
17. W. P. Stevens, G. J. Meyers, and L. L. Constantine, "Structured Design," *IBM Systems Journal*, 1974.
18. M. A. Jackson, *Principles of Program Design*, Academic Press, New York, 1975.
19. D. J. Farber and F. R. Heinrich, "The Structure of a Distributed Computer System—The File System," *Proceedings of International Conference on Computer Communications*, Oct. 1972, pp. 364–370.
20. C. V. Ramamoorthy, K. M. Chandy, and M. J. Gonzalez, "Optimal Scheduling Strategies in a Multiprocessor System," *IEEE Transactions on Computers* C-21, Feb. 1972, pp. 137–146.
21. E. B. Fernandez and B. Bussell, "Bounds on the Number of Processors and Time for Multiprocessor Optimal Schedules," *IEEE Transactions on Computers*, (C-22), Aug. 1973, pp. 745–751.
22. K. M. Chandy and J. R. Dickson, "Scheduling Unidentical Processors in a Stochastic Environment," *COMPCON 1972 Proceedings*, Sept. 1972, pp. 171–174.
23. T. L. Booth and Y. Chien, *Computing: Fundamentals and Applications*, Hamilton Publishing Co., Santa Barbara, 1974, Chapter 4.
24. Yourdon and Constantine, *Structured Design*, Chapter 10.
25. G. M. Schneider, S. W. Weingart, and D. M. Perlman, *An Introduction to Programming and Problem Solving with PASCAL*, Wiley & Sons, New York, 1978, Chapter 2.
26. C. V. Ramamoorthy and H. H. So, "Software Requirements and Specifications: Status and Perspectives," *Tutorial: Software Methodology*, in C. V. Ramamoorthy and Raymond T. Yeh (eds.), IEEE Computer Society, EHO 142-0, 1978, pp. 43–164. Also reprinted in Mariani and Palmer (eds.), *Tutorial: Distributed System Design*.
27. D. L. Parnas, *Use of Abstract Interfaces in the Development of Software for Embedded Computer Systems*, NRL Report 8047, Washington, D.C., June 3, 1977.
28. R. C. Holt, et al., *Structured Concurrent Programming with Operating Systems Applications*, Addison-Wesley, Reading, Mass., 1978.
29. P. B. Hansen, "Concurrent Programming Concepts," *Computing Surveys*, vol. 5, no. 4, Dec. 1973, pp. 223–245.
30. M. Abramowitz and I. A. Segun (eds.), *Handbook of Mathematical Functions*, Dover Publications, Inc., New York, 1965, Table 24.4, p. 835.
31. A. F. Bond and P. C. Belford, "An Approach to a Distributed Data Processing Architecture Methodology," *Proc. Sixth Texas Conf. on Computing Systems*, 1B-13-1B-35, University of Texas, Austin, Tex., Nov. 1977.
32. B. P. Buckles and D. M. Hardin, "Partitioning and Allocation of Logical Resources in a Distributed Computing Environment," in M. P. Mariani and D.

F. Palmer (eds.), *Tutorial: Distributed System Design,* pp. 247–276.

33. V. B. Gylys and J. A. Edwards, "Optimal Partitioning of Workload for Distributed Systems," *Proc. COMPCON/76 FALL,* 76CH1115-5C, IEEE Computer Society, 1976, pp. 353–357. Also reprinted in Mariani and Palmer (eds.), *Tutorial: Distributed System Design.*

34. H. L. Morgan and K. D. Levin, "Optimal Programs and Data Locations in Computer Networks," *Com. ACM,* vol. 20, no. 5, May 1977, pp. 315–322. Also reprinted in Mariani and Palmer (eds.), *Tutorial: Distributed System Design.*

35. K. D. Levin and H. L. Morgan, "Optimizing Distributed Data Bases—A Framework for Research," *AFIPS Conf. Proc.,* vol. 44, 1975, pp. 473–478. Also reprinted in Mariani and Palmer (eds.), *Tutorial: Distributed System Design.*

36. R. R. Boorstyn and H. Frank, "Large Scale Network Topological Optimization," *IEEE Trans. on Communications,* vol. COM-25, no. 1, Jan. 1977, pp. 37–55. Also reprinted in Mariani and Palmer (eds.), *Tutorial: Distributed System Design.*

37. H. S. Stone, "Multiprocessing Scheduling with the Aid of Network Flow Algorithms," *IEEE Trans. on Software Engineering,* vol. SE-3, no. 1, Jan. 1977, pp. 85–93. Also reprinted in Mariani and Palmer (eds.), *Tutorial: Distributed System Design.*

38. K. Arvind, P. Gostelow, and W. Plouffe, *An Asynchronous Programming Language and Computing Machine,* Report No. 114A, Department of Information and Computer Science, University of California, Irvine, Dec. 1978.

39. W. F. Cote and R. F. Riccelli, "The Design of a Data Driven Processing Element," *Proc. 1978 International Conf. on Parallel Processing,* 78CH1321-9C, IEEE Computer Society, Aug. 1978, pp. 173–183.

40. A. L. Davis, "DDN's—A Low-Level Program Schema for Fully Distributed Systems," *Proc. First European Conference on Parallel & Distributed Processing,* AFCET, CNRS, IEEE, Section Française, Toulouse, France, Feb. 1979, pp. 1–7.

41. N. DeFrancesco, et al., "On the Feasibility of Nondeterministic and Interprocess Communications Constructs in Data-Flow Computing Systems," *Proc. First European Conf. on Parallel & Distributed Processing,* AFCET, CNRS, IEEE, Section Française, Toulouse, France, Feb. 1979, pp. 93–100.

42. J. B. Dennis, "The Varieties of Data Flow Computers," *Proc. First International Conf. on Distributed Computing Systems,* 79CH14456C, IEEE Computer Society, Oct. 1979, pp. 430–439.

43. J. C. Syre, et al., "Pipelining, Parallelism and Asynchronism in the LAU System," *Proc 1977 International Conf. on Parallel Processing,* 77CH1253-4C, IEEE Computer Society, Aug. 1977, pp. 87–92.

44. D. Teichroew and E. A. Hershey III, "PSL/PSA: A Computer-Aided Technique for Structured Documentation and Analysis of Information Processing Systems," *IEEE Trans. on Software Engineering,* vol. SE-3, no. 1, Jan. 1977, pp. 41–48.

45. M. W. Alford, "A Requirements Engineering Methodology for Real-Time Processing Requirements," *IEEE Trans. on Software Engineering,* vol. SE-3, no. 1, Jan. 1977, pp. 60–69.

46. C. Mohan, *A Perspective of Distributed Computing Models, Constructs, Methodologies and Applications,* Working Paper DSG-8001, University of Texas, Austin, Tex., Jan. 15, 1980.

47. Yourdon and Constantine, *Structured Design,* Chapter 20.

Index